Vegetable Love

Vege~ table Love

BARBARA KAFKA

WITH CHRISTOPHER STYLER

PHOTOGRAPHS BY CHRISTINA CORNISH

ARTISAN

Published by Artisan
A Division of Workman Publishing, Inc.
708 Broadway
New York, New York 10003-9555
www.artisanbooks.com

Library of Congress Cataloging-in-Publication Data
Kafka, Barbara.
Vegetable love : Barbara Kafka with Christopher Styler.
  p. cm.
Includes bibliographical references and index.
ISBN-13: 978-1-57965-168-8
ISBN-10: 1-57965-168-2
1. Cookery (Vegetables). 2. Vegetables.
I. Styler, Christopher. II. Title
TX801.K33 2005
641.6'5—dc2   2005047818

Printed in the United States of America
10 9 8 7 6 5 4 3 2 1
Book design by Mark Lerner

This book is for Barbara Tropp, who is not a memory,
but a living presence in every day of my life.

We ate tofu, shopped for shoes, shared hugs,
laughter and information.

I owe her one.

This is a picture of the most recent and loved addition
to my life, Lily Anna Kafka, who, as her wonderful
brother, Oliver, pointed out, was not around to have
her picture alongside his in *Soup, A Way of Life*.

CONTENTS

WHY   ix

HOW   x

WHO   xii

Vegetables of the New World   3

Vegetables of the Mediterranean Basin,
Europe and the Arab World   153

Vegetables of Asia and Africa   295

Citizens of the World   371

Basic Recipes and Techniques   447

Cook's Guide   523

SOURCES   668

BIBLIOGRAPHY   670

INDEX   673

WHY

THIS IS A BOOK ABOUT PLEASURE, not a moral tract. I love the sweet seductive perfume of slowly sautéing onions, the impossibly vivid red of roasted peppers, the slow dance of eating an artichoke, the crunch of pale young romaine lettuce between my teeth, the surprise of gourds and squash I had not known and the practically infinite world of recipes using them—ones that exist and others that I can invent.

I find that I am eating more vegetables and that I will often select from a menu or my repertoire a group of compatible vegetable dishes—much like an eclectic meze (the Greek and Turkish first course)—rather than conventional first and main courses. There are, of course, times when a more conventional main course—sometimes all vegetable, sometimes with meat, fish or chicken—is exactly what I want. It is all here.

There is plenty for the vegetarian and even the vegan; but I feel free to use broths—some vegetable, some meat—and butter and cream as they seem good to me. Ignore the recipes that do not fit your pleasure. Invent your own using the Cook's Guide, which starts on page 523, with its descriptions of vegetables, buying and storing information, modes of cooking along with timings, and even some gardening tips.

At the end, the truth must out: I love food of all kinds, lean and meaty, acid and sweet, elegant and down to earth. I hope I can give my readers some of my pleasure, my love.

Barbara Kafka

HOW

I'M SLIGHTLY ECCENTRIC and so is my book, but I hope it is useful and even a pleasure. The easiest and most usual way to have organized the material in the book would have been alphabetically by vegetable. I started out that way; but as I worked, I found that there were things I wanted to say and ideas that I wanted to discuss that did not fit happily into that format. The recognition that most of us, myself included, have only the sketchiest idea of where most vegetables originated and how they relate to one another was the impetus. While this may seem very abstract, it highlights cooking facts and timings that would otherwise be disassociated, such as the differences between beans and peas—minimal except for their shape and cooking times. In truth it is fun. Also, knowing which vegetables are indigenous to which part of the world, in great measure, explains the inhabitants' cooking repertoire, even their culture. Therefore, I have organized the book by regions of the world. However, it is easy to find any vegetable that is of interest. The Contents lists the parts of the world and the vegetables of each. The Index easily will guide the searcher, and the Cook's Guide is largely alphabetical by vegetable and is cross-referenced to other parts of the guide and to recipe sections.

The Cook's Guide, easily turned to with the colored edges of its pages, has the facts related to how to buy, methods of cooking, cooking times, amounts produced by cutting the vegetable raw or when cooked. I put this last batch of information in this separate section for easy reference. As someone pointed out, it could be a book on its own. I think it will be useful to both the new cook and the expert. I refer to it all the time—too much to keep in my head.

The recipes are of many sorts representing a lifetime of cooking and growing vegetables. There are many recipes new to this book and some that have followed me like loyal friends from earlier books. They, and what I have to say about them, are not to be seen as orphaned children, but rather as cherished old friends. This is one of the reasons that there are still microwave recipes cropping up, as well as my belief that there are certain dishes or just vegetables—asparagus, for example—that are better cooked in this way than in any other.

Vegetable recipes are much like dishes in a home-style Chinese family meal; placement may be all together or a matter of whim. Each section does more or less follow traditional meal order; but mix and match as you choose. There are dishes that can be side dishes, first courses or parts of a main course. There are some dishes that are evidently main courses and some that are just as clearly desserts. Enjoy.

The information on growing reflects only my own plot of green in Vermont; but I consider it important because growing-your-own provides fresher, better-tasting vegetables, as well as chemical-free ones that are good for our families and the environment. Similarly, I am not an expert in all nationalities of food. I can give recipes for that which I enjoy and the vegetables I can find. I would love to have written a true encyclopedia. This is a love letter instead.

WHO

FIRST I MUST THANK ANDREW MARVELL, from whose wonderful and elegantly sexy poem "To His Coy Mistress" I borrowed my title.

Most of all I thank Christopher Styler, who has worked with me on and off for many years and been a good friend. I had been ill, and it is certainly true that I could not have put myself, let alone this book, together without his support. I also thank Joseph Seoane, his partner, who had to share so much. Everybody says "without whom . . ."; in this case it is true.

Ann Bramson has been my editor and now my publisher for more books than I choose to count. She has been, as always, astute, loving and a maker of beautiful books; but this time she has been patient beyond the limits of reason.

Esti Marpet has been a loyal assistant and researcher for some fifteen years. While I have had many assistants over the years who deserve credit for work on this book, I must above all thank Cindy Yeh and Amanda Cropper.

Elsa Tobar makes my life livable and has developed into a fine kitchen assistant in her own right.

No book this big and fact-filled could have been written without recourse to the works of many who have gone before me and whose works are mentioned in the Bibliography, and others who do not write but do share. I should also mention Farmer Jones of the red tie, who is always available to help with questions.

In the present, there are no better-informed friends than Penny and Paul Levy, whose sharing of life and information is extraordinary. They also shared their friend, the delightful photographer Christina Cornish. Eric Shearing has been of invaluable help with the vegetable gardens, as has Clarence Boston with the fruit trees.

Recently there was Barbara Tropp, to whom this book is dedicated. We shared an obscene passion for research and arcana. I miss her more than I can say.

Skip Dye, a vegetarian, was the first to suggest that I do a vegetable book. I hope he will not be upset by the nonvegetarian recipes and pleased to remember some of the recipes that I have brought along with me from previous books. I thank all of my friends and supporters at William Morrow/HarperCollins for whose editions of my books I did some of the original research and development for this compendium of my knowledge and thoughts.

A special thanks is due to Judith Sutton, who under great pressure did a fine job of copyediting this book, and to Vivian Ghazarian for the book jacket. Thanks also to Barbara Peragine, who typeset this behemoth with speed and finesse.

Over the years, there have been many editors at publications to whom I owe much. Foremost was my love, Leo Lerman. I am proud to have been one of his girls. Jane Montand of *Gourmet* was a very special supporter. Corby Kummer has never been my official editor, but he has done much to improve my work. Jim Beard didn't edit me, but we taught together and in the process he, like James Villas, taught as much about style as food.

Books have been the special delights of my life, not least in cookery. The Bibliography records some of my debts.

But just as man does not live by bread—or even vegetables—alone, my life is really a part of my family and friends. First there were my parents, Jack and Lillian Poses, at whose table I ate the brilliant cooking of Rachel Wellman. Most important, there is my partner, my love, my supporter and eating and wining companion, Ernest Kafka, without whom life would be unimaginable and without whom I would not have grown to take on challenges I didn't think I could master. Besides, we laugh. Our children, Nicole and Michael and, now, Jill, and Michael and Jill's children, Oliver and Lily, are delights and enrichments.

I mention no friends. There are too many and the fear of omitting someone beloved is painful. I do mention Bob and Barbara Haas, who taught me so much about wine and who are fine partners, and the restaurateurs with whom I worked, particularly Joseph Baum and Stephen Spector. More recently, the Kirkmans shared their Mexico and the expertise of their cook, Maria Auxillo Rodriguez.

Avocados 4   Beans of the New World Green Beans, Haricots Verts, Romano Beans,

Wax Beans, Black Beans, Cranberry Beans, Lima Beans, Navy Beans and Pink Beans 10

Cactus Pads (Nopales) 28   Corn Fresh Corn, Cornmeal, Hominy, Grits and Popcorn 30

Peanuts 49   Promiscuous Peppers 53   Potatoes 69

Summer Squash Pattypan, Zucchini and Yellow Squash 83

Tomatillos 92   Poison Tomatoes 95

Winter Squash Acorn, Delicata, Chayote, Pumpkin, Calabaza, Red Kuri,

Hubbard, Butternut, Jarrahdale and Kabocha 117   Sweet Potatoes and Yams 137

American Roots Jerusalem Artichokes, Jicama, Yautía and Yuca 142

Vegetables of the New World

MANY PEOPLE FIND IT HARD TO BELIEVE that all of the staples and treats in this section of the book are American and only began to play their part on the world stage of cooking, eating and agriculture with the arrival here of Europeans. Indeed, I have been repeatedly challenged by the incredulous, the Doubting Thomases, who take my assertions as insults to their familial or favorite kinds of cooking.

It is hard to imagine what European, Asian and even African food was like before the arrival of the New World vegetables and their seeds.

Like all novelties, they were greeted by some with suspicion bordering on panic and by others with hosannas of praise. In part, the reception depended on what arrived. It is a truism if not a truth that Columbus set out to find alternate sources for spice peppers that then had to come all the way from India, or in the form of a long pepper, a grape-shaped bunch of seeds from Africa. He found American pod peppers, such as bell peppers, that grow easily all around the globe.

Other vegetables took longer to integrate, especially as many, such as the tomato, were part of a poisonous family. However, enter onstage they did, often taking the starring role. They were constantly modified by the vagaries of nature and the careful work of growers until now when it can truly be said that there are indeed Mediterranean, Asian and African versions of almost all.

Avocados

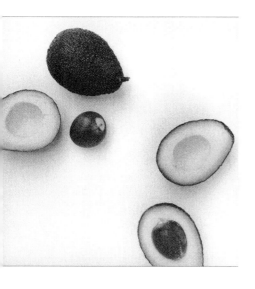

Yes, I know it grows on a tree and is probably a fruit. I eat it mainly as a vegetable, so here it is. The big trees grow in the tropics, have large shiny dark green leaves and are very handsome. If I lived in the proper climate, I would certainly grow some for their beauty as well as their succulent fruit, rich in monounsaturated fats.

They are a wonderful addition to a salad, are the makings of guacamole and purée into a kind of butter or the base of a cold soup or a sweet dessert. While I generally don't like them hot, they can serve as a counterpoint to a hot main course, sautéed liver, for instance. Some of the salads here are substantial enough to be used in a larger portion as a luncheon main course. All avocados have a brilliant affinity with seafood and curry.

That is why they so often come stuffed with shrimp, lobster or crabmeat salad. In this guise, they are typically a first course or a summer lunch. Try any of these for stuffing avocado halves: Curried Chicken Salad (page 499), Quintessential Tuna Salad (page 499), Velvet Smoked Trout (page 500) or Salad of Tiny Shrimp, Celery and Dill (page 500). Avocados would also be a colorful and succulent alternative to bananas or plantains in cooked dishes.

Unless peeled and sliced at the very last minute, avocados require acid, usually citrus juice and/or garlic, to keep from darkening. They are happy with hot peppers, Thai or biblical basil, and cilantro.

And that is not all—avocado leaves are used as a seasoning, much as banana leaves lend their flavor to rice. See Zarela Martinez's Puréed Black Beans (page 23).

To choose avocados, do not pinch them, which will only bruise them. Push gently on the stem end, which should give. Generally, really ripe Hass avocados—my favorites—are dark, almost black in color.

Turn to **AVOCADOS** in the Cook's Guide
for how-tos and to the Index for more recipes.

Avocado, Pink Grapefruit and Papaya Salad

The colors of the ingredients are a pleasure. The pink grapefruit provides the acid that avocados crave with somewhat less bite than those acids typically used.

1 1/2 medium Hass avocados, pitted and peeled, each half sliced crosswise into 6 slices (18 slices total)

1 medium yellow-skinned papaya (about 7 inches long), halved, peeled and seeded, each half sliced crosswise into 9 slices (18 slices total)

2 pink grapefruits, peeled and sections removed from white membrane (18 segments; see Note)

1 recipe Poppy Seed Blood Orange Vinaigrette (page 450)

6 small sprigs fresh purple or Thai basil, mint or cilantro

Arrange 3 pieces each of avocado, papaya and grapefruit on six plates. Whisk the dressing and spoon some over each. Top each plate with an herb sprig and serve. **Serves 6 as a first course**

NOTE: *To prepare citrus segments:* Cut away the peel and white pith, removing as little of the fruit as possible. Holding the fruit over a bowl to catch the juices, free the segments from the membranes with a paring knife.

Tomato Avocado Salad

This salad can be served on its own, but it is a good choice with simply prepared white-fleshed fish or chicken.

VINAIGRETTE

1 tablespoon fresh lemon juice

1/4 cup olive oil

1/8 teaspoon dry mustard

Scant 1/2 teaspoon kosher salt

Freshly ground black pepper to taste

2 medium tomatoes, cored and cut into 1 1/2-inch chunks

continued

1 medium Hass avocado, halved, pitted, peeled and cut into 1 1/2- to 2-inch chunks

1/2 small red onion, thinly sliced

2 tablespoons chopped fresh parsley, cilantro or basil

Kosher salt and freshly ground black pepper to taste

For the vinaigrette, whisk together the lemon juice, olive oil, dry mustard, salt and pepper. Set aside.

Toss the tomatoes, avocado, onion and parsley together in a bowl. Sprinkle with salt and pepper and toss with 1/4 cup dressing.

Serves 4 as a first course, 6 as a side dish

Shrimp and Avocado Salad on Lettuce and Sorrel

Here part of the citrus acid is replaced by the acid of sorrel. The salad is very pretty and, with the portion size increased, makes a good hot-day main course.

1 pound shrimp, cooked, peeled and cut into quarters

2 1/4 cups cubed Hass avocados

2 tablespoons chopped cilantro

4 1/2 tablespoons fresh lemon juice

6 tablespoons olive oil

2 teaspoons soy sauce

1/8 teaspoon minced garlic

2 1/2 teaspoons kosher salt

Freshly ground black pepper to taste

8 large leaves romaine lettuce, cut across into 1/4-inch strips

1/2 pound sorrel, stems removed and cut across into 1/4-inch strips

Put the shrimp, avocados and cilantro in a bowl.

Whisk together the lemon juice, olive oil, soy sauce, garlic, salt and pepper. Pour over the shrimp and avocado and gently toss. Put in the center of a large plate.

Mix together the lettuce and sorrel and arrange around the border of the plate. Of course, the portions can be plated individually, but that is less dramatic.

Serves 8 as a first course, 4 as a light lunch

Cold Lobster and Avocado Salad

Replace the shrimp with 1 pound frozen lobster tails. Omit the sorrel and use 3 or 6 large leaves romaine or Boston lettuce; do not slice the leaves.

Steam the lobster over boiling water for 18 minutes. Allow to cool. Remove the meat from the shells and slice crosswise into 1/4-inch slices.

Core a medium tomato and cut it into 12 wedges. Set aside.

Halve, pit and peel 2 medium avocados. Cut one half lengthwise into 6 slices. Sprinkle with some lemon juice to prevent discoloration and set aside for plating.

Slice the remaining avocado halves crosswise into 1/4-inch slices.

Whisk the dressing. Toss with the lobster and 1 cup celery cut across into 1/2-inch slices. Add the avocados and gently toss.

To serve as a first course, line six plates with a lettuce leaf. Place a mound of lobster salad in the middle of each. Place 2 tomato wedges and a reserved avocado slice on each plate. For a main course, line three plates with lettuce. Place a mound of lobster salad in each, and place 4 tomato wedges and 2 avocado slices on each plate.

Serves 6 as a first course, 3 as a main course

Chinese Shrimp and Avocado

Well, it is not really Chinese, but the seasonings are. They work very well.

- **1 1/2 tablespoons Chinese salted black beans**
- **1 pound shrimp**
- **1/2 lemon**
- **1 medium-large Hass avocado**
- **2 teaspoons cornstarch**
- **3 tablespoons vegetable oil**
- **1/2 teaspoon minced garlic**
- **1 1/2 teaspoons minced peeled fresh ginger**
- **1 small dried red chili peppers, crushed (about 1/4 teaspoon)**
- **3 scallions, trimmed and cut into thin 3 x 1/4 -inch strips**
- **2 tablespoons soy sauce**
- **1 1/2 teaspoons rice wine vinegar**

In a small dish, soak the black beans in 1/2 cup water for 15 minutes.

Meanwhile, peel the shrimp, leaving the tail shell on. Slice the shrimp down the back to devein, cutting almost all the way through to butterfly. Set aside.

Squeeze the juice of the lemon half into a quart of water and drop in the lemon. Halve, pit and peel the avocado. Cut each half lengthwise into 10 slices, then cut each slice in half crosswise. Drop the avocado into the acidulated water to prevent discoloration.

Drain the black beans, reserving 1/4 cup of the liquid. Mix the reserved liquid with the cornstarch.

Heat the oil in a wok or large skillet. Add the garlic, ginger and crushed chili pepper and stir-fry for about 10 seconds. Add the shrimp and fry for about 1 minute. As the shrimp cooks, push the more cooked pieces to the sides.

Drain the avocado. Add it to the wok, with the scallions, and stir-fry for 10 seconds. Add the soy sauce, vinegar and dissolved cornstarch. Stir and cook until the sauce thickens, about 30 seconds. Serve immediately.

Serves 4 as a first course or, with jasmine rice, as a main course

Liver and Avocado Sauté

Ready-made meat glaze (sometimes called demi-glace) can nowadays be purchased in specialty food stores and some groceries and butcher shops. It can also be made from scratch by reducing homemade beef stock until syrupy; chicken stock will work too. The dryness of liver can be moistened with avocado, and its fat is better than the more usual bacon or chicken fat. It is also more attractive. Rice would be the accompaniment of choice; if something more is desired, try sautéed spinach. The recipe can easily be multiplied.

- **1 medium-large Hass avocado**
- **3 1/2 tablespoons fresh lemon juice**
- **3/4 pound calves' liver, outer membrane and veins removed**
- **3 tablespoons unsalted butter**
- **3 tablespoons Meat or Chicken Glaze (page 505)**
- **3/4 teaspoon kosher salt**
- **Freshly ground black pepper to taste**

Halve, pit and peel the avocado. Cut each half lengthwise into 10 slices. Place them in a bowl and pour the lemon juice over them. Toss gently so all the avocado slices are coated with lemon juice to prevent discoloration.

Cut the liver into 20 thin slices, each about the same size as an avocado slice. Pat the pieces dry.

continued

Heat 2 tablespoons of the butter in a 10-inch skillet until it is foaming but not brown. Add half the liver and cook for about 2 minutes. Turn and cook 2 minutes more on the other side. Remove the liver to a plate and keep warm.

Add the remaining tablespoon of butter to skillet. Add the remaining liver and cook as above. Add to the first batch of liver.

Stir the meat glaze into the liquid remaining in the skillet. Add the avocados with the lemon juice and stir gently so the avocados do not break, to mix. Season with the salt and pepper to taste. Let cook until the liquid has thickened slightly, about 1 minute. Return the liver to the skillet and gently toss. Cook just to heat through, then serve. **Serves 2 as a main course**

Guacamole

So much green glop masquerades under this name that I hesitate to recommend it, but it is worth rescuing if made with really ripe dark-skinned Hass avocados that have been mashed, not puréed. This version is pleasant, mild and fresh. If guacamole is desired hotter, add more peppers. To further adorn this recipe, stir in a tablespoon of grated onion and two of chopped cilantro. The guacamole will keep for the length of a party, because of the amount of lime juice and garlic.

Don't add tomato to guacamole: Tomato makes it watery. Instead, consider making one of the salsas (see page 114 or 435, for example) and serving it with the guacamole and tortilla chips. Or, dice any type of firm ripe tomato into ¼-inch dice. Do the same to half a large white onion. Mix them and serve in a bowl next to the guacamole for guests to add as they like. (Blue corn chips make a beautiful color contrast.) On my last trip to Mexico, I prepared guacamole to serve, along with diced tomato and onion, with soft scrambled eggs.

It was smashing. This recipe will make enough to serve eight in that way.

If fresh hot chili peppers aren't available, substitute a third the amount of a green bell pepper and hot red pepper sauce to taste. Do not use dried peppers or pepper flakes.

If multiplying the recipe several times, purée the flavoring mixture in a blender.

> **1 tablespoon kosher salt**
>
> **5 medium cloves garlic, smashed and peeled**
>
> **3 small fresh hot peppers, such as jalapeños, halved, seeded and deribbed**
>
> **5 tablespoons fresh lime juice**
>
> **3 large Hass avocados**

Sprinkle the salt over the garlic cloves and mince very fine, pressing them into the salt with the flat of the knife from time to time until they form a paste. Add the peppers and mince them, pressing on the mixture to make a fine paste that retains all the pepper juices. Scrape into a small bowl, stir in 2 tablespoons of the lime juice and set aside.

Just before serving, cut the avocados in half lengthwise. Remove the pits and scoop the meat from the skin with a teaspoon. In a nonmetallic serving bowl, mash the avocados with a fork. Stir in the garlic mixture and the remaining 3 tablespoons lime juice. **Makes 2¼ cups**

Avocado Dressing

Into anybody's life a little luck must fall from time to time. I was reading some pretty dry information about fats and oils when I stumbled over the fact that avocado fat—caloric though it may be—is entirely monounsaturated, like olive oil. I decided to make a salad dressing using avocado instead of oil, but found that I had to add a lot of liquid to the avocado purée or it was too thick. Imagine my delighted surprise when the nutritional analysis came back and I found that there were only fourteen calories in a tablespoon of dressing. Use two tablespoons or more for a portion of salad.

1 large Hass avocado, halved, pitted and peeled

3 tablespoons fresh lemon juice

2 cloves garlic, smashed and peeled

1 teaspoon hot red pepper sauce

1 cup buttermilk

1 teaspoon kosher salt

Put all the ingredients in a blender. Add 1 cup water. Cover and blend until smooth. Store tightly covered and refrigerated. **Makes 3 cups**

Spicy-Cool Avocado Sauce

This very pleasant sauce is the invention of my dear coauthor Chris Styler, from his book *Smokin'*.

1 ripe but not mushy Hass avocado

4 to 5 teaspoons fresh lime juice

1/4 cup sour cream

1 teaspoon hot red pepper sauce, or to taste

Kosher salt to taste

Halve the avocado and remove the pit. Scoop the flesh into a bowl. Add the lime juice and toss well. Purée in a food processor, stopping twice to scrape down the sides of the bowl, until very smooth.

Scrape the mixture back into the bowl. Beat in the sour cream. Season with the hot red pepper sauce and salt to taste. The sauce can be prepared up to 1 day in advance and refrigerated with a piece of plastic wrap pressed directly against the surface to prevent browning. Bring to room temperature before serving. **Makes 2 cups**

NOTE: This makes a thick, dollopy kind of sauce with a velvety texture. For a thinner sauce, better suited for drizzling or dipping, beat in 1 to 2 tablespoons water just before serving. Check the seasonings and step up the salt and pepper sauce if needed.

Avocado Ice Cream

While an avocado-flavored dessert may seem strange to North Americans, South Americans have long considered the avocado an ideal ingredient for sweet desserts. Try this recipe and understand why.

4 medium Hass avocados (8 ounces each)

3/4 teaspoon kosher salt

1 cup superfine sugar

6 tablespoons fresh lemon juice

1 cup heavy cream

Halve, pit and peel the avocados. Cut into chunks and put in a food processor or a blender. (If using a blender, it may be necessary to work in 2 batches.) Process until fairly smooth. With the machine running, add the salt, sugar and then lemon juice. Process until smooth.

With the machine running, slowly pour in the cream. Continue processing until the mixture is smooth and fluffy.

Transfer to a metal bowl, cover and freeze.

When the mixture is completely frozen, dip the bowl briefly in hot water to loosen the mixture, and unmold it in one piece into a shallow bowl.

Cut the mixture into 2-inch cubes and put into the food processor. Pulse on and off to break up large lumps and then process until smooth. Serve immediately. **Makes about 1 quart**

NOTE: This dessert is best served fresh. Do not begin more than 1 day before you plan to serve it.

Beans of the New World

Green Beans, Haricots Verts, Romano Beans, Wax Beans, Black Beans, Cranberry Beans, Lima Beans, Navy Beans and Pink Beans

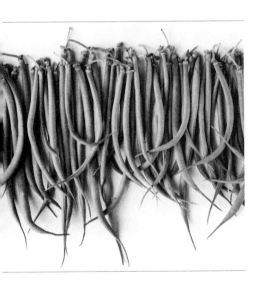

Beans are eaten in two distinct ways. Some are eaten in the shell, such as our ordinary green beans. Then there are the seeds that grow inside the shell, getting larger as the shell grows. Most of the shell beans can be shelled when they get large enough, and then we have the familiar kidney- or lima bean–shaped delights that can be cooked fresh when available or, more commonly, reconstituted from dried.

Beans are some of my favorite eating and I can enjoy them knowing that they help the soil by setting nitrogen. Perhaps my favorite way to eat green beans is as a salad with really ripe tomatoes and a lemon vinaigrette. Sometimes I add slivers of red onion. The salad should not be cold: I want to taste the beans. Nor should they be al dente, so that they crack. I don't like them limp in this dish, but I do like them thoroughly cooked. This is one of the great delights of summer, with good bread to sop up all the wonderful juices.

I am as fond of gigantes, the huge Greek shell beans, or their white Italian equivalent, coronas. Fresh flageolets, a pale celadon just out of the shell, usually with leg of lamb, and fresh cranberry beans with a handful of herbs and olive oil are delights—as are the non-American beans such as favas and soy.

Beans are delicious, nutritious and easy to grow, but they are confusing. There are the true beans, such as green beans, that are strictly of New World origin, members of the family Phaseolus, and there are Old World beans, such as favas, and Asian beans, which are members of several different families.

New World beans have been adopted and changed in all parts of the world. The English, for example, are great growers of red runner beans that climb and are very attractive. Sadly, by the time they are long and decorative, they are overgrown from the point of view of the eater, adding unfairly to the traditional—but certainly no longer true—view of the English as good gardeners and bad cooks.

The original beans were all climbers. American and Central American Indians grew them to climb up cornstalks. Providentially, the corn and beans combined to make a whole protein. The French and then the Italians adapted these vining beans to create bush beans, which are low growing. The French call them "nain" (literally, dwarf) and for years I thought that meant thin little beans such as haricots verts. It doesn't; it only means bush beans. The Italian is also confusing. If one doesn't know, it is impossible to tell which is the fastest train: the diretto, direttissimo,

accelerato or rapido. Similarly, each type of bean has numerous names, though all beans (dried and fresh) are called fagioli (green beans are called fagiolini).

All beans meant to be eaten in the shell must be picked constantly to keep on producing. This is hard, as they are past masters of deception. Just when I have looked under every leaf and think that I have picked them all, I go around again and find handfuls more. In any case, it is a good idea to succession-plant beans. I can grow two crops even in Vermont. More sympathetic climates can provide beans for the greater part of the year.

All beans do well with members of the onion family, tomatoes and, among the herbs, fresh sage in particular. Try cutting some sage into thin strips and heating it in olive oil or butter before tossing with the beans. Recently, I tried fresh lemon balm and marjoram in hot green bean dishes, and they worked very well. Despite their adaptability, there is one way I do not like them, and that is pickled as dilly beans. Go to another author if you must make them.

When winter is about to hit my last crop of beans in the shell or the plants are clearly exhausted, I pick all the remaining beans and boil them, uncovered, in a lot of salted water for about three minutes after the water has returned to the boil. I drain them and run them under cold water (the only time I use cold water, other than for some salads, such as Green Bean Salad, page 12). I put them in about one-cup amounts in plastic bags and freeze them.

A nice way to eat these—I had them for lunch just yesterday—is to put about three tablespoons chopped white onions to simmer in two tablespoons of good butter. While they were becoming translucent, I defrosted the beans in the microwave for about three minutes. I stirred them together, added salt and pepper and ate.

We have taken to calling thin green beans in the shell "French beans" or "haricots verts." So, if that is what is called for in a recipe, the thinnest, rather short, about four inches long beans are what is meant.

Turn to BEANS OF THE NEW WORLD in the Cook's Guide for how-tos and to the Index for more recipes.

EATEN IN THE SHELL

As I said before, these beans were originally American, but they have spread all over the world in both their vining and bush varieties. Most of these beans may be left to grow large and then shelled and eaten fresh or dried and reconstituted.

Mostly, I first slightly undercook beans in boiling water and then let them continue to cook as they are tossed in butter or added to other preparations. Most writers call for refreshing the beans—running them under cold water in a sieve to stop the cooking. I prefer to avoid this, as it tends to leach out flavor. I make an exception when parcooking beans for salad or before freezing, as I don't want them to get mushy from the retained cooking heat. Many people, myself included, prefer to salt the water before boiling beans. It is not essential, and salting them after cooking gives a little more control. But the salt in the water tends to help retain the color.

One of my favorite summer first courses—even a main course—is a salad of French beans and chunks of tomato, with or without thinly sliced red onions. I eat it at home, in Italy, or the South of France. The vegetables must be impeccably fresh and the beans still slightly crisp but cooked through.

Not all bean recipes are for lightly cooked, crisp beans. The Italians especially will stew green beans for a long time, and very good they are. They have their own varieties of green beans, such as Romanos (see the Cook's Guide, page 537). Some are broader than the typical French kind, some are somewhat curly and there is a wide variety of colors. They tend to be meatier than other beans in the shell and do very well in long-cooked recipes. When cooks fall into the trendy mode of cooking beans al dente, the beans are often undercooked and taste grassy.

Green Bean Salad

If lovage is unavailable, use cilantro, chervil or tarragon.

Kosher salt

1 1/2 pounds haricots verts (French green beans), tipped and tailed

1/3 cup thinly sliced red onion

1/3 to 1/2 cup chopped fresh lovage

1/3 cup Soy-Sesame Vinaigrette (page 449)

Bring a large pot of salted water to a boil. Add the beans. Cook for 1 to 2 minutes, until bright green and crisp-tender. Drain, rinse under cold running water and drain.

Combine the beans, onion and lovage in a bowl. Add the dressing. Toss to combine.
Makes 4 1/2 cups

Midsummer Green Bean Salad

The reason this is a midsummer salad is that the larger beans welcome stronger seasonings.

1/4 cup plus 2 tablespoons kosher salt

2 pounds haricots verts (French green beans), tipped and tailed

1 1/2 pounds ripe tomatoes, cored and cut into 1-inch chunks

1/2 cup scallions, white parts only, thinly sliced on the diagonal

1/2 cup olive oil

Generous amount of freshly ground black pepper

1/2 cup coarsely chopped fresh dill

1/2 lemon (optional)

Bring 3 quarts water plus the 1/4 cup of salt to a rolling boil in a large pot. Add the beans. Bring the water back to a boil and boil for 5 minutes. While the beans cook, prepare a very cold ice water bath in a large bowl. Drain the beans and plunge into the ice water. Stir and toss.

While the beans are chilling, combine the tomatoes with the remaining 2 tablespoons salt and the scallions in a bowl. Toss and allow to sit for 20 minutes.

Add the olive oil and pepper to the tomatoes. Drain the beans. Toss thoroughly with the tomatoes. Allow to sit until ready to serve, or for up to 1 hour.

Toss in the dill and, if desired, squeeze lemon over the salad. **Makes 8 cups**

Green Bean Salad with Vinaigrette

A jazzier version of the basic green bean salad, this shouldn't be served too cold or the various flavors won't show up.

1 pound green beans, tipped and tailed

VINAIGRETTE

2 tablespoons any wine vinegar

6 tablespoons olive oil

1 teaspoon capers, drained and rinsed

1 teaspoon chopped fresh parsley

1 teaspoon chopped fresh tarragon

1 teaspoon chopped fresh chervil

1 teaspoon chopped fresh chives

1 tablespoon finely chopped hard-boiled egg (slice the rest of the egg for topping)

Kosher salt and freshly ground black pepper to taste

Bring a large pot of salted water to a boil. Drop in the beans and cook, uncovered, until they are cooked but still slightly crisp. Drain well.

While the beans are cooking, make the vinaigrette: Combine the vinegar, olive oil, capers, chopped herbs and chopped egg and salt and pepper in a medium bowl.

Mix the warm drained beans with the vinaigrette. Cover and place in the refrigerator to chill slightly. Mix occasionally to distribute the sauce evenly.

Top with the sliced hard-boiled egg and serve. **Makes 4 2/3 cups**

Salade Less-Gastronomique

In the first wave of nouvelle cuisine, when a first-course salad was still a novelty to the French, the "salade gastronomique" made its appearance at the fanciest restaurants. It was comprised of cool cooked beans, slices of foie gras and the tail meat of crayfish (écrevisses) topped with vinaigrette and thinly sliced black truffles. It was delicious—and expensive—but isn't around much anymore—a cliché.

Here it's a variant with shrimp and avocado, cheaper, more today, less work than the fancy salade gastronomique—worth trying. The nicely fatty avocado replaces the smooth and sexy texture of the foie gras. Shrimp replace the écrevisses, for less money and less work. Remember, we are talking shelled weight. I just omitted the truffles.

> 1/2 cup kosher salt
>
> 1 pound haricots verts (French green beans), tipped and tailed
>
> 1 pound shelled and deveined shrimp
>
> **DRESSING**
>
> 1/2 cup excellent olive oil
>
> 2 tablespoons tarragon vinegar
>
> 1 1/2 teaspoons balsamic vinegar
>
> Kosher salt and freshly ground black pepper to taste
>
> 2 ripe Hass avocados
>
> 1/4 pound mâche (lamb's lettuce) or other light green such as pale green frisée or baby spinach

Bring two 8-quart pots of water to a boil. Add the salt to one pot and add the beans to that pot. Add the shrimp to the other pot. Cook the beans for 3½ minutes and the shrimp for 4 minutes. Drain separately and allow to cool.

Combine the dressing ingredients and reserve.

Just before serving, halve, pit and peel the avocados. Cut each half lengthwise into 6 slices, keeping the halves together. Arrange the slices of one half in a circle near the rim of each plate. Toss the shrimp and the beans with the dressing and allow to sit 1 minute.

Lift the shrimp and beans out of the dressing and pile in the center of each avocado ring. Tuck some of the greens—sparsely—in and around the avocado slices. Serve.

Serves 4 as a first course

Green Beans, Tuna, Potatoes and Niçoise Olives with Tomatoes and Anchovy Cheese Vinaigrette

Here is the conventional salade Niçoise.

> 4 pounds waxy new potatoes
>
> 1 pound haricots verts (French green beans), tipped and tailed
>
> 1 recipe Anchovy Cheese Dressing (page 450)
>
> 1 head young romaine lettuce, leaves torn into bite-size pieces
>
> 2 large tomatoes, each cored and sliced into 8 wedges
>
> 12 ounces solid white tuna (about 1 1/2 cans), drained, in large chunks
>
> 24 Niçoise olives
>
> 4 eggs, cooked until just under hard-boiled, peeled and quartered

Cook the potatoes in boiling salted water until just tender. Drain and let cool slightly.

Meanwhile, bring a large pot of salted water to a boil. Add the beans and cook, uncovered, until cooked but still slightly crisp. Drain.

As soon as the potatoes are cool enough to handle, peel and slice them. In a large bowl, toss the warm potatoes with half of the vinaigrette; let cool. Divide the romaine among four plates. Add the beans, tomatoes and tuna to the potatoes. Spoon more dressing over the ingredients and toss again. Place on top of the romaine leaves. Top each plate with one-quarter of the olives and eggs. **Serves 6 as a main course, 8 as a starter**

Haricots Verts with Crème Fraîche

Easy to make and delightful to eat, this is a great way to prepare green beans. The beans can be blanched ahead of time and stored in the refrigerator, then heated a few minutes before serving. It is particularly good with roasted chicken.

2/3 cup kosher salt, plus 1 tablespoon, or to taste

2 1/2 pounds haricots verts (French green beans), tipped and tailed

3 tablespoons unsalted butter

1 cup crème fraîche

In an 8-quart pot, bring 5 quarts water and the 2/3 cup salt to a boil. Add the green beans and cook, uncovered, for 5 minutes; the beans will be tender and cooked through but still bright green. Drain the beans in a colander and immediately rinse under cold running water, tossing the beans with your hands to cool them.

Melt the butter in the same pot over medium heat. Add the beans. Tossing them with a wooden spoon, cook the beans until heated through, about 8 minutes. Remove from the heat and stir in the crème fraîche and remaining 1 tablespoon salt.

Makes 6 1/2 cups

Long-Cooked Italian Green Beans

This is my favorite exemplar of why not all vegetables and not even all beans in the pod should be served al dente, crisp. I tend to make big batches, as the dish keeps very well, covered, in the refrigerator. It can be served hot or at room temperature, used as a first course, side dish or pasta sauce. It can turn into a main course as an omelet filling, or alongside sliced ham or topped with lightly fried eggs. Or chop up leftovers and add enough stock to make a quick bowl of hot soup.

1/3 cup olive oil

1 pound yellow onions, halved from root to tip and sliced across into 1/4-inch strips (about 4 cups)

3 pounds large green beans or Romano beans, tipped and tailed

3 cups peeled, seeded and chopped ripe tomatoes, sterile-pack chopped tomatoes, or chopped canned American-style tomatoes (not in purée)

8 cloves garlic, smashed and peeled

TO FINISH

1/2 cup packed fresh sage leaves, cut across into strips and chopped

3 large cloves garlic, peeled and smashed, finely chopped

Kosher salt and freshly ground black pepper to taste

Heat the oil in a large heavy pot with a lid over low heat. Add the onions and cook uncovered, stirring from time to time, until soft and translucent, about 20 minutes.

Add the beans and toss until thoroughly coated with oil. Add the tomatoes and garlic. Cover and cook over the lowest heat for 5 hours.

continued

Uncover, bring to a boil and boil for 5 minutes. Reduce the heat to medium and stir in the "finishing" ingredients. The amount of salt will depend on the tomatoes used. Cook for 15 minutes.

Serve hot or cold or as a pasta sauce.

Makes 8 ample cups

Long-Cooked American Green Beans

In both New England and the South, green beans cooked with bacon are traditional. They are long cooked.

> 1/4 pound bacon (4 thick strips), cut across into 1/2-inch pieces
>
> 1 pound green beans, tipped and tailed
>
> Kosher salt and freshly ground black pepper to taste
>
> 1 1/2 tablespoons fresh sage leaves cut across into thin strips (optional)

Render the bacon in a medium pot over low heat. Add the beans and toss to coat with fat. Add 1 cup water. Bring to a boil. Reduce the heat, cover and simmer for 1 hour.

Most of the water should have evaporated; if not, bring back to a boil and cook it off. Season with salt and pepper to taste. Toss with the sage if desired. **Makes 2 2/3 cups**

Braised Wax Beans with Herbs

Serve this with roast chicken, fish, lamb or veal. The deglazing sauce from the meat mingles delectably with the juices of the vegetables.

> 1 tablespoon olive oil
>
> 1 small onion, thinly sliced (about 1 cup)
>
> 2 pounds wax beans, tipped and tailed
>
> 1 1/2 pounds plum tomatoes, cored and quartered lengthwise, cut crosswise in half if long
>
> 1/4 cup loosely packed chopped fresh lovage or 1/4 cup loosely packed chopped fresh parsley with either 1/2 teaspoon dried summer savory or 1/4 teaspoon dried Greek oregano
>
> 2 teaspoons kosher salt
>
> Freshly ground black pepper to taste

Heat the oil in a large deep skillet. Add the onions and cook over high heat until translucent. Add the beans. Toss and cook for 3 minutes. Reduce the heat to medium and cook for 10 minutes, stirring occasionally.

Add the tomatoes and ½ cup water. Bring to a boil. Cover, reduce the heat and simmer for 20 minutes. Add the herbs. Cover and cook at a low boil for 40 minutes. Add the salt and pepper and cook, uncovered, until most of the liquid has evaporated.

Makes 3 cups; serves 4 as a side dish

Szechwan Green Beans

The classic Chinese preparation would call for long beans, blanched in oil to soften the skin and evaporate the moisture inside. The older and tougher green beans one finds here in winter can be seamlessly substituted. In place of oil-blanching, I provide three other methods that achieve similar effects. My favorite is the microwave; it is the easiest (to prepare and clean up) and shrinks the vegetables least. Serve the beans hot or at room temperature.

2 scallions, trimmed and cut into 2-inch pieces

2 quarter-size slices peeled fresh ginger

6 cloves garlic, smashed and peeled

1 tablespoon soy sauce, preferably tamari

1 tablespoon rice wine vinegar

1 pound green beans, tipped and tailed

1 tablespoon canola oil

1/2 teaspoon hot red pepper flakes

Put the scallions, ginger and garlic in a food processor. Process until finely chopped. Set aside.

Combine the soy sauce and vinegar in a small bowl. Set aside.

Oven method: Preheat the oven to 500°F.

Toss the beans with 2 teaspoons of the oil. Arrange in a single layer on a baking sheet. Roast for 13 to 15 minutes, stirring every 5 minutes, until the skin is shriveled and browned. Set aside.

Heat a 12-inch skillet or wok over high heat. Add the remaining 1 teaspoon oil. When the pan is smoking, add the beans, scallion mixture and red pepper flakes and stir-fry for 1 minute. Add the soy mixture and stir-fry briefly until all the liquid is absorbed.

Stovetop method: Heat a 12-inch skillet or wok over high heat. Add the oil. When the pan is smoking, add the green beans. Stir-fry for 13 to 15 minutes, until the skin is shriveled and browned. Add the scallion mixture and red pepper flakes and stir-fry for 1 minute. Add the soy mixture and stir-fry briefly until all the liquid is absorbed.

Microwave method: Put the scallion mixture in a 14 x 11 x 2-inch dish. Add the oil and pepper flakes. Cook, uncovered, at 100% for 3 minutes. Remove from the oven and stir in the remaining ingredients. Cook, uncovered, at 100% for 15 minutes, stirring 4 or 5 times. Remove from the oven. **Makes 4 cups**

Green Bean Frappé

This is a fresh, light sauce good in summer with fish and fish pâtés.

1 1/2 pounds green beans

1/4 cup olive oil

Kosher salt and freshly ground black pepper to taste

Bring a large pot of salted water to a boil. Drop in the beans and cook, uncovered, until they are cooked but still slightly crisp. Drain well.

Purée the beans in a food processor until smooth. Force the mixture through a fine sieve. Stir in the olive oil, then add salt and pepper.

Serve immediately. **Makes enough to sauce 4 servings**

EATEN SHELLED: FRESH, DRIED AND CANNED

It is one of life's little annoyances that beans that are fairly easy to digest when young and eaten in their shells become a source of flatulence or discomfort to many when adult and shelled, whether fresh or dried. Fortunately, today there are pills that can be taken to reduce the problem. This needs to be done with the non-American varieties as well.

Canned shelled beans are available in many varieties. While cooking our own generally gives a better product, there is no doubt that canned beans are quick and convenient. I do use them occasionally. I don't use them if I need the cooking liquid to make a dish.

Some dried beans, like giant limas, need a good long soaking—overnight works for me. Others need only a briefer—three- to four-hour—bath. Some need no soaking at all. For help sorting all this out, see the Cook's Guide.

Corn and Black Bean Salad

This is an extremely attractive salad—lots of color—that makes a wonderful addition to a late summer buffet. It goes well with barbecued and grilled fish and chicken, and it makes a splendid starter. It is also a complete protein.

1 cup fresh corn kernels, blanched (see the Cook's Guide, page 572)

1 cup canned black beans, rinsed and drained, or 1 cup cooked black beans

1 large ripe tomato, cored and cut into $1/4$-inch dice (about 1 cup)

$1/3$ cup finely diced onion

1 cup lightly packed cilantro leaves, coarsely chopped

1 to 2 jalapeño peppers (fresh or canned), seeded and very finely chopped

2 tablespoons fresh lime juice

2 tablespoons olive oil

1 teaspoon kosher salt, or more if using home-cooked beans

Freshly ground black pepper to taste

Combine all the ingredients in a serving bowl and toss well. Allow to stand for 30 minutes.

Taste and adjust the seasoning if necessary. Serve. **Makes 3$1/4$ cups**

Black Bean Salad

Unlike the prior salad, this one has no tomato and can be made in the winter.

1 cup cooked black beans or canned black beans, rinsed and drained

$1/4$ cup peeled celery, cut into $1/4$-inch-wide lengths, then across into $1/4$-inch diagonal pieces

$1/4$ cup ($1/4$-inch dice) onion

$1/4$ cup ($1/4$-inch dice) green bell pepper

2 tablespoons chopped fresh dill

2 tablespoons fresh lime juice

$1/2$ teaspoon kosher salt

Freshly ground black pepper to taste

Put all the ingredients into a bowl and toss to combine. Let stand for 20 to 30 minutes.

Toss and taste for seasonings before serving. **Makes 1$3/4$ cups**

Fresh Cranberry Bean Soup

Bean soups are the ones that give soup a he-man reputation. This small lady loves them.

Fresh shelling beans in the pod and the last of the summer's tomatoes usually are plentiful at the same time. If the beans are available and good tomatoes are not, use the tomato base. When cooked, the cranberry beans or other fresh beans are creamy without being floury. If other fresh beans are findable, they could be substituted, but I wouldn't waste fresh flageolets (small shelled French green beans) on this. Top the soup with a drizzle of very good olive oil.

3 tablespoons olive oil

1 medium onion, cut into $1/2$-inch dice (about 1 cup)

2$1/2$ pounds ripe tomatoes, cored and cut into 1-inch cubes, or 5 cups Chunky Tomato Base (page 460) or sterile-pack chopped tomatoes

1 pound fresh cranberry beans, shelled

4 leaves fresh holy basil or Italian basil, minced

2 leaves fresh sage, minced, or a pinch of dried

1 teaspoon minced fresh oregano or $1/4$ teaspoon dried

1 teaspoon minced fresh lemon thyme

1 1/2 teaspoons kosher salt

Very good olive oil for serving

Freshly ground black pepper to taste

In a medium saucepan, warm the olive oil over low heat. Stir in the onion. Cook, stirring occasionally, for 12 minutes, or until translucent.

Raise the heat and stir in the fresh tomatoes, if using. Bring to a boil; lower the heat and simmer, stirring occasionally, for 20 minutes, or until the tomatoes are soft and liquid. Or, raise the heat, stir in the tomato base or sterile-pack tomatoes and bring to a boil.

Stir in the beans and 1¾ cups water. Bring to a boil. Lower the heat and simmer for 10 minutes. If using dried herbs, stir them in now. In either case, simmer for another 10 minutes.

If using fresh herbs, stir them in and simmer for 1 minute. Season with the salt. Remove from the heat and let rest for at least 30 minutes before serving. I like it at this temperature. If you insist, reheat, stirring to be sure it doesn't stick.

Serve the soup drizzled with good olive oil and a grind of black pepper.

Makes 6 cups; serves 4 generously as a first course

Cod Soup with Fresh Cranberry Beans

This soup can be made a lighter dish without the cranberry beans, with the addition of cucumber.

5 cups Basic Fish Stock (page 505)

1 cup dry white wine

1 pound small waxy new potatoes, scrubbed and cut in half

2 medium shallots, minced

1¾ pounds fresh cranberry beans, shelled, or 1 medium hothouse cucumber, peeled and cut across into 1/2-inch slices

1/2 pound peas in the pod, shelled (about 2/3 cup)

Four 7-ounce cod fillets, pinbones removed

1 small bunch dill, tough stems removed, minced

Kosher salt to taste

In a medium-large saucepan, bring the stock and wine to a boil. Stir in the potatoes, shallots and, if using, the beans. Return to a boil. Lower the heat and simmer for 8 minutes. If using the cucumber, stir it in now. Simmer for 5 minutes longer.

Stir in the peas and simmer for 2 minutes. Add the fish and bring to a boil. Lower the heat and simmer for 6 minutes. Stir in the dill and season with salt.

Makes 10 cups; serves 5 to 6 as a main course

Doug Rodriguez's Black Bean Soup

This is my very favorite black bean soup, from a wonderful chef. He graciously let me use it, though he should really have asked his Cuban mother—whose recipe it originally was.

Notice that the beans are not soaked first or parboiled. This is very typical of Cuban and Central American soups.

1 pound dried black beans

2 bay leaves

1 cup extra-virgin olive oil

2 large red bell peppers, cored, seeded, deribbed and cut into 1/4-inch dice

2 medium shallots, coarsely chopped

2 medium onions, coarsely chopped

8 medium cloves garlic, smashed, peeled and coarsely chopped

1 tablespoon ground cumin

continued

2 tablespoons dried oregano

2 tablespoons chopped fresh oregano

1 1/2 tablespoons sugar, or to taste

2 tablespoons kosher salt, or to taste

FOR SERVING

1 medium red onion, thinly sliced

1 cup sour cream (optional)

In a medium stockpot, bring 12 cups water, the beans and bay leaves to a boil. Lower the heat and simmer, stirring frequently, for 2 hours and 30 minutes to 3 hours, until the beans are tender. Add more water if necessary to keep the beans covered.

Meanwhile, in a medium frying pan, heat the oil over medium heat. Stir in the peppers, shallots and onions. Cook, stirring frequently, for 8 minutes, or until the onions are translucent. Stir in the garlic, cumin and dried and fresh oregano and cook for 2 minutes. Remove from the heat and allow to cool slightly. Purée in a blender.

When the beans are almost done, stir in the purée, sugar and salt. Continue to simmer until the beans are very tender, another 20 to 30 minutes. Adjust the seasonings.

Serve with the sliced red onion and sour cream, if desired, on the side.

Makes 10 cups; serves 8 to 10 as a first course

Curried Lima Beans

I had always thought that lima beans were a small version of favas. It turns out that they are a true (*Phaseolus*) bean, also American. Limas should be small to be tender; otherwise their skin will be tough. My favorites are Fordhooks, originating at the farm of the same name. The frozen ones are usually perfectly satisfactory.

3 1/2 cups fresh baby lima beans or two 10-ounce packages frozen baby lima beans, defrosted in a sieve under warm running water and drained

4 tablespoons unsalted butter

1 medium onion, chopped

4 teaspoons curry powder

4 teaspoons fresh lemon juice

1/4 cup plain nonfat yogurt

1 tablespoon kosher salt

Freshly ground black pepper to taste

Place 1 cup water and the lima beans in a medium saucepan. Bring to a boil over high heat. Cover, reduce the heat to low and cook for 6 minutes. Drain.

While the lima beans are cooking, melt the butter in a medium saucepan. Stir in the onion and curry powder. Cook, stirring occasionally, until the onion is soft, about 3 minutes.

Stir the lima beans into the onion mixture. Reduce the heat to low and stir in the remaining ingredients. **Serves 4 as a side dish**

Succotash

Succotash is the New England version of the all-in-one-pot stew. Winter succotashes were made with dried corn and dried lima beans. Summer succotashes were made with fresh kernels scraped off the cob and tiny, sweet beans.

1 tablespoon unsalted butter

1/2 teaspoon minced garlic

3 1/2 cups fresh baby lima beans or two 10-ounce packages frozen baby lima beans, defrosted in a sieve under warm running water and drained

1 cup fresh corn kernels (cut from 2 medium ears of corn)

1 cup heavy cream, or as needed

2 tablespoons chopped fresh chives

3/4 teaspoon kosher salt

Freshly ground black pepper to taste

1 1/2 tablespoons fresh lemon juice

Heat the butter in a large skillet over medium heat. Add the garlic and cook for about 30 seconds. Add the lima beans, corn and cream. Simmer over low heat for 10 minutes.

Stir in the chives, salt, pepper and lemon juice. Serve immediately or let the flavors mellow overnight in the refrigerator. Reheat before serving; if the mixture is too thick, add a little more cream. **Makes 4 2/3 cups**

Curry Stew with Lamb and Cranberry Beans

An almost irresistible stew to delight the hearty of appetite. The recipe can easily be doubled and if its filling qualities are doubted, a side of rice can be added.

2 tablespoons canola oil

1 pound lamb stew meat, cut into 1/2-inch dice (about 2 1/2 cups)

1 medium onion, cut into 1/4-inch dice (about 1 cup)

4 cloves garlic, smashed, peeled and minced

2 tablespoons curry powder

3 1/2 pounds fresh cranberry beans, shelled (about 5 cups)

1 cup coconut milk

2 tablespoons tamarind paste

1 1/2 teaspoons kosher salt

Freshly ground black pepper to taste

Chopped cilantro (optional)

Heat the oil in a medium saucepan over high heat. Add the lamb, in 2 batches if necessary, and brown lightly. (Return all the lamb to the pan if necessary.) Add the onion, reduce the heat to medium and cook until translucent, about 3 minutes. Add the garlic. Cook for 1 minute. Add 1 cup water, bring to a boil and cover. Reduce the heat and simmer for 45 minutes.

Stir in the curry powder and beans. Bring to a boil. Cover, reduce the heat and simmer for 25 minutes, stirring occasionally.

Add the coconut milk, tamarind paste, salt and pepper. Simmer, uncovered, for 10 minutes. Top with chopped cilantro before serving, if desired. **Makes 6 cups; serves 4 as a main course**

Giant Lima Beans Simmered with Onion and Garlic

Good with a green salad of any sort or as a side to roasted or grilled meats.

1 medium white onion, cut into chunks (about 1 cup)

2 large cloves garlic, smashed and peeled

2 tablespoons olive oil

2 cups dried giant lima beans (gigantes) or corona beans, soaked

3 cups Basic Chicken Stock (page 501) or commercial chicken broth, or as needed

2 teaspoons kosher salt

1 large pinch dried sage, crumbled

1/2 teaspoon dried thyme

Freshly ground black pepper to taste

Combine the onion and garlic in a food processor and pulse until the onion is very finely chopped.

continued

Heat the olive oil in a heavy 2- to 3-quart saucepan. Add the onion mixture and cook until translucent. Drain the beans and add to the pan. Add the chicken stock and bring to a boil. Lower the heat to a simmer. Cook, uncovered, until the beans are tender, about 2 hours. Keep an eye on the beans as they cook; there should always be enough liquid to cover them. Add more broth or water as necessary.

Drain the beans; reserve the liquid. Return the liquid to the pan and stir in the salt, sage and thyme. Bring to a boil and cook until reduced by about one-third. Add the beans and cook a minute or two (or add the beans, cool and refrigerate overnight). Stir in pepper to taste. Serve at room temperature or chilled.

Makes 3 1/2 cups

Seafood Succotash

Yes, there are a lot of beans—I have never found them to go begging. If an even more lavish version of this New Age succotash is wanted, use two lobsters. Serve with soupspoons and seafood forks. Crusty bread is almost a necessity.

> 6 ears corn, shucked and silk removed
>
> 3 tablespoons unsalted butter
>
> 1 1/2 teaspoons minced garlic
>
> Six 10-ounce packages frozen baby lima beans, thawed and drained in a sieve under warm running water, or 9 cups shelled fresh lima beans
>
> 3 cups heavy cream
>
> 6 tablespoons chopped fresh chives
>
> 2 1/4 teaspoons kosher salt
>
> Freshly ground black pepper to taste
>
> 4 1/2 tablespoons fresh lemon juice

FOR THE SEAFOOD

> One 1 1/2-pound live lobster
>
> 1 tablespoon unsalted butter
>
> 1 tablespoon olive oil
>
> 1/2 teaspoon minced garlic
>
> 12 large shrimp, peeled but tails left on
>
> 2 tablespoons bourbon
>
> 4 cups peeled, cored, seeded and roughly chopped tomatoes
>
> 1/2 cup chopped fresh parsley
>
> 1 1/2 to 2 teaspoons kosher salt
>
> Freshly ground black pepper
>
> Pinch of cayenne pepper
>
> 18 mussels, well scrubbed, debearded if need be

Using a sharp knife, scrape all the kernels from the corncobs into a bowl. Set aside.

Heat the butter in a large deep skillet over medium heat. Add the garlic and cook for about 30 seconds. Add the lima beans, corn and cream. Simmer over low heat for about 10 minutes. Stir in the chives, then season with salt, pepper and lemon juice. Remove from the heat and let sit while you prepare the seafood. (The succotash can be refrigerated for up to a day.)

Cut the lobster into 16 pieces as follows (or ask the fishmonger to do it). (If you absolutely must, kill the lobster before cutting it up by plunging it in a large pot of boiling water for 2 minutes. Drain and rinse briefly under cold water.) Place the lobster on its stomach, holding it securely against your work surface. With a large cook's knife, cut the tail from the body in a single hard, downward motion. (If your knife isn't heavy enough, tap it firmly with a hammer.) Cut the tail in half lengthwise. Cut each half crosswise into 4 pieces. Set aside.

Grasp the lobster body firmly in one hand and grasp a claw securely in the other hand. Twist and pull off the claw. Repeat with the other claw. Cut off the very end of each claw (the "knuckle") if necessary—it won't always come away with the claw. Break the claw at the joint into two pieces. Remove the plug or band holding the claws together, then cut each claw in half crosswise.

Finally, place the lobster body bottom up on the work surface. Place your knife in position to split the lobster in half lengthwise. Using a hammer, tap on the top of the knife to cut the lobster evenly in half. Remove and discard the stomach and the small yellow sac.

Heat the butter and oil in a large skillet. When hot, add the garlic, lobster and shrimp. Cook, stirring or shaking the pan often, for about 1 minute. Pour on the bourbon and carefully ignite. When the flames die down, remove the shellfish to a plate.

Add the tomatoes, parsley, salt, a generous amount of black pepper and the cayenne to the pan. Cover and cook over high heat for about 3 minutes, or until the tomatoes begin to give off liquid.

Add the mussels, lobster and shrimp with any liquid that has accumulated on the plate. Cover the pan and cook for about 2 minutes, shaking the pan occasionally, until the mussels have opened. Taste the sauce and season with more salt and pepper if necessary.

Meanwhile, reheat the lima and corn mixture to simmering. Spoon some succotash into a ring on each plate. Spoon the seafood mixture into the center. **Serves 8 as a side dish**

Zarela Martinez's Puréed Black Beans
Frijoles Negros Colados

Zarela is a charming woman, an excellent cook, a writer of fine cookbooks and the owner of a fabulous restaurant in New York. If that isn't enough, one of her sons is also a fine chef.

Zarela says: "This is an exciting variation on the theme of refried beans. The taste immediately brings Oaxaca to my mind—the fragrant, anise-y avocado leaves and the delicate spiciness of the chilies are so characteristic. Made with oil, this is an excellent vegetarian dish. However, I usually use home-rendered lard for deeper flavor."

1 pound dried black beans

1 whole head garlic, unpeeled

4 medium onions, 1 left unpeeled

2 teaspoons to 1 tablespoon kosher salt, or to taste

3 árbol chilies, stemmed

12 dried avocado leaves (see the Cook's Guide, page 535)

1/2 cup lard (preferably home-rendered) or vegetable oil

Put the (unsoaked) beans, garlic and unpeeled onion in a large saucepan. Pour in enough water to cover by 2 inches. Bring to a boil. Lower the heat to simmering. Cover and cook for 1 hour and 30 minutes.

Add the salt and cook until the beans are tender, about 30 minutes. Remove the onion and garlic. Let the beans cool in the cooking liquid.

Meanwhile, griddle-roast the chilies (see page 626). Place in a small bowl and cover well with boiling water. Let soak for 20 minutes.

continued

Lightly toast the avocado leaves on the hot griddle (just a few seconds, until the aroma is released). Crumble when cool enough to handle; set aside.

Drain the beans, reserving about 1½ cups of the cooking liquid. Drain the soaked chilies. Working in batches as necessary, purée the beans, chilies and avocado leaves together in a blender, adding enough of the reserved cooking liquid to facilitate blending. The mixture should be about the consistency of peanut butter.

Alternatively, process in a food processor, adding enough liquid to achieve the right consistency. With a wooden spoon or pusher, force the mixture through a medium-mesh sieve into a bowl; discard any fibrous parts that will not go through.

Cut the remaining 3 onions into thin slices. In a large heavy saucepan or Dutch oven, heat the lard over medium-high heat until rippling. Add the onions. Cook, stirring frequently, until they are well browned, about 8 minutes; do not let scorch. Scoop out and discard the onions, letting as much fat as possible drain back into the pan. Add the puréed beans to the seasoned fat, stirring vigorously to mix. Reduce the heat to low and cook, covered, for 30 minutes, stirring frequently to prevent sticking.

Makes 4½ cups

Basic Boston Baked Beans

Nobody ever said Bostonians weren't frugal. Here we see how little of a really cheap meat they can use. It still tastes delicious. The more spendthrift of us can use this as a side dish rather than a main course. These "baked" beans can also be prepared on the stovetop or in a slow cooker (see the Cook's Guide, page 541).

1 pound dried navy beans, soaked

½ pound salt pork

1 medium onion, diced

⅓ cup packed brown sugar

⅓ cup molasses

3 tablespoons pure maple syrup

1 tablespoon dry mustard

Kosher salt to taste

Preheat the oven to 250°F.

Drain the beans and put them in a pot large enough to hold them comfortably. Pour in enough water to cover by 2 inches. Bring to a boil.

Meanwhile, cut half the salt pork into ¼-inch dice. Slice the remaining salt pork ¼ inch thick. Set aside.

Remove the beans from the heat and scoop them into a covered 1½-quart casserole; set the liquid aside. Stir in the diced salt pork and onion. Whisk the brown sugar, molasses, maple syrup and mustard into the bean water, then pour over the beans. Lay the slices of salt pork over the top. Cover and bake for 4 hours.

Continue baking the beans, adding hot water if necessary to keep them covered, until tender, 1 to 2 hours. Season with salt.

Makes 7 cups; serves about 8 as a side dish

Pink Beans

These are unusual and delicious. It is always worth making a whole recipe, as any leftovers can be the basis of the bean cakes or feijoada that follow. All of the pink bean recipes were developed with the help of Kathi Long, who worked with me for several years and is a very good cook.

One 1-pound bag dried pink beans, soaked

4 cups Basic Chicken Stock (page 501) or
   Vegetable Broth (page 506)

2 cups diced canned or sterile-pack tomatoes

2 medium onions, finely diced

4 medium cloves garlic, smashed and peeled,
   plus 4 medium cloves garlic, smashed,
   peeled and finely minced

1 1/4 cups peeled and finely diced celery

1/2 cup diced carrots (1/4-inch cubes)

1 tablespoon kosher salt

1 tablespoon tarragon vinegar or
   white wine vinegar

2 teaspoons pure chili powder

1/2 teaspoon ground cumin

Scant 1/4 teaspoon freshly ground black pepper

3 to 4 drops hot red pepper sauce

Drain the beans and put in a 4-quart pot. Add the chicken stock and tomatoes. Bring to a boil, then reduce the heat to a simmer. Add the onions and the smashed whole garlic cloves. Cook for 3 hours, topping off with water if necessary to keep the beans submerged.

Add the celery, carrots, minced garlic, salt, vinegar, chili powder, cumin, black pepper and hot pepper sauce. Cook until the vegetables are tender, about 20 minutes.

Makes about 9 cups; serves 8 as a side dish

Panfried Bean Cakes

Make these with any amount of pink beans on hand. A full recipe will make about thirty cakes. Serve two or three per person for a main course, one for a first course.

1 recipe Pink Beans (page 24)

Vegetable oil

Sour cream

Fresh Tomato Mint Salsa
   (made with cilantro; page 114)

Cilantro sprigs

Drain the beans thoroughly (save the liquid for soup). Spread the beans out on a baking sheet to dry and cool.

Working with about 2 cups at a time, coarsely grind the beans in a food processor. Cover and refrigerate.

When chilled, form the bean mixture into 3-inch cakes, using about 1/4 cup for each.

Pour enough oil into a large skillet to coat the bottom. Heat over medium heat until rippling. Add as many cakes as fit without touching and cook, turning once, until browned on both sides, about 3 minutes on each side. Slip the spatula completely under each cake before turning to prevent the cake from falling apart.

Serve warm, topping each cake with a dollop of sour cream, a spoonful of salsa and a sprig of cilantro.

Bean Cakes with Crab or Shrimp
After grinding the beans, stir in 1/4 cup diced cooked shrimp or lump crabmeat, picked over for shells and cartilage, per cup of beans. Proceed as above.

Pink Bean Feijoada over Spicy Rice

No Brazilian would recognize this—no pig's ears, for one thing—but I think it is delicious.

1 recipe Pink Beans (page 24)

FOR THE RICE

1 onion, chopped

3 cloves garlic, smashed, peeled and minced or put through a press

2 tablespoons olive oil

1 tablespoon unsalted butter

2 tomatoes, peeled, cored and coarsely chopped

2¹/₂ cups cooked brown rice

SAUCE

Juice of 1 lemon

2 tomatoes, peeled

1 small onion, quartered

2 cloves garlic, smashed and peeled

1 teaspoon chili sauce

1 fresh hot green chili (optional)

¹/₄ cup wine vinegar or cider vinegar

Kosher salt to taste

When the pink beans are almost cooked, make the rice: Sauté the onion and garlic in the olive oil and butter in a large skillet until the onion is tender and golden. Add the tomatoes and simmer for a few minutes, then stir in the cooked rice and mix well. Keep warm over low heat until ready to serve (or reheat over medium heat shortly before serving).

Just before serving, put the sauce ingredients in a blender and liquefy. Add some bean cooking liquid to make a smooth sauce.

Serve the beans and rice side by side, spooning some of the sauce over the rice.
Serves 6 to 8 as a main course

Large Lima Beans with Garlic and Fennel

For many years, I thought that gigantes were a large fava bean. When I checked with the invaluable Aglaia Kremezi, the author of several books on Greek cooking, a fine photographer and a former magazine editor, I found that the beans are actually giant (gigante) lima beans. They can be used fresh or dried, but dried is more common. I love their meaty flavor and rich texture, which serves them so well all over Greece during Lent, when meat is not eaten. Any time I find them on a menu, I will have a dish as a first course.

Here is a recipe from Aglaia, who sometimes makes these beans with chopped fresh dill instead of the fennel.

1 pound giant lima beans (gigantes), soaked

2 tablespoons dried oregano

²/₃ to 1 cup olive oil, to taste

2 medium onions, sliced

³/₄ cup finely diced fennel, plus ¹/₄ cup finely chopped fennel fronds

¹/₂ to 1 teaspooon finely chopped fresh chili pepper or ¹/₃ to ¹/₂ teaspoon hot red pepper flakes, to taste

6 cloves garlic, smashed, peeled and coarsely chopped

1 cup dry white wine

1 tablespoon dry mustard

Sea salt to taste

Drain the beans and put in a pot. Cover with cold water by 2 inches and bring to a boil. Skim the foam from the surface, reduce the heat to simmering and sprinkle with 1 tablespoon oregano. Simmer until the beans start to become tender, about 1 hour. Drain the beans; reserve the liquid.

Preheat the oven to 300°F.

In a large skillet, heat the olive oil over medium heat. Add the onions, diced fennel, and chili pepper or pepper flakes. Cook until the onions are softened, about 5 minutes. Remove from the heat.

Stir the garlic, wine, mustard, the remaining 1 tablespoon oregano and the beans into the onions. Mix well and season with salt. Scrape into a covered earthenware or glass casserole that holds the beans comfortably. Add enough of the bean liquid to cover the beans, about 1½ cups; reserve the remaining liquid.

Cover and bake until the beans are tender and most of the liquid has been absorbed, about 1 hour. Add more bean cooking liquid if all the liquid is absorbed before the beans are tender.

Sprinkle the chopped fennel fronds over the beans and serve.

Serves 6 generously as a first course or a side dish

Giant Lima Bean Salad with Mexican Flavors

Taste the cilantro before adding it to the salad. When testing this, I had a bunch of cilantro with huge leaves and virtually no flavor.

> **1 cup giant lima beans (gigantes), soaked, cooked and drained**
>
> **2 tablespoons olive oil**
>
> **1 to 2 serrano peppers, seeded and finely chopped**
>
> **Handful of chopped cilantro**
>
> **Kosher salt to taste**

In a serving bowl, toss the beans, olive oil, serranos and cilantro together. Add salt to taste. Let stand at room temperature about 30 minutes.

Toss the salad and taste again for seasoning before serving. **Makes about 3 cups**

Cactus Pads (Nopales)

Now that there are Hispanic groceries all over the country, nopales are fairly easy to find. I found them in a regular supermarket. Like everything else, they are seasonal.

Turn to **CACTUS PADS** in the Cook's Guide for how-tos.

Cactus Pad Salad

This dish can be served warm, at room temperature or chilled. It will be even better served cold the day after it is made. It is very much like a string bean salad, which is flavored the same way and found throughout Chile.

FOR THE COOKING LIQUID

1 medium onion, peeled and halved

2 cloves garlic, peeled

10 large cilantro sprigs

1 tablespoon kosher salt

1 pound (about 5) cactus pads, rough ends trimmed and spines removed (see the Cook's Guide, page 559), cut across into 1/4-inch strips

SEASONINGS

About 1/2 cup finely diced white onion

1 medium tomato, cored and cut into 1/4-inch dice (about 3/4 cup)

1 ounce cilantro leaves and small tender stems, chopped medium fine (about 1/2 cup)

2 tablespoons olive oil

1 teaspoon kosher salt

FOR SERVING

1/2 lime per person

In a large pot, combine 9 cups water, the onion, garlic, cilantro and salt. Bring to a boil, then reduce to a low boil and cook for 20 minutes.

Add the cactus pads. Continue to boil gently for 20 minutes, or until the strips are cooked through.

Drain and toss with the seasoning ingredients. Serve cold or warm, with a ½ lime for each eater. **Makes 4 cups**

Corn

Fresh Corn, Cornmeal, Hominy, Grits and Popcorn

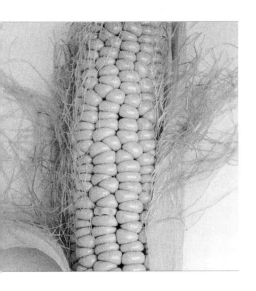

A steaming ear of corn, butter melting into its crevices and lightly sprinkled with salt, is surely the most iconographic of American foods. While many American foods have made it to the big time on world tables, corn has remained primarily American. In recent years, a cautious sprinkling of kernels has found its way into fancy French salads. Of course, the Italians now think that cornmeal is their property—as in polenta. I will admit that it is a nicer word than "mush"; but polenta doesn't predate mush as a dish made with corn—polenta made with millet, yes, it is earlier.

Corn is truly a grass and a grain, not a vegetable. This has led to a lot of the confusion in Europe over its name and to an actual distaste for what is one of the bounties of the late summer garden. To Europeans, all grains are corn. For our corn, the Europeans use the name "maize," which is fairly close to the American Indian name and the botanical name. For them maize is primarily cattle feed. When Eliza Leslie wrote a pamphlet on "Indian meal" to aid charity to Ireland during the potato famine and advocated that the Irish replace the potato—another American food—with corn, she was disdained.

While all corn is the same species, there are basically six different types—sweet corn, flour (soft or squaw) corn, dent corn, popcorn, Chinese miniature corn and flint—and these may come in a variety of colors.

In any case, the corn we eat is a hybrid. The colorful corn, red, almost black and blue, that we tend to decorate with at Thanksgiving is close to the original Central American corn.

I don't grow corn. I used to, but too many times, the morning after the evening I decided it would be perfect for picking the next day, I would go out and find the cobs picked, stripped of their husks and neatly piled up, all facing in the same direction—raccoons! No fence, even electric, kept them at bay. Now, I buy from local farm stands that get fresh supplies every few hours. I don't buy the hyper-sweet hybrid corn. I find it unpleasant. I miss some of the old-fashioned varieties of my childhood. I can only hope that a change in the tide of fashion and preservationist groups will return us to better corn. My preference is for ears with small white niblets. My husband, on the other hand, prefers large yellow kernels on big ears. I usually buy some of each. If I cook more than is eaten, I cut off the niblets and have a perfect start on a salad or soup the next day.

I am often asked how to tell if corn is good to buy. I don't pull down the husk to look—unfair to the market. I note whether the silk at the top is luxuriant and glossy; dry is a bad sign. I pick up the ear to see if it seems heavy for its size, then pinch the silk end lightly to see if the husk is well filled out with corn. Sometimes I am wrong, but I have a pretty good track record.

When the Spaniards and Portuguese came to Central and South America, they found vines of beans growing around the corn stalks. The practice made the best use of the land, but it is also an ideal nutritional combination that is perpetuated to this day in dishes like corn tacos with beans. Corn is at its best freshly picked in summer. In winter, substitute canned corn niblets, which I find better than the frozen.

Corn is also sold as hominy, kernels that have been treated with lye so that the white insides pop out, and grits, which are dried and ground hominy (the best is stone ground with flecks of black—the germ). Corn flour, including masa, is used for tortillas, and cornstarch is an all-purpose thickener.

The various forms of corn go well with the other Central American ingredients, such as tomatoes, beans, achiote and both sweet and chili peppers.

This chapter is divided into two sections: corn and dried corn, the latter sometimes reconstituted (popcorn, cornmeal, grits and hominy). The soufflé is made with both cornmeal and real corn.

Butters may be flavored, such as those on pages 35 and 443. And the ears are very nice if the husks are peeled back and the butter spread on, then the husks replaced and tied with string before grilling.

Turn to **CORN** in the Cook's Guide
for how-tos and to the Index for more recipes.

Corn Fritters

These slightly sweet, all-American fritters are delicious. Serve with Plum Tomato Purée (page 459), Tartar Sauce (page 457) or Tomato Cranberry Salsa (page 114). While the recipe seems to make a great deal, I find that they disappear rapidly. However, the recipe can be halved.

4 medium ears corn, shucked and silk removed

2 tablespoons sugar

2 teaspoons kosher salt

Pinch of sweet paprika

Freshly ground black pepper to taste

3 large eggs, separated

¼ cup sifted all-purpose flour

½ teaspoon baking powder

3 cups vegetable oil

Run a sharp knife lengthwise through each line of kernels to score them. Grate the corn from the cob or cut off the kernels with a very sharp knife. If the corn is grated or very young and fresh, it can be left raw. Otherwise, place the cut kernels in a sieve and dip in boiling water for 30 seconds; drain.

In a large bowl, mash the corn lightly with a potato masher until the milky liquid is exuded. Add the sugar, salt, paprika and pepper, then add the egg yolks, flour and baking powder; stir to combine. Beat the egg whites until stiff. Fold into the corn mixture.

Heat the vegetable oil to 375°F in a large deep skillet. Drop the batter into the oil by the tablespoonful, frying only as many spoonfuls at a time as will float in a single layer without touching. Fry until the fritters are golden brown. Remove with a slotted spoon to paper towels to drain. Serve hot. **Makes 25 to 30 fritters**

Mini Corn Crêpes

Each mouthful of these fabulous little crêpes is a blend of crispy edges, creamy center and luscious sweet corn flavor. Be sure to use the freshest corn available. Canned creamed corn just will not do.

These crêpes are also very versatile. Arranged five on a plate and topped with queso blanco, mild chèvre or American large-curd cottage cheese and sour cream, they are an elegant first course. The same combination on single crêpes morphs them into an hors d'oeuvre. Change the topping from savory to sweet, and the crêpes become a delicious twist on the traditional breakfast pancake or a light dessert. For dessert, try the curry variation that follows. The same peach topping and/or a little whipped cream would not be amiss.

2 cups fresh creamed corn (see Note)

¾ cup heavy cream

¾ cup milk

5 large eggs

¾ cup all-purpose flour

½ teaspoon sugar

1 teaspoon kosher salt

2 scant teaspoons baking soda

4 tablespoons unsalted butter, melted

CHUNKY PEACH SAUCE

3 large or 4 medium ripe peaches, peeled, pitted and diced

2 to 3 tablespoons sugar, depending on sweetness of peaches

3 tablespoons unsalted butter, more if needed

In a mixing bowl, combine the creamed corn, cream, milk, eggs, flour, sugar, salt, baking soda and melted butter. Whisk until the flour is no longer visible. (Makes 4½ cups batter)

For the sauce, put the peaches and sugar in a saucepan and cook over low heat, stirring occasionally, until the sugar dissolves. Continue to cook until the peaches release their juices and the sauce is warm. Cover the pan and keep warm.

Line a baking sheet or ovenproof plate with parchment paper.

Melt ½ tablespoon butter in a large skillet over low heat. Drop the batter a tablespoon at a time into the pan. The batter will run slightly and form crêpes that are more oval than round. Cook for 3 minutes. The crêpes will be slightly puffed and lightly browned on the bottom. Flip the crêpes and cook the other side for 3 minutes. Remove the cooked crêpes to the baking sheet or plate. Keep warm, lightly covered with a kitchen towel or in a 200°F oven, while cooking the rest, adding more butter to the pan as necessary. (If the butter gets brown, pour it out and use fresh.) Keep the crêpes warm until ready to serve. (The crêpes can be made ahead of time and reheated in a 350°F oven for 5 minutes, or until warmed through.)

Makes approximately 50 mini crêpes; serves 8 to 10 as a first course

NOTE: *To make fresh creamed corn:* Remove the pulp from as many ears of corn as you'd like to cream (see the Cook's Guide, page 573; each medium ear of corn will yield a scant ¼ cup pulp). Leave the skin of the kernels on the cobs and discard. *Alternatively,* grate the corn against the large-hole side of a box grater. This method results in a smoother consistency but slightly less volume. The creamed corn can be used as is since it cooks so quickly.

Curry Corn Crêpes

Curry powder adds an elusive, warm spiciness to this dessert version of the corn crêpes. Add ¼ cup packed brown sugar and a scant ¼ teaspoon curry powder to the batter. Make the crêpes as in the basic recipe. Serve the warm crêpes topped with the warm sauce and whipped cream.

Makes approximately 50 mini crêpes; serves 8 to 10 as a first course

Southwestern Mini Corn Crêpes

Corn kernels that are fresh, young and tender will cook through in the same short amount of time it takes to cook the crêpes, so you can add them to the batter raw. If the corn is less fresh, cook it briefly with the peppers before adding to the batter.

Increase the salt to 2 teaspoons and add it, along with freshly ground black pepper to taste, to the batter. Cook ½ cup chopped red bell pepper and 2½ tablespoons finely chopped seeded jalapeño pepper in ½ teaspoon vegetable oil or unsalted butter for 1 minute. Add to the batter, along with ½ cup fresh corn kernels, and stir to distribute evenly.

Preheat the broiler. Line a baking pan with parchment.

Cook the crêpes as instructed in the basic recipe, removing them to the parchment as they are ready. Just before serving, top each crêpe with a rounded ¼ teaspoon of grated manchego cheese (you will need about ½ pound cheese). Place the baking pan under the broiler until the cheese is just melted. Serve immediately.

Makes 60 to 65 mini crêpes; serves 10 as a first course

Velvet Corn Soup

This is by now a regular Chinese-American soup. I have never known a Chinese cook to make it at home with anything other than canned corn, but if purism is the order of the day, a fresh purée can be made. Smithfield ham comes closest to the taste and texture of Chinese ham. Prosciutto or serrano ham cut ⅛ inch thick makes a good substitute.

2 tablespoons canola oil

2¹/₂ teaspoons chopped peeled fresh ginger

2 tablespoons chopped scallions
(green and white parts), plus additional
for topping

2 ounces ham, coarsely chopped
(about 6 tablespoons)

2 tablespoons Chinese rice wine
or dry sherry

4 cups Basic Chicken Stock (page 501),
Roasted Chicken Stock (page 502) or
commercial chicken broth

1²/₃ cups fresh creamed corn (page 33)
or one 15-ounce can creamed corn

4 teaspoons kosher salt (less if using a salty ham
such as Smithfield or Chinese)

1 teaspoon rice wine vinegar

2 teaspoons toasted sesame oil

1 tablespoon cornstarch

2 egg whites

In a large saucepan, warm the oil over medium heat. Add the ginger and scallions and cook for 30 seconds, or until fragrant but not brown. Add the ham and cook until it changes color. Add the rice wine and let it sizzle and evaporate slightly. Stir in the stock and corn. Bring to a boil.

Stir in the salt, rice wine vinegar and sesame oil and bring back to a boil. Meanwhile, dissolve the cornstarch in 2 tablespoons water to make a slurry. When the soup comes to a boil, pour in the slurry and boil, stirring for 1 minute. The soup will thicken.

Lightly whisk the egg whites in a bowl to break them up, but not until they become frothy. Position the bowl a few inches above the saucepan and pour the whites into the soup in a steady spiral. Immediately turn off the heat and gently stir up once from the bottom. The egg whites will "flower" attractively.

Ladle the soup into bowls and top with scallions. **Makes 6 cups**

Corn Chowder

This is a satisfying American classic. Served over common crackers, it makes a meal.

1 pound floury potatoes, peeled and
cut into ¹/₃-inch dice

1 medium red bell pepper, cored, deribbed,
and seeded, cut into ¹/₄-inch dice

1 medium green bell pepper, cored,
deribbed and seeded, cut into ¹/₄-inch dice

1 small onion, chopped

2 cups fresh corn kernels
(cut from 4 medium ears corn)

4 scallions, trimmed and thinly sliced

2 stalks celery, peeled and thinly sliced

1¹/₂ cups milk

¹/₂ cup heavy cream

1 tablespoon kosher salt

3 drops hot red pepper sauce

Freshly ground black pepper to taste

2 tablespoons unsalted butter
(optional)

Place the potatoes, bell peppers, onion and 1 cup water in a 5-quart casserole dish with a tightly fitting lid. Cook in the microwave, covered, at 100% for 12 minutes. Stir in the corn, scallions, celery, milk and cream. Cook, covered, for 9 more minutes.

Remove from the oven, uncover, and stir in the salt, pepper sauce and black pepper. Cool slightly before serving, then stir in the butter, if desired. **Makes 7 cups; serves 6 as a first course**

Thick Potato Soup with Corn

A delicious vegetarian Ecuadoran soup with a lovely golden color from pumpkin and annatto, accented by the red kidney beans and the yellow corn.

ANNATTO BUTTER

$^1/_2$ cup annatto (achiote) seeds

8 tablespoons (4 ounces) unsalted butter or $^1/_2$ cup vegetable oil

REFRITO

2 tablespoons unsalted butter

1 small red onion, finely chopped

2 teaspoons reserved Annatto Butter

$3^1/_2$ pounds soup pumpkin or acorn or Hubbard squash, cut into 8 wedges, seeded, peeled and each section cut across into $^1/_4$-inch slices

$1^1/_2$ cups milk

2 ears corn, shucked, silk removed and each cob cut across into 6 pieces

1 pound waxy potatoes, peeled and cut into $^1/_4$-inch dice

$^1/_3$ cup dried kidney beans, soaked and cooked, or 1 cup canned kidney beans, drained and rinsed (optional)

1 tablespoon kosher salt, or to taste

Freshly ground black pepper to taste

$^1/_2$ pound queso blanco (white cheese) or mozzarella cheese, coarsely grated, for serving

For the annatto butter, in a small saucepan, combine the annatto and 2 tablespoons butter or oil. Cook over low heat for 5 minutes. Strain through a fine sieve into a small heatproof bowl. Repeat the process three more times, using the same annatto and 2 tablespoons of the remaining butter or oil each time. Heat the mixture a little less each time, to avoid burning, and strain the butter or oil into the same bowl. Reserve 2 teaspoons for the refrito. Refrigerate the rest for another use. (Makes about $^1/_3$ cup)

For the refrito, in a small saucepan, melt the unsalted butter over medium heat. Stir in the onion and cook for 10 minutes, stirring occasionally. Stir in the reserved annatto butter until melted. Remove from the heat.

Meanwhile, in a medium stockpot, bring 6 cups water and the pumpkin to a boil. Lower the heat and simmer, covered, for 25 minutes, or until the pumpkin is very soft.

In a blender, purée the refrito with $^1/_2$ cup milk. Stir into the pumpkin, along with the corn. Cook for 10 minutes. Stir in the remaining 1 cup milk and the potatoes. If using beans, add them now. Simmer, covered, over low heat for 20 minutes. The pumpkin will disintegrate, thickening the soup and turning it yellow-to-gold. Season with the salt and pepper. The soup can be made ahead to this point and refrigerated for up to 3 days.

If the soup has been refrigerated, reheat it. Stir in the cheese just before serving and allow it to melt. **Makes 10 cups; serves 9 as a first course**

Southwestern Corn

1 tablespoon vegetable oil

2 medium red bell peppers, cored, seeded, deribbed and chopped

3 cups fresh corn kernels, blanched (cut from 6 medium ears corn), two 10-ounce packages frozen corn kernels, thawed, or 3 cups canned corn kernels, drained

2 jarred jalapeño peppers, seeded and minced

1/2 cup chopped cilantro or fresh parsley

2 teaspoons kosher salt

Freshly ground black pepper to taste

Heat the oil in a medium saucepan over medium heat. Add the red peppers and cook for 2 minutes, stirring occasionally. Stir in the corn and the remaining ingredients. Cook until heated through, about 1½ minutes.
Makes 4 servings as a side dish

Santa Fe Corn Salad

If using fresh corn kernels, boil or steam them and cool under cold running water. Omit the step of cooking the vegetables in oil. Combine the corn, bell peppers, jalapeño and cilantro in a bowl with ½ cup thinly sliced scallions (white and green parts).

Whisk together ¼ cup white wine vinegar, ¼ to ⅓ cup vegetable oil (to taste), 1 tablespoon freshly ground cumin seeds, 1 to 2 teaspoons kosher salt and freshly ground white pepper to taste. Pour the dressing onto the vegetables and toss.

Corn and Feta Cheese Omelet

For sophisticated friends, try this as a first course (cut the omelets in half to serve eight). I find that many of my friends don't understand eggs as a first course—unless the eggs are in a cheese soufflé.

A little jalapeño pepper and cilantro will jazz this up.

4 tablespoons unsalted butter

2 cups peeled, seeded and chopped tomatoes

2 cups fresh corn kernels, blanched (cut from 4 medium ears corn), frozen corn kernels, thawed, or canned corn kernels, drained

1 cup sliced scallions (white and green parts)

1 teaspoon kosher salt

Freshly ground black pepper to taste

6 ounces feta cheese, crumbled (about 1 1/2 cups)

12 eggs

Heat the butter in a large skillet and add the tomatoes. Cook over medium-high heat for about 3 minutes, or until the tomatoes begin to give off liquid. Add the corn, scallions, salt and pepper and cook for 1 more minute over low heat. Remove the pan from the heat and stir in the cheese.

One at a time, make four 3-egg omelets in a 9-inch skillet. Before folding them over, spoon in some of the filling. Slide the omelets onto plates and spoon the remaining filling over the tops. **Makes 4 omelets**

Cazuela de Elsa Tobar

This Chilean recipe closely resembles the Ecuadoran sancocho. It is very beautiful, but it does require that guests not be persnickety about eating with their fingers—the corn, that is. I suppose the kernels could be removed from the cobs and added during the last few minutes of cooking, but the flavor would not be the same. To cut slices across the cob, slam the sharp blade of a heavy knife into the cob. Lift the knife and cob together and slam down on a cutting board.

2 medium carrots, peeled, halved lengthwise and cut across into 2-inch lengths

1 medium yellow onion, cut into 1-inch wedges

1 medium sweet potato, peeled and cut across into $1/4$-inch slices

One $2^1/2$- to 3-pound chicken, cut by a butcher (or see Note) into 14 serving pieces (wing tips and backs reserved for stock, if desired)

6 medium cloves garlic, smashed and peeled

4 teaspoons kosher salt, or to taste

1 large green bell pepper, cored, seeded, deribbed and cut into 2-inch pieces

1 medium tomato, cored and cut into 2-inch chunks

2 ears corn, shucked, silk removed and cut across into 2-inch rounds

$1/4$ cup finely chopped cilantro

Freshly ground black pepper to taste

In a tall narrow stockpot, bring the carrots, onion, sweet potato, chicken, garlic, salt and 5 cups water to a boil. Lower the heat and simmer for 15 minutes.

Stir in the bell pepper, tomato and corn. Cover and bring to a boil. Lower the heat and simmer, partially covered, for 5 minutes.

Stir in the cilantro and pepper. Simmer for 2 more minutes.

Makes 13 cups; serves 6 to 8 as a main course

NOTE: *To cut up chicken:* The easiest way to cut a chicken into 14 pieces is to buy a chicken already cut into eighths. Cut the breasts in half crosswise with a sharp heavy knife. Do the same to the thighs. Cut off and discard the wing tips (or save them for stock). Cut the wings in half at the joint.

Scallops, Baby Corn and Asparagus Sauté

Resist the temptation to pair this dish with rice. The sweetness of the scallops combines with the fresh spring vegetables in a manner so gentle and elegant it stars on its own. If an accompaniment is absolutely needed, try a little Fried Bread (page 510).

I used a nonstick pan, so very little oil is needed. If making this in a regular pan, increase the oil slightly.

$2^1/2$ pounds fresh baby corn (4 dozen ears), shucked and trimmed (about 3 cups)

1 pound large sea scallops

4 pounds medium asparagus, 2-inch tips only (stalks reserved for another use)

Scant 1 tablespoon canola oil

12 scallions, green parts only, cut across into $1/4$-inch pieces (about 1 cup)

$1/2$ teaspoon grated fresh ginger

4 teaspoons rice wine vinegar

1 teaspoon kosher salt

To cook the corn, bring a large pot of water to a boil. Add the corn (in 2 batches if necessary) and boil for 2 minutes. Drain; rinse under cold running water. Set aside.

Remove any small muscles on the sides of the scallops. Cut the scallops into $1/4$-inch-thick rounds: Place each scallop flat on the cutting board. With one hand, firmly press down on the scallop. With the other hand, slice horizontally across, cutting the scallop into halves or thirds, depending on its size. Set aside.

Peel any of the stalks that remain on the asparagus tips.

Heat the oil in a medium nonstick skillet. Add the asparagus tips and cook over medium heat for 4 minutes, or until they are not soft but a knife can be inserted into the stalk without resistance. Add the scallops. Reduce the heat to medium-low and cook for 1 minute, gently stirring to separate the slices. Add the corn, scallions and ginger. Cook, stirring for 1 minute. Add the rice vinegar and salt. Cook and stir for 3 minutes, or until all the vegetables are heated through. **Makes 8 cups; serves 6 as a first course**

Shrimp and Corn Curry

This is a very pretty and good combination. Rice would be a plus here.

- 2 tablespoons vegetable oil, preferably canola
- 3 tablespoons curry powder
- 1 medium onion, chopped (about 1 cup)
- 1 tablespoon black mustard seeds
- 2 medium tomatoes, cored and chopped
- 2 cups fresh corn kernels, blanched (cut from 4 medium ears corn), frozen corn kernels, thawed, or canned corn kernels, drained
- 1 1/2 pounds shrimp, peeled and deveined
- 1 tablespoon grated peeled fresh ginger
- 1 to 2 tablespoons fresh lemon juice
- 1/4 cup chopped cilantro
- 1 1/2 teaspoons kosher salt
- Freshly ground black pepper to taste

Heat the oil in a 12-inch skillet. Add the curry powder, onion and mustard seeds. Cook over medium-low heat for 4 minutes, or until the onions are translucent and the spices are fragrant.

Increase the heat to medium. Add the tomatoes and corn. Cook for 5 minutes. Stir in the shrimp. Cook for 5 minutes. Remove from the heat and stir in the remaining ingredients. **Makes 5 cups; serves 4 as a main course**

Microwave Variation
Place the oil, curry, onion and mustard seeds in a 2 1/2-quart casserole dish with a tight-fitting lid. Cook, uncovered, at 100% for 4 minutes. Stir in the shrimp. Cook, covered, at 100% for 3 minutes. Stir in the tomatoes, corn and ginger. Cook, covered, at 100% for 5 minutes. Remove from the oven and stir in the remaining ingredients.

Summer Corn Pudding

This is a light and pretty dish that can be a first course, main course or side dish.

- 1 tablespoon unsalted butter
- 2 cups fresh corn kernels (cut from 4 medium ears corn)
- 3 scallions, trimmed and thinly sliced
- 1/4 pound radishes, trimmed and thinly sliced (about 3/4 cup)
- 2 tablespoons chopped fresh dill
- 8 ounces small-curd creamy cottage cheese
- 3/4 cup plain yogurt
- 1/4 cup heavy cream
- 4 large eggs
- 3 large egg yolks
- 2 teaspoons kosher salt
- Freshly ground black pepper to taste

Preheat the oven to 300°F.

Melt the butter in a large skillet over medium heat. Add the corn, scallions and radishes. Cook, stirring, just until the corn is softened, about 4 minutes. Scrape into an 11 x 8 x 2-inch baking dish and smooth into an even layer. Sprinkle the dill over the vegetables. Set aside.

Put the cottage cheese, yogurt, cream, eggs, egg yolks, salt and pepper in a food processor or blender. Blend well. Pour over the vegetables. Bake until the edges are lightly browned and the center is firm, about 45 minutes. Serve hot or at room temperature.

Serves 6 to 8 as a side dish, 4 to 6 as a brunch dish

Microwave Variation

Omit the butter. Toss the corn, scallions and radishes in the dish. Cook, uncovered, at 100% for 5 minutes.

Meanwhile, blend the cottage cheese, yogurt, cream, eggs, egg yolks, salt and pepper in a food processor or blender. Sprinkle the dill over the vegetables. Pour the egg mixture over and stir to combine. Cook, uncovered, at 100% for 3 minutes. Stir thoroughly, especially at the edges of the dish (where it cooks most rapidly). Cook, uncovered, at 100% for 3 minutes. Stir again. Cover tightly and cook at 100% for 2 minutes. Prick the plastic. Release the steam and uncover. Serve hot or at room temperature.

Corn Custard

An old southern favorite, this is a delight. It is light enough to serve with a simple main course, from fish to meat. It can stand on its own as an egg dish at a brunch or luncheon. It can be spiced up, but try it this way at least once.

2 tablespoons unsalted butter

2 cups corn kernels (cut from 4 medium ears corn)

$^1/_2$ small onion, chopped (about $^1/_4$ cup)

$^1/_3$ cup sliced scallion greens

4 large eggs

1 $^1/_4$ cups milk

$^3/_4$ cup heavy cream

2 teaspoons kosher salt

$^1/_4$ teaspoon hot red pepper sauce

Preheat the oven to 325°F.

Heat the butter in a large skillet over medium heat until foaming. Add the corn, onion and scallions; stir until softened, about 4 minutes. Scrape into an 11 x 8 x 2-inch baking dish.

Whisk together the remaining ingredients. Pour over the corn mixture. Bake until the edges are lightly browned and the center is firm, about 30 minutes.

Remove from the oven and heat the broiler. Broil 5 inches from the heat until the top is golden brown, about 2 minutes. Serve hot.

Serves 8 as a side dish, 4 to 6 as a brunch dish

Microwave Variation

Combine the butter, onions, scallions and corn in an 11 x 8 x 2-inch dish. Cook, uncovered, at 100% for 3 minutes. Remove from the oven and stir well.

Whisk together the remaining ingredients. Pour over the corn mixture. Cook, uncovered, at 100% for 3 minutes. Stir well and cook at 100% for 3 minutes more. Without removing the dish from the oven, cover tightly with microwave plastic wrap. Cook at 100% for 1 minute and 30 seconds. Prick the plastic to release the steam.

Meanwhile, preheat the broiler. Uncover the dish and broil 5 inches from the heat source until the top is golden brown. Serve hot.

continued

South of the Border Corn Custard

Add ½ cup peeled, seeded and diced (¼ inch) tomato and ¼ cup each diced (¼ inch) deribbed green and red bell pepper, along with the scallions. If using the microwave, increase the cooking time to 4 minutes. Add ½ cup grated aged cheddar cheese and 1 teaspoon hot red pepper sauce to the egg mixture. Cook as in the basic recipe or the microwave variation.

Maple Corn Jalapeño Relish

This makes enough to bottle and keep for winter. (See page 91 for canning instructions.)

$^1\!/_4$ cup peeled and diced ($^1\!/_8$ inch) fresh ginger

1 cup dark pure maple syrup

2 tablespoons Dijon mustard

$1^1\!/_2$ cups white vinegar

8 large cloves garlic, smashed, peeled and minced

4 bell peppers, cored, seeded, deribbed and cut into $^1\!/_4$-inch dice (about 4 cups)

6 jalapeño peppers, seeded, deribbed and cut into $^1\!/_8$-inch dice

2 cups finely diced (not minced) sweet onions

8 cups yellow corn kernels (cut from 16 medium ears corn)

In a large nonreactive saucepan, bring the ginger, maple syrup, mustard, vinegar and garlic to a boil and boil for 5 minutes. Add the bell peppers, jalapeños and onions. Return to a boil and cook for 3 minutes. Add the corn. Return to a boil and cook for 2 to 3 minutes, or until just tender but not mushy. **Makes 5 to 6 pints**

Spicy Corn Relish

This doesn't make enough to be worthwhile putting up. It will keep for up to two weeks in the refrigerator. If multiplying the recipe, though, see page 91 for sterile canning instructions.

Choose the peppers according to your love of heat. (See the Cook's Guide, page 626.)

1 medium onion, cut into chunks

2 hot peppers, halved and seeded

6 cloves garlic, smashed and peeled

$^1\!/_2$ cup tightly packed cilantro leaves

1 tablespoon tightly packed fresh oregano leaves

$1^1\!/_2$ cups fresh corn kernels (cut from 3 medium ears corn) or canned corn kernels, drained

1 large red bell pepper, cored, seeded, deribbed and cut into $^1\!/_2$-inch dice

3 stalks celery, peeled and chopped (about $^3\!/_4$ cup)

1 tablespoon kosher salt

1 tablespoon sugar

$1^1\!/_2$ teaspoons ground cumin

$^3\!/_4$ cup white vinegar

$^1\!/_2$ cup dark Mexican beer

Place the onion, hot peppers, garlic, cilantro and oregano in a food processor. Process until coarsely chopped. Tranfer to a 12-inch skillet. Add the remaining ingredients. Bring to a boil over high heat. Reduce to medium-high heat and cook, stirring, for 10 minutes, or until the liquid is mostly evaporated. **Makes 4 cups**

DRIED CORN
AND HOMINY

The first identity of corn is fresh corn on the cob, and it must be eaten as soon after picking as possible. But it is also a valuable staple in that it dries very well, to be used as a ground grain and to be made into hominy. Canned hominy is one of the more usable preserved products. I always have grits, plain cornmeal or polenta, and cornstarch on hand; they are essentials. Usually there is a packet of popcorn hanging around waiting to be made—often for children, and often as a diet snack for me.

I'm not southern or a big maker of corn pone or corn dodgers, but I do love grits, which I eat as breakfast with indecent amounts of butter and sometimes cream. Grits are also good as a side dish instead of mashed potatoes. Very much like polenta, they can be cooled in a mold or on a slick sheet pan and then cut into pieces and fried.

Pumped-Up Popcorn

Consider serving this at large informal parties, such as a group watching a football game. It is terribly simple to do with popcorn you have just popped or with store-bought popped popcorn. Try to buy unsalted air-popped popcorn, and then salt the final product to taste.

3/4 cup vegetable oil

8 medium cloves garlic, smashed, peeled and minced

2 1/4 teaspoons chili powder

Scant 1/4 teaspoon cayenne pepper

12 cups unsalted popcorn or one 4-ounce bag plain popcorn

Kosher salt to taste

Place the oil, garlic, chili powder and cayenne in a small saucepan over very low heat. Cook, stirring occasionally, for 5 minutes.

Place the popcorn in a large bowl. Pour the spice mixture over and toss to coat; hands are best. Season with salt to taste. **Makes 12 cups**

Creamy Polenta

Somehow we managed to give the credit for our birthright, cornmeal mush, to the Italians. Let's take it back and eat it.

This can be eaten as breakfast or as a side dish or a starter. A spoon is helpful. Consider stirring in a cheese such as Gorgonzola (see the variation that follows), or flavor it to the limits of imagination.

Several books and many recipes later, I still make polenta in the microwave: freedom from lumps and a shoulder that survives, avoiding excess stirring. I know it is heresy to many Italians, with their image of their grandmother, large wooden paddle in hand, stirring endlessly.

Incidentally, polenta was not originally a dish made from sweet corn, but instead was made from lentils and other grains as sustenance for the Italian army.

6 1/2 cups cold water

2 teaspoons kosher salt, or to taste

1 cup yellow or white cornmeal

3/4 to 1 cup heavy cream

6 tablespoons unsalted butter, melted

Freshly ground black pepper to taste

Bring 5 cups of the water to a boil in a 3-quart saucepan. Add the salt.

In a large bowl, stir the cornmeal into the remaining 1 1/2 cups cold water. Pour the cold water and cornmeal all at once into the boiling water. Reduce the heat and cook at a low boil, stirring frequently, for about 30 minutes. The polenta should pull away from the sides of the pan and be able to hold its shape.

Reduce the heat to low and stir in the cream and butter. Continue to stir until the polenta is smooth and creamy. Add pepper and additional salt, if desired. Serve immediately.

Serves 6 as a side dish or first course, or for breakfast

Creamy Gorgonzola Polenta

Make the polenta using ½ cup heavy cream. When stirring in the cream and melted butter, add ½ cup crumbled Gorgonzola cheese.

Monterey Jack or fresh goat cheese can be used instead of Gorgonzola. If desired, add 1 jalapeño pepper, seeded and chopped.

Microwave Variation

Increase the cornmeal to 1¼ cups. Use ¾ cup heavy cream and 3 tablespoons unsalted butter.

Combine 4 cups water, the cornmeal, and the 2 teaspoons salt in a 2-quart soufflé dish. Cook, uncovered, at 100% for 12 minutes, stirring once. Remove from the oven, stir in the heavy cream and butter and add ⅛ teaspoon pepper. Let stand for 3 minutes. Serve hot.

Fried or Grilled Polenta

Prepare Creamy Polenta or the microwave version above, omitting the heavy cream. Lightly grease an 8 x 4 x 2-inch loaf pan with 2 to 3 teaspoons softened butter. Pour the polenta into the pan and brush lightly with 1 to 2 teaspoons butter. Let stand until cool, then cover and refrigerate until chilled.

To serve, unmold the polenta and slice about ½ inch thick. Brush both sides of the slices with melted butter or olive oil, and panfry or grill. Serve the slices as is, or spread with butter, drizzle with olive oil or top with Tomato Basil Dipping Sauce (page 464), Baby Food Tomato Sauce (page 461) or Herbed Tomato Sauce (page 462). **Serves 8 as part of a first course or as a side dish**

Hominy Soup

The Ecuadorans are great soup makers. Just as the Chinese ask, "Did you have rice today?" meaning, "Have you eaten?" Ecuadorans will ask, "Have you had soup today?" They make fabulous soups, mostly vegetarian, except for the use of lard—replaced here by butter. Achiote, coriander and tamarillo (tree tomatoes) are frequent ingredients or accompaniments. Of course, one can cook dried hominy, but frankly I seldom bother. I use canned. (I might if I were going all out and making a stew with squirrel or raccoon.)

One thing I did learn in Ecuador is that the tender top stems of cilantro have as much flavor as the leaves and are usually used, saving a lot of work for a lot of flavor.

3 tablespoons unsalted butter

1 medium-large yellow onion, minced

12 cloves garlic, smashed, peeled and coarsely chopped

1 teaspoon ground cumin

1 small red onion, minced

5 cups water

Two 30-ounce cans hominy, rinsed and drained

1½ pounds fresh cranberry beans, shelled (about 2 cups)

One 10-ounce package frozen baby lima beans, defrosted in a sieve under warm running water and drained

3 cups fresh corn kernels (cut from 6 medium ears corn)

2 red bell peppers, cored, seeded, deribbed and cut into ¼-inch dice

2 tablespoons kosher salt

Freshly ground black pepper to taste

6 sprigs cilantro, plus chopped cilantro for serving

In a tall stockpot, melt the butter over low heat. Stir in the yellow onion, garlic and cumin. Cook, stirring, for 5 minutes, or until all the liquid has been absorbed.

Stir in the red onion, water, hominy and cranberry beans. Bring to a boil. Lower the heat and simmer, covered, for 20 minutes, or until the beans are cooked.

Stir in the lima beans, corn, bell peppers, salt, pepper and cilantro sprigs. Simmer for 5 minutes.

Serve with a small bowl of chopped cilantro.

Makes 14 cups; serves 10 to 12 as a first course

Rich Lamb and Hominy Soup

Delicious as is, or with a few diced carrots, leeks and/or tomatoes tossed in during the final simmering. Hominy, even canned, is absorptive, so feel free to thin the finished soup a little if it seems too thick.

- 4 medium lamb shanks (about 2 1/2 pounds)
- 1 tablespoon kosher salt, or to taste
- 1/2 teaspoon freshly ground black pepper, or to taste
- 3 tablespoons olive oil
- 4 cups Basic Chicken Stock (page 501) or commercial chicken broth, or as needed
- Two 15-ounce cans hominy, rinsed and drained (about 4 cups)

Rub the lamb shanks thoroughly with the salt and pepper. In a deep skillet or casserole with a tight-fitting lid large enough to hold the shanks comfortably, heat the oil over high heat. Add the shanks and cook, turning as necessary, until well browned on all sides, about 12 minutes.

Pour in the stock and bring to a boil. Adjust the heat so the liquid is simmering. Cover and cook, turning the shanks a few times, until the lamb is very tender, about 2 hours. Remove the shanks from the liquid and cool. Set the pan aside.

Remove the lamb from the bones, discarding the fat and gristle and very coarsely shredding the meat as you go. Skim any fat from the surface of the cooking liquid. Stir in the lamb and hominy. Bring to a simmer. Add chicken stock to thin the soup as desired. Cook for 4 to 5 minutes. Season with salt and pepper. Serve hot. **Makes 8 cups; serves 4 as a main course**

Faux Pho

Pho is a traditional Vietnamese beef and noodle soup. A delicious version can be made with the above soup. Just before serving, stir in 4 ounces cooked and drained angel hair pasta or 4 ounces cooked rice stick noodles (prepared according to the package directions). Ladle into bowls and pass sliced scallions, chopped cilantro and sliced hot chilies (such as serranos or jalapeños).

Corn-Chili Soufflé

This is one of my all-time favorite cornmeal dishes. The whole corn kernels give it an interesting texture, and the spicy ingredients complement the other flavors. I like to serve this with pork dishes.

- 1 cup yellow or white cornmeal
- One 17-ounce can corn kernels, drained, or 1 3/4 cups fresh corn kernels
- 1 cup milk
- 6 large eggs, separated
- 1 1/2 teaspoons chili powder
- 1 teaspoon kosher salt
- 1 teaspoon freshly ground black pepper
- 2 teaspoons baking powder

continued

1 cup pimiento-stuffed olives, chopped

1 jalapeño or serrano pepper, seeded, deribbed and finely chopped

1 1/2 cups crumbled crisp-cooked bacon (from about 6 slices)

3/4 cup freshly grated Parmesan cheese

Soak the cornmeal and corn in the milk in a medium saucepan for 30 minutes.

Heat the mixture over low heat, stirring constantly, until it just comes to a boil and starts to thicken. Transfer to a large bowl. Stir in the egg yolks, seasonings, baking powder, olives and chili, mixing thoroughly. Add the bacon and cheese. Stir well until thoroughly incorporated.

Preheat the oven to 375°F.

Beat the egg whites until stiff but not dry. Fold about one-quarter of the whites very thoroughly into the corn mixture. Add the remaining whites and stir and fold until no white shows.

Pour into a well-buttered 2-quart baking dish or soufflé dish. Bake for 35 minutes or until set. **Serves 4 to 6 as a side dish**

Individual White Cheddar Corn-Chili Soufflés

A nice recipe for a party.

1/2 cup yellow or white cornmeal

3/4 cup milk

5 large eggs, separated

1 cup fresh corn kernels (cut from 2 medium ears corn)

1 teaspoon chili powder

1 teaspoon kosher salt

3 large canned green chilies, finely chopped

1/2 pound bacon, fried until crisp, drained and crumbled into small pieces

1/4 pound white cheddar cheese, grated, plus 12 thin 2-inch squares cheese

1 large egg white

Generously butter twelve 4-ounce (1/2-cup) ramekins or soufflé dishes. Set aside.

Stir the cornmeal into the milk in a saucepan. Heat the mixture, stirring constantly, until it just barely comes to a boil and starts to thicken. Transfer to a large bowl.

Stir in the egg yolks, corn, chili powder, salt and chilies, mixing thoroughly. Add the bacon and grated cheese. Stir well, until thoroughly incorporated.

Preheat the oven to 400°F.

Beat the egg white in a large bowl until stiff but not dry. Stir about one-quarter of the white very thoroughly into the corn mixture. Add the remaining white and stir and fold until no white shows. Divide the mixture evenly among the twelve ramekins. Top each with a slice of cheese.

Bake for about 20 minutes, or until set. **Serves 12 as a side dish**

Spoon Bread

An inspired cook, a Mrs. Wayne Begnaud, gives a recipe in *Talk About Good*, from the Service League of Lafayette, Louisiana, to which I owe this most unusual technique. The cornmeal is not cooked first, but the recipe turns out perfectly and very quickly.

I would eat spoon bread on its own; but it is usually an accompaniment to a main course such as fried chicken with a mess of greens on the side.

**6 tablespoons unsalted butter,
cut into 6 pieces and softened**

1 cup yellow cornmeal

3 cups milk

2 teaspoons kosher salt

3 large eggs

Place a rack in the center of the oven and preheat to 375°F.

Grease an 8 x 8 x 2-inch glass baking dish with 1 tablespoon of the butter. Set aside.

Place the cornmeal in a food processor.

In a small saucepan, bring the milk and salt to a rolling boil. With the food processor running, quickly pour the hot milk into the cornmeal. Process for 1 minute, or until there are no visible lumps. With the processor running, add the remaining 5 tablespoons butter to the cornmeal mixture. Process briefly, until completely incorporated.

In a small bowl, whisk the eggs until they are light and frothy, about 1 minute. With the processor running, scrape in the eggs and process briefly.

Pour the batter into the greased dish and bake for 40 minutes, or until the top is golden brown. **Makes sixteen 2-inch squares**

Grits

Start with yellow or white quick-cooking, not instant, grits. This is a treat for those who have sampled only watery, underseasoned instant grits.

Use ¼ cup quick-cooking grits, 1 cup water and ¼ teaspoon kosher salt for each serving; stir together in a saucepan. Bring to a boil over medium heat, then adjust to simmering. Cover and cook, stirring once or twice, for 4 to 5 minutes, or until the grits mound on

a fork and are tender but not mushy. Stir in 2 teaspoons unsalted butter per serving if desired. Serve hot.

Cheese Grits
Stir in 3 tablespoons finely grated cheddar cheese (mild or sharp) per serving after removing the pan of grits from the heat; stir until melted.

Lee Ann Cox's Classic Corn Bread

Lee Ann Cox comes from the South and makes both this corn bread and the corn bread dressing that follows.

1 ¼ cups yellow cornmeal

½ cup all-purpose flour

4 teaspoons baking powder

1 tablespoon sugar

1 teaspoon kosher salt

1 large egg

1 cup milk

3 tablespoons vegetable oil

Position a rack in the center of the oven. Preheat the oven to 350°F.

Grease a 9 x 2-inch round cake pan.

Combine the dry ingredients in a small bowl.

Whisk together the egg, milk and oil in a medium bowl. Stir in the dry ingredients.

Scrape the mixture into the prepared pan. Bake for 25 minutes, or until the center is firm to the touch. Remove from the oven and place on a rack to cool. **Makes one 9-inch round bread**

continued

Southwestern Corn Bread

Generously grease a 9 x 9 x 2-inch glass baking dish. Line the bottom with a square of parchment paper and generously grease the paper.

To the prepared corn bread batter, add 4 ounces Monterey Jack cheese, shredded, 2 jalapeño peppers, seeded and diced, and ½ red bell pepper, seeded, deribbed and cut into small dice. Mix to distribute evenly. Pour into the baking dish. Bake for 30 minutes, or until the center is firm to the touch.

Allow the corn bread to cool for about 10 minutes in the pan. Turn out onto a rack, remove the parchment liner and turn right side up to finish cooling on the rack.

Makes sixteen 2-inch squares

NOTE: *To freeze the corn bread:* Allow to cool completely. Wrap tightly in plastic wrap, then in foil. To serve, thaw for at least 1 hour at room temperature before reheating. Unwrap and place on a baking sheet in a 300°F oven for 10 minutes, or until thoroughly heated through.

The southwestern corn bread stays very moist due to the cheese and peppers. If necessary, reheat more than once.

Lee Ann Cox's Corn Bread Dressing

Here is a dressing made with Lee Ann's corn bread, great for stuffing a turkey. The dressing takes almost the whole loaf. To have enough corn bread to eat warm with a stew or slathered with butter, make a double batch and place the two pans catty-corner on a baking sheet. Then save one for the next day to turn into the crumbs.

4 tablespoons unsalted butter

2 medium onions, chopped (about 2 ½ cups)

4 stalks celery, peeled, cut lengthwise in half and across into ¼-inch pieces (about 1 ⅓ cups)

¼ cup celery leaves, finely chopped

3 cups Dried Bread Crumbs (page 510) made from Lee Ann Cox's Classic Corn Bread (page 45), plus ½ cup dried bread crumbs made from white bread

1 ¼ cups cracker crumbs (hard dry ship's biscuits are best, but saltines will do)

2 large eggs if using as a stuffing, 5 large eggs if using as a dressing

2 cups turkey stock, Basic Chicken Stock (page 501), Roasted Chicken Stock (page 502) or commercial chicken broth

4 teaspoons dried sage

1 ½ teaspoons kosher salt

Freshly ground black pepper to taste

Melt the butter in a large sauté pan over medium heat. Add the onions and cook until they become limp. Add the celery and celery leaves and cook until the onions begin to color, about 10 minutes. Remove from the heat.

Combine the bread crumbs and and cracker crumbs in a large bowl. Stir in the onion mixture. Whisk the eggs together in a small bowl and add to the crumb mixture. Stir in the stock and ½ cup hot water. Add the sage, salt and pepper and mix well.

Fill the cavity of the turkey with the stuffing or place it in an ungreased 2-quart soufflé dish.

To bake the dressing, preheat the oven to 350°F. Cover the soufflé dish with a lid or foil and bake for 45 minutes. Uncover and bake 30 minutes longer.

Makes 6 cups; serves 6 to 8 as a side dish

Spoon Bread with Raisins

This is a dessert variant of spoon bread and just as easy. The milk may curdle when boiled with the liquor and fruit, but this is not a disaster; the milk solids just get scraped into the mixture, and the processor will smooth them out. For true self-indulgence, consider some unsweetened whipped cream to spoon onto this almost-soufflé.

6 tablespoons unsalted butter, cut into 6 pieces, softened

1 cup yellow cornmeal

2 1/2 cups milk

3/4 cup brandy

1 cup sultana or golden raisins

1 teaspoon kosher salt

4 large eggs

1/3 cup sugar

Place a rack in the center of the oven. Preheat the oven to 375°F.

Grease an 8 x 8 x 2-inch glass baking dish with 1 tablespoon of the butter. Set aside.

Place the cornmeal in the work bowl of a food processor.

In a medium saucepan, bring the milk, brandy, raisins and salt to a boil. Strain the milk into a glass measure; reserve the raisins.

With the processor running, quickly pour the hot milk into the cornmeal. Process for 1 minute, or until there are no visible lumps. Add the remaining 5 tablespoons butter. Process briefly.

In a small bowl, whisk the eggs and sugar until light and frothy, about 1 minute. Scrape the egg mixture into the food processor and process briefly. Add half the raisins and pulse briefly to mix.

Pour the batter into the greased dish and sprinkle the remaining raisins on top. Bake for 45 minutes, or until the top is golden brown.

Makes sixteen 2-inch squares

Cornmeal Cookies

A staple that keeps well.

1 1/4 cups all-purpose flour

1 1/4 cups yellow cornmeal

1/2 teaspoon baking powder

1/2 teaspoon kosher salt

1/2 pound (8 ounces) unsalted butter, softened

3/4 cup sugar

Grated zest of 2 oranges

2 large eggs

1 teaspoon vanilla extract

Confectioners' sugar

Stir the flour, cornmeal, baking powder and salt together in a small bowl. Set aside.

In the bowl of an electric mixer or another large bowl, using a handheld mixer, beat the butter until smooth. Gradually add the sugar, beating until light and fluffy. Beat in the zest. Add the eggs one at a time, beating constantly. Beat in the vanilla. Stir in the dry ingredients until no trace of flour remains. Wrap the dough in plastic wrap and chill for at least 2 hours.

Preheat the oven to 350°F.

Using a level tablespoon measure for each, make balls of dough and set them 2 inches apart on two greased or nonstick cookie sheets. Press the balls with the bottom of a glass to flatten them slightly.

continued

Bake until golden brown on the bottom, about 15 minutes. Cool completely on a rack.

Sprinkle the cookies with confectioners' sugar before serving. **Makes about 48 cookies**

Popcorn Crunch

Some cooks are daunted by the prospect of cooking sugar; it's easy to understand why. The traditional stovetop method often includes studious watching of a thermometer and continuous brushing down of the sides of the pan. It is both easier and cleaner in the microwave. Try it once, and be a convert. This is a variation on peanut brittle. Watch your teeth.

> **2 cups sugar**
>
> **1 cup light corn syrup**
>
> **1 1/2 cups pecans**
>
> **4 cups unsalted popcorn**

Preheat the oven to 350°F. Generously oil a large baking sheet and a large spoon. Set aside.

Stir the sugar, corn syrup and 1 cup water together in a 2½-quart soufflé dish. Cook, uncovered, in a microwave at 100% for 4 minutes. Stir. Cover tightly with microwave plastic wrap. Cook at 100% for 24 minutes. Prick the plastic to release the steam.

While the syrup is cooking, place the pecans on an ungreased baking sheet. Bake for 10 minutes, stirring once. Set aside.

Uncover the cooked syrup and let stand for 2 minutes. Use the spoon to carefully stir in the popcorn and nuts. Let stand for 5 minutes, turning the popcorn over in the mixture from time to time to ensure that the popcorn and nuts are well coated.

Spoon the mixture out onto the oiled baking sheet; use the back of the spoon to spread the mixture into an even layer. Let it completely cool and harden.

When cool, break into chunks with a wooden mallet or rolling pin. Store in an airtight container.

Makes 1 1/2 pounds, or about 8 cups, depending on the chunk size

Peanuts

Of course peanuts aren't really a usual vegetable, but a legume—they certainly aren't nuts; but Africa would have a great nutritional lack without them, and we would be impoverished. George Washington Carver did us all a great service by inventing myriad ways to use peanuts.

Imagine American children without peanut butter and jelly sandwiches, or peanut butter and sliced banana sandwiches. Peanuts are very nutritious and make a fine ingredient in cooking. The only problem is that there are people who are violently allergic to peanuts, and it is better to know one's own nuts—friends—before putting peanuts on the menu or even out around the house. Many schools and airlines have already banned them.

In the American South—I've eaten them with Greek fishermen along the Florida coast—peanuts in the shell are boiled in heavily salted water as long as overnight. In Africa, peanuts are used in many soups and stews just as we use them here. Often we take a shortcut and use prepared peanut butter. Many people won't touch peanut butter that isn't organic or reduced in fat. I like the creamy kind, in jars, that is quite ordinary. Sadly, it is true that peanuts, like all oil-rich foods, are fattening.

Turn to **PEANUTS** in the Cook's Guide
for how-tos and to the Index for more recipes.

Chicken Peanut Butter Stew

This is a variation on an African stew. For more authenticity, use yams instead of sweet potatoes.

- 2 tablespoons peanut oil
- $1/2$ cup coarsely chopped onion
- One 2- to 3-pound chicken, cut into 8 pieces
- Kosher salt and ground black pepper to taste
- $2/3$ cup crunchy peanut butter from a jar
- 2 cups Basic Chicken Stock (page 501) or commercial chicken broth
- 3 cloves garlic, smashed and peeled
- 1 dried red chili pepper or $1/4$ teaspoon hot red pepper flakes
- 2 medium sweet potatoes, peeled and cut into eighths
- Juice of $1/2$ lemon
- $1/2$ pound spinach leaves (4 cups loosely packed), cut crosswise into very thin strips
- 2 cups Basic White Rice (page 489)

Heat the oil in a 3-quart saucepan over medium heat. Add the onion and cook, stirring, until soft but not brown, about 6 minutes. Season the chicken with salt and pepper. Add to the pan. Cover loosely and cook, turning once, for 15 minutes, or until lightly browned on both sides.

While the chicken is cooking, blend the peanut butter and chicken stock in a blender until smooth. Set aside. In the blender, a food processor or a mortar and pestle, chop the garlic and red pepper to almost to a paste.

Uncover the pan and add the peanut butter mixture and the garlic–red pepper mixture. Stir to blend and cook for 10 minutes more.

Add the sweet potatoes, $1\frac{1}{2}$ teaspoons salt and $1/4$ teaspoon pepper and continue cooking for 15 to 30 minutes, or until the sweet potatoes and chicken are cooked. Add the lemon juice and spinach and cook, stirring, for 2 minutes, or until the spinach is wilted.

Serve over the rice. **Serves 4 as a main course**

Peanut-Ginger Lace Cookies

Tuiles are the French lace cookies that are formed by being draped over a rolling pin while still warm to take on the shape of French roof tiles (tuiles). A version combining American peanuts and Asian ginger is a lovely variation.

- $2/3$ cup unsalted dry-roasted peanuts
- $2/3$ cup sugar
- $1/2$ cup all-purpose flour
- $1/3$ cup packed candied ginger pieces
- 1 teaspoon ground ginger
- $1/2$ teaspoon salt
- 6 tablespoons unsalted butter, melted and cooled
- 3 large egg whites
- 3 tablespoons milk

Place a rack in the middle of the oven. Preheat the oven to 400°F.

Combine the peanuts, sugar, flour, candied and ground ginger and salt in a food processor. Pulse until the peanuts and ginger are finely ground.

Beat the butter, egg whites and milk together in a bowl until blended. Stir in the flour mixture.

Scrape 1 tablespoon batter onto a nonstick baking sheet. With the back of a teaspoon, spread into a more or less even 4-inch circle. Fit as many cookies as possible on the sheet, leaving 1 inch between them. Bake until lacy golden brown, about 6 minutes. Remove and cool for 1 minute.

Slide a flexible metal spatula under each cookie and transfer them to a cooling rack. Alternatively, for a tuile shape, drape the cookies hot from the baking sheet over a rolling pin. They take shape and cook quickly, so can be removed to make room for more. Repeat with the remaining batter.
Makes about 30 cookies

Peanut Butter Cookies

Peanut butter cookies are a standard and still good.

1 ¹/2 cups sifted all-purpose flour

³/4 teaspoon baking soda

8 tablespoons (4 ounces) unsalted butter, softened

¹/2 teaspoon pure vanilla extract

¹/2 cup granulated sugar

¹/2 cup packed dark brown sugar

1 large egg

¹/2 cup plus 2 tablespoons crunchy peanut butter from a jar

Place a rack in the center of the oven. Preheat the oven to 375°F.

Sift the flour and baking soda together. Set aside.

Beat the butter in a large bowl with an electric mixer until pale and fluffy. Add the vanilla and both sugars and beat until smooth. Beat in the egg. Beat in half the flour mixture, then the peanut butter, then the rest of the flour.

Drop the dough by rounded teaspoons onto an ungreased cookie sheet. Press each cookie down with the back of a fork, making a cross-hatch pattern. Bake for 12 minutes or until lightly browned. Cool on a rack. Repeat with the remaining dough. **Makes about 72 cookies**

Oatmeal or Coconut Peanut Butter Cookies
Add ¹/2 cup rolled oats or ¹/2 cup shredded coconut. Beat in with the second half of the flour.

Peanut Brittle

The recipe for this treat, which works well in a microwave oven, first appeared in my book *Microwave Gourmet*. The microwave is a miracle with sugar.

1 cup granulated sugar

¹/2 cup light corn syrup

1 ¹/2 cups blanched or unblanched raw peanuts

Vegetable oil for baking sheet

Combine the sugar, corn syrup and ¹/2 cup water in an 2-quart glass measure. Cook, uncovered, at 100% for 3 minutes.

Remove from the oven and stir thoroughly. Add the peanuts; stir again. Cover tightly with microwave plastic wrap. Cook at 100% for 15 minutes.

continued

Lightly coat a spatula and a large baking sheet or a 16 x 12-inch marble slab with vegetable oil. Remove the syrup from the oven. Pierce the plastic to release the steam and uncover carefully. Pour the mixture onto the oiled surface. With the oiled spatula, spread the peanuts to distribute them evenly through the cooling syrup. Let cool and harden.

When the brittle is cool, break into chunks with a wooden mallet or rolling pin. Store in an airtight container. **Makes 1 1/2 pounds**

Promiscuous Peppers

Peppers are flirts; they are not to be trusted. Plant a nice mild frying pepper in the garden and it is as likely as not to mix and mingle with some other plant's mate. A sweet variety may turn out to have a tinge of spice. I buy a serrano to give a blast of spice to a dish and find out that the bed it has been lying in was too easy and accommodating, leaving my food bland. What is a cook to do?

Despite the problems, we are seduced. In late summer and fall, roadside stands are piled with multicolored peppers: "yellow, and black, and pale and hectic red," as well as green, orange and purple. They used to be almost exclusively bell peppers in the Northeast. Latterly, we of New England have been catching up with the rest of the world, and I have found pale green thin-skinned

Italian frying peppers, squashed orbs of orange and yellow Scotch bonnets, dark green jalapeños, thin hot Asian peppers and numerous others. New ones keep appearing on the market. Recently I found peppers that looked like serranos but were mild with thin skins like frying peppers, and they came in a multitude of colors. Look for them.

Even with my short Vermont growing season, I can grow bird peppers and then dry them by hanging the entire plant upside down. I grow Scotch bonnets and several others. If I lived in the Southwest, I would have ristras of red peppers hanging from my eaves to dry.

The whole world has adopted American peppers, grateful for their spice and seemingly never daunted by their membership in the otherwise-suspect family of the Solanaceae. Columbus set off to find a spice route. He didn't get to India and black pepper, but he brought back pod peppers.

The seeds, normally removed except in dried hot pepper flakes, are the hottest part of the pepper. The hotness of peppers is rated on the Scoville scale, named for the man who first devised the rating system. The system has been heavily altered since his day. Technically, it has to do with how much alcohol it takes to neutralize the pepper's heat, capsaicin. It is measured in parts per thousand. From the cook's point of view, the less technical rating is the ranking of 1 through 10+.

Peppers are not poisonous, but they can badly burn the fingers and lips of unwary users. The solution for the cook is wearing rubber gloves and for the eater, sipping milk. Some people have trouble digesting peppers— particularly raw ones with their skins on. This must be why there are so many ways of peeling peppers. I find that peppers roasted the Greek way (page 56) with their skins on are delicious as well as digestible.

Some peppers come fresh, some dried (for instance, ancho) and some smoked (for instance, chipotle). Each has a different use. Some are main ingredients and some are mainly for seasoning. The hotter the pepper, the more likely it is to be a seasoning. Dried peppers are almost always soaked (and sometimes toasted before soaking) before using.

Since peppers have seasons (late summer and fall) like other vegetables, buy them when they are good, plentiful and cheap. Peter Piper shouldn't be the only one with a peck of pickled peppers for winter use.

Today bell peppers come in a bewildering variety of beautiful colors; all of them can be cooked in a variety of ways—in the oven or microwave oven, over a flame or under the broiler—and used in many more. Roasted peppers are good just after preparation, with salt and either a little vinegar or olive oil. In addition to being a classic part of an Italian antipasto, they can be used in endless simple first-course preparations with a little vinaigrette. Strips of roasted peppers make attractive garnishes for canapés. They can be chopped and seasoned to make dips. Or use roasted peppers instead of out-of-season tomatoes in a salad with mozzarella and a leaf or two of fresh basil, and make the vinaigrette with a little prepared mustard. Shred some Belgian endive lengthwise, put roasted peppers over it and top with a few capers. Or put them over some arugula and top with anchovies, small black olives or very thin slices of Parmesan.

As our cooking has gotten more and more international, there is an increasingly confusing variety of regional names for peppers especially as the same pepper may have different names when fresh, dried or powdered as a spice. Additionally, the original confusion between the seeds that we put in mills and the fruit has provided another set of overlapping names.

All sweet Spanish peppers are called pimientos. More particularly, the word describes a pointy, thin-skinned, medium-size relatively sweet pepper. From it we take the English word "pimento"; pimientos are available in jars and olives. To further confuse things, "pimenta" is the Spanish word for peppercorn, while "chili" is the Spanish word for hot peppers and the spice made from them.

The French distinguish between "poivrons," the fresh vegetable, and "poivre," the spice, a term they apply equally to peppercorns and to ground dried pod peppers.

Turn to **PEPPERS** in the Cook's Guide
for how-tos and to the Index for more recipes.

ROASTED PEPPERS

Most people like to roast peppers before eating them. It's easier to remove the skin and the flavor changes, gaining a smoky aura.

Marinated Roasted Peppers

These recipes are made with roasted peppers (see the Cook's Guide, page 628) that have been cored, seeded, peeled and cut into 1- to 1½-inch-wide strips. Each recipe makes enough marinade for six roasted peppers.

Roasted Peppers in Oil (Sott' Olio)

Whisk ⅓ cup extra-virgin olive oil, 1 teaspoon minced fresh sage, 2 teaspoons kosher salt and ¼ teaspoon freshly ground black pepper in a medium bowl until the salt is dissolved. Add the peppers and their liquid and toss to coat.

Let marinate, tossing occasionally, for 2 hours at room temperature or up to 2 days in the refrigerator. Bring to room temperature and check the seasoning before serving.

Roasted Peppers in Vinegar

Stir ¼ cup balsamic vinegar, 1½ teaspoons kosher salt and freshly ground black pepper to taste in a mixing bowl until the salt is dissolved. Add the peppers and their liquid and toss to coat. Let marinate at room temperature for 1 to 4 hours, or store in the refrigerator for up to 4 days. Bring to room temperature and check the seasoning before serving.

Roasted Peppers with Fresh Thyme

Whisk ¼ cup extra-virgin olive oil, 2 tablespoons red wine vinegar (or fresh lemon juice), 2 teaspoons chopped fresh thyme leaves, 1½ teaspoons kosher salt and ¼ teaspoon freshly ground black pepper in a medium bowl until the salt is dissolved. Add the peppers and their liquid and toss to mix. Let marinate for 2 hours at room temperature or for up to 2 days in the refrigerator. Bring to room temperature and check the seasoning before serving.

Roasted Peppers with Anchovies and Chives

Use any of the preceding marinated peppers; feel free to mix the colors. Lay the strips out flat or overlapping on a large platter. Rinse the anchovies from three 2-ounce cans in warm water and top the peppers in an attractive pattern. Dribble the marinade over the anchovies and peppers. Sprinkle with the petals from 6 or 7 chive flowers. To separate the petals from the flower, hold the petals in one hand and the green base in the other; twist and pull.

Roasted Red Pepper Spread

Very pretty, very good and a last-minute savior if you use jarred roasted red peppers, which are quite satisfactory. This is easily multiplied and keeps well, covered, in the refrigerator; it is good on Crostini (page 510).

6 red bell peppers, roasted, cored, seeded and peeled, or two 7-ounce jars roasted red peppers, drained

2 tablespoons extra-virgin olive oil

2 tablespoons minced fresh parsley

1 tablespoon fresh lemon juice

2 teaspoons capers, drained

1 medium clove garlic, smashed, peeled and mashed to a paste with $1/4$ teaspoon kosher salt

Arrange the roasted peppers on a double layer of paper towels and let them drain and dry.

Process the remaining ingredients in a food processor until the capers and parsley are very finely chopped. Add the peppers and pulse until coarsely chopped. Stop several times to scrape down the sides of the bowl. Check the seasonings and adjust as necessary.

Refrigerate in a covered container for up to 5 days. Let come to room temperature at least 30 minutes before serving. **Makes 2 cups**

Roasted Red Pepper Spread with Anchovies
Substitute 4 flat anchovy fillets for the capers and 6 fresh basil leaves for the parsley.

Roasted Red Pepper and Mushroom Salad

This simple dish can be turned to many uses. It can be spooned onto Crostini (page 510) or endive leaves. At another meal, it makes a

good accompaniment to grilled fish or chicken. A quarter cup is an attractive topping for a portion of pasta or a slice of fried or grilled polenta (page 42). A tablespoon makes a taste, three a serving. The whole will make forty tastes, enough for about a dozen people.

3 medium red bell peppers, roasted, cored, seeded, peeled and cut into $1/8$-inch-wide strips

$1/4$ pound mushrooms, trimmed and thinly sliced (about 1 cup)

$1 1/2$ tablespoons fresh lemon juice

$1 1/2$ tablespoons anchovy paste

1 tablespoon chopped fresh parsley

6 tablespoons olive oil

1 tablespoon capers, rinsed and drained (optional)

Kosher salt and freshly ground black pepper to taste

Combine the pepper strips and mushrooms in a medium bowl. In a small bowl, combine the remaining ingredients. Mix well, and toss with the peppers and mushrooms. Let marinate for at least 1 hour before serving. The salad keeps for up to 1 day if covered and refrigerated. Serve at room temperature. **Makes 2 1/2 cups**

Greek Garlic Roasted Peppers

I first had these peppers at my friend Marilia's home in Greece. They are unbelievably simple, and the prolonged cooking makes the skin digestible, so they don't need to be peeled.

A very good pasta sauce can be made by simply puréeing the peppers with the garlic or by adding the purée to tomato sauce and heating it with a little Greek oregano. Marilia made the recipe with green bell peppers and then I tried it with the sweeter yellow bell peppers. Made with a mixture of pepper colors, this is beautiful.

Serve it as part of a mixed first course or as a side dish. Typically, a pepper per person should do. However, I find that people can eat enormous amounts of these and it might be wise to allow as many as three per person for hearty eaters. You can easily multiply the recipe. Any extras will keep for a week in the refrigerator or can be puréed for use in a pasta sauce, as described above, or in the Ratatouille Pasta Sauce (page 338). Leftovers can also be placed in a narrow plastic storage container and covered with balsamic or other red wine vinegar.

The garlic is as good to eat as the peppers are. Feel free to stir a teaspoon or so of good dried Greek oregano into the pepper juices just before serving.

If small bell peppers are all that is available, add two more and cook the peppers and garlic together for 20 minutes instead of 30.

2 tablespoons olive oil

8 meaty bell peppers, a mix of colors if available, cored and seeded but left whole

1 to 1 1/2 heads garlic, cloves separated, smashed and peeled

Place a rack in the upper third of the oven. Preheat the oven to 350°F.

Coat a 16 x 13-inch roasting pan with a little oil. Add the peppers and drizzle with the remaining oil. Roast for 30 minutes. Turn over the peppers and rotate the pan. Cook for another 30 minutes.

Turn the peppers and rotate the pan again. Add the garlic to the center of the pan. Cook for 15 minutes. Turn the garlic over. Cook for another 15 minutes, or until the peppers are soft and collapsed. (Add 10 minutes for very large peppers.)

Remove the peppers and garlic to a plate. Loosen the caramelized juices from the pan with a wooden spoon. Pour over the peppers.

Cover loosely with a cloth and let cool. Serve at room temperature.

The peppers can be roasted a day ahead. Cover tightly with plastic wrap and refrigerate. Bring to room temperature before serving. **Serves 3 to 8 as part of a first course or as a side dish**

Garlic Roasted Pepper Purée
Follow the instructions using 1 3/4 pounds large red (or any single color) bell peppers. Put the garlic and peppers into a food processor. Process until smooth. **Makes 3/4 cup**

Garlic Roasted Peppers with Mozzarella and Anchovies
Follow the instructions using any color(s) pepper you like. Drain the oil from one 2-ounce can anchovy fillets and reserve it. Set the fish aside.

Just before serving, drain the liquid from the peppers into a small saucepan. Stir in 1 teaspoon dried Greek oregano and the reserved anchovy oil. Add 2 (or more) chopped anchovy fillets and cook over low heat, stirring, until the anchovy dissolves. Taste for saltiness. Add freshly ground black pepper and additional salt, if desired. Let cool.

To serve, slice two 10-ounce rounds buffalo milk mozzarella (or other fresh mozzarella) lengthwise. Arrange the peppers and garlic on a platter, overlapping the peppers with the mozzarella slices. Top each mozzarella slice with 1 or more anchovy fillets. Drizzle the dressing on top. **Serves 6 to 8 as part of a first course**

Roasted Yellow Bell Peppers and Tomatoes

With the new (not so new) ready availability of yellow peppers, I have been having a wonderful time creating new recipes and adapting old ones. Their thick flesh has a rich, fresh sweetness that is positively voluptuous. Eat this tepid; when this is made ahead, allow enough time for it to come back to room temperature. Bake it in an attractive earthenware dish so it can be served as is.

- **3 medium yellow bell peppers**
- **3 medium ripe tomatoes**
- **1/4 cup olive oil**
- **2 teaspoons minced garlic**
- **2 teaspoons fresh thyme leaves or**
  - **1/2 teaspoon dried, crumbled**
- **1 teaspoon kosher salt**
- **1/4 teaspoon freshly ground black pepper**

Preheat the oven to 400°F.

Cut the yellow peppers in half lengthwise. Remove the cores and seeds, then cut the peppers into 1-inch-wide strips. Core the tomatoes. Cut them into ½-inch-thick slices. Arrange the peppers and tomatoes, overlapping, in an oval baking dish.

In a small bowl, blend the oil, garlic, thyme, salt and pepper. Pour over the peppers and tomatoes. Bake for 1 hour and 15 minutes, or until the peppers are tender. Baste occasionally with the juices during baking. Cool to tepid or room temperature before serving.

Serves 6 as a first course

MORE PEPPER RECIPES

Silky Pepper Strips

These can be made with peppers of any color, but red and yellow will be the prettiest. Homemade, they are much less expensive than those bought jarred, and they have almost no sodium. Plus they are not restricted to one color of pepper. Cover leftover pepper strips with a good vinegar and store in the refrigerator virtually indefinitely to use later as needed. The pepper strips break easily, so peel them first, if desired, then cook them.

Using a microwave oven saves a lot of work, particularly when making a purée. It is also useful if the peppers will be served with the skin on.

- **1 pound red, yellow or green bell peppers**
  - **(3 small or 2 large)**

Peel the peppers, if desired, with a vegetable peeler. Cut small peppers lengthwise into quarters and large peppers into sixths. (If necessary, finish peeling the pepper strips at this point.) Core the peppers and remove the seeds and ribs.

Arrange the pepper strips, skinned side down, in a 13 x 9 x 2-inch oval dish, with the tapered ends toward the center. Cover tightly with microwave plastic wrap and cook in the microwave at 100% for 7 minutes, or until tender. Prick the plastic to release the steam.

Remove from the oven. Let stand for 1 minute, then uncover. Remove the peppers and drain on paper towels. **Makes 1 cup**

Bell Peppers and Sardines with Balsamic Vinegar

I'm not sure that I can convince myself or anyone else to eat the bones of the sardines, but my more robust friends assure me that they provide a rich source of calcium. They also provide the good kind of fish oil.

The sardines used in this recipe are rather small and often come ten to a can. If using large sardines—four to a can—use only half a sardine for each portion. Use leftover sardines in the Fennel Sardine Sauce (page 215).

This first course feels right served before a pasta main course, especially when you consider the dividends: all of your vitamin A and masses of vitamin C, as well as potassium, phosphorus, iron and calcium. It's also easy to make if the pepper strips are habitually on hand.

1 recipe Silky Pepper Strips (page 58) using 2 large peppers

4 whole small sardines packed in oil (¹/₂ ounce each), split and boned or left whole, 4 teaspoons oil reserved

4 sprigs fresh basil

4 teaspoons balsamic vinegar

1 small clove garlic, smashed, peeled and minced

Freshly ground black pepper to taste

Arrange the pepper strips on four small serving plates, overlapping the strips.

Wipe away any scales from the sardines. Arrange 2 fillets, skin side up, or 1 whole fish, on each plate and garnish with the basil sprigs.

Whisk together the reserved sardine oil, the vinegar and garlic in a small bowl. Drizzle over the sardines and peppers. Sprinkle with black pepper. **Serves 4 as a first course**

Golden Pepper Potato Purée

I found some wonderful meaty yellow peppers and decided to try a new way of making them. It worked wonderfully. A lot got eaten.

3 pounds yellow bell peppers, cored, seeded, deribbed and cut into 1-inch pieces

1 pound red bell peppers, cored, seeded, deribbed and cut into 1-inch pieces

3 medium white potatoes, peeled and cut into 1-inch chunks

4 tablespoons unsalted butter

3 tablespoons ground cumin

Kosher salt and freshly ground black pepper to taste

In a large saucepan, bring 3 quarts water to a boil. Stir in the peppers and reduce the heat to a high simmer. Cook for about 20 minutes, uncovered, or until the peppers are thoroughly softened. Drain the peppers and put through the fine disc of a food mill into a bowl.

In the meantime, put the potatoes in a microwave-safe bowl and tightly cover with plastic wrap. Cook at 100% for 15 minutes. Pierce the plastic to release the steam, then uncover and drain the potatoes. Alternatively, cook the potatoes in boiling salted water until tender, then drain.

Put the potatoes through the food mill and stir them into the peppers.

Heat 1 tablespoon of the butter in a small pan. Gently cook the cumin until all the fat is absorbed. Stir into the pepper mixture. In a regular blender or with an immersion blender, purée the pepper mixture until absolutely smooth.

When ready to serve, reheat the purée, stirring in the remaining 3 tablespoons butter and salt and pepper to taste. **Makes 8 cups**

Chilies Rellenos

No Mexican is going to recognize these— wrong peppers, wrong cheese—but they are small enough to handle at a stand-up party without a knife and fork, and they are puffy and delicious. Serve with a salsa such as Fresh Tomato Mint Salsa (page 114), if desired.

continued

One 11-ounce jar peperoncini (Italian pickled hot peppers) or Greek Salonika peppers

4 1/2 ounces feta cheese, crumbled and drained (about 1 cup)

2 1/2 ounces mozzarella cheese, preferably fresh, shredded (about 1/2 cup)

1/4 teaspoon freshly ground black pepper

All-purpose flour for dredging

Vegetable oil for shallow-frying

1 recipe Egg White Batter (page 516)

Drain the peppers and rinse. Cut a slit down each pepper from stem end to tip. Scrape out the seeds from each pepper, leaving the stem intact. Be careful not to tear or cut the peppers, or the filling will leak out during frying. Drain the peppers well on a double thickness of paper towels.

Stir the feta, mozzarella and black pepper in a small bowl until well blended. Working with 1 pepper at a time, form an oval of the cheese mixture roughly the size of the pepper and carefully fill the pepper. The cheese should fill the pepper solidly but not to overflowing. Make sure both sides of the slit meet over the cheese filling. The peppers may be prepared ahead to this point and refrigerated.

Dredge the filled peppers in flour, making sure all surfaces are coated. Tap off excess flour.

Heat about ½ inch of oil in a large skillet. Working in batches, dip the coated peppers in the batter and shallow-fry (see page 512 for more information on frying), increasing the heat slightly each time after putting the peppers in the pan, then lowering it. Fry until the underside is dark golden brown, about 4 minutes. Turn and fry until completely browned, another minute or so. Drain on paper towels. Serve hot. **Makes about 15 pieces**

Chilies Rellenos with Corn

Many people don't like to deep-fry. Here is a version of chilies rellenos that eliminates that step. If you can't get farmer cheese, use half again as much small-curd cottage cheese and drain it in a sieve, pressing lightly.

2 tablespoons unsalted butter

1/2 cup chopped onion

1 teaspoon minced garlic

1 small dried red pepper, crumbled

2 cups fresh corn kernels (cut from 4 medium ears corn), or canned corn, drained

1/4 teaspoon ground cumin

1/2 pound farmer cheese, crumbled

1 egg, lightly beaten

2 tablespoons chopped cilantro

1 1/2 teaspoons kosher salt

12 to 20 poblano chilies, depending on size, roasted, slit down one side, cored, peeled and seeded (see the Cook's Guide, page 628)

1 to 1 1/2 cups sour cream, lightly beaten

1/3 cup grated cheddar cheese

Heat the butter in a medium skillet. Add the onion, garlic and red pepper. Cook over medium-high heat until soft, stirring occasionally. Stir in the corn, 2 tablespoons water and the cumin. Cover the pan and cook until the corn is tender, 10 to 20 minutes, depending on the type used. Remove the pan from the heat and let cool.

Stir the farmer cheese, egg, cilantro and salt into the corn.

Preheat the oven to 350°F. Lightly oil a baking dish.

Stuff the chilies with the filling and place in the baking dish. Spoon the sour cream over the chilies and sprinkle with the grated cheese.

Bake for about 20 minutes, or until heated through. **Serves 6 as a first course**

Pork Chops with Cherry and Bell Peppers

There are many variations on this Italian-American combination of pork and cherry peppers. This one tames the cherry peppers' heat with sweet peppers.

Two 10-ounce loin pork chops, about 1 inch thick

Kosher salt and freshly ground black pepper

3 tablespoons olive oil

4 cloves garlic, smashed, peeled and sliced

1 each large red and yellow bell pepper, cored, seeded, deribbed and cut into $^1/_4$-inch strips (about 4 cups)

1 medium red onion, cut into $^1/_2$-inch strips

2 to 3 bottled hot cherry peppers, cored, seeded and coarsely chopped

$^1/_3$ cup dry red wine

$^1/_2$ cup Basic Chicken Stock (page 501) or commercial chicken broth

1 tablespoon liquid from bottled hot cherry peppers (optional)

Rub the pork chops with salt and pepper. Heat 2 tablespoons oil in a medium deep skillet over medium-high heat. Cook the pork chops, turning once, until browned on both sides and just a slight trace of pink remains near the bone, about 14 minutes. Transfer the chops to a plate and cover with aluminum foil to keep warm.

Pour off the oil from the pan. Add the remaining 1 tablespoon oil and the garlic.

Cook until the garlic starts to change color, about 1 minute. Stir in the bell peppers, onion and cherry peppers. Season lightly with salt and pepper. Cook until the vegetables are wilted, about 4 minutes.

Pour in the wine. Bring to a boil and cook until almost evaporated. Add the stock and cherry pepper liquid, if using. Bring to a boil. Cook, stirring, until the liquid is syrupy and just enough of it remains to coat the vegetables. Spoon the vegetables and sauce over the chops and serve. **Serves 2 as a main course**

Tabbouleh with Red and Hot Peppers

Tabbouleh, made with bulgur—processed cracked wheat—is instantaneous and fresh tasting. It can be served with chicken or fish but is delicious on its own, or with raw vegetables or leftover cooked vegetables on the side. Serve as a first course with sliced tomatoes and watercress sprigs or fresh cilantro. It also makes a good stuffing.

When asparagus is in season, serve tabbouleh with cooked tips sprinkled with olive oil and lemon juice. Cucumber strips, red radishes, slices of raw variously colored peppers, carrot sticks and raw mushroom slices are other good accompaniments.

Tabbouleh is usually a version of a parsley salad (page 444). Here, the leaves are mint and the result is wonderful.

1$^1/_2$ cups fine bulgur

$^1/_4$ cup olive oil

$^1/_2$ cup chopped fresh mint

3 cloves garlic, smashed, peeled and minced

2 red bell peppers, cored, seeded, deribbed and cut into $^1/_4$-inch dice

continued

2 hot green peppers, seeded and thinly sliced

1 bunch scallions, trimmed and thinly sliced

1 tablespoon kosher salt

Juice of 2 lemons

Bring 4 cups water to a simmer. Place the bulgur in a bowl and add the simmering water. Let sit for 15 minutes.

Meanwhile, bring another 3 cups water to a simmer. Drain the bulgur and return to the bowl. Add the simmering water. Let sit for 10 minutes. Drain well.

In a medium bowl, toss the bulgur with olive oil to coat, then stir in the remaining ingredients. Let sit at room temperature for at least 30 minutes (see Note).

Serves 6 as a first course, 8 as a side dish

NOTE: To serve this before it rests for 30 minutes, increase the seasonings. To make it spicier, leave in the seeds from the hot peppers.

Pickled Jalapeño Peppers

This handy work of Peter Piper—pickled peppers—requires canning jars with their lids and rings. The recipe makes four quarts, about thirty-two peppers. I use four quart jars with eight peppers in each jar, but eight pint jars with four peppers each are fine also. I know official guidelines suggest to boil these after canning them, but I don't. Burning oneself in the process is more likely than getting poisoned, with all the vinegar.

Four 1-quart or eight 1-pint canning jars with
  two-piece lids

2 pounds jalapeño peppers

5 quarts white vinegar

Put the canning jars, lids and rings in a large pot filled with enough water to cover the jars by 2 inches. Boil for 5 to 10 minutes to sterilize. Keep the jars warm in the water until ready to put up the peppers. (For more about canning, see page 91.)

Put the vinegar and 5 quarts water in a nonreactive 12-quart pot. Cover and bring to a boil. Reduce the heat slightly. Add the peppers to the pot. Cover and boil for 20 minutes, or until the skins split and start to detach from the peppers. Remove the pot from the heat. Using tongs, a slotted spoon or a skimmer, take the peppers out of the liquid and run them under cold water to loosen the skins. Peel the skins from the peppers, either with fingers or a small paring knife.

Bring the vinegar and water back to a boil. Place the peppers in the jars. One by one, fill each jar up to the lip with the boiling vinegar and water (it helps to use a wide-mouthed funnel to avoid spills), then immediately cover with its lid and loosely secure the ring. When all the jars are filled, tighten the rings. **Makes 4 quarts**

Fried Peppers and Tomatoes
for Pasta

This is currently my hands-down favorite pasta sauce, bar none—very Amalfi Coast. It is clear in taste, sinus-clearing and mildly addictive. Make more than needed: People always take seconds. The flavor is a balance of sweet, hot and fresh-fruit flavors, Keats's "a beaker full of the warm south" that gets any meal off to a joyous start.

Perhaps the best version of this dish is made with sweet ripe yellow bell peppers, cut in strips, instead the frying peppers, and with three-quarters of the tomatoes being yellow and fleshy sweet.

1/2 cup olive oil

16 hot green peppers (about 4 to 5 inches long), stemmed

3 large Italian frying peppers, cored, seeded and quartered

8 cloves garlic, smashed, peeled and thinly sliced

5 medium tomatoes, cored and cut into 1-inch dice (about 6 cups)

Kosher salt and freshly ground black pepper to taste

Heat the oil in a large heavy skillet over medium heat until very hot. Carefully add the hot and sweet peppers to the oil, shaking the pan to distribute them evenly. Cook, tossing, until the peppers are wilted, about 4 minutes. Add the garlic and cook until fragrant, about 30 seconds.

Add the tomatoes and cook just until softened, 4 to 6 minutes. (Longer cooking will make the sauce watery.) Add salt and pepper to taste. Serve over linguine or spaghettini. **Serves 8 as a first course, 4 as a main course**

Roasted Italian Frying Peppers and Chunky Tomatoes

for Pasta

Try this not overly spicy sauce over a pound of cooked ziti.

8 Italian frying peppers (1 pound), cored and seeded but left whole

4 large tomatoes (2 pounds), cored and quartered lengthwise

6 cloves garlic, smashed, peeled and thinly sliced lengthwise

2 tablespoons olive oil

1 1/2 teaspoons kosher salt

Freshly ground black pepper to taste

1/4 cup wine, stock or water for deglazing

1/2 bunch fresh basil (1 1/2 ounces), leaves only, stacked 4 or 5 at a time, rolled up and cut across into thin strips (optional)

Place a rack in the center of the oven. Preheat the oven to 500°F.

Put the peppers, tomatoes and garlic in an 18 x 13 x 2-inch roasting pan. Pour the oil into the pan and rub it over the bottom of the pan and all over each pepper, tomato and slice of garlic. Roast for 10 minutes.

Shake the pan to move things around. Roast for 10 minutes more. There should be plenty of juice in the pan from the tomatoes, but if things look dry and the garlic is too dark, add up to 1/4 cup water. Scrape the roasted vegetables into a medium bowl. Add the salt and pepper.

Place the roasting pan over medium-high heat. Add the wine and bring to a boil, using a wooden spoon to scrape up any blackened and cooked-on bits. Reduce the heat to a simmer and let the liquid reduce by half. Add to the vegetables in the bowl.

With a small knife, roughly cut through the peppers and tomatoes in the bowl. Do not cut too much; leave in large chunks. Add the basil, if desired, after mixing with pasta. **Makes 4 cups**

Romesco Sauce

This is a standard and very good Catalan recipe. For slightly different versions, see Colman Andrews's *Catalan Cuisine* (see the Bibliography). The sauce evidently derives from a combination of Spanish and Arabic foods, just as Creole cooking in America has roots in African, Spanish and Italian cooking, with American ingredients. The ground nuts that are used as the base show the Arabic influence. The peppers and tomatoes were all pounded with the nuts in a mortar with a pestle.

Traditionally, Romesco is stirred into fish soups, as in Ten-Minute Fish Soup (see the variation), or used as a sauce to accompany grilled fish and meats. I serve it as a simple dipping sauce with boiled shrimp, marinated grilled shrimp or skewers of vegetables, chicken or meat, or use it as a topping for Crostini (page 510).

There is no shortcut around the grilling; it is essential to the flavor. If making this ahead, cover it with a little olive oil and then put some plastic wrap directly on top of the Romesco before covering the container. Wonderful as this sauce is, it discolors when exposed to the air for any length of time. So serve it in a smallish bowl and refill with fresh sauce as needed.

3 ancho chilies

2 small ripe tomatoes (about 4 ounces each)

1 medium-large red bell pepper (about 7 ounces)

¼ cup plus 1 teaspoon olive oil

1 ounce blanched whole almonds (about 40)

1 ounce whole hazelnuts (about 20)

2 slices (about 1 ounce each) French or Italian bread, crusts removed

6 medium cloves garlic, smashed and peeled

1 jalapeño pepper, seeded

2 tablespoons red wine vinegar

2½ teaspoons kosher salt

Freshly ground black pepper to taste

Preheat a grill or broiler with the rack about 4 inches from the heat.

Place the anchos and 1 cup water in a 1-quart soufflé dish, cover tightly with microwave plastic wrap and microwave at 100% for 4 minutes.

Prick the plastic to release the steam, remove from the oven and uncover. Or place the chilies and water in a small saucepan and simmer, covered, until softened. Allow the chilies to stand, covered with a plate or the lid, until cool enough to handle.

Meanwhile, rub the tomatoes and bell pepper with the 1 teaspoon oil. Grill or broil them for 10 to 15 minutes, turning frequently so that the skin is evenly charred all over. Remove and place in a bowl. Cover with a plate and allow to steam for about 10 minutes.

Drain the chilies and remove the seeds. Place in a food processor. Peel, core and seed the tomatoes. Add to the food processor. Core, seed and peel the pepper. Add to the processor.

Heat a heavy skillet over medium to high heat for about 2 minutes. Add the almonds and cook, stirring continuously, for about 5 minutes, until golden brown all over. Transfer to the food processor. Add the hazelnuts to the pan and cook in the same manner. Gather them up in a kitchen towel and rub them on a hard surface to remove the skins. Add to the food processor.

Brush the bread with about 3 tablespoons of oil. Broil about 3 inches from the heat for 2 minutes on each side or cook in a skillet over moderate heat, turning once, for about 5 minutes, or until golden brown. Break up into pieces and add to the food processor along with the garlic, jalapeño and vinegar. For a chunky sauce, process until coarsely chopped. Or process until very smooth. Season with the salt and pepper. **Makes 2½ cups**

Ten-Minute Fish Soup

For 1 main-course serving or 2 first-course servings: Cut ½ pound firm white-flesh fish fillets, such as halibut or cod, into 1-inch slices. (If the fillets narrow toward the tail end, cut the slices wider—about 2 inches—as they near the tail.) Put in a saucepan with 2 cups Basic Fish Stock (page 505) (choose a pan that allows the stock to cover the fish; a 6-inch-diameter pan works perfectly for a single serving). Bring to a simmer. Cook until the fish is opaque in the center, about 8 minutes. Remove from the heat, add ¼ cup Romesco sauce and gently stir until blended into the broth. Season to taste with kosher salt and freshly ground black pepper.

Letcho

Letcho is an omnipresent "ingredient" or sauce in Hungary. It is served with eggs at breakfast, and with meat (often pork chops or sausage or both), fish or chicken at lunch and dinner. Two strips of grilled or fried Polenta (page 42) or a cup of cooked pasta can be topped with half a cup. Or top small rounds of toasted bread (Croutons or Crostini, pages 510–511) with a tablespoon of letcho to make an Italian sort of hors d'oeuvre, a succulent snack with drinks.

Using hot paprika or chili powder makes a relatively spicy dish; for a milder one, ordinary paprika can be substituted. If a stronger tomato flavor is desired, increase the amount of tomato paste. Note, however, that commercial paste tends to be salty; if using it, adjust the salt in the recipe accordingly. In Hungary, this dish would traditionally have been made with lard.

This can be the base for many Hungarian main dishes. See the recipe for Chicken Paprikás on page 66 and its chicken livers variation.

2 tablespoons canola oil

1 tablespoon hot paprika or chili powder without cumin

1½ mild or sweet onions, such as Vidalia, thinly sliced (about 5½ cups)

1 pound red bell peppers (2 to 3), cored, seeded, deribbed and cut into thin strips (about 3½ cups)

1 pound tomatoes, cored and cut into ¼-inch dice (about 1⅔ cups)

2 tablespoons Fresh Tomato Paste (page 459) or commercial tomato paste

1 tablespoon kosher salt (less if using commercial tomato paste)

Put the oil and paprika in a deep wide skillet. Cook over low heat for 1 minute. The paprika will be very fragrant; do not let it burn.

Add the onions and toss to coat with the paprika oil. Cook over medium heat for 10 minutes, stirring occasionally, or until soft and translucent. Add the peppers. Cook for 10 minutes, stirring occasionally. Add the tomatoes. Cook for about 20 minutes, stirring occasionally, until the tomatoes break down.

Stir in the tomato paste and salt. Cook for 10 more minutes. The vegetables will be very soft and the flavors well blended.

Makes a generous 4 cups

Microwave Variation

Reduce the canola oil to 1 tablespoon and the paprika or chili powder to 1 teaspoon. Omit the tomatoes.

Combine the oil and paprika or chili powder in a 13 x 9 x 2-inch oval dish. Cook, uncovered, at 100% for 1 minute. Stir in the onions, coating them with the paprika oil. Cook, uncovered, at 100% for 6 minutes.

Remove from the oven. Stir the onions and mound the peppers on top. Cover tightly with microwave plastic wrap. Cook at 100% for 8 minutes. Prick the plastic to release the steam, remove from the oven and uncover.

Stir well and cook, uncovered, at 100% for 6 minutes. Stir in tomato paste and cook, uncovered, for 18 minutes more, stirring twice. Season with the salt. **Makes 4 cups**

Chicken Paprikás

If my prediction is correct, letcho will become a staple in homes across this country as it is across Hungary. Here it is in a simple dish, packed with flavor. Serve with boiled potatoes or buttered egg noodles.

One 4-pound chicken, cut into 8 pieces, wing tips cut off

4 cups Basic Chicken Stock (page 501) or commercial chicken broth

1¹/₂ teaspoons kosher salt

1 cup Letcho (page 65)

2 to 3 tablespoons sour cream (optional)

Put the chicken pieces in a pot large enough to hold them snugly in a singler layer. Pour the stock over the chicken. Bring to a boil over medium heat. Adjust the heat to simmering. Cover and cook until no trace of pink remains near the bones, about 30 minutes for breast and wing pieces and 40 minutes for thigh and leg pieces; remove the pieces as they are cooked and let stand until cool. Set the pot aside.

Remove the skin from the chicken (except the wing pieces). Pour all but 1 cup of the chicken cooking liquid into a container for another use. Stir the letcho and salt into the liquid remaining in the pot. Tuck the chicken into the sauce, bring to a simmer and cook, turning the chicken pieces in the sauce, for 10 minutes.

Transfer the chicken to a serving platter. Remove the sauce from the heat and stir in the sour cream, if using, just until blended. Spoon over the chicken. **Serves 4 as a main course**

Chicken Livers Paprikás

Trim the fat and connective tissue from ¾ pound chicken livers (both are found where the lobes of the livers meet). Pat the livers dry with paper towels and season them with salt and freshly ground black pepper. Pour enough canola oil into a large heavy skillet to film the bottom. Heat over medium-high heat until very hot. Add the livers. Cook, turning once, until browned on both sides but still pink in the center, about 5 minutes. Remove from the pan.

Pour ½ cup Basic Chicken Stock (page 501) or commercial chicken broth into the pan and bring to a boil, scraping the bottom of the pan. Add ½ cup letcho and, if desired, whisk in 1 tablespoon sour cream. Return the livers to the pan and turn to coat with the sauce. Serve immediately. **Serves 2 as a main course**

Pepper Relish

This is perfect with hamburgers. The recipe can be multiplied and the result put up in jars (see page 91).

3 large bell peppers—one each red, yellow and green—(about 8 ounces each), cored, seeded, deribbed and cut into 2-inch chunks (about 4¹/₂ cups)

1 large yellow onion, cut into 2-inch chunks (about 2 cups)

1 cup cider vinegar

¹/₂ cup pure maple syrup

1¹/₂ teaspoons dry mustard

¹/₂ teaspoon hot red pepper flakes or 3 small dried red peppers

1 tablespoon finely chopped peeled fresh ginger

4 medium cloves garlic, smashed, peeled and minced

2 teaspoons cardamom seeds

Place the peppers and onion in a food processor. Pulse until finely chopped but not puréed or mushy (a few larger pieces are fine).

Scrape into a 2½-quart soufflé dish. Add the remaining ingredients and stir to combine. Cover tightly with microwave plastic wrap. Cook in the microwave at 100% for 4 minutes, or until the vegetables are cooked but firm. Prick the plastic with the tip of a sharp knife to release the steam. Uncover and stir. Cook, uncovered, at 100% for 2 minutes longer, or until the liquid is reduced to the consistency of a relish. **Makes 3½ cups**

Hot-and-Sweet Pepper Jelly

This is a different approach to hot pepper jelly from that found in most recipes. Puréeing and straining a mix of red and yellow peppers produces an opaque, not crystal clear, pale orange jelly that wiggles on the spoon. It is also less sweet than most red pepper jellies. Add another ½ cup of sugar if you like it sweet.

- 2 large meaty red bell peppers (about 1 pound), cored, seeded, deribbed and cut into 1-inch pieces
- 1 large meaty yellow bell pepper (about 8 ounces), cored, seeded, deribbed and cut into 1-inch pieces
- 3 jalapeño peppers, sliced into ½-inch rings
- 1 cup cider vinegar or white vinegar
- Liquid or powdered pectin as needed
- 1¼ cups sugar, or to taste

Place the bell peppers, jalapeños and vinegar in a food processor or blender and process until the peppers are chopped as fine as possible, 1 to 2 minutes. Line a large strainer with a jelly bag or with several layers of cheesecloth; set it over a bowl. Pour about half the pepper mixture into the sieve and let drain for a minute.

Lift the jelly bag or cheesecloth and gently squeeze out as much of the liquid as possible. Discard the solids and repeat with the remaining pepper mixture. Measure the strained liquid; there will be about 3 cups. Measure the pectin needed to set that amount of liquid, based on the package directions; set aside.

Bring the pepper liquid to a boil. Lower to a slow boil and cook for 5 minutes. Stir in the sugar and thicken with the pectin according to the package directions. Pour into jars, cool, cover and refrigerate. (Optionally, prepare canning jars, pour the hot jelly into them and boil as described on page 91.) **Makes 3 cups**

Golden Pepper Ice Cream

This may sound bizarre, but it is truly good. It has no cream—just skim milk—a hint of ginger and a generous sweetness. Peppers are fruits, so maybe it isn't so odd after all.

- 2½ pounds large meaty yellow bell peppers, oven-roasted (see the Cook's Guide, page 628), cored, seeded and peeled
- 2 cups skim milk
- 1 cup sugar
- One 2 x ½-inch slice peeled fresh ginger
- 5 egg yolks

Pass the peppers through a food mill fitted with the fine disc into a bowl. You will have about 1½ cups purée. Set aside.

Heat the milk, sugar, and ginger to simmering in a heavy medium saucepan. Simmer for 10 minutes.

continued

Beat the egg yolks in a medium bowl. Slowly strain the milk mixture into the egg yolks, whisking constantly. Pour the mixture back into the saucepan and cook over medium-low heat, stirring constantly, until thick enough to lightly coat a spoon. Remove from the heat and stir in the pepper purée.

Chill thoroughly, then freeze in an ice cream machine according to the manufacturer's directions. **Makes 4 1/2 cups**

Red Pepper Sorbet

This beautiful sorbet looks as if it were made with strawberries. The taste comes as a surprise—not a shock. With the addition of hot peppers, chopped fine and cooked, this makes a unique first course.

1 1/4 pounds red bell peppers, roasted in the microwave oven (see the Cook's Guide, page 628)

3 cups One-to-One Simple Syrup (page 511), or as needed

3 tablespoons fresh lemon juice

Pass the peppers through a food mill fitted with the fine disc into a bowl. Measure the purée; you will have about 3 cups. Add an equal amount of simple syrup and the lemon juice and stir well.

Chill thoroughly, then freeze in an ice cream maker according to the manufacturer's directions. **Makes 5 cups**

Potatoes

It is hard to imagine any of the world, let alone Ireland, without potatoes, and yet there they were, leading their provincial lives in Central America, unknown to international stardom, until the arrival of the Spaniards. Once seen and tasted, the potatoes' diva authority asserted itself and there was no country that did not have them planted. This was despite their belonging to a suspect family of poisonous vegetables (see page 97).

It is true that their leaves and stems are poisonous and, after picking, care must be taken to shield them from the light, lest they turn green. Actually, a whole class at one of Britain's better public schools was afflicted mortally by green potatoes.

Sadly, although there are hundreds of potato varieties, from white with brown skins through white with pale beige skins, white with red skins and yellow- and golden-fleshed potatoes to red, purple and blue ones, up until recently a very limited group has been grown. This is despite the fact that England has a potato museum preserving a great variety of potatoes.

None of them are, however, sweet potatoes or yams. For these, see the recipes on pages 136–141, and the Index. Elizabeth Schneider is particularly good on these subjects (see the Bibliography).

While potatoes are valued partly because they store so well, they are better and sweeter when newly dug. I have been to markets in Ecuador where women sit on the ground surrounded by their crops. If a customer seems interested, the women will jab a fingernail into a potato to show the juice spurting out, illustrating its freshness.

Potatoes fall into three categories: waxy, medium-waxy and floury, going from low to high starch. Different types are good for different preparations. Some waxy potatoes are Carola, Russian Banana (also called yellow-fleshed banana fingerlings), Rose Gold, La Rouge and La Soda (the last two are both small and red). The red fingerlings—Ruby Crescent and Ruby—are also waxy. La Ratte is an old variety of waxy fingerling that is all the rage in France and England. Joël Robuchon uses it to make his fabulous mashed potatoes. Unfortunately, since Rattes have very little starch, which is what holds the fat, the mashing and beating in of unbelievable amounts of butter can be done only at the last minute, because they cannot be reheated: The lack of starch means that they will ooze out their butter.

Among the medium-waxy potatoes are Carib (white flesh and purple skin), Yukon Gold (yellowish flesh), Red Cloud (red skin and somewhat dry white flesh), the standard Eastern potatoes (superior, Kennebec, Maine, Delaware and Long Island) and Peruvian blue (blue inside and out). Medium-waxy potatoes can become more floury with age. Floury potatoes include Red Bliss, Belrus, Green Mountain, russet and older Maine and Long Island potatoes.

There are hundreds more varieties, and the enterprising gardener can have a field day trying them out. Potatoes are quite easy to grow, which is what gave the Irish a reputation as lazy farmers. Normally, an eye with some surrounding flesh is dug out of a potato in the spring—when it may even have begun sprouting—and stuck in the ground to form a vigorous plant that will send forth enchantingly perfumed white or lavender flowers. Actually, long before the French would eat the vegetable, they wore the flowers at court as exotic bouquets. The potatoes themselves grow underground, attached to what I think of as the mother tuber by thin filaments.

I grow them somewhat differently. I prepare the soil, moving the bed each year to avoid blight as much as possible. Then I scatter the eyes and cover the whole bed with about a four-inch-thick layer of straw. This means that I do not have to dig the potatoes, which always risks scarring them. I just lift some straw and see if they are ready.

I don't go for big potatoes—cheap and easy to buy—unless they are exotica. I go for very small potatoes, about an inch to an inch and a half in diameter, with thin fragile skins. These are a real delicacy. I wash them carefully—no scrubbing—to leave the skin intact and gently steam them whole in butter, covered. High heat will fry them, which is not what is wanted at all. The cooked potatoes should be served immediately. A sprinkling of chives and/or a lavishly expensive sprinkle of fleur de sel is all that is needed. With a salad, I find this an ideal summer meal. Those who want protein should choose something mild, such as a white-fleshed fish or other summer vegetables of sweet, mild taste such as string beans, baby carrots and peas.

Leftover cooked potatoes are turned into myriad preparations, from hashed browns and cottage fries to mashed potato cakes and all sorts of hashes.

Think of all the mashed potatoes—with skins, without, with oil or butter, creamy, chunky and silky—that have shown up on restaurant menus in recent years as part of the comfort-food bonanza. Think of the mountains of French fries that are consumed with glee. Potatoes are probably America's favorite vegetable.

Quick! What food comes to mind when I say vitamin C? If you are like me, you think of orange juice; but America gets much more C from potatoes. It's all those French fries. If we ate the skins, we would get even more vitamins. I have always loved potatoes, both as an eater and as a cook; but now I have a moral justification for promoting them.

Moreover, the potato is versatile. It can be combined with almost any herb or vegetable to make a delicious soup or add body to stews. The kinds of potatoes used for this are the floury varieties. I call them mashing potatoes in my book *Soup, A Way of Life,* where they figure prominently. Waxy potatoes hold their shape when cooked and are usually used when their firmer texture is desired.

Another nice quality of potatoes is their ability to make soups that are equally good for eating cold or hot. It just means avoiding the butter. Usually it is the puréed soups that do best cold. Here, I give a recipe for a soup so simple and delicious even when you use water instead of stock that you will want to make it often.

No, I did not neglect potato leek soup. It is with leeks, page 387.

Turn to **POTATOES** in the Cook's Guide for how-tos and to the Index for more recipes.

Basic Potage

The potage has been the basic French day-to-day and meal-to-meal soup ever since the natives took to the potato. These potages are not the English potages with meat. One of my family's favorites is Basic Potage. Here is a formula that permits the cook to combine, vary and change the soup at will; Garlic Broth (page 507) can be used instead of stock or water. The vegetables may be solid, leafy or a combination of both; see the list at the end of the recipe. Start with about 1¼ pounds solid vegetables, cleaned, peeled, trimmed and cut into 1-inch cubes (to make about 3 cups), or about 2 pounds leafy vegetables, stemmed, washed and cut across into wide strips (to make 5 to 8 cups). Or use 1 pound solid vegetables and 1 pound leafy vegetables.

2 tablespoons unsalted butter (optional)

6 to 8 ounces onion, leek, shallot or garlic, or a mixture, coarsely chopped

³/₄ pound floury potatoes, peeled and cut into chunks

3 to 4 cups any stock (pages 501–507) or water

Cut-up vegetables, per lists on page 72 (see the headnote for quantities)

Kosher salt and freshly ground black pepper to taste

If using the butter, melt it in a medium saucepan or a tall narrow stockpot (a taller pot is good for a soup using a lot of leafy greens) over medium heat. Stir in the onion, leek, shallots and/or garlic. Cook, stirring frequently, for about

10 minutes, or until translucent. Add the remaining ingredients except the seasoning and bring to a boil. Or, if not using the butter, place all the ingredients except the salt and pepper in the saucepan or pot and bring to a boil.

In either case, lower the heat and simmer until the vegetables are tender. Pass through the medium disc of a food mill or, with more effort, a potato ricer. Or skim the solids from the cooked soup and pulse them in batches in a food processor to a coarse purée; return them to the liquid. Season with salt and pepper and reheat if necessary.

Solid vegetables: broccoli, broccoli di raab, carrots, cauliflower, celery, celery root, fennel, green beans, parsnips, peas, turnips.

Leafy vegetables: cabbage, chard, escarole, kale, spinach, sorrel. **Makes about 6 cups**

Potato Soup

This is a simple potato soup that is not puréed, but slightly thickened as the potatoes disintegrate. It can be made vegetarian by substituting Garlic Broth (page 507) for the chicken broth.

1 tablespoon unsalted butter

1 medium onion, finely chopped

2 pounds floury potatoes, peeled and cut across into $1/4$-inch slices

6 cups Basic Chicken Stock (page 501), Roasted Chicken Stock (page 502) or commercial chicken broth

$1/4$ teaspoon celery seeds

Kosher salt and freshly ground black pepper to taste

Buttermilk or extra stock, if desired

In a medium saucepan, melt the butter over medium heat. Stir in the onion. Toss to coat

in the butter and cook for 5 minutes, stirring occasionally. Stir in the potatoes and stock. Bring to a boil. Lower the heat and simmer for about 15 minutes, stirring frequently, until the potatoes are almost cooked though.

Stir in the celery seeds and simmer for 5 minutes, stirring to break up the potato slices.

Gently whisk the soup with a balloon whisk so that it becomes a little smoother. There will still be small pieces of potato remaining. Season to taste with salt and pepper. The soup can be made 2 hours ahead and reheated from room temperature, or refrigerated for up to 2 days and then reheated.

If not serving the soup immediately, add a little buttermilk, if desired, or extra chicken stock, because the soup will get thicker as it stands. **Makes 6 cups; serves 5 as a first course**

Pommes Vapeur

These are basically steamed potatoes usually served with fish. The French somewhat derisively call them or their plainer cousins, ungilded with butter, pommes anglaise (English potatoes).

2 pounds waxy new potatoes, peeled, or larger waxy potatoes, peeled and cut into halves or quarters

2 tablespoons unsalted butter

$1/4$ cup chopped fresh parsley

Put the potatoes in a single layer in the top of a two-part steamer, on a steaming rack or on a plate in a bamboo steamer. Fill the bottom of the steamer, or a pan large enough to hold the steaming rack without the water touching it, with water. Bring to a boil over medium heat. Place the potatoes on top, cover and steam for 25 to 30 minutes, or until tender when pierced with a toothpick. Toss with the butter and parsley. **Serves 4 to 6 as a side dish**

Mashed Potatoes

There is little that I like as much as mashed potatoes. There are hundreds of variants, such as what the English call smashed potatoes, meaning lumpy and broken up with a fork, and whipped potatoes that contain the maximum amount of butter and milk. The amounts of butter and fat can be changed to match one's pleasure. Waxy potatoes can be used, but they cannot hold the fat for any length of time. I once made them for my editor, Ann Bramson, and thought I really had mastered the Joël Robuchon invention (page 70). They were made smooth in the food processor, which does work for super buttery waxy potatoes made at the last minute. I reheated them later, though, and had a mess.

> 2 1/2 pounds floury potatoes, peeled and
>   cut into 1/4-inch slices
>
> 1/2 pound (8 ounces) unsalted butter,
>   1 cup whole milk or 3/4 cup low-fat milk
>
> 1/2 teaspoon kosher salt
>
> Freshly ground black pepper to taste

Place the potatoes and 2 quarts water in a large saucepan. Cover and boil over high heat until the potatoes are tender, about 15 minutes; drain.

Pass the potatoes through a food mill fitted with a medium disc. Scrape into a medium saucepan and place over medium heat. Stir in the butter or milk and cook, stirring, until hot. Season with the salt and pepper. Serve warm. **Serves 4 to 6 as a side dish**

Microwave Variation

Use 4 large floury potatoes (about 3 pounds), scrubbed and each pricked twice with a fork; 1/2 pound (8 ounces) unsalted butter, 1/2 pound butter plus 1 1/4 cups whole milk, 2 cups whole milk or 1 1/2 cups low-fat milk; 1 teaspoon kosher salt if using butter, 2 teaspoons if using milk; and freshly ground black pepper to taste.

Place 1 potato in the center of the microwave oven and arrange the remaining potatoes spoke-fashion around it. Cook, uncovered, at 100% for 21 minutes.

Remove from the oven. Peel the potatoes and pass through a food mill fitted with a medium disc. Scrape into a medium saucepan and place over medium heat. Stir in the butter or milk and cook, stirring, until hot. Season with the salt and pepper. Serve warm.

Microwave Olive Oil Mashed Potatoes

Use 2 floury potatoes (7 to 8 ounces each), scrubbed and pricked several times with a fork; 2 tablespoons very good olive oil; and kosher salt and freshly ground black pepper to taste.

Place the potatoes on a double thickness of paper toweling in the microwave oven. Cook, uncovered, at 100% for 11 minutes. Remove from the oven with a kitchen towel.

Holding the potatoes in the towel, peel them and cut into chunks. Pass through the fine disc of a food mill or a potato ricer. Scrape the potatoes into a dish and stir in the remaining ingredients. Cook, uncovered, at 100% for 1 minute, or until hot. **Serves 2 to 3**

Roasted Red New Potatoes with Garlic and Rosemary

If the guests like garlic, add more. Pair the potatoes with a simple dish such as roast lamb.

The potatoes can be peeled or not. Peeling takes extra time, but something very nice happens to roasted peeled potatoes: They turn an excellent dark brown color and puff up on the outside. But peeled potatoes can stick a bit to the pan. Be sure to scrape the bottom of the pan to get up any browned bits.

continued

Larger potatoes will need to roast longer. To increase the amount, increase the pan size.

3 pounds waxy red new potatoes (1 1/2 to 2 inches in diameter), peeled if desired (see headnote)

2 tablespoons olive oil

Kosher salt and freshly ground black pepper to taste

5 to 6 cloves garlic, unpeeled

1 tablespoon chopped fresh rosemary

Place a rack in the center of the oven. Preheat the oven to 500°F.

Place the potatoes in a 12 x 8 x 1½-inch roasting pan. Drizzle the oil over the potatoes, then rub it over the potatoes and the bottom of the pan. Sprinkle the potatoes with salt and pepper.

Roast for 15 minutes. Turn the potatoes over with a metal spatula. Scrape along the pan bottom to scoop up any crisp bits. Scatter the garlic around the potatoes. Roast for 15 more minutes.

Sprinkle on the rosemary. Turn the potatoes and garlic with the spatula so that the rosemary mixes in. Roast for 10 minutes more, or until the potatoes are easy to pierce with the tip of a sharp knife. **Serves 4 to 5 as a side dish**

Melting Potatoes
Not on Your Diet

One of the best, this is the most sinful recipe from a nutritional point of view. I would gladly sacrifice fat and butter for several days to eat as many of these potatoes as I could. The problem with preparing them is that people tend to eat the potatoes rather than the main dish; friends have begged me to make these. Half of this recipe—a pound and a half of potatoes—serves four people and can be made in a small roasting pan. But that seems like a waste of effort. If I really thought the larger amount of potatoes wouldn't be eaten, I would probably finish just those I thought would get eaten with the last fifteen minutes of extra-butter roasting. The next day, I would indulge myself by letting the leftover potatoes come to room temperature while the oven heated, and then finish cooking them. Goodness knows, these potatoes plus a green salad and a glass of wine would make me happy.

The cooking time will be the same for red new potatoes and baking potatoes; either can be used. The wedges of baking potatoes will get a crisper crust that contrasts adorably with the floury insides. The red new potatoes are good, but firmer. All the liquid and fat gets absorbed during the cooking, and the potatoes still shrink.

I frequently make this dish on a rack at the bottom of the oven while chicken roasts, especially if I am making more than one chicken and the potatoes cannot fit around them in the pan. A smallish bird roasts for fifty minutes, like the potatoes. The potatoes can wait outside the oven while a larger chicken continues. Finish off the potatoes while deglazing the chicken's roasting pan.

For the ultimate flavor and glazing, use six tablespoons of goose fat instead of the butter and olive oil; do not use the extra tablespoon of butter for the final heating. If using all butter rather than olive oil and butter combination, the potatoes will brown and roast more quickly. Follow the alternate times in the recipe.

3 tablespoons unsalted butter, cut into 6 pieces, plus 1 tablespoon reserved in refrigerator

3 tablespoons olive oil or 3 tablespoons additional butter

6 large floury potatoes (3 pounds)

1 teaspoon kosher salt

Freshly ground black pepper to taste

2 cups Basic Chicken Stock (page 501),
Roasted Chicken Stock (page 502) or
commercial chicken broth (see Note)

Place a rack in the top third of the oven. Preheat the oven to 500°F.

Put the 3 tablespoons butter into an 18 x 12 x 2-inch roasting pan. Set the pan over medium heat just until the butter has melted. Remove from the heat and add the olive oil.

Peel the potatoes. Cut in half lengthwise, then cut each half crosswise in half. Cut each quarter into 3 wedges. Put them in the roasting pan and roll in the butter and oil until evenly coated. Arrange so that they touch each other as little as possible. Sprinkle with the salt and pepper.

Roast for 15 minutes. Turn the wedges with a pancake turner. Roast for another 10 minutes. Turn again. Roast for 10 minutes more. Remove the pan from the oven. Turn the wedges again so the cut sides of each wedge face up. Add the stock. Return to the oven for 15 minutes. (If using all butter, roast for 10 minutes, then 5 minutes, 5 minutes; add the stock and roast for 15 minutes.) The potatoes can be made to this point and held for 4 to 6 hours at room temperature.

When ready to serve, dot the potato wedges with small pieces of the reserved butter. (It is much easier to break up the butter into teeny pieces when it is cold.) If the potatoes have been at room temperature, roast for 15 minutes. If they are still warm, 5 minutes or so will do nicely. Remove the potatoes to a platter right away or they will stick to the pan.

Serves 8 to 10 as a side dish

NOTE: Canned broth lacks the gelatin that makes this dish so sumptuous in texture. *To enrich canned broth with gelatin:* Put the broth into a heatproof measuring cup. Sprinkle ½ envelope gelatin over it and let sit for 10 minutes. Place the measuring cup in a small saucepan. Fill the pan with just enough water to come halfway up the sides of the measuring cup. Heat until the broth is warm and the gelatin has dissolved. (Or melt in the microwave oven.)

Seaside Melting Potatoes

This is a variation of Melting Potatoes that roasts in the same way. A hint of the ocean comes through with the fish stock and a fresh taste with the dill. Perfect to serve with a whole roasted fish.

Substitute 4 tablespoons olive oil for the butter and Basic Fish Stock (page 505) for the chicken stock. Start with 6 tablespoons oil in the roasting pan, the wedges sprinkled with the salt and pepper. Combine ½ teaspoon dill seed with the fish stock before adding it. Drizzle the last tablespoon of the oil over the potatoes at the end, when returning them to the oven for reheating. To serve, top the potato wedges with finely chopped fresh dill. Squeeze on the juice from 1 large lemon wedge, if desired.

Greek Island Potatoes

If there are any of these addicting potato slices left over, they can be reheated in a single layer in a roasting pan in a 400°F oven for 10 minutes, or until crisp again. I learned this at my friend Marilia Aisenstein's Greek island home.

3 pounds floury potatoes, peeled and cut into
⅓-inch slices (about 8 cups)

1¼ cups olive oil

3 tablespoons paprika

2 tablespoons dried oregano

2 tablespoons kosher salt

Freshly ground black pepper to taste

3 tablespoons fresh lemon juice

continued

Put one oven rack in the bottom position, another at the top. Preheat the oven to 350°F.

In a large bowl, combine the potatoes with the oil, paprika, oregano and salt, coating the potatoes thoroughly. Place in a single layer in a large roasting pan (or use two 17 x 12-inch pans and divide the potatoes evenly between the two). Cook for 30 minutes on the bottom rack.

Move the pans to the top rack and turn the heat to broil. Cook for 15 minutes, or until crispy and browned but not burned.

Remove the potatoes to a large platter. Sprinkle with the pepper and lemon juice while still hot. Let sit for 5 minutes and serve. **Serves 5 as a side dish**

Potato Pancakes

This is the most basic of potato pancakes. The Jewish variation that follows makes latkes for Chanukah.

> **3 pounds floury potatoes, peeled and coarsely grated (about 6 cups)**
>
> **5 teaspoons kosher salt**
>
> **Freshly ground black pepper to taste**
>
> **2 to 4 tablespoons vegetable oil, or as needed**

Pat the potatoes dry and toss with the salt and pepper in a large bowl. Heat 2 tablespoons oil in a 12-inch nonstick frying pan (use the larger amount of oil if you do not have a nonstick pan) over high heat. Spread the potatoes evenly in the pan and cook, without stirring, until they begin to brown on the bottom, about 5 minutes. Turn the heat to low, cover and cook until the potatoes are golden brown on the bottom, about 20 minutes.

Invert the potatoes onto a large flat plate or the lid of the pan. Add more oil if the skillet appears dry. Slide the potatoes back into the

skillet on their bottoms. Turn the heat to high and cook until the potatoes begin to brown on the bottom, about 3 minutes. Turn the heat to low, cover and cook until the potatoes are golden brown on the bottom, about 7 minutes. Slide the pancake out onto a large plate and serve warm. **Serves 10 as a side dish**

NOTE: *To make 6 servings:* Use 1½ pounds potatoes, 2½ teaspoons kosher salt, pepper to taste and 1½ to 3 tablespoons vegetable oil, or as needed. Cook in a 9-inch skillet.

Jewish Potato Pancakes

> **1 3/4 pounds floury potatoes, peeled**
>
> **1 medium onion, coarsely chopped**
>
> **1 tablespoon kosher salt**
>
> **1/2 teaspoon baking soda**
>
> **1/2 cup all-purpose flour**
>
> **5 large eggs, lightly beaten**
>
> **Oil or rendered chicken fat for frying**

Coarsely grate the potatoes with a grater or in a food processor. Place the potatoes in a food processor and process until creamy but still gritty to the touch. Drain off as much liquid as possible and scrape the potatoes into a medium bowl.

Place the onion in the food processor and process until finely chopped. Scrape into the bowl with the potatoes. Stir in the salt, baking soda, flour and eggs.

Add enough oil to a 12-inch frying pan to come to a depth of ¼ inch and heat over medium-high heat until hot but not smoking. Working in batches, pour in ⅓ cup batter for each pancake (about 2 pancakes at a time) and cook until brown on the bottom, about 2 minutes. Turn the pancakes and cook until brown on the

bottom, about 2 minutes. Remove from the pan with a slotted spatula and drain on paper towels. Keep them warm in a 200°F oven while cooking the remaining pancakes. Serve warm.
Serves 12 as a side dish

Swiss Potato Pancakes
Rösti

Swiss potato pancakes, or rösti, are usually made large and thick in big quantities for hearty cold-weather appetites. I like them small and crisp as a base for sour cream and chives or smoked salmon, caviar or smoked trout. The crisper cakes are easier for guests to pick up. These can also be made ahead, frozen and reheated.

> 1 1/2 pounds waxy potatoes, peeled
>
> 2 tablespoons kosher salt
>
> 1/4 teaspoon freshly ground black pepper
>
> Vegetable oil for frying

Grate the potatoes lengthwise on a coarse grater into a mixing bowl; or use the julienne blade on a mandoline. Press the potatoes firmly against the grater, to get thicker strips that will make rösti that hold together more firmly (about 4 cups). Add the salt and pepper and toss to mix.

Pour a thin film, about ⅛ inch, of oil into a large nonstick frying pan. Heat over medium-high heat until wavy. Working in batches, form 2-inch pancakes, using 1 tablespoon of the potato mixture for each one. Don't overcrowd the pan; leave enough room to turn the rösti easily. Cook, turning once, until golden brown on both sides, about 6 minutes. Drain the rösti on a double thickness of paper towels. Keep them warm in a 200°F oven while cooking the remaining rösti, or until needed. Serve warm.
Makes thirty-six 2-inch rösti

NOTE: The pancakes can be made up to 4 weeks in advance and frozen. Freeze in a single layer. When they've frozen, set them in a container, separating the layers of pancakes with wax paper. Cover the container tightly with aluminum foil and a lid. To serve: Place the pancakes in a single layer on a baking sheet and heat in a 375°F oven until warmed through and crisp, about 6 minutes; flip once. (Do not thaw the pancakes before heating, or they will get soggy.)

Mashed Potato Cakes

I make lots of mashed potatoes. Rarely, there are some left over. It is better to make these than reheat the mash.

> 2 cups Mashed Potatoes (page 73) made with whole milk
>
> 1 large egg
>
> 1 tablespoon freshly grated Parmesan cheese
>
> Kosher salt to taste
>
> 2 teaspoons unsalted butter
>
> 2 teaspoons vegetable oil

Stir together the potatoes, egg, cheese and salt in a small bowl. Refrigerate until very cold.

Heat the butter and oil in a 12-inch frying pan over medium-high heat. Divide the potatoes into 6 portions, form into flat rounds and place in the pan, leaving space between them. Allow the potatoes to set, about 2 minutes, then turn the heat to low and cook until the potatoes are golden brown on the bottom, about 6 minutes. Raise the heat, turn the potatoes over, and cook until they set, about 2 minutes. Lower the heat and cook until the potatoes are well browned, about 5 minutes. Remove the potatoes from the pan with a spatula and drain on paper towels. Serve warm. **Serves 6 as a side dish**

The Art of the Fry

With the exception of shoestring fries, all French fries are cooked twice: once at lower heat to cook them through and evaporate much of their water and once at higher heat to crisp them up and turn them golden. Shoestring potatoes, because of their thinness, can be cooked through, browned and crisped in one frying.

Whatever the type of fries, keep an eye on the temperature of the oil. When the potatoes go in, the temperature goes down. Raise the heat slightly until the temperature returns to its starting point. That usually happens just before the potatoes are cooked through (first frying) or crisp (second frying).

Shoestring and regular fries can be cut on a mandoline or similar slicing tool, or by hand. The more even the cut, the better the end result.

Homemade French fries are an excellent reason to make Better Than Ketchup (page 114), and vice versa.

For Frying: Cook no more at a time than the fries cut from two 8-ounce baking potatoes. Pour 2 quarts vegetable oil into a heavy 4- to 5-quart pot. Heat over medium heat to the desired temperature. Use a wire skimmer to separate the potatoes as they cook and to remove them. Drain them on a baking sheet lined with several thicknesses of paper towels. Potatoes may be fried up to 2 hours before the second frying.

Shoestring Fries

Heat the oil to 360°F. While it is heating, peel the potatoes and cut them lengthwise into ³⁄₁₆-inch-thick strips. Spread out on paper towels and blot dry. Carefully slip the potatoes into the oil, a handful at a time. Immediately stir gently to keep the potatoes from sticking. Fry, stirring occasionally, until golden brown and crisp, about 5 minutes. Remove with the wire skimmer, draining excess oil back into the pot, and drain on paper towels. Sprinkle with kosher salt.

French Fries

Heat the oil to 300°F. While the oil is heating, peel the potatoes and cut lengthwise into ³⁄₈-inch-thick strips. Slip the potatoes a handful at a time into the oil; immediately stir to keep them from sticking. Fry, stirring occasionally, until the potatoes are tender when poked with the tip of a paring knife and the ends are just beginning to brown, 4 to 5 minutes. Remove with the wire skimmer, draining excess oil back into the pot, and drain on paper towels.

To serve: Heat the oil to 360°F. Return the potatoes to the oil, stirring gently to separate them. Fry, stirring occasionally, until golden brown and crisp, about 4 minutes. Drain and sprinkle with kosher salt.

Steak-House Fries

Steak-house fries will not be as crispy as regular or shoestring fries. The abundant delicious exterior and fluffy interior make up for that.

Heat the oil to 275°F. While it is heating, cut peeled or unpeeled potatoes (scrub and dry well if using unpeeled potatoes) lengthwise into large strips no more than ⅝ to ¾ inch on any side. Slip the potatoes into the oil; immediately stir to separate them. Fry, stirring occasionally, until the potatoes are tender when poked with a fork and the ends are just beginning to brown, about 8 minutes. Remove with the wire skimmer, draining excess oil back into the pot, and drain on paper towels.

To serve: Heat the oil to 360°F. Return the potatoes to the oil, stirring gently to separate them. Fry, stirring occasionally, until golden brown and firm, about 5 minutes. Drain and sprinkle with kosher salt.

Angel Potatoes

These are the quickest and probably the most dramatic deep-fried potatoes.

2 pounds floury potatoes, peeled and rinsed

Corn oil for deep-frying

Kosher salt to taste

Using a food processor with a shredding disc, shred the potatoes in two batches. Turn out onto kitchen toweling and pat dry.

Pour the oil into a deep-fat fryer or fill a 10-inch wok with oil to within 2 inches of the rim. Heat until smoking. Add half the potatoes and stir constantly with a wooden spoon until they are golden; this will take very little time. With a skimmer, remove the cooked potatoes to paper toweling to drain. Repeat with the remaining potatoes. Sprinkle with salt and serve. **Serves 4 to 6 as a side dish**

Potato Gratin

Pommes Lyonnaise

This is the perfect potato gratin. Decadent and beautiful, it cooks up with a fantastic brown crust and just enough liquid to keep the potatoes moist and creamy. It can be made ahead; dot another tablespoon of butter (cut into small pieces) on top before putting it in a 375°F oven to reheat for 10 minutes.

2 tablespoons unsalted butter

6 medium floury potatoes (about 2 3/4 pounds), peeled and cut into 1/8-inch slices (about 7 cups)

1 cup heavy cream

2 cloves garlic, smashed, peeled and minced

2 teaspoons kosher salt

Put a rack in the center of the oven. Preheat the oven to 450°F.

Coat the bottom of a 12 x 8-inch oval baking dish with 1 tablespoon butter. Arrange the potato slices in layers evenly in the dish. Mix the cream, garlic and salt together and pour over the potatoes.

Cover with aluminum foil and bake for 20 minutes. Remove the foil and cook for another 20 minutes.

Cut the remaining tablespoon of butter into small pieces and scatter over the gratin. Reduce the oven temperature to 375°F and cook for 20 minutes longer, or until about half the liquid is absorbed and a golden brown crust has formed on top. Remove from the oven and let cool for 15 minutes. **Serves 6 to 8 as a side dish**

Sage Potatoes

This recipe—impossible to stop eating—from Chef Francesco Antonucci at Remi, a very good Italian restaurant in New York, really had me confused. When I first tested it, I thought it was made with a batter and fried; I couldn't duplicate it. I threw myself on Francesco's mercy, and he gave me the recipe, which included neither batter nor frying. The potatoes can be reheated for five minutes in a 350°F oven, or they can be cooked ahead and frozen, then reheated for about five minutes (do not thaw first). Allow at least five ovals per person, and multiply the recipe as need be. You can have the sheets of potatoes all ready to go in the oven. They need not be eaten hot.

Vegetable oil for greasing pan

1 large baking potato (about 10 ounces), peeled

4 tablespoons unsalted butter, melted, or 1/4 cup olive oil

25 fresh sage leaves, stems removed

Kosher salt to taste

continued

Preheat the oven to 350°F. Generously oil a baking sheet (not air-cushioned).

Cut the potato lengthwise into paper-thin slices (this is easily done on a mandoline). Trim the slices into ovals slightly larger than the sage leaves. Place the ovals in a medium bowl, add the butter and toss to coat.

Place 1 potato slice on a work surface. Put a sage leaf in the center and sprinkle with a little salt. Cover with another potato slice. Place on the baking sheet. Repeat with the remaining potato slices and sage leaves.

Bake until browned on the edges, about 12 minutes. Transfer to a plate lined with paper towels. Sprinkle with additional salt, if desired. **Makes 25 pieces**

Pommes à l'Huile

This is a French version of potato salad, served tepid or at room temperature. It is a favorite accompaniment to sausage along with a sharp Dijon mustard. This recipe will feed six; but it is well worth doubling or tripling, as it is sure to disappear from the refrigerator behind your back. To serve it a second time, take it out of the refrigerator far enough in advance of mealtime for it to warm up to room temperature all the way through.

1 ½ pounds waxy red or white new potatoes

1 teaspoon kosher salt

3 grinds fresh black pepper

1 ½ tablespoons tarragon vinegar

¼ cup olive oil

¼ teaspoon dry mustard

1 tablespoon good stock (optional)

1 tablespoon chopped fresh parsley

1 teaspoon chopped fresh chives

Boil the potatoes in their skins in salted water until they can be pierced with a toothpick. Drain.

As soon as the potatoes can be handled, slip off the skins. Slice ⅛ inch thick and place in a china or glass bowl. Combine the remaining ingredients except the herbs. Toss with the potatoes until they are well coated and shiny. Put to one side, covered by a plate, to cool to room temperature. Fold in the chopped herbs. Serve. **Serves 6 as a side dish**

Potato and Truffle Salad

This may be the world's most opulent potato salad. As can be imagined, it comes from France.

6 pounds waxy white new potatoes

3 cups dry white wine

3 tablespoons kosher salt

¼ cup very thinly sliced black, white or winter truffles (2 small truffles)

1 ½ tablespoons minced shallots

1 ½ tablespoons vegetable oil

3 tablespoons heavy cream

Generous amount of freshly ground black pepper

Cook the potatoes in a large quantity of boiling salted water until tender. Drain in a colander.

Peel the potatoes as soon as they are cool enough to handle. Slice into ⅛-inch-thick rounds and place in a large mixing bowl. Pour over 2 cups wine and ½ tablespoon oil and add 2 tablespoons salt. Toss gently to coat. Let the potatoes cool, adding more wine as it is absorbed.

When the potatoes are cool, add the remaining ingredients, including the remaining 1 tablespoon oil. Refrigerate, covered, at least 8 hours before serving. **Makes 4 quarts**

Potato Salad
with Capers and Bacon

Yum!

- 1 1/2 pounds waxy new potatoes, preferably red
- 2 tablespoons olive oil
- 1 tablespoon tarragon vinegar
- 2 tablespoons coarsely chopped fresh parsley
- 2 tablespoons coarsely chopped fresh dill
- 4 scallions, trimmed and thinly sliced on the diagonal
- 1 tablespoon salt-packed or drained jarred capers
- 2 tablespoons crisply fried diced bacon
- Kosher salt and freshly ground black pepper to taste

Boil the potatoes in salted water to cover generously until just cooked through. Drain.

As soon as they are cool enough to handle, cut the potatoes into 1/2-inch-thick pieces with the skins on. Place in a bowl and, while they are still warm, add the oil, vinegar, herbs, scallions, capers and bacon, tossing thoroughly. Season with salt and pepper to taste. Serve at room temperature. **Serves 6 as a side dish**

Creamy Potato Salad

A rich and spicy basic potato salad.

- 2 1/2 pounds waxy red new potatoes
- 5 to 6 stalks celery (about 6 ounces), peeled, halved lengthwise and cut across into 1/4-inch slices
- 1/2 red onion, cut into 1/4-inch dice
- 10 hard-boiled eggs, peeled and coarsely chopped
- 3 tablespoons dried basil
- 1/2 bunch fresh parsley, leaves only, coarsely chopped
- 4 cups Classic Mayonnaise (page 455), Cooked-Yolk Mayonnaise (page 455) or commercial mayonnaise
- 1/4 cup Zatarain's or other Creole mustard
- 5 anchovy fillets
- 1/4 cup tarragon vinegar
- 1/4 cup fresh lemon juice
- Kosher salt and freshly ground black pepper to taste

Boil the potatoes in salted water to cover generously until just done. Drain.

As soon as the potatoes are cool enough to handle, cut them into 1-inch cubes, leaving the skin on. Place in a bowl and, while the potatoes are still warm, add the celery, onion, eggs, basil and parsley. Toss to combine.

In a food processor, combine the remaining ingredients and process for 1 minute. Pour the dressing over the potatoes and mix well. Let sit for 1 hour before serving to allow the flavors to meld. **Makes 2 quarts**

Salade Russe

Although called "Russe" ("Russian"), this is really a classic French dish used as a first course or as a side dish with cold meats or fish.

1/2 pound floury potatoes, peeled and cut into 1/4-inch dice

1/2 pound carrots, peeled and cut into 1/4-inch dice

1/2 pound turnips, peeled and cut into 1/4-inch dice

1/4 pound green beans, tipped, tailed and cut into 1/4-inch pieces

1 cup fresh peas

1/3 cup Classic Mayonnaise (page 455), Cooked-Yolk Mayonnaise (page 455) or commercial mayonnaise

2 tablespoons tarragon vinegar

2 tablespoons chopped fresh tarragon

6 cornichons, thinly sliced (optional)

Kosher salt and freshly ground black pepper to taste

Combine the potatoes and 2 tablespoons water in a 1-quart soufflé dish. Cover tightly with microwave plastic wrap. Microwave at 100% for 4 minutes 30 seconds. Prick the plastic to release the steam.

Remove from the oven and uncover. Drain the potatoes.

Place the carrots in a ring around the edge of a 13 x 9 x 2-inch oval dish. Form a ring of turnips inside the ring of carrots. Place the green beans in the center of the dish; place the peas on top.

Cover tightly with microwave plastic wrap. Cook at 100% for 5 minutes. Prick the plastic to release the steam.

Remove from the oven and uncover. Stir the vegetables. Re-cover and cook at 100% for 3 minutes longer. Prick the plastic to release the steam.

Remove from the oven and uncover. Add the vegetables to the potatoes. Gently stir in the mayonnaise, vinegar, tarragon and cornichons, if using. Season to taste with salt and pepper. Allow to cool. Serve at room temperature.

Serves 4 as a side dish

Summer Squash

Pattypan, Zucchini and Yellow Squash

The summer squash come in all shades of yellow, white and green. They range from little scalloped pattypans to zucchini (courgettes) to the lemon yellow of what is actually called "summer squash." All are best young and small, when their seeds are unformed and their flesh is firm, not pulpy. All have edible skins that add color and nutrition. The one exception to the small-is-best rule is the Italian cucuzza, which is long and twisted. Cut it up and use it as zucchini.

The very smallest squash may be hard to find when they are growing, as they hide under the huge dark green leaves and mimic the look of the stalks. A few always get away from me and grow to an exaggerated size before discovery.

If confronted with one of these, check the skin for blemishes and gouge them out with the tip of a sharp knife. Cut the squash lengthwise into quarters. Place each quarter, skin side down, and run a knife down its length to cut out the large seeds and pulpy interior. Proceed to cook as with common squash, but do check the weight.

Turn to **SQUASH, SUMMER** in the Cook's Guide for how-tos and to the Index for more recipes.

Pattypan-Potato Soufflés

These are very pretty. It is important to drain the squash thoroughly.

Serve them with a light tomato sauce or on a bed of Parsley Salad (page 444). The chewy deep green leaves are a good color and textural contrast to the pale and creamy squash.

As a variation, the soufflés can be baked in four-ounce ramekins that have been buttered and dusted with bread crumbs, then turned out onto a plate for serving.

6 medium pattypan squash (5 ounces each)
   or 3 large pattypans (12 ounces each)

Kosher salt

Oil for brushing pattypans

1 medium floury potato (7 ounces)

1 1/2 teaspoons grated onion

1 teaspoon fresh thyme leaves or
   1/4 teaspoon dried

Freshly ground black pepper to taste

2 large eggs, separated

2 tablespoons grated Swiss cheese

2 large egg whites

Place a rack in the center of the oven. Preheat the oven to 350°F.

Cook the pattypans in boiling water until softened but still firm enough to hold their shape once the insides have been scooped out, 11 to 12 minutes for medium pattypans, 20 minutes for large. Rinse under cold running water. Cut a lid from the flat end of each pattypan, and carefully remove the pulp with the small end of a melon baller. There will be about 1 1/2 cups pulp. Reserve.

Sprinkle the inside of each pattypan with a pinch of salt. Brush the outside of each with oil and arrange on a baking sheet.

Chop the pulp and drain it in a sieve set over a bowl; push down on the solids to remove as much liquid as possible and reduce the volume by half. While the pulp is draining, boil the potato until a knife easily slips into the flesh. Rinse under cold running water. Peel and place in a large bowl. Mash with a fork until smooth.

Purée the drained pulp in a food processor and add to the potato. Stir in the onion, thyme, 1 1/2 teaspoons salt, pepper, egg yolks and cheese.

In a clean metal bowl, beat the egg whites until stiff but not dry. Stir about one-quarter of the egg whites into the pattypan mixture, then fold in the remaining whites. Spoon the soufflé into the pattypans, mounding a generous amount on top. Do not worry if there is a little extra soufflé remaining.

Bake for 45 minutes, or until the soufflés are puffed and golden brown. Serve immediately.
**Serves 6 as a first course if using medium pattypans,
3 as a main course if using large pattypans**

Green Gazpacho with Citrus Fruit and Yellow Squash

There are so many gazpachos in Spain I thought there could be no objection if I added a slightly freaky one of my own. I love the colors, the rich aromas of citrus fruits, the garlic and cilantro. The taste has a rich balance too.

- 1 medium onion, peeled and quartered
- 2 medium green bell peppers, cored, deribbed and seeded, cut into 1-inch pieces
- 2 medium cucumbers, peeled and thickly sliced
- 1/2 cup packed fresh parsley leaves
- 1/2 cup packed cilantro leaves
- 1 cup Spanish olive oil
- 3 medium to large cloves garlic, smashed and peeled
- 2 small fresh hot green peppers, cut into 1/4-inch rings
- Kosher salt
- 3 slices soft bread, crusts removed, torn into pieces
- 1 medium yellow summer squash, trimmed and thickly sliced
- 2 lemons
- 1 navel orange

In a food processor, process—one at a time—the onion, then the green peppers, cucumbers, parsley and cilantro, pulsing until finely chopped. Stop the machine frequently to scrape the sides of the bowl. Transfer each ingredient as it is chopped to a bowl large enough to hold them all. Put the olive oil, garlic, hot peppers, 1½ tablespoons salt and bread into the processor and process until finely puréed. Add to the chopped ingredients. Process the squash until coarsely chopped; add to the bowl.

Cut 1 lemon and the orange into quarters. Reserve one-quarter of the orange for another use. Remove the seeds from the remaining citrus quarters and place, peel and all, in the food processor. Process until minced, frequently scraping the sides of the bowl. Stir into the rest of the soup.

Squeeze the remaining lemon and add the juice to the soup. Add salt to taste. Refrigerate until ready to serve.

After refrigerating, the soup may need to be thinned with water, since oil thickens as it gets cold. **Serves 4 as a first course**

Zucchini Custard

This is one of my all-time best—a sort of crustless quiche. The quality comes from letting the zucchini drain until there is no liquid left to disrupt the texture of the custard. The peeled zucchini virtually disappears into the custard.

- 2 pounds small firm zucchini, trimmed, peeled and cut into strips 2 inches long and 1/4 inch thick
- 1 1/2 cups heavy cream
- 3 large eggs, beaten
- 1/3 to 3/4 cup freshly grated Parmesan cheese
- Freshly ground black pepper to taste

Bring about 6 cups heavily salted water to a boil in a medium saucepan. Add the zucchini, return to the boil and boil for 30 seconds; drain well. Spread the zucchini in a single layer on kitchen towels and let dry for several hours or all day.

Place a rack in the lower third of the oven. Preheat the oven to 450°F.

Mix the zucchini with the cream, eggs, cheese and pepper. Pour the mixture into a 9- or 10-inch pie plate or ceramic quiche pan. Bake for 40 minutes, or until puffed, brown, custardy and set.

Serve immediately. **Serves 8 as a side dish**

NOTE: If individual servings are preferred, divide the mixture among eight 6-ounce ceramic quiche pans and bake for 15 to 20 minutes.

Roasted Yellow Squash in a Mint Bath

This is as fresh tasting as summer and just as attractive. I like it best at room temperature as an addition to an antipasto platter or as part of a vegetarian main course.

The preparation can be done up to eight hours ahead, with the squash left to marinate, covered, at room temperature. It is extremely important to have the oven rack in the top position.

4 medium yellow summer squash (2 pounds), trimmed, cut across in half and each half cut lengthwise into 4 pieces, seeds scooped out

1/4 cup fresh lemon juice

1/4 cup olive oil

1/4 cup tightly packed fresh mint leaves, chopped medium-fine

1 teaspoon kosher salt

Place a rack in the top of the oven. Preheat the oven to 500°F.

Check the slices of squash to see that pieces are no larger than 5 x 1¼ inches. Any larger, and the squash will not cook evenly; trim if necessary.

In a small bowl, combine the lemon juice, oil, mint and salt. Pour into a 14 x 12 x 2-inch roasting pan. Arrange the squash in the pan, with the thinner pieces in the center of the pan and larger pieces around the edges so that the squash fits tightly and doesn't leave a lot of surface space showing. Roll the squash in the oil mixture. Roast for 30 minutes.

Use a fork or a spatula to turn the squash pieces over. Roast for 15 minutes more. Serve warm from the oven or at room temperature.
Serves 6 to 8 as part of a first course or as a side dish

Sautéed Zucchini with Dill

Quick and flavorful, this can be made with yellow summer squash in the fall. Sometimes I like to cover the pan and cook the zucchini until meltingly soft. Very different. The shrunken zucchini serves only four.

5 tablespoons unsalted butter

2 pounds young zucchini, trimmed and cut into 1/4-inch-thick rounds

1/2 cup chopped fresh dill

Juice of 1 lemon

Kosher salt to taste

Heat the butter in a 12-inch sauté pan. Add the zucchini, dill and lemon juice. Cook over medium heat, stirring, until the zucchini is cooked but still slightly crisp. Add salt to taste.
Serves 6 to 8 as a side dish

Zucchini Chunks with Citrus and Mint

A zesty summer treat, particularly good with fish.

5 medium zucchini (2 pounds), trimmed, quartered lengthwise and cut across into 1 1/2-inch chunks

1 tablespoon canola oil or other neutral oil

1 teaspoon kosher salt, or to taste

2 tablespoons fresh orange juice

2 teaspoons fresh lemon juice

2 tablespoons chopped (medium-fine) fresh mint

Freshly ground black pepper to taste

Place a rack in the center of the oven. Heat the oven to 500°F.

Toss the zucchini chunks with the oil and salt in a 14 x 12 x 2-inch roasting pan.

Roast for 10 minutes. Shake the pan vigorously to move the squash pieces around. Roast for 10 minutes more—if not planning to serve immediately, roast for slightly less time, as the retained heat will continue to cook the zucchini chunks, making them soft and mushy.

Transfer the zucchini and roasting liquid to a medium bowl. Add the orange juice, lemon juice, mint and pepper. Stir to combine. Taste and add salt, if necessary. **Serves 4 as a side dish**

Buttery Zucchini and Summer Squash

This simple recipe tastes buttery without being greasy. The vegetables absorb all of the butter, becoming tender and delicious but not mushy.

1 tablespoon unsalted butter

1 medium yellow squash, trimmed, quartered lengthwise and cut across into $^1/_2$-inch slices (about 1 $^3/_4$ cups)

1 medium zucchini, trimmed, quartered lengthwise and cut across into $^1/_2$-inch slices (about 1 $^3/_4$ cups)

1 teaspoon kosher salt

In a small pot (about 8 inches across), melt the butter over medium heat. Add the squash and zucchini. Cook, stirring regularly, for 10 minutes, or until the insides are tender but the outsides are still firm and slightly crunchy. Mix in the salt. Cook for 1 minute longer, stirring. Serve. **Make 2 cups; serves 2 as a side dish**

Oven-Grilled Zucchini

This method gives attractive grill marks without the hassle of firing up the grill.

4 medium zucchini, trimmed and cut lengthwise into $^1/_2$-inch slices

$^1/_2$ cup olive oil

Kosher salt and freshly ground black pepper to taste

Place a rack in the top of the oven. Preheat the oven to 500°F. Place a metal wire cooling rack (not a mesh rack) on a baking sheet and heat in the oven for at least 20 minutes.

With a pastry brush, cover both sides of the zucchini slices with olive oil. When the wire rack and baking sheet have preheated, brush the rack generously with olive oil. Place the zucchini slices on the wire rack, laying them perpendicular to the wires for proper marking (cook in batches if necessary). Cook for 10 minutes on each side. Remove from the oven and let cool. Season with salt and pepper to taste.
Makes 16 slices; serves 4 as a side dish

Green Curry of Summer Squash

The recipe, green with spinach, makes more spice powder than needed. Store the remainder in an airtight jar and use it to flavor chicken, pork and fish or a variety of vegetables.

SPICE POWDER

2 tablespoons coriander seeds

2 tablespoons mustard seeds

2 teaspoons cumin seeds

2 teaspoons fennel seeds

$^1/_2$ teaspoon hot red pepper flakes

continued

SQUASH

2 tablespoons vegetable oil

1 medium onion (8 ounces), thinly sliced

1 clove garlic, smashed, peeled and minced

1 teaspoon Spice Powder (page 87)

Large pinch of cayenne pepper

4 cups stemmed and washed spinach
   (about 1 pound before cleaning)

3 scallions, trimmed and coarsely
   chopped

3 tablespoons chopped fresh dill

1/4 cup Basic Chicken Stock (page 501),
   Roasted Chicken Stock (page 502) or
   commercial chicken broth

1 teaspoon kosher salt

2 small zucchini (about 8 ounces), trimmed,
   cut into 2-inch lengths and each round
   cut into eighths

2 small yellow squash (about 8 ounces),
   trimmed, cut into 2-inch lengths and
   each round cut into eighths

Spread the spice powder ingredients in an even layer in a flat dish. Cook, uncovered, at 100% for 6 minutes, shaking the dish once. Let cool completely. Grind the spices to a fine powder in a spice grinder or clean electric coffee mill. (Makes 1/4 cup)

Reserve 1 teaspoon of the spice powder for use in this recipe; store the remainder in an airtight container.

Microwave the oil in a 2-quart soufflé dish, uncovered, at 100% for 2 minutes. Add the onion, garlic, spice powder and cayenne. Cook, uncovered, at 100% for 4 minutes.

Add the remaining ingredients except the zucchini and yellow squash. Cover tightly with microwave plastic wrap. Cook at 100%

for 5 minutes. Carefully uncover and stir in the squash. Cover again and cook at 100% for 5 minutes more, stirring once. Prick the plastic to release the steam.

Remove from the oven. Uncover and let stand for 3 minutes before serving.

Serves 4 as a side dish

Summer Vegetable Bonanza

This is terrific in early summer when the first of the vegetables start coming in. For a meal, add eggs or stir in ¾ pound feta cheese or tofu, rinsed and cut into ½-inch cubes, at the last minute. Serve lots of chunky bread, please.

1 tablespoon kosher salt

8 grinds fresh black pepper

1 teaspoon dried thyme

6 tablespoons olive oil

2 pounds baby eggplants (4 1/2 to 5 inches long)
   or Chinese eggplants (5 to 6 inches long),
   trimmed and cut lengthwise into quarters,
   or 2 pounds larger eggplants, trimmed and
   cut into 2 x 2 x 3-inch pieces

1/2 pound baby zucchini (3 to 4 inches long),
   trimmed, or larger zucchini, trimmed and
   cut into 1 x 1 x 3-inch pieces

1/2 pound baby yellow squash (3 to 4 inches long),
   trimmed, or larger squash, trimmed and
   cut into 1 x 1 x 3-inch pieces

2 pounds plum tomatoes (about 12), cored and
   cut in half lengthwise

12 cloves garlic, smashed and peeled

1 cup packed fresh basil leaves,
   plus extra for serving if desired

Combine the salt, pepper and thyme in a small bowl. Set aside.

Heat the oil in a deep pan wide enough to hold the eggplant in a single layer. Add the eggplant. Cover and cook for 5 minutes over low heat. Turn the eggplant over. Cover; cook for another 5 minutes. Sprinkle some of the salt mixture over the eggplant.

Arrange the zucchini and yellow squash on top of the eggplant. Sprinkle with more of the salt mixture. Top with the tomatoes, cut side up. Sprinkle with the remaining salt mixture. Tuck the garlic and basil among the vegetables. Cover. Cook over low heat for 20 minutes, or until a knife inserts easily into the vegetables but they are not falling apart.

Transfer the vegetables to a platter. Pour any juices in the bottom of the pan over the vegetables. Serve with extra basil sprigs scattered on top, if desired.

Serves 12 as a side dish or a first course, 6 as a vegetarian main course

Microwave Variation

If using baby or Chinese eggplants, trim each one and prick 4 times with a fork. Leave the plum tomatoes whole. Core and prick each one four times with a fork.

Arrange the eggplants around the rim of a 14 x 12 x 2-inch dish. Place the zucchini and yellow squash in the center. Arrange the tomatoes in a ring on top. Tuck the garlic and basil among the vegetables. Sprinkle the thyme, salt and pepper over all. Drizzle with the oil.

Cover tightly with microwave plastic wrap. Cook at 100% for 20 minutes. Prick the plastic to release the steam.

Remove from the oven. Uncover and let stand for 3 minutes. Serve with extra basil sprigs scattered on top, if desired.

Midsummer Squash

The quality of olive oil is particularly important in this dish. If not using an exceptionally fruity oil (which can also be exceptionally expensive), double the amount of oil and reduce the cooking time by 1 minute. If small tomatoes are not available, core and quarter large tomatoes.

This combination was devised at the height of summer, when I had returned from Vermont with a bounty of perfect produce. There are alternatives for some of the ingredients, but one that is indispensable is fresh basil. Best of all was a version using half bush basil and half large-leaf basil.

At once refreshing and comforting, this is one of my favorite recipes from a ripened garden on a warm day. The oil from the peppers is absorbed into all the other vegetables— delightful. Serve with cold leftover meat or an omelet. It is also good over pasta.

- 1 pound very small yellow squash (8 to 10 squash), with flowers intact if possible; or 1 pound larger yellow squash, trimmed and cut into 3 x 1 x1-inch pieces

- 4 medium Hungarian peppers, or 4 medium frying peppers plus 1 teaspoon hot red pepper flakes

- 1 pound small tomatoes (2 inches in diameter), each pricked 3 or 4 times

- 1/4 cup fresh basil leaves

- 2 tablespoons fruity olive oil

- 1 teaspoon kosher salt

Arrange the squash spoke-fashion in a 2-quart soufflé dish, with the flowers, or narrower ends, pointing toward the center. Place the peppers in the center and arrange the tomatoes on top of the squash. Tuck the basil between the vegetables. Pour 2 tablespoons water, then the oil over all; sprinkle with the salt. Cover the dish tightly with microwave plastic wrap. Cook at 100% for 12 minutes and 30 seconds, or until the vegetables are tender. Prick the plastic to release the steam.

Remove from the oven and uncover. Cut the peppers in half. Serve hot or let cool to room temperature. **Serves 8 as a first course or a side dish**

Zucchini Bread-and-Butter Pickles

These are good to make when the garden has more zucchini than one could possibly imagine. Serve with any roast meat or hamburgers.

> **3 pounds medium zucchini (6 to 8 ounces each), cut into $^{1}/_{2}$-inch rounds with a ripple potato slicer, the ripple blade of a mandoline or with a food processor (about 12 cups)**
>
> **$^{3}/_{4}$ cup thinly sliced onion**
>
> **2 medium cloves garlic, smashed and peeled**
>
> **3 tablespoons kosher salt**
>
> **3 cups ice cubes**
>
> **Four 1-pint canning jars with two-piece lids**
>
> **2 tablespoons black mustard seeds or yellow mustard seeds**
>
> **2 cups white vinegar**
>
> **1$^{1}/_{2}$ cups sugar**
>
> **Three 2 x $^{1}/_{2}$-inch pieces orange zest**
>
> **1 teaspoon dill seeds**
>
> **1 teaspoon ground cumin**

Combine the zucchini, onion, garlic and salt in a large bowl. Add the ice cubes and stir to combine. Let stand for 3 hours.

Place the jars, lids and rings in a deep stockpot. Fill with enough water to cover the jars by 2 inches. Bring to a boil and boil for 5 to 10 minutes to sterilize. Use clean tongs to remove the jars from the water (for more about canning, see page 91).

Drain the vegetables; discard the liquid.

Place the mustard seeds in a 5-quart casserole dish. Cook in the microwave, uncovered, at 100% for 2 minutes. Remove from the oven and stir in the vinegar, sugar, zest, dill seeds and cumin. Stir well and cook, uncovered, at 100% for 6 minutes.

Add the zucchini mixture and stir to combine. Cover tightly with a lid or microwave plastic wrap. Cook at 100% for 12 minutes. Prick the plastic, if using, to release the steam.

Remove from the oven. Divide the zucchini among the sterilized jars, making sure it is covered with liquid. Use tongs to remove the lids from the water and carefully place on top of the jars. Screw onto the jars. **Makes 4 pints**

Canning

Most of the recipes for pickles or preserves in this book contain enough vinegar or sugar so that, when refrigerated, there is no threat of spoilage. For those recipes that require heat sterilization or for added security, follow these steps:

Always use canning jars with two-piece lids. (Never reuse the lids; replacements are sold separately.)

Place the jars and lids in a deep pot. Fill with enough water to cover the jars by 2 inches. Boil for 5 to 10 minutes to sterilize. Keep in hot water until needed.

Prepare the item(s) for canning. Remove the jars and lids with tongs. Fill the jars, leaving $1/2$ inch of headroom in pint and quart jars, $1/4$ inch in half-pint jars.

Fit together the two-piece lids and screw onto the jars just enough to close securely. Do not twist the lids on too tightly.

Stand the filled jars in the hot water. Bring to a boil and boil for 10 minutes for half-pint jars or for 15 minutes for pint or quart jars.

Remove the jars; let cool. When the jars are cool, check the seals.

Tomatillos

It is true that at the uppermost reaches of their family tree tomatillos are related to tomatoes and we tend to think of them as a sort of green tomato—especially as they come from Central America and are often used in salsas. However, they have a husk and are much more closely related to another fruit, the ground cherry, which often has the sections of its husk folded back to make a handle and the fruit itself is dipped into white fondant, to serve as part of a petits fours tray, especially in England.

There is a delicious combination of sweetness and mild acidity to tomatillos, of which I am particularly fond. It works spectacularly well in Fish Swimming in Vegetables, making enough sauce to flourish rice.

Turn to **TOMATILLOS** in the Cook's Guide
for how-tos and to the Index for more recipes.

Fresh Tomatillo Salsa

In northern climes, tomatillos—the green tomato-shape fruits with the brown papery husks—are easier to find than they used to be. They are nicely astringent. Serve tomatillo salsa along with a more conventional red tomato salsa. If fresh tomatillos are unavailable, skip right to the next recipe.

Finely chopped green bell pepper will improve the color of this dish. Multiply as needed.

2 medium cloves garlic, smashed and peeled

1 small jalapeño pepper, seeded and deribbed

$1/2$ pound tomatillos, husks removed, rinsed well, cored and coarsely chopped

2 scallions, trimmed and cut into 2-inch lengths

2 tablespoons chopped cilantro

1 tablespoon fresh lime juice

1 teaspoon kosher salt

Freshly ground black pepper to taste

Place the garlic and jalapeño in a food processor and chop very fine. Add the tomatillos and scallions and process until finely chopped but not puréed.

Transfer the mixture to a bowl and stir in $1/3$ cup water and the remaining ingredients. Allow to stand for about 30 minutes, then adjust the seasoning and serve. **Makes 1$1/2$ cups**

Canned Tomatillo Sauce

For those times (or places) when fresh tomatillos are not available. This is quite good.

2 medium cloves garlic, smashed and peeled

2 jalapeños, seeded; deribbed for a milder sauce

$3/4$ cup loosely packed fresh parsley leaves

$3/4$ cup loosely packed cilantro leaves

One 18-ounce can tomatillos, drained

1 small onion, chopped (about $1/3$ cup)

1 teaspoon fresh lemon juice

Pinch of sugar

$1/2$ teaspoon kosher salt

Place the garlic, peppers, parsley and cilantro in a food processor. Process until finely chopped. Add the tomatillos and process until smooth. Scrape the mixture into a small bowl. Stir in the onion, lemon juice, sugar and salt. **Makes 1$1/4$ cups**

Fish Swimming in Vegetables

This is beautiful to taste and beautiful to look at. The inspiration came from the sudden appearance in my market of some peppers I had never had before. They looked like jalapeños but were sweet and had thin skins like Italian frying peppers. They were a mix of red, yellow, orange and green and came in one-pint plastic containers. I still don't know what they are, but next year I will try to find seeds and grow them. (A good friend tells me that they were in the farmers' market last year, so it should be possible.)

The same market yielded tomatillos and baby Russian banana potatoes. My luck was in. The potatoes were good but mainly attractive with the small peppers; any firm potato or rice could be substituted.

continued

I made two three-pound snappers for four hearty eaters rather than cooking one big fish. That way, the fish and vegetables finished cooking at the same time. The roasting pan should be just large enough to hold the fish so the vegetables can be tucked between and around. The recipe can be made with a larger fish and the vegetables added twenty minutes before the fish is ready to come out of the oven.

2 red snappers, about 3 pounds each and 2 inches thick

2 pounds tomatillos, husks removed, rinsed well and quartered or cut into 6 wedges, depending on size

1 pound mini peppers (see headnote, page 93)

1/2 cup robust olive oil

1 scant cup fresh lemon juice

3 tablespoons kosher salt

Freshly ground black pepper to taste

Place a rack in the center of the oven. Preheat the oven to 500°F.

With a sharp knife, cut several diagonal slashes about 2 inches apart on each side of the fish. Put in a roasting pan and tuck the vegetables all around. Pour over the olive oil and lemon juice. Sprinkle with the salt and pepper. Turn the fish over and swirl the vegetables in the liquid. Put the fish in the oven and cook for 20 minutes, or until just cooked through.

Put the fish on a large platter so that it can be filleted with no bones ending up in mouths. Put the vegetables and sauce in a capacious bowl. Serve 2 pieces of fillet smothered with vegetables and liquid to each guest. Glorious.

Serves 4 as a main course

Poison Tomatoes

Poison? Those gorgeous fruits of the vine, the delights of a warm summer's day, the ravishment of a salad, the base of a hundred sauces—Italian and Hispanic—and the foundation of soups, cozy, robust and as elegant as can be? Yet there persists the legend that an English cook in General Washington's kitchen claimed to have poisoned him by adding tomatoes to a prepared dish. It wasn't until the eighteenth century that tomatoes really took off in North America.

Certainly, when they came to England from their home in Central America, *Gerard's Herbal* thought of them as poisonous and another herbal called them "cold and unhealthy." It is partly guilt by association; they are relatives of poisonous plants.

In their own right, their leaves and stems are poisonous.

Tomatoes came to Europe through Spain—but even there, where they eventually became extremely popular, it took over a century. In Italy, where they have practically become a religion, it took two centuries.

Today, if labor is a proof of love, then the tomato is America's food of love, as it was to the French—"pomme d'amour" (love apple), not related to the Italian "pomodoro," or golden apple. (The first tomatoes in Italy were gold in color, hence "oro.") In a world in which gardening is the nation's largest outdoor activity, the tomato is the most widely homegrown and plentiful crop.

It is also, if less obviously, our favorite flavor. Tomatoes are ubiquitous, so you may not notice that they pervade almost everything we eat. America's gift to world cooking shows up in foods Italian, Chinese and Thai. It may be concealed by the basil or coriander, hot peppers or garlic, fermented black beans or cream; but, just under the surface, there it is, America's favorite taste. It got a hold on us in childhood slathered on pizza, dripped onto hamburgers as ketchup, hugging pasta and helping salsas burn our mouths. Which is not to mention tomato juice, Bloody Mary mix and sun-dried tomatoes. Now it tops blue cornmeal pasta.

I love tomatoes. To my mind, one of the best reasons to put in the work of planting a vegetable garden and maintaining it all season long is to have sun-warm, vine-ripened tomatoes in a broad range of colors, sizes, textures and flavors available in one sense-startling glut—and the joy of putting them up in so many guises for winter-long pleasure!

I plant as many kinds as I have room for and buy what I don't. I have even come to be fond of tomato plants with their fuzzy leaves and the strange pungent perfume they give off in the hot summer sun. This smell at the stem end of a tomato—even in a store—is the sign of ripeness. It is acrid and tonic, not at all sweet.

Today we have a vast selection of tomatoes from which to choose, thanks to seed savers and importers of seeds from Europe. We no longer have to settle for the grocer's ubiquitous glossy red rounds of anonymity bred more for ease in shipping and shelf life than flavor. I like the tomato varieties from France whose tops are not smooth but evenly bumpy. Among the heirlooms from the saved seeds, I particularly like Brandywine, Paul Robeson and some of the extremely decorative tiger-stripe varieties—some orange and green and tawny red even when ripe. The tastes are all different, so it is fun to experiment.

I plant plum tomatoes for sauce and paste; large beefsteaks, hoping that they will ripen before the frost; and cherry tomatoes, yellow and red. I have even located seed for the yet smaller, sweeter, round tomatoes that look like a bunch of grapes, which Italians dry in the sun upended on the plant as peppers are dried in our Southwest. Some thumbnail-size tomatoes can be tossed into salads—watch out, they spurt juice when bitten into—or they can be sautéed with olive oil, garlic and basil as a quick vegetable. I welcome the small pear-shape, shmoo-like red and yellow tomatoes that pop with juice as I crunch them in my mouth. I slice the golden yellow tomatoes—normal except for their sweetness and extra color. I plant a quick-ripening tomato variety for first pleasure. I even grow tomatillos (see page 92), husk tomatoes, for acid green sauces. At summer's end, I pickle all the fruit that remains green.

This year I cheated. I supplemented the seedlings that cluttered my windowsills with large, vigorous plants bought at a local nursery, which set fruit almost the minute they went into the ground.

Tomatoes should be planted in full sun, with a tomato cage put around them so they will not

Dangerous Vegetables

SOLANACEAE

Poison Tomatoes, Promiscuous Peppers, Enemy Eggplants, Perilous Potatoes, Tempestuous Tomatillos

By now we all have been warned that tobacco, a prominent member of this family, can be lethal even though some chefs have taken to using it as a flavoring. We may be less aware that many edible members of this glorious family may be poisonous under the wrong conditions.

Under proper conditions, these mainly New World gifts to the table and even the pharmacopoeia are wonderful. We should never eat the leaves of any of these plants. The flowers of members of this family, such as aconite and digitalis (foxglove), should be consumed only properly prepared as medicines on a doctor's orders. They contain vast amounts of potentially toxic alkaloids. When Stubbs, my Portuguese water spaniel, was a tiny puppy, he was badly poisoned by eating some of these enticingly beautiful flowers in the garden. Owners of pets and children beware!

On the other hand, the beneficial qualities of decoctions of these flowers have been known and some have been used as hallucinogens and witches' ingredients. Since Roman times in the West and perhaps even earlier in China and India, they were early ways of putting people to sleep for operations and as heart medications. Women in their never-ending search for beauty used liquid henbane and belladonna as eyedrops, as well as to enlarge their pupils.

I find it interesting that, despite eggplants having been known and eaten in Europe and Asia for centuries, the fear engendered by the poisonous and medicinal drugs made from solanaceae overwhelmed all other ideas when the other edible plants of the family were discovered in America.

The edible group is so large and important that it would hardly fit in one chapter if many of the recipes were not in the sauces section of Basics, and in recipes in other chapters. See the Index.

fall over when they become large and heavy. Water as need be, but not too much or the skins will crack. I plant basil between the plants, as the two go together so well and the tomatoes provide needed shade for the basil.

While tomatoes are used frequently in this book, I have restrained myself. Wanting the book to be as usable as possible with commonly available ingredients, I do not call for glorious reddish-golden tomatoes or firm zebra-striped green tomatoes, or for the wonderful little Italian tomatoes that dry and sweeten as they hang from the drying racks. I do recommend trying them when available.

Tomato Salads

The sine qua non of a tomato first course is a salad. An emblematic tale is of Robert Courtine, one of the great French food writers. When he used to review restaurants, it was said he ordered a salade tomate as the first course no matter where he went, no matter how elegant the restaurant, feeling that it was a true test of a restaurant's devotion to good ingredients and proper technique.

The French typically use small, even, round tomatoes with bumpy shoulders. When they make salade tomate, they peel the tomatoes after a brief dip in simmering water. (When it's really ripe, all that is required is to run the back of the blade of a dinner knife over the entire tomato. Slip a sharp knife under the skin and pull; it will pull off.) The tomatoes are sliced, sprinkled with salt, overlapped on a plate and topped with a vinaigrette (pages 448–450). Recipes in nineteenth-century French cookbooks for the housewife do not call for peeling the tomato but otherwise are identical to today's usage.

The Italians approach great tomatoes informally but carefully. They don't add acid (lemon or vinegar), because they feel ripe tomatoes have enough. They slice the tomatoes about a quarter of an inch thick, overlap the slices and add only olive oil, basil, salt and pepper. The dressing that forms from the tomato juices and olive oil is then spooned on top. With the same mixture and Crostini (page 510), they make bruschetta as an equally easy first course.

In early fall, when the acrid smell of late tomatoes is in the air and they can be bought by the inexpensive bushel, do at least consider putting up some—canned or frozen—for winter use; it is easy. When tomatoes are cheap and mine are less than splendid, I buy a lot. They can be the imperfect, oddly shaped ones. I remember that the pink cardboard of winter tomatoes lies ahead. I spend time freezing, putting up and drying. Whole perfect tomatoes can be frozen in individual freezer containers. Do not defrost the tomatoes totally before using. Let them thaw just enough so that they can be cut up and cooked.

I also make tomato purée and tomato paste to freeze—no salt or added preservatives. See page 459.

"One hot tomato" was a compliment when I was young, if, albeit, a slightly vulgar one, on the order of "she's a good-looking broad." In summer and fall, the season of the tomato's glory, we enjoy tomatoes hot and cold.

After midwinter's indifferent tomatoes, the contents of salty cans and overpriced hothouse tomatoes with a taste a lot less hefty than their price, it is a delight to welcome field-grown, vine-ripened tomatoes. Just picked, they are sun-warm. Tomatoes should never be refrigerated.

Tomatoes obviously like basil, garlic and onions; but they are equally happy with oranges, parsley, fennel, dill and olives. Simply changing the herbs can vary a recipe. Stores don't normally sell tomatoes that weigh a

They make insalata caprese by interspersing overlapping tomato slices with similar slices of buffalo mozzarella. By the by, where is all the buffalo-milk mozzarella coming from? I've been to the south of Italy, and only a few buffalo (water buffalo, not American bison) were to be seen.

Italians use many different tomato varieties. Sometimes basil, shredded or in whole leaves, lends its tang. When tomatoes are combined with sweet onions and tiny blanched green beans for one of the best summer salads, the red fruit is cut in wedges, and, when beans are used, lemon juice is added.

I often delight in a tomato salad, sometimes with lettuce, sometimes with just cucumbers and onions, and sometimes with whatever is good in the garden tossed in. Usually I cut up the tomatoes, and cucumbers, if using, and toss them with some kosher salt and let them sit for at least fifteen minutes. This draws the juices from the vegetables, making a good base for the dressing and letting me use less oil—good for the diet and good to taste.

Unless obligatory, do not use plum tomatoes; they are relatively juiceless. Do use good olive oil, but not the most assertive one in the cupboard, which would overwhelm the taste of the tomatoes. In the same way, use a small amount of seasoning or dressing. More can always be added if desired. Use a serrated knife to slice tomatoes, preferably a tomato knife, but a bread knife will work. This way, the tomatoes can be sliced through their resistant skins without smashing the pulp. Most tomatoes need to be cored.

pound each, but I can't resist boasting a little about those from my garden. I simply slip the skins off these and serve them sliced, one per person, slathered with herbs, salt, pepper and a tiny bit of olive oil on a bed of watercress.

Note that salting and spooning on of the sauce warms cold tomatoes. That is as it should be. The appropriateness of room-warm tomatoes is also true of salsa cruda, which is nothing other than our friend the Italian tomato salad in chopped form. Sometimes chopped sweet onions or garlic is added. It is served over hot pasta.

Sometimes I crave one of my favorite recipes, Melting Tomatoes Provençal (page 108), learned years ago from a friend whose almost lone culinary triumph it was. It typifies the virtues of slow-cooking. The tomatoes can be cooked entirely ahead and eaten at room temperature or cooked ahead up until they need to go under the broiler to serve hot. Even in winter, this recipe can make tomatoes taste good; but try it in season.

I like thick red slices salted and topped with chopped chives, black pepper, very good olive oil and tiny whole bush–basil leaves (spicier than the large-leaf kind).

My favorite low-life tomato treat is Kitchen Sink Sandwiches. I slather a slice of commercial white bread—mainly fluff—with mayonnaise out of the jar, lay on sliced ripe tomatoes, sprinkle with salt and pepper and cover with another mayonnaised slice of bread. I bend over the sink and eat the dripping glory with fine abandon.

I make pasta sauces both raw and cooked. By the time the yellow tomatoes are ripe, the hot and semi-hot peppers will be, too. Cooked quickly together, they make a marvelous sauce (page 62). I guarantee that this will become a warm-weather favorite.

It must be fate that just when the summer is broiling hot and we crave something cool and soothing, the best tomatoes come along to be made into cold soups. They can be chunky or smooth, icy or tepid. All are good. Dried chipotle peppers add a mysterious background flavor to almost any of the tomato soups here. See the Cook's Guide, page 626, for information on reconstituting them.

There is a deadening uniformity in an increasingly lower standard of commercial tomatoes. Do not despair. I enjoy them within their limits. I use commercial canned tomatoes, packed whole, in juice or paste; tomatoes canned as juice; paste (better in tubes); purée; crushed; commercial pasta sauces and even ketchup. If they are all that is reasonably available, add some lemon juice to any preparation using them. The heat of cooking and packing robs these of the natural tomato acidity, and a tomato cannot taste sweet without acid.

Despite prevailing snobbery, when using canned, I tend to use American-style tomatoes rather than the Italian, except when making Italian-style pasta sauces. American tomatoes, to me, have a fresher, more acid taste with less hint of the can.

Turn to **TOMATOES** in the Cook's Guide for how-tos and to the Index for more recipes.

Basic French Tomato Salad

Use medium-size tomatoes, preferably a Marmande type with a bumpy top. If desired, peel. Allow about two tomatoes per person. Slice across in ⅛- to ¼-inch slices. Arrange, slightly overlapping, on individual plates. Sprinkle with kosher salt or fleur de sel and freshly ground black pepper. Drizzle with olive oil. A tiny amount of white wine vinegar is optional, as is a dusting of finely chopped fresh parsley.

Basic Italian Tomato Salad

Use ox-heart (cuor di bue) or other pointed-bottom Italian-style tomatoes, but not plum types such as Romano. Allow one to two per person, depending on other ingredients used. Do not peel. Slice crosswise into quarter-inch-thick slices or into wedges about one-quarter- to one-half inch wide (at the skin side). Dress with good olive oil, kosher salt and freshly ground black pepper and, if desired, basil leaves cut crosswise into thin strips or whole leaves of the tiny-leaved bush basil—about a tablespoon per person. If the tomatoes are sliced, overlap on a plate and put the dressing (and basil) on top. If the tomatoes are in wedges, toss and serve immediately, before the salt dissolves them.

Insalata Caprese

Use only one tomato per person. Dress as above. Slice enough of the freshest mozzarella findable into as many thick slices as there are tomato slices. Overlap the tomato and mozzarella slices on a serving platter.

American Steak-House Tomato Salad

Peter Luger in Brooklyn, New York, is the paradigm of the American steak house. There, they serve a tomato salad of beefsteak tomatoes sliced about half an inch thick and plated with overlapping layers of onion slices almost as thick. The sauce is their own, the same that they use on the steak. It can be ordered online, or a reasonable facsimile can be made by jazzing up Better Than Ketchup (page 114) with vinegar and additional horseradish.

Barbara's Tomato Salad

For a mainly tomato salad, my distinguishing technique is the way that I cut the tomatoes. Instead of slicing or wedging, I chunk. This is done by inserting the tip of a paring knife about an inch into the tomato and then twisting the knife and wrist so as to get a chunk that is about an inch square at the skin end and tapers into the center of the tomato. This method allows as much skin as possible for each chunk by taking advantage of the natural shape of the tomato. This is after first coring the tomato deeply enough to remove all the hard whitish center.

I do salt, leaving the tomatoes for about ten to fifteen minutes. This provides a nice ration of juice and I can then use less olive oil. It's not just to be thinner, although that is not to be despised, but to have a lighter, fresher flavor. I do use some lemon, particularly when the tomatoes are not from my garden and need some acid. Given a choice, I prefer Meyer lemons, which have a sweet-acid balance and a lovely aroma that emphasize the fruitiness of good tomatoes. I have taken to growing them in tubs and bringing them indoors in the winter. A nice alternative is the juice of the tiny Key limes, which, incidentally, are ripe when they fall from the tree and are no longer bright green, but before they shrivel.

I vary the herbs, which I chop medium-fine. Basil is the obvious choice; but lemon balm, marjoram, oregano, lovage and parsley are all good. Dried herbs do not make it. A half teaspoon of chopped fresh herbs per tomato is about right.

I tend to avoid garlic, much as I love it, finding it overwhelming with tomatoes. However, one-half garlic chive or young scallion per tomato, the green and white parts cut across into very thin slices, is often a fine addition. Sweet red onion can be used instead.

At the very end, I grind on black pepper.

Miniature Tomato-Basil Quiches

More elegant and formal than a pizza, this quiche shares much of pizza's flavor and pleasure. Since the tomato sauce in this recipe uses only half a can of tomatoes, I often double the recipe—or just the sauce, to have some for another day.

10 medium cherry tomatoes, each cut across into 3 slices

1 1/2 tablespoons kosher salt

TOMATO SAUCE

1 teaspoon olive oil

1/2 medium onion, coarsely chopped (1/2 cup)

Half a 14.5-ounce can Italian plum tomatoes, drained and chopped

1/4 teaspoon fresh lemon juice

1 large egg, lightly beaten

1/4 cup heavy cream

continued

2 tablespoons chopped fresh basil

Kosher salt and freshly ground black pepper
to taste

24 miniature pastry shells made with Flaky Tart
Dough (page 477), partially baked

Place the sliced cherry tomatoes in a single
layer on a double layer of paper toweling.
Sprinkle with the kosher salt and allow to
drain for at least 15 minutes.

Place a rack in the middle of the oven.
Preheat the oven to 375°F.

For the tomato sauce, heat the oil in a small
skillet over medium heat. Stir in the onion and
cook, stirring occasionally, for about 10 minutes,
until golden brown. Stir in the canned tomatoes.
Cover, reduce the heat to low and cook, stirring
occasionally, for about 10 minutes.

Remove the lid and cook for 4 minutes
longer, or until almost all the liquid has
evaporated. Stir in the lemon juice. Remove
from the heat and allow to cool.

In a small mixing bowl, combine the egg
with the cream and basil. Season to taste with
salt and pepper. Stir in the tomato sauce (or
half of it if you doubled the recipe). Fill the
partially baked pastry shells with the mixture
and top each one with a slice of cherry tomato.

Bake for 10 minutes. Remove from the oven
and allow to cool slightly on a wire rack before
serving. **Makes 24 miniature quiches**

Shirred Eggs with Herbs, Tomatoes and Cream

When trying to think of a last-minute first
course, I don't ignore the loyal eggs waiting
in the refrigerator. These shirred (baked with
liquid) eggs can be prepared with nothing
more exotic than parsley if other fresh herbs
are hard to find.

1 teaspoon unsalted butter

8 eggs, at room temperature

1/4 cup chopped mixed fresh herbs

1/4 to 1/2 cup peeled, seeded and chopped tomato

Kosher salt and freshly ground black pepper
to taste

About 1/4 cup heavy cream

Preheat the oven to 450°F.

Butter four small gratin dishes and put them
on a baking sheet. Break 2 eggs into each.
Scatter the chopped herbs and tomatoes over
them. Season to taste with salt and pepper.
Spoon the cream on to cover the surface evenly.

Bake just until set, 8 to 10 minutes; don't
overcook. Remove from the oven and turn on
the broiler.

Place the eggs under the broiler for a
moment to brown lightly. Serve immediately,
setting each gratin dish on a plate or doubled
napkin. Give each eater a soupspoon.

Serves 4 as a first course

Gazpacho

This gazpacho first appeared in a cookbook
that James Beard wrote with Carl Jerome for
Cuisinart. Jim asked me for a recipe, and,
flattered, I came up with this. I still like it and
so, it seems, do many readers.

It is the paradigm of a raw soup originally
made by farm workers, using what they had in
the fields around them as well as a little olive
oil. It is not meant to be a purée, but chunky,
and for that the food processor, for those as lazy
as I am (or a large knife, for the vigorous),
is the best tool. The vegetables are cut up to
process evenly but not to purée. Be sure to
make this far enough ahead so that it gets really
cold. I often double the recipe.

It is only one of the many Spanish gazpachos (in Barcelona I had a version that was not only puréed, but also sieved), but it is probably the most familiar to today's eaters.

- 1 small Bermuda or other sweet onion, cut into chunks
- 2 firm small cucumbers, peeled and cut into chunks
- 2 small green bell peppers, cored, seeded, deribbed and cut into chunks
- 6 medium-large ripe tomatoes, cored, peeled and cut into eighths
- 5 large cloves garlic, smashed and peeled
- 1 cup tomato juice, or as needed
- 1/2 cup olive oil
- 1/4 teaspoon pure chili powder or 1 small fresh chili pepper, halved
- 1 tablespoon kosher salt, or to taste

Finely chop the onion in a food processor, stopping occasionally to scrape down the sides of the bowl. Scrape into a large metal bowl. Repeat the process with the cucumbers, then with the green peppers, adding each to the onions. Process 5 of the tomatoes until finely chopped but not puréed. Add to the other chopped vegetables.

Process the remaining tomato with the garlic, tomato juice, oil and chili powder until a smooth liquid has formed. Combine with the chopped vegetables. Cover and refrigerate until chilled.

Before serving, add the salt. If the soup is too thick, add more tomato juice (or a combination of tomato juice and beef broth).

Makes about 6 cups; serves 4 as a first course

Cold Moroccan Tomato Soup

This requires only two minutes of cooking, and the rest is easy, provided that the tomatoes are good. Use a food mill, which removes both skin and seeds. Lacking a food mill, peel the tomatoes, cut them in half and, with a small spoon, scoop out the seeds. Pulse in a food processor until puréed, being careful not to create tomato juice.

- 5 medium cloves garlic, smashed, peeled and very finely chopped
- 2 1/2 teaspoons paprika
- 1 1/2 teaspoons ground cumin
- Large pinch of cayenne pepper
- 4 teaspoons olive oil
- 2 1/4 pounds ripe tomatoes, cored and cut into 1-inch cubes
- 1/4 cup packed cilantro leaves, coarsely chopped, plus 4 small sprigs
- 1 tablespoon white wine vinegar
- Juice of 1 medium lemon
- 5 teaspoons kosher salt
- 4 medium stalks celery, peeled and coarsely chopped
- 3 tablespoons olive oil for drizzling (optional)

In a small saucepan, stir together the garlic, paprika, cumin, cayenne and olive oil. Cook over low heat, stirring constantly, for 2 minutes. Remove from the heat and set aside.

Pass the tomatoes through the large disc of a food mill into a medium bowl. Stir in the cooked spice mixture, 2 tablespoons water and the chopped cilantro, vinegar, lemon juice and salt. Refrigerate until cold.

Pour the soup into bowls and top with the cilantro sprigs, chopped celery and, if desired, a drizzle of oil. **Makes 4 cups; serves 4 as a first course**

Tomato and Bread Soup

This soup is usually served at little more than room temperature. It is comfort food to the max.

    Four 3/4-inch-thick slices peasant bread

    1/3 cup olive oil

    3 medium cloves garlic, smashed, peeled and sliced

    1 medium onion, very finely chopped

    14 large fresh basil leaves, cut across into
        narrow strips

    1 3/4 pounds plum tomatoes, peeled and
        cut into 1/4-inch dice

    4 cups Basic Chicken Stock (page 501),
        Roasted Chicken Stock (page 502) or
        commercial chicken broth

    2 teaspoons kosher salt (less if using
        commercial broth)

    Freshly ground black pepper to taste

    Good olive oil for serving

Preheat the oven to 225°F.

Place the bread directly on the middle rack of the oven. Bake for 20 to 30 minutes, just to dry the bread out; do not brown. Break the bread into large pieces.

In a medium saucepan, heat the oil over medium heat. Add the garlic and onion and cook, stirring, for 5 minutes. Stir in the basil and cook for 1 minute. Stir in the tomatoes and bring to a boil. Reduce the heat and cook at a low boil for 13 to 15 minutes, stirring frequently.

Stir in the stock, bread, salt and pepper. Return to a boil. Lower the heat and simmer, stirring and breaking up the bread with the back of a spoon, for 15 minutes. The bread should break down to a mush. Remove the pan from the heat, cover and let sit for 10 minutes.

Serve with a few grinds of fresh pepper and a drizzle of some good olive oil.

Makes 6 cups; serves 6 as a first course

Tomato and Dill Soup with Crème Fraîche

For the virtues of different kinds of tomatoes or purées for soups, see the Cook's Guide (pages 659–663). If using a commercial product, reduce the salt called for in the recipe.

This simple soup is delightful hot or cold. When I serve it, I whisk in the crème fraîche right before I put it on the table. Otherwise, the acidity of the tomatoes will break down the cream. Crème fraîche is best for this recipe because its high acidity works with the tomatoes. If crème fraîche is not available, use half heavy cream and half sour cream in its place. Nonfat yogurt or nonfat sour cream can be used by those concerned about fat content, but the result will not be as sumptuous.

    4 cups American Tomato Purée (page 460)

    1/2 cup chopped fresh dill

    2 tablespoons kosher salt

    1 cup crème fraîche

In a 4-quart nonreactive pot, bring the purée to a simmer over high heat. Stir in the dill and salt. Cook for 2 minutes. Remove from the heat. Whisk in the crème fraîche and serve immediately. Or, to serve cold, chill the soup thoroughly, then whisk in the crème fraîche just before serving. **Makes 5 cups; serves 4 as a first course**

Tomato Basil Soup

This is simply a salad turned into a soup, and very good it is.

> 3¹/₂ cups Basic Chicken Stock (page 501), Roasted Chicken Stock (page 502) or commercial chicken broth
>
> 2¹/₂ cups Plum Tomato Purée (page 459), puréed canned plum tomatoes or sterile-pack strained tomatoes
>
> 3 cloves garlic, smashed and peeled
>
> 2¹/₂ teaspoons kosher salt
>
> 1 medium bunch fresh basil, leaves only
>
> About 1 tablespoon olive oil for serving

In a medium saucepan, bring the chicken stock and tomato purée to a boil.

Meanwhile, in a blender, or using the side of a large knife, make a paste of the garlic and salt; add a little stock mixture if using the blender.

Whisk the paste into the stock. Lower the heat and simmer, covered, for 10 minutes. Coarsely chop half of the basil. Stir into the soup and simmer for 5 minutes. The soup can be made ahead to this point and refrigerated for up to 2 days; reheat before proceeding.

Stack the remaining basil leaves, about 4 or 5 at a time, roll them up tightly and cut across into thin shreds. Stir into the soup. Serve immediately, drizzled with a little olive oil.

Makes 5 cups; serves 4 as a first course

Curry Tomato Soup

This is a wonderful soup hot or cold. Made with the garlic broth, it is vegetarian.

> 2 tablespoons unsalted butter
>
> 1 small onion, finely chopped
>
> 3 tablespoons curry powder

> 1 tablespoon sweet paprika
>
> 2¹/₂ cups Plum Tomato Purée (page 459), puréed canned plum tomatoes or sterile-pack strained tomatoes
>
> 2 cups Beef Stock (page 502), Basic Chicken Stock (page 501), Roasted Chicken Stock (page 502), commercial chicken broth or Garlic Broth (page 507)
>
> 1 tablespoon kosher salt (less if using commercial broth)
>
> 1 tablespoon fresh lemon juice
>
> Freshly ground black pepper to taste

In a medium saucepan, melt the butter over low heat. Stir in the onion and cook until it is limp and completely translucent, about 10 minutes. Stir in the curry powder and paprika and cook, stirring constantly, for 3 minutes.

Stir the tomato purée and stock into the onions. Bring to a boil. Lower the heat and simmer for 5 minutes. Stir in the salt. The soup can be made ahead to this point and refrigerated.

To serve the soup cold, refrigerate for 2 hours, or overnight, then stir in the lemon juice and pepper. To serve hot, reheat if necessary, then stir in the lemon juice and pepper.

Makes 4 cups; serves 4 as a first course

Southwestern Corn and Tomato Soup

For me, this is a delightful summer main course.

> 2 ounces slab bacon, cut into 1 x ¹/₂ x ¹/₂-inch matchstick strips
>
> 1 small onion, cut into ¹/₄-inch dice
>
> 4 medium cloves garlic, smashed and peeled

continued

1 teaspoon hot red pepper flakes

$^1/_3$ cup diced ($^1/_2$ inch) green bell pepper

$^1/_3$ cup diced ($^1/_2$ inch) red bell pepper

1 pound waxy potatoes, peeled and cut into
$^1/_2$-inch dice

3 cups Plum Tomato Purée (page 459),
puréed canned plum tomatoes or
sterile-pack strained tomatoes

3 cups corn kernels (cut from 6 medium
ears of corn)

1 tablespoon kosher salt

Freshly ground black pepper to taste

2 tablespoons coarsely chopped cilantro

2 medium scallions, white part only, thinly sliced

Hot red pepper sauce to taste

In a medium saucepan, cook the bacon over medium heat until it is crisp, about 20 minutes.

Stir in the onion, garlic, red pepper flakes, peppers, potatoes, tomato purée and 1½ cups water. Bring to a boil. Lower the heat and simmer for 10 minutes.

Stir in the corn and simmer for 10 minutes, or until the potatoes are tender. Season with the salt and pepper. The soup can be made ahead to this point and refrigerated for up to 2 days; reheat before proceeding.

Stir the cilantro, scallions and hot red pepper sauce into the soup. Serve hot.

Makes 8 cups; serves 8 as a first course, 4 as a main course

All-American Stewed Tomatoes

Typical of American tomato dishes, this one is sweet. If less sweet is desired, reduce the sugar to 2 tablespoons and add an additional tablespoon of lemon juice at the end. Try to use smaller tomatoes for this; they have a greater ratio of pulp to seeds.

4 tablespoons unsalted butter

4 quarter-size slices peeled fresh ginger,
cut into matchstick strips

$^1/_4$ teaspoon sweet paprika

Pinch of ground cloves

1 medium onion, thinly sliced

3 pounds ripe tomatoes, 2 to 2$^1/_2$ inches in
diameter, cored and cut into 1-inch wedges
(6 pieces if smaller tomatoes, 8 pieces if larger)

$^1/_4$ cup sugar

2 teaspoons kosher salt

2 tablespoons cornstarch

2 tablespoons fresh lemon juice

Freshly ground black pepper to taste

Melt the butter in a 12-inch skillet over medium-low heat. Add the ginger, paprika and cloves. Cook for 1 minute. Add the onion. Cook for 5 minutes, or until translucent. Lower the heat. Add the tomatoes, sugar and salt. Cook for 15 minutes, gently turning and moving the outer cooked pieces toward the center as necessary.

Dissolve the cornstarch in ¼ cup water. Pour into the tomatoes. Gently stir and turn until the sauce is thickened and clear. Stir in the lemon juice and pepper.

Makes 6 cups; serves 8 to 10 as a side dish

Microwave Variation

In an 14 x 11 x 2-inch dish, combine the butter, ginger, paprika, cloves, onion, sugar and salt. Cook, uncovered, at 100% for 4 minutes. Stir in the tomatoes, then push them to the edges of the dish, leaving an open area in the center. Cover tightly with microwave plastic wrap. Cook at 100% for 8 minutes. Carefully uncover (because of steam) and stir in the dissolved cornstarch. Cover and cook at 100% for 3 minutes longer. Pierce the plastic wrap to release the steam.

Uncover and stir in lemon juice and pepper to taste. Serve immediately.

To make 3 cups stewed tomatoes: Halve all the ingredients (dissolve the cornstarch in 2 tablespoons water). Use an 11 x 8-inch oval dish and cook the onion mixture for 3 minutes at 100%. Add the tomatoes and cover tightly with microwave plastic wrap. Cook at 100% for 6 minutes. Stir in the dissolved cornstarch as above, cover and cook at 100% for 2 minutes longer. Finish as above.

Chilled Stewed Tomato Soup

To make cold soup, pass the stewed tomatoes through the medium disc of a food mill. For each 2 cups of purée, add ½ cup Basic Chicken Stock (page 501) or commercial chicken broth. Chill. Correct the seasonings before serving.

Chinese Stewed Tomatoes

Make all of this. You will never regret it. If there's any left over, it is good in an omelet or with scrambled eggs. Cook fish or chicken in it. Or use it as a sauce for angel hair pasta. Serve with a sandwich or sliced ham instead of coleslaw. Serve as a vegetable with almost any main course that does not have tomatoes or sauce. Think of it as a relish for a robust pâté. You may have gathered that I like it. If you want to start small, there are directions for making less at the end of the recipe.

Chinese salted black beans (sometimes called fermented black beans) can be purchased in Asian groceries and specialty stores. Store leftovers in a covered jar in a cool, dry place. If the beans become dry from prolonged storage, soak them in water for ten minutes, then drain before using.

6 cloves garlic, smashed, peeled and coarsely chopped

2 scallions, trimmed and cut into 2-inch lengths

½ cup cilantro sprigs (including 2 inches of the stems)

1 tablespoon vegetable oil

3 pounds ripe tomatoes (2 to 2½ inches in diameter), cored and cut into 1-inch wedges (6 pieces if smaller tomatoes, 8 pieces if larger)

¼ cup Chinese salted black beans

2 tablespoons cornstarch

2 tablespoons soy sauce, preferably tamari

1 tablespoon rice wine vinegar

Chop the garlic, scallions and cilantro together or process coarsely in a food processor. Set aside.

Heat the oil in a 12-inch skillet over low heat. Add the garlic mixture and cook, stirring, for 8 minutes. Increase the heat to medium-high and add the tomatoes and black beans. Cook for 10 minutes, gently turning.

Dissolve the cornstarch in the soy sauce and vinegar. Pour into the tomatoes. Gently stir and turn until the sauce is thickened and clear.

Makes 6 cups; serves 8 to 10 as a side dish

Microwave Variation

Scoop the garlic mixture into a 14 x 11 x 2-inch dish. Add the oil. Cook, uncovered, at 100% for 3 minutes. Add the tomatoes and beans and stir to coat. Cover tightly with microwave plastic wrap. Cook at 100% for 10 minutes. Prick the plastic wrap to release the steam.

Dissolve the cornstarch in the soy sauce and vinegar. Remove the tomato mixture from the oven. Uncover and stir in the cornstarch mixture. Cook, uncovered, at 100% for 3 minutes.

Serve hot.

continued

To serve 2: Chop ½ scallion (white part only), 1 clove garlic smashed and peeled, and 2 tablespoons coriander leaves in a food processor. Scrape into an 8-inch square dish and stir in 1 teaspoon oil. Cook at 100% for 2 minutes. Add 2 tomatoes, cut into wedges, and 1 tablespoon black beans. Cover and cook at 100% for 3 minutes. Dissolve 2 teaspoons cornstarch in 2 teaspoons soy and 1 teaspoon vinegar. Stir in. Cook, uncovered, at 100% for 2 minutes.

Fried Tomatoes

Fried green ones are a southern classic, and this is a basic recipe for which many variations are possible. Bacon fat, my fat of choice, gives the tomatoes a smoky quality. I got used to bacon grease during World War II, when every kitchen had a can into which to pour the fat. Some of it went to the government to make munitions and some of it was substituted for tightly rationed butter. Canola or olive oil can be substituted.

Then there is the crumb coating. Cornmeal produces a firm and crisp crust. Crushed crackers form a softer crust, one with an addictively satisfying wheat flavor that goes particularly well with the tomatoes. Either will do, so long as the crumbs are well seasoned.

Most important, of course, are the tomatoes themselves. They must be very firm. My garden provides me with an ample supply. Those without a garden may find green tomatoes more difficult to come by except for their brief late-summer appearance at farmers' markets.

CORNMEAL CRUMB COATING

(per every 4 to 5 tomato slices)

¹/₃ cup yellow cornmeal

**¹/₂ teaspoon kosher salt, or to taste
(less if the bacon fat is salty)**

Generous amount of freshly ground black pepper

CRACKER CRUMB COATING

(per every 4 to 5 tomato slices)

10 salted crackers, such as saltines

Generous amount of freshly ground black pepper

Rendered bacon fat, canola oil or olive oil

Large green or very firm tomatoes, cored and sliced across into ¹/₃-inch rounds

For the cornmeal crumb coating: Mix together the cornmeal, salt and pepper. Pour onto a sheet of parchment or wax paper.

Or, for the cracker crumb coating: Put the crackers between two sheets of parchment or wax paper. Crush with a rolling pin to produce a fine crumb. Remove the top sheet. Season with the salt and pepper, mixing well. Leave on the paper.

For either, pour ¼ inch fat of choice into a large frying pan. Place the pan over high heat until the fat is smoking. Dredge a few tomato slices in the crumb mixture, turning once or twice, until both sides are amply coated. Cook 1 to 1½ minutes per side, or until golden brown. Drain on paper towels or a brown paper bag. Repeat with the remaining slices.

**Makes enough for 4 to 5 slices per recipe;
12 slices serve 4 as a side dish**

Melting Tomatoes Provençal

Ever since a French friend, the artist Jeanette Leroy, made these for me years ago, they have been a staple in my kitchen. They can be made even in the middle of winter when tomatoes are terrible. The slow cooking drives out the water and intensifies the flavor. Make the whole recipe even if there are only four guests. I serve them with roast leg of lamb and eat my leftovers with eggs.

3 ripe tomatoes (2 to 3 inches in diameter), cored

1 tablespoon olive oil plus more for the
    baking sheet

2 cloves garlic, smashed, peeled and minced

6 fresh basil leaves, finely chopped

1 teaspoon kosher salt

Freshly ground black pepper to taste

2 tablespoons Dried Bread Crumbs (page 510)
    or commercial bread crumbs

Cut the tomatoes crosswise in half. Seed them and, with a small spoon, pierce a few holes in the skin side of each half. Put the tomatoes, cut side down, on paper towels to drain for 30 minutes.

Put 1 tablespoon olive oil in a 12-inch skillet. Add the tomatoes, cut side down. Cook over very low heat for 20 minutes. Turn the tomatoes, skin side down, and cook, uncovered, over the lowest possible heat for 1½ to 2 hours longer.

Heat the broiler.

Place the tomatoes, skin side down, on an oiled baking sheet. Sprinkle with the garlic, basil, salt and pepper. Sprinkle the bread crumbs evenly over them. Pour the skillet juices over the top. Broil the tomatoes for 2 to 3 minutes, or just until they brown and the bread crumbs form a crust. Serve hot or at room temperature.

Serves 6 as a side dish

Roasted Cherry Tomatoes with Basil

Medium to large cherry tomatoes make an extraordinary vegetable when roasted; garlic lovers can add six unpeeled cloves to the roasting pan. Thinly sliced strips of basil, tossed in after the tomatoes have cooked, wilt and give a welcome peppery taste.

The tomatoes will be soft and have a smoky, roasted flavor. Consider using this as a pasta sauce.

1½ pounds cherry tomatoes, stemmed
    (about 4 cups)

1½ tablespoons olive oil

Scant ½ teaspoon kosher salt

2 tablespoons fresh basil leaves, stacked 4 or 5
    at a time, rolled up and thinly sliced across

Place a rack in the center of the oven. Preheat the oven to 500°F.

Place the tomatoes in the smallest pan that will hold them comfortably. Drizzle the oil over them. Rub the oil over the tomatoes and pan. Sprinkle with the salt. Roast for 10 minutes. Shake the pan to move the tomatoes around. Roast for 15 minutes more. Add the basil and toss lightly. Serve warm. **Serves 3 as a side dish**

Roasted Cherry Tomato Purée

Place a food mill fitted with the finest disc over a bowl or pot. Force the roasted cherry tomatoes through the mill. From time to time, stop to scrape the bottom of the disc with a rubber spatula to allow all the tomatoes to pass through the mill. The purée may be used as is or reduced over very low heat to thicken further. It can be stored in the freezer in airtight containers for 3 to 4 months. **Makes about 3 cups**

Big Tabbouleh

"Big" describes both flavor and quantity. I make big quantities of this because it is good for parties, where it seems to go quickly. If desired, halve or even quarter the amounts for a smaller group.

continued

2 pounds medium bulgur (cracked wheat; about 5 cups)

8 ripe tomatoes, cored and cut into 1/4-inch dice (about 2 1/2 cups)

2 bunches scallions, trimmed and thinly sliced on the diagonal

2 bunches fresh Italian parsley, leaves only, coarsely chopped

1 bunch fresh mint, leaves only, coarsely chopped

2 teaspoons ground cumin

4 teaspoons kosher salt

2 teaspoons freshly ground black pepper

3/4 cup olive oil, or as needed

3/4 cup fresh lemon juice, or as needed

4 tablespoons unsalted butter

1/4 cup olive oil

1 cup finely diced yellow onion (about 8 ounces)

2 tablespoons finely minced garlic (about 4 large cloves)

2 cups arborio rice

4 cups Roasted Cherry Tomato Purée (page 109), puréed canned Italian plum tomatoes or sterile-pack strained tomatoes

4 cups Basic Chicken Stock (page 501), Roasted Chicken Stock (page 502) or commercial chicken broth

Kosher salt and freshly ground black pepper to taste

2/3 cup freshly grated Parmesan cheese

Soak the bulgur in hot water to cover for 30 minutes. If the water is not completely absorbed, drain the bulgur and squeeze dry.

In a large bowl, combine the bulgur, tomatoes, scallions, parsley and mint. Toss to combine. Add the cumin, salt, pepper, olive oil and lemon juice. Mix well. Taste and adjust the seasoning. Add more olive oil and/or lemon juice as needed. Let the mixture stand for at least 1 hour before serving.

Serves 18 as a first course, 24 as part of a buffet

Stovetop Tomato Risotto

Risotto of all stripes is marvelous made in a microwave oven, but regardless of how quick and easy it is, I know there are some people who just won't be able to bring themselves to make it in the microwave. For them, here is a traditional version.

Melt the butter with the oil in a large shallow pan. Add the onion and garlic. Cook over medium-low heat for 3 minutes, or until translucent. Add the rice. Increase the heat to medium-high. Cook, stirring continuously, for 3 minutes, or until the rice turns white and loses its translucence. Reduce the heat slightly. Add the tomatoes. Cook, stirring continuously, turning the rice up from the bottom, for 5 to 6 minutes, or until most of the liquid has been absorbed.

Increase the heat to medium-high. Add 1/2 cup stock. Cook, stirring well, until the rice has absorbed most of the stock. Add another 1/2 cup stock and repeat the process, making sure the liquid is mostly absorbed before each addition of stock. Continue until the rice has cooked, about 20 to 25 minutes, and is creamy with a slight chew. Season with salt and pepper to taste. Serve with the grated Parmesan on top.

Serves 6 as a first course, 12 as a side dish

Stuffed Tomatoes with Rice and Basil

This recipe can be easily divided to make as few as two tomatoes. However, it's so good cold that I always like to make the whole quantity.

8 small tomatoes (3 ounces each),
  2¹/₄ to 2¹/₂ inches wide

About 1¹/₂ tablespoons olive oil

1 medium onion (4 ounces), finely chopped

¹/₂ cup long-grain white rice

¹/₄ cup packed fresh basil leaves,
  sliced across into thin strips

Kosher salt and freshly ground black pepper
  to taste

Place a rack in the center of the oven.

Deeply core the tomatoes. Cut off a ¼-inch slice from the top of each tomato; reserve. Using a spoon, scoop out the seeds and pulp; reserve. Using the spoon, remove the ribs from the tomatoes; reserve.

Finely chop the tops and ribs. Combine with the seeds and pulp in a small saucepan. Cook over low heat until liquefied and reduced to 1 cup. Set aside.

Preheat the oven to 350°F.

Heat 1 tablespoon oil in a small pan. Cook the onion over low heat until translucent. Stir in the tomato liquid, rice and basil. Add salt and pepper to taste.

Stuff the tomato shells with the tomato-rice mixture, mounding it slightly on top. Place in a 12 x 8 x 2-inch glass baking dish greased with 1 teaspoon oil. Lightly oil the shiny side of a piece of aluminum foil. Place loosely over the tomatoes, shiny side down.

Bake for 30 minutes. Uncover and pour 1 tablespoon water on top of each tomato. Re-cover with foil. Bake for another 20 minutes.

Repeat twice more with water, covering the tomatoes and baking for 20 minutes each time.

Uncover. Pour 2 tablespoons water on top of each tomato. Re-cover with foil. Bake for 30 minutes. Turn off the oven. Allow the tomatoes to sit in the warm oven for 30 minutes. **Serves 8 as a first course or a side dish**

Tomatoes Stuffed with Tabbouleh

Since tomatoes retain their vivid color and do not burst when cooked in the microwave oven, the microwave is ideal for cooking stuffed tomatoes. This dish, good hot or cold, has an intense tomato flavor. It is good as a vegetarian first course or as part of a stuffed vegetable main course or as an accompaniment to grilled fish or roast lamb or chicken. The juice from the cooked tomatoes can become a vegetarian base for soup or, mixed with lemon juice and a minimum of olive oil, a light salad dressing.

8 small (2¹/₂ to 3 inches wide) or 6 medium
  (4 inches wide) tomatoes

Kosher salt to taste

¹/₂ cup bulgur

2 cups fresh or canned tomato juice

¹/₄ cup plus 3 tablespoons olive oil, and
  more for oiling the tomatoes

¹/₄ cup chopped fresh mint

1 tablespoon minced garlic

¹/₂ teaspoon hot red pepper flakes

¹/₂ teaspoon chopped scallion
  (green and white parts)

2 tablespoons fresh lemon juice

Freshly ground black pepper to taste

continued

Cut a small slice from the top of each tomato. Scoop out the inside of the tomatoes, preferably with a silver spoon, leaving a ⅛-inch-thick shell. Chop the flesh and set aside together with the seeds and juice.

Sprinkle the inside of each tomato with salt. Prick the skin of each two or three times and rub with oil. Place the tomatoes, cut side down, on paper toweling to drain.

Combine the bulgur, tomato juice, oil, mint, garlic, pepper flakes and scallions in a bowl. Let stand for 15 minutes.

Sauces, Purées and Ketchups

Despite my love of tomato salads and the endless BLTs, bowls of tomato soup and grilled cheese sandwiches that I have consumed, I venture to assert that, like most people, much of my tomato consumption has been in sauces of one kind or another. Here are a few more evolved ones:

Tomato Frappé (page 452), Tomato Sauce for Stuffed Vegetables (page 461), Pacific Tomato Dipping Sauce (page 463), Spicy Middle Eastern Tomato Sauce (page 464), Tomato Basil Dipping Sauce (page 464), Baby Food Tomato Sauce (page 461), Herbed Tomato Sauce (page 462) and the Roasted Cherry Tomato Purée (page 109).

Pour the bulgur mixture into a sieve set over a bowl. Drain for 20 minutes, stirring several times; reserve the liquid.

Pour the bulgur mixture into a clean bowl. Stir in the lemon juice, salt and pepper to taste and the reserved tomato flesh, seeds and juice.

Arrange the tomato shells, cut side up, around the edge of a 9-inch glass pie plate. Fill the shells with the bulgur mixture, mounding it slightly. Pour the reserved drained liquid around the tomatoes. Cover tightly with microwave plastic wrap. Cook at 100% for 7 to 9 minutes, until the tomatoes are tender when pricked with the tip of a sharp knife. Prick the plastic to release the steam.

Remove from the oven and uncover. With a slotted spoon, transfer the tomatoes to a serving plate. (Save the tomato liquid to use as a base for soup or a salad dressing, if desired.)

Serves 6 as a first course or a side dish

Bucatini with Tomato, Pancetta and Onion Sauce
all'Amatriciana

Traditionally this sauce is served with bucatini or perciatelli—think fat spaghetti with a hole running through the center. Penne or rigatoni would be good substitutes. This is enough to sauce a pound of pasta.

2 tablespoons olive oil

½ pound pancetta or lightly smoked lean slab bacon, cut into ½-inch cubes

1 medium onion, finely chopped (about 1 cup)

3 cups sterile-pack diced tomatoes, with their liquid

Kosher salt and freshly ground black pepper to taste

1 pound bucatini, perciatelli or penne pasta

Freshly grated Pecorino Romano

Heat the olive oil in a wide saucepan over medium heat. Add the pancetta and cook, stirring, until lightly browned on all sides, about 6 minutes. Add the onion and stir until softened and starting to pick up the color from the bottom of the pan, a minute or two. Pour in the tomatoes and bring to a boil. Lower the heat to simmering and cook until the onion is tender, about 10 minutes. Season with salt and pepper.

Meanwhile, bring a large pot of salted water to a boil. Stir in the pasta and cook until al dente.

Reserve about a cup of the pasta cooking liquid. Drain the pasta, return it to the pot and add the sauce. Stir to coat the pasta with sauce, adding some of the reserved cooking liquid if necessary to help the sauce coat the pasta. Remove from the heat, stir in a handful of Pecorino and scrape the pasta into a serving bowl. Pass additional grated Pecorino at the table. **Serves 4 to 6 as a main course**

Early American Tomato Ketchup

Most of us have never thought of making ketchup; but our ancestors used to do it all the time with all sorts of ingredients, from oysters to mushrooms. Tomato ketchup came along very late; but when it did, oh my!

I first got a version of this recipe from Jennie June's *American Cookery Book,* published in New York in 1878. Her recipe made gallons. This one makes much less, but it has a wonderful texture and lots of flavor. It is easy to make. It has no salt and has sugar only as desired; I don't think either will be missed. I like mine fairly spicy, so I use the larger amounts of red pepper flakes and black pepper; but start with the smaller amounts and see how spicy it gets.

2 1/2 pounds plum tomatoes, cored and cut into quarters (about 6 cups)

1 cup cider vinegar

1/2 teaspoon dry mustard

1/4 to 1/2 teaspoon hot red pepper flakes

1/4 to 1/2 teaspoon freshly ground black pepper

1/2 teaspoon ground mace

1 to 2 tablespoons medium brown muscovado or other brown sugar

Coarsely chop the tomatoes in a food processor; in a small food processor, this can be done in two batches. (There will be about 4½ cups chopped tomatoes.)

Stir together the tomatoes and remaining ingredients in a 4-quart nonreactive saucepan. Cover and bring to a boil. Reduce the heat slightly and cook, uncovered, at a slow boil, for about 70 minutes.

Pass the tomato mixture through a food mill fitted with the medium disc. Return to the pan. Cook, uncovered, for 15 minutes.

Transfer the tomato mixture to a blender. Whirl until smooth. Allow to cool, then place in clean glass jars with tightly fitting lids and refrigerate. **Makes 3 cups**

Better Than Ketchup

This sauce is wonderful on a bland vegetable such as cauliflower. It also makes a good, very low fat salad dressing and even ketchup. The flavor and texture will vary somewhat depending on the type of tamarind concentrate available.

One 2.8-ounce can anchovy fillets (about 17) packed in olive oil

1 1/2 tablespoons prepared horseradish, drained

3 large cloves garlic, smashed, peeled and coarsely chopped

1/2 cup unsweetened tamarind concentrate

1/4 teaspoon hot red pepper flakes

1/2 teaspoon kosher salt

1 cup Simple Stovetop Cherry Tomato Stew Base (page 461)

Freshly ground black pepper to taste

In a blender, combine all the ingredients except the tomato stew base and black pepper and blend until smooth, adding a little of the tomato from time to time as needed to blend. Scrape into a 1-quart nonreactive saucepan and stir in the remaining tomato stew base. Bring to a boil, then reduce the heat to a simmer. Cook for 4 minutes. Season with pepper. Allow to cool slightly, or refrigerate. **Makes 1 3/4 cups**

Tomato Cranberry Salsa

This is certainly not traditional, but it is a godsend in winter, when the tomatoes are faded.

2 cups (8 ounces) fresh cranberries

1/2 cup coarsely chopped red onion

3/4 pound ripe tomatoes, cored, seeded and cut into 1/2-inch dice (about 1 3/4 cups), or 3/4 cup drained and coarsely chopped canned tomatoes

1 jalapeño pepper, seeded and deribbed, or 1 canned jalapeño pepper, rinsed and drained

2 teaspoons kosher salt

2 tablespoons fresh lemon juice

1/2 teaspoon ground cumin

Place the cranberries and onion in a food processor and pulse until coarsely chopped. Add the tomatoes and jalapeño. Pulse 2 or 3 times in short bursts just to combine.

Scrape the mixture into a ceramic or glass bowl. Stir in the salt, lemon juice and cumin. Allow to ripen for 45 minutes at room temperature, or overnight in the refrigerator. **Makes 3 1/2 cups**

Fresh Tomato Mint Salsa

This is a salsa I made for a friend who loathes cilantro. Cilantro can replace the mint, using only a cup's worth. Mint keeps its color in lime juice better than cilantro does.

2 cups loosely packed fresh mint leaves, finely chopped (about 1 cup)

3/4 pound ripe tomatoes, cored and finely chopped (about 1 1/4 cups)

2 medium cloves garlic, smashed, peeled and minced

1 to 2 small jalapeño peppers, seeded, deribbed and finely chopped

2 tablespoons finely chopped yellow onion

2 tablespoons fresh lime juice

1 teaspoon kosher salt, or to taste

Freshly ground black pepper to taste

Place all the ingredients in a small bowl and mix until thoroughly combined. Allow to stand for about 30 minutes, then adjust the seasonings to taste. **Makes about 3 1/2 cups**

Bruschetta Topping
Omit the jalapeño, substitute basil for the mint and spoon onto Crostini (page 510).

Sweet Tomato Tart

This is a bit of a surprise. But both in classes and at the table it has proved successful—pretty too.

- **2 cups all-purpose flour**
- **7 tablespoons unsalted butter, cut into 1/2-inch slices**
- **Pinch of kosher salt**
- **1 egg, mixed with 1 teaspoon water**
- **2 tablespoons blanched julienned orange zest**
- **2 tablespoons blanched julienned lemon zest**
- **2 tablespoons brown sugar**
- **4 ripe beefsteak tomatoes, thinly sliced, drained and patted dry**
- **2 tablespoons currant jelly**

Place the flour, butter and salt in a food processor. Pulsing in short bursts, blend only until the pieces of butter are evenly distributed and coated with flour. Do not overprocess. With the machine running, again pulsing in short bursts, add about 6 tablespoons ice water; add only enough water to form a cohesive, but not sticky, mass.

Remove the mixture from the processor and press the pastry together, using the heel of your hand. Gently pat the pastry into an 12 x 8-inch rectangle. Fold in thirds as for a business letter. Wrap in plastic wrap and chill for an hour.

Preheat the oven to 400°F.

Roll the dough out on a lightly floured board into an even 18 x 10-inch rectangle. Cut four 1/2-inch-wide strips from one long side of the rectangle. Brush the edges of the rectangle with the egg and place a dough strip on top of each long side to make a rim. Place the remaining strips on the short sides, trimming them as necessary.

Place the tart shell on a baking sheet. Prick the bottom with a fork. Bake for 15 to 20 minutes, or until golden brown. Set aside on a rack.

Lower the oven temperature to 350°F.

Mix the orange zest, lemon zest and brown sugar in a bowl. Arrange a layer of one-third of the tomatoes, slightly overlapping, over the bottom of the tart shell. Sprinkle half the zest mixture over the tomatoes. Repeat with another layer of tomatoes, then the rest of the zest. End with a third layer of tomatoes.

Bake for 30 minutes. Remove and let cool slightly.

Heat the broiler. Melt the currant jelly in a small pan over low heat. Brush gently over the tart. Broil just until the jelly bubbles. Remove from the broiler and cool slightly before serving. **Serves 12**

Tomato Jam

Tomato jam may not be everybody's idea of a morning treat, but I love its spicy sweetness and relish the scantiness of calories. If you don't welcome the thought at breakfast, consider it as teatime snack with toast.

4 pounds tomatoes (about 8 large)

Four 1/2- pint canning jars with two-piece lids

1 lemon, quartered, seeded and cut into 1-inch chunks

1 large juice orange (8 ounces), quartered, seeded and cut into 1-inch chunks

3 cloves garlic, smashed and peeled

5 quarter-size slices peeled fresh ginger

1/2 cup packed dark brown sugar

1/2 teaspoon ground mace

1/2 teaspoon freshly grated nutmeg

2 teaspoons kosher salt

1 tablespoon fresh lemon juice

Core the tomatoes and cut an X in the bottom of each. Place in a 2½-quart soufflé dish or casserole. Cook in the microwave, uncovered, at 100% for 20 minutes, stirring halfway through cooking.

Remove from the oven. Pass the tomatoes through the medium disc of a food mill. Return to the dish and cook, uncovered, at 100% for 45 minutes, or until you have a thick tomato purée.

Meanwhile, place the jars, lids and rings in a deep pot. Add enough water to cover the jars by 2 inches. Boil for 5 to 10 minutes to sterilize. (For more about canning, see page 91.)

Place the lemon, orange, garlic and ginger in a food processor. Process until coarsely chopped.

Remove the tomatoes from the oven. Stir in the chopped lemon mixture, the sugar, mace, nutmeg and salt. Cook, uncovered, at 100% for 5 minutes.

Remove from the oven and stir in the lemon juice. Divide among the sterilized jars and process according to the instructions on page 91. **Makes 4 cups**

Tomato Granita

Yes, it is good.

2 1/4 pounds ripe tomatoes, peeled, cored and seeded

6 tablespoons fresh lemon juice

1 1/2 teaspoons kosher salt

3/4 cup One-to-One Simple Syrup (page 511)

1 1/2 tablespoons tomato paste

Purée the tomatoes in a food processor or blender or put through a food mill. You will have 3½ cups purée. Mix the purée with the remaining ingredients.

Shortly before serving, churn the tomato mixture in an ice cream maker according to the manufacturer's instructions. Because of the low sugar, it will get icy if done ahead. Transfer to a container and hold in the freezer for no more than 30 minutes before serving. **Makes 1 quart**

Winter Squash

Acorn, Delicata, Chayote, Pumpkin, Calabaza, Red Kuri, Hubbard, Butternut, Jarrahdale and Kabocha

The difference between summer and winter squash is a matter of usage rather than botanical species. Summer squash are eaten when immature, whereas winter squash are allowed to mature fully—developing a firmer and drier texture best appreciated fully cooked. Winter squash also have tough woody stems and hard rinds, allowing them to keep for weeks to months if stored in a cool, dry location. Certain varieties (acorn, butternut, spaghetti) can be found in stores year-round, but, as the name indicates, winter squash are most abundant from September through December.

Pumpkins are among these squash, but they are generally coarser in texture and less flavorful.

The list in the Cook's Guide includes some of the common eating pumpkins. The best ones weigh no more than a few pounds. Remember that pumpkins can be used with pasta and other nonsweet dishes as well as in pie. Larger pumpkins are dry and flavorless, better used as decoration.

When choosing how to cook a winter squash, it is important to note the texture as well as taste. Squash range from moist and delicate with fine flesh to slightly dry and medium coarse to starchy and very dense, sometimes unpleasantly fibrous. All winter squash will not be equally available. Many of them are new introductions from abroad. If using a different squash from that called for in a recipe, choose one of similar texture. In soup, for instance, a light moist squash purée will require less liquid and a dense starchy squash purée, such as Hubbard, will require more.

Delicata and chayote are classified as winter squash, but I usually cook them like summer squash. While I usually use chayotes when they have turned yellow on the vine, I found that in Mexico they are used green, puréed with some chunks left in and served as a light soup.

Many of my recipes call for acorn squash, as that is the one that has been most readily available in the markets. It is far from my favorite. Looking at the chart on page 653 makes it easy to substitute another kind of squash in any recipe.

All winter squash have seeds that can be cleaned and roasted for a snack (see page 652).

Many of the winter squash recipes begin with steamed squash. (See the Cook's Guide, page 653, for steaming instructions.)

Turn to **SQUASH, WINTER** in the Cook's Guide for how-tos and to the Index for more recipes..

Stuffed Acorn Squash

This makes a substantial winter meal to satisfy the bold.

> 2 large acorn squash (about 2 pounds each), halved lengthwise, seeds and fibers removed
>
> 2 tablespoons olive oil
>
> 1 recipe Lamb Curry Stuffing (page 493), rice cooked for just 5 minutes

Place a rack in the middle of the oven. Preheat the oven to 425°F.

Slice ¼ inch from each squash half so that it will sit steadily on the baking sheet.

Brush the cavities of the squash with the olive oil. Put ½ cup stuffing in each squash half. Place the squash on a baking sheet and bake for 40 minutes. **Serves 4 as a first or a main course**

Delicata Stuffed with Shrimp

This is an elegant, appropriately delicate first course for the end of summer.

> 1 large egg
>
> ¼ cup heavy cream
>
> 1 tablespoon finely minced scallions or snipped fresh chives, plus more for garnish
>
> 1 tablespoon chopped fresh dill, plus additional for topping
>
> 3 drops hot red pepper sauce
>
> ½ teaspoon kosher salt, plus additional to taste
>
> 2 ounces peeled and deveined medium shrimp, chopped
>
> 3 small delicata squash (7 ounces each), steamed, halved lengthwise, seeds and fibers removed

Place a rack in the center of the oven. Preheat the oven to 325°F.

Put the egg and cream in a small bowl. Beat lightly to break up the egg so strands are no longer visible. Mix in the scallions, dill, red pepper sauce, salt and shrimp.

Arrange the squash halves, cut side up, in a 13 x 9 x 2-inch glass baking dish. Lightly sprinkle the cavities with salt. Evenly distribute the shrimp filling among the squash halves. Bake for 40 minutes.

Top with additional scallions before serving.

Serves 6 as a first course

Chayotes au Gratin

Chayote—also known as cho cho, christophene and mirliton—is a vine-growing perennial gourd with beautiful flowers and makes some of the Caribbean's richest dishes.

> **2 chayotes, halved lengthwise, seeded and steamed**
>
> **4 tablespoons plus 2 teaspoons unsalted butter**
>
> **1 small onion, thinly sliced**
>
> **1 clove garlic, smashed, peeled and minced**
>
> **1 tablespoon minced fresh parsley**
>
> **1/4 teaspoon dried thyme**
>
> **1 cup milk**
>
> **1/2 teaspoon kosher salt**
>
> **Freshly ground black pepper to taste**
>
> **Pinch of cayenne pepper**
>
> **1 cup grated Gruyère cheese**
>
> **1/2 cup Dried Bread Crumbs (page 510) or store-bought dried bread crumbs**

Scoop out the flesh from each chayote half, leaving a 1/4-inch-thick shell. Reserve the shells. Mash the flesh with a fork. Drain, then squeeze dry between doubled paper towels.

Melt the 4 tablespoons butter in a large frying pan over medium heat. Add the onion and garlic and cook until the onion just begins to turn golden. Add the parsley, thyme and drained chayote. Cook, stirring constantly, until the mixture is fairly dry. Stir in the milk little by little until all is absorbed. Season with the salt, pepper and cayenne. Simmer gently for 5 minutes.

Divide half the chayote mixture among the reserved shells. Cover with half the Gruyère. Mound the remaining chayote over the cheese. Top with the remaining Gruyère. The chayote may be prepared to this point up to 1 day ahead; cover and refrigerate. Bring to room temperature before proceeding.

Just before serving, position an oven rack as close as possible to the heat source and preheat the broiler. Sprinkle the bread crumbs over the chayote. Dot with bits of the remaining 2 teaspoons butter. Broil until browned and bubbly. **Serves 4 as a first course or a side dish**

Jamaican Stuffed Cho Cho

Serve each stuffed squash to eat with a knife and fork. The thin skin is edible, although cho chos are usually peeled.

> **2 ripe cho chos (chayotes), halved lengthwise, seeded and steamed**
>
> **1 tablespoon plus 2 teaspoons raw rice**
>
> **1 tablespoon canola oil**
>
> **1 small onion, finely chopped (about 1/2 cup)**
>
> **2 cloves garlic, smashed, peeled and minced**
>
> **2 teaspoons Caribbean curry powder**
>
> **Good pinch of ground cloves**
>
> **2 jalapeño peppers, seeded and finely chopped (about 1/4 cup), or 1 Scotch bonnet or habanero pepper, seeded and finely chopped**

continued

¼ pound ground beef

½ teaspoon fresh thyme leaves

1 teaspoon kosher salt

Freshly ground black pepper to taste

3 ounces Gruyère cheese, grated (about ¾ cup)

Scoop out the flesh from each squash half, leaving a ¼-inch-thick shell. Reserve the shells. Mash the flesh with a fork. Let stand in a sieve set over a bowl for 1½ hours; the liquid will separate out.

Drain the squash well, pushing down with fingers until ½ cup pulp remains.

Place a rack in the center of the oven. Preheat the oven to 350°F.

Bring ½ cup water to a boil in a small saucepan. Add the rice. Cover and simmer over very low heat for 12 minutes. Drain in a sieve, rinse with cold water and drain again. Set aside.

Heat the oil in a small saucepan. Add the onion. Cook over low heat for 3 minutes, or until translucent. Add the garlic and cook for 2 minutes. Add the curry powder, cloves and chili peppers. Cook for 1 minute. Increase the heat to medium-low. Add the beef and cook, scraping the bottom of the pan, just until the beef loses its raw color. Stir in the thyme, cooked rice, drained chayote, salt, pepper and ¼ cup Gruyère.

Arrange the squash in an 8 x 8 x 2-inch glass baking dish. Fill each shell with one-quarter of the stuffing, mounding it on top. The dish can be made to this point up to 1 day ahead. Cover with plastic wrap and refrigerate. Bring to room temperature before proceeding.

Bake for 10 minutes, or until the squash is warmed through. Top with the remaining cheese in an even layer. Bake for 5 to 10 minutes, until the cheese is melted.

Serves 4 as a first course or a side dish

Kadoo Bichak

Baked Pumpkin and Onion Dumplings

This recipe appears in *Sephardic Cooking* by Copeland Marks (see the Bibliography).

DOUGH

1 package (¼ ounce) active dry yeast or
  2 ounces fresh yeast

1 cup warm water

4 cups all-purpose flour

1 teaspoon salt

1 egg yolk beaten with 1 tablespoon water

STUFFING

2 pounds cut-up pumpkin or calabaza squash, seeds and fibers removed, cut into ½-inch cubes

1 pound onions, chopped

½ teaspoon hot red pepper flakes

For the dough, dissolve the yeast in ½ cup of the warm water and let stand in a warm place for 10 minutes.

Put the flour in a large bowl. Mix in the salt and yeast mixture, then gradually add the remaining ½ cup warm water, or enough to prepare a soft, moist dough. Turn the dough out and knead for 5 minutes, sprinkling with flour if necessary for easy handling. Return the dough to the bowl, cover with a kitchen towel and let rise for 1 hour.

For the stuffing, mix the pumpkin and onions together in a large pan. Cover and cook over low heat for 30 minutes or more to reduce the bulk and soften the vegetables; considerable liquid may accumulate. Uncover the pan and cook for 10 minutes to evaporate all the liquid. Turn out into a bowl and stir in the pepper flakes. Cool.

Space two racks evenly in the oven. Preheat the oven to 325°F. Have two large baking sheets oiled and ready.

Punch down the dough. Roll it out into a long sausage shape about 3 inches in diameter. Pull off ⅓ cup dough (about 2 ounces), and roll it out into a pancake 4 inches in diameter and ¼ inch thick. Put 1 generous tablespoon stuffing into the center and fold over the top toward the center. Then fold the bottom left and right sides over toward the center to shape a closed triangle. Pinch the folds together to seal. Place on an oiled baking sheet. Repeat with the remaining dough and filling.

Brush the egg over the dumplings. Bake for 20 minutes, or until browned on top. Serve warm. **Makes 20 dumplings**

NOTE: The dumplings may be frozen in plastic bags after baking and cooling. To serve, allow them to thaw at room temperature for 1 hour. Reheat in a 350°F oven for 10 minutes.

Red Kuri Rice Paper Packets

Inspired by Asian spring rolls, these bite-size snacks look like small puffed pillows. Rice paper, available in Asian markets, creates a light and crisp exterior for the creamy squash. Serve them as a first course or pass around as part of a mixed hors d'oeuvre.

Five 8-inch-round sheets rice paper

1¼ cups Asian-Flavored Red Kuri Purée (page 128)

About 2 cups canola oil for frying

Soak 1 sheet of rice paper in a broad shallow dish of warm water for 1 to 3 minutes, or until thoroughly pliable. Carefully remove the sheet and place on a flat surface. Set another sheet of rice paper in the dish to soak.

Using a very sharp knife or scissors, cut the soaked rice paper into 6 wedges. If necessary, use a paper towel to blot excess moisture from the wedges before proceeding. Put a rounded ½ teaspoon purée on each wedge, about ½ inch from the curved bottom edge of the rice paper. Fold the bottom over the filling. Fold the left and right sides in over the filling and roll up tightly. Repeat with the remaining rice paper and filling. Put the packets, seam side down, on a plate or baking sheet and cover with barely damp paper towels. Let stand for at least 15 minutes.

Pour enough oil into a 10-inch frying pan to measure ½ inch deep. Heat the oil to 325°F. With a slotted spoon, lower the packets, a few at a time, into the oil. Turn them over immediately. Do not crowd the pan—if the packets touch, they will stick together. Fry for 1 minute, or until golden brown. Remove and drain on paper towels. Serve hot. The packets can be made ahead. To serve, arrange in a single layer on a parchment-lined baking sheet and reheat in a 350°F oven for 5 minutes.
Makes 30 packets; serves 5 as a first course, 10 or more as an hors d'oeuvre

Fried Squash Nuggets

All of the firm winter squashes described on page 653 can be deep-fried. This particular batter gets light and puffy and can withstand the frying time needed for the squash to cook through. Serve as an hors d'oeuvre or as part of a Fritto Misto (page 516).

continued

Vegetable oil for deep-frying

Squash of choice (half of a 1 1/2-pound acorn squash or 3/4 pound calabaza squash will yield enough pieces), peeled, seeds and fibers removed, cut into 22 rough pieces about 1 x 1 x 1/2 inch—size is important; the squash will not cook through if they are too large

Flour for dredging

1 recipe Egg White Batter (page 516)

Pour enough oil into a deep 11- or 12-inch pot to come to a depth of 1½ to 2 inches. Heat the oil to 350°F. (See page 512 for more information on frying.)

Roll the squash in the flour, making sure all surfaces are coated, then put in a sieve and tap gently to remove excess flour. Working in batches of 4 or 5, dip the cubes in the batter and then fry for 3 minutes, or until golden brown. The squash is best if served immediately, but it can be reheated: Place on a parchment-lined baking pan and reheat in a 350°F oven for 10 minutes. The nuggets will recrisp but will also shrink slightly due to deflating egg whites.

Makes 22 nuggets

Acras de Christophene

These small spicy balls are often served with a spicy tomato sauce such as the Spicy Middle Eastern Tomato Sauce (page 464) for dipping.

1 envelope (1/4 ounce) active dry yeast

2 cups sifted all-purpose flour

1/2 cup minced onion

4 cloves garlic, smashed, peeled and minced

3 tablespoons minced fresh parsley

2 teaspoons crumbled dried thyme

1 tablespoon kosher salt

1/2 to 1 1/2 teaspoons cayenne pepper

2 large eggs, lightly beaten

4 christophenes (chayotes), halved lengthwise, pitted and steamed

Vegetable oil for deep-frying

In a large bowl, dissolve the yeast in ¼ cup warm water and let stand in a warm place for 10 minutes. Add the flour, onion, garlic, parsley, thyme, salt and cayenne to taste. Slowly stir in more water as necessary, up to 1½ cups, to make a fairly thick batter. Add the eggs and stir just to combine. Cover loosely with a damp towel and let stand in a warm place for 4 to 5 hours.

Meanwhile, scoop out the flesh from the chayotes and mash with a fork. Drain in a sieve, then squeeze dry between doubled paper towels. Set aside.

Stir the chayote into the batter. Pour 3 inches of oil into a large, deep pot and heat to 375°F. Drop 1 teaspoonful of the batter into the hot oil and fry for 1½ to 2 minutes, until golden. Drain on paper towels and taste. Correct the seasoning with additional cayenne if desired. Continue to fry, adding only as many spoonfuls at a time as will float in a single layer and without touching. If desired, the fritters may be fried several hours in advance; recrisp in a 400°F oven for 5 to 7 minutes, or until heated through and crisp.

Makes about 36 pieces; serves 4 to 6 as a first course, more as an hors d'oeuvre

Squash Tortelli with Sage-Butter Sauce

Tortelli mantovani di zucca, a stuffed pasta sweetened with mostarda and amaretti, is a traditional dish from Mantova (Mantua) in the north of Italy. "Tortelli" is a general word for pasta with filling. The filling can be layered between circles of dough, as it is here. Variously, the pasta may be folded over the filling into half-moons or made as one-and-a-half-inch square ravioli.

This recipe is adapted from the *Grande Enciclopedia Illustrata della Gastronomia* (see the Bibliography), which uses, traditionally, Marina di Chioggia squash. As it is difficult to find in this country, I have substituted the similar calabaza squash.

Mostarda is a kind of sweet sticky fruit pickle. It is very good and any extra can be served with cold or boiled meat.

One 1¼-pound wedge calabaza squash, steamed

Six 1½-inch-wide amaretti cookies, finely crushed in a mortar or spice mill

6 tablespoons minced mostarda (also called mostarda di Cremona; see headnote)

¼ cup freshly grated Parmesan cheese, plus additional for topping

Generous grating of nutmeg

¼ cup plus ½ teaspoon kosher salt, plus additional to taste

Freshly ground black pepper to taste

1 recipe Basic Pasta Dough (page 469) or Green Pasta Dough (page 472)

¾ cup (6 ounces) unsalted butter

24 fresh sage leaves, stacked 4 at a time, rolled up lengthwise and sliced into thin strips (about ¼ cup)

Peel the squash and cut into chunks. Place in a food processor and purée until smooth, stopping occasionally to scrape down the sides of the bowl. (Makes 1½ cups purée)

In a medium bowl, combine the purée with the amaretti, mostarda, Parmesan, nutmeg, the ½ teaspoon salt and pepper to taste. Mix well and set aside.

Divide the pasta dough into sixths. Using a pasta machine or a rolling pin (see page 470 for instructions), roll the dough into thin sheets.

With a glass or a sharp cookie cutter, cut each sheet of pasta into 2-inch circles. Reroll the scraps quickly and cut out more circles for a total of 48. Place the circles on a kitchen towel dusted with cornmeal or flour.

Place 1 level tablespoon of the squash filling in the center of half the circles; brush the edges lightly with water. Cover with another circle, and press the edges together to seal. Repeat with the remaining filling and circles of dough, setting the finished tortelli on another kitchen towel dusted with cornmeal or flour. At this point the tortelli may be put aside, covered with plastic wrap, for 1 hour, or frozen (see Note).

Bring 4 quarts water and the ¼ cup salt to a boil in a large pot. Slip 8 tortelli into the boiling water. Stir gently until the water returns to a boil, then cook for 3 minutes. With a slotted spoon, remove to a platter. Repeat with the remaining pasta. Reserve ¾ cup of the cooking water.

To make the sage-butter sauce: Melt the butter in a saucepan. Stir in the sage and reserved pasta cooking water; bring to a boil. Season with salt to taste.

Transfer the tortelli to a serving bowl. Toss with the hot sauce. Sprinkle with grated Parmesan cheese. Serve immediately.

Makes 32 tortelli; serves 8 as a first course, 4 as a main course

NOTE: To freeze the tortelli, place them on a parchment- or waxed paper–lined baking sheet in a single layer. Freeze just until solid, about 1 hour. Transfer to plastic freezer bags and seal tightly. Frozen tortelli can be stored for up to 3 months. They can be cooked right out of the freezer, without defrosting; add about 1 minute to the cooking time.

Buttercup Squash Gnocchi

Moisture from the squash and just enough flour to bind give these fluffy gnocchi an ethereal texture. However, the dough is very sticky, so flour hands liberally. Serve gnocchi with an equally light sauce—either the ricotta-parsley sauce here or, for a classic Italian take, the sage-butter sauce (see page 123). A larger pot may accommodate more gnocchi and reduce the overall cooking time; a smaller pot, though, will result in a more flavorful cooking liquid for the sauce.

> A 14-ounce wedge buttercup or butternut squash, seeds and fibers removed, steamed
>
> 3/4 cup all-purpose flour
>
> 2 1/2 tablespoons kosher salt, or to taste
>
> 1 large egg
>
> Olive oil for greasing spoons
>
> 1 cup ricotta cheese
>
> 1/2 bunch fresh parsley, leaves only (about 1/4 packed cup)
>
> Freshly ground black pepper to taste
>
> 5 tablespoons freshly grated Parmesan

Peel the squash and cut into chunks. Place in a food processor and purée until smooth, stopping occasionally to scrape down the sides of the bowl. Cool. (Makes 1 cup purée)

Transfer the purée to a medium bowl and add the flour, 1/2 teaspoon salt and the egg. Mix to the consistency of a thick batter; the dough will be very sticky.

Set out a small bowl of olive oil and two flatware teaspoons. Bring 2 quarts water and 2 tablespoons salt to a boil in a medium saucepan.

Cook the gnocchi in three batches: Dip the spoons into the oil, coating generously, then shake off the excess. Dip one spoon into the batter, scooping up a rounded teaspoonful. Use the other spoon to help shape the batter into a rounded oval, then scrape the gnocchi into the boiling water. Make 10 to 12 more gnocchi, greasing the spoons often. Simmer for 10 minutes. With a slotted spoon, remove the gnocchi to a platter. Repeat for remaining batches. Reserve 1/2 cup of the cooking water.

To make the sauce, put the ricotta, parsley and reserved cooking liquid into a blender and purée until smooth. Add the pepper and the remaining salt, or to taste. Stir to combine.

Preheat the broiler. Divide the gnocchi among five 6-inch round gratin dishes. Pour 1/4 cup sauce over each and top with 1 tablespoon Parmesan. Alternatively, arrange all the gnocchi in a single layer in a 12-inch oval gratin dish. Top with the sauce and Parmesan. Just before serving, run the gnocchi under the broiler for 4 minutes, or until puffed and golden brown.

Makes about 35 gnocchi; serves 5 as a first course

Hubbard Squash Risotto

This recipe is adapted from the *Grande Enciclopedia Illustrata della Gastronomia* (see the Bibliography). The amount of squash specified allows for a variable amount left for cutting into cubes after grating what is needed. There may be some waste, depending on the amount of fibers and seeds. This is a classic Italian dish, though traditionally it would be made with Marina di Chioggia.

Commercial broths can be salty. If using one, taste first and adjust the amount of additional salt (if any) accordingly. If using salted broth, do not add the salt until the end.

- 1 1/2 pounds Hubbard squash, peeled, seeds and fibers removed, or 1 1/4 pounds butternut squash, peeled, seeds and fibers removed

- 1 tablespoon unsalted butter

- 1 tablespoon olive oil

- 2 cups arborio or other risotto rice

- 1 small onion, very finely chopped (about 1/2 cup)

- 1 clove garlic, smashed, peeled and chopped

- 1 cup dry vermouth

- 4 1/2 to 5 cups Beef Stock (page 502), Fake Beef Stock (page 504) or commercial beef broth

- 1 1/2 tablespoons kosher salt, plus more to taste

- Freshly grated nutmeg to taste

- 1/2 cup chopped fresh parsley (optional)

- Freshly ground black pepper to taste

- Freshly grated Parmesan cheese for serving

Grate enough of the squash (about ¾ pound) to get 3 cups. Cut the remaining squash into ½-inch cubes.

Melt the butter with the oil in a large shallow pan. Add the rice. Cook over medium-high heat, stirring continuously, for 3 minutes, or until the rice turns white and loses its translucence. Add the onion and garlic. Reduce the heat slightly and cook for 1 minute. Add the grated squash. Stirring continuously, turning the rice up from the bottom, cook for 5 minutes. Add the vermouth. Reduce the heat to medium and cook until the vermouth is absorbed.

Increase the heat to medium-high and add ½ cup stock. Cook, stirring well, until the rice has absorbed most of the stock. Add another ½ cup stock and repeat the process, making sure the stock is mostly absorbed before each addition. Continue until the rice has cooked about 15 minutes and absorbed 4 cups stock.

Add the salt and nutmeg, then the parsley, if using. Add the squash cubes and ½ cup more stock, or 1 cup stock for a looser risotto. Cook, stirring, for 10 minutes, until creamy with a slight chew. Season with pepper and, if necessary, salt. Serve with Parmesan on top. Makes 6 1/2 cups

Hubbard Squash Silk

This is an extremely elegant soup from simple ingredients, except for a surprise one that makes all the difference. Pale ivory in color and beautiful in patterned double-handled consommé cups, this soup can be made in a food processor but is silkier and better using a blender. It is rich, and a cup to a cup and a half per person should be a good amount.

- One 3-pound Hubbard squash, cut lengthwise in half and seeds scraped out with a spoon

- 3 cups Basic Chicken Stock (page 501) or commercial chicken broth

- 1/2 cup Dijon mustard (surprise!)

- 1 tablespoon kosher salt

- 1 pint heavy cream

- Freshly ground black pepper to taste

- 1/3 cup fresh lime juice

Place a rack in the center of the oven. Preheat the oven to 350°F.

Place the squash halves side by side on a heavy baking sheet. Cover loosely with aluminum foil. Bake for 1½ hours, or until a knife slips easily into the thickest part of the flesh. Remove from the oven.

Holding the halves one at a time in a pot holder, pour off any extra liquid. Scoop the flesh, scraping it from the skin, into a bowl or large glass measure. Mash the flesh and whisk in the chicken stock. In batches, purée in a blender. The soup base can be made ahead and refrigerated.

When ready to serve, transfer the soup base to a saucepan and whisk in the remaining ingredients except the lime juice. Heat to the desired temperature; I prefer it not too hot. Stir in the lime juice and serve.

Makes 8 cups; serves 5 to 8 as a first course

Acorn Squash and Mint Soup

This soup is a nice surprise, with the sweet squash and refreshing mint. The recipe can be doubled.

1 tablespoon canola oil

2 medium shallots, coarsely chopped

1 acorn squash, halved, seeds and fibers removed, steamed or cooked in the microwave (see the Cook's Guide, pages 653 and 655)

1 cup American Tomato Purée (page 460) or sterile-pack strained tomatoes

1 cup Basic Chicken Stock (page 501) or commercial chicken broth

$1/3$ cup chopped fresh mint (about $1/2$ bunch)

$1 1/2$ teaspoons kosher salt

Freshly ground black pepper to taste

$1 1/2$ tablespoons fresh lime juice

Heat the oil in a medium saucepan. Cook the shallots for 2 to 3 minutes, until soft. Meanwhile, scoop the squash flesh from the skin and put in a blender.

Add the shallots, tomato purée and chicken stock to the blender. Purée until smooth. Transfer to a medium saucepan. Add the mint. Cook for 10 minutes over low heat. Stir in the salt, pepper and lime juice. **Makes $2 1/2$ cups**

Butternut Squash Soup with Glazed Chestnuts

The chestnuts and the pomegranate may sound unusual, but the recipe is well worth doing.

2 tablespoons unsalted butter

1 medium onion, cut into $1/4$-inch dice (about 1 cup)

2 stalks celery, peeled and cut into $1/4$-inch dice (about $2/3$ cup)

1 large floury potato (10 ounces), peeled and cut into 1-inch cubes (about $1 1/2$ cups)

$1/2$ large or 1 medium butternut squash ($2 1/4$ pounds), peeled, seeds and fibers removed, cut into 1-inch chunks (about 6 cups)

3 cups Roasted Chicken Stock (page 502) or commercial chicken broth

2 teaspoons kosher salt, or to taste

Freshly ground black pepper to taste

1 recipe Glazed Chestnuts (page 508)

Seeds from 1 medium pomegranate (optional)

In a medium saucepan, melt the butter over medium heat. Add the onion and turn the heat to medium-high; cook, stirring frequently, for 5 minutes, or until the onion begins to brown. Add the celery. Lower the heat and cook, stirring occasionally, for 5 minutes. Add the potato and cook, stirring, for 1 minute.

Add the squash and the stock. Bring to a boil. Lower the heat and simmer for 15 minutes, or until all the vegetables are very tender. Strain and return the liquid to the pan. In a food processor, purée the solids with a little of the liquid. Pass the purée through a sieve into the pan. Whisk to combine. Season with the salt and pepper. Reheat gently.

Serve topped with the glazed chestnuts. If desired, sprinkle with pomegranate seeds.

Makes 7 cups; serves 6 as a first course

Jarrahdale-Lemongrass Soup

Lemongrass is wildly misunderstood in the north of America and Europe. The greens are not meant to be used, unless added to a vegetarian stock. It is the bottom end, which has a softish interior, cut up finely, that is used. The flavor is wonderful. If fresh is unavailable, look for dried and powdered lemongrass, sometimes labeled sereh powder, in specialty shops.

> $^1/_2$ Jarrahdale squash (3 $^1/_4$ pounds), seeds and fibers removed, steamed, or 2 large acorn squash (2 pounds each), seeds and fibers removed, steamed
>
> 1 tablespoon unsalted butter
>
> 1 small onion, finely chopped (about $^1/_3$ cup)
>
> 1 $^1/_2$ teaspoons ground cumin
>
> Pinch of cayenne pepper
>
> One 3-inch piece bulb end lemongrass, tender interior stalk only, finely chopped (about $^1/_4$ cup)
>
> 2 cups Basic Chicken Stock (page 501) or commercial chicken broth
>
> 2 tablespoons kosher salt, or to taste

Peel the squash and cut into large chunks. Place in a food processor and purée until smooth, stopping occasionally to scrape down the sides of the bowl. (Makes 4 cups purée)

Melt the butter in a large saucepan. Add the onion and cook over medium-low heat until translucent. Stir in the cumin and cayenne. Cook for 1 minute. Mix in the purée and the remaining ingredients. Bring to a boil. Reduce the heat and simmer for 5 minutes. Season with additional salt, if desired. **Makes 6 cups**

Simple Kabocha Purée

With its firm texture and sweet, nutty flavor, kabocha needs only a little butter and salt to make a light, silky purée. Serve it with game as an orange-gold alternative to the traditional chestnut purée.

> 1 kabocha squash (2 pounds), halved, seeds and fibers removed, steamed
>
> 1 tablespoon unsalted butter
>
> $^1/_4$ teaspoon kosher salt

Peel the squash and cut into chunks. Place in a food processor and purée until smooth, stopping occasionally to scrape down the sides of the bowl.

Transfer the purée to a medium saucepan. Add the butter and salt. Heat over low heat. **Makes 2 cups**

Simple Acorn Squash Purée

Acorn squash tends to be watery, so I use cooked rice as a thickener. Golden acorn squash is less bitter than its green sibling.

> $^1/_4$ cup raw rice
>
> 1 large golden or regular acorn squash (1 $^1/_2$ pounds), halved, seeds and fibers removed, steamed
>
> 2 tablespoons unsalted butter
>
> $^1/_2$ teaspoon kosher salt

Bring $^1/_2$ cup water to a boil in a small saucepan. Add the rice. Cover and simmer for 15 minutes, or until the rice is cooked.

Peel the squash and cut into chunks. Place in a food processor and purée until smooth, stopping occasionally to scrape down the sides of the bowl.

continued

Transfer the purée to a blender. Add the rice and purée until smooth. The suction from the blender will create a funnel in the purée that is visible from the top. For the best texture, use a rubber spatula to slowly and continuously smooth the top of the purée over the suction funnel while the blender is running.

Transfer the purée to a medium saucepan. Add the butter and salt. Heat over low heat.

Makes 2 cups

Asian-Flavored Red Kuri Purée

The starchy red kuri squash makes a smooth and thick purée that can be served on its own as a side dish or used as a filling (see Red Kuri Rice Paper Packets, page 121). If using the more watery acorn squash, add cooked rice to thicken the purée; see the variation.

> 2 1/2 pounds red kuri squash, halved,
>   seeds and fibers removed, steamed
>   (see the Cook's Guide, page 654)
>
> 2 tablespoons canola oil
>
> 1/4 cup Semi-Thai Sauce (page 467)

Peel the squash and cut into chunks. Place in a food processor and purée until smooth, stopping occasionally to scrape down the sides of the bowl.

Transfer the purée to a medium saucepan. Add the oil and sauce. Heat over low heat.

Makes 2 1/2 cups

Asian-Flavored Acorn Squash Purée

Bring 2/3 cup water to boil in a small saucepan. Add 1/4 cup plus 2 tablespoons rice. Cover and simmer for 15 minutes, or until the rice is cooked.

Replace the red kuri with 2 acorn squash (1 1/4 pounds each), halved, seeds and fibers removed, steamed. Peel the squash and cut into chunks. Purée in a food processor as above.

Transfer the purée to a blender. Add the rice and purée until smooth. The suction from the blender will create a funnel in the purée that is visible from the top; for the best texture, use a rubber spatula to slowly and continuously smooth the top of the purée over the suction funnel while the blender is running. Heat the purée as directed.

Delicata with Mixed Fresh Herbs

Think of these starchy, golden-edged cubes as a healthier version of hash browns.

> 3 tablespoons unsalted butter
>
> 3 delicata squash (about 1 1/2 pounds), trimmed,
>   halved, seeds removed and cut into 1/2-inch dice
>   (about 4 cups)
>
> 1 1/2 teaspoons chopped fresh savory
>
> 1 1/2 teaspoons chopped fresh thyme
>
> 1 1/2 teaspoons chopped fresh sage
>
> 1/2 teaspoon kosher salt, or to taste
>
> Freshly ground black pepper to taste

Melt the butter in a large skillet. Cook the squash over medium-high heat, stirring occasionally, until lightly browned and tender, 7 to 12 minutes. Add the herbs. Cover, reduce the heat to low and cook for 3 minutes. Season with the salt and pepper to taste. **Makes 3 cups**

Roasted Buttercup Squash with Chili Oil

These small green squash, deeply ribbed, with a paler green topknot like a brioche, may be dappled with orange. Cut across into slices, they make a pretty and unusual roasted vegetable. Slicked with a little fat before roasting and sprinkled with salt and pepper, they are simple and good. Add a little more fat and more seasonings, and they are a standout. While I have used chili powder to season the slices when serving with roast pork, good alternatives are ground cumin, ground anise to accompany fish, or a little bit of ground cinnamon and nutmeg to go with southern Mediterranean food.

1 buttercup squash (1 pound), halved lengthwise, seeds and fibers removed, each half cut across into 8 slices

3 to 4 tablespoons canola oil or other neutral oil

1 1/2 teaspoons chili powder

1/2 teaspoon kosher salt

Freshly ground black pepper to taste

Place a rack in the center of the oven. Preheat the oven to 500°F.

Peel the squash slices with a sharp knife. Place in a 12 x 8 x 1½-inch roasting pan. Combine the oil, chili powder, salt and pepper. Toss with the squash slices.

Roast for 5 minutes. Shake the pan to turn the pieces. Roast for 5 minutes more. Shake the pan again. Roast for 5 to 10 minutes more, until the squash is tender. **Serves 3 to 4 as a side dish**

Braised Calabaza with Mushrooms

Served with brown rice and a dark green such as kale, this dish makes a hearty vegetarian main course. It can be reheated, but only on the same day.

1 tablespoon canola oil

1 tablespoon toasted sesame oil

1 small onion, cut into 1/4-inch dice (about 1/2 cup)

6 large white mushrooms (6 ounces), trimmed and cut into 6 wedges each (about 2 cups)

3 cloves garlic, smashed, peeled and finely chopped

2 teaspoons grated peeled fresh ginger

1 1/4 pounds calabaza or acorn squash, peeled, seeds and fibers removed, cut into 1 x 1 x 1/2-inch pieces (about 4 cups)

1/2 ounce dried porcini (*Boletus*) mushrooms, soaked in 1/3 cup boiling water for 15 minutes; soaking liquid strained and reserved

1 tablespoon soy sauce, preferably tamari

Heat the canola and sesame oils in a large saucepan. Cook the onion over medium-low heat until translucent. Add the white mushrooms. Cook for 5 minutes, stirring occasionally. Add the garlic and ginger. Stir and cook for 1 minute.

Add the calabaza, soaked mushrooms and mushroom soaking liquid. Cover, reduce the heat and simmer for 10 minutes, or until the calabaza is cooked through but not mushy. Stir in the soy sauce.

Makes 4 1/2 cups; serves 4 as a main course, as described, 6 as a side dish or a first course

Acorn Squash Stew

With the addition of the protein-rich soybeans (edamame), this squash stew is a great meal for vegetarians.

2 tablespoons canola oil

1 medium onion, finely chopped (about 1 cup)

3 cloves garlic, smashed, peeled and minced

2 tablespoons curry powder

continued

₁/4 teaspoon cayenne pepper

2 cups Plum Tomato Purée (page 459) or
sterile-pack strained tomatoes

3 cups shelled fresh or frozen soybeans
(edamame)

2 large acorn squash (about 1 ^{3}/4 pounds each),
seeds and fibers removed, steamed, peeled
and cut into ^{1}/2 x 1 x 1-inch pieces
(about 5 ^{1}/2 cups), or 5 ^{1}/2 cups peeled raw
calabaza squash in 1 x 1 x ^{1}/2-inch pieces
(about 2 pounds squash)

1 teaspoon kosher salt

Freshly ground black pepper to taste

1 tablespoon fresh lemon juice

In a large nonreactive saucepan, combine the oil, onion, garlic, curry powder and cayenne pepper and cook over medium-low heat for 10 minutes, or until the onion and garlic are soft and translucent. Add the tomato purée and edamame. Increase the heat to medium. Simmer for about 5 minutes, or until the edamame are cooked through.

Stir in the squash. Cook for 10 minutes (12 minutes if using calabaza), or until the squash is tender. Remove from the heat. Season with the salt and pepper and stir in the lemon juice. **Makes 7 cups**

Coconut-Jarrahdale Vegetable Stew

Serve this on top of plain white rice or, omitting the cardamom, Rice Pilaf (page 489). Made with garlic broth, it becomes vegetarian.

3 tablespoons unsalted butter

2 medium onions, cut into ^{1}/2-inch dice
(about 2 cups)

2 medium carrots, peeled and cut into ^{1}/2-inch
dice (about ^{1}/2 cup)

1 bunch broccoli, florets only (stems reserved
for another dish), in 1- to 1 ^{1}/2-inch pieces
(about 5 cups)

^{1}/2 Jarrahdale squash (2 ^{1}/4 pounds), peeled,
seeds and fibers removed, cut into
1- to 1 ^{1}/2-inch chunks, or 3 acorn squash
(1 ^{1}/4 pounds each), peeled, seeds and fibers
removed, cut into 1- to 1 ^{1}/2-inch chunks
(about 6 cups)

1 cup coconut milk

^{1}/2 cup Basic Chicken Stock (page 501),
Garlic Broth (page 507) or commercial
chicken broth

Seeds from enough white cardamom pods
(about 24) to make 1 tablespoon ground
cardamom, or 1 tablespoon ground cardamom

2 tablespoons celery seeds

1 tablespoon kosher salt

Freshly ground black pepper to taste

Melt the butter in a large saucepan over medium heat. Add the onions. Cook for 3 minutes, or until limp and translucent. Increase the heat to high. Add the carrots, broccoli and squash. Cook for 5 minutes, stirring occasionally.

Reduce the heat to medium-high. Add the coconut milk and chicken stock. Bring to a boil. Stir in the cardamom and celery seeds. Continue to boil for 3 minutes. Cover, reduce the heat to medium and simmer for 10 minutes, or until the squash is cooked through.

Remove the lid and cook over high heat to reduce and thicken the sauce. Season with the salt and pepper. **Makes 6 ^{1}/2 cups**

Calabaza Stew with Lamb

Serve this stew over cooked orzo or rice.

- 1 tablespoon olive oil

- 1 medium onion, cut into $1/4$-inch dice (about 1 cup)

- $1/2$ pound ground lean lamb

- 2 cloves garlic, smashed, peeled and chopped

- $1 1/2$ pounds calabaza squash, peeled, seeds and fibers removed, cut into $3/4$- to 1-inch chunks, or 1 large acorn squash ($1 1/2$ to $1 3/4$ pounds), peeled, fibers and seeds removed, cut into $3/4$- to 1-inch chunks (about 5 cups)

- $1 1/2$ tablespoons crushed dried Greek oregano

- 1 teaspoon kosher salt, or to taste

- $1/3$ cup Plum Tomato Purée (page 459) or sterile-pack strained tomatoes

- 2 tablespoons fresh lemon juice

- Freshly ground black pepper to taste

Heat the olive oil in a large saucepan. Add the onion and cook over medium-low heat for 2 to 3 minutes, or until translucent. Add the lamb, breaking it up with a wooden spoon. Cook for 5 minutes, or until the lamb has lost most of its raw color. Add the garlic and cook for 1 minute. Add the squash, oregano and salt. Stir and cook for 2 minutes. Pour in ¼ cup water; stir. Cover, reduce the heat and simmer for 15 minutes.

Add the tomato purée. (If not serving immediately, turn off the heat; reheat just before serving.) Cook, uncovered, at a low boil for about 5 minutes, until the liquid reduces and the squash is meltingly tender. Stir in the lemon juice, additional salt, if desired, and pepper. **Makes 4 cups**

Thanksgiving Squash Muffins

Butternut will produce a fluffier and lighter-colored muffin than buttercup. Both result in a moist and exceptionally tender muffin, fragrant with spices. These muffins were quickly devoured by all, including the one with the most finicky of palates, our dog, Stubbs.

- $1/2$ buttercup or butternut squash (1 pound), halved, seeds and fibers removed, steamed

- 9 tablespoons unsalted butter, slightly softened

- $1 1/2$ cups plus 2 tablespoons cake flour

- 1 teaspoon baking soda

- $1/2$ teaspoon baking powder

- $1/2$ teaspoon ground allspice

- $2/3$ teaspoon ground cinnamon

- $1/2$ teaspoon kosher salt

- 1 cup packed dark brown sugar

- $1/3$ cup milk

- 1 teaspoon vanilla extract

- 2 large eggs

Peel the squash and cut into chunks. Place in a food processor and purée until smooth, stopping occasionally to scrape down the sides of the bowl. Allow to cool. (Makes 1 cup purée)

Place a rack in the center of the oven. Preheat the oven to 350°F. Grease and flour one 12-cup or two 6-cup muffin tins, using 1 tablespoon butter and 2 tablespoons flour. Place in the refrigerator until needed.

Whisk together the 1½ cups flour, the baking soda, baking powder, spices and salt.

Using a mixer set on medium speed, beat the remaining 8 tablespoons butter and the sugar in a large bowl until fluffy. Add the squash purée, milk and vanilla. Mix until ell combined, scraping down the sides of the bowl as necessary. Add the eggs one at a time, mixing well after each addition. Stir in the dry ingredients by hand until just combined, being careful not to overmix.

Spoon the batter into the prepared tin(s). Bake for 28 to 30 minutes, or until a tester inserted in a muffin comes out clean. Loosen the muffins from the tin(s) while still warm and cool in the tin(s) on a rack.

Serve or wrap well and freeze. Defrost and serve at room temperature. **Makes 12 muffins**

Pickled Chayote

This is often made in New Orleans, where it is known as pickled mirliton. Paul Prudhomme fills a jar with the pickles and then with martinis—lethal.

> 1 tablespoon plus 1 teaspoon kosher salt
>
> 2 chayotes (10 to 11 ounces each), halved lengthwise, peeled, seeded, cut lengthwise into $^1/_3$-inch-thick sticks and halved across
>
> 1 medium onion (6 ounces), cut lengthwise into $^1/_4$-inch-thick strips
>
> 2 cups white vinegar
>
> 1 tablespoon sugar
>
> 4 cloves garlic, smashed and peeled
>
> 6 small dried chili peppers (pequín or bird)
>
> 1 tablespoon celery seeds
>
> 1 tablespoon coriander seeds
>
> 2 tablespoons mustard seeds
>
> Two 1-pint canning jars with two-piece lids

In a narrow 3-quart bowl, dissolve the 1 tablespoon salt in 4 cups water. Add the chayotes and onion; the water should just cover them. Allow to sit at room temperature for 3 hours. Drain.

Combine the 1 teaspoon salt, $^1/_2$ cup water, the vinegar, sugar, garlic, chilies and spices in a 4-quart nonreactive saucepan. Bring to a boil. Reduce the heat and simmer for 10 minutes.

Add the chayote and onions. Cook for 20 minutes, stirring occasionally. The vegetables will be slightly wilted and translucent.

While the vegetables are cooking, prepare the canning jars. Place the jars, lids and rings in a deep stockpot. Fill with enough water to cover the jars by 2 inches. Boil for 5 to 10 minutes to sterilize them. Bring a small saucepan of water to a boil. Keep it ready to top off the jars if necessary. (For more about canning, see page 91.)

When the vegetables are cooked, use clean tongs to remove the jars from the water. Divide the vegetables evenly between the jars, packing them down (a large-mouthed funnel is helpful here). Divide the cooking liquid, garlic, chilies and spices among the jars. If more water is required to barely cover the vegetables, add some of the reserved boiling water.

Use tongs to remove the lids from the water one at a time, and carefully place them on top of the jars. An airtight seal will form. Remove the rings from the water and screw them onto the jars. **Makes 2 pints**

Kabocha with Cumin, Raisins and Almonds

Serve this dessert with a thick yogurt—Greek style or sheep's milk—or vanilla ice cream.

> $^1/_2$ cup raisins
>
> 2 tablespoons unsalted butter
>
> 2 teaspoons ground cumin
>
> 1 pound kabocha or butternut squash, peeled, seeds and fibers removed, cut into 1-inch chunks (about 3 cups)

1/2 cup slivered almonds

1/2 cup turbinado sugar or raw sugar

1/2 teaspoon grated peeled fresh ginger

2 tablespoons fresh lemon juice

Freshly ground black pepper to taste

Soak the raisins in 1 cup boiling water for 30 minutes. Drain; reserve the soaking liquid.

Melt the butter in an 11- or 12-inch frying pan. Add the cumin and cook 1 minute over medium heat. Stir in the squash. Cook for 5 minutes. Add the raisins and almonds. Reduce the heat slightly and cook for 7 minutes, stirring occasionally. Add the reserved soaking liquid. Cover. Cook for 5 minutes.

Add the sugar and ginger. Stir to combine. Cover and cook for 5 to 8 minutes, or until the squash is tender. Uncover, increase the heat to high and cook for a few minutes to reduce and thicken the liquid. Stir in the lemon juice and pepper. **Makes 3 cups**

Candied Coconut-Acorn Squash Balls

Coconut and sweet squash or pumpkin are a natural couple in savory dishes such as Coconut-JarrahdaleVegetable Stew (page 130). Here dried unsweetened coconut adds crunch as well as flavor. Look for it in specialty markets or health food stores. Stick these little candies with toothpicks and serve on a platter as an end to a meal, or sprinkle them on sundaes.

1 cup dried (dessicated) unsweetened shredded coconut, finely chopped

1 golden or regular acorn squash (1 1/2 pounds), halved lengthwise, seeds and fibers removed

4 tablespoons unsalted butter

1/4 cup sugar

Spread the coconut on a pie plate. Line a 10 x 15-inch baking sheet with parchment paper. Set aside.

Use the small end of a melon baller to scoop balls from the squash. Melt the butter in a 12-inch frying pan. Add the squash in a single layer. Cook over medium-low heat, shaking and swirling the pan regularly to toss the squash; or use a heatproof spatula to gently turn the squash without mashing it. After 10 minutes, or when the squash is tender but still retains its shape, add the sugar. Cook for 3 minutes, gently turning the squash, or until the sauce browns and a glaze forms.

Scrape the squash onto the pie plate with the coconut. Roll the balls in the coconut until well covered. Remove to the baking sheet, keeping the balls separate, and cool. **Makes about 55 balls**

Spiced Squash Pudding

Using fresh squash in a baked pudding is a revelation. Unlike canned pumpkin, which must be heavily spiced and sweetened to make up for its lack of flavor, the squash makes a pudding sweet, nutty, and voluptuously creamy.

This is a time-intensive dessert but worth the effort. The slow-cooking of the squash purée evaporates excess liquid, improving its texture and intensifying the flavor. The cooking of the entire dish can be done the day before serving.

4 3/4 pounds calabaza squash, seeds and fibers removed, steamed, or two 2 1/2-pound sugar pie pumpkins, halved, seeds and fibers removed, steamed

1/2 tablespoon unsalted butter

1 tablespoon all-purpose flour

3/4 cup packed brown sugar

1/2 teaspoon ground cinnamon

continued

1/2 teaspoon ground ginger

1/2 teaspoon ground cloves

2 large eggs

1 cup heavy cream

1 cup heavy cream, softly whipped, for topping
  (optional)

To make squash or pumpkin purée: Peel the squash or pumpkin and cut into large chunks. Place in a food processor and purée until smooth, stopping occasionally to scrape down the sides of the bowl. (Makes 6¼ cups purée.)

Cook the purée in a 12-inch nonstick pan over medium heat, stirring often, for 30 minutes. Reduce the heat to medium-low. Cook and stir for 15 minutes.

Reduce the heat to low. Cook and stir the squash for 1 hour and 45 minutes, until it is reduced to 1½ cups. The squash will be caramel brown and very thick with all its moisture evaporated. Allow to cool.

Place a rack in the middle of the oven. Preheat to 425°F. Butter and flour a 9-inch glass pie plate.

Transfer the squash to a medium bowl. Add the sugar, spices, eggs and 1 cup cream, mixing well after each addition. Pour into the pie plate. Bake for 30 to 35 minutes, until a knife inserted in the center comes out clean. The edges will be golden brown and the center will puff. Cool.

Serve with whipped cream, if desired.

Serves 8

Spiced Squash Pie

Prepare a 9-inch Basic Pie Crust (page 476), and partially bake it. Pour the pudding mixture into the crust and bake as above. Turn the pie plate halfway through the bake time to ensure even cooking. If the crust rim browns too much before the filling is cooked, cover the rim with foil. Cool before serving.

Pumpkin Pudding

This was developed as a low-fat recipe, but whole milk can be substituted; I prefer to use skim. It's a lovely dessert for Thanksgiving, when richer pies may make one rue the festivities for days. It is so good I don't think anyone will feel deprived; it tastes rich. In any case, it can be served with heavy cream floated on top.

1 1/2 cups squash or pumpkin purée
  (see previous recipe)

2 large eggs

1/4 cup cornstarch

1/2 cup packed light brown sugar

1/2 teaspoon ground cinnamon

1/2 teaspoon ground ginger

1/4 teaspoon freshly grated nutmeg

1/4 teaspoon ground cardamom

2 cups skim or whole milk

2/3 cup fresh orange juice

Beat together the pumpkin and eggs in a large heavy saucepan. In a small bowl, combine the cornstarch, brown sugar, and spices and stir into the pumpkin mixture. Add the milk and juice.

Cook over medium heat, whisking continuously—be sure to get the corners, where lumps can hide—until the pudding is very thick. Reduce the heat and give the pudding a few quick whisks to remove any lumps.

Divide the pudding among eight 4-ounce (½-cup) ramekins or place in a serving bowl. Cover with plastic wrap and refrigerate until chilled. **Makes 3 1/3 cups; serves 8**

Microwave Variation

Heat the milk in a 2-quart glass measure, uncovered, at 100% for 6 minutes. Whisk in the remaining ingredients. Cover tightly with plastic wrap. Cook at 100% for 8 minutes. Prick the plastic to release the steam.

Remove from the oven and uncover. Divide among ramekins or place in a serving bowl. Cover and refrigerate until chilled.

NOTE: *To serve 4:* Use ¾ cup purée, 1 egg, 2 tablespoons cornstarch, ¼ cup packed light brown sugar, ¼ teaspoon cinnamon, ¼ teaspoon ginger, ⅛ teaspoon nutmeg, ⅛ teaspoon cardamom, 1 cup milk, 5 tablespoons orange juice. If using the microwave, cook for 3 minutes, then for 4 minutes.

To serve 12: Use 2¼ cups purée, 3 eggs, 6 tablespoons cornstarch, ¾ cup packed light brown sugar, ¾ teaspoon cinnamon, ¾ teaspoon ginger, ½ teaspoon each nutmeg and cardamom, 3 cups milk, 1 cup orange juice. If using the microwave, cook for at 100% for 9 minutes, then for 15 minutes.

Thanksgiving Pudding

I love steamed puddings and their moist texture somewhere between cake and pudding. Until the microwave oven, I made them infrequently, as they were too fussy for me, requiring long steaming in a hot water bath that needed to be constantly checked and have more water added. Now they are no more difficult or time-consuming than any other dessert.

I devised this steamed pudding to replace the more traditional rich pies associated with Thanksgiving. It is equally good but less heavy. Pumpkin can be substituted for the acorn squash, if desired. Place 2 cups (12 ounces) 1-inch cubes pumpkin flesh in a large glass measure and cook, tightly covered with microwave plastic wrap, for 8 minutes.

Unsweetened whipped cream is a welcome topping. Under Queen Victoria, people would have served hard sauce, but these days that's a lot of butter (even for me).

14 tablespoons (7 ounces) unsalted butter

1 acorn squash (about 1 pound), halved, seeds and fibers removed

1 cup packed dark brown sugar

5 large eggs

½ cup heavy cream

⅓ cup cake flour, sifted

1 teaspoon vanilla extract

¾ teaspoon ground cinnamon

¼ teaspoon ground allspice (optional)

TOPPING

Candied orange peel

2 tablespoons pomegranate seeds

Unsweetened whipped cream, for serving (optional)

Butter a 4-inch-deep 9-inch ceramic bowl or a 4-cup pudding basin with 2 tablespoons butter.

Wrap the squash halves tightly in microwave plastic wrap. Cook in the microwave at 100% for 7 minutes. Pierce the plastic to release the steam.

Remove from the oven and uncover. Let cool to room temperature.

Cut the remaining 12 tablespoons butter into 1-tablespoon pieces, put it in a food processor with the sugar and blend. Scrape the cooked squash from its shell into the processor. Add the remaining pudding ingredients and blend until smooth.

Pour into the prepared bowl. Cover tightly with microwave plastic wrap. Cook at 100% for 9 minutes, until set; if the pudding looks moist in the center, that is fine.

continued

Remove from the oven. Pierce the plastic with the tip of a sharp knife and cover the bowl with a heavy plate; this will keep the pudding hot. Let stand for 15 minutes.

Unmold the pudding onto a serving plate. Garnish with the candied orange peel and pomegranate seeds. Serve with whipped cream, if desired. **Serves 8**

To make individual servings: Divide the pudding mixture among eight 4-ounce ramekins. Cook in 2 batches of 4 at 100% for 2 minutes each.

To make a single, smaller pudding: Halve the ingredients and the cooking time; cook in a 7-inch bowl or 3-cup pudding basin. From this quantity 4 individual puddings can be prepared.

Basic Seeds

This works for any seeds, but timing varies with the kind of seed and the amount of moisture. Peek from time to time to make sure the seeds are not getting too brown. If time allows, letting them dry first will shorten the roasting time. The ideal result is a golden toasty color with the seeds cooked through. The amount of salt is subjective. To serve as a snack with a drink, more salt gets more drinkers.

As soon as the seeds have been removed from the squash, put them into a sieve and run cold water over them, rubbing them gently to remove as much of the sticky surrounding fiber as possible. This can be done while the squash is cooking or before; if the seeds are left sitting around too long, it is hard to remove the fiber. Drain and place on several sheets of paper toweling. Rub with more paper towels if need be to remove the remaining fiber. Allow to dry.

Seeds from a 1-pound buttercup squash, or ³/₄ cup other seeds, such as pumpkin or Hubbard, fibers removed, rinsed

1 tablespoon canola oil

Kosher salt to taste

Place a rack in the center of the oven. Preheat the oven to 400°F.

Remove the fibers from the seeds, rinse and dry (see headnote). Use the smallest baking pan that will hold the seeds comfortably in a single layer. Slick the seeds and pan with the oil.

Roast for 10 minutes. Turn the seeds. Roast for 5 minutes more. If necessary, turn again and roast for 5 to 10 minutes more. Sprinkle with salt. **Makes ¹/₂ to ³/₄ cup**

Adelle's Favorite Roasted Seeds

Throughout Mexico, this is a favorite salty snack with sangria and margaritas. Cut limes in a small saucer are brought with these spicy seeds to squeeze over them. Don't squeeze the juice on ahead of time; the seeds get soggy. Multiply the recipes as needed.

1 recipe Basic Seeds (at left)

¹/₂ to ³/₄ teaspoon pure chili powder

1 lime, halved

Mix the seeds and chili powder and proceed as directed in Basic Seeds. Keep at room temperature for a day or refrigerated up to a month. If they were refrigerated, reheat the seeds in a microwave just until warm. To serve, squeeze lime juice over them. **Makes ³/₄ cup**

Sweet Potatoes and Yams

In the whole world of vegetables there is perhaps no confusion as great as the common one between sweet potatoes and yams. I have put them both here in order to try to clarify their differences. First of all, they belong to different families—as can be seen by looking in the Cook's Guide on page 656.

Sweet potatoes are actually roots, not potatoes (tubers) at all. To add to the confusion, some kinds of sweet potatoes have been given "yam" as part of their common name. Sweet potatoes have traveled the world over and have even—to a great extent—replaced the African igname (a true yam, and where the word "yam" comes from).

Sweet potatoes are American by derivation, and they are what are eaten in their orange-gold glory at Thanksgiving; but, to confuse things further, some sweet potatoes are white. White sweet potatoes are less common, are drier than yellow or orange and take slightly longer to cook. The white are also sweeter than the orange ones. Both do well in purées, a use to which they are frequently put in the Caribbean, but white sweet potatoes need much more butter and cream than regular potatoes to become smooth.

Another version is the boniato (aka batata), sometimes thought of as a different vegetable entirely rather than what it is—a variant of sweet potato. It is drier and mealier than other sweet potatoes.

My favorite way of preparing and serving the orange-fleshed sweet potatoes is to cook them in the microwave oven, where they hold their shape better than when they're boiled. I peel them, cut them into wedges and serve them with either Aïoli or Rouille (page 456 or 457). This pairing derives from a grand aïoli that I had in the South of France.

Yams, on the other hand, may come from Asia or Africa. They are frequently eaten in the Caribbean and come in a range of colors. Yams go by so many names around the world that it is hard to know what one is buying or eating.

All of the following recipes are for sweet potatoes. I don't cook yams often, but often enough to know yams cannot be substituted for sweet potatoes and vice versa.

Turn to **SWEET POTATOES AND YAMS** in the Cook's Guide
for how-tos and to the Index for recipes.

Purée de Batata

Batatas, white sweet potatoes from the Caribbean islands, are hard and quite floury in texture.

- 1 pound batata, unpeeled, cut into 2-inch chunks
- 12 tablespoons (6 ounces) unsalted butter, softened
- 1/4 cup heavy cream
- 1/4 to 1/2 cup milk
- 1 1/2 teaspoons kosher salt

Put the batata in the top of a two-part steamer or on a steaming rack or plate in a bamboo steamer. Fill the bottom of the steamer pan or a pan large enough to hold the bamboo or steaming rack with water; the water should not touch the rack. Bring to a boil over medium heat. Place the batata on top, cover and steam for 1 hour, or until very soft.

Sieve or rice the batata into a bowl. Stir in the softened butter and cream. Add 1/4 cup milk and let sit for 5 minutes. If necessary, add additional milk to obtain a smooth, creamy purée. Season with the salt. Serve hot. **Makes 2 cups**

Sweet Potato Terrine

This is an extremely easy recipe with an autumn taste and color. Spread the terrine onto Crisp Vegetable Chips (page 514) or a good bread.

- 2 pounds sweet potatoes, peeled and cut into 1-inch pieces (about 6 1/3 cups)
- 2 medium cloves garlic, smashed, peeled, and halved
- 1/4 cup agar-agar flakes (see page 501)

1 cup Vegetable Broth (page 506)

Pinch of ground cinnamon

Pinch of freshly grated nutmeg

Kosher salt and freshly ground white pepper
   to taste

Combine the potatoes with the garlic in a
13 x 9 x 2-inch oval dish. Cover tightly with
microwave plastic wrap and cook at 100% for
16 minutes, stirring once during cooking.
Prick the plastic to release steam. Alternatively,
steam, covered, on top of the stove until tender
(see the Cook's Guide, page 657).

Transfer the sweet potatoes to a food
processor and process until finely chopped
(leave in the processor).

Stir the agar-agar and ½ cup vegetable
broth together in a 2-cup glass measure or a
bowl. Cook, uncovered, at 100% for 2 minutes,
or until the agar-agar is dissolved. Or, stir
the agar-agar and the 1 cup vegetable broth
together in a small saucepan. Heat to simmering
over low heat, then simmer, stirring occasionally,
until the agar-agar is dissolved, about 4 minutes.

With the food processor motor running,
pour in the dissolved agar-agar, along with the
remaining vegetable broth (if any). Process until
completely smooth. Season to taste with the
cinnamon, nutmeg, salt and white pepper.

Prepare a 3½-cup mold (a loaf pan will do)
by rinsing it with ice water just before filling;
do not dry. Scrape in the sweet potato mixture.
Cover and refrigerate for at least 3 hours.

To unmold: Put the mold in a large bowl.
Pour in hot water to just below the rim of the
mold. Let sit 30 seconds. Remove and invert
onto a serving platter. If the mold doesn't lift
easily from terrine, repeat.

Makes one 3½-cup terrine; serves 20 or more
as part of an hors d'oeuvre selection

Puffed Sweet Potato Slices with Crisp Red Onion Rings

This recipe combines two vegetables, which
can be made separately. Together their contrast
in taste, texture and color makes the dish an
instant hit. Use three large roasting pans and
three oven racks. If two pans and racks are all
that are available, halve the sweet potatoes (and
remember there will be less). Everything cooks
for 50 minutes, so once it's in the oven, it's easy.
Delicious with roast venison.

SWEET POTATOES

5 tablespoons olive oil

6 medium sweet potatoes (about 3 pounds), peeled
   and cut on the diagonal into long ½-inch slices

½ teaspoon kosher salt

ONIONS

¼ cup olive oil

5 red onions (about 1¾ pounds), cut into
   ¼-inch rings

¼ teaspoon kosher salt

The sweet potato slices will fill two 18 x 13 x
2-inch roasting pans; a third pan of the same
dimensions will be fine for the onions. Place
one rack in the center of the oven, another in
the lower third and one in the bottom. Preheat
the oven to 500°F.

For the sweet potatoes, pour half the oil into
one of the roasting pans. Smear it around.
Using half of the sweet potato slices, take each
one and swish both sides quickly through the
oil—do not blot or soak the pieces in the oil—
and arrange the slices in the pan so that they do
not touch. Repeat with the remaining oil and
potatoes in the second pan. Sprinkle ¼ teaspoon
of salt over each panful of slices.

continued

For the onions, pour the oil into the roasting pan. Swirl the pan until the oil evenly covers the bottom. Gently pull apart the rings of each onion slice; as the rings are separated, put them into the oiled pan. Toss the rings in the oil until all are coated, then arrange them so they touch as little as possible. Sprinkle with the salt.

Place the onions on the lowest oven rack and the sweet potatoes on the other two. Roast for 25 minutes. Remove one pan at a time from the oven and use a spatula to turn over each sweet potato slice and each onion ring. Return the pans to the oven, back to front, putting the pan of sweet potatoes that was on the highest rack on the middle one and vice versa. Roast for 25 minutes more.

Pile the sweet potatoes on a serving platter. Top with the red onion rings, sprinkle with salt and serve. **Serves 8 as a side dish**

Maple-Glazed Roasted Sweet Potatoes

A Texan friend feels that the syrup on these richly brown wedges transports her down memory lane: "It tastes like when I was a child and got to eat masses of sweet potatoes with brown sugar and—even better—with marshmallows toasty and fluffy on top." To get even more southern, use cane or dark corn syrup in place of the maple syrup. Add some marshmallows on top for the last five minutes of cooking if you must.

> 3 or 4 small sweet potatoes
> (about 1 1/2 pounds total), peeled
>
> 3 tablespoons unsalted butter
>
> 3 tablespoons maple syrup

Place a rack in the center of the oven. Preheat the oven to 500°F.

Cut the sweet potatoes in half lengthwise, then across. Cut each section lengthwise into 3 wedges.

Use the smallest pan that will hold the sweet potatoes comfortably. Melt the butter in it on top of the stove. Remove from the heat, place the sweet potatoes in the pan and turn the wedges in the butter.

Roast for 15 minutes. Remove the pan from the oven and toss the sweet potatoes with the maple syrup. Roast for about 15 minutes more. The sweet potatoes should be easy to pierce with the tip of a sharp knife. Immediately remove to a serving plate, or the sweet potatoes will stick to the pan. Soak the pan.
Serves 3 or 4 as a side dish

Balsamic Root Vegetables

A nice side dish for boiled meat or hash.

> 1 pound sweet potatoes, peeled and
> cut into 1/4-inch dice (about 3 1/2 cups)
>
> 1 pound beets, trimmed, peeled and
> cut into 1/4-inch dice (about 1 1/2 cups)
>
> 1 large onion, finely chopped
>
> 2 medium stalks celery, peeled and
> cut into 1/4-inch dice (about 1 cup)
>
> 1/4 pound mushrooms, trimmed and
> cut into 1/4-inch dice (about 1 1/2 cups)
>
> 3 tablespoons unsalted butter
>
> 1 teaspoon balsamic vinegar
>
> 1/4 teaspoon kosher salt

Put the sweet potatoes and the beets next to each other in the top of a two-part steamer or on a steaming rack or a plate in a bamboo steamer. Fill the bottom of the steamer pan or a pan large enough to hold the bamboo or steaming rack with water; the water should not touch the rack. Bring to a boil over medium heat. Place the vegetables on top, cover and steam for 15 minutes. Set aside.

In a 2-quart saucepan, slowly cook the onion, celery and mushrooms in the butter over very low heat until wilted, about 15 minutes. Add the sweet potatoes, beets, balsamic vinegar and salt. Stir to combine; heat for a minute or so.

Makes 4 cups

Sweet Potato Pie

This is extremely attractive with its white whipped cream top sprinkled with grated dark chocolate and orange zest. However, the cream will do a good job on its own.

1 1/4 pounds sweet potatoes, peeled and cut into 1/4-inch dice (about 3 1/2 cups)

3/4 cup milk

1/2 cup sugar

1/2 cup heavy cream

3 large eggs

2 large egg yolks

One 9-inch pie shell made from Basic Pie Crust (page 476), partially baked

TOPPINGS

1 cup heavy cream, chilled

1 ounce bittersweet chocolate, grated (optional)

1 teaspoon finely grated orange zest (optional)

Preheat the oven to 350°F.

Put the sweet potatoes, milk and sugar in a 2-quart saucepan. Bring to a boil over medium heat. Reduce the heat to a simmer, cover and cook, stirring occasionally, for 20 minutes, or until the sweet potatoes are very tender.

Put the potatoes, with their cooking liquid, and heavy cream in a food processor. Purée until very smooth. Add the eggs and yolks. Purée until combined. Pour into the partially baked piecrust.

Bake for 35 to 40 minutes, until the center no longer jiggles. Turn the pie plate halfway through the bake time to ensure even cooking. Cool. Refrigerate if making a day ahead.

To serve, allow the pie to come to room temperature if necessary. Beat the cream until it holds soft peaks. Spread the whipped cream over the pie and sprinkle with chocolate and/or orange zest, if desired. **Makes one 9-inch pie; serves 8**

American Roots

Jerusalem Artichokes, Jicama, Yautía and Yuca

Well, I admit defeat. I have spent many pleasant mornings and afternoons in Central and South American, as well as Caribbean, markets and seen women surrounded by piles of dark tubers and roots. I have never managed to really sort them out, and all my wonderful books haven't given me the answers either.

I will describe only four that I have somewhat tamed; and I give warning that, in southern climes, each root has a multitude of names that can only cause more confusion. Most of them can be peeled and cooked like potatoes. Good luck.

Only one of these vegetables is North American, the Jerusalem artichoke, a Native American food being promoted as the "sunchoke." This is a tuber that is neither from Jerusalem nor an artichoke. It grows prolifically and has often been used as cattle feed. In France, during World War II, Jerusalem artichokes were one of the few readily available foods. Cattle and famine have probably given them a bad name, along with the fact that these ovoid tubers used to be knobby and hard to peel. In their new sunchoke incarnation, they have become quite smooth.

They are at their best during cold weather, and they store well. The season is from late September through February. These starchy little tubers serve the same purpose on a plate as potatoes but have a more assertive flavor. Like turnips, they balance rich foods such as duck.

Moving south, we come to jicama and yautía. Jicama has become so popular that it is now also grown in Texas. It is a dark brown flattened ball that can be eaten raw or cooked. Raw, it is nicely crisp but has a slightly starchy feel on the tongue. Even when using it in salad, I prefer to cut it into the size I want and plunge it into boiling water for about a minute; I then run it under cold water. It is still crisp, but the floury feel on the tongue is gone. Jicamas make a very pleasant substitute for potatoes in salad.

Yautía is also known as malanga and is either white or yellow. The latter is cultivated for its corm (root) and often substitutes for yams. More confusing yet, there are places in the Americas where the root is called taro, another tuber that belongs to the same family. All of these vegetables must be cooked or they are acrid and sometimes poisonous. The corm is slightly hairy, longish and thin, sort of the shape of a summer squash, with visible rings. It must be peeled and should be used quickly, as the flesh tends to darken like a potato when exposed to air.

Perhaps the best known of the Caribbean–Central American roots is the yuc(c)a. When

I first went to the new and exciting Miami, a primarily Cuban world with a mix of Haitians, Nicaraguans, Europeans and a remainder of retirement Americans, I was introduced to an excellent restaurant called Yuca. This was not a reference to the vegetable but an acronym for "young upwardly mobile Cuban American."

But whether it was there or in any other Cuban restaurant, yuca was sure to be on the menu as a basic starch—and very good it is, too. It is long and thin and starchy, like the other tubers and roots of the region.

Turn to **JERUSALEM ARTICHOKES, JICAMA** and **TROPICAL TUBERS** in the Cook's Guide for how-tos and to the Index for more recipes.

Roasted Jerusalem Artichokes in Tomato-Olive Sauce

I like to use firm, briny green olives with their pits firmly in place. If pits in cheeks is not the guests' or family's idea of fun, use small pitted green Spanish olives.

If possible, bake this dish in a pan that will set off the handsome golden brown vegetables.

Served hot or at room temperature, the Jerusalem artichokes go particularly well with simply prepared chicken or fish. This dish can also be served on its own as a first course or as a main dish with ham or prosciutto.

2 pounds Jerusalem artichokes, peeled and cut into 1-inch wedges

2 tablespoons olive oil

1 1/2 pounds medium shallots, peeled and trimmed

continued

3/4 cup Enriched Chicken Stock (page 502) or Garlic Broth (page 507)

1 1/2 pounds tomatoes, cored and chopped into large pieces (about 3 cups)

1/4 pound drained medium green olives (about 3/4 cup), preferably Picholine

1 tablespoon kosher salt

Freshly ground black pepper to taste

Place a rack in the center of the oven. Preheat the oven to 500°F.

Place the Jerusalem artichoke wedges in a 17½ x 12 x 2-inch roasting pan. Slick with the olive oil, then arrange them in a single layer in the pan. Roast for 5 minutes. Flip the Jerusalem artichokes over and rotate the pan. Roast for another 5 minutes.

Flip the artichokes over and rotate the pan. Add the shallots in a single layer. Roast for 5 minutes. Flip the vegetables over and rotate the pan. Roast for another 5 minutes.

Flip the vegetables over and rotate the pan. Add the chicken stock and tomatoes. Roast for 10 minutes. Stir in the olives. Roast for 20 minutes, or until the vegetables are nicely browned. Season with salt and pepper and serve.

Makes 7 1/2 cups; serves 6 as a first course, 6 to 8 as a side dish

Baked Halibut with Jerusalem Artichokes and Leeks

The light taste of halibut goes well with the mild flavor of Jerusalem artichokes, which serve as a starch in this meal. Eat the fish and vegetables along with the brothy sauce out of a bowl with a fork and spoon. The recipe may be doubled and prepared in a 14 x 8-inch roasting pan.

1/2 cup dry white wine

1/2 teaspoon saffron threads

1 teaspoon kosher salt, plus additional for seasoning the vegetables

1/4 teaspoon coarsely ground black pepper

1/4 teaspoon anise seeds

2 teaspoons olive oil

Two 8-ounce halibut steaks, each about 1 inch thick

1 1/2 cups Basic Chicken Stock (page 501) or commercial chicken broth

2 teaspoons tomato paste

1/2 to 3/4 pound Jerusalem artichokes, peeled and cut across into 1/4-inch slices

2 small leeks, white parts only, washed well and cut across into 1/2-inch slices

Place a rack in the center of the oven. Preheat the oven to 425°F.

Combine the wine and saffron in a medium nonreactive saucepan. Set aside to steep.

Grind the salt, pepper and anise seeds in a spice mill or clean coffee grinder until the anise is coarsely ground. Stir into the oil in a small bowl. Rub spice mixture onto both sides of the steaks. Put the fish in a 13 x 9-inch baking dish, arranging them so there is room between them and the sides of the dish. Set aside.

Add the stock and tomato paste to the wine; whisk until the tomato paste is dissolved. Add the Jerusalem artichokes and bring to a boil over medium-high heat. Cook for 5 minutes. Add the leeks. Cook for 5 minutes, stirring occasionally.

Season the vegetables with salt. Spoon around the fish. Bake until the steaks are opaque near the bone and the Jerusalem artichokes are tender, about 15 minutes. Transfer the steaks to warm shallow bowls and spoon the vegetables and sauce over and around them.

Serves 2 as a main course

Julienne of Jicama, Red Peppers and Pear with Cilantro Dressing

Crunchy jicama, juicy pear and bright red pepper make a seductive salad. It can be made a little less starchy by dipping the jicama in boiling water for 30 seconds prior to soaking in ice water.

- 1 small jicama (1 pound), peeled, halved lengthwise, cut into 1/4-inch strips (about 4 cups) and soaked in ice water
- 1 large Bosc pear, peeled, cored, cut into 1/4-inch strips (about 1 cup) and tossed in fresh lemon juice
- 1 small red bell pepper, cored, seeded, deribbed and cut into 1/4-inch strips (about 1 cup)

DRESSING

- 1 cup grapefruit juice
- 2 to 3 tablespoons sugar
- 1/2 teaspoon kosher salt
- 3 tablespoons coarsely chopped cilantro
- 1/2 cup olive oil

- 6 bunches mâche (see the Cook's Guide, page 602), stemmed

Drain the jicama and dry with paper towels. Toss with the pear and the red pepper.

Just before serving, whisk the grapefruit juice, sugar, cilantro and salt together in a medium bowl until the sugar is dissolved. Slowly pour the oil into the bowl, whisking constantly.

Arrange the salad on individual plates or a serving dish. Scatter the mâche leaves over or around the salad. Spoon the dressing over the top and serve. **Serves 6 as a first course, 12 as a side dish**

Chicken and Jicama Salad with Green Goddess Dressing

Poaching the chicken breasts and dressing them before they see the inside of a refrigerator gives them a moist and creamy texture. A simpler version can be made with boneless skinless chicken breasts (use about 1 1/4 pounds) and a simpler one still with 3 cups of diced leftover cooked chicken. The nice thing about going the extra step of poaching bone-in chicken is the resulting enriched broth—a bonus with multiple uses.

- 3 large bone-in chicken breast halves with skin (about 2 pounds)
- 4 to 5 cups Basic Chicken Stock (page 501) or commercial chicken broth
- 1 small jicama (1 pound), peeled and cut into 1/2-inch cubes
- 2 spears broccoli (about 12 ounces), florets cut into bite-size pieces, stems peeled and sliced into coins (about 4 cups)
- 1 1/2 cups Green Goddess Dressing (page 452)
- Kosher salt to taste
- Freshly ground black pepper to taste

Put the chicken breasts in a pot large enough to hold them comfortably in a single layer. Pour enough broth over them to barely cover. Bring to a boil over high heat. Lower the heat to simmering. Cover the pot and cook until no trace of pink remains near the bone, about 25 minutes. Remove the chicken to a plate and cool.

Meanwhile, bring a large pot of salted water to a boil. Add the jicama and cook for 1 minute after the water returns to a boil. With a skimmer, transfer to a colander and rinse briefly under cold water. Cool completely.

continued

Stir the broccoli into the boiling water. Cook until tender but not mushy, about 4 minutes. Drain and rinse briefly under cold water. Cool completely.

Remove the skin and bones from the chicken. (If desired, return the skin and bones to the broth, cover and simmer for an additional 30 minutes before straining; reserve the broth for another use.) Cut the chicken into 1-inch cubes.

Toss the chicken, jicama and broccoli with the dressing. Season with salt and pepper. Let stand for 30 minutes before serving. **Makes about 8 cups; serves 6 as a main course**

Yautía Fritters

Simplicity itself and a wonderful introduction to the subtle flavor of yautía (malanga). These fritters should be eaten as hot as possible; their crisp coating will soften quickly. They'll still be good later, just not as.

1 pound yautía, peeled and cut into 1-inch chunks

Vegetable oil for deep-frying

1/4 cup finely chopped fresh chives

2 tablespoons all-purpose flour

1 1/2 teaspoons kosher salt, plus additional for sprinkling if desired

1/2 teaspoon baking powder

2 large eggs, beaten

Cook the yautía in a medium saucepan of boiling water until tender, about 10 minutes. Drain. While still warm, pass through a food mill fitted with a fine disc or, with more effort, a ricer into a bowl. Let cool.

Meanwhile, pour 3 to 4 inches of vegetable oil into a wide medium saucepan. Heat over medium heat to 360°F.

Scatter the chives, flour, salt and baking powder over the yautía. Pour in the eggs and stir with a fork just until blended. Fry the fritters in 2 batches: Slip the fritters by slightly mounded tablespoonfuls into the oil and fry, turning the fritters once, until deep golden brown, about 6 minutes. Remove with a slotted spoon or skimmer to paper towels to drain. Allow the oil to return to 360°F if necessary between batches. Sprinkle with salt before serving, if desired. **Makes about 20 fritters**

Yuca Croquettes

These are very rich and very filling.

3/4 pound yuca, peeled, halved lengthwise, fibrous center removed and each half cut into 3 pieces

2 1/2 tablespoons olive oil

1 small onion, diced

1 small red bell pepper, cored, seeded, deribbed and diced

1 small green bell pepper, cored, seeded, deribbed and diced

1 medium clove garlic, smashed, peeled and chopped

1/4 pound smoked ham, diced

1 1/4 cups all-purpose flour

2 teaspoons kosher salt

Freshly ground black pepper to taste

FILLING (optional)

2 tablespoons olive oil

1 1/2 ounces kale leaves, finely chopped (about 1 1/3 cups)

1 small onion, finely chopped

1 large clove garlic, smashed, peeled and minced

¹/₂ cup cracker meal (see Note)

1 large egg

Vegetable oil for deep-frying

Put the yuca in a medium saucepan and cover with water by 2 inches. Bring to a boil. Reduce the heat and simmer for 15 minutes, or until a knife is easily inserted into the flesh.

While the yuca is cooking, heat the olive oil in a medium frying pan over medium heat. Add the onion, bell peppers, garlic and ham and cook until the onion is translucent, about 5 minutes.

Remove from the heat and stir in ¾ cup flour. Place in a food processor and process until the mixture forms a paste. Scrape into a medium bowl. Reserve.

Place the yuca in the food processor and process until smooth. With moistened hands, work the yuca purée, salt and pepper into the vegetable mixture. Refrigerate for 1 hour.

If using the filling, heat the olive oil in a small skillet over medium heat. Add the kale, onion and garlic and sauté until the vegetables are softened, about 5 minutes. Drain and set aside.

Form the yuca mixture into 20 rounds, using a heaping tablespoonful for each. If using the filling, make a well in each round with a thumb. Put a scant ½ teaspoon of the kale mixture in each well. Re-form the croquette mixture around the filling to enclose it completely and pinch to seal.

Place the remaining ½ cup flour and the cracker meal in separate small bowls. Lightly beat the egg in another small bowl. One at a time, roll each croquette first in flour, then in egg, then in cracker meal. Place on a tray. Refrigerate for 1 hour.

Pour enough oil to come to a depth of 3 inches into a medium pot. Heat the oil to 375°F. Carefully drop 5 croquettes into the oil and fry until golden brown, about 30 seconds. Drain on paper towels. Repeat with the remaining croquettes. Serve hot. These may be cooked ahead and reheated on a baking sheet in a 350°F oven for 3 minutes. **Makes 20 croquettes**

NOTE: To make ½ cup cracker meal, place 20 plain unsalted crackers in a food processor and pulse until finely ground.

Yuca con Mojo Criollo

The garlic sauce is adapted from *Memories of a Cuban Kitchen* by Mary Urrutia Randelman and Joan Schwartz (see the Bibliography). The addition of the Scotch bonnet and cumin seeds were inspired by Norman Van Aken and his book *Norman's New World Cuisine* (see the Bibliography).

Fresh sour oranges, also called Seville oranges, can be difficult to find. Bottled juice can be purchased from Latin grocery stores. A mixture of orange juice, lemon juice and lime juice is a good substitute.

The sauce can be made in a much larger quantity and kept refrigerated. Caribbeans cook yuca almost daily and keep mojo on hand to serve along with it.

2 yuca (1 ¹/₂ pounds), peeled, halved, fibrous center removed and each half cut into 3 pieces

GARLIC SAUCE

1 teaspoon cumin seeds

3 cloves garlic, peeled and smashed

1 teaspoon kosher salt

¹/₄ cup sour orange juice or substitute a combination of 2 tablespoons fresh orange juice, 1 tablespoon fresh lemon juice and 1 tablespoon fresh lime juice

continued

¼ cup good Spanish olive oil

1 to 2 teaspoons chopped and seeded Scotch
   bonnet pepper

Put the yuca in a medium saucepan and cover
with water by 2 inches. Bring to a boil. Reduce
the heat and simmer for 15 minutes, or until a
knife is easily inserted into the flesh.

While the yuca is cooking, make the sauce:
Place the cumin seeds under a cloth. Pound
with a heavy flat-bottomed pot to release flavor;
they will not be ground. Reserve.

Using a mortar and pestle or the side of
a large knife, mash the garlic and salt into a
coarse paste. Alternatively, finely chop the garlic
and combine with the salt.

Transfer the garlic paste to a small saucepan.
Whisk in the juice and oil. Cook for 1 minute,
or just enough so that garlic no longer tastes
raw. Stir in the Scotch bonnet and cumin seeds.
(Makes ½ cup sauce)

Drain the cooked yuca. Transfer to a serving
dish. Spoon about 1½ teaspoons sauce over
each wedge. **Serves 6 as a side dish**

Coconut-Yuca Custard Cake

This traditional Southeast Asian dessert is so
sweet as to be almost a candy. A dense and
creamy cake is topped with an even creamier
layer of custard.

Traditionally the cake is baked in a pan lined
with banana leaves—an excellent nonstick surface
that also imparts a subtle grassy flavor. Banana
leaves can be found frozen in Southeast Asian
or specialty food stores. Greased aluminum foil
is an adequate substitute.

The recipe also calls for pandan, or pandanus,
the leaves of the screwpine tree, whose fragrance
evokes a combination of vanilla, coconut and
hazelnut. Frozen pandan can sometimes be

found in Latin, Southeast Asian or specialty
food stores. I prefer these over the more
available pandan extract, which colors
everything green.

On its own, small portions of this cake will
satisfy. Increase the portions if serving with
the rhubarb sauce—it balances the sweet for
a beautiful, untraditional dessert.

Banana leaves to line pan (optional)

2 tablespoons plus ½ cup melted butter
   (and a scant 1 tablespoon to grease
   aluminum foil, if using)

Two 13.5-ounce cans unsweetened coconut milk,
   allowed to sit undisturbed for several hours or
   overnight so it separates into 2 layers

4 pandan (pandanus) leaves or 4 to 5 drops
   pandan extract or 2 teaspoons vanilla extract

3 large eggs

2 cups sugar

1 teaspoon kosher salt

1⅓ pounds yuca, peeled and grated
   (about 3½ cups)

1 large egg yolk

One 14-ounce can sweetened condensed milk

1 recipe Basic Rhubarb Sauce (page 348),
   made with ½ cup sugar (optional)

Place a rack in the upper third of the oven.
Preheat the oven to 375°F.

Line a 13 x 9-inch pan or two 9 x 9-inch
pans with banana leaves, cutting them to fit.
Alternatively, line with aluminum foil and
grease the foil with butter.

Without shaking them, open the cans of
coconut milk. Scoop out the thick "cream" that
has risen to the surface. Measure 1 cup thick
coconut "cream" and 2 cups thin coconut milk.

If using pandan leaves, put in a medium saucepan with the thin coconut milk. Bring to a boil. Cover, turn off the heat and let steep for 20 minutes. Remove and discard the leaves.

If using pandan or vanilla extract, mix into the thin coconut milk without heating it.

In a large bowl, whisk the whole eggs with the sugar, salt and the 2 tablespoons melted butter. Add the yuca and thin coconut milk. Combine well. Pour into the prepared pan.

Bake for 20 minutes or until almost set.

Meanwhile, mix together the egg yolk, sweetened condensed milk, ½ cup butter and thick coconut milk. Pour onto the cake. Bake for 25 minutes, or until the custard is set and lightly browned. Allow to cool.

Cut each square cake into 12 pieces, or 9 if serving with sauce. Or, cut the rectangular 13 x 9-inch cake into 18 pieces, or 12 if serving with sauce. Using a spatula, remove the pieces from the pan. Serve at room temperature or cold, with the optional sauce on the side.

Makes one 13 x 9 x 2-inch cake or two 9 x 9 x 2-inch cakes

A Satin of Oysters and Tapioca

It is not an exaggeration to call this semi-solid soup a satin. It has an elegant lightness and a texture of pure pleasure. It is based on a dish of chef Rick Moonen's. It can be served warm, not hot, or tepid, not cold. It is thicker when cool than when hot. If reheating it, do not add the oysters until the end, or they will toughen. The oysters are not really cooked.

Buy fresh shucked oysters with their liquor (juices) or shuck your own. I wouldn't use Belons or Kumamotos for this; that would be a waste. (Canned oysters will not do.) They need to be cut in pieces. The easiest way is with scissors. Drain the oysters in a sieve, retaining the liquor. Cut them into roughly quarter-inch-wide pieces. How many pieces each will make

will depend on the size of the oyster. Be careful with the salt: Oysters vary remarkably in their saltiness, and if commercial broth is used, it may add salt as well.

The parsley is purely aesthetic. I don't use it, but some may feel that the grayish color of the soup needs some decoration. Some chopped chives can be used as well. Rick put caviar on his cool soup. It was wonderful in a gala restaurant, but I find it hard to justify the expense. I might spring for fresh salmon roe, again being very careful with the salt in the soup.

This recipe does not make a great quantity, but it can easily be multiplied. The flavor is rich, which makes it filling.

The recipe needs to be started the day before serving, as the tapioca needs to soak overnight.

½ cup small pearl tapioca (see page 150)

4 cups Basic Chicken Stock (page 501) or commercial chicken broth; if there is some fish stock on hand, 1 cup of the chicken stock can be advantageously replaced with it

1 pint shucked oysters, drained (liquor reserved) and cut into roughly ¼-inch-wide pieces (see headnote)

Kosher salt and freshly ground black pepper to taste

2 tablespoons finely minced fresh parsley (optional)

Put the tapioca in a small bowl with 2 cups water. Let it soak overnight. Drain; there will be 1⅓ cups.

Bring the stock to a boil in a large heavy saucepan. Add the tapioca and reduce to a simmer; stir to avoid clumping. Should clumps form, gently press them against the side of the pan to break them up. Cook for 10 minutes.

continued

Tapioca

I grew up detesting tapioca, concurring with its epithet, "fish eyes and glue." It was a common school dessert. Later, I learned that the French use it in classic recipes as a thickener for soup. I could see no earthly reason why. Time changed me and my response. Basically, this was due to chef Rick Moonen's soup that had oysters swimming in it. I never got his recipe, so do not blame him; the recipe on page 149 is my own responsibility.

Tapioca is yuca (see page 142) that is processed and formed into flakes or balls. The balls are known as pearl tapioca. The smaller pearls come in various sizes, and one is somewhat at the mercy of the producers.

There are also some instant tapiocas in which the balls are even smaller, but I find them less attractive. They do have the virtue, however, of cooking in the microwave oven in ten minutes.

The other tapiocas need, like beans, to soak. They absorb a great deal of liquid, about four times as much liquid as tapioca by volume. For instance, a half cup of tapioca requires about two cups of liquid. The slightly larger pearl tapioca will soak up more liquid; two tablespoons becomes two-thirds of a cup. The small pearl tapioca become about a half cup. Any extra liquid can be strained off, and then the cooking can begin.

If serving the soup right away, stir in the oysters and their liquor. Taste and add salt if necessary and pepper. Or, if serving the soup cold or warm at a later time, cool and refrigerate; the soup will thicken as it cools. Reheat, if desired. Stir the oysters and liquor into the reheated or chilled soup. Taste and add salt if necessary and pepper.

To serve, ladle the soup into a serving dish or into cups or bowls and sprinkle on the parsley, if using. **Makes about 4 cups**

Piquillo Peppers with Olive-Cheese Stuffing

I had fun with this very unclassic use of tapioca. It worked well.

$1/2$ cup small pearl tapioca (see box)

One 12-ounce jar piquillo peppers (see the Cook's Guide, page 631)

1 cup coarsely grated Monterey Jack cheese

$1/4$ cup finely chopped pitted Spanish olives

A few dashes of hot red pepper sauce (optional)

Pour 2 cups water over the tapioca in a small bowl. Let soak in the refrigerator for at least 6 hours, or up to 1 day.

Place a rack in the center of the oven. Preheat the oven to 350°F.

Drain the peppers and blot dry with paper towels. Drain the tapioca and place in a small bowl. Stir in the cheese, olives and pepper sauce, if using. Fill the peppers with the cheese mixture, using about 1½ tablespoons for each. Lay the peppers on a parchment paper–lined or nonstick baking sheet.

Bake just until the cheese is melted and the peppers are warmed through, about 5 minutes. Serve immediately. **Makes about 14 peppers**

Cranberry Tapioca Parfait

This pretty dessert, pink from cranberries, with flecks of orange, is a festive end to a meal.

2/3 cup small pearl tapioca (see box)

1 cup dried cranberries

1/2 cup cranberry juice

2/3 cup sugar

3 large eggs

1/2 teaspoon salt

1 quart milk

2 teaspoons vanilla extract

Grated zest of 1 orange

Whipped cream (optional)

Pour 2 cups water over the tapioca in a small bowl. Let soak in the refrigerator for at least 6 hours, or up to 1 day.

Just before preparing the tapioca and bring the cranberries and juice to a boil in a small saucepan. Remove from the heat.

Drain the tapioca. Whisk the sugar, eggs and salt in a 3-quart saucepan with a very heavy bottom. Add the tapioca gradually pour in the milk, whisking constantly. Cook over medium-low heat, stirring constantly with a wooden spoon, until the tapioca is tripled in size and the custard is thickened enough to coat the spoon generously, about 30 minutes. Remove from the heat and ladle into a bowl.

Stir the cranberries and their juice, the vanilla and orange zest into the tapioca. Place a sheet of plastic wrap directly against the surface of the tapioca and refrigerate until thoroughly chilled.

Spoon the mixture into parfait glasses or bowls. Top with whipped cream, if desired. **Makes 6 servings**

Asparagus 154   Beets 163   Chard 177   Carrots 182

Parsnips 194   Celery 199   Celery Root 204   Fennel 208

Chicories: Chicory, Escarole, Frisée, Puntarelle, Endive and Radicchio 217

Fava Beans 224   Thistles: Artichokes, Cardoons and Nettles 229

Spinach 246   Broccoli and Cauliflower 254

Of Cabbages and Sprouts: Green, Red and Savoy Cabbages and Brussel Sprouts 266

Cabbages Without Heads: Broccoli di Raab, Kale, Mustard Greens and Collards 279

Cabbages with Roots: Turnips, Kohlrabi and Radishes   289

Vegetables of the Mediterranean Basin, Europe and the Arab World

THESE REGIONS ARE THE CRADLE of our culinary supplies. Most of our fruits, many of our herbs and a great percentage of our vegetables come from this part of the world (along with many legumes, humankind and many of its languages). Some of our vegetables derive in the distant past from Asia and farther south in Africa. It is hard to sort out, but I have done my best.

Asparagus

I've had many surprises as I learned things for this book. Perhaps the oddest is that asparagus are lilies. Unable to believe that those stalks and what later seem to be waving, fernlike fronds could be lilies, I called Paul Levy in England. He is a fine source of information and, with his wife, Penny, a fine gardener. Although their growing season is slightly out of sync with mine in Vermont, Penny rushed out into the garden and did indeed find some pale lavender little lily trumpets. As my asparagus went to seed, I had them as well.

Asparagus basically grow in two colors, green and purple—which is, as in broccoli, a variant of green. However, we see and eat white asparagus too. These are shoots that have been blanched—darkness provided in one form or another until the vegetable is ready to eat.

Even the fussiest of manners didacts allow for fingers as the best tool for green asparagus. In Victorian times, there were tongs—one pair per person—for picking up asparagus. They looked rather like the tongs that Gloria Swanson used to hold her cigarettes in *Sunset Boulevard*. (The last time I saw a pair used was about the last time I saw a man, my father, in pearl gray spats.) This is true only of green asparagus. White asparagus tend to be fibrous and require cutting with a knife.

Asparagus have always been considered a treat. Feasts of them are a spring festivity. All manner of special dishes—plates, not cooking—have been created to show them off. My favorites are French majolica in tones of pale pink and green with flowers—on one set, carnations; on the other, nasturtiums. There are also double-whammy plates that have designs with artichokes as well as asparagus spears; there are indentations to hold sauce. Some lucky collectors have serving dishes to hold large bunches of asparagus. Often they are pierced with holes to drain into a second dish set below the asparagus cradle. Sometimes there is a design of a napkin on the dish, presumably to echo the actual napkins sometimes placed under cooked asparagus as they drain.

There are also sauceboats to match. I have an artichoke one embellished with its own attached saucer.

Jim Beard used to declare that the best white asparagus were canned. I think that is probably because he was eating them in America. In his day, there really was no white asparagus grown in America. Now there are thin white asparagus with telltale lavender tips. The lavender tips come for two reasons. The strain of asparagus used for white asparagus both here and in Europe is purple, which gives a sweeter result than the green. The second reason is that the asparagus stalks are cut before they are fully blanched and so the tips have gone purple.

At that point, they must be cut, or they will go to seed. This also means that we never get the huge—an inch or more across—asparagus that are the basis of the festivals of eating in Austria, Germany, Holland, Spain and France.

I grow green asparagus and have never tried white; too much work. While asparagus take up a lot of space and must be weeded and fertilized with manure (heavy feeders), they are well worth growing. They have a natural sweetness that disappears shortly after cutting. They should be cut beneath the soil so that they don't get crown rot. I snap off the woody part—the asparagus chooses where the snap should come—and I peel the remainder all the way from the tip to the bottom. Peeling is work but not much if the asparagus is laid flat and a vegetable peeler is used. This way, the asparagus are incomparable.

I always cook my asparagus in the microwave oven; the asparagus are far better than when cooked in water, although I do sprinkle the surface of the spears with a little water to get things going.

My knowledge of growing white asparagus was learned from Bob Jones, "Farmer Jones," of the overalls and red bow tie, who has the Chef's Garden in Milan, Ohio (see the Bibliography for the Web site). Cooking them is restricted to the thin ones usually grown in America. Farmer Jones tells me that the difference in size has to do with the age of the crowns (the part with the roots attached), enough space between the plants, the variety, not being greedy (only cutting for four weeks) and, of course, proper blanching after a full growth. He has developed a special technique in which he constructs a black plastic tunnel rather than mounding dirt, and the picking is done by workers with miner's lamps on their heads. He says that this keeps the asparagus from absorbing bitter tastes from the mounding soil and keeps the thin skin on the outside soft and supple. He also says that they don't need peeling, but I suspect I would peel. After the four weeks of cutting, sometimes twice a day, when the temperature in the tunnel gets very hot, the plastic is removed and the plants are allowed to go to seed, so as to feed the plants for the coming year. Farmer Jones says he is already growing white asparagus as thick as his not inconsiderable thumb, and that they will increase along with the age of the plants. I look forward to the future.

In the meantime, I have given cooking times and instructions in the Cook's Guide for the white asparagus I can buy. Even well cooked, white asparagus can be difficult to chew. Serve them with a knife and fork. Several attempts have let me understand what the asparagus cookers of my childhood were about. Tall and thin, the green asparagus could be put in water but with the tips exposed only to steam for their rather prolonged cooking. I didn't find that this helped with white asparagus.

Until I can get some of Farmer Jones's asparagus, or eat the fresh ones abroad, I think I will agree with Jim that the canned are better. Try ordering from La Tienda (see Sources) and be sure that you specify the largest size. I don't usually eat or serve canned vegetables except for tomato sauce and pickles; but I did the other night serve a jar of very large white asparagus that a friend brought me from Spain, along with the customary boiled new potatoes and hollandaise. Everybody loved them. They took about four minutes to reheat in the microwave oven with most of the canning liquid removed. Until we esteem white asparagus as much as Europeans do, they will be hard to come by. They will always be expensive.

In recent years, something called wild asparagus has cropped up in the stores. Asparagus that are picked in the wild are garden escapees. In either case, the best substitute is pencil-thin asparagus.

Turn to **ASPARAGUS** in the Cook's Guide for how-tos and to the Index for more recipes.

Asparagus Soup with Caramelized Leeks

One spring day, I was at Paul Levy's house outside Oxford. He was making a wonderful soup base from his wintered-over leeks and a plentiful supply of asparagus. I promptly stole the notion and made this soup with it. The vegetarian asparagus stock base is best made ahead, as it takes quite a long time. I make it with the stems and peelings left over after I have cooked a lot of asparagus for a feast. It can be used as the stock in many spring vegetable soups. Paul makes the stock in the lower oven of his Aga. It can be made in a low oven or a slow cooker. A large amount of base can even go overnight.

The finished soup cannot be made too far ahead or the asparagus tips and tender stems will shrivel.

2 pounds asparagus, trimmed and peeled, stem ends and peelings reserved for the stock

1 recipe Asparagus Stock (page 506)

1/2 cup long-grain white rice

1 tablespoon unsalted butter

4 small leeks, trimmed, cut in half lengthwise, washed, green parts cut into 2-inch lengths and reserved for the stock, white parts cut into 2-inch lengths and then lengthwise into hair-thin strips

1/2 teaspoon very finely chopped fresh tarragon or a pinch of dried

4 teaspoons kosher salt

Freshly ground black pepper to taste

Cut the peeled asparagus stalks into 1-inch lengths and reserve. Reserve the tips separately.

Make the asparagus stock, using the reserved asparagus peelings and stem ends and the leek greens.

In a small saucepan, bring 1¼ cups lightly salted water to a boil. Stir in the rice and cover. Lower the heat and simmer for 13 minutes, or until the rice is almost done. Reserve.

For the soup, in a large frying pan, melt the butter over medium-high heat. Add the whites of the leeks and cook, stirring frequently, for 5 minutes, or until they are nicely browned. Add the peeled asparagus stalks and cook, stirring, for 4 minutes. Stir in the asparagus tips. Cook for 1 minute. Scrape into a medium saucepan.

Pour a little of the asparagus stock into the frying pan and bring to a boil, scraping up the browned bits from the bottom of the pan. Pour this over the vegetables. Stir in the rest of the asparagus stock.

Bring the soup to a boil. Add the cooked rice and tarragon. Return to a boil. Reduce the heat and simmer for 4 minutes. Season with the salt and pepper. **Makes 7 cups; serves 6 as a first course**

Light Spring Soup with Peas and Asparagus

Nothing says spring like early peas and asparagus or fiddlehead ferns. In this soup, they shine in all their freshness, with little competition from the other ingredients. The colors are pretty too.

5 cups Basic Chicken Stock (page 501), Roasted Chicken Stock (page 502) or commercial chicken broth

¹/₃ cup long-grain white rice

4 large shallots, finely chopped

2 pounds peas in the pod, shelled (scant 2 cups)

1 tablespoon kosher salt (less if using commercial broth)

Freshly ground black pepper to taste

1 pound asparagus, tips only (reserve stems for another use, such as Asparagus Stock, page 506), or ¹/₄ pound fiddlehead ferns

In a small saucepan, bring 1 cup stock and rice to a boil. Cover, lower heat and simmer for 13 minutes. Remove from heat; set aside.

In a medium saucepan, bring the remaining 4 cups stock, the shallots and half the peas to a boil. Lower the heat and simmer for 5 minutes. Drain, reserving the liquid.

In a blender, purée the cooked peas and shallots. Return to the saucepan and whisk in the reserved liquid. Season with the salt and pepper. The soup can be made ahead to this point and refrigerated for up to 2 days.

Return the soup to the stove and bring to a boil. Stir in the uncooked peas (add the fiddlehead ferns now, if using). Return to a boil. Lower the heat. Simmer for 3 minutes. Stir in the rice (add the asparagus tips now, if using). Simmer for 2 minutes. Serve immediately.

Makes 6 cups; serves 4 to 6 as a first course

Asparagus with Ham and Vinaigrette

In their increasingly long season, asparagus make a perfect first course, cold or warm. They can be served with Classic Mayonnaise (page 455); with Everyday Vinaigrette (page 449), plain or enriched with hard-boiled eggs, capers, parsley and dill; with Hollandaise Sauce (page 454); with browned butter (page 453) and capers with a touch of vinegar; or with this somewhat unusual sauce. With a poached egg on top, this also makes a good light lunch. Or does anybody make lunch anymore?

continued

1 1/2 pounds asparagus, trimmed and peeled

1/4 pound thinly sliced smoked ham

1/3 to 1/2 cup Soy-Sesame Vinaigrette (page 449)
or Everyday Vinaigrette (page 449)

Boil or steam the asparagus (see the Cook's Guide, page 532) until tender but still firm. Place in a colander and rinse very briefly under cold running water. Drain well. Arrange on a serving platter.

While the asparagus is cooking, stir the sliced ham into the vinaigrette.

Spoon the dressing and ham over the center of the asparagus, leaving the tips and ends exposed. Serve. **Serves 6 as a first course**

Asparagus with Sesame Dressing and Tofu
Omit the ham; use the Soy-Sesame Vinaigrette. Cut 1/2 pound very firm tofu into 1-inch cubes and drain well on paper towels. After dressing the asparagus, pour 1/2 inch vegetable oil into a large nonstick skillet and heat over medium heat. Dredge the tofu cubes in cornstarch, tap off the excess and add the tofu to the oil. Fry, turning gently, until lightly browned on all sides, about 6 minutes. Drain on paper towels and spoon over the asparagus. Spoon the dressing over.

Asparagus with Poached Egg and Browned Butter

The asparagus are first steamed or boiled, then simmered in the browned butter while the eggs poach. In this way, both ingredients finish cooking at about the same time.

The steps remain the same if the recipe is halved. If multiplying the recipe, it is easier to poach the eggs and hold them in some warm water while the asparagus finish cooking.

1 pound medium-thick asparagus, trimmed
and peeled

1/2 cup Clarified Butter made from 1 cup butter
(page 453)

4 large eggs

2 tablespoons capers, rinsed and dried

Kosher salt and freshly ground black pepper
to taste

4 slices Fried Bread (page 510; optional)

Steam or boil the asparagus (see the Cook's Guide, page 532). Place in a colander and rinse under cold running water. Drain and blot dry.

To make the browned butter, pour the clarified butter into a 12-inch frying pan. Cook over medium heat for about 7 minutes, until deeply brown with a nutty aroma; do not burn. Set aside while you prepare the eggs.

Break each egg into a demitasse cup with a rounded bottom. Bring 2 inches of water to a boil in a medium saucepan or sauté pan.

Gently reheat the browned butter. Stir in the capers. Add the asparagus and cook for 2 minutes.

Meanwhile, lower the rim of each demitasse cup to the surface of the boiling water and invert the egg into the water in a smooth motion. Poach the eggs for 2 minutes. The whites will be firm, but the yolks still soft and runny. With a slotted spoon, remove the eggs to a paper towel or cloth to drain.

Divide the asparagus among four plates. Top each plate with a poached egg and a generous 2 tablespoons of the caper sauce. Salt and pepper to taste. Serve immediately, with the optional fried bread alongside. **Serves 4 as a first course**

Asparagus with Morels

This is a star dish. Do not serve it with anything else, not even rice or pasta.

2 ounces dried morels

1 tablespoon olive oil

³/₄ pound medium asparagus (about ¹/₂-inch-thick spears), peeled and trimmed, cut into 1¹/₄-inch pieces, stems and tips reserved separately

1 heaping tablespoon chopped fresh tarragon

1 tablespoon cornstarch

¹/₂ cup Enriched Beef Stock (page 504) or 1 cup unsalted beef stock, reduced by half

Kosher salt and freshly ground black pepper to taste

Bring 3 cups water to a boil in a medium saucepan. Add the morels and boil for 1 minute. Turn off the heat. Allow the morels to sit for 20 minutes. Drain, reserving the liquid.

Strain the morel liquid through a fine sieve, or a sieve lined with a clean kitchen towel, into a medium saucepan. Reduce over low heat to 1 cup. If the liquid appears gritty, strain once more through a coffee filter.

Cut the morels into 1-inch pieces, or leave whole if small. Rinse briefly.

Heat the oil in a 10- to 12-inch frying pan. Add the asparagus stems. Cook for 1 minute over high heat. Reduce the heat to medium. Add ¹/₂ cup of the morel liquid. Cook for 2 minutes.

Add the asparagus tips, morels and tarragon. Dissolve the cornstarch in ¹/₄ cup of the beef stock. Add to the pan and stir for 1 minute. Add the remaining mushroom liquid and stock. Cook until the asparagus tips are just tender to a knife tip and the sauce is a shiny glaze. Salt and pepper to taste.

Makes 3 cups, serves 4 as a first course

Asparagus Custard

This makes a wonderful first course for a springtime meal. With a spoonful or two of the Tomato Sauce for Stuffed Vegetables (page 461) or Aïoli with Potato (page 456), it is lunch. If the chives are picked from the garden, their blossoms can be sprinkled alluringly on top. Simply hold the petals in one hand, pull off the bottom with the other and sprinkle away.

1 tablespoon kosher salt

4 cups 1-inch pieces trimmed and peeled asparagus

1 tablespoon unsalted butter

1 medium sweet onion, cut into thin strips

7 large eggs

1¹/₄ cups heavy cream

³/₄ cup freshly grated Parmesan cheese

1¹/₂ tablespoons finely chopped fresh chives

Bring 2 quarts water and the salt to a boil in a 7- to 8-quart pot. Throw in the asparagus. Return the water to a boil and cook for 2 minutes. Drain the asparagus in a colander and let sit for 1 hour to remove excess water.

Position a rack in the middle of the oven. Preheat the oven to 450°F.

Melt the butter in a small nonstick pan. Add the onion. Cook over medium-low heat until the onion is soft and translucent. Remove from the heat.

In a large bowl, beat the eggs until blended. Beat in the heavy cream, cheese and chives. Mix the asparagus and onion with the heavy cream mixture. Pour into a 10-inch quiche pan. Place the pan on a cookie sheet to catch any spills. Bake for 35 minutes, or until the top is brown and puffed up and the custard has set.

Serves 6 to 8 as a first course or a light lunch

Wild Asparagus and Ramp Frittata

The combination of wild asparagus (*Ornithogalum pyrenaicum;* see the Cook's Guide, page 532) or pencil-thin asparagus and ramps (wild leeks) is irresistible.

> 1/4 pound ramps, ends trimmed, outer papery layer removed if necessary
>
> 1/4 pound wild asparagus or pencil-thin fresh asparagus, ends trimmed
>
> 6 large eggs
>
> 1 teaspoon kosher salt
>
> Freshly ground black pepper to taste
>
> 3 tablespoons unsalted butter or a good olive oil (not a mighty Tuscan, which is too strong here)
>
> 2 tablespoons freshly grated Parmesan cheese (optional)

Place a rack in the top of the oven. Preheat the oven to 425°F.

Cut across the ramps to separate them into the white bulbs, pink stems and green leaves. Wash them, keeping the bulbs, leaves and stems separate. Cut the leaves across into 1-inch slices. Chop the stems into ¼-inch pieces and put with the leaves. Reserve the bulbs separately.

Cut the tips from the asparagus. Chop the stems into ¼-inch pieces. Reserve.

Beat the eggs with the salt and pepper. Reserve.

Melt the butter or heat the oil in a 12-inch ovenproof (not nonstick) frying pan. Tilt the pan to grease the sides and bottom completely. Put in the ramp bulbs. Cook for 1 minute over low heat. Add the asparagus and ramp leaves and stems. Cook, stirring, until the ramp leaves are wilted and bright green.

Spread the vegetables in an even layer, leaving a 1-inch border around the edge of the pan. Pour in the eggs. Increase the heat to high. As the eggs set, run a spatula around the edges of the frittata to loosen it from the pan; repeat as necessary to prevent the frittata from sticking. Cook until the bottom is fairly firm. The top should be loose and runny.

Sprinkle with the Parmesan, if desired. Bake for 5 minutes, or until the frittata is puffy and browned. Shake the pan to loosen the frittata. Use a spatula to slide the frittata onto a serving dish. Cut into wedges and serve.

Serves 6 as a first course, 4 as a light main course

Asparagus and Tarragon Quiche

This crustless quiche makes a delicious first course or main dish for lunch or one of several dishes at a buffet. It can be served hot—my preference—or at room temperature.

> 2 tablespoons unsalted butter, plus additional for greasing the pan
>
> 1 cup minced yellow onion
>
> 1 1/2 teaspoons dried tarragon
>
> 1 tablespoon white wine vinegar
>
> 1/4 pound asparagus, trimmed and peeled, cut into 1-inch pieces (about 2/3 cup)
>
> 4 large eggs
>
> 1 cup heavy cream
>
> 1 cup milk
>
> 1/4 pound Gruyère cheese, grated (about 1 cup)
>
> 1 1/2 teaspoons kosher salt
>
> Pinch of freshly grated nutmeg
>
> Freshly ground black pepper to taste

Place a rack in the center of the oven. Preheat the oven to 375°F.

Butter a 10-inch quiche pan and set aside.

Melt the butter in a large skillet. Add the onion. Cook for 3 minutes over medium heat, or until translucent. Add the tarragon, vinegar and asparagus. Cook for 1 to 2 minutes, until the asparagus turns bright green. Set aside.

Whisk together the remaining ingredients in a large bowl. Stir in the asparagus mixture. Pour into the quiche pan. Bake for 25 to 30 minutes, until lightly browned and puffed and set in the center. **Serves 8 as a first course, 6 as a main course**

Pasta with Asparagus Sauce

The elegance of asparagus comes through in this dish with a minimum of ingredients.

- 1 pound asparagus, trimmed and peeled, stem ends and peelings reserved
- One 8.8-ounce package dried Italian egg noodles or 1 recipe Basic Pasta Dough (page 469), cut into fettuccine
- 2 teaspoons kosher salt
- Freshly ground black pepper to taste
- 1 tablespoon good olive oil
- Freshly grated Parmesan cheese (optional)

Separate the asparagus tips from the stems. Cut the stems into 1½-inch pieces. Reserve the stems and tips individually.

Bring about 1 quart water to a boil in a medium saucepan. Add the asparagus stems. Cook for 7 to 8 minutes, until a knife easily slips into the flesh. Remove with a slotted spoon and reserve. Add the asparagus tips to the water. Cook for 2 to 3 minutes, just until tender. With the slotted spoon, remove to a strainer or colander; rinse under cold running water. Drain; reserve.

Add the trimmings to the water. Cook for 20 to 25 minutes, or until the broth is reduced to 1 cup and tastes strongly of asparagus. Strain the broth, pressing down on the solids to extract as much flavor as possible. Discard the solids.

Put the reserved stems through a food mill fitted with the medium disc to remove the fibers; there will be a generous ½ cup liquid. Strain through a fine sieve to remove any remaining fibers. Reserve.

Bring a large pot of salted water to a boil. Add the noodles and cook for 2 minutes, or until softened but still quite firm. Drain.

Combine the asparagus broth and liquid in the pot. Bring to a boil. Stir in the pasta. Cook over low heat, stirring continuously, until the liquid is mostly absorbed. Stir in the salt, pepper, oil and asparagus tips. Cook for a few minutes longer, until the liquid is fully absorbed. Serve immediately, topped with Parmesan, if desired. **Makes 5 cups; serves 4 as a first course**

Fettuccine with Wild Asparagus and Ramps

Once again, what I mean by wild asparagus is *Ornithogalum pyrenaicum* (see the Cook's Guide, page 532).

- ½ pound ramps, ends trimmed, outer papery layer removed if necessary
- 8 to 10 ounces dried fettuccine or a double recipe fresh fettuccine (page 469)
- 3 tablespoons olive oil
- ¾ pound wild asparagus or pencil-thin asparagus, ends trimmed, cut into 3-inch pieces
- Kosher salt and freshly ground black pepper to taste

continued

Slice the ramps to separate them into the whites and leaves. Wash them separately and thoroughly. Cut the greens across into 1-inch pieces. Separate the greens and whites.

Bring a medium pot of salted water to a boil. Add the fettuccine. Boil until just undercooked; drain.

While the pasta is cooking, heat the oil in a 5-quart pot. Add the ramp whites. Cook for 1 minute over medium heat. Add the ramp greens. Cook until wilted.

Add the pasta to the ramps. Add the asparagus. Toss and cook until the asparagus is soft but not mushy, and the pasta is tender. Salt and pepper to taste.

Serves 3 to 4 as a main course, 5 to 6 as a first course

Fettuccine with Asparagus and Leeks

Substitute 1 medium leek, white and light green parts only, for the ramps. Wash and slice into ½-inch pieces. Substitute medium asparagus, trimmed and peeled, cut into ½-inch lengths, for the wild asparagus. Before boiling the pasta, cook the leek in the oil until wilted. Stir in the asparagus, reduce the heat to low and cover the pan. Cook, stirring, until the asparagus is tender, about 4 minutes. Cook the fettuccine until tender but firm, about 2 minutes for fresh, 8 minutes for dried. Reserve about 1 cup of the cooking water. Drain the pasta, add to the asparagus sauce and toss, adding a little of the reserved water if the pasta looks dry. Season and serve, passing freshly grated Parmesan cheese, if you like.

Asparagus and Beef Stir-fry

¼ cup Basic Chicken Stock (page 501) or commercial chicken broth

1 tablespoon soy sauce, preferably tamari

1 tablespoon hoisin sauce

¾ pound beef tenderloin, cut into ¾ x ¾ x 1½-inch strips

2 tablespoons vegetable oil or peanut oil

3 quarter-size peeled ginger slices, minced

3 cloves garlic, smashed, peeled and minced

4 scallions, trimmed and minced

½ pound asparagus, trimmed and peeled, cut diagonally into 1- to 1½-inch pieces (about 1¼ cups)

6 ounces oyster mushrooms, thick stems removed, torn into 1-inch strips (about 3 cups)

Toasted sesame oil (optional)

In a small bowl, stir together the stock and the soy and hoisin sauces. Set aside.

Pat the beef dry with paper towels. Heat the oil in a large nonstick skillet over medium-high heat until very hot. Add the beef and cook, turning, until well browned but still rare, about 4 minutes. Scoop out onto a plate.

Add the ginger, garlic and scallions to the pan and stir-fry until fragrant, about 30 seconds. Add the asparagus and toss until bright green, about 2 minutes. Add the mushrooms and toss until wilted, about 1 minute.

Pour in the chicken stock mixture, bring to a boil and cook until the sauce is thick enough to lightly coat the vegetables. Remove from the heat and stir in the beef to coat it with sauce. Serve immediately, drizzling sesame oil over the top if desired. **Serves 2 as a main course**

Beets

Beets are the arriviste members of their family. Their near relatives, chards (see page 177), were the first version brought in from the wild and tamed from the shoreline plant *Beta maritima*. Beets were originally grown mainly for their leaves. Like carrots, they came in a wide variety of colors: crimson, red, yellow and white. Being of Russian descent, I thought of them in connection with borscht—and the north. They do grow well in cold climates, but it turns out they are, like many European plants, of Mediterranean origin.

The most commercially valuable members of the family are sugar beets, which must be planted far from the eating vegetable, or they will intermarry— and not to their advantage. My favorite version of the family, almost for its name alone, is the cattle feed mangelwurzel, which can grow to a huge size and was used before the discovery of the Americas to carve and illuminate as we do pumpkins.

The flavor of beets varies with age and size almost more than for any other vegetable. Very young ones, such as those I sometimes pull from my garden in Vermont as thinnings from the row, can be eaten, greens and all, with their well-scrubbed skins left on after cooking—roasted, sautéed or grilled. The tops (greens) of somewhat older spring and summer beets should be saved for simple sautéing (see Beet Greens with White Beans, Bacon and Walnuts, page 173). Very small beets, about an inch to an inch and a half in diameter, are also wonderful, stems removed, cleaned, boiled until tender (about fifteen minutes) and the skins rubbed off.

Freshly dug beets will keep for months—not washed—in the refrigerator, or cooked beets can be kept for several days refrigerated in their cooking liquid or, if not boiled, in plastic wrap. To serve, peel and reheat in some butter, about one tablespoon per portion. Add kosher salt to taste, about a quarter teaspoon of sugar per portion and a few drops of red wine vinegar. If there is some dill hanging around, a little chopped on top will not be amiss. This is not a formal recipe because the presence of such beets is a gift of the gardening gods and quantities are as capricious as the gods.

As they get older, beets are less sweet and the skin is less pleasant. It will need to be removed after cooking. It's best to peel beets as soon as they are cool enough to touch, or the skin sort of sticks on. After peeling, to avoid having burgundy-toned fingers, wash immediately with a mildly abrasive powder. *Alternatively,* wear gloves while peeling, or use paper towels (see the Cook's Guide, page 545)). It is better to peel beets after cooking, as they lose too much juice if cooked peeled.

If the beets have been boiled, always save the cooking liquid. Strain it through a very fine sieve and keep it refrigerated or frozen to have a step up on the way to soup.

The huge beets sold as "roasted" in European markets are really baked like potatoes in their skins on a cookie sheet at about 325°F until they can be easily pierced with a sharp knife.

Perhaps the most prevalent use of beets is in salad. At first, it was with endive and walnuts. Today, they are liable to turn up in any salad or can be a salad on their own.

If preparing beets ahead, put a little vinegar or oil on them to keep them from drying out after cooking, or replace them in the strained boiling liquid. Vinegar keeps the color vivid, undarkened. A disadvantage of roasting is that beets are less vibrant in color than if boiled or steamed.

Turn to **BEETS** in the Cook's Guide for how-tos and to the Index for more recipes.

Beet Sorbet

Beets leave their imprint on everything. Even the cooking water takes on their characteristic sweetness and rosy hue. This sorbet, more like a granita, makes a festive starter to a special-occasion meal. Use the cooked beets in Beet and Endive Salad (page 165) or Beet and Potato Purée (page 170).

1 pound beets, trimmed and scrubbed

2 1/2 teaspoons white vinegar

2 tablespoons fresh lemon juice

$^3/_4$ teaspoon citric acid crystals (see Note, page 167)

$^1/_2$ to $^3/_4$ cup sugar

$2^1/_4$ teaspoons kosher salt, or to taste

TOPPING

Sour cream

Chopped fresh dill

Boil the beets in a medium saucepan with plenty of water to cover until a knife easily slips into the flesh, 30 to 45 minutes.

Reserve the beets for another use (see headnote); strain the beet liquid through a fine-mesh strainer into a pan.

Measure the beet liquid and add enough warm water to make 4 cups. While the liquid is still hot, add the vinegar, lemon juice, citric acid, sugar and salt. Stir to dissolve. Taste and correct the seasoning if necessary; the effect should be sweet and sour.

Cool the liquid thoroughly.

Shortly before serving, churn the mixture in an ice cream maker according to the manufacturer's instructions, 20 to 25 minutes. (Because of the low sugar, the sorbet will get icy if done ahead.) Transfer to a container and hold in the freezer for up to 30 minutes before serving.

Top each serving with a dollop of sour cream and a sprinkling of fresh dill. **Makes 4 cups**

Beet and Endive Salad

This classic French salad, with a hint of sweetness and lots of color from the beets, is often used as a first course. It provides a little sweetness at the beginning of the meal, which may help reduce the appetite. Using precooked beets left over from Beet Sorbet (page 164) or cooking them in the microwave will save time.

4 medium beets (4 ounces each), trimmed and scrubbed, or leftover cooked beets

2 tablespoons olive oil

2 tablespoons balsamic vinegar

Kosher salt and freshly ground black pepper to taste

4 heads endive ($3^1/_2$ ounces each), cut lengthwise into 8 wedges, core removed

If using raw beets, cook them by steaming, boiling, or microwaving (see the Cook's Guide, page 545). When just cool enough to touch, slip off the skins. Cut into $^1/_3$-inch-thick slices.

In a large bowl, whisk together the oil, vinegar, 2 tablespoons water, and salt and pepper to taste. Add the beets. Toss to coat well. Mix in the endive. **Serves 4 as a first course**

Shredded Beet and Orange Salad

While everything can be prepared several hours before serving, keep the components—dressed beets, orange segments and chives—separate, or everything will turn the same shade of purple. Nice served with slices of room-temperature goat cheese, especially if you dress and then serve the beets while still warm.

1 pound medium beets, trimmed and scrubbed

2 navel oranges, plus additional orange juice (fresh or store-bought) if needed

3 tablespoons extra virgin olive oil

1 teaspoon kosher salt

1 teaspoon Dijon mustard

$^1/_2$ teaspoon ground cumin

$^1/_4$ teaspoon freshly ground black pepper

3 tablespoons 1-inch lengths fresh chives

continued

Cook the beets by steaming, boiling, or microwaving (see the Cook's Guide, page 545). Peel or scrape the skins off while the beets are still quite warm.

While the beets are cooking, make the dressing. With a paring knife, cut away the peel and white pith from the oranges. Working over a bowl, remove the segments by cutting between the membranes. When all the segments are removed, squeeze the juice from the membranes into a separate bowl. Drain the juice from the segments into the bowl of juice. Add orange juice if necessary to measure ¼ cup. Add the olive oil, salt, mustard, cumin and pepper to the juice and whisk thoroughly. Set aside.

Coarsely grate the beets into a serving bowl. Toss with the dressing. Finish the salad now to serve warm, or cool to room temperature.

Add the orange segments to the beets and toss gently. Scatter the chives over the top and serve. The salad is best served without refrigerating, but it can be made up to 3 hours in advance. **Serves 4 to 6 as a first course or a side dish**

Rainbow Beets with Celery, Capers and Dill

Use a single variety of beet if that's all that's available, but it is nicer to mix them up for a rainbow effect. It is a terrific accompaniment to grilled or roasted fish.

This is a good make-ahead salad, but do not add the celery until just before serving, or it will discolor.

2 pounds medium beets (about 3 ounces each), mixed varieties (red, golden, Chioggia), trimmed and scrubbed

7 teaspoons rice wine vinegar, plus additional for chilling the beets

2 tablespoons plus 2 teaspoons olive oil

3 large ribs celery, trimmed, peeled and cut across into ¼-inch diagonal pieces (about 1 cup)

¼ cup coarsely chopped fresh dill

½ teaspoon kosher salt

Freshly ground black pepper to taste

Place each variety of beet in a different saucepan. Cover with water by 2 inches and bring to a boil. Lower the heat and simmer for 30 minutes, or until a knife slips easily into the flesh; add water as necessary to keep the beets covered. Drain and rinse under cold running water. Rub off the skins. Cut into ½-inch wedges.

Place each beet variety in a separate bowl. Add 1 teaspoon rice wine vinegar to each; mix well. Cover and chill for several hours or overnight.

Combine the beets in a large bowl. Add the remaining 4 teaspoons rice vinegar and then the remaining ingredients. Mix well.

Makes 4 cups; serves 4 as a first course, 6 as a side dish

Cold Beet Borscht

This may be one of the world's most glamorous-looking soups. It turns a brilliant magenta as the cream is added to the cooked beets and beet liquid. I like to serve it in a large white bowl surrounded by smaller bowls containing the toppings. I ladle out the soup and invite the eaters to serve themselves with the toppings. I frequently double or triple the recipe and keep it in the refrigerator. A large bowl of soup plus bread and a salad is an ideal summer lunch.

1 pound beets, trimmed and scrubbed

2 teaspoons white vinegar, or to taste

4 teaspoons fresh lemon juice

3/4 teaspoon citric acid powder (see Note)

1/2 cup plus 1 tablespoon sugar

1 1/2 teaspoons kosher salt

1/2 cup sour cream

2/3 cup heavy cream

AD-LIB TOPPINGS

Chopped onion, chopped cucumber, chopped
fresh dill, lemon wedges, sour cream, heavy
cream, reserved grated beets, chopped hard-
boiled egg, cold boiled very small waxy potatoes

In a small saucepan, bring the beets and water
to cover by 2 inches to a boil. Lower the heat
and simmer until the beets are tender when
pierced with the tip of a knife, 30 to 45 minutes
(depending on the size and age of the beets).

Drain the beets in a sieve lined with a damp
cloth; reserve the cooking liquid. Run the beets
under cold water to cool, then peel. In a food
processor, grate the beets with the grating disc
(this can also be done on a box grater).

Return half of the grated beets to the cooking
liquid. Reserve the rest of the beets for topping
or for another use. Season the soup with the
vinegar, lemon juice, citric acid, sugar and salt
and stir until everything is dissolved. Chill.

Just before serving, whisk in the sour cream
and heavy cream. Pass small bowls of the ad lib
toppings.

Makes 7 cups; serves 6 (or more, depending on the amount
of garnish used) as a first course.

NOTE: Citric acid in crystals or powder used to
be easily available. Today, it can be found online or in packets meant for aid in jelly making.
Vitamin C is citric acid; crushed tablets can
be used.

Jellied Borscht

Well, no, caviar isn't essential. The sour cream
topping can be topped with thin shreds of the
cooked beets and some tufts of dill. But think
of the colors and flavors of the acid-sweet ruby
red soup, the stark white sour cream and the
pearly, lightly salty, black pop of the caviar.

The soup can easily be made vegetarian by
substituting agar-agar for the gelatin.

In any case, there will be beets left over.
Grate and make them into a salad, good with
cold meats or fish. Use a lemon vinaigrette and
some chopped dill. The beets could be added
to a cucumber salad. Peel the beets and cube
them. They can be refrigerated for two to three
days or frozen.

1 pound beets, trimmed and scrubbed

5 teaspoons gelatin or 1 tablespoon finely ground
agar-agar (see page 501)

2 tablespoons fresh lemon juice

2 1/2 teaspoons white vinegar

3/4 teaspoon citric acid powder (see Note at left)

8 to 10 tablespoons sugar

2 1/4 teaspoons kosher salt

FOR SERVING

Sour cream

Caviar or chopped fresh dill

In a medium saucepan, bring the beets and
5 cups water to a boil. Cover. Lower the heat
and simmer until the beets can easily be pierced
with a skewer, 30 to 45 minutes (cooking time
depends on the size and age of the beets).

Strain the cooking liquid through a fine-
mesh sieve set over a small saucepan. Reserve
the beets for another use. Measure the liquid
and add enough water to make 4 cups.

continued

If using gelatin, sprinkle it over the liquid and let it sit for 2 minutes to soften. Whisk to combine, then heat the soup to just under a boil, stirring frequently. If using agar-agar, combine it with the liquid and bring to a boil. Lower the heat and simmer for 5 minutes.

Stir in the lemon juice, vinegar, citric acid, sugar and salt and continue stirring until everything is dissolved. Remove from the heat. Correct the seasoning with salt, sugar and/or lemon juice if necessary. The soup should be distinctly sweet and sour. (Remember that flavors fade when cold.) Refrigerate until set, about 6 hours.

Serve the soup chilled, topped with a dollop of sour cream and caviar or chopped dill.

Makes about 4 cups; serves 4 as a first course

Red Russian Vegetable Soup

I made this borscht variation to start a Thanksgiving dinner. I wanted something hot with a lot of flavor but not too heavy. It got raves. It is also beautiful, and my little granddaughter, who loves everything pink, took it as a compliment. The aim is a balanced sweet-and-sour soup. The seasonings can be played with.

4 bunches (about 4 pounds) beets, trimmed and scrubbed

6 tablespoons goose fat or duck fat, or olive oil for a vegetarian version

2 medium red onions, thinly sliced

2 cups canned tomatoes

1 medium red cabbage, cored and thinly sliced

1 cup red wine vinegar

2 cups sugar, or to taste

2 tablespoons citric acid powder (see Note, page 167)

3 tablespoons kosher salt

$1/8$ teaspoon freshly ground black pepper

Fresh lemon juice to taste (about $1/4$ cup)

FOR SERVING

1 pint heavy cream

Sour cream

1 large bunch fresh dill, fronds only, coarsely chopped

Place the beets in a deep pot with water to cover by 2 inches. Bring to a boil. Reduce the heat and simmer until the beets can be easily pierced with a knife, 30 to 45 minutes.

Strain the cooking liquid through a sieve lined with cheesecloth; reserve. Trim the beets and remove the skins. Grate them.

Melt the fat or heat the olive oil in a large pot. Add the onions and cook, stirring, over medium heat until soft. Add the tomatoes, cabbage and enough beet liquid to cover the ingredients by 4 inches. Bring to a boil, reduce the heat and simmer until the cabbage is tender, about 45 minutes.

Add the beets and cook for 20 minutes longer. Add enough of the remaining beet liquid to make the desired consistency. Add the vinegar, sugar and citric acid. Bring to a boil. Season with the salt and pepper. The aim is to get a balanced sweet-and-sour taste, but leave it a little sweet. Add the lemon juice.

Allow the flavors to blend off the heat for an hour.

To serve, reheat the soup. Place the heavy cream in a pitcher. Place the soup in individual bowls. Drizzle each serving with a circle of heavy cream poured from the pitcher. Spoon a dollop of sour cream in the center. Sprinkle with the dill. **Makes about 4 quarts**

Red Russian Soup—

the Meat Version

This is a version of a soup I originally made for my father, who was from Slutzk, one of the disappeared shtetls near Minsk. It appears with variations in all the surrounding areas. Using red cabbage seems to be my own idea. It gives it, in combination with vinegar and beets and tomatoes, a wonderful rich red color. Look for an appropriate sweet-and-sour balance: Taste the finished soup and add more sugar, vinegar or salt if needed.

In my family we love to eat, and my leftovers are quickly snatched up by the first person in the kitchen. However, the recipe can be halved (especially as the 5½ quarts made does not even include the potatoes).

2¹/₂ pounds beef short ribs, cut into pieces between the bones

2 pounds beets, trimmed and scrubbed

4 cups canned tomatoes (not plum) with their juices

³/₄ pound carrots, peeled, trimmed and cut into ¹/₂-inch rounds

1 medium onion, coarsely chopped

1 medium red cabbage, cored and cut into 1¹/₂-inch square pieces

1 large bunch fresh dill, fronds only, coarsely chopped

1 cup red wine vinegar

³/₄ cup sugar, or to taste

3 tablespoons kosher salt

¹/₈ teaspoon freshly ground black pepper

FOR SERVING

Smallish waxy potatoes, boiled, peeled and halved

Sour cream

Coarsely chopped fresh dill—lots

Place the short ribs and 8 cups water in a large stockpot. Bring to a boil over high heat, then reduce the heat to a slow simmer. Cook, skimming occasionally, for 1½ to 2 hours, or until the meat is tender.

Remove the short ribs from the liquid. When cool, separate the meat from the bones and trim off any fat. Cut the meat into cubes and reserve. Skim the liquid, then measure it and add enough cold water to equal 7 cups. Skim any fat that rises to the surface, and return to the pot.

While the short ribs are cooking, cook the beets. Place them in enough water to cover by 2 inches in a large pot. Bring to a boil, then reduce the heat to a simmer and cook until the beets can easily be pierced with a knife, 30 to 45 minutes. Strain the cooking liquid. You want 5 cups liquid; add water if necessary. Set aside. Slip the skins from the beets. Cut into 1 x ¼ x ¼-inch sticks. Set aside.

Add the tomatoes, with their liquid, the carrots, onion and cabbage to the short rib cooking liquid. Add half the chopped dill. Bring to a simmer and cook until the carrots are almost tender, about 20 minutes.

Add the beet sticks and cook for 20 minutes longer. Add the 5 cups reserved beet liquid, the vinegar, sugar, remaining dill, the short ribs, salt and pepper. Remove from the heat and allow the flavors to blend for 1 hour, or overnight.

To serve, reheat the soup.

Place a boiled potato half in each bowl. Ladle in 1 cup hot soup. Float 1 tablespoon sour cream on top and sprinkle with additional chopped dill. **Serves 10 as a main course**

Pickled Beets

I like these beets. Serve them with cold fish or roast pork.

- 4 pounds beets, trimmed and scrubbed, or three 15-ounce cans sliced beets, drained
- 20 whole black peppercorns
- 12 allspice berries
- 12 whole cloves
- 1 1/2 cups dry red wine
- 3/4 cup red wine vinegar
- 3/4 cup sugar
- 3 tablespoons kosher salt

If using raw beets, cook (see the Cook's Guide, page 545). When cool enough to handle, slip off the skins and slice. Place the beets in a deep 2-quart container (a soufflé dish works well).

In a 2 x 2-inch square of cheesecloth, tie up the peppercorns, allspice and cloves. Combine the red wine, 1 cup water, vinegar, sugar and salt in a 4-quart nonaluminum saucepan. Add the spice bag and heat to boiling over medium heat. Boil for 2 minutes. Pour the spice mixture over the beets and cool to room temperature.

Cover the beets securely and store in the refrigerator at least 2 days, or up to 1 week, before serving. **Makes 8 cups**

Beet and Potato Purée

This is not only a recipe; it is also a model for countless combined vegetable purées. Other good combinations are turnip and potato, celery root and potato, carrot and potato, broccoli and potato and cauliflower and potato—vary the seasonings to suit.

- 3/4 pound floury potatoes, peeled and coarsely chopped
- 3 tablespoons sugar
- 1 tablespoon kosher salt
- 1 teaspoon ground cumin (optional)
- 1 pound beets, trimmed, peeled and coarsely chopped, or cooked beets from Beet Sorbet (page 164), peeled, trimmed and coarsely chopped
- 6 tablespoons unsalted butter
- 1/2 cup heavy cream

Put the potatoes in a saucepan with 2 cups water, the sugar, 2 teaspoons salt and the cumin, if using. If using raw beets, add to the pan, along with another 1 cup water. Simmer over medium heat for 30 minutes, or until the vegetables are tender.

Drain the vegetables and place in a food processor. If using precooked beets, add them now. Pulse until the mixture is nearly smooth but small pieces of beet still show. Pulse in the butter 1 tablespoon at a time, then the cream and the remaining teaspoon of salt.
Serves 4 to 6 as a side dish

Golden Surprise

No butter is needed for this light, slightly sweet and altogether unusual purée.

- 8 small to medium golden beets (about 1 pound 2 ounces), trimmed
- 1 pound small to medium carrots (about 8), peeled and trimmed
- 2 large yellow bell peppers (1 pound)
- 1 teaspoon kosher salt

Steam the beets (see the Cook's Guide, page 545) for 40 minutes, or until a knife easily slips into the flesh. Add the carrots during the last 15 minutes of cooking. Let cool slightly. When the beets are cool enough to touch, slip off the skins. Cut into chunks.

While the beets are cooking, roast and peel the peppers via the fire-roasting or broiler method (see the Cook's Guide, page 629).

In a food processor, purée the vegetables until fairly smooth. Add the salt and pulse to blend. **Makes 4²/₃ cups**

Golden Soup

In a medium saucepan, combine 3 cups Golden Surprise with 3 cups Basic Chicken Stock (page 501), Roasted Chicken Stock (page 502) or commercial chicken broth. Cook over medium heat until warmed through. Add freshly ground black pepper to taste. Remove from the heat. Stir in 3 tablespoons fresh lemon juice and ¾ cup sour cream. Whisk to combine. Serve. **Makes 6 cups; serves 4 as a first course**

Orange Glazed Beets

Although sweet in and of themselves, beets are often sweetened in cooking to compensate for the large amount of tannin. This is a variant of the old-time standard Harvard beets, but much better. By the way, I think they were Harvard beets because crimson is Harvard's color, not because they were particularly served there.

Nothing can stop one from boiling beets for this recipe, but sometimes it is nice to have a canned shortcut that still tastes excellent.

> **Two 16-ounce cans sliced beets, drained, or 1¹/₂ pounds raw whole beets (5 to 7 beets, 3 to 5 ounces each), trimmed and scrubbed**
>
> **1 large orange**

> **¹/₂ cup packed light brown sugar**
>
> **³/₄ teaspoon fresh lemon juice**
>
> **Small pinch of ground cloves**
>
> **Pinch of kosher salt**
>
> **1 tablespoon cornstarch**

If using fresh beets, bake them in foil (see the Cook's Guide, page 545) until a knife easily slips into the flesh. When just cool enough to touch, slip off the skins. Cut into ¹/₄-inch-thick slices.

Using the large holes of a grater, remove the zest from the orange in long thin strips. Set aside. Juice half of the orange to get 4 teaspoons juice. Stir the orange juice and brown sugar together until well combined. Stir in the lemon juice, cloves and salt.

Put the beets in a pot or deep frying pan large enough to hold them comfortably. Pour the juice mixture over the beets. Using a rubber spatula, fold the beets into the liquid until well coated. Cook over medium heat for 5 minutes. Turn the beets over in the liquid. Cook for 5 to 10 more minutes.

While the beets are cooking, stir the cornstarch and 1 tablespoon water together in a small dish. Mix a little of the hot cooking liquid into the cornstarch mixture. Fold the cornstarch mixture and orange zest into beets. Cook until the sauce thickens. **Makes 2 cups; serves 6 as a side dish**

Microwave Variation

Place the sliced beets in a 9-inch pie plate. Pour the juice mixture over them. Using a rubber spatula, fold the beets into the liquid until well coated. Cook, uncovered, at 100% for 2 minutes 30 seconds. Turn the beets over in the liquid. Cook, uncovered, at 100% for 3 minutes.

While the beets are cooking, stir the cornstarch and 1 tablespoon water together in a small dish. Fold the cornstarch mixture and orange zest into the beets. Cook, uncovered, at 100% for 3 minutes. Remove from the oven. Turn the beets over so that each is coated with liquid. Serve.

Meatless Red Flannel Hash

At Thanksgiving, this is an unusual side dish unlikely to duplicate anything else being served. It also has enough flavor to serve as a main dish for any chance vegetarians. If they eat eggs, top each portion with a fried egg and add some barely wilted spinach or another green such as a salad. The hash can be reheated in a 350°F oven for fifteen minutes.

Two 8 1/4-ounce cans sliced beets or 3/4 pound raw whole beets (3 to 4 beets, 3 to 5 ounces each), trimmed and scrubbed

2 large floury potatoes (1 1/4 pounds), scrubbed

2 tablespoons unsalted butter, plus 1 tablespoon, melted

2 tablespoons vegetable oil

2 medium onions, coarsely chopped

16 fresh sage leaves, stacked 4 or 5 at a time , rolled up and cut across into thin strips (about 1/4 cup)

2 teaspoons kosher salt

7 to 8 grinds fresh black pepper

1 tablespoon red wine vinegar

If using canned beets, stick a small paring knife into the opened cans of beets, running it back and forth several times to coarsely cut the slices into irregular 1/4-inch pieces. Drain the beets, reserving 1/2 cup of their liquid. If using fresh beets, roast (see the Cook's Guide, page 545) until a knife easily slips into the flesh. When just cool enough to touch, slip off the skins.

Cut into 1/4-inch slices, then coarsely chop into irregular 1/4-inch pieces.

Place the potatoes in a 3-quart pot with water to cover. Bring to boil over high heat. Cook until just tender, about 25 minutes. Drain and refrigerate until cold (if in a hurry, plunge the potatoes into a water bath with lots of ice until cool enough to handle). Remove the skins and cut into 1/2-inch cubes.

Heat the 2 tablespoons butter and the oil in a 10-inch nonstick frying pan over medium-high heat. Add the onions and cook until translucent, about 5 minutes. Add the sage and cook until wilted. Add the potatoes and cook until brown, about 15 minutes. As the potatoes begin to brown, use a spatula to turn the mixture over occasionally, rather than stirring, so that the cubes do not break up and turn into mush.

When the potatoes have browned, add the beets, salt and pepper, folding them in with the spatula. Continue to cook for about 10 minutes.

Pour in the vinegar and 1/4 cup beet liquid or water (or stock). Cook for about 2 minutes, until the liquid is absorbed. Pour in the remaining 1/4 cup beet liquid or water (or stock) and cook until the liquid has been absorbed once more. Press the hash down into an even layer over the bottom of the pan, like a pancake. Remove from the heat.

Place an oven rack on the second level from the top. Set the oven to broil.

Center a 9- to 10-inch glass pie dish over the skillet. Holding the pie dish in place, flip the skillet over, turning the hash out into the pie dish. Press down into an even layer. The hash can be made ahead to this point and refrigerated. Bring to room temperature before continuing.

Brush the top of the hash with the melted butter. Broil for 10 minutes, or until the top is crusty and nicely browned. **Serves 4 as a side dish**

Beet Greens with White Beans, Bacon and Walnuts

A good grocery store will sell beets still attached to vigorous and leafy greens. Save them; they have the pleasant bitterness of winter greens tempered with some of the beets' sweetness. Treat them like chard or kale: Cook them, minus their stems, in a pan with a touch of oil to make a simple side dish; add them to soups and stews; or pair them with strong-flavored ingredients such as bacon and walnuts.

A single bunch of beets will yield an average of five to six ounces leaves and stems.

> 5 ounces (about 1 cup) dried cannellini beans, soaked, or one 19-ounce can cannellini beans, drained (about 2 cups) and rinsed
>
> 1 recipe Bacon Lardons (page 509), fat reserved
>
> 2 tablespoons walnut oil
>
> Greens from 6 bunches beets (leaves only), cut across into 1/4-inch strips (about 7 packed cups)
>
> 3 tablespoons sherry vinegar
>
> Kosher salt to taste
>
> 1/2 cup chopped walnuts
>
> Freshly ground black pepper to taste

If using dried beans, drain them. Put in a pot and add fresh water to cover by 2 inches. Bring to a boil. Lower the heat and simmer for 1 to 3 hours, depending on the age of the beans, until soft but not bursting.

Drain the beans in a colander; rinse with cold water to stop the cooking. Set aside.

Prepare the lardons. Very meaty bacon will leave only 2 teaspoons fat; if the bacon has rendered a lot of fat, remove all but 2 teaspoons. Or, for bacon cooked in the microwave, transfer 2 teaspoons fat to a medium saucepan.

Add the walnut oil to the pan and increase the heat to medium-high. Add the greens in 3 batches, cooking for 1 minute each time and letting the volume shrink before adding the next batch. With a wooden spoon, scrape the leaves against the bottom and sides of the pan to deglaze and get the flavors. Turn the heat to low. Cook for 5 minutes.

Stir in the vinegar and salt. Add the beans, bacon, walnuts and pepper. Toss gently. Cook for a few minutes, until heated through.

Makes an ample 4 cups

Tuna and Beets Niçoise Bâtarde

The popular salade Niçoise is traditionally made up of tuna, potatoes, haricots verts (French green beans) and eggs. Inspired by the classic dish and the tender farm-fresh beets at hand, I came up with this variation.

The beets can be red, yellow or Chioggia or any combination. Keep them separate to preserve their color.

The vinaigrette is made with ume-boshi vinegar, a Japanese plum vinegar with a delicate floral quality that brings out the sweetness in beets. Red wine vinegar can be used; balsamic it is too sweet and too strong.

> 2 medium red or yellow beets and 2 medium Chioggias (3 to 5 ounces each), trimmed and scrubbed
>
> 1 teaspoon rice wine vinegar
>
> 1/3 cup thinly sliced sweet onion, cut across into 1/2-inch pieces
>
> 1 1/2 to 2 tablespoons ume-boshi (Japanese plum) vinegar or red wine vinegar (quantity depends on acidity of the vinegar)
>
> 1/4 cup olive oil

continued

Kosher salt and freshly ground black pepper
to taste

One 9-ounce can tuna packed in water, drained
and lightly flaked

4 heads Bibb lettuce or 2 heads young romaine,
dark or yellowed leaves removed, leaves
separated, washed and ripped into bite-size
pieces (about 3 to 4 cups)

2 to 4 Oeufs Mollets (page 480), depending on
number of servings

Place each beet variety in a separate saucepan.
Cover with water by 2 inches. Bring to a boil,
then lower the heat and simmer until a knife
slips easily into the flesh, 30 to 45 minutes.
Drain and rinse under cold running water.
Rub off the skins. Cut into ½-inch wedges.

Place each beet variety in a separate bowl.
Add ½ teaspoon rice wine vinegar to each.
Mix well. Cover and chill several hours, or
overnight.

Put the beets and onion in a bowl. Whisk
together the ume-boshi or red wine vinegar, oil
and salt and pepper. Pour over the vegetables
and toss. Add the tuna and lettuce. Gently toss.

Serve in the bowl, with the eggs halved
lengthwise and placed on top, or divide evenly
among plates and top with the eggs.

Serves 4 as a first course, 2 to 3 as a main course

Beet Biscuits

These ruby-red beet biscuits are denser than
regular biscuits and not as high. They will be
sizzling when removed from the oven because of
fat and moisture. Let them sit; they will absorb
the butter. Serve them with cream cheese.

Dough left over after cutting the first round
of biscuits can be patted again to cut a second
round, which will not be as tender as the first.

3 small beets (²/₃ pound), trimmed and scrubbed

¹/₄ cup buttermilk

2 cups all-purpose flour, plus additional for
flouring the board

1 teaspoon kosher salt

¹/₂ teaspoon baking soda

8 tablespoons (4 ounces) cold unsalted butter,
cut into small cubes

In a medium saucepan, cover the beets with
water by 2 inches. Bring to a boil, then lower
the heat and simmer until a knife slips easily
into the flesh, 30 to 45 minutes. Drain and cool
10 minutes. Rub off the skins and quarter.

In a food processor, purée the beets; there
should be 1 cup purée. Transfer to a bowl.
Whisk in the buttermilk.

Place a rack in the center of the oven.
Preheat the oven to 500°F.

Sift the dry ingredients into a medium
mixing bowl. Cut in the butter until the largest
pieces are the size of small peas. Place in the
freezer or refrigerator until the butter is hard,
10 to15 minutes.

Scrape the purée into the flour mixture and
stir with a wooden spoon just until the dough
comes together around the spoon. This will be
a very moist, sticky dough; there should still
be whole pieces of butter visible in the dough.

Turn the dough out onto a well-floured
surface. Knead about 10 times, incorporating
enough flour so the dough no longer sticks to
hands. Keep the board well floured.

Pat the dough out ½ inch thick. Using a
biscuit cutter or a glass, cut into 2-inch rounds.
Place on an ungreased air-cushioned cookie
sheet or a heavy baking sheet, preferably
black. Bake for 9 to 11 minutes, or until cooked
through. Let sit for a few minutes, then serve.

Makes 16 biscuits

Beet Caraway Sauce

This unusual sauce is one of my favorites for white-fleshed fish, which it sets off to admiration.

3/4 pound beets, trimmed and scrubbed

1 tablespoon unsalted butter

1 teaspoon caraway seeds

1/2 teaspoon kosher salt

2 tablespoons sherry vinegar

Roast the beets (see the Cook's Guide, page 545) until a knife easily slips into the flesh. When they're just cool enough to touch, slip off the skins. Cut into 1/4-inch slices.

Melt the butter with the caraway in an 11- or 12-inch frying pan. Cook over low heat for 1 minute, or until fragrant. Add the beets in a single layer. Cook for 3 minutes. Turn the beets over. Add the salt and vinegar. Cook for 2 minutes. Transfer the beets to a blender.

Add 1/2 cup water to the pan and scrape the bottom. Pour into the blender. Purée until smooth. **Makes 1 1/2 cups**

Beet Ice Cream

This is really good and lovely looking. Candied rose petals on top would be lavish.

4 pounds beets, trimmed, peeled and cut into 1/4-inch dice (about 6 cups)

1 cup milk

2/3 cup sugar

1 2/3 cups crème fraîche

3/4 cup fresh lemon juice

Combine the beets, milk and sugar in a 4-quart saucepan. Bring to a boil over medium heat. Reduce the heat to a simmer. Cover and cook for 30 minutes, or until the beets are very tender, stirring occasionally.

Put the beets, with the cooking liquid and crème fraîche, in a blender. Purée until very smooth. Transfer the mixture to a metal bowl and stir in the lemon juice. Cover and chill for 2 hours or until cold.

Churn the beet mixture in an ice cream maker according to manufacturer's instructions, for about 25 minutes. Transfer to a container and store in the freezer. **Makes 2 1/2 pints**

Beets for Dessert

While beets may seem to be odd for dessert—they are certainly unusual—a little reflection will remind us that sugar beets are grown for extracting sugar. Ordinary beets are still very sweet, and the color is always spectacular. I find these well worth making.

Beet and Apple Strudel

This recipe was developed by the fabulous Chris Styler. When shopping, make sure to buy packages with full-size sheets of pastry (sometimes spelled filo), not half-size (see Note). Unused dough can be tightly wrapped and refrozen.

1/2 cup walnut pieces

1/4 cup Dried Bread Crumbs (page 510) or store-bought dried bread crumbs

8 tablespoons unsalted butter

1/2 pound red or golden beets, trimmed, peeled and coarsely shredded (about 1 3/4 cups)

1 large Gala or Granny Smith apple (about 8 ounces), peeled and coarsely shredded

1/4 cup packed light or dark brown sugar

1 tablespoon fresh lemon juice

1/4 teaspoon ground cinnamon

1/8 teaspoon ground allspice or cloves

1/8 teaspoon freshly ground black pepper

4 sheets phyllo dough (see Note)

Confectioners' sugar

Preheat the oven to 350°F.

Spread the walnuts and bread crumbs out on a baking sheet. Bake, stirring once or twice, until the bread crumbs are lightly toasted, 10 minutes. Cool completely. (Leave the oven on.)

Grind the nuts and crumbs in a food processor until the walnuts are very finely chopped. Set aside.

Melt the butter in a large skillet. Pour half into a bowl and keep warm. Stir the beets into the remaining butter. Stir over medium-low heat until steaming. Cover the skillet and cook, stirring occasionally, until the beets are tender with a little bite, about 12 minutes.

Scrape the beets and butter into a mixing bowl. Stir in the apple, sugar, lemon juice, cinnamon, allspice and pepper.

Brush one of the phyllo sheets with melted butter. Top with a second sheet and butter that. Repeat and top with a last sheet. Butter the top sheet and spread the nut mixture in an even layer over it. Starting 1 inch from one of the long sides, make a 3-inch-wide strip of beet filling along the long edge. Fold the edge of the phyllo over the filling, then carefully roll up to enclose the filling entirely in phyllo.

Place the phyllo roll, seam side down, on a baking sheet. Brush the top with butter. Make a few slits 1 inch apart with a paring knife. Bake until the phyllo is golden brown and crisp, about 30 minutes. Cool for 10 to 15 minutes.

To serve, sprinkle liberally with confectioners' sugar. Cut diagonally into 1 1/2-inch slices.

Makes 8 servings

NOTE: This recipe was developed using sheets of phyllo that measure 12 x 6 inches. Lately, phyllo sheets of approximately half that size have become available. If using these smaller sheets, double the amount called for; overlap two of them along one of their longer edges to create larger sheets, and proceed as above.

Beet and Carrot Strudel

Substitute 1/2 pound carrots, peeled and coarsely shredded, for the apple. Cook the carrots along with the beets, and proceed as above.

Chard

Swiss chard and ruby chard are available
throughout most of the year, but late summer
into winter is their natural season. They are
particularly liked in Provence and along the
Ligurian coast of Italy, where they are known
as bette, blette and biete, which stresses their
relationship to beets, which they are—but without
the large roots. All their value is in their leaves
and stems. While the stems and leafy parts can be
cut up and cooked together like spinach, usually
the green leafy part is separated from the stem
and the two are cooked as separate vegetables.

Red chard has red stems, ribs and veins. Green
chard is milder in taste. The red reveals a darker,
more beetlike flavor. Some like it; some prefer the
green. There is also a yellow or golden chard,

which is particularly pretty, especially mixed in with the others, but I find it relatively less intense in taste. I like all three.

Roughly speaking, a bunch of chard will give the same weight of stem and leaf; but once the leaves are cooked, they shrink like spinach to a small quantity. It is seldom that leaves and stems will come out evenly for recipes. Extra leaves can always be cut into strips and added to bean or legume soups. Extra stems can be blanched and served like asparagus.

Turn to **CHARD** in the Cook's Guide for how-tos and to the Index for recipes.

Ruby Chard Tart

These can also be transformed into mini-tarts, suitable for hors d'oeuvre; see the variation.

1 recipe Flamiche Crust (page 481)

Oil for greasing the ring

FILLING

1/2 pound ruby chard leaves (reserve the stems for another use), roughly chopped (about 8 cups)

1/4 cup long-grain rice, cooked in boiling water for 8 minutes, or until barely firm, then drained

2 large eggs

One 3 1/2-ounce button fresh soft goat cheese

1/4 pound thinly sliced prosciutto

1/4 teaspoon kosher salt

6 grinds fresh black pepper

GLAZE

1 egg, beaten with 1 teaspoon water, milk or cream

Make the dough, then make the filling while the dough is rising: Put all the filling ingredients in a food processor. Pulse until well combined, scraping down the sides of the bowl once or twice. The mixture should still be a little lumpy with some texture, not a pureé. Reserve.

Place a rack in the center of the oven. Preheat the oven to 375°F.

Lightly oil a 1-inch-high 10-inch pastry ring. Place the ring on a baking sheet (not air-cushioned).

Lightly oil the section of the sheet enclosed by the ring. Set aside.

Divide the dough in half. On a well-floured surface, roll out one piece to a 12-inch circle, using extra flour as needed. Twirl the dough onto the rolling pin and set into the oiled ring. Using fingers, tuck the dough down snugly into the ring. If necessary, press the dough against the sides of the ring to create a small overhanging lip of dough. Using the tines of a fork, lightly prick the dough so that it will not rise too much while cooking. Scrape the filling onto the dough. Using a spatula, spread it out evenly.

Roll out the second half of the dough into a 10-inch circle. Place on top of the filling; smooth out with fingers. Fold the edge of the bottom crust over the top crust to seal in the filling. Trim the flap to about 1/4 inch wide. Pat the edges down gently with a fork to make a firmer seal.

Brush the crust with the glaze. Using the tip of a sharp knife, make 3 slashes in the crust to act as steam vents. Bake for 40 minutes.

Gently slide the tart onto a flat plate. Delicious warm, but it may be served at room temperature as well. **Makes one 10-inch tart**

Tiny Chard Tarts for Hors d'oeuvre

Roll out the dough and cut into 2-inch rounds. Place on a lightly greased baking sheet. Prick the dough lightly with a fork. Top each round with 1 tablespoon of the filling. Brush the edges with the glaze, if desired. Bake for 15 to 18 minutes. Serve warm.

Chard and Lentil Soup

Just when I am beginning to get chilly in the evenings and the days are getting shorter, the chard in the garden is at its most flourishing. It is time for a robust soup. A couple of bowls of this, and I am ready to face the dark.

1/4 cup olive oil

1 teaspoon sweet paprika

1 teaspoon ground cumin

2 bunches small scallions (about 14), trimmed, white parts cut across into 1/4-inch pieces (about 3/4 cup), enough green parts cut across in 1/4-inch pieces to make 1/2 cup

1 pound brown lentils, rinsed (about 3 cups)

5 1/2 to 6 cups Basic Chicken Stock (page 501) or commercial chicken broth

3 small cloves garlic, smashed and peeled

6 ounces green chard leaves, roughly chopped (about 3 cups)

1 bunch fresh cilantro, leaves and tender stems only, coarsely chopped (about 1 cup)

Freshly ground black pepper to taste

1 tablespoon fresh lemon juice

In a large soup pot, heat the olive oil, paprika and cumin over low heat for 3 to 4 minutes. Add the scallion whites. Cook until wilted, about 5 minutes. Add the lentils, chicken stock and garlic. Raise the heat to high; cover and

bring to a boil. Lower the heat to a simmer and cook for 20 minutes, or until the lentils are soft but not mushy. (Cooking time will vary depending on the age of the lentils.)

Stir in the scallion greens, chard, cilantro, pepper and lemon juice. Cook for 5 to 10 minutes, until the chard is cooked through. Serve warm. **Makes 8 cups**

Warm Ruby Chard Stems and Anchovy Sauté

There are not too many things you can cook with such a beautiful color. Use plates that will set off this rich red shade. Even better, there is hardly any fat in this vegetable dish.

1 pound ruby chard stems trimmed and cut across into 3/4-inch pieces (about 4 cups)

1/4 cup dark raisins

2 cloves garlic, smashed and peeled

1 teaspoon kosher salt

One 2-ounce can anchovy fillets, rinsed

1 tablespoon fennel seeds

1 teaspoon olive oil

1 cup roughly chopped pulp from canned whole tomatoes (drain and squeeze dry the tomatoes before chopping)

3 grinds fresh black pepper

Bring a pot of water to a boil. Add the chard stems. Cover until the water returns to a boil, then uncover and cook for 10 to 12 minutes. Drain in a colander, reserving 1/2 cup cooking liquid. Rinse the stems under cold running water. Leave in the colander for 10 to 15 minutes to drain. The stems may be prepared 3 to 4 hours ahead to this point.

continued

Soak the raisins in the reserved cooking liquid: Put in the microwave. Cook at 100% for 1 minute. Drain the raisins.

Mash together the garlic and salt in a mortar to form a paste. Add the anchovies and fennel seeds. Mash until fairly smooth.

Heat the oil in a medium saucepan. Add the blanched stems, garlic paste, raisins and tomatoes. Cook over low heat, stirring, until warm throughout. Season with pepper.

Makes 2 1/2 cups

Elegant Chard Gratin

Elegance is richness in this soothing gratin.

1 pound white chard stems, trimmed and cut across into 3/4-inch pieces (about 4 cups)

3 large eggs

1 1/2 cups heavy cream

3/4 teaspoon kosher salt

8 grinds fresh black pepper

1/2 cup grated Gruyère cheese

1 teaspoon unsalted butter

Place a rack in the lowest level of the oven. Preheat the oven to 450°F.

Put the chard stems in a pot of boiling water. Cover until the water returns to a boil, then uncover and cook for 10 to 12 minutes. Drain in a colander and rinse under cold water. Leave the stems in the colander for 10 to 15 minutes to drain. The stems may be prepared to this point up to a day in advance; wrap and refrigerate.

In a medium bowl, combine the eggs, cream, salt, pepper and cheese. Add the stems. With hands, mix ingredients together until very well combined.

Grease a 9-inch glass pie pan with the butter. Pour the mixture into the pan, making sure to scrape out the bowl completely. Carefully place in the oven. Bake for 35 minutes or until the top is golden brown.

Remove and let cool for 5 minutes to allow the juices to collect. Invert onto a flat serving dish and serve warm.

Serves 6 as a side dish, 4 as a main course

Chard and Veal Tortelloni

These tortelloni are particularly nice with my Baby Food Tomato Sauce (page 461). The delicate and smoky flavor of the sauce offsets the sharpness of the chard and veal filling. If making the sauce, use some of it in place of the Plum Tomato Purée called for in the filling. I prefer to make my own fresh pasta, but if I am pressed for time and can find good fresh pasta sheets, those work also. Cooking times for the pasta depend on its freshness. My own fresh pasta cooks up quickly, while I find that store-bought pasta sheets take longer to cook. I always test a small piece of pasta on its own before I cook the tortelloni.

2 shallots, finely minced (about 1/4 cup)

2 tablespoons olive oil

1/4 pound ground veal

4 cups chopped yellow chard leaves

2 1/2 tablespoons Plum Tomato Purée (page 459)

2 tablespoons balsamic vinegar

1/2 teaspoon kosher salt

Freshly ground black pepper to taste

1 recipe Basic Pasta Dough (page 469) or four 12 x 9-inch fresh pasta sheets

Cornmeal or flour for dusting

In a 12-inch nonreactive frying pan, cook the shallots in the oil over medium heat for 4 minutes, or until they have softened. Add the veal. Stirring regularly, cook for 2 minutes, or until the veal has just started to brown. Mix in the chard. Cook for 10 minutes, or until the chard is wilted and cooked through. Stir in the tomato purée and vinegar. Cook for 5 minutes longer. Remove from the heat. Add the salt and pepper.

If using homemade dough, divide it into 4 equal pieces. Using a pasta machine or a rolling pin (see page 470 for instructions), roll the dough into thin sheets.

With a glass or a sharp cookie cutter, cut each sheet of pasta into 3-inch circles. Quickly reroll and cut the scraps, to make a total of 48 circles. Place the circles on a kitchen towel dusted with cornmeal or flour.

Put 1 teaspoon filling in the center of each circle of pasta. Using a small pastry brush, wet the edges of a pasta circle with water. Fold the circle over to form a semicircle. Using either a fork or fingertips, press the edges together to seal the filling inside. Repeat with the remaining circles of dough, setting the finished tortelloni on a kitchen towel dusted with cornmeal or flour.

In a large covered pot, cook the tortelloni in boiling salted water for 5 to 7 minutes. Drain in a colander and cover with a wet paper towel or dishcloth. Let sit for 10 minutes.

If using the Baby Food Tomato Sauce (see headnote), use ½ cup for each 8-tortelloni serving.

Makes about 48 tortelloni; serves 5 to 6 as a main course, 8 as a first course

Yellow Chard, Roasted Tomatoes and Penne

If your friends have an affinity for anchovies, slice them into small pieces and stir them directly into the dish. If not, serve the anchovies on the side and let everyone add to taste.

4½ tablespoons olive oil

1½ pounds yellow cherry tomatoes

6 to 8 cloves garlic, smashed and peeled

2 pounds yellow chard, trimmed, leaves cut across into ½-inch strips (about 12 cups), stems cut across into ¼-inch strips (about 5 cups)

1 pound penne pasta

Three 2-ounce cans anchovies packed in oil, drained and fillets separated

Kosher salt and freshly ground black pepper to taste

Place a rack in the center of the oven. Preheat the oven to 500°F.

Use 3 tablespoons of the olive oil to grease the smallest pan that will hold the tomatoes comfortably in a single layer. Put the tomatoes in the pan, interspersing them with the garlic cloves. Roast for 45 minutes, stirring every 15 minutes.

While the tomatoes are roasting, bring a large pot of water to a boil. Add the chard stems. Cook for 8 to 10 minutes, or until a knife easily pierces the flesh. Remove with a skimmer and drain. Toss the stems with the remaining 1½ tablespoons olive oil.

Add the leaves to the pot. Cook for 5 to 10 minutes, or until tender. Drain. Add to the chard stems.

Once the tomatoes and chard are cooked, bring a fresh pot of water to a boil. Cook the pasta according to the package directions until just done. Drain. Return the pasta to the pot. Add the chard stems, leaves, roasted tomatoes with the garlic and their juices, and anchovies, if using. Toss over medium-low heat until well combined. Season with salt if necessary, depending on the saltiness of the anchovies, and pepper to taste. **Serves 6 as a main course**

Carrots

It was only in the relatively recent past, when they became orange and sweet, that carrots became so popular, surpassing their previously preeminent cousins, the parsnips. Their newfound fame may also have had to do with the arrival of refrigeration. Parsnips had had the advantage that they could be stored for long periods of time in root cellars or in piles of cool sand. Carrots wilted rapidly. Refrigeration changed all that, giving carrots a long storage life. As they were frequently eaten raw—carrot sticks for diets— they came up trumps.

Carrots fresh from the garden are more tender and sweeter than carrots of comparable size bought from the market. Freshly pulled, they will also need only scraping. If I can get the seed,

Under One Umbrella

THE UMBELLIFERAE FAMILY

After buttercups—held under the chin to create a golden glow—daisies and dandelions, perhaps the first wildflower I could name was Queen Anne's lace. I was drawn to the delicate collection of little white flowers whose threadlike stems spread out into a tiny parasol. This looked like an umbrella, and that accounts for the family name of many plants with similar flower heads.

Some of them are poisonous (Queen Anne's lace, for one). Many are eaten primarily for their vegetables, often roots. The most common are probably the carrots, followed by parsnips, celery root and—above the ground—celery and bulb fennel. That brings us to the other culinary contributors, the vast array of umbelliferous herbs such as parsley (including a rooted kind, good for chicken soup, called Hamburg parsley), chervil, cumin, coriander (whose seed is used as a spice), anise, dill, angelica and lovage. For more on those, see Lettices and Herbes (page 416).

I plant some variety of Nantes carrot, as their straight shape makes them easy to pull.

When buying small carrots, check to see if they are real babies, or midgets or dwarves. The two latter kinds are genetically small but full grown; peel and cook them as other carrots. True baby carrots, about three-quarter inch wide at the top and three to five inches long, are sweet and tender, needing only the briefest cooking; or they can be savored raw.

When cooking with carrots as an ingredient, I am particularly careful if using onions, long-cooked garlic and/or parsnips. All are sweet and the effect can be overwhelming. Carrots often welcome the acidity of lemon or ginger, the sharpness of chilies or the roundness of cumin for balance.

Carrots make a cheerful start to a meal with their smiling orange color, cooked or raw. Older carrots have a darker winter flavor shown off in Carrot Leek Soup (page 186), while young carrots are a summer flavor.

It is typically Swiss to have a plate of various grated raw vegetable salads. With carrots, consider celery root and jicama or beets if very young beets are available. Carrots on their own just need a nice leaf or two of lettuce to help contain the dressing.

Two cups of grated carrots combined with a simple mustard dressing of 1 tablespoon Dijon mustard, 3 tablespoons olive oil, 1 tablespoon red wine vinegar and a large pinch of salt make a light and simple first course. Or another vinaigrette such as Orange Wheat Germ Dressing (page 451) can be used.

Cumin Carrots (page 191) pair well with Cumin Mushrooms (page 403) as a warm, spicy first course.

Carrots are also a prime soup ingredient. They are almost ubiquitous in chicken soups and meat soups. They add luster to lentil soup and a wide variety of vegetable soups, and they can star in soups hot and cold. I consider some carrots in the refrigerator a staple, as I am always making soup.

As for side and main dishes, carrots are eyeliner for a plate, making almost any one look better. The Carrot Sauce on page 186 is all the simplest food needs to star. I serve the Braised Carrots (page 189) with wild rice as a main dish. The variation of braised carrots made with roast arctic char (page 190) is an obvious main course, as is the Lemon Glazed Carrots served with eggs (see headnote, page 188), although I often just make the carrot part and serve it as a relish.

Carottes Vichy, a French classic very similar to Lemon Glazed Carrots but without the lemon, is "Vichy" by virtue of using Vichy water, which would replace the juice.

Turn to **CARROTS** in the Cook's Guide for how-tos and to the Index for more recipes.

Carrot Cumin Salad

Carrots and cumin are good buddies. Here they meet in a light salad that can be used on a buffet or served as a summer accompaniment to cold meats or fish. The recipe can be multiplied ad lib.

- 1 clove garlic, smashed and peeled
- 1 pound carrots, peeled, trimmed and cut on the diagonal into $1/8$-inch slices (about $1 1/2$ cups)
- $1/8$ teaspoon ground cinnamon
- $1/4$ teaspoon ground cumin
- $1/2$ teaspoon sweet paprika
- Pinch of cayenne pepper
- Juice of 1 lemon
- $1/8$ teaspoon sugar
- Kosher salt to taste
- Olive oil to taste
- 1 tablespoon chopped fresh parsley

Fill a medium saucepan with water, add the garlic and bring to a boil. Add the carrots and cook until just barely tender. Drain; discard the garlic. Transfer the carrots to a bowl.

Mix together the spices, lemon juice and sugar. Salt to taste. Pour over the carrots. Chill.

Sprinkle with olive oil and the chopped parsley just before serving. **Makes 1 $1/2$ cups**

Carrot Salad with Currants and Almonds

Do not substitute nonfat yogurt; the creaminess of whole-milk yogurt wonderfully tempers the sharpness of the vinegar. Coconut milk can be used by those avoiding milk.

Reserve the salad and dressing separately if making this ahead of time. Toss just before serving. Multiply if desired.

- $1/2$ cup dried currants
- $1/4$ cup red wine vinegar
- $3/4$ teaspoon kosher salt
- 1 pound carrots, peeled, trimmed and coarsely grated (about 4 cups)
- $1/4$ cup slivered almonds
- 1 tablespoon honey
- $1/4$ cup plain whole-milk yogurt

Place the currants in a small bowl. Combine the vinegar, ¼ cup water and ¼ teaspoon salt in a small saucepan. Bring to a boil. Pour over the currants. Allow to soak for 20 minutes.

Drain the currants; reserve the liquid. Put the currants, carrots and almonds in a bowl. Whisk together the reserved soaking liquid, the honey and yogurt until smooth. Pour over the carrot mixture and toss until combined. Add the remaining ½ teaspoon salt. Toss until thoroughly mixed. **Makes 1 ¹/₃ cups**

Creamy Carrot Soup

Cumin and carrots find themselves together again in this dietetic but sumptuous soup that can be eaten hot or cold. Stovetop multiplication is easy. To multiply the microwave version, see the cooking times in the Cook's Guide, page 563.

2 teaspoons canola oil

1 ¹/₂ teaspoons ground cumin

³/₄ pound carrots, peeled, trimmed and cut across into 1-inch rounds (about 2 cups)

2 ³/₄ cups Basic Chicken Stock (page 501), Roasted Chicken Stock (page 502) or commercial chicken broth

1 cup part-skim ricotta cheese

1 teaspoon kosher salt

1 tablespoon fresh lemon juice

Cook the oil and cumin in a medium saucepan over medium heat (be careful not to overheat, or the cumin will burn) for 1 minute to release the flavor of the cumin. Add the carrots and stock. Cover and bring to a boil. Lower the heat and simmer for 30 minutes, or until the carrots are very soft. Remove from the heat.

Place the ricotta in a blender with a small amount of the cooking liquid. Blend to combine. Remove the carrots from the pan with a slotted spoon and add to the blender. Blend until smooth. Return the purée to the pan of liquid; stir to combine. Season with the salt and lemon juice. Serve hot. Or, to serve chilled, refrigerate for at least 3 hours, or overnight.

Makes 4 cups; serves 4 as a first course

Microwave Variation

Place the carrots, ³/₄ cup stock and cumin in a 9-inch pie plate. Cover tightly with microwave plastic wrap. Cook at 100% for 15 minutes, or until the carrots are easily pierced with the tip of a knife. Remove from the oven. Prick the plastic to release steam and uncover. Proceed as above. If serving hot, reheat, covered, in a bowl at 100% for 4 minutes, then add the lemon juice.

Potage of Turnip and Carrot

This soup can be made ahead up to the point of adding the celery seed and butter. Celery seed tends to get bitter with prolonged sitting. The butter will, of course, separate from the soup if the soup isn't served as soon as it is stirred in.

1 medium floury potato (8 ounces), peeled and cut into 1-inch dice (about 2 cups)

1 medium-large turnip (10 ounces) trimmed, peeled and cut into ¹/₂-inch dice (about 2 cups)

3 medium carrots, trimmed, peeled and sliced crosswise into ¹/₂-inch rounds (about 2 cups)

1 small onion, cut into ¹/₂-inch dice (about ³/₄ cup)

4 medium cloves garlic, smashed and peeled

2 medium stalks celery, sliced crosswise into ¹/₂-inch pieces (about ³/₄ cup)

2 cups roughly chopped fresh parsley

1 heaping tablespoon kosher salt

¹/₄ teaspoon celery seeds

1 tablespoon unsalted butter (optional)

continued

Put all the vegetables except the parsley in a 4-quart saucepan. Add 4 cups water. Cover and bring to a boil. Lower the heat and simmer, uncovered, for 10 minutes. Add the parsley and simmer for 10 minutes more. Stir in the salt.

Pass all the vegetables and liquid through a food mill fitted with a medium disc. The soup can be made ahead to this point and refrigerated for up to 3 days.

Return the soup to the pan. Add the celery seeds and heat through. Remove from the heat. If using the butter, stir it in. Serve immediately. **Makes 6¹/₂ cups**

Carrot Leek Soup

This quickly made soup is very full flavored on its own, but the color of the soup matched the color of some rouille I had on hand, so I put a dollop on top. The saffron and garlic of the rouille added a surprising dimension that jazzed up the carrots without overwhelming them.

> 4 tablespoons unsalted butter
>
> 3 medium leeks (1 pound), trimmed, white parts only, washed and cut across into ¹/₂-inch slices (about 3 cups)
>
> 1 pound carrots, peeled, trimmed and cut into ¹/₄-inch rounds (about 3 cups)
>
> 3¹/₂ cups Basic Chicken Stock (page 501), Roasted Chicken Stock (page 502) or commercial chicken broth
>
> ¹/₂ cup heavy cream
>
> 1 ¹/₂ teaspoons kosher salt
>
> Freshly ground black pepper to taste
>
> ¹/₂ recipe Rouille (page 457; optional)

Melt the butter in a 4-quart saucepan. Cook the leeks for 10 minutes over medium heat, or until wilted but not browned. Add the carrots and

chicken stock. Cover and bring to a boil. Reduce the heat and simmer for 10 minutes.

Drain the vegetables; reserve the liquid. In 2 batches, purée the vegetables with some of the liquid in a blender. Return the purée to the saucepan, along with any remaining cooking liquid. Add the cream, salt and pepper to taste. Cook over low heat until warmed through.

Serve each bowl topped with a small dollop of rouille, if desired. **Makes 6 cups**

Microwave Variation

Place the butter in a 2¹/₂-quart casserole with a tightly fitting lid. Cook, uncovered, at 100% for 4 minutes.

Remove from the oven and stir in the leeks. Cover with the lid and cook for 8 minutes at 100%, stirring once during cooking.

Remove from the oven. Stir in the carrots and 1 cup of the stock. Cover and cook at 100% for 13 minutes. Transfer to a blender or food processor and purée until smooth.

Return the purée to the casserole and stir in the remaining 2¹/₂ cups broth and the cream. Season to taste with salt and pepper. Serve each bowl with a small dollop of rouille, if desired.

Carrot Purée or Sauce

There was a time when fancy restaurants served every main course with an assortment of variously colored purées. Now that the time is past, we can still serve the purées when the spirit moves us. The recipe is easily doubled; increase the cooking time if needed.

I'm particularly fond of this attractive and unusual sauce variation on cauliflower, fish or chicken.

> ³/₄ cup Basic Chicken Stock (page 501) or commercial chicken broth

³/₄ pound carrots, peeled, trimmed and cut across into 1-inch rounds (about 2 cups)

Kosher salt to taste

A squeeze of lemon (optional)

Put the stock in a medium saucepan and bring to a boil. Add the carrots. Cover, reduce the heat and simmer for 30 minutes, or until very tender.

Transfer to a blender and purée until completely smooth. Season with salt and the lemon juice, if using. **Makes 1 cup**

Microwave Variation
Combine the carrots and stock in a 2½-quart soufflé dish. Cover tightly with microwave plastic wrap. Cook at 100% for 15 minutes (increase the cooking time to 20 minutes if doubling the recipe). Prick the plastic to release the steam. Remove from the oven and uncover. Transfer the mixture to a blender and purée until completely smooth. Season with salt and the lemon juice, if using.

Creamy Carrot Sauce with Sage
After puréeing the carrots, add 1 cup fromage blanc (a fat-free white cow's milk cheese; or use an equal amount of cottage cheese blended until smooth), 16 to 18 fresh sage leaves and ¼ cup Basic Chicken Stock or commercial broth to the blender. Purée until smooth and combined. Transfer to a saucepan and cook over low heat until heated through. Serve hot. **Makes 2 cups**

Carrot Potato Purée

This is a thicker and more conventional purée than the previous one. The vegetables can be boiled, but they absorb less water with steaming.

2 pounds carrots, peeled, trimmed and cut across into 1-inch rounds (about 6 cups)

1 pound floury potatoes, peeled and cut into 1-inch cubes (about 3 cups)

8 tablespoons unsalted butter, softened

Kosher salt and freshly ground black pepper to taste

Put the carrots and potatoes in the top of a two-part steamer or on a steaming rack or a plate in a bamboo steamer. Fill the bottom of the steamer pan or a pan large enough to hold the rack or bamboo with water; the water should not touch the rack. Bring to a boil over medium heat. Place the carrots and potatoes on top, cover and steam for 15 minutes, or until very tender.

Purée the vegetables through the coarse disc of a food mill into a large bowl. Beat in the butter and salt and pepper to taste. **Makes 3½ cups**

Baby Carrots with Tiny Green Beans Sautéed in Mint Butter

Unlike the conventionally paired peas and carrots, which do not come into season together, the especially delightful baby carrots and tiny French green beans, haricots verts, are ready for picking at the same time. I know: Picking the beans can break the back. With young mint, they make a classic combination. I tend to use the fuzzy leaves of apple mint, being gentle in flavor.

The dish can be divided or multiplied. The boiling can be done ahead and the frothing in butter at the last minute.

2 pounds baby carrots, trimmed and cleaned by scraping with the back of a paring knife or a green scouring pad

½ pound haricots verts (French green beans), tipped and tailed

½ pound (8 ounces) unsalted butter, softened

¼ cup lightly packed fresh mint leaves

continued

1/4 cup lightly packed fresh mint leaves

1 1/2 teaspoons fresh lemon juice

1 teaspoon kosher salt

Bring a large pot of salted water to a boil. Add the carrots and cook for 7 minutes, or until crisp-tender. Remove the carrots to a sieve and rinse under cold running water. Drain thoroughly. Repeat with the haricots verts, cooking for 3 minutes. Toss the vegetables together until mixed.

Put the butter, mint, lemon juice and salt in a food processor. Process, scraping the sides occasionally, until the butter is smooth and the mint is finely chopped.

Scrape the butter into a large skillet and heat until foaming. Add the vegetables. Toss to coat with the butter and cook until heated through, about 4 minutes. Serve hot.

Serves 12 as a side dish

Lemon Glazed Carrots

This is very lemony in flavor, almost jamlike with its balance of sweet and tang.

While the preparation of the baby carrots takes longer than usual, the cooking time is brief and the carrots, especially when sprinkled with freshly chopped parsley or chervil, are important enough to make a company lunch out of the simplest scrambled eggs.

8 bunches baby carrots (2 pounds with greens), trimmed and cleaned by scraping with the back of a paring knife or a green scouring pad (about 5 cups)

1 scant cup sugar

2 tablespoons salt

4 tablespoons unsalted butter

1/3 cup fresh lemon juice

If the carrots are thicker than 1/2 inch, cut lengthwise in half to ensure even cooking.

Bring 3 quarts water, 1/2 cup sugar and the salt to a boil in a large saucepan over medium-high heat. Add the carrots and cook for 8 to 9 minutes, until just tender. Drain.

Melt the butter and the remaining scant 1/2 cup sugar in a 12-inch frying pan. Add the lemon juice. Add the carrots and mix carefully, then cook over high heat for 5 minutes, or until the sauce is reduced to a syrupy glaze. **Makes 4 cups**

Lemon-Light Carrots

The lemons, whose zests are removed to use in the recipe, can be squeezed for plenty of juice for this dish.

4 tablespoons unsalted butter

1/4 teaspoon cayenne pepper

10 medium carrots (3 pounds), peeled, trimmed and cut into 3 x 1/4 x 1/4-inch matchsticks

1 large sweet onion, thinly sliced

Zest of 2 lemons—removed with a vegetable peeler and thinly sliced into long strips (about 3 tablespoons)

1 teaspoon Chinese five-spice powder

4 teaspoons fresh lemon juice

1/2 teaspoon kosher salt

Melt the butter in a nonreactive 4-quart pot over low heat. Stir in the cayenne pepper. Add the carrots, onion and lemon zest and mix well. Cover the pot. Cook, stirring occasionally, until the carrots are tender but not mushy and the onions have softened and turned light yellow, about 45 minutes.

Stir in the five-spice powder, lemon juice and salt and cook for 30 seconds more.

Makes 5 cups; serves 8 as a side dish

Braised Carrots and Potatoes

Simple, excellent and addictive, these carrots and potatoes practically melt on the inside.

3/4 **pound carrots, peeled, trimmed and cut into 1-inch pieces**

1 **pound floury potatoes, peeled and cut into 1-inch pieces**

2 **tablespoons unsalted butter, melted**

1/2 **cup Basic Chicken Stock (page 501), Roasted Chicken Stock (page 502) or commercial chicken broth**

1/2 **teaspoon kosher salt**

Freshly ground black pepper to taste

Place a rack in the bottom third of the oven. Preheat the oven to 500°F.

Toss the carrots and potatoes with the butter in a 12 x 10-inch roasting pan. Spread out in a single layer. Roast the vegetables for 30 minutes, stirring midway through cooking, until lightly browned.

Reduce the oven temperature to 350°F. Pour the stock into the roasting pan. Cover tightly with foil. Bake for 15 minutes. The liquid will be mostly absorbed by the vegetables. Season with the salt and pepper. **Makes 3**1/2 **cups**

Braised Carrots

There are some vegetables that reward one with special flavors and melting textures when cooked for a prolonged time. Carrots are one. I find that I always eat more than my share of the carrots from the pot roast. Here is a way of making those delicious carrots on their own to serve with less fatty meats or as part of a vegetarian spread. I would always make more rather than less, as people

like these a lot. Leftovers are good to have cold as a first course or vegetarian lunch on another day.

1 **pound carrots, peeled, trimmed and cut into 5 x** 1/2 **x** 1/2 **-inch sticks**

1 **tablespoon olive oil**

6 **cloves garlic, smashed and peeled**

2 **medium tomatoes (about 1 pound), cored and coarsely chopped (about 2 cups), or 2 cups drained, seeded and chopped canned tomatoes**

1/4 **cup chopped fresh mint**

3 **slices lemon, seeds removed, plus juice from rest of lemon**

1/4 **teaspoon ground cumin**

1/2 **teaspoon anise seeds**

1 **tablespoon sugar**

1 **teaspoon kosher salt**

Freshly ground black pepper to taste

Put the carrots and oil in a heavy 10-inch skillet. Cook over high heat for about 10 minutes, stirring and shaking the pan often; scrape the pan from time to time with a wooden spoon to collect the browned bits.

Once the carrots have browned nicely, add all the other ingredients except the lemon juice and pepper. Mix well. Bring to a boil, then reduce the heat to low. Cover tightly. Cook for 20 minutes.

Turn the carrots and stir the mixture. Cover and cook for 20 minutes, or until the carrots are very soft. Add the lemon juice and salt and pepper to taste. Serve hot or at room temperature.

Makes 23/4 **cups; serves 4 to 5 as a first course, 6 as a side dish**

continued

Oven-Roasted Version

Note that only the first step is truly roasting; the rest—still in the oven—is braising.

Preheat the oven to 500°F.

Place the carrots in a 12 x 6 x 1½-inch roasting pan. Drizzle with the oil. Rub the carrots and pan with the oil. Roast for 10 minutes. Use a spatula to turn the carrots. Roast for 10 minutes more.

Remove the pan from the oven and turn the heat down to 325°F. Add all the other ingredients except the lemon juice and pepper. Mix well. Cover tightly with aluminum foil. Roast for 15 minutes.

Turn the carrots and stir the mixture. Roast for 15 minutes more. The carrots should be very soft. If they are not, roast for 5 to 10 more minutes.

Add the lemon juice, pepper to taste and more salt if desired. Serve hot or at room temperature. **Makes 2¹/₂ cups; serves 4 as a side dish**

Braised Carrots in Orange Cherry Tomato Sauce

Freshness of ingredients is of particular importance here, as there are only two. I make this with tomatoes just plucked from my garden at the end of summer and carrots just pulled from the ground.

I am partial to orange cherry tomatoes—even sweeter than the regular red. They pair divinely with carrots to create a dish that is lightly sweet, slightly acidic and bright. It makes a terrific side dish to roast fish or pork. I once served it as a sauce over arctic char to rave reviews; see the variation.

1 pound very fresh carrots, peeled, trimmed and cut into 1-inch chunks (about 3 cups)

1 recipe Simple Stovetop Cherry Tomato Stew Base (page 461), made with orange cherry tomatoes

Kosher salt to taste

Put the carrots and tomato base in a pot small enough so that the base covers the carrots. Bring to a boil. Reduce the heat to low. Simmer for 30 to 33 minutes, or until the carrots are very tender and flavors are completely blended. Salt to taste. **Makes 3¹/₂ cups**

Roast Arctic Char with Braised Carrots in Orange Cherry Tomato Sauce

Order a 3½- to 4-pound whole arctic char (2¼ inches at its thickest point), scaled, gutted and cleaned, from the fish store. If char is unavailable, use Atlantic salmon, whitefish or a very young and fresh bluefish. With its small head and light bones, arctic char yields enough meat for 5 to 6 people. If the fish has a larger head or larger bones, it will serve 3 to 4 people.

Prepare the carrots as directed. Set aside.

Preheat the oven to 500°F.

With a large sharp knife, cut 3 parallel diagonal slashes into each side of the fish, cutting 1 to 1½ inches into the flesh. Place the fish on a diagonal in an 18 x 13 x 2-inch roasting pan; it is okay if the head and tail jut out slightly over the edges. Rub 2 tablespoons each olive oil and fresh lemon juice into the sides, slits and cavity of the fish. Sprinkle on both sides with 2 tablespoons kosher salt and freshly ground black pepper to taste. Roast the fish for 22 minutes (or 10 minutes for each inch of thickness). The fish is cooked when a knife inserted in its thickest point to the backbone reveals that the flesh is opaque, not translucent. Use two large spatulas to carefully remove the fish to a serving platter.

Put the roasting pan on top of the stove over low heat. Pour the carrots and sauce into the pan. Use a wooden spoon to scrape up any brown bits stuck to the pan. Loosen the sauce with a little water if too thick. Pour the carrots and sauce over the fish. Serve immediately.

Serves 5 to 6 as a main course (see headnote if using a fish other than arctic char)

Cumin Carrots

The recipe on page 184 is for a carrot and cumin salad. This is a cooked version.

> $1/2$ cup olive oil
>
> 3 pounds carrots, peeled, trimmed and cut into 3 x $1/4$ x $1/4$-inch sticks
>
> $1/4$ teaspoon kosher salt
>
> Freshly ground black pepper to taste
>
> $2 1/2$ teaspoons ground cumin

Heat two large skillets over medium heat. Divide the oil between them. Add half the carrots, the salt, pepper to taste and 1 teaspoon cumin to each skillet. Reduce the heat to low. Cook uncovered, turning the carrots occasionally, for 25 to 30 minutes, until they are golden and shriveled looking. Five minutes before the end of cooking, combine the carrots in a single skillet. Stir in the remaining $1/2$ teaspoon cumin.

Taste and adjust the seasoning if necessary. Transfer the carrots to a bowl and cool to room temperature, tossing occasionally. Serve at room temperature. **Makes 4 cups**

Fall Vegetable Sauté

A second sowing of carrots will give babies in the fall. Instead of the lighter tastes of summer, the warm flavors of cumin and chestnut are welcome.

> 6 ounces baby carrots, trimmed and cleaned by scraping with the back of a paring knife or a green scouring pad (about 1 cup)
>
> 1 cup pearl onions
>
> 4 tablespoons unsalted butter
>
> 2 teaspoons ground cumin, or to taste
>
> Small pinch of cayenne pepper
>
> 1 teaspoon kosher salt
>
> $1/4$ teaspoon freshly ground black pepper
>
> 1 teaspoon sugar
>
> 1 medium yellow bell pepper, cored, seeded, deribbed and cut into 1-inch squares (about 1 cup)
>
> 1 cup Roasted Peeled Chestnuts (page 508)
>
> 2 tablespoons fresh lemon juice

Bring a 2-quart saucepan of salted water to a boil.

If any of the carrots are thicker than $1/2$ inch, cut them lengthwise in half so each piece is approximately the same thickness. Boil for 3 minutes, or until half cooked. Drain and rinse under cold running water; drain again. Set aside.

Bring a 1-quart saucepan of salted water to a boil. Cut the root ends off the onions. Boil for 3 minutes. Drain and rinse under cold running water. Drain again. Pinch each onion at the top so that it pops out of the skin at the root end. Set aside.

Cut off the mushroom stems flush with the caps. Quarter the caps. Set aside.

continued

Melt the butter in a medium frying pan over medium heat. Add the cumin, cayenne, salt, black pepper and sugar. Cook for 1 minute. Add all the vegetables. Stir for 2 minutes.

Add the chestnuts and stir to combine. Add the lemon juice and ¾ cup water. Raise the heat and bring to a boil. Cook, uncovered, over high heat until the liquid is reduced to a syrupy glaze and the carrots and onions are tender. If the vegetables are not tender when the sauce has become thick and syrupy, add another ¼ cup water and reduce again.

Taste for seasoning; add additional salt, cayenne or black pepper and cumin as desired. If adding cumin or cayenne, cook for another minute, taking care not to let the glaze burn.

Makes 3 cups; serves 4 to 6 as a side dish

Carrot Bread

In the sixties, carrot and zucchini breads were staples of the commune and vegetarian kitchens. It is worth reviving them today.

Vegetables used as a major component in bread making keep the bread moist for a long time. Carrots add attractive tweedy flecks of orange. A half cup of shredded carrots can be added to almost any nonsweet loaf with good results.

> 3 cups all-purpose flour
>
> 1½ tablespoons baking soda
>
> ½ teaspoon kosher salt
>
> 8 tablespoons chilled unsalted butter, cut into pieces
>
> ⅔ cup sour cream
>
> 1 medium carrot, peeled, trimmed and grated (about 1 cup)
>
> ¼ cup milk

Place a rack in the center of the oven. Preheat the oven to 375°F.

Sift the flour, baking soda and salt into a bowl. Cut in the butter with a pastry cutter or two butter knives until the butter is in pea-size pieces. Stir in the sour cream, carrot and milk. Mix until just combined. Form the dough into a neat loaf and place in a 9 x 5-inch loaf pan. Make 3 diagonal slashes in the dough, each ¼ inch deep.

Bake for 50 minutes, or until a wooden skewer inserted in the center comes out clean.

Makes 1 loaf

Carrot-Honey Ice Cream

There aren't a million vegetable desserts. The sweetness of carrots lends itself to two that I like and that surprise guests—this ice cream and the sorbet that follows. Serve a spoonful of each and top with some orange sections and even grated chocolate for a dessert that will please any but the confirmed cake eater.

The color of the ice cream is divine.

> 2 pounds slender young carrots, peeled, trimmed and cut into ¼-inch dice (about 6 cups)
>
> 1 cup milk
>
> ⅔ cup honey
>
> ½ teaspoon Chinese five-spice powder
>
> 1 cup heavy cream
>
> 1½ tablespoons fresh lemon juice

Combine the carrots, milk, honey and five-spice powder in a 4-quart saucepan. Bring to a boil over medium heat. Reduce the heat to a simmer. Cover and cook, stirring occasionally, for 20 minutes, or until the carrots are very tender.

Put the carrots, cooking liquid and heavy cream in a blender. Purée until very smooth. Transfer the mixture to a metal bowl. Stir in the lemon juice. Chill, covered, for 2 hours, or until cold.

Churn the carrot mixture in an ice cream maker, according to manufacturer's instructions, for about 25 minutes. Transfer to a container and store in the freezer. **Makes about 2 1/2 pints**

Carrot Sorbet

This is the most extraordinarily beautiful color and takes advantage of the natural sweetness of carrots. Fresh ginger and lemon juice are the counterbalances.

I buy fresh carrot juice from health food stores. Those with juicers can make their own. Carrot juice can also be bought, already in containers, in supermarkets; but it is not as lively in taste or as fresh in color.

While this recipe makes only three and a half cups, it will be plenty on its own for three people, as the flavor is so intense. Paired with lemon sorbet or vanilla ice cream, it will serve six to eight. A thin ginger cookie would not be amiss.

1 cup sugar

3 ounces fresh ginger, peeled and thinly sliced (about 14 thin slices)

2 tablespoons fresh lemon juice

2 cups carrot juice (see headnote)

Combine the sugar, ½ cup water and ginger in a small saucepan. Bring to a strong simmer over low heat. Cook for 20 minutes. Strain and refrigerate. There will be about 1 cup syrup.

Stir the lemon juice into the syrup to liquefy it. Combine with the carrot juice. Churn the carrot mixture in an ice cream maker according to manufacturer's instructions until it has the texture of soft ice cream. Transfer to a container and place in the freezer for 1 hour. Or, if no machine is available, put the mixture in ice cube trays and freeze until almost hard throughout. Put in a food processor and process until just smooth. Store in a container in the freezer. **Makes 3 1/2 cups**

Parsnips

When carrots, only recently orange, were pushy newcomers, parsnips were already a treasured standby in the kitchen. Fashion's vagaries have promoted the carrot to quasi-universality while making the parsnip an occasional visitor. Maybe the coming of refrigeration hastened the carrot's dominance. It used to be that parsnips were prized because they would last virtually forever in a root cellar or in a mound of cool sand.

After the carrots have all been pulled, the parsnip members of the family live on in the garden through first frost, or even until spring. Where the ground doesn't freeze hard, they can be dug right through the winter. I dig them again in early spring, as soon as the earth can be turned in my gelid Vermont garden. The frost intensifies their sweetness and reduces any fibrousness.

A delightfully old-fashioned vegetable that used to turn up in every greengrocer's soup bunch, the parsnip—and its sweet, nutty flavor—deserves to be reintroduced to common use. Add some puréed cooked parsnips to mashed potatoes, or stir them into a winter vegetable soup or, cooked and cubed, into a winter version of chicken fricassee.

In winter, when racking my brain for a side dish, I sometimes have the wit to come up with "parsnips." Parsnips can be elegant as in the Parsnip Flan (page 197) or hearty and down to earth. Elegant, think smoked salmon, smoked eel or even caviar. Hearty, think sausage, roast pork or boiled beef. And don't forget them in chicken soup. Just don't be overgenerous, especially if using carrots and onions too, or there may be more than a desired amount of sweetness.

The French consider parsnips—under the name panais—an essential part of a pot-au-feu. It should be noted in passing that in Italian they are called pastinaca, after their Latin name. Perversely—considering their history—the Italians also call them carota bianca. They use them mainly to ferment into alcohol.

I'm sure there are numerous stews and other soups, such as lentil, that would benefit from small cubes of parsnip cooked in them.

Turn to **PARSNIPS** in the Cook's Guide
for how-tos and to the Index for more recipes.

Parsnip Soup

Parsnips are another root often included in soup, particularly beef soups. As a main ingredient of soup, they are perhaps less common but more delicious.

The sweetness of parsnips that have been in frozen ground is very special. The five-spice powder is an unusual counterpoint.

> 4 large parsnips, peeled, trimmed and cut in half lengthwise and then across into $1/2$-inch pieces
>
> 5 cups Basic Chicken Stock (page 501), Roasted Chicken Stock (page 502) or commercial chicken broth
>
> 1 teaspoon Chinese five-spice powder
>
> 1 tablespoon kosher salt (less if using commercial broth)
>
> Freshly ground black pepper to taste
>
> 4 tablespoons unsalted butter, cut into $1/2$-inch pieces
>
> 3 tablespoons snipped fresh chives (optional)

In a medium saucepan, bring the parsnips, stock and five-spice powder to a boil. Lower the and heat simmer, uncovered, for 15 minutes, or until the parsnips are very soft.

Drain the parsnips in a sieve, reserving the liquid. Purée the solids in a food processor with a little of the reserved liquid, then whisk the purée into the remaining liquid. Or pass the whole thing through the fine disc of a food mill. Scrape the purée back into the pan and bring to a boil. Season with the salt and pepper to taste. Remove from the heat. Stir in the butter and, if using, the chives.

Makes 8 cups; serves 6 as a first course

Roasted Vegetable Combination

This uses carrots, turnips and parsnips and is a wonderful way to save time in the kitchen because these three vegetables roast remarkably well together. The combination can be used in a variety of ways: as a vegetable dish (see Balsamic Root Vegetables, page 140), simmered with

PARSNIPS   195

leftover roasted meat for a stew or puréed for a side dish or as the base of a soup, to be thinned with stock.

> **2 tablespoons unsalted butter, melted**
>
> **1 pound medium carrots, peeled, trimmed, cut in half lengthwise and then across into $1/2$-inch pieces (about 3 cups)**
>
> **1 pound parsnips, peeled, trimmed, cut in half lengthwise and then sliced across into $1/2$-inch pieces (about 3 cups)**
>
> **1 pound turnips, trimmed, peeled and roughly cut into $1/2$-inch pieces (about $2 1/2$ cups)**
>
> **Kosher salt to taste**

Place a rack in the lowest level of the oven. Preheat the oven to 500°F.

Put the melted butter, carrots, parsnips and turnips in a 14 x 12 x 2-inch roasting pan. Toss until the vegetables are lightly coated with butter. Roast for 15 minutes.

Use a spatula to toss and turn the pieces well. Move the pieces nearest the edges of the pan into the center and those in the center to the outer edges, to allow the maximum browning. Roast for 15 minutes more. Most pieces will be nicely browned. Season with salt. Serve warm. **Makes 5 cups; serves 8 to 10 as a side dish**

Vegetable Combination Salad

This room-temperature side dish cum salad makes good use of the Roasted Vegetable Combination. The balsamic vinegar warms up the colors of the parsnips and turnips, making them look like water chestnuts in a Chinese dish. The trio is perfect for a buffet, or for serving over quickly sautéed bitter greens as a vegetarian main course.

When the vegetables are cooked, remove from the roasting pan to a medium bowl. Pour $1/3$ cup balsamic vinegar and $1 1/2$ teaspoons

kosher salt over the vegetables. Using a slotted spoon, toss gently. Let cool to room temperature, tossing occasionally.

Roasted Vegetable Combination with Kielbasa

Putting a kielbasa sausage in the center of the oven halfway through the vegetable cooking time turns the vegetable combination into a hearty, hot dinner to serve with beer, or a Cahors or Barbera red wine, and mustard. Simply slice the sausage and season the vegetables with vinegar and salt.

Place a second rack in the center of the oven. Prick a ring of kielbasa sausage in about 6 different spots with the tip of a sharp knife. Put in a small roasting pan. After the vegetables have roasted for 15 minutes, place the sausage on the center rack. Roast for the remaining 15 minutes, or until warm throughout.

To serve, slice the ring of sausage on the diagonal into 10 to 20 pieces. Arrange the sausage on top of the vegetables. Serve warm. **Serves 4 as a main course**

Oven-Braised Parsnips

I don't remember what brought this somewhat nutty combination to my mind, but it works splendidly.

> **2 medium tangerines (6 to 7 ounces each)**
>
> **1 pound medium parsnips, peeled, trimmed and cut crosswise into thicker and thinner halves**
>
> **2 tablespoons unsalted butter**
>
> **$3/4$ cup Basic Chicken Stock (page 501), Roasted Chicken Stock (page 502) or commercial chicken broth**
>
> **1 tablespoon tarragon vinegar**
>
> **1 teaspoon kosher salt**
>
> **Freshly ground black pepper to taste**

Place a rack in the center of the oven. Preheat the oven to 350°F.

Grate the zest from 1½ tangerines, or enough to make 1 tablespoon. Squeeze 1 tangerine to get ¼ cup juice. Set aside.

Slice the thickest part of the parsnips lengthwise into quarters or halves so that they are the same thickness as the thinner halves.

Put the butter in a 12 x 10 x 2-inch roasting pan. Place the pan in the oven for 1 minute to melt the butter. Remove from the oven. Toss the parsnips in the pan, turning to coat evenly with butter. Spread out in a single layer.

Combine the stock, zest, juice, vinegar, salt and just a touch of pepper. Pour over the parsnips. Bake for 40 minutes, turning the vegetable over every 10 minutes.

Bake for about 20 minutes more without turning the parsnips. The parsnips will be tender and the sauce reduced to a glaze.

Serves 4 to 5 as a side dish

Parsnip Flan

This is one of the best of the flans. As a first course, it is sensational counterpointed by a thin slice of smoked salmon.

1/2 pound parsnips, peeled, trimmed and cut into chunks

1 shallot, chopped

1 1/2 teaspoons unsalted butter, cut into bits

1/2 cup Basic Chicken Stock (page 501), Roasted Chicken Stock (page 502) or commercial chicken broth

Vegetable oil for greasing molds

1/4 cup heavy cream

2 large egg yolks

Kosher salt and freshly ground black pepper to taste

Put the parsnips, shallot, butter and chicken stock in a small saucepan. Bring to a boil. Reduce the heat and simmer, covered, for 20 minutes, or until the parsnips are very soft. Cool slightly.

Preheat the oven to 350°F. Lightly grease eight 4-ounce (½-cup) ramekins with oil. Line a baking pan large enough to hold the ramekins with several thicknesses of newspaper. Set aside.

Transfer the parsnip mixture to a food processor. Process until smooth. Add the cream and egg yolks. Process until well combined. Season with salt and pepper.

Divide the mixture evenly among the ramekins. Place the ramekins in the lined pan and add enough hot water to come halfway up the sides of the ramekins. Bake for 35 minutes, or until a knife inserted into a flan comes out clean. Remove from the water bath; cool slightly.

Run a knife around each flan and unmold onto a serving platter or individual dishes. Serve immediately. **Serves 8 as a side dish or first course**

Microwave Variation
Lightly grease eight 4-ounce (½-cup) ramekins with oil. Set aside.

Place the parsnips and shallot in a 2-quart soufflé dish. Add the butter and stock. Cover tightly with microwave plastic wrap. Cook at 100% for 5 minutes. Pierce the plastic to release the steam.

Uncover and transfer the mixture to a food processor. Process until smooth. Add the cream and egg yolks. Process until well combined. Season with salt and pepper.

Pour ¼ cup of the mixture into each ramekin. Place the ramekins in a 14 x 11 x 2-inch dish. Add water to come to a depth of 1 inch. Cover tightly with microwave plastic wrap. Cook at 100% for 8 minutes.

Pierce the plastic with the tip of a sharp knife. Remove the ramekins from the oven. Let stand for 3 minutes.

continued

Uncover, and unmold the flans onto a serving platter or individual dishes. Serve immediately. **Serves 8 as a side dish or a first course**

Parsnip Purée

Cooking the parsnips in the milk, instead of separately in water, retains all their flavor.

> 2¹/₄ pounds parsnips, peeled, trimmed and
> cut into ¹/₄-inch dice (about 6 cups)
>
> 1 cup milk
>
> 1 cup heavy cream
>
> Kosher salt to taste

Combine the parsnips and milk in a 4-quart saucepan. Bring to a boil over medium heat. Reduce the heat to a simmer. Cover and cook, stirring occasionally, for 20 minutes, or until the parsnips are very tender.

Put the parsnips, cooking liquid and heavy cream in a food processor. Purée until very smooth. Season with salt. **Makes 5 cups**

Parsnip Potato Purée

Parsnips have a sweet and spicy taste that will come as a surprise to eaters of what looks like mashed potatoes.

To make this dish on the stovetop, simmer the parsnips and potato (peeled and cut into chunks) in the water, covered, for twenty minutes, or until very tender. Proceed with the recipe.

> 1 pound parsnips, peeled, trimmed and cut into
> 1¹/₂-inch chunks
>
> 1 floury potato, baked, peeled and riced
>
> 4 tablespoons unsalted butter
>
> 1 to 1¹/₂ cups heavy cream, heated until hot

> 2 teaspoons kosher salt
>
> ¹/₂ teaspoon freshly ground black pepper

Combine the parsnips and 1 cup water in a 4-cup glass measure. Cover tightly with microwave plastic wrap. Cook at 100% for 8 minutes.

Pierce the plastic to release the steam. Uncover and place the parsnips and water in a food processor. Process until smooth. Add the remaining ingredients and process until well combined. **Makes 4 cups**

Parsnip Ice Cream

I know, I'm pushing it; but sometimes when I do, there is a good outcome. Try it. It is wonderful, if unconventional.

> 2¹/₄ pounds parsnips, peeled, trimmed and
> cut into ¹/₄-inch dice (about 6 cups)
>
> 1¹/₂ cups milk
>
> ²/₃ cup sugar
>
> 1 cup heavy cream

Combine the parsnips, 1 cup milk and the sugar in a 4-quart saucepan. Bring to a boil over medium heat. Reduce the heat to a simmer. Cover and cook, stirring occasionally, for 20 minutes, or until the parsnips are very tender.

Put the parsnips, cooking liquid, the remaining ½ cup milk and heavy cream in a blender. Purée until very smooth. Transfer the mixture to a metal bowl. Chill, covered, for 2 hours, or until cold.

Churn the parsnip mixture in an ice cream maker according to manufacturer's instructions, for about 25 minutes. Transfer to a container and store in the freezer. **Makes 1¹/₂ quarts**

Celery

This lovely vegetable, traditionally an herb, is massively ignored except in chicken soup or chicken or tuna fish salad, or for display in a cut-glass bowl with olives. There used to be special dishes just the length of a trimmed celery stalk with its top edges curling in. Even in these simple forms, it tends to be misused: Celery needs to be well washed and then strung thoroughly by peeling with a vegetable peeler.

Two-and-a-half-inch pieces make good containers at a cocktail party for seasoned cream cheese, salads with everything in small dice or purées such as chicken liver.

Considering that it is almost entirely water and cellulose, celery has a surprisingly elegant and delicate taste. Try cooked celery, leaves included, mixed with basic béchamel. If desired, top with grated mozzarella or Swiss cheese and brown under the broiler. Add a cup of cooked celery to two cups cooked potatoes before mashing them. For a spectacular soup, puréed or not, combine a cup of cooked celery, a cup and a half of chicken stock and a cup of cooked cubed potatoes. A touch of cream would not be wrong. Salt and pepper to taste.

Turn to **CELERY** in the Cook's Guide for how-tos and to the Index for more recipes.

Braised Celery

Braised celery is a gentle dish of palest greenish yellow. Cooked celery has a fine, but not intense, flavor. Made with oil, this can be served at room temperature with a vinaigrette that is not overwhelming. Rather than the anchovies that accompany the look-alike fennel, try adding some good sardines, grilled fresh ones or canned ones in olive oil and drained.

Basically, I braise celery in two ways. One is in the oven and takes time but is easy. The other is in the microwave; it takes much less time and is also easy (see page 565). In the microwave, I use trimmed-down hearts, which requires more hearts to serve the same number of people: four pieces per person versus two for a first course or one for a side dish from the regular oven. In the regular oven, I have a slight preference for butter over olive oil. If using vegetable stock, dissolve a packet of gelatin in it.

Beware when adding salt; celery is naturally salty. This is something I learned to my astonishment when checking the nutritional analysis for *Microwave Healthstyle Cookbook*. The

liquid from the braising is delicious. Even if I don't serve it, I keep the liquid for a soup or stew.

Either method will leave a plentiful supply of stalks to be used in soups, salads or stews. The large bunches used here will result in about a pound of stalks each.

> 3 tablespoons olive oil or unsalted butter
>
> 2 bunches celery (about 2 1/2 pounds each)
>
> 1 cup stock—my favorite, Beef Stock (page 502), or after that, Roasted Chicken Stock (page 502), Vegetable Broth (page 506) or commercial broth (no bouillon cubes— too salty)
>
> Kosher salt to taste
>
> 1 1/2 teaspoons cornstarch to thicken cooking liquid (optional)
>
> 1/2 teaspoon fresh lemon juice (if using olive oil)

Place a rack in the bottom third of the oven. Preheat the oven to 325°F.

Thoroughly grease a glass or ceramic baking dish about 12 x 10 inches with 1 tablespoon of the oil or butter. (I use a glass oval dish.)

Cut off a very small slice at the base of each celery to clean but not separate the stalks. Cut across the tops so as to have a heart about 4 inches long. Retain the stalks for another use; reserve the leaves. With a vegetable peeler, remove as much of the fibrous outside of each heart as possible. Cut each heart in quarters lengthwise. Remove any leaves at the center; they may scorch. Chop enough of the reserved leaves to make about 2 tablespoons; set aside.

Arrange the quarters of heart in the baking dish so that they do not overlap. Pour on the stock. Cover tightly with aluminum foil. Place in the oven and cook for 30 minutes. Uncover and, using tongs, turn each piece over. Cover again and cook for another 30 minutes.

Remove the foil. Turn the pieces once more and cook for 30 minutes. Turn again and top each piece with a little of the remaining 2 tablespoons oil (and ½ teaspoon lemon juice) or butter.

Serve as is with an even share of the cooking liquid, with or without salt as needed. If a thicker sauce is preferred, let the liquid cool down. Place the cornstarch in a small saucepan and slowly stir in the cooking liquid, avoiding lumps. Bring to a boil. Add the reserved leaves, reduce the heat and simmer for 3 to 5 minutes, stirring constantly, until the sauce is thickened. Taste and season with salt and the optional lemon juice. Spoon over the celery and serve. If not thickening the sauce, scatter the leaves over the celery before serving.

Serves 4 as a first course, 8 as a side dish

Stovetop Braised Celery Hearts

While this certainly makes a nice light side dish, you can also use it as a first course. For a true indulgence, make the version with meat glaze and serve it with slices of marrow or perhaps under foie gras.

> **4 celery hearts, trimmed to 4-inch lengths (each heart should have about 7 ribs and weigh 4 to 6 ounces)**
>
> **¹/₂ cup Basic Chicken Stock (page 501), Roasted Chicken Stock (page 502) or commercial chicken broth**

Cut a very thin slice from the base of the celery hearts; without separating the stalks, peel the outer ribs. Cut lengthwise into halves or quarters.

Put the celery in the top of a two-part steamer or on a steaming rack or a plate in a bamboo steamer. Fill the bottom of the steamer pan or a pan large enough to hold the bamboo or steaming rack with water; the water should not touch the rack. Bring to a boil over medium heat. Place the celery on top and cover. If the celery is cut into quarters, steam for 4 minutes, turn the pieces over and steam for 3 minutes more. If it is cut into halves, steam 5 minutes, turn the pieces over and steam for 5 to 6 minutes more. The celery should be cooked but retain some crunch. Rinse under cold running water. Drain.

Arrange the celery in a single layer in a 12-inch skillet. Add the stock, cover and cook for 20 minutes over medium-low heat. Uncover and cook until the liquid has evaporated.

Serves 4 as a side dish

Braised Celery Hearts with Meat Glaze
Preheat the broiler. Combine 6 tablespoons Enriched Beef Stock (page 504), 1½ teaspoons unsalted butter and a pinch each of kosher salt and freshly ground black pepper in a small saucepan. Cook over low heat until reduced to a glaze. Arrange the braised celery in a single layer in an ovenproof dish. Brush with the glaze. Broil for 6 minutes, or until there is a hint of color.

Celery Slaw

This is a variation on coleslaw with some extra crunch. Serve it as coleslaw, with anything from hamburgers to simple festive foods.

> **¹/₄ cup sour cream**
>
> **¹/₄ cup plus 2 tablespoons Classic Mayonnaise (page 455), Cooked-Yolk Mayonnaise (page 455) or commercial mayonnaise**
>
> **1 tablespoon red wine vinegar**
>
> **¹/₂ teaspoon kosher salt**
>
> **¹/₈ teaspoon freshly ground black pepper**
>
> **¹/₄ teaspoon sugar**
>
> **2 drops hot red pepper sauce**

continued

Pinch of paprika

5 cups thinly sliced celery, cut on the diagonal

3 tablespoons slivered pimientos or roasted red
  peppers (see the Cook's Guide, page 628)

Mix together all the ingredients except the celery and pimientos or roasted peppers. Place the celery and peppers in a bowl and toss with the dressing. **Makes about 3 cups**

Celery Soup

It is absolutely amazing to me just how much flavor and pleasure utter simplicity can give. Basically, this recipe has only two ingredients. Salt can be added, but I don't think it is necessary; celery has so much salt on its own. A light chicken stock is all that is needed. However, even chicken broth right from the can does extremely well.

I prefer this as a hot soup with its pale green color and light flavor. It can be served as a cold soup with some sour cream swirled in. I tried yogurt and sweet cream, and neither one worked as well.

The soup can be puréed in two ways. The easiest is in the food processor. I prefer it put through a food mill; it retains just enough texture. With the food mill, just keep turning until there is almost nothing left besides strings.

2 1/2 pounds celery, preferably with leaves,
  trimmed and cut into 1-inch pieces
  (about 12 cups)

3 cups Basic Chicken Stock (page 501) or
  commercial chicken broth

Combine the celery and stock in a pot and bring to a boil, covered. Reduce to a simmer and cook for 30 minutes.

Put through the fine disc of a food mill. Or drain, reserving the liquid. Purée the solids in a food processor, and combine with the reserved liquid. **Makes 6 to 7 cups**

Celery Purée

This is a pale, pale green purée that is aromatic.

1 pound celery, peeled and cut across into
  1/4-inch pieces (about 2 cups)

2 tablespoons chopped celery leaves,
  if available

1 floury potato, cooked, peeled and riced

1/2 cup heavy cream

3 tablespoons unsalted butter, softened

Kosher salt and freshly ground black pepper
  to taste

Put the celery in the top of a two-part steamer, or on a steaming rack or a plate in a bamboo steamer. Fill the bottom of the steamer pan or a pan large enough to hold the bamboo or steaming rack with water; the water should not touch the rack. Bring to a boil over medium heat. Place the celery on top, cover and steam for 7 minutes, or until very tender.

Transfer to a food processor. Add the celery leaves, potato, cream and butter and process until well combined. Season to taste. **Makes 1 1/2 cups**

Microwave Variation

Place the celery in a microwave-safe plastic bag with 1 tablespoon water and close tight. Cook at 100% for 5 to 6 minutes, until tender. Unwrap and place in a food processor. Process until smooth. Add the remaining ingredients except the salt and pepper and process until well combined. Season to taste.

Celery Soup

Add 1½ cups Basic Chicken Stock (page 501), Roasted Chicken Stock (page 502) or commercial chicken broth to the purée. Stir to combine and serve hot. **Serves 4 as a first course**

Fillet of Sole over Celery

In this recipe, the sole is cut into strips that curl up alluringly when cooked. The dish looks like spring, all white and pale green, and has a light but especially good flavor.

- 8 center stalks celery with leaves, peeled and thinly sliced across, leaves left whole

- 4 sole fillets (about 6 ounces each), each sliced crosswise into 4 strips

- ¼ cup Basic Fish Stock (page 505), Basic Chicken Stock (page 501), Roasted Chicken Stock (page 502) or commercial chicken broth

- 3 tablespoons unsalted butter, cut into pieces

- 4 teaspoons green peppercorns in brine, drained

- 1 teaspoon kosher salt

- 2 teaspoons fresh lemon juice

- ¼ teaspoon celery seeds

Put the celery in the top of a two-part steamer or on a steaming rack or a plate in a bamboo steamer. Fill the bottom of the steamer or a pan large enough to hold the bamboo or steaming rack with water; the water should not touch the rack. Bring to a boil over medium heat. Place the celery on top, cover and steam for 4 minutes, or until just underdone. Transfer to a skillet.

Place the fish on top of the celery. Pour the broth or stock into the pan. Top the fish evenly with the remaining ingredients. Bring to a boil. Reduce the heat to low. Cook, covered, until the fish is barely opaque, about 2 minutes. Gently spoon celery, fish and sauce onto serving plates. **Serves 4 as a main course**

Celery Root

Celery root (aka celeriac) is most famous for the classic French dish céléri rémoulade, where it is tossed—cooked or raw—with a mayonnaise. I have found a few other uses that I like. To deal with its obdurate exterior, see the information in the Cook's Guide, page 565.

All of the rémoulades and salads here make good first courses on their own or paired with prosciutto, ham, smoked salmon, smoked eel or other fish. They are also invaluable for picnics, as they don't get soggy as they sit.

Turn to **CELERY ROOT** in the Cook's Guide
for how-tos and to the Index for more recipes.

Celery Root Salad

Instead of mayonnaise, this salad uses a mustard-intense vinaigrette.

3 tablespoons Dijon mustard

1 tablespoon red wine vinegar

3 tablespoons olive oil

2 teaspoons chopped fresh parsley

$1/4$ teaspoon kosher salt

Good pinch of freshly ground black pepper

$3/4$ pound celery root, peeled and trimmed, cut into 2 x $1/4$ x $1/4$-inch matchsticks (about 3 cups)

Put the mustard in a medium bowl and whisk in the vinegar. Gradually whisk in the oil, beginning with drops and increasing to a steady stream. Add the parsley and season with the salt and pepper. Whisk again and toss in the celery root. **Serves 4 as a first course**

Celery Root, Smoked Mozzarella and Prosciutto Salad

Insalata caprese, interspersed slices of mozzarella and tomato dribbled with basil vinaigrette, is a classic of summer. This is a similar invention for winter.

2 tablespoons Dijon mustard

3 tablespoons red wine vinegar

$1/2$ cup olive oil

Pinch of kosher salt

Freshly ground black pepper to taste

$1/3$ cup celery root cut into matchsticks

24 very thin slices smoked mozzarella

24 very thin slices prosciutto

2 tablespoons chopped fresh flat-leaf parsley

Place the mustard in a small bowl and whisk in the vinegar. Gradually whisk in the oil, beginning with drops and then increasing to a steady stream. Season with the salt and pepper. Fold in the celery root.

Overlap 4 mozzarella and 4 prosciutto slices across each of six salad plates. Strew the celery root and dressing over the middle. Sprinkle with the parsley. **Serves 6 as a first course**

Celery Root Rémoulade

This is a classic of French cooking, a good first course on its own. A smaller portion can be served to accompany another vegetable first course. It is also a perfect counterpoint to cold fish or chicken, or for grilled meats or fish.

For variation, substitute for the dressing a quarter cup of the Spicy Rémoulade (page 458) or New Orleans Spicy Rémoulade Sauce (page 458). (Freshly grated horseradish added at the last minute gives an intriguingly spicy note to the salad. Paul Levy got this idea from Eva Chadwick, widow of the sculptor Lynn Chadwick.)

1 celery root (about 12 ounces), peeled and trimmed

$1/4$ cup Classic Mayonnaise (page 455), Cooked-Yolk Mayonnaise (page 455) or a good mayonnaise made with lemon

1 tablespoon Dijon mustard

1 tablespoon fresh lemon juice

$1/2$ teaspoon kosher salt

Coarsely shred the celery root in a food processor, or julienne by hand.

Place the celery root in a 10-inch quiche dish or pie plate. Cover tightly with microwave plastic wrap. Cook in a microwave at 100% for 2 minutes.

continued

Remove from the oven. Prick the plastic to release the steam and uncover. Stir in the remaining ingredients. Chill before serving.

Makes 4 cups, serves 4 as a first course

Cream of Celery Root Soup

It's hard to believe that this soup has its origins in a truly ugly vegetable. If there is a little extra celery root, cut it into matchstick strips and put them in water to cover with a little lemon juice. When ready to serve, stir in the raw root for a pleasant crunch.

1 1/2 pounds celery root, peeled and trimmed, cut into chunks

2 3/4 cups Basic Chicken Stock (page 501), Roasted Chicken Stock (page 502) or commercial chicken broth

1/2 cup heavy cream

1 tablespoon kosher salt

Freshly ground black pepper to taste

Freshly grated nutmeg for serving (optional)

In a medium saucepan, bring the celery root and stock to a boil. Lower the heat and simmer, covered, for 20 minutes.

In a blender, working in batches of no more than 2 cups, purée the celery root with the stock. Return to the pan, stir in the cream and heat through. Season with the salt and pepper.

Sprinkle nutmeg over each serving, if desired. **Makes 4 cups**

Puréed Celery Root with Apples

An unusual fall or winter purée, this goes brilliantly with roast pork or grilled sausages. For a quick and simplified purée without apples, see the recipe that follows.

1 pound celery root, peeled and trimmed, cut into chunks

1 quart milk

3/4 pound Golden Delicious apples

2 to 4 tablespoons heavy cream

Kosher salt and freshly ground black pepper to taste

In a medium saucepan, bring the celery root and milk to a simmer over medium heat. Cover and cook for 10 minutes.

Meanwhile, peel, core and quarter the apples. Add to the celery root and cook together for 10 minutes longer, or until the celery root is tender.

Drain, reserving the milk. Purée the celery root and apples in a food processor for 3 minutes adding the cream and about 1/2 cup of the reserved milk. Season to taste with salt and pepper.

If the purée is not completely smooth, push it through a fine sieve. Warm, if necessary, before serving. **Makes a scant 2 cups**

Celery Root Purée

This very simple purée has its celery flavor boosted with an optional sprinkling of celery seeds.

1 1/4 pounds celery root, peeled and trimmed, cut into 1/2-inch dice (about 2 1/2 cups)

2 tablespoons unsalted butter

Kosher salt and freshly ground black pepper to taste

1/2 teaspoon celery seeds (optional)

Put the celery root in the top of a two-part steamer or on a steaming rack or a plate in a bamboo steamer. Fill the bottom of the steamer pan or a pan large enough to hold the bamboo or steaming rack with water; the water should not touch the rack. Bring to a boil over medium heat. Place the celery root on top, cover and steam for 10 to 12 minutes, or until tender. Cool slightly.

Transfer the celery root to a food processor. Add the butter and process until smooth. Season with salt and pepper.

Serve sprinkled with the celery seeds, if desired. **Makes 1 cup**

Microwave Variation
Place the celery root in a glass or ceramic bowl just large enough to hold it. Tightly cover with plastic wrap. Cook at 100% for 9 minutes. Prick the plastic to release the steam. Remove from the oven and transfer to a food processor. Proceed as directed.

Celery Root and Potato Purée
Cook the celery root. Cook a medium floury potato (about 7 ounces). Peel. Purée with the celery root and butter, adding ¼ cup heavy cream. Add salt to taste. **Makes 2 cups**

Winter Vegetable Purée
Combine the Celery Root and Potato Purée with 1 cup Parsnip Purée (page 198). Season to taste. **Makes 3 cups**

Three-Vegetable Winter Cream Soup
Combine the Winter Vegetable Purée with 2½ cups Basic Chicken Stock (page 501), Roasted Chicken Stock (page 502) or commercial chicken broth in a 2-quart glass measure. Add ½ cup heavy cream and 1 teaspoon kosher salt. Tightly cover with microwave plastic wrap. Heat in a microwave at 100% for 5 minutes. Or heat on top of the stove until warmed through.
Makes 6 cups; serves 6 as a first course

Gratin of Celery Root

Now this is a truly elegant dish. The celery root simmering in the stock provides a heady perfume. The finished browned and bubbling gratin goes with any roast or can be served with a group of other vegetable dishes. Substitute a good vegetarian stock for the chicken stock to make the gratin vegetarian.

> 3 cups Basic Chicken Stock (page 501), Roasted Chicken Stock (page 502) or commercial chicken broth
>
> 1½ teaspoons kosher salt, or to taste
>
> 2½ pounds celery root, peeled and trimmed, quartered lengthwise, each wedge cut in ¼-inch slices (about 8 cups)
>
> 1½ cups heavy cream
>
> Freshly ground black pepper to taste
>
> ½ cup Dried Bread Crumbs (page 510) or store-bought
>
> ½ cup finely grated Gruyère cheese
>
> ¼ cup freshly grated Parmesan cheese

Place a rack in the center of the oven. Preheat the oven to 400°F.

Heat the chicken stock to boiling in a medium saucepan. Add the salt. Add half the celery root and boil until tender but still firm, about 6 minutes. Remove with a slotted spoon. Repeat with the remaining celery root. Spread evenly in a 12-inch oval gratin dish.

Pour the cream into the chicken stock. Boil until reduced to 1 cup. Taste; season with pepper and with additional salt, if desired. Pour the cream mixture over the celery root.

Stir together the bread crumbs, Gruyère and Parmesan. Sprinkle evenly over the celery root.

Bake until golden brown and bubbling, about 25 minutes. Allow to cool slightly before serving.
Serves 12 as a side dish

Fennel

Fennel is a variety of things to the cook. There are the bulbs, which are actually swellings of the stalk above the ground. Large ones are about three to four inches across. Baby versions of the same plant have bulbs that are only about an inch and a half to two inches wide. This kind of tame fennel is often called Florence fennel. Wild fennel is a tall, terrific weed with tough stalks and attractive green fronds. The tame fennel also has similar fronds. Both are delicious flavorings.

The stalks can be used to stuff and flavor fish or chicken as they roast or they can be dried and flamed under fish that is being grilled outdoors, as is done in the South of France.

It used to be that fennel bulbs could be found only in Italian enclaves of large cities for very limited seasons. Today, fennel is generally available. It is one of my favorite dippers among crudités with a well-seasoned dip (see Index for recipes.)

I grow it, but my fennel will not be the envy of commercial growers. It gets to a reasonable—not large—size late in my short season. When I first grew it, I had no idea what to expect. I didn't realize that the goiter-like swelling of the stalks that forms the bulb grows above the ground, but close to it. The first year, I didn't space the plants and ended up dwarfing them. Small is good for braising, but these were ridiculous.

Although this is the vegetable variety, do not discard the tops; they are very decorative and full of flavor. They can be strewn on top of whatever dish is being made or chopped and added raw to a salad.

Recently, attractive flat and expensive tins that contain "fennel pollen" have arrived on the market from Italy. It is a nice thing to have on hand and comes in a variety of flavoring mixtures. It was originally rubbed into meat and fish before roasting. Fennel seeds, which look much like dill seeds, are very good in their own right. They can be powdered in a spice mill to give a somewhat less subtle version of the pollen. (Who ever said subtlety was my strong suit?)

Almost all of the fennel recipes, with their mildly licorice flavor, make wonderful first courses or parts of first courses. Fennel has a rich full taste and is at the same time light. There are vegetarian dishes here as well as those that are clearly not.

The licorice flavor will be more pronounced in the crisp raw recipes. It is mellower in the cooked dishes. Essentially a Mediterranean vegetable, fennel combines well with olive oil, lemon, garlic, tomatoes and olives.

Turn to **FENNEL** in the Cook's Guide for how-tos and to the Index for more recipes.

Kalamata Antipasto

Various Mediterranean countries make lightly pickled antipasto mixtures of vegetables to use ad lib. Bread—such as pita—toothpicks or small forks are all the equipment needed. Chunks of feta that have been rinsed in water may be added. Pass an attractive bottle or cruet of good Kalamata olive oil for guests to dribble on top if they want.

On a hot summer evening, serve a half cup of this to each of six guests with the cheese and the olive oil. The recipe is easily multiplied. At a cocktail party, allow a quarter cup per person.

I like this as a vegetable with cold lamb, fish or chicken.

10 ounces Kalamata olives in brine

$1/2$ medium fennel bulb, trimmed and cut into 2 x $1/4$-inch strips (about 1 cup)

$1/2$ cup roasted peppers (see the Cook's Guide, page 628) or bottled roasted red peppers (about half a 7-ounce jar), cut into $2^1/2$ x $1/4$-inch strips

2 tablespoons minced fennel fronds

$1/4$ cup red wine vinegar

$1/4$ teaspoon freshly ground black pepper

Combine all the ingredients, including the olive brine, with ¼ cup water in a large bowl. Spoon into a jar with a tight-fitting lid. There should be enough liquid to cover all the ingredients. Cover and store in the refrigerator, shaking occasionally, for at least 3 days, and up to 1 week.

continued

Bring to room temperature and drain the brine before serving; reserve the brine. If there is any of the antipasto left, put it back in the brine and store in the refrigerator. **Makes 3 cups**

Anchovies with Fennel Marinade

Anchovies and fennel seem destined for each other, whether the fennel is raw or cooked. Use whole salted anchovies soaked in water and filleted or canned anchovy fillets packed in olive oil. Rinse them under warm water before using.

Small plates, bread and intense flavor make this enough on its own; but olives and prosciutto can be added to the plate for those who cannot bear the idea of seeming sparseness.

> **12 ounces whole, salt-packed anchovies or 8 ounces canned anchovy fillets**
>
> **2¹/₂ ounces fennel, trimmed and cut lengthwise into slivers (about ³/₄ cup)**
>
> **Freshly ground black pepper to taste**
>
> **³/₄ cup olive oil**
>
> **¹/₂ cup fresh lemon juice**
>
> **¹/₄ cup chopped fennel fronds**

If using whole, salt-packed anchovies, fillet them by pulling off the heads and running a thumbnail along the backbone to separate them into two fillets. Pull or scrape off as many of the little bones as possible and soak the fillets in a bowl with plenty of cold water to cover until softened, about 20 minutes. Rinse under warm water briefly to remove scales and remaining bones. Pat dry.

Lay half the anchovies in the bottom of a small dish. Top with half the fennel slivers and some pepper. Repeat with the remaining anchovies and fennel; season with pepper.

Whisk the olive oil and lemon juice. Pour over the layers. Refrigerate for at least 12 hours.

Sprinkle with the fennel fronds before serving. **Makes about 1 cup; serves 4 as a first course**

Roasted Fennel with Caramelized Tomato Sauce

Yummy and particularly good just with potatoes or with roast chicken, fish, lamb or pork.

> **2 large fennel bulbs (1¹/₄ pounds each), trimmed, fronds reserved, and each bulb cut through the core into 6 wedges**
>
> **3 tablespoons unsalted butter, cut into 3 pieces**
>
> **³/₄ cup Plum Tomato Purée (page 459), sterile-pack strained tomatoes or puréed canned plum tomatoes**
>
> **¹/₄ cup Basic Chicken Stock (page 501), Roasted Chicken Stock (page 502) or commercial chicken broth**
>
> **1 tablespoon fresh lemon juice**
>
> **¹/₄ teaspoon kosher salt, or to taste**

Place a rack in the center of the oven. Preheat the oven to 500°F.

Chop enough of the reserved fennel fronds to get 2 tablespoons. Set aside.

Put the butter in a 12 x 10 x 2-inch roasting pan. Place the pan in the oven for 1 minute to melt the butter. Remove from the oven. Toss the fennel into the pan, turning to coat evenly with butter.

Roast the fennel for 17 minutes. Turn the fennel over and roast for another 10 minutes, or until golden brown. Remove the pan from the oven.

Reduce the oven temperature to 350°F.

Pour the tomato purée and stock over the fennel. Return the pan to the oven and bake for 25 minutes, or until tender, turning the fennel once halfway through cooking. Remove the fennel to a platter with a slotted spoon. Add the lemon juice and salt to the sauce in the pan. Pour over the fennel and sprinkle with the fennel fronds.

Makes 2 cups; serves 4 as a first course, 6 as a side dish

Eggplant, Tomato and Fennel

This is a sensational first course, major vegetable course or vegetarian main dish that cannot be made anywhere as well as in the microwave oven, which permits the vegetables to stay whole and still lend their juices.

- 4 small Japanese eggplants (about 3^1/$_2$ inches long), calyx removed and each pricked 4 times with a fork
- 4 large plum tomatoes (about ^{2}/$_3$ pound), each pricked 4 times with a fork
- ^{1}/$_2$ fennel bulb, trimmed and quartered lengthwise
- 4 large cloves garlic, smashed and peeled
- 3 sprigs fresh basil
- ^{1}/$_4$ teaspoon fresh thyme leaves
- ^{1}/$_4$ teaspoon olive oil
- 1 teaspoon kosher salt
- Freshly ground black pepper to taste

Arrange the eggplants spoke-fashion, stems toward the center, around the rim of a 2-quart soufflé dish. Place the tomatoes in the center. Scatter the fennel on top of the eggplants. Tuck the garlic, basil and thyme among the vegetables. Pour the oil, 1 tablespoon water, the salt and pepper over all.

Cover tightly with microwave plastic wrap. Cook at 100% for 15 minutes.

Remove from the oven. Prick the plastic to release the steam. Uncover and let stand for 3 minutes before serving.

Serves 4 as a first course, 2 as a main course

Roasted Fennel and Pepper Salad

This delicious cold first course contrasts the smoky anise flavor of the fennel with the rich, seemingly oily sweetness of roasted peppers. The peppers can roast at the same time as the fennel—or use jarred peppers. The juices from the two vegetables marry to make the dressing.

- 3 large red bell peppers (8 ounces each) or 1^1/$_2$ cups bottled roasted peppers, drained and rinsed
- 2 to 3 tablespoons olive oil
- 1 large fennel bulb (1^1/$_4$ pounds), trimmed, fronds reserved, and cut lengthwise through the core into ^{1}/$_4$-inch-thick slices so that the pieces stay together
- ^{1}/$_2$ cup balsamic vinegar
- 1^1/$_2$ tablespoons rinsed capers
- ^{1}/$_8$ teaspoon kosher salt
- 1 tablespoon chopped reserved fennel fronds
- Freshly ground black pepper to taste

Place a rack on the top level of the oven, if roasting the peppers, and another rack on the lowest level. Preheat the oven to 500°F.

Put the raw peppers in a 12 x 8 x 1½-inch roasting pan and rub the peppers and pan with 1 tablespoon olive oil. Put the fennel slices in a 14 x 12 x 2-inch roasting pan. Drizzle 1 tablespoon oil over the slices and gently rub them until evenly coated. Arrange the slices so they touch as little as possible.

continued

Roast the peppers on the top rack and the fennel on the bottom rack for 15 minutes. Use a spatula to turn the peppers and fennel, trying to keep the fennel intact. Roast for 15 more minutes.

Remove the fennel slices. Turn the peppers again. Roast them for 15 minutes more. Meanwhile, let the fennel cool, then place in a bowl and drizzle with the remaining 1 tablespoon oil to keep from drying out. Refrigerate the fennel.

After the peppers have roasted a total of 45 minutes, the skins will be scorched and black, which is exactly how they should be. Cool, peel and core them as described on page 628. Tear them into 1-inch wide strips.

Pack the peppers into a clean glass jar. Cover with the balsamic vinegar. Seal tightly. Let marinate in the refrigerator for 2 to 3 hours. The recipe may be prepared several days ahead up to this point.

Before serving, allow the peppers and fennel to come to room temperature. Arrange 2 pieces of fennel with the root ends pointing toward each other in the center of each plate (set the fennel bowl aside). Place 2 large or several small pieces of red pepper across from each other in the two open spaces. Divide any remaining fennel and peppers among the plates, and sprinkle the capers evenly over the salads.

Add 1 tablespoon of the marinade from the peppers and the salt to the liquid remaining in the fennel bowl. Mix. Pour over each serving. Top with a sprinkling of chopped fennel fronds and a grind of black pepper.

Serves 4 as a first course

Fennel Salad

This salad makes a good opener for a meal with pasta as the main course, or use it to follow a tomato-based fish or chicken dish. I also like it on a buffet—it's pretty and doesn't wilt. The recipe can easily be multiplied.

> 1 medium fennel bulb (about 1 pound), trimmed, fronds reserved, halved, cored and cut across into 1/8-inch slices (about 3 cups)
>
> 2 tablespoons fresh lemon juice
>
> 1 small red onion, cut across into 1/8-inch-thick slices (about 1 cup)
>
> 1/4 cup fresh orange juice
>
> 4 teaspoons chopped reserved fennel fronds
>
> 1 tablespoon olive oil
>
> Kosher salt and freshly ground black pepper to taste

In a large bowl, toss the fennel with the lemon juice. Add the remaining ingredients and mix well to combine. **Serves 3 as a first course**

Fennel Soup

This pale soup has an intriguing sweetness from the ricotta behind the lightly anise flavor of the fennel. It can be served hot or cold.

> 4 cups Basic Chicken Stock (page 501), Roasted Chicken Stock (page 502) or commercial chicken broth
>
> 5 medium fennel bulbs, trimmed and fronds reserved, cut into 1-inch cubes
>
> 1 cup part-skim ricotta cheese, cottage cheese or fromage blanc
>
> 2 tablespoons fresh lemon juice

1 tablespoon kosher salt
  (less if using commercial broth)

Freshly ground black pepper to taste

In a medium stockpot, bring the stock to a boil. Add the fennel, cover and return to a boil. Lower the heat and simmer, covered, for about 25 minutes, until the fennel is soft. Pour into a sieve set over a bowl. Reserve the liquid and fennel separately.

Purée the fennel in a food processor until smooth. Add the cheese, lemon juice and enough of the reserved liquid to make a smooth purée; pulse to combine. Scrape into a large bowl and whisk in the remaining liquid. Season with the salt and pepper.

To serve the soup hot, return to the saucepan and heat through. To serve chilled, refrigerate for 2 hours, or overnight. Coarsely chop the reserved fennel tops and sprinkle over the top.

Makes 9 cups; serves 8 as a first course

Roasted Sliced Fennel

This is an unusual side dish that can be served hot or cold. When serving it hot, consider replacing the olive oil with melted butter and the lemon juice with a quarter cup of rich stock.

1 large fennel bulb (1 1/2 pounds), trimmed and
  fronds reserved, cut lengthwise through the
  core into 1/4-inch-thick slices so that the pieces
  stay together

3 tablespoons olive oil

1 tablespoon fresh lemon juice

Kosher salt and freshly ground black pepper
  to taste

Place a rack in the lowest oven position. Preheat the oven to 500°F.

Put the fennel slices in a 14 x 12 x 2-inch roasting pan. Drizzle 1 tablespoon oil over the slices. Gently toss until all slices are evenly coated. Spread the slices out in a single layer so that they touch as little as possible.

Roast for 15 minutes. Turn carefully with a spatula, trying to keep the slices intact. Roast for 15 minutes more.

Drizzle with the remaining 2 tablespoons oil, the lemon juice, salt and pepper. Serve hot or allow to cool.

Chop the reserved fennel fronds. Sprinkle over the slices just before serving.

Makes 1 1/4 cups; serves 4 as a side dish

Braised Fennel

Serve this as an accompaniment to any meat or fish. I especially like it with a lemony veal scaloppini and the Carrot Potato Purée (page 187).

2 tablespoons olive oil

4 small to medium fennel bulbs, trimmed and cut
  through into 4 to 8 wedges, depending on size
  (wedges should be about 2 inches wide at most)

1 teaspoon kosher salt

2 teaspoons fresh lemon juice

2 cups Basic Chicken Stock (page 501),
  Roasted Chicken Stock (page 502) or
  commercial chicken broth, or as needed

Freshly ground black pepper to taste

In a medium pan, heat the olive oil over low heat. Add the fennel pieces and salt. Cook gently for about 10 minutes, turning occasionally, until the fennel is softened. Add the lemon juice. Cook for 10 minutes.

Pour in enough chicken stock to cover the fennel. Simmer gently, partially covered, about 1 hour, until the fennel is very tender. The liquid should be reduced to a glaze. Taste; add pepper and more salt, if desired. To serve, toss the fennel with the glaze to coat.

Serves 6 as a side dish

Double-Garlic Braised Baby Fennel

Whole cloves of garlic braised alongside the fennel add a soft, mellow background note. Chopped garlic added in the last few minutes of cooking provides the balance of a sharp foreground note. While the recipe was developed for simple fish, roasted or broiled, the baby fennel would be just as happy starring with an omelet or other egg dish.

The fish stock can be replaced with chicken stock (page 501) but not with vegetable stock, which lacks the gelatin that makes the sauce so sumptuously good.

12 baby fennel bulbs (about 2 pounds), stems and root ends well trimmed, fronds reserved

¼ cup olive oil

6 cloves garlic, smashed and peeled, plus 4 teaspoons chopped garlic

¼ cup Fresh Tomato Paste (page 459) or commercial tomato paste

1 cup Fish Stock (page 505)

½ teaspoon white wine vinegar

Kosher salt and freshly ground black pepper to taste

2 tablespoons chopped reserved fennel fronds

Cut any large fennels bulbs in half lengthwise so that all pieces are no more than 1½ to 2 inches thick.

Heat the oil in the smallest pan that will hold the fennel in a single layer. Add the fennel. Cook gently over low heat for 10 minutes, turning from time to time, just until the fennel is softened but not browned.

Add the garlic cloves, tomato paste and stock. Bring to a boil. Cover; reduce the heat and simmer for 25 minutes, turning the fennel over every 10 minutes. The fennel will be soft but not mushy and a knife will easily insert into the flesh.

Stir in the chopped garlic. Boil, uncovered, to thicken the sauce. Add the vinegar, salt and pepper. Sprinkle with the fennel fronds.

Serves 4 as a first course, 6 as a side dish

Fennel Compote

This recipe comes from San Domenico restaurant in New York. When I first tasted it, I thought it was eggplant, which just shows how fallible I am and how smooth the fennel gets with slow and gentle cooking, melting it in its own juices. At San Domenico, they use wild fennel seed. That is usually hard to get unless the cook lives in California and can pick fennel by the roadside.

2 medium fennel bulbs (about 2 pounds), trimmed and cut into ¼-inch dice (about 5 cups)

1½ tablespoons olive oil

2 tablespoons Basic Chicken Stock (page 501), Roasted Chicken Stock (page 502) or commercial chicken broth

¼ teaspoon fennel seeds

¾ teaspoon kosher salt

Freshly ground white pepper to taste

In a medium saucepan, toss the fennel with the oil to coat. Add the stock and fennel seeds. Cover. Cook over the lowest heat, stirring two or three times, for 2 hours 15 minutes, or until the fennel is easily mashed by a fork.

Using a potato masher or a fork, mash the fennel into a chunky purée. Season with the salt and pepper. **Makes 2¼ cups**

Basic Fennel with Butter

To make this on the stovetop, steam the fennel according to the instructions on page 583 and then continue with the recipe as instructed.

> **2 large fennel bulbs (about 3 inches in diameter), trimmed, fronds reserved if desired, and cut into 6 wedges each**
>
> **2 tablespoons finely chopped feathery tops of fennel (optional)**
>
> **1 tablespoon unsalted butter, cut into small pieces**
>
> **Kosher salt and freshly ground black pepper to taste**

Place the fennel in an 8-inch soufflé dish or 8-cup glass measure. Top with the fennel tops, if desired. Cover tightly with plastic wrap. Put in the microwave and cook at 100% for 5 minutes. Remove from the oven. Let stand, still wrapped, for 2 minutes. Pierce the plastic with the tip of a sharp knife; uncover the fennel and remove to a serving platter. Top or toss with the butter, salt and pepper. Serve hot. **Serves 4 as a side dish**

NOTE: *To serve 1:* Use 1 small fennel bulb or ½ large bulb and a scant 1 teaspoon butter. Cook for 2 minutes 30 seconds.

To serve 2: Use 1 large fennel bulb and half the amount of butter. Cook for 3 minutes 30 seconds.

Fennel with Lemon Butter
Add 1 teaspoon fresh lemon juice with the other seasonings.

Fennel with Olive Oil and Lemon
Combine 1½ tablespoons olive oil, 1 tablespoon fresh lemon juice, ¾ teaspoon kosher salt and ¼ teaspoon freshly ground black pepper. Add the oil mixture instead of the butter to the warm fennel. Let stand until cool, and serve at room temperature.

Fennel Sardine Sauce

In Sicily, they make rich layered pastas with unusual combinations of flavors. One classic dish is pasta con le sarde, pasta with sardines and wild fennel. This version is robust and I prefer it on substantial pasta such as rigatoni. Use 1½ pounds dry pasta; if you can find it, green rigatoni will add color to the dish. Also look for fennel with lots of bushy fronds to finish the dish.

> **2 medium fennel bulbs (1 pound each), trimmed and cut into 1-inch cubes (about 8 cups), fronds reserved and finely chopped**
>
> **1 head garlic, separated into cloves, cloves smashed and peeled**
>
> **1½ teaspoons fennel seeds**
>
> **1 cup Basic Chicken Stock (page 501), Roasted Chicken Stock (page 502) or commercial chicken broth**
>
> **¼ cup olive oil**
>
> **One 3¾-ounce can sardines packed in olive oil, split and boned**
>
> **One 3-ounce bottle capers, drained**
>
> **Kosher salt and freshly ground black pepper to taste**

continued

Put the fennel, garlic, fennel seeds and stock in a pot just large enough to hold them. Cover. Bring to a boil. Reduce the heat to medium-low and simmer about 15 minutes, turning the fennel occasionally, until it is easily pierced with the tip of a knife. Remove half the fennel with a slotted spoon and reserve.

Transfer the remaining fennel and broth to a food processor. Add the olive oil and sardines and process until fairly smooth. Scrape the mixture into a bowl. Stir in the reserved fennel, the capers, fennel fronds, salt to taste and a generous amount of pepper.

Makes 4 1/4 cups; serves 8 with 1 1/2 pounds pasta, cooked, as a main course

Fennel Sauce

Fennel's gentle licorice scent and taste hint their way into this pale green sauce that can be made with chicken or vegetable broth. It adds a minimum of calories and a nice little boost of nutrition. Its delicate flavor and color would set off scallops or salmon to perfection.

> 1 large fennel bulb (1 1/2 pounds), trimmed and cut into 1-inch chunks (about 4 cups)
>
> 1 1/2 cups Basic Chicken Stock (page 501), Roasted Chicken Stock (page 502), commercial chicken broth or Vegetable Broth (page 506)
>
> 1 tablespoon olive oil
>
> Kosher salt and freshly ground black pepper to taste

Place the fennel and broth in a 2½-quart soufflé dish or casserole. Cover with a lid or microwave plastic wrap. Cook in a microwave at 100% for 15 minutes, or until the fennel is tender. If using plastic, prick it to release the steam.

Uncover and transfer to a blender. Add the oil and blend until smooth. Add salt and pepper to taste. **Makes 2 cups**

Chicories

Chicory, Escarole, Frisée, Puntarelle, Endive and Radicchio

One day many years ago when I was more innocent, I was in Sutton's, the famous English seed house in London, buying seed for the season to come. After much looking, I went up to the counter and complained that I couldn't find any frisée seed. The rather superior young clerk asked me where I had looked. I pointed to the lettuce section. Very condescendingly, he readdressed me to the chicories, where I found what I wanted.

Since then, I have realized that many of my favorite vegetables are actually chicories, whether they be sprawling greens such as escarole, what we call chicory, frisée or puntarelle. Others come in second growths, sometimes blanched. That means that the first growth is cut off and the plant then produces chicons, thin, firm heads, the kind we know best being endive. If they are white endive, they will have been grown in the dark, which blanches them. Others are red and grown in daylight. Among these are most of the Italian varieties of radicchio, such as Verona (a red lettucelike head), Treviso (like a red endive) and Chioggia (a red-and-green mottled lettucelike head).

There is much to be said about the large family of red chicories. Some are like endive second growths, forced in a cold (slightly above freezing), dark environment. Other species of radicchio are field grown. All are early-spring or late-fall-to-winter vegetables due to their need for cold weather. The kind most commonly available in this country, Rosso da Verona, looks like an undernourished red cabbage except that it is softer and costs more.

Other heads of radicchio are more oval in form. Some are quite loose; some are splotched like cranberry beans or red on green; some have pointed leaves. All radicchio are natives of the Veneto around Venice; there they are so varied and important (grown for cooking as vegetables more than for use in salads) that whole cookbooks have been written about them. The most desirable radicchio for cooking is Treviso.

Puntarelle is probably the least known of the chicories in America. In Italy, it is a much prized early spring green. It is much like frisée but upright, with long thin leaves that are whitish to yellow green in color. It is usually served raw with a vinaigrette or just with a dish of good olive oil, through which the leaves are swished by the eater. I first had it served to me by Tony May, the owner of San Domenico in New York and a great supporter of his native Italian foods. It can be tossed in with a hot thin pasta like spaghettini, but that seems a shame.

Turn to **CHICORY, ESCAROLE, FRISÉE, PUNTARELLE, ENDIVE** and **RADICCHIO** under **CHICORIES** in the Cook's Guide for how-tos and to the Index for more recipes.

Bistro Salad

Often in a French bistro I will have this instead of a meal. It is a classic recipe and, with the optional eggs very substantial.

    4 Oeufs Mollets (page 480; optional)

    1 medium head frisée (about 6 ounces), trimmed, cored and washed

    1/2 recipe Bacon Lardons (page 509)

    8 Croutons (page 510), crumbled

    1/2 cup Everyday Vinaigrette (page 449)

    Freshly ground black pepper to taste

Just before serving, make the oeufs mollets, if desired.

While the eggs are cooling, toss the frisée, lardons, croutons and vinaigrette in a bowl until the frisée is coated. Season with pepper. Divide among four plates.

Top each with a peeled egg, if using. Serve immediately. **Serves 4 as a first course**

Frisée with Walnuts and Walnut Oil

Walnut oil, while delicious, can also be expensive. Steeping unsalted walnuts in canola oil for one week will produce a similar tasting substitute at a fraction of the cost. Store any remaining oil in the refrigerator.

DRESSING

DRESSING

1/2 cup walnut oil (see headnote)

1 tablespoon white wine vinegar

1/2 teaspoon kosher salt

2 grinds fresh black pepper

1/2 teaspoon chopped fresh chives

4 cups trimmed and washed frisée
    (small, light leaves only)

6 walnut halves, split lengthwise

Whisk together all the ingredients for the dressing in a wide bowl.

Pass the frisée leaves through the dressing and arrange them like an open flower on a serving plate. Arrange the walnuts in the center. Alternatively, divide the dressed frisée among four individual plates and top each with 3 walnut pieces. **Serves 4 as a first course**

Bitter Greens with Lardons

This recipe makes a lot of salad. To pare it down, make the full amount of dressing, as it stores well and can be reheated. Then, for each serving, toss 2 cups greens with 2 tablespoons dressing and top with 4 lardons.

DRESSING

1 1/2 pounds slab bacon, turned into lardons
    (see page 509)

3/4 cup plus 2 tablespoons malt vinegar

4 teaspoons salt (or to taste, depending on the
    saltiness of the bacon)

1/2 teaspoon freshly ground black pepper

24 cups trimmed and washed assorted bitter
    greens, such as chicory, dandelions, arugula,
    turnip greens and/or escarole

Make the lardons. Reserve the fat.

Pour the vinegar into the hot fat. Boil for 1 minute, scraping the bottom of the skillet. Add the salt and pepper.

Toss with the greens and lardons in a large bowl. **Serves 12 as a first course**

Toasty Treviso with Mozzarella and Anchovies

What a wonderful complexity of flavors—salty, bitter, sweet and unctuous. I serve this as a first course or after the main course instead of salad and cheese. Used this way, two small radicchio halves or three large quarters make a serving.

The number of anchovies used depends on the size of the Treviso and whether the guests are really wild for them. Quarters of large heads will need three anchovy fillets to run the length of each piece. Smaller heads will need only two anchovies per half. Different-size heads can be mixed, but don't stint on the toppings. A half pound of mozzarella may be enough if sliced very thin.

No Treviso? Use endive or Verona radicchio cut in half lengthwise, putting as many as will fit comfortably in the pan.

1 1/4 pounds Treviso radicchio (2 to 5 heads,
    depending on size)

1 teaspoon kosher salt

2 cloves garlic, smashed and peeled

1/4 cup olive oil

16 to 24 anchovy fillets (two to three 2-ounce cans)

3/4 pound fresh mozzarella, cut into 1/8-inch-thick
    slices (2 to 3 slices per piece of Treviso)

Place a rack in the lower level of the oven. Preheat the oven to 500°F.

continued

Trim the Treviso, removing any wilted or discolored leaves. If the heads are large (10 ounces each), cut lengthwise into quarters, leaving stems intact; if small (4 ounces each), cut lengthwise into halves.

Put the salt, garlic and oil in a blender; blend to a smooth purée. (Alternatively, the garlic and salt may be smushed in a mortar with a pestle, and the oil whisked in.)

Place the Treviso in an 18 x 13 x 2-inch roasting pan. Pour the garlic mixture over it. Turn to coat each piece well. Roast for 10 minutes. Turn. Roast for 5 minutes.

Place the anchovy fillets lengthwise in strips down the center of each piece of Treviso. Cover with the mozzarella. Roast for 5 minutes more, or until the mozzarella is brown and melting at the edges. Remove to a platter or plate.

Serves 4 as a first course

Risotto with Radicchio and Vermouth

When Venice was lord of the seas and a great power, it controlled most of the Po Valley spreading northward. Naturally, there developed an extensive repertoire of risottos made with its rice, arborio.

2 tablespoons unsalted butter

2 tablespoons olive oil

¹/₃ cup minced yellow onion

1 cup arborio rice

3 cups Basic Chicken Stock (page 501), Roasted Chicken Stock (page 502) or commercial chicken broth, heated to a simmer

1¹/₂ teaspoons kosher salt

¹/₄ cup minced fresh parsley

2 cups packed cored and shredded (across the white veins) radicchio, any kind

2 tablespoons aged red Italian vermouth or bitter vermouth such as Punt e Mes

Freshly ground black pepper to taste

¹/₄ cup freshly grated Parmesan cheese

In a medium saucepan, melt the butter with the olive oil. Add the onion and cook, stirring, over medium heat until completely translucent but not at all browned. Stir in the rice and cook until white and coated with oil, 3 to 4 minutes. Add ¹/₄ cup simmering stock and cook, stirring constantly, until all liquid is absorbed. Add another ¹/₄ cup and stir until absorbed. Continue in this fashion until 1 cup stock remains. Stir in the salt. Stir in another ¹/₂ cup stock as above, ¹/₄ cup at a time. Remove from the heat and add the parsley, radicchio, vermouth and pepper. Allow the flavors to mellow in a warm place for 15 minutes.

Just before serving, add the remaining stock over medium heat, stirring until the risotto is creamy and heated through. Add the Parmesan and serve.

Serves 4 as a first course or a side dish (pigging quantity for 2)

Scallop and Endive Soup

This is a delicate and unusual soup, good enough to start the most festive of dinners. It could also be dinner for four people with bread and a salad.

2 pounds sea scallops, small connective muscle removed and reserved

3 medium shallots, coarsely chopped (about ¹/₂ cup)

1 cup dry white wine

3 large Belgian endive, trimmed and cut across into ¹/₂-inch pieces (about 4¹/₂ cups)

¹/₄ cup fresh tarragon leaves

1 cup heavy cream

1 tablespoon cornstarch

2 teaspoons kosher salt

Freshly ground black pepper to taste

Place the connective muscle from the scallops, the shallots, wine and 3 cups water in a small pot. Bring to a boil. Lower the heat and simmer for 15 minutes. Strain and discard the solids.

Pour the liquid into a medium pot. Bring to a boil. Add the endive and return to a boil. Add the scallops and tarragon; stir once to separate the scallops. Return barely to a simmer, without stirring again.

Add ½ cup of the heavy cream. Mix the cornstarch with the other ½ cup cream. Ladle a few spoons of the hot soup into the cornstarch mixture. Pour the cornstarch mixture back into the soup, stirring gently to incorporate. Add the salt and pepper. Cover and return to a boil; as soon as it returns to a boil; uncover the pot, or the soup will overflow. Lower the heat and simmer, uncovered, for 3 minutes.

Makes 9 cups; serves 8 as a first course

Chicory Potage

I doubt if any one of the guests will guess that it's chicory, but they will enjoy it.

2 pounds chicory, cored, separated into leaves and washed

1 quart milk

8 tablespoons unsalted butter

2 carrots, peeled, trimmed and cut into 1/3-inch dice

1 large onion, cut into 1/3-inch dice

1 medium (1/2 pound) floury potato, peeled and cut into 1/3-inch dice

1/4 cup all-purpose flour

Kosher salt and freshly ground black pepper to taste

3 cups Basic Chicken Stock (page 501), Roasted Chicken Stock (page 502) or commercial chicken broth

Bring a large pot of salted water to a boil. Drop the chicory leaves into the boiling water. Cook for about a minute to soften. Drain in a colander and rinse under cold running water. Drain again, squeeze dry and chop. Set aside.

Heat the milk in a medium saucepan over medium-low heat until steaming. Set aside.

Melt 4 tablespoons butter in a large pot. Add the chicory and cook, stirring, until all the water has evaporated. Set aside.

Melt the remaining 4 tablespoons butter in a 3-quart pan. Add the carrots, onion and potato. Cook, stirring, until the onion is translucent. Stir in the flour and cook for 4 to 5 minutes. Stir in the milk and bring to a boil. Add salt and pepper to taste. Simmer for 30 minutes to obtain a thick, smooth béchamel sauce.

Meanwhile, add 1 cup stock to the chicory and simmer until the vegetable is almost dry again.

Pour the béchamel sauce into the chicory mixture. Mix well. Transfer to a food processor and purée until smooth.

Pour the soup into a clean pot. Add the remaining 2 cups stock. Reheat. Season to taste with salt and pepper. **Serves 8 as a first course**

Mahogany Roasted Endives

Mahogany refers to the glorious color the pale green heads achieve after roasting, not to any woody texture. They become meltingly soft. The rich flavor goes well with almost any roasted meat or fish. Change the type of stock according to what the endive is served with. In a pinch, chicken broth out of a can would probably be neutral enough to go with anything. Vegetarians can use a vegetable stock; this is a great friend to grains such as bulgur or quinoa.

The fat can vary as well. I use goose fat and goose stock to go with roast goose. The result is divine.

¼ cup goose fat or other fat

2 tablespoons unsalted butter

12 endive (about 4 ounces each), trimmed

¼ teaspoon kosher salt

Freshly ground black pepper to taste

⅓ cup stock (see headnote)

Place a rack in the bottom of the oven. Preheat the oven to 500°F.

Melt the fat and butter in a 14 x 12 x 2-inch roasting pan on the stovetop over low heat. Turn off the heat. Put the endives in the pan and turn each in the melted fat. Arrange the endive in 2 rows, alternating the positions so the top of one endive is next to the bottom of another. Salt and pepper lightly.

Put in the oven and roast for 15 minutes. Shake the pan, remove from the oven and turn each endive over. Roast for 15 minutes more. Pour or spoon off the fat. Pour a little of the stock onto each endive. If making ahead, reserve at this point; leave in the pan until ready to serve. Reheat briefly if needed or desired. **Serves 6 to 12 as a side dish**

Gratin of Radicchio

With a larger baking dish, this can be doubled for a larger party. It is definitely party food, say with roast veal.

2 heads Chioggia or Treviso radicchio, quartered lengthwise, or red (Verona) radicchio, cut into 2-inch-wide wedges

2 tablespoons unsalted butter, plus butter for pan

2 tablespoons all-purpose flour

1½ cups milk

1 teaspoon kosher salt

Freshly ground black pepper to taste

¼ cup freshly grated Parmesan cheese

8 very thin slices prosciutto

Trim any stalks from the Chioggia or Treviso radicchio to ½ inch. Fill a large deep frying pan with salted water. Bring to a boil; lower to a simmer. Place the radicchio in the water in a single layer. Cover with a clean tea towel. Cook in barely simmering water for 30 minutes.

While the radicchio is simmering, prepare the béchamel sauce: Melt the butter in a 2-quart saucepan. Add the flour and cook, stirring, over low heat for 5 minutes. Slowly add the milk, whisking briskly to prevent lumps; be sure to scrape the corners, where lumps can hide. Increase the heat to medium. Cook for several minutes, stirring occasionally, until thickened. Stir in the salt and pepper. Remove from the heat and stir in the Parmesan.

Preheat the oven to 350°F.

Butter an 8 x 8-inch baking dish. Drain the radicchio. Wrap each quarter in a slice of prosciutto. Or, if using Verona radicchio, divide the prosciutto as necessary to wrap each piece.

Arrange in a single layer in the buttered pan. Spread with the béchamel, making sure to reach into the corners of the pan. Bake for 15 to 18 minutes, or until bubbly.

Serves 4 as a side dish

Endive Sweet-and-Sour Sauce

The sweet, bitter and sour flavors of this sauce are a perfect match for squash-filled tortelli (page 122) or a similar vegetable pasta. It also goes well with simply cooked chicken or pork.

- **2 medium beets (5 ounces each), trimmed and scrubbed**

- **2 tablespoons olive oil**

- **2 large shallots (2 ounces each), thinly sliced crosswise (about 1 cup)**

- **3 large endive, cored and cut crosswise into $^1/_8$-inch strips (about 5 $^1/_2$ cups)**

- **$^2/_3$ cup orange juice**

- **Ample $^1/_4$ cup dark raisins**

- **$^1/_4$ teaspoon kosher salt, or to taste**

- **2 tablespoons balsamic vinegar**

- **Freshly ground black pepper to taste**

Place a rack in the center of the oven. Preheat the oven to 450°F.

Wrap each beet in foil and place in a small baking pan. Bake for 20 to 30 minutes, or until a knife easily slips into the flesh. Allow to cool. Peel the beets and grate. There should be 2 cups.

Heat the olive oil in a 2-quart saucepan. Add the shallots and cook, stirring, over high heat for 1 minute. Add the endive. Cook, stirring constantly, for 7 minutes, or until the mixture is uniformly beige. Pour in the orange juice. Cook for 1 minute. Mix in the raisins and beets. Reduce the heat to low. Add the salt and simmer for 5 minutes, or until the raisins are soft. Add the balsamic vinegar and cook for an additional minute. Season with pepper and more salt, if desired. **Makes 1 $^1/_2$ cups**

Fava Beans

These are the only true European bean antedating the New World beans (see pages 10 to 27). I love them but I haven't been in the habit of using them a great deal because, in addition to having to be shelled, unless they are very young and small, each bean has a skin that needs to be removed.

Most European countries use these beans. The Spanish word "habas" technically means broad bean, but it is used generically just to mean beans. Fresh ones are called habas verdes. Whether the beans are fresh or dried, in French, they are fèves or haricots larges; in German, grosse Bohnen or Pferdebohnen; and in Italian, fave. These names hold whether the beans are fresh or dried. In England, the fresh beans are called broad beans, horse beans or shell beans. They are sometimes cut up in the shell, cooked and eaten. I don't like them.

Oddly, considering how many Central American beans there are, favas have become very popular in Mexico. Recently, I discovered that Mexican markets sell dried peeled favas, making them a lot more seductive to use than those that are sold unpeeled. (See "Rich" Peasant Stew with Favas, page 227, for how to peel dried unpeeled favas.) I also found peeled, split giant favas. All favas have two halves. I prefer the whole favas to the split ones, as the beans easily get overcooked and mushy. However, the split favas cook more quickly. Generally, favas double in volume when cooked. Halved favas will give a little more.

The best use for cooked dried favas is puréed in soup. Favas go well with most herbs, members of the onion family, hot and sweet peppers and tomatoes.

Tiny fresh favas are delicious raw in salads. They can be simply stewed in olive oil or butter with a little sea salt. They can also be substituted for or combined with peas in Piselli alla Romana (page 301). This is not a use for dried beans. Small lima beans can be substituted for fresh favas.

Turn to **BEAN OF THE OLD WORLD** in the Cook's Guide for how-tos and to the Index for more recipes.

Fava Bean Soup

Sopa de Habas

This is an adaptation of a wonderful recipe from Maria Auxillo Rodriguez, who cooks for our friends the Kirkmans. It is richly round in taste and full bodied. Her soup calls for fresh favas. Sadly, they are seldom available to me, and they are a great deal of work. In addition, when I had this soup at Restaurant 1810 in the main plaza of Querétaro, it was made with dried beans, which added texture and thickening that was very welcoming. I am sometimes tempted to double the recipe and serve it as a meal. (I wouldn't freeze it; freshness is important.) But don't be tempted to replace the water with more chicken stock. If anything, replace the stock with water.

Fussy cooks may want to seed the tomatoes. I don't. I like a little crunch. It probably is better to fish out the two pieces of chili pepper, though, so no one gets burned.

2 tablespoons olive oil

1 medium white onion, cut into $1/4$-inch dice (about 1 cup)

1 tablespoon minced garlic

1 serrano chili, halved lengthwise and seeded

$3/4$ pound tomatoes, peeled, cored and cut into $1/4$-inch dice (about $3/4$ cup)

Large pinch of dried oregano, preferably Greek

2 cups Basic Chicken Stock (page 501) or commercial chicken broth

2 cups dried split fava beans or $2^1/2$ cups dried whole fava beaans

$1/2$ cup packed cilantro leaves and tender stems, coarsely chopped

2 teaspoons kosher salt

Freshly ground black pepper to taste

continued

Put the oil in a 4-quart pot over low heat. Add the onion, garlic and chili. Cook, stirring from time to time, until the onion is translucent. Add the tomatoes, oregano and stock. Bring to a boil. Stir in the favas and bring back to the boil. Reduce the heat to a low boil and cook for 30 minutes.

Add 2 cups water. Cook for another 30 minutes, or until the favas are cooked through. Stir in the cilantro, salt and pepper. Allow to sit for about 15 minutes before serving; reheat if need be. **Makes 4¹/₂ cups**

Persian Fava Bean Omelet
Kookoo-ye Baghala

I love the name kookoo. It appeals to the child in me. I suppose that is as an American child. A Persian child wouldn't even notice it, but take it for granted as the name of this cross between a European flat omelet and a cake. The beans in the recipe are rather like the potatoes in many European flat omelets. The fava version needs to be started well ahead of mealtime.

> 10 ounces shelled fresh fava beans (from about 3 pounds in the shell), outer skin removed (see the Cook's Guide, page 542), or one 10-ounce package frozen lima beans, defrosted in a sieve under warm running water (about 1³/₄ cups)
>
> 4 tablespoons unsalted butter
>
> 1 cup chopped onion
>
> ¹/₃ cup chopped fresh dill
>
> 6 large eggs
>
> 1¹/₂ teaspoons kosher salt
>
> ¹/₂ teaspoon baking soda
>
> ¹/₄ teaspoon freshly ground black pepper

If using fava beans, bring a medium saucepan of water to a boil. Drop in the favas and simmer for 5 minutes. Drain.

Pass the favas or limas through a food mill into a mixing bowl. Let cool if necessary.

Preheat the oven to 500°F. Butter a round 1-quart baking dish.

Heat 2 tablespoons butter in a small skillet. Add the onion. Cook over medium heat, stirring occasionally, until tender, about 3 minutes. Stir in the dill and cook for another minute. Remove from the heat and cool slightly.

In a medium bowl, whisk together the eggs, salt, baking soda and pepper. Whisk in the bean purée. Stir in the cooled onion and dill.

Pour the mixture into the baking dish. Bake for 35 to 45 minutes, or until the bottom and edges are brown and crispy. Remove from the oven and invert onto a plate. Cut into wedges. **Serves 4 to 6 as a first course or a light main course with a salad**

NOTE: Two cups dried peeled fava beans can replace the fresh. Place the dried beans in a large pot and cover with water. Bring to a boil. Cover the pot and remove from the heat; let stand for 1 hour.

Drain the beans, rinse and return to the pot. Cover with fresh water and add 1 teaspoon salt. Cook until tender, about 1 hour (timing depends on the age of the beans). Drain.

"Rich" Peasant Stew with Favas

Bold and lusty, this rustic dish is immensely satisfying served with a chunk of good crusty bread or white rice.

Mushrooms, red wine and a good meat stock add richness to this meat-free dish. To make it truly meat free, use Mushroom Broth (page 507). To make it vegetarian, substitute a strong vegetable stock enhanced with agar-agar.

6 ounces dried fava beans (about 1 cup) or
    1 1/2 cups dried peeled favas

1/3 cup olive oil

1 small onion, coarsely chopped (about 1/3 cup)

2 ounces mushrooms, trimmed and coarsely
    chopped (about 3/4 cup)

1/4 pound mustard greens, cut across into 1/4-inch
    strips (about 1 1/2 cups)

1/2 pound beet greens, cut across into 1/4-inch
    strips (about 2 1/2 cups)

1 cup Basic Chicken Stock (page 501),
    Roasted Chicken Stock (page 502), Beef Stock
    (page 502), or commercial chicken or beef
    broth or Vegetable Broth (page 506) enhanced
    with agar-agar (see page 501)

1/2 cup dry red wine

Kosher salt and freshly ground black pepper
    to taste

If using unpeeled dried favas, bring 2½ cups water to a boil in a medium saucepan. Add the favas. Bring back to a boil. Reduce the heat and simmer for 15 minutes. Drain and rinse under cold running water. Peel the favas. There should be 1½ cups. Set aside.

Heat the oil in a medium pot. Add the onion. Cook over medium-low heat until translucent. Add the mushrooms. Cook until they appear very soft and melted, about 5 minutes. Add the mustard and beet greens. Toss until the greens are wilted.

Stir in the beans and stock. Bring to a boil. Cover, reduce the heat to low and simmer for 25 minutes, stirring once or twice.

Stir in the red wine. Cover. Cook for 20 minutes, or until the liquid has completely evaporated and the favas are soft. (As this is a rustic dish, do not worry if the beans break up when stirred.) Salt and pepper to taste. Makes 3 cups

Golden Fava Soup, Latin Style

We have been told that turmeric is good for us, here it is a star.

2 cups dried split fava beans, soaked

2 large onions (about 14 ounces), cut into chunks

1 serrano chili

1 tablespoon turmeric

4 teaspoons kosher salt

2 tablespoons fresh lime juice

1/4 cup coarsely chopped cilantro

Drain the beans and put in a 3-quart saucepan. Pour in enough water to cover by 1 inch. Bring to a boil, then lower the heat to simmering and cook until the beans are almost tender, about 25 minutes.

Add the onions, whole chili, turmeric and salt to the beans. Bring to a boil. Reduce the heat to simmering. Cover and cook until the onions are tender, about 45 minutes.

Remove the chili and stir in the lime juice and cilantro. Serve hot. Makes 4 cups

Great Green Fava Bean Fritters

The beans are ground after soaking but before cooking, which leaves enough starch in them to hold the fritters together. The green color and flavor come from cilantro, parsley and dill.

2 cups dried split fava beans

1 small yellow onion, cut into 1-inch chunks

1 small leek, white and light green parts only, cleaned (see the Cook's Guide, page 600) and sliced across into $^1/_2$-inch pieces

$^1/_2$ cup (lightly packed) cilantro leaves and thin stems

$^1/_2$ cup (lightly packed) fresh dill

$^1/_2$ cup (lightly packed) fresh flat-leaf parsley leaves

$2^1/_2$ teaspoons kosher salt

1 teaspoon baking soda

1 teaspoon ground cumin

$^1/_4$ teaspoon cayenne pepper

Vegetable oil

Sesame seeds (optional)

Lemon wedges (optional)

Soak the beans in cold water to cover by 4 inches until softened, for 4 to 8 hours, depending on the age and size of the beans. When a fully soaked bean is snapped in half, the interior should be evenly colored, without a lighter center.

Drain the beans and pat completely dry with paper towels. Pass through a meat grinder fitted with the finest disc into a medium bowl.

Put the onion, leek, cilantro, dill and parsley in a food processor and process until very finely chopped. Stir into the ground beans. Stir in the salt, baking soda, cumin and cayenne. Let stand at room temperature for 30 minutes to 1 hour.

Pour 2 inches of vegetable oil into a medium heavy skillet. Heat over medium heat to 350°F. Meanwhile, if using the sesame seeds, spread them out on a plate. Using a level tablespoon for each fritter, gently roll the batter between moistened hands into balls. Roll the balls in the sesame seeds, if using.

Slip as many fritters into the oil as will fit comfortably. Fry, turning if necessary, until deep golden brown on all sides, about 3 minutes. Remove with a slotted spoon to a paper towel–lined baking sheet. Repeat with the remaining fritters. Serve hot with the lemon wedges, if desired. **Makes about 50 fritters**

Thistles

Artichokes, Cardoons and Nettles

Thistles sound hostile and many are fiercely defended with spiky leaves both along the stem and as the base of their flowers, but they are beauties in the garden. The loveliest have the form of the Scotch national symbol with a rounded bottom and a sort of shaving brush of filaments, usually a shade of lavender or even bright yellow.

I love them, realizing that this group contains the various artichokes and cardoons that make such good spring and summer eating. Even nettles can be and are eaten.

ARTICHOKES

Artichokes are a kind of thistle. When grown in a mild climate (I have grown them in Vermont, but it is an unnatural act involving burying the plant just before frost under a bushel basket and immuring them in dirt), those that escape and go to seed develop a beautiful purple bristle shaped like an old-fashioned shaving brush. What we eat is the flower of this plant, before the thistle top emerges or, in the case of baby artichokes, before it truly forms in the shape of a choke. The choke, what the French call foin ("hay"), is the immature bristle that lies, pale cream color, on top of the heart or base of the artichoke and under the leaves. It can literally choke. If there is any doubt as to its immaturity, it should be scraped out with a knife or a spoon. The leaves, whose rich goodness we skim off with our teeth, are actually the petals.

Turn to **ARTICHOKES** in the Cook's Guide for how-tos and to the Index for more recipes.

White Salad

To serve, top each salad of raw sliced artichokes with three thinly sliced sheets (do not use grated) of Parmesan or grana cheese, easily made with a vegetable peeler. Alternatively, reserve the fennel fronds, chop them coarsely and sprinkle over each plate.

    4 large artichokes (about 10 ounces each)

    6 tablespoons fresh lemon juice, plus 2 lemons for preparing artichoke bottoms

    1/2 small fennel bulb, trimmed and thinly sliced crosswise (about 1 cup)

    6 tablespoons olive oil

    1 teaspoon kosher salt

    Freshly ground black pepper to taste

    2 large endives (4 to 5 ounces each), cored and thinly sliced lengthwise (about 3 cups)

    12 thin slices Parmesan or grana padano

Prepare artichoke bottoms (see the Cook's Guide, page 527), using a cut lemon and lemon water.

With a knife or the slicing side of a box grater, cut the artichoke bottoms into 1/8-inch-thick slices. Immediately toss with the 6 tablespoons lemon juice, coating thoroughly. Mix in the fennel, oil, salt and pepper.

Divide the endive among four plates. Place one-quarter of the artichoke-fennel mixture in the center of each plate. Top each with 3 slices Parmesan or grana, or fennel fronds, if using.
Serves 4 as a first course

Marinated Artichokes

While jarred marinated artichokes are fairly satisfactory, they are easily made at home if frozen or canned artichoke hearts are available. There are about as many hearts in a tin as there are in a box. Be sure to rinse these well before marinating.

    One 9-ounce box frozen artichoke hearts, defrosted in a sieve under warm running water

    1/2 cup olive oil

    1/2 teaspoon dried thyme

    1/2 teaspoon dried oregano

    A grind of fresh black pepper

    2 teaspoons kosher salt

    1 tablespoon fresh lemon juice

Combine the artichokes, oil, herbs and pepper in a small saucepan. Place over very low heat and cook, covered, for 10 minutes. Remove from the heat and stir in the salt. Let cool.

Stir in the lemon juice. Keep the artichokes refrigerated. Bring to room temperature before serving. **Makes 1 1/2 cups**

Artichokes Filled with Snails in Cream

This is a sensational recipe that requires time. However, it can be made less painful: All the component preparations can be done ahead. Then reheat the artichoke hearts and snails at the end, just before beating the cold beurre blanc into the cream reduction. I have written this as an elegant meal introduction for four, but the recipe doubles easily.

28 snails canned in brine

1 cup dry white wine

3 lemons, 2 for preparing artichoke bottoms and 1 for cooking artichokes

4 medium to large artichokes

2 cups heavy cream

1 1/2 teaspoons Dijon mustard

1 recipe Beurre Blanc (page 453) made with fresh herbs, chilled and cut into pieces

Drain the snails. Put them in a bowl with the wine for at least an hour. Drain the snails again, reserving the wine; set aside.

Put ¾ cup of the snail-flavored wine in a small saucepan and boil over moderate heat until reduced to 4 teaspoons. Set aside.

Squeeze the juice of 1 lemon into a pot of water and bring to a boil. Meanwhile, prepare the artichoke bottoms (see the Cook's Guide, page 527), using 2 cut lemons and lemon water.

Cook the artichoke bottoms in the boiling lemon water until a knife easily slips into the flesh, about 20 minutes. Drain and keep warm.

Place the cream and mustard in a medium saucepan and cook over medium to high heat until slightly reduced, about 5 minutes. Stir in the reduced snail wine, then add the beurre blanc bit by bit, stirring until you have a smooth sauce. Lower the heat and add the snails. Cook just to heat through.

Place a warm artichoke bottom, hollow side up, on each of four individual plates. Divide the sauce and snails evenly among the plates, spooning them over the artichokes. Serve immediately. **Serves 4 as a first course**

Roasted Young Artichokes with Garlic

Try to buy small artichokes that are fairly uniform in size so they will roast evenly. If you have a choice, buy ones with longer stems. They look prettier arranged on a platter for serving and the stems are good to eat. Use a roasting pan that is flat on the bottom and just large enough to hold the halved vegetables, or the liquid will pool in the center of the pan and the artichokes will not cook evenly. The garlic cloves cook right along with the artichokes, flavoring them and becoming delightfully creamy. Be sure to add at least one clove garlic per guest.

These artichokes are best served as a first course. They combine well with roasted peppers.

1/2 cup fresh lemon juice

15 small artichokes (2 1/2 to 3 ounces each), rinsed well if sandy

2 tablespoons olive oil

2 teaspoons kosher salt

continued

10 to 12 cloves garlic, unpeeled

1 1/2 cups Basic Chicken Stock (page 501), Roasted Chicken Stock (page 502) or commercial chicken broth

Freshly ground black pepper to taste

Place a rack in the center of the oven. Preheat the oven to 500°F. Pour the lemon juice into an 18 x 13 x 2-inch roasting pan.

Prepare the baby artichokes, keeping the stems (see the Cook's Guide, page 527); omit the cut lemon and lemon water. One at a time, cut the artichokes in half lengthwise and immediately put the halves, cut side down, in the pan of lemon juice. Then, using a small knife, cut the small choke out of each half and discard; return the artichoke halves to the lemon juice. Continue until all the artichokes are prepared.

Brush each artichoke half with a small amount of the olive oil. Arrange in 6 tightly packed rows in the pan. Sprinkle with the salt and snuggle the garlic among the artichokes. Roast for 20 minutes.

Remove the pan from the oven. Add the stock and cover tightly with foil. Roast for 20 to 25 minutes more.

Sprinkle the artichokes with pepper. Serve warm from the oven, or serve at room temperature. **Serves 8 to 10 as a first course**

Presentation of Whole Cooked Artichokes

Boiled, steamed or microwaved artichokes (see the Cook's Guide, pages 527–528) can just be plopped down in the middle of a largish plate after they have been turned upside down on paper towels or a cloth to drain, so as not to present a puddle of water. A largish plate gives room for the gnawed leaves and for cleaning the heart once the bottom has been achieved. An extra plate per person or a large one for the center of the table is useful as well.

The next step up in elegance is to gently spread the cooked leaves outward, without detaching them, until a cone of light green or yellow leaves is exposed. With a small knife, cut out the cone. Scrape away the choke with a spoon or a melon baller, which I find helpful. Sauce can be poured into the hollow now formed in the heart. The cone of yellow leaves can be placed over the sauce or not. In any case, the bottom will not hold enough sauce for a greedy person like me.

The fanciest presentation of the simple artichoke that I know is served at Elaine's restaurant in New York. Each portion arrives with the cleaned bottom in the center of the plate and the leaves in circles radiating out from it like the petals of a flower.

Bacon-Wrapped Artichokes

This substantial dish can make a meal out of a simple main course such as an omelet or be served on its own.

6 medium artichokes (about 8 ounces each),

2 lemons for preparing artichoke shells

24 thin slices bacon

1/2 pound mushrooms, trimmed and finely chopped (about 2 cups)

6 large fresh sage leaves, cut across into thin shreds

1/3 cup finely chopped freshly parsley

1 teaspoon kosher salt

Freshly ground black pepper to taste

Prepare the artichoke shells (see the Cook's Guide, page 529) using a cut lemon and lemon water.

Place a rack in the bottom third of the oven. Preheat the oven to 500°F.

Wrap each artichoke around the base with 3 overlapping bacon slices, securing them with a toothpick. Stand them in a roasting pan just large enough to hold them so they do not touch.

Cut the remaining bacon slices into small pieces with sharp scissors. Combine with the remaining ingredients. Pack the hollow bottoms of the artichoke shells with the mixture, then top each artichoke with an even layer of the remaining mixture.

Bake for 30 minutes or until a knife pierces the bottom easily. Serve hot or warm.

Serves 6 as a first course or a light lunch

Artichokes Filled with Artichoke Soufflé

Artichoke purée adds flavor and color to the golden clouds that billow out from the center of this artichoke first course.

When there is neither the time nor inclination to be fancy, bake the artichoke soufflés in four-ounce ramekins, greased with butter and lightly coated with bread crumbs. The ramekin versions can even be prepared ahead and stored overnight in the freezer, well wrapped. To cook: Unwrap, space evenly on a baking sheet and bake (directly from the freezer) for 28 minutes.

ARTICHOKE SOUFFLÉ

3 tablespoons unsalted butter

1/4 cup finely chopped onion

3 tablespoons all-purpose flour

I cup Artichoke Purée (page 236)

4 large egg yolks

1 1/4 teaspoons kosher salt

Freshly ground black pepper to taste

6 drops hot red pepper sauce

5 large egg whites, at room temperature

6 large artichokes (9 to 12 ounces each), prepared as artichoke shells and cooked (see the Cook's Guide, page 529), using 2 lemons for preparing shells

Melted butter for brushing artichokes

Place a rack in the center of the oven. Preheat the oven to 425°F.

To prepare the soufflé, melt the butter in a medium saucepan over medium heat. When it is foamy, add the onion. Cook until translucent, about 5 minutes. Add the flour, stirring constantly to avoid lumps. Let the mixture cook for 1 minute; do not let it brown. Gradually whisk in the artichoke purée. Cook for 4 to 5 minutes, stirring constantly to avoid scorching and to eliminate all lumps. Remove the pan from the heat.

Place the egg yolks in a small bowl. Whisk in ½ cup of the artichoke mixture. When it is well blended, whisk it back into the remaining artichoke mixture. Cook over low heat for 1 to 3 minutes until thick. Remove from the heat; let cool for 5 minutes. Stir in the salt, pepper, and hot red pepper sauce.

In a clean stainless steel or glass bowl, beat the egg whites until stiff but not dry. Stir about one-quarter of the egg whites into the artichoke base, then fold in the remaining whites.

Using a ½-cup measuring cup, gently scoop the mixture into the artichoke centers, filling them up to the top or a little higher. Brush the artichokes with melted butter. Place on a baking sheet.

Bake for 10 minutes. The tops will be browned and slightly firm to the touch. Serve immediately. **Serves 6 as a first course**

Marinated Shrimp, Mussel and Artichoke Salad

This picture-perfect pink-and-white-and-green dish can start any party, find a home on any buffet.

³/4 pound medium shrimp, shelled and deveined

18 large mussels (about 1¹/2 pounds), scrubbed and debearded

3 stalks celery, peeled and cut across diagonally into ¹/4-inch slices (about 1 cup)

1 small onion, quartered and thinly sliced (about ¹/2 cup)

Two 10-ounce packages frozen artichoke hearts, defrosted in a sieve under warm running water

1 tablespoon olive oil

2 tablespoons fresh lemon juice

Scant 1 teaspoon kosher salt

Pinch of freshly ground black pepper

Lettuce leaves for serving

Cook the shrimp in boiling water for 2 minutes and drain or in a microwave oven in a 1½-quart casserole with a tightly fitting lid. Cover tightly and cook at 100% for 2 minutes 30 seconds, or until cooked through.

Steam the mussels over boiling water or in a microwave, hinge side down, in a 2-quart casserole. Cover tightly and cook at 100% for 5 minutes, or until all the mussels are open.

When the mussels are cool enough to handle, remove the mussel meat from the shells and reserve. Strain the juices through a cloth-lined sieve; reserve ¼ cup.

Combine the shrimp, mussels, celery, onion and artichoke hearts in a bowl.

Whisk together the remaining ingredients and the reserved mussel juice. Pour over the salad. Toss well to combine. Cover loosely and refrigerate until chilled.

Serve on lettuce-lined plates.
Serves 8 as a first course, 16 as part of a buffet

Artichoke Soup

The first—and best—artichoke soup that I ever ate was at the Stanford Court Hotel in San Francisco when the brilliant Jimmy Nassikas was its leader. You will find my attempt at it further along as Artichoke Hazelnut Soup (page 236). This is a simpler soup altogether but still very good. I make it when I have trimmed a lot of artichokes for bottoms or hearts and have a plethora of leaves to provide the purée.

As this is rich, serve only a small amount to each person, in a demitasse cup.

1½ cups Artichoke Pureé (page 236)

1 cup Basic Chicken Stock (page 501), Roasted Chicken Stock (page 502) or commercial chicken broth

1 rounded teaspoon kosher salt

1 cup heavy cream

2 egg yolks

1 teaspoon fresh lemon juice

Freshly ground white pepper to taste

Place the artichoke purée, chicken stock and salt in a medium nonreactive saucepan. Bring to a boil. Reduce heat and simmer for 10 minutes.

In a small bowl, combine the cream and egg yolks, beating lightly until smooth. Whisk some of the hot soup into this mixture, then whisk it into the saucepan with the soup. Cook over low heat until slightly thickened, about 30 seconds. Season with the lemon juice and pepper.

Makes 3 cups

Potato and Artichoke Soup

Zuppa di Patate e Carciofi

I am often asked what my favorite restaurant is. I tend to answer that it is the one closest to my house. In my case, I am fortunate that it is a very good simple Italian restaurant, Vico. They kindly shared this excellent vegetarian recipe with me.

This is exactly the sort of recipe that results in a great many leaves to make purée (page 236).

Omit the Parmesan if making the soup a day ahead; add it after reheating. A small bowl of grated cheese can also be passed around the table for those to wish to add more.

4 large artichokes (about 9 ounces each)

2 lemons for preparing artichokes bottoms

1 tablespoon olive oil

1 tablespoon chopped onion

1 clove garlic, smashed, peeled and minced

¾ pound floury potatoes, peeled and cut into ½-inch dice (about 2 cups)

1 tablespoon chopped fresh parsley

1 teaspoon kosher salt

Freshly ground black pepper to taste

1½ tablespoons grated Parmesan cheese

Prepare artichoke bottoms (see the Cook's Guide, page 527), using a cut lemon and lemon water. Cut the bottoms into ½-inch dice. Reserve in the lemon water.

Heat the oil in a medium saucepan. Add the onion and garlic. Cook for 2 minutes over low heat. Add the potatoes. Cook and stir for 2 minutes. Add 2 cups water and bring to a boil. Reduce the heat and simmer for 15 minutes.

Drain the artichokes and add to the pan. Bring to a boil. Reduce the heat and simmer for 15 minutes. Add 1 cup water, if necessary, to bring the soup up to 4 cups. Simmer for 5 minutes.

Add the parsley. Cook for 2 minutes. Stir in the salt, pepper and Parmesan. Taste for seasoning, and adjust if desired.

Makes 4 cups; serves 4 as a first course

Artichoke Hazelnut Soup

An automatic spice mill and a hand-crank cheese grater are both effective for turning whole hazelnuts into a powder. The spice mill produces a finer but oilier consistency; oiliness will not affect the end result here.

1 cup plus 2 tablespoons hazelnuts

2 tablespoons unsalted butter

2 large shallots, finely chopped (about ³/₄ cup)

3 cups Artichoke Purée (at right)

2 cups Basic Chicken Stock (page 501),
   Roasted Chicken Stock (page 502) or
   commercial chicken broth

1 tablespoon kosher salt
   (less if using commercial broth)

¹/₃ cup heavy cream

Place a rack in the center of the oven. Preheat the oven to 375°F.

To skin the hazelnuts: Spread them in a single layer on a cookie sheet and toast for 10 to 15 minutes, until the skins have cracked. Immediately wrap the warm nuts in a terry-cloth towel. Rub vigorously to remove the skins.

Once the nuts are cool enough to handle, any remaining skin can be scraped off with fingernails or the back of a paring knife. Chop enough of the hazelnuts to make 2 tablespoons. Grind the remaining hazelnuts in a spice grinder until very fine; or use a cheese grater. Set aside.

Melt the butter in a medium saucepan. Add the shallots and cook over medium heat for 5 minutes, or until translucent. Reduce the heat. Cook for 5 minutes more, or until the shallots are completely soft.

Add the ground hazelnuts, artichoke purée, chicken stock and salt. Bring to a boil. Reduce the heat. Stir in the cream. Heat until warmed.

In 2 batches, purée the soup in a blender until completely smooth. The soup can be prepared in advance. Store covered in the refrigerator; reheat slowly over low heat to prevent scorching.

Ladle the soup into serving bowls. Sprinkle with the chopped hazelnuts and serve.

Serves 4 as a first course

Artichoke Purée

When preparing artichoke bottoms, save the flavorful leaves and stems trimmed from the whole to make this deep green purée. Then use it in Artichokes Filled with Artichoke Soufflé (page 233), Artichoke-Chervil Ravioli (page 239), or Artichoke Hazelnut Soup (at left) or as a soup base.

The consistency of the purée depends on several things: First is how much water the leaves soak up. Waterlogged leaves will yield a thinner purée. Cook the leaves in an equal volume of water and be sure to drain well afterwards. Second, whole leaves and stems (left over from making artichoke bottoms or hearts) will yield a better purée than leaf tips (left over from making stuffed artichokes). Most important is to work the leaves long enough in the food mill. Artichoke leaves are immensely fibrous. It takes a little muscle and a lot of patience to extract all the flesh, and it may take ten minutes or longer per batch. The purée will at first be thin. Continue turning, and the mill will slowly begin to extract thick pulp. The finished purée should be the consistency of an overly thick soup.

1 pound leaves, trimmings, and stems from
   artichokes (about 11 cups)

Put the leaves and trimmings in a large deep pot. Peel the stems and add to the pot. Pour in 11 cups water, or enough to cover by ½ inch.

Cover the pot loosely with the lid or an otoshi-buta (see Note). Bring to a boil. Reduce the heat. Simmer for 1 hour 30 minutes, or until the artichoke leaves are completely soft and limp. Drain very well (any water clinging to the leaves will dilute the purée).

In 2 batches, put the leaves through a food mill fitted with a medium-coarse disc: Turn the crank about 20 times, then reverse-turn to loosen the leaves, use a fork to stir the leaves up and repeat. The artichokes will splatter slightly as the leaves give off their juices. Be patient and work the food mill until the leaves are completely shredded and dry.

The purée can be made ahead and frozen. Defrost and whirl in a blender before using.

Makes 1¹/₂ to 1²/₃ cups

NOTE: Otoshi-buta are Japanese wooden lids meant to fit inside a pot, leaving about ½ inch around them. They keep simmering or boiling items submerged in liquid. A similar-sized metal pot lid can be used.

Baby Artichokes, Jewish Style
Carciofi alla Giudia

Follow this two-step method, and the artichoke petals will open dramatically to resemble roses in full bloom. If artichokes with stems are available, the stems can be trimmed and peeled, adding to the flowerlike allure.

The Romans, whose recipe this is, always use olive oil.

To prepare both baby and young artichokes, see the Cook's Guide, page 527.

1 pound baby artichokes (1 to 1¹/₂ ounces each; 13 to 16 pieces)

Kosher salt and freshly ground black pepper to taste

Olive oil or canola oil for deep-frying

Prepare the artichokes, leaving the stems on.

Use fingers to loosen the artichoke leaves, gently pulling them away from the center and opening up each artichoke as much as possible without breaking. Turn the artichokes, leaf side down, and press against a flat surface to flatten them further.

Turn the artichokes, leaf side up. Sprinkle with salt and pepper. Use fingers and the flat surface to open leaves and flatten artichokes.

Pour 1½ to 3 inches of oil into a deep 11- to 12-inch pan or pot. Heat the oil to 250°F.

Fry the artichokes a few at a time: Cook for 5 minutes, or until the leaves are light brown and a knife will easily slip into the flesh. Remove from the oil and place, leaf side down, on a paper towel–lined baking sheet. Gently push down on the artichokes to flatten as much as possible. They can be done ahead to this point.

Increase the oil temperature to 300°F. Have a small bowl of cold water nearby.

Moving quickly, return a few artichokes to the oil. The leaves will immediately open up. Cook briefly, 20 to 30 seconds, then dip fingers into cold water, stand back and shake water into the hot oil. The oil will splatter loudly for several seconds. As soon as the splattering dies down, remove the artichokes to another paper towel–lined pan. Repeat with the remaining artichokes. Serve immediately.

Serves 5 to 6 as a first course

Young Artichokes, Jewish Style
Prepare 2 pounds small artichokes (2½ to 3 ounces each; about 12 pieces) and heat the oil.

Fry the artichokes a few at a time, cooking for 8 minutes. Remove from the oil and flatten as above; the tip of a paring knife is helpful for separating the leaves in the center. The artichokes can be done ahead to this point.

Fry again for 1 to 3 minutes, until golden brown, before shaking water into the hot oil.

Tangy Artichokes and Olives

Artichokes and celery are slowly cooked until wilted but still crunchy in this exceptional side dish inspired by the Artichoke Caponata from *Many Beautiful Things* by Vincent Schiavelli. Serve at room temperature with toothpicks.

2 pounds baby artichokes (about 1 1/2 ounces each; 20 to 22 pieces)

2 lemons for preparing artichokes

6 ounces drained medium green olives, such as manzanilla or picholine (about 1 cup)

1/4 cup olive oil

4 large ribs celery, peeled and thinly sliced crosswise (about 2 1/2 cups)

2 tablespoons capers, rinsed

2 to 3 tablespoons red wine vinegar

Kosher salt and freshly ground black pepper to taste

Prepare the baby artichokes, leaving the stems on (see the Cook's Guide, page 527), using a cut lemon and lemon water.

To pit the olives, place close together on a work surface. Cover with a towel. Smash with a heavy-bottomed pan. The pits will loosen and can be removed easily. The olives can also be smashed individually with the side of a large heavy knife.

Heat the oil in a 12-inch skillet. Drain the artichokes well and pat dry. Add to the pan. Cook over medium heat for 5 minutes, stirring from time to time. Reduce the heat slightly. Cook for 5 minutes more.

Add the celery. Increase the heat to medium and cook for 5 minutes. Add the olives and capers. Reduce the heat slightly. Cook for 5 minutes. Pour in the vinegar. Stir and cook for 1 minute, allowing the vinegar to evaporate. Salt and pepper to taste.

Serve hot or at room temperature. The dish can be made up to 3 days ahead and refrigerated; bring to room temperature to serve. **Makes 5 1/2 cups**

Tangy Artichoke and Olive Pasta Sauce
Add 1 1/3 cups Plum Tomato Purée (page 459), sterile-pack strained tomatoes or puréed canned tomato to the finished artichokes. If desired, add 2 tablespoons fresh basil leaves cut across into thin shreds. Simmer for a few minutes to allow the flavors to blend. Serve hot over pasta. **Makes about 6 cups**

Artichoke Bottoms Stuffed with Duxelles

This is a delicious reward for preparing ahead staples such as cooked artichoke bottoms and duxelles. The microwave oven makes short work of the whole thing and provides a gala first course. If making this for a party, prepare the artichoke bottoms, stuff them and refrigerate. If the artichoke bottoms have been chilled, cook at 100% for 3 minutes when ready to serve.

It is easy to multiply or divide this recipe, using the times given for artichoke cooking in the Cook's Guide (page 528). Allow 1 1/2 tablespoons of duxelles and 1 1/2 teaspoons of Parmesan cheese per serving.

Serve the artichokes on a bed of watercress tossed with balsamic vinegar, if desired.

4 large artichokes (about 10 ounces each)

2 lemons for preparing artichoke bottoms

1/2 cup Mushroom Duxelles (page 405)

2 tablespoons freshly grated Parmesan cheese

Prepare artichoke bottoms (see the Cook's Guide, page 527), using a cut lemon and lemon water, saving the leaves for purée (page 236).

Place the bottoms in a circle without touching, in a dish just large enough to hold them, such as a 10-inch pie plate. Cover tightly with microwave plastic wrap. Cook at 100% for 14 minutes. Prick the plastic wrap to release the steam.

Remove from the oven and uncover. Let stand until cool enough to handle.

Combine the duxelles and cheese in a small bowl. Divide the mixture among the artichoke bottoms. Place in a circle on a dinner plate or in a 10-inch quiche dish. Cover with plastic wrap.

Cook at 100% for 1 minute. Prick the plastic wrap, if using. Remove from the oven and uncover. **Serves 4 as a first course**

Artichoke-Chervil Ravioli

When making this, it's important that the artichoke purée be very thick. The filling will be too loose and runny otherwise.

1 1/2 cups Artichoke Purée (page 236)

3/4 cup part-skim ricotta cheese

Kosher salt and freshly ground black pepper to taste

1 recipe Chervil Pasta Dough (page 472)

Flour for dusting surface

Cornmeal for dusting (optional)

4 tablespoons unsalted butter

Fresh chervil sprigs for topping

Combine the artichoke purée and ricotta in a bowl. Salt and pepper to taste. Set aside.

Divide the pasta dough into eighths. Using a pasta machine or a rolling pin (see page 470 for instructions), roll each piece out very thin into a 15 x 5-inch sheet. Each sheet will make seven 2-inch square ravioli.

Place 1 pasta sheet horizontally on a lightly floured surface. Use the dull edge of a knife to mark a horizontal centerfold line and seven 2-inch squares beneath it.

Drop 1 slightly rounded teaspoon of artichoke filling in the center of each square. Brush the pasta sheet with water along the edges and in between the mounds of filling. Fold the top half of the pasta sheet over the bottom. Seal the pasta along the edges and in between the filling. Trim the ravioli into 2-inch squares. Place on a kitchen towel dusted with cornmeal or flour. Repeat with the remaining pasta sheets and fillings. At this point, the ravioli may be cooked or put aside, covered with plastic wrap, for an hour.

Bring a large pot of salted water to a boil. Cook the ravioli, in batches if necessary, for 5 to 6 minutes. Remove with a slotted spoon and keep warm.

To serve, melt the butter in a large skillet. Salt and pepper to taste. Add the ravioli. Toss gently to coat.

Divide the ravioli among plates. Top each with chervil. Serve immediately.
Makes 56 ravioli; serves 6 to 7 as a first course, 4 as a main course

Artichokes à la Grecque

Large globe artichokes are more frequently cooked in Greece than the tiny ones.

4 large artichokes (about 12 ounces each), leaves trimmed, quartered through the stem and choke removed (see the Cook's Guide, page 526)

8 small (1 to 1 1/2 inches diameter) white onions, peeled and trimmed

continued

Juice of 2 lemons, lemon shells reserved

2 cups Basic Chicken Stock (page 501) or
commercial chicken broth

$^1/_2$ cup olive oil

1 tablespoon kosher salt

4 fresh dill sprigs

$^1/_4$ cup chopped fresh mint or dill

Arrange the artichokes, cut side down, in a
12 x 7½ x 2-inch dish, with the fat stem ends
pointing out. Tuck the onions and lemon shells
among the artichokes. Add the stock, oil, salt
and dill sprigs. Cover tightly with microwave
plastic wrap.

Cook at 100% for 12 minutes. Remove from
the oven. Prick the plastic to release the steam,
carefully uncover and turn the artichokes over.
Cover tightly and cook at 100% for 8 minutes
more. Remove from the oven. Let stand,
covered, until cool.

Just before serving, stir in ¼ cup lemon juice
(reserve the rest for another use) and salt to
taste. Sprinkle with the mint or dill.
**Serves 4 to 6 by itself, 8 to 16 as part of a mixed
hors d'oeuvre**

NOTE: If using ½-pound artichokes, use five.
Cut them in half lengthwise, and plan on
serving at least one half per person.

Late Fall Artichokes à la Grecque
Add ½ teaspoon cardamom pods, crushed, and
a pinch of dried oregano to the stock before
cooking.

Baby Artichokes à la Grecque

Serve these artichokes as part of a mixed
vegetable hors d'oeuvre or double the recipe—
it keeps very well—to have on hand as a starter
or side. Serve at room temperature.

1 pound baby artichokes
(1 to 1½ ounces each; 13 to 16 pieces)

2 lemons for preparing artichokes,
plus 2 tablespoons fresh lemon juice

$^1/_4$ pound pearl onions, peeled and trimmed
(about 1 cup)

3 medium carrots, peeled, trimmed and
cut into ¼-inch rounds (about 1 cup)

3 cloves garlic, smashed and peeled

$^1/_2$ teaspoon coriander seeds

$^1/_2$ teaspoon cardamom seeds

$^1/_4$ teaspoon mustard seeds

$^1/_4$ cup olive oil

About 2 cups Basic Chicken Stock (page 501) or
commercial chicken broth

$^1/_4$ teaspoon dried Greek oregano

1 teaspoon kosher salt

Prepare the baby artichokes (see the Cook's
Guide, page 527) using a cut lemon and lemon
water; trim the stems to ½ inch.

Put the artichokes, onions and carrots in a pot
just large enough to hold them. Add the garlic,
coriander, cardamom, mustard seeds and oil.
Pour in chicken stock to just cover the artichokes.
Bring to a boil. Loosely cover (an otoshi-buta
works very well; see Note, page 237), reduce the
heat and simmer for 20 minutes.

Reduce the heat to a bare simmer. Cook for
10 minutes more.

Stir in the lemon juice, oregano and salt. Allow
the artichokes to cool in the liquid. **Makes 4 cups**

Stuffed Artichokes

The Italians frequently stuff artichokes by poking the stuffing in between the petals instead of hollowing them out to make a shell. However, bottoms can profitably be stuffed; allow about three tablespoons of this stuffing per bottom. (For artichokes made into shells and stuffed, see the Cook's Guide, page 529.)

The instructions call for steaming the artichokes; they can just as easily be boiled or cooked in the microwave (see pages 527 and 528). Steaming and microwaving are preferable, though, as boiled artichokes often become soggy.

4 medium artichokes (about 8 ounces each)

1 lemon, halved

1 recipe Garlic and Parsley Stuffing (page 498) or 2 recipes Salt Pork and Sage Stuffing (page 498, cooked in 2 batches, then combined)

1 tablespoon olive oil, plus more for brushing artichokes

2 tablespoons Basic Chicken Stock (page 501), Roasted Chicken Stock (page 502) or commercial chicken broth

Prepare the artichokes (see the Cook's Guide, page 527), using a cut lemon and lemon water.

Put the artichokes in the top of a two-part steamer or on a steaming rack or a plate in a bamboo steamer. Fill the bottom of the steamer or a pan large enough to hold the bamboo or steaming rack with water; the water should not touch the rack. Bring to a boil over medium heat. Place the artichokes on top, cover and steam for 30 to 40 minutes, or until a knife easily inserts into the bottom. Cool slightly.

Remove the purple-tipped leaves and choke from the center of each artichoke. The artichokes may be prepared ahead up to this point; refrigerate, tightly wrapped, for up to 1 day.

Place a rack in the center of the oven. Preheat the oven to 375°F.

Divide the stuffing evenly among the artichokes, placing most of it in the cavities and sprinkling about 2 tablespoons between the leaves of each. Arrange the artichokes in a 10 x 8-inch oval baking dish, or any dish that holds them snuggly. Brush the sides of the artichokes with oil. Stir together the stock and oil and drizzle evenly over the artichokes.

Bake for 15 minutes, or until the stuffing is warmed through. Serve hot.

Serves 4 as a first course

Microwave Variation

Rub the trimmed artichokes with the lemon halves to keep them from discoloring. Wrap each artichoke tightly in microwave plastic wrap. Cook at 100% for 15 minutes, or until the bottoms are tender. Remove from the oven. Pierce the plastic to release the steam and let the artichokes stand, still wrapped, for 5 minutes.

Unwrap. Remove the purple-tipped leaves and choke from the center of each artichoke. The artichokes may be prepared ahead up to this point; refrigerate, tightly wrapped, for up to 1 day.

Divide the stuffing equally among the artichokes, placing most of it in cavities and sprinkling about 2 tablespoons between the leaves of each. Arrange the artichokes in a 10 x 8-inch oval dish. Stir together the stock and oil and pour over the artichokes.

Cover tightly with microwave plastic wrap. Cook at 100% for 5 minutes. Prick the plastic to release the steam.

Remove from the oven, uncover and serve hot.

CARDOONS

There is some question as to which came first—the chicken or the egg, artichokes or cardoons. The consensus, though, seems to be that the cardoons came first, growing wild on the southern shores of the Mediterranean. It is hard to see exactly how they morphed into artichokes. Cardoons are white or ivory in color and have a conical shape. The stems of very young cardoons are often eaten. The whole heads can be very fibrous and need fairly long cooking, and I find that they do better when cut in pieces. They are easier to eat that way as well.

Turn to **CARDOONS** in the Cook's Guide for how-tos and to the Index for more recipes.

Cardoons with Parsley, Anchovies and Olive Sauce

This is a dish with very rich flavors. Serve with a simple, light fish—no sauce.

- 3 tablespoons olive oil
- 1 small bunch cardoons (1 1/2 pounds), trimmed, peeled, cut into 3-inch lengths and boiled (see the Cook's Guide, page 560), then sliced lengthwise into 3/4- to 1-inch strips (about 3 cups)
- 1/2 cup chopped fresh parsley
- 2 tablespoons all-purpose flour
- 1 1/2 cups Roasted Chicken Stock (page 501), Enriched Chicken Stock (page 502) or commercial chicken broth

- 2/3 cup Kalamata olives (4 ounces), pitted and chopped (about 6 tablespoons)
- 3/4 teaspoon anchovy paste
- 2 tablespoons fresh lemon juice
- Kosher salt and freshly ground black pepper to taste

Heat the oil in a medium pan. Add the cardoons and parsley. Stir briefly over medium heat. Add the flour, tossing to coat. Stir in the chicken stock. Bring to a boil. Reduce the heat, cover and cook for 10 minutes.

Stir in the olives and anchovy paste. Cook for 1 minute, uncovered, to thicken and reduce the sauce. Add the lemon juice and salt and pepper to taste. **Makes 3 cups; serves 6 as a side dish**

Creamy Gratin of Cardoons with Fontina

For a luxurious, and still vegetarian, variation, tuck thin slices of white truffles underneath the cheese and replace 1/2 teaspoon of the butter with truffle oil. Add a simple green salad if serving as a main course.

- 1/2 bunch cardoons (1 pound), trimmed, peeled and cut into 3-inch lengths and boiled (see the Cook's Guide, page 560; about 2 1/2 cups)
- 2 tablespoons unsalted butter
- 2 tablespoons all-purpose flour
- 1 cup milk
- 1/2 teaspoon salt
- Small pinch of cayenne pepper
- Freshly ground white pepper to taste
- 2 ounces Fontina cheese, cut into thin pieces

Place a rack in the center of the oven. Preheat the oven to 400°F.

Arrange the cardoons in a 9-inch glass pie plate.

Melt the butter in a 2-quart saucepan. Add the flour and cook over low heat, stirring, for 5 minutes. Slowly add the milk, whisking briskly to prevent lumps; be sure to scrape the corners, where lumps can hide. Increase the heat to medium. Cook for several minutes, stirring occasionally until thickened. Add the salt, cayenne pepper, and white pepper.

Pour the sauce over the cardoons. Top with the cheese. Bake for 10 minutes, or until bubbly. **Serves 6 as a side dish, 4 as a main course**

Gratin of Cardoons with Meat Sauce

Cardoons are very popular in Italy, and here they are presented in a very Italian style.

1 tablespoon olive oil

1 small onion, chopped (about 1/2 cup)

1/2 pound ground beef, crumbled

1 cup Plum Tomato Purée (page 459), sterile-pack strained tomatoes or puréed canned tomatoes

1 tablespoon dry white wine

1/2 ounce dried porcini, soaked in 3/4 cup hot water for 15 minutes, drained, rinsed and chopped

1 teaspoon kosher salt, plus a pinch

Freshly ground black pepper to taste

1 tablespoon unsalted butter

1/2 bunch cardoons (1 pound), trimmed, peeled, cut into 3-inch lengths and boiled (see the Cook's Guide, page 560; about 2 1/2 cups)

6 tablespoons grated Parmesan cheese

Place a rack in the center of the oven. Preheat the oven to 325°F.

Heat the oil in a medium saucepan. Add the onion. Cook over medium-low heat until translucent. Increase the heat and add the beef. Cook until the beef has lost its raw color. Add the tomato purée, wine and mushrooms. Bring to a boil. Reduce the heat and simmer for 15 minutes.

Stir the 1 teaspoon salt and pepper to taste into the sauce. Set aside.

Grease a 9-inch round glass pie plate with 1/2 tablespoon of the butter. Sprinkle with the pinch of salt. Arrange half the cardoons in an even layer in the pie plate. Top with half the meat sauce and 2 tablespoons cheese. Layer with the remaining cardoons. Top with the remaining meat sauce and 1/4 cup cheese. Dot the top with the remaining 1/2 tablespoon butter.

Bake for 30 minutes. Increase the oven temperature to 350°F. Bake for an additional 10 minutes. **Serves 6 as a side dish, 4 as a main course**

NETTLES

Anyone who gardens has had a hostile confrontation with that invasive weed with hairy stems and unpleasant jagged leaves, the nettle. Strangely enough, when cooked, nettles lose their sting; but until it is time to put them in the pot, it is best to handle them with care and gloves. I find a strange consolation—as I do with wild sorrel—in knowing that the pests can be made useful in spite of themselves. Use only the leaves. The stems are too stringy. The best way to pull them is to grasp the stem near the bottom before giving an even gentle tug.

Nettles are clearly not the food of the rich, but it is well worth cooking them as ancestors and gatherers have for centuries.

In England, there are numerous recipes for nettle soup in the earliest cookbooks. Small nettles appear early in the spring and can be used as one would spinach later in the season. In Italy and Greece, other wild greens are collected to the same end. However, most of those greens can also be used raw in salad.

Just look in the Index and put young nettle weedings into spinach recipes, such as soups.

Turn to **NETTLES** in the Cook's Guide for how-tos and to the Index for more recipes.

Nettle Soup

Cooking the nettles prior to adding them to the soup concentrates their earthy flavor.

> 2 tablespoons unsalted butter or olive oil
>
> Leaves from 1/4 pound nettles, cut across into 1/4-inch strips (see the Cook's Guide, page 614; about 1 1/2 cups packed)
>
> 3 medium floury potatoes (1 1/4 pounds), peeled and cut into 1/4-inch dice (about 3 cups)
>
> 5 cups Basic Chicken Stock (page 501), Roasted Chicken Stock (page 502) or commercial chicken broth
>
> 1/2 cup heavy cream
>
> 1 teaspoon kosher salt
>
> Freshly ground black pepper to taste

Melt the butter or heat the oil in a large pot. Add the nettles. Cook, stirring, over medium heat for 5 minutes. Add 1/2 cup water. Reduce the heat and simmer for 10 minutes, stirring occasionally; the water will be almost evaporated.

Add the potatoes. Pour in the chicken stock. Bring to a boil. Reduce the heat and simmer for 8 minutes, or until the potatoes are tender. Stir in the cream.

Pass the soup through a food mill fitted with a medium-coarse disc. Season with the salt and pepper to taste. Serve hot. **Makes 6 1/2 cups**

Nettles with Olive Oil and Lemon

This is a Greek-flavored dish to accompany a simple fish or chicken or as part of a first course.

Leaves from 1 pound nettles (see the Cook's Guide, page 614; about 6 cups packed)

3 tablespoons fresh lemon juice

6 tablespoons olive oil

3/4 teaspoon kosher salt

Freshly ground black pepper to taste

Bring a large pot of water to a boil. Add the nettle leaves. Boil, partially covered, for 25 minutes, or until tender. Drain. Toss with the lemon juice, olive oil, salt and pepper.

Makes 3 cups

Nettle and Ricotta Filling

Use as a filling for ravioli or to replace a favorite filling for baked stuffed shells or manicotti.

2 tablespoons olive oil

1 medium leek, white and light green parts only, cleaned and cut into 1/2-inch dice

2 cups lightly packed coarsely chopped nettles (see the Cook's Guide, page 614)

One 15-ounce container ricotta cheese

1 cup coarsely grated mozzarella cheese, preferably fresh (about 4 ounces)

1/4 cup freshly grated Parmesan cheese

1/8 teaspoon freshly grated nutmeg

Kosher salt and freshly ground black pepper to taste

1 egg

Heat the oil in a medium skillet over medium heat. Add the leek and stir until softened, about 4 minutes. Stir in the nettles and cook just until wilted, about 2 minutes. Lower the heat, cover the pan and cook, stirring until nettles are softened, about 6 minutes. Scrape into a bowl and cool.

Stir the ricotta, mozzarella, Parmesan and nutmeg into the nettle mixture. Add the salt and pepper, then beat in the egg. The filling can be made up to 1 day in advance; cover and refrigerate until needed.

Makes 2 3/4 cups; enough to fill 40 stuffed shells, 12 store-bought manicotti or 96 homemade ravioli (page 473)

Spinach

It's hard to understand how spinach—especially with Popeye as a spokesperson—got such a bad rap. Maybe it's because we recoil from constantly being told how good it is for us, even though that is the truth. Badly overcooked and canned spinach are indeed rather repulsive, and very small children may have a problem with this vegetable's tannin. Adults usually love, as I do, well-prepared leaf spinach and Creamed Spinach (page 249). Recently there has appeared on the market what is called baby spinach. It is tender and clean, a great boon for the cook. Like all spinach, it makes a fine addition to salads. On the other hand, just as with other kinds of spinach, it takes a great volume to make a small amount of cooked spinach.

Ordinary crinkly spinach is usually cooked just in the water adhering to the leaves after washing it. Such spinach takes a great deal of washing. I usually remove the heavy stems and plunge the leaves into a sink full of cold water and then lift it and let it drain in a colander. After carefully cleaning the sink, I repeat the process two times, then drain the spinach or dry it depending on how it is to be used.

The bagged baby spinach requires no such careful washing, as the leaves are flat and don't retain dirt. It also has tender little stems that do not require removal. I usually cook it by starting with a small amount of olive oil or melted butter in a large nonreactive pan. I toss in the leaves in batches, adding more as each bunch reduces in volume. I continue until all of the spinach is wilted and cooked. Put the spinach in a colander to drain.

Turn to **SPINACH** in the Cook's Guide for how-tos and to the Index for more recipes.

Spinach Soup

Spinach requires very little to become soup. A little fat if none has been used to cook it and some chicken stock or garlic broth. Puréeing is usual. Cream is optional. The only needed seasonings are salt and pepper.

This is a somewhat more exotic version, with a distinctly Russian twist provided by the pickles and dill. It is good hot or cold.

2 pounds spinach, stemmed and washed

$1/4$ cup loosely packed fresh dill fronds

1 scallion, trimmed and thinly sliced

$1/2$ pound good dill pickles, cut into $1/4$-inch dice (if good pickles are unavailable, substitute peeled and seeded cucumbers)

One 12-ounce bottle light beer

$1/4$ teaspoon peeled, grated fresh horseradish or 1 teaspoon prepared horseradish

Kosher salt to taste

1 tablespoon unsalted butter (optional)

6 bunches sorrel (1 $1/2$ pounds), leaves cut across into $1/8$-inch strips (optional)

$1/2$ cup sour cream, or 1 $1/2$ cups if adding sorrel

$1/2$ cup plain yogurt, or 1 $1/2$ cups heavy cream if adding sorrel

1 tablespoon cider vinegar

Place the washed spinach in a large skillet with the water adhering to it. Cover and cook over medium heat just until wilted. Drain.

Place the spinach and dill in a food processor and process until finely chopped. Scrape into a metal bowl. Stir in the scallion, pickles, beer, horseradish and salt. Add 1½ cups water.

If using the optional sorrel, melt the butter in a large skillet over medium heat. Add the sorrel and cook just until the color turns. Remove from the heat. Stir the sorrel, and 1½ cups each sour cream and heavy cream into the spinach mixture. If not using sorrel, stir in ½ cup each sour cream and plain yogurt. Refrigerate until cold or reheat over low heat.

Just before serving, stir in the vinegar. Add more salt if needed.

Without sorrel, serves 8 as a first course; with sorrel, serves 12

Spinach Potato Soup

There are times when dealing with fresh spinach may be too much. Use frozen: It will be fine.

continued

One 10-ounce package frozen spinach or
   2 pounds fresh spinach, stemmed, washed
   and steamed until wilted

6 cups Roasted Chicken Stock (page 502) or
   commercial chicken broth

1/2 cup thinly sliced scallions

1/2 teaspoon minced garlic

4 tablespoons unsalted butter

1 medium floury potato, washed, peeled and
   sliced (1 cup)

1/2 cup heavy cream

1/4 teaspoon hot red pepper sauce

Juice of 3/4 lemon

1 tablespoon kosher salt

Freshly ground black pepper to taste

If using frozen spinach, cook it in about ½ cup stock until defrosted. Drain fresh or frozen, reserving the liquid, if any, and squeeze dry.

In a large nonreactive pot over low heat, cook the scallions and garlic in the butter for 10 minutes. Stir in the spinach and cook for 3 minutes longer. Pour in the remaining stock and the reserved spinach liquid (if any).

Add the potatoes, cream, hot pepper sauce, lemon juice, salt and pepper. Bring to a boil. Reduce the heat and simmer until the potatoes are soft and cooked through, 15 to 20 minutes.
Serves 6 as a first course

Brodo con Stracciatelle

Stracciatelle are little rags or strings, which is what the eggs look like when they are cooked. It is these gentle shreds that make this soup so comforting. The essentials of the soup are the stock, or brodo (which must be full flavored), the eggs and cheese. The spinach or other greens are variants, as is the prosciutto. Cooked

peas can be used instead of the greens, and if Garlic Broth (page 507) is substituted for the brodo and serrano ham for the prosciutto, this will be a distinctly Spanish soup.

The technique in this recipe is stolen, with gratitude, from Pellegrino Artusi, a brilliant cook and gastronome who wrote *The Art of Eating Well* (see the Bibliography).

Although this soup is often found in restaurants, it is infinitely better made at home. In restaurants, the eggs seldom get to the table soft enough, as they continue to cook as they wend their way from kitchen to table. Use a pot that is large enough to hold the colander above the stock without touching it so that the egg can flow freely into the soup to form the strings.

2 eggs

4 teaspoons finely grated Parmesan cheese

1 1/2 teaspoons kosher salt plus a pinch

A pinch of freshly grated nutmeg

1 tablespoon all-purpose flour

4 cups Enriched Chicken Stock (page 502) or
   Beef Stock (page 502)

1 pound spinach or Swiss chard, stemmed,
   washed and leaves cut across into narrow strips

Freshly ground black pepper to taste

In a small bowl, gently stir together the eggs, cheese, pinch of salt, nutmeg and flour; try not to get the eggs all frothy.

In a medium saucepan, bring the stock to a boil. Place a colander with widely spaced holes over the stock. Pour the egg mixture through the colander. Remove the colander and stir the soup once or twice. Lower the heat and stir in the spinach or chard just to heat through. Remove from the heat and season with the 1½ teaspoons salt and the pepper. Serve immediately. **Makes 5 cups; serves 4 as a first course**

Spinach Jade Soup

Some of the most opulent jade is a very dark green. Equally rich is this smooth dark green soup even though it has no cream and very little butter.

The soup is scrumptious hot or cold. If it is chilled and good homemade chicken broth has been used—as it should be—the soup will thicken. It may be attractive and taste yummy to swirl a little heavy cream on the surface of each portion or plop in a spoonful of sour cream. Staying lean is good too.

> 2 tablespoons plus 2 teaspoons unsalted butter
>
> 4 pounds young or baby spinach, stemmed and washed
>
> $3/4$ pound Vidalia onions, finely chopped
>
> $3^1/2$ cups Basic Chicken Stock (page 501) or commercial chicken broth
>
> $1^1/2$ to 2 tablespoons kosher salt

Heat 2 tablespoons butter in a large pot over medium heat. Stir the spinach a large handful at a time into the butter, waiting for each addition to wilt before adding another. Cook until thoroughly wilted. Purée in batches in a blender, and pour into a 4-quart pot.

In a small pot, melt the 2 teaspoons butter over medium-low heat. Add the onions; stir until translucent. Pour in ¾ cup water and cook until the onions are very tender. Purée the onions in the blender. Stir into the spinach purée.

Add the stock and salt to taste. Chill the soup thoroughly or heat to simmering before serving. **Makes 6 cups; serves 6**

Cold Spinach Sauce
To make a quick, delicious sauce for fish or chicken breasts, stir together equal parts of chilled Spinach Jade Soup and mayonnaise.

Spinach Aglio Olio

This basic can be multiplied as needed.

> 4 cloves garlic, smashed, peeled and quartered
>
> 2 tablespoons olive oil
>
> 1 pound 14 ounces (three 10-ounce bags) spinach, stemmed and washed (about 15 cups)
>
> $1^1/4$ teaspoons kosher salt
>
> $1/4$ teaspoon hot red pepper flakes
>
> Freshly ground black pepper to taste

In a large nonreactive pan, cook the garlic in the oil over medium-low heat for 5 minutes; do not allow the garlic to brown. Add as much of the spinach as will fit and increase the heat to medium. As the spinach wilts, add the remainder, in batches, turning the leaves over with a wooden spoon so that the spinach cooks evenly. Stirring occasionally, cook for 15 minutes. Remove from the heat.

Mix in the salt and red pepper flakes. Season lightly with black pepper. **Makes about $2^1/2$ cups**

Spinach Goyesca
Omit the garlic and hot red pepper flakes. Use unsalted butter and heat in the pan over medium heat until foaming, and proceed as directed.

Creamed Spinach

Even children will probably accept this version of spinach. Some people add nutmeg. I don't.

> 5 tablespoons unsalted butter
>
> 2 tablespoons all-purpose flour
>
> 1 cup heavy cream
>
> $1/2$ teaspoon kosher salt
>
> $1^1/4$ pounds spinach, stemmed, washed and cut across into thin strips (about 10 cups packed)

continued

To make the béchamel sauce: Melt 2 tablespoons butter in a medium saucepan. Add the flour and cook over low heat, stirring, for 5 minutes. Slowly add the cream to the roux, whisking briskly to prevent lumps; be sure to scrape the corners, where lumps can hide. Add ¼ teaspoon salt. Increase the heat to medium. Cook for several minutes, stirring occasionally, until thickened. Set aside.

Melt the remaining 3 tablespoons butter in a large nonreactive saucepan. Add the spinach, cover and cook until just wilted. Transfer the spinach to a food processor. Add the remaining ¼ teaspoon salt and béchamel. Process until mixed. The spinach can be made ahead and reheated. **Makes 2½ cups**

Spinach Soufflé

Scrape the creamed spinach into a large bowl. Cool to tepid, stirring often.

Preheat the oven to 400°F. Butter a 1½-quart soufflé dish. Coat the dish with grated Parmesan cheese.

Beat 4 egg yolks into the creamed spinach. Stir in 1 cup grated Gruyère or Swiss cheese and ¼ cup freshly grated Parmesan cheese. In a separate bowl, beat 4 egg whites until they hold stiff peaks. Using a rubber spatula, fold about one-quarter of the whites into the spinach mixture. Fold in the remaining whites. Scrape the batter into the prepared dish.

Bake until the top is well browned and the soufflé is risen, 25 to 30 minutes. Serve immediately, including some of the browned exterior and creamy interior in each serving.

Creamed Spinach Polenta Sandwiches

   1 recipe Creamed Spinach (page 249)

   1 loaf firm polenta (page 41)

   3 ounces Parmesan cheese, grated (about ¾ cup)

   Olive oil

   Kosher salt and freshly ground black pepper
      to taste

In a 4-quart nonreactive saucepan, cook the creamed spinach over low heat until it has thickened significantly, about 20 minutes.

Place a rack in the upper third of the oven. Preheat the oven to 400°F.

To assemble the sandwiches, cut the polenta into 10 slices. Arrange 5 slices on a large baking sheet. Put 2 tablespoons creamed spinach on each slice. Sprinkle about 1 tablespoon cheese on top of the spinach and cover with another slice of polenta. Brush the tops lightly with olive oil and sprinkle with salt and pepper. Bake until heated through, about 12 minutes. **Makes 5 sandwiches**

Eggs Florentine

This classic dish nestles poached eggs in a bed of creamed spinach. It has been made even more luscious by enriching the béchamel sauce with cheese. I serve the eggs and spinach over English muffins or, more festively, on artichoke bottoms (see the Cook's Guide, page 527).

   4 eggs

   2 pounds spinach, stemmed and washed,
      or 1½ ten-ounce packages frozen chopped
      spinach

   2½ tablespoons plus ½ teaspoon unsalted butter

   ⅓ cup all-purpose flour

   2 cups whole milk, skim milk or half-and-half

   ½ teaspoon kosher salt

   Freshly ground black pepper to taste

   Pinch of freshly grated nutmeg

   ¾ cup grated Gruyère cheese

Poach the eggs (page 479) and keep in a bowl of warm water until needed.

If using fresh spinach, add it, in batches, to a large heavy pan over medium heat and cook until limp; wait until each batch wilts before adding another. Drain thoroughly in a sieve, pressing to remove as much water as possible. Pulse in a food processor until coarsely chopped and drain again. If using frozen spinach, defrost in a sieve under warm running water. Press with the back of a spoon to remove as much water as possible.

Butter a 9-inch pie plate or quiche dish with the ½ teaspoon butter. Set aside.

To make the sauce, melt the butter in a medium saucepan. Add the flour and cook over low heat for 5 minutes, stirring. Slowly add the milk, whisking briskly to prevent lumps; be sure to scrape the corners, where lumps can hide. Increase the heat to medium. Cook for several minutes, stirring occasionally, until thickened.

Transfer the sauce to a food processor and process until completely smooth. Combine half the sauce with the spinach, salt, pepper and nutmeg. Stir ½ cup of the cheese into the remaining sauce.

Preheat the broiler, placing the rack at the highest level. Make a smooth layer of the spinach in the buttered pan. With the back of a kitchen spoon, make 4 separate depressions about 1 inch from the edge of the pan.

Drain the eggs; place 1 in each depression. Divide the sauce over the eggs; do not let any sauce touch the sides of the pan. Sprinkle the remaining ¼ cup cheese all over the top. Place the pie pan on a cookie sheet, and broil for 4 minutes. **Serves 4 as a brunch or a lunch dish**

Easy Eggs Florentine

Eggs Florentine can be made for one or many people. When I have a little creamed spinach left over, I make an egg for myself.

5 teaspoons unsalted butter

1 recipe Creamed Spinach (page 249)

5 eggs

5 teaspoons heavy cream

5 tablespoons freshly grated Parmesan cheese

Kosher salt

Place a rack in the middle of the oven. Preheat the oven to 300°F.

Grease five shirring dishes or other individual heatproof dishes (1 inch deep and 4 inches across) with 1 teaspoon butter each. Line each dish with ½ cup creamed spinach, making a depression in the middle for the egg. Put 1 egg in each dish. Spoon 1 teaspoon of heavy cream over each yolk and sprinkle 1 tablespoon of grated cheese and a pinch of salt over the egg.

Place the dishes on a baking sheet. Cook for 20 minutes, or until the egg whites are opaque but not solid. **Serves 5 as a brunch or a lunch dish**

Spinach and Mushroom Lasagna

A lovely green vegetarian lasagna. Cut into two-inch squares, it is a first course for sixteen. It is a substantial main course for six.

1 tablespoon olive oil

Four ready-made 8 x 8-inch sheets spinach lasagna noodles (8 ounces) or eight 8 x 4-inch sheets spinach lasagna noodles made from 1 recipe Green Pasta Dough (page 472; see page 470 for instructions on rolling out dough)

6 tablespoons unsalted butter

3 tablespoons all-purpose flour

2 cups milk

Pinch of cayenne pepper

continued

Kosher salt and freshly ground black pepper to taste

¹/₂ cup (1 ounce) dried mushrooms, such as porcini

¹/₂ cup heavy cream

³/₄ pound mushrooms, trimmed

³/₄ pound spinach leaves, stemmed and washed

¹/₂ cup fresh flat-leaf parsley leaves

1 medium onion, thinly sliced (about 1 ¹/₃ cups)

¹/₂ pound Emmenthaler cheese, grated (about 2 cups)

Bring a large pot of water to a boil. Add the olive oil. Prepare a large bowl of ice-cold water. Slip 2 large or 3 small pasta sheets into the boiling water. Cook for 1 to 2 minutes, until the pasta is softened but still very firm. Remove with a wire skimmer to the cold water. Repeat with the remaining pasta. Drain and lay out on kitchen towels.

For the béchamel sauce, melt 3 tablespoons butter in a medium saucepan. Add the flour and cook over low heat for 5 minutes, stirring. Slowly add the milk, whisking briskly to prevent lumps; be sure to scrape the corners, where lumps can hide. Increase the heat to medium and bring the sauce to a boil, stirring regularly. Season with the cayenne, salt and black pepper. Remove half of the sauce to a small bowl to cover the finished lasagna. Continue to cook the remaining sauce, stirring, over low heat until thickened, about 3 minutes. Remove from the heat and set aside.

Place the dried mushrooms in a small bowl and cover with 1 cup boiling water, or enough to immerse the mushrooms. Allow to stand for about 10 minutes, until the mushrooms are very soft.

Remove the mushrooms from the liquid and rinse under cold running water. Strain the soaking liquid through a fine sieve lined with a coffee filter or a piece of paper towel. Transfer the liquid to a small saucepan. Add the heavy

cream and bring to a boil over medium heat. Reduce the heat to low. Simmer, uncovered, for 20 minutes, or until the mixture has reduced and thickened considerably. Set aside.

Place the softened dried mushrooms in a food processor and add the fresh mushrooms. Finely chop.

Melt 2 tablespoons butter in a medium frying pan over moderate heat. Stir in the chopped mushroom mixture and cook for about 8 minutes, or until most of the liquid has evaporated. Remove from the heat. Stir in the reduced cream mixture and about half of the thick béchamel sauce.

Bring a large pot of salted water to a boil. Add the spinach and cook for about 2 minutes, or until completely wilted. Drain and rinse under cold water. Squeeze out the excess water but do not squeeze the spinach completely dry. Place the spinach and parsley in the food processor and finely chop.

Melt ½ tablespoon butter in a small frying pan over medium heat. Add the onion and cook for about 5 minutes, or until soft. Stir in the spinach and cook until heated through. Remove from the heat and stir in the remaining thickened béchamel.

To assemble, place a rack in the middle of the oven. Preheat the oven to 350°F. Grease the bottom of an 8 x 8 x 2-inch baking dish with the remaining ½ tablespoon butter.

Place 2 large or 4 small sheets of pasta in the bottom of the dish. Spread the mushroom mixture over the pasta and sprinkle with about a third of the grated cheese. Place 1 large or 2 small pasta sheets on top. Spread the spinach mixture over the pasta and cover with half of the remaining cheese. Cover with the remaining pasta and pour the reserved béchamel sauce over the top. Cover with the remaining cheese. Cover the dish with aluminum foil. Bake for 35 minutes. Remove from the oven and preheat the broiler.

Remove the aluminum foil from the dish and place under the broiler for about 5 minutes, or until browned evenly. Allow to stand for about 10 minutes before serving. **Serves 9 as a first course, 6 as a main course**

Gala Meat Loaf with Spinach

This meat loaf is gala because it tastes so good and looks attractive, with the green spinach splashes throughout. It is a quick microwave dish. I serve it with Olive Oil Mashed Potatoes (page 73) and Red Pepper Purée (page 629). Leftovers are good cold and make great sandwiches.

> 1 pound fresh spinach, stemmed and washed (6 loosely packed cups), or two 10-ounce boxes frozen spinach, defrosted in a sieve under warm running water
>
> 1 medium onion (about 6 ounces), peeled and quartered
>
> 3 cloves garlic, smashed and peeled
>
> 1 1/2 cups Dried Bread Crumbs (see page 510)
>
> 2 tablespoons soy sauce, preferably tamari
>
> Freshly ground black pepper to taste
>
> 1 1/2 pounds lean ground beef, preferably top round

If using fresh spinach, place it in a 10-inch quiche dish or pie plate. Cook in microwave, uncovered, at 100% for 5 minutes 30 seconds. Remove from the oven and let stand until cool.

Coarsely chop the spinach in a food processor. squeeze the excess moisture from the spinach. Transfer to a mixing bowl and reserve.

Finely chop the onion and garlic in the food processor. Add to the spinach. Add the bread crumbs, soy, pepper and ground beef and mix well.

Transfer the mixture to a 9 x 5 x 3-inch glass loaf pan, making sure there are no air pockets. Cook, uncovered, at 100% for 14 minutes.

Remove from the oven. Let stand, covered with a kitchen towel, for 10 minutes before serving. **Serves 6 as a main course**

Virginia Ham, Spinach and Rosemary Pasta

This unusual sauce looks like pesto but tastes very different.

> 1/2 pound Virginia ham, cut into 1/2-inch cubes (about 2 cups)
>
> 1 pound spinach, stemmed, washed and cooked (see the Cook's Guide, page 646; about 3 cups)
>
> 2 to 2 1/2 teaspoons fresh rosemary
>
> 1/4 teaspoon freshly grated nutmeg
>
> 1 tablespoon Dijon mustard
>
> 1/2 cup Basic Chicken Stock (page 501), Roasted Chicken Stock (page 502) or commercial chicken broth, or more as needed
>
> 3/4 pound tomato fettuccine, or substitute spaghettini or shell pasta

Process the ham, spinach, spices and mustard in a food processor for about 30 seconds, until coarsely chopped. Scrape down the sides and continue to process the mixture to a thick, smooth paste. With the motor running, add enough chicken stock so the mixture becomes a thick sauce. (Makes 3 1/3 cups)

Cook the pasta in a large pot of boiling salted water. (Remember fresh pasta will be done a few seconds after the water returns to a boil.) Drain.

Transfer to a heated serving bowl and top with the sauce. Toss briskly to mix, and serve immediately. Grated cheese is not recommended with this dish. **Serves 4 as a main course**

Broccoli and Cauliflower

While most people were laughing, I was very sympathetic when George Bush Senior confessed to a dislike of broccoli. I like broccoli, but I think I understood why he felt that way. There was almost no broccoli, green and with stems, around when he was a kid. There was plenty of its kin cauliflower; but broccoli was a novelty, an import from Italy, which still produces the widest range of different kinds of broccoli and, by extension, cauliflower, since they are basically the same vegetable in different outfits and flavors.

My husband was a small child in Vienna and doesn't remember any broccoli, although he fondly remembers his mother's cauliflower soup (page 257). Novelty is not always a recommendation for a food, particularly one such as broccoli that easily can be badly cooked and smell very strong when overdone. I would offer to make him some; but I think I would be rejected.

For a sampling of this enormous group, see the Cook's Guide.

Turn to **BROCCOLI AND CAULIFLOWER** in the Cook's Guide for how-tos and to the Index for more recipes.

Cauliflower Bavarian

When Joël Robuchon had the legendary restaurant Jamin in Paris, he created a soup that was essentially a cauliflower Bavarian cream covering a layer of aspic imbued with caviar. It was spectacular. I was proud that I had made a less spectacular dish, a cauliflower Bavarian cream, all on my own. Cream of cauliflower soup is a classic and taking it a step further by setting it with gelatin seemed perfectly logical. Oddly, a rather gently flavored soup doesn't get effaced by the chilling.

The toppings are in part for presentation. Don't add anything too strong. A dollop of caviar on top would be very festive.

All the preparation may be done a day ahead, and the Bavarian unmolded and garnished just before serving.

3 envelopes (^{1}/4 ounce each) unflavored gelatin or 2 tablespoons agar-agar (see page 501 for information on substituting agar-agar for gelatin)

^{1}/4 cup milk

^{1}/2 small head cauliflower, or as needed to yield 2^1/2 cups (^{3}/4-inch chunks) and ^{3}/4 cup tiny (^{1}/4-inch) florets

2 teaspoons fresh lemon juice

2 teaspoons sugar

^{1}/8 teaspoon freshly grated nutmeg

^{1}/8 teaspoon cayenne pepper

^{1}/4 teaspoon freshly ground white pepper

1 tablespoon kosher salt

1^1/4 cups heavy cream

TOPPINGS

1 lemon

1 orange

12 to 18 snow peas, stems and strings removed

Tomato Sauce for Stuffed Vegetables (page 461) or Baby Food Tomato Sauce (page 461)

Bring a large pot of salted water to a boil.

Meanwhile, in a glass measuring cup, sprinkle the gelatin, if using, over ¼ cup cold water. When the gelatin has absorbed the water, place the cup in a saucepan with enough water to reach halfway up the sides of the cup. Warm the saucepan over medium heat until the gelatin dissolves, occasionally scraping the sides of the cup with a rubber spatula. Remove from the heat. Add the milk to the gelatin. Stir well and set aside.

Cook the cauliflower florets in the boiling water until barely done, about 2 minutes. Remove. Put in ice water and drain for garnish.

Cook the cauliflower chunks in the boiling water for 4 minutes, or until tender. Drain well. Transfer to a food processor and purée until smooth. Add the lemon juice, sugar, nutmeg, cayenne pepper, white pepper and salt. Process to blend well. Leave the mixture in the food processer.

Check the gelatin mixture. If every granule of gelatin is not dissolved, pour through a fine sieve into the cauliflower purée. Otherwise, add the dissolved gelatin directly to the purée. Process for 1 minute, or until thoroughly blended.

Transfer the purée to a stainless steel bowl. Place it in a larger bowl filled with ice. Stir occasionally and run the spatula around the sides of the bowl until the mixture begins to thicken; it will thicken quickly. Remove from the ice bath.

Fill a 3-cup porcelain ring mold with ice and water. Set aside. Whip the cream to soft peaks. Fold the whipped cream, in 3 batches, into the thickened purée.

Drain the ice water from the mold but do not dry. Pour the purée into the mold. Cover with plastic wrap and chill until set, 3 to 4 hours, or overnight.

To prepare the toppings, bring a medium pot of water to a boil. Using a vegetable peeler, remove 3-inch-long strips of zest from the lemon and orange; be careful not to get any white pith. Cut the zest into very thin strips. Place in a small strainer and dip for a minute into the boiling water for 30 seconds. Rinse under cold running water. Drain well and set aside.

Cook the snowpeas in the boiling water for 1 minute. Drain and rinse under cold running water; set aside.

If the Bavarian was made the day before, allow it to stand at room temperature for 15 minutes before serving.

Briefly dip the mold in a large bowl of very hot water. Invert a white or yellow serving plate over the mold, then turn over the mold and plate together. Lift off the mold.

Spoon a ring of sauce around the mold, then spoon about an inch of it into the center. Arrange the snow peas around the mold, tips in the sauce, leaning them against the mold and overlapping. Sprinkle the zest over the snow peas. Arrange

the cauliflower florets in the sauce around the mold, leaving about an inch between the pieces. Serve any extra sauce in an attractive bowl with a large spoon. **Serves 6 as a first course**

Cabbages and Kin(gs)
ROOTS, HEADS, LEAVES AND STALKS

There is probably no larger or more valuable group of vegetables, particularly in winter when greens are scarce. There are even more than show up in this section of the book. The Asians have a group all their own.

Of course, spring cabbage, delicate and sweet, and early broccoli are delights in their own right, as is the more tender, crinkly savoy cabbage, which is particularly good for stuffed cabbage.

Although we don't always recognize it, the cauliflower-broccoli group is part of the cabbage family.

Pickled Vegetable Antipasto

An Italian-inspired red wine–brined vegetable antipasto, a cousin of the Kalamata antipasto (page 209), this is good with pâtés or simply with focaccia (page 475) and slices of mozzarella.

1 bunch thin carrots (about 1 1/4 pounds),
   peeled, trimmed and cut into 2 x 1/4-inch strips
   (about 3 cups)

1 small head cauliflower, cored and
   cut into pieces no larger than 1/2 inch
   (about 3 cups)

1 medium fennel bulb, trimmed and cut into
   2 x 1/4-inch strips (about 2 cups)

6 small or 4 large bottled peperoncini,
   halved lengthwise, seeded and cut across
   into 1/2-inch slices

3 cups dry red wine

1 1/2 cups red wine vinegar

1/4 cup kosher salt

Three 1-pint canning jars with two-piece lids
   (optional; see below)

Bring a large pot of salted water to a boil over
high heat. Add the carrots and boil just until
softened but still quite firm, about 2 minutes.
With a wire skimmer, remove to a colander
and run under cold water until cool. Cook
the cauliflower in the boiling water for about
3 minutes; drain and rinse under cold water.

Drain the vegetables very well. Combine
with the fennel and peperoncini in a large
bowl. Toss to mix the vegetables. Transfer to
the canning jars, dividing the vegetables and
peperoncini evenly among the jars, or a tall
narrow 1½-quart container.

Bring the wine, vinegar and salt to a boil
in a small saucepan over high heat. Boil for
1 minute. Pour the wine mixture over the
vegetables. Cool to room temperature.

Cover and store in the refrigerator for at
least 1 day, or up to 2 weeks, before serving.

Makes 6 cups

Creamy Cauliflower Soup

This is as close as I could get to my mother-in-
law's soup. Risking family memory is always
dangerous. My husband informs me that there
should be some small pieces of cauliflower
floating in the soup. Try it both ways.

With its creamy color, this looks particularly
pretty served at the table from a tureen. I find
that a bouillon-size soup bowl is just enough for
each guest. Have the chives in a separate bowl
on the side and sprinkle them over the soup in
each bowl as it is served.

Do not substitute commercial broth; the
gelatin from the bones is needed to add body.
This soup can be made ahead and reheated.

1 medium head cauliflower, cored and
   cut into 1-inch florets (about 5 cups)

6 cups Basic Chicken Stock (page 501) or
   Roasted Chicken Stock (page 502)

2 medium leeks, white parts only, split lengthwise
   in half, cut across into thin slices (about 3/4 cup)

2 large floury potatoes, washed and peeled and
   cut into thin slices (about 3 cups)

1 1/2 cups heavy cream

1 1/2 teaspoons kosher salt

2/3 bunch fresh chives (about 1/4 ounce),
   snipped into small pieces

Put the cauliflower in the top of a 10- to 12-inch
two-part steamer or on a steaming rack or a
plate in a bamboo steamer. Fill the bottom of
the steamer pan or a pan large enough to hold
the bamboo or steaming rack with 4 cups
chicken stock; the stock should not touch the
rack. (If 4 cups is too much broth, reserve the
remainder.) Bring to a boil over medium heat.
Place the cauliflower on top. Cover and steam
for 15 to 20 minutes until very tender.

continued

Transfer the cauliflower and ¾ cup of the steaming liquid to a food processor. Purée until completely smooth, stopping two or three times to scrape down the sides of the bowl. Reserve.

Add the remaining chicken stock, leeks and potatoes to the steaming liquid in the pot. The potatoes should be completely submerged; add more stock or water if necessary. Cover and bring to a boil. Reduce the heat to medium and cook for 1 hour and 15 minutes, or until the potatoes are falling apart.

Transfer the leeks, potatoes and ½ cup cooking liquid to the food processor. Purée until completely smooth, stopping two or three times to scrape down the sides of the bowl; add more liquid if necessary.

Combine the potato and cauliflower purées with the remaining cooking liquid in a narrow pot. Stir in the cream and salt. Heat slowly over a low flame so the soup does not scorch. Sprinkle each serving with chives. **Serves 8 to 10 as a first course**

Simpler Creamy Cauliflower Soup

Omit the potatoes, leeks and chives. Steam the cauliflower as directed above or simmer in the chicken stock until very soft. Transfer the cauliflower and stock to a food processor and purée until completely smooth, stopping two or three times to scrape down the sides of the bowl.

Melt 3 tablespoons unsalted butter in a 3-quart saucepan. Add 3 tablespoons all-purpose flour and cook over low heat for 5 minutes, stirring. Slowly add the cream, whisking briskly to prevent lumps; be sure to scrape the corners, where lumps can hide. Add the cauliflower purée and all the stock. Increase the heat to medium and cook until thickened. Season to taste with salt, freshly ground white pepper and freshly grated nutmeg. **Serves 6 as a first course**

Light Cauliflower Soup

This soup uses no thickeners and it is so white and creamy that people cannot believe no cream has been added.

> 2 medium heads cauliflower, cored and cut into 1-inch florets (about 10½ cups)
>
> 2¾ cups milk
>
> 2¾ cups Basic Chicken Stock (page 501) or commercial chicken broth
>
> 1 tablespoon kosher salt, or to taste
>
> Freshly ground white pepper to taste

Put the cauliflower, 2 cups milk and 2 cups chicken stock in a deep stockpot. The cauliflower will not be submerged. Bring to a boil, watching carefully, as the soup is prone to bubble over. Reduce the heat to low and cook for 20 minutes, or until the cauliflower breaks up easily when mashed with a wooden spoon.

Strain through a sieve; reserve the cauliflower and liquid separately. In 2 batches, purée the cauliflower in a food processor with some of the liquid until completely smooth. Return to the pot. Stir in the remaining cooking liquid, ¾ cup milk and ¾ cup stock. Cook over low heat until warmed through. Season with the salt and pepper. **Makes 8 cups**

Broccoli Potato Soup

Obviously this soup is green, not white. It is also somewhat sweet due to the ricotta.

    2 large floury potatoes, peeled and cut into
        1-inch cubes

    1 head broccoli, florets only, in 1 1/2-inch pieces
        (about 5 cups)

    1 cup part-skim ricotta

    6 cups Basic Chicken Stock (page 501),
        Roasted Chicken Stock (page 502) or
        commercial chicken broth

    1 tablespoon kosher salt

    Freshly ground black pepper to taste

Put the potatoes in the top of a two-part steamer or on a steaming rack or a plate in a bamboo steamer. Fill the bottom of the steamer pan or a pan large enough to hold the bamboo or steaming rack with water; the water should not touch the rack. Bring to a boil over medium heat. Place the potatoes on top, cover and steam for 25 minutes, or until soft. Set aside. Repeat with the broccoli, steaming for 10 to 13 minutes.

Transfer the potatoes to a food processor. Purée until smooth. Pour into a medium saucepan. Transfer the broccoli to the food processor and purée until smooth. Add the ricotta and pulse until just incorporated. Add 2 cups of the stock and purée until smooth.

Pour the mixture into a medium saucepan. Add remaining stock. Heat over medium heat until hot. Season with the salt and pepper.

Makes 10 cups

Viennese-Style Cauliflower

Not only did my husband relish his mother's soup, he was also fond of her typically Viennese way of serving cauliflower with buttered crumbs.

    1 medium-large head cauliflower (2 1/2 pounds),
        cored

    1 tablespoon kosher salt

    1/4 cup Clarified Butter (page 453)

    1/2 cup Dried Bread Crumbs (page 510)

    Freshly ground black pepper to taste

Place a rack in the center of the oven. Preheat the oven to 350°F.

Sprinkle the top and bottom of the cauliflower with 1 teaspoon salt each; rub to get the salt inside the cracks. Put the cauliflower in the top of a two-part steamer or on a steaming rack or a plate in a bamboo steamer. Fill the bottom of the steamer pan or a pan large enough to hold the bamboo or steaming rack with water; the water should not touch the rack. Bring to a boil over medium heat. Place the cauliflower on top, cover and steam for 18 to 20 minutes. Let cool for 10 minutes.

While the cauliflower is cooking, melt the clarified butter in a 1-quart saucepan. Cook over medium heat for 3 minutes, or until deeply brown with a nutty aroma; do not burn. Reduce the heat. Add the bread crumbs, the remaining 1 teaspoon salt and pepper to taste. Cook over low heat for 2 minutes, stirring occasionally. The bread crumbs will be a rich golden brown. Spread in a pie plate or other deep plate.

Roll the cauliflower in the bread crumbs until well covered. Use hands to pack on any loose crumbs.

Place the cauliflower, stem side down, in a 9-inch pie plate and bake for 30 minutes.

Serves 4 to 6 as a side dish

Cauliflower Cheddar Gratin

No, it's not mac and cheese, but it is delicious and substantial enough to be a veggie meal.

**1 large head cauliflower, cored and cut into
³/₄- to 1-inch florets (about 5 cups)**

3¹/₂ teaspoons kosher salt

4 tablespoons unsalted butter

¹/₂ cup all-purpose flour

2¹/₂ cups milk

³/₄ cup heavy cream

¹/₈ teaspoon cayenne pepper

1¹/₂ cups grated sharp yellow cheddar cheese

Place a rack in the center of the oven. Preheat the oven to 400°F.

Toss the cauliflower with 2 teaspoons salt. Put in the top of a two-part steamer or on a steaming rack or a plate in a bamboo steamer. Fill the bottom of the steamer pan or a pan large enough to hold the bamboo or steaming rack with water; the water should not touch the rack. Bring to a boil over medium heat. Place the cauliflower on top, cover and steam for 10 minutes. Set aside.

Melt the butter in a 2-quart saucepan. Add the flour and cook over low heat for 5 minutes, stirring. Slowly add the milk, whisking briskly to prevent lumps; be sure to scrape the corners, where lumps can hide. Add the cream, cayenne and remaining 1¹/₂ teaspoons salt. Increase the heat to medium. Cook, stirring occasionally, for 12 minutes, or until thickened. Add the cheese. Stir until melted.

Arrange the cauliflower in a single layer in a 12 x 7¹/₂ x 2-inch glass baking dish. Pour the cheese sauce on top. Bake for 45 minutes, or until bubbly and browned.

Serves 4 to 6 as a main course

Cauliflower Pasta Sauce with Anchovies and Garlic

Back to its Italian roots, cauliflower makes a very good and somewhat unusual pasta sauce. Try it tossed with medium shells or penne.

**One 2-ounce can anchovies packed in oil,
drained, oil reserved, and chopped**

**6 large cloves garlic, smashed, peeled and
chopped**

¹/₃ cup olive oil

**1 medium-large head cauliflower, cored
and cut into ³/₄- to 1-inch florets (about 5 cups)**

Kosher salt if necessary

Freshly ground black pepper to taste

Put the anchovies, reserved oil and the garlic in a 1-quart saucepan. Cook for 5 minutes over low heat, stirring until the anchovies have dissolved. Set aside.

Heat the olive oil in an 11- to 12-inch frying pan. Add the cauliflower and cook for 5 minutes over high heat, stirring constantly. Reduce the heat to low. Add the anchovy mixture. Cook for 3 minutes.

Depending on the saltiness of the anchovies, add salt and pepper if needed.

Makes 5 cups, enough to sauce 1¹/₂ pounds of pasta

Cauliflower with Bacon and Mushrooms

Cauliflower, like all the cabbages, is a big winner in the Germanic countries. This dish is robust enough to stand up to a northern winter.

**¹/₄ pound slab bacon, cut into ¹/₄-inch slices,
then across into ¹/₄-inch-wide strips**

2 tablespoons unsalted butter

1/2 medium head cauliflower, cored and cut into
   1/2- to 3/4-inch florets (about 4 cups)

5 ounces mushrooms, trimmed and cut into
   1/4-inch slices, then across into 1/4-inch-wide
   strips (about 2 cups)

3 medium shallots, chopped (about 1/2 cup)

1/2 cup chopped fresh parsley

1 teaspoon kosher salt

Freshly ground black pepper to taste

In an 11- to 12-inch frying pan, cook the bacon over low heat for 13 minutes, or until crisp, stirring occasionally. Remove the bacon with a slotted spoon; leave the fat in the pan.

Add the butter to the pan. Add the cauliflower and mushrooms. Cook for 5 minutes over high heat, stirring constantly. Add the shallots. Cook for 2 minutes, stirring. Reduce the heat to low. Add the bacon and parsley. Cook for 2 minutes, stirring. Add 1/4 cup water and use a spatula to scrape up the brown bits. Cook for a minute or so, until the water has evaporated. Add the salt and pepper. **Makes 4 cups**

Vegetable Curry

This is a slightly unusual curry mellowed with sweet potato. The colors are vibrant.

SPICE MIXTURE

2 teaspoons ground coriander

1/4 teaspoon ground fenugreek

1/4 teaspoon celery seeds

1 to 2 small dried chili peppers, such as pequín

1/4 teaspoon yellow mustard seeds

1/4 teaspoon seeds from green cardamom pods

1/4 teaspoon ground cumin

Pinch of ground cinnamon or 1 1/2 tablespoons
   good imported curry powder

FOR THE CURRY

1 tablespoon canola oil

1 medium onion, roughly chopped (about 1 cup)

2 cloves garlic, smashed, peeled and minced

1 cup tomato juice

1 cup Plum Tomato Purée (page 459), sterile-pack
   strained tomatoes or puréed canned tomatoes

1 medium sweet potato, peeled and cut into
   1-inch cubes (about 2 cups)

2 small carrots, peeled, trimmed and cut across
   into 1/4-inch rounds (about 1 cup)

5 ounces (about 3/4 cup) fresh shelled peas or
   frozen peas, defrosted in a sieve under warm
   running water

6 ounces cauliflower, cut into 1-inch florets
   (about 1 1/2 cups)

3 small stalks celery, peeled and cut across into
   1/4-inch slices (about 3/4 cup)

6 ounces broccoli, cut into 1-inch florets
   (about 2 cups)

1/4 pound mushrooms, trimmed and cut into
   1/4-inch slices

2 teaspoons kosher salt

Freshly ground black pepper to taste

1 1/2 tablespoons fresh lime juice

1 recipe Rice Pilaf (page 489)

If making the spice mixture, place all spices in a spice mill or clean coffee grinder and grind to a powder.

Heat the oil in a medium pot. Add the onion and cook over low heat, stirring occasionally, until soft, about 3 minutes. Add the garlic and spice mixture or curry powder. Cook, stirring, for 1 minute. Add the tomato juice, tomato purée, sweet potato, carrots, and fresh peas, if using. Bring to a boil. Cover, reduce the heat to low and cook for 20 minutes, stirring occasionally.

Add the cauliflower and celery. Cover and cook for 5 minutes. Add the broccoli and mushrooms. Cover. Cook for 10 minutes. Add the defrosted peas, if using. Cover and cook for 5 more minutes.

Stir in the salt, pepper and lime juice.

Serve with the rice. **Makes 6 cups**

Microwave Variation

Pour the spice mixture or curry powder into a 2½-quart casserole dish with a tightly fitting lid. Stir in the onion, garlic and oil. Cook, uncovered, at 100% for 3 minutes.

Remove from the oven and stir in the sweet potatoes, carrots, fresh peas, if using, and ½ cup tomato juice. Cover with the lid and cook at 100% for 8 minutes.

Remove from the oven and uncover. Arrange the cauliflower florets in a ring around the edge of the dish. Put the celery slices in the center. Re-cover and cook at 100% for 3 minutes.

Remove from the oven and uncover. Stir in remaining ½ cup tomato juice. Arrange the broccoli florets around the edge of the dish. Re-cover and cook at 100% for 3 minutes.

Remove from the oven and uncover. Stir in the tomato purée. Place the mushroom slices and defrosted peas, if using, over the vegetables. Re-cover and cook at 100% for 4 minutes. Remove from the oven and stir in the remaining ingredients.

Cauliflower Stew with Lamb

This is a substantial meal; serve it in bowls.

> **1 tablespoon unsalted butter**
>
> **10 ounces pearl onions, peeled and trimmed (see the Cook's Guide, page 616)**
>
> **1 pound ground lamb, crumbled**
>
> **1 medium-large head cauliflower (2½ pounds), cored and cut into 1-inch florets**
>
> **3 medium stalks celery, peeled and cut across into ¼-inch slices**
>
> **6 medium waxy new potatoes (1 pound), peeled and quartered**
>
> **4 teaspoons kosher salt**
>
> **½ cup cornstarch**
>
> **3 tablespoons fresh lemon juice**
>
> **2 tablespoons chopped fresh sage**
>
> **Freshly ground black pepper to taste**

Melt the butter in a medium stockpot. Add the pearl onions and cook over medium-low heat, stirring occasionally, for 8 minutes to lightly brown. Add the lamb and cook for 4 minutes over high heat, or until no longer pink.

Add the cauliflower, celery, potatoes, salt and 3 cups water; the vegetables will not be completely covered with liquid. Cover and bring to a boil. Lower the heat and simmer with the cover ajar, poking the vegetables down into the liquid occasionally, for 20 minutes, or until the potatoes are cooked.

Ladle out ¼ cup stew broth and let cool slightly. Combine with the cornstarch, stirring to make a smooth paste. Stir the mixture into the stew and return to a boil. Lower the heat and boil gently for about 2 minutes, until thickened and the starch flavor has cooked off. Taste for salt and add more if necessary. Stir in the lemon juice, sage and pepper. **Makes 9 cups**

Persian Cauliflower Kookoo

A kookoo is similar to an Italian frittata or Spanish tortilla. This particular version was inspired by Najimieh Batmanglij's *Silk Road Cooking* (see the Bibliography). The generous amount of fragrant spices can adhere to the pan, causing the kookoo to stick slightly. Not to worry. Just run a spatula around the pan to loosen the kookoo—or make this dish in a nonstick pan.

1/4 cup canola oil

1 small red onion, thinly sliced (about 1 cup)

1/4 medium head cauliflower (8 ounces), cut into 1/4-inch dice (about 1 1/2 cups)

1/4 cup chopped fresh parsley

2 cloves garlic, smashed, peeled and chopped

1 tablespoon kosher salt

2 teaspoons ground cumin

1 teaspoon sweet paprika

1 teaspoon turmeric

1/2 teaspoon freshly ground black pepper

1/4 teaspoon cayenne pepper

6 large eggs

1/2 cup whole milk

1 tablespoon all-purpose flour or rice flour

1/2 teaspoon baking powder

1 ounce Parmesan cheese, grated (about 1/2 cup)

Heat an 11- or 12-inch ovenproof frying pan. Add the oil and tilt to coat the entire bottom and sides of the pan. Add the onion. Cook over medium-low heat for 3 minutes, or until translucent. Increase the heat to medium. Add the cauliflower, parsley, garlic and spices. Cook for about 10 minutes, stirring occasionally, until the cauliflower is tender. Spread in an even layer in the pan.

Whisk together the eggs, milk, flour and baking powder. Stir in the cheese. Pour the egg mixture over the cauliflower mixture. Reduce the heat to low. Cook for 12 minutes. The sides will be set but the center still runny.

Meanwhile, preheat the broiler. Place the pan under the broiler for 1 to 2 minutes, until the center is set and the top is nicely browned. Loosen the edges of the kookoo, slide onto a plate and cut into wedges.

Serves 6 for lunch, 8 to 10 servings as a first course

Broccoli Purée

This purée may be frozen. It makes a good soup or sauce base; see the variation. It uses the stems when florets have been used for something else.

4 heads broccoli (about 5 pounds), stems only (see Index for floret recipes)

8 tablespoons (1 stick) cold unsalted butter

Kosher salt to taste

Peel the tough skin from the broccoli stems with a paring knife or a vegetable peeler. Trim the ends and cut the stems into 1-inch slices.

Bring a large pot of salted water to a rolling boil. Drop in the broccoli stems and cook until just tender. Drain in a colander and rinse under cold running water. In batches, purée the broccoli in a food processor until smooth.

Cut the cold butter into small chunks. Return the purée to the pan and set over medium-low heat. Stir in the butter. Beat with a wooden spoon until warm. Adjust the seasoning to taste with salt—pepper is not recommended.

Makes 2 2/3 cups

continued

Light and Tangy Broccoli Soup

The tanginess of this creamless soup is light but becomes more pronounced if it is made a day or so in advance and allowed to rest in the refrigerator.

Combine the Broccoli Purée, ⅔ cup buttermilk, and 1⅓ cups Basic Chicken Stock (page 501), Roasted Chicken Stock (page 502) or commercial chicken broth in a medium saucepan. Heat slowly until warmed through. Taste and adjust the salt if necessary. Serve warm or refrigerate, covered, for 2 to 3 days to allow the flavor to develop. **Makes 3¼ cups**

Broccoli Baked in Light Cheese Sauce

Unlike the richer, more fattening cauliflower version (page 260), this is a true side dish.

- 2 heads broccoli, florets cut into ¾- to 1-inch pieces, stems peeled, trimmed and cut across into ½-inch coins
- 3 tablespoons cornstarch
- 1 quart nonfat milk
- 4 teaspoons curry powder
- 2¾ teaspoons kosher salt
- 5 dashes hot red pepper sauce
- 9 ounces part-skim mozzarella cheese, grated (about 2¼ cups)

Place a rack in the center of the oven. Preheat the oven to 400°F.

Put the broccoli florets in the top of a two-part steamer or on a steaming rack or a plate in a bamboo steamer. Fill the bottom of the steamer pan or pan large enough to hold the bamboo or steaming rack with water; the water should not touch the rack. Bring to a boil over medium heat. Place the broccoli florets on top, cover and

steam for 4 minutes. Set aside. Repeat with the broccoli stems, steaming them for 2 minutes.

In a small bowl, dissolve the cornstarch in ⅓ cup milk. Put the remaining 3⅔ cups of milk, the curry powder and salt in a medium saucepan. Bring to a boil. Add the cornstarch slurry and whisk well. The mixture will be very thick. Remove from the heat. Stir in the red pepper sauce and 1½ cups cheese.

Arrange the florets and stems evenly in a 12 x 8¾ x 2-inch glass baking dish. Pour the cheese sauce over the broccoli. Sprinkle on the rest of the cheese.

Bake for 38 to 40 minutes, until bubbly and browned.

Serves 10 as a side dish, 6 as a vegetarian main course

Roasted Broccoli Stems with Lemon-Garlic Bath

Be sure to peel the entire length of the broccoli stems well, or there will be woody patches that will result in uneven cooking. This dish can be made up to eight hours ahead and loosely covered with foil.

- 2 heads broccoli, stems only, peeled, trimmed and cut into 2 x ½ x ½-inch sticks
- 2 cloves garlic, smashed and peeled
- 1 teaspoon kosher salt
- Freshly ground black pepper to taste
- ¼ cup fresh lemon juice
- ¼ cup olive oil

Place a rack on the lowest level of the oven. Preheat the oven to 500°F.

Arrange the broccoli stems in a 12 x 8 x 2-inch roasting pan; it is fine if they are close together.

In a mortar with a pestle, or on a cutting board using the back of a heavy knife, smash the garlic with the salt and pepper to make a smooth paste. Put the lemon juice in a small bowl. Whisk in the garlic paste and olive oil until smooth. Pour the mixture evenly over the broccoli. Turn the broccoli until all sides are coated.

Roast for 7 minutes. Turn. Roast for 8 minutes more. The broccoli is done when the stalks are easily pierced with the tip of a sharp knife. Thinner pieces will cook more quickly; remove them and roast the remaining pieces for 5 to 10 more minutes.

The broccoli may be served warm from the oven, or made ahead and served at room temperature or reheated in a 500°F oven for about 7 minutes. **Makes 2 cups**

Roasted Broccoli Stems with Spaghettini

While the broccoli is roasting, bring a large pot of salted water to boil. Cook 1 pound spaghettini. Drain, reserving 3 to 4 tablespoons of the cooking water in the pot.

Return the pasta to the pot. Toss with ½ cup freshly grated Parmesan cheese to melt slightly. Add 2 tablespoons olive oil and the roasted broccoli stems. Toss over low heat. Add ½ teaspoon hot red pepper flakes, if desired, salt and freshly ground black pepper to taste.

Or, for a smooth sauce, purée the roasted broccoli stems in a food processor, with 2 tablespoons olive oil and ½ teaspoon red pepper flakes, if desired. Add the broccoli purée to the pasta and toss over low heat. Season with salt and freshly ground black pepper to taste.

Of Cabbages and Sprouts

Green, Red and Savoy Cabbages and Brussels Sprouts

I would wager that in America most cabbage is eaten in the form of coleslaw. In Europe, it is often eaten as sauerkraut, which preserves it through the winter and preserves its vitamins as well. I do have one friend, Paula Frosch, who makes her own sauerkraut. It is excellent. I beg some from her or buy plastic sacks at the store. There is some good kraut sold in jars. I find the canned kind less good. It is worth testing and seeing what is best. Sauerkraut makes a great accompaniment to sausages, most resplendently as the Alsatian choucroute (sauerkraut) garni (lots of meats).

I seldom use red cabbage, except in soup. Otherwise it is too tough, and raw, it reminds me of all the hideous fast-food salads into which it is cut to add color. Now radicchio is used the same way, and I don't like it any better, even though it is much more costly.

Sprouts here are Brussels sprouts. I would have thought that I would have roasted Brussels sprouts when I wrote *Roasting*. I didn't, but my daughter-in-law, Jill, got me to try. They roast splendidly at 500°F in melted butter, being shaken from time to time until they are browned. Timing is difficult, as it depends on the size and age of the sprouts. A knife tip should slip in when they are done.

Turn to **CABBAGES, EUROPEAN** and **BRUSSELS SPROUTS** in the Cook's Guide for how-tos and to the Index for more recipes.

Hot Shrimp and Cabbage Slaw

Double this for a party or summer main course. Eat with pleasure.

> 3 cups thinly shredded green cabbage
>
> $^1/_2$ cup good olive oil
>
> 1 red bell pepper, peeled with a vegetable peeler, cored, seeded, deribbed and cut lengthwise into $^1/_4$-inch strips (about $^3/_4$ cup)
>
> 1 green bell pepper, peeled with a vegetable peeler, cored, seeded, deribbed and cut lengthwise into $^1/_4$-inch strips (about $^3/_4$ cup)
>
> 4 strips lemon zest
>
> 2 pounds shrimp, peeled and deveined
>
> $^1/_3$ cup fresh lemon juice
>
> 2 teaspoons kosher salt
>
> Freshly ground black pepper to taste

Bring 6 cups water to a boil. Place the cabbage in a colander in the sink. Pour the boiling water over the cabbage. Set aside.

Heat the oil in a 10- to 12-inch frying pan over medium heat. When it is hot, add the red and green pepper strips. Toss to coat with oil. Add the lemon zest. Stir to mix. Add the shrimp and cook, stirring, for 1 minute. Add the lemon juice, salt and a generous amount of pepper. Continue to cook until the shrimp is barely done. With a slotted spoon, remove the shrimp and peppers to a bowl, leaving the liquid.

Place the pan back over high heat. Add the cabbage, toss to coat and cook for 30 seconds. With a slotted spoon or skimmer, remove the cabbage and divide it among four serving plates, making a neat layer. Arrange a quarter of the shrimp and pepper mixture in the center of each cabbage layer. Divide any liquid remaining in the pan among the four plates, pouring it over the shrimp.

The salads may be served immediately or left at room temperature for up to half an hour.

Serves 4 as a first course

Stuffed Brussels Sprouts

If a head of cabbage can be stuffed, why not a Brussels sprout? The centers are easier to hollow out than one would think and the results make for a visually dynamic first course. Or they can be passed along with other hors d'oeuvre.

> 18 medium Brussels sprouts (about 11 ounces)
>
> 2 tablespoons unsalted butter
>
> 1 medium onion, finely chopped (about 1 cup)
>
> 1 teaspoon sweet paprika
>
> 1$^1/_2$ teaspoons kosher salt, or to taste
>
> 2 tablespoons Basic Chicken Stock (page 501) or commercial chicken broth

continued

1/4 pound ground lamb

Freshly ground black pepper to taste

1/2 cup dry white wine

1/2 cup Plum Tomato Purée (page 459) or
sterile-pack strained tomatoes

1/4 cup sour cream

Place a rack in the center of the oven. Preheat the oven to 350°F. Prepare the Brussels sprouts for stuffing (see the Cook's Guide, page 552). Reserve the shells.

Chop the removed centers very fine.

Melt the butter in an 8-inch frying pan. Cook the onion over low heat for 1½ minutes, or until translucent. Add the chopped Brussels sprouts and cook for 5 minutes, stirring occasionally. Add the paprika and 1 teaspoon salt. Cook for 35 to 40 minutes, stirring occasionally, until the vegetables are very soft and reduced.

Remove from the heat and add the chicken stock. Scrape any brown bits from the bottom of the pan. Add the ground lamb, the remaining ½ teaspoon salt and a generous amount of pepper. Mix well. Remove from the heat. (Makes 1 cup stuffing.)

Stuff the shells with the lamb filling, packing it in well and mounding any extra filling on top. Arrange the Brussels sprouts in an 8 x 8 x 2-inch glass baking dish so they are not touching each other or the sides of the dish. Pour ¼ cup white wine and ¼ cup tomato purée into the dish.

Bake for 35 minutes. Combine ¼ cup each white wine and tomato purée. Spoon over each Brussels sprout to moisten. Bake for 25 minutes.

With a slotted spoon, remove the Brussels sprouts to a plate. Scrape the sauce into a 1-quart saucepan. Mix in the sour cream. Cook over low heat just until heated through; be careful not to overheat, or the sauce may separate. Add salt and pepper to taste.

Arrange 3 Brussels sprouts on each plate. Top each sprout with about 1½ teaspoons sauce.
Serves 6 as a first course or as an hors d'oeuvre course with sauce on the side for dipping

Vegetarian Borscht

There are many different kinds of borscht. The very first recipe I wrote for print was an attempt to make one that my father spoke of. This borscht takes into account the many fasting days on the old Russian calendar and also the Jews who liked to use sour cream but couldn't include it if the soup had a meat base. The flavor is so intense that I don't miss the meat.

If the beets are nice and small and the greens look good, wash them, cut them across into narrow strips and add them to the soup along with the cabbage. A small whole boiled potato can be added to each bowl of soup.

1 ounce dried porcini mushrooms

2 tablespoons vegetable oil

1/4 pound mushrooms, trimmed and
cut into 1/4-inch slices

1 large onion, cut into 1/4-inch dice

10 small or 7 to 8 medium beets (about 1 1/2 pounds,
with greens—see headnote), trimmed, peeled,
quartered and cut across into 1/4-inch slices

2 medium carrots, peeled, trimmed and
cut across into 1/4-inch rounds

1 medium parsnip, peeled, trimmed and
cut across into 1/4-inch rounds

1 medium celery root (12 ounces), peeled,
trimmed and cut into 1/2-inch cubes

1 1/2 pounds floury potatoes, peeled and
cut into 1/2-inch cubes

1/2 small green cabbage (12 ounces), cored and
shredded

3 large cloves garlic, smashed, peeled and
  very finely chopped

3 tablespoons tomato paste

1 medium bunch fresh dill, fronds only,
  coarsely chopped

1/4 cup sugar

1/2 cup cider vinegar

2 tablespoons kosher salt

Freshly ground black pepper to taste

FOR SERVING

Coarsely chopped dill

Sour cream

Soak the dried mushrooms in 1 cup hot water
for 15 minutes. Drain, reserving the liquid,
and squeeze out the excess liquid. Strain all
the soaking liquid through a fine-mesh sieve.
Reserve the liquid and mushrooms separately.

In a tall narrow stockpot, heat the oil over
medium heat. Stir in the fresh mushrooms
and cook, stirring occasionally, for 4 minutes.
Stir in the onion and cook, stirring occasionally,
for 8 minutes.

Add the beets, carrots, parsnip, celery root,
2 quarts water and the mushroom soaking
liquid. Bring to a boil. Lower the heat and
simmer for 5 minutes. Stir in the potatoes,
cabbage, garlic and, if using, the beet greens.

Dissolve the tomato paste in 1/2 cup of the
liquid and stir it into the soup. Return to a boil.
Lower the heat and simmer for 5 minutes. Stir
in the reconstituted dried mushrooms and
simmer for 5 minutes, or until all the vegetables
are tender.

Remove from the heat. Stir in the dill, sugar,
vinegar, salt and pepper.

Pass bowls of chopped dill and sour cream at
the table. **Makes 19 cups; serves 8 as a main course**

Cabbage Risotto

This unusual risotto is good on its own, but
with the cabbage it makes a great vegetable
dish. I never make a small quantity of this,
because it hardly seems worth shredding
the cabbage for a small amount. This risotto
takes a little less than the usual amount of
liquid because of the juices from the cabbage.

2 3/4 cups Basic Chicken Stock (page 501),
  Roasted Chicken Stock (page 502) or
  commercial chicken broth

2 tablespoons unsalted butter

2 tablespoons olive oil

1/3 cup minced yellow onion

1 cup arborio rice

1 cup shredded green cabbage

1/4 cup packed chopped fresh parsley

2 teaspoons kosher salt

Freshly ground black pepper to taste

1/4 cup freshly grated Parmesan cheese

Heat the stock in a small saucepan; keep warm.

Melt the butter with the oil in a large shallow
pan. Add the onion. Cook for 3 minutes over
medium-low heat, or until translucent. Add the
rice. Cook over medium-high heat, stirring
continuously, for 3 minutes, or until the rice
turns white and loses its translucence. Reduce
the heat slightly.

Add 1/2 cup stock. Cook, stirring well, until
the rice has absorbed most of the stock. Add
another 1/2 cup stock and repeat the process,
making sure the liquid is mostly absorbed
before each addition of stock. Continue until
half the stock is used. Add the cabbage and
parsley. Cook until the cabbage begins to
wilt, adding some stock if necessary. Continue
adding stock by the 1/2 cup, cooking until the

liquid is mostly absorbed each time. The risotto should be creamy with a slight chew. Stir in the salt and pepper. Serve with grated Parmesan on top. **Serves 4 as a first course**

Microwave Variation

Heat the butter and oil in a 14 x 11 x 2-inch dish, uncovered, at 100% for 2 minutes. Add the onion and stir to coat. Cook, uncovered, at 100% for 2 minutes. Add the rice and stir to coat. Cook, uncovered, for 2 minutes. Uncover and stir in the stock. Cook at 100% for 9 minutes.

Add the cabbage and parsley and stir well. Cook, uncovered, for 9 minutes longer.

Remove from the oven. Stir in the salt and pepper. Serve with the grated cheese on top.

Crisp Slaw

The Germans, although we often forget it, were once the largest ethnic group in America. Their ancestors certainly brought coleslaw with them when they came here. By now, it is a heavily naturalized citizen on display at picnics and barbecues all summer long, and it accompanies sandwiches throughout the year. We have tried numerous dressings and ingredients. This version is one of my favorites. Presoaking the cabbage in salt water keeps it crisp, but this step can be omitted. The red onion, green pepper and orange carrot slivers mimic the cabbage and add color, flavor and crunch. Multiply the recipe as much as you want—and as much as your guests can eat. If the cabbage is soaked first, this keeps very well, so leftovers are no problem.

$^1/_2$ small green cabbage (12 ounces), cored and finely shredded (about 4 cups)

2 tablespoons kosher salt

1 medium red onion, thinly sliced (about 1 cup)

1 to 2 carrots, peeled, trimmed and grated lengthwise on the largest holes of a box grater (about $^1/_2$ cup)

1 medium green bell pepper, cored, seeded, deribbed and thinly sliced (about 1 cup)

DRESSING

2 tablespoons cider vinegar

$^1/_2$ cup Classic Mayonnaise (page 455), Cooked-Yolk Mayonnaise (page 455) or commercial mayonnaise

2 teaspoons sugar

2 teaspoons kosher salt

Freshly ground black pepper to taste

$^1/_2$ teaspoon celery seeds

$^1/_4$ teaspoon mustard seeds

In a medium bowl, toss the cabbage with the salt. Cover with cold water. Add a handful of ice cubes. Refrigerate for 5 to 6 hours, or up to overnight.

Drain the cabbage in a sieve and rinse well. Toss with the other vegetables in a bowl. Combine the dressing ingredients and toss with the vegetables. Refrigerate for at least 1 hour, or up to 4 days. **Makes 6 cups**

Coleslaw for the Slender

Replace half the green cabbage with shredded red cabbage. Replace the bell pepper with ½ cup green beans, tipped, tailed and, unless very thin, cut lengthwise into strips; drop briefly into boiling water and rinse under cold water. For the dressing omit the mayonnaise; increase the cider vinegar to ¾ cup and the sugar to 1 tablespoon; whisk in ¼ cup water. Combine the slaw with the dressing in a bowl. Cover the slaw with plastic wrap and set a weight on top. Refrigerate for 24 hours. Drain before serving.

Vegetable Slaw with Asian Dressing

This is a refreshing and colorful warm-weather dish. Serve it alongside roast or grilled chicken, and spoon the extra dressing over it.

Shredding the zucchini, yellow squash and carrots lengthwise against a box grater will produce the long spaghettilike strands called for here.

1 medium zucchini, trimmed and finely shredded into long strips; center seedy part discarded (about 1 1/2 cups)

1 medium yellow squash, trimmed and finely shredded into long strips; center seedy part discarded (about 1 1/2 cups)

1/4 small green cabbage, cored and sliced into long thin strips (about 2 cups)

1 medium red onion, halved lengthwise and thinly sliced (about 1 cup)

1 large carrot, peeled, trimmed and shredded into long strips (about 1 1/4 cups)

DRESSING

5 tablespoons vegetable oil

5 tablespoons rice wine vinegar

3 tablespoons fresh lime juice

1 tablespoon plus 2 teaspoons toasted sesame oil

2 teaspoons soy sauce

1/2 cup loosely packed cilantro leaves, chopped

1/2 hot red or green pepper, seeded and minced, or 1/4 teaspoon hot red pepper sauce

1 tablespoon peeled, grated fresh ginger

1 large clove garlic, smashed, peeled and chopped

1/4 teaspoon kosher salt

Before preparing the vegetables, fill a large bowl with ice water. Add the vegetables to the bowl as they are prepared. Keep them in the water until ready to use.

Whisk together all the dressing ingredients.

No more than 30 minutes before serving, drain the vegetables and pat them dry. Transfer to a bowl, pour 1/2 cup of the dressing over the vegetables and toss to coat. Remaining dressing can be refrigerated for up to 1 week.

Makes 6 cups; serves 6 as a side dish

Mildly Cardamom Cabbage

The sweet taste of cabbage comes through with these mild Indian seasonings, and they leave my mouth feeling very fresh. This goes with any roasted bird or fish. To double, see roasted green cabbage in the Cook's Guide (page 555).

1/2 medium green cabbage, quartered, cored and cut across into 1/2-inch-wide strips (6 cups)

3 tablespoons unsalted butter, melted

1 teaspoon kosher salt

1/4 cup dry white wine

3 tablespoons heavy cream

Seeds from 4 cardamom pods

Place a rack in the upper level of the oven. Preheat the oven to 500°F.

Put the cabbage and butter in a 14 x 12-inch roasting pan. Toss the cabbage until lightly coated; the butter will not entirely coat each piece.

Roast for 15 minutes. Use a spatula to toss and turn the cabbage pieces. They will still be very moist, particularly those in the center of the pan. Be sure to scoop up the center pieces and redistribute them around the pan for even cooking. Roast for 15 minutes more. About half the pieces will be nicely browned. Sprinkle with the salt. The cabbage may be held at this stage in the refrigerater for up to 24 hours; bring to room temperature before continuing.

Combine the wine, cream and cardamom in a small bowl. Place the roasting pan with the cabbage over medium heat. Pour in the wine mixture. Stirring with a wooden spoon, deglaze the pan, turning the pan from time to time to dissolve all the brown glaze in the bottom. Cook for 5 minutes, or until hot. **Makes 1 1/2 cups; serves 3 as a side dish**

Hungarian Roasted Cabbage
Substitute 1/4 cup sour cream, 2 tablespoons mild paprika and 2 teaspoons caraway seeds for the heavy cream and cardamom. Do not let boil during final stovetop cooking, or the sour cream will curdle.

Slow-Braised Cabbage with Garlic

Whenever I roast a goose, I make sure to save the immensely flavorful fat, which adds a meaty dimension to any dish. A 12-pound goose will yield about 4 cups of fat. To store the fat, let it cool slightly and then pour through a paper coffee filter. The fat will keep virtually indefinitely in the freezer.

1/4 cup goose fat

2 cloves garlic, smashed, peeled and minced

2 heads savoy cabbage, outer leaves removed, deeply cored to remove the thickest ribs and cut into 1-inch chunks (about 24 cups)

1 teaspoon kosher salt, or to taste

Freshly ground black pepper to taste

Melt the fat in a deep 11- to 12-inch frying pan over low heat. Add the garlic and cook until it is just beginning to brown. Break up the cabbage leaves and add to the pan, turning until well coated with fat. Add the salt. Cook for 5 minutes, stirring occasionally.

Add 1/2 cup water. Cook for about 30 minutes, stirring occasionally, until the water has evaporated and the cabbage is completely wilted. Taste for seasoning. Add pepper and additional salt, if desired. **Makes 5 cups; serves 4 to 6 as a side dish**

Curried Cabbage

This is a spectacular and surprising side dish. It's mildly spicy and quite smooth.

1 tablespoon vegetable oil

1 1/2 teaspoons curry powder

1 medium onion, thinly sliced (about 1 cup)

4 cups shredded green cabbage (about 12 ounces)

1 1/2 teaspoons fresh lemon juice or 1 tablespoon fresh lime juice

2 tablespoons regular or nonfat yogurt

Heat the oil in a 10- to 11-inch skillet over medium heat. Add the curry powder. Cook for 30 seconds, just until fragrant. Add the onion. Cook until translucent. Add the cabbage. Cook, stirring occasionally, until wilted and soft to the bite. Remove from the heat. Stir in the lemon juice and yogurt until the cabbage is coated. Serve hot. **Serves 4 as a side dish**

Microwave Variation
Stir together the oil and curry powder in a 13 x 10 x 2-inch oval dish. Cook, uncovered, at 100% for 2 minutes. Remove from the oven

and add the cabbage and onion. Stir well to coat with the oil. Cover tightly with microwave plastic wrap. Cook at 100% for 12 minutes, stirring once halfway through cooking. Prick the plastic to release the steam.

Remove from the oven and uncover. Stir in the remaining ingredients and serve.

Deli Pizza

14 ounces sliced bacon, cut into $1/2$-inch squares (about $2^1/3$ cups)

A double recipe Basic Focaccia dough (page 475; omit the toppings)

$3^1/2$ cups sauerkraut, drained and coarsely chopped

14 ounces Swiss cheese, grated (about $3^1/2$ cups)

Kosher salt and freshly ground black pepper to taste

Preheat the oven to 400°F. Grease two large baking sheets.

Cook the bacon squares in a large frying pan over medium-high heat for 5 minutes, or until cooked through and no longer soft but not browned at all. Remove the bacon and drain on paper towels.

Divide the dough into seven ⅓-pound pieces, each about the size of a tennis ball. On a lightly oiled surface, roll each piece of dough into a circle about ¼ inch thick. Shape each one into a scant 7-inch circle with an edge that is ½ inch wide and ¾-inch deep. Place on the greased baking sheets.

Spread the sauerkraut evenly on the dough. Sprinkle the cheese on top and cover with the bacon. Bake for 20 to 25 minutes, or until the crust is golden, the cheese is melted and the bacon is crisp. **Makes 7 individual pizzas**

White Noodles, Green Cabbage, String Beans and Cream

This is a wonderfully elegant first-course pasta, simple to make and with an original combination of unexpected ingredients. Be sure the cabbage is young and, if possible, pale green, so that it has a delicate taste. The creamy fettuccine is pale but for hints of green beans (the cabbage and onions disappear), so serve it on plates with a colorful rim.

3 tablespoons unsalted butter

2 cups thinly sliced (about $1/8$ inch) onions

3 cups sliced ($1/8$-inch thick) green cabbage

1 pound string beans, tipped, tailed, cut lengthwise into quarters and blanched for 2 minutes in boiling salted water

$1/2$ pound dried fettuccine

$2^1/2$ cups heavy cream

2 tablespoons fresh lemon juice

$2^1/4$ teaspoons kosher salt

Freshly ground black pepper to taste

A tiny squeeze of Hungarian paprika paste (optional)

Bring a large pot of salted water to a boil.

Melt 2 tablespoons butter in a large skillet over medium heat. Add the sliced onions and cook until soft and translucent but not browned. Add the remaining tablespoon of butter and let melt. Add the cabbage and beans and toss to mix with the onions. Remove from the heat.

Cook the pasta in the boiling salted water until done but still firm. Drain and immediately toss with the onion mixture. Place the skillet over medium heat. Add the cream, lemon juice, salt, pepper and paprika paste, if you want a hint of sharpness. Toss until heated through.
Serves 8 as a first course

Creamy Brussels Sprouts and Pearl Onions

Small to medium Brussels sprouts work best in this dish; they cook in the same amount of time as the onions. If only larger Brussels sprouts are available, steam them separately and increase the cooking time by a few minutes.

The sauce can be made with milk, stock or even half of each, depending on how much richness is preferred.

> $3/4$ pound small to medium Brussels sprouts, trimmed (about $2 1/2$ cups)
>
> 6 ounces pearl onions, peeled and trimmed (see the Cook's Guide, page 616; a generous $1 1/2$ cups)
>
> 2 tablespoons unsalted butter
>
> 2 tablespoons all-purpose flour
>
> 1 cup milk, Basic Chicken Stock (page 501), Roasted Chicken Stock (page 502) or commercial chicken broth, or $1/2$ cup milk plus $1/2$ cup chicken stock
>
> 1 teaspoon kosher salt
>
> Pinch of cayenne pepper
>
> 2 tablespoons chopped fresh parsley (optional)

Put the Brussels sprouts and onions in the top of a two-part steamer or on a steaming rack or a plate in a bamboo steamer. Fill the bottom of the steamer pan or a pan large enough to hold the bamboo or steaming rack with water; the water should not touch the rack. Bring to a boil over medium heat. Place the vegetables on top, cover and steam for 10 to 11 minutes, or until a knife easily slips into the flesh. Set aside.

Melt the butter in a medium saucepan. Add the flour and cook over low heat for 5 minutes, stirring. Slowly add the milk, whisking briskly to prevent lumps; be sure to scrape the corners, where lumps can hide. Add the salt and cayenne. Increase the heat to medium. Cook for several minutes, stirring occasionally, until thickened.

Add the Brussels sprouts, onions and optional parsley. Cook over low heat until fully heated through. **Makes 3 cups**

Basic Roasted Brussels Sprouts

Multiply this recipe as many times as desired.

> 1 tablespoon olive oil or unsalted butter
>
> $1/2$ to $3/4$ pound Brussels sprouts, ends trimmed (about 2 cups)
>
> Kosher salt to taste
>
> 1 teaspoon fresh lemon juice

Place a rack in the bottom third of the oven. Preheat the oven to 500°F.

Put the oil or butter in the smallest baking pan that will hold the Brussels sprouts in one layer; if using the butter, melt it by placing the pan in the oven for 1 minute.

Roll the Brussels sprouts in the fat. Roast for 7 to 15 minutes, depending on size. Salt to taste. Toss with the lemon juice. **Makes a scant 2 cups**

Roasted Brussels Sprouts and Chestnuts

In a pinch, vacuum-packed chestnuts can be used. But fresh chestnuts are better and worth the extra effort.

> 2 tablespoons unsalted butter
>
> $3/4$ pound medium Brussels sprouts, trimmed (about $2 1/2$ cups)
>
> 1 cup Roasted Peeled Chestnuts (page 508)
>
> Kosher salt to taste

Place a rack in the bottom third of the oven. Preheat the oven to 500°F.

Put the butter in an 8 x 12-inch baking pan. Melt the butter by placing the pan in the oven for a minute.

Add the Brussels sprouts and chestnuts to the pan. Toss to coat well. Roast for 7 minutes. Turn the pieces over. Roast for another 7 minutes, or until the Brussels sprouts are crisp and browned. Add the salt. Mix well. **Makes 3 cups**

Brussels Sprouts with Caraway and Sour Cream

A dish with Hungarian antecedents. Serve as a side dish with roast chicken, pork or game or pair with boiled potatoes as a main course. The recipe can be easily doubled.

- 1 tablespoon unsalted butter
- 1 small onion, finely chopped (about $1/2$ cup)
- 1 tablespoon sweet paprika
- $3/4$ pound medium Brussels sprouts, trimmed (about $2 1/2$ cups)
- $2/3$ cup sour cream
- 2 teaspoons caraway seeds
- $3/4$ teaspoon kosher salt
- 1 teaspoon fresh lemon juice

Melt the butter in a medium pan. Cook the onion over medium-low heat until translucent. Add the paprika; cook for 30 seconds. Add the Brussels sprouts. Toss to coat with the paprika-onion mixture. Pour in $1/3$ cup water. Bring to a boil. Loosely cover the pan. Reduce the heat to medium-low. Simmer 12 to 17 minutes, or until a knife inserts easily into the Brussels sprouts. The liquid will be mostly evaporated. The dish can be made ahead up to this point. Slowly rewarm before proceeding.

Add the sour cream, caraway and salt. Cook over low heat to warm through; do not let boil. Turn off the heat and stir in the lemon juice. **Makes 2 cups; serves 4 as a side dish**

Sweet-and-Sour Red Cabbage

I eat this straight from the fridge, but it was intended to go with a rich meat such as venison. Warm, it makes a meal with Potato Pancakes and Fresh Applesauce with Horseradish (pages 76 and 413).

- $1 1/2$ tablespoons rendered chicken fat or vegetable oil
- 1 medium onion, thinly sliced (about 1 cup)
- Scant 1 cup red wine vinegar
- 2 teaspoons sugar
- $1/2$ teaspoon kosher salt
- $1/2$ teaspoon freshly ground black pepper
- 4 cloves
- 1 large European bay leaf
- 6 juniper berries
- 1 medium red cabbage, cored and shredded (about 8 cups)

Heat the chicken fat in a large saucepan. Cook the onions over low heat until translucent. Add 1 cup water, the vinegar, sugar, salt, pepper, cloves, bay leaf and juniper. Bring to a boil.

Add the cabbage. Stir to mix well, and bring the mixture back to the boil. Reduce the heat to a simmer. Cover the pan and simmer for 45 minutes, or until the cabbage is tender. **Makes 4 ample cups; serves 6 as a side dish**

Stuffed Whole Cabbage

This dramatic presentation can be set off by a tomato sauce and sour cream.

4 cloves

2 European bay leaves

3 tablespoons olive oil

1 large onion, finely chopped (about 2 cups)

3 cloves garlic, smashed, peeled and minced

1 head savoy cabbage (1 3/4 pounds), prepared
  for stuffing whole (see the Cook's Guide,
  page 556), interior cabbage reserved and finely
  chopped

3/4 cup chopped fresh mint

3/4 pound ground lamb

1 1/2 tablespoons kosher salt

Freshly ground pepper to taste

3/4 cup dry red wine

3/4 cup Basic Chicken Stock (page 501),
  Roasted Chicken Stock (page 502) or
  commercial chicken broth

Place a rack in the middle of the oven. Preheat the oven to 350°F.

Wrap the cloves and bay leaves in a small piece of cheesecloth. Set aside.

Heat the olive oil in a large pan over medium heat. Add the onion and cook for 5 minutes or until translucent. Add the garlic, chopped cabbage and the spice packet. Cook for 30 minutes, or until the cabbage is very soft and reduced.

Remove from the heat. Discard the spice packet. Add the mint, ground lamb, salt and pepper. Mix well.

Slice a small piece from the rounded top of the cabbage so it can stand upright when it's served. Fill the cabbage with the stuffing; pack well. Place stuffing side up in a 10 x 12 x 2-inch roasting pan. Add the wine and chicken stock to the pan. Bake for 1 hour 15 minutes.

Turn upside down into a deepish round platter. Let cool slightly and cut in wedges with a bread knife to serve. **Serves 4 to 6 as a main course**

Stuffed Cabbage Rolls

This is a slightly Romanian version. I prefer it to the more common sweet one.

1 large head savoy cabbage (2 1/2 to 3 pounds)

1/4 recipe Bacon Lardons (page 509; made from
  2 ounces bacon), fat reserved

1 tablespoon canola oil, or as needed

1 1/4 cups drained sauerkraut, 3/4 cup liquid
  reserved (if sauerkraut is very salty,
  rinse with cold water and drain)

1 medium onion, thinly sliced crosswise
  (about 1 cup)

2 teaspoons sweet paprika

1/4 teaspoon caraway seeds

1/2 pound ground beef

1/4 cup long-grain white rice

2 teaspoons kosher salt, or to taste

Freshly ground black pepper to taste

2 small European bay leaves

1 cup Plum Tomato Purée (page 459),
  sterile-pack strained tomatoes or puréed
  canned tomatoes, or as needed

FOR SERVING (optional)

1 recipe Beet Caraway Sauce (page 175)

Sour cream

Prepare 8 cabbage leaves for stuffing (see the Cook's Guide, page 556).

Prepare the lardons; remove the bacon to a paper towel to drain. Add the oil to the pan (a very meaty bacon will leave only ½ teaspoon fat; use less oil if the bacon has rendered a lot of fat). Add ¼ cup sauerkraut liquid to the pan. Increase the heat to medium. Continuously stir and scrape the brown bits from the pan bottom until the liquid has evaporated. Reduce the heat to low. Add the onion. Cook until limp and the volume has reduced by half. Add the paprika. Cook for 2 to 3 minutes over very low heat. Add ¾ cup sauerkraut; mix well. Remove from the heat and stir in 20 caraway seeds and the bacon. Set aside.

Place a rack in the bottom third of the oven. Preheat the oven to 350°F.

Cook the beef in a small nonstick pan over medium heat, breaking up chunks with a wooden spoon, just until the beef loses its raw color. Combine with the onion-sauerkraut mixture. Add the rice and ¼ cup sauerkraut liquid; mix well. Taste for saltiness; add up to 1 teaspoon salt and pepper to taste.

To assemble the rolls, overlap the cut ends of each leaf and place about ⅓ cup filling in the center. Tuck in the sides and carefully roll up the leaf—not too tight, so the rice has room to expand. If the rolls will not stay together by simply tucking in the edges, secure each roll with a toothpick. About ⅓ cup filling will be left.

Carefully place the rolls seam side down in a 10 x 12 x 2-inch baking pan. Tuck the bay leaves among the rolls. Stir together the remaining ½ cup sauerkraut and ¼ cup sauerkraut liquid, remaining beef filling and enough tomato purée (about 1 cup) to make 2 cups sauce. Taste for saltiness; add up to 1 teaspoon salt and pepper to taste. Pour evenly over the cabbage rolls.

Bake for 1 hour. Add 1 cup water to the pan. Rotate the pan and spoon some sauce over each cabbage roll. Bake for another hour.

Reduce the oven temperature to 300°F. Add ½ cup water to the pan. Rotate the pan and spoon some sauce over each cabbage roll. Bake for 1 more hour. The cabbage rolls should be browned and the liquid evaporated.

Serve with the beet sauce and sour cream, if desired. **Serves 8 as a first course, 4 as a main course**

Stuffed Cabbage Rolls with Beef Glaze

Here is a stovetop variation of the recipe above that finishes cooking in the oven. In place of the tomato sauce, I use a meat sauce flavored with bits of tomato and wine-soaked raisins.

Preheat the oven to 350°F.

Omit the ingredients for the tomato sauce. Add ¼ teaspoon ground ginger and a dash of nutmeg to the stuffing. Follow the instructions above for preparing the cabbage rolls. Place seam side down in a deep heavy ovenproof saucepan with 1 cup Beef Stock (page 502) or 1 cup beef bouillon with 1 package gelatin dissolved in it. The stock should barely cover the rolls. Add about 3 ripe tomatoes, peeled, seeded and diced.

Cover tightly and cook over medium heat for 30 minutes. Reduce the heat and add more stock if needed. Simmer for 20 minutes.

Meanwhile, soak ½ cup raisins in ¼ cup Tokay or other sweet wine or dark port.

Add the soaked raisins to the pan. Bake, uncovered, for 20 minutes, turning the rolls after 10 minutes so the top and bottom brown evenly.

Roast Turkey with Sauerkraut Stuffing

Think of a turkey as a large chicken without much fat of its own. I cook turkey in a rather unorthodox way: quickly at high heat. Not only is this the way I do most roasting, but I also find that it gives a much juicier turkey. As with chicken, I do not truss and I do not rack. I do baste: The skin is thin; the bird is large. It still stays crisp.

Make the extra effort of finding a fresh turkey. It usually only requires ordering ahead. Make sure it has not been injected with anything. Turkey is one of those fortunate ingredients with a low enough price so that we can afford the best. Injected turkeys are tougher, and you are paying for water.

When I invented this stuffing, I felt very original; then I was told that in Maryland they serve turkey with sauerkraut. Well, a good idea for them seems a great idea to me—but as a stuffing.

For those who want more stuffing, simply double the amounts given below. Bake extra in a buttered heatproof casserole, moistening it with additional chicken stock and bacon fat as required.

One 15-pound turkey, preferably fresh, giblets removed

4 cups Basic Chicken Stock (page 501) or commercial chicken broth, or as needed

Freshly ground black pepper to taste

1 pound bacon

4 medium onions, thinly sliced (about 4 cups)

1 to 1 1/4 pounds sour rye bread with seeds, crusts left on, cut into 1/2-inch cubes

1 tablespoon caraway seeds

Two 16-ounce bags, jars or cans sauerkraut, drained in a sieve

Kosher salt to taste

Reserve the turkey liver for another use. In a small saucepan, combine the remaining giblets, turkey neck and enough stock to cover. Simmer for 4 to 5 hours over low heat; replenish the stock as necessary.

Meanwhile, about 2½ hours before serving, preheat the oven to 500°F. Rinse the turkey body cavity. Pat dry with paper towels. Sprinkle the outside with pepper.

In a large heavy frying pan, cook half the bacon over medium heat for about 6 minutes; it should be just crisp, but not dry. Drain on paper towels. Repeat with the remaining bacon. Crumble coarsely.

Pour off all but 3 tablespoons of the fat from the bacon pan; reserve the extra fat. Add the onions to the pan. Cook over medium heat, stirring frequently, until wilted and golden brown, about 10 minutes.

In a large bowl, toss the bread, bacon, onions, caraway, and ¼ teaspoon pepper until mixed. Add the sauerkraut a handful at a time, mixing well after each addition. Carefully add salt to taste; the bacon and sauerkraut will have plenty of salt. Moisten with about ½ cup chicken stock.

Stuff the body cavity and crop of the turkey. Secure the crop with a long metal skewer, if desired. Roast the turkey until the leg joint near the backbone wiggles easily, about 2 hours. Baste the turkey with the reserved bacon grease every 20 minutes during roasting. Let the turkey rest at least 10 minutes before removing the stuffing and carving.

While the turkey is resting, remove the giblets and neck from the stock. Slice the heart, gizzard and neck meat and return to the stock. Season with salt and pepper. Keep hot over low heat until ready to serve. This is your gravy, and wonderful it is. I have been known to skip the turkey and just have stuffing and gravy, grits and gravy, or mashed potatoes and gravy.
Serves 12 as a main course, with leftovers

Cabbages Without Heads

Broccoli di Raab, Kale, Mustard Greens and Collards

Broccoli di raab is primarily Italian, kale is European, but much used in North America. Mustard greens pop up on every continent and collards—so called—are the province of the American South, but show up in other places under other names.

Specific information about each of these greens is in the Cook's Guide. They are all strong in taste and fairly fibrous. This means longish cooking and strongish flavorings.

Turn to **BROCCOLI DI RAAB, KALE, MUSTARD GREENS** and **COLLARD GREENS** in the Cook's Guide for how-tos and to the Index for more recipes.

Kale Pissaladière

This is a nice variation on the traditional pissaladière. The saltiness of the anchovies pairs well with the sharp flavor of the kale.

DOUGH

4 cups all-purpose flour

14 tablespoons (7 ounces) unsalted butter, cut into ¹/₂-inch pieces

¹/₄ teaspoon kosher salt

TOPPING

2 tablespoons olive oil

1 large sweet yellow onion, finely chopped (about 1²/₃ cups)

4 cups braised kale leaves (see the Cook's Guide, page 598), finely chopped (about 2¹/₂ cups)

1 teaspoon kosher salt

Freshly ground black pepper to taste

¹/₄ cup dark raisins

Two 2-ounce cans anchovy fillets in olive oil

GLAZE

1 egg, beaten with 2 tablespoons water

Place the flour, butter and salt in a food processor and pulse only until the pieces of butter are evenly distributed and coated with flour; do not overprocess. With the machine running, again in on-and-off pulses, add only enough ice water—about ¾ cup—to form a cohesive, but not sticky, dough. Wrap in plastic wrap and refrigeate until needed.

In a large pan, heat the olive oil. Add the onion and cook over medium heat until translucent, 5 to 10 minutes. Add the kale. Cook for 20 minutes, stirring occasionally; the mixture should be moist but not wet, and the kale cooked through. Mix in the salt and season with pepper. Set aside to cool.

Preheat the oven to 425°F.

In a covered dish, soak the raisins in boiling water for 15 minutes. Drain and put aside.

Roll out the dough into a 9 x 18-inch rectangle. Cut into six 9 x 3-inch strips. Place on two baking sheets. Cut partway through the dough to make a border ¼-inch from the edges of each strip. Brush the egg glaze onto the edges of the dough.

Bake the pastry strips for 4 minutes. Remove from the oven. Spread 3 tablespoons of the kale mixture evenly down in the center of each strip. Brush the egg wash on the ¼-inch edge. Crisscross 6 anchovies diagonally across the filling on each dough strip, forming three crosses. Place a soaked raisin in the center of each cross.

Bake for 10 minutes, or until the pastry is golden brown but not until the filling is crisp.

Makes 6 strips

Chickpea and Lentil Soup

When I'm not feeling lean and mean, I dribble on some good olive oil right before serving.

4 cups liquid from "Braised" Collards with Vegetables (page 286)

³/₄ cup French green lentils, rinsed

1 cup drained canned or cooked chickpeas

²/₃ cup chopped fresh parsley

Kosher salt and freshly ground black pepper to taste

Good olive oil for dribbling (optional)

In a medium saucepan, bring the liquid to a boil. Add the lentils. Simmer until just tender, 20 to 25 minutes. Add the chickpeas. Simmer for

1 minute. Add ⅓ cup of the parsley. Simmer for 3 minutes. Salt and pepper to taste.

Serve with the remaining parsley and a drizzle of olive oil over the top, if desired. (If making ahead, do not add the parsley until reheating.) **Makes 4 cups**

Bean and Broccoli di Raab Soup

3 or 4 anchovy fillets

¼ teaspoon dried rosemary

¼ cup olive oil

½ teaspoon minced garlic

½ pound broccoli di raab, trimmed and cut into 1-inch pieces (about 4 cups packed)

5 cups Basic Chicken Stock (page 501), Roasted Chicken Stock (page 502) or commercial chicken broth

½ cup small elbow macaroni or shell macaroni

¾ cup canned navy beans or small white beans, rinsed and drained

2½ teaspoons kosher salt

Freshly ground black pepper to taste

Freshly grated Parmesan cheese for serving

Chop the anchovies and rosemary together into a paste.

Heat the oil in a medium saucepan. Add the anchovy-rosemary paste and garlic. Cook until the garlic just begins to brown. Add the broccoli di raab and toss to coat with the oil. Cook, stirring frequently, until the greens are wilted.

Add the stock and bring to a boil. Reduce the heat, add the macaroni and simmer for 8 minutes. Stir in the beans, salt and pepper. Simmer for 1 to 2 minutes more, until the pasta is cooked through and the flavors are melded. Serve with the cheese. **Makes 6 cups**

Creamy Broccoli di Raab Soup

This somewhat unusual potage contrasts the slight, but pleasant, bitterness of the broccoli di raab with the richness of the cream.

1 tablespoon olive oil

1 bunch broccoli di raab, trimmed and cut across into 1-inch pieces

1 medium floury potato, peeled and cut into 1-inch chunks

4 cups Basic Chicken Stock (page 501), Roasted Chicken Stock (page 502) or commercial chicken broth

½ cup heavy cream

1 tablespoon kosher salt, or to taste

Freshly ground black pepper to taste

In a medium saucepan, heat the oil over medium heat. Add the broccoli di raab and turn to coat with oil. Cook, turning, for 3 minutes, or until wilted. Cover again and cook for 3 minutes.

Add the potato and stock. Bring to a boil. Lower the heat and simmer for 15 minutes, or until the raab and potatoes are very soft.

Strain the liquid from the solids; reserve the liquid. In a blender, working in batches of no more than 2 cups, purée the solids with some of the liquid. Scrape the soup back into the pan; add the remaining liquid. Whisk in the cream. Heat through, and season with the salt and pepper. **Makes 6 cups**

Broccoli di Raab, Greens and Chicken Soup

Think of this as Italian comfort food. The recipe interests me because of a certain prissiness in it. I developed it years ago and put it in *Food for Friends*. I obviously thought whole floating cloves of garlic were unacceptable and tied them up in a cloth so that they could be removed. Today, I would probably add two more cloves and let them all float, prizes for the eaters. Certainly, the cook should suit the occasion and the friends.

2 tablespoons olive oil

1/2 cup minced onion

1 small bunch broccoli di raab, trimmed and cut across into 2-inch pieces

8 cups Basic Chicken Stock (page 501), Roasted Chicken Stock (page 502) or commercial chicken broth

4 to 6 medium cloves garlic, unpeeled—tied in a cheesecloth bag if desired

Kosher salt and freshly ground black pepper to taste

1/2 cup pastina

4 teaspoons fresh lemon juice

Freshly grated Parmesan cheese for serving

In a medium saucepan, heat the oil over medium heat. Stir in the onion and cook, stirring occasionally, for 10 minutes. Stir in the broccoli di raab and cook for 2 minutes.

Add the chicken stock and the garlic cloves. Bring to a boil. Lower the heat and simmer for 30 minutes.

Remove and discard the garlic cloves or untie the bag and drop the cloves into the broth. Season with salt and pepper. The soup can be made ahead to this point and refrigerated for up to 2 days.

Return the soup to a boil. Stir in the pastina and simmer for 1 to 2 minutes, until just tender. Stir in the lemon juice.

Pass the Parmesan at the table.

Makes 10 cups; serves 8 as a first course

Escarole and Chicken Soup

Substitute 1 head escarole for the broccoli di raab. Wash in several changes of water, then cut across into 2-inch strips. Proceed as directed.

Green Soup

Double the recipe and keep the extra to eat cold the next day. When made with a vegetarian broth (page 506), it is good for all but vegans.

2 tablespoons unsalted butter (if serving hot) or canola oil (if serving cold)

1/4 pound tender mustard greens or kale, cut across into narrow strips

4 cups Basic Chicken Stock (page 501), Roasted Chicken Stock (page 502) or commercial chicken broth

1 cup sorrel leaves, cut across into narrow strips

8 egg yolks

1 cup heavy cream

3 small zucchini, trimmed and cut into matchstick strips

6 tablespoons Pesto Sauce (page 467)

1/2 cup thinly sliced (cut across the leaf) fresh basil

1 teaspoon kosher salt, or to taste

Freshly ground black pepper to taste

In a medium saucepan, melt the butter or warm the oil over medium heat. Stir in the greens, toss to coat with butter or oil and cook for about 1 minute. Stir in the stock and bring to a boil. Lower the heat and simmer for 15 to 20 minutes, or until the greens are tender.

Stir in the sorrel and simmer for 5 minutes. The soup can be made ahead to this point and refrigerated for up to 2 days.

If the soup has been refrigerated, reheat it. In a small bowl, beat the egg yolks with the cream. Whisk in about one-third of the soup, a ladleful at a time, to slowly bring up the temperature of the yolks. Whisk the egg yolk mixture back into the soup. Stir in the zucchini, pesto, basil, salt and pepper. Cook, stirring, over medium heat until the soup has slightly thickened and coats the back of a wooden spoon. Serve immediately, or chill for at least 5 hours and serve cold.

Makes 6 cups; serves 4 or 5 as a first course

Braised Broccoli di Raab

This is the classic Italian way of making this dish. I often have it as a main course. If the raab is finely chopped, it is also a splendid pasta sauce.

> **2 tablespoons olive oil**
>
> **3 medium cloves garlic, smashed, peeled and thinly sliced**
>
> **1¹/2 pounds broccoli di raab, rinsed, trimmed, patted dry and cut across into 1-inch pieces (about 16 cups)**
>
> **¹/4 teaspoon hot red pepper flakes**
>
> **2¹/2 teaspoons kosher salt**
>
> **Freshly ground black pepper to taste**

Heat the oil in a large frying pan over medium-high heat. Add the garlic and cook until just beginning to brown. Add the broccoli di raab and cook, stirring frequently, for 5 minutes.

Pour ¹/2 cup water into the pan. Cover, reduce the heat to low and simmer for 20 minutes, or until the stalks are tender. Toss with the red pepper flakes, salt and black pepper. **Makes 4 cups**

Broccoli di Raab with Italian Sausage

This takes the previous recipe one step further. It is definitely a main dish.

> **³/4 cup olive oil**
>
> **2¹/4 pounds broccoli di raab, trimmed, stems cut in half lengthwise if large**
>
> **15 medium garlic cloves, smashed, peeled and thinly sliced**
>
> **³/4 teaspoon hot red pepper flakes**
>
> **1 tablespoon kosher salt**
>
> **Freshly ground black pepper to taste**
>
> **6 hot Italian sausages (about 1¹/4 pounds)**

Heat the olive oil in a large frying pan over medium-high heat. Place the broccoli di raab in the pan with the leaves toward the edge of the pan and the stems in the center. Add the garlic and cook for 7 minutes, frequently shaking the pan or moving the raab with a wooden spoon.

Pour in ¹/2 cup water. Cover, turn the heat to very low and cook until the stems are tender, about 30 minutes. Remove from the heat and toss with the red pepper, salt and black pepper.

While the broccoli di raab is cooking, prick the sausages with a fork. Place in a medium frying pan with ¹/4 cup water. Cover and cook over high heat for 4 minutes. Uncover and cook for 15 minutes, turning occasionally to brown on all sides. Turn the heat to low and cook for 8 minutes, or until cooked through, turning occasionally. Remove and place on paper towels to drain.

Divide the broccoli di raab among six plates. Top each with a sausage. Serve hot.

Serves 6 as a main course

Boiled Variation

Bring 4½ quarts water and 1 tablespoon salt to a boil in a large pot. Add the broccoli di raab. When the water returns to a boil, cook for 3 minutes longer. Drain and refresh under cold running water.

Heat the olive oil in a large frying pan over medium-high heat. Place the broccoli di raab in the pan with leaves toward the edge of the pan and the stems in the center. Add the garlic. Cook for 5 minutes, frequently shaking the pan or moving the raab with a wooden spoon. Remove from the heat and toss with the red pepper, salt and black pepper.

Meanwhile, cook the sausages as directed. Divide the broccoli di raab among the plates and top with the sausages.

Barley Risotto with Broccoli di Raab

This dish is best with a strong stock and some good Parmesan cheese.

> 6 cups Basic Chicken Stock (page 501), Roasted Chicken Stock (page 502), Vegetable Broth (page 506), or commercial chicken or vegetable broth
>
> ¹/₂ cup olive oil
>
> 1 medium onion, minced
>
> 8 large cloves garlic, smashed, peeled and minced
>
> 2 cups medium pearl barley
>
> 1 pound broccoli di raab, trimmed and cut into ¹/₂-inch pieces
>
> 2 teaspoons kosher salt
>
> Freshly ground black pepper to taste

Heat the stock in a 2-quart saucepan; keep warm.

Heat the oil in a 3-quart saucepan over medium heat. Add the onion and garlic. Cook for 5 minutes or until softened, stirring occasionally.

Add the barley. Stir for 1 to 2 minutes to coat with oil. Add ½ cup warm stock. Cook, stirring well, until the barley has absorbed most of the stock. Add another ½ cup stock and repeat the process, making sure the liquid is mostly absorbed before each new addition, until the barley has cooked for 20 minutes.

Add the broccoli di raab. Continue cooking, adding stock ½ cup at a time and stirring, for 20 more minutes. The barley should be creamy with a slight chew. Add the salt and pepper.

Makes 7 cups

Braised Kale

Kale can be cut and eaten well into the winter. It may be an acquired taste—but once acquired, it becomes a favorite.

> 2 tablespoons olive oil
>
> 4³/₄ pounds kale, stems removed
>
> 1 head garlic (about 10 plump cloves), separated into cloves, smashed, peeled and chopped medium
>
> 2 teaspoons kosher salt
>
> Freshly ground black pepper to taste

Heat the olive oil in a 12-inch-wide pot over low heat. Take a handful of kale leaves and roughly stack them into a pile. With a large kitchen knife, cut across into approximately ½-inch strips. Throw the leaves into the pot. Continue until all the kale is cut and cooking.

Increase the heat to medium and stir the kale around in the pot. Cook for 10 minutes. At this point, the kale will have begun to shrink dramatically. Lift and turn the kale so that the pieces on the bottom move to the top; it is easy to do this using tongs, or use a wooden spoon. Reduce the heat to low. Cook for 5 minutes.

Add the garlic. Stir to mix. Simmer for 25 minutes. Add the salt and pepper. Serve. **Makes 8 cups; serves 8 to 10 as a side dish**

Tamari-Garlic Kale

The slight harshness of kale seems to have an affinity to the sweetness of soy.

2 tablespoons olive oil

2 pounds kale leaves (about 2^1/$_2$ pounds kale with stems), heavy veins removed and leaves cut across into ^{1}/$_2$-inch strips (about 14 packed cups)

2 tablespoons coarsely chopped garlic

2 tablespoons soy sauce, preferably tamari

^{1}/$_2$ teaspoon kosher salt

Freshly ground black pepper to taste

Heat the oil in a large deep pot. Add the kale, in batches if necessary, and toss and cook over medium heat until it has wilted and the volume has shrunk by one-quarter.

Add the garlic. Cover and reduce the heat to a simmer. Cook for 2 hours, stirring every 30 minutes and adding a little water if necessary to prevent the kale from browning.

Stir in the soy. Add the salt and pepper to taste. **Makes 3 cups; serves 6 as a side dish**

Garlic Kale with Yogurt

This can be served warm or at room temperature. To serve warm, stir 1½ cups Strained Yogurt (page 511), strained for 24 hours, into the cooked kale. Cook over low heat until warmed through; do not boil. To serve cold or at room temperature, stir in 1½ cups yogurt that has been strained for 3½ hours.

Kale Stew with Chickpeas and Mushrooms

For those who love Asian seasonings but do not want to stir-fry, this is a nice alternative. The hot pepper oil adds a subtle spiciness.

2 tablespoons olive oil

1^1/$_2$ pounds mushrooms, trimmed and cut into eighths (about 7 cups)

2 pounds kale, stems removed and leaves cut across into ^{1}/$_2$-inch strips (about 11 cups)

^{1}/$_2$ head garlic, smashed, peeled and chopped

One 19-ounce can chickpeas, rinsed and drained

2 tablespoons soy sauce, preferably tamari

2 tablespoons toasted sesame oil

3 tablespoons sesame seeds

Freshly ground black pepper to taste

1 tablespoon hot pepper oil (optional)

In a 7-quart pot, heat the oil. Add the mushrooms and cook over medium heat until they begin to give off liquid, about 5 minutes. Add the kale. Cook for 15 minutes, stirring occasionally.

Mix in the garlic. Cook for 20 minutes.

Add the chickpeas; reduce the heat to low. Stir in the soy sauce, sesame oil, sesame seeds, pepper, and, if spiciness is desired, hot pepper oil. Heat through. **Makes 6 cups**

"Braised" Collards with Vegetables

Almost all braised collard recipes flavor the greens with side meat, a southern cut of pork. This recipe is a rare and very good vegetarian version. Those who eat meat can replace some of the water with a good meat stock. Pork or ham stock works especially well.

Traditional cooked collards require hours of long simmering. The results are good but usually mushy and gray. Vertamae Smart-Grosvenor, author of the clever and sassy cookbook-memoir *Vibration Cooking or the Travel Notes of a Geechee Girl* (see the Bibliography), writes about using residual heat to gently cook the greens. It has become a favorite technique of mine. It's incredibly simple, and the greens cook up a rich dark green, perfectly tender and chewy.

Save the cooking liquid—pot likker—to make Herbed Rice (page 490) or Chickpea and Lentil Soup (page 280).

> 4 sprigs fresh parsley
>
> 1 clove
>
> 2 small dried chili peppers, such as pequín
>
> 2 European bay leaves
>
> 1 medium onion, cut into 1-inch chunks (about 1 1/2 cups)
>
> 2 medium carrots, peeled, trimmed and cut into 1/4-inch rounds (about 1 cup)
>
> 2 large stalks celery, peeled and cut into 1/4-inch slices (about 1 1/2 cups)
>
> 3 cloves garlic, smashed and peeled
>
> 1 pound collard leaves (from about 2 pounds collard greens); cut across into 1 1/2- to 2-inch pieces (about 13 cups)
>
> 1 tablespoon canola oil
>
> 2 teaspoons kosher salt

Tie the parsley, clove, chili peppers and bay leaves together in a square of cheesecloth. Put into a large pot. Add the onion, carrots, celery, garlic and 3 quarts water. Bring to a boil. Reduce to a strong simmer. Cook for 1 hour.

Strain the broth; reserve the vegetables, and discard the cheesecloth bundle.

Measure the broth and add enough water to get 7 1/2 cups. Return the liquid to the pot. Bring to a boil. Add the collards. Cook for 15 minutes, stirring occasionally. Cover, turn off the heat and allow to sit for 1 hour.

Drain the collards. Return to the pot and toss with the oil to keep the pieces from sticking together. Mix in the reserved vegetables, and reheat. Add the salt.

Makes 5 1/2 cups; serves 6 as a side dish

Timbale of Collards, Mushrooms and Ham

Other dark leafy greens, such as Swiss chard, kale or spinach, can replace the collards in both the stuffing and the timbale. To make this with chard or kale, cook the leaves in boiling water for several minutes until tender. Drain and rinse under cold running water. If using spinach, choose large leaves—baby spinach will not work here—and barely cook it in boiling water. Rinse under cold running water.

> 12 to 16 large collard leaves—enough to line eight 1/2-cup (4-ounce) ramekins—stems removed and cut lengthwise in half
>
> Vegetable oil for greasing ramekins and brushing leaves
>
> 1 recipe Collard, Mushroom and Ham Stuffing (page 496)

Bring a large wide pot of water to a boil. Add the collard leaves, laying them flat in overlapping layers. Cook for 15 minutes, periodically pushing down on the leaves to keep them submerged. Cover, turn off the heat and allow to sit for 1 hour.

Place a rack in the center of the oven. Preheat the oven to 350°F.

Bring water to a boil in a medium saucepan; keep the water at a low simmer. Oil eight ½-cup (4-ounce) ramekins.

Drain the collard leaves. Line each ramekin with 3 or 4 leaf halves, or enough to cover the bottom and sides with at least a 1½-inch overhang. Divide the stuffing evenly among the ramekins, packing it down to fit. Fold the leaves over toward the center; the stuffing should be completely covered. Brush the tops with oil.

Arrange the ramekins in two 9 x 9 x 2-inch glass baking dishes or a single large pan. Pour boiling water into the dish(es) to reach halfway up the sides of the ramekins. Place a piece of foil loosely over the ramekins. Bake for 20 minutes.

Remove the ramekins from the water bath. Turn the timbales out onto individual plates or a serving platter. Use a paper towel to blot away excess liquid around the timbales.

Serves 8 as a side dish

Braised Mustard Greens

This is a nice, somewhat Italian variant of a traditional southern dish.

> 5 pounds mustard greens, stem ends snapped off and large stems removed
>
> 2 tablespoons olive oil
>
> 6 plump garlic cloves, smashed, peeled and sliced lengthwise
>
> 1¼ cups sliced scallions (about 12 whole; use both white and green parts)
>
> 1 cup fresh basil leaves, cut across into thin strips
>
> 2 teaspoons kosher salt
>
> Freshly ground black pepper to taste

Put the olive oil and garlic in a 12-inch pot over low heat. Take a handful of mustard greens and roughly stack them into a pile. With a large kitchen knife, cut across into approximately ½-inch strips. Throw them into the pot. Continue until all the greens are cut.

Increase the heat to medium. Stir the greens around in the pot. Cook for 10 minutes. At this point, the greens will have begun to shrink dramatically. Lift and turn the greens, moving the pieces on the bottom to the top; it is easy to do this using tongs, or use a wooden spoon. Reduce the heat to low. Cook for 10 minutes.

Add the scallions, basil, salt and pepper. Mix well. Heat just until warm throughout.

Makes 4 cups

Fresh Greens

Use this as a base for steamed scallops or fish.

- 1 1/2 pounds collard greens (about 2 bunches)
- 1 tablespoon peanut oil
- 14 ounces mustard greens (about 2 bunches)
- 1 cup port
- 1/2 cup mirin
- 2 tablespoons soy sauce, preferably tamari
- Kosher salt and freshly ground black pepper to taste

Strip the tough center stalk from the middle of each collard leaf; discard the stalks. Stack the leaves in 2 or 3 piles. Using a large kitchen knife, cut across into roughly ½-inch strips.

Put 1½ teaspoons oil in a 10-inch skillet. Add the collard greens and cook over medium heat for 5 minutes, turning frequently. Add ⅓ cup of water. Reduce to low heat. Cook for 30 minutes.

Meanwhile, strip the center stalk out of each mustard leaf. Stack the leaves the same way as for collards and cut across into roughly ½-inch strips. Cook separately in the same way as the collard greens, using the remaining 1½ teaspoons oil, for 30 minutes.

The greens may be held at this stage for 1 day if you like. Combine and refrigerate.

Put the greens in a small pot. Add the port, mirin and soy sauce. Cook over low heat until hot. Add the salt and pepper.

Serves 10 to 12 as a side dish

Cabbages with Roots

Turnips, Kohlrabi and Radishes

The large cabbage and cauliflower families contain a number of vegetables that are grown for their roots rather than their leaves. All are better when young and small. I particularly like the oval French breakfast radishes—half red, half white—that are served raw with sweet butter and salt as a snack or hors d'oeuvre.

Turn to **TURNIPS, KOHLRABI** and **RADISHES** in the Cook's Guide for how-tos and to the Index for more recipes.

Warm Vegetable Salad

Using some frozen vegetables makes this quick and easy. Of course, fresh can be used.

> 1 1/2 cups peeled small white turnips cut into wedges
>
> 1 1/2 cups julienned peeled carrots
>
> 1 tablespoon unsalted butter
>
> 18 small scallions, trimmed and cut into 2- to 3-inch lengths
>
> 1/4 cup Basic Chicken Stock (page 501), Roasted Chicken Stock (page 502) or commercial chicken broth
>
> 1/4 cup tarragon vinegar
>
> 3 tablespoons olive oil
>
> Kosher salt and freshly ground black pepper to taste
>
> 18 frozen baby artichokes, defrosted
>
> One 10-ounce package frozen tiny green peas, defrosted in a sieve under warm running water
>
> 1 yellow bell pepper, cored, seeded, deribbed and cut lengthwise into thin strips
>
> 12 nice lettuce leaves

Cook the turnips and carrots separately in boiling salted water until crisp-tender. Drain and rinse under cold running water. Set aside.

Heat the butter in a large skillet over medium heat until it foams. Add the scallions. Reduce the heat to low and cook the scallions until bright green and wilted, about 5 minutes. Add the chicken stock. Bring to a bare simmer and cook until the scallions are tender, 3 to 5 minutes. With a slotted spoon, remove the scallions.

Add half of the vinegar to the skillet. Heat to a boil. Gradually whisk in the remaining vinegar and the oil. Season with salt and pepper.

Add the artichokes and heat over very low heat until warmed through. Add the peas, turnips, carrots and bell pepper and toss until warmed through.

Line six plates with the lettuce leaves. Using a slotted spoon, arrange the warm vegetables on the lettuce. **Serves 6 as a first course**

Stuffed Kohlrabi

Briefly cooked in the microwave oven, kohlrabi is revealed to be a wholly new vegetable, elegant and pale jade green. Premicrowave, kohlrabi had to be cooked so long that it became white, watery and fibrous.

> 8 small kohlrabi, peeled and trimmed
>
> 2 tablespoons anchovy paste
>
> 1 tablespoon olive oil
>
> 1/2 cup cooked rice
>
> Freshly ground black pepper to taste

Using a melon baller, remove the center of each kohlrabi, leaving a 1/2-inch shell, and set aside. Place the kohlrabi in a ring around the edge of a pie plate.

Finely chop the reserved centers. Combine with the remaining ingredients. Divide the stuffing among the kohlrabi, mounding it slightly. Pour 1 tablespoon water into the center of the pie plate. Cover tightly with microwave plastic wrap. Cook at 100% for 7 minutes. Prick the plastic to release the steam. Uncover and serve. **Serves 8 as a first course**

NOTE: To double the recipe, double all the ingredients. Use a 14 x 11 x 2-inch dish or oval platter and increase the cooking time to 10 minutes

To cook 2 kohlrabi, use 2 small kohlrabi, 1½ teaspoons anchovy paste, ¾ teaspoon olive oil, 2 tablespoons cooked rice and freshly ground black pepper. Proceed as directed, using a small plate. Pour 1 teaspoon water into the center of the plate. Cook for 3 to 4 minutes.

Pastina Salad with Radish and Mint

Quick, pretty and vegetarian, this is given an unexpected jolt by the ginger.

2^1/$_2$ tablespoons kosher salt

1^1/$_2$ cups pastina (8 ounces)

DRESSING

2 teaspoons grated lemon zest

^{1}/$_4$ cup fresh lemon juice

5 tablespoons vegetable oil

1^1/$_2$ tablespoons grated peeled fresh ginger

1 teaspoon kosher salt

Freshly ground black pepper to taste

1^1/$_2$ cups sliced radishes

^{3}/$_4$ cup diagonally sliced scallions

Bring 2 quarts water and the salt to a boil in a large pot. Stir in the pastina and cook for 2 minutes. Pour the pastina into a fine-mesh strainer, rinse under cold running water and shake several times to rid the pastina of excess water. Remove to a large bowl.

Mix together the dressing ingredients in a small bowl. Toss the pastina with 2 tablespoons dressing. Let stand for 30 minutes to an hour. Fluff from time to time with a fork to prevent compacting.

Just before serving, add the radishes, scallions and remaining dressing to the salad. Toss well and serve. **Makes 5 cups; serves 6 as a first course**

Radish Soup

This soup is also good cold.

^{3}/$_4$ pound red radishes, trimmed and thinly sliced across

2 tablespoons red wine vinegar

10 ounces floury potatoes, peeled and cut into 1-inch cubes

2^1/$_2$ cups Basic Chicken Stock (page 501), Roasted Chicken Stock (page 502) or commercial chicken broth

3 scallions, trimmed and thinly sliced

Kosher salt and freshly ground black pepper to taste

Toss 2¼ cups of the radish slices with the vinegar in a bowl.

In a medium saucepan, bring the potatoes and stock to a boil. Lower the heat and simmer for 3 minutes. Add the radish slices and vinegar. Cover and return to a boil. Lower the heat and simmer until the potatoes and radishes are tender, about 15 minutes.

In a blender, working in batches of no more than 2 cups, purée the soup until smooth. Scrape the purée back into the saucepan.

Cut the remaining radish slices into thin strips. Stir them into the soup. Bring to a boil. Lower the heat and simmer for 5 minutes. Remove from the heat. Stir in ½ cup water, the scallions and salt and pepper. Serve hot, or refrigerate until thoroughly chilled and serve cold. **Makes 4 cups; serves 4 as a first course**

Cold Radish Soup with Cucumber

Refrigerate the soup until cold. Stir in 1 medium cucumber, peeled, seeded and cut in ¼-inch dice, and, if desired, ½ cup plain yogurt. Taste for salt and adjust if necessary.
Makes about 5 cups; serves 4 as a first course

Oven-Braised Turnips with Garlic

This takes turnips from a boring slightly woody vegetable to a star.

- 2¼ pounds turnips, trimmed, peeled and cut into ½-inch wedges
- 2 tablespoons olive oil
- 1½ heads garlic, separated into cloves, smashed and peeled
- 2½ European bay leaves, whole leaves broken in half
- 1½ cups Enriched Beef Stock (page 504)
- ¼ teaspoon dried thyme
- ¼ teaspoon rubbed sage
- ¼ teaspoon dried oregano, preferably Greek
- ¾ teaspoon kosher salt, or to taste
- Freshly ground black pepper to taste

Place a rack in the center of the oven. Preheat the oven to 500°F.

Place the turnips in a 12 x 17½ x 2-inch roasting pan and slick with the oil. Spread out in a single layer. Roast for 15 minutes.

Flip the turnips over and rotate the pan. Add the garlic. Roast for 5 minutes. Flip the turnips and garlic over and rotate the pan. Tuck the bay leaves under the turnips. Add the stock and herbs. Roast for 10 minutes.

Flip the turnips and garlic over and rotate the pan. Roast for 10 more minutes. The liquid will be mostly absorbed. Remove the bay leaves. Add the salt and pepper to taste. **Makes 3¾ cups**

Radishes with Parsley Butter

We don't usually think of radishes as a hot dish; but properly made they are a fine contrast to somewhat bland foods. They lose much of their sharpness with cooking.

- 1 pound red radishes, trimmed and cut in half
- 1 teaspoon red wine vinegar
- 4 tablespoons unsalted butter, cut into small pieces
- 3 tablespoons chopped fresh parsley
- Kosher salt and freshly ground black pepper to taste

Mix the radishes with the vinegar in a 2½-quart soufflé dish. Cover tightly with microwave plastic wrap. Cook in a microwave at 100% for 6 minutes. Prick the plastic to release the steam.

Remove from the oven and uncover. Stir in the butter, parsley and salt and pepper to taste. Cook, uncovered, for 1 minute more.

Remove from the oven and stir well. Serve immediately, or the radishes will toughen.
Serves 4 as a side dish

Radish Greens Pasta Sauce

This unusual use of radish greens avoids waste and tastes very good.

- ¼ cup olive oil
- 3 cloves garlic, smashed, peeled and minced
- 4 cups radish greens (from about 3 bunches radishes), stemmed and washed
- Kosher salt and freshly ground black pepper to taste

Place the oil and garlic in a 2½-quart soufflé dish. Cover tightly with microwave plastic wrap. Cook at 100% for 3 minutes.

Remove from the oven and carefully uncover. Stir in the greens. Re-cover and cook at 100% for 3 minutes more. Prick the plastic to release the steam.

Remove from the oven and uncover. Transfer the mixture to a food processor and process until coarsely chopped. Add 3 tablespoons water and salt and pepper to taste; process to blend.

Serve hot over pasta, or scrape into a jar and store, covered, in the refrigerator. Reheat before serving. **Makes 1 cup; serves 4**

Spicy Papaya Salsa with Daikon

The golden yellow cubes of papaya bathe in a bright jade-green sauce that is hot to taste, not killing. Daikon adds the perfect crunch. Substitute jicama if daikon is not available.

Make this up to 2 hours before serving, but no longer; stir and serve.

2 jalapeño peppers, seeded and cut into strips

6 medium cloves garlic, smashed and peeled

1 cup loosely packed cilantro leaves

3 tablespoons fresh lime juice

1 1/2 pounds ripe papaya, peeled, seeded and cut into 1/4-inch dice (about 2 1/2 cups)

3/4 cup peeled diced (1/4-inch) daikon

Combine the jalapeños, garlic, cilantro and lime juice in a blender or mini chopper. Let the machine run until a smooth green sauce forms.

Put the papaya in a bowl, pour the sauce over and stir. Stir in the daikon. Let stand at room temperature for 15 minutes before serving. **Makes about 3 cups**

Radish Pickles

A crisp and mildly spicy pickle to have with a drink, or before a party to stave off hunger. It can be put up as well in six 1-pint jars, but I find that a half-pint is usually what gets eaten.

Twelve 1/2-pint canning jars with two-piece lids

4 1/2 to 5 pounds daikon radishes (or white or black radishes), peeled and trimmed

2 tablespoons coriander seeds

2 tablespoons yellow mustard seeds

1 tablespoon celery seeds

2 1/4 cups tarragon vinegar

2 tablespoons kosher salt

1 teaspoon dried tarragon

6 shallots, peeled and halved

Sterilize the canning jars (see page 91).

Cut the radishes into 2 1/2 x 1/2 x 1/2-inch sticks (or, if using young white radishes, leave whole).

Place the coriander, mustard and celery seeds in a mound on one side of a kitchen towel. Fold the towel over the seeds. Pound with a heavy saucepan until the spices are crushed. Pour into a 2-quart glass measure. Add the vinegar, 2 1/4 cups water, the salt and tarragon. Cover tightly with microwave plastic wrap. Cook in a microwave at 100% for 7 minutes, or until boiling. Prick the plastic to release the steam.

Remove from the oven and uncover. Divide the radishes evenly among the jars, fitting the pieces snugly, upright, in them. Place half a shallot in the center of each jar. Pour enough vinegar mixture over the radishes to cover, leaving 1/2 inch headroom in each jar.

Arrange the filled jars around the edge of the carousel. Cook at 100% for 12 minutes, or until just tender. Remove from the oven and cover with the lids. Let cool slightly.

Refrigerate at least overnight, or up to several months. Serve chilled. **Makes 6 pints**

Peas: Sweet Green Peas, Snow Peas, Sugar Snaps, Pea Shoots,

Split Peas, Cowpeas, Black-eyed Peas and Long Beans 296

Beans from Asia: Adzuki and Soybeans 310

Asian Cabbages: Bok Choy, Pak Choy, Tatsoi, Napa Cabbage and Chinese Broccoli 315

Eggplants 322   Okra and Malokhei 339   Rhubarb 346

Cucumbers and Gourds 350

Lovely Roots and Hearts: Taro, Lotus Root, Hearts of Palm and Bamboo Shoots 362

Vegetables of
Asia and Africa

IT MAY SEEM STRANGE TO COMBINE these two continents into one section of this book, but at least as long ago as there was the Silk Road, there was a brisk trade among sub-Saharan Africa, Turkey and Asia. It goes back to a time before there were even records of vegetables. However, members of the gourd family are edible on both of these continents, differentiating them from the American gourds, which are purely ornamental. We can see that there is a connection even if we do not know exactly what it is and how far it goes. Eggplants are also used on both continents, and then there are surprises.

Peas

Sweet Green Peas, Snow Peas, Sugar Snaps, Pea Shoots,
Split Peas, Cowpeas, Black-eyed Peas and Long Beans

It was a shock to discover that sweet green peas originally came from Asia. They are seldom used there fresh, and I have always seen them referred to as English peas, sweet peas or green peas. In their dried, often split form, they are used in India to make dahl. Pea tendrils are used in Chinese stir-fries. The African-Asian connection can be recognized in the cousinship of sweet green peas to cowpeas, which are shelled long beans, and black-eyed peas. (Although black-eyed peas are technically a subspecies of cowpeas—see the Cook's Guide—to the cook the difference is indistinguishable, and the two names are used interchangeably.) Their relationship to green peas shows in their rapid cooking time when fresh and relatively short cooking time—compared to those of *Phaseolus* beans—when dried.

Cowpeas and black-eyed peas found their way to America along with the slaves. The long beans traveled from western Asia to as far east as China. Cowpeas and black-eyed peas are often used dried—not so my favorites, the sweet green peas.

To understand or multiply the confusion, also see the introduction to Beans in the Cook's Guide (page 536). It should be noted that the recipes in this section are grouped by type of vegetable, not by the part of the meal as in some other chapters.

SWEET GREEN PEAS

Spring delights us with its bounty of fresh, sweet green vegetables: artichokes, asparagus, baby leeks and—above all—tiny peas, with their crunchy pods and delicate curling tendrils of vine. Peas have a long and ancient history. Most of the early peas were eaten dried or cooked into a form of mush called pease porridge. The English developed and promulgated fine varieties of sweet peas, which are also called garden or English peas. These are the peas we commonly eat when they're young and tender and green. Colonial settlers brought them to North America. Cultivating the first peas of the season was a vigorous annual competition engaged in by the likes of President Thomas Jefferson, who grew more than thirty varieties at Monticello; indeed, none other than the pea was one of his favorite vegetables.

Tiny peas can be quickly cooked or blanched by boiling for about three minutes, but they can also benefit from longer, slow cooking, as for Peas with Peppers and Tomatoes (page 302).

Depending on how fresh they are, they vary considerably in cooking time.

When fresh peas are not good, the best alternative is frozen tiny (petite) peas. Simply place frozen peas in a sieve and separate under warm running water; use as designated in the desired recipe.

No matter how sweet, peas are still a starch. As soon as they are picked, their sugars begin to break down into starch, which lessens the sweetness. As the ol' wives' tale says, peas—like corn—should be shucked on the way from the garden; fresher is better.

As a starch, peas love fat. Two excellent examples are Peas with Mint (page 301), a classic French preparation that typically uses butter, and the very similar Italian preparation Piselli alla Romana (page 301), which calls for olive oil and prosciutto.

Turn to **PEAS** in the Cook's Guide for how-tos and to the Index for more recipes.

Miniature Scallion-Pea Quiches

A pretty vegetarian quiche, this can even be made in winter if small frozen peas are used. Fresh peas can be used—just look at page 624 for yields.

2 tablespoons unsalted butter

1 bunch scallions, trimmed and cut across into $1/4$**-inch slices (about 1 cup)**

1 large egg

$1/4$ cup heavy cream

$1/4$ cup cooked peas or small frozen peas, defrosted in a sieve under warm running water, or tender fresh peas

continued

Kosher salt and freshly ground black pepper
to taste

24 partially baked tartlet shells (page 478)
made with Quiche Crust (page 481)

1/4 cup freshly grated Parmesan cheese

Preheat the oven to 375°F.

Melt the butter in a small skillet over medium heat. Stir in the scallions and 3 tablespoons water. Cook, stirring, for about 8 minutes, or until the scallions are very soft and almost all the liquid has evaporated. Remove from the heat and allow to cool slightly.

In a medium bowl, lightly beat the egg. Stir in the cream. Add the peas and season to taste with salt and pepper.

Fill the pastry shells on a baking sheet with the pea mixture. Sprinkle the cheese over the top. Bake until set and golden, for about 10 minutes.

Remove from the oven and allow to cool slightly on a wire rack before serving.

Makes 24 individual quiches

Large Scallion Pea Quiche

Prepare a 10-inch baked quiche shell (see page 477). While it is cooling, prepare the filling, tripling all the ingredients. Increase the oven temperature to 375°F.

Put the shell, still in its pan, on a baking sheet on the center oven rack. Pour in the filling and sprinkle the cheese over the top. Bake until the center is set and the top is golden brown, for about 25 minutes. Serve warm or at room temperature. **Serves 8 to 10 as a first course**

Pea Pod Soup

I hate waste. When I was shelling a mountain of peas for a party one day, it occurred to me that pea shells are very sweet in their own right. I made this soup, which I found very satisfying.

The soup base—no cream, no eggs—can be frozen and then used as a pleasant midwinter surprise. Seasoned with salt, the base can double as a pleasant sauce for a strong-tasting first course such as Horseradish Custards (page 410). The peas are no problem; use them in any recipe or sprinkle into a stew.

Pods from 2 pounds fresh peas

6 cups Basic Chicken Stock (page 501),
Roasted Chicken Stock (page 502) or
commercial chicken broth

2 egg yolks

1/2 cup heavy cream, plus extra for decoration
if desired

Kosher salt and freshly ground black pepper
to taste

Pull the strings and shell the peas. Discard the tops and strings; set the pods aside. Reserve the peas for another use.

Bring the stock to a boil in a large saucepan. Add the pods, stirring them in well to immerse them. Reduce the heat to a low boil and cook for 45 minutes, or until the pods are extremely tender. Remove from the heat and cool.

In 2 or 3 batches, purée the pods with the stock in a food processor. Strain and return the purée to the saucepan and heat until hot.

In a small bowl, beat the egg yolks lightly with the cream. Stirring constantly, pour about 1 cup of the hot soup into the egg-cream mixture to help prevent the eggs from curdling when added to the soup. Stir this mixture into the soup. Cook over medium heat, stirring constantly, until the soup thickens slightly and coats the back of the spoon. Season to taste with salt and pepper.

Ladle into warm bowls. If desired, swirl a little cream on top of each serving for decoration.

Serves 4 as a first course

Fresh Pea Soup Base

Peas are good for only a short period of time when freshly picked. I use this purée for Quick Pea Soup, which follows. I am sure that good cooks will find other uses. Be warned, shelling the peas takes time.

- 6³/₄ pounds fresh peas in the pod, shelled (about 5¹/₂ cups)
- 5 cups Basic Chicken Stock (page 501), Roasted Chicken Stock (page 502) or commercial chicken broth

In a medium saucepan, bring the peas and stock to a boil. Lower the heat and simmer for 8 to 10 minutes, or until the peas are tender. Remove from the heat and cool.

In a blender, working in batches of no more than 2 cups, purée the mixture. Use immediately or refrigerate for up to 3 days or freeze, tightly covered, in 1-cup batches. **Makes about 8 cups**

Quick Pea Soup

If the pea soup base is not on hand in the freezer, fresh or frozen peas can be substituted and puréed with chicken stock to make the base. Serve with Cubed Croutons (page 511).

- 7 cups Fresh Pea Soup Base (above) or 6 pounds fresh peas in the pod, shelled (about 5¹/₂ cups), or 5¹/₂ cups frozen peas (about three 10-ounce boxes), defrosted in a sieve under warm running water
- 4¹/₂ cups Basic Chicken Stock (page 501), Roasted Chicken Stock (page 502) or commercial chicken broth, or as needed— if not using the pea soup base

- ³/₄ cup loosely packed fresh dill sprigs or ¹/₂ cup loosely packed fresh mint leaves plus 3 sprigs dill (see below)
- Kosher salt and freshly ground black pepper to taste

IF USING MINT
- ¹/₂ teaspoon freshly grated nutmeg
- 1 cup milk
- ¹/₂ cup heavy cream

If using the pea soup base, heat it in a medium saucepan over medium heat. Or, to make a soup base with fresh or frozen peas, bring the peas and stock to a boil in a medium saucepan. Lower the heat and simmer until the peas are tender, for about 8 minutes for fresh peas, 4 minutes for frozen. Drain, reserving the peas and stock separately.

In a blender, working in batches of no larger than 2 cups each, purée the cooked peas with a little of the stock. Scrape into a medium saucepan. Stir in the remaining stock.

If using only dill: Stir it into the soup base. Season with salt and pepper and heat through. If it's necessary, add additional stock to achieve the desired consistency. Serve.

If using mint: Chop the mint and dill with the salt and nutmeg in a blender. With the machine running, slowly pour in 2 cups of the soup base. Whisk back into the pan with the remaining soup base. Stir in the milk, cream and additional stock if necessary to achieve the desired consistency. Bring to a boil. Lower the heat and simmer for 3 to 4 minutes. Serve immediately.
Makes 7 cups without cream and milk, 8¹/₂ cups with; serves 6 to 8 as a first course

Chilled Curried Pea Soup

This gentle green soup has a surprisingly rich flavor. For a somewhat lighter soup, substitute Basic Chicken Stock (page 501) for the beef stock. As this is a cold soup, it must be made ahead.

1 medium onion, cut into $^1/_2$-inch cubes

1 tablespoon vegetable oil

1 $^1/_2$ tablespoons curry powder

Two 10-ounce packages frozen peas, defrosted in a sieve under warm running water and drained (about 3 $^1/_2$ cups), or 3 $^1/_2$ cups shelled fresh peas (about 4 pounds in the pod)

3 cups Beef Stock (page 502), Vegetable Broth (page 506) or commercial beef broth

1 $^1/_2$ teaspoons kosher salt, or to taste

Freshly ground black pepper to taste

2 teaspoons fresh lime juice

$^1/_2$ cup plain low-fat yogurt

In a medium saucepan, cook the onion in the oil over medium heat until wilted. Add the curry powder and cook, stirring constantly to avoid scorching, for 1 minute. Stir in the peas and stock. Cover and bring to a boil. Lower the heat and simmer until the peas are soft, 8 to 10 minutes for fresh, 4 minutes for frozen.

Pass the mixture through the fine disc of a food mill or a fine sieve to remove the pea skins. Season with the salt and pepper. Refrigerate for at least 2 hours, or overnight.

Stir the lime juice and yogurt into the chilled soup. Adjust the seasoning if necessary.

Makes about 5 cups; serves 4 as a first course

"Soup" of Small Peas with Fresh Herbs

Soupe de Petits Pois aux Herbes Fraîches

This recipe Pierre Gagnaire, the famous and fabulous Parisian, gave me after I had eaten this. There is a question of definition as well as technique. I would not call it a soup. He certainly served it as a side dish. The somewhat prosaic British would probably look at it as a variation of the traditional mushy peas. I think it is simply wonderful—but it is at its very best when the peas are fresh and young and small. I have made the dish as well with frozen tiny peas and it is very, very good, if not sublime.

2 tablespoons kosher salt

2 $^1/_4$ pounds fresh peas in the pod, shelled (about 2 cups), or two 10-ounce packages frozen tiny peas, defrosted in a sieve under warm running water (scant 4 cups defrosted)

1 large bunch fresh flat-leaf parsley, leaves and small stems only

1 bunch cilantro, largest stems removed

$^1/_4$ pound spinach, stemmed and washed

About 2 ounces fresh lemon balm, leaves only (a small handful), 3 leaves reserved for decoration

$^1/_2$ cup fresh mint leaves (from about 1 small bunch), 3 leaves reserved for decoration

$^1/_4$ pound arugula (about 5 cups)

1 $^1/_2$ cups milk, plus a little extra if desired

2 tablespoons good but not overpowering olive oil

Kosher salt and freshly ground black pepper to taste

1 $^1/_2$ tablespoons unsalted butter

In a large saucepan, bring 5 cups water to a boil with the salt. Add the peas and cook for 3 minutes. Remove the peas from the water, put in a sieve and cool under cold running water. Pierre pops the skins; I don't—too much work. In the same boiling water, cook the herbs, spinach and arugula for about 7 minutes. Drain and cool under cold running water. Press the ball of herbs to remove as much water as possible.

Put the herbs in a food processor or blender. Gradually add the milk and olive oil, then add salt and pepper and process until a very smooth sauce is formed.

At the last minute, cut the reserved mint and balm leaves into thin strips. Warm the peas in the butter; season with salt and pepper to taste. Add the green sauce to the peas, and add a little more milk if desired. Sprinkle with the herb strips and serve immediately.

Makes about 4 cups

Peas with Mint

The combination of lettuce, peas and mint is a French classic. Sugar is optional in this recipe, depending on how sweet and fresh the peas are. The recipe can be easily multiplied.

> 4 tablespoons unsalted butter
>
> 2 cups fresh or frozen peas
>   (about 2^1/$_2$ pounds in the pod)
>
> ^{1}/$_4$ cup fresh mint leaves cut across into thin strips
>
> ^{1}/$_2$ head Boston lettuce, cut across into ^{1}/$_4$-inch
>   strips (about 1 ^{1}/$_2$ cups)
>
> ^{1}/$_4$ teaspoon kosher salt
>
> ^{1}/$_2$ teaspoon sugar (optional)

Melt the butter in a small pan over high heat. Add the peas and cook for 2 minutes. Cover,

reduce the heat to medium and cook for 3 minutes, or until the peas are tender. Stir in the mint. Cook for 2 minutes longer. Add the lettuce. Cook until the lettuce has wilted. Remove from the heat and add the salt and sugar, if desired. **Makes 2 cups**

Piselli alla Romana

Italians make this dish with prosciutto. I prefer serrano ham, which is meatier and less likely to be dry. Prosciutto also varies more in saltiness. If using it, taste it first and adjust the amount of salt accordingly.

This recipe is also excellent made with fresh, very young, green fava beans. A restaurant that I love in New York called Sistina makes the dish with a combination of peas and favas. I have been known to make a whole meal of it, along with a crisp, dry white wine.

> 3 large shallots, minced
>
> 3 tablespoons extra virgin olive oil,
>   plus more for drizzling
>
> 4 pounds fresh peas in the pod, shelled
>   (about 3^1/$_2$ cups)
>
> 6 cups shredded romaine lettuce (ribs removed)
>
> 2 slices prosciutto or serrano ham, cut into thin
>   strips, then crosswise into small squares
>
> ^{1}/$_2$ teaspoon kosher salt
>
> Freshly ground black pepper to taste

In a 12-inch frying pan, slowly cook the shallots in the olive oil over very low heat until wilted, 3 to 4 minutes. Increase the heat to low. Add the peas. Cook for 15 minutes, stirring a few times.

Add the lettuce and ham. Cook for 10 minutes. Season with the salt and pepper. Drizzle with olive oil. **Makes 4 cups**

Peas with Peppers and Tomatoes

This side dish is not spicy, but smoky. If a spicier flavor is desired, add Fiery Pepper Sauce (page 629) or finely chopped fresh chili peppers when cooking or store-bought chili pepper sauce at the end. Serve hot, warm or cool.

  3 dried Catarina or cascabel peppers

  3 dried ancho peppers

  1 medium onion, finely chopped (about 1 1/2 cups)

  1 tablespoon canola oil

  4 cups shelled peas, preferably fresh
    (but frozen will do)

  1 cup American Tomato Purée (page 460) or
    sterile-pack strained tomatoes

  Kosher salt and freshly ground black pepper
    to taste

Bring 4 cups water to a boil. Pour over the peppers in a medium bowl. Cover and soak for 1½ hours.

Drain the peppers. Remove the seeds and stem ends. Purée the peppers very well in a blender.

In a large nonreactive saucepan, cook the onion in the canola oil over medium heat until softened, about 5 minutes. Stir in the peas and cook for 2 minutes. Add the chili pepper purée and tomato purée. Cook for 30 to 45 minutes, or until the peas are very soft.

Remove from the heat and add salt and pepper to taste. **Makes 4 cups**

Venetian Rice with Peas

Risi Bisi

Much like risotto but soupier, risi bisi is a Venetian favorite. Be sure to have the extra stock in case it is needed to make this soupy— but not soup. Serve with a spoon.

  1/2 pound scallions, white and half the green
    parts only, cut into 2-inch pieces

  2 cups packed spinach leaves

  2 tablespoons packed fresh parsley leaves

  1 cup arborio rice

  1/4 cup olive oil

  4 to 5 cups Basic Chicken Stock (page 501),
    Roasted Chicken Stock (page 502) or
    commercial chicken broth

  1 1/2 cups fresh or frozen peas (about 2 pounds
    in the pod)

  Kosher salt and freshly ground black pepper to taste

  Freshly grated Parmesan cheese (optional)

In a food processor, finely chop—but do not purée—the scallions, spinach and parsley.

In a large pan, stir the rice in the olive oil over high heat for 2 minutes. Reduce the heat to medium. Add the chicken stock bit by bit, stirring until it is absorbed. Continue adding the broth and cooking for 15 minutes. Stir in the peas and the scallion mixture. Continue to cook, adding broth little by little, until the peas are tender but the rice is still soupy, about 10 minutes. Season with salt and pepper to taste.

Ladle into warm bowls and pass grated Parmesan, if desired. **Makes 5 to 6 cups**

Green Seafood Stew with Peas and Spinach

This is one of the prettiest new dishes that I have made. It is light and fresh tasting and worthy of being the centerpiece of a party. Pass a big bowl of simple white rice, letting people help themselves as they see fit.

  3 quarts Basic Fish Stock (page 505)

  3/4 cup olive oil

1 1/4 pounds baby spinach, washed

36 littleneck or other small hard-shell clams, scrubbed

3 pounds skinless firm white-fleshed fish fillets, such as halibut

6 to 8 cloves garlic, smashed and peeled

3 cups fresh peas (about 4 pounds in the shell)

36 mussels (about 1 1/2 pounds), scrubbed and debearded if necessary

Kosher salt and freshly ground black pepper to taste

8 cups Basic White Rice (page 489)

Bring the stock to a boil in a 5-quart pot.

Meanwhile, heat half the oil in a large skillet over medium heat. Add the spinach in batches, waiting for each one to wilt before adding the next. When all the spinach is wilted, scrape into a bowl and set aside; wipe out the skillet with paper towels.

When the stock is boiling, add the clams. Meanwhile, heat the remaining oil in the same pan over medium-high heat. Add the fillets and garlic. Cook, turning the fillets once, for 5 minutes, or until opaque on both sides.

When the clams start to open, add the peas, fish and garlic to the pot. Cook for 5 minutes. Add the mussels and cook until opened, about 2 minutes. Add the spinach, salt and pepper and cook just until the spinach is heated through. Ladle into warm deep bowls. Serve with the rice. **Serves 6 as a main course**

Sweet Pea Ice Cream

Hardly traditional, anything but, yet it is clearly green—yes, Kermit—and good. Peas are sweet, so that this works shouldn't be a shock.

3 pounds peas in the pod, shelled (about 3 cups)

1/2 cup milk

1/3 cup sugar

1/2 cup heavy cream

Combine the peas, milk and sugar in a 2-quart saucepan. Bring to a boil over medium heat. Reduce the heat to a simmer. Cover and cook, stirring occasionally, for 1 hour, or until the peas are very tender. The liquid will be mostly absorbed.

Put the peas and heavy cream in a blender and purée until very smooth. Transfer the mixture to a metal bowl. Chill, covered, for at least 2 hours, or until cold.

Churn the pea mixture in an ice cream maker according to the manufacturer's instructions, about 25 minutes. Transfer to a container and store in the freezer. **Makes 3 1/2 cups**

SNOW PEAS, SUGAR SNAPS AND PEA SHOOTS

We use snow peas, frequently in stir-fries, whole or cut lengthwise into thin strips. These need to have their strings removed, as do the newer sugar snap peas, which have actual peas in their edible shells. Both are better young, when the shells are less fibrous.

Pea shoots are a relative reintroduction to ingredients available for cooking. They were used in Evelyn's (see page 416) time. Now they have reappeared as an elegant garnish. They are the tendrils (and their leaves) that hold the vines to whatever they are growing up.

Turn to **PEAS** in the Cook's Guide for how-tos and to the Index for more recipes.

Stir-fried Chicken and Snow Peas in Mustard-Soy Sauce

This one is healthy, quick and easy to prepare. It can also be made a few hours ahead, in which case, use the lesser amount of chicken stock. The vegetables will give off juice as they sit, making the dish saucier. And do not add the cashews until reheating; they will become soggy.

The samphire (see the Cook's Guide, page 640) adds a pleasant saltiness but can be difficult to find. Make the dish anyway, using more snow peas in place of the samphire and seasoning with additional salt to taste.

1/4 cup cornstarch

1/2 to 1 1/4 cups Basic Chicken Stock (page 501), Roasted Chicken Stock (page 502) or commercial chicken broth

2 tablespoons mirin

2 tablespoons rice wine vinegar

2 tablespoons canola oil

1/2 pound snow peas, strung, tips and tails removed and cut lengthwise into thin strips or on the diagonal into 1/4-inch strips (about 2 cups)

3/4 pound skinless, boneless chicken breasts, cut into thin strips (about 1 1/2 cups)

1/4 pound unsalted cashews (about 2/3 cup)

2/3 cup samphire, plus additional as topping (optional)

3 tablespoons soy sauce, preferably tamari

2 teaspoons Dijon mustard

1 1/3 cups cilantro leaves

Dissolve the cornstarch in 1 cup of the stock (use only 1/2 cup if making ahead). Mix in the mirin and rice vinegar. Set aside.

Heat the oil in a large skillet or a wok. Add the snow peas; toss to coat with oil. Add the chicken. Toss and cook for 2 minutes, or until the outside of the chicken is white. Stir in the cashews. Add the samphire, if using; toss for 30 seconds.

Pour in the cornstarch mixture. Cook for 2 to 3 minutes, stirring, until thickened. Add 1/4 cup stock (or water, if the sauce already has a strong flavor), soy, mustard and half the cilantro. Stir until combined. Serve topped with the remaining cilantro and, if desired, some samphire. **Makes 2 cups; serves 2 as a main course**

Chicken, Beef and Vegetable Soup

Here is an unusual soup that brings together several deep-flavored root vegetables and is finished off with the bright green flavor of snap peas. This makes a lot, so it needs a lot of seasoning. Don't balk when it comes to adding salt and pepper, especially if starting with unseasoned homemade stock.

Grated fresh horseradish passed separately makes a big difference and is universally appreciated. Mustard, which I also offered the first time I made this, came in a distant second.

One 4-pound chicken

2 quarts Basic Chicken Stock (page 501) or commercial chicken broth

2 cups Beef Stock (page 502) or commercial beef broth

2 small carrots, peeled, trimmed and cut into 1-inch pieces (about 1 1/2 cups)

1/2 small Vidalia or other sweet onion, cut into strips about 2 inches long (about 3/4 cup)

2 pounds calabaza, Hubbard or other orange-fleshed squash, peeled, seeds and fibers removed (about 1 1/2 pounds) and cut into 1-inch pieces (about 5 cups)

2 medium pieces yautía (a scant pound; see the Cook's Guide, page 663), peeled, trimmed and cut into 1-inch cubes (about 3 cups)

Kosher salt and freshly ground black pepper to taste

Ten 2-inch cubes filet mignon (about 1 1/2 pounds)

1/2 pound large dried lima beans, soaked and cooked (see the Cook's Guide, page 542; about 3 cups)

1 pound sugar snap peas, preferably small and young (about 2 1/2 cups, more if larger), strings removed

One 4-inch piece horseradish, peeled and finely grated, preferably using a Microplane

Prepared mustard (optional)

Put the chicken in a 4-quart stockpot (or any pot of similar size that is taller than it is wide). Pour in the chicken stock. Bring to a boil. Lower the heat to a slow simmer. Weight the chicken with an otoshi-buta (see Note, page 237) or a plate to keep it submerged during cooking. Cook until no trace of pink remains near the thigh bone, about 1 hour.

Carefully transfer the chicken to a large bowl; let stand until cool enough to handle. Set the broth aisde.

Remove the chicken skin and remove the meat from the bones; reserve both skin and bones. Shred the meat very coarsely. Set aside half the meat for the soup; refrigerate the remaining meat for another use. Return the bones and skin to the broth and simmer until it is reduced by about half.

Strain the broth; return to the pot. Add the beef stock, carrots and onion. Bring to a simmer. Cook for 10 minutes. Add the calabaza, malanga and reserved chicken. Cook for 10 minutes. Season liberally with salt and pepper.

Stir in the beef. Cook for 10 minutes, or until cooked through. Stir in the lima beans and snap peas. Cook until the limas are heated through and the snap peas are bright green, about 1 minute.

To serve, place a piece of beef and some chicken in each bowl. Ladle in the broth and vegetables. Pass the horseradish and mustard, if desired, separately. **Serves 10 as a main course**

Creamy Baby Corn, Chanterelles and Pea Shoots

A clearly Chinese-influenced dish, this can be made only in the spring when the ingredients are incredibly fresh. Even then it may be hard to find some of them. Check the local Chinatown markets for corn shoots, the tender new growth of the corn plant. The only substitution I can recommend is grapevine tendrils for pea tendrils. Pea tendrils are better and easier to find. Even a few years ago, they were never sold. Now, they have become trendy. They are the curls of stem, with the top leaves, that hold the pea vines to their supports. Although new to me, they were common in Roman times as well as in the Chinese past. They have the allure of a baby's curls.

1 3/4 pounds fresh baby corn (about 3 dozen ears), husked and trimmed (about 2 1/4 cups), or two 15-ounce cans or jars baby corn, drained

3/4 pound chanterelles, trimmed (about 3 cups)

3 tablespoons unsalted butter

3 medium-large shallots (about 4 1/2 ounces), finely chopped (about 3/4 cup)

1 1/2 cups heavy cream

3/4 teaspoon kosher salt

Freshly ground black pepper to taste

3/4 ounce yellow corn shoots (scant 1/2 cup), plus more for topping (optional)

1 1/2 ounces pea shoots (scant 2 cups), plus more for topping

continued

Bring a large pot of water to a boil. Add the corn and boil for 2 minutes. Drain and rinse under cold running water. Reserve. (Do not cook canned corn.)

Cut the chanterelles lengthwise into quarters, or into sixths if large. Each piece should be about ¼ inch wide at the top.

Melt the butter in a large pan. Add the shallots and cook over low heat for 3 minutes, or until translucent. Increase the heat to medium. Add the chanterelles. Cook, stirring, for 2 to 3 minutes. Reduce the heat to low. Add the corn. Cook and stir for 1 to 2 minutes. Pour in the cream, increase the heat to high and bring to a boil. Cook for 1 to 2 minutes, or until the corn is tender. Add the salt and pepper. The dish can be made ahead of time to this point; reheat slowly before proceeding.

Reduce the heat to low. Add the corn shoots, if using, and pea shoots. Toss for 30 seconds, or until wilted. Serve topped with additional shoots. **Makes 4½ cups; serves 4 as a first course**

SPLIT PEAS

I am not very fond of split peas. When I was a child I went to a progressive school, and boys and girls alike had cooking classes. We made split pea soup. Proudly, I came home to announce this feat. I was told I could make it, but it was a disaster, and I was never able to smell or tolerate split pea soup thereafter. For those who like it, and there are many, here are two recipes. Kielbasa or frankfurters in slices are traditional additions.

Turn to **PEAS** in the Cook's Guide for how-tos and to the Index for more recipes.

Yellow Split Pea and Ham Hock Soup

This makes quite a bit of soup, perfect for eating some now and freezing some. Or cut the recipe in half. Without the ham and with half the amount of water, this makes an excellent dahl, especially good with vegetable curries.

> 2 large smoked ham hocks (about 1½ pounds)
>
> 3 European bay leaves
>
> 1 tablespoon vegetable oil
>
> 1 tablespoon unsalted butter
>
> 2 medium carrots, peeled, trimmed and cut into ¼-inch dice
>
> 2 celery ribs, peeled, trimmed and cut into ¼-inch dice
>
> 2 medium onions, cut into ¼-inch dice
>
> 2 pounds yellow split peas
>
> Kosher salt and freshly ground black pepper to taste

Put the ham hocks, bay leaves and 4 quarts water in a large pot. Bring to a boil. Adjust the heat to simmering and cook until the meat is barely tender, about 1 hour. Remove the hocks and cool. Set the broth aside.

Pull the meat from the bones and shred coarsely; reserve the skin. Return the bones and skin to the pot and simmer for 30 minutes to 1 hour.

Strain the broth into a heatproof bowl. Wipe out the pot and heat the oil and butter over medium heat until the butter is foaming. Add the carrots, celery and onions; cook, stirring occasionally, until lightly browned, about 10 minutes.

Add the split peas and pour in the ham broth. Bring to a boil. Cover and cook, stirring occasionally, until the peas are tender, about

20 minutes. Season to taste with salt and pepper about halfway through cooking.

Serve the soup as is or remove about one-quarter of the soup and cool slightly, then blend until smooth and return to the soup. Reheat if necessary before serving.

Makes about 12 cups; serves 12 to 15 as a first course, 6 as a main course

Yellow Split Pea Soup with Smoked Turkey
Substitute 2 small smoked turkey wings (about 1¾ pounds) for the ham hocks.

Purée of Split Peas with Caramelized Onions

Again, this makes an excellent dahl, prepared as is without reducing the liquid.

> 6 cups Basic Chicken Stock (page 501) or commercial chicken broth
>
> 1 pound green split peas
>
> 1 medium carrot, peeled, trimmed and grated
>
> Kosher salt to taste
>
> 4 tablespoons unsalted butter
>
> 2 small yellow onions, cut into ¼-inch dice
>
> Freshly ground black pepper to taste

Stir the stock, peas and carrot together in a heavy 3-quart saucepan. Bring to a boil over medium heat. Adjust the heat to simmering, cover and cook, stirring occasionally, until the peas are tender and almost all of the liquid is absorbed. Season to taste with salt about halfway through the cooking.

While the peas are cooking, heat the butter in a large heavy skillet over medium heat until foaming. Stir in the onions. Cook, stirring often, until they start to brown, about 10 minutes. Reduce the heat to low. Cook, stirring often,

until the onions are a deep golden brown, for 10 to 15 minutes. Set aside.

Remove the cooked peas from the heat. Let stand, covered, for 10 to 15 minutes.

With a handheld mixer or an immersion blender, beat the peas, at low speed if using a mixer, until the consistency of lumpy mashed potatoes. Stir in the onions and season to taste with pepper and salt if necessary. Serve hot.

Makes about 6 cups; serves 6 as a side dish

Green Split Pea Soup, Greek Style
Stir 2 cups of the split pea purée (with onion), 1 cup milk and ½ teaspoon dried oregano, preferably Greek, together over medium-low heat until simmering. Serve hot.

Makes about 3 cups; serves 2 to 3 as a first course

COWPEAS OR BLACK-EYED PEAS

Black-eyed peas are a New Year's Day ritual in the southern United States. They originally came from Africa, most probably with slaves. Despite their lurid historical association, they are delicious and cook relatively quickly compared to other beans; do not overcook. They are often served with baked ham.

Turn to **PEAS** in the Cook's Guide for how-tos and to the Index for more recipes.

Black-eyed Peas and Collard Greens

Two soul food staples, usually enjoyed side by side, here share a pot. Pot likker—what's left in the pot after cooking the greens—soaks into and flavors the beans.

  1/2 pound (about 1 1/2 cups) black-eyed peas

  1 pound smoked pork neck bones or ham hocks

  2 dried cayenne peppers

  1 pound collard greens, stems removed, cleaned
    and cut into 1-inch strips

  Kosher salt and freshly ground black pepper
    to taste

Soak the peas in water to cover at room temperature for 6 hours. Drain.

In a 4-quart pot, bring 3 cups water and the neck bones to a boil. Lower the heat to simmering. Cover and cook for 30 minutes.

Add the drained peas and the peppers. Cover and cook for 30 minutes.

Stir in the collard greens. There should be enough liquid to cover the greens; if not, add water as needed. Simmer, stirring, until the greens and peas are tender, about 20 minutes. Remove the peppers and pork bones or ham hocks; let the pork cool slightly. Set the pot aside.

When the pork is cool enough to handle, remove the meat and coarsely shred it. Return it to the pot and season with salt and pepper.

This can be made up to 3 days ahead; reheat over low heat, adding water and seasoning as needed.

Makes 6 to 7 cups; serves 8 as side dish, 4 as a main course

Smooth Black-eyed Pea Soup
Prepare as directed, omitting the collard greens. When the peas are tender, about 45 minutes, remove the pork or ham (the meat may be shredded and returned to the finished soup if desired). Purée the peas with the cooking liquid, in batches, in a blender, adding a small amount of water to make a smooth, loose soup. Season with salt and pepper. Reheat before serving.

Hoppin' John

This is the New Year–welcoming southern special.

  1 pound black-eyed peas

  1/2 pound salt pork or fatback, in 1 piece

  1 medium onion, finely diced

  Kosher salt and freshly ground black pepper
    to taste

  6 cups Basic White Rice (page 489)

  Hot red pepper sauce (optional)

Soak the peas in water to cover at room temperature for 6 hours. Drain.

In a 4-quart pot, bring 5 cups water and the salt pork or fatback to a boil. Lower the heat to simmering, cover and cook for 30 minutes.

Stir in the peas. Return to a simmer, cover and cook until the peas are almost tender, about 40 minutes. Remove the pot from the heat. Remove the salt pork or fatback and cool.

Cut the salt pork or fatback into 1/2-inch dice. Put in a medium skillet and set over medium heat. When the pork begins to render its fat, stir in the onion and season lightly with salt. Cook, stirring occasionally, until the onion is softened, about 10 minutes. Stir into the peas.

Return to a simmer over medium-low heat. Season with salt and pepper. There should be enough liquid to barely cover the peas; if not, add water as needed. Stir the cooked rice into the peas until thoroughly mixed. Check the seasoning and serve, passing hot red pepper sauce separately, if desired.

Makes 10 cups; serves 6 generously as a main course

LONG BEANS

As noted above, these are simply cowpeas in the shell. As they have grown for centuries in China, they are much used there; I vastly prefer New World green beans (see page 10), finding long beans starchy and chewy. Perhaps they are an acquired taste. They are also called yard-long beans, and I guess they make a dramatic statement cooked whole. I use them to replace green beans only when those are less than good, cutting them into green-bean lengths and cooking them slightly longer.

Beans from Asia

Adzuki and Soybeans

Non-American beans—non-*Phaseolus*—have long been staple crops in Asia. They comprise beans primarily meant for shelling, such as soybeans. Soybeans are a rich source of protein and are made into myriad products and sauces. Fresh, they are called edamame and are usually boiled in the shell in salted water; my grandchildren adore them.

ADZUKI

Adzuki beans often find their way into a dark red sweetened paste that can be bought canned and is put into pastries. I hate the sweetened paste. But used as an alternate to *Phaseolus* beans, adzuki cook more quickly and their maroon color—lighter tan than kidney beans—is very attractive. Canned adzuki that are not sweetened and puréed can be very helpful.

Turn to **ADZUKI** under **BEANS FROM ASIA** in the Cook's Guide for how-tos and to the Index for more recipes.

Red Beans and Rice, Japanese Style

The lovely color and the relatively small size of adzuki beans make a very attractive combination that tastes good as well.

- 1 cup dried adzuki beans, soaked
- 2 tablespoons vegetable oil
- 1 medium onion, cut into 1/2-inch dice
- 1 small clove garlic, smashed, peeled and finely chopped
- 2 teaspoons kosher salt, or as needed
- 3 to 4 cups Basic White Rice (page 489)

Put the beans into a small saucepan and pour in enough water to cover by 2 inches. Bring to a boil. Lower the heat to simmering. Skim the foam from the surface and cook, uncovered, until the beans are tender, about 50 minutes.

Meanwhile, heat the oil in a small skillet over medium heat. Add the onion and cook until wilted, about 4 minutes. Add the garlic and cook until the onion is tender, about 5 minutes.

When the beans are tender, scrape the onion mixture into the pan and add the salt. Cover to keep hot.

Scrape the rice into a large serving bowl. Pour in the beans and stir to mix. Season with salt if necessary. Serve hot.

Makes 7 cups; serves 6 generously as a side dish

Braised Short Ribs with Adzuki and Celery

Canned adzuki beans are easier to find than dried in some places. If dried are on hand, soak and cook 1 cup (see the previous recipe) and substitute them for the canned. The sauce is thickened with the pot vegetables, which gives the dish a pleasantly coarse texture; it is not thick. Serve with rice, buttered noodles or mashed potatoes.

- 4 pounds beef short ribs, cut into 2 to 2 1/2-inch pieces
- 2 teaspoons kosher salt, or as needed
- 1/2 teaspoon freshly ground black pepper, or as needed
- 2 tablespoons vegetable oil
- 6 stalks celery
- 2 carrots, peeled, trimmed and cut into 1-inch pieces
- 2 leeks, trimmed and cleaned, cut into 1-inch pieces
- 8 cloves garlic, smashed and peeled
- 4 cups Basic Chicken Stock (page 501), Beef Stock (page 502) or commercial chicken or beef broth
- 3 tablespoons soy sauce, preferably tamari

continued

**2 tablespoons rice wine vinegar or
red wine vinegar**

2 tablespoons sugar

2 teaspoons dry mustard

**Two 15-ounce cans adzuki beans,
rinsed and drained**

Pat the short ribs dry with paper towels. Rub the salt and pepper into the meaty sides of the ribs.

Heat the oil in a 4- to 5-quart heavy pot over medium-high heat. Add as many short rib pieces as fit comfortably. Cook, turning as needed, until well browned on all sides, about 15 minutes. Lower the heat if the bottom of the pan darkens past deep golden brown. Remove to a plate and repeat with the remaining beef if necessary.

Meanwhile, prepare the celery: Remove all the small branches and leaves from stalks. Coarsely chop the leaves and branches and 2 of the stalks. Trim and peel the remaining 4 stalks, then cut on the diagonal into ½-inch slices. Refrigerate until needed.

Spoon off all but 2 tablespoons fat from the pot. Add the chopped celery, carrots, leeks and garlic. Cook, stirring, until the vegetables are browned, about 5 minutes. Pour in the stock. Bring to a boil. Lower the heat to simmering and stir in the soy sauce, vinegar and sugar. Return the beef to the pot and cook, covered, until the beef is barely tender but still clinging to the bone, about 1½ hours.

Transfer the beef to a plate. Pass the vegetables and liquid through a food mill fitted with the fine disc and return the sauce to the pot. Whisk in the dry mustard until no lumps remain. Return the beef to the pot. Add the reserved sliced celery. Bring to a simmer, cover and cook until the celery is softened, about 15 minutes.

Stir in the beans and heat through. Add salt and pepper if necessary. Serve in deep bowls.
Serves 4 as a main course

SOYBEANS

Tofu and soy sauce are probably the forms in which we are most familiar with soybeans.

There was a period of time when I was a tofu addict. I would arrive in San Francisco, and, at the first opportunity, Barbara Tropp and I would go to Chinatown for tofu. I think my favorite version was served at a tiny Hakka restaurant. Rectangles of tofu were split in half lengthwise. A semi-spicy meat hash was layered between two halves, which were then bound together with a knotted ribbon of thinly sliced scallion. The whole was simmered gently in the rich juices that oozed from a roasted chicken. It was not stock.

It wasn't until the arrival in America of a flotilla of Japanese restaurants—mainly sushi— that I was exposed to actual soybeans. There they are boiled in the shell in salted water and known as edamame.

Although I knew that they existed and were a major crop in the United States as well as Japan, primarily for the oil, for many years I didn't really think of soybeans as real things. I knew only their derivatives: soy sauce from different nations (thick, dark, sweet Chinese and various Japanese soy sauces, of which my favorite is tamari made with no wheat) and tofu in its many forms: ordinary square blocks, silken square blocks and brown crinkly sheets often masquerading as meat. (See Shurtleff in the Bibliography for all that anyone would ever need to know about soybeans.)

Today, soy comes in a life-saving formula for babies who cannot tolerate milk. And soy "milk" has become a major product for adults.

Edamame at this point are more expensive than peas, but if fresh peas aren't good, use edamame in a risi bisi or risotto. Why not? They are less starchy and contain more protein and can often be bought satisfactorily cooked and shelled, sometimes frozen.

Keep in mind that the soybeans I am discussing and using in this chapter are the green-seeded type. Many other varieties exist. Also remember that raw or undercooked soybeans inhibit tryespin—an enzyme vital to the digestion of protein.

Turn to **SOYBEANS** under **BEANS FROM ASIA** in the Cook's Guide for how-tos and to the Index for more recipes.

Quadruple Soy Threat

Quadruple because it contains soybeans as tofu, sprouts, edamame and sauce.

One 14-ounce block firm tofu, drained

2 tablespoons vegetable oil

¼ cup cornstarch

4 quarter-size slices peeled ginger, very finely chopped

2 scallions, trimmed and very finely chopped

1½ pounds fresh edamame in the shell, cooked and shelled (about 1 cup), or 1 cup frozen shelled and cooked edamame, defrosted in a sieve under warm running water and drained

¼ cup Vegetable Broth (page 506), Chicken Stock (page 501) or commercial vegetable or chicken broth

2 tablespoons soy sauce, preferably tamari

1 cup soybean or mung bean sprouts

Cut the tofu crosswise into 8 even slices (about ½ inch each). Drain on several thicknesses of paper towels until dry to the touch.

Heat the oil in a large skillet, preferably nonstick, over medium-high heat. Coat the tofu on both sides with the cornstarch, tapping off excess. Add the tofu to the pan and cook, turning once, until golden brown on both sides, about 9 minutes. Remove and drain on paper towels.

Reduce the heat to medium. Add the ginger and scallions and stir until fragrant. Add the edamame and toss to coat with the seasonings. Remove the pan from the heat and add the broth and soy sauce. Slip in the tofu. Return to a simmer over medium-low heat, turning the tofu once. Cook for a minute or two longer, until the liquid is lightly thickened.

Divide the tofu among plates. Toss the sprouts with the edamame and sauce just until warmed through. Top the tofu with the sprout-edamame mixture and sauce.
Serves 4 as a first course, 2 as a main course

Roasted Edamame

These should be eaten warm, or at least freshly roasted. If they sit—especially covered or in the refrigerator—they will lose their crunch and become rather nasty. They can be made without the oil, but will not be as good. They are a good snack with drinks and healthier than the dried salted edamame that come in tins.

Preheat the oven to 400°F.

Toss each cup of shelled and cooked edamame with 1 teaspoon vegetable oil and ½ teaspoon salt. (About 2½ cups of edamame fit on a standard baking sheet.) Roast until well browned in spots and crispy, about 14 minutes. Cool slightly before serving. **Makes 1 cup**

Orzo, Edamame and Shrimp Sauté

Edamame with Italian-style Greek pasta (usually called riso in Italy), shrimp and Asian seasonings make for a lovely dish. It can be made with rice and peas, but I prefer this lighter version.

1 cup orzo

2 tablespoons toasted sesame oil

1/2 pound shelled and deveined medium shrimp

2 scallions, trimmed and very finely chopped

1 1/2 pounds fresh edamame in the shell, cooked and shelled (about 1 cup), or 1 cup frozen shelled and cooked edamame, defrosted in a sieve under cold running water

1/2 cup loosely packed chopped cilantro

1 tablespoon soy sauce, preferably tamari

1 to 2 teaspoons grated peeled fresh ginger

Cook the orzo in a medium saucepan of boiling salted water just until very al dente, about 5 minutes. Drain and rinse under cold water. Drain well.

Heat the oil in a large skillet over medium-high heat. Add the shrimp and scallions and toss just until they turn uniformly pink, about 2 minutes. Add the edamame, orzo and cilantro and toss until the edamame are warmed through. Add the soy sauce, scraping the bottom of the pan. Remove the pan from the heat, add the ginger and mix well. The orzo should be creamy; if not, add a tablespoon of water and toss again. Serve hot. **Serves 2 as a main course**

Asian Cabbages

Bok Choy, Pak Choy, Tatsoi, Napa Cabbage and Chinese Broccoli

We are now entering the more evidently Asian part of the vegetable world. The Chinese have a love of cabbage as great as my own and that of Europeans. The European species are all variants of *Brassica oleracea*. The Asian are of several species with an enormous number of names, even in the United States. Sorting out the names is almost as difficult as dealing with the broccoli-cauliflower confusion. In part, this is because most of the first Chinese arrivals in the Americas spoke Cantonese, but now Mandarin is the official language. Additionally, as Americans absorbed these greens into their diet, they often provided new names of their own. For example, what we usually call "napa cabbage" or "Chinese cabbage"

is officially *Brassica pekinensis*, variety *cylindrica*, paak ts'oi. It is often called bok choy in Cantonese, and in Mandarin it has names I have never even heard. I will continue to call it napa cabbage. Another large group is *Brassica chinensis*. Elizabeth Schneider's *Vegetables from Amaranth to Zucchini* has excellent photographs of this group, often called bok choy or pak choy in Mandarin, although the kind that is grown in flat rosettes is called tatsoi. Herklots, my guide to all such complexities, seems as confused as I, although more erudite. Since Herklots's time, things have only gotten worse as local agricultures have created more and more subspecialties.

For the purposes of this book, I am limiting myself to napa cabbage, bok choy, pak choy and tatsoi, as well as Chinese broccoli (page 549). There will be references in this chapter and in the Cook's Guide to other members of the family, but I will try to describe them as I go along. Pak choy also have different names depending on their size and the amount of green in what I call their leaves—and are more precisely petioles. I will differentiate by description and think that the cook's results will be good no matter if a slight variation is made. The Japanese and the Taiwanese also use pak choy, using their own names—fair enough. This does not begin to include Korean, Malaysian and assorted other parts of that vast mass we call Asia. Those interested in going further can go online to the Web site evergreenseeds.com. I think learning it all would be as difficult as learning Chinese.

Turn to **BOK CHOY, PAK CHOY, TATSOI** and **NAPA CABBAGE** under **CABBAGES, ASIAN** and to **BROCCOLI, CHINESE** in the Cook's Guide for how-tos and to the Index for more recipes.

Deep-fried Baby Bok Choy

Use the smallest baby bok choy available, about two inches in length and thirty-four to thirty-six pieces per half pound. Because no batter is used, the bok choy comes out light, crisp and utterly delicious.

2 quarts canola oil, or as needed

1 cup rice flour, sifted

1 tablespoon kosher salt

Pinch of cayenne pepper

¹/₂ pound baby bok choy, washed and mostly dried (see headnote; about 5 cups)

1 lemon, cut into wedges

Line a baking sheet with parchment paper and set aside. Pour 1½ to 2 inches of oil into a deep 11- or 12-inch pan and heat the oil to 350°F.

Mix together the rice flour, salt and cayenne in a bowl. Quickly toss half the baby bok choy in the flour mix to coat lightly. Then turn each bok choy upside down and press into the flour mix to cover as much as possible. The slight moisture remaining on the bok choy will help the flour cling.

Standing at a safe distance to avoid splatters, slip the bok choy one by one into the oil, being careful to keep them from touching each other. Fry for 3 minutes, or until golden brown, turning halfway through to ensure even cooking. With a slotted spoon, remove to the parchment-covered baking sheet. Bring the oil temperature back to 350°F and repeat with the remaining bok choy.

Serve immediately, with the lemon wedges, or hold in a preheated 350°F oven for up to 20 minutes. **Serves 4 as a first course or a side dish**

Fried Feelers

While this combination may at first seem unusual, baby bok choy and baby octopus have a similar shape when fried. Their contrasting textures go together well. Baby octopus, one and a half to two inches in length, are common in Italian seafood markets or can be ordered from the local fishmonger.

> 1 pound baby octopus (16 to 18 pieces)
>
> Ingredients from Deep-fried Baby Bok Choy (page 316)

Place one rack in the top third of the oven and one in the lower third. Preheat the oven to 350°F. Line two baking sheets with parchment paper.

To clean the octopus: Separate the heads from the tentacles. Remove any black bits found in the heads. The white goo is fine.

Pour 1½ to 2 inches of oil into a deep 11- or 12-inch pan and heat the oil to 350°F.

Mix together the rice flour, salt and cayenne in a bowl. Toss half the octopus quickly and lightly in the flour mix. Standing at a safe distance to avoid splatters, drop the octopus one by one into the oil, being careful to keep them from touching each other. Fry for 3 to 4 minutes, until golden brown, turning halfway through to ensure even cooking. Remove to a parchment-covered baking sheet. Bring the oil temperature back to 350°F and repeat with the remaining octopus. Keep warm in the oven.

Bring the oil temperature back up to 350°F. Coat and fry the bok choy as directed on page 316; keep the first batch warm in the oven while you cook the second batch.

Combine octopus and bok choy on a platter and serve immediately with the lemon wedges. **Serves 10 as a first course, 6 as a main course**

Shredded Napa Salad

Make this in winter when the selection of other greens is limited. It has a lightly Asian flavor and is very pretty. It's as good a side dish as it is a first course. It goes very well with fish dishes.

> 1 ounce dried shiitake mushrooms (about 5 medium mushrooms)
>
> 1/3 cup rice vinegar
>
> 1/8 teaspoon hot red pepper sauce
>
> Freshly ground black pepper to taste
>
> 1/2 pound napa cabbage, shredded (about 4 cups)
>
> 2 scallions, trimmed and sliced (about 1/3 cup)
>
> 1/3 cup Soy-Sesame Vinaigrette (page 449)
>
> 1 ounce red or daikon radishes, trimmed and cut into 1/8-inch slices (about 1/4 cup)

Combine the mushrooms, vinegar, hot pepper sauce, ½ cup water and black pepper in a 2½-quart soufflé dish or casserole with a tightly fitted lid. Cover tightly with microwave plastic wrap or the lid. Cook at 100% for 5 minutes. If using plastic wrap, prick to release the steam.

Remove from the oven and uncover. Allow to stand until cool enough to handle. Using scissors, remove the mushroom stems and discard. Cut the mushrooms into ½-inch strips.

In a large serving bowl, combine the mushrooms with the cabbage, scallions and dressing. Toss to coat, and scatter the radish slices over. **Serves 8 as a first course or a side dish**

Very Spicy Asian Vegetable Salad

8 snow peas (about 2 ounces) strung,
 tips and tails removed (about 1 cup)

6 large leaves bok choy (about 8 ounces),
 cut across into $1/4$-inch strips

1 cup shredded ($1/4$ inch) napa or Chinese
 cabbage (about 1 cup)

4 ounces daikon, peeled and cut into
 2 x $1/8$ x $1/8$-inch sticks (about $2/3$ cup)

1 medium yellow bell pepper, cored, seeded,
 deribbed and cut into 2 x $1/4$-inch strips
 (about $2/3$ cup)

2 fresh shiitake mushrooms, stemmed and
 thinly sliced

4 scallions, trimmed and thinly sliced on the
 diagonal (about $2/3$ cup)

TOPPING

$1/4$ cup unsalted cashews (optional)

1 small bunch enoki mushrooms

DRESSING

$1/4$ cup soy sauce, preferably tamari

$1 1/2$ tablespoons rice wine vinegar

1 tablespoon sugar

$1/2$ to 1 tablespoon hot chili oil

1 tablespoon toasted sesame oil

Up to 2 tablespoons untoasted sesame oil

Bring a 1-quart saucepan of water to a boil over medium heat. Add the snow peas and cook for 30 seconds, or until bright green. Drain and rinse under cold running water. Thinly slice on the diagonal. Set aside.

Toss together the bok choy and napa cabbage and place in the center of a platter or bowl. Toss together the daikon and yellow bell pepper and place on top of the cabbage. Top with the snow peas, sliced shiitakes and scallions. Sprinkle with the cashews, if using. Place the enoki mushrooms in the center.

Combine the soy sauce, rice wine vinegar and sugar in a small bowl. Stir until the sugar is dissolved. Whisk in the hot chili oil, toasted sesame oil, and enough untoasted sesame oil to equal $1/2$ cup dressing. Serve the dressing on the side. **Makes 8 cups; serves 4 to 6 as a first course**

Radiant Bok Choy

This is one of my proudest recipes, with a minimum of ingredients and a maximum of flavor and beauty. The white part of the bok choy turns the brilliant color of Asian mendicants' robes and the green stays intensely emerald.

The vegetable does very well on its own with rice. As a vegetarian dish, it can have soaked dried shiitake, stemmed and cut into strips, added during the final six minutes of cooking. It can be a succulent sauce and side dish for chicken or fish—or shreds of either can be added for the final six minutes of cooking time.

1 tablespoon canola oil

2 tablespoons turmeric

1 tablespoon kosher salt

2 pounds bok choy (about 4 pieces),
 halved lengthwise

1 can coconut milk, plus enough water to
 make 3 cups liquid

1 tablespoon fresh lime juice or 4 lime wedges

In an 8- or 9-inch saucepan, heat the oil over low heat. Stir in the turmeric and salt and cook for about 1 minute. Add the pieces of bok choy, laying them on their sides and cramming them in so as to make them as compact as possible.

Pour in the coconut-water mixture, cover the pan and bring to a boil over medium heat. Cook for 6 minutes. The bok choy should sink into the sauce and cook evenly. If some of the bok choy is not covered with liquid, turn the pieces. Re-cover and cook for 6 more minutes.

Stir in the lime juice, if using. Or serve hot, accompanied with lime wedges, if desired. This is also good tepid. **Serves 4 as a side dish**

Ginger and Garlic Baby Bok Choy

This is a perfect side dish with fish, or serve on a mixed vegetable platter that has no other vegetables using vinegar. It is good hot or cold.

> 1 $^1/_2$ tablespoons vegetable oil
>
> $^1/_2$ pound baby bok choy (about 35; 5 cups)
>
> 2 quarter-size slices peeled fresh ginger, cut into matchstick pieces (about 2 tablespoons)
>
> 1 clove garlic, smashed, peeled and cut into thin strips
>
> 1 teaspoon rice wine vinegar
>
> $^3/_4$ teaspoon kosher salt, or to taste

In a 10-inch frying pan, heat the oil over medium heat for 3 minutes, or until very hot. Add the bok choy, ginger and garlic. Cook, tossing regularly with two wooden spoons, for 15 to 20 minutes, or until the leaves are completely wilted but the whites are still slightly crunchy. Keep the heat between medium and medium-high so that the pan is sizzling but the oil is not sputtering.

Add the vinegar and salt. Cook for 1 minute more. Remove from the heat and serve.

Makes 2 cups

Braised Small Bok Choy

A lovely side dish or first course, these bok choy are a nice Asian variation on the classic French preparation of Belgian endive.

> 2 cups Beef Stock (page 502), Fake Beef Stock (page 504) or, as a last resort, commercial chicken broth
>
> 8 to 10 dried shiitake mushrooms (about $^3/_4$ ounce)
>
> 2 tablespoons unsalted butter
>
> 1 shallot, thinly sliced (about 3 tablespoons)
>
> 6 small bok choy (1 $^1/_2$ pounds), quartered lengthwise
>
> 1 teaspoon kosher salt
>
> Freshly ground black pepper to taste
>
> 1 tablespoon cornstarch

In a small saucepan, bring all but 2 tablespoons of the stock to a boil. Pour into a small bowl with the dried mushrooms. Cover and let sit for 5 minutes, or until the mushrooms have softened.

Remove the mushrooms from the broth and let cool. Pass the broth through a fine strainer lined with a coffee filter or a piece of paper towel and set aside. Cut off the mushroom stems with scissors and cut the caps into thin strips.

Melt 1 tablespoon butter in a 12- to 14-inch skillet. Stir in the shallot and cook over medium heat, stirring regularly, for 4 minutes, or until soft and translucent. Add the broth and mushrooms. Arrange the bok choy in a single layer in the pan. Cover with an otoshi-buta (see Note, page 237) or a pot lid that is a few inches too small for the pan. Cook for 5 minutes. Remove the lid and turn over the bok choy. Cook, covered, for another 5 minutes.

continued

Turn the bok choy over once more and cook for 5 minutes longer. Sprinkle with the salt and season with pepper to taste.

Mix the cornstarch with the reserved 2 tablespoons stock and 1 tablespoon water. Stir the cornstarch mixture into the liquid in the pan. Cook over low heat for 3 minutes, stirring occasionally, until the liquid is thickened. Swirl the remaining tablespoon butter into the sauce. **Serves 6 as a side dish, 4 as a first course**

Bok Choy Provençal

While I prefer white bok choy to the greener variety (see the Cook's Guide, page 557) in quick-cooked stir-fries and sautés, the flavor of the green holds up better when slow-cooking, as in this recipe.

$^1\!/_3$ **cup olive oil**

6 small bok choy (1 $^1\!/_2$ pounds), cut into sixths lengthwise, washed and dried well

3 cloves garlic, smashed, peeled and finely chopped

1 cup sterile-pack or fresh diced tomatoes

4 strips lemon zest (each about 3 x $^1\!/_8$ inch)

4 strips orange zest (each about 3 x $^1\!/_8$ inch)

$^1\!/_3$ **cup Niçoise olives**

1 European bay leaf

2 teaspoons anchovy paste

Kosher salt and freshly ground black pepper to taste

Heat the oil in a 4-inch-deep 12-inch-wide pan over high heat for 2 minutes. Add the bok choy; be careful, as the oil may splatter. Cook, tossing with a wooden spoon, for 5 minutes, or until the leaves have wilted. Stir in the garlic. Cook for 3 minutes longer. Add the tomatoes, lemon and orange zests, olives and bay leaf. Reduce the heat to low. Simmer, stirring occasionally, for 5 minutes.

Dissolve the anchovy paste in $^1\!/_2$ cup water, stirring so that there are no lumps remaining. Add the anchovy mixture to the pan and stir well. Season with salt and pepper to taste. Cook, stirring occasionally, for 25 minutes, or until the white hearts can be cut easily with a paring knife.

Makes 4 cups; serves 4 as a first course, 6 as a side dish

Tatsoi Vegetarian Feast

Tatsoi is one of the most attractive vegetables. It grows close to the ground, a rosette of crinkly dark green leaves about eight inches in diameter. This growing habit means that it must be carefully washed, since it is liable to retain dirt. Usually the leaves are torn off and added to stir-fries or used like spinach. I like to use it whole as a base for steaming other vegetables—an edible dish. Generally, enough cut-up vegetables can be laid on top of it to serve four. It can be put on a plate, mounded with the vegetables and cooked in a bamboo or other steamer (see page 521 for information on steaming). As the tatsoi takes only about ten minutes to cook, vegetables that take longer can be briefly stir fried or steamed on their own before adding.

Don't overseason. Let the vegetables sing. Serve rice on the side.

Stir-fried Chinese Broccoli

I prefer the sausage sold loose from a Chinatown butcher to the packaged version that is more readily available. This is an incredibly quick and easy dish to prepare.

1 tablespoon peanut oil

1 clove garlic, smashed, peeled and sliced

One 1-inch chunk fresh ginger, peeled and
cut into strips (a scant 3 tablespoons)

3 links Chinese pork sausage (each about
5 inches long; 2 1/2 ounces total), cut on an
extreme diagonal into 1/2-inch slices

1 bunch Chinese broccoli (about 1 pound),
trimmed, stems discarded if tough and
cut into 2-inch pieces (about 10 cups)

2 tablespoons hoisin sauce

Heat the oil in a wok or a 12-inch heavy skillet over high heat until very hot. Add the garlic and stir-fry briefly until light brown; do not allow it to blacken. Remove and discard the garlic.

Add the ginger and sausage. Stir-fry for 1 to 2 minutes. Add the greens and hoisin sauce. Stir-fry for 1 minute longer. Serve immediately. **Makes 5 1/2 cups; serves 4 as a first course, 6 as part of a meal**

Steamed Chinese Broccoli with Mustard-Soy Sauce

If black or dark Chinese soy sauce is available, use it here. Its natural sweetness is perfect for this sauce. In any case, use a good-quality soy sauce (i.e., fermented; see the Cook's Guide, page 543).

1 pound Chinese broccoli, trimmed,
stems peeled

2 tablespoons soy sauce, preferably black
or dark Chinese

2 teaspoons spicy prepared mustard

4 teaspoons turbinado sugar, or to taste

Put the Chinese broccoli in the top of a two-part steamer or on a steaming rack or a plate in a bamboo steamer. Fill the bottom of the steamer pan or a pan large enough to hold the steaming rack with water; the water should not touch the rack. Bring to a boil over medium heat. Place the Chinese broccoli on top, cover and steam until the stems are tender when poked with the tip of a paring knife, about 7 minutes.

While the broccoli is steaming, stir together the soy, mustard and turbinado in a small glass bowl. Microwave at 100% for 1 minute. Remove and stir until the sugar is dissolved.

Remove the broccoli from the steamer, draining off excess water, and arrange on a platter. Drizzle the sauce over the broccoli stems and leaves. **Serves 4 as a side dish**

Eggplants

Glossy, deep-tasting eggplant, the boon of vegetarian diets with its rich, meaty flesh, has been a favorite vegetable (really a fruit) in Mediterranean cuisines and almost every Asian cuisine since before time. It was the first of the Solanaceae to break the poison-fear barrier, so long ago that there is no record. However, like all of its family, the leaves and stems are poisonous, and, if stomachs are not to be badly upset, eggplant must be thoroughly cooked.

I thought I knew a decent amount about eggplant, having eaten it in America, Italy ("melanzana" and many related regional names), France ("aubergine," from the Arabic "al-badinjân"), Spain ("berenjena"), Turkey, Greece and Japan; in Thai, Vietnamese and Chinese (according to

Barbara Tropp, my authority on Mandarin, "ch'ieh tsu") restaurants; and even in England, where culinary experts now call it aubergine but where it was eggplant until fairly recent times.

Yet it wasn't until I lost myself for a day in my treasured hoard of reference books and gardening catalogs while trying to sort out the many shapes, sizes, colors and names of eggplants that I learned all of the above names. When I finally got to the out-of-print but brilliantly written, helpful and chock-full of information *Vegetables in South-East Asia* by the ardent gardener and botanist G.A.C. Herklots (see the Bibliography), I finally figured out the sonic boom that tied all the names together. I learned about varieties I will probably never see and got a better handle on the history of this extraordinary food.

Eggplants grow wild in Southeast Asia and India and have done so since time immemorial. At some point, they underwent selective cultivation. They don't crop up in Chinese literature until the fifth century, or in Europe until sometime between the thirteenth and sixteenth centuries. It seems that one of the many Indian names for eggplant is "bengen." From there, it is easy to see how the name followed the customary trade route to the Arab-speaking world and onward, being modified according to the pronunciation of each language, just as the fruit itself was modified by the climates, growing seasons and tastes of each culinary tradition.

I undertook the search not just for the pure joy of learning but to sort out the confusion brought on by the market-to-market variation of names for the relatively newly arrived Japanese and other far more exotic—to me—eggplants. They are all *Solanum*. Most are *Solanum melongena*, but there are many subvarieties as well.

In 1946, Vilmorin, the great French seed house, issued a dictionary and called the very large purple ones "l'aubergine monstreuse de New York." The "monster" name persists in many gardening catalogs. There are many other large eggplants in addition to the large purple ones. Two of the best are agora, or larga, which is creamy white blushed with reddish-pink splotches, and violetta di Firenze, which can be dark oxblood in color and is notable for its odd lobed shape, like Cinderella's carriage pumpkin. These lobes give the slices a seductive scalloped shape.

My favorite eggplants are medium to small—but not tiny—weighing at most eight ounces but usually only three to four. Many eggplants are long and slender, such as Chinese eggplants, which go from a narrow stem end to slightly wider and rounded at the other end, curving on the way. The ones in Chinese paintings tend to start out white and flush to lavender at the round end. One such is Asian Bride, which fruits in small clusters of two or three. Barbara Tropp had the experience of getting all-white Asian Brides. The kind available in Chinese markets is a bright lavender, which unfortunately—like all colors of eggplant—darkens to almost beige in cooking.

The Chinese eggplants are very similar to the Turkish, which can be pale or purple, the Neapolitan "violetta lunga" and the French "violette longue." The French violet is more purple than the Italian, and I have no idea what it means. All can be used in recipes calling for Chinese eggplant.

The French have cultivated a delicious thin-skinned purple eggplant that is absolutely straight, like a zucchini. A recent development is a dark pink cultivar, which I haven't seen. There are many offspring of the French eggplant. All will be called "de Barbentane" (Barbentane style). They are six to eight inches long and about two inches in diameter. They are very good for sautéing or using in stews with their skin on. They can be used in recipes calling for Chinese eggplant, although they may sometimes be slightly heavier and require a little longer cooking.

In this country, we have recently begun to grow, under the name "fingerlings," an Asian variety that is purple and straight like the de Barbentane, but smaller: three to seven inches long and three-quarters to one and a quarter inches in diameter. They grow in clusters. I have had great luck with them in Vermont, as they have a short growing season. I prefer them at the four-inch length.

The Japanese use Chinese eggplants; but the true Japanese eggplant is small, shaped like an asymmetrical pear and purple. These weigh three to four ounces and are four inches long, very similar to the baby eggplant, which is about three inches long and weighs about three ounces. Smaller Japanese eggplants and the babies can be used interchangeably. The larger Japanese eggplants can be used like the Chinese.

The baby should not be confused with the Italian "bambino," which is very small—one to one and a half inches long—like our dwarf eggplant. Bambinos are usually used for pickling, like the truly tiny pea eggplants of Southeast Asia, which are very bitter.

Any of the shapes and sizes of these many eggplants can be white; but it is small white, ovoid ones looking like chicken fruit that gave us the name eggplant. There are many other colors. I have cooked orange eggplants. Mine were round and about three and a half inches in diameter. I understand there are also egg-shape orange ones, but I have not run off to search for them because I found the ones I did cook to have tough skins and big seeds. I have read of light green eggplants with yellow markings, called Madras, in a European catalog; but little other information was given. I will try planting them and see how they are. Future experimentation seems endlessly possible.

To cook eggplants whole in the microwave for all of the following dips, see the Cook's Guide, page 581.

Turn to **EGGPLANTS** in the Cook's Guide for how-tos and to the Index for more recipes.

Eggplant Caviar
Baba Ganoush

Almost all cultures that use eggplants have figured out that eggplants can be cooked and mashed to be seasoned and mixed with oil to make part of a first course, a sauce or a dip.

This was the one dish that my mother's mother made that we all really liked. As she was Romanian, she created the variation that follows. While roasting the eggplant is traditional and lends a flavor of its own, I usually cook it in the microwave, which leaves the flesh pale green instead of brown.

> 1 medium eggplant (1 to 1 1/4 pounds), roasted or cooked whole in the microwave
>
> 3 tablespoons olive oil
>
> 1 medium clove garlic, smashed, peeled and minced
>
> 1 teaspoon kosher salt
>
> 1 teaspoon fresh lemon juice

Cut the still-warm eggplant in half and scoop out all the flesh; discard the skin. Roughly chop the flesh and put it in a bowl. Stir in the olive oil while the eggplant is still warm; let stand for about 10 minutes.

Stir in the remaining ingredients. **Makes 3 1/2 cups**

Eggplant Caviar with Onions and Peppers
Drain 1 cup canned plum tomatoes, crush them by hand and add to the eggplant caviar. In a small skillet, heat 2 teaspoons olive oil over medium heat. Add 3 tablespoons chopped

onion and 2 tablespoons finely chopped green bell pepper. Let soften slowly, but do not brown. Add to the tomato-eggplant mixture; stir in ½ to 1 teaspoon fresh lemon juice.
Makes about 4 ½ cups

Romanian Eggplant Dip
Prepare the eggplant caviar, using 2 garlic cloves, if desired. Season with freshly ground black pepper. Stir in ¼ cup packed chopped fresh parsley. Store, covered, in the refrigerator at least overnight to let the flavors develop.
Makes about 3 cups

Russian Eggplant Dip
Prepare the eggplant caviar, adding ⅓ cup Plum Tomato Purée (page 459) or sterile-pack strained tomatoes, 3 tablespoons tomato paste and a pinch of cayenne pepper. Process in a food processor until smooth. Stir in 2 roasted red or green bell peppers (see the Cook's Guide, page 628) that have been cored, seeded, deribbed and diced. **Makes about 4 cups**

Classic Eggplant Appetizer
These dips have a fresh appealing look and a flavor that is delicious with raw vegetables or warm pita bread. They are terrific for cocktail parties.

This wonderfully garlicky dish would demand one and a half hours of baking in a conventional oven but takes only twelve minutes in the microwave oven.

- 1 medium eggplant (about 1 pound), cooked whole in the microwave
- 1 small onion, finely chopped
- ¼ cup coarsely chopped fresh parsley
- 1 clove garlic, smashed, peeled and minced
- 1 teaspoon kosher salt
- ¼ teaspoon freshly ground black pepper
- 2 tablespoons olive oil
- 2 teaspoons fresh lemon juice

When the eggplant is cool enough to handle, cut it in half and scoop out the flesh. Place the flesh in a food processor. Add the onion, parsley, garlic, salt and pepper and process just until the mixture is coarsely chopped.

Transfer to a serving bowl. Stir in the oil and lemon juice. Serve at room temperature.
Makes 2 cups

Russian Eggplant Orientale
While waiting for the eggplant to cool, core, seed and derib 1 green bell pepper; chop fine. Place in a 1-cup glass measure with 1 tablespoon olive oil. Cover tightly with microwave plastic wrap. Cook in the microwave at 100% for 3 minutes. Pierce the plastic to release steam; remove from the microwave.

Prepare the chopped eggplant mixture, then stir in the pepper, along with ½ cup chopped tomatoes, 3 tablespoons tomato paste, 2 tablespoons fresh lemon juice and a pinch of cayenne pepper. Serve with lemon wedges.
Makes about 3 cups

Eggplant with Asian Seasoning
Cook the eggplant as directed, but omit all the seasonings except the garlic and lemon juice. After puréeing the eggplant, add 2 chopped scallions, ¼ cup chopped cilantro, 1 tablespoon minced peeled fresh ginger, 2 teaspoons soy sauce and 2 teaspoons toasted sesame oil along with the garlic. Proceed as directed.
Makes about 3 cups

East of the Pacific Eggplant Dip

I've never had an eggplant dip in the Far East, but I have had many wonderful eggplant dishes there. I adopted some of their seasonings for this dip made with fat purple eggplants rather than their slim lavender ones or the short, curved purple ones. If they're findable consider thin Asian rice-flour crackers as the dippers.

To make a greater quantity, simply multiply, using the eggplant cooking times in the Cook's Guide (page 581).

1 medium eggplant (about 1 pound), cooked whole in the microwave

2 teaspoons rice wine vinegar

1 medium clove garlic, smashed, peeled and minced

2 scallions, trimmed and chopped

1/4 cup chopped cilantro

1 tablespoon grated peeled fresh ginger

2 teaspoons soy sauce, preferably tamari

2 teaspoons toasted sesame oil

When the eggplant is cool enough to handle, cut it in half lengthwise and scoop out the flesh. Place the flesh in a food processor, along with the remaining ingredients. Process until coarsely chopped.

Transfer to a serving bowl. The dip may be refrigerated, covered, for 2 to 3 days, but be sure to let it come to room temperature before serving. **Makes 2 cups**

Eggplant Moroccan

One day, I had peeled eggplant left after testing the Caponata (page 327) and I needed a dip for a party. I made this, and everybody seemed to like it. The "Moroccan" in the title is purely honorary. This is a large batch that will easily serve thirty-six to forty people, but it's worth making the whole thing since it keeps so well and so a long in the refrigerator. To make a smaller amount, halve or quarter the recipe.

This would make an untraditional but good topping for crostini (see Croutons, page 510). Top each with a couple of extra pine nuts. It would also be a good sauce for a robust pasta such as ziti.

3/4 to 1 cup olive oil

1 small onion, finely chopped (about 2/3 cup)

6 ounces garlic cloves, smashed, peeled and finely chopped (about 1/3 cup)

1 large eggplant (1 1/2 pounds), trimmed, peeled and finely chopped

One 28-ounce can Italian plum tomatoes, drained and excess juice squeezed out, 2 cups juice reserved

2 European bay leaves

1/2 teaspoon ground cinnamon

1 teaspoon ground cumin

1 teaspoon red pepper flakes

1 1/2 cups golden raisins

One 3-ounce jar pine nuts (2/3 cup)

Two 1-gram vials saffron threads

2 tablespoons kosher salt

1/2 cup fresh orange juice

1/3 cup fresh lemon juice

Heat 1/4 cup olive oil in a 12- to 14-inch skillet or braising pan. Add the onion and cook over low heat until translucent, about 20 minutes. Add one-third of the garlic and cook over low heat for 10 minutes.

Stir in the eggplant and ¼ cup olive oil. Increase the heat to medium. Cook until the eggplant is translucent but not brown. Add the tomatoes, bay leaves, cinnamon, cumin, red pepper flakes and half of the remaining garlic. Cook over low heat for 1 hour, stirring occasionally.

While the eggplant mixture is cooking, place the raisins in a medium saucepan for stovetop cooking or a 1-quart soufflé dish for microwaving. Separate the raisins if they are sticking together. Stir in the reserved tomato juice. Cook, covered, in the pan over very low heat until plumped; or cover the soufflé dish tightly with microwave plastic wrap and cook at 100% for 10 minutes. Prick the plastic to release steam.

Add the raisin mixture, ¼ cup olive oil, the pine nuts, saffron, salt and orange juice to the eggplant mixture. Cook for 10 minutes. Taste and add the remaining garlic and another ¼ cup olive oil, if desired. Cook over medium-low heat, stirring occasionally, until the mixture has a thick dip consistency, about 45 minutes. Remove the bay leaves.

Remove from the heat and stir in the lemon juice. The dip can be stored in the refrigerator, tightly covered, for up to 3 weeks. **Makes 9 cups**

Eggplant dishes are a perfect example of the usefulness of a vegetable in a variety of courses. The dips here are served on their own or as part of a mixed hors d'oeuvre such as a meze. The other dishes can be first courses, parts of first courses or sometimes summer meals on their own.

Caponata

This is a delicious sweet-and-sour southern Italian stewy vegetable dish meant to be served at room temperature as a first course or side dish. Olives are traditional in caponata. Using them does mean the additional work of pitting them. It is very important to use good-quality olives, not the canned California sort or the somewhat bitter dry oil-cured ones.

This recipe can easily be doubled or tripled. Packed into sterile jars (see page 91), it will keep in the refrigerator for up to two months.

¹/₃ cup olive oil

2 small onions, finely diced (about 1¹/₂ cups)

2 stalks celery, trimmed, halved lengthwise and cut crosswise into ¹/₂-inch slices (about 1¹/₂ cups)

1 medium eggplant (about 1¹/₄ pounds), trimmed, peeled and cut into ¹/₂-inch cubes (about 4¹/₂ cups)

¹/₄ cup sterile-pack strained tomatoes

2 canned Italian plum tomatoes, squeezed of excess liquid and chopped (about ¹/₄ cup), or an equivalent amount of peeled and chopped ripe tomatoes

1 ounce pitted olives, chopped (about ¹/₄ cup)

2 tablespoons dark raisins, soaked in warm water for 10 minutes and drained

¹/₄ cup red wine vinegar

2 tablespoons capers, rinsed

2 tablespoons tomato paste

1 tablespoon sugar

1 tablespoon pine nuts

2 teaspoons kosher salt

Freshly ground black pepper to taste

continued

Heat the oil in a heavy 4-quart saucepan over medium heat until rippling. Add the onions and celery; cook, stirring, until wilted, about 4 minutes. Stir in the eggplant and cook, stirring occasionally, until lightly browned, about 8 minutes. Stir in the remaining ingredients. Heat to simmering. Reduce the heat to low and simmer, covered, until the eggplant is very tender and the flavors are blended, about 30 minutes.

Cool the caponata to room temperature and let stand at least 3 hours before serving. It can be stored in the refrigerator for up to a week. Bring to room temperature and check the seasoning before serving. **Makes 4 cups**

Eggplant and Chickpea Fritters

These are delicious passed with toothpicks to go with drinks. They can also be put into a tomato pasta sauce. They pair well with Baby Food Tomato Sauce (page 461), given a little kick of extra spice if desired. Use a thin dry pasta, such as spaghettini or vermicelli.

> One 15 1/2-ounce can chickpeas, rinsed and drained (about 1 1/2 cups)
>
> 1 cup Microwave Eggplant Purée (page 581)
>
> 1 tablespoon kosher salt
>
> 1/2 teaspoon cayenne pepper
>
> Freshly ground black pepper to taste
>
> 1 egg
>
> 2 cups canola oil

Purée the chickpeas in a food processor until slightly grainy. Add the eggplant, salt, cayenne and black pepper and process to blend. Transfer to a bowl.

Separate the egg. Stir the yolk into the chickpea and eggplant mixture. Beat the white until soft peaks form. Fold into the eggplant mixture.

Heat the oil in a 4-quart pot to 325°F. With an oiled spoon, drop teaspoonfuls of the chickpea mixture, in batches, into the oil. Cook for 2 minutes, or until golden brown, turning the fritters over every 30 seconds. Drain on paper towels. **Makes about 50 fritters**

Marinated Roasted Baby Eggplant

These are spectacularly good. The only problem is that they must be started the day before needed. If that's not convenient, make them a day or two ahead; they keep well once cooked. Good hot, good cold, good as a first course, good as a side dish—no problems.

> 2 pounds baby eggplants, small Japanese eggplants or long thin Chinese eggplants
>
> 1/2 cup fruity olive oil, preferably California
>
> 1/3 cup soy sauce, preferably tamari
>
> 1/4 cup vegetable oil
>
> 6 to 8 medium cloves garlic, smashed and peeled

Cut each eggplant in half lengthwise, leaving the stem attached. With the skin side down, use a paring knife to score the flesh diagonally, then crisscross to form a diamond pattern; cut as deep as possible without piercing the skin.

In a food processor, blend the olive oil, soy sauce, vegetable oil and garlic until the garlic is finely chopped. Pour the marinade into a deep baking dish. Place the eggplants, cut side down, in the baking dish. Marinate at least overnight— up to 2 days is fine—in the refrigerator. Before roasting, let the eggplants come to room temperature.

Heat the oven to 250°F.

Bake the eggplants, in the marinade, for 20 minutes. Turn the eggplants over and bake for an additional 20 to 25 minutes, until softened. Let the eggplants cool in the liquid.

Remove the eggplants with a slotted spoon and serve at room temperature.

Serves 8 as a first course or a side dish

Stuffed Eggplant

Eggplants are perfect candidates for stuffing, but large ones provide altogether too much food for an attractive portion and have a nasty tendency to be bitter. Make this when smallish Japanese eggplants—the kinds that look like miniatures of our ordinary large purple ones—are available, or use the long thin Chinese or Middle Eastern eggplants in any shade from purple to almost white. The flesh combines with the stuffing to luscious effect.

6 small purple eggplants (each about 4 inches long)

Kosher salt to taste

1/2 cup Mushroom Duxelles (page 405)

1 small onion (about 4 ounces), peeled and quartered

3 tablespoons freshly grated Parmesan cheese

1/2 teaspoon ground cumin

3 tablespoons fresh lemon juice

1 tablespoon Basic Chicken Stock (page 501), Roasted Chicken Stock (page 502) or commercial chicken broth

Freshly ground black pepper to taste

CRUMB MIXTURE

3/4 cup fresh bread crumbs

1/4 cup coarsely chopped fresh parsley

3 tablespoons freshly grated Parmesan cheese

2 to 3 tablespoons extra virgin olive oil

Prepare uncooked eggplant shells (see the Cook's Guide, page 581). Generously salt the inside of the shells and the reserved pulp.

Place a sheet of paper toweling in a 9-inch pie plate. Arrange the shells spoke-fashion on the paper towel, cut side down, with the narrow ends toward the center of the dish. Place the pulp in the center of the dish. Cover tightly with microwave plastic wrap. Cook in a microwave at 100% for 3 minutes. Prick the plastic to release the steam.

Remove from the oven. Uncover and rinse both the shells and pulp well. Pat dry with paper toweling, pressing on the pulp to remove excess moisture. Set the shells aside.

Place the pulp and the remaining ingredients (except the crumb mixture) in a food processor. Process until the mixture is thoroughly combined and the pulp is finely chopped.

Spoon the mixture loosely into the shells and arrange spoke-fashion in the pie plate, this time with the narrow ends toward the outside of the dish. Cover with a sheet of paper toweling and then cover tightly with microwave plastic wrap. Cook at 100% for 4 minutes. Prick the plastic to release the steam.

Remove from the oven. Remove the plastic, but let stand for 3 minutes before removing the paper toweling.

Preheat the broiler. Toss together the ingredients for the crumb mixture. Sprinkle 1 to 2 teaspoons of the mixture over each eggplant half and broil until lightly browned. Serve immediately. **Serves 6 as a first course**

Eggplant Stuffed with Greek or Moroccan Stuffing Omit the crumb mixture. Prepare and cook the eggplant shells as above. Coarsely chop the pulp and combine with 1/2 recipe either Greek

Stuffed Eggplant

There are many sorts of stuffed vegetables in this book. General instructions are under each vegetable in the Cook's Guide and on pages 491–500. The reason the eggplants are not included there is that generally they are cooked and the pulp removed before the shells are stuffed. The pulp that has been removed is used in the stuffing: different method.

or Moroccan Stuffing (page 494). Cook the shells and stuffing for 10 minutes, tightly covered, at 100%. Stuff the eggplant shells. Continue as in the basic recipe, but without the paper towel on top.

Stuffed Eggplant with Lamb and Orzo

This is another recipe that truly works best in the microwave.

- 2 large eggplants (about 1¹/₂ pounds each)
- 6 ounces ground lamb
- 1 medium onion (about 6 ounces), coarsely chopped
- 2 cloves garlic, smashed, peeled and sliced
- 2 tablespoons olive oil
- One 14-ounce can Italian plum tomatoes, drained and liquid reserved
- ¹/₃ cup cooked orzo (cook according to the instructions on the box)
- 1¹/₂ teaspoons kosher salt
- 1 teaspoon dried thyme
- 1 teaspoon dried oregano, preferably Greek
- Freshly ground black pepper to taste
- 1 tablespoon cornstarch
- 1¹/₂ tablespoons fresh lemon juice

Prepare cooked eggplant shells for stuffing (see the Cook's Guide, page 582), using the microwave and cooking the eggplants uncovered at 100% for 12 minutes.

Place the eggplant shells in a 14 x 11 x 2-inch ceramic dish and set aside. Coarsely chop the pulp and reserve.

Combine the lamb, onion, garlic and 1 tablespoon oil in a 2½-quart soufflé dish. Cook, uncovered, for 5 minutes, stirring once. Transfer to a food processor. Add the tomatoes and process just until the meat is finely chopped.

Return the mixture to the soufflé dish and stir in the reserved eggplant, the orzo, salt, thyme, oregano and black pepper to taste. Mound ½ cup stuffing in each eggplant shell.

Combine the cornstarch with the reserved tomato liquid in a small bowl, stirring well. Stir in the lemon juice and the remaining 1 tablespoon oil. Pour the mixture over the eggplants. Cover with microwave plastic wrap and cook for 9 minutes. Prick the plastic to release steam.

Remove from the oven. Uncover and serve hot. **Serves 8 as a first course, 4 as a main course**

Eggplant with Confetti Vegetarian Stuffing

This stuffing is well worth making, despite the many ingredients. Try it in other vegetables and combine them to make a festive meal. The recipe makes five cups, enough to fill fifteen small eggplant halves, ten medium zucchini boats or ten medium bell peppers.

1/2 cup coarse-ground bulgur

2 large eggplants (about 1 1/2 pounds each)

2 tablespoons olive oil, plus additional
   if necessary, for cooking eggplant pulp

3/4 pound sweet onion, finely chopped
   (about 1 1/2 cups)

3/4 pound mushrooms, trimmed and cut into
   1/4-inch pieces (about 3 1/2 cups)

4 cloves garlic, smashed, peeled and minced

2 medium yellow squash, trimmed and cut into
   1/4-inch pieces (about 3 1/2 cups)

1 small green bell pepper, cored, seeded,
   deribbed and cut into 1/4-inch pieces
   (about 1/2 cup)

2 medium tomatoes, cut into 1/4-inch pieces
   (about 1 cup)

1/2 cup finely chopped fresh mint

1/4 cup finely chopped fresh parsley

1/4 cup dried currants

2 1/2 teaspoons fresh lemon juice

2 1/2 teaspoons kosher salt

A generous amount of freshly ground black
   pepper

TOPPING

1/4 cup olive oil

1/4 cup finely chopped fresh mint

Grind the bulgur in a spice mill until about as coarse as sand.

Prepare cooked eggplant shells for stuffing (see the Cook's Guide, page 582), using either the conventional oven or microwave method. Reserve the shells.

Coarsely chop the eggplant pulp. If the eggplant was cooked in a conventional oven, cook the pulp in a small amount of the oil until softened, about 5 minutes. Purée the pulp in a blender. (Makes 1 cup)

Preheat the oven to 350°F.

In a 7-quart nonreactive pot, heat the 2 tablespoons oil over high heat. Reduce the heat to medium. Add the onion and mushrooms. Cook, stirring frequently, for 5 minutes, or until the mushrooms start to give off liquid. Stir in half the garlic, the squash and bell pepper. Cook for 6 minutes. Add the bulgur. Cook for 1 minute, stirring frequently. Mix in 1/2 cup water. Cook for 2 minutes, or until the mixture is hot and steaming. Remove from the heat. Stir in the tomatoes, mint, parsley, currants, lemon juice, the remaining garlic and the eggplant purée. Season with the salt and pepper.

Fill the eggplant shells with the stuffing, about 1 1/4 cups in each. Place in a baking pan with space in between, and bake for 25 minutes.

Drizzle the tops of the eggplants with the oil. Top with the mint. Bake for 15 minutes longer. Serve warm or at room temperature.

Serves 4 as a main course

Eggplant Stuffed with Minted Rice

This is a very basic recipe, but it can be varied in myriad ways. Possible additions include pine nuts, small plumped raisins, sunflower seeds, feta or another firmish cheese in small cubes or pitted and minced olives.

1 large eggplant (about 1 1/2 pounds)

1 tablespoon olive oil, if necessary, plus olive oil
   for brushing eggplant

1 recipe Minted Rice Stuffing (page 496)

1 1/2 teaspoons kosher salt

continued

Preheat the oven to 350°F.

Prepare cooked eggplant shells for stuffing (see the Cook's Guide, page 582), using either the conventional oven or microwave method. Reserve the shells. Coarsely chop the eggplant pulp to get 1 cup.

If the eggplant was cooked in a conventional oven, heat the oil in a small pan. Add the eggplant pulp and cook over medium heat for 5 to 7 minutes, or until completely soft.

Combine the eggplant pulp with the rice stuffing and salt. Mix well. (Makes 3 cups stuffing)

Place the eggplant halves in a baking pan, with space between them. Divide the stuffing equally between the eggplant halves. Brush the tops and sides of the halves with oil. Bake for 20 minutes.

Cut the eggplant into pieces. (Note that the filling will become more solid as it cools.) Serve warm or at room temperature.

Serves 6 as a side dish

Eggplant with Italian Sausage Stuffing

Cooked stuffing can easily be substituted for the raw. Just cook the eggplant pulp in a bit of oil until completely softened before mixing it in. As all of the ingredients are then cooked, the assembled dish needs to bake only until it is completely warmed through.

5 small Japanese eggplants (about 5 ounces each)

Olive oil for brushing eggplants

1 recipe Italian Sausage Stuffing (page 493), raw

Place a rack in the center of the oven. Preheat the oven to 350°F.

Prepare uncooked eggplant shells for stuffing (see the Cook's Guide, page 581). Reserve the pulp.

Brush the eggplant shells with oil. Place the shells on a baking sheet. Bake for 15 minutes. Allow the shells to cool before stuffing them. (Leave the oven on.)

Mix the chopped eggplant pulp with the stuffing. Divide evenly among the shells, mounding the stuffing on top. Place in 1 or 2 baking pans, keeping a little space between each eggplant. Brush the outside of the eggplants with oil. Bake for 25 minutes.

Serves 10 as a side dish or a first course, 4 as a main course

Eggplant with Middle Eastern Spiced Rice

The warmly aromatic stuffing makes this a gala opening for a simple meal.

1 large eggplant (about 1 1/2 pounds)

1/4 cup dark raisins

1/4 teaspoon ground cinnamon

1/4 teaspoon ground allspice

1/4 teaspoon ground ginger

1/8 teaspoon freshly grated nutmeg

1/4 cup long-grain rice

2 tablespoons olive oil, plus additional for brushing eggplants

1 large onion, cut into 1/3-inch dice (about 1 1/2 cups)

1 1/2 cups zucchini flesh (scooped from about 6 small zucchini), coarsely chopped (reserve the zucchini shells for use in another recipe; see Stuffings, pages 491–500)

1/4 teaspoon chili powder

1 teaspoon kosher salt

Freshly ground black pepper to taste

Preheat the oven to 350°F.

Prepare cooked eggplant shells for stuffing (see the Cook's Guide, page 582), using either the conventional oven or microwave method. Reserve the shells.

Coarsely chop the eggplant pulp to get 1 cup. Reserve.

Put the raisins in a small saucepan. Add the cinnamon, allspice, ginger, nutmeg and 1 cup water. Bring to a boil. Cook until the liquid is reduced to ¾ cup. Reserve.

In a separate small saucepan, bring 1 cup water to a boil. Add the rice. Cook for 9 minutes. The rice will be just undercooked. Drain and rinse under cold water. Drain and reserve.

Heat the oil in an 8- or 9-inch frying pan. Add the onion. Cook slowly, stirring occasionally, until lightly browned, about 25 minutes. Increase the heat to medium-high. Stir for 2 to 3 minutes until the onion is very browned. Add the eggplant pulp. Reduce the heat to medium and cook for 5 minutes, or until the eggplant is very soft. Add the zucchini flesh. Cook for 5 to 7 minutes more. Reduce the heat and simmer for 5 minutes. Stir in the chili powder; cook for another minute.

Add the raisins and their soaking liquid to the pan. Cook over high heat for 2 minutes. Add the rice; mix well. Cook several minutes, until the liquid has been absorbed by the rice. Season with salt and pepper. (Makes 2½ cups)

Place the eggplant halves in a baking pan, leaving space between them. Divide the stuffing equally between the halves. Brush the tops and sides of the eggplant halves with oil. Bake for 20 minutes.

Let stand for 10 minutes. Cut the eggplant into 6 slices. Serve warm or at room temperature. **Serves 6 as a first course**

Parmesan-Breaded Fried Eggplant

These can serve on their own as snacks with drinks or be tossed in at the last minute to pasta sauces (see the Index). They also make a good alternative to meatballs.

1 medium eggplant (about 1 pound), trimmed, peeled and cut into 1-inch cubes (about 3½ cups)

Flour for dredging

2 eggs

1 cup Dried Bread Crumbs (page 510) or store-bought dried bread crumbs

½ cup freshly grated Parmesan cheese

Vegetable oil for frying

Soak the eggplant cubes in salted water for 30 minutes. Drain and pat dry.

Spread the flour on a plate. Beat the eggs thoroughly in a wide bowl. Stir the crumbs and Parmesan cheese together on a plate.

A few at a time, toss the eggplant cubes with flour until coated; bounce them in a sieve to remove excess flour. Add to the eggs and stir with a skimmer to coat. Lift the cubes with the skimmer, letting excess egg drip back into the bowl, drop them into the seasoned crumbs and turn them, patting gently, until coated with crumbs. Place on a baking sheet.

Pour ¾ inch of oil into a large deep skillet. Heat over medium heat until one of the breaded cubes sizzles when dipped into the oil. Slip half the cubes into the oil and fry, turning occasionally, until golden brown and tender, about 6 minutes. Drain on paper towels and repeat with the remaining eggplant. Serve hot or warm. **Serves about 8 as a snack**

continued

Anise-Scented Eggplant Cubes

Stir 1 tablespoon kosher salt and 2 teaspoons anise seeds together in a small heavy skillet over low heat until the anise is fragrant, about 5 minutes. Cool completely, then grind to a fine powder in a spice mill. Prepare the eggplant as directed, omitting the Parmesan cheese. Dust the fried eggplant lightly with the anise salt. Serve hot.

Pasta with Hidden-Depth Eggplant

This is a complex-tasting—not -making—pasta dish. The caper and anchovy taste gives a surprising depth of flavor and enough salt so that the dish needs no more. The recipe can be doubled and made ahead.

> 8 cloves garlic, smashed, peeled and finely chopped (about 3 tablespoons)
>
> 1/4 cup olive oil
>
> 1 large eggplant, roasted and fork-shredded (see the Cook's Guide, page 580)
>
> 1/2 cup capers, rinsed
>
> 3 tablespoons anchovy paste
>
> 1/2 cup dry red wine
>
> 1/4 cup red wine vinegar
>
> Freshly ground black pepper to taste
>
> 1 pound dried rigatoni or bucatini
>
> 1/2 cup toasted pine nuts (optional)

Put the garlic in a 1½-quart saucepan with the oil and cook over lowish heat until softened.

Add the eggplant and capers to the garlic; stir. Add the remaining ingredients except the pasta and pine nuts. Cook until warm throughout. Remove from the heat. The sauce can be set aside for an hour or refrigerated, covered, for up to a day. Reheat before serving. (Makes 4 cups)

Meanwhile, bring a large pot of salted water to a boil. Cook the pasta until tender but firm. Drain, reserving a few tablespoons of the cooking water.

Return the pasta to the warm pot with the reserved water. Add the sauce. Toss. Serve warm, topped with the pine nuts, if using.

Serves 4 to 6 as a first course, 2 or more as a main course

Summer's Bounty Stew

By mid-August, the generous yield from my garden has left me with an abundance of eggplant, onion, squash and tomato. This colorful dish is the happy outcome.

Cook the vegetables individually for best results (this can be done a day ahead), then combine and simmer them just long enough to blend the flavors.

> 5 tablespoons olive oil
>
> 1 pound long and thin Chinese eggplants, trimmed and cut into 1-inch pieces (about 6 cups), or other small eggplants
>
> Bottoms (6 to 8) from 4 ounces Egyptian onions (see the Cook's Guide, page 616), trimmed
>
> 1 pound summer squash, trimmed, halved lengthwise and cut into 1-inch pieces (about 3 cups)
>
> 1 pound tomatoes, cored and cut into 1-inch chunks
>
> 1 sprig fresh oregano
>
> 5 fresh sage leaves, cut across into thin strips
>
> 7 fresh basil leaves, cut across into thin strips
>
> Kosher salt and freshly ground black pepper to taste

Heat 2 tablespoons oil in a deep skillet. Add the eggplant. Cook and stir over medium heat for 10 minutes, or until the eggplant has shriveled to half its original volume but is not fully cooked. Remove from the skillet and reserve.

Add 1 tablespoon oil to the pan, then the onions. Cover and cook over medium heat until just tender, about 3 minutes. Remove from the skillet and reserve.

Add 1 tablespoon oil to the pan, then the squash. Cook over medium-high heat until lightly browned, 10 to 12 minutes. Remove from the skillet and reserve.

Add the remaining 1 tablespoon oil to the pan, then add the tomatoes. Cook over medium heat until fairly dry. Add the cooked eggplant, onions and squash, along with all the herbs. Season with salt and pepper. Simmer until the eggplant is fully cooked. Remove the oregano. **Makes 5 to 6 cups**

Winter-y Lamb Stew with Eggplant and Red Peppers

Cook the lamb, eggplant and peppers separately, then combine at the end for a short simmer to marry the flavors. Meltingly tender and slightly rich, this is a good cold-weather dish that will feed four to six people, depending on what else is served. Serve with rice.

4 pounds lamb on the bone, preferably neck or shoulder, cut into 2- to 3-inch pieces (best done by the butcher)

Cornstarch for dusting (if using oven method)

3 to 5 tablespoons canola oil

1 cup Basic Chicken Stock (page 501), commercial chicken broth or water

4 cups Plum Tomato Sauce (page 462)

1 medium eggplant (about 1 1/4 pounds), trimmed, peeled and cut into 1/2 x 2-inch pieces

3 large red bell peppers, cored, seeded, deribbed and cut into 2-inch pieces

Kosher salt and freshly ground black pepper to taste

Brown the lamb in one of two ways.

For the oven method: Preheat the oven to 500°F. Dust the lamb with cornstarch. Arrange in a single layer in an 18 x 13 x 2-inch roasting pan; do not crowd. Roast for 15 minutes. Turn the pieces with tongs or a spoon. Roast for 15 minutes more. The pieces will be crusty and brown. Transfer the lamb to a large pot or Dutch oven.

For the stovetop method: Heat a 12-inch skillet over high heat. Add 2 tablespoons oil. Brown the lamb in 2 to 3 batches, about 10 minutes per batch, turning as necessary; do not crowd. Transfer the lamb to a large pot or Dutch oven.

Pour or spoon off any extra fat from the roasting pan or skillet. Add the stock or water and bring to a boil over medium-high heat, scraping vigorously with a wooden spoon. Let reduce by half. Pour into a glass measuring cup. Allow to settle for 5 minutes. Remove any fat that rises to the top, then add to the lamb.

Add the tomato sauce and enough water to just cover the lamb. Bring to a boil. Reduce the heat and simmer for 1½ to 2 hours, or until the lamb is tender.

While the lamb is cooking, heat 2 tablespoons oil in a 12-inch skillet. Add the eggplant. Cook, stirring occasionally, until completely softened. Remove and set aside.

Heat the remaining 1 tablespoon oil in the same skillet. Add the bell peppers. Cook until soft. Set aside.

When the meat is cooked through and tender, add the eggplant and peppers. Cook for 15 minutes. Season with salt and pepper. **Serves 4 to 6 as a main course**

Eggplant Lasagna

No pasta; eggplant slices instead. This makes a main course for four or a first for eight—if there are no squabbles over seconds.

1 large eggplant (1 1/2 pounds), trimmed and
    cut lengthwise into 1/4-inch slices

2 tablespoons unsalted butter

2 tablespoons all-purpose flour

1 cup milk

1/8 teaspoon kosher salt

Freshly ground black pepper to taste

1 cup Herbed Tomato Sauce (page 462)
    or jarred pasta sauce

1/2 pound mozzarella cheese, grated

Soak the eggplant slices in salted water for 30 minutes. Drain and pat dry. Cook according to the instructions for Oven-Grilled Eggplant (see the Cook's Guide, page 580).

To make the béchamel sauce: Melt the butter in a medium saucepan. Add the flour and cook over low heat for 5 minutes, stirring. Slowly add the milk, whisking briskly to prevent lumps; be sure to scrape the corners where lumps can hide. Increase the heat to medium and cook for several minutes, stirring occasionally, until thickened. Add the salt and the pepper. Reserve.

Preheat the oven to 375°F.

Spread 1/4 cup tomato sauce in the bottom of a 13 x 10 x 2-inch ceramic dish. Arrange one-third of the eggplant slices over the sauce. Cover with 1/4 cup tomato sauce, 1/3 cup béchamel sauce and half of the mozzarella. Repeat with the remaining eggplant and sauces, making 2 more layers of eggplant and finishing with béchamel sauce. Sprinkle over the remaining mozzarella.

Bake for 30 minutes, or until bubbly. If desired, brown for a moment under the broiler.

Serves 4 as a main course

Microwave Variation

Place one-third of the eggplant slices in a single layer in a 13 x 10 x 2-inch dish and sprinkle with 1 teaspoon salt. Cook, uncovered, at 100% for 4 minutes. Remove from the oven, rinse the slices with cold water and pat dry. Repeat, in 2 batches, with the remaining eggplant and 2 more teaspoons salt. Reserve.

To make the béchamel sauce: Place the butter in a 1-quart glass measure. Cook in the microwave, uncovered, at 100% for 30 to 45 seconds. Remove from the oven and whisk in the flour, making sure that there are no lumps. Cook, uncovered, at 100% for 1 minute.

Remove from the oven and slowly whisk in the milk. Cook, uncovered, at 100% for 3 minutes to bring to a full boil, stirring once. Remove from the oven. Add 1/8 teaspoon salt and black pepper to taste.

Spread 1/4 cup tomato sauce in the bottom of the 13 x 10 x 2-inch dish. Arrange one-third of the eggplant slices over the sauce. Cover with 1/4 cup tomato sauce, 1/3 cup béchamel and half of the mozzarella. Repeat with the remaining eggplant and sauces, making 2 more layers of eggplant and finishing with béchamel sauce. Sprinkle over the remaining mozzarella.

Cover with microwave plastic wrap and cook at 100% for 10 minutes, or until the eggplant is cooked through and the cheese is melted. Prick the plastic to release the steam.

Remove from the oven and uncover. If desired, brown the lasagna under a hot broiler for 3 to 4 minutes.

Mock Eggplant Parmesan

It isn't the eggplant that is mock, but the technique, which uses much less oil than the conventional method and includes no Parmesan.

1 large eggplant (about 1 1/2 pounds), trimmed and cut lengthwise into 1/4-inch slices (20 slices)

1 recipe Plum Tomato Sauce (page 462)

5 ounces mozzarella cheese, shredded

Kosher salt and freshly ground black pepper to taste

Soak the eggplant slices in salted water for 30 minutes. Drain and pat dry. Follow the instructions for Oven-Grilled Eggplants (see the Cook's Guide, page 580), but cook at 500°F for 10 minutes, with one side marked. Reduce the oven temperature to 400°F.

Arrange half the eggplant slices on a baking sheet. Spread 2 tablespoons tomato sauce and 2 tablespoons cheese on each slice. Season with salt and pepper. Top with the remaining eggplant slices.

Bake for 10 minutes, or just until the cheese is bubbly but before the eggplant has browned.

Remove from the oven and let cool slightly so the cheese won't burn anyone's mouth; or serve at room temperature. **Makes 10 sandwiches**

Eggplant Rollatini

This makes enough filling for eight slices, which is what should be the yield of a small eggplant. Leftover fried slices, if any, are a good in a sandwich.

SAUCE

2 tablespoons olive oil

2 cloves garlic, smashed, peeled and minced

2 cups canned or sterile-pack chopped tomatoes in liquid

Hot red pepper flakes (optional)

Kosher salt to taste

Vegetable oil for frying

3 large eggs

2 teaspoons kosher salt

Freshly ground black pepper

1 small eggplant (about 1 pound), trimmed, peeled and cut lengthwise into 1/4-inch slices

One 15-ounce container whole-milk ricotta

1/2 pound whole-milk mozzarella, cut into 1/4-inch dice

1/4 cup freshly grated Parmesan cheese

2 cups coarsely shredded Muenster cheese (about 6 ounces)

To make the sauce, heat the olive oil in a small saucepan over medium heat. Add the garlic and cook, shaking the pan, until aromatic, about 30 seconds. Stir in the tomatoes and bring to a boil, then reduce to a simmer. Season to taste with red pepper flakes, if using, and salt. Cook for 10 minutes. Remove from the heat.

Preheat the oven to 375°F.

Pour ¾ inch of vegetable oil into a large skillet. Heat over medium heat. Meanwhile, beat 2 eggs, the salt and ½ teaspoon pepper together in a shallow bowl until blended.

Dip 2 of the eggplant slices in the egg to generously coat both sides. Lay them carefully in the oil. Cook, turning once, until golden brown on both sides, about 6 minutes. Drain on a baking sheet lined with paper towels. Repeat with the remaining eggplant.

While the eggplant is frying, beat the ricotta, mozzarella and Parmesan together in a large bowl. Add pepper and, if necessary, salt to taste. Beat in the remaining egg.

Spoon a thin layer of sauce over the bottom of an 11-inch oval baking dish (or any dish into which the rolls will fit comfortably). Put a scant ¼ cup of the filling on the narrower end of a fried eggplant slice. Roll the eggplant up around the filling and place, seam side down, in the baking dish. Repeat with the remaining eggplant and filling. Spoon the remaining sauce over the rolls and top with an even layer of the Muenster cheese.

Bake until the cheese is golden brown and the sauce is bubbling in the center, about 40 minutes. Let stand for 10 minutes before serving. **Makes 8 rolls; serves 8 as a first course, 4 as a main course**

Ratatouille Pasta Sauce

There are many kinds of ratatouille. This one is a blend of purées that can be made on different days. It would be ideal on freshly made egg pasta ribbons, but dried medium egg noodles would also work well. The sauce is emphatic and should be enough for six to eight servings. I think this tastes fresher without Parmesan cheese, but it could be passed on the side.

2 cups Microwave Eggplant Purée (page 581)

3 1/2 cups Baby Food Tomato Sauce (page 461) made with 4 cloves garlic

1/4 cup Garlic Roasted Pepper Purée (page 57)

1 teaspoon fresh lemon juice

1 teaspoon kosher salt

Freshly ground black pepper to taste

Whisk together all the ingredients in a medium saucepan. Just before serving, heat over low heat until hot. **Makes 5 3/4 cups**

Roasted Eggplant, Cumin and Yogurt Sauce

The intriguing flavor of this sauce goes well with grilled lamb chops, roast salmon or sautéed chicken.

1 medium eggplant (1 1/4 pounds), roasted (see the Cook's Guide, page 580)

3 tablespoons olive oil

4 large garlic cloves, smashed, peeled and coarsely chopped

1 teaspoon ground cumin

1/2 cup chopped fresh parsley

1 cup whole-milk yogurt

Kosher salt and freshly ground black pepper to taste

Halve the eggplant and scoop the flesh from the skin while it is still hot. Discard the skin.

Heat the oil in a medium skillet over medium heat. Add the garlic and cook, shaking the pan, until the garlic just starts to change color, about 2 minutes. Stir in the cumin and let it sizzle a few seconds, then stir in the parsley. Remove from the heat.

Scrape the mixture into a food processor. Add the eggplant pulp and process until smooth. Scrape into a serving bowl, stir in the yogurt and season with salt and pepper. Serve at room temperature. **Makes about 2 1/2 cups**

Okra and Malokhei

There are people who hate okra and then there are people like me who love it. In at least one case, I know that the man who hated okra had always had it badly cooked by his mother. When it appeared in my food fresh from the garden, he didn't even know what it was and ate it.

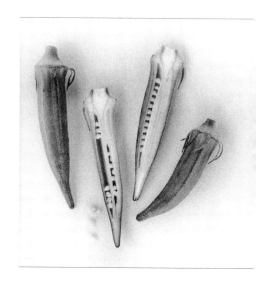

I love the plants as well as the food. They are little bushes on which the okra grow upright like small pointed candles. Okra come in green and purple. The purple is, as with other purple vegetables, actually a supersaturated green that turns bright green with cooking. Purple okra have purple flowers and purple stems—very decorative.

The problem with much okra is that it has a gelatinous fluid inside. Proper preparation—

slicing off the top of the okra very thinly so as not to expose the tiny tubules that hold the liquid—and proper cooking can minimize this. It should be noted that there are culinary cultures—particularly the Chinese—that like this texture, as do the French, in pigs' feet and tripe. Incidentally, this is a thickener that is useful in gumbos and soups.

Other problems with okra are that it is often picked when it is too big and too old and tough. Sometimes it is overcooked and becomes stringy. In good Turkish restaurants, the okra served are usually two inches long or shorter. Buy the smallest and freshest available. That means firm and plump, without dark spots. I find it hard to steel myself to pick what seem to be babies, but they are better. As okra get older on the plant, the candles turn upside down.

Another plant that was for centuries listed as belonging to the same family (see the Cook's Guide) is malokhei, in English known as Jew's mallow. I have seen at least ten different spellings of the name, which is a transliteration from Arabic, although the plant is equally popular in India, Lebanon and southern Africa.

It was totally unknown to me and I came across it by one of the nicest accidents. I was walking the dog in the park, and another woman who regularly walks her large brown poodle, Sinatra, at the same time overheard me telling someone about this book. She volunteered that she had a friend who, although American, loved Egyptian food. She volunteered to find out for me about this soup she had tasted. She came back true to her word but with the sketchiest of descriptions. Intrigued, I called a good friend and excellent cook—an immigrant to France, an Egyptian Jew. She gave me a better description. I then had to think how I was going to find the green leaf that was the mysterious and essential ingredient. I called Kalustyan's (see Sources) and they said "of course" they had malokhei. I asked in what form, as I had been told that it was also sold dried. Chris Styler went and found frozen, canned whole, canned chopped and dried. Obviously it is popular.

We tried some of each. Hands down, go for the frozen if it is findable. If not, go for the canned whole. Do not try the dried, which smells like a particularly nasty tea.

The obvious connection to okra is the gelatinous quality, though it's less stringy and pronounced than okra. It makes divine soup.

Turn to OKRA and MALOKHEI in the Cook's Guide for how-tos and to the Index for more recipes.

Okra with Basil

Most people don't think of okra as a salad ingredient, but it is small and ripe just when the days are hottest. Consider serving this with simply grilled or cold poached fish.

This salad may be made up to four hours before serving; longer and it tends to get soggy.

1/2 pound okra, stems trimmed to 1/4 inch

2 tablespoons fruity olive oil

1 tablespoon fresh lemon juice

1/2 teaspoon kosher salt

1 tablespoon finely shredded loosely packed small fresh basil leaves (preferably tiny bush basil leaves)

In a medium stockpot, bring 2 quarts heavily salted water to a boil. Add the okra and cook for exactly 5 minutes. Drain and rinse the okra under cold running water for 5 minutes. Drain well.

Whisk together the olive oil, lemon juice and salt in a small bowl. Add the okra and basil. Toss well. Let marinate for 30 minutes before serving. **Serves 4 as a side dish**

Pickled Okra

I don't like dilly beans, but when I have lots of small okra or can buy it—generally in a Turkish market—I love pickled okra. If I'm making it for a party, I don't put it in jars. If I do want to put it up, I boil the okra for only a minute before packing it in sterile jars (see page 91). This is not a long-lasting pickle. Use it within a couple of months. If this is too much, halve the recipe.

2 quarts tarragon vinegar

2 cups sugar

8 small dried red chili peppers

6 cloves garlic, smashed and peeled

25 whole black peppercorns

3 European bay leaves

5 pounds okra, stems trimmed to $1/4$ inch

In a large pot, combine all the ingredients except the okra; add 4 cups water. Bring to a boil. Add the okra and simmer for 5 minutes. Remove from the heat and cool to room temperature. Refrigerate for 2 to 3 days before using. **Makes about 8 quarts**

Fried Okra

Cooked this way, okra is crunchy and delicious. Serve it, immediately, with drinks.

3 cups canola oil

1 pound baby okra, cut across into $1/4$-inch slices (about 4 cups)

Kosher salt to taste

In a 2-quart sauté pan, heat the oil over high heat to 350°F. When the oil is hot, fry the okra in $1/2$-cup batches, for 1 minute each. Remove from the oil with a skimmer and place on a baking sheet lined with paper towels. Salt to taste. **Makes about 3 cups**

Spring Vegetable Gumbo

I proudly think this recipe is a triumph. Please try it. It is very different from the Summer Vegetable Gumbo (page 343).

2 tablespoons unsalted butter

$1/2$ cups diced onions

$1/4$ teaspoon minced garlic

2 cups drained canned whole tomatoes, crushed, or $1 1/2$ cups sterile-pack chopped tomatoes

4 cups Beef Stock (page 502)

4 cups Basic Chicken Stock (page 501), Roasted Chicken Stock (page 502) or commercial chicken broth

2 to $2 1/2$ tablespoons kosher salt

Freshly ground black pepper to taste

Cayenne pepper to taste

Hot red pepper sauce to taste

2 cups thinly sliced fresh (preferably) or frozen okra

$1/3$ cup diagonally sliced scallions (white and green parts), plus additional for topping

$1/4$ cup carrots cut into $2 1/2$- to 3-inch long strips, $1/8$ inch across

$1/3$ cup 1-inch pieces asparagus spears, blanched

$1/4$ cup cooked fresh peas

In a heavy 4- to 5-quart nonreactive pot, melt the butter over medium heat. Add the onions and garlic and cook until translucent; do not brown. Add the tomatoes, stocks, salt, black pepper, cayenne and hot pepper sauce. Simmer the mixture for about 30 minutes.

Add the okra and cook until tender, for roughly 3 minutes. Meanwhile, in a bowl, mix together the ⅓ cup scallions, carrots, asparagus and peas.

When serving, stir a small amount of the scallion mixture into each portion. Sprinkle with scallions and serve immediately.

Makes about 10 to 12 cups; serves 10 to 12 as a first course

Okra and Roasted Pepper Stew with Rice

Our great friends the Bankers are both excellent cooks. One evening they served us this as a starter. I think it would make an excellent light meal. The Italian flag colors are a cheerful introduction to a meal. If there is no ring mold around, simply form the rice into a loose circle, leaving the center of the serving dish empty to be filled with the vegetables.

1 ½ cups long-grain white rice

2 tablespoons olive oil

¾ pound okra, cut into 1-inch lengths (about 3 cups)

2 medium red bell peppers roasted, cored, seeded, peeled and cut into ¼-inch strips

1 teaspoon kosher salt

½ cup Basic Chicken Stock (page 501) or commercial chicken broth

Freshly ground black pepper to taste

Cook the rice (see Basic White Rice, page 489). Using vegetable oil, lightly oil a 4-cup ring mold, if using.

While the rice is cooking, heat the olive oil in a large heavy skillet over medium heat. Add the okra. Cook, stirring, until bright green, about 4 minutes; do not brown. Add the roasted pepper strips and salt. Toss to mix. Pour in the chicken stock, bring to a boil and cook until the okra is tender but still crisp and the stock is reduced by about half, about 4 minutes. Season to taste with pepper.

Pack the rice lightly into the prepared mold, then invert onto a serving plate. (Or arrange the rice in a ring shape on the plate.) Spoon the stew into the center of the rice and serve immediately.

Serves 4 as a first course or a light main course

Eggplant and Okra Stew

I serve this over spaghetti, but it can be a side dish.

3 tablespoons canola oil

1 tablespoon ground cumin

1 medium sweet onion, finely chopped (about 1 ½ cups)

4 cups American Tomato Purée (page 460)

2 cups Fried Okra (page 340)

4 cups Fried Eggplant Cubes (page 581)

1 teaspoon kosher salt

Freshly ground black pepper to taste

In a 4-quart nonreactive pan, heat the oil with the cumin over high heat. Stir in the onion. Cook for 2 minutes. Add the tomato purée, reduce to a simmer and cook, stirring occasionally, for 10 minutes.

Stir in the okra and eggplant. Cook for 3 minutes. Season with the salt and pepper.

Makes 8 cups

Middle Eastern Eggplant and Okra Stew
For more of a Middle Eastern flavor, add 1 teaspoon fresh lemon juice, ½ teaspoon grated lemon zest and ½ teaspoon ground cinnamon at the end.

Mysterious Pasta Sauce

This vegetable sauce is particularly nice with tomato pasta, for both the color and the flavor it lends.

- **¼ cup plus 1 tablespoon olive oil**
- **½ pound okra, cut across into ¼-inch slices (about 2 cups)**
- **1 pound fingerling eggplants, cut across into ¼-inch slices (about 4½ cups)**
- **1¼ pounds plum tomatoes, cut across into ½-inch slices (about 2½ cups)**
- **5 medium garlic cloves, smashed and peeled, 2 cloves quartered, 3 cloves finely chopped**
- **1½ pounds fresh or 1 pound dried fettuccine, preferably tomato-flavored**
- **1 tablespoon ground cumin**
- **1 cup chopped fresh parsley**
- **½ teaspoon kosher salt**

In a large nonreactive pot, heat the ¼ cup olive oil over high heat. Add the okra and cook, stirring regularly, for 3 minutes. Mix in the eggplant. Cook for 9 minutes. Add the tomatoes, the quartered garlic and 1½ cups of hot water. Reduce the heat to medium and cook for 20 minutes.

Meanwhile, bring a large pot of salted water to a boil. Cook the pasta until just tender. Drain, reserving 1¾ cups of the pasta cooking water. In a large bowl, toss the pasta with the 1 tablespoon oil until coated. Cover to keep warm.

Turn the heat to low and stir the cumin into the sauce. Cook for 5 minutes. Add the parsley and chopped garlic cloves. Stir and let simmer for 2 minutes. Remove from the heat and stir in the salt. (Makes 3½ cups)

Pour the sauce over the pasta and toss to coat, adding some of the remaining pasta water if the sauce is too thick to coat the pasta evenly.

Serves 8 as a side dish, 4 as a main course

Summer Vegetable Gumbo

Somewhere there must exist Creole vegetarians, although I have yet to meet one. If there are any, this soup's for them; otherwise, it's for me. I like it so much that I have played with two versions, both in this recipe—one with a roux and one without. Try both and tell me which is better. The non-roux version is good cold.

- **½ cup plus 2 tablespoons vegetable oil if using roux; 6 tablespoons olive oil if not using roux**
- **¼ cup all-purpose flour, if using roux**
- **1 large onion, cut into ¼-inch dice**
- **10 medium cloves garlic, smashed, peeled and very finely chopped**
- **3 medium dried hot red peppers, crumbled**
- **2 medium bunches kale, leaves only, cut across into ½-inch strips**

continued

1 1/2 pounds fresh cranberry beans, shelled,
   or one 19-ounce can cannellini beans,
   rinsed and drained

4 cups Chunky Tomato Base (page 460), lightly
   crushed canned tomatoes (not plum), with their
   juice, or sterile-pack chopped tomatoes

1 pound okra, cut across into 1/4-inch slices

Kernels from 2 ears corn

2 pounds fava beans, shelled, blanched and
   peeled (about 1 cup; see the Cook's Guide,
   page 542), or 1 cup frozen lima beans,
   defrosted in a sieve under warm running
   water and drained

Kosher salt to taste

1/2 cup red wine vinegar if using roux;
   1 tablespoon vinegar if not using roux

Freshly ground black pepper to taste

Hot red pepper sauce to taste

If using a roux: Heat the vegetable oil in a large
wide pot over medium-high heat. Stir in the
flour and cook, stirring continuously, for
15 minutes. At this point, the mixture should
begin to take on a lot of color. Lower the heat
to medium-low and continue to cook until
the roux is a warm brown, like milk chocolate.
This will take 20 to 30 minutes from the time
flour is added.

Stir the onion into the brown roux. Remove
from the heat and continue to stir; the mixture
will be hot enough to continue cooking to the
point where the roux is a rich chocolate brown
and the onion is wilted without burning. When
the onion and roux have stopped sizzling,
return to medium heat.

If not using a roux: Heat the olive oil in a large
wide pot over medium heat. Stir in the onion
and cook, stirring occasionally, for 10 minutes
or until translucent.

With or without the roux, stir half of the
garlic, the red peppers and kale into the
onion. Cook over medium-low heat, stirring
occasionally, until the kale is wilted, about
10 minutes. Stir in 5 cups water and the
cranberry beans, if using. Bring to a boil.
Lower the heat and simmer, partially covered,
for 20 minutes.

Stir in the tomatoes, okra and 2 cups water.
Return to a boil. Lower the heat and simmer
for 8 minutes.

Stir in the corn, cannellini beans, if using,
and fava beans. Add the remaining garlic
and season with the salt, vinegar, pepper and
hot pepper sauce. Let the soup sit at room
temperature for at least 30 minutes or up to
1½ hours.

Reheat and serve.

Makes 13 cups; serves 8 as a main course

Malokhei

Light Chicken, Malokhei and Rice Soup

Versions of this soup made with rabbit, seafood
or lamb can be found around the Persian
Gulf and on into Lebanon, Syria and beyond.
Malokhei is the name of both the green and the
soup made from it. Like okra, it thickens liquid
lightly and lends a pleasant texture.

One 4 1/2-pound chicken with the neck and
   gizzards (no liver)

4 cups Basic White Rice (page 489)

One 400-gram (about 14-ounce) bag defrosted
   frozen malokhei leaves or one well-drained
   27-ounce can malokhei, cut into 1-inch strips

4 teaspoons kosher salt

1 tablespoon vegetable oil

2 tablespoons ground cumin

Put the chicken, neck and gizzards into a deep pot narrow enough to hold the chicken snugly (a small stockpot, 11 inches deep by 8 inches wide, works well). Pour enough cold water over the chicken to cover it completely. Cover and bring to a boil over high heat. Skim the foam and fat from the surface. Adjust the heat to a steady simmer. Cook until no trace of pink remains near the joint where the thigh meets the backbone, about 1 hour 15 minutes.

Using a large skimmer, lift the chicken into a large bowl. (It's fine if the chicken breaks apart while removing.) Let stand until cool enough to handle. Set the broth aside.

Remove the chicken meat from the bones. (Discard the neck and gizzards and use the broth as is, or enrich it if desired; see Note.) Shred the meat very coarsely. Combine the meat, 2 quarts of the strained cooking liquid, the rice, malokhei and salt in a pot large enough to hold them comfortably. Heat to simmering.

While the soup is heating, stir the oil and cumin together in a very small pot or skillet over medium-low heat. When the cumin changes color and is fragrant, scrape the mixture into the soup. Serve hot.

Makes 16 cups; serves 8 as a main course

NOTE: For a richer broth, return the chicken skin and bones to the broth and simmer for 1 hour; strain.

Rhubarb

Early in chilly northern spring, one of the most decorative of perennial food plants pushes up year after year. Its pink-to-red stalks and dark green leaves are inviting indeed. Originally a plant from the eastern part of Russia, rhubarb has been used all over Europe and North America to make spring tonics—a wise move in earlier times, since it is rich in vitamins that would have been lacking all through the dark winter. Be careful, though, of the leaves; they contain too much oxalic acid to be human fodder. Incidentally, if someone in the family is prone to the insult of kidney stones, it's a good idea to omit rhubarb from the menu.

Vitamin C in pill form and the winter arrival of warm-climate citrus have vitiated the need for rhubarb, but it still merits a place in garden and kitchen for its taste. Fibrous like celery, it is best cooked by first being cut across the stalk into one-quarter-inch diagonal slices. Then it can be cooked rapidly, retaining more color and flavor than when cooked, as traditionally, for a longer time. Add it to early strawberries for jam and pie. New Englanders called it "pie plant"; every garden had one. It still makes good strawberry-rhubarb pies.

Rhubarb freezes beautifully if it is first blanched: Cook each cup of cut stems for 1 minute in 1½ cups of One-to-One Simple Syrup (page 511). Freeze in half-pint microwave-safe plastic containers. To defrost in a microwave, uncover the container; cover tightly with microwave plastic wrap. Cook at 100% for 4 minutes. Allow to sit until completely defrosted. Use as for fresh rhubarb.

Turn to **RHUBARB** in the Cook's Guide
for how-tos and to the Index for more recipes.

Duck Breast with Rhubarb Sauce

Every once in a while I want to make an all-out sensational dish. This fills the bill. It occurred to me that it is classic to combine duck with an acid flavor, usually a fruit such as an orange. "Why not rhubarb?" I asked myself, and responded, "Why not indeed."

Buy duck breasts, if available, but I prefer to start with whole ducks. The legs can be used in my Duck Gumbo in *American Food and California Wine* (page 50) or braised in the fashion of lamb shank (page 197) in *Roasting, A Simple Art*.

The reason for the two sets of rhubarb is that, like celery, rhubarb is very salty and the marinade becomes too salty to use in the finished dish.

Begin this recipe the day before you plan to serve it.

Breasts from four 5-pound ducks or
   8 boneless (skin-on) duck breasts
   (about 4½ pounds)

8 cups diagonally sliced rhubarb
   (cut into pieces about 2 inches long)

4 cups diagonally sliced, trimmed scallions
   (cut into very thin slices about 1 inch long)

2 tablespoons kosher salt

1 teaspoon freshly ground black pepper

1 recipe Rhubarb Sauce (page 348)

Only the boned breasts from the ducks are needed. Cut each breast in half through the breastbone and remove all the bones, including the complete wings; save them all for stock.

Leave the skin on the breasts, but trim off the excess skin and fat that hang over and do not cover the meat.

Combine the sliced rhubarb, scallions, salt and pepper. Place half in an 13 x 9-inch baking dish. Place the duck breasts in one layer over the mixture. Top with the remaining rhubarb mixture. Cover the dish and refrigerate overnight.

Let the duck breasts reach room temperature before continuing. Preheat a broiler or grill.

Remove the duck breasts from the marinade and pat dry. Score the skin of each piece, cutting crosswise 4 or 5 times through the skin but not into the meat.

If broiling, place the breasts, skin side up, on the broiling pan and cook for 5 to 6 minutes; then turn and cook for 1½ to 2 minutes on the flesh side. The meat should be pink and juicy. If grilling, the timings are the same, but begin with the breasts skin side down so that side cooks first.

Slice the breasts crosswise, holding the knife at a 45-degree angle to the cutting board. Serve with the rhubarb sauce. **Serves 8 as a main course**

Rhubarb Sauce

I invented this sauce to go with the duck dish on page 347; but it would be just as delicious on a pork roast. Make duck stock with the bones from the duck following the guidelines for chicken stock. Or use one of the other suggested stocks. Make the duck glaze following the chicken glaze guidelines.

> 2 cups duck stock (see headnote), Basic Chicken Stock (page 501), Roasted Chicken Stock (page 502) or commercial chicken broth
>
> 5 to 6 tablespoons duck glaze, Chicken Glaze (page 505) or commercial chicken glaze (demi-glace)
>
> 1/4 cup Cabernet Sauvignon vinegar or other red wine vinegar
>
> 1 1/2 teaspoons kosher salt
>
> Freshly ground black pepper
>
> 3/4 pound (12 ounces) unsalted butter, cut into 1-inch pieces
>
> 1 1/3 cups diagonally sliced rhubarb (pieces should be 3/4 inch long and very thin)
>
> 1 cup sliced trimmed scallions (cut into very thin pieces about 1/4 inch long)
>
> 1 cup very thinly sliced radishes

Pour the stock and glaze into a medium saucepan. Boil gently over medium heat until 1 cup remains.

Add the vinegar, salt and a generous amount of pepper. Gradually beat in the butter, piece by piece, until the sauce is smooth. Stir in the rhubarb, scallions and radishes. Let sit off the heat while cooking the duck breasts. Or, if serving with a pork roast, make the sauce after removing the pork from the oven. Before serving, taste for salt and pepper, keeping in mind that rhubarb tends to be salty. **Makes 3 cups**

Basic Rhubarb Sauce

This is a more expectable rhubarb sauce, a sweet one, but not too sweet, and as simple as it gets. Like it sweeter? Add another quarter cup of sugar. This is wonderful served with the Coconut-Yuca Custard Cake (page 148).

> 1 pound rhubarb (stalks only), rinsed, trimmed and cut into 1/4-inch diagonal slices (about 4 cups)
>
> 1/2 cup sugar

Put the rhubarb in a medium saucepan, add the sugar and toss to coat. Cook over low heat, stirring occasionally. After 5 minutes the sugar should be melted. Continue to cook, stirring gently from time to time, until the rhubarb pieces are limp and the volume is reduced by about half. Serve warm, at room temperature or cold. **Makes 2 cups**

Rhubarb Energy Beets

My pleasure on finding out that rhubarb was a vegetable galvanized me into action, especially as I have two very prolific plants in the garden. I had the thought of combining the acidity of rhubarb with the sweetness of beets—especially as they are both red. It worked very well, with the acidity helping to keep the bright color. The rhubarb also obviated the need for salt as, like its cousin celery, it has lots of salt.

The leftover beet cooking liquid can be used in Beet Sorbet (page 164) or to replace part of the cooking liquid in Red Russian Vegetable Soup (page 168) or Red Russian Soup—the Meat Version (page 169).

3 pounds trimmed beets (without greens), well washed

1¹/₂ pounds rhubarb (stalks only), rinsed, trimmed and cut on the diagonal into ¹/₄-inch slices (about 6 cups)

2 tablespoons unsalted butter

Put the beets in a large stainless steel pot. Cover with water (about 6 cups) and bring to a boil. Reduce to a simmer and cook until the beets are tender, about 45 minutes. Drain, reserving the liquid. Allow the beets to cool.

Peel the beets. Cut in half and then into scant ¼-inch slices; there will be about 7 cups.

Combine the rhubarb, beets, 1 cup of the reserved beet liquid and the butter in a saucepan. Cook until heated through. **Makes about 6 cups**

Rhubarb Strawberry Jam

Strawberry flavor dominates this jam. Don't worry about stringing the rhubarb; just remove any strings that really get in the way while slicing. If the jam seems stringy once it's cooked, pass it through a food mill fitted with a medium disc. This can be made into a very good pie filling (see the variation).

In my house, this disappears in a few days; I don't bother to process the jars in boiling water. In fact, if the jam is put into hot sterilized jars and sealed with paraffin, it doesn't have to be processed.

1 pound rhubarb (stalks only), rinsed, trimmed and cut into ¹/₄-inch diagonal slices

1 pint strawberries, wiped clean and hulled

2¹/₂ cups sugar

Combine all the ingredients in a 2½-quart soufflé dish. Cover with microwave plastic wrap. (If your microwave oven does not have a carousel, place the soufflé dish on a large plate.) Cook at 100% for 10 minutes. Prick the plastic to release the steam, uncover and cook for 10 minutes longer. If any liquid bubbles out of the dish during cooking, simply scrape it off the carousel (or plate) and back into the dish at the end of cooking.

Remove from the oven. Divide the jam among sterilized jars. Seal with ⅛ inch of melted paraffin, if desired. **Makes 2¹/₂ cups**

Rhubarb-Strawberry Pie

Make the jam, reducing the uncovered cooking time to 6 minutes. Add 2½ tablespoons instant tapioca, cover tightly and cook for 4 minutes longer. Pour into a baked 8-inch pie shell made with Basic Pie Crust (page 476); let cool. Cover with meringue or whipped cream, if desired. **Makes one 8-inch pie; serves 6 to 8**

Cucumbers and Gourds

Aside from learning by reading, my first sense of cucumbers as an Asian vegetable came from their plentiful use in raitas and other side dishes in Indian cooking.

The cucumbers that show up most plentifully in the stores are large, dark green and shiny. If it's possible, these should be avoided in favor of their dowdier relative the Kirby, smaller, less shiny and bumpier, with smaller seeds and more flavor. The shine on the big ones frequently comes from wax, which means that the skins must be scrubbed or peeled. It is possible to tell by running a fingernail down the skin and seeing if any wax comes off. Generally, I prefer Kirbys. I used to use hothouse cucumbers—English tea cucumbers—for sandwiches, but I now find them to be somewhat overgrown and a bit flabby. It is hard to tell, as they come shrink-wrapped in plastic. Use a knife to peel off the plastic. These cucumbers should have no true seeds but rather a sort of honeycomb texture in the center, where the seeds would have been tucked in a normal cucumber.

There are also specialty cucumbers that I have grown, such as lemon cucumbers and round cucumbers. I have found them flabby too, and without much taste. I no longer grow them.

I do, however, grow cornichon cucumbers. Oh well, here I am displaying my prejudices. To me these are French, even though we have the perfectly good word "gherkin" for the same very small variety of cucumber, picked at 1½ to 2½ inches. (To me, jarred "gherkins" are cloyingly sweet and unpleasant.) These tiny gems need to be picked constantly, as they are very prolific and tend to get too big too quickly. The vines are hairy and prickly. I have been known to resort to gloves—long—when picking them. It's a good use for ball gown gloves that are no longer worn. Cornichons are pickled and used primarily by the French and Russians as a condiment with pâté and boiled meats.

All cucumbers grow on vines and need strong trellises or other supports.

Cucumbers are generally served as a salad or as part of a salad. Cut in pieces—peeled if they are not Kirbys—and salted along with tomatoes, they add a lot of flavor to a dressing. They have a cool taste and are used in Indian raitas and Greek tzatziki (see page 352) to contrast with hot curry spices. Their coolness used to be a beauty aid for belles who laid thin slices of cucumber on tired, red or puffy eyes before going out.

Cucumbers are almost never part of a main dish, but I do have one (see page 357). They make very good side dishes, as with the salads that follow. A few hot versions do not come amiss.

Often cucumbers are salted before being used to remove some of their very high percentage of water and, in some cases, to avoid thinning the dressing. Also, some cucumbers are slightly bitter and the salting removes that taste. They can be sliced and soaked in salted water, which leaves them crisper than simply salting them.

For both pickled and fresh cucumbers, dillweed seems to be the most consistently used flavoring, followed by coriander seeds, garlic and dill seeds.

Turn to **CUCUMBERS** and to **GOURDS** in the Cook's Guide for how-tos and to the Index for more recipes.

Gourds

Some come from Africa, more from Asia. While not yet widely available, they are beginning to show up. As with most vegetables since time immemorial, the more they are used, the more they are used. They can be planted; see the Cook's Guide, page 587, for seed information.

Any or all of the following four recipes can be used as part of a mixed hors d'oeuvre, as an accompaniment or as a salad.

Cucumber Tzatziki

I make this dip when cucumbers in the garden grow to giants without my discovering them. It can be made with normal cucumbers. It is a traditional Greek first course, often served as part of a meze spread and eaten on little plates when the diners are seated. Without a plate, it is best served with dunkers such as focaccia (see page 475) or crudités, as it has the texture of a chunky sour cream. It is virtually identical to an Indian raita. Divide the recipe if it makes too much.

> 12 medium cucumbers (about 5 1/4 pounds), trimmed, peeled, quartered lengthwise, seeds removed and cut into 2-inch lengths (about 10 cups)
>
> 2 tablespoons kosher salt
>
> 20 medium cloves garlic, smashed and peeled
>
> 1 cup packed fresh mint leaves
>
> 1 quart yogurt, preferably sheep's milk
>
> Freshly ground black pepper to taste

Working in batches, place the cucumbers in a food processor and process until medium fine. Scrape each batch as it is done into a large bowl. Stir in the salt. Let stand 1 1/2 hours.

Drain the cucumber in a medium sieve, pressing lightly. Discard the liquid. There will be a scant 4 cups cucumber.

Place the garlic and mint in a food processor and process until finely chopped. Scrape into a large bowl. Stir in the cucumber, yogurt and pepper to taste. Refrigerate, covered, for at least 1 hour before serving. The tzatziki will keep for up to 4 days. **Makes 6 cups**

Cucumber Dill Salad

This is very Hapsburg Empire and was practically ubiquitous until the nouvellization of Austrian cooking. (Others would say German.) Even though I am not a delighter in sweet salads, I like this particularly with boiled foods such as chicken or beef, where spiciness is liable to crop up in a condiment such as mustard or horseradish. It is a classic with cold poached salmon.

> 1/2 bunch fresh dill, fronds only, coarsely chopped
>
> 6 medium scallions, white parts only, thinly sliced
>
> 4 medium cucumbers, trimmed, peeled, and thinly sliced
>
> 1/2 cup cider vinegar
>
> 1 1/2 teaspoons sugar
>
> 1 teaspoon kosher salt
>
> 1/4 teaspoon freshly ground black pepper

Combine all the ingredients in a serving bowl, add 1 tablespoon water and toss well. Let sit for at least 30 minutes to wilt the cucumbers before serving. **Makes 5 cups**

Food Processor Variation
Start with whole dill sprigs, trimmed whole scallions and cucumbers cut crosswise into thirds. Place the dill in a food processor and process with 7 or 8 short pulses. Remove the blade, leaving the dill in the bowl. Fit the machine with the slicing disc. Put the scallions in the feed tube, white parts down. Turn the machine on and gently push the scallions through the slicing disc until you can no longer hold them. Stop the machine and reserve the uncut greens for another use. Place the cucumber pieces in the feed tube and slice, using medium pressure on the pusher.

Transfer the contents of the work bowl to a serving bowl and toss with the remaining ingredients plus 1 tablespoon water. Let sit for at least 30 minutes to wilt the cucumbers.

Cucumber Pachadi

This Indian dish is usually served at the beginning of a meal with hot bread. Come summer, it is a delightful side dish with an omelet, cold salmon or grilled foods.

> **2** medium cucumbers, trimmed, peeled, halved lengthwise, seeded and coarsely chopped
>
> **1** teaspoon salt
>
> **1** onion, finely chopped
>
> **1** large ripe tomato, peeled, seeded and finely chopped
>
> **3** small fresh green chilies, seeded and finely chopped
>
> **1** bunch cilantro, leaves only, finely chopped
>
> **3/4** cup plain yogurt

Place the cucumbers in a bowl and sprinkle the salt over them. Let stand for 15 minutes.

Squeeze out the cucumbers by hand and dry on a clean kitchen towel; discard the cucumber liquid.

Just before serving, return the cucumbers to the bowl, add the remaining ingredients and mix well. Do not do ahead or the whole thing will get soupy. **Serves 8 as a first course or a side dish**

Food Processor Variation

Start with cucumbers cut into 1-inch lengths, a quartered (peeled) onion, quartered tomato, chilies cut in half and whole cilantro leaves. Add the cucumbers to a food processor and process with 6 or 7 pulses. Transfer to a bowl. Sprinkle with the salt. Reserve.

Place the onion, tomato, chilies and cilantro in the processor and process until everything is in small pieces.

Squeeze out the cucumbers by hand. Wrap them in a dish towel to dry briefly. Place in a serving bowl. Add the tomato mixture and the yogurt and mix well.

Cucumber Salad

This is a rather Tex-Mex version of cucumber salad. I really like it. Without the sour cream, it makes a fine salsa.

> **6** cucumbers (about 2$\frac{1}{2}$ pounds), trimmed, peeled, halved lengthwise, seeded and cut across into $\frac{1}{2}$-inch slices
>
> **1$\frac{1}{2}$** tablespoons plus 1 teaspoon kosher salt
>
> **$\frac{1}{2}$** bunch cilantro, leaves only, coarsely chopped
>
> **$\frac{1}{4}$** bunch mint, leaves only, coarsely chopped
>
> **1$\frac{1}{2}$** cloves garlic, smashed, peeled and minced
>
> **$\frac{1}{2}$** cup sour cream
>
> **$\frac{3}{4}$** cup plain yogurt
>
> **2** tablespoons fresh Key lime juice or 1 tablespoon fresh lemon juice
>
> **$\frac{1}{4}$** teaspoon cayenne pepper

Place the cucumber slices in a colander set on a plate and sprinkle with 1½ tablespoons salt. Toss and let drain for 45 minutes.

Squeeze the excess liquid from the cucumber slices and combine in a bowl with the remaining ingredients, including the 1 teaspoon salt. Mix well. Serve chilled. **Makes 4 cups**

Cucumber Vichyssoise

This needs to be made ahead and refrigerated to get thoroughly chilled.

4 pounds cucumbers, trimmed, peeled, halved lengthwise, seeded and cut into $1/2$-inch pieces (about 4 cups)

4 cups Basic Chicken Stock (page 501), Roasted Chicken Stock (page 502) or commercial chicken broth

1 pound floury potatoes (such as russet or Yukon Gold), peeled and cut into 1-inch cubes

$1/2$ cup fresh mint leaves

$1/2$ cup fresh oregano leaves

Kosher salt to taste

In a large pot, bring the cucumbers and 1 cup of the stock to a boil. Cover, reduce to a simmer and cook for 15 minutes.

Remove 1 cup of the cucumber cooking liquid to another large pot and add the remaining

3 cups chicken stock and the potatoes. Cover both pots. Cook both pots over high heat until the cucumbers and potatoes are very tender but not falling apart. Remove from the heat. Allow the cucumbers and potatoes to cool slightly.

In a food processor or a blender, purée the cucumbers and then the potatoes in small batches, adding the mint and oregano. Mix the two purées together. Salt to taste.

Chill thoroughly before serving.

Makes 9 cups; serves 8 as a first course

Cucumber Gazpacho

This is a delightfully aromatic soup with cucumber and mint—very fresh. Puréeing the cucumbers provides the liquid base, a nice little trick. One of the best restaurants I have been at in recent years is improbably enough in Bray, as in "the Vicar of Bray, sir." It is called the Fat Duck and the chef is Heston Blumenthal, who also turns up on English television. His book, *Family Food, a New Approach to Cooking*, is a delight. In it, he puts crabmeat into his cucumber gazpacho. I would too, but I am allergic to crab. As to the gazpacho, great minds think somewhat alike.

5 medium Kirby cucumbers (about 1 pound), trimmed, peeled, halved lengthwise and seeded

1 medium Vidalia or other sweet onion, cut into 2-inch chunks

2 large red bell peppers, cored, seeded, deribbed and cut into 2-inch squares

1 medium jalapeño pepper, seeded and deribbed

4 medium cloves garlic, smashed and peeled

6 slices firm white bread, crusts removed

2 medium bunches mint, leaves only ($3/4$ cup), a few small sprigs or leaves reserved for serving

$3/4$ cup olive oil

Cucumber Soups

———

Cucumbers make excellent soups on their own or with other vegetables, as in Cucumber Gazpacho (at right). As they are very liquid when puréed, they are almost a soup on their own. It is amazing that, given the coolness of cucumbers, they are not more used in summer soups. These are a few of my favorites. If cucumbers are largely ignored for cold soups, they are even rarer in hot soups— in which they do very well.

3 tablespoons fresh lemon juice

2 tablespoons kosher salt

Cubed Croutons (page 511) for serving

Purée the cucumbers in a food processor until very liquidy, almost like water. Remove to a large bowl. Add the onion to the processor and pulse until coarsely chopped. Add to the cucumbers. Repeat with the red peppers. Add to the cucumbers and onion.

Put the jalapeño, garlic, bread and ¾ cup mint leaves in the processor and process to a paste while slowly pouring the oil through the feed tube. Stir into the vegetables. Stir in the lemon juice, salt and 2 cups water. Refrigerate for 2 hours, or until cold. The soup can be made up to 1 day ahead.

Serve the soup chilled, with croutons and a sprig (or a few leaves) of mint on top of each serving. **Makes about 7 cups**

Chilled Cucumber Soup

Brightly soothing, with a texture almost like a granita, this soup was made for balmy summer evenings.

I like to top each bowl with a dollop of sheep's-milk yogurt.

5 pounds cucumbers, trimmed, peeled, quartered lengthwise, seeded and cut across into 1-inch lengths (12 cups)

2 cups Basic Chicken Stock (page 501) or commercial chicken broth

Kosher salt and freshly ground black pepper to taste

Plain yogurt, preferably sheep's milk, for topping

Put the cucumbers and chicken stock in a large saucepan. Bring to a boil. Reduce the heat and simmer for 20 minutes, or until the cucumbers are very tender. Put the mixture through a food mill fitted with the fine disc. (Do not use a blender—the soup should have some texture.) Salt and pepper to taste.

Transfer the soup to a stainless steel bowl. Chill several hours until very cold. Top each serving with a dollop of yogurt.
Serves 8 as a first course

Okroshka

Okroshka, a cold Russian soup, undoubtedly has the oddest-sounding set of ingredients of all of these soups, more like a salad than a soup, and yet it works wonderfully well.

The sourovetz is an actively fermenting brew. It needs to be made two weeks in advance, so think ahead if it must be authentic. It is a pain, though, and can be replaced by light beer. Neither the sourovetz nor beer should be added to the other ingredients until the soup is ready to serve, or the soup is liable to turn. The best thing to do is to have all the ingredients ready and then just combine them at the last minute.

Soups such as this were obviously made in great houses that could be counted on to have a wonderful group of leftovers. Today, the best thing to do is to get the meats from a delicatessen.

1 pound Russian pumpernickel or black bread for the sourovetz, if using

1 hard-boiled egg

¼ teaspoon dry mustard

¼ cup sour cream

continued

4 cups light beer if not using the sourovetz

1 medium cucumber, trimmed, peeled, halved lengthwise, seeded and cut into ¼-inch dice

5 leaves Bibb lettuce, trimmed and thinly sliced across

1 medium scallion, trimmed and thinly sliced

½ pound cold roast beef, chicken, veal and/or ham, cut into ½-inch dice

Kosher salt to taste

For the sourovetz (bread kvass), if using: Cut the bread into 2-inch chunks. Place in a 1-gallon glass or ceramic container. Cover with 4 cups boiling water. Cover the container with a double layer of cheesecloth. Allow to stand in a cool, dark place for 2 weeks.

Skim any foam from the liquid. Drain the bread, reserving the liquid in a bowl. Squeeze the bread over the bowl to remove all the liquid, and discard. There should be about 6 cups liquid. Refrigerate it until chilled.

For the soup: Separate the yolk and white of the egg. Mince the white and reserve. With a fork, mash the yolk with the mustard in a small bowl. Slowly work in the sour cream until smooth and creamy. This can be made a day ahead and refrigerated.

Pour 4 cups of the sourovetz or the beer into a soup tureen. Stir in the cucumber, lettuce, scallion and meat. Whisk in the sour cream mixture. If no ham was used, taste for salt and adjust if necessary. Serve immediately. **Makes about 6 cups; serves 6 as a first course**

Elegant Cucumber Bean Soup

I like to swirl a few drops of heavy cream onto each bowl of warm soup when serving it to guests.

½ pound green beans, tipped and tailed (about 2 cups)

3 cups Cucumber Purée (page 357)

1 cup Basic Chicken Stock (page 501), Roasted Chicken Stock (page 502) or commercial chicken broth

½ cup heavy cream, plus extra for decoration

1 teaspoon kosher salt

Bring a pot of salted water to a boil. Add the green beans. Simmer for 8 minutes, or until completely cooked. Drain. Rinse under cold running water. Drain.

Put the beans in a food processor and purée until smooth. (Makes 1 cup)

Put the green bean purée, cucumber purée and chicken stock in a blender and blend together. Transfer to a saucepan and stir in the heavy cream and salt. Heat until lukewarm. Serve, swirling a few drops cream onto each bowl. **Makes 5½ cups; serves about 5 as a first course**

Cucumber Curry Soup

Since cucumbers are so often used as a side with curry, I thought the flavors might combine well as a soup. They did. It's a good use for somewhat overly large cucumbers. I use a blender for a smooth soup; but if a soup with a little more texture is preferred, use a food mill.

2 tablespoons unsalted butter

2 tablespoons curry powder

2 medium onions (about 12 ounces), coarsely chopped

1 double recipe of Cucumber Purée (page 357)

2 tablespoons fresh lemon juice

2 tablespoons fresh lime juice

Kosher salt and freshly ground black pepper
to taste

1 cup plain nonfat yogurt

3 tablespoons finely chopped cilantro (optional)

Melt the butter in a 4-quart pot over medium heat. Stir in the curry powder and cook for 1 minute. Stir in the onions and cook, stirring, until translucent. Add ½ cup water; bring to a boil. Reduce to a simmer and cook until the water is evaporated and the onions are lightly browned, about 8 minutes. Transfer to a blender and purée until smooth. The recipe can be made ahead to this point.

Return the onion purée to the pot. Stir in the cucumber purée and reheat through. Add the lemon and lime juices, salt and pepper. Whisk in the yogurt and cilantro, if using. Serve immediately. **Makes 8½ to 9 cups**

Cucumber Purée

This isn't really a recipe on its own, but, as I use it in several recipes, it had to go someplace.

1 pound cucumbers, trimmed, peeled, halved
lengthwise, seeded and cut into large chunks

1 cup Basic Chicken Stock (page 501),
Vegetable Broth (page 506) or commercial
chicken broth

In a 4-quart pot, bring the cucumbers and chicken stock to a boil over medium heat. Reduce to low heat and cook, covered, for 30 minutes, or until the cucumbers are mushy but not falling apart. Allow to cool for 10 minutes.

In small batches, purée the cucumbers in a food processor, and combine with the broth remaining in the pan; or put through the fine disc of a food mill. **Makes 1½ cups**

Crab and Cucumber Curry

Serve with white or black rice. If there is tamarind paste, an intriguing acid often used in curries, in the house, use it sparingly in place of the lime juice. The bigger the crabmeat lumps, the better.

1 pound lump crabmeat

1 large Kirby cucumber, trimmed, peeled,
halved and seeded

2 tablespoons unsalted butter

4 large scallions, trimmed, white parts finely
chopped, green parts thinly sliced

4 teaspoons minced peeled fresh ginger

4 teaspoons curry powder

1 cup coconut milk

3 to 4 teaspoons fresh lime juice or
unsweetened tamarind paste

½ teaspoon salt

Hot red pepper sauce or Fiery Pepper Sauce
(page 629) to taste (optional)

2 tablespoons chopped cilantro

Pick over the crabmeat to remove bits of shell and cartilage; work gently to keep the crab lumps as large as possible. Transfer to a bowl. Cut the cucumber halves lengthwise into ½-inch strips; cut crosswise on the bias into pieces the size of the crabmeat lumps. Add to the crab and set aside.

In a large skillet, heat the butter over medium heat until foaming. Add the scallion whites, ginger and curry powder. Stir until the scallions are softened, about 2 minutes. Pour in the coconut milk. Add the lime juice or tamarind, salt and hot pepper sauce or purée, if using. Bring to a boil, adjust the heat to simmering and cook until any lumps in the coconut milk are dissolved.

continued

Stir the crab and cucumber gently into the sauce and cook until heated through. Add the scallion greens and cilantro and serve immediately. **Serves 4 as a main course with rice**

Sesame Noodles with Cucumber

A Chinese take-out standard, but never as good as this. The cucumbers lighten the somewhat cloying texture of peanut butter. What did the Chinese do before peanut butter? Sesame paste? If you can find fresh Chinese egg noodles, use them here.

To cut the cucumbers as close as possible to the thickness of the noodles, use a mandoline—a large (and expensive) contraption for cutting and slicing; it would do the trick nicely. So would one of the less expensive, smaller plastic versions from Japan.

1/4 cup toasted sesame oil

3 tablespoons soy sauce, preferably tamari

3 tablespoons smooth peanut butter

1 tablespoon rice wine vinegar or white wine vinegar

2 teaspoons sugar

1/2 teaspoon salt

1/2 teaspoon minced garlic (optional)

8 ounces dried Chinese noodles or vermicelli

2 large Kirby cucumbers, trimmed, peeled, halved and seeded

2 tablespoons toasted sesame seeds

In a large serving bowl, whisk together the sesame oil, soy, peanut butter, vinegar, sugar, salt and garlic, if using, until smooth. This can be done up to 2 hours before serving.

Cook the noodles in a large pot of boiling salted water until tender but firm. Drain. Rinse under cool water just until they stop steaming. Drain thoroughly and add to the dressing. Toss to coat. Cool completely, tossing once or twice.

While the noodles are cooling, cut the cucumber halves lengthwise into strips as thin as possible; the strips should match the thickness of the cooked noodles.

To serve, put the cucumber strips over the center of the noodles. Sprinkle the sesame seeds over the cucumbers. Bring to the table, toss thoroughly and serve.
Serves 4 as a first course or as part of a larger meal

Garlic or Dill Pickles

Even if adding the dill, leave the garlic in, unless there are anti-garlic persons in your circle. If growing dill, add three dried umbrels in place of the store-bought fresh dill.

6 pounds small (about 4 to 5 inches) Kirby cucumbers (about 18)

1/3 cup plus 1/2 cup kosher salt

4 to 8 sprigs fresh dill (optional)

1/2 cup good white wine vinegar plus more if needed

12 cloves garlic, smashed and peeled

In a large bowl, toss the cucumbers with 1/3 cup salt. Cover with plastic wrap and refrigerate until the salt is dissolved and the cucumbers turn bright green, about 2 days.

Drain and rinse the cucumbers. (Eat them now, or continue with pickling.)

Put the cucumbers in a crock in which they fit comfortably. If using the dill, add the larger amount for new pickles (to be eaten after about 4 days), the smaller amount for old pickles

Pickles

When I was quite a small child, my maternal grandmother had a kind of general store and deli in Far Rockaway, the same Far Rockaway of Woody Allen's *Radio Days*. The family was socialist, like that in the film; but practicality—marginal—kept my grandfather constructing and renting bungalows and my far-from-good-cook grandmother minding the store. The great and rare treat was to be taken there and allowed to pluck a briny dill pickle from the barrel. There was a faint white scum from the fermentation and a wooden lid that sat right on the brine, leaving a margin of liquid around it.

Most culinary cultures have a pickle repertoire, though not all of them are cucumber. I was surprised during my first stay at a Japanese hotel to be served pickles for breakfast.

Cucumbers are pickled all over Europe. The pickling medium changes from country to country and varies with different cultures. Russia and Central Europe make garlic pickles. Semi-pickles are the German and Austrian sugared salads of very thinly sliced, peeled cucumbers with some white vinegar and salt that are often served as a side vegetable. French cornichons are made with shallots or small white onions, coriander and tarragon. Americans make bread-and-butter pickles and piccalilli.

Non-cucumber pickles will show up in the sections that deal with their main ingredient; look at the Index.

(eaten after about a week or so); lay the sprigs over the cucumbers when the crock is half-filled. Bring 6 cups water, the vinegar, the ½ cup salt and the garlic to a boil in a large saucepan, stirring to dissolve the salt. Cool to room temperature.

Pour the liquid and garlic over the cucumbers. To keep the cucumbers submerged, use a pot lid that fits inside the crock to weight them. Set in a cool place. For new pickles, eat after 4 days. For old pickles, continue fermenting until the surface is coated with a milky white layer, a week or two.

Makes about 3 quarts or 18 pickles

Cornichons

These are my favorites, and I always make a large amount. Of course, the recipe can be divided.

7 pounds cornichon cucumbers

¹/₃ cup kosher salt

3 cups good white wine vinegar (tarragon vinegar can be used)

3 cloves garlic, smashed, peeled and sliced

15 pearl onions, trimmed and peeled (see the Cook's Guide, page 616)

continued

Salting

One of the basic techniques in the pickle making of many culinary styles starts with salting. Sometimes it ends there, although a later rinsing and preserving in vinegar may take place. Salt is a powerful preservative. Whole small cucumbers, usually Kirbys, are put into salt and tossed and refrigerated and left for one to two days, or they may be put in a heavy brine. It is essential to use pickling or kosher salt, or they will turn a terrible color.

10 black peppercorns

10 coriander seeds

Large bunch of fresh tarragon

Eight 1-pint canning jars with two-piece lids

Soak the cucumbers in the salt and 4 cups water for 24 hours.

Sterilize the canning jars (see page 91).

Drain and rinse the cucumbers; set aside. Bring the vinegar and remaining ingredients to a boil. Let simmer for 10 minutes.

Pack the jars tightly with the cucumbers, filling the jars. Pour the hot vinegar over to ½ inch from the top. If necessary, quickly bring additional vinegar to a boil and top off the jars. Evenly distribute the seasonings and vinegar among the jars. Seal the jars and process according to the directions on page 91.

Store in a dark place for 3 months before using. **Makes about 8 pints**

Sweet-and-Sharp Cucumbers

These are wonderful with cold meats and fish.

2 firm cucumbers (about 1½ pounds), trimmed, peeled, halved lengthwise, seeded and cut into 2 x ¼ x ¼-inch matchsticks, or 5 Kirby cucumbers, trimmed, peeled and cut into matchsticks

1 teaspoon kosher salt

2½ teaspoons vegetable oil

¼ teaspoon hot red pepper flakes

½ teaspoon chopped garlic (optional)

1 tablespoon thin soy sauce

¼ to ½ cup sugar

1 scant tablespoon cider vinegar

Toss the cucumbers with the salt in a bowl. Cover and let sit for 8 to 10 hours.

Drain and rinse the cucumbers under cold running water. Gently press the remaining water from the cucumbers with your hands or a lint-free kitchen towel.

Heat a wok or medium skillet over high heat until hot. Add the oil and reduce the heat to low. Swirl the pan to coat the bottom evenly with oil and wait 3 seconds. Add the red pepper flakes and garlic, if using, to the pan. Adjust the heat so that the pepper just sizzles gently and doesn't blacken. After 3 seconds, add the cucumbers and stir for 5 seconds. Add the soy, ¼ cup sugar and the vinegar and stir for 2 minutes. Taste for sweetness and add more sugar if necessary. Don't be afraid; this pickle really loves to be sweet. Raise the heat to medium-high for 10 seconds. Stir the cucumbers and remove to a bowl to cool. Stir occasionally while cooling, then chill before serving.

The cucumbers will keep under refrigeration for 2 weeks. Their flavor grows hotter as they sit. **Makes about 2 cups**

Bread-and-Butter Pickles

An American classic, a sweet-and-sour pickle. The cucumbers are often sliced with a ripple cutter.

3 pounds Kirby cucumbers, trimmed and sliced ¼ inch thick

¾ cup sliced onion

1 large clove garlic, smashed and peeled

3 tablespoons kosher salt

Five ½-pint canning jars with two-piece lids

2¼ cups sugar

¾ teaspoon turmeric

¾ teaspoon celery seed

1 tablespoon mustard seeds

1½ cups white vinegar

Combine the cucumbers, onion, garlic and salt in a large bowl. Cover with two trays of ice cubes or crushed ice and stir well. Let stand for 3 hours.

Sterilize the canning jars (see page 91).

Drain the cucumbers; set aside.

Combine the remaining ingredients in a large skillet and bring to a boil. Add the cucumbers. Return to a boil and cook for 3 minutes.

Divide the pickles among the sterilized jars. Seal the jars and process according to the directions on page 91. **Makes about 5 cups**

Cucumber Granita

The freshness and cooling qualities of cucumbers are particularly appreciated in summer. Oddly, the cucumbers turn out to be strong enough to have flavor here. If desired, sprinkle each portion with a few celery seeds.

Remember, granitas are not meant to be smooth.

3 pounds cucumbers, trimmed, peeled, halved, seeded and cut into ¼-inch dice (about 5½ cups)

1 tablespoon Pernod

1½ cups One-to-One Simple Syrup (page 511)

Purée the cucumbers in a food processor until smooth; stop the machine from time to time to scrape down the sides. There should be 3 cups. Transfer to a bowl.

Warm and flame the Pernod in a small saucepan. When the flame dies down, stir the Pernod into the cucumber purée, along with the simple syrup. Cover and chill.

Shortly before serving, churn the cucumber mixture in an ice cream maker according to the manufacturer's instructions until it has the consistency of a Sno-Kone, not smooth. (Because of the low amount of sugar, it will get icy if done ahead.) Transfer to a container and hold in the freezer for up to 30 minutes before serving. **Makes 2½ pints**

NOTE: To make granita without an ice cream maker, pour the cucumber mixture into a rectangular baking dish or nonstick cake pan. (An 11 x 9-inch pan works well.) Place in the freezer and stir periodically whenever the edges begin to freeze, every 30 minutes or so. When all the syrup is frozen into coarse crystals, the granita is ready to serve.

Lovely Roots and Hearts

Taro, Lotus Root, Hearts of Palm and Bamboo Shoots

There seem to be fewer different roots used in Asian cooking than in the West. This may be due to the ubiquity of taro or to the ample supply of other starches such as rice, soy and even wheat. The two exceptions are lotus roots, with their beautiful shape and pleasant crunch, and the three-inch-long tuber called Chinese or Japanese artichoke, also called "crosne," supposedly after the French town where it was first grown in Europe. Its taste is not exceptional, fairly akin to Jerusalem artichoke. It is rarely available, but when it is, it is well worth buying, as it is so beautiful. It is creamy white and has a shape rather like a lamp finial, with stacked rings descending in size to a point at one end.

Like roots, hearts are hidden from casual view until opened up for the cook. Deep in the heart of many stems, tree trunks, grasses and vegetables live edible delights with different textures and flavors. I used to feel very guilty about eating hearts of palm, but now they are grown specially and forests are not being decimated for my pleasure. Canned hearts of palm are adequate, but for real pleasure, try to find the fresh, which have a light crispness, a little like endive strips. I usually save them for salad. Bamboo shoots are no risk to the environment, as the plants start out new each year. They can, rarely, be found fresh in Chinese markets. More often they are completely trimmed and ready for slicing in vacuum-sealed packages or in cans.

It is hard to imagine Asian cooking without these ingredients.

Turn to **TROPICAL TUBERS, LOTUS ROOTS, HEARTS OF PALM** and **BAMBOO SHOOTS** in the Cook's Guide for how-tos and to the Index for more recipes.

TARO

Taro seems to have come originally from India, but it has spread all over the semitropical world: the Caribbean, the Pacific Islands, Australia and beyond. It is the kind of ingredient that can drive this writer batty. Each area has its own name for taro, and for the greens—best known in the Caribbean as "callaloo"—as well. Here are a few of its names: "eddo," "coco yam," "satoimo," "dasheen" and "kalo."

Made into a purée called poi that is often allowed to ferment, it is virtually a Hawaiian religion. With the best will in the world, I cannot honestly give a recipe for poi, since I hate it.

Otherwise, taro is used in almost all the ways that potatoes are used: mashed, boiled, roasted, fried, steamed and made into chips.

My best advice is to read cookbooks of the regions that interest you and to experiment.

Deep-fried Taro Horns

Taro horns, called "yu tou jiao" in Mandarin, are a Chinese dim sum staple. Traditionally served in small paper cups, these deep-fried snacks are crunchy and flaky on the outside, creamy and starchy on the inside. The classic filling is composed of pork and shrimp. Chinese food authority and cookbook author Eileen Yin-Fei Lo offers an alternate vegetable filling in *The Dim-Sum Book*. She also uses wheat starch (wheat in which the proteins are removed) in her dough. It is an ingredient difficult to find outside of Chinese specialty stores, so I have adapted a dough from the *Chinese Snacks* book (see the Bibliography), which is much simpler. The recipe is somewhat adapted as well.

Large taro (see page 664) has a flavor and texture ideal for the dough. Fried, it becomes light, airy and riddled with tiny holes. The small eddo taro (see page 664) makes a smoother but less traditional crust.

The filling can be made a day ahead, but form the taro horns no more than a few hours before cooking, or they become soggy. These are best cooked and eaten the same day but can be refrigerated overnight and reheated next day: Arrange a single layer on a baking sheet and bake for fifteen minutes in a 350°F oven.

continued

1 1/2 tablespoons oyster sauce

1 teaspoon toasted sesame oil

1 teaspoon sugar

1 teaspoon Shao Hsing wine or sherry

1 teaspoon light soy sauce

2 1/2 teaspoons tapioca starch or cornstarch

Pinch of freshly ground white pepper

1 tablespoon canola oil

1 clove garlic, smashed and peeled

1/8 teaspoon kosher salt

1/4 pound snow peas, strung, tipped and tailed,
   cut across into 1/4-inch pieces (about 1 cup)

2 scallions, trimmed and thinly sliced
   (about 1/3 cup)

3 shiitake mushrooms, stems removed, caps
   steamed for 3 minutes, then cut lengthwise into
   1/2-inch strips and crosswise into 1/8-inch
   pieces (about 1/4 cup)

DOUGH

1 pound taro (see headnote, page 363),
   peeled and cut into large chunks

5 tablespoons lard or margarine, softened

6 tablespoons tapioca starch or cornstarch
   (plus 2 teaspoons if using eddo), plus additional
   for dusting surface

1 tablespoon sugar

1/2 teaspoon kosher salt

Canola oil for deep-frying

To make the filling, mix together the oyster sauce, sesame oil, sugar, wine or sherry, soy, starch, white pepper and 1/4 cup cold water in a small bowl. Set aside.

Heat the oil in a medium pan. Add the garlic and cook until brown; remove and discard. Add the salt, snow peas and scallions; stir and cook for 30 seconds. Add the mushrooms; stir and cook for 1 minute. Give the oyster sauce mixture a stir and add to the pan. Cook and stir until thickened. Transfer to a shallow dish. Cool to room temperature, then refrigerate for 4 hours, uncovered, or overnight, covered.

To make the dough, put the taro in the top of a two-part steamer or on a steaming rack or a plate in a bamboo steamer. Fill the bottom of the steamer pan or a pan large enough to hold the bamboo or steaming rack with water; the water should not touch the rack. Bring to a boil over medium heat. Place the taro on top, cover and steam for 30 minutes, or until very soft.

In a medium bowl, mash the taro with a fork. Allow to cool.

Mix the lard or margarine, starch (including the extra 2 teaspoons if using eddo), sugar and salt into the taro. Knead into a smooth dough. Roll into a log and cut into 16 equal pieces.

On a surface dusted with tapioca starch or cornstarch, flatten each piece of dough into a 3-inch circle. Place 1 scant tablespoon filling in the center of each circle, fold the dough over and pinch the edges to seal. Use fingers to smooth over any large cracks. Place on a baking sheet and let rest for 15 minutes.

Pour 1 1/2 to 2 inches oil into a deep pan. Heat the oil to 350°F. Lower in the taro horns one at a time—be careful, the oil will bubble vigorously. Cook no more than 4 at a time. Fry for 3 to 4 minutes, until golden brown, turning halfway through to ensure even cooking. Remove to a parchment-covered baking sheet. Bring the oil temperature back to 350°F between batches. Serve warm. **Makes 16 pieces**

Callaloo Soup with Dumplings

Callaloo is probably one of the most popular soups in the Caribbean. If callaloo (taro leaves) are not available, you can use spinach, watercress, young kale or Swiss chard.

SOUP

3/4 pound salt pork, cut into 1/4-inch cubes

1 large onion, chopped

2 cloves garlic, smashed, peeled and minced

1 stalk celery with leaves, chopped

1 pound callaloo (taro leaves) with stems, washed and finely chopped

1 teaspoon cayenne pepper

1/4 teaspoon fresh thyme, crushed

1 tablespoon tomato paste

2 medium sweet potatoes, peeled and sliced

1/4 pound pumpkin or calabaza squash, peeled and sliced

Kosher salt and freshly ground black pepper to taste

DUMPLINGS

1 cup all-purpose flour

1/4 cup cornmeal

2 teaspoons baking powder

1/2 teaspoon kosher salt

1/4 teaspoon ground cinnamon

1 teaspoon sugar

1 large egg

1/2 cup milk

2 tablespoons unsalted butter, melted

In a large skillet, fry the salt pork until crisp. With a slotted spoon, remove to a soup pot.

In the same skillet, sauté the onion, garlic and celery for about 5 minutes, or until the onion is tender. With a slotted spoon, remove the vegetables to the soup pot. Add to the pot the callaloo, 4 quarts water and the remaining soup ingredients except the salt and pepper. Bring to a boil. Reduce the heat and simmer, covered, for 45 minutes.

Season the soup with salt and pepper. Turn off the heat and let sit for at least 1 hour. Reheat to a simmer just before serving.

While the soup is reheating, make the dumplings: Stir the flour, cornmeal, baking powder, salt, cinnamon and sugar in a large bowl. Beat the egg, milk and melted butter in a small bowl. Pour over the dry ingredients and stir just until the dry ingredients are evenly moistened.

Drop the dumpling batter by heaping teaspoonfuls onto the surface of the soup. Cover tightly and simmer for 15 minutes.

Serves 8 as a main course

NOTE: Smoked turkey necks or wings or a ham bone can be substituted for the salt pork. Substitute 2 tablespoons vegetable oil for the rendered pork fat and add the turkey or bone with the callaloo.

LOTUS ROOTS

Shrimp and Lotus Root with Lemongrass and Lime

If baby bok choy are unavailable (though the bok choy does add lovely color and texture to this light, zippy dish), use an equal amount of regular bok choy or spinach cut into one-quarter-inch strips, or omit altogether. Serve over an interesting green as a first-course salad or with rice as a main course.

2 tablespoons canola oil

1 bunch scallions, white parts cut into 2-inch lengths, enough of the greens sliced on the diagonal into $^1/_4$-inch pieces to make $^1/_2$ cup

1$^1/_2$ pounds medium shrimp, peeled and deveined

$^1/_2$ pound lotus root, peeled and cut into $^1/_8$-inch slices (about 1$^1/_3$ cups)

$^1/_2$ stalk lemongrass, tender part only, thinly sliced (about 3 tablespoons)

1 ounce fresh ginger, peeled and grated (about 1 tablespoon)

$^1/_4$ pound baby bok choy (17 to 18, each 2 inches in length; optional)

2 tablespoons fresh lime juice

$^1/_2$ teaspoon kosher salt

Heat the oil in an 11- or 12-inch frying pan over high heat. Add the scallion whites and cook briefly, 30 seconds to 1 minute, until sizzling. Add the shrimp. Toss and cook for 1 to 1$^1/_2$ minutes, just until they turn pink but are not yet cooked through. Add the lotus root and cook for 1 minute, tossing to coat with oil. Add the lemongrass and ginger. Cook for 1 minute, stirring vigorously to prevent sticking.

Stir in the bok choy, if using, the scallion greens, lime juice and salt. Continue to cook and toss until the bok choy leaves begin to wilt, about 1½ to 2 minutes. Or, if not using bok choy, cook for 1 minute longer to blend the flavors. If the ingredients stick to the pan bottom, add 1 tablespoon water. Add another tablespoon water if a saucier dish is desired. (The starch from the lotus root will help thicken and bind the ingredients.) **Makes 6 cups**

Braised Napa Cabbage with Lotus Root, Snow Peas and Bamboo

The large amount of napa cabbage fills even a big deep stockpot to the brim. Cooked, it wilts and shrinks enormously to create a light and saucy Asian-inspired dish.

$^1/_4$ cup canola oil

5 ounces lotus root, peeled and cut across into $^1/_8$-inch rounds (about 1 scant cup)

$^1/_4$ pound fresh bamboo shoots, peeled, or 2 ounces vacuum-packed whole bamboo shoots, cut across into $^1/_4$-inch slices (about 1 cup)

2 ounces fresh ginger, peeled and cut into strips (about $^1/_3$ cup)

2 cloves garlic, smashed, peeled and coarsely chopped

1 head napa cabbage (3$^1/_4$ pounds), cut across into $^1/_4$-inch strips (about 19 cups)

$^1/_4$ pound snow peas, strung, tipped and tailed (about 1 cup)

$^1/_3$ cup soy sauce, preferably tamari

1$^1/_2$ tablespoons rice wine vinegar

2 tablespoons cornstarch

Kosher salt to taste

Heat the oil in a large deep stockpot over high heat. Add the lotus root and cook for 2 minutes. Add the bamboo and cook for 1 minute. Add the ginger and cook for 3 minutes. Stir in the garlic.

Add the cabbage. Using two wooden spoons, carefully toss the cabbage as if it were a salad. When the volume of cabbage has reduced by half, add the snow peas. Continue to cook and toss for about 4 minutes, until the snow peas are bright green and soften slightly. Add the soy sauce and rice wine vinegar. Cook several minutes to release the liquid from the vegetables.

Reduce the heat to low. Dissolve the cornstarch in 1½ tablespoons water and some of the vegetable liquid. Stir into the vegetables. Continue stirring for 3 minutes, or until the sauce is thickened and the cornstarch no longer tastes raw. Season to taste with salt and serve.

Makes 7½ cups; serves 6 as a side dish, 4 as a main course

Chinese Artichokes

CROSNES

These beautiful tubers cook very quickly—about five minutes of boiling. They can be served on their own with a little butter or sesame oil or fried or stir-fried. They beautify any plate or dish in which they are included.

HEARTS OF PALM
AND BAMBOO SHOOTS

Hearts of Palm Salad

While this is best made with fresh hearts of palm, canned are quite satisfactory.

½ pound trimmed fresh hearts of palm or one 14-ounce can hearts of palm, rinsed and drained

3 tablespoons dry white wine

1 tablespoon thinly sliced scallion greens

Shred the hearts of palm by cutting them lengthwise into very thin strips. Toss with the white wine and scallion greens in a bowl. Marinate for 30 minutes before serving.

Serves 4 as a first course

Miso Soup with Shiitake and Shiso

There is a rich tradition of vegetarian dishes in Japanese monasteries and convents. I have taken the liberty of devising my own version of one of their typical recipes. Serve in small bowls.

3 cups Konbu Dashi (page 507)

1 tablespoon dark soy miso (see page 544)

6 small dried shiitake mushrooms

2 ounces cleaned fresh bamboo shoots or good-quality canned or vacuum-sealed bamboo shoots, cut lengthwise into ⅛-inch slices and across into ¼-inch strips (about ¼ cup)

Two 1-ounce pieces silken tofu, each piece cut in half

4 shiso (perilla) leaves (see the Cook's Guide, page 531), cut across into ⅛-inch strips

1 scant tablespoon lemon zest sliced into very fine strips

Heat 2¼ cups of the dashi in a small pot. Dissolve the soy miso in 1 to 2 tablespoons of the hot dashi. Stir back into the broth in the pot. Remove from the heat.

Bring the remaining ¾ cup dashi to a boil. Pour over the mushrooms in a small bowl. Allow to soak for 15 minutes, or until softened. Remove the mushrooms and squeeze the excess liquid back into the bowl. Strain and reserve the liquid. Discard the mushroom stems and slice the caps across into ⅛-inch strips.

continued

Place the bamboo shoots and mushroom soaking liquid in a small pot. Bring to a boil. Add the tofu, simmer for 1 minute and turn it over; simmer for 1 minute more. Add the shiso leaves and mushrooms and cook for 10 seconds. Add to the miso and dashi base.

Ladle into bowls and top each bowl with a few pieces of lemon zest. **Serves 4 as a first course**

Soothing Asian Vegetable Salad

The silken tofu will crumble when it is tossed and combined with the oil-free dressing to hold this light and fresh salad together.

- **3 ounces lotus root, peeled and cut into $1/8$-inch rounds (about $1/2$ cup)**

- **7 fresh water chestnuts (about 6 ounces), peeled**

- **3 ounces snow peas, strung, tips and tails removed (about $1/2$ cup)**

- **$3^1/2$ ounces trimmed fresh bamboo shoots (see the Cook's Guide, page 536) or good-quality canned bamboo shoots, cut across into $1/8$-inch slices (about $1/2$ cup)**

- **8 scallions, white parts only, cut into 2-inch lengths, then quartered lengthwise (about $1/2$ cup)**

- **$1/2$ stalk lemongrass, tender part only, finely chopped (2 tablespoons)**

- **$1/4$ cup Semi-Thai Sauce (page 467)**

- **2 tablespoons coarsely chopped cilantro**

- **6 ounces silken tofu, rinsed and cut into $1/4$-inch cubes**

Put the lotus slices in the top of a two-part steamer or on a steaming rack or a plate in a bamboo steamer. Fill the bottom of the steamer pan or a pan large enough to hold the steaming rack with water; the water should not touch the rack. Bring to a boil over medium heat. Place the lotus root on top, cover and steam for 2 minutes. Remove and rinse under cold running water; drain and set aside.

Repeat the procedure with the water chestnuts: Steam for 3 to 4 minutes, until no longer starchy but still sweet and crunchy. Rinse under cold running water. Drain and set aside.

Half fill a 1-quart saucepan with water and bring to a boil. Add the snow peas and cook for 1 minute. Drain. Rinse under cold running water; drain. Cut lengthwise into long strips.

Put the bamboo, scallions, lemongrass, lotus root, water chestnuts and snow peas in a bowl. Add the sauce and cilantro and toss to combine. Then add the tofu and toss again. **Makes 3 cups**

Spicy Bamboo Stir-fry

When there is nothing else in the house, a can of bamboo grabbed from the pantry can provide a quick and easy accompaniment to chicken or fish. This dish is so addictive I can eat it all by myself.

- **1 tablespoon canola oil**

- **2 cups cleaned fresh bamboo shoots, blanched (see Cook's Guide, page 536) and cut into 2 x $1/2$ x $1/8$-inch strips, or two 8-ounce cans sliced bamboo shoots, rinsed and drained**

- **3 tablespoons Shao Hsing rice wine**

- **2 tablesoons soy sauce**

- **2 teaspoons turbinado or demerara sugar, sifted free of lumps**

- **1 teaspoon chili paste, or to taste**

- **$1/2$ teaspoon rice wine vinegar**

Heat the oil in a wok or large skillet over high heat. Add the bamboo shoots and stir-fry for 1 to 2 minutes. Add the remaining ingredients. Stir-fry for 2 to 3 minutes, until the bamboo shoots are tender and the sauce is thick enough to coat them. **Makes 2 cups; serves 4 as a side dish**

Bamboo-Détente Lamb

While the ingredients are Asian, I call this "détente" because the resulting dish has a rather Western feel.

Half a bone-in loin of lamb (1 1/2 pounds after trimming), bones reserved

2 cups Basic Chicken Broth (page 501), Roasted Chicken Broth (page 502) or commercial chicken broth

Vegetable oil

1 tablespoon hot chili oil

1 clove garlic, smashed, peeled and halved

1/2 pound fresh bamboo shoots, peeled, sliced and blanched (about 2 cups), 1/4 pound vacuum-packed whole bamboo shoots, sliced, or 2 cups drained good-quality canned sliced bamboo shoots

2 cups red, green and yellow bell pepper strips

1 tablespoon hoisin sauce

2 tablespoons oyster sauce

1 fresh hot pepper, seeded and thinly sliced

1 bunch scallions, trimmed and cut diagonally into 1 1/2-inch pieces (about 2 cups)

1 tablespoon mirin

1 teaspoon cornstarch, dissolved in 2 tablespoons cold water

1 recipe Basic White Rice (page 489)

Using a heavy cleaver, chop the lamb bones into 3-inch pieces. Put in a saucepan, cover with the chicken broth and simmer for 35 minutes. Strain and reserve the broth.

Trim the lamb loin of any fat. Using a very sharp knife, slice across the grain to get 1/8-inch-thick ovals of meat. Reserve.

Coat a wok or a 12-inch heavy skillet with a very thin layer of vegetable oil (most easily done by pouring about 1/2 teaspoon oil onto a paper towel and wiping the pan). Heat to smoking over high heat. Add the chili oil and garlic. Stir to heat through. Add the lamb and quickly stir-fry just to seal in the juices, 1 1/2 to 2 minutes.

Add the bamboo shoots and bell peppers. Stir to coat with the oil and heat through, about 2 minutes. Pour in the hoisin, oyster sauce and 1/4 cup reserved lamb broth. Stir-fry until the bamboo shoots and peppers are tender but crisp. Toss in the hot pepper and the scallions. Cook until the scallion greens are wilted.

Quickly add the mirin and dissolved cornstarch. Cook, stirring constantly, until the sauce is thickened and the lamb and vegetables are coated. Serve with the rice.

Serves 6 to 8 as a main course

Onions 372   Leeks 383   Scallions and Ramps 390   Mushrooms 396

Odd Roots: Burdock, Horseradish, Scorzonera and Salsify 409   Lettuces 414

Weeds and Odd Leaves: Amaranth, Purslane, Samphire, Sorrel, Arugula,

Dandelion Greens, Chrysanthemum Greens and Fiddlehead Ferns 422

Herbs and Their Flowers 433

Citizens
of the World

I AM SURE WE ALL THINK OF OURSELVES as incredibly
urbane, sophisticated citizens of the world. Increasingly,
so are our vegetables. What were once exotica are either
shipped to us from many points around the globe or have
been naturalized and become staples. In other parts of the
world, the same process occurs. However, there are some
vegetable families that have always been widely spread out
among the continents and nations. I certainly have no wish
to corral them into one location.

Onions

Onions and their relatives—the shallot, leek, garlic, scallion and chive—are cooking staples, as much a flavoring as a major ingredient. Flavor depends on the onion variety and the soil it grows in—and, in the case of Maui, Walla Walla and Vidalia onions, on their age as well.

The onion may be our most-used culinary vegetable. It is hard to imagine Creole, Cajun, Italian, Spanish and Central and South American cooking without its almost ubiquitous use in refritos and soffritos, the aromatic sautés that form the basis of most dishes. Hungarian cooking would be impoverished without onions. We use them raw in salads and on hamburgers, fry them into crisp rings, enjoy onion soup and soubise types of sauces (which have onions as the

Lilies of the Field

I think Matthew was very hard on "the lilies of the field." Despite their glorious array, the Liliaceae—figuratively—do toil and spin. The members of this very large family serve us well in the cooking of every country that I know. There are the alliums—the onions, etc.—and the various asparagus (see page 531), but even the beautiful flowering kinds serve our palates. Barbara Tropp once gave me a jar of day lily buds sweetly preserved in China to be used as a condiment, especially with rice. While many lily bulbs are poisonous, the bulbs of the tiger lily and the Hong Kong lily are eaten as a vegetable. I had never tasted one. According to Herklots (see the Bibliography), they are somewhat like parsnips. Oddly enough, shortly after I started research on the lilies, I went to a Chinese restaurant where they served a soup with lily bulbs in it. I found them totally without interest.

The invaluable Charmaine Solomon, in her *Encyclopedia of Asian Food* (see the Bibliography), gives information I find a good deal more enticing. She suggests picking day lily (*Hemerocallis fulva*) buds when still tightly furled and brightly yellow and cooking them briefly in a stir-fry. Their brilliant color accounts for their Chinese soubriquet, golden needles. They are even called this when they are sold dried and tan, which is most of the year. They can be rehydrated for about thirty minutes in warm water. Cut them into pieces before adding to a dish; they are somewhat chewy.

predominant component), pickle them and put them into Gibsons.

It is astonishing that in recipes so little attention is paid to onions' diversity in color, size, type and flavor. Although much attention has been drawn in recent years to the sweetness of some onions (Vidalias, Mauis and Walla Wallas), aside from an occasional reference to color—red, white or yellow—or size, few specifications are normally given.

At different times of the year, plain yellow or white onions can vary wildly in strength. They also vary according to variety. A whole dish can be ruined by following the quantities in a recipe but using onions that are excessively strong. How can you tell? Tasting is the best test; but if you find your eyes streaming when cutting onions, that is a good clue. What does the cook do? Use fewer onions, or substitute leeks or shallots. Avoid those that are sprouting, green at the core or have brown mushy rings or spots inside. They will have unpleasant off flavors.

Large onions with thick layers will give a coarse chop, unless mashed—which makes them almost impossible to brown because so much of their juice has been released. For a fine chop or mince, use smaller onions with thinner layers. For the same reason, try to avoid chopping onions in the food processor, which tends to mash them but is a good way out if there are lots to chop. Large onions will also make thicker rings.

Turn to **ONIONS** in the Cook's Guide
for how-tos and to the Index for more recipes.

Orange and Onion Salad with Cumin Vinaigrette

In Morocco and Algeria, they make this salad of brilliant colors with the mysterious background flavor of cumin. This and prosciutto with melon or figs are virtually the only primarily fruit first courses I tolerate, let alone like. It is a marvelous meal introduction on a gray winter night, bringing hints of warmth and tropical vacations just when I need them most.

This salad is a pretty red when made with blood oranges.

VINAIGRETTE

$^1/_4$ cup olive oil

2 tablespoons fresh orange juice (squeezed from the reserved ends of the oranges below)

1 $^1/_2$ tablespoons fresh lemon juice

$^1/_2$ teaspoon kosher salt

$^1/_4$ teaspoon packed ground cumin

2 thin-skinned (juice) oranges, very thinly sliced and seeds removed, ends reserved for juice

1 $^1/_2$ to 2 red onions, very thinly sliced

$^1/_4$ cup Niçoise olives

In a small bowl, mix the olive oil, orange juice, lemon juice, salt and cumin. Let stand for about 10 minutes to develop the flavors.

Meanwhile, arrange the orange and onion slices alternately and overlapping on a platter. Sprinkle the olives around. Pour the dressing over the oranges and onions.

Let marinate at room temperature for 30 minutes before serving. From time to time, spoon some of the dressing that accumulates in the bottom of the platter over the slices.
Serves 4 to 6 as a first course

Pissaladière

One of the delights of the French Riviera is a little strip of an onion-anchovy tart, normally served warm and cut into pieces to eat before the first course or as a snack. I have had it made with puff pastry and with bread dough. The bread dough version is probably more authentic and is certainly easier to pick up with your fingers. The puff pastry version is more gala, more fragile and easier to make, using store-bought dough. The main recipe here uses puff pastry. At the end are instructions for using focaccia dough instead.

FILLING

6 tablespoons olive oil

3 pounds yellow onions, coarsely chopped in a food processor (about 4 cups)

1 $^1/_4$ teaspoons anchovy paste

$^1/_4$ teaspoon red wine vinegar

Freshly ground black pepper to taste

1 package (16 to 18 ounces) frozen puff pastry, defrosted (usually 2 sheets)

One 2-ounce can anchovy fillets in oil, cut lengthwise into thin strips

24 Niçoise olives, pitted and halved

GLAZE

1 egg yolk beaten with 1 tablespoon cold water

The Onion and His Friends

The alliums are one of the largest, smelliest and most useful of the vegetable families, as well as being among my favorites. Additionally, they are good for the health. There is a chemical, allicin, in them that works as an anticlotting and blood pressure–reducing agent. Several years ago, a medical study was done giving male patients with elevated blood pressure a raw onion per day. The researchers were about to give up after several months when, to their astonishment, the numbers began to go toward normal. Note that the onions were raw; it will work with cooked onions, too, but less efficiently.

This same chemical gives the alliums their strong taste and is killed—the alliums are bulbs, living plants waiting to happen—when garlic is crushed before using.

One of the great advantages of the alliums is that they keep well, but they should be kept in the dark, not only of their impending fate, but also to keep them from sprouting. All members of the onion family are sensitive to light and benefit from proper storage (see the Cook's Guide, page 615).

When using garlic, shallots and onions that are not at the height of their season, it is best to cut them in half from stem to root end and see if any green or yellow sprout is forming. If so, pry it out with the tip of a knife. If the garlic has been crushed, this will be easy. Thoroughly washed and trimmed (see the Cook's Guide, page 600) leeks will keep, if well wrapped, for more than a month in the refrigerator.

William Woys Weaver is excellent on onions in his book *Heirloom Vegetable Gardening* and well worth the reading (see the Bibliography).

For the filling, heat 2 tablespoons oil in a medium skillet over medium heat. Add the onions and stir to coat with oil. Reduce the heat to very low and cook for about 50 minutes, stirring occasionally so the onions do not stick, until they are soft and golden brown.

Increase the heat to high and cook, stirring constantly and gradually adding the remaining ¼ cup oil, for about 10 minutes, so that the onions become slightly darker brown.

Remove from the heat and stir until the onions have cooled slightly. Stir in the anchovy paste and vinegar and season with pepper.

Place a rack in the center of the oven. Preheat the oven to 425°F.

On a lightly floured surface, roll each sheet of dough out to a 12 x 9-inch rectangle (if necessary). Cut each sheet across into 4 strips, each about 9 x 3 inches. Place 4 strips on each of two baking sheets (not air-cushioned).

Spread about 2 tablespoons of the onion mixture down the center of each dough strip, leaving about ¼ inch free all around the edges.

continued

Crisscross the anchovy strips diagonally across the filling, forming 4 crosses on each strip. Arrange 6 olive halves, evenly placed, on top of each strip. Brush the pastry edges with the egg glaze. Bake one sheet for 15 minutes (keep the other sheet in a cool place). Remove from the oven and allow to cool on a wire rack while baking the remaining strips.

These can be baked a day ahead, cooled and refrigerated. Reheat in a 350°F oven for 5 minutes before serving.

To serve, slice each strip across into 6 pieces.

Makes 48 hors d'oeuvre

Pissaladière with Basic Focaccia Dough

Use 1 recipe Basic Focaccia (page 475), risen for 1 hour. Preheat the oven to 350°F. Divide the dough into 4 equal pieces and form each into a long sausage shape. With the fingers, flatten each piece into a strip about 14 x 2 inches. Place on a large baking sheet (not air-cushioned) that has been sprinkled with 1 tablespoon cornmeal. With the thumb and index finger, form ridges down the edges of each strip. Divide the filling mixture among the strips, spreading it down the center of each one. Top as above. Bake for 20 minutes. To serve, cut off the ends and slice each strip across into 10 pieces.

Makes 40 hors d'oeuvre

Stuffed Onions

In Turkey and in many other countries on both sides of the Mediterranean, onions are often included in platters of mixed stuffed vegetables. This nonvegetarian onion dish is substantial enough to be a first course on its own.

There is no need to mound the stuffing on top: It will rise naturally as the onions shrink during cooking.

6 onions (6 to 7 ounces each) 2$^1/_2$ to 3 inches in diameter

2 tablespoons unsalted butter

1 tablespoon vegetable oil

$^2/_3$ cup finely chopped mushroom stems

$^1/_4$ cup finely diced ham

2 teaspoons chopped fresh dill

3 tablespoons heavy cream

1 tablespoon Dried Bread Crumbs (page 510) or unseasoned store-bought bread crumbs

1$^1/_4$ teaspoons kosher salt, or to taste

Freshly ground black pepper to taste

1 to 2 cups Basic Chicken Stock (page 501), Roasted Chicken Stock (page 502) or commercial chicken broth

Place a rack in the center of the oven. Preheat the oven to 350°F.

Prepare onion shells for stuffing (see the Cook's Guide, page 619); chop the scooped-out onion.

Melt the butter with the oil in a large skillet. Add the chopped onions and mushrooms and cook over medium heat for 5 to 7 minutes, until very soft. Stir in the ham, dill, cream, bread crumbs, salt and pepper. Adjust the seasonings if necessary. (Makes 2 cups)

Fill each onion with about ⅓ cup stuffing. Place the onions, stuffing side up, in a baking pan just large enough to hold them comfortably. Pour in enough stock to come about one-third of the way up the onions.

Bake for 1½ to 1¾ hours, basting with the chicken stock every 15 to 20 minutes. The onions should be tender when pierced with a skewer. **Serves 6 as a side dish**

James Beard's Onion Sandwiches

When James Beard and I taught at James Nassikas's Stanford Court in San Francisco, we used to ride up and down from our contiguous rooms to Fournou's Ovens, the restaurant in which we taught, in the service elevator. At the end of the day, we would pass carts set up with hors d'oeuvre ready to go into the bar. I would often sneak one of Mr. Beard's famous onion sandwiches. He had originally made the recipe for the catering company that he owned with friends in New York. Here they are once again.

Using a 2½- to 3-inch wineglass or biscuit cutter, cut thin slices of brioche or firm white bread into circles. Spread one side of each circle with mayonnaise, store-bought or homemade (page 455). Cut a mild onion, yellow or white, into very thin slices. Remove some of the outer rings if necessary to match the size of the slices to the size of the circles. Sandwich an onion slice between two of the bread slices. Coat the edges of the sandwiches very lightly in mayonnaise and roll them in finely chopped fresh parsley.

Onion Soup

When my daughter was a child, she loved a bubbling bowl of cheese-crusted onion soup better than almost anything. For her, I made it without wine. The idea of using Champagne comes from the legend that onion soup was invented by Henry IV one evening after hunting. He was supposed to have stopped at a peasant hut and asked for something to eat. Embarrassed, the wife replied that she had only onions, stale bread and a little fat. The king replied that he would make a soup, using the Champagne that he had left.

I would use Champagne only if I had some left and getting flat after a party. (Onion soup is a famous hangover remedy.) Usually I would substitute a somewhat acid white wine—no sweetness, since the onions are so sweet. Any single stock can be used, although I like the balance of beef and chicken, or just water. I remember Jacques Pépin once made a soup (in *A French Chef Cooks at Home*) where he broke the crust of a soup that was almost solid with layered bread, slid in a ladle filled with egg yolks and port and swished it around in the soup. Vary at will.

There are pale onion soups, but for this one, cook the onions slowly so they get very dark but do not burn. When the pot is deglazed, the caramelized coating on the onions comes off into the liquid, leaving the onions clear and the soup very dark. The pot must be large enough so that the onions glaze rather than stew in the juices.

The soup can be served without the bread and cheese (the gratin). If so, it will make more servings; the bread absorbs a great deal of soup.

6 tablespoons unsalted butter

4 large onions, thinly sliced

1 cup dry white wine or flat Champagne

1 cup Beef Stock (page 502)

5½ cups Basic Chicken Stock (page 501), Roasted Chicken Stock (page 502) or commercial chicken broth

continued

By now, I have made it clear that I love soup. If I have some member of the allium family around, I need not be deprived. Oddly, leeks, which are a winter vegetable, often turn up in summer's cold soups, while onions, which can be picked in warmer weather, usually bespeak a winter soup.

1 tablespoon kosher salt (less if using
   commercial broth), or to taste

Freshly ground black pepper to taste

FOR SERVING (optional)

Twelve 1/4-inch diagonal slices Italian or
   French bread, toasted

5 ounces Gruyère cheese, coarsely grated
   (about 1 1/2 cups), plus 1 cup freshly grated
   Parmesan cheese; or 1/2 pound low-fat
   mozzarella cheese, sliced across into 32 slices

In a large wide pot, melt the butter over
medium heat. Add the onions. To keep them
from stewing rather than browning, spread
them in as close to a single layer as possible.
Cook, stirring occasionally, until they are very
brown and soft, for about 30 minutes; they will
need more frequent stirring toward the end.

Stir in the wine and bring to a boil, scraping
the bottom of the pot vigorously with a wooden
spoon to get up all of the browned bits. Continue
scraping while pouring in the beef stock. Then
pour in the chicken stock. Season with the salt
and pepper. Bring to a boil. Lower the heat and
simmer for 10 minutes. Can be made ahead to
this point and refrigerated for up to 3 days.

To gratinée, preheat the broiler. If necessary,
return the soup to a simmer.

Lay 2 slices of toast in the bottom of each
of six ovenproof bowls or crocks, or make two
layers of bread in a large earthenware casserole.
If using, mix together the Gruyère and Parmesan.
Pour the soup over the bread. Sprinkle the
cheese over the soup; or, lay 4 thin slices
mozzarella over each serving or all the slices
over the casserole. Broil for 3 to 4 minutes,
until bubbling and brown.

**Makes 9 cups; serves 6 as a first course if gratinéed,
8 if not**

Curried Onion Soup

The onions are not browned in this soup.
For an elegant soup, add a cup of heavy
cream, and additional salt to taste.

8 tablespoons (4 ounces) unsalted butter,
   cut into pieces

1/4 cup curry powder

4 large onions, cut into chunks

4 cups Basic Chicken Stock (page 501),
   Roasted Chicken Stock (page 502) or
   commercial chicken broth

1 tablespoon fresh lime juice

1 tablespoon kosher salt (less if using
   commercial broth), or to taste

1 cup heavy cream (optional)

In a medium saucepan, melt the butter over
medium-low heat. Stir in the curry powder and
cook, stirring, for 2 minutes. Stir in the onions
and cook, stirring occasionally, for 10 minutes.

Pour in the stock. Bring to a boil. Lower the
heat and simmer for 10 minutes, or until the
onions are very soft.

In a blender, working in batches of no more
than 2 cups, purée the soup until very smooth,
stopping once or twice to scrape down the sides
of the jar. The soup can be made ahead up to
this point and refrigerated.

Scrape the purée back into the pan. Heat the
soup through. Remove from the heat and whisk
in the lime juice, salt and, if using, the heavy
cream.

**Makes 7 cups without cream, 8 cups with;
serves 6 to 8 as a first course**

Roasted Onion Soup with Cannellini Beans

This soothing, smoky-flavored soup is welcome during winter. Make an extra batch of the soup base, using just the first two ingredients, and freeze for another time. The whole soup freezes well for about three weeks. Canned cannellini beans make it extra easy.

> 3 cups Basic Chicken Stock (page 501), Roasted Chicken Stock (page 502) or commercial chicken broth
>
> 1 cup leftover roasted onions (see the Cook's Guide, page 617) or Roasted Onion Flowers (at right)
>
> 1²/₃ cups cooked cannellini beans or one 19-ounce can, rinsed and drained
>
> 2 teaspoons kosher salt (less if using commercial stock)
>
> 2 tablespoons red wine vinegar
>
> ¹/₂ bunch (1¹/₂ ounces) fresh basil, leaves only, stacked 4 or 5 at a time, rolled and cut across into thin strips (about ³/₄ cup)
>
> ¹/₄ cup freshly grated Parmesan cheese (optional)

In a blender, combine 1 cup of the stock with the onions. Blend until smooth, stopping once to scrape down the sides of the blender.

Scrape the contents of the blender into a medium saucepan. Add the remaining 2 cups stock, the beans, salt and vinegar. Heat until just warmed throughout. Stir to combine the ingredients completely.

Stir in half the basil and the Parmesan, if using. Serve, and sprinkle the remaining basil and cheese over the soup.

Makes 4²/₃ cups; serves 4 as a first course

Roasted Onion Flowers

On their own or as an ingredient, browned onions are used in many forms in the kitchen. Roasting onions is a simple way to brown them with a minimal amount of fat and attention. It is frequently done for stocks and stews.

There are fashions even in vegetable preparation. There was a fad at one time for deep-fried onions looking like flowers. They were a lot of work and the fat sputtered alarmingly. This is an improved substitution that not only looks spectacular on the plate but also is fun to eat and loved by guests. I often put each onion on a separate plate next to the main course plate. Onion devotees will like them as a first course.

These may be scary because the tips sometimes get very brown, almost black, and look burned. Be reassured. After one taste, everybody will enjoy them.

This works equally well with red or white onions. Smaller onions are best. They open up and brown evenly, and they fit nicely on the dinner plate. Leftovers, if there are any, are perfect for Roasted Onion Soup with Cannellini Beans (at left).

> 6 small-medium red or white onions (4 to 6 ounces each), peeled and cut through in an X from the top just down to the root, root end left intact
>
> 4 tablespoons olive oil

Place a rack in the center of the oven. Preheat the oven to 500°F.

Cut just enough off the root end of each onion so the onions will stand up in the pan. Pour 2 tablespoons of the oil into a 14 x 12 x 2-inch roasting pan. Rub the oil around the bottom and sides of the pan. Add the onions to the pan and rub with the oil. Arrange the onions as far away from one another as possible so they will have room to open up. Roast for 30 minutes. Remove the pan from the oven to check its dryness, which will depend on the age and size of the onions. If the pan is dry, drizzle the remaining 2 tablespoons oil over and around the onions. Roast for 15 more minutes. The onions should be browned and soft.

If some of the tips are too black, just snip them off with kitchen scissors. Serve right away.

Serves 6 as a side dish

Crisp Red Onion Rings

Roasting onion rings uses much less fat than deep-frying and is more enjoyable. The crisped rings will look very dark—mahogany-brown. Don't worry, they are not burned. Roasting them this long is what gives them their smoky flavor. For fried onion rings, see page 517.

¼ cup olive oil

1 ¾ pounds (about 5) small red onions, sliced into ¼-inch-thick rounds

¼ teaspoon kosher salt

Place a rack on the lowest level of the oven. Preheat the oven to 500°F.

Pour the oil into an 18 x 13 x 2-inch roasting pan. Swirl the pan until the oil evenly covers the bottom. Gently pull apart the onion rings; as they are separated, put them in the oiled pan. Toss the rings in the oil until all are coated. Pile loosely.

Roast for 25 minutes. Remove from the oven and turn the rings over with a spatula. Roast for 25 minutes more. Remove to a platter. Sprinkle with the salt and serve.

Serves 8 as a side dish

Roasted and Marinated Cippolini

I love these. They are sweet-and-sour without the addition of any honey or sugar, because the onions are so sweet. I usually keep some in the refrigerator. The only problem in counting on them as emergency guest rations is that they seem to disappear mysteriously. I may be the culprit, since they are just as good cold as warm, which makes them ideal on a buffet or as part of a mixed hors d'oeuvre plate. Warm, they can be part of a vegetable medley main course or a side dish with roasted birds or meats.

Due to the amount of sugar in the onions, it is very important to remove them from the roasting pan as soon as they are done, or they will stick. If cippolini are not available, small onions (pearls) can be substituted.

Eight to nine ½-pint or four 1-pint canning jars with two-piece lids

¼ cup olive oil

3 pounds cippolini, peeled and trimmed (10 to 11 cups)

½ cup balsamic vinegar or red wine vinegar, or as needed

1 tablespoon kosher salt

Place a rack on the lowest level of the oven. Preheat the oven to 500°F.

Sterilize the canning jars (see page 91).

Pour the oil into a 14 x 12 x 2-inch roasting pan. Roll each cippoline in the oil, then spread out in a single layer. Roast for 15 minutes.

Turn the onions and roast for another 15 minutes more. Immediately remove from the pan with a slotted metal spoon and transfer to a large bowl. (The cippolini may be used at this point as a side dish or in a stew.)

Put the roasting pan over medium-high heat. Pour in the vinegar and ⅔ cup water. Bring the liquid to a boil, scraping up the brown glaze on the bottom of the pan. Add the salt. Cook for 5 minutes. Pour the liquid over the cippolini. Let cool.

Pack the cippolini into the sterilized jars. Cover with the liquid. If the liquid does not completely cover, top off with more vinegar.

Once the onions are completely cooled, they may be stored in the refrigerator, where they will keep for several months.

Makes 4 ¹/₂ cups; serves 6 to 8 as a side dish

Cippolini Riviera

In times that are far from antique and that I remember with great fondness, almost every restaurant along the French Riviera presented a seductive table of hors d'oeuvre variés, or the staff would parade by your table, bringing first the vegetable hors d'oeuvre, then the fish, and finally the meats and sausages. I still go to the Colombe d'Or, in St. Paul-de-Vence, because—in addition to having a spectacular view—they preserve this custom.

A standard and always welcome element to these "cascades" of hors d'oeuvre was this dish (sometimes made with other small onions). The name would vary according to the town, the birthplace of the chef or the supposed celebrity of the locale; "Monegasque," after Monaco, was a favorite name.

It may be harder to find the "cascade," but I can make the onions and have them at home in their sweet-and-sour sauce of an alluring orangey red.

3 pounds cippolini, peeled and trimmed (10 to 11 cups)

¹/₄ cup olive oil

MARINADE

³/₄ cup white wine vinegar

²/₃ cup golden raisins

One ¹/₂-gram vial saffron threads

3 tablespoons Fresh Tomato Paste (page 459) or commercial tomato paste

Freshly ground black pepper to taste

Roast the cippolini as above, using the olive oil. During the last 15 minutes, combine all the marinade ingredients in a small saucepan. Bring to a boil over medium heat, then reduce to a simmer. Simmer until the cippolini come out of the oven.

Place the roasting pan of cippolini on the stove over medium heat. Pour the simmering liquid into the pan. Stir with a wooden spoon, scraping up the brown glaze on the bottom of the pan.

Fill the sterilized jars with the hot cippolini and marinade. If the liquid does not cover the onions, top off with more white wine vinegar. Let cool completely. Refrigerate for at least 2 days to let the flavor develop. These will keep for several months in the refrigerator.

Creamed Onions

For those who want something leaner and don't mind meat, substitute chicken stock for the cream. Frozen pearl or mini onions can be used.

1 ¹/₂ pounds small pearl onions, peeled and trimmed

³/₄ cup milk

¹/₄ cup heavy cream

1 European bay leaf

¹/₂ teaspoon dried oregano

¹/₄ teaspoon dried thyme

1 ¹/₂ tablespoons cornstarch

continued

¼ cup loosely packed chopped fresh parsley

1 ½ teaspoons kosher salt, or to taste

Freshly ground black pepper to taste

Combine the onions, milk, cream, bay leaf, oregano and thyme in a medium saucepan. Bring to a boil. Reduce the heat and simmer, covered, for 10 to 15 minutes, or until a knife easily slips into flesh. Meanwhile, mix the cornstarch with 1 tablespoon water to make a slurry.

Add the cornstarch mixture and parsley to the onions. Cook for 5 more minutes. Remove the bay leaf. Season with the salt and pepper. **Serves 6 as a side dish**

Microwave Variation

Combine the onions, milk, cream and dried herbs in a 2½-quart casserole dish with a tightly fitting lid. Cook, covered, at 100% for 12 minutes. While the onions are cooking, stir the cornstarch and 1 tablespoon water together in a small dish.

Stir the cornstarch mixture and parsley into the onions. Cook, covered, for 8 minutes. Remove from the oven. Remove the bay leaf. Stir in the salt and pepper.

Sweet-and-Sour Onions

This is a healthy dish with robust flavor.

¾ pound pearl onions or one 12-ounce package frozen pearl onions, defrosted in a sieve under warm running water

5 tablespoons Orange Wheat Germ Dressing (page 451)

2 tablespoons dark raisins

¼ teaspoon turmeric

¼ teaspoon kosher salt

¼ teaspoon sugar

If using fresh onions, peel, trim and steam or microwave them (see the Cook's Guide, page 616).

Place all the ingredients except the onions in a medium saucepan and heat until hot. Add the onions and cook just to heat through. Remove from the heat and cool. Serve at room temperature or chilled. **Makes 3 cups**

Pickled Egyptian Onions

To find out about Egyptian, or "walking," onions, see the Cook's Guide, page 616. Allow these to sit for two weeks before opening. Once opened, they will keep for two years stored in the refrigerator. Pearl onions may be substituted, but they will not keep as well.

This recipe may be multiplied to accommodate as many Egyptian onions as are available.

¼ pound Egyptian onions, peeled and trimmed

One ½-pint canning jar with a two-piece lid

½ cup white vinegar

¼ teaspoon kosher salt

In a small bowl, cover the onions with water. Soak overnight; drain.

Sterilize the canning jar (see page 91).

In a small saucepan, bring the vinegar and salt to a boil. Add the onions. Simmer for 2 minutes. Immediately pour into the sterilized jar; a large-mouthed funnel is helpful here. Push down on the onions to submerge them in the liquid. Seal the jar and process according to the directions on page 91. **Makes 1 cup**

Leeks

Even in the coldest of climes, leeks can be pulled or dug from the ground through a good part of the winter. I have a son who believes that there is no Thanksgiving or Christmas without my braised leeks. One year, a very harried year, I skipped the leeks. He walked into the house, took a look around the kitchen, didn't see any leeks and moaned. A compulsive mother, I hurried across the street to an open store and bought some leeks. Fortunately, I had previously mastered the technique of cooking leeks in the microwave oven and so was able to have them on the table in time for dinner.

Leeks are like slightly flattened thin candles early in the season, and as much as an inch and a half in diameter toward the end of the season.

They always need to be cooked, even when tiny. Since the cooking produces a richly flavored broth, save it to drink or use as an ingredient in soups or sauces.

Leeks can be made ahead of time. Serve at room temperature. Or, to reheat, add some more stock and cook for 10 minutes in a 500°F oven.

Turn to **LEEKS** in the Cook's Guide for how-tos and to the Index for more recipes.

Braised Leeks

I love braised leeks. They can be eaten hot or cold, as a first course or as a side dish. Put a thin slice of Virginia or Vermont ham over each portion (three leeks) and a half cup of grated cheddar over that; place under the broiler until bubbly, and voilà, a light main course.

12 small leeks, trimmed and cleaned

About 1 1/2 cups Basic Chicken Stock (page 501), Roasted Chicken Stock (page 502) or commercial chicken broth

Kosher salt to taste

6 tablespoons unsalted butter

Preheat the oven to 350°F.

Place the leeks in a pan or pot wide enough to hold them flat in one or two layers. Add enough stock to almost cover the leeks; then add salt to taste. (The amount of salt needed will vary according to the saltiness of the stock.) Bring to a boil and cook at a slow boil for 10 minutes.

Butter a baking dish wide enough to hold the leeks in a single layer. Place the leeks in the dish and pour the cooking liquid over them. Dot with the remaining butter. Bake for 30 minutes, or until the leeks are lightly browned and liquid is almost evaporated.

Serves 4 as a side dish, 6 if using larger leeks

NOTE: If only large leeks are available, cook them longer, about 10 minutes more both when on top of the stove and in the oven.

Roasted, Then Braised Leeks

These leeks are a beautiful rich brown, which gives added sweetness and beauty. The leeks can be browned by sautéing them in batches, turning from time to time, rather than roasting. Then bake for 45 to 55 minutes, turning once.

6 tablespoons unsalted butter, melted

3 tablespoons olive oil

12 medium leeks (5 to 6 pounds), trimmed and cleaned

3 cups Basic Chicken Stock (page 501), Roasted Chicken Stock (page 502) or commercial chicken broth

Kosher salt to taste

Place a rack in the center of the oven. Preheat the oven to 500°F.

Swirl the butter and oil in a 14 x 12 x 2-inch roasting pan so that the bottom is coated. Arrange the leeks in a single layer in the pan. Roast for 15 minutes. Turn the leeks over with tongs. Roast for 7 minutes more.

Turn the leeks again so that their palest sides are up. Return the pan to the oven and pour in the stock. Roast for 10 minutes. For maximum browning, turn over again. Roast for 10 minutes longer (or up to 20 minutes for really large leeks). Season with salt.

Serves 6 as a first course, 12 as a side dish

Braised Leeks with Lemon

I make these each year for Thanksgiving, using some jealously guarded turkey stock made the year before. (A recipe for turkey stock is in my book *Soup, A Way of Life*.) These stay pale in color and can be happily prepared using canned chicken broth. They are good for vegetarians and excellent hot or cold. The leeks vinaigrette variation is a traditional French bistro dish made with non-meat stock. Using the leek broth will give a more intense leek flavor and a completely vegetarian dish.

1/2 cup olive oil

5 pounds leeks, trimmed to 6 to 7 inches and cleaned

10 cups Basic Chicken Stock (page 501), Leek Broth (see box), Vegetable Broth (page 506) or commercial chicken or vegetable broth

1 lemon, sliced very thinly and seeded

Kosher salt and freshly ground black pepper to taste

Preheat the oven to 350°F.

Using some of the oil, grease a roasting pan large enough to hold the leeks comfortably in a single layer. Arrange the leeks in a single layer and pour over the stock.

Bake until very tender, for about 2 hours. Fifteen minutes before the leeks are done, arrange the lemon slices over them and add the remaining olive oil.

Season with salt and pepper, and serve hot or cold. **Serves 6 as a first course, 6 to 8 as a side dish**

Microwave Variation

Place the leeks in 2 layers in a 14 x 9 x 2-inch oval dish. Pour in 2 cups stock. Arrange 2 lemons, sliced as above, in an even layer over the leeks. Drizzle with the olive oil.

Leek Broth

Leek greens need not be discarded. When washed, cut into 2-inch pieces and put in a stockpot, they make an excellent broth. Add liquid—about 6 cups broth or water for the greens from 4 pounds of leeks. Bring to a boil. Cover; reduce the heat and simmer for 3 hours. Strain.

Cover tightly with microwave plastic wrap or a lid. Cook at 100% for 50 minutes. Prick the plastic, if using, to release the steam.

Remove from the oven and uncover. Season with salt and pepper. Serve hot or cold.

Leeks Vinaigrette

Prepare the leeks using either the conventional or microwave version, omitting the lemon. Serve cool or chilled, spooning Everyday Vinaigrette (page 449) over each serving. Chop 1 or 2 hard-boiled eggs and stir into the vinaigrette if desired.

Warm Vegetable Compote

This is a quick sort of vegetables à la Grecque. It is very pretty because of the pink color lent by the beets. Make it three or four days ahead and refrigerate, or make it early on the day you wish to serve it. Either way, serve at room temperature, not too warm and not chilled. This is great to keep on hand in case company drops in unannounced.

continued

1 cup sliced (¼-inch) peeled seedless cucumber

2 teaspoons kosher salt, or to taste

4 small leeks, roots trimmed and only 2 inches of greens removed, cleaned

8 small red radishes

2 cups Basic Chicken Stock (page 501), Roasted Chicken Stock (page 502) or commercial chicken broth

½ cup olive oil

Freshly ground black pepper to taste

1 small beet, peeled, trimmed and cut into ¼-inch rounds (about ¾ cup)

2 small waxy red new potatoes, peeled and cut into ¼-inch rounds (about ½ cup)

¾ cup fresh shelled peas or frozen peas, defrosted in a sieve under warm running water

3 small carrots, peeled, trimmed and cut into ¼-inch rounds (¼ cup)

12 small green beans, tipped and tailed

½ cup sliced (¼-inch) peeled daikon or other white radishes

2 small white turnips, trimmed, peeled and cut into ¼-inch rounds (about ½ cup)

¾ cup sliced red onion (¼-inch rounds)

1 packed cup sliced (¼ inch) fennel

½ cup fresh lemon juice

Toss the cucumbers and salt together in a bowl. Set aside. Cut a ½-inch-deep cross into the bottom of each leek; set aside.

Bring a large pot of water to a boil. Add the red radishes and cook for 1 minute. Remove with a slotted spoon and plunge immediately into a bowl of ice water. Set aside. Cook the leeks in the boiling water for 3 minutes. Drain and plunge into the ice water.

Meanwhile, bring the chicken stock to a boil in a 4-quart pot. Add the olive oil and pepper. Add the beet and bring to a rolling boil. Cook for 1½ minutes. Add the potatoes; cook for 1 minute. As the vegetables cook, skim off any foam that rises to the top. Add the fresh peas, if using. After another minute, add the carrots. Cook for 2 minutes. Add the green beans. Let cook for a minute. Add the white radish, turnips, onion, fennel, lemon juice and frozen peas, if using.

Drain and rinse the cucumbers and add to the pot. Let everything boil for 1 minute longer. Taste the liquid. Season with salt and pepper to taste. Remove from the heat.

Drain the leeks and red radishes and arrange them in a large serving bowl. Pour the other vegetables and their liquid over them and stir gently. Cool to room temperature.

Serves 4 generously; to serve 6, add more leeks

Grilled Baby Leeks
or Large Scallions

Leeks to be grilled need to be partly cooked first. They can be steamed (see the Cook's Guide, page 600) if preferred.

> 25 baby leeks or large scallions, trimmed to 8 inches and cleaned
>
> ¼ cup olive oil

Place the leeks and ⅓ cup water in a 13 x 9 x 2-inch oval dish. Cover tightly with microwave plastic wrap. Cook in the microwave at 100% for 4 minutes. Prick the plastic to release the steam.

Remove from the oven and uncover. Drain and rinse the leeks under cold water. Pat dry.

Heat a grill until very hot.

Brush the leeks lightly with the olive oil. Grill for 5 to 15 minutes, turning often, until all sides are brown. (Timing varies depending on the size of the leeks or scallions and the heat of the grill.) **Serves 5 to 6 as a side dish**

Leek Gratin

Salt can make or break this lovely side dish. I always taste my ham and cheese before adding them to the gratin. If either is particularly salty, I leave out the extra salt altogether.

> 1 teaspoon unsalted butter
>
> 2 ounces thinly sliced serrano, prosciutto or Smithfield ham, trimmed and cut into slivers (about $^1/_2$ cup)
>
> $^1/_2$ cup freshly grated Parmesan or Gruyère cheese
>
> 7 to 9 medium leeks, trimmed, cleaned, cut across into $^1/_8$-inch pieces and boiled or steamed (see the Cook's Guide, page 600; about 2$^1/_2$ cups cooked)
>
> 1 teaspoon kosher salt, or to taste
>
> $^3/_4$ cup heavy cream

Place a rack in the center of the oven. Preheat the oven to 400°F. Grease a 9-inch glass pie plate with the butter.

Sprinkle half of the ham and 1 tablespoon cheese over the bottom of the pie plate. Lay out the leeks evenly in the plate. Cover with the remaining ham and sprinkle with the salt. Pour the heavy cream over the leeks. Sprinkle the top with the remaining cheese.

Bake for 30 minutes, or until brown and bubbling well. **Serves 4 to 5 as a side dish**

Leek and Potato Soup

Potage Parmentier (if hot), Vichyssoise (if cold)

My mother worked for the government in midtown New York. As a great treat, she would take me out to lunch. I was most impressed by the dining room of the Ritz, controlled by the famous chef Louis Diat. One entered by carefully (I was a child) walking down a carpeted semicircular flight of steps into a formal dining room. It was for this space that Diat invented vichyssoise, based on the homely leek and potato soup of his French childhood.

> 1 $^1/_2$ pounds floury potatoes, peeled and cut into 1-inch cubes
>
> 4 medium leeks, white and 1 inch of pale green parts only, cleaned and cut across into $^1/_4$-inch lengths
>
> 4 cups Basic Chicken Stock (page 501), Roasted Chicken Stock (page 502), commercial chicken broth or Leek Broth (page 385)
>
> $^1/_2$ cup heavy cream, plus $^1/_2$ cup for the chilled version
>
> Kosher salt and freshly ground black pepper
>
> 1 tablespoon finely snipped fresh chives, for the chilled version

In a medium saucepan, bring the potatoes, leeks and stock to a boil. Lower the heat and simmer, covered, for 20 minutes.

In a blender, working in batches of no more than 2 cups, purée the soup; or pass everything through the fine disk of a food mill.

Return the soup to the pot, stir in the ½ cup cream and heat through. Season with salt and pepper. The soup can be made ahead to this point and refrigerated for up to 2 days.

continued

If the soup has been refrigerated and it is to be served hot, reheat. If serving cold, stir in the additional cream. Taste and add salt and pepper to taste if necessary. Top each serving with chives. **Makes 7 cups; serves 5 to 6 as a first course**

Quiche with Leeks

The rich custard and meltingly sweet leeks form such a convincing partnership as to make the traditional addition of cheese unnecessary. However, for those who insist that more is better, crisp-cubed bacon and shredded Gruyère will make this dish more substantial; see the variation that follows

> 2 tablespoons unsalted butter
>
> 3/4 pound leeks, white parts only, cleaned and sliced thinly across (about 3 1/2 cups)
>
> 1 1/2 teaspoons kosher salt
>
> 3 large eggs
>
> 3/4 cup heavy cream
>
> One 10-inch Quiche Crust (page 481), fully baked

Place a rack in the center of the oven. Preheat the oven to 375°F.

Melt the butter in a large skillet. Add the leeks and 1/2 teaspoon salt. Cook over medium heat for 5 minutes, or until wilted. Reduce the heat to low. Cook for 20 minutes, stirring occasionally, until the leeks are very soft but not browned. Set aside.

Whisk together the eggs, cream and remaining 1 teaspoon salt in a medium bowl. Stir in the leeks. Pour into the prepared crust.

Bake for 20 minutes, or until set and slightly puffed. **Serves 8 as a first course, 6 as a main course**

Quiche with Leeks, Bacon and Gruyère
Cook 1/4 pound thick-cut bacon, cut into 1/4-inch dice, until lightly browned. If desired, cook the leeks in the rendered bacon fat. Stir 3 ounces Gruyère cheese, grated (about 3/4 cup) and the bacon into the custard base. Pour into the prepared crust and bake as directed.

Leek Sauce

Leeks make a light and elegant sauce with a minimum of ingredients and fuss. Consider it under poached chicken breasts or fish, or with rice and poached eggs (see page 479). A handful of chopped herbs such as tarragon, chervil or lovage stirred in at the end makes a cheerful addition.

> 6 to 8 medium-large leeks, trimmed, cleaned and boiled or steamed until very tender (see the Cook's Guide, page 600)
>
> 1 cup Basic Chicken Stock (page 501), Roasted Chicken Stock (page 502), Leek Broth (page 385) or commercial chicken broth
>
> 3/4 cup heavy cream
>
> Kosher salt and freshly ground black or white pepper to taste
>
> 1/2 cup finely chopped fresh herbs (optional)

Coarsely chop the leeks. Purée all the ingredients in food processor or blender. Add 1/2 cup water and salt and pepper to taste. Heat to serve and stir in the herbs, if using. **Makes 3 1/2 cups**

Leek Sauce with Red Wine

This is a more complicated and elegant sauce than the previous one. It can take the plainest ingredient and turn it into a feast. In many cases, I prefer a leek broth or vegetable broth for sauces and soups. Here the richness of chicken stock is welcome. Consider serving it over noodles topped with steamed mushrooms, asparagus steamed with broccoli and new potatoes, string beans over boiled rice or almost any ingredient the cook is interested in: chicken, fish or veal. Have fun.

2/3 cup boiled or steamed sliced leeks
   (1 medium leek; see the Cook's Guide,
   page 600)

1/3 cup dry red wine

1 tablespoon Worcestershire sauce

1 tablespoon olive oil

2 tablespoons dried wild mushroom powder
   (see the Cook's Guide, page 610)

1 cup Basic Chicken Stock (page 501),
   Roasted Chicken Stock (page 502) or
   commercial chicken broth

Kosher salt and freshly ground black pepper
   to taste

Purée all the ingredients except the chicken stock and seasonings in a blender.

Put the mixture in a small nonreactive saucepan and set over low heat. Gradually add the chicken stock, stirring constantly until the sauce is uniform. Add salt and pepper to taste.

Makes 2 cups

Scallions and Ramps

The Chinese, the Japanese and Americans use scallions. It was a shock when I had previous books converted for the British market to find that the British do not. They happily use spring (green) onions, which form bulbs; baby leeks, which are straight like American scallions but flatter and tougher and need to be cooked, like big leeks; and wild onions or wild leeks, which many of us call ramps. I think it's a shame to be deprived of the crisp freshness of raw scallions, with the white and the green parts often used differently.

Ramps can smell and taste somewhat rank when raw. Cooked, they are sweet and delicious. Cover the green leaves with some foil for part of the time so they don't dry out.

Roasted, green onions, ramps and scallions will cook in the same way. The only thing to keep in mind is the necessity of choosing a pan just big enough to hold them flat. Turn on the exhaust fan or open a window here. Once again, onions, members of the Allium family, have a lot of sugar, which may caramelize and smoke.

The sweet brownness is delicious whether they are roasted or sautéed or grilled. Roasting is easier and uses less fat than trying to get the same effect in a skillet. A grill may char scallions before they cook through.

The Chinese make delicious scallion pancakes, rolled in oil, not flour. The recipe is long and complicated; I decided not to include it here. If you want to try it, look in my book *Party Food*.

The various chives belong in this family, but they are really seasonings rather than main ingredients, except for sauces. (See pages 431 and 590.)

Turn to **SCALLIONS** and **RAMPS** in the Cook's Guide for how-tos and to the Index for more recipes.

Parsley and Scallion Dip

Much like scallion cream cheese, but looser in texture, a good last-minute solution for a small party.

   4 ounces ($^1/_2$ cup) cream cheese

   $^1/_4$ cup plain yogurt

   $^1/_2$ cup loosely packed 1-inch pieces trimmed
      scallions

   $^1/_2$ cup loosely packed fresh parsley leaves, chopped

   $^1/_4$ cup fresh lemon juice, or as needed

   Kosher salt and freshly ground black pepper
      to taste

In a food processor, combine the cream cheese, yogurt, scallions and parsley. Process until the mixture is smooth and light green. Season with the lemon juice and salt and pepper.

Pour the dip into a bowl and whisk to smooth out any lumps of cream cheese. **Makes 1 cup**

Scallion Soup

Scallions are up early sometimes, the product of fall planting. They are the makings of the most delicate of the Allium family soups.

   $3^1/_2$ cups Basic Chicken Stock (page 501),
      Roasted Chicken Stock (page 502) or
      commercial chicken broth

   4 medium bunches scallions, trimmed and
      cut across into 1-inch lengths

   $^1/_4$ cup cornstarch

   $^1/_8$ teaspoon freshly ground black pepper

   Kosher salt to taste

In a medium saucepan, bring 3 cups stock to a boil. Stir in the scallions. Return to a boil. Lower the heat and simmer, partially covered, for 10 minutes, or until the scallions are very soft.

In a blender, working in batches of no more than 2 cups, purée the soup. Scrape back into the pan.

In a small bowl, dissolve the cornstarch in the remaining ½ cup stock. Whisk the cornstarch mixture into the soup. Bring to a boil. Lower the heat and simmer for 2 minutes, or until the soup is slightly thickened. Season with the pepper and salt to taste.

Makes 4 cups; serves 4 as a first course, 2 as a main course

Scallion and Radish Soup

This is a perfect early spring soup made from the first promising notes out of the garden. It is pretty too. It can be served hot or cold.

4 cups Basic Chicken Stock (page 501), Roasted Chicken Stock (page 502) or commercial chicken broth

3 bunches scallions, trimmed, white parts chopped (about 1 1/2 packed cups), green parts sliced (about 1 cup) and kept separate

1/4 cup heavy cream

1 1/2 teaspoons fresh lemon juice

1/4 teaspoon kosher salt

3 breakfast or other early red radishes, very thinly sliced and blanched for 15 to 20 seconds in boiling water

Sprigs of fresh dill (optional)

Cucumber slices, preferably young Kirby (optional)

In a medium saucepan, heat the stock to boiling. Stir in the scallion whites and boil for 15 minutes.

Purée the cooked scallions with 1 cup of the stock in a food processor. Return the purée to the saucepan and place over medium heat. Stir in the cream, lemon juice and salt. Just before serving, stir the scallion greens into the soup. Return to simmer if serving hot. Chill thoroughly if serving cold.

Divide the radish slices among six small bowls and pour in the soup. Garnish with sprigs of dill and cucumber slices, if desired.

Serves 6 as a first course

Scallions, Bok Choy and Shiitake Mushrooms in Broth

4 medium dried shiitake mushrooms

3 small bok choy (about 12 ounces)

2 cups Basic Chicken Stock (page 501) or Mushroom Broth (page 507)

2 bunches medium scallions (about 8 per bunch), trimmed and cut into 2-inch lengths

3 slices peeled fresh ginger

2 teaspoons rice wine vinegar or white wine vinegar

Kosher salt to taste

2 teaspoons cornstarch (optional)

Cilantro leaves

Toasted sesame oil

Pour enough boiling water over the mushrooms in a small bowl to cover them. Let stand until softened, about 20 minutes.

Meanwhile, trim any wilted or yellow leaves and stalks from the bok choy. Cut each head lengthwise into quarters. Wash and drain.

Drain the mushrooms. Cut off and discard the stems. Cut the caps into 1-inch strips. Combine the stock, scallions, ginger, vinegar, bok choy, and mushrooms in a saucepan. Bring to a boil. Adjust the heat to simmering. Add salt to taste. Cook until the bok choy is crisp-tender, for about 6 minutes; turn it if necessary for even cooking.

Discard the ginger. To thicken the cooking liquid, if desired, stir the cornstarch together with enough cold water to dissolve it in a small bowl. Stir into the liquid, bring to a simmer and cook for 30 seconds.

Spoon the soup into serving bowls. Scatter cilantro leaves over and pass sesame oil.

Serves 4 as a main course with rice, 6 as a side dish

Ants on a Scallion Tree

I came up with this idea as a variation of Barbara Tropp's version of the Chinese classic dish in which the "ants" (bits of ground pork) climb up rice stick noodles. Chris Styler made the actual recipe. He advises that it is relatively mild and the seeds of the peppers can be left in for more kick, if desired.

3 bunches small scallions
   (about 12 per bunch), trimmed

1 pound lean ground pork

3 tablespoons soy sauce, preferably tamari

2 teaspoons sugar

2 teaspoons cornstarch

2 tablespoons vegetable oil

4 slices peeled fresh ginger,
   finely chopped

1 small hot chili pepper, such as serrano or
   jalapeño, seeded and finely chopped

Toasted sesame oil

Finely chop 2 of the scallions and set aside. Thoroughly dry the remaining scallions.

Crumble the pork onto a cutting board. Sprinkle the soy sauce, sugar and cornstarch over the pork. Rock a large knife or cleaver back and forth over the pork to incorporate the seasonings and break up any clumps. Set aside.

Heat the oil in a large heavy skillet over medium heat. Lay the whole scallions in the oil. Cook, turning once, until bright green and wilted, for about 1 minute. Transfer to a warm serving bowl, holding them over the skillet to drain off excess oil.

Add the chopped scallions, ginger and hot pepper to the oil in the pan. Stir until fragrant, for about 1 minute. Add the pork and stir to break it up. Cook, stirring to prevent sticking, until the liquid given off by the pork has evaporated and the pork begins to brown, for about 4 minutes.

Spoon the pork over the scallions and toss well. Drizzle sesame oil over and serve.

Serves 4 as a main course

Ramps

The so-called wild leeks, ramps have long been a spring favorite in the southern United States, inspiring whole festivals during their brief season. I remember when they became a "foodie" fad, a touchstone of the local-food movement, treated as if a rare delight. Now, I do like ramps and relish them in season, but I also know that they grow wild in Vermont; that is north.

Find somebody who knows how to pick ramps. They look like lily of the valley, same shape leaves. Nowadays they can be bought in an increasing number of stores and at roadside stands. Uncooked, they taste rather strong. Cooked, they taste mellow and lovely.

Grilled Ramps

These are bound to be a favorite with friends who are not afraid to get their fingers greasy. Some very fancy stores may sell ramps; scallions can be substituted. These are good cold and I find that people devour them, so prepare more than you think you will need.

1 1/2 pounds ramps

1 cup olive oil

Kosher salt and freshly ground black pepper
    to taste

Wash the ramps well. Pull off the thin outermost layers.

Preheat a grill until the coals are white-hot. Brush the ramps with oil. Place in a single layer crosswise on the grill so that they cannot fall through the rack and so that the green parts are not actually over the heat. When the white parts of the ramps start to turn brown, turn them over with a pancake turner and move them toward the center of the grill so that the greens are over the heat. Continue to brush the ramps with the remaining oil as necessary while they cook.

When the ramps are fully cooked and quite soft, remove from the grill with the pancake turner. Season to taste with salt and pepper.

Serves 4 to 8 as a side dish

Roasted, Then Braised Scallions

If we think of the relationship between scallions and leeks or, indeed, use baby leeks, this recipe makes instant sense. I often add a little bit of lemon juice after the cooking, especially if serving the scallions cool at the start of a spring meal, much the way one serves asparagus.

1 tablespoon unsalted butter, melted

1 tablespoon olive oil

4 bunches large scallions (about 5 per bunch),
    trimmed to 8 inches

1/2 cup Basic Chicken Stock (page 501),
    Roasted Chicken Stock (page 502) or
    commercial chicken broth

1/4 teaspoon kosher salt (omit if using commercial
    broth), or to taste

Place a rack in the center of the oven. Preheat the oven to 500°F.

Put the butter, oil and scallions in a roasting pan that is 14 x 12 x 2 inches. Turn the scallions so that they are lightly coated. Roast for 8 minutes.

Remove from the oven. Use a fork to turn the scallions over. Rotate the pan and return to the oven. Roast for 3 minutes more. Add the stock and salt, if using, and roast for 3 to 4 minutes more. Or, if serving hot but not immediately, remove from the oven after adding the stock. Then, just before serving, roast for 4 minutes longer. Serve warm or at room temperature. **Serves 5 to 6 as a side dish**

Fettuccine with Roasted Scallions and Tomato Sauce

This starts life with some leftovers of roasted scallions. To serve more people, use a full recipe of scallions and double the amount of tomatoes. Or, if there are no leftover roasted scallions, roast the scallions and tomatoes in two pans at the same time. If the pan isn't big enough for all of the tomatoes, either add a third rack to the oven or cook them separately.

The richness of egg noodle fettuccine is smooth and sexy with the sauce, but leaner non-egg linguine or even angel hair is fine, although the angel hair needs a little extra oil to keep the thin strands from clumping. Don't move to a heavier pasta; the sauce is light and elegant. It can be made ahead.

2 teaspoons olive oil

6 medium ripe tomatoes (5 to 6 ounces each), cored and cut into 4 wedges each

1 cup roasted scallions (see the Cook's Guide, page 641), roughly snipped into 1- to 2-inch-long pieces

Kosher salt and freshly ground black pepper to taste

$^1/_2$ pound dried fettuccine

Place a rack in the upper section of the oven for the tomatoes. (If making roasted scallions now, place another rack in the center of the oven and proceed as directed on page 641.) Preheat the oven to 500°F.

Put the oil and tomatoes in a 14 x 12 x 2-inch roasting pan. Rub the tomatoes with the oil until lightly coated and rub some of the oil onto the sides of the pan. Arrange the wedges, with a flat side down, so they touch as little as possible.

Roast for 8 minutes. Remove the pan from the oven. Use a small spatula or fork to turn each wedge onto its unbrowned flat side. Rotate the pan and return to the oven. Roast for 7 minutes more.

Meanwhile, bring a large pot of salted water to a boil for the pasta.

In a medium saucepan, combine the tomatoes, with all the juices, and the scallions, with all their juices. Heat until warmed throughout. Season with salt and pepper.

Meanwhile, cook the pasta; drain. Toss with the sauce. **Serves 4 as a main course, 6 as a first course**

Mushrooms

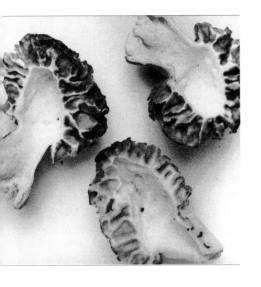

There is an enormous world of mushrooms out there to buy in shops and to forage. I don't know of a single culinary culture that doesn't prize at least one kind of mushroom as either a staple or a treat. They are earthy. The traditional English come perilously close to gentrifying them under glass.

Mushrooms are not vegetables, but we use them that way. They are fungi—which sounds extremely unappealing.

There is a common fallacy that mushrooms in one part of the world are not the same as in others. While a few may be rare in certain locations and a very few found only in a certain place, by and large, mushrooms are the same from continent to continent. The rare and expensive matsutake of Japan is much more common on the U.S. Pacific Coast as "pine mushroom." A chanterelle is a prize no matter where you find it.

Normally generous and sharing people, among whom I count myself, become secretive and possessive about the locations of their picking sites.

Unfortunately, one needs to learn a lot about wild mushrooms before picking them; but it is great fun, and wild mushrooms truly have a stronger, better taste than cultivated ones. In France, pharmacists must be trained to judge mushrooms, and all the forager has to do is take the haul to the nearest pharmacy to find out whether the mushrooms are edible and what type(s) they are. In any case, never eat mushrooms raw that grow in forests where there are beavers. You can get what Vermonters call "beaver fever," an acute case of the runs that must be cured by a doctor's strong medicine. In this book, I have restricted my recipes to those using store-bought mushrooms.

The world seems to divide itself into mushroom and non-mushroom cultures, especially when it comes to wild mushrooms (and even more so when it comes to hallucinogenic mushrooms). John Evelyn (see the Bibliography) gives several cautionary tales about the eating of wild mushrooms. Generally, there are certain mushrooms that are favored in different cultures.

As the world of available mushrooms has grown, a strange problem has cropped up to confront the recipe writer. What do we call what used to be simply called mushrooms? I have had people suggest calling them "store-bought mushrooms"; but as many of the mushrooms formerly found only in the wild are now available farmed and in stores, this seems inaccurate and confusing. Some people call them "button mushrooms," but as most of them are much larger than buttons, this equally doesn't work. There was a time when mushrooms came primarily in cans and they were indeed the size of a large bombé button. I think that I will settle for calling the most common mushrooms "mushrooms" and calling all other kinds by more precise names.

Fear of creating mass poisonings keeps me from giving picking information, but on pages 605–607 in the Cook's Guide, there is information about the more available kinds of domesticated mushrooms.

In the happy times when hunting has provided me with more magic than I can foresee using in the quite near future, I dry the surplus. I spread a large table (not outdoors—the wind would blow the mushrooms away, as they get lighter as they dry—and not in direct sunlight) with newspaper, which I cover with a layer of paper toweling. Small mushrooms can be dried whole. Larger ones should be sliced about an eighth of an inch thick. I spread them in a non-touching, single layer and turn them over during the course of a day or two until they are totally dry. See the Cook's Guide for more specific information on drying mushrooms, including microwave drying. They go into a jar with a tight screw top. They are a treasure for other seasons in risottos, soups and stews. They cannot be used as if fresh; the texture is wrong.

Along with soy products, mushrooms have long been a staple of vegetarian diets. They have a fleshy texture and a rich, warm taste that goes well with grains and other vegetables. Doubling the portions of the mushroom side dishes included here and adding cracked wheat, brown rice or barley will turn them into a main course.

Turn to **MUSHROOMS** in the Cook's Guide for how-tos and to the Index for more recipes.

Mushrooms with Yogurt and Dill

The mushrooms virtually cook in the dressing and can be spooned into fully baked tartlet shells made from Cheddar Cheese Tart Dough (page 478). Or spoon over lettuce leaves for a simple first course. Multiply this recipe as many times as wanted. Since it takes about a tablespoon to fill each small tart shell, the basic recipe will make thirty-two hors d'oeuvre, enough for ten guests. They go very nicely with thinly sliced ham, which would make this serve more as a first course.

1/2 pound mushrooms, trimmed, quartered and cut into 1/4-inch slices (2 1/3 cups)

2 tablespoons fresh lemon juice

3 tablespoons plain yogurt

1 1/2 tablespoons Dijon mustard

2 tablespoons chopped fresh dill

1/2 teaspoon kosher salt

2 to 4 drops hot red pepper sauce

Freshly ground black pepper to taste

Toss the mushrooms with the lemon juice in a medium bowl. Set aside.

In a small bowl, whisk together the remaining ingredients. Pour over the mushrooms and toss to combine. Let stand for at least 1 hour to let the flavor develop. Packed into a crock and refrigerated, these will keep for several days.

Makes 2 cups; serves 4 as a first course

Mushroom Dumplings

I think these are a fine creation. Serve in mushroom broth, moistened but not swimming; or in seasoned beef stock or clear vegetable broth.

1 tablespoon unsalted butter

2 medium shallots, very finely chopped

1 pound mushrooms, trimmed and finely chopped

1 1/4 teaspoons kosher salt

1 tablespoon finely minced fresh parsley

1/2 cup whole-milk ricotta

1/2 cup all-purpose flour, plus 2 to 3 tablespoons for rolling

2 large egg yolks

Freshly ground black pepper to taste

3 to 4 cups Mushroom Broth (page 507) or Beef Stock (page 502)

In a medium frying pan, melt the butter over medium heat. Stir in the shallots and cook for 5 minutes, or until they are wilted. Stir in the mushrooms and salt. Cook, stirring occasionally, for 10 minutes. Stir in the parsley. Continue cooking, stirring frequently, for 15 minutes, or until the mushrooms and shallots are dark golden brown and dry. Remove the mixture to a bowl and allow to cool to room temperature.

Add the ricotta, 1/2 cup flour, egg yolks and pepper to the mushroom mixture. Mix thoroughly to create a very moist dough.

Sprinkle a work surface with 2 tablespoons flour. Divide the dough in two. Roll each piece into a log approximately 15 inches long and 1 inch in diameter, using additional flour as necessary to keep the dough from sticking. Cut across into small dumplings about 1/2 inch thick.

Bring a large pot of lightly salted water to a boil. Working in batches if necessary, add the dumplings and simmer for 5 minutes, or until they are floating and the centers are cooked; the dumplings will be moist in the center and slightly chewy.

Meanwhile, heat the broth. Divide the dumplings among warm bowls and ladle the broth over them.

Makes 60 dumplings; serves 6 to 8 as a first course

Miniature Mushroom Quiches

This is basically a very simple quiche jazzed up with a faintly anise flavor, which blends into the mushrooms, intensifying the flavor rather than concealing it. If, like me, you are a mushroom hunter, wild mushrooms take this up a definite notch in flavor. You can use fresh farmed shiitakes, but I think other store-bought wild or semi-wild mushrooms (such as oyster mushrooms) are really too expensive to be worth it here.

2 tablespoons unsalted butter

6 ounces small mushrooms, trimmed and coarsely chopped (about 2^1/$_2$ cups)

^{2}/$_3$ cup heavy cream

1 tablespoon Pernod

2 large eggs

4 teaspoons chopped fresh dill or fennel fronds

Kosher salt and freshly ground black pepper to taste

36 individual pastry shells made from Quiche Crust (page 481), partially baked (see Flaky Tart Dough, page 477, for instructions for shaping and partially baking individual shells)

Melt the butter in a small skillet over medium heat. Stir in the mushrooms and cook for about 2 minutes, or until they just start to give off some liquid. Stir in the cream and Pernod and cook for about 2 minutes, or until the mixture comes to a boil.

Remove from the heat and allow to cool to room temperature.

Preheat the oven to 375°F.

Lightly beat the eggs in a small mixing bowl. Stir in the mushroom mixture and dill or fennel. Season to taste with salt and pepper.

Fill the partially baked pastry shells with the mushroom mixture. Bake until the centers are set and the tops are lightly browned, for about 10 minutes. Remove from the oven and allow to cool slightly on a wire rack before serving.

Makes thirty-six 2-inch quiches

Large Mushroom Quiche

Prepare the filling as above. Prepare a 10-inch prebaked Quiche Crust (page 481). Add filling and bake until the center is set and the top is lightly browned, about 35 minutes.

Crustless Spring Quiche

Divine, rich and lighter than it would be with a crust. I spoon it out to serve, or cut it.

^{1}/$_3$ pound waxy new potatoes, peeled and cut into ^{1}/$_4$-inch slices

3 tablespoons unsalted butter

^{1}/$_3$ pound chanterelles, trimmed and halved lengthwise, or mushrooms, trimmed and cut into ^{1}/$_4$-inch slices

2 scallions, trimmed and cut into ^{1}/$_4$-inch slices (about ^{1}/$_2$ cup)

^{1}/$_3$ cup chopped fresh parsley

^{3}/$_4$ cup shelled fresh peas, cooked, or frozen small peas, defrosted in a sieve under warm water and patted dry

Kosher salt and freshly ground black pepper

4 large eggs

1 cup heavy cream

^{1}/$_4$ pound Gruyère cheese, grated (about 1 cup)

continued

Place a rack in the center of the oven. Preheat the oven to 375°F. Butter a 10-inch quiche pan.

Put the potatoes in a single layer in the top of a two-part steamer or on a steaming rack or a plate in a bamboo steamer. Fill the bottom of the steamer pan or a pan large enough to hold the bamboo or steaming rack with water; the water should not touch the rack. Bring to a boil over medium heat. Place the potatoes on top, cover and steam for 3 minutes; they will still be crunchy. Set aside.

Melt the butter in a 12-inch skillet. Add the mushrooms; cook over medium-high heat for 5 minutes, or until browned and softened. Reduce the heat to medium. Add the scallions and parsley. Cook for 2 minutes. Remove from the heat. Add the potatoes, peas, salt and pepper; toss to combine.

Whisk together the eggs and cream in a medium bowl. Stir in the cheese and vegetable mixture. Pour into the quiche pan.

Bake for 20 to 25 minutes. The quiche should be lightly browned and puffed and set in the center. **Serves 6 to 8 as a first course**

Mushroom Barley Soup

This is a vegetarian barley soup—no stock. Barley, an ancient grain, swells a lot as it sits. If not serving the soup right away, use a third less barley. For a richer soup, use the mushroom broth instead of water.

8 cups Mushroom Broth (page 507; optional)

¹/₂ ounce dried porcini mushrooms

1 cup pearl barley

1 medium carrot, peeled, trimmed and cut into ¹/₄-inch dice

2 small stalks celery, peeled and cut into ¹/₄-inch dice

1 tablespoon unsalted butter

1 small onion, minced

¹/₄ pound mushrooms, trimmed and thinly sliced

3 medium cloves garlic, smashed, peeled and minced

1 tablespoon coarsely chopped celery leaves

¹/₄ cup coarsely chopped fresh dill

4 teaspoons kosher salt

Freshly ground black pepper to taste

In a small saucepan, bring 1 cup mushroom broth or water to a boil. Pour it over the dried mushrooms in a small bowl. Soak for 15 minutes. Remove the mushrooms from the water and squeeze out the excess liquid. Strain the soaking liquid through a fine-mesh sieve. Reserve the mushrooms and liquid separately.

In a medium saucepan, bring the barley, carrot, celery, rehydrated mushrooms and 7 cups mushroom broth or water to a boil. Lower the heat and simmer, covered, for 30 minutes.

Meanwhile, in a medium frying pan, melt the butter over medium heat. Stir in the onion; cook, stirring occasionally, for 8 minutes, or until soft. Stir in the fresh mushrooms and cook for 5 minutes. Scrape the mushroom mixture into the soup.

Return the frying pan to the burner, pour the reserved mushroom soaking liquid into the pan and raise the heat. Bring to a boil, stirring and scraping the bottom of the pan with a wooden spoon to release any brown bits stuck there. Add to the soup. Return to a boil. Lower the heat and simmer, covered, for 10 minutes. Stir in the garlic. Simmer, covered, for 5 minutes. Remove from the heat and stir in the remaining ingredients.
Makes 8 cups; serves 6 as a first course

Winter Mushroom Soup

Porcini are *Boletus,* which can be found in American woods if one knows what one is doing. Last summer, I found myself with more than I could use and I restricted myself to *Boletus edulis,* the choicest ones. As this soup uses dried mushrooms, it can be made at any time, but it is robust and particularly welcome in winter months. The mushroom broth is a nice alternative to water.

3 quarts Mushroom Broth (page 507; optional)

2 ounces dried porcini mushrooms (about 2 cups)

2 tablespoons unsalted butter

1 pound mushrooms, trimmed and thinly sliced

1 large onion, cut into 1/4-inch dice

2 large leeks, white parts only, cut in half lengthwise, cleaned and cut across into 1 1/2-inch lengths

2 medium carrots, trimmed, peeled and cut across into thin slices

1/2 pound parsnips or celery root, trimmed, peeled and cut into 1/2-inch dice

4 medium cloves garlic, smashed and peeled

4 European bay leaves

1 cup pearl barley

1/2 pound waxy potatoes, peeled and cut into 1-inch cubes

1 tablespoon kosher salt, or to taste

Freshly ground black pepper to taste

1/2 cup snipped fresh dill

Sour cream for serving (optional)

In a small saucepan, bring 1 1/2 cups mushroom broth or water just to a boil. Place the dried mushrooms in a small bowl and pour the hot broth over them. Soak for 15 minutes. Drain the mushrooms, reserving the liquid; squeeze out the excess liquid and set aside. Strain the mushroom soaking liquid through a coffee filter rinsed with hot water; reserve.

In a large stockpot, melt the butter over low heat. Stir in the fresh mushrooms and cook until they soften and give off their liquid, about 10 minutes. Stir in the remaining broth (or 10 1/2 cups water), the soaked mushrooms and their liquid, the onion, leeks, carrots, parsnips, garlic and bay leaves. Bring to a boil. Skim the top as necessary. Lower the heat and simmer for 30 minutes.

Stir in the barley and simmer for 20 minutes. Stir in the potatoes. Simmer for 30 minutes, or until the barley and potatoes are tender. Remove from the heat. Discard the bay leaves. Season with the salt, pepper and dill.

Swirl a dollop of sour cream into each serving, if desired.

Makes 15 cups; serves 10 as a first course, 6 as a main course

Wild Mushroom Soup

I first met friend and fine chef Greg Parks of The Four Columns Inn in Newfane, Vermont, when he came to live with us as a house sitter and to help with the gardens. He was a painter and thought ours would be a peaceful place to work. To make some extra money, he got a job as a chef's assistant. When the inn was sold and I was asked what should be done about the food, I recommended Greg and helped with the menu and recipes. He has worked out splendidly.

Greg started using wild mushrooms because of guest interest and demand. He notes that "this is a wonderfully flexible and fun recipe. You can use as many different kinds and combinations of wild mushrooms as you please." He uses a vegetable stock to soak the dried mushrooms. I don't find it to be needed.

continued

1 1/2 ounces dried morels (about 1 1/2 cups)

1 1/2 ounces dried porcini (about 1 cup)

5 tablespoons unsalted butter

1 1/2 cups finely chopped onions

1/2 pound cremini mushrooms, trimmed
 and sliced

1/2 pound mushrooms, sliced

2 1/2 cups Vegetable Broth (page 506) or
 Mushroom Broth (page 507)

1/2 cup brandy

1/2 cup half-and-half

Kosher salt and freshly ground pepper to taste

In a small bowl, pour enough boiling water
over the dried morels and porcini to cover.
Soak until soft, about 20 minutes. Drain,
reserving the liquid. Rinse the morels and
porcini briefly under warm running water.
Strain the soaking liquid through a coffee
filter or a sieve lined with double thickness
of cheesecloth and reserve.

Melt the butter in a 3-quart saucepan
over low heat. Add the onions. Cook until
translucent, about 10 minutes, stirring often;
do not brown. Stir in the fresh mushrooms
and cook until the liquid they give off is
evaporated, about 20 minutes.

Add the broth, brandy, dried morels and
porcini and their soaking liquid. Simmer,
covered, 45 minutes.

Strain the soup. Return the liquid to the
pot. Purée the solids with the half-and-half
in a blender until smooth. Stir the purée into
the liquid in the pot. Heat to simmering and
season with salt and pepper.

Makes about 7 cups; serves 6 as a first course

Chanterelle Omelet

If feeling flush, increase the mushrooms by
another quarter cup or so.

2 tablespoons unsalted butter

1 small shallot, finely chopped

1/2 cup chopped chanterelles (about 2 ounces)

Kosher salt and freshly ground black pepper to taste

3 large eggs

Melt 1 tablespoon of the butter in a nonstick
or well-seasoned omelet pan over medium
heat. Add the shallot and cook, stirring, until
softened, about 3 minutes. Add the chanterelles
and salt and pepper, and stir until lightly cooked
and the butter absorbed, about 4 minutes.
Scrape into a bowl.

In a small bowl, beat the eggs thoroughly.
Season lightly with salt and pepper. Melt the
remaining 1 tablespoon butter in the same pan.
Make a rolled omelet (see page 483), adding
the mushroom mixture just before folding.

Serves 1 as a main course

Roasted Portobello Mushrooms with Garlic Marinade

Try to find caps of the same size. If they're
unavailable, don't worry; the size (diameter)
of the caps will not affect the cooking time.

Partner these with steak. For a quick dinner,
put them on toasted country-style bread for a
smashing first course or use them as part of
a vegetable dinner medley. Vary the flavor
of the marinade by adding two teaspoons of
chopped fresh herbs. A combination of thyme,
oregano and savory works well, as do sage and
parsley. Consider dropping in two teaspoons
of sherry vinegar, or tarragon vinegar mixed
with chopped tarragon.

4 portobello mushrooms ($^3/_4$ to 1 pound),
   caps wiped clean

6 cloves garlic, smashed, peeled and roughly
   chopped

$^1/_2$ cup olive oil

1 teaspoon kosher salt

Freshly ground black pepper to taste

Using a small kitchen knife, cut the stems off
the mushroom caps. (Reserve the stems in the
refrigerator in a sealed plastic bag or container
for stock, if desired.)

Put the garlic in a blender with 2 tablespoons
oil. Blend until smooth. Scrape down the sides
with a rubber spatula. Add the remaining ¼ cup
oil, the salt and pepper. Blend until smooth.

Put the mushrooms in a 12 x 8 x 1½-inch
roasting pan. Using the spatula, scrape all the
garlic purée into the pan. Rub the purée onto
both sides of each mushroom cap. Leave to
marinate for at least 30 minutes, or up to 5 to
6 hours, turning occasionally.

Place a rack on the second level from the
bottom of the oven. Preheat the oven to 500°F.

Arrange the mushrooms in the pan, stem
sides down, so that they touch as little as
possible. Roast for 6 minutes. Turn. Roast for
6 minutes more. Serve warm or at room
temperature. **Serves 4 as a side dish**

Cumin Mushrooms

Speared on toothpicks, these make a great
cocktail snack. As a vegetable, they go
particularly well with fish. Carrots can be
prepared the same way and are also very
good with fish or alongside a green vegetable
such as broccoli.

$^1/_2$ cup vegetable oil

2 pounds firm medium mushrooms,
   stems removed

2 to 2$^1/_2$ teaspoons ground cumin

$^1/_4$ teaspoon kosher salt, or to taste

Freshly ground black pepper to taste

In a skillet large enough to hold all the
mushrooms in a single layer, heat the oil
over medium heat. (If one skillet will not
hold all the mushrooms, use two skillets
and divide the ingredients equally between
them.) Set the mushrooms in the pan, stem
side down. Sprinkle with 1½ teaspoons
cumin, the salt and several grindings of
pepper. Reduce the heat to low. Cook the
mushrooms uncovered, turning occasionally,
for 1½ to 2 hours, until very dark brown.

Five minutes before removing the mushrooms
from the heat, stir in the remaining ½ teaspoon
cumin. Taste and adjust the seasonings.

Transfer the mushrooms to a bowl. Cool to
room temperature, tossing occasionally; serve.
Serves 4 as a side dish, more as a cocktail snack

Sautéed Mushrooms
with Lemon and Mustard

These are at their best with a thick broiled
steak. When served, the steak juices run into
the mushrooms to make a sauce.

12 tablespoons (6 ounces) unsalted butter

2 pounds medium mushrooms, trimmed and
   cut in half

4 teaspoons kosher salt

1 teaspoon freshly ground black pepper

2 tablespoons prepared mustard

2 tablespoons fresh lemon juice

continued

Melt the butter in a large skillet. Add the mushrooms and cook, stirring, until they are just heated through, for about 5 minutes. Add the salt, pepper, mustard and lemon juice. Cook for a few minutes, until the liquid is reduced enough to lightly coat the mushrooms. **Serves 6 as a side dish**

Morels with Rhubarb and Asparagus

This is an extravagantly delicious and beautiful early spring dish—and a little odd, like me. Some rice or fresh egg noodles would turn this into a main course.

    2 tablespoons vegetable oil

    1 tablespoon toasted sesame oil

    1 pound asparagus, woody stems snapped off, stalks peeled and cut across into 1 1/2-inch pieces (about 2 cups)

    1/3 pound medium fresh morels, trimmed (if the mushrooms are large, cut them in half lengthwise), or 1/3 pound oyster mushrooms, trimmed and cut lengthwise into 2 pieces for small clusters, 3 pieces for large (2 cups)

    4 medium stalks rhubarb (a little over 8 ounces), trimmed and cut across diagonally into 1/4-inch pieces (about 2 cups)

    1/2 teaspoon kosher salt

    1/2 teaspoon sugar

    Lots of freshly ground black pepper

In a large straight-sided frying pan, heat the vegetable and sesame oil over high heat. Stir in the asparagus and, if using, oyster mushrooms. Cook, stirring, for 2 minutes. Stir in the morels, if using, and rhubarb. Cook, stirring, for 3 more minutes.

Remove from the heat and stir in the salt, sugar and pepper. Let sit for 5 minutes before serving. **Serves 4 as a first course or a side dish**

Mushroom-Vegetable Stew

While I first made this as a side dish, piled on well-seasoned barley or couscous, it would make a very good main course for four.

    1 tablespoon olive oil

    2 ounces cremini mushrooms, trimmed and cut across into 1/4-inch slices (about 1 1/2 cups)

    2 ounces shiitake mushrooms, trimmed and cut across into 1/4-inch slices (about 2 cups)

    2 ounces oyster mushrooms, trimmed and cut across into 1/4-inch slices (about 2 1/2 cups)

    1/2 cup chopped fresh parsley

    3 cloves garlic, smashed, peeled and minced

    1/2 teaspoon celery seeds

    1/4 teaspoon dried thyme

    Pinch of dried oregano

    One 16-ounce can black beans, rinsed and drained

    6 ounces frozen peas (about 1 cup), defrosted in a strainer under warm running water

    1 tablespoon cornstarch

    1 cup V-8 vegetable juice

    3 cups small cauliflower florets (about 8 ounces), steamed (see the Cook's Guide, page 548)

    Kosher salt and freshly ground black pepper to taste

Heat the olive oil in a large deep skillet over medium heat. Stir in the cremini. Cook 1½ to 2 minutes, until they start to wilt. Add the shiitakes; cook 3 minutes, or until barely wilted.

Add the oyster mushrooms; stir for 2 minutes. Stir in the parsley, garlic, celery seeds, thyme and oregano; cook until fragrant.

Add the beans and peas and stir gently until warmed through. Dissolve the cornstarch in the vegetable juice, then stir into the skillet. Bring to a boil. Add the cauliflower and simmer until the sauce is thickened. Season to taste with salt and pepper.

Makes about 5³/4 cups; serves 6 as a side dish

Microwave Variation

Do not steam the cauliflower. Stir together the mushrooms, parsley, garlic and oil in a 2½-quart casserole dish with a tightly fitting lid. Cover and cook at 100% for 2 minutes.

Remove from the oven and uncover. With a large spoon, move the mushroom mixture to the center of the dish and arrange the cauliflower and peas around the edges. Re-cover and cook at 100% for 3 minutes.

Remove from the oven and uncover. Place the cornstarch and dried herbs in a small bowl and gradually stir in the juice. Stir into the vegetables along with the drained black beans. Re-cover and cook at 100% for 4 minutes.

Remove from the oven and uncover. Season with salt and pepper to taste.

Honey Mushroom Sauté

While honey mushrooms will make this special, it is a good basic recipe for almost any vigorous-tasting mushroom. If store-bought mushrooms are used, choose cremini or oyster mushrooms.

¹/4 cup olive oil

6¹/2 cups (about 1 pound) honey mushrooms or other mushrooms, preferably wild, trimmed and coarsely chopped

2 teaspoons chopped fresh thyme

4 large cloves garlic, smashed, peeled and minced

¹/4 cup chopped fresh parsley

1 teaspoon kosher salt

Freshly ground black pepper to taste

Heat the oil in a large deep skillet. Stir in the mushrooms, thyme, garlic and parsley and cook, stirring, over medium heat for 5 minutes. Stir in ½ cup water, the salt and pepper and cook until the liquid has completely evaporated.

Serves 4 as a side dish

Mushroom Duxelles

Duxelles, a standard of the French kitchen, is remarkably versatile. It can be used for stuffing meats and vegetables or—perhaps with extra herbs and/or seasonings such as parsley, oregano, chopped cooked spinach, turmeric, celery seed or fennel—with pastas. Egg pastas such as fettuccine can be sauced after adding a little cream to the duxelles, and lasagna can be layered with duxelles and cheese and then sauced with tomato or other sauces.

1 medium sweet white onion or 4 shallots, finely chopped (about ¹/2 cup)

¹/4 cup olive oil or 6 tablespoons unsalted butter

1 pound mushrooms, trimmed and finely chopped (about 4¹/2 cups)

³/4 teaspoon kosher salt

Freshly ground black pepper to taste

In a large saucepan, cook the onions or shallots in the olive oil or butter over medium-low heat until translucent, for about 10 minutes. Stir in the mushrooms. Cook until they begin to give off liquid. Turn the heat up to medium-high. Stirring constantly, cook until there is no water remaining in the pan but the mushrooms are still moist, for about 15 minutes. Remove from the heat and season with the salt and pepper.

Makes 1 1/2 cups

Morels in Rich Lamb Sauce

A festive dinner party special if ever there was one. Serve with rice or egg noodles.

> **7 ounces small fresh morels (about 2 1/2 cups) or 1 1/2 ounces dried morels, soaked in warm water until softened (see the Cook's Guide, page 610), water strained through a cloth or coffee filter and kept for another use, if desired**
>
> **1 1/2 tablespoons unsalted butter**
>
> **1 small onion (4 ounces), finely chopped**
>
> **6 ounces lean ground lamb**
>
> **1/2 cup heavy cream**
>
> **3 tablespoons chopped fresh tarragon**
>
> **Kosher salt and freshly ground black pepper to taste**

Cut off the stems of the morels flush with the caps; chop the stems. Reserve the caps and stems separately.

Melt the butter in a medium saucepan over low heat. Add the onion. Cook until thoroughly translucent, for about 3 minutes. Add the chopped stems and lamb. Cook, breaking up the meat with a wooden spoon, until the lamb has lost almost all of its pink color. Add the morel caps, cream and tarragon. Bring to a boil. Cook for 2 to 3 minutes, until thickened. Season with salt and pepper.

Serves 6 as a first course

Stuffed Mushrooms

Choose the mushrooms for this dish based on how they will be served. Medium to large mushrooms are good singly for a first course or buffet. Serve four to five medium mushrooms per person if this is a main course. Medium to small mushrooms can be a passed hors d'oeuvre. In which case, the combined yogurt and mint can be served as a sauce.

> **15 to 22 mushrooms, depending on size (see headnote), stems removed**
>
> **2 tablespoons olive oil**
>
> **1 teaspoon kosher salt**
>
> **1 recipe Lamb Curry Stuffing (page 493)**
>
> **Plain yogurt (optional)**
>
> **Chopped fresh mint (optional)**

Place a rack in the center of the oven. Preheat the oven to 350°F.

In a large bowl, toss the mushroom caps with the olive oil and salt. Fill the caps with the stuffing, mounding it on top.

Arrange the mushrooms in a baking pan. Cover the pan with foil. Bake small mushrooms for 15 minutes, extra-large mushrooms for up to 30 minutes. The stuffing should be firm, the mushrooms soft.

Serve with the yogurt and mint, if desired.

Makes 15 to 22 mushrooms

Braised Stuffed Morels

When morels are in season, they are the most luxurious of the mushrooms to stuff. Their pouchlike shape makes it seem as if this was their destiny. Look for large morels, about two to three inches long and one and a half inches wide. The shape is also important. Plump round morels will be easier to stuff than flat ones.

5 ounces morels (23 to 27)

2 ounces Brie, rind removed, roughly chopped

1/2 cup Dried Bread Crumbs (page 510) or store-bought

3 tablespoons plus 2 teaspoons unsalted butter

1 large shallot (2 ounces), finely chopped

1/4 cup finely chopped fresh parsley

2 tablespoons finely chopped fresh tarragon

3/4 teaspoon kosher salt

Freshly ground black pepper to taste

Trim the stems from the morels; finely chop the stems. Reserve the stems and caps separately.

Process the Brie and bread crumbs in a food processor until well mixed and resembling a rough dough. Reserve.

Melt the 2 teaspoons butter in a small frying pan over low heat. Add the shallot. Cook until soft and translucent, for about 5 minutes. Add the chopped morel stems. Cook for 2 minutes. Add the parsley and tarragon. Cook for 1 minute. Transfer to a medium bowl.

Add the bread crumb mixture to the shallot-herb mixture. Season with 1/4 teaspoon salt and a generous amount of pepper. Mix well.

With a demitasse spoon, ice tea spoon or other small spoon, stuff the morels, packing the mixture in gently; do not break the morels.

Melt the remaining 3 tablespoons butter in the smallest frying pan that will hold the morels comfortably in a single layer. Add the morels; turn to coat in butter. Sprinkle with the remaining 1/2 teaspoon salt. Cook over low heat for about 13 minutes, occasionally turning to cook all sides.

Add 3 tablespoons water. Cook for 2 minutes, or until the morels are tender and the stuffing melted.

Serves 4 to 5 as a first course or 10 to 12 as a side dish

Braised Stuffed Mushrooms

Replace the morels with 1 pound medium mushrooms (20 to 22); put 2 teaspoons stuffing in each cap. Melt the 3 tablespoons butter in the smallest frying pan that will hold the mushrooms comfortably. Sprinkle with 1/4 teaspoon salt. Add the mushroom caps, stuffed side up. Cook over low heat for 7 minutes. Add 3 tablespoons water. Cover and cook for 5 to 8 minutes. The mushrooms should be tender and the stuffing melted.

Serves 6 to 7 as a first course, 10 to 12 as an accompaniment

Poached Eggs on Mushroom Duxelles with Hollandaise Sauce

4 large eggs

1 recipe Hollandaise Sauce (page 454)

1 recipe Mushroom Duxelles (page 405)

1/2 teaspoon unsalted butter

Preheat the oven to 325°F.

Poach the eggs according to the directions on page 479. Keep them in a bowl of warm water until needed.

Make the hollandaise sauce. Keep warm. Heat the duxelles.

Butter a 9-inch pie plate or quiche dish with the butter. Make a smooth layer of the duxelles in the pan. With the back of a kitchen spoon, make 4 depressions, each large enough to hold an egg; space them equally from one another and about 1 inch from the edge of the pan.

Drain the eggs; place 1 in each depression. Spoon the sauce over the eggs. Reheat in the oven for a couple of minutes. Spoon some of the hollandaise over each egg and serve, scooping up some of the mushroom with each egg. **Serves 4 as a first course**

Cremini Mushroom Sauce with Cream and Tarragon

In the absence of cremini, make this with regular mushrooms or small portobellos. For an opulent vegetarian meal for four, double the recipe and serve with bulgur and sautéed leaf spinach (page 646). It is a good pasta sauce to start a meal for six people or to serve as a main course for four.

1 tablespoon unsalted butter

1 1/3 pounds cremini mushrooms, stems removed, trimmed and chopped; caps halved and then sliced (about 4 1/2 cups)

2 cups heavy cream

1/4 cup packed fresh tarragon leaves, finely chopped

1 teaspoon kosher salt

Freshly ground black pepper to taste

In a 9-inch skillet, heat the butter over high heat until it starts to foam; do not brown. Add the mushrooms. Cook, stirring regularly, until they brown and release some liquid, about 10 minutes. Reduce the heat to medium-low. Add the heavy cream and tarragon. Cook for 10 minutes, or until the sauce is thick enough to coat a spoon. Remove from the heat. Add the salt and pepper. **Makes 2 cups**

Odd Roots

Burdock, Horseradish, Scorzonera and Salsify

The word "root" is odd, with many meanings and associations—good and bad, and sometimes the opposite of each other. If an animal roots around looking for food, it is a pig. Yet if one roots, it can be that one is establishing permanency in a community. If one is rootless, a settled location or function in life is missing. Words are roots in languages. People who live on roots are metaphorically poor and deprived. However, it is time to root for roots. They are on the food team.

The roots most ordinarily eaten, such as beets, carrots, and parsnips, are discussed in Vegetables of the Mediterranean Basin, Europe and the Arab World. There are many less known that are used in various parts of the world.

Burdock is from northern Europe and Asia, but I have eaten it in Japan, Italy and the United States. Salsify and scorzonera are often confused with each other, even by excellent chefs, although the roots come from different families. This confusion was even rampant in Evelyn's time (see page 416) and is now perpetuated by distributors who mark bags of scorzonera "salsify."

Salsify, also known as oyster plant, is white, while scorzonera, which is primarily Italian, is externally black. Both have the same long pointed shape, which they share with burdock. All of them are very hard to dig, as they cling deeply and tenaciously to the soil. All need to be scrubbed and peeled. Additionally, there is a great similarity in flavor, rather like an artichoke, with burdock having the mildest taste. All can be and are used interchangeably in recipes.

The easiest way to serve horseradish is simply to spoon it out of a jar. The next easiest is to combine prepared horseradish—white, not the red, which is sweet—with whipped cream or sour cream. I am particularly fond of the whipped cream version, which is less caloric because of all the air beaten in. The slight sweetness of the cream also tempers the bite of the horseradish.

Of course, horseradish was not born in a jar, and it is most definitely worth the effort to seek it out fresh. The flavor difference is remarkable. To use, peel the root and grate it on a box grater—or in a food processor, which offers better protection for sensitive eyes. Three tablespoons of freshly grated horseradish will replace a drained four-ounce jar.

Turn to **BURDOCK, HORSERADISH** and **SCORZONERA AND SALSIFY** in the Cook's Guide for how-tos and to the Index for more recipes.

Burdock Tempura

For an all-Asian menu, pair this with the Deep-fried Baby Bok Choy (page 316) and serve with a light sauce on the side. The Japanese Dipping Sauce on page 465 goes well with both.

This does not work well as a side dish; it is better as a first course or hors d'oeuvre. It can be part of a Japanese fritto misto, with other vegetables cooked in tempura, such as lotus root, snow peas, Japanese eggplant, etc.

Vegetable oil for deep-frying

1 recipe Tempura Batter (page 516)

3 burdock roots (about 8 ounces), trimmed and cut into 1-inch pieces (about 1 1/2 cups)

Pour 1½ to 2 inches of oil into a deep saucepan (see Frying, page 512). Meanwhile, make the tempura batter. Dip several pieces of burdock into the batter at a time and drop gently into the oil. Fry for 2 to 3 minutes, until golden brown, turning halfway through to ensure even cooking. With a slotted spoon, remove to a parchment-covered baking sheet. Serve immediately. **Makes about 36 pieces**

Horseradish Custards

Do not try this with prepared horseradish. The pungent sharpness of fresh horseradish is needed to balance the richness of the cream. Surround these unusual and delicate custards with warm asparagus pieces or spears for an elegant first course. A drizzle of Baby Food Tomato Sauce (page 461) is equally good.

If serving the custards as a side dish, pair them with Piselli alla Romana (page 301) or any other simply prepared vegetable to go with meat or fish.

The custard base can be prepared ahead of time, but do not cook until just before serving.

6 ounces fresh horseradish, peeled and grated (about 1½ cups)

1 cup heavy cream

1 cup milk

1 teaspoon kosher salt

6 large egg yolks

1 teaspoon unsalted butter

Place a rack in the center of the oven. Preheat the oven to 325°F.

Put the horseradish, cream and milk in a medium saucepan. Bring to a boil. Reduce the heat and simmer for 10 minutes. Strain through a fine-mesh sieve, pressing down on the pulp to extract as much liquid as possible; discard the pulp. Cool the cream mixture to body temperature so that the yolks will not curdle when added.

Whisk in the salt and yolks. Set aside.

Butter six 2-ounce (¼-cup) ramekins. Line a 12 x 7½-inch glass baking dish with a few pages of newspaper. Set the ramekins on the newspaper and divide the cream mixture evenly among them. Put the baking dish in the oven and pour in enough boiling hot water to reach halfway up sides of the ramekins. Bake for 30 minutes.

Remove the ramekins from the water bath. Run a knife around the edge of each and gently unmold onto a serving platter or individual dishes. Serve immediately.

Serves 6 as a first course or a side dish

Horseradish Custard in Ramekins

This custard is softer and cannot be unmolded. Reduce the horseradish to 4 ounces and the egg yolks to 3. Follow the instructions above for cooking. Serve in the ramekins.

Burdock Kinpara

Kinpara is a traditional Japanese dish made of thinly cut burdock and/or carrots cooked in soy sauce. This unusual version omits the carrots and uses burdock cut into pieces resembling small branches. It's also not as salty. Add more tamari if salt is your preference.

The Japanese commonly wrap burdock inside very thin slices of marinated beef and grill them over charcoal using skewers. Rare roast beef, sliced deli thin, is easier. For a quick hors d'oeuvre, roll the burdock kinpari in the beef, slice the rolls into 1-inch pieces and fasten each with a toothpick (this makes 72 pieces). Serve the sauce alongside in a small bowl for dipping.

3 tablespoons toasted sesame oil

6 burdock roots (about 1 pound), trimmed, each cut crosswise into 3 pieces, and steamed (see the Cook's Guide, page 553)

¼ cup soy sauce, preferably tamari

6 tablespoons mirin

⅛ teaspoon cayenne pepper

3 tablespoons rice wine vinegar

1 tablespoon sesame seeds, toasted

Heat the sesame oil in a pan just large enough to hold the burdock in a single layer. Add the burdock. Cook over high heat, shaking the pan to brown all sides, for about 3 minutes. Add the tamari, mirin and cayenne. Reduce the heat and simmer, turning the burdock from time to time, until the liquid is mostly evaporated and the burdock is covered with a deep brown glaze; this may take up to 30 minutes. Remove the burdock to a bowl.

Add the rice wine vinegar to the pan, scraping up any brown bits. Add the sesame seeds. Simmer a few seconds, then pour over the burdock. Toss to coat. Cool to room temperature. **Makes 2½ cups**

Roasted Burdock and Onions

Both raw and steamed burdock will yield the same results when roasted, making this a convenient way to use up leftovers of this vegetable.

Burdock is a fine substitute for potatoes as a side dish. Garlic cloves can be added or substituted for the onions. The cloves should roast for fifteen minutes if peeled, fifteen minutes longer if unpeeled.

1 pound pearl onions (26 to 30), trimmed
    and peeled

1/4 cup olive oil

9 burdock roots (about 1 1/2 pounds), raw or
    steamed (see headnote), cut crosswise into
    1-inch pieces (about 4 1/2 cups)

Kosher salt and freshly ground black pepper
    to taste

Place a rack in the center of the oven. Preheat the oven to 500°F.

Place the onions in a medium roasting pan. Slick the onions and pan with 3 tablespoons oil. Roast for 15 minutes. Shake the pan vigorously to turn the onions. Roast for another 15 minutes.

Toss the burdock with the remaining 1 tablespoon oil. Add to the pan. Roast for 8 minutes. Turn the burdock and onions. Roast for 8 minutes more, or until tender. Salt and pepper to taste.

Makes 4 to 5 cups; serves 4 to 6 as a side dish

Scorzonera in Lemon-Parsley Sauce

This is a classic Italian method for cooking scorzonera. The egg yolks give the lightly tangy sauce a velvety texture that is rich without being heavy. Serve immediately, as it is very hard to reheat the dish without curdling the yolks.

3 tablespoons olive oil

1 medium onion, finely chopped (about 1 cup)

3/4 cup finely chopped Italian parsley

1 1/2 pounds scorzonera, peeled, trimmed,
    cut across into 1-inch pieces and steamed
    (see the Cook's Guide, page 642)

2 tablespoons all-purpose flour

1 1/2 cups Basic Chicken Stock (page 501),
    Vegetable Broth (page 506) or commercial
    chicken broth

3 egg yolks

2 tablespoons fresh lemon juice

3/4 teaspoon kosher salt

In a medium skillet, heat the oil over medium-low heat. Add the onion. Cook until translucent, for about 4 minutes. Add the parsley and cook for 1 minute. Add the scorzonera and cook for 15 minutes, stirring occasionally.

Stir in the flour, then chicken stock. Cook a few minutes until thickened and the flour no longer tastes raw. Beat the yolks with the lemon juice and salt. Reduce the heat to very low. Stir the yolk mixture into the pan. Cook, stirring, until the sauce is thickened; be careful not to let it curdle. **Makes 3 cups; serves 6 as a side dish**

Braised Scorzonera with Tarragon

This is a French version of the previous scorzonera dish.

3 tablespoons unsalted butter

2 medium shallots, finely chopped (scant 1/2 cup)

1 1/2 pounds scorzonera, peeled, trimmed, cut into
    1-inch pieces and steamed (see the Cook's Guide,
    page 642)

3 tablespoons all-purpose flour

1 1/2 cups Enriched Beef Stock (page 504)

2 tablespoons chopped fresh tarragon

3/4 teaspoon kosher salt

Freshly ground black pepper to taste

In a medium saucepan, melt the butter over medium-low heat. Add the shallots. Cook until translucent. Add the scorzonera, then stir in the flour. Stir in the stock. Cook for 15 minutes, stirring occasionally, until the sauce is reduced and thickened.

Add the tarragon, salt and pepper. **Makes 3 cups; serves 6 as a side dish**

Horseradish Sauce

All of these sauces are excellent accompaniments to beef. The whipped cream horseradish is traditional with smoked or poached fish or chicken.

One 4-ounce bottle prepared horseradish or
3 tablespoons grated peeled fresh horseradish

1 cup heavy cream or sour cream

Place the horseradish in a fine-mesh sieve and set over a bowl and let drain for 15 minutes.

If using heavy cream, whip it to stiff peaks. With a fork, gently combine the whipped cream or sour cream with the horseradish. If making more than an hour ahead, refrigerate. **Makes 1 cup if using sour cream, 2 cups if using whipped cream**

Horseradish Sauce 2
Purée the drained or fresh horseradish with 4 teaspoons white wine vinegar and 4 teaspoons heavy cream. Whip 2 cups heavy cream until it forms soft peaks. With a fork, gently combine the whipped cream with the horseradish purée. **Makes 4 cups**

Horseradish Hollandaise Sauce
Now, this is truly spiffy and I think an invention.

Purée the drained or fresh horseradish with 1½ tablespoons white wine vinegar and 1½ tablespoons heavy cream. Reserve.

Prepare 1 recipe Hollandaise Sauce (page 454) in the food processor, omitting the mustard, pepper and lemon juice. Scrape the sauce into a bowl and whisk until body temperature.

Whisk in the horseradish purée. Serve immediately. **Makes 2½ cups**

Beef in Horseradish Dressing
Mix together the drained horseradish, 1½ teaspoons lemon juice and 1 cup Classic Mayonnaise (page 455), Cooked-Yolk Mayonnaise (page 455) or commercial mayonnaise. Add kosher salt and freshly ground black pepper to taste. Toss the dressing with 3 cups cooked beef cubes and 2 tablespoons chopped fresh chives. Serve over 3 cups washed and trimmed spinach leaves. **Serves 2 as a first course**

Fresh Applesauce with Horseradish

This is a quick and good applesauce. Greening or early acidic Macs are best.

8 apples, cored, peeled and cut into eighths

4 tablespoons unsalted butter

1 scant teaspoon kosher salt

1/2 cup prepared horseradish, drained

In a large saucepan, cook the apples with the butter and 2 tablespoons water for 15 to 20 minutes, or until tender.

Place the apple mixture in a food processor and purée. When smooth, add the salt and horseradish and pulse to mix. **Makes about 5 cups**

Lettuces

Salads, crisp and summery, deep tasting and rewarding, as first courses, on the side and as main dishes, are some of my favorites. The wide array of lettuces are their most usual starting point. There are many other ingredients and ideas for salads scattered throughout the book, in particular for tomatoes, cucumbers and chicories.

Other elements commonly enjoyed in salads are beets; carrots; celery; members of the onion family, especially onions, chives and garlic; peppers; pea tendrils; hops and vine tendrils; and radishes. Turn to their individual chapters in the book, to specific vegetables in the Cook's Guide and to the Index.

Bibb Lettuce
with Soy-Sesame Vinaigrette

This is one of my favorite salads. Toss the leaves so as not to crush them or make them soggy.

VINAIGRETTE

1/4 cup olive oil

2 1/2 tablespoons tarragon vinegar

2 1/2 tablespoons soy sauce, preferably tamari

Scant 1/8 teaspoon toasted sesame oil

1/8 teaspoon kosher salt

Freshly ground black pepper to taste

1/8 teaspoon dry mustard

1/4 teaspoon tightly packed chopped fresh
   tarragon leaves (optional)

6 heads Bibb lettuce, leaves separated,
   washed and dried

Combine all the vinaigrette ingredients and mix well. Pour over the lettuce and toss to coat.

Serves 6 as a first course

Iceberg Lettuce Wedges
with Blue Cheese Dressing

If serving fewer people, buy a smaller head of iceberg and cut the dressing recipe in half, or make all the dressing and keep the leftover for another day.

DRESSING

2/3 cup commercial mayonnaise

1/4 cup sour cream

2 tablespoons white wine vinegar

2 teaspoons Worcestershire sauce

Large pinch of cayenne pepper

1/2 cup finely crumbled blue cheese, plus,
   if desired, more coarsely crumbled blue cheese
   for serving

Kosher salt if needed

1 large head iceberg lettuce

Stir together the mayonnaise, sour cream, vinegar, Worcestershire and cayenne pepper in a small bowl. Stir in the 1/2 cup blue cheese. Taste and add salt if necessary. The dressing keeps, refrigerated, for up to 1 week.

Remove any wilted or yellow leaves from the lettuce. Cut out the core with a paring knife. Cut the head into 8 wedges. Serve the lettuce wedges on individual plates, spooning some of the dressing over each. Scatter a little crumbled blue cheese over each, if desired.

Serves 8 as a first course

Salmon Wrapped
in Lettuce Leaves

It isn't even necessary to fuss with a fancy filling, as this recipe shows. Serve with Southeast Asian Dipping Sauce (page 465) or Semi-Thai Sauce (page 467).

4 medium heads Boston lettuce
   (about 8 ounces each)

1 pound salmon fillet

Prepare the lettuce: Carefully separate the lettuce leaves. Cut each leaf in half, removing the center rib. Trim the heavy white sections from each half, leaving a circle of lettuce approximately 3 1/2 inches in diameter. Set aside (do not blanch).

Cut the salmon into 1 x 1 x 1/2-inch pieces. Place a piece of salmon on each piece of lettuce

The World of John Evelyn: Lettices and Herbes

One of the authors of the past whom I would like to have known is John Evelyn. He had a wide range of interests, was instrumental in establishing the Royal Society, wrote a brilliant diary of many volumes that rivals the better-known one of Samuel Pepys in recording the life of his times and published in 1699 *Acetaria: A Discourse of Sallets*. He traveled widely, avoiding the political upheavals of his time, and learned much about plants and gardening in all the places to which he went. As far as we know, he was always a passionate gardener, and when his older brother died, leaving him the family property, he had ample space and resources to indulge that passion.

He wrote about trees and other plants as well, but the *Acetaria,* of which I am lucky enough to have a first edition, is a slim volume rich in information about edible plants. To a great extent it follows in the older tradition of the herbal, explaining, as he knew them, the effects of the various plants on the human system. He was a child of his own age, or perhaps a slightly earlier one, in that he still saw the body as made up of humors that could be balanced by foods. It was a system not so different from the Chinese one.

His book is dense with classical quotations. It is not a recipe book, although it has many indications as to the proper combination of ingredients and dressings. Evelyn writes: "Sallets in general consist of certain esculent [edible] plants and herbs, improved by culture, industry and art of the gard'ner: or, as others say, they are composition of edule [softened, made more palatable] plants and roots of several kinds to be eaten raw or green, blanch'd or candied; simple, and per se [on their own], or intermingl'd with others according to the season." Although he here restricts the meaning to raw plants, in the book he mentions plants, such as beets, that are cooked before being added to salad and talks about wild plants that have not been civilized.

While he gives several derivations of the word "acetaria," it is commonly used in Italian cookery for salads with vinegar (acid) in the dressing, which seems to make a good deal of sense.

We have hybridized many plants and imported many from other countries and climates, but the vast array of plants Evelyn mentions puts us to shame in their variety of local and seasonal. While there has just been a recent trend to use pea shoots in salads or as garnishes, for example, Evelyn mentions them along with a number of other tendrils as salad components.

He also mentions a variety of lettuces among the salad greens. While there is a clear distinction between herbs and lettuces, the distinction between them was not as sharp at that time, and herbs were not seen as seasonings but themselves as part of the salads. It gives one to understand the pun in the title of the play *Lettice and Lovage* by Peter Shaffer.

The distinction between lettuces and chicories was more fluid than that between herbs and lettuces. I keep them apart; see the Index for chicory recipes.

M. Grieve was a lady whose *Culinary Herbs and Condiments* came out in 1931; I use the 1933 edition. Although ostensibly writing about herbs, she also pays attention to the lettuces. She has more modern information with some recipes and much information on growing. I recommend it highly.

G.A.C. Herklots's *Vegetables in South-East Asia*, published in 1972, is a mine of information that also credits the sources of his prodigious research. He touches on vegetables of other than Asian origins as well, commenting on their suitability for being grown in his chosen climate.

Evidently, with Evelyn we entered a period in which salads were taken as a fit subject for good minds. Perhaps the best-known piece of writing is Sydney Smith's "A Recipe for Salad," of 1796, which gives a fine recipe for dressing and ends with the famous lines:

"Serenely full, the epicure would say,
'Fate cannot harm me, I have dined to-day.'"

Poet William Cowper can talk of "a cheap but wholesome salad from the brook." With *The Tale of Flopsy Bunnies* of 1909, Beatrix Potter returns us to the world of Evelyn's properties of the ingredients for salads: "It is said that the effect of eating too much lettuce is soporific." In fact, the bunnies, charming plagues of the garden, are correct, as is proverbial usage. The milky sap of lettuce stems is soporific, which is why salad was traditionally served at the end of the meal. I still prefer it there, but I know that I am bucking a trend. Salad is either now the fancy *salade composé* or a way for a restaurant to slow us down and fill us up between first and main courses.

This section of my book is not poetry or philosophy or medicine, but testimony to my love of salads.

leaf. Fold the edges of the leaf over the salmon. Place seam side down in the top of a two-part steamer, or in a bamboo steamer rack or on a plate in a bamboo steamer. Fill the bottom of the steamer pan or a pan large enough to hold the bamboo or steaming rack with water; the water should not touch the rack. Bring to a boil. Place the salmon on top, cover and steam until the salmon is completely cooked, for about 10 minutes.

Makes about 48 pieces (can be divided easily)

Caesar Salad

Multiply the salad by only as many servings as you need. Because of the egg, this dressing should be used the same day it is made.

DRESSING

1 egg

$^1/_2$ cup olive oil

$^3/_4$ teaspoon fresh lemon juice

1 teaspoon kosher salt

$^1/_2$ teaspoon crushed garlic, or to taste

$^1/_2$ teaspoon tarragon vinegar

$^1/_8$ teaspoon anchovy paste

Freshly ground black pepper to taste

4 cups loosely packed torn romaine lettuce

2 tablespoons coarsely grated Parmesan cheese

3 Garlic Croutons (page 511)

For the dressing, place the egg in a saucepan of water to cover. Bring to a boil. Turn off the heat and let sit for 2 minutes. Immediately run the egg under cold water.

Peel the egg; discard the egg white. Beat the coddled egg yolk in a mixing bowl until smooth. Beat in the oil, lemon juice, salt, garlic,

vinegar, anchovy paste and pepper. Let stand for at least 20 minutes for the flavors to blend.

For the salad, toss the romaine, Parmesan and croutons with the dressing until thoroughly blended. **Serves 2 as a first course**

Julienne of Five Lettuce Soup

Just before my lettuce bolts in the hot August sun, I have more lettuces of different kinds than I can use. The Haitians recommend lettuce soup to calm the stomach and the nerves. This soup does that and uses up the extra lettuce as well. If lettuce isn't growing, excellent varieties can be found in the stores. Different lettuces can be substituted, but try to preserve the ratio of bitter to sweet and soft to firm.

1 cup packed romaine lettuce leaves (ribs removed)

1 cup packed Boston lettuce leaves

1 cup packed leaf lettuce

1 cup packed escarole leaves

$^1/_2$ cup packed chicory leaves

2 tablespoons unsalted butter

5 cups Basic Chicken Stock (page 501), Roasted Chicken Stock (page 502) or commercial chicken broth, heated until hot

$^1/_2$ cup heavy cream

6 egg yolks

1$^1/_2$ teaspoons kosher salt

$^1/_4$ teaspoon freshly ground black pepper

Wash the lettuces and dry well. Cut into $^1/_8$-inch strips: This is easiest to do if you stack several leaves at a time, roll into a tight wad and slice them across. You can also use the medium slicing disk of a food processor.

Melt the butter in a medium saucepan. Add the lettuces and toss with the butter. When the lettuces are wilted, add the chicken stock and cook over medium heat for about 10 minutes, or until the toughest leaves are tender.

In a small bowl, mix the cream with the egg yolks. Gradually stir a small amount of the hot soup into the cream mixture to slowly raise the temperature of the egg yolks. Keep adding soup until the mixture is warm. Whisk the egg yolk mixture into the soup and cook, stirring constantly, without letting the soup boil, until it thickens enough to coat the back of the spoon. Season with the salt and pepper.

Serves 6 to 8 as a first course

Braised Lettuce

Lettuce is another of those vegetables like cucumbers that Americans use mainly in salads. It is surprisingly good cooked, something the clever French have known for a long time. Here is a dish that looks and tastes so much better made in the microwave oven than conventionally and is so much quicker that I really cannot imagine doing it any other way ever again.

If using meat glaze, note that ready-made meat glaze (sometimes called demi-glace) can nowadays be purchased in specialty food stores and some groceries and butcher shops. It can also be made from scratch by reducing homemade beef or chicken stock until syrupy.

4 tablespoons unsalted butter

1 cup Basic Chicken Stock (page 501), Roasted Chicken Stock (page 502) or commercial chicken broth

$^1/_2$ cup Meat or Chicken Glaze (page 505) or commercial meat or chicken glaze (optional)

1 $^1/_2$ teaspoons kosher salt

4 heads Boston lettuce (8 ounces each), large outer leaves removed and discarded, washed and heads cut in half lengthwise

1 tablespoon cornstarch, dissolved in 2 tablespoons cold water

Microwave the butter and broth in a 14 x 11 x 2-inch dish, uncovered, at 100% for 3 minutes. Remove from the microwave oven. Stir in the meat glaze, if using, and salt. Arrange the lettuce halves in the dish with the core ends pointing toward the outside of the dish. Cover tightly with microwave plastic wrap. Cook at 100% for 15 minutes. Prick the plastic to release steam.

Remove from the oven. Uncover and remove lettuce to a warmed serving platter, folding any ragged leaf edges under. Stir the cornstarch mixture into the liquid in the dish. Cook, uncovered, at 100% power for 7 minutes.

Remove from the oven. Spoon the sauce over the lettuce and serve immediately.

Serves 8 as a side dish

NOTE: *To serve 4:* Halve all the ingredients and omit the cornstarch. Cook the lettuce in an 11 x 8½ x 2-inch dish for 8 minutes. Finish cooking the sauce for 4 minutes.

To serve 2, Quarter all the ingredients and omit the cornstarch. Cook the lettuce in a 9½ x 7 x 1¾-inch oval dish for 5 minutes 30 seconds. Finish cooking the sauce for 4 minutes.

Iceberg Lettuce

Bravely, I admit I like iceberg (Simpson) lettuce. I buy it; I eat it. I eat it the way I did as a child, cut into crisp wedges and slathered with delicious tacky Russian dressing made with about two parts commercial mayonnaise to one part commercial chili sauce. I eat this salad with a knife and fork. I wouldn't think of putting another kind of lettuce on my tuna sandwich.

Even worse from the food snobs' point of view, I often enjoy a salad, made in winter, with torn chunks of iceberg lettuce, lots of thinly sliced white onions and a dressing of olive oil, lemon juice, salt and pepper. This salad is even better after it is allowed to get a little soggy for twenty minutes or so. If you want to add some Boston lettuce, feel free.

By this point, I have probably lost all my credentials as a gourmet or even a good cook. In my defense, I note that while iceberg lettuce has lost all cachet as a salad green, even the snobbiest still seem willing to use it to wrap Chinese minced squab or Thai specialties, or, shredded, as a garnish for Southwestern food.

Aside from the carefully shielded red radicchios, blanched endive and expensively transported lettuce from distant soils, by late fall most of us can look forward only to deficiencies in the salad greens department. Lettuce that has been packed in ice for shipping has strange tastes and textures. Plastic-encased baby lettuce leaves are very expensive although a work saver as they don't need washing.

Maybe this salad situation will get some people to look at iceberg lettuce again. Because it keeps very well, it is available all winter. It is almost never dirty. All that has to be done to it is to insert a sharp knife at the stem end and make a deep conical incision so that the core can be removed—as if cleaning a cabbage. Then remove any browned, limp or faded external leaves. The lettuce should be torn apart or separated into leaves, depending on the way it is to be used. The only time it is cut with a knife is for those old-fashioned hearts-of-lettuce wedges.

Of course, one can go too far with iceberg lettuce. It should not be ubiquitous. In a very trendy, resuscitated restaurant in London, I was served a Caesar salad with iceberg lettuce. No, no, no . . . I am a purist here at least. It must be romaine or, as the Brits would call it, Cos. Midwinter, romaine gets very large and darkly green. This does not make an ideal Caesar salad either. Self-restraint must be exercised. Use only the inner pale and crisp leaves. The dark leaves that are left over make a terrific soup if finely shredded, wilted in a little butter with some thinly sliced onion and then simmered with good chicken broth. It can be puréed if desired and salt and pepper added as wanted. Cream-soup freaks can stir in some cream whisked with an egg yolk and then simmer until thickened.

While a Caesar would never be a health food salad, it can be made relatively safe by using vinegar instead of lemon juice, then using one egg and thinning the egg mixture, after cooking, with a little water.

Speaking of fat-loaded dressings, I have another far-from-fashionable favorite that does wonderfully on iceberg lettuce wedges. Again, it's based on mayonnaise from the jar. Just whisk in some good creamy blue cheese, leaving some chunks but no large cubes. Use a midwestern blue like Navoo, or some Gorgonzola. Don't use Roquefort—it's too salty—or Stilton (a waste).

Having burned my respectability bridges, I will now defend American mayonnaise. It isn't olive oil–rich and eggy like homemade and respectable mayonnaise, but, on that tuna sandwich—yes, canned tuna—I want my

childhood mayo. The same holds true for deviled eggs, egg salad, many kinds of chicken salad, BLTs, club sandwiches and my summer favorite, the eaten-over-the-sink sliced tomato and mayo sandwich on soft white commercial bread. It's more than nostalgia—it still tastes wonderful.

If I could peek in the refrigerators of my purist friends, I wonder how many would reveal the familiar fat jar. Before I learned about canning, I used to boil the jars and lids and save them for summer preserves. Now I use them only for refrigerator storage; I never throw them out.

Even if I convince no one to go for iceberg lettuce and mayo, I may give heart to those, like me, still sneaking these delights in private. Would I serve the hearts-of-lettuce-with-Russian at a dinner party? No, I am not retro enough for that. I probably wouldn't serve it to my family either, because of the fat; but they have often eaten the iceberg lettuce salad in winter. Bravely, if there is no reason not to, let's make "Eat Iceberg" buttons and wear them in public.

Weeds and Odd Leaves

Amaranth, Purslane, Samphire, Sorrel, Arugula, Dandelion Greens, Chrysanthemum Greens and Fiddlehead Ferns

Someone—sadly I do not remember who—wrote that weeds were simply plants growing in the wrong place. Emerson said a weed is "a plant whose virtues have not yet been discovered." In America, those of us with lawns certainly consider dandelions as weeds. But English settlers nostalgic for their garden green, the dandelion, imported it to put in salads and to cook as a spring green. Some such as dock and plantain (the weed, not the relative of the banana) were clearly, to me, invasive commoners.

When I was growing up, spring was sure to bring small crowds of black-clad ladies to roadsides.

I didn't know then that they were looking for wild plants to harvest.

Obviously, almost all the basic vegetables started out as weeds and were brought in from the wild only to be married to other weeds or selectively bred in a historical eugenics program. A few weeds were left to fester in the wild—see Thistles, page 229.

All around the Mediterranean, in India and in parts of America where natives of these areas have settled, spring will find foragers moving along roadsides, combing the new growth for young weeds. In Greece, a whole dish, particularly enjoyed during Lent, is made from wild greens and is called horta. There is a special dish for them in Italy, too, torta pasqualina, an Easter speciality.

Turn to AMARANTH, PURSLANE, SAMPHIRE, SORREL, ARUGULA, DANDELION GREENS, CHRYSANTHEMUM GREENS and FIDDLEHEAD FERNS in the Cook's Guide for how-tos and to the Index for more recipes.

Chinese Soup

Not really Chinese, but very good.

> 4 cups Basic Chicken Stock (page 501), Roasted Chicken Stock (page 502) or commercial chicken broth
>
> 2 Chinese eggplants (each 5 inches long), trimmed and cut on the diagonal into 1/4-inch slices
>
> 2 packed cups red amaranth leaves
>
> 1 teaspoon plum sauce
>
> 2 teaspoons light soy sauce
>
> 1 1/2 cups diced (3/4-inch) soft silk tofu, at room temperature

Put the stock in a medium saucepan and heat over low heat. Add the eggplant. Simmer gently until the marbling pattern in the eggplant is clearly discernible on both sides. Stir in the amaranth. Continue simmering gently for 3 minutes.

Stir in the plum sauce and soy sauce, then the tofu. Serve in white bowls.

Serves 4 as a first course

Salad of Potatoes and Purslane with a Tahini-Citrus Dressing

This unusual salad makes a festive first course, or it can be doubled to make a lovely main course for four.

> 2 small or 1 1/2 medium-large floury potatoes (12 to 13 ounces total), peeled and cut into 1/4-inch dice (about 2 cups)
>
> 1 recipe Tahini-Citrus Dressing (page 452)
>
> 1 pound purslane, roots trimmed, tough stems discarded and cut into 1-inch pieces (about 8 cups)
>
> 4 Oeufs Mollets (page 480)
>
> 4 teaspoons black sesame seeds

Put the potatoes in a medium saucepan. Cover with water by 2 inches. Bring to a boil, reduce the heat and simmer for 8 minutes, or until the potatoes are tender. Drain. Cool to room temperature.

Toss the potatoes with the dressing. Divide the purslane evenly among four plates. Place one-quarter of the dressed potatoes in the center of each plate. Slice the eggs in half lengthwise and place 2 halves on each plate. Sprinkle with the sesame seeds.

Serves 4 as a first course

Simple Soup with Purslane

It is said that purslane can be used as a soup thickener in the same manner as okra. In actuality, its thickening effect is very slight. Use it for the flavor instead. It imbues soup with a delicate leafy quality.

As there are only two ingredients plus seasonings in this recipe, a good-flavored stock is essential.

> 4 cups Basic Chicken Stock (page 501), Vegetable Broth (page 506) or Konbu Dashi (page 507)
>
> 1/4 pound purslane, roots trimmed, tough stems discarded and cut into 1-inch pieces (about 2 cups)
>
> Kosher salt and freshly ground black pepper to taste

In a medium saucepan, bring the stock to a boil. Add the purslane. Cook for 1 to 3 minutes, until wilted and tender. Salt and pepper to taste. **Makes 4 1/4 cups**

Pickled Samphire

While it is sometimes possible to buy samphire (see the Cook's Guide, page 640), usually I get it by picking it. In either case, it is useful to preserve—pickle—as much as is not being used immediately. The pickled samphire can be kept for up to a year. It should be rinsed well under cold running water and blotted dry before using. Serve it at room temperature or use it in any recipe that calls for it. This recipe is easily multiplied.

> One 1-pint canning jar with a two-piece lid
>
> 1 1/2 cups tarragon vinegar
>
> 1/4 pound samphire (about 1 1/3 cups)

Sterilize the canning jar (see page 91).

In a small saucepan, bring the vinegar to a boil. Add the samphire. Stir briefly to submerge it in the liquid. Remove from the heat. Pour into the jar, pushing down on the samphire; a large-mouthed funnel is helpful here.

Cover and process the jar according to the directions on page 91. Store for at least 1 day before using; it will keep for up to a year. **Makes 1 pint**

Risotto with Asparagus, Sorrel and Samphire

The asparagus will not be crisp in this green-hued risotto. The tart sorrel, the salty samphire and the rich asparagus all melt into a delightful whole.

Be sure to use only unsalted stock.

> 5 tablespoons olive oil
>
> 1/2 cup thinly sliced scallion whites, plus 3/4 cup thinly sliced scallion greens
>
> 2 cups arborio or other risotto rice
>
> 1/2 cup slightly acidic white wine or flat Champagne
>
> 5 1/2 cups Basic Chicken Stock (page 501), Asparagus Stock (page 506) or unsalted commercial chicken broth, heated
>
> 8 cups packed sorrel leaves, cut across into 1/4-inch strips (about 1 1/4 pounds)
>
> 1 pound asparagus, woody stems snapped off, stalks peeled and cut across into 1-inch pieces
>
> 4 1/2 ounces samphire (about 1 1/2 cups)
>
> Kosher salt and freshly ground black pepper to taste
>
> 1 cup freshly grated Parmesan cheese (optional)

Put the oil and scallion whites in a large deep unreactive pan. Wilt the scallions slowly over medium heat. When the scallions begin to sizzle but not brown, increase the heat to high. Add the rice; toss to coat with oil. Cook and stir until the grains turn white and opaque. Add wine; cook until absorbed. Reduce heat to medium-high.

Add ½ cup stock. Cook, stirring well, until the rice has absorbed most of the stock. Add another ½ cup stock and repeat the process, making sure the liquid is mostly absorbed before each addition of stock. Continue until the rice has cooked for about 10 minutes and absorbed 3 cups stock.

Add the sorrel in 3 batches, stirring from the bottom and scraping the corners of the pan to prevent sticking (using two utensils is easiest). Add ½ cup stock to keep the rice moist. Cook and stir until the sorrel has turned color and is limp. Add the asparagus. Continue to cook and stir for 4 minutes, adding small amounts of stock as necessary and scraping the pan bottom. Add 1 cup of the samphire. Cook and stir for 2 minutes. Either stop cooking at this point and reheat later or continue to cook, stirring and adding remaining broth ½ cup at a time.

If reheating, place the pan over low heat and warm the risotto, stirring. Increase heat to medium-high. Add remaining broth ½ cup at a time.

Season with salt and pepper. Mix in the scallion greens. Serve with the remaining samphire on top and Parmesan on the side, if desired.

Makes 9 cups; serves 8 as a first course, 4 as a main course

Rich Sorrel Soup

Serve this soup hot or cold. I find that if I try to keep it in quart jars in the refrigerator, it disappears behind my back. In any case, the soup tastes better after a full twenty-four hours in the refrigerator.

Homemade stock without fat is preferred for this recipe, but a good commercial one may be used.

2 handfuls sorrel leaves (about 2 cups loosely packed)

3 tablespoons unsalted butter

5 cups Basic Chicken Stock (page 501), Roasted Chicken Stock (page 502) or commercial chicken broth

5 egg yolks

1¹⁄₂ cups heavy cream

Roll the sorrel leaves up 4 or 5 at a time and cut them by hand into thin strips. Or bundle them into a compact ball and place in the feed tube of a food processor fitted with the thin slicing blade. With the plunger in place, process quickly.

Melt the butter in a 1-quart nonreactive saucepan. Add the sorrel and stir with a spoon until limp and concentrated. Pour in the chicken stock. Bring to a boil, then lower the heat to a simmer Let cook gently for 20 minutes.

If planning to serve the soup hot, do this just before you are ready to serve; if serving it cold, continue without stopping: Beat the egg yolks and cream together in a bowl. Slowly spoon in some of the hot soup, whisking constantly, until about one-third of the soup has been added and has raised the temperature of the egg yolks. Now, while whisking the soup, slowly pour in the egg yolk mixture. Cook just until the soup thickens slightly. Serve immediately, or, to serve the soup cold, stir frequently while it cools, then refrigerate. **Makes 6 cups**

Sorrel Soup with Potato

Instead of being thickened with eggs, this more robust soup uses flour (in the béchamel sauce) and potatoes.

4 tablespoons unsalted butter

1/2 cup chopped onion

1/2 pound sorrel leaves

4 cups Basic Chicken Stock (page 501), Roasted Chicken Stock (page 502) or commercial chicken broth

1 1/2 cups diced (1/2-inch) peeled floury potatoes (about 8 ounces)

1 recipe Sorrel Béchamel Sauce (page 428)

1 cup heavy cream

1/2 teaspoon kosher salt

1/8 teaspoon freshly ground black pepper

Melt the butter in a medium nonreactive saucepan. Add the onions and cook until soft and translucent. Add the sorrel leaves and cook until wilted, for 6 to 8 minutes. Add the chicken stock and bring to a boil. Reduce the heat to a simmer. Add the potatoes. Cook until the potatoes are tender, for about 15 minutes.

With a slotted spoon, remove the potatoes to a food processor. Add 1/2 cup of the cooking liquid, and process until smooth. Return the purée to the pan and mix well. Add the béchamel sauce and cream, stir and bring to a simmer. Add the salt and pepper.

Serves 6 to 8 as a first course

Salmon with Sorrel Soup

Not necessarily a soup in the true sense of the word, this dish certainly has too much sauce to be served any other way than in a bowl with a spoon. Make sure to cut the sorrel across the leaves, not along the grain, so that the ribs are cut into small pieces.

One 18-ounce salmon head, cut into 4 or 5 pieces

1 small onion (about 4 ounces), cut into quarters

2 cloves garlic, smashed and peeled

1 pound salmon fillet, about 1 inch thick, any pinbones removed with a pair of pliers

1/4 pound sorrel, stems removed and cut into very thin strips (about 1 1/2 cups packed)

1 teaspoon kosher salt

Freshly ground black pepper to taste

1/2 cup heavy cream

Place the salmon head and 6 cups water in a medium nonreactive saucepan. Bring to a boil. Lower the heat and simmer for 1 hour.

Add the onion and garlic and simmer for another 50 minutes, or until the salmon head is falling apart.

Place the salmon fillet flesh side down in the pan. Cover and simmer for 8 minutes. The fish will be medium-rare. Remove it to a plate, using a flat spatula to keep the piece whole; set the pan aside. Allow the salmon to cool for a few minutes and remove the skin. Cut into 4 pieces.

Strain the stock through a sieve; there should be 2 cups. Return to the pan, along with the sorrel and salt. Bring to a boil. Lower the heat and simmer for 5 minutes. Add the pepper and cream. Simmer for 2 minutes.

Place a piece of fish in the bottom of each bowl and pour 1/2 cup sauce over the fish.

Serves 4 as a first course

Spring Vegetable Stew with Sorrel

The sorrel gives a small acid surprise to the stew. Be careful to avoid using an aluminum pan.

To serve as a main course for two, double the recipe and serve with rice.

- 1/4 cup confectioners' sugar
- 1 teaspoon kosher salt
- 6 baby white turnips (each about 1 1/2 inches wide), trimmed and peeled
- 5 very young carrots, peeled, trimmed and each cut crosswise into 4 equal pieces
- 6 very small waxy new potatoes (7 to 8 ounces total), cut in half or quartered, depending on size
- 3 large shallots, peeled and halved, or 6 small shallots, peeled and trimmed
- 3 tablespoons unsalted butter
- 6 very young radishes, trimmed and halved lengthwise
- 1/2 pound sorrel, stemmed and cut across into 1/4-inch strips (about 3 cups packed)
- Freshly ground black pepper to taste

Combine the sugar and salt in a paper bag. Put in the turnips, carrots, potatoes and shallots. Close the bag and shake vigorously to coat the vegetables.

Melt the butter in a large skillet. Add the coated vegetables. Cook over high heat, stirring continuously and scraping the bottom and sides of the pan to prevent burning, until the vegetables are browned, for about 10 minutes. Pour in 1/2 cup water. Scrape up any brown bits stuck to the pan. Add the radishes. Cover, reduce the heat to low and simmer for 10 minutes, or until the vegetables are soft.

Add the sorrel and 1/4 cup water. Gently toss over high heat until the sorrel has wilted and turned color. Season with pepper.

Makes 3 cups; serves 6 as a side dish

Sautéed Spinach and Sorrel

Don't call me at 9 P.M. to tell me that your wonderful vegetable is a noxiously colored mess. I am issuing a warning: Only nonreactive surfaces—i.e., not aluminum—need apply.

After washing the spinach, shake off any excess water, but do not blot it dry. The excess water clinging to the spinach will evaporate over heat and cook the spinach without the addition of oil.

This versatile side dish is very light. Add some crème fraîche to make it more substantial. It also freezes well and makes a flavorful soup base.

- 1 shallot, finely chopped (about 3 tablespoons)
- 2 tablespoons olive oil
- 1 bunch fresh parsley, leaves only, chopped (a generous 1/2 cup)
- 2 pounds sorrel, stemmed and cut across into 1/4-inch strips (about 10 cups packed)
- 1 teaspoon kosher salt
- 2 pounds curly spinach, stemmed and cut into 1/4-inch strips (about 12 1/2 cups packed)

In a large nonreactive pan, cook the shallots in the oil over medium-low heat until translucent. Add the parsley and sorrel. Increase the heat to medium-high. Cook until the sorrel has just wilted and changed color, for 5 to 6 minutes. Add 1/2 teaspoon salt. Reserve.

Put a large saucepan over medium heat and add the spinach in 3 batches, continuously turning it up from the bottom and allowing each batch to wilt before adding the next. Remove from the heat as soon as all the leaves have wilted and turned a bright green. Drain in a sieve, pushing down on the spinach until mostly dry.

Add the spinach to the sorrel mixture. Add the remaining ½ teaspoon salt, and heat through. **Makes 3⅓ cups**

Creamed Spinach and Sorrel
If the vegetables were made ahead of time, gently heat through in a saucepan. Stir in ⅔ cup crème fraîche, ¾ teaspoon kosher salt and freshly ground black pepper to taste. Cook over low heat until the crème fraîche is completely absorbed. **Makes 3⅓ cups**

Shrimp and Asparagus with Sorrel

The acidity of the sorrel enlivens this simple spring dish.

3 tablespoons unsalted butter

5 ounces sorrel, stemmed and cut across into very thin strips (about 3 cups)

2 pounds asparagus, woody stems broken off, stalks peeled and cut across into 1½-inch lengths

1½ pounds medium shrimp, peeled and, if desired, deveined, or 1¼ pounds cleaned medium shrimp

1 teaspoon kosher salt

Freshly ground black pepper to taste

4 cups hot Basic White Rice (page 489)

Melt the butter in a large nonreactive frying pan over low heat. Add the sorrel and cook, stirring occasionally, for 2 to 3 minutes, until it is completely wilted.

Increase the heat to medium. Add the asparagus and shrimp. Cook for 2 minutes, stirring, or until the shrimp begin to change color. Add ½ cup water and cover. Cook, stirring once, for 5 minutes. The shrimp should be cooked through but not tough, and the asparagus tender.

Season with the salt and pepper. Serve over the rice. **Serves 4 as a main course**

Sorrel Béchamel Sauce

A terrific sauce with simply cooked chicken, a start on sorrel soup or, with a vegetarian broth, a summer topping for steamed vegetables.

4 tablespoons unsalted butter

2 cups sorrel leaves, stemmed and cut across into very thin strips

¾ cup Basic Chicken Stock (page 501), Roasted Chicken Stock (page 502) or commercial chicken broth, or as needed

2 tablespoons all-purpose flour

¾ cup milk

⅛ teaspoon cayenne pepper

½ teaspoon kosher salt

⅛ teaspoon freshly ground black pepper

In a nonreactive skillet, melt 2 tablespoons of the butter over medium-low heat. Add the sorrel and cook, stirring occasionally, until wilted, for about 10 minutes. Add the chicken stock and simmer over low heat for 20 minutes, or until the stock is almost completely evaporated.

Meanwhile, in a small saucepan, melt the remaining 2 tablespoons butter. Add the flour and cook over low heat for 5 minutes, stirring. Slowly add the milk, whisking briskly to prevent lumps; be sure to scrape the corners, where lumps can hide. Increase the heat to medium. Cook for several minutes, stirring occasionally, until thickened. Add the cayenne, salt and pepper.

Stir the sorrel mixture into the sauce. If the mixture is too thick, add a little more chicken stock. **Makes 1 1/2 cups**

Arugula, Fennel and Hazelnut Salad

Use the kind of baby arugula sold in bags or the curliest young, tender arugula, torn into small pieces.

1/3 cup hazelnuts

1/3 cup olive oil

2 tablespoons fresh lemon juice

1 teaspoon kosher salt

1/4 teaspoon freshly ground black pepper

6 cups (about 5 ounces) baby arugula

1 small fennel bulb, trimmed, quartered, cored and very thinly sliced

1 cup Parmesan shards (made by shaving a chunk of Parmesan cheese with a vegetable peeler)

Toast and peel the hazelnuts (see Artichoke Hazelnut Soup, page 236). Whack them, a few at a time, with the bottom of a small saucepan to smash them coarsely. Set aside.

Whisk the olive oil, lemon juice, salt and pepper together in a serving bowl. Add the arugula, fennel and hazelnuts and toss to coat with dressing. Add the Parmesan, toss again and serve. **Serves 4 as a first course**

Arugula, Tuna and White Bean Salad

This is a large amount of salad, good for a party. Make only half the amount for a smaller group.

3/4 cup small white beans, such as navy beans or Great Northern, soaked and cooked (see the Cook's Guide, page 540), seasoned with salt and cooled to tepid, or one 19-ounce can cannellini beans, rinsed and drained

Two 6-ounce cans tuna, preferably Italian packed in olive oil, drained and flaked

1/2 small red onion, very thinly sliced

1/2 cup chopped roasted plum tomatoes (see the Cook's Guide, page 661) or 1 cup diced ripe tomatoes

1/2 cup thinly sliced inner celery stalks and leaves

1/3 cup olive oil

3 tablespoons fresh lemon juice

Kosher salt and freshly ground black pepper to taste

One 5-ounce bag baby arugula, washed and dried

Drain the beans and transfer to a large serving bowl. Add the tuna, red onion, tomatoes, celery, olive oil and lemon juice. Toss gently to coat the beans and vegetables with the dressing. Season with salt and pepper. The salad can be prepared to this point up to 2 hours before serving. Cover and let stand at room temperature.

Add the arugula to the bowl. Season lightly with salt and pepper and toss. Serve immediately. **Makes 12 cups; serves 12 as a first course or a side dish, 6 as a main course**

Penne with Dandelion Greens and Garlic

3 cups (8 ounces) penne pasta

1/4 cup olive oil

3 cloves garlic, smashed, peeled and coarsely chopped

1/4 to 1/2 teaspoon hot red pepper flakes

2 bunches (about 1 1/2 pounds) dandelion greens, thick stems removed, washed and cut crosswise into 1-inch strips

Kosher salt to taste

Freshly grated Parmesan or Pecorino Romano cheese for serving

Cook the penne in a large saucepan of boiling salted water until tender but firm, for about 9 minutes.

Meanwhile, heat the olive oil in a large skillet over medium heat. Add the garlic and cook, stirring, just until it begins to brown. Stir in the red pepper and cook just until it sizzles. Stir in the dandelions and cook, stirring, until bright green and wilted, for about 3 minutes. Ladle about 1/3 cup of the pasta cooking water into the skillet, bring to a boil and cook until reduced by half. Season with salt.

Drain the pasta and add to the skillet. Toss until coated with sauce. Add salt if necessary. Divide among warm serving bowls, and sprinkle some grated cheese over each.

Serves 6 as a first course, 2 as a main course

Chrysanthemum Leaves with Chorizo

The chorizo used here is a hard Spanish smoked sausage about an inch in diameter. There are chorizos from various Hispanic countries, which vary in degree of spiciness and seasonings; some are fresh, others are dried. See the Cook's Guide, page 570, for a description of the type of chrysanthemum leaves to use in cooking.

2 tablespoons olive oil

3 cloves garlic, smashed, peeled and thinly sliced

2 ounces firm dried chorizo, cut into 1/8-inch slices (about 1/2 cup)

2 pounds chrysanthemum leaves, thick stem ends discarded, long leaves or bunches of leaves broken up (about 16 cups packed)

2 tablespoons sherry vinegar

1/2 teaspoon kosher salt

Heat the oil in a large deep pot. Add the garlic. Cook for 1 minute over low heat; do not brown. Add the chorizo. Cook for 2 minutes.

Increase the heat to medium. Add the leaves in 3 batches, allowing each batch to wilt before adding the next and continuously turning the leaves up from the bottom of the pot, until all the leaves are bright green and wilted.

Add the sherry vinegar and salt. Cook and stir for 1 to 2 minutes.

Makes 3 2/3 cups; serves 4 as a first course or a side dish

Fiddlehead and Chanterelle Risotto

This is a risotto full of the freshness of spring. It is liable to be expensive unless there is a good forager around. The colors are green and gold set off by the lavender flecks that are chive flowers—separated from their clumps—and sprinkled on top after all the stirring.

Either Italian arborio rice, which is white, or Ambra, which is gold, can be used. It is essential to have a really rich chicken stock. The easiest way to grate the cheese is with a food rasp (microplane). The amount of salt will depend heavily on the cheese.

4 tablespoons unsalted butter

$^1/_2$ cup finely minced shallots (about 3 ounces)

5 cups chanterelles (about 1 $^1/_4$ pounds), trimmed and coarsely chopped (about 4 cups)

$^3/_4$ cup coarsely chopped fresh tarragon

$^1/_2$ cup olive oil

1 pound (2 cups) arborio or Ambra rice

1 cup leftover dry Champagne or other medium-acid white wine

6 cups Enriched Chicken Stock (page 502), heated

1 $^1/_2$ cups peas (from about 1 $^1/_4$ pounds peas in the pod)

2 cups (about 5 ounces) trimmed fiddlehead ferns

1 $^1/_2$ cups finely grated Parmesan cheese

Kosher salt and freshly ground black pepper to taste

Flowers from about 12 chives

Chives

Chives are the thinnest and smallest members of the onion family. There are several different kinds. There are very thin chives; garlic chives, which are thicker and sometimes curled; and then there are Chinese chives, which are quite a bit thicker and have a flavor between the sharpish oniony flavor of regular chives and the distinctly garlicky flavor of garlic chives. Remember that each leaf pair is a plant. Just snipping off tops isn't a good idea. It is better to take as many leaves as are needed and then snip them into small bits. A pair of scissors is the most efficient tool.

Chives don't have recipes of their own in this book, as they are used as a seasoning. Their flowers, which come in clumps, are a delightful topping for pale-colored dishes. Hold the chive by its base and pull off the flowers.

Melt the butter in a 10-inch skillet over medium heat. Add the shallots and cook, stirring, until translucent, for about 3 minutes. Add the mushrooms and stir until well coated with butter. Cook over medium-low heat for 5 minutes. Add the tarragon and cook for 8 to 10 minutes. The mushrooms should be reduced to about 2 cups. Set aside.

In a heavy 12-inch casserole, heat the olive oil over medium-high heat. Add the rice and cook, stirring fairly constantly, until all the grains have become opaque—white if using arborio. Pour in the Champagne or wine. Cook, stirring, until the liquid is almost evaporated. Add 1 cup of the stock and cook, stirring, until almost absorbed. Continue to add the stock in 1-cup amounts, stirring and letting the rice absorb the liquid each time. After 4 cups have been added, stir in the peas, then add another cup of stock. When it has been absorbed, stir in the fiddleheads. Add the remaining cup of stock and the chanterelle mixture. When the liquid is almost absorbed, add the Parmesan, salt and pepper. Serve from the pan or transfer to serving dishes. Sprinkle with the chive flowers. **Makes about 12 cups; serves 8 as a main course**

Warm Spring Vegetable Salad

When picking fennel at the market, look for a bulb with lots of bushy, fresh fronds. Good chicken stock is a must.

> **$1/4$ pound radishes, trimmed, halved and cut into $1/8$-inch slices (about 1 cup)**
>
> **$1 1/4$ pounds (about 60 stalks) pencil asparagus, trimmed**
>
> **48 ramps (about $1 1/2$ pounds), cleaned**
>
> **4 cups Basic Chicken Stock (page 501) or Enriched Chicken Stock (page 502)**
>
> **Kosher salt to taste**
>
> **Olive oil (light in flavor, preferably from Puglia)**
>
> **1 medium beet, trimmed, peeled, halved and cut into $1/8$-inch slices (12 slices)**
>
> **12 to 18 baby carrots, trimmed, with a small bit of top left on, peeled and cut in half lengthwise**
>
> **1 pound haricots verts (French green beans) or very thin green beans, topped and tailed**
>
> **24 fiddlehead ferns, trimmed and cleaned**
>
> **1 fennel bulb, trimmed, fronds reserved, and cut crosswise into $1/8$-inch crescents**
>
> **1 cup peas (from about $3/4$ pound peas in the pod)**
>
> **Freshly ground black pepper to taste**
>
> **Flowers from about 20 chives**

Bring a large pot of salted water to a boil. Add the radish slices and cook just until the centers of the slices change color but the outside is still bright red, for about 30 seconds. Remove with a skimmer and plunge into a bowl of ice water. Drain and set aside. Add the asparagus to the boiling water and cook until fully tender, for about 3 minutes. Remove with a skimmer and drain. Submerge the white parts of the ramps, leaving the greens above the water (holding the ramps with tongs or tying them into a bundle with kitchen twine helps) and cook for 2 minutes. Then submerge the whole ramps and cook until fully tender, about 4 minutes. Drain and set aside.

Bring the chicken stock to a boil in a large deep skillet. Add salt to taste, then the oil and sliced beets. Cook until the beets are just beginning to soften, for about 5 minutes. Add the carrots and green beans; cook for 2 minutes. Add the fiddleheads; cook for 1 minute. Add the fennel and peas. Cook until tender but not overcooked, about 3 minutes. Remove from the heat.

Divide the asparagus and ramps among six large serving plates, lining them up on either side of the plate and leaving the center of the plate open. Remove the vegetables from the skillet with a slotted spoon and place them in between the asparagus and ramps, dividing them evenly. Spoon some broth over the vegetables. Sprinkle with salt and pepper to taste. Scatter the fennel fronds and chive flowers over the vegetables. Serve immediately. **Serves 6**

Herbs and Their Flowers

In Evelyn's time (see page 416), herb leaves and their flowers were routinely included in salads. Today we tend to use the leaves more as seasonings in cooked dishes. The flowers are still used raw, often as decoration. To use flower petals in salads, firmly grasp the petals in one hand and pull them away from their anchor to the plant.

Turn to **HERBS AND THEIR FLOWERS** in the Cook's Guide , then locate specific herbs by name for how-tos and the Index for more recipes.

Chervil Pesto

This is really not too exact a name, but it is the best that I can do. It is milder than pesto and has neither nuts nor cheese. It uses shallots. They complement chervil's flavor better than harsher garlic. It should be served at room temperature with grilled fish, poached chicken or steamed vegetables. Unlike real pesto, it needs to be cooked and then cooled.

The recipe can be easily doubled or tripled.

$1/4$ cup olive oil

$1/2$ cup finely chopped shallots
(about $2^1/2$ ounces)

$2/3$ tightly packed cup fresh chervil, including
about 1 inch of stem (about 4 ounces)

$1/4$ teaspoon kosher salt, or to taste

In a small pan, heat 3 tablespoons oil over low heat. Add the shallots and cook until soft, for about 5 minutes. Add the chervil and cook for 5 minutes longer.

Transfer to a blender. Blend, poking down as need be, until fairly smooth. Stir in the remaining tablespoon of olive oil, and let come to room temperature. Season with the salt. **Makes $1/3$ cup**

Warm Chervil Sauce or Stew Base

This novelty has become one of my favorites. It is a delight in spring with favas or asparagus and as the base of a chicken stew.

1 cup finely chopped shallots (about 5 ounces)

3 tablespoons unsalted butter

$1^1/2$ cups packed fresh chervil, including about
1 inch of tender stems (about 8 ounces)

$1/2$ cup Basic Chicken Stock (page 501) or
commercial chicken broth, or as needed

Kosher salt to taste

Cook the shallots in the butter in a small pan until limp. Stir in the chervil until wilted. Transfer to a blender and purée, adding chicken stock as needed to keep the blender going. Add enough of the remaining stock to make a scant cup of sauce. Salt to taste. Heat until warm to use as a sauce, or add to a stew as is. **Makes 1 scant cup**

Chervil Chicken Stew

This is a terrific main course that would be equally good made with shrimp, bay scallops or strips of sole in place of the chicken. If making it with seafood, use Basic Chicken Stock (page 501), commercial broth or Basic Fish Stock (page 505) made quickly from light nonoily fish bones and/or heads.

Feel free to substitute asparagus tips or peas for the beans. If using either of these, do not boil them first. Add to the stew at the same time as the chervil slurry.

1 tablespoon unsalted butter

$1/2$ pound cremini or ordinary mushrooms,
stemmed and cut into $1/4$-inch slices

$1^1/2$ tablespoons kosher salt, plus additional
to taste

$1^1/2$ cups (about 6 ounces) small haricots verts
(French green beans), tipped and tailed

One 4- to 5-pound chicken, cut into 8 to
12 pieces and skinned

2 quarts Basic Chicken Stock (page 501)

1 double recipe of Warm Chervil Sauce or Stew
Base (at left), warm

2 tablespoons rice flour, potato flour or cornstarch

3/4 to 1 pound waxy white new potatoes, halved or quartered into bite-size pieces, cooked in the microwave or boiled (see the Cook's Guide, pages 633 and 634) until just cooked but still firm

1 pound tiny white onions, trimmed and peeled (see the Cook's Guide, page 616)

Freshly ground black pepper to taste

In a large skillet, heat the butter over medium heat until foaming. Add the mushrooms and cook, stirring, just until cooked through. Reserve.

Bring 3 quarts water and the salt to a boil in a medium saucepan. Throw in the beans and cook until bright green but firm. Drain and run under cold water for 30 seconds; do not soak.

Put the chicken in a 6-quart pot. Cover with the stock. Bring to a boil. Reduce the heat to a simmer and cook until chicken is opaque all the way through, for about 15 minutes.

Meanwhile, stir the warm sauce into the rice flour to make a slurry.

Add the potatoes, onions, mushrooms and beans to the chicken. Heat through over medium heat. (If there seems to be too much liquid, remove some and save for another use; but I love sauce and serve this dish with spoons, using all the liquid.) Stir some of the warm liquid into the chervil slurry and stir it back into the stew. Cook for 4 to 5 minutes, or until there is no starchy taste. Season with salt and pepper. **Serves 4 to 6 as a main course**

Cilantro Salsa

1 cup loosely packed cilantro leaves, finely chopped

3/4 pound ripe tomatoes, cored and finely chopped (about 1 1/4 cups)

2 medium cloves garlic, smashed, peeled and minced

1 to 2 small jalapeño peppers, seeded, deribbed and finely chopped

2 tablespoons finely chopped yellow onion

2 tablespoons fresh lime juice

1 teaspoon kosher salt, or to taste

Freshly ground black pepper to taste

Place all the ingredients in a small bowl and mix until thoroughly combined. Allow to stand for about 30 minutes. Adjust the seasonings to taste. **Makes 2 cups**

Creamy Asian Dip

I used tofu "pillows"—the smallish ravioli-shaped pieces. A similar amount of regular tofu can be substituted. Serve as a sauce with lightly cooked vegetables.

3 tofu pillows (3 ounces each)

1/2 ounce peeled fresh ginger, cut into small pieces (1 heaping tablespoon)

1 cup loosely packed cilantro leaves, plus 1/4 cup chopped cilantro

3/4 teaspoon wasabi paste (see the Cook's Guide, page 666)

3 tablespoons soy sauce, preferably tamari

2 to 3 tablespoons toasted sesame oil to taste

2 to 3 tablespoons rice wine vinegar to taste

2 tablespoons coarsely grated peeled daikon or very thinly sliced fennel bulb

Place all the ingredients except the chopped cilantro and daikon or fennel in a blender or food processor, add 2 tablespoons water and process until very smooth. Refrigerate for at least an hour to let the flavor develop. Stir in the chopped cilantro. The dip may be made up to 2 days ahead. Just before serving, sprinkle with the daikon or fennel. **Makes 2 cups**

Cilantro-Marinated Shrimp

A rich green marinade enlivens this first course, or serve each shrimp on a toothpick as an hors d'oeuvre.

1/2 cup cilantro leaves and tender stems

2 jalapeño peppers, seeded, deribbed and
    cut into chunks

2 1/2 tablespoons fresh lime juice

1 tablespoon olive oil

1 pound medium shrimp (26 to 30 per pound),
    peeled and deveined

Kosher salt to taste

Purée the cilantro, peppers, lime juice and oil in a blender until completely smooth. Transfer to a bowl and toss the shrimp in this mixture. Marinate at room temperature for 30 minutes.

Preheat the broiler. Place the shrimp in a single layer in a 14 1/2 x 12 1/2 x 2-inch roasting pan. Broil for 1 1/2 minutes. Turn the shrimp and broil for 1 1/2 minutes more. Sprinkle with salt. **Makes 26 to 30 shrimp; serves 8 as a first course**

Cayenne Quail on a Cilantro Nest

This is an absolutely smashing first course once guests are convinced that fingers are the best tool. The dish needs advance planning because of the marinating.

1/3 cup cayenne pepper

2 cups vegetable oil

8 quail (4 ounces each)

Kosher salt and freshly ground black pepper to taste

5 cups loosely packed cilantro sprigs

8 lemon wedges

In a heavy saucepan, stir together the cayenne pepper and oil. Heat over medium-low to low heat for 1 hour; the oil should not get so hot that the cayenne changes color. Cool to room temperature. Strain the oil through cheesecloth.

Cut the quail into quarters. Remove the feet, if necessary, at the ankle joints. Cut away any innards from the body cavity. Remove the backbones. (If desired, reserve the bones, hearts and gizzards, if any, to cook in a chicken stock; see page 501). The liver can be sautéed with a few mushrooms and some sliced shallots, seasoned with salt and pepper and used to fill an omelet for 4 people for another day's first course.

Place the quail pieces in a large shallow dish. Cover with the cayenne oil. Marinate for 2 to 3 days in the refrigerator if you can. If you are in a hurry, marinate overnight at room temperature; the pepper acts as a preservative.

Remove the quail from the marinade. Allow the oil to drip off; do not wipe them—this is easily done by placing a cake rack on top of a baking sheet and putting the quail on the rack. Sprinkle with salt and pepper.

The birds can be grilled over a very hot charcoal or gas fire or cooked under the broiler. If grilling, lightly grease the grill rack and arrange the quail in a single layer, bone side down, over the fire. If broiling, lightly grease the perforated rack and arrange the quail, bone side up. In either case, cook for 1 minute. Turn the quail over and cook for about 2 minutes more, until the skin is crisp. The meat will be rare in the center.

While the quail are cooking, make a nest of cilantro on each of eight plates. Neatly arrange two breasts and two legs on each nest. Place a lemon wedge in the center of each plate. Make sure guests have large napkins and encourage them to use their hands to eat. This is a time for finger bowls, if desired. **Serves 8 as a first course**

Green Shrimp Curry

Spinach mixes with cilantro to make this green and flavorful unspicy curry.

1 1/2 pounds spinach, stemmed, washed and dried (about 8 cups loosely packed)

1 cup loosely packed cilantro leaves

1/2 cup loosely packed fresh parsley leaves

1 tablespoon vegetable oil

2 teaspoons fennel seeds

4 teaspoons cumin seeds

2 teaspoons yellow mustard seeds

6 cloves garlic, smashed, peeled and minced

1 small onion (about 4 ounces), coarsely chopped

1 medium green bell pepper (about 6 ounces), stemmed, seeded, deribbed and cut into 1-inch pieces

1 large Granny Smith apple (about 8 ounces), peeled, cored and cut into 1-inch pieces

2 pounds large shrimp (21 to 25 per pound), peeled and deveined

3/4 cup Basic Fish Stock (page 505), Basic Chicken Stock (page 501) or commercial chicken broth

1 tablespoon grated peeled fresh ginger

5 ounces frozen baby lima beans, defrosted in a sieve under warm running water (about 3/4 cup)

1 1/2 teaspoons hot red pepper sauce

2 tablespoons fresh lime juice

Kosher salt to taste

Place the spinach, cilantro and parsley in a food processor and finely chop. Reserve.

Combine the oil, fennel seeds, cumin seeds and mustard seeds in a 5-quart casserole dish with a tightly fitting lid. Cook, uncovered, in the microwave at 100% for 3 minutes.

Remove from the oven and stir in the garlic and onion. Cover, return to the oven and cook at 100% for 4 minutes.

Remove from the oven and uncover. Stir in the bell pepper and apple. Cover and cook at 100% for 3 minutes.

Remove from the oven and uncover. Push the vegetables into the center of the dish. Place about half of the reserved spinach mixture around the edge of the dish. Arrange the shrimp in a single layer over the spinach and cover with the remaining spinach. Pour over the stock. Cover and cook at 100% power for 6 minutes.

Remove from the oven and uncover. Stir in the grated ginger. Scatter the lima beans over. Re-cover and cook at 100% for 3 minutes.

Remove from the oven and uncover. Stir in the hot pepper sauce, lime juice and salt to taste. **Serves 8 as a main course**

Mexican Lasagna with Cilantro-Jalapeño Pasta

This attractive dish uses the cilantro-jalapeño dough to great advantage.

2 tablespoons canola oil

1 small sweet onion, cut into 1/8-inch dice (about 1/2 cup)

1 small-medium zucchini, trimmed and cut into 1/8-inch dice (about 1/2 cup)

1 medium yellow bell pepper, cored, deribbed, seeded and cut into 1/8-inch dice (about 1 cup)

1 jalapeño pepper, seeded and finely chopped

1 1/2 cups Plum Tomato Purée (page 459), sterile-pack strained tomatoes or puréed canned tomatoes

2 teaspoons kosher salt, plus more to taste

Freshly ground black pepper to taste

continued

6 tablespoons unsalted butter, plus more for greasing the pan

6 tablespoons all-purpose flour

1 1/2 cups milk

10 ounces queso fresco (Mexican fresh cow's milk cheese), finely crumbled (about 2 cups)

5 1/2 ounces Manchego cheese, grated (generous 1 1/3 cups)

Six 8 x 4-inch lasagna noodles made from Cilantro-Jalapeño Pasta Dough (page 472; see page 470 for instructions on rolling out pasta dough)

For the vegetable sauce, heat the oil in a medium saucepan. Add the onions. Cook over medium-low heat until translucent, for about 4 minutes. Add the zucchini. Cook for 2 minutes, stirring occasionally. Add the yellow and jalapeño peppers. Cook for 10 minutes, stirring occasionally. Reduce the heat to low and cook, stirring, until the vegetables are completely soft, for 4 to 5 minutes. Mix in the tomato purée, 1/2 teaspoon salt and pepper to taste. Taste for seasoning.

For the béchamel sauce, melt the butter in a medium saucepan. Add the flour and cook over low heat for 5 minutes, stirring. Slowly add the milk, whisking briskly to prevent lumps; be sure to scrape the corners, where lumps can hide. Increase the heat to medium. Cook for several minutes, stirring occasionally, until thickened. Stir in 1 cup queso fresco, 1/4 cup Manchego, 1 teaspoon salt and pepper to taste. Whisk until smooth. Set aside, covered with plastic wrap to prevent a skin from forming.

Place a rack in the center of the oven. Preheat the oven to 350°F.

Bring a large pot of water to a boil. Prepare a large bowl of ice-cold water. Slip 3 pasta sheets into the boiling water. Cook for 1 to 2 minutes,

until the pasta is soft but still very firm. Using a wire skimmer, remove to the cold water. Repeat with the remaining pasta.

Drain the pasta on kitchen towels. Lightly butter an 8 x 8 x 2-inch baking dish. Arrange 2 sheets of pasta in the bottom of the pan so that it is completely covered. Spoon one-third of the béchamel sauce over the pasta. Cover with half the vegetable sauce. Sprinkle with 1/3 cup Manchego cheese and 1/2 cup queso fresco. Repeat with another layer of pasta, béchamel, vegetable sauce and Manchego cheese. Cover with the remaining 2 sheets of pasta. Top with the remaining béchamel and Manchego cheese. Sprinkle with the remaining queso fresco.

Place the pan on a baking sheet to prevent spills. Bake for 40 minutes, or until the filling is bubbling and top is golden brown. Let stand for 10 minutes before serving.

Serves 6 as a main course, 9 as a first course

NOTE: This dish improves in texture if made a day ahead. To reheat, bake in a 350°F oven for 20 minutes, or until warmed through.

Gravlax

This is one of Scandinavia's great contributions to world eating. I have a less traditional one in *Party Food* that is also worth trying.

Start curing the fish two days before serving. Use one recipe of cure for each pound and a half of fish to be cured. Multiply as needed.

CURE

1/4 cup coarsely chopped fresh dill

3 tablespoons kosher salt

1/2 teaspoon freshly ground black pepper

3 tablespoons sugar

1 1/2 pounds fresh fish, such as salmon, bluefish, mackerel or catfish, in 2 matching (if possible) skin-on fillets (skinless can be used), pinbones removed

Sweet Mustard Sauce (page 441)

For the cure, combine all the dill, salt, pepper and sugar. (Makes ½ cup)

Place a wire rack over a large baking dish and cover with cheesecloth. Rub equal amounts of the cure mixture on both sides of the fillets and place on the cheesecloth, sandwiching the fillets together, skin sides out. Or, if stuck with a single fillet or with mismatched ones, rub each with the cure mixture and roll up. Tie with string and place on the cheesecloth. Cover the fish with plastic wrap.

Place a baking sheet on top of the plastic wrap. Place a heavy weight on top and refrigerate for a day.

Turn the fish over. Re-cover the fillets and continue curing for at least 1 day, turning over one more time.

When ready to serve, unwrap the fillets and scrape off all of the cure. Slice across on the diagonal into ⅛-inch slices, making the pieces as large as possible. Divide the slices among individual plates, and serve with the mustard sauce (about 1 tablespoon per serving).

Alternatively, cut the sliced gravlax into smaller pieces, put them on crackers, crostini (page 510) or pita chips and top each with a small dab of mustard sauce.

Serves 8 as a first course; makes at least 25 finger-food portions

Pot Cheese and Vegetable Salad

When summer comes, I crave this salad that my grandmother used to make. The flavors, colors and textures are all perfectly varied. For me this salad is lunch, with a good rye bread. If real pot cheese is unavailable, use the driest uncreamed large-curd cottage cheese you can find.

2 cucumbers, peeled, seeded and cut into ½-inch dice

2 tomatoes, cored, seeded and cut into ½-inch dice

1 green bell pepper, cored, seeded, deribbed and cut into ½-inch dice

2 bunches dill, fronds only, roughly chopped

1 bunch scallions, white parts only, chopped

Kosher salt and freshly ground black pepper to taste

2 cups pot cheese

2 cups sour cream

Mix the vegetables, dill and scallions together in a bowl; season with salt and pepper to taste. Place them in the center of a platter. Place the pot cheese and sour cream on either side.

Guests can mix the salad to their own taste, using either pot cheese or sour cream or both.

Serves 4 normal people, 2 people like me

Chicken Soup with Dill, Gelled or Hot

Cold, this is a lovely way to start a summer meal, perhaps before a whole poached fish, a big salad and fresh berries with sorbet. It is also delightful hot. The recipe can be multiplied ad lib.

continued

4 cups Basic Chicken Stock (page 501)

1 small onion, quartered

1 small carrot, peeled and coarsely chopped

Freshly ground black pepper to taste

1 tablespoon gelatin, if preparing gelled version

2 tablespoons fresh lemon juice

3/4 teaspoon kosher salt

2 tablespoons coarsely chopped fresh dill,
   plus 4 sprigs for serving

4 lemon wedges

Sour cream if serving gelled

In a medium saucepan, bring the stock (reserve
½ cup if using gelatin), onion, carrot and
pepper to a boil. Lower the heat and simmer
for 20 minutes.

If using the gelatin, sprinkle it over the
reserved ½ cup stock. Let sit for 2 minutes to
soften. Stir into the soup and cook over medium
heat, stirring constantly, until it is dissolved.

For either version, pour the stock through a
damp-cloth–lined sieve; discard the solids.
Season with the lemon juice and salt.

If serving hot, stir in the chopped dill and
serve immediately. If serving cold, refrigerate
until cool and slightly thickened, then stir in the
chopped dill and serve. Or, if serving gelled,
stir in the dill, divide among four bowls and
chill until set.

Top each portion with a dill sprig and serve
with a wedge of lemon. Serve sour cream on
the side if the soup is gelled.

Makes 4 cups; serves 4 as a first course

Veal and Artichoke Heart Stew

This is the first recipe I can remember inventing,
and I still make it today. It can be made with an
inexpensive cut of veal or pieces of chicken. I
think it is as good as a blanquette de veau and it
is certainly a lot lighter. Since veal cooks quickly,
it is rather rapidly done. The artichoke hearts
lend a festive touch and an unusual flavor. Being
frozen, they require no work except shopping.
Cook the artichokes in the same way but without
the veal for an almost instant and unexpected
vegetable to go with roasted chicken.

Incidentally, this stew is pale. Choose
colorful plates.

3 1/2 tablespoons unsalted butter

2 pounds veal cubes (1 1/2 inches), trimmed

2 medium onions (6 ounces each), cut into
   1-inch chunks

4 cups Basic Chicken Stock (page 501) or
   commercial chicken broth, or as needed

1 teaspoon kosher salt, or to taste

1/4 teaspoon freshly ground black pepper,
   or to taste

Two 9-ounce boxes frozen artichoke hearts,
   defrosted in a sieve under warm water and
   drained

3 tablespoons fresh lemon juice

1/2 cup coarsely chopped fresh dill

1 1/2 tablespoons all-purpose flour

In a large skillet, melt 2 tablespoons butter
over medium-low heat. Add the veal cubes and
onions. Toss until they are coated with the
butter. Cook, stirring occasionally, until the
veal is uniformly gray and the onions are wilted,
for about 10 minutes. Scrape the contents of the
skillet into a pot that will hold the veal and
artichokes comfortably.

Add enough chicken stock to just cover the
veal and onions. Add the salt and pepper.
Heat to simmering. Simmer, partially covered,
for 1 hour, or until the veal is almost tender.

Add the artichoke hearts. Cook for about 10 minutes, until the artichokes are tender when pierced with a knife point. The stew can be made ahead to this point; reheat when ready to proceed.

Just before serving, stir in the lemon juice, dill and additional salt and pepper to taste. In a small bowl, beat the remaining 1½ tablespoons butter and the flour until smooth to make a beurre manié. Pour in ½ cup of the hot liquid from the pot. Beat until incorporated. Stir into the stew. Cook 5 minutes. Adjust the seasonings.

Serve the stew with rice. **Serves 6 as a main course**

NOTE: For an even lighter dish, the final 1½ tablespoons butter and the flour can be omitted and 2 tablespoons cornstarch dissolved in 3 tablespoons water used instead.

Hot Dilled Cucumbers

Most of us think of cucumbers in salad and leave it at that, although they make an interesting hot vegetable, whose smell freshens the air of the kitchen when they are being prepared and delights the dining room when they are served. They go very well with fish and chicken. I make them in the microwave, but they can be made on top of the stove.

2¹/₂ pounds medium cucumbers (6 to 7), trimmed, peeled, quartered lengthwise, seeds removed and cut into 1- to 1¹/₂-inch pieces

¹/₂ cup snipped (¹/₄-inch pieces) fresh dill

2 teaspoons cornstarch

2 tablespoons unsalted butter

2 teaspoons kosher salt

Combine the cucumbers and dill in a 1-quart glass measure. Cover tightly with microwave plastic wrap. Cook in the microwave at 100% for 6 minutes. Prick the plastic to release the steam.

Remove from the oven and uncover. Pour ¼ cup of the liquid into a small bowl. Stir in the cornstarch and mix well; pour back over the cucumbers. Add the butter and salt and stir until the butter melts. Cook, uncovered, at 100% for 4 minutes.

Remove from the oven. Stir well and serve hot. **Serves 4 as a side dish**

NOTE: *To serve 2:* Halve all ingredients. Cook the cucumbers for 4 minutes. Add the cornstarch, butter and salt and cook for 4 minutes more.

Sweet Mustard Sauce

If this were a sauce only for Gravlax (page 438), it would live on the same page, but I like this cinnamon-heightened variation so much that I use it in a number of other preparations. I spread it on bread before topping with smoked salmon. I serve it with boiled potatoes and it makes a great potato salad. Let the potatoes cool before tossing them in the sauce, and add some thinly sliced red onion.

As it keeps so well, multiply the recipe.

¹/₂ cup spicy German mustard

2 teaspoons dry mustard

6 tablespoons sugar

¹/₄ cup white wine vinegar

1 teaspoon ground cinnamon

²/₃ cup vegetable oil

6 tablespoons finely chopped fresh dill

In a medium bowl, combine the mustards, sugar, vinegar and cinnamon. Slowly whisk in the oil. Stir in the dill. The sauce will keep in a closed jar in the refrigerator up to 1 month. Before serving, allow to come to room temperature and stir briskly. **Makes 1¹/₂ cups**

A Victorian Tale:
"The Green Menace, or Virtue Reclaimed"

This is edifyingly told in three parts: being parsley, its dangers; parsley addiction; and parsley, redemption through restraint. When I first began my green temperance league, the signs of parsley abuse were already widespread. Sprigs showed up in the strangest places. I feared the day a cooking student would proudly show me a chocolate cake luridly wreathed in parsley, "for a little color." As cooks have become more aware of the possibilities inherent in contrasts and arrangements of food on the plate, this danger has faded. Abstinence is not the solution. Remember that parsley is a wonderful herb with very good flavor, an important seasoning in its own right.

There are two principal kinds of parsley, common curly parsley and Italian flat-leaf parsley. Both are delicious. Contrary to popular supposition, curly parsley is stronger-tasting than flat leaf. Young parsley of either kind will be better and more delicate than the older, tougher sprigs and the quantity may need to be increased. For maximum flavor, parsley needs to be cooked; this is particularly nice when done in the microwave oven, since the parsley will keep its color. The stems can be saved for soup whenever only the leaves are called for. I dislike the quantity "a bunch of parsley" (though I'm guilty of the mistake myself); no two bunches are ever the same.

Parsley has long been one of the chief components in simple, delicious sauces. For the puréed sauces, I prefer flat-leaf, or Italian parsley. Oddly, considering the rage for all things Italian, I prefer curly parsley with its stronger flavor and less leathery texture for butter sauces and in rolled omelets (see page 483).

Lovage Pesto

If my campaign to get people to grow lovage has had success, one reward for the large plant is this bright green and fragrant sauce. While the sauce can be made in a food processor, it will be more satiny if made in a blender. It gets used as any other pesto.

3 large cloves garlic, smashed, peeled and coarsely chopped

1/4 pound lovage leaves (no stems; about 6 cups)

1 1/4 cups full-flavored olive oil, or as needed

1/2 pound walnuts (pieces are fine; about 2 cups)

2 teaspoons kosher salt, or to taste

Put the garlic in a blender. Top with the lovage leaves. Add half the oil. Blend until the mixture is liquid smooth; add more oil if needed. Add the walnuts and, with the blender running, gradually pour in the remaining oil until it is absorbed. Add the salt.

Allow the pesto to mellow for an hour or so. It will keep refrigerated for about 2 weeks; serve at room temperature. **Makes about 3 cups**

Gremolata

This raw chopped-up topping (also spelled gremolada) traditionally arrives sprinkled over osso buco. I also like it on top of steamed or roasted vegetables such as sweet potatoes, beets (beautiful colors) and carrots.

> 1 bunch fresh flat-leaf parsley
> (1 cup packed leaves)
>
> 5 medium cloves garlic (4 if not using almonds),
> smashed and peeled
>
> 5 strips lemon zest (3 x 1/4 inch)
>
> 7 strips orange zest (3 x 1/4 inch)
>
> 1/3 cup sliced blanched almonds (optional)

Separate the parsley leaves from the stems. Discard the stems or save for making stock.

Chop together (medium-fine) the parsley, garlic and orange and lemon zests. Chop the almonds, if using, and add to the mixture. **Makes 3/4 cup with almonds, a generous 1/2 cup without almonds**

Parsley Pesto

This is another all-purpose version of pesto that stays green. It is milder in taste than conventional pesto, as it uses shallot instead of garlic.

> 3 tablespoons olive oil
>
> 1 shallot, minced (about 2 tablespoons)
>
> 2 bunches fresh parsley, leaves only,
> finely chopped (about 1 cup)
>
> 1/2 teaspoon kosher salt

In a medium skillet, heat 1 tablespoon oil. Add the shallot and cook over medium heat for 5 minutes, or until soft but not brown. Add the parsley and reduce the heat to low. Cook, stirring regularly, for 5 minutes. Remove from the heat.

Scrape into a bowl and mix in the remaining 2 tablespoons olive oil and the salt. **Makes 3/4 cup**

Beurre Maître d'Hôtel

The two simplest parsley sauces are little more than finely chopped—minced—parsley and butter. One is hot, the other cold.

This butter is often formed into a small log about an inch in diameter and wrapped in waxed paper, foil or plastic wrap so that it can be refrigerated or frozen and slices cut off as desired. Quarter-inch slices are often put on plainly grilled steak, fish, chicken or steamed vegetables. I particularly like to put several slices copiously sprinkled with freshly ground black pepper and doused with Worcestershire sauce under a thick broiled steak. The heat of the steak melts everything together to make a sauce that is enriched with the meat juices when the steak is sliced. Another slice can be slicked over the top of the steak to give it a fine shine.

> 8 tablespoons (4 ounces) unsalted butter, softened
>
> 2 tablespoons minced fresh parsley
>
> 1/2 teaspoon fresh lemon juice

continued

1/4 teaspoon kosher salt

A small amount of freshly ground black pepper
(optional)

Beat all the ingredients together in a bowl until thoroughly blended. Wrap and refrigerate or freeze if not using immediately: Spoon onto a sheet of waxed paper, forming a very rough roll about an inch in diameter. Wrap tightly in the waxed paper, making a more even roll, then wrap tightly in aluminum foil.

Slice off thin rounds to top hot foods, or bring to room temperature before using as a spread.

Hot Parsley Butter Sauce

Heat the butter and parsley in a small skillet over low heat until the butter is foaming. Remove from the heat and add the lemon juice, salt and pepper. Use immediately.

Parsley Salad

I prefer to use curly parsley here. It holds up remarkably well, making this a rare green salad that can be tossed hours ahead of time and left at room temperature without fear of wilting. It will even keep for several days in the refrigerator. Flat-leaf parsley can be substituted if it is young and tender.

Top with some chopped hard-boiled egg or raw white mushrooms tossed with lemon juice to make this more substantial fare. The egg version makes an exceptional accompaniment to smoked salmon.

3 cups packed curly parsley leaves
(about 4 ounces)

1/4 cup olive oil

1 tablespoon fresh lemon juice

Large pinch of kosher salt

1 small red or sweet onion, finely chopped
(about 5 tablespoons)

Freshly ground black pepper to taste

Coarsely chop the parsley, to get about 4 cups; transfer to a bowl. With a fork, toss the parsley with the olive oil, lemon juice and salt. Divide among four plates.

Top each plate with a quarter of the onions and a generous grind of pepper.

Makes 4 cups; serves 4 as a first course

Parsley Soup

I developed this recipe for a class that I was giving with James Beard at the Stanford Court in San Francisco. I wanted students to realize that parsley is not a tasteless garnish but a taste-rich ingredient. It worked; they loved the soup.

3 bunches fresh flat-leaf parsley

3 bunches fresh curly parsley

6 tablespoons unsalted butter

3/4 teaspoon ground coriander

3 cloves garlic, smashed and peeled

3 cups Basic Chicken Stock (page 501),
Roasted Chicken Stock (page 502) or
commercial chicken broth

3/4 cup cottage cheese

Fresh lemon juice to taste

Freshly ground black pepper to taste

Kosher salt to taste

Remove and discard the parsley stems. Rinse the leaves well under cold running water. Drain well and squeeze dry.

Melt the butter in a medium saucepan over medium heat. Add the drained parsley leaves and toss to coat well. Lower the heat and cook for 5 minutes, stirring occasionally. Add the coriander and garlic and cook until the garlic becomes fragrant, 1 to 2 minutes. Add the chicken stock and bring to a boil. Lower the heat and simmer for 7 minutes. Remove from the heat and stir in the cottage cheese.

Let the soup cool slightly, then purée in a food processor in batches of no larger than 2 cups until it is smooth and the parsley is chopped fine.

Return to the pan and season to taste with lemon juice, pepper and salt, if needed. Heat through before serving. **Serves 6 as a first course**

Deep-fried Parsley

Glossy, deep green with a crisp, papery texture, deep-fried parsley is a classic topping in French cuisine. Either flat-leaf or curly parsley can be used. Just be sure it is completely dry or the oil will splatter.

**$^1/_2$ bunch fresh parsley, washed and
dried very well**

Canola oil for deep-frying

Break the parsley into clusters of 3 to 4 leaves with just a bit of stem. Pour 1½ to 2 inches of oil into a deep 11- or 12-inch pot. Heat the oil to 375°F.

Standing at a safe distance to avoid splatters, drop a handful of parsley into the oil. Fry for 5 to 10 seconds. Remove to a parchment-covered baking sheet. Repeat with the remaining parsley. **Makes enough to decorate 8 plates or 1 platter**

Vinaigrettes and Salad Dressings 448   Sauces 453

Doughs and Pastries 469   Egg Dishes 479   Rice 489   Stuffings 491

Stocks, Broths and Soup Bases 501   Odds and Ends 508   Methods 512

Basic Recipes and Techniques

"INTO EACH LIFE" A LITTLE STOCK MUST FALL, or the need to get one's peas into an omelet. Many basic instructions for peeling, coring and boiling and other modes of cooking appear with their own vegetables in the Cook's Guide. Here are the ones that are somewhat more general, or more like recipes. I hope that they help.

Vinaigrettes and Dressings

I love salads of many kinds and using many kinds of ingredients. In this section are the goos that lave the leaves. Many other dressings are sprinkled—or spooned—through the book in sections such as those on tomatoes and on green beans. Look in the Index to locate them.

If I say so myself, I make one mean salad dressing. People love it. Nevertheless, I have found over the years that the simplest vinaigrette is the hardest thing to teach. Not only are all kinds of olive oil different, but there will be, as there is with wine, a variation from one year's crop to another, even from bottle to bottle; hence I do not specify a special kind of olive oil. Taste is the only answer. Certainly vinegars are wildly disparate. Even something as simple as a lemon will have its own character. Obviously, a Meyer lemon will be more aromatic and less acid than an everyday lemon, but everyday lemons themselves vary in amount of juice and acidity. Salt is a major issue. I use and call for kosher salt as the most reliable in flavor. The amounts may look large, but the crystals are larger, taking up more room than crystals of table salt. I actively dislike the taste of the iodine that is added to most table salt, and I have never understood paying a lot of extra money for sea salt to use in a dish that has nothing of the sea about it. Also, salts from different seas have different flavors.

This leads us finally to pepper and other seasonings such as mustard. Peppers are not only white and black—and despite the usual prejudice, white pepper is stronger than black. Peppers are named for the port from which they are shipped. It is not so much that they are different kinds but rather that they are cured and dried differently. This doesn't even take into account long pepper, looking like a bunch of grapes rather than a pellet for a BB gun, or green, or pink pepper (not a pepper at all).

As a cautionary tale, I will describe a class that I gave with the late James Beard at the Stanford Court, with many of the ingredients provided by Chuck Williams of Williams-Sonoma. On a long table, I arranged a large series of little bowls. Each contained a different oil or vinegar. The students were encouraged to taste these, rinsing their mouths with water and chewing bread between samples. Then, with only salt and pepper available, they were asked to make a salad dressing. Except for two out of some twenty-odd, the results were ghastly. The usual error was the choice of a favorite oil—usually a killer dark green Tuscan—that was then coupled with a favorite vinegar, without any thought given to their compatibility. Almost all the students used what they believed to be the standard ratio of the two ingredients.

My advice: Taste carefully. Learn what you like and try combining a bit of it with something else you like. See what happens before making a batch.

Don't overdress salads; they will get soggy. Instead, add a little at a time and toss. Really toss, lifting the greens into the air while turning them over. Repeat. Try not to bruise the leaves. None of this holds true for salads with wilted lettuce such as chicory (frisée) or dandelion with hot bacon lardons (page 219).

VINAIGRETTES

Everyday Vinaigrette

This is the basic French sauce. The mustard helps to hold the ingredients together. Try to use imported—but not coarse-grain—mustard made in France. Much of what is called Dijon is actually made in this country. Dry English mustard can be used instead. Be careful; the dry tends to be hotter.

1/4 teaspoon Dijon mustard

1 teaspoon kosher salt

1/8 teaspoon freshly ground black pepper

3 tablespoons red wine vinegar (can be part fresh lemon juice) or tarragon vinegar

1/2 cup olive oil that is not a killer

1/2 cup vegetable oil

In a small bowl, whisk together all the ingredients. The vinaigrette can be stored, covered, in the refrigerator for up to 2 weeks. Whisk well each time before using. **Makes about 1 1/4 cups**

Soy-Sesame Vinaigrette

This is a knockoff of the salad dressing that used to be on Trader Vic's limestone lettuce salad. It's not a perfect reproduction, but it's very good over Bibb lettuce leaves. The garlic can be omitted.

1 1/2 tablespoons tarragon vinegar

1/8 teaspoon dry mustard

1/8 teaspoon kosher salt

Freshly ground black pepper to taste

2 1/2 tablespoons soy sauce, preferably tamari

1/4 cup olive oil

Scant 1/8 teaspoon toasted sesame oil

1/4 teaspoon packed chopped fresh tarragon

1/4 teaspoon finely minced garlic

Put the vinegar, mustard, salt, pepper and soy sauce in a small bowl. Whisk until smooth. While whisking, add the olive oil, then the sesame oil, tarragon and garlic. At this point, the dressing can keep for an hour—longer, and the garlic will get too strong. **Makes about 1/2 cup**

Anchovy Vinaigrette

Try these dressings on a simple romaine salad; they're also very good on potatoes.

1/2 cup olive oil

2 tablespoons red wine vinegar

3/4 teaspoon anchovy paste

3/4 teaspoon Dijon mustard

4 sprigs fresh parsley, leaves only

1/4 cup fresh basil leaves

1/4 teaspoon kosher salt

1/4 teaspoon freshly ground black pepper

continued

Blend all the ingredients together in a food processor or blender. **Makes 3/4 cup**

Anchovy Cheese Dressing
Add 1 tablespoon freshly grated Parmesan cheese to the vinaigrette.

Blood Orange Vinaigrette

Serve this with a salad of watercress tops— leaves and slim stems. Add endives slivered lengthwise, six to seven cups altogether. Toss well and let sit for at least ten minutes before serving. The endives will turn a delectable pink.

For variation, add poppy seeds (see below). Their light crunch contrasts perfectly with the creaminess of the avocado in the Avocado, Pink Grapefruit and Papaya Salad (page 5).

> 2/3 cup fresh blood orange juice
>
> 2/3 cup balsamic vinegar
>
> 2/3 cup olive oil
>
> 2 1/2 teaspoons kosher salt
>
> Freshly ground black pepper to taste

In a small bowl, whisk together all the ingredients. Whisk well again before using. **Makes a scant 2/3 cup**

Poppy Seed Blood Orange Vinaigrette
Mix in 2 teaspoons poppy seeds. Whisk well before each use.

Walnut Vinaigrette

This is particularly good with bitter greens and chicory (frisée) leaves (page 567) arranged like an open flower on the plate, with some walnuts in the center. Be careful: Buy all nut oils in small quantities and store in a cool, dark place; they tend to go rancid.

> 1/2 cup walnut oil
>
> 1 tablespoon white wine vinegar
>
> 1/2 teaspoon kosher salt
>
> 2 grinds black pepper
>
> 1/2 teaspoon chopped fresh chives

Whisk all the ingredients together. **Makes a generous 1/2 cup**

SALAD DRESSINGS

Yogurt Dressing

This is a tart and healthful dressing that is low in calories. It is good on fruit salads as well as vegetable salads. Prepare it at least a day before using.

> 1/2 teaspoon ground cumin
>
> 1/2 teaspoon vegetable oil or canola oil
>
> 2 cups plain yogurt
>
> 1/4 cup fresh orange juice
>
> 1/16 teaspoon minced garlic
>
> 1 teaspoon kosher salt
>
> Pinch of freshly ground black pepper

In a small glass bowl, microwave the cumin in the oil at 50% until fragrant, about 1 minute. Transfer to a blender. Add the remaining ingredients and blend on low speed until mixed. Store, covered, in the refrigerator for at least 1 day before using. **Makes about 2 1/4 cups**

Pseudo-Indian Dressing

This flavorful sauce is good with cooled steamed broccoli or fennel. Amchoor is a pleasantly acidic powdered mango.

Spoon the seeds from the dressing (they will rise to the top) over the cooked vegetables, then pour the dressing over all. Allow the vegetables to marinate for at least one to two hours, or longer, occasionally spooning the dressing over them.

2 tablespoons amchoor (see Sources)

2 tablespoons sesame seeds

1 1/2 teaspoons black mustard seeds

3 tablespoons toasted sesame oil

1/4 teaspoon cardamom seeds

4 large cloves garlic, smashed, peeled and
    coarsely chopped

Small pinch of hot red pepper flakes

1 tablespoon kosher salt

In a 1-quart saucepan, dissolve the amchoor in 1 cup water. Bring to a boil. Remove from the heat and let sit.

Put the sesame seeds in a separate 1-quart saucepan and stir over low heat for 2 minutes. Add the mustard seeds. Stir for 1 minute, or until the sesame seeds brown lightly and the mustard seeds begin to pop. Add the sesame oil and cardamom; stir and heat for 2 minutes. Add the garlic and red pepper flakes. Cook for 1 minute to lightly brown. Stir in the salt and amchoor liquid.

Makes 1 1/4 cups, enough for 2 pounds vegetables

Microwave Variation

Combine the amchoor and 1 cup water in a 1-quart measure. Cover tightly with microwave plastic wrap. Cook at 100% for 5 minutes. Prick the plastic to release the steam. Remove from the oven. Uncover and set aside.

Place the sesame seeds in a 1-quart soufflé dish. Cook at 100%, uncovered, for 4 minutes. Stir in the mustard seeds. Cook, uncovered, for 2 minutes. Stir in the sesame oil and cardamom seeds. Cook, uncovered, for 2 minutes. Stir in the garlic and red pepper flakes. Cook, uncovered, for 2 minutes. Remove from the oven. Stir the amchoor liquid into the seed mixture. Stir in the salt. Allow to cool.

Orange Wheat Germ Dressing

In this light dressing, gelatin adds body to replace much of what would normally be oil. Toss with three cups (half a pound) grated carrots to make grated carrot salad.

1/2 cup orange juice

1/2 teaspoon plain gelatin

2 tablespoons fresh lemon juice

2 tablespoons wheat germ

2 tablespoons vegetable oil

1 teaspoon toasted sesame oil

1/4 teaspoon Dijon mustard

1/4 teaspoon plus 1/8 teaspoon kosher salt

1/4 teaspoon grated orange zest

Put 1/4 cup orange juice in a small saucepan. Sprinkle the gelatin over the top and let stand to soften, about 5 minutes. Place over medium heat and stir until the gelatin is dissolved. Remove from the heat and let cool, then whisk in the remaining ingredients. **Makes a scant 1 cup**

Tahini-Citrus Dressing

Fresh sour oranges, also called Seville oranges, can be difficult to find. Bottled juice can be purchased from Latin grocery stores. A mixture of half regular orange juice, one-quarter lemon juice and one-quarter lime juice is a good substitute.

    6 tablespoons tahini (stirred to incorporate
        the oil before measuring)

    3/4 cup sour orange juice or above mixture
        (see headnote)

    6 tablespoons olive oil

    1 1/2 teaspoons kosher salt

In a small bowl, vigorously whisk the tahini with ¼ cup juice until well blended. Slowly whisk in the remaining ½ cup juice, the oil and salt. **Makes 1 1/2 cups**

Tomato Frappé

This comes from an idea of the Troisgroses. They are great geniuses. It is more a sauce for vegetable dishes than a dressing. An example is Cauliflower Bavarian (page 255).

    1 1/4 pounds ripe tomatoes, peeled, cored
        and seeded

    1 generous teaspoon tomato paste

    1/4 cup fresh lemon juice

    1 1/2 teaspoons kosher salt

    Freshly ground black pepper to taste

    1 1/2 tablespoons chopped fresh parsley

    1 tablespoon coarsely chopped fresh basil

    1/4 cup olive oil

Place the tomatoes in a food processor and pulse until puréed. Press them through a fine sieve into a small bowl. Add the tomato paste, lemon juice, salt, pepper and herbs.

Just before serving, whisk in the oil, a few drops at a time. **Makes about 1 3/4 cups**

Green Goddess Dressing

Anybody who has read James Beard or Helen Evans Brown will be familiar with this San Francisco dressing.

    1 cup Classic Mayonnaise (page 455),
        Cooked-Yolk Mayonnaise (page 455) or
        commercial mayonnaise

    1 cup sour cream

    One 2-ounce can anchovies,
        drained and chopped

    1 tablespoon fresh lemon juice

    3 tablespoons tarragon vinegar

    2 teaspoons chopped fresh tarragon

    3 tablespoons chopped fresh chives

    1/2 cup chopped fresh Italian parsley

    1/2 teaspoon kosher salt

    Freshly ground black pepper to taste

Combine all the ingredients in a food processor and process until smooth. Chill. **Makes 2 1/4 cups**

Sauces

A great deal of the food that I make is very simple—roasted, grilled, boiled or steamed. Sometimes a little something extra is welcome.

BUTTER SAUCES

Clarified Butter

8 tablespoons (4 ounces) unsalted butter

In a 1-quart saucepan, melt the butter over low heat. Pour it into a small bowl. Allow 5 to 6 minutes for the butter to settle into three layers: The solids will float to the top and the water will sink to the bottom.

Carefully skim off the top layer. Chill the bowl until the middle layer solidifies. Lift off the clarified middle layer and blot the underside with a paper towel. Reserve for use in recipes. **Makes 1/4 cup or so, depending on the quality of the butter**

Browned Butter

While this is typically used with fish or brains, it is very good with the lighter-color, blander vegetables such as cauliflower or steamed Brussels sprouts. With the simple addition of a single element, it can turn into a sauce. Consider adding a teaspoon of any or several of the following: capers, bread crumbs (toasted or plain), one or two herbs chopped together, fresh lemon juice, vinegar (especially malt) or slivered almonds (toasted or plain).

1/4 cup Clarified Butter (at left)

Pour the clarified butter into a small pan. Cook over medium heat until deep brown with a nutty aroma, about 7 minutes. Stir in any extra ingredients. Do not burn. Allow to cool slightly before using. **Makes 1/4 cup, enough for 1 to 2 servings**

Beurre Blanc

This is called a woman's sauce, probably because it was invented by two sisters and doesn't require other basic preparations, such as stock. It is usually used with white-fleshed fish or chicken. I like it with young peas and carrots.

1/4 cup chopped shallots

1/4 cup chopped fresh parsley

1 tablespoon dried tarragon

continued

6 tablespoons tarragon vinegar, or as needed

6 tablespoons dry white wine

Fresh lemon juice (optional)

3/4 pound (12 ounces) chilled unsalted butter, cut into pieces

1/4 teaspoon kosher salt

1/4 teaspoon freshly ground black pepper

Cayenne pepper to taste

1 tablespoon chopped fresh tarragon plus
2 tablespoons chopped fresh parsley, or
3 tablespoons chopped parsley (optional)

Place the shallots, ¼ cup parsley, dried tarragon, vinegar and wine in a nonaluminum pan. Begin reducing the liquid over low heat, which will permit some of the sharp odors and tastes of vinegar to escape. After 10 minutes, increase the heat and reduce rapidly. When the reduction looks fairly dry, remove it from the heat. Tilting the pan and pressing on the mixture with a spoon should show about 2 tablespoons of liquid remaining.

At this point, the reduction can be put through a sieve into a clean pan. Unsieved, it will make a somewhat textured, rather more peasanty sauce. In either case, taste the reduction: It should be quite acid. If it isn't, add some lemon juice or extra vinegar and heat for a second or two.

Place the pan over low heat and whisk in the butter a few pieces at a time, adding more butter only as the preceding batch is absorbed. When all the butter is absorbed, remove the pan from the heat. Stir in the salt, both peppers and the fresh herbs, if desired. Use promptly. Or, if using this as an ingredient in Artichokes Filled with Snails in Cream and Beurre Blanc (page 231), chill until firm. **Makes about 1 1/2 cups**

Hollandaise Sauce

The classic accompaniment to fresh asparagus, this is wonderful with other vegetables or over fish, and it is an essential ingredient in eggs Benedict. It can be varied as mayonnaise can, with fresh herbs, curry powder or any of the meat or chicken glazes on page 505. Instead of eggs Benedict, consider artichoke bottoms filled with creamed spinach, each topped with a poached egg and slathered with the sauce.

1 pound unsalted butter

3 egg yolks

1/2 teaspoon dry mustard

1 teaspoon kosher salt

1/4 teaspoon freshly ground black pepper

2 teaspoons fresh lemon juice

Melt the butter in a saucepan. Keep hot over low heat.

Place the egg yolks, mustard, salt and pepper in a food processor. Turn the machine on and let it run for 90 seconds. With the machine still running, slowly but steadily pour the butter through the feed tube. The sauce will thicken until it has the consistency of mayonnaise. Pour in the lemon juice through the feed tube.

Scrape the sauce into a serving bowl and serve immediately. Or, keep the sauce warm in the top of a double boiler over simmering water or in a thermos. Do not let it get too hot, or the butter will separate out of the sauce.
Makes about 2 cups

MAYONNAISE AND MAYO-BASED SAUCES

After ketchup, mayonnaise may be our most ubiquitous sauce, on its own or as the base for Tartar Sauce (page 457), Rémoulade (page 458) and so on. Mayonnaise is a cold sauce, most often made with egg yolks that are beaten with oil to form a stable emulsion. Mayonnaise-type sauces are rich and almost infinitely variable.

All the mayonnaises keep well, covered, in a glass jar in the refrigerator for up to a month, so you may want to multiply the recipes.

Classic Mayonnaise

This is the classic mayonnaise, but the dried mustard can be omitted, vinegar used instead of lemon juice and all olive oil used instead of part vegetable oil. I use a strong-tasting olive oil and cut it with vegetable oil—usually canola oil—to save money and to avoid an overwhelmingly olivey sauce. Adjust according to the oils on hand.

Mayonnaise made in a food processor will be a little more stable—less likely to separate—than that made by hand. Classic mayonnaise is less satisfactory when made in a blender, as it quickly gets too stiff to accept all the oil needed.

> 3 egg yolks
>
> 4 teaspoons fresh lemon juice
>
> 1 1/2 teaspoons kosher salt
>
> Freshly ground white pepper
>
> 1 teaspoon dry mustard
>
> 1 cup vegetable oil
>
> 1/2 cup olive oil

Place the egg yolks in a food processor and process for 1 minute. Add the lemon juice, salt, white pepper and mustard and process to blend. With the machine running, gradually add the oil through the feed tube, beginning with droplets and working up to a thin stream as the mayonnaise begins to set up.

Or, in a large nonreactive bowl, work with a large whisk in the same manner. **Makes 2 cups**

Cooked-Yolk Mayonnaise

This technique was developed by Harold McGee, author of *The Curious Cook*. To learn more about it, read his book (see the Bibliography). The yolks cook sufficiently so that they are no longer possibly contaminated. The mayonnaise has a slight taste of cooked yolks, but it is eminently satisfactory.

Put 2 large egg yolks in a 2-cup glass measure and whisk thoroughly with 2 tablespoons plus 1 teaspoon each water and fresh lemon juice. Wash the whisk with very hot soapy water. Cover the measure tightly with microwave plastic wrap. Cook in the microwave at 100% for 45 seconds to 1 minute, or until the yolks just begin to boil (when the first bubbles appear). Prick the plastic to release the steam.

Remove from the oven. Uncover and whisk with the cleaned whisk. Return to the oven, uncovered, and cook for 20 seconds.

Remove from the oven and whisk with a clean whisk—yes, another one—until cool. Now continue by whisking in the oil as if making any other mayonnaise; use 1 1/2 cups of the oil of your choice, seasoning with salt, pepper and mustard, if desired. **Makes 1 3/4 cups**

Sweet Garlic "Mayonnaise"

This mayonnaise has no eggs whatsoever. It is thickened by the sticky texture of long-cooked garlic. The long cooking also gentles the taste of the garlic. It still is not a sauce for those who loathe garlic, but it is very good in fish soups, with cold fish preparations and with strong vegetables such as broccoli.

1 1/2 medium heads garlic, cloves separated, smashed and peeled

1 1/2 cups Basic Chicken Stock (page 501), Roasted Chicken Stock (page 502) or commercial chicken broth

2 cups olive oil or a combination of olive and vegetable oil

Kosher salt and freshly ground black pepper to taste

Fresh lemon juice (optional)

Prepared mustard (optional)

Combine the garlic and chicken stock in a medium saucepan, cover with a lid and bring to a boil over medium heat. Reduce the heat to low. Simmer, covered, for 25 minutes. Remove from the heat.

Transfer the softened garlic and broth to a food processor or blender. Process until completely smooth. With the motor running, gradually add the oil in a thin, steady stream. When fully combined, add the seasonings and optional flavorings, if desired. **Makes 3 cups**

Aïoli with Potato

This eggless version is bound with potato. It can also be made with an equal amount of bread soaked in water and squeezed dry.

10 ounces floury potatoes, peeled and cut into 1-inch cubes (about 1 3/4 cups)

6 medium cloves garlic, smashed and peeled

1/2 cup olive oil

4 teaspoons fresh lemon juice

1 teaspoon kosher salt

Freshly ground black pepper to taste

Aïoli

Aïoli is a sauce that turns up all along the Mediterranean with its name spelled variously. It is made in three different ways: The simplest and yet the hardest is to pound the garlic with the salt in a mortar until it becomes a smooth purée. Then the oil is dripped in very slowly, working the pestle constantly—good luck. The most common today is to add garlic to a classic mayonnaise. If making the mayonnaise in a food processor, just throw in the garlic cloves about halfway through adding the oil. Use 8 medium cloves garlic, or to taste. Remember, the garlic flavor will become more intense as the aïoli sits. The third way is to use a cooked potato as a base.

Aïoli is known as the butter of Provence, and it is spread on bread or served with steamed fish, steamed chicken or meat or with many steamed vegetables as a grand aïoli.

Put the potatoes in the top of a two-part steamer or on a steaming rack or a plate in a bamboo steamer. Fill the bottom of the steamer pan or a pan large enough to hold the bamboo or steaming rack with water; the water should not touch the rack. Bring to a boil over medium heat. Place the potatoes on top, cover and steam until a knife easily pierces the flesh. Put through a food mill into a bowl.

Place the garlic and ¼ cup oil in a food processor and process until smooth.

Stir the garlic mixture into the potato until thoroughly incorporated. Gradually add the remaining ¼ cup oil, stirring well after each addition. Stir in the lemon juice and add the salt and pepper to taste. **Makes 1 cup**

Microwave Variation

Put the potatoes and ¼ cup water in a 1½-quart soufflé dish. Cover tightly with microwave plastic wrap and cook at 100% for 10 minutes. Prick the plastic to release the steam.

Remove from the oven and uncover. Drain off any remaining liquid and pass the potatoes through a mill fitted with the fine disc. Continue as directed.

Rouille

"Rouille" means "rust-colored," as in the term "tâches de rousseur," which means "freckles." Traditionally, this is made with a mortar and a pestle, first pulverizing the solids and then slowly adding the oil while rotating the pestle in one direction. If small hot peppers in their dried form are unavailable, use the flakes that come from a jar. Rouille is the classic partner of bouillabaisse. Try it with steamed sweet potatoes—special. Saffron soaked in a little white wine can be added.

4 egg yolks

1 teaspoon kosher salt

¼ teaspoon dry mustard

2 teaspoons white wine vinegar

12 medium cloves garlic, smashed, peeled and cut into chunks

3 small dried hot red chili peppers

1 cup extra-virgin olive oil

1 cup vegetable oil

¼ cup coarsely chopped roasted red peppers, homemade (see the Cook's Guide, page 628) or drained jarred

In a food processor, pulse the yolks, salt, mustard, vinegar, garlic and dried peppers to combine. With the machine running, pour in the oil: Add it a few drops at a time at first; as the sauce begins to look like mayonnaise, add the oil in a slow, steady stream and process until all the oil is incorporated and the sauce is thick. Add the roasted peppers and process until smooth. **Makes 3½ cups**

Tartar Sauce

Pair this with fried foods including cauliflower, broccoli and potatoes as well as with fish and seafood.

2 cups Classic Mayonnaise (page 455), Cooked-Yolk Mayonnaise (page 455) or commercial mayonnaise

2 tablespoons white wine vinegar

3 sweet gherkins, minced

3 scallions, trimmed and minced

6 tablespoons small capers, drained

Combine all the ingredients in a small bowl. Refrigerate, covered, until cold. **Makes 2 cups**

Rémoulade Sauce

While very similar to American tartar sauce and good on similar foods, this sauce has an extremely French air. It really needs homemade mayonnaise, which I would make with tarragon vinegar. The recipe is easily multiplied and will keep, covered, in the refrigerator for at least a week.

 3 tablespoons minced cornichons

 3 tablespoons rinsed minced capers

 1/4 cup minced fresh herbs (such as flat-leaf parsley, chervil, chives and tarragon)

 1/2 teaspoon anchovy paste

 1 1/2 cups mayonnaise, preferably Classic Mayonnaise (page 455) or Cooked-Yolk Mayonnaise (page 455)

In a medium bowl, beat the flavorings into the mayonnaise. **Makes about 1 1/2 cups**

Spicy Rémoulade

In the South, there are many sauces called rémoulade that the French would never recognize. They are spicy and go well with boiled seafood, among other things. Try this in place of the classic rémoulade dressing on celery root (page 205).

I would make this with homemade mayonnaise, but the seasonings are sufficiently sharp that one should be able to get away with commercial mayonnaise; just make sure it's not sweet.

 1 cup Classic Mayonnaise (page 455), Cooked-Yolk Mayonnaise (page 455) or commercial mayonnaise

 2 tablespoons Dijon mustard or spicy Creole mustard, preferably Zatarain's

 2 tablespoons prepared horseradish, drained

 1 tablespoon fresh lemon juice

 1/4 cup chopped celery

 1/4 cup chopped scallions

 1/2 teaspoon cayenne pepper

 1 tablespoon sweet paprika

 1 medium clove garlic, smashed, peeled and minced

Mix everything together, blending well. Refrigerate for several hours before using. **Makes 1 1/2 cups**

New Orleans Spicy Rémoulade

Now this is clearly not authentic, as it uses Sweet Garlic "Mayonnaise." I think it is very good. To be more authentic, substitute Classic Mayonnaise (page 455) made with tarragon vinegar and add at least four minced garlic cloves to the food processor along with the parsley and other ingredients. The spicy rémoulade may not seem very hot when first made, but its true flavor will show as it sits in the refrigerator for a few hours. It's famous with fried foods (which would negate all the health benefits of non-egg mayonnaise), but grilled foods, including vegetables, can be successfully substituted.

 1 cup loosely packed fresh parsley leaves

 2 scallions, trimmed and cut into 1-inch pieces (about 1/2 cup)

 2 slices peeled fresh horseradish (about 1/2 ounce), cut into small pieces

 1 stalk celery, peeled and cut into 1-inch pieces (about 1/2 cup)

 2 tablespoons tarragon vinegar

 1 tablespoon sweet paprika

2 teaspoons soy sauce, preferably tamari

2 teaspoons dry mustard

¹/₄ teaspoon hot red pepper sauce

³/₄ cup unseasoned Sweet Garlic "Mayonnaise" (page 456)

Kosher salt to taste

Combine all the ingredients except the mayonnaise and salt in a food processor and process until finely chopped. Add the mayonnaise and salt and process to combine. Scrape into a container and store, tightly covered, in the refrigerator. **Makes 1¹/₂ cups**

TOMATO PURÉES, BASES AND SAUCES

Plum Tomato Purée

I really dislike most canned plum tomatoes. They seem to taste of the tin and they are very salty. If buying them, try to get the ones without purée. For many purposes, canned ordinary tomatoes, if they are good, will have a less heavy flavor. Plum tomatoes are normally used for sauce, as they are meatier, with less liquid. A good alternative is sterile-pack strained tomatoes.

This is used in Tomato Basil Soup (page 105), Curry Tomato Soup (page 105) and Southwestern Corn and Tomato Soup (page 105), as well as many other recipes. See the variation for a version with oil and garlic.

5 pounds ripe plum tomatoes, cored and cut into 1-inch cubes

Cook the tomatoes in a medium nonreactive stockpot over high heat until steam appears. Cover and lower the heat. Cook, stirring occasionally, for 30 minutes, or until the tomatoes are very soft.

Pass the tomatoes through the medium disc of a food mill. Return to the pot. Bring to a boil. Lower the heat and simmer, uncovered, stirring frequently to prevent scorching, for 1 hour, or until the purée is thick.

Use immediately, or refrigerate for up to 3 days or freeze. **Makes 8 cups**

Italian Plum Tomato Purée
Add 1 cup olive oil and, if desired, 12 medium cloves garlic, smashed and peeled, to the uncooked tomatoes and proceed as directed.

Fresh Tomato Paste

The color will not be the same dark red as the stuff from cans. Nor will it be as thick. The flavor, however, will be far superior.

Use a heat diffuser underneath the saucepan if possible to prevent scorching during the long reduction process.

2¹/₂ cups Plum Tomato Purée (at left)

In a small nonreactive saucepan, preferably over a heat diffuser, bring the purée to a boil. Reduce the heat to low. Simmer until the purée reduces to 1 cup, about 2 hours. Stir and scrape the sides of the pan from time to time; as the purée reduces, it will need to be stirred more frequently. **Makes 1 cup**

American Tomato Purée

A thicker version of this base makes a fine sauce. Once the purée is made, continue to cook it slowly over low heat for about two hours, or until the volume is reduced by half. Stir occasionally and use a heat diffuser, if available, to keep the sauce from scorching.

5 pounds American tomatoes

Core the tomatoes deeply, removing the hard centers. Remove any bad spots on the skins or mushy flesh. Cut the tomatoes into 1-inch pieces. In a covered nonreactive 7- or 8-quart pot, bring the tomatoes to a boil over low heat, stirring occasionally, and cook for about 45 minutes.

Uncover and simmer the tomatoes over low heat until all the pieces are soft and the mixture is mostly liquid (about 1 hour).

Pass the tomatoes through a food mill, using the finest disc. The purée will be extremely runny. Return the purée to the pot and simmer, uncovered, over low heat for about 3 hours, stirring occasionally. When finished, the purée will still be runny but no longer watery, and it will have a substantial amount of tomato pulp—as thick as a light sauce or a soup base. **Makes 5 cups**

Chunky Tomato Base

for Soups

A base is not a stock, but a wonderful way of carrying the sun into winter, of using the prodigal produce of spring, summer and fall when it is cheap and plentiful.

This works well for peasanty-type soups such as minestrone, in Summer Vegetable Gumbo (page 343)—or any soup that calls for lightly crushed canned whole tomatoes. Sterile-pack strained tomatoes would be the best alternative.

2 medium onions, cut into $1/2$-inch cubes

6 tablespoons olive oil

5 pounds ripe tomatoes, cored and cut into 1-inch cubes

In a medium nonreactive stockpot, cook the onions in the olive oil over low heat, stirring occasionally, for 8 minutes.

Raise the heat and stir in the tomatoes. Bring to a boil. Lower the heat and simmer for 20 minutes, or until the tomatoes are soft and liquid.

Use immediately, or refrigerate for up to 3 days or freeze. **Makes 10 cups**

Cherry Tomato Stew Base

This goes in my microwave to avoid browning and to gentle the garlic.

4 pounds cherry tomatoes, quartered (about 10 cups)

2 cups tightly packed fresh basil sprigs (about 2 ounces)

1 head garlic (about $3^1/4$ ounces), cloves separated, smashed and peeled

$1/2$ cup olive oil

Toss the tomatoes with the basil, garlic and olive oil in a 13 x 9 x 2-inch oval dish. Cover tightly with microwave plastic wrap. Cook in the microwave at 100% for 25 minutes. Prick the plastic wrap to release steam.

Uncover and cook for 15 minutes.

Pass the tomato base through a food mill fitted with the medium disc. **Makes $5^1/4$ cups**

NOTE: To make 8 cups, use 6 pounds tomatoes, 3 cups tightly packed basil, 5 ounces garlic (about 1½ heads) and ½ cup olive oil. In batches, purée the tomatoes in a food processor and scrape into a 5-quart dish. Stir in the remaining ingredients and cook, covered, for 30 minutes. Pierce the plastic to release the steam.

Uncover and cook for 35 minutes. Finish the recipe as directed.

Simple Stovetop Cherry Tomato Stew Base

Use 2 pounds orange or regular cherry tomatoes, quartered (about 5½ cups). Cook the tomatoes in a nonreactive pot, uncovered, over high heat until sizzling. Cover, reduce the heat to medium and cook for 10 minutes. Uncover and cook for 15 minutes. Pass the tomatoes through a food mill fitted with the medium disc. **Makes 2½ cups**

Tomato Sauce for Stuffed Vegetables

This is a complex and interesting sauce that can stand up to the taste of green peppers or most vegetables. It can also be used for pizza.

   ¼ cup olive oil

   ¾ cup chopped onion

   1¼ teaspoons minced garlic

   3 cups peeled, seeded and chopped ripe tomatoes, one 26-ounce package sterile-pack strained tomatoes or one 35-ounce can American tomatoes, passed through the fine disc of a food mill

   ½ cup dry white wine

   One 2-inch strip of orange zest

   ¾ teaspoon kosher salt

   ¼ teaspoon freshly ground black pepper

   ⅛ teaspoon cayenne pepper

   ½ cup Basic Chicken Stock (page 501), Vegetable Broth (page 506) or commercial chicken broth

   2 to 3 tablespoons brown sugar

   1 to 2 tablespoons red wine vinegar

   2 tablespoons chopped fresh parsley

Heat the oil in a nonreactive saucepan. Add the onion and garlic and cook for 1 to 2 minutes over medium-high heat, until the onion is soft but not brown. Add the tomatoes, wine, orange zest, salt and both peppers. Cover and simmer for 20 minutes.

Add the remaining ingredients. Correct the seasoning with more salt, pepper, sugar and vinegar, as needed. **Makes about 2½ cups**

Baby Food Tomato Sauce

This gentle and flavorful sauce is especially delicious on fresh noodles.

   4 medium-large tomatoes (about 2 pounds), deeply cored (with hard centers removed)

   ¼ large sweet onion, cut into ½-inch chunks

   1 clove garlic, smashed, peeled and quartered

   ¼ cup olive oil

   Kosher salt to taste

Place a rack in the upper third of the oven. Preheat the oven to 500°F.

Put the tomatoes in a pan just large enough to hold them snugly. Spread the onion and garlic around the tomatoes. Pour the olive oil over the tomatoes, onion and garlic. Roast until the tomatoes have collapsed and the skin is lightly charred, 15 to 30 minutes, depending on the firmness and ripeness of the tomatoes. Remove from the oven and let sit for 15 minutes.

Purée the tomatoes in a food processor or blender until smooth. Season with salt to taste. **Makes 3½ cups**

Herbed Tomato Sauce

Another all-purpose tomato sauce with gusto. It is good with dried pasta.

1/2 small yellow onion

1/2 cup fresh parsley leaves

3 cloves garlic, smashed and peeled

1/4 cup olive oil

1/2 teaspoon dried thyme

1/2 teaspoon dried oregano

1/4 teaspoon anise seeds

2 cups canned tomato purée (preferably Italian), sterile-pack strained tomatoes or Plum Tomato Purée (page 459)

Place the onion, parsley and garlic in a food processor and process until finely chopped.

Heat the oil in a nonreactive medium saucepan. Add the onion mixture. Cook over low heat until translucent, stirring occasionally; do not brown.

Add the thyme, oregano, anise and tomato purée. Bring to a boil. Reduce the heat to low and simmer for 20 minutes, stirring occasionally.

Makes 2 cups, enough for 1 pound pasta

Microwave Variation

Scrape the chopped onion mixture into a 2½-quart soufflé dish. Stir in the oil and toss to coat. Cook, uncovered, at 100% for 5 minutes.

Remove from the oven and stir in the remaining ingredients. Cover tightly with microwave plastic wrap. Cook at 100% for 5 minutes. Prick the plastic to release steam.

Remove from the oven.

Plum Tomato Sauce

The base for the dipping sauces and as many pasta sauces as you wish to invent.

2 pounds plum tomatoes, cored and cut into 1-inch pieces (about 6 cups)

5 medium cloves garlic, smashed and peeled

1/4 cup fruity olive oil

Kosher salt and freshly ground black pepper to taste

Stovetop method: Combine all the ingredients in a nonreactive pan and cook over low heat, covered, for 45 minutes, or until the tomatoes get soft and break down.

Put the mixture through a food mill fitted with the medium disc. Pour into another nonreactive saucepan and cook, uncovered, over low heat, stirring frequently so the sauce does not scorch, until reduced to 4 cups. It will take about 1½ hours; the exact time will depend on the tomatoes used and the amount of water they contain.

Microwave method: Combine all the sauce ingredients in a 2½-quart casserole dish with a tightly fitting lid. Cover and cook at 100% for 15 minutes.

Remove from the oven and uncover. Pass the mixture through a food mill fitted with the medium disc. Discard the pulp and return the purée to the casserole. Cook, uncovered, at 100% for about 25 minutes, until reduced to 4 cups.

Remove from the oven and allow to cool.

Makes 4 cups

Basic Pizza Sauce

1 clove garlic, smashed, peeled and minced

1 tablespoon olive oil

3 cups Plum Tomato Purée (page 459)

1/4 teaspoon dried oregano

1/2 teaspoon kosher salt

Freshly ground black pepper to taste

In a 4-quart nonreactive saucepan, cook the garlic in oil over medium heat for 5 minutes, or until soft but not browned. Add the tomato purée. Simmer for 20 minutes over low heat, stirring occasionally. Remove from heat; stir in the oregano, salt and pepper. **Makes 2 cups**

Even-More-Basic Pizza Sauce

One 28-ounce can whole tomatoes in juice (not purée)

1 small clove garlic, smashed, peeled and minced

1/2 teaspoon dried oregano

Large pinch of hot red pepper flakes

Kosher salt to taste

Pass the tomatoes and juice through a food mill fitted with the fine disc into a medium nonreactive saucepan. Add the garlic, oregano and red pepper. Simmer over medium heat for 5 minutes. Add the salt. **Makes 2 1/2 cups**

DIPPING SAUCES

Of course, many sliced raw vegetables are dipped into sauces at cocktail parties. It really is a matter of individual taste as to what one wants to use. Usually a slightly thicker sauce is less messy. I find that Green Goddess Dressing (page 452) is always welcome. Tempura and fried food can be dipped in the Asian-flavored sauces. Acras de Christophene (page 122) and other small balls of fried delight can go with a spicy tomato sauce or a flavored hollandaise.

Many dipping sauces can also be used as pasta sauces. The Asian ones are good with rice noodles. For the rest, I counsel experimentation.

Pacific Tomato Dipping Sauce

This sauce is unexpected but good with vegetables fried in tempura batter (page 516) or Corn Fritters (page 32)

1 cup Plum Tomato Sauce (page 462) or puréed canned plum tomatoes (with their liquid)

1/2 ounce fresh ginger (about 1 x 1-inch piece), peeled

1/2 cup loosely packed cilantro leaves

5 medium cloves garlic, smashed and peeled

2 tablespoons soy sauce, preferably tamari

2 teaspoons rice wine vinegar

1/4 teaspoon hot red pepper sauce

Combine all the ingredients in a blender and process until smooth. Let stand for at least 1 hour to let the flavors develop. **Makes 1 1/4 cups**

Spicy Middle Eastern Tomato Sauce

Use this as a dipping sauce with Acras de Cristophene (page 122), or serve with stuffed vegetables with a Middle Eastern flavor.

2 1/2 cups Plum Tomato Sauce (page 462) or puréed canned plum tomatoes (with their liquid)

15 medium cloves garlic, smashed and peeled

2 teaspoons ground cumin

2 teaspoons ground coriander

2 teaspoons sweet paprika

1 teaspoon ground cardamom

1 teaspoon kosher salt

1/2 teaspoon cayenne pepper

Pinch of ground cinnamon

Pinch of ground cloves

2 tablespoons fresh lime juice (if serving warm)

1 cup plain yogurt (if serving cold)

Place all the ingredients except the lime juice and yogurt in a blender and process until completely smooth. Allow the sauce to stand for at least an hour for the flavors to blend.

If using as a warm sauce, heat gently on top of the stove, then stir in the lime juice. Or, if using as a cold dipping sauce, stir in the yogurt. **Makes 2 1/2 cups, 3 1/3 cups with optional yogurt**

Tomato Basil Dipping Sauce

I love the fresh taste of this sauce. Try stirring some into eggs as they scramble.

1 cup Plum Tomato Sauce (page 462) or puréed canned plum tomatoes (with their liquid)

2/3 cup medium-packed fresh basil leaves

10 medium cloves garlic, smashed and peeled

2 tablespoons tomato paste

1 tablespoon fresh lemon juice

6 tablespoons olive oil

2 teaspoons kosher salt

Freshly ground black pepper to taste

Place all the ingredients in a food processor and process until smooth. **Makes 1 2/3 cups**

Peanut Dipping Sauce

There are two basic kinds of peanut dipping sauce used in the Malay Straits area and the rest of Southeast Asia. One is thin with flecks of peanuts and spices floating in it (such as Southeast Asian Dipping Sauce, page 465). This is the other kind—smooth, creamy and mildly spicy.

5 ounces unsalted roasted peanuts (about 1/2 cup)

2 slices (1/8-inch) peeled fresh ginger (about 1/4 ounce)

1 medium clove garlic, smashed and peeled

2 teaspoons sugar

1/2 teaspoon hot red pepper flakes

4 teaspoons soy sauce, preferably tamari

1 tablespoon rice wine vinegar

5 teaspoons fresh lime juice

Combine all the ingredients except the lime juice in a food processor. Process until smooth. With the motor running, add 1 cup warm water in a thin stream and process until incorporated. Add the lime juice and process to blend. Serve at room temperature. **Makes 1 2/3 cups**

Southeast Asian Dipping Sauce

This sauce can be made even prettier by stirring in a tablespoon of thinly shredded peeled carrot and shredded, peeled seeded cucumber. This is a good salad dressing as well.

Make a large quantity to store (covered, in the refrigerator) for months by omitting the scallion and fresh cilantro; add them proportionately about thirty minutes before serving, along with the carrot and cucumber, if desired.

> $1/2$ cup Thai or Vietnamese fish sauce (nam pla or nuoc nam)
>
> $1/3$ cup fresh lime juice
>
> $1/4$ cup soy sauce, preferably tamari
>
> $1/4$ cup coarsely chopped unsalted roasted peanuts
>
> 1 scallion, trimmed and sliced very thin on the bias (about $1/4$ cup)
>
> 2 tablespoons sugar
>
> 2 tablespoons chopped cilantro
>
> 1 small jalapeño pepper, very finely diced (about 1 $1/2$ tablespoons)

Combine all the ingredients in a jar with a tight-fitting lid. Shake vigorously until the sugar is dissolved. Let stand at room temperature for up to 4 hours, or in the refrigerator for up to 2 days. Bring to room temperature if necessary and shake vigorously before serving. **Makes 1 $1/4$ cups**

Chinese Dipping Sauce

This is a simple all-purpose sauce for fried vegetables, dumplings and other Asian finger foods. Those who like hot food can add up to twice as much chili paste. Those who want a milder sauce can use Japanese Dipping Sauce (at right).

> $3/4$ cup dark Chinese soy sauce with molasses
>
> 1 tablespoon Chinese chili paste with garlic
>
> $3/4$ teaspoon sugar

Whisk all the ingredients together in a small bowl. **Makes a scant 1 cup**

Japanese Dipping Sauce

Ponzu is a standard Japanese sauce for fried foods. I have adapted it for ease of preparation. The original recipe calls for heating the mirin and adding bonito flakes and konbu (dried kelp), a kind of seaweed. That mixture is then allowed to mellow for a month or more. I really like this easily made adaptation, which is good with tempura and other semi-spicy fried foods.

> $1/4$ cup mirin
>
> $1/2$ cup soy sauce, preferably tamari
>
> 2 tablespoons Ginger Juice (page 509)
>
> $1/4$ cup rice wine vinegar
>
> 2 tablespoons fresh lemon juice

Combine all the ingredients in a small bowl. **Makes 1 cup**

Harissa Sauce

This pungent red sauce can be made as spicy as desired or as guests might enjoy by upping the quantities of sambal and harissa; increase the other seasonings to taste so as to maintain the flavor balance. Harissa is added to Moroccan dishes as they are eaten and the palate numbs. It is a good sauce for any cold steamed vegetable as well. Its spiciness can be diluted—nontraditionally—and the texture thickened with a good mayonnaise.

continued

The ingredient list looks long, but it is mainly composed of spices that require no work beyond purchase.

- 1 cup tomato juice
- 3/4 cup chopped tomatoes, either drained canned or seeded fresh (about 8 ounces)
- 1 teaspoon sambal olek (see the Cook's Guide, page 628)
- 1 teaspoon harissa paste (the best is French, in tubes)
- 3/4 teaspoon anise seeds
- Pinch of ground allspice
- Pinch of freshly grated nutmeg
- 1/4 teaspoon ground coriander
- 1/8 teaspoon ground cinnamon
- 1/4 teaspoon ground cardamom
- 2 teaspoons ground cumin
- 1/2 teaspoon ground ginger
- 2 tablespoons fresh lemon juice
- 2 tablespoons fresh lime juice
- 3 medium cloves garlic, smashed, peeled and finely chopped
- 1 tablespoon olive oil
- 1 cup Classic Mayonnaise (page 455), Cooked-Yolk Mayonnaise (page 455) or commercial mayonnaise (optional)

Combine all the ingredients except the olive oil and optional mayonnaise in a heavy nonaluminum pot and bring to a boil. Reduce the heat to a simmer and cook for 5 minutes. Turn off the heat and stir in the olive oil. Serve warm, stirring in the mayonnaise first, if desired. **Makes 2 cups**

Bagna Cauda

"Bagna cauda" is, literally, a "warm bath" in Italian—in this case, of seasoned olive oil. Dig the old fondue pot out of the back of the closet and use it to keep this warm on the table. Put the pot in the middle of a large platter and surround with pieces or slices of vegetables and chunky bread. Make the slices long enough (leave some stem on the broccoli) so that friends don't get their fingers in the oil. This can be made ahead and reheated, but not in a plastic container if using the microwave—it gets too hot. The recipe can easily be multiplied.

- One 3-ounce jar anchovy fillets (about 18 fillets) or an equal amount of canned anchovy fillets, drained
- 1/2 cup milk
- 8 tablespoons (4 ounces) unsalted butter
- 35 medium cloves garlic, smashed, peeled and thinly sliced
- 1/2 cup olive oil

Place the anchovies in a small bowl. Cover with the milk and let stand for 1 hour. Drain and pat dry.

Melt the butter in a medium pan over low heat. Stir in the anchovies, garlic and oil. Simmer gently over very low heat, stirring occasionally, for about 15 minutes, or until the garlic is very soft.

Transfer the mixture to a blender and blend until the anchovies are puréed. Return to the saucepan and reheat. **Makes 1 cup**

Microwave Variation
Soak the anchovies as above; drain and dry. Place the butter, garlic and oil in a 2½-quart soufflé dish. Add the anchovies. Cover tightly with microwave plastic wrap. Cook at 100% for 8 minutes. Prick the plastic to release steam.

Remove from the oven and uncover. Transfer the mixture to a blender and blend until until the anchovies are puréed. Return to the soufflé dish or a ceramic serving bowl. Reheat, uncovered, for 30 seconds, or until hot.

Anchovy Dip

Anchöiade, the Provençal delight, is not a sauce to give friends who hate anchovies, but I love it—and I pick the anchovies out of Caesar salad. It is particularly good with fennel, Belgian endive and radishes and is an intensely flavorful dip for crudités. It's also good on bread, either dipped up with or spread on crostini (see Croutons, page 510), and it makes a terrific salad dressing; use a quarter cup for three cups torn-up romaine (for a lighter variation, see Bagna Cauda, page 466).

> Four 2-ounce cans anchovy fillets
>   packed in olive oil
>
> 25 medium cloves garlic, smashed and peeled
>
> 1 cup olive oil
>
> 1 cup packed fresh basil leaves
>   (about 2 1/4 ounces)
>
> 4 teaspoons red wine vinegar
>
> Freshly ground black pepper to taste

Combine the anchovies (with their oil) and garlic in a blender and process until smooth. With the motor running, add the olive oil in a thin, steady stream. Add the remaining ingredients and process until thoroughly combined and smooth.

Transfer to a container and store, covered, in the refrigerator for up to 5 days. Let come to room temperature before serving. **Makes 2 cups**

OTHER SAUCES

Semi-Thai Sauce

Don't put this on a delicate, mild-tasting ingredient; it will overwhelm light-tasting vegetables or other foods. However, it can make almost anything taste delicious. I have added oil and used it as a salad dressing.

> 4 medium cloves garlic, smashed and peeled
>
> 1 ounce fresh ginger, peeled and cut into small
>   pieces (about 1/4 cup)
>
> 3 tablespoons sugar
>
> 2 tablespoons soy sauce, preferably tamari
>
> 6 tablespoons fresh lime juice
>
> 1/2 cup Thai or Vietnamese fish sauce
>   (nam pla or nuoc nam)

Place all the ingredients in a blender and process until smooth, stopping once or twice to scrape the sides of the jar. **Makes 1 cup**

Pesto Sauce (Pistou)

"Pesto" is Italian, "pistou" is French. Either can be made with or without pine nuts and cheese. It depends on the dish, tradition and personal preference. In soup, it is usually without nuts or cheese. One version or another is used for Green Soup (page 382). This is delicious in its ubiquitous use as a sauce for pasta. I prefer it on fresh egg pastas or slender dried pasta such as spaghettini. This recipe makes enough sauce for about one pound pasta. I give no amount for salt, as its presence, absence or quantity will depend on the cheese.

continued

2 tablespoons pine nuts (optional)

2 large bunches basil, leaves only, washed well and dried

2 medium cloves garlic, smashed and peeled

1/4 cup olive oil

3 tablespoons freshly grated Parmesan (optional)

Kosher salt to taste

If using the pine nuts, toast in a small skillet over medium-low heat for about 4 minutes, tossing frequently, until evenly lightly browned. Immediately remove them from the pan and cool completely.

Finely chop the basil and garlic in a food processor. With the machine running, pour in the olive oil in a slow, steady stream. Add the cheese and pine nuts, if using. Process until fairly smooth. Salt to taste. **Makes 3/4 cup**

Olive Oil and Garlic Sauce

This can be used instead of the garlic sauce given with the yuca on page 147. It is equally good with other bland roots and vegetables, from steamed potatoes to cauliflower.

1 cup olive oil

1 cup fresh lemon juice

2 tablespoons crushed garlic

2 teaspoons kosher salt, or to taste

1/2 teaspoon freshly ground black pepper

Whisk together all the ingredients in a bowl. Refrigerate, covered, for at least 4 hours before using. **Makes 2 cups**

Blood Orange Sauce

A smooth spoon of this tangy citrus sauce will add bright color to the plate. It goes especially well with Pumpkin Pudding (page 134).

1/3 cup fresh blood orange juice

1/3 cup sour cream or crème fraîche

1 tablespoon sugar

Whisk the ingredients together in a bowl until no streaks are visible. **Makes a scant 2/3 cup**

Doughs and Pastries

James Thurber wrote that "containers for the thing contained" are very important. In this part of the book, they are both literal containers or, like pasta, transporters.

PASTA DOUGHS

Pasta is one of the most useful and delectable things to make at home. All of the following can go in soups or in clear meat, chicken or vegetable stocks or broths; see pages 501–507. Also, all can be used immediately or frozen (see page 471 for freezing directions).

All the yields given below and after each recipe are accurate to a point: Depending on whether they are rolled by hand or machine, or with which machine, the pasta sheets here may come out longer and thinner or shorter and fatter than mine.

Roll, fill and cut the pasta of choice according to the instructions on pages 470–471 or in the individual recipe.

For stuffed pastas, the lighter the filling, the lighter the sauce—such as Baby Food Tomato Sauce (page 461), alone or with veggies and cream for light fillings. For more robust fillings, use a more robust sauce, such as Herbed Tomato Sauce (page 462).

Basic Pasta Dough

This dough has no salt, which makes it more tender than salted dough. Do remember to salt the boiling water or the sauce more heavily than usual.

> **2 large eggs**
>
> **1 tablespoon olive oil**
>
> **1 1/2 cups all-purpose flour,**
>   **plus additional as needed**

Beat the eggs and oil in a small bowl. Put 1¼ cups of the flour in a food processor. While the motor is running, pour the egg and oil through the feed tube and process until a stiff dough forms. Add 2 to 3 tablespoons more flour if necessary.

Remove the dough to a lightly floured board. Knead for about 5 minutes, adding 2 to 3 tablespoons flour as necessary, until the dough is very smooth and elastic. Wrap the dough in plastic wrap and let it rest at room temperature for 15 minutes.

Makes about 12 ounces, or six 15 x 5-inch sheets, enough for sixty 2-inch tortelli, thirty-six 2 1/2-inch square ravioli, forty-two 3-inch round ravioli or 4 first-course servings with 1 cup thick sauce or slightly less of a thinner sauce

How to Roll Out, Shape and Fill Pasta

Divide the pasta dough into portions as specified in the recipe.

To roll out with a machine: Dust each portion lightly with flour. Start rolling with the machine on the widest setting and work down one setting at a time to the third-smallest setting if making lasagna, the second-smallest setting if making a stuffed pasta or fettuccine. While rolling, lightly dust the pasta as necessary to prevent it from sticking to the machine. Store the rolled-out sheets of pasta between kitchen towels dusted with cornmeal or flour.

To roll out by hand: On a lightly floured board, roll each piece out very thin. It should be possible to read a magazine through the pasta. (Don't use the traditional newspaper; the print will smear onto the dough.) Store the rolled-out sheets of pasta between kitchen towels dusted with cornmeal or flour.

To Make Fettuccine

If using a machine: Run the sheets of pasta through the $1/2$-inch (or so) cutters.

If rolling by hand: Flour the sheets well and roll them up, starting at one of the short ends. With a pizza cutter or very sharp knife, cut the rolls crosswise into $1/2$-inch strips.

In either case, separate the strips immediately, keeping the ends in line (for neatness). Dust the fettuccine lightly with fine semolina or cornmeal. Roll each strip's worth (or dozen or so fettuccine) up into little nests. Store on a semolina- or cornmeal-dusted baking sheet until needed.

To Make Cappelletti

Cut the pasta sheets into 2-inch squares. Place 1 teaspoon filling in the center of each square. Moisten the edges of the squares with a brush dipped in water, fold into triangles and press the edges to seal. Wrap the two bottom corners of each triangle around the tip of the index finger and press together to seal. Set the finished cappelletti on a kitchen towel dusted with cornmeal or flour.

To Make Tortelli

With a sharp biscuit cutter or a glass, cut the sheets of pasta into 2-inch circles. Quickly reroll and cut the scraps. Place the circles on a kitchen towel dusted with cornmeal or flour.

Place a level teaspoon filling in the center of half the circles. Brush the edge of one circle lightly with water, cover with a plain circle and press the edges together to seal. Repeat, setting the finished tortelli on a kitchen towel dusted with cornmeal or flour.

To Make Ravioli

For square ravioli made by hand or by machine:
Roll the dough into 15 x 5-inch sheets. Divide each sheet into twelve 2¹/₂-inch squares and place 2 teaspoons filling in the center of each. Moisten the edges of each "square" with a brush dipped in water. Cover with another sheet, matching the edges and pressing the air out from around the mounds of filling to seal the two sheets together. Cut into ravioli with a sharp knife or fluted pastry cutter.

For round ravioli, using a sharp biscuit cutter or a glass: Cut 2¹/₂- to 3-inch circles from the dough sheets. Place 1¹/₂ teaspoons filling in the center of half of them. Moisten the edge of one circle with a brush dipped in water, cover with a plain dough circle, matching up the edges, and press the air out from around the filling. Repeat with the remaining circles. Reroll the scraps, working quickly, before they dry. Or cut them into random "spoon-size" pieces and spread them out to dry; add to soups in place of small diced pasta or rice.

Store the ravioli on a baking sheet lined with a lightly floured kitchen towel. If it's necessary, separate layers with more lightly floured towels. Refrigerate until needed.

Pasta Fillings

Artichoke Purée (page 236)—1 cup will fill 48 cappelletti, 36 ravioli or 16 tortelli

Mushroom Duxelles (page 405)—1 recipe will fill 72 cappelletti, 48 ravioli or 36 tortelli

Nettle and Ricotta Filling (page 245)—¹/₂ recipe will fill 72 cappelletti, 36 ravioli or 24 tortelli

Pasta Pointers

Two ounces (a packed but level ¹/₄-cup measure) of fresh pasta yields one 15 x 5-inch sheet, on which the yields following each pasta recipe are based. Weight yields are given with each recipe, too. Divide or multiply as needed.

All filled pasta shapes may be frozen. Place a single layer of pasta on a parchment-paper-lined baking sheet and freeze until solid. Transfer the frozen pasta in single or multiple servings to sealable plastic bags and freeze until needed, or for up to 6 weeks.

A typical hand-cranked pasta machine can make strips up to 5 inches wide. To make the widest possible strips, roughly shape each 2-ounce portion of dough into a 5 x 3-inch rectangle and begin feeding it through the machine with one of the wide ends first.

If not overfloured or overworked, pasta scraps can be rerolled to get the most out of each batch.

Green Pasta Dough

A particularly beautiful version of basic pasta dough, this too is made without salt. It is important to squeeze out as much water as possible from the spinach.

    1/4 pound spinach, stemmed
        (about 4 cups packed leaves)

    2 cups all-purpose flour, plus additional
        as needed

    3 large eggs

Wash the spinach leaves well in several changes of water. Transfer them to a large pot. Using only the water clinging to the leaves, steam over high heat for about 4 minutes, or until wilted but still bright green. Drain in a sieve. Rinse under cool running water. Hand-squeeze as much water as possible from the spinach. Coarsely chop.

Place the flour and spinach in a food processor and process until the spinach is very finely chopped and mixed with the flour. With the motor running, add the eggs all at once and process until a stiff dough forms.

Transfer the dough to a lightly floured surface. Knead, adding a tablespoon or two more flour as necessary, until the dough is smooth and elastic. Wrap the dough in plastic wrap and let it rest at room temperature for at least 30 minutes.

Makes about 18 ounces, or nine 15 x 5-inch sheets, enough for ninety 2-inch tortelli, fifty-four 2¹/₂-inch square ravioli, sixty 3-inch round ravioli or 8 to 10 first-course servings with 2¹/₄ cups thick sauce or slightly less of a thinner sauce

Chervil Pasta Dough

This dough is best if made no longer than a few hours in advance.

    2 cups all-purpose flour, plus additional
        as needed

    1¹/₄ ounces chervil sprigs, with tender stems
        (about 1¹/₂ cups loosely packed)

    2 teaspoons kosher salt

    3 large eggs

Place the flour, chervil and salt in a food processor and process until the chervil is very finely chopped and mixed with the flour. With the motor running, add the eggs all at once and process until a stiff dough forms.

Transfer the dough to a lightly floured surface. Knead, adding a tablespoon or two more flour as necessary, until the dough is smooth and elastic. Wrap the dough in plastic wrap and let it rest at room temperature for at least 1 hour.

Makes about 14 ounces, or seven 15 x 5-inch sheets, enough for seventy 2-inch tortelli, forty-two 2¹/₂-inch square ravioli, forty-eight 3-inch round ravioli or 6 to 8 first-course servings with 1³/₄ cups thick sauce or slightly less of a thinner sauce

Cilantro-Jalapeño Pasta Dough

Use only the leaves and the top half of the tender cilantro stems, and be sure they are completely dry. Even a hint of moisture will alter the texture of the dough. This is used in Mexican Lasagna (page 437), but I often double it and save half in the refrigerator or freezer to turn into fettuccine.

1 scant cup all-purpose flour, plus additional
    as needed

$3/4$ cup loosely packed cilantro sprigs,
    with tender stems (about $1 1/4$ ounces)

1 small jalapeño pepper, halved and seeded

1 teaspoon kosher salt

1 large egg plus 1 yolk

Place the flour, cilantro, jalapeños and salt in a food processor and process until the cilantro is very finely chopped and mixed with the flour. With the motor running, add the egg and yolk and process until a stiff dough forms.

Transfer the dough to a lightly floured surface. Knead, adding a tablespoon or two more flour as necessary, until the dough is smooth and elastic. Wrap the dough in plastic wrap and let it rest at room temperature for at least 1 hour.

Makes about 8 ounces, or four 15 x 5-inch sheets, enough for forty 2-inch tortelli, twenty-four $2^1/2$-inch ravioli, twenty-eight 3-inch round ravioli or 4 first-course servings with 1 cup thick sauce or slightly less of a thinner sauce

PIZZA AND FOCACCIA

Pizza Dough

Italy, its off islands and the French Riviera serve up multitudes of different pizzas. Originally they were inexpensive ways for poor people to make delicious, filling food. Here is a basic pizza dough sturdy enough to hold a variety of toppings. It can be made into a thicker nine-inch square Sicilian-style pizza. Done as such, it will hold roughly the same amount of toppings, but in a thicker layer. Allow five extra minutes' baking time.

For another version of pizza, see Pissaladière (page 374) and Kale Pissaladière (page 280). Of course, in addition to the vegetable toppings suggested on page 474, there is a meaty world out there to choose from, including sliced pepperoni, crumbled cooked Italian sausage or anchovies—those packed in oil, which need only draining, or in salt, which need soaking in cold water and boning before use. While I'm on the topic, some canned anchovies can be overly salty. Soak them briefly in cold water after draining off the oil.

$3/4$ cup warm (110° to 115°F) water

2 tablespoons olive oil or vegetable oil,
    plus more for the bowl and baking sheet

One $1/4$-ounce envelope active dry yeast

2 cups all-purpose flour, plus more as needed

1 teaspoon kosher salt

1 tablespoon coarse cornmeal (optional)

Stir the water, oil and yeast together in a medium bowl until the yeast is dissolved. Cover with a towel and set aside in a warm place until the yeast is foamy.

Add the flour and salt. Stir until a firm but rough dough is formed. If necessary, add additional flour, 1 tablespoon at a time. Turn the dough out onto a generously floured board. Knead, adding flour as necessary to prevent the dough from sticking to the board, until it is smooth and elastic.

Wash out the bowl, dry it well and pour in enough oil to film the bottom. Turn the dough in the bowl until lightly coated with oil. Cover with a towel and let rise until doubled, about 45 minutes.

To form the pizza crust, punch down the dough, keeping it in a rough circular shape. Let it rest for a few minutes. Lightly oil a baking sheet (even if using a nonstick sheet). Sprinkle the optional cornmeal over the sheet.

Put the dough in the center of the baking sheet. Working from the center toward the edges, stretch the dough with your fingertips to make a circle about 12 inches in diameter with slightly thicker edges.

Let the dough rest while the oven is preheating; however, the dough shouldn't rise at all before baking. Place a rack in the lower third of the oven and preheat the oven to 425°F. **Makes one 12-inch crust**

Basic Pizza

This is a basic pizza. An untraditional but delicious variation is made using 1½ cups Ratatouille Pasta Sauce (page 338), Mushroom Duxelles (page 405) or Caponata (page 327) in place of pizza sauce. Top with cheese (Gruyère goes well with the duxelles) and bake a little longer.

The classic cheese for pizza is mozzarella. Choose between fresh and the much firmer, but gooier, supermarket brands. Shred it coarsely on a box grater; avoid the preshredded kind.

Generous ¹/₂ cup Basic Pizza Sauce (page 463) or Even-More-Basic Pizza Sauce (page 463)

1 unbaked crust made from 1 recipe Pizza Dough (page 473)

1 cup shredded mozzarella cheese

¹/₄ cup coarsely grated Parmesan cheese

Just before baking, spread the sauce over the dough, leaving the edge uncovered. The dough may appear only lightly coated in places; that is fine. Scatter both cheeses over the sauce.

Bake until the mozzarella and the underside of the crust are golden, about 18 minutes. Cool for a few minutes before serving.
Makes one 12-inch pizza, 8 slices

Vegetable Pizza

After topping pizza with the sauce and cheese, scatter 1 cup of any of the following over the cheese: sautéed mushrooms (see page 608); coarsely chopped sautéed spinach or broccoli di raab (see page 646); red and/or yellow bell peppers cut into ½-inch dice; coarsely chopped steamed or boiled broccoli florets (see the Cook's Guide, page 548); oil-blanched eggplant cubes (page 580) or grilled eggplant cut into ½-inch squares (see page 581); or coarsely chopped sautéed artichoke hearts (see the Cook's Guide, page 529). Half a cup or so thinly sliced red onion would go nicely with any of the above.

Deep-Dish Pizza

1 recipe Pizza Dough (page 473)

1¹/₂ cups coarsely grated Swiss cheese (about 4 ounces)

1¹/₃ cups coarsely grated whole-milk mozzarella (packaged, not fresh; about 4 ounces)

¹/₂ cup freshly grated Parmesan cheese

1¹/₂ cups thick tomato sauce, such as Herbed Tomato Sauce (page 462), or a thick store-bought sauce (do not use either of the pizza sauces on page 463; they are too thin)

Make the dough. While it is rising, toss together the Swiss, mozzarella and Parmesan cheeses.

Place a rack in the center of the oven. Preheat the oven to 400°F. Lightly oil a 1½-inch deep 8-inch round cake pan.

Punch down the dough into a rough 12-inch circle. Using fingertips, stretch the dough until it covers the bottom and sides of the pan; it is fine if the dough comes above the sides of the pan in places. The dough needn't be perfectly even, but it should be of relatively even thickness.

Scatter ¾ cup of the cheese mix evenly over the crust. Spread the sauce in an even layer over the cheese. Top with the remaining cheese.

Place on a baking sheet and bake until the cheese and crust are golden brown and the edge is bubbling, about 30 minutes. Cool for 10 minutes before cutting. **Makes one 8-inch pizza, 6 slices**

Caponata Pizza

Substitute 2 cups Caponata (page 327) or an equal amount of store-bought caponata for the tomato sauce.

Pizza Amalfitana

In their homeland—the stretch of coast just south of Naples—these are often done as miniatures, with the dough rolled out in circles just large enough to accommodate a smallish slice of tomato. Tuck the basil underneath the tomato and top with small pieces of sliced fresh mozzarella. That is how they make them at San Pietro in Positano. The individual pizzas are slipped into the brick oven to order and served immediately—no chance to sit around and get tired.

> 1 crust made from 1 recipe Pizza Dough (page 473)
>
> 2 ripe large tomatoes, cored and cut into ½-inch slices
>
> ¾ pound fresh mozzarella, cut into ¼-inch slices
>
> 1 cup roughly torn fresh basil leaves
>
> 2 tablespoons olive oil
>
> Kosher salt and coarsely ground black pepper to taste

Place a rack in the lower third of the oven. Preheat the oven to 425°F.

Cover the dough, except the thick edge, with the tomato slices. It is fine to leave some space between them; cut some slices in half to fit into tight spaces. Lay the sliced mozzarella over the tomatoes, again leaving spaces.

Bake for 10 minutes. Scatter the basil over the cheese and drizzle the oil over everything. Season with salt and pepper. Bake until the underside of the crust is golden brown and the cheese is bubbling, about 8 minutes. **Makes one 12-inch pizza, 8 slices**

Basic Focaccia

These days many things are called focaccia. Many of them aren't. It is not a cakelike creation, but a robust, thick version close to a pizza that is eaten as a bread, sometimes with rosemary on the top.

> One ¼-ounce package active dry yeast
>
> ¾ cup lukewarm (110°F) water
>
> ¼ cup olive oil, plus additional for greasing pan
>
> 2 tablespoons kosher salt
>
> 2¼ cups all-purpose flour
>
> **TOPPING**
>
> ½ teaspoon olive oil
>
> ½ teaspoon kosher salt
>
> Freshly ground black pepper to taste

Food processor method: Place the yeast and water in a food processor and process for a few seconds. Let stand for 5 minutes.

Add the olive oil, salt and 1 cup flour to the yeast mixture. Process for 30 seconds. Add the remaining 1¼ cups flour. Process for 1½ minutes to knead the dough.

continued

Heavy-duty mixer method: Place the yeast and water in a mixer fitted with the paddle attachment and mix a few seconds to blend. Let stand for 5 minutes.

Add the olive oil, salt and 1 cup flour to the yeast mixture. Mix on low speed until smooth. Replace the paddle with the dough hook. Add the remaining 1¼ cups flour. Mix on medium speed for 1½ minutes to knead.

Regardless of the mixing method, allow the dough to rise once (see Note).

Lightly coat a rolling pin and work surface with olive oil and shape the dough.

To make a round: Roll the dough into a 10½-inch circle (it will shrink to about 9½ inches). Place it on an oiled baking sheet (not air-cushioned).

To make a rectangle: Oil an 11½ x 8 x 2-inch or 11 x 7 x 2-inch baking dish. Roll the dough into a rectangle slightly larger than the dish. Place it in the dish.

Allow the dough to rise until doubled.

Place a rack in the lower third of the oven. Preheat the oven to 400°F.

Make small indentations all over the dough with a skewer or the handle of a wooden spoon. Gently spread the ½ teaspoon olive oil over the dough with fingers. Sprinkle with the salt and pepper. Bake for 45 minutes. Remove from the oven, cut into slices and serve hot.

NOTE ON RISING THE DOUGH: Form the dough into a ball and put it in a lightly greased bowl. Turn the dough until lightly coated with oil. Cover with a kitchen towel and let rise in a warm location until doubled in bulk (looking twice as large). Or place the dough to double in a 2-quart measure, which will show its progress.

Punch down the dough—push a hand into it once or twice. If more than one rising is called for, repeat, including the punching down.

Makes one 9½-inch round loaf (16 small wedges) or one 11 x 8-inch rectangular loaf (24 small squares)

PASTRY AND PIE DOUGHS

Basic Pie Crust

In the good old days, this would have been made with lard for a flakier dough. Today most of us do not keep fresh lard on hand and many are leery of the dietary implication. However, lard can be substituted one for one for the butter. This can be a crust for a sweet filling or a savory one. Do not use with a wet filling, which could make the dough soggy.

If making the dough by hand, keep fingers cool by dipping them in cold water from time to time if need be.

> 1 cup all-purpose flour
>
> 6 tablespoons cold unsalted butter, cut into 4 to 5 pieces
>
> 1 tablespoon sugar
>
> ½ teaspoon kosher salt
>
> 1 large egg, beaten with 1 tablespoon milk for glaze

Food processor method: Place the flour, butter, sugar and salt in a food processor and pulse until the mixture resembles coarse meal. Add 2 tablespoons cold water and process until a ball of dough forms on top of the blade. Carefully gather the dough together and shape into a disc about 4 inches in diameter. Wrap the dough in wax paper or plastic wrap and refrigerate for 30 minutes.

Hand method: Place the flour, sugar and salt in a medium bowl. Add the butter and, with fingertips, rub it into the flour until the mixture resembles coarse meal. Add 2 tablespoons cold water and work the mixture together until it forms a ball. Carefully gather the dough together and shape into a disc about 4 inches in diameter. Wrap the dough in wax paper or plastic and refrigerate for 30 minutes.

To roll out the dough: On a lightly floured work surface, roll the dough into a 12-inch circle ⅛ inch thick. Fit it into a 9-inch glass pie plate, making sure there are no air pockets trapped underneath. Run a sharp knife around the edge of the plate to trim off any excess dough. Prick the bottom of the crust every ½ inch with the tines of a fork. Refrigerate for 30 minutes to 1 hour.

Place a rack in the center of the oven. Preheat the oven to 425°F.

To partially bake the pie shell (for fillings that will need further cooking): Line the crust with aluminum foil and fill with dried beans or rice. Bake for 12 minutes. Remove from the oven and carefully lift out the foil lining and weights.

Brush the bottom, sides and edges of the crust with the egg glaze. Add the filling of choice and bake according to the recipe instructions.

To completely bake the pie shell (for fillings that do not require further cooking): Line the crust with aluminum foil and fill with dried beans or rice. Bake for 12 minutes. Remove from the oven and carefully lift out the foil lining.

Brush the bottom, sides and edges of the crust with the egg glaze. Return the crust to the oven and bake until nicely colored, about 6 minutes. Turn the pie plate once or twice while baking so the crust browns evenly. Cool completely before filling.

Makes enough for one 9-inch pie shell or about twenty-four 2-inch tartlet shells (for instructions for tartlet shells, see page 478)

Basic Tart Dough

Much like the basic pie dough crust, but firmer and not at all sweet. Doughs made in a food processor do not need refrigeration before they are rolled out. If making the dough by hand (see page 476), wrap it in plastic wrap and refrigerate it for an hour or so before rolling.

> **4 cups all-purpose flour**
>
> **14 tablespoons cold unsalted butter, cut into ¹/₂-inch pieces**
>
> **¹/₄ teaspoon kosher salt**

Place the flour, butter and salt in a food processor and pulse only until the pieces of butter are evenly distributed and coated with flour. Do not overprocess. With the machine running, again in on-and-off pulsing motions, add approximately ¾ cup ice water to the flour mixture; add only enough water to form a cohesive, not sticky, mass. The dough can be rolled out now or shaped into a disc, wrapped and refrigerated until ready to use. Proceed following specific recipe instructions or turn to Making Tartlet Shells, page 478.

Makes about 2 pounds

Flaky Tart Dough

This is the basic French tart dough, pâte brisée. It holds up very well. If desired, fill the fully baked shells several hours before a party; after they have come out of the oven but before unmolding, brush the insides of the shells with a little lightly beaten egg white. Put the baking sheet of shells back in the oven for 2 minutes, then remove and unmold them. This seals the shells so that they don't get soggy. These are the shells used for individual quiches or tarts.

continued

1 1/2 cups all-purpose flour

3/4 teaspoon kosher salt

8 tablespoons (4 ounces) cold unsalted butter, cut into small pieces

1 large egg, lightly beaten

1 teaspoon milk

Combine the flour and salt in a medium bowl. Add the butter and rub it into the flour until the mixture resembles coarse meal. Add the beaten egg and milk and gently work the mixture together until it forms a ball. Shape the dough into a disc, wrap it in plastic wrap and refrigerate for at least 2 hours.

Makes 14 ounces, enough for about twenty-eight 2- to 3-inch tartlet shells

Cheddar Cheese Tart Dough

This is very good with the Mushrooms with Yogurt and Dill (page 398) used as filling. Increase the salt to 1 teaspoon and add to the flour, along with ¾ teaspoon dry mustard, ⅛ teaspoon cayenne pepper, ¼ teaspoon caraway seeds (optional) and ⅓ cup grated cheddar cheese. Increase the milk to 1 tablespoon.

Making Tartlet Shells

Place a rack in the center of the oven. Preheat the oven to 350°F.

On a lightly floured surface, roll out the dough to about 1/8 inch thick. Cut out rounds to fit the tartlet pans and press the pastry into the pans, using knuckles. Prick the base of the pastry in each pan twice with a fork. Place the filled pans on baking sheets. Reroll the pastry scraps to make more rounds.

Place the shells in the oven and bake for 12 minutes for partially baked and 17 minutes for fully baked crusts. Remove from the oven; tip the shells out of the pans and transfer to a wire rack to cool completely. Fully baked shells can be used immediately, or they can be carefully packed in airtight containers and kept at room temperature for up to 2 days. Do not fill until shortly before using. Partially baked shells can be filled and baked as directed in the individual quiche recipes such as Miniature Tomato Basil Quiches (page 101). Or they can be carefully packed in plastic bags and stored in the refrigerator for a week or in the freezer for up to a month.

Frozen or refrigerated partially baked shells should be replaced in the tins and allowed to come to room temperature before filling and baking. Or, to use frozen or refrigerated partially baked shells for precooked mixtures, place them (in the tins) on a baking sheet (not air-cushioned) preheated in a 350°F oven: From room temperature, the shells take about 4 minutes; directly from the freezer, they take about 6 minutes. Frozen fully baked shells are not as good as thawed; they never crisp up fully.

Egg Dishes

Eggs have a love affair with vegetables. A few eggs from the refrigerator, with odds and ends of raw or cooked vegetables, will provide the makings of omelets, frittatas, soufflés and scrambled eggs. A little grated cheese couldn't hurt.

My husband makes the best scrambled eggs I know; but scrambled egg texture is so much a question of taste that I give no recipe. Milk will harden them. I like them soft, glistening and moist.

BASIC EGG PREPARATIONS

Poached Eggs

When I first started to cook, I was terrified of poaching eggs because I had heard so many tales about how things could go wrong. Since I was following standard practices of the day, horrible results were almost inevitable.

For example, my first scantily equipped kitchen came with an aluminum device with five circular depressions. Eggs were cracked one by one into the hollows and then the contrivance was set over boiling water. The resulting poached eggs were tough and ghastly.

A noted food writer suggested creating a series of whirlpools in a pot of boiling water by vigorously stirring the water in a circle and then dropping an egg into the maelstrom, then repeating this risky undertaking for each egg in turn. Many attempts at this still left egg whites broken apart pathetically in the water.

The standard chefs' trick is to add vinegar to the water. This does help congeal the whites, but all the rinsing in the world does not eliminate the vinegar taste.

Happily, much experimentation over the years has led to a regimen for perfectly poached eggs. First of all, use large eggs (small ones will cook too quickly and harden) and make sure they are as fresh as possible (though not laid the same day). It is also very important to crack each egg into a small container that has a rounded bottom. I find that demitasse cups serve nicely. The egg seems to take on the nice rounded form of the cup and, therefore, holds together in that shape in the water. The cups also have handles, making them safe to hold as the eggs are slipped into the water as close to the surface as possible (in a pinch, though, flat-bottomed old-fashioned custard cups or miniature soufflé dishes will do).

Use a nonaluminum pan that is just large enough to hold the number of poached eggs desired. Put 2 inches of water in the pan (more than that will just give the whites more opportunity to float away from the yolks). Bring to a boil.

Crack an egg into a cup. When the water is at full boil, lower the rim of the cup to the surface of the water and invert the egg in a smooth motion. Repeat with each egg.

Set a timer: Two minutes will give formed whites and runny yolks; 3 minutes, medium yolks. Beyond that, it's not poached but hard-boiled. The eggs will start to set as the water returns to a boil. A little of the white will float loosely, but most will form around the yolk. When the water has returned to a boil, lower the heat and simmer for the remaining time.

Remove the eggs with a slotted spoon. Drain on a cloth and use, or put in a bowl of warm water until needed. The eggs can be reheated by putting them back very briefly into boiling water.

Oeufs Mollets (Coddled Eggs)

"Oeufs mollets" is a French term for eggs poached in the shell. They are softer than hard-boiled eggs, the yolks slightly runny and the whites coagulated just enough to hold their shape.

Put the desired number of eggs in a pan large enough to hold them comfortably. Cover with water by 2 inches. Bring to a boil, then reduce the heat and simmer for exactly 5 minutes. Drain. Rinse under cold running water until the eggs are cooled.

Carefully crack the shells, and peel. Handle gently; the eggs will be soft. If the eggs are cooked and peeled ahead of time, cover with warm water to prevent them from drying out.

QUICHES AND CRUSTLESS QUICHES

Quiches are savory baked custards composed of three main ingredients: eggs, cream and cheese. Even the traditional crust is unnecessary. Any shallow bowl-shaped vessel that will hold liquid can be used. One of my favorite quiche recipes is baked in hollowed-out squash halves, and miniature quiches baked in muffin tins make for fine hors d'oeuvre.

With its fluted edge and straight side, the classic quiche pan is designed to encourage even cooking. A 10-inch quiche pan will hold about 3 cups of filling with crust, 4 cups without. If a quiche pan is not available, a glass pie plate will suffice. Just be mindful that the amount of filling pie plates can hold will vary and thus affect the cooking time.

Like all custards, a quiche can overcook. Bake only until the center is set and the surface slightly puffed.

Almost anything imaginable (including last night's leftovers) can be added to a quiche. However, keep the following in mind when choosing filling ingredients:

Meats—but not seafoods—should be precooked before adding.

Vegetables that cook quickly do not need to be precooked. These include corn, peas, scallions and asparagus, along with all frozen vegetables, which should be defrosted in a sieve under warm running water, then blotted dry before use.

Vegetables that exude liquid or whose flavor and texture improve when softened over heat should be precooked. These include onions, peppers, eggplants, mushrooms, celery, fennel, beets and chard. The exception is tomatoes, which can be added raw or cooked.

Vegetables that cook slowly but remain dry will benefit from partial cooking before adding to the quiche mixture. These include potatoes and winter squashes.

The crustless quiches can be found in their respective vegetable chapters:

Zucchini Custard (page 85)

Asparagus Custard (page 159)

Asparagus and Tarragon Quiche (page 160)

Crustless Spring Quiche (page 399)

The other quiches can be found in their respective vegetable chapters:

Miniature Tomato-Basil Quiches (page 101)

Miniature Mushroom Quiches (page 399)

Miniature Scallion-Pea Quiches (page 297)

Quiche with Leeks (page 388)

Quiche with Leeks, Bacon and Gruyère (page 388)

Quiche Crust

The light and floury crust that is traditional to quiche is simple to make and easy to work with. This is great for less experienced bakers.

2 cups all-purpose flour

7 tablespoons cold unsalted butter, cut into $^1/_4$-inch cubes

Pinch of kosher salt

Place the flour, butter, and salt in a food processor and pulse only until the pieces of butter are evenly distributed and coated with flour. Do not overprocess.

With the motor running, again in on-and-off pulsing motions, add enough ice water to the flour mixture to form a cohesive, but not sticky, mass, about 6 tablespoons.

Remove the mixture from the processor and press the pastry together, using the heel of the hand. Gently pat the pastry into a 12 x 8-inch rectangle. Fold into thirds as with a business letter and refrigerate for at least 1 hour, or until needed.

To bake the quiche crust: Preheat the oven to 400°F.

Roll out the dough on a lightly floured surface to a 12-inch circle. Fit it into a 10-inch quiche pan. Trim the edge. Prick the bottom in several places with a fork. Line the shell with aluminum foil and weight with dried beans or rice. Bake for 15 minutes, or until partially set. Remove the foil and weights and bake for 5 to 8 minutes longer, or until baked through and light golden brown. **Makes one 10-inch quiche shell**

Flamiche Crust

The Flemish quiche called a "flamiche" replaces the pastry crust with a yeast-risen dough. This recipe makes one that is easy to handle, similar to pizza dough. Plain bread dough makes a suitable substitute.

To accommodate the longer cooking time of the crust, it is best to fill the flamiche with a custard that contains a greater proportion of liquid and therefore will not overcook. Try the Zucchini Custard (page 85), or about 3 cups of any similar mixture.

1 teaspoon plus $^1/_8$ teaspoon ($^1/_2$ package) active dry yeast

$^1/_4$ teaspoon kosher salt

continued

1/2 lightly beaten large egg

1/2 teaspoon canola oil, plus extra for oiling the
pastry ring

1/2 cup plus 2 tablespoons all-purpose flour,
plus extra for rolling out the dough

1 large egg, beaten with 1 teaspoon water,
milk or cream for glaze (optional)

Sprinkle the yeast over ¼ cup warm water in a
cup and let sit for 5 minutes, or until bubbling.
(If nothing happens, the yeast is old and needs to
be replaced with fresh.) Combine the remaining
ingredients except the egg glaze in a small bowl.
When it is ready, add the yeast-water mixture and
stir to make a rough dough. Then knead by hand
on a work surface just until combined. If the
dough is wet and sticky, add a little more flour.
Form the dough into a ball, put it in the bowl and
cover with a kitchen towel. Let rise in a warm
place for 1 hour, or until doubled in volume.

About 20 minutes before baking, place a rack
in the center of the oven and preheat the oven
to 375°F. Lightly oil a 10-inch pastry ring. Place
the ring on a baking sheet (not air-cushioned).
Lightly oil the section of sheet enclosed by the
ring. Set aside.

On a floured surface, roll out the dough to
a 12-inch circle, using extra flour as needed.
Twirl the dough up onto the rolling pin and
set it in the oiled ring. Using fingers, tuck the
dough snugly down into the ring; leave the
edge up above the side of the ring. Lightly
prick the dough with a fork so that it will not
rise too much while cooking.

Add the filling of choice and spread it evenly.
Brush the dough rim with the egg glaze, if
desired. Bake for 40 minutes, or until the crust is
light golden brown and the filling is set Remove
and gently slide the tart off onto a flat plate.
Delicious warm, but may be served at room
temperature as well. **Makes one 10-inch round tart**

OMELETS,
FRITTATAS AND
TORTILLAS

People's opinions of the humble omelet can
best be described as highly divided. There are
two main schools of thought: One prefers that
omelets be browned. The other prefers pale.
The pale omelet is more commonplace in
France. In America, the browned omelet reigns
supreme. Interestingly, the great French chef
Escoffier preferred his omelets browned. I like
them both.

Simple, inexpensive and adaptable to many
flavors, the omelet is popular not just in this
country, but worldwide. In Spain, it is flat and
called a tortilla, traditionally filled with fragrantly
sautéed potatoes and onions and served warm
or at room temperature as a snack or tapa. The
Italian frittata and Persian kookoo (or kuku)
are similar except for the inclusion of regional
ingredients and flavorings. Even the Chinese
love omelets in the form of egg foo yung, wok-
fried and served with a side of white rice and
gravy over the top.

Omelets require no specialized equipment—
especially not one of those hinged omelet pans
resembling two half-moons with a handle on
either side. A heavy-bottomed pan with a well-
seasoned or nonstick finish will do the trick. If
the dish will be baked, the handle should also
be ovenproof.

The pale omelet, more commonly known as
the French rolled omelet, takes some practice to
learn. Jacques Pépin likes to say that he often
judges how good a chef is by his mastery of this
basic dish.

A perfect rolled omelet is plump and pale,
with small barely discernible curds on the

outside, a slightly underdone center the French call baveuse and a surface glistening from a light brushing of butter. Sprinkle on some chopped fresh herbs, accompany with a small salad and a glass of wine and lunch is served.

BASIC TECHNIQUE FOR A ROLLED (OR FOLDED) OMELET Have any filling ready, and keep warm off to the side.

Whisk the eggs together in a bowl and season with salt and freshly ground black pepper. Heat a well-seasoned or nonstick pan over medium-low heat. Melt some butter. Pour in the eggs and quickly whisk with a fork, pulling the sides in toward the center. Stop before the eggs are fully cooked. The omelet will appear mostly solid on the bottom, wet on top. When in doubt, stop sooner rather than later. (How firm or loose to serve the finished omelet is a matter of personal preference. The French as a rule prefer theirs fairly runny, but many others opt for firmer centers.)

Spread the eggs evenly in the pan and quickly rap the pan against the burner to help the omelet settle. At this point it should be solid enough to slide around inside the pan (if necessary, add more butter to the pan). Jerk the pan with one hand, allowing the base of the handle to run up against the heel of the other hand. This will shift the omelet to one side and force part of it up the sloping side of the pan, forming a lip. Put in the filling. Fold both sides over the filling and turn the finished omelet out onto a plate, seam side down. Brush with melted butter, if desired.

Rolled omelets are best made in a single-serving size. Larger ones become difficult to handle and turn. They can, however, be cooked in pans as large as 10 to 12 inches in diameter.

Number of eggs	Pan size	Servings
3	8 inches	1
6	10 inches	2

FILLINGS FOR OMELETS Fillings should be precooked and warmed if necessary before using. Allow ¼ to ⅓ cup filling per person. Suggestions include:

Caponata (page 327)

Marinated Roasted Peppers (page 55)

Silky Pepper Strips (page 58)

Mushroom Duxelles (page 405)

Parsley Pesto (page 443)

BASIC TECHNIQUE FOR A FLAT OMELET OR FRITTATA Unlike the French rolled omelet, flat omelets have two sides to worry about. The traditional technique for making one involves cooking the first side on the stovetop, then flipping the omelet out onto a platter and sliding it back into the pan to cook the other side over the heat. But I often prefer to finish the dish in the oven or under a broiler. There is less mess and the omelet puffs more attractively.

To start, heat a deep well-seasoned or nonstick pan well. (If the omelet is to be finished in the oven, the pan and handle must be ovenproof.) Add the oil or butter—it should be sizzly—and tilt to coat the bottom and sides of the pan thoroughly. Cook the filling according to the recipe. Pour the eggs over the filling and continue with one of the following methods.

Flip method: Pull the edges of the omelet toward the center as they set. Stop before the eggs are completely cooked and allow the bottom of the omelet to solidify and form a golden brown crust.

To release the omelet from the pan, run a thin flexible spatula around the edge, inserting it far enough to also loosen the bottom center. Shake the pan to make sure the omelet holds together and will move in one piece. Invert a platter over the top. Hold pan and platter together and flip. Slide the omelet back into the pan. Cook until the bottom is browned. Slide onto a platter and serve.

Bake or broil method: After adding the eggs, rotate the pan around the burner to prevent scorching and encourage even cooking, until the eggs are set on the bottom and sides. Finish the omelet in a preheated 400°F oven or under a hot broiler, cooking until lightly browned and puffy on top.

To release the omelet from the pan, run a thin flexible spatula around the edge, inserting it far enough to also loosen the bottom center. Shake the pan to make sure the omelet holds together and will move in one piece. Slide it onto a platter.

Italians often serve frittatas cool, cut into wedges, along with tomato sauce.

The following recipes for omelets and frittatas appear elsewhere in the book. They can be found in their respective vegetable chapters.

Corn and Feta Cheese Omelet (page 36)

Wild Asparagus and Ramp Frittata (page 160)

Persian Cauliflower Kookoo (page 263)

Persian Fava Bean Omelet (Kookoo-ye Baghala) (page 226)

Vegetable Frittata

In addition to the wonderful combination I offer here, I encourage you to try any of the many vegetable medley recipes in this book. Among them are Vegetable Curry (page 261), Caponata (page 327), Summer's Bounty Stew (page 334) and Summer Vegetable Gumbo (page 343). Drain excess liquid from them and heat in the skillet before adding the eggs.

2 tablespoons unsalted butter

1/4 pound small zucchini (about 1 inch in diameter), trimmed and cut across into 1/4-inch slices (about 1 1/4 cups)

1/4 pound yellow summer squash (about 1 inch in diameter), trimmed and cut across into 1/4-inch slices (about 1 cup)

1/2 small green bell pepper (about 2 ounces), diced

1/4 cup fresh peas, boiled in salted water for 3 minutes and drained

1/4 cup Egyptian bulb onions, peeled and thinly sliced, or 2 scallions, trimmed and thinly sliced

1 tablespoon finely chopped fresh parsley

Kosher salt and freshly ground black pepper to taste

7 large eggs

Melt the butter in a 10-inch nonstick or well-seasoned cast-iron pan (ovenproof if using the oven method for finishing the frittata) over medium-low heat. Add the zucchini, yellow squash, green pepper, peas, onions or scallions and parsley. Cook, stirring, until the vegetables are tender, about 15 minutes. Season with salt and pepper.

Whisk the eggs together in a bowl and stir into the vegetables, then follow one of the basic frittata techniques on page 483.

Serves 3 to 4 as a main course, 6 or more as a first course

Party Frittata (Tortilla)

Into every life a large party will fall. This whole concoction will make three large frittatas if I think in Italian, tortillas if I think in Spanish—enough for a crowd as either a main course or a starter. It is rich with vegetables and vegetarian. Of course, it can be divided. The whole thing makes fourteen cups of glop. (A twelve-inch-wide, two-inch-deep pan will hold seven cups comfortably. If using a different-size pan, measure its capacity to get an idea of how many batches to make or how to divide the ingredients. Two cups fits well in a ten-inch pan and will feed four to six as a first course. Leftover frittata can be served at room temperature with a tomato sauce or with Lovage Pesto (page 442), if there is the good fortune of having lovage around.

Vegetarians and the health-minded may want to avoid butter, but it does make a browner, richer frittata. Small zucchini and long thin Chinese eggplants will make a most attractive dish, since the slices can be left whole. Otherwise the vegetables have to be cut in quarters lengthwise and then cut across. There should be nothing in the frittata that needs to be cut to be eaten.

Use a nonstick pan if at all possible. It is then easier to flip out the frittata or simply slide it onto a large round serving dish. Cut it into wedges. If serving a sauce, put it on the side.

6 tablespoons unsalted butter or olive oil, plus a little extra for the pan

2 pounds zucchini, trimmed and cut across into ¼-inch slices, or, if using larger zucchini, first cut lengthwise into quarters, then sliced (about 6 cups)

2 pounds Chinese eggplants, cut as for zucchini (about 9 cups; Japanese eggplants can be substituted, but they must first be quartered lengthwise)

1 pound yellow bell peppers, cored, seeded, deribbed and cut into ¼-inch dice (about 3 cups)

1 pound red onions, cut into ¼-inch dice (about 3 cups)

4 pounds baby leaf spinach or stemmed regular spinach

Kosher salt and freshly ground black pepper to taste

18 large eggs (or as needed)

Put 4 tablespoons of the butter or oil in a very large ovenproof sauté pan, preferably nonstick, over medium heat (see headnote for pan sizes and amounts needed to fill each). Allow to get hot. Add all the vegetables except the spinach. Cook, tossing, until soft but not soggy. Remove to a bowl.

Return the cleaned pan to the burner and add the remaining 2 tablespoons butter or oil. Add the spinach a few cups at a time, turning so that it all wilts and fits in the pan. Once it is all wilted, turn out into a sieve or colander. Squeeze to remove as much liquid as possible. (The spinach juices can be saved for soup; see pages 247 and 249.) Coarsely chop the spinach, or leave whole if the leaves are very small.

Combine the spinach with the reserved vegetables. Salt and pepper to taste. Normally I would taste the mixture after I added the eggs, but these days raw eggs are sadly a no-no. Remember that the eggs will dilute the seasonings and add more than the vegetables alone would call for.

Preheat the broiler with the rack in the top position.

Whisk the eggs in a bowl until thoroughly combined but not beaten. Stir into the vegetables. (There should be about 14 cups; if need be, add more eggs.)

Slick the cleaned pan with a small amount of butter or oil and heat over high heat. Pour half the mix into the skillet; it should fill the pan about three-quarters full. If the oven is really large, 2 frittatas can be made at once, using two pans. Do not stir. Smooth the top and from time to time lift the edges of the frittata and let the loose eggs drool into the space. Turn the heat to medium and continue to cook until the eggs are almost set and the bottom—peek—is a lovely brown. Put the pan (or pans) under the broiler for about 5 minutes, until the eggs are fully set.

The most attractive presentation is achieved by placing a large round serving dish over the pan and flipping the whole thing over together, leaving the browner surface on top. However, if using a nonstick pan, the frittata can just be slid out onto the serving dish. (See headnote for serving suggestions and amounts.)

SOUFFLÉS

It is too bad that most cooks are afraid to make soufflés. They are really very easy. When I was much younger, I went to the house of a man who was a great connoisseur of books, art, furniture and the good life in general. Every Sunday lunch was the same, a cheese soufflé followed by a leg of lamb with haricots verts.

Here are two basic types of soufflé: one made in a traditional French style, starting with béchamel, and one starting with a thickish vegetable purée, which has the advantage of being flourless. The sweet potato variation would be a good substitute. Try doubling the amount of cheese.

Both can be prepared completely ahead, spooned into the prepared dish and refrigerated for up to 6 hours before baking. Add 5 minutes or so to the baking time.

Just as with omelets, the French prefer their soufflés baveuse, creamy in the middle. This semiliquid center serves almost as a sauce.

A note on soufflé dishes: Some dishes billed as "6-cup" hold 6 cups when filled to the brim. Others hold 6 cups when filled to the inside lip, 8 cups when filled to the brim. These soufflés may be baked in either. The true 6-cup dish produces a soufflé that rises well above the lip. The larger dish yields one that rises slightly above the rim. Both are good.

Vegetable-Cheese Soufflé Master Recipe

This is the basic mixture for a number of vegetable soufflés, the specifics for which follow. For Spinach Soufflé, see page 250.

1 1/2 cups milk

3 tablespoons unsalted butter, plus more for greasing dish

3 tablespoons all-purpose flour

3/4 teaspoon kosher salt

1/4 teaspoon freshly ground black or white pepper

4 large eggs, separated, at room temperature

Vegetable mixture of your choice (page 487), at room temperature

1 cup grated Swiss, Gruyère or Emmenthaler cheese

1/4 cup freshly grated Parmesan cheese, plus more for soufflé dish

Heat the milk in a small saucepan over low heat until steaming. Set aside.

To make the béchamel: Melt the butter in a 1 1/2- to 2-quart saucepan. Add the flour and cook over low heat for 5 minutes, stirring. Slowly add the milk, whisking briskly to prevent lumps; be sure to scrape the corners, where lumps can hide. Increase the heat to medium and cook for several minutes, stirring occasionally, until thickened. Add the salt and pepper.

Pour the béchamel into a medium bowl. Let stand, whisking often, until no longer steaming but still warm.

Beat in the egg yolks one at a time. Stir in the vegetable mixture, then the Swiss and Parmesan cheeses.

Place a rack in the center of the oven. Preheat the oven to 400°F.

Butter a 6-cup soufflé dish. Lightly coat with Parmesan cheese.

In the bowl of a stand mixer, or in another large bowl, using a handheld mixer, beat the egg whites until they hold stiff peaks. Scoop up some of the beaten whites with a rubber spatula and fold them into the cheese mixture to lighten it, then fold in the remaining whites just until a few streaks of white remain. Scrape the mixture into the prepared dish and set on a baking sheet.

Bake for 25 minutes, or until puffed, deep golden brown and only slightly wiggly in the center. Serve immediately, spooning some of the crisp edges and moister center onto each plate. **Serves 6 as a first course**

Mushroom Soufflé

1 pound mushrooms, cremini mushrooms or other firm-textured mushrooms, trimmed and cut into 1-inch pieces

3 tablespoons unsalted butter

1 teaspoon kosher salt

1/4 teaspoon freshly ground black pepper

While the béchamel is cooling, process the mushrooms in 3 batches in a food processor until finely chopped. Heat the butter in a 12-inch skillet over medium heat until foaming and just beginning to brown in places. Add the mushrooms, salt and pepper and stir until the mushrooms give up all their liquid, about 4 minutes. Increase the heat to medium-high and cook, stirring, until the liquid evaporates and the mushrooms begin to brown, about 8 minutes.

Proceed as described in the master recipe, adding the mushrooms after the egg yolks.

Broccoli Soufflé

1/2 teaspoon dried Greek oregano or 2 teaspoons finely chopped fresh thyme

1 1/2 cups cooked broccoli cut into rough 1/2-inch pieces

Whisk the oregano or thyme into the béchamel and let cool as above.

Proceed as described in the master recipe, adding the broccoli after the egg yolks.

Hot-and-Sweet Pepper Soufflé

Substitute ¾ cup roasted red bell pepper purée (see the Cook's Guide, page 629) for ¾ cup of the milk in the soufflé base.

1/2 teaspoon ground cardamom

2 poblano peppers, roasted (see the Cook's Guide, page 628), peeled, seeded, deribbed and cut into 1/4-inch dice (about 2/3 cup)

1 yellow bell pepper, roasted (see the Cook's Guide, page 628), peeled, seeded, deribbed and cut into 1/4-inch dice (about 1/2 cup)

Whisk the cardamom into the béchamel and let cool as above.

Proceed as described in the master recipe, adding the roasted peppers after the egg yolks.

Vegetable Purée Soufflé

Without Flour

There has been a rebellion in recent years in France against the use of flour. I don't agree, but when it comes to vegetable soufflés, the taste of the vegetable is often more pronounced without the use of flour.

> Unsalted butter, softened
>
> ¼ cup freshly grated Parmesan cheese, plus more for soufflé dish
>
> 1½ cups vegetable purée (see suggestions at right), at room temperature
>
> 1 cup milk, heated until hot
>
> 4 large eggs, separated, at room temperature
>
> 1 cup grated Swiss, Gruyère or Emmenthaler cheese
>
> 1 teaspoon kosher salt
>
> ¼ teaspoon freshly ground black pepper

Place a rack in the center of the oven. Preheat the oven to 400°F.

Butter a 6-cup soufflé dish. Lightly coat with Parmesan cheese.

Whisk the vegetable purée and milk in a large bowl until smooth. Beat in the egg yolks, Swiss cheese, the ¼ cup Parmesan cheese, salt, and pepper.

In the bowl of a stand mixer, or in another large bowl, using a handheld mixer, beat the egg whites until they hold stiff peaks. Scoop up some of the beaten whites with a rubber spatula and fold them into the cheese mixture to lighten it, then fold in the remaining whites just until a few streaks of white remain. Scrape the mixture into the prepared dish and set on a baking sheet.

Bake for 25 minutes, or until puffed, deep golden brown and only slightly wiggly in the center. Serve immediately, spooning some of the crisp edges and moister center onto each plate. **Serves 6 as a first course**

Sweet Potato Purée

Bake or microwave one 12-ounce sweet potato, preferably yellow (see the Cook's Guide, page 658). Let stand until cool enough to handle. Split the sweet potato lengthwise and strip off the peel with the fingers. Purée the sweet potato in a food processor. Measure out 1½ cups of purée.

Celery Root Purée

Peel 2 medium (about 10-ounce) celery roots and cut them into ¾-inch dice. Steam until tender (see the Cook's Guide, page 566). Spread out on a baking sheet to cool. Purée in a food processor until smooth. Measure out 1½ cups of purée and beat in 1 tablespoon grainy mustard and ¼ cup thinly sliced fresh chives.

Acorn or Butternut Squash Purée

Preheat the oven to 400°F.

Cut a 1½-pound acorn squash in half. Scoop out the seeds and fibers. Lightly oil the flesh with vegetable oil. Put the squash, cut side down, on a baking sheet. Bake until tender, about 1 hour. Cool until tepid. Peel the squash and purée in a food processor. Measure out 1½ cups.

Rice

Many of the world's vegetarian cuisines are rice-based. Knowing how to make good rice is essential to their enjoyment. It is also important to know what kind of rice to use. Short-grain Italian rice with a sort of white dot in the center is essential for risotto. Basmati rice is the rice of choice for Indian foods. Brown rice is essentially a modern-day health food. Latinos, Turks and Iranians like rice that does something that is a no-no in most other cultures. They like the bottom layer of rice to stick to the bottom of the pan, making a crisp cake. Puerto Ricans call this "pegao"; Cubans, "raspa"; Dominicans, "concon."

Wild rice isn't rice, but a grass. Basic white rice is best for vegetable stuffings, whereas parcooked rice is good as a side dish. Think about it and select.

Basic White Rice

1 1/2 teaspoons kosher salt

1 tablespoon unsalted butter or olive oil (optional)

1 cup long-grain white rice

Bring 1¾ cups water, the salt and butter or oil, if using, to a boil in a small saucepan. Immediately stir in the rice. Return to a boil, lower the heat to a bare simmer, cover and cook for 15 minutes. Let stand for 5 minutes off the heat.

Fluff the rice with a fork before serving.

Makes 3 cups

Rice Pilaf

Pilaf is related to risotto, but the liquid is added all at once and the pot is covered.

3/4 cup dark raisins or dried currants

1/2 cup ghee or Clarified Butter (page 453)

1 large onion (about 12 ounces), sliced (about 3 cups)

3 cinnamon sticks

3 whole cloves

Seeds from 3 cardamom pods

3 cups long-grain white or basmati rice

1 tablespoon kosher salt

3/4 cup slivered almonds

Bring 6 cups water to a boil. Soak the raisins or currants in 1½ cups of the boiling water for several minutes, until plump.

Heat the ghee or butter in a large saucepan. Add the onions, cinnamon, cloves and cardamom seeds. Cook over high heat until the onions are softened and just beginning to color.

continued

Return the remaining 4½ cups water to a boil. Add the rice and salt to the onions and stir until the rice is coated with ghee or butter. Pour in the boiling water. Cover and cook over medium heat for 15 to 20 minutes, or until the rice has absorbed three-quarters of the water and is almost done. Taste for salt, and add more if necessary. Stir in the almonds and raisins with their soaking liquid. Continue to cook until the liquid is absorbed.

Makes 8 cups; serves 8 as a side dish

Herbed Rice

Don't be fooled by the fanciful name: "Pot likker," the leftover liquid from cooked greens, is a rich and flavorful stock, wonderful for enhancing dishes such as soups and rice. I happened to have both the dark-emerald pot likker from "braised" collards with vegetables and the Madeira cooking liquid from a roasted ham when developing this dish. Roasting a ham, while one would certainly be a good accompaniment to the rice, is not necessary. Just use a meat stock that matches the meat being served.

> 5½ cups cooking liquid from "Braised" Collards with Vegetables (page 286), Vegetable Broth (page 506) or pot likker from cooked greens
>
> 2½ cups meat stock, such as Basic Chicken Stock (page 501), Roasted Chicken Stock (page 502) or Beef Stock (page 502)
>
> 4 cups long-grain white rice
>
> 3 bunches fresh parsley, leaves only, chopped
>
> 2 bunches fresh sage, leaves only, chopped
>
> Kosher salt and freshly ground black pepper to taste

Combine the liquids in a large stockpot and bring to a boil. Add the rice, stir and bring to a boil. Reduce the heat and simmer for 13 minutes.

Add the herbs, salt and pepper. Simmer for 3 more minutes over low heat. Cover and turn off the heat. Allow the rice to stand for 10 minutes, or until all the liquid is absorbed.

Makes about 10 cups

Brown Rice

Brown rice takes longer to cook than white rice. It is also chewier and nuttier in flavor. If brown rice is preferred, use it wherever rice is called for in a recipe's serving suggestions. However, brown rice cannot be substituted for white rice in recipes, such as Stuffed Tomatoes with Rice and Basil (page 111), that call for "long-grain rice" to be cooked along with other ingredients. The timings of those recipes depend on long-grain white rice.

> ¾ tablespoon salt
>
> 1 tablespoon butter or oil
>
> 1 cup long-grain brown rice

Bring 2½ cups water, the salt and butter or oil to a boil in a 2-quart saucepan. Stir in the rice, return to the boil and reduce the heat to low. Cover and cook until the rice is tender, about 40 minutes. (Like white rice, the timing will depend on the age of the grain.) Do not uncover or stir for the first 35 minutes. At that point, peek and check. If the rice is not tender and the water is almost all absorbed, add 1 to 2 tablespoons water, cover and continue cooking until the rice is tender.

Makes a scant 4 cups

Stuffings

I've always liked stuffed vegetables, and they are a handy way to use up leftovers. I fell in love with them, however, one day in Turkey when I saw a child about ten years old leaving the bread baker's, where he had picked up a tray of vegetables made earlier in the day after the bread had finished baking. Many Middle Eastern homes did not have their own ovens, and the retained heat in the baker's oven was perfect for slow-cooking the stuffed vegetables.

Each recipe here lists how many of a certain vegetable each stuffing will fill. See the Cook's Guide for how to prepare the vegetable and how to cook the vegetable once stuffed.

PARTIALLY COOKED OR RAW STUFFINGS

Basic Rice Stuffing

This stuffing is perfect for stuffed vegetables served cold. For hot stuffed vegetables, reduce the lemon juice to two tablespoons.

1 cup long-grain white rice

1 tablespoon kosher salt

$1/4$ cup fresh lemon juice

2 teaspoons dried oregano

1 teaspoon kosher salt

Freshly ground black pepper to taste

Bring 3 cups water to a boil in a covered 4-quart pot. Add the rice and salt. Reduce the heat to medium, cover and cook for 6 minutes. Drain the rice in a colander.

In a bowl, mix the rice with the lemon juice, oregano, salt and pepper.

Makes $2^1/3$ cups, enough to fill:

Six 6- to 7-ounce (3-inch) onions

6 boats made from 5-ounce (6- to 7-inch) zucchini

Four to five 8-ounce tomatoes

2 halves of a $1^1/2$-pound eggplant or 6 to 8 uncooked shells made from Japanese eggplants

Two 8-ounce bell peppers, four 6-ounce peppers or 4 halves of 8-ounce bell peppers

7 to 10 savoy cabbage leaves or a $1^3/4$-pound savoy cabbage

Stuffed Vegetable Pointers

There are four types of stuffings in this chapter: fully cooked, partially cooked, altogether raw and those salad-y stuffings meant to be served cold in raw (or lightly cooked) vegetables. Following is information on how to deal with each. Look up the vegetable being stuffed in the Cook's Guide for directions on preparing and cooking the vegetable shells and the times and temperatures for baking the stuffed vegetables, if applicable.

Suggestions for suitable vegetables follow each stuffing recipe.

Bell peppers, tomatoes, and onions are best stuffed when raw; cooking them first makes them hard to deal with. When stuffing peppers or onions, choose partially cooked stuffings, which need additional cooking, instead of fully cooked stuffings, which may overcook by the time the vegetable is tender.

Partially Cooked/Raw Stuffings

Spoon partially cooked stuffings into uncooked vegetable shells. See the Cook's Guide for baking each type of vegetable after stuffing.

> Basic Rice Stuffing (page 491)
>
> Pork Stuffing (*not* the variation; page 493)
>
> Lamb Curry Stuffing (page 493)
>
> Greek Stuffing (page 494)
>
> Moroccan Stuffing (page 494)
>
> Pork Stuffing Variation (page 493)

Fully Cooked Stuffings

Spoon fully cooked stuffings into cooked vegetable shells and serve them at room temperature or heat them on a baking sheet in a 350°F oven until warmed or heated through.

> Collard, Mushroom and Ham Stuffing (page 496)
>
> Orzo Stuffing (page 495)
>
> Minted Rice Stuffing (page 496)
>
> Mushroom-Bulgur (or Quinoa) Stuffing (page 497)

Cold Stuffings

Mound cold stuffings into uncooked tomato, cucumber or avocado shells or lightly cooked zucchini boats. See the Cook's Guide for directions for making each vegetable.

> Curried Chicken Salad (page 499)
>
> Quintessential Tuna Salad (page 499)
>
> Velvet Smoked Trout (page 500)
>
> Salad of Tiny Shrimp, Celery and Dill (page 500)

Pork Stuffing

Use for peppers, onions, mushrooms or anything else. Cook this stuffing if using it to fill partially cooked shells. The variation that follows is raw and is meant for filling uncooked vegetable shells.

2 tablespoons olive oil

1/2 cup chopped onion

1 teaspoon minced garlic

3/4 pound ground pork

1 1/2 tablespoons tomato paste

1 teaspoon kosher salt

1/8 to 1/4 teaspoon freshly ground black pepper

Pinch of cayenne pepper

1/2 cup Dried Bread Crumbs (page 510) or store-bought plain bread crumbs

3 tablespoons milk

1/2 lightly beaten egg

1/2 cup roughly chopped toasted pine nuts

2 tablespoons chopped fresh basil

1 tablespoon chopped fresh parsley

1/4 cup freshly grated Parmesan cheese (optional)

Heat the oil in a medium skillet over low heat. Add the onion and garlic; cook until soft but not brown, about 3 minutes. Add the pork, breaking it up as it browns. Stir in the tomato paste, salt and both peppers. Remove the mixture to a bowl and cool.

Meanwhile, stir the bread crumbs and milk together in a small bowl.

When the pork mixture is cool, stir in the moistened bread crumbs, the egg, pine nuts, basil, parsley and cheese, if using.

Makes 3 cups, enough to fill:

Nine to ten 6- to 7-ounce (3-inch) onions

8 to 9 uncooked boats made from 5-ounce (6- to 7-inch) zucchini or 6 boats made from 8-ounce zucchini

2 halves of a 1 1/2-pound eggplant or 6 to 8 uncooked shells made from 5-ounce Japanese eggplants

Three 8-ounce bell peppers, six 6-ounce bell peppers or 6 halves of 8-ounce bell peppers

10 to 12 savoy cabbage leaves or one 1 3/4-pound savoy cabbage

Six 8-ounce tomatoes (use the cooked version only; the tomatoes will overcook before a raw stuffing is fully cooked)

Variation

To prepare as a raw stuffing, omit the oil. Combine all the ingredients in a bowl and mix well. Use in uncooked vegetables.

Italian Sausage Stuffing

Substitute 3/4 pound Italian sausages, casings removed, for the ground pork. Proceed as in main recipe for a partially cooked stuffing, or as in the variation for a raw stuffing.

Lamb Curry Stuffing

1 cup Basic Chicken Stock (page 501), Roasted Chicken Stock (page 502) or commercial chicken broth

1/4 cup long-grain white rice

1 small onion, diced (about 2/3 cup)

1 pound ground lamb

2 cloves garlic, smashed, peeled and minced

1 tablespoon curry powder

continued

1/4 teaspoon cayenne pepper

1 1/2 teaspoons kosher salt

Bring the chicken broth to a boil in a small covered pan. Add the rice, reduce the heat to medium and cook for 7 minutes. The rice can be cooked up to 1 hour in advance.

Mix the rice and chicken broth with the rest of the ingredients in a large bowl.

Makes 2 2/3 cups, enough to fill:

Eight 6- to 7-ounce (3-inch) onions

8 uncooked boats made from 5-ounce (6- to 7-inch) zucchini or 5 boats made from 8-ounce zucchini

2 halves of a 1 1/2-pound eggplant or 6 to 8 uncooked shells made from 5-ounce Japanese eggplants

2 (generously filled) 8-ounce bell peppers, six 6-ounce bell peppers or 5 to 6 halves of 8-ounce bell peppers

10 to 12 savoy cabbage leaves or one 1 3/4-pound savoy cabbage

Greek Stuffing

There was a time when this would have been made with lamb in Greece. Sadly, lamb is in short supply there today; imported beef is used instead. The flavors are fairly straightforward, much like those in Italian cooking.

1/3 cup long-grain white rice

1/4 cup olive oil

1 large onion, minced (about 1 1/2 cups)

6 ounces ground beef or lamb (about 2/3 cup)

One 14-ounce can Italian plum tomatoes, drained and finely chopped

2 teaspoons kosher salt

1 teaspoon dried thyme

1 teaspoon dried oregano, preferably Greek

1/4 teaspoon freshly ground black pepper

In a small saucepan, bring 1 cup water to a boil. Add the rice. Reduce the heat and simmer for 9 minutes. The rice should be slightly undercooked. Drain and rinse under cold running water. Drain and reserve.

Heat the oil in a medium skillet. Add the onion and cook over medium heat for 5 minutes, or until wilted and translucent. Add the beef or lamb. Increase the heat to high and cook, stirring to break up the meat, until the meat is no longer pink, about 4 minutes. Stir in the rice and the remaining ingredients. Remove from the heat.

Makes 3 cups, enough to fill:

Nine to ten 6- to 7-ounce (3-inch) onions

8 to 9 uncooked boats made from 5-ounce (6- to 7-inch) zucchini or 6 boats made from 8-ounce zucchini

2 halves of a 1 1/2-pound eggplant or 6 to 8 uncooked shells made from 5-ounce Japanese eggplants

Three 8-ounce bell peppers, six 6-ounce bell peppers or 6 halves of 8-ounce bell peppers

10 to 12 savoy cabbage leaves or one 1 3/4-pound savoy cabbage

Six 8-ounce tomatoes

Moroccan Stuffing

This is less an authentic Moroccan dish than an evocation of characteristic Moroccan flavors.

2 tablespoons olive oil

1 large onion, minced (about 1 1/2 cups)

6 ounces ground lamb (about 2/3 cup)

2 cloves garlic, smashed, peeled and chopped

1/2 cup couscous (or slightly undercooked rice)

1/4 cup dark raisins

2 tablespoons dried mint

2 tablespoons fresh lemon juice

1 teaspoon kosher salt

1 teaspoon ground cumin

1/4 teaspoon freshly ground black pepper

Heat the oil in a large skillet over medium heat. Add the onion, lamb and garlic. Cook, stirring to break up the lamb, until the onion is softened and the lamb is fully cooked, 5 minutes.

Pour off all but 1/4 cup drippings from the pan. Scrape into a mixing bowl and add the remaining ingredients.

Makes 2 1/2 cups, enough to fill:

Seven to eight 6- to 7-ounce (3-inch) onions

7 to 8 precooked boats made from 5-ounce (6- to 7-inch) zucchini or 5 boats made from 8-ounce zucchini

2 halves of a 1 1/4-pound eggplant or 6 to 8 uncooked shells made from 5-ounce Japanese eggplants

2 (generously filled) 8-ounce bell peppers, five 6-ounce bell peppers or 5 halves of 8-ounce bell peppers

7 to 10 savoy cabbage leaves or one 1 1/2-pound savoy cabbage

Five 8-ounce tomatoes

FULLY COOKED STUFFINGS

Orzo Stuffing

Vegetables stuffed with this make a nice vegetarian appetizer. The cheese holds everything together, though, so it is not for vegans. Chill the cheese thoroughly or put it in the freezer for five minutes so it will be easier to shred it.

4 large shallots (about 3 ounces), sliced

4 mushrooms (about 3 ounces), sliced

2 tablespoons unsalted butter

2 tablespoons olive oil

1 teaspoon kosher salt

Freshly ground black pepper to taste

1/3 cup orzo

2 canned Italian plum tomatoes, drained and diced (about 1/4 cup)

2 teaspoons minced fresh thyme or 1 scant teaspoon dried thyme

1/2 cup Basic Chicken Stock (page 501), Vegetable Broth (page 506), commercial chicken broth or water

2 tablespoons minced fresh parsley

1/2 cup shredded mozzarella cheese (about 2 ounces)

Combine the shallots and mushrooms in a food processor and chop fine, using on/off pulses. Or chop with a sharp knife.

Heat the butter and oil in a medium skillet over medium heat until the butter is foaming. Add the mushroom mixture and sprinkle with the salt and pepper to taste. Sauté, stirring occasionally, until the shallots are tender, about 5 minutes. Add the orzo and toss to coat. Add the remaining ingredients except the cheese and heat to boiling. Reduce to a simmer, cover and cook until the orzo is tender, about 6 minutes. Uncover and let cool to room temperature.

Stir in the cheese and check the seasoning.

Makes 1 1/2 cups, enough to fill:

4 cooked boats made from 5-ounce (6- to 7-inch) zucchini or 3 boats made from 8-ounce zucchini

continued

Half of a 1 1/2-pound eggplant (cooked) or
   4 cooked eggplant shells made from
   5-ounce Japanese eggplants

5 savoy cabbage leaves or one 1-pound
   savoy cabbage

Collard, Mushroom and Ham Stuffing

Any hearty dark leafy green, such as kale or Swiss chard, will work in place of the collard greens. Spinach can also be used, but cook it just until it turns bright green.

1/2 pound leaves from collard greens, cut across
   into 1/4-inch pieces (about 4 cups)

1 recipe Mushroom Duxelles (page 405)

1/4 pound Gruyère cheese, grated (about 1 cup)

1/4 pound sliced lean ham, finely chopped

Kosher salt and freshly ground black pepper
   to taste

Bring a medium saucepan of water to a boil. Add the chopped collards and cook for 5 minutes. Drain in a colander or sieve and rinse under cold water. Squeeze dry.

Combine the collards with the duxelles, cheese and ham in a bowl. Salt and pepper to taste.

Makes 3 cups, enough to fill:

8 to 9 cooked boats made from 5-ounce
   (6- to 7-inch) zucchini or 6 boats made from
   8-ounce zucchini

2 halves of a 1 1/2-pound eggplant (cooked) or
   6 to 8 cooked shells made from 5-ounce Japanese
   eggplants

10 to 12 savoy cabbage leaves or one 1 3/4-pound
   savoy cabbage

Minted Rice Stuffing

Simple, savory and thrifty, with a mildly Greek taste.

2 tablespoons olive oil

1 small onion, finely diced (about 2/3 cup)

3/4 cup long-grain white rice

1 tablespoon chopped fresh mint or
   1 1/2 teaspoons dried mint

1 1/2 cups Basic Chicken Stock (page 501),
   Vegetable Broth (page 506), commercial
   chicken broth or water

1 teaspoon kosher salt

2 teaspoons fresh lemon juice

Heat the olive oil in a 2-quart saucepan over low heat. Add the onion and cook, stirring, until wilted, about 5 minutes. Add the rice and mint and stir until the rice is coated with oil. Add the stock and salt. Increase the heat to medium and heat to boiling. Reduce the heat to a bare simmer, cover and cook until the rice is tender and the liquid is absorbed, about 15 minutes.

Stir in the lemon juice off the heat.

Makes 1 1/2 cups, enough to fill:

4 cooked boats made from 5-ounce (6- to 7-inch)
   zucchini or 3 boats made from 8-ounce zucchini

Half of a 1 1/2-pound eggplant (cooked) or
   4 cooked eggplant shells made from 5-ounce
   Japanese eggplants

5 savoy cabbage leaves or one 1-pound savoy cabbage

Lamb-Tomato Stuffing

This is absolutely delicious. I got the idea for the recipe from Elsa, who works with me. She, a Chilean, uses it to stuff grape leaves, so in addition to using it in vegetables, I use it in grape leaves.

- $1/2$ pound ground lamb

- 1 small onion, finely diced (about $1/2$ cup)

- 2 medium cloves garlic, smashed, peeled and minced

- $1/8$ teaspoon cayenne pepper

- 2 tablespoons long-grain white rice

- $1/2$ cup diced canned plum tomatoes, with their liquid

- $1/2$ cup Basic Chicken Stock (page 501), commercial chicken broth or water

- 2 tablespoons loosely packed chopped cilantro

- $1 1/2$ teaspoons red wine vinegar

- $1/8$ teaspoon ground cinnamon

- 1 teaspoon kosher salt

- $1/8$ teaspoon freshly ground black pepper

Crumble the lamb into a large saucepan. Place over medium heat and sauté, stirring, until no trace of pink remains. Stir in the onion, garlic and cayenne pepper. Sauté until the lamb is browned and the onion is tender, about 8 minutes.

Stir in the rice, then add the tomatoes, stock, cilantro, vinegar, cinnamon, salt and pepper. Heat to simmering. Cover the pan and cook until the rice is tender and the liquid is absorbed, about 15 minutes. Check occasionally and adjust the heat if necessary. If the liquid evaporates before the rice is tender, add a little water or stock.

Makes about 1 $3/4$ cups, enough to fill:

- 5 to 6 cooked boats made from 5-ounce (6- to 7-inch) zucchini or 3 boats made from 8-ounce zucchini

- Half of a 1 $1/2$-pound eggplant (cooked) or 5 cooked eggplant shells made from 5-ounce Japanese eggplants

- 5 savoy cabbage leaves or one 1-pound savoy cabbage

Moussaka Stuffing

Cool the stuffing slightly. In a small bowl, whisk together $1/2$ cup loosely packed grated Parmesan cheese, $1/4$ cup ricotta cheese and 2 large eggs until blended. Fold into the stuffing.

Makes about 2 cups

Mushroom-Bulgur (or Quinoa) Stuffing

Stuffed into vegetables, this makes a perfect dish for vegans and vegetarians. Those who want meat should use the variation.

- 1 ounce dried mushrooms (about $3/4$ cup)

- 2 tablespoons unsalted butter

- 1 small onion, diced (about $2/3$ cup)

- 1 tablespoon chopped garlic

- 5 ounces mushrooms, trimmed and chopped (about 1 $1/4$ cups), mixed with 1 teaspoon fresh lemon juice

- 2 $1/4$ teaspoons chopped fresh thyme leaves or $3/4$ teaspoon dried thyme

- 2 $1/4$ teaspoons kosher salt

- 10 ounces coarse-grain bulgur (1 $1/2$ cups) or quinoa (scant 1 $1/2$ cups)

- Freshly ground black pepper to taste

Put the dried mushrooms in a small saucepan, crumbling any large mushrooms. Pour in 1 cup boiling or very hot tap water. Soak for 20 minutes.

Bring the mushrooms and their liquid to a boil. Reduce the heat to a simmer and cook, uncovered, for 10 minutes.

With a slotted spoon, skim the mushrooms out of the broth; reserve. Strain the mushroom liquid through a sieve lined with a dampened piece of cheesecloth or a coffee filter. Pour a little hot water through the filter to extract as much mushroom flavor as possible; there should be ¾ cup total liquid. Reserve.

Melt the butter in a small pan. Add the onion and cook over low heat until translucent, for 8 to 10 minutes; do not brown. Add the garlic. Cook until the garlic softens and becomes translucent, 5 to 7 minutes. Add ¾ cup of the fresh mushrooms and cook over medium heat, stirring occasionally, until cooked through but not colored, 8 to 10 minutes. Add the thyme and plumped mushrooms and cook for 2 minutes. Reserve.

Put 3 cups water (or 2¼ cups for quinoa), the remaining fresh mushrooms and the reserved mushroom liquid in a medium saucepan. Bring to a boil. Reduce the heat and simmer for 5 minutes. Add the salt and bring back to a boil. Add the bulgur or quinoa and stir well. Cook, uncovered, for 10 minutes at a light boil. Remove from the heat, stir well and let cool for 15 minutes.

Add the mushroom-onion mixture to the bulgur. Mix well. Add the pepper. If making the stuffing ahead of time, cover tightly and refrigerate; bring to room temperature (about 1 hour) before using.

Makes 5 cups, enough to fill:

> 16 cooked boats made from 5-ounce (6- to 7-inch) zucchini or 8 boats made from 8-ounce zucchini
>
> 4 halves of 1½-pound eggplants (cooked) or 16 cooked shells made from 5-ounce Japanese eggplants
>
> 16 to 20 savoy cabbage leaves or two 1¾-pound savoy cabbages

Bulgur–Chicken Liver Stuffing

Melt an additional 2 tablespoons butter in a medium skillet over medium heat. Add 6 ounces chicken livers, trimmed of fat and connective tissue, and cook just until they lose their external color, about 4 minutes; they should not harden or brown. Remove the livers from the pan and transfer to a bowl. Add the 2 tablespoons butter

for cooking the onion to the skillet and proceed as above. Chop the livers medium-fine and add to the pan of mushrooms along with the thyme and plumped mushrooms.

Salt Pork and Sage Stuffing

> 6 ounces salt pork, cut into ½-inch cubes
>
> 1 small onion (about 4 ounces), peeled and quartered
>
> 1 large stalk celery, trimmed, peeled and cut into 2-inch lengths
>
> ½ teaspoon dried sage
>
> ½ cup dried bread crumbs, homemade (page 510) or store-bought

Place the salt pork in a 10-inch glass pie plate and cook, uncovered, in a microwave at 100% for 4 minutes. Remove from the oven and set aside.

Place the onion and celery pieces in a food processor. Process until coarsely chopped. Add the vegetables to the salt pork and stir to coat. Cook, uncovered, at 100% for 2 minutes.

Remove from the oven and stir in the sage and bread crumbs. Cook, uncovered, at 100% for 2 minutes.

Makes 1 cup, enough to fill two 8-ounce globe artichokes

Garlic and Parsley Stuffing

> 1½ cups (loosely packed) fresh Italian parsley leaves
>
> 6 cloves garlic, smashed and peeled
>
> ¾ cup olive oil
>
> 2¼ cups dried bread crumbs, homemade (page 510) or store-bought
>
> 3 tablespoons fresh lemon juice

3 teaspoons kosher salt

³/4 teaspoon freshly ground black pepper

Put the parsley and garlic in a food processor and pulse until chopped. Add the remaining ingredients. Pulse to combine.

Transfer the stuffing to a skillet. Cook, stirring, over low heat for a few minutes, until the garlic no longer tastes raw; do not let it brown.

Makes 3 cups, enough to fill six 8-ounce globe artichokes

COLD STUFFINGS

See individual entries in the Cook's Guide for preparing vegetables for cold stuffings.

Curried Chicken Salad

The curry has to be cooked before it is added to the mayonnaise, or the flavors won't develop and it will taste raw.

This salad also makes a good summer meal if the chicken is in half-inch dice. Walnuts or grapes can be mixed in and chutney served on the side.

1¹/2 teaspoons olive oil

³/4 teaspoon curry powder

1 drop hot red pepper sauce

³/4 cup Classic Mayonnaise (page 455), Cooked-Yolk Mayonnaise (page 455) or commercial mayonnaise

1¹/2 cups cooked chicken cut into ¹/4-inch cubes

6 tablespoons finely chopped peeled celery

1¹/2 tablespoons finely chopped onion

1¹/2 tablespoons chopped cilantro

³/4 teaspoon fresh lemon juice

Kosher salt and freshly ground black pepper to taste

Heat the olive oil in a small pan. Add the curry powder and cook over low heat for about 2 minutes, or until it is well browned. Remove from the heat and let cool.

Add the curry mixture and hot pepper sauce to the mayonnaise. Put the chicken, celery, onion and cilantro in a bowl. Add the mayonnaise; mix well. Stir in the lemon juice and season with salt and pepper.

Makes 1³/4 cups, enough to fill:

7 cucumber boats made from 5-ounce Kirby cucumbers

Shells made from three 8-ounce or five 6-ounce tomatoes

6 to 7 halves of 8-ounce Hass avocados

5 cooked boats made from 5-ounce zucchini

Quintessential Tuna Salad

Another of my low tastes, canned tuna American style.

1 small onion, quartered, or ¹/4 large onion (4 ounces)

2 stalks celery, trimmed, peeled and cut into 1-inch pieces

¹/2 cup Classic Mayonnaise (page 455), Cooked-Yolk Mayonnaise (page 455) or commercial mayonnaise

2 to 3 tablespoons fresh lemon juice

One 12¹/2-ounce can tuna packed in water, drained

1¹/2 teaspoons dill seeds

Kosher salt and freshly ground black pepper to taste

Coarsely chop the onion and celery in the food processor. Add the mayonnaise and process just until combined. Add the lemon juice and tuna. Process with 5 to 6 on-off pulses. Transfer to a bowl. Stir in dill seeds, salt and pepper.

Makes 2 1/4 cups, enough to fill:

    9 cucumber boats made from 5-ounce Kirby cucumbers

    Shells made from four 8-ounce or six 6-ounce tomatoes

    9 halves of 8-ounce Hass avocados

Velvet Smoked Trout

This can be stuffed into any cooked vegetable, served with crudités, spread on crostini (see Croutons, page 510) or tucked into fully baked miniature tart shells.

    One 8-ounce whole smoked trout

    1/4 cup minced celery

    1/4 cup minced yellow onion

    1 tablespoon unsalted butter

    1/4 teaspoon freshly ground black pepper

    6 tablespoons very cold heavy cream

Remove the skin, head and tail from the trout. Gently pull the fillets from the bones, leaving even the very fine bones attached. In a mixing bowl, gently shred the fillets with two forks; remove any fine bones now. Set aside.

Cook the celery and onion in butter over medium-low heat until softened, about 5 minutes. Add, with pepper, to the fish. Cool.

Beat the cream until it holds soft peaks. Gently fold into the trout. Refrigerate for at least 3 to 4 hours, or up to 2 days, before using.

Makes 1 1/4 cups, enough to fill:

    6 cucumber boats made from 5-ounce Kirby cucumbers

    Shells made from three 7-ounce or four 6-ounce tomatoes

    5 halves of 8-ounce Hass avocados

    4 cooked boats made from 5-ounce zucchini

Salad of Tiny Shrimp, Celery and Dill

Bay or TT shrimp, very tiny shrimp about the size of a fingernail, are perfect for mixed salads. They are sweet and firm textured and can be used whole. They come bottled, brined, frozen or, occasionally, fresh. Rinse brined shrimp well before use; taste and add salt only if needed. If only canned shrimp is available, substitute chopped regular shrimp cut into little pieces.

DRESSING

    2 tablespoons olive oil

    1 tablespoon vegetable oil

    1/8 teaspoon dry mustard

    1/8 teaspoon kosher salt, or to taste

    Freshly ground black pepper to taste

    1 1/2 teaspoons chopped fresh dill

    1 cup tiny shrimp (see headnote), peeled and cooked

    1/2 cup diced (1/4 inch) peeled celery

Whisk together the dressing ingredients. In a small bowl, combine the shrimp and celery. Add 3 tablespoons dressing, or to taste. Toss.

Makes 1 1/3 cups, enough to fill:

    4 halves of 8-ounce Hass avocados

    5 to 6 boats made from 5-ounce Kirby cucumbers

    Shells made from four 7-ounce or five 6-ounce tomatoes

    4 boats made from 5-ounce zucchini

Stocks, Broths and Soup Bases

Here at last are the stocks. I know that you have heard it all before, but homemade stock is really better than what comes out of a can, a sterile pack or—worst of all—a stock cube. Yes, commercial stocks can be used, and where I think that they are not a disaster, I have so indicated. I always have a lot of stock frozen. I make a roast chicken at least once a week and use the carcass and innards to make stock that I then freeze. When the freezer is overloaded, I use defrosted stock instead of water to make new—now double-strength—stock.

The worst and saltiest commercial stocks are the vegetarian ones. They also have no mouth feel. There are many vegetarian stocks in this book, such as mushroom and asparagus; look in the Index.

TO GIVE BODY TO VEGETARIAN STOCKS Meat, poultry and fish stocks get a rich texture from the gelatin in the bones. The Garlic Broth (page 507) is silk on its own; to add consistency to Vegetable Broth (page 506), Mushroom Broth (page 507) or Asparagus Stock (page 506), ½ cup agar-agar flakes, 8 teaspoons powdered agar-agar or 5 tablespoons tapioca powder may be cooked into the finished broth. If using agar-agar, mix with the broth and bring to a boil. Lower the heat and simmer until the agar-agar dissolves,

about 5 minutes. If using tapioca, mix with ¾ cup cold broth. Bring the rest of the broth to a boil, whisk in the tapioca, return to a boil, then remove from the stove. Both of these are good; the agar-agar sets up at room temperature.

Basic Chicken Stock

As I roast chicken frequently, I break up the leftover carcass and add it, along with any gizzards, hearts and bones from the plate, to my freezer bag or to my pot. Stock made with bones from a roast will have a somewhat darker, deeper flavor. I don't bother to roast fresh parts or bones when I get them; I simply cover them with water and proceed as in this recipe.

Even though the stocks made in the oven and in the slow-cooker cook for more than twice as long as stock made on the stove, the gelling quality and flavor are the same. This is due to the gentle cooking methods, which extract flavor and gelatin at a slower rate.

NOTE: To make this in a slow-cooker, the recipe must be halved.

> **5 pounds chicken backs and necks, roasted carcasses or other bones**

continued

To make the stock on top of the stove: In a tall narrow stockpot, bring the bones and 3 quarts water to a boil. Skim the fat. Lower the heat and simmer gently, so bubbles are barely breaking the surface of the liquid, for at least 4 hours and up to 12; add water as needed to keep the bones covered. Skim as necessary to remove as much fat as possible.

To make the stock in the oven: Place a rack on the lowest level of the oven (remove any other racks) and heat the oven to 250°F.

In a tall narrow stockpot, bring the bones and 3 quarts water to a boil. Skim the fat. Place in the oven for 4 hours; add water if needed. Remove and skim the fat. Return to the oven for at least 5 hours, and up to 8.

To make the stock in a slow-cooker: Start with 2½ pounds bones and 6 cups water for a 4-quart cooker. Place the bones in the slow-cooker and pour the water over. Cover and turn the heat on low. Cook for 11 to 12 hours.

In all methods the bones will be falling apart when the stock is done. Strain the stock through a fine-mesh sieve. Skim the fat and cool to room temperature. Refrigerate for 3 hours.

Remove the fat from the top of the stock and the sediment from the bottom. Use immediately or refrigerate for up to 3 days or freeze.

Makes 10 cups on top of the stove, 8 cups in the oven, 6 cups in the slow-cooker

Roasted Chicken Stock

Use the bones left over from roasting a chicken. Cover with water in a tall narrow stockpot and simmer until the bones fall apart. The bones from one 5-pound chicken will make about 6 cups stock.

Enriched Chicken Stock

Place the necks, hearts, gizzards, backs and wing tips from two 3-pound chickens in a saucepan. Add 3 quarts Basic Chicken Stock or Roasted Chicken Stock. Bring to a boil. Reduce the heat to a low simmer and cook as long as time allows—up to 18 hours. Top up the liquid from time to time with water, and skim regularly. Strain.

Makes about 10 cups, depending on how long it cooks

Beef Stock

While commercial chicken stock can be used instead of homemade, there is really no adequate substitute for homemade beef stock. My English friends tell me, in their days of wrath, the time of banned beef on the bone, that game bird stock can be used. Game birds are cheap and readily available to them, but not to us.

Canned beef consommé or broth is, at best, unfortunate. In desperation, it is possible to use canned beef madrilène, which at least has some gelatin in it. All over Europe, even in Italy, stock (bouillon) cubes are used. In general, I don't like these compressed bits of flavoring, which are heavy with salt. The beef variety is almost the least successful, though some cheating is possible (see Fake Beef Stock, page 504).

This recipe, with its variations for cooking in the oven (those with an Aga can use it) and in a slow-cooker, shows how important beef stock is to me. Many people may be more comfortable leaving an oven or a slow-cooker on for prolonged periods of time.

Once all the lovely stock is made, freeze whatever is not being used immediately. It keeps virtually forever.

Please note that this is a two-stage recipe. The first is a bone broth. The way it is treated determines whether the final stock will be brown and hearty or lighter (traditionally a white stock). For the slightly lighter effect, the bones are not browned and carrots and celery are used rather than tomatoes and garlic. The bone broth is always strained at the end of stage one to allow enough room for adding the beef shin in stage two.

The finished stock made with these bone broths, using either the stovetop or oven method, will gel when cold. However, since the stock made in the slow-cooker doesn't reduce or extract as much gelatin, it will not gel unless it is boiled to reduce by a cup and a half—and even then it will be a weak gel. For either method, if the yield after the second stage is somewhat higher than the mentioned one, once the stock has been strained, reduce it to fourteen cups for a richer, gelling stock.

With any method, the process can be stopped after stage one and refrigerated. To continue with the recipe, bring the refrigerated broth to a boil and simmer for ten minutes, then proceed.

NOTE: To make this in a slow-cooker, the recipe must be halved.

3½ pounds veal knuckle, split
   (see bone broth in headnote)

3 large tomatoes, for brown stock

6 cloves garlic, for brown stock

2 medium onions, cut in half

2 medium ribs celery, for white stock

3 medium carrots, for white stock

4½ pounds beef shin with bone, cut across
   by the butcher into 2- to 3-inch lengths

STAGE 1: BONE BROTH If preroasting the bones for a brown stock, place the rack in the center of the oven and preheat the oven to 500°F.

Place the veal knuckle, tomatoes, garlic and onions (half the amounts if using a slow-cooker) in a large roasting pan. Roast for 20 minutes. Turn the bones and vegetables and roast for 25 minutes or more.

Transfer the bones and vegetables to a large stockpot (or the slow-cooker). Place the roasting pan on top of the stove over high heat, add 1 cup water and bring to a boil, scraping all the browned bits from the bottom and sides of the pan. Pour into the stockpot (or slow-cooker).

To make the stock on top of the stove: For brown stock, add 15 cups water to the stockpot, or enough to cover the ingredients by 2 inches.

For white stock, place the veal knuckle, onions, celery and carrots in a large stockpot. Add 4 quarts water, or enough to cover by 2 inches.

For either, bring to a boil. Lower the heat to a simmer so that gentle bubbles break the surface, and cook for 8 hours. Skim and check the level of the water every few hours; it should remain about 2 inches above the bones. Six to 8 cups more water will be needed in the 8-hour cooking time unless an otoshi-buta (see Note, page 237) or pot lid is used.

To make the stock in the oven: Adjust the oven temperature (or preheat the oven) to 300°F. The rack should be at the lowest possible level, with no other racks above it.

For brown stock, add 15 cups water to the stockpot, or enough to cover the ingredients by 2 inches.

For white stock, combine the veal knuckle, onion, celery and carrots in a large stockpot. Add 2 quarts water, or enough to cover by 2 inches.

For either, bring to a boil. Transfer the pot to the oven. Cook for 1 hour. Lower the heat to 250°F and cook for 11 hours. Check the water level every few hours. It should remain about 2 inches above the bones. Approximately 8 cups more will be needed in a 12-hour cooking period unless an otoshi-buta (see Note, page 237) or pot lid is used.

To make the stock in a 4- to 5-quart slow-cooker: For brown stock, add 7 cups water.

For white stock, place the half quantity of veal knuckle, onion, celery and carrots in the slow-cooker and add 8 cups water.

continued

For either, turn the slow-cooker on to low and cook for 12 hours.

For all methods: Strain the broth and discard the solids. Skim the fat. Add enough water to the liquid to make 16 cups for the stovetop and oven methods, 8 cups for the slow-cooker method.

STAGE 2: THE STOCK *On top of the stove:* Return the liquid to the stockpot and add the beef shin. Bring to a boil. Lower the heat and simmer so bubbles are gently breaking the surface, for 2½ hours. The meat should be tender.

Remove the beef shin from the pot and separate the meat from the bones; reserve the meat. Poke or scoop the marrow out of the bones and reserve. Return the bones to the pot and cook for 30 minutes.

In the oven: Return the liquid to the stockpot and add the beef shin. Bring to a boil on top of the stove. Place the pot back in the oven. Cook for 3 hours. The meat should be tender.

Remove the shin from the pot and separate the meat from the bones; reserve the meat. Scoop or poke the marrow out of the bones; reserve (it is wonderful spread on toast or stirred into sautéed mushrooms or in Stovetop Braised Celery Hearts, page 201). Return the bones to the pot and cook for 1 hour.

In a slow-cooker: Return the liquid to the slow-cooker and add the half quantity of beef shin. Cook on low for 5 hours.

For all methods: When the meat is cool enough to handle, tear or cut it into bite-size pieces; reserve for use in soups. Strain the stock through a fine-mesh sieve. Skim the fat. Cool to room temperature. Refrigerate for 3 hours.

Remove the fat from the top and the sediment from the bottom of the stock. Use immediately, or refrigerate for up to 3 days or freeze.

Makes 14 cups on top of the stove or in the oven, 8 cups in a slow-cooker

Enriched Beef Stock
Roast an additional 1½ pounds split veal knuckles during stage one; set aside. Make the stock using either the stovetop or the oven method. At the end of stage two, after the meat has been removed from the shins and the bones added back to the pot, add the reserved knuckles. Simmer until the broth has reduced to 6 cups. **Makes 6 cups**

Fake Beef Stock

Although this beef stock will gel, I would serve it on its own, as cold starter soup, only if seasoned with a lot of lemon or lime juice and fresh pepper. It still has a lot of salt. It does not gel hard enough to support dilution with other ingredients. The fake stock is meant to be used in soups—but in any recipe in which it is used, be very careful when adding salt, as the cubes are salty.

This recipe can easily be multiplied as needed.

Beef bouillon cubes

½ pound lean ground beef

One ¼-ounce package gelatin

Bring 4 cups of water to a boil in a medium saucepan. Dissolve as many beef bouillon cubes as are called for on the package in the boiling water. Crumble in the ground beef and bring to a boil. Reduce the heat to a simmer and cook for 30 minutes.

While the beef is cooking, sprinkle the gelatin (1 tablespoon) over ½ cup water and let sit for 1 minute.

Strain the broth through a damp-cloth-lined sieve into a small saucepan. Stir in the softened gelatin and cook, stirring, at just below a simmer, for 3 minutes to dissolve the gelatin.

Makes 4 cups

Meat or Chicken Glaze

This is the prototype for all glazes. It is very simple. The only things to watch out for are, on the one hand, that it gets thick enough and, on the other, that you go very slowly at the end so the glaze doesn't scorch. You can tell that the glaze is thick enough when, as the pan is tilted from side to side, it has an oceanlike undercurrent: It is still sliding in one direction as you reverse the tilt. The glaze thickens as it cools. Keep it refrigerated if you are going to use it fairly soon. Otherwise, freeze it in small portions. As you will see, the yield is very small. You should start with the most profligate amount of stock that you can manage.

Decent-quality meat glaze can now also be purchased in specialty stores and from some butchers. Glaze can be omitted in any of the recipes that call for it here. Don't substitute.

4 cups Beef Stock (page 502), Basic Chicken Stock (page 501) or Roasted Chicken Stock (page 502)

Pour the stock into a 2-quart saucepan. Bring to a boil. Lower the heat and simmer until deep brown and syrupy. It may be necessary to transfer the contents to a smaller pan as it reduces; watch so it does not burn.

When the glaze has reduced to about ½ cup, pour it into a small container or an ice-cube tray. Make sure to scrape all the rich, syrupy glaze into the container. Refrigerate or freeze until firm.

Remove the glaze from the container or ice-cube tray sections. Wrap tightly in plastic wrap. Store indefinitely in the freezer. **Makes ½ cup**

Basic Fish Stock

There is a myth that comes from French cooking that fish stock must not be cooked for more than twenty to forty minutes. As an ignorant young cook, though, for many years, I cooked my fish stocks for long hours, just as I did my other stocks. When I learned more, I persisted in my very satisfactory habit. It was not until years later, when I began to work with restaurants, that I understood the shibboleth. French restaurant chefs use the frames of flatfish, flounder and sole for their stock. These bones do give a bitter stock if cooked longer than twenty minutes, or forty at the outside. But if no flatfish bones are used, the stock can cook for four to six hours, extracting all the gelatin to make a wonderfully rich stock. (I would have thought that any country that invented bouillabaisse, dependent on the gelatin to bind the ingredients together, would have figured this out.)

I use fish bones and heads, and cod collars, if available. These are free or very cheap. When I order fish fillets, I always ask for the heads and bones, since I have paid for them. It is better not to use the heads and bones from oily fish such as mackerel and bluefish or salmon, which will make heavy stock. Bones and heads of white-fleshed fish such as snapper, bass and cod (including the cod collar) can be used, as can the bones and heads from previously cooked fish.

All the gills should be cut out of the heads and the bones thoroughly rinsed to remove any blood, which could make the stock bitter.

The stock can be frozen to use as wanted.

In general, unless it is required in the dependent recipe, it is better not to use wine or to season the stock when making it. Such elements can always be added later. A neutral stock provides more flexibility.

continued

5 pounds nonoily fish heads and bones, such as cod, red snapper, grouper and/or bass

1 cup dry white wine (optional)

Wash the fish heads and bones very well to eliminate all traces of blood. Cut out the oil-rich gills with scissors. Put the fish heads and bones in a medium stockpot and cover with 11 cups water and, if using, the white wine. Bring to a boil. Skim off the scum that rises to the top. Lower the heat and simmer the stock, skimming as necessary, for 4 hours.

Strain through a fine-mesh sieve. Use immediately or cool to room temperature and refrigerate for up to 3 days or freeze.

Makes 8 cups

Roasted Fish Stock
Replace the uncooked bones with bones left from roasted fish. Use the same ratio of water to bones.

Vegetable Broth

For a smoother, more unctuous mouth feel, agar-agar or tapioca powder may be added to the finished broth (see page 501). Leek Broth (page 385) is another vegetarian alternative.

2 cloves garlic, smashed and peeled

2 medium-large onions, quartered

3 medium carrots, peeled and cut into 1-inch lengths

3 medium tomatoes, coarsely chopped

3 medium leeks, white parts only, split in half lengthwise, cleaned and cut into 1-inch lengths

2 tablespoons olive oil

1 medium bunch spinach, stemmed, washed well and cut across into 2-inch strips

1 cup celery leaves

Stems from 2 bunches fresh parsley (reserve the leaves for another use)

2 European bay leaves

For roasted vegetable broth: Place a rack in the middle of the oven and preheat the oven to 500°F.

Place the garlic, onions, carrots, tomatoes, and leeks in a large roasting pan. Add the olive oil and toss to coat. Roast for 15 minutes. Turn the vegetables and roast for 15 more minutes.

Move the vegetables around in the pan and roast them for 10 more minutes, or until the vegetables are all nicely browned and the tomatoes are collapsing.

Transfer the roasted vegetables to a tall narrow stockpot. Add the spinach, celery leaves, parsley stems and bay leaves to the pan. Place the pan on the stovetop and add 7 cups water. Bring to a boil, scraping up any browned bits from the sides and bottom of the pan with a wooden spoon. Pour this liquid over the vegetables in the stockpot.

For plain vegetable broth: Place all the ingredients plus 8 cups water in a tall narrow stockpot. Bring to a boil. Lower the heat and simmer, partially covered, for 45 minutes.

For either method: Strain the broth through a damp-cloth-lined sieve. Use immediately or refrigerate for up to 3 days or freeze.

Makes 8 cups

Asparagus Stock

Easy, quick, and I have the asparagus detritus anyhow.

Woody stems and peelings reserved from 2 pounds asparagus

4 small leeks, green parts only (white parts reserved for another use), split in half lengthwise, cleaned and cut into 2-inch lengths (4 cups)

Place the asparagus stems, peels, leek greens and 2½ quarts water in a medium pot. Cover and bring to a boil. Lower the heat and simmer, uncovered, for 2½ hours.

Strain the stock through a sieve, pushing down on the solids to extract as much liquid as possible. Use right away, or refrigerate for up to 3 days or freeze. **Makes 4½ to 5 cups**

Garlic Broth

This is a base for other soups that can also be served on its own—but in that case, consider adding some jalapeño pepper, cilantro and lime juice; diced tomatoes, chopped parsley, matchsticks of zucchini and thinly sliced basil; cooked peas and small leaves of spinach; curry leaves, lemongrass, and lime juice; or any other seasoning group that seems enjoyable.

Do not make this with sprouting garlic in the spring. The taste will be nasty.

3 small heads garlic, cloves separated, smashed and peeled

1 tablespoon olive oil

Kosher salt and freshly ground pepper to taste (optional)

Cut the garlic cloves in half lengthwise. If necessary, remove the green germ growing through the center.

In a medium saucepan, heat the oil over low heat. Stir in the garlic cloves and cook, stirring often, until the outside of the garlic is translucent and the cloves are soft, about 20 minutes. Don't let the garlic brown.

Pour in 9 cups water. Bring to a boil. Lower the heat and simmer, uncovered, for 40 minutes. The garlic will be very tender.

If using as an ingredient, strain. To serve the broth on its own, season with salt and pepper to taste. **Makes 8 cups; serves 8 as a first course**

Mushroom Broth

To make this base into a soup, add 1 tablespoon salt. It is also nice with Mushroom Dumplings (page 398) and some chopped tarragon or dill. Or use instead of water in Mushroom Barley Soup (page 400) and Winter Mushroom Soup (page 401).

1½ pounds mushrooms, broken into large chunks

½ ounce dried porcini

1 ounce dried shiitake mushrooms

In a food processor, working in batches if necessary, chop the fresh mushrooms to a coarse paste, stopping a couple of times to scrape down the sides of the bowl.

Combine the fresh and dried mushrooms in a tall narrow stockpot. Add 3 quarts water and bring to a boil. Lower the heat and simmer, uncovered, for 30 minutes.

Strain through a fine-mesh sieve, then through a damp-cloth-lined sieve. Use immediately or refrigerate for up to 3 days or freeze. **Makes 9 cups**

Konbu Dashi

One 1¾-ounce package konbu (dried kelp)

Wipe the konbu with a damp cloth. Cut it into 4-inch pieces. Place in a medium saucepan with 8⅔ cups water. Cover and bring to a boil. Lower the heat to medium-low and simmer, partially covered, for 1 hour, or until the liquid has reduced to about 4⅓ cups.

Strain through a fine-mesh sieve. The dashi will keep 3 to 4 days refrigerated. **Makes 4⅓ cups**

Odds and Ends

These are the recipes I use often but that do not fit into any known category. However, they can take a simple dish and make it special.

Roasted Peeled Chestnuts

My husband adores roasted chestnuts. They are one of the few things other than divine scrambled eggs that he will cook for himself—especially since he has discovered the microwave. They can be bought in season from vendors on the streets of New York, but home roasted are better. Due to the hideous chestnut blight, most of the chestnuts for sale come in a short fall season from Italy.

Chestnuts are a classic addition to Brussels sprouts and to stuffings for birds and, chopped, for pork roast. In Italy and in France, chestnuts are sold candied at a great price.

¹/₂ pound chestnuts in the shell (14 to 15 pieces)

Preheat the oven to 350°F.

On the flat side of each chestnut, cut an X through the shell large enough to reach the edges. Place the chestnuts on a cookie sheet in a single layer, flat side up. Roast for 20 minutes, or until a knife easily slides into the nut meat. Peel while still warm. **Makes 1 cup**

Microwave Variation

On the flat side of each chestnut, cut an X through the shell large enough to reach the edges. Place the chestnuts in a single layer on a plate just large enough to hold them. Cover tightly with plastic wrap and cook for 2½ minutes at 100%, just until the cut edges of the shells curl open wide enough to peel easily. Be careful not to overcook, or the chestnuts will become tough. Prick the plastic with the tip of a sharp knife to release steam.

Remove from the oven and uncover; peel while warm.

Glazed Chestnuts

As a vegetable on their own to replace another starch, chestnuts are delicious done this way, with a little salt. They also add more flavor to dishes in which they are used—such as roasted or braised Brussels sprouts (see the Cook's Guide, page 552). As a topping, consider them on cauliflower, carrots or onions.

1 tablespoon unsalted butter

1 recipe Roasted Peeled Chestnuts (at left)

¹/₂ cup Roasted Chicken Stock (page 502)

Kosher salt and freshly ground black pepper to taste

In a small saucepan, melt the butter over medium heat. Add the chestnuts and toss to coat. Add the stock and bring to a boil. Lower the heat so the liquid is gently bubbling. Cook for 11 to 13 minutes, stirring occasionally, or until almost all of the liquid is gone.

Season with salt and pepper. Cook for 30 to 90 seconds more, stirring constantly, until the liquid is all but gone. There will be a thick syrupy glaze at the bottom of the pan and covering the nuts. Let cool, then coarsely chop the nuts if using as a topping. Or leave whole if serving on their own or mixed with other vegetables. **Makes 1 cup**

Bacon Lardons

Many classic recipes call for lardons, thick match-shape strips of crisp bacon. It is easy to make them.

The best lardons are made from lean, meaty slab bacon. Buy it from a local butcher, who will slice it to order in the appropriate thickness.

If slab bacon is unavailable, regular store-bought bacon can be substituted with varying results. Groceries carry three basic types: Standard bacon is sliced thin and heavily marbled with fat; thick-cut bacon, also well marbled, is thicker than standard sliced bacon but thinner than the preferred ¼-inch cut; lean bacon, not always labeled as such, has much less fat and is prone to crumble when sliced thin. All three bacons will make crisp and tasty lardons. They also give off more fat, allowing for higher heat and faster cooking.

Once they are cooked, remove the lardons from the fat with a slotted spoon. Save the fat for use in other recipes, or for roasting potatoes or panfrying chicken. Most classically the fat (warm) and the lardons are used with a little vinegar and salt as a dressing for a frisée salad (see page 218) with or without Croutons (page 510) and sometimes a soft-boiled egg. I like it so much I eat it as a meal.

> **¹/₂ pound very lean slab bacon (see headnote), sliced into ¹/₄-inch-thick slices, then cut across into ¹/₄-inch strips (about 1 ¹/₃ cups)**

Put the bacon in a medium saucepan. Cook, turning occasionally, over very low heat until the fat is rendered and the bacon is browned. This can take up to 35 minutes if the bacon is very lean. (For fattier, store-bought bacon, increase the heat to decrease the cooking time.)

Remove the bacon to a paper towel to drain. **Makes ²/₃ cup (with about 2 teaspoons fat if using very lean slab bacon, more if using fattier bacon)**

Microwave Variation

For ¹/₄-inch-thick lean slab bacon: Place the sliced bacon strips in a single layer on a plate, cover loosely with a paper towel and cook at 100%.

4 ounces	7 minutes
8 ounces	9 minutes

For thinner-cut store-bought bacon: Place the bacon strips in a single layer on a plate, cover loosely with a paper towel and cook at 100%.

4 ounces	3 minutes 30 seconds

Microwave bacon will render less usable fat, as much of it is absorbed by the paper towel.

Ginger Juice

This is a first-rate Chinese trick that I learned only recently. It is a good way to keep the flavor of ginger virtually indefinitely (refrigerated in a closed container), although the juice will darken and the flavor will get a little weaker with age. The juice can be added to soups or any other dish where you want the flavor of ginger but may not want to bite a piece.

¹/₂ pound fresh ginger, trimmed, peeled and thinly sliced (6 ounces)

Place the ginger and ⅔ cup water in a blender. Blend until a smooth paste forms, stopping several times to scrape down the sides.

Cut two 9-inch squares of cheesecloth. Put one on top of the other, dampen and wring out; place in a sieve over a storage container. Pour in the ginger mixture. Gather up the edges of the cheesecloth and wring out all the liquid from the ginger. Discard the dry pulp. Refrigerate.

Stir well before using. **Makes 1 cup**

Dried Bread Crumbs

Most of us have leftover bread. It shouldn't be wasted. I routinely make dried bread crumbs and keep them in a tightly covered jar to use as need be. They are a classic Austrian topping—tossed in butter—for a number of vegetables such as cauliflower and even boiled potatoes.

One day-old 1-pound loaf Italian bread, with crust, or day-old 1-pound loaf sliced white bread, with crust

If using Italian bread, cut it into pieces. Lay the bread pieces or slices in a single layer on a tray and allow to dry, uncovered, at least overnight. In humid weather, it may take a day and a half. The bread should be completely dry. The longer the bread has dried, the finer and more uniform the crumbs and the smaller their measure.

Pulse the bread in a food processor. Italian bread may also be grated on the smallest holes of a four-sided grater. (Grating works well if the bread was left over uncut and is now too hard to cut into pieces.) Sieve all crumbs to get rid of overly large ones. Store in a brown paper—not plastic—bag.
Makes 4 cups if using Italian bread, 3 cups if using white bread

Croutons

(Fried Bread or Crostini)

These are thin, flat croutons that the British used to call "sippets" and cut into fanciful shapes—hearts and diamonds. When made with olive oil, they turn into Italian crostini. They can go on top of a wide variety of soups or be served on the side for people to add as wanted.

1 narrowish loaf good Italian bread, cut across on a slight diagonal into ¹/₄-inch slices

About 8 tablespoons (4 ounces) unsalted butter, melted, or ¹/₂ cup good olive oil

Oven method: Place a rack in the center of the oven and preheat the oven to 350°F.

Place as many of the bread slices as will fit in a single layer on a large (not air-cushioned) cookie sheet. Brush the tops with a generous amount of butter or olive oil. Toast for 15 to 17 minutes, or until the bread is brown around the edges and crisp. Let cool. Repeat with any remaining bread.

Stovetop method: Pour enough melted butter or oil into a large frying pan to lightly coat the bottom. Heat over medium heat. Add as many slices of bread as will fit in a single layer and cook over medium heat until golden brown on the first side. Turn the slices over. Cook until golden brown on the other side. Remove to paper towels to drain. Repeat with the remaining slices, adding butter or olive oil to the pan as needed. **Makes about 24**

Garlic Croutons

Mash 1 clove garlic into the melted butter or olive oil. Follow the oven method.

Cubed Croutons

Cubed croutons are more typically French. They are sprinkled on cream soups such as Tomato and Dill Soup with Crème Fraîche (page 104) or Creamy Cauliflower Soup (page 257), where they provide a satisfying contrast of crunch.

Cubed croutons can be baked or fried and different fats can be used. Fried croutons yield a fattier, more satisfying product; baked are leaner. Suit the fat to that of the soup they are to go with.

> **3 cups vegetable oil if frying the croutons; or 2 tablespoons unsalted butter, melted, or 2 tablespoons olive oil if baking**
>
> **6 slices white sandwich bread, crusts removed and cut into $1/2$-inch squares**

To fry the croutons: Heat the oil to 375°F in a medium saucepan.

Working in small batches, fry the bread cubes for 20 to 25 seconds, turning once, until golden brown. Remove with a slotted spoon and drain on paper towels.

To bake the croutons: Preheat the oven to 350°F.

Toss the bread cubes in butter or oil and spread in a single layer on a baking sheet. Bake for 7 minutes. Turn the croutons and bake for 8 more minutes, or until golden brown. Let cool. **Makes 2 cups fried croutons, 1 $3/4$ cups baked croutons**

Strained Yogurt

It's easier now to find rich, thick strained Greek yogurt in local groceries. It's just as easy to make the equivalent.

> **2 cups plain whole-milk yogurt**

Put the yogurt in a sieve lined with cheesecloth or a thick paper towel and place the sieve over a bowl to catch the liquid.

Refrigerate until the yogurt has drained to the consistency desired. After 3½ hours, the yogurt will be twice as thick and the volume reduced by half. After 24 hours, the yogurt will be the consistency of softened cream cheese. **Makes about 1 cup**

One-to-One Simple Syrup

I'm very proud of the wide selection of sweet desserts and even cookies that I have developed for this book; turn to the Index to locate them. Where sauces are appropriate, they are given. Here is the one lonely sweet thing that is a general need (for sorbets).

> **4 cups sugar**

Put the sugar and 4 cups water in a 4-quart saucepan. Have on hand a pastry brush and some water to wash down the sides of the pan should crystals form. Stir over very low heat, letting the sugar dissolve before allowing the mixture to come to a boil. Once the mixture boils, cover and cook for 3 to 5 minutes. Remove from the heat and cool. **Makes 6 cups**

Methods

FRYING

Frying is, usually, cooking foods—coated or not—in enough fat so that they are sealed and crisped as they cook. Some Chinese shallow-frying is a combined technique, where food such as dumplings sets a firm surface in the fat and then steams, covered, until cooking is completed. Deep-fat frying is generally used when there is quite a lot of food that needs to float freely so as not to stick or when the pieces of food are fairly bulky. As food fries, it will generally rise to the surface. Sometimes it will need to be turned so that all sides brown.

Deep-frying

Select a pan: For a gas stove, a large wok, 12 to 14 inches in diameter, with a stand (ring) to hold it securely over the burner is best. A wok can also be used on a wood stove by setting it directly in the hole that appears when one of the round lids over the firebox is removed. In some cases a deep skillet can be used, which will require less oil. Otherwise, use a large pot or Dutch oven of the same diameter, which will require more oil. In any case, allow enough room in the pan for the oil to bubble up. And do not fry in copper; the tin lining cannot withstand the high temperature. For a deep-fat fryer, follow the manufacturer's instructions.

Items that take a minute or more to cook can be done in two or three pans at a time, in staggered batches. Items that cook in a few seconds should be fried one batch at a time in one pan.

Any neutral vegetable oil, such as canola, safflower, grapeseed or peanut, can be used.

Place the pan over the burner and pour in oil to a depth of 2 to 4 inches, just enough to float the items being fried. A wok filled to a depth of 2 inches will take about 6 cups of oil. A 12-inch skillet filled 1 inch deep will take about 4½ cups oil.

Turn the heat to medium-high. To ensure good results, use a deep-fat thermometer. Place the thermometer in the oil—it can usually hang securely over the side of the pan. Do not let the thermometer touch the bottom of the pan. If necessary, place a chopstick across the rim of the pan, under the head of the thermometer, to prop the tip up and prevent it from touching the bottom.

Normal frying temperature is 375°F; the temperature may vary 5 to 10 degrees in either direction. The temperature should be monitored at all times and the heat adjusted as necessary. Oil can get too hot very quickly and takes a long time to cool down. On the other hand, putting in a large batch of food tends to cool the oil. Raise or lower the heat as needed.

If you do not have a thermometer, test the oil by placing a wooden chopstick in the center of the pan. When the oil is hot enough, bubbles will form vigorously around the chopstick from the ambient humidity retained by the wood. This method is not ideal, because it is difficult to monitor the temperature between or during batches.

There are a few other items to have ready before beginning. A skimmer (particularly a large-mesh Chinese one), with its wide shallow basket, is ideal for removing fried food from oil, but a slotted spoon is fine. You will need baking sheets lined with parchment paper, paper towels (better for the environment) or brown paper bags for draining. Have pot holders nearby. You may want to wear an apron.

Once the food is prepared, the other items are at hand and the oil is at the correct temperature, begin frying. When adding items to the pan, hold them as close to the oil as possible before easing them in (use tongs if you like). Foods with stems, such as stuffed peppers, can be held by a bit of stem. This prevents splashing hot oil on your hands. Drop in only as many pieces as will float freely in the oil; do not crowd or the food will not cook properly and the oil will cool down. If you have trouble with splattering caused by wet foods, slide the items off an oiled pancake turner or a slotted spoon.

Turn the pieces over only if instructed to in the recipe. In some cases, you will need to lift a piece slightly out of the oil with the skimmer to check the color. When the desired color is reached, scoop up the pieces and transfer them to a lined baking sheet. To keep the first fried items warm while you work, place them in a 200°F oven.

Check the oil temperature (even if using an electric pan). If the oil is too hot or too cool, adjust the heat and wait until the proper temperature is reached again. Drop in more pieces and continue in the same manner until all of the items have been fried.

Turn off the heat. Leave the pan on the burner or set it aside in a safe place, such as the back of the stove, to cool completely. Serve the fried food hot or store as recommended in the recipe.

When cleaning up, pour the cool oil through a coffee filter into a container with a tightly fitting lid (empty coffee cans are good for this). The strained oil will keep indefinitely at room temperature and can be reused for frying until it turns dark or develops an off odor. Do not reuse oil that has been used for frying fish for any other food, or the food will taste fishy. Sometimes the fish taste can be cleared from the oil by frying potatoes in it, but the potatoes will not be good to eat except as part of fish and chips.

Shallow-frying

The basic techniques for shallow-fat frying are fundamentally the same as those for deep-fat-frying. The amount of oil needed for shallow-frying varies from a thin coating of oil to ½ inch. Heat the oil. If the oil is deep enough, use a thermometer, propped up off the bottom of the pan, to check the temperature. If not, use the chopstick method mentioned earlier. Place the items in the pan, avoiding overcrowding. Cook as directed in the recipe.

Naked Frying

It should be noted that there are things that can be fried without any batter or coating of any kind. The only trick, beyond following the basic techniques in deep-frying, is to make sure that you pat the things to be fried thoroughly dry. Resist the temptation to dip vegetables in water; you will get a terrible and dangerous spatter. It is that spatter that prompts me to caution strongly as I give you directions for my favorite garnish, fried herb, celery and spinach leaves. To try them, wash the herbs well and pluck off attractive sprigs or—as in spinach—individual leaves. Dry the leaves as well as humanly possible. Heat the oil (see Deep-frying, page 512). Standing well back from the stove, throw two handfuls of leaves into the oil. As soon as it has stopped spitting, advance on the pan and, with a skimmer, remove the leaves to a paper to drain. Repeat. The leaves should be crisp and only lightly browned. See also Deep-fried Parsley (page 445).

Crisp Vegetable Chips

Here are traditional chips, made into multicolored delights by using all kinds of vegetables. They are so good that they may not even get dipped. Of course, you can make regular potato chips the same way.

Certain vegetable peelers will work fine with this. Choose one that will make very thin chips without tearing the slices. Or use a mandoline.

At the end of the recipe, I give a way of making the chips ahead (up to three days in advance) and then reheating them shortly before serving that keeps you away from the fryer in your good clothes.

Vegetable sticks can be made in the same way. Peel the vegetables and cut them into matchstick strips. Think mandoline. Salt after frying. Do not bother to reheat; they are good at room temperature.

> **1 pound small (3-inch) beets, white turnips, celery root, sweet potatoes, floury potatoes or Jerusalem artichokes, peeled, or 1 medium rutabaga or yam (1 pound), peeled and quartered**
>
> **Vegetable oil for deep-frying**
>
> **Kosher salt to taste**

Slice the vegetables to the thickness of a penny on a mandoline or with a vegetable peeler; do not store in cold water. Blot dry.

Heat 4 inches of oil (see Deep-frying, page 512). Carefully slip about 20 of the slices into the oil and fry, stirring with a skimmer to separate, until cooked through. Some vegetables will not be crisp at this point and each will be a different color: Turnips should be white with dark brown markings; celery root, Jerusalem artichokes, yams and sweet potatoes should be dark brown; beets will be deep purple with golden brown highlights; and rutabagas will be light brown. Skim out, drain and let stand until cool and crisp. Sprinkle with salt to taste. Repeat with the remaining vegetables.

The chips can be fried up to 3 days in advance. Do *not* salt them.

Store in an airtight container at room temperature. Up to 3 hours before serving, spread the chips in a single layer on a baking sheet and heat in a 375°F oven until hot, about 3 minutes. (The chips will not be crisp at this point.) Drain on paper towels until crisp, and salt to taste before serving. **Makes about 6 cups**

Fried Zucchini

These are absolutely the best, if not the most typical, of fried zucchini. Instead of being fried after coating with egg and crumbs or batter, these long, very thin matchstick-size strips are fried naked to make crisp handfuls. People will eat more than you think. Make in batches as needed, or reheat cooled zucchini for one minute in a 350°F oven. If making in batches, do not succumb to the temptation to keep the zucchini strips in water—they will spatter when fried. Keep them on paper towels, covered with a barely moistened paper towel.

You can use the large holes of a four-sided grater to cut these, but you will get a better result with a mandoline. Remove the ends and grate lengthwise, without peeling.

If you are using large—seedy—zucchini, grate or slide through the mandoline, turning on all four sides, then discard the center part with all the seeds; buy about one-third more weight of zucchini to allow for these discards.

Vegetable oil for deep-frying

6 medium zucchini, trimmed, halved across and finely shredded or grated

Kosher salt to taste

Heat the oil (see Deep-frying, page 512) in a large skillet.

Add about 1½ cups zucchini to the hot oil. Stir. The oil will foam up and bubble vigorously. When the bubbles die down and the zucchini turns golden brown, skim from the oil and drain on paper towels. Repeat with the remaining zucchini.

Sprinkle with salt. Serve warm or at room temperature. **Makes 6 cups**

Five Batters for Frying

There are many batters for deep-fat-frying, and many countries use the technique to embellish little bits of food. Beer adds a certain lightness to batter. The vinegar batter is particularly nice with sage leaves and vegetables but requires a slightly different technique. The buttermilk batter is blander and good with seafood as well.

It is better to sift flour for batters. Mix up to two hours ahead of time. The vinegar batter will need a full two hours in the refrigerator before the beaten egg whites are added. Whisk the batter from time to time as it sits to keep it smooth.

The beer, buttermilk and vinegar batters make 1 cup each, good for an average of 24 pieces, depending on the size of the item being fried. Multiply the batter recipes as desired and the ingredients accordingly. To serve, choose a dipping sauce (pages 463–467).

Beer Batter

3/4 cup (6 ounces) light beer

1 cup all-purpose flour, sifted

1½ teaspoons kosher salt

1½ teaspoons sweet paprika

Whisk together all the ingredients in a medium bowl just until blended. Cover and refrigerate for 1 to 2 hours before using.

Buttermilk Batter

    1/2 cup all-purpose flour, sifted

    1/2 cup buttermilk

    2 teaspoons olive oil

    1/2 teaspoon kosher salt

Whisk together all the ingredients in a medium bowl just until blended. Cover and refrigerate for 1 to 2 hours before using.

Vinegar Batter

    2/3 cup all-purpose flour, sifted

    6 tablespoons white wine vinegar

    1 egg, separated

    1 tablespoon vegetable oil

    Pinch of kosher salt

Combine the flour, vinegar, egg yolk, oil and salt in a medium bowl, mixing to form a smooth batter. Cover with plastic wrap and refrigerate for at least 2 hours.

Beat the egg white until soft peaks form. Gently fold into the batter until completely incorporated.

Tempura Batter

This is very good but, unfortunately, last-minute. You may want to save it for an all-tempura party with beer. Put out a bowl of Japanese Dipping Sauce (page 465).

    2 cups rice flour

    1/2 teaspoon paprika

    1 large egg

Just before ready to cook, place all the batter ingredients in a medium bowl. Pour in 1 cup ice water (plus an additional 1½ tablespoons if cooking shrimp). Stir very lightly (chopsticks are good for this) so that the batter is barely combined; there should be lumps of flour in the batter and around the rim of the bowl.
Makes enough for about 90 pieces, depending on size

Egg White Batter

    4 large eggs, separated

    1/3 cup all-purpose flour, plus more for dredging

Beat the egg whites in a large bowl with a wire whisk (or in the bowl of an electric mixer) until they form stiff peaks. Stir one-third of the whites into the yolks in another large bowl. Sprinkle this mixture with the ⅓ cup flour and top with the remaining whites. Fold the whites and flour in until no streaks of whites remain. A few lumps of flour may remain.

To fry, coat the items to be fried with batter and dredge in flour, making sure all surfaces are coated, then tap off excess flour.
Makes about 1½ cups, enough for 15 Chilies Rellenos (page 59)

Fritto Misto

"Fritto misto" is Italian for "mixed fried." Seafood is often involved, as are brains, but it can just as easily be made vegetarian. Choose any combination of herbs, vegetables and/or seafood that follows and match with any of the batters (pages 515–516) and dipping sauces (pages 463–467). Spicy mayonnaises are a common pairing (see page 458).

The best vegetables are those that are not watery (water creates splatter) and need minimal cooking. Quick cooking is further encouraged by thinly slicing the vegetables. Denser vegetables such as sweet potatoes and winter squash can be successfully fried so long as they are precooked.

Vegetable oil for deep-frying

A selection of herbs, vegetables or seafood (see below and box)

Heat the oil to 350°F (see Deep-frying, page 512). Dip the herbs, vegetables or seafood in the batter so that they are generously coated. Use herb stems or shrimp tails as handles; other foods go on a slotted spoon. Dredge in flour.

Working in batches, fry until golden brown, about 2 minutes on each side for vegetables or seafood, less for herbs.

HERBS

Leaves of sage, lovage, flat-leaf parsley and basil and edible flowers (leave about $1/4$ inch of stem attached)

VEGETABLES

Red and yellow bell peppers, cored, seeded and deribbed, cut into $1/2$-inch strips

Zucchini or yellow squash, trimmed and cut into $1/2$-inch slices, sprinkled generously with salt and allowed to drain for at least 30 minutes

Cauliflower, in small florets or thin slices, blanched in boiling water so that they are still a little crunchy.

SEAFOOD

Shrimp, peeled but tails left on

Oysters, shucked and patted dry

Medium scallops, left whole, or large scallops, halved crosswise

Fish (such as sole): 6-ounce fillets, halved lengthwise and center membranes removed, cut on a sharp diagonal into $2^1/2$ x $1/2$-inch strips

Some Suggested Items for Frying

Carrots, peeled, trimmed and cut into long ribbons with a vegetable peeler (1 medium carrot makes about 48 pieces)

Turnips, trimmed, peeled and sliced into thin rounds (1 medium turnip makes about 24 pieces)

Green beans, slit lengthwise into quarters left attached at one end (4 ounces green beans makes about 24 pieces)

Small sprigs of celery

Shrimp (20 to 24 per pound), peeled and deveined

Fried Onion Rings

Serve hot or at room temperature, but do not attempt to reheat—the onions get soggy in the oven. If making in batches, have the onions sliced and the seasoned flour prepared, but do not flour the onions until just before frying.

1 cup all-purpose flour

$1/4$ cup kosher salt

1 tablespoon finely ground black pepper

Vegetable oil for deep-frying

1 pound red or white onions, cut into very thin rings

Combine the flour, salt and pepper in a medium bowl. Heat the oil (see Deep-frying, page 512).

continued

Add the onion rings to the flour mixture and toss well to coat evenly. Remove about half the onion rings from the flour and shake off any excess flour. Fry, stirring occasionally, until crisp and golden brown, about 5 minutes. Drain on paper towels. Repeat with the remaining onion rings. **Makes 6 cups**

GRILLING

Some vegetables—summer squash, eggplants and leeks—lend themselves to grilling without a lot of fuss. Others must be coaxed. Firm vegetables such as potatoes, winter squash and fennel should be softened up first by steaming or a trip to the microwave oven (see the Cook's Guide for preparation of each vegetable). Most vegetables, parcooked or not before grilling, are cut into pieces or thicknesses that cook through quickly, appropriate for the high temperatures over which they're cooked.

Cutting vegetables into quick-cooking pieces and threading them onto skewers of metal or wood (wood should be soaked in plenty of water before grilling to prevent them from burning) is a way to handle both firmer vegetables and those that would, literally, slip through the cracks.

The vegetables that I deem suitable for the grill as listed at right. The individual sections in the Cook's Guide discuss preparation and cooking times for each.

To grill vegetables: Always start with a clean grill. Clean the grill itself with a sturdy wire brush or, in a pinch, a tightly wadded ball of aluminum foil. After scraping, wipe the grill clean with a lightly oiled wad of paper towel; continue wiping, using new towels as necessary, until there is no trace of black residue. If using a gas grill, clean the briquets regularly according to manufacturer's directions to prevent a buildup

of grease, which can cause flare-ups and off flavors. If using a charcoal grill, clean the grate that holds the coals and the inside of the grill after each use for better air circulation and more even burning.

Firm-textured vegetables that hold their shape (leeks and larger pieces of other vegetables) go directly on the grill. Some vegetables—quartered bell peppers, slices of eggplant or summer squash—can be placed directly on the grill as well. Others with soft textures, such as slices of tomatoes or oyster mushrooms, or those that are small enough to slip through the grill, such as slices of fennel or asparagus, should be placed in a hinged grill basket. (Soft-textured or smaller vegetables can also be threaded onto skewers before grilling, but a basket is easier, holds more and requires less attention.) Use a nonstick grill basket or spray the basket with vegetable cooking spray before using. Other than the basket, a pair of long tongs and/or a wide metal spatula are all that is needed. A spray bottle filled with water comes in handy for taming flare-ups.

Just before grilling, brush all sides of the vegetables lightly with peanut or canola oil (save expensive olive oil for drizzling over the vegetables after grilling) and season with salt and pepper. When practical, as with quartered bell peppers or sliced (blanched) fennel, it is faster to toss the vegetables with oil to coat and salt and pepper to taste. Alternatively, prepare one of the following marinades (page 519) and brush or toss to coat lightly.

All of the instructions in the Cook's Guide for grilling vegetables call for grilling over a fire that meets "the four-second test": If you can hold your palm two inches above the grill—not the coals—for a full four seconds, but no longer, before having to remove it, the grill is ready for cooking.

When grilling, lay the vegetables on the grate with a little space around them for even cooking. If the coals begin to flare up often (one or two little flare-ups is no cause for alarm), remove the vegetables and wait for the coals to cool a little. Grilled vegetables are good hot from the grill or at room temperature.

Marinades

Many vegetables, and meats and fish as well, are improved by marinating before grilling. Vegetables should not be left in the wet marinades for more than half an hour, or they will get soggy.

Each marinade makes $1/2$ cup, enough to marinate:

Eight 6-ounce bell peppers

Eight 6-ounce zucchini or yellow squash (cut lengthwise into $1/3$-inch slices)

2 pounds mushrooms or cremini mushrooms

2 pounds medium asparagus

Two 1-pound acorn squash

6 medium leeks

Two 1-pound eggplants (cut into $1/3$-inch slices)

8 large Belgian endives

2 large fennel bulbs (cut into $1/2$-inch wedges)

3 large red or yellow onions (cut into $1/3$-inch slices)

2 pounds small new potatoes

4 small sweet potatoes (halved)

2 pounds plum tomatoes (halved)

Fresh Herb Marinade

$1/3$ cup vegetable oil

2 tablespoons chopped fresh thyme

1 tablespoon chopped fresh rosemary

2 tablespoons chopped fresh sage

2 tablespoons fresh lemon juice or orange juice, fresh or store-bought

2 teaspoons kosher salt

$1/2$ teaspoon freshly ground black pepper

Stir the oil, thyme, rosemary and sage together in a small skillet. Heat over very low heat for 5 minutes. If the herbs start to sizzle, remove from the heat and wait until sizzling stops.

Scrape the herb mixture into a bowl. Whisk in the lemon juice, salt and pepper. Let stand at room temperature for 1 hour or refrigerate overnight before using.

Asian Marinade and Brushing Sauce

3 cloves garlic, smashed and peeled

2 slices (each the size of a quarter) peeled ginger, smashed

$1/4$ cup soy sauce, preferably tamari

$1 1/2$ teaspoons brown sugar

1 tablespoon rice wine vinegar or white wine vinegar

$1 1/2$ tablespoons tamarind purée or grated zest and juice of 1 lemon

$1/2$ teaspoon ground coriander

1 tablespoon fresh lemon juice

$1/2$ teaspoon hot red pepper sauce

continued

Bring the garlic, ginger and ½ cup water to a boil in a small saucepan. Reduce the heat to very low and simmer until almost all the liquid has evaporated. Add the soy, sugar, vinegar, tamarind or lemon and coriander. Bring to a simmer and cook for 5 minutes.

Remove from the heat and stir in the lemon juice and hot red pepper sauce. Cool before using. The marinade can be refrigerated for up to 1 week.

Citrus-Garlic Marinade

4 cloves garlic, smashed, peeled and finely chopped

Grated zest of 1 orange

Grated zest of 2 lemons

2 tablespoons fresh orange juice

2 tablespoons fresh lemon juice

2 tablespoons vegetable oil

Kosher salt and freshly ground black pepper to taste

Combine all the ingredients in a small jar with a tight-fitting lid. Shake vigorously. Let stand at room temperature for 1 hour, or refrigerate overnight, before using.

Maple Mustard Glaze

This is ideal for sweeter, firm vegetables such as acorn squash and sweet potatoes, which feel right when the weather gets cool (but not cool enough to stow the grill for the season).

3 tablespoons pure maple syrup

2 tablespoons prepared mustard

2 tablespoons liquid from a jar of bottled hot peppers (such as peperoncini or cherry peppers) or 2 tablespoons white vinegar plus 1 teaspoon hot red pepper sauce

Beat all the ingredients together with 1 tablespoon water in a small bowl until smooth. The glaze can be made up to a week in advance and refrigerated.

SAUTÉING

"Sauté" means "to jump," and the foods in a pan are often made to jump by being tossed around. The fat should be heated in the pan over medium-high heat. It is ready when the fat begins to wrinkle and turn slightly blue; it should not smoke. Just enough food should be put in at one time to make a layer or a layer and a half. Reduce the heat slightly and continue to cook, stirring until the food is cooked to the desired texture—either fully or partially if more cooking will be done.

STEAMING

Steaming takes place when food is cooked over boiling water. I have done it in specially made metal steamers with tiers, the bottom for water, upper ones with holes pierced in the bottom, and lids to keep the steam in. I have also used traditional Chinese bamboo steamers and steamer inserts—usually metal—that are specially made for certain pots such as couscous pots or, more conventionally, made with little feet or rims that permit them to be in the pot but above the water. And then there are the simplest devices: perforated footed metal trays with wings that fold over and can be flattened out and resemble a flower.

To steam, it is important that the water be at a boil before the food is added and timing begins. Make sure to use enough water so that the pot doesn't dry out before the cooking is done. Add more as needed but be careful; steam is very hot. The water should not touch the level where the food sits.

MICROWAVE COOKING

Directions for cooking vegetables in the microwave oven are given as part of many of the individual entries in the Cook's Guide, and there are recipes using the microwave throughout the book. For most recipes, the containers or dishes are covered.

If cooking covered, there are two options. Choose a cooking container, such as a casserole, with a tight-fitting lid or cover the container with microwave plastic wrap. If using the plastic wrap, by the end of cooking, the plastic will expand and the container will fill with steam. With the container still in the oven, pierce the plastic with the tip of a paring knife to allow the steam to escape; this will help prevent burns. Before completely uncovering the dish, poke the knife into a piece of vegetable to check for doneness. If further cooking is required, patch the hole in the plastic with a small piece of plastic rather than replacing it all. Continue cooking for a minute or two.

Microwave ovens are continually evolving. Use the cooking times here as a guideline. All the recipes included here are cooked at 100% unless otherwise specified. Some ovens may take a minute longer or shorter than indicated. After cooking a few vegetables, it should be simple to figure out how a particular oven performs.

Cook's Guide

ALL RECIPES, INCLUDING MINE, are guidelines, no matter how often and carefully I test them. Recipes call for quantities, but that doesn't always help when shopping. Additionally, an ingredient may be unavailable or disliked and a substitution must be made. Also, we like to make up our own recipes but need some information as to quantities, flavors, cooking methods and times. An unfamiliar ingredient chanced upon in a store may create similar questions. It is my hope that this section will help answer these questions and liberate the cook from a rigid adherence to the printed page.

Here is where I have stashed much of what I know about the vegetables and herbs mentioned in the book. There is information as to their botanical families and genera, how they should be bought and stored and how much they make when cut up and/or cooked. There are timings for the different modes of cooking such as boiling, steaming, roasting, grilling, micro-waving and sautéing. (For detailed information on each of these cooking techniques, turn to the Preparation and Methods sections throughout this guide for the specific vegetable that is of interest.) There are entries that are abbreviated recipes, many for braising. Enjoy.

I have also tried to describe something of their attributes as to taste, texture, compatibility with other flavors or ingredients and, when I know, something about how they grow.

Obviously, I cannot include all the edible plants in the world; nevertheless, I still get nightmares thinking of omissions. For example, just the other day, Penny Levy told me she had a plant called para (*Spilanthes acmella* or *Acmella oleracea*). In Brazil, it is "jambu"; in England, "Brazilian or Australian cress." It is used in salads and, in Brazil, to flavor rice and tacaca—a soup made with yuca, chilies, dried shrimp and jambu. This information is from the invaluable Chiltern Seeds Web site (see Sources). I know no more, but I have gotten it off my conscience.

We may never see or use some of the vegetables here—but I wouldn't bet on it. Various vegetables unknown only a few short years ago have spread around the globe and into local supermarkets and restaurants as well as specialty stores.

Some vegetables are listed independently and alphabetically. Some, however, are grouped, as much of the information about them seems to me best stated in a clump. This is the case with mushrooms and herbs. I also grouped together some less familiar vegetables under a single

heading, such as yuca, malanga and taro under Tropical Tubers. All of the exotic types of mustard greens, such as mizuna, have a logical home in Mustard Greens. However, finding them should not be a problem, as there are cross-references under the correct alphabetical placement throughout the text, or any item desired can be looked up in the Index.

I know that my ambition is greater than my knowledge. I have included a Bibliography so that other authors can be consulted. My life and the book have been made more complicated by the tendency of authorities to change the botanical names of ingredients or sometimes allowing two disparate names—such as calling a child both Alice and Susan. I have chosen to list first the name with which I am most familiar and follow it in parentheses with the alternate name.

I have avoided the "what is a vegetable?" discussion, since it is clear that many of what are fruits, such as peppers and tomatoes, are regarded by most eaters, cooks and myself as vegetables.

I am weakest when it comes to Asian growths and cannot pretend to be an expert in their preparation or in general knowledge about them. I have done what I can, hoping it will be of help. I particularly direct attention to two wonderful books listed in the Bibliography, one by G.A.C. Herklots that is certainly out of print, and one by Charmaine Solomon that sometimes shares the same fate. The Web and libraries can help. I was introduced to Herklots by Barbara Tropp, and we had many good conversations in his praise.

ACORN SQUASH see Squash, Winter

ADANKA see Beans from Asia under Beans

ADZUKI see Beans from Asia under Beans

ADZUKI SPROUTS see Sprouts

ALFALFA SPROUTS see Sprouts

ALLIUMS see Onions

Amaranth

Amaranthus cruentus

Most of us are accustomed to thinking of amaranth as a grain, and very healthy it is too. However, one part of amaranth that fits in this book is the leaves. Some are green, shaped like roundish arrowheads with uneven edges and slightly frilly. My favorite kind is red amaranth, in which the edges are green and the heart red. It is used in Chinese cooking in stir-fries or served as an alternative to spinach. I first came across it in a Chinese market. Not knowing what it was, I simply steeped it in some light chicken stock (page 501). It turned the soup a beautiful color and added a light flavor. In summer, the Greeks use the shoots to make horta (see page 577).

Methods

BUYING AND STORING

Store like spinach, loosely wrapped in plastic in the refrigerator. Use as fresh as possible.

WASHING/WAYS OF CUTTING

Basically this doesn't need soaking, just a light rinse. It is quite clean when bought. I use the leaves whole, as they are tender whether in soup or for stir-frying, but they can be cut in strips across the leaves if desired. The flavor is very mild and shouldn't be swamped with very strong seasonings.

Yields and Equivalents

3 ounces amaranth leaves = 6 cups = 4 cups cut into thin strips

AMERICAN PINE MUSHROOMS see Mushrooms, Fresh

ANCHOS see Peppers

ANGELICA see Herbs and Their Flowers

Anise

Pimpinella anisum

Anise is one of the many herbs that has a licoricelike flavor. It is mainly the seeds, small and light brown, that are used in liqueurs and other infusions, but the frond-y leaves can be chopped and used in salads or desserts. It is important to know for crossword puzzle solvers, as it is a frequent answer. All versions of anise make a pleasant addition to pasta sauces, particularly those with sausage or other meat. A bit of anise seed ground to a powder will marry the pasta sauce to the sausage.

Methods

BUYING AND STORING

Usually the seeds are bought, in bottles or other containers. The herb itself must be grown, as it is not commercially available. The seeds can be replaced by fennel seeds.

If a powder is desired, the seeds can be ground in a coffee grinder or spice mill or the smallest food processor.

Yields and Equivalents

WHOLE SEEDS

1 tablespoon anise seeds = $1/4$ ounce = 2 teaspoons ground

APPLE MINT see Mints under Herbs and Their Flowers

Artichokes

Cynara scolymus

"I have been faithful to thee, Cynara! in my fashion." When I came to the Latin name for artichokes, I was reminded of the famous line by Ernest Dowson. It seems to relate (in the poem) to the myth that Zeus in one of his many capricious affairs made Cynara an immortal and took her up to live with the gods. She became lonesome for her family and visited the world of men. For revenge, Zeus turned her into an artichoke—not his most poetic transformation.

Varieties

What we think of as the leaves are actually the petals of a thistlelike flower. The choke, the furry strawlike leaves under the real petals, is inedible. These actually choke and must be removed by either the cook or the eater.

There are a number of related plants among the artichokes. In some, leaves are rounded with rather sharp spines at the tip. These are the globe artichokes, and although I have not found them suitable for roasting, I do like them in almost every other preparation, as well as the raw bottoms thinly shaved in salad. Other petals may have a more pointed shape and may be green or flushed with violet. These need to be small, and there should be no choke, or it should be so small that when the artichoke is halved or quartered lengthwise, the little bit at the bottom can be cut out with a spoon or a knife.

GLOBE Rounded, compact shape with round-tipped leaves sporting sharp tips. The largest artichokes, and hence bottoms, come from Brittany. The baby artichokes, round, of this variety are usually growths of side shoots after the main artichoke has been removed.

PURPLE (petit violet in France) Tapered toward the tip with pointy, purple-tinged leaves.

SMALL (2 to 3 inches long and about $2^1/2$ ounces each) Versions of purple artichokes, these should be relatively free of choke.

BABY (about 1 ounce each) These really do not have a choke.

Methods

BUYING AND STORING

Whether globe, purple, small or baby, artichokes should be tightly furled and firm and feel heavy for their size. Stems should be firm and not discolored; their bottoms should not be woody. An old saw says freshly picked artichokes will squeak when rubbed together. Store artichokes in a plastic bag in the refrigerator and use as soon as possible.

STRIPPING THE ARTICHOKE

Most vegetables are the Lili St. Cyrs or Gypsy Rose Lees of the plant world, needing stripping before they are edible. Pods and skins, outer leaves and cores, stems and husks may all be cast aside with seductive abandon. Artichokes, too, need to be undressed before or after cooking. An artichoke is a thistle and can—like its relatives—scratch. How much and in what way the stripping takes place depends on the size of this nascent flower and the way it is cooked.

See page 230 for more on artichokes. They are reputed to be terrible with wine. They do change the palate. I don't mind. Try a Grüner Veltliner.

All artichokes, no matter what their size, should have the tips of their leaves cut off with scissors or a strong knife. These tips are part of the defensive system of the artichoke and can prick. For how to continue with small or baby artichokes, see page 527. The thoughts here about preparing artichokes pertain to the artichokes commonly available in American stores, large round globe artichokes. (For thoughts on how to present them, see page 232.) Have a cut lemon or some lemon juice at the ready to prevent discoloration. Wipe the exposed surfaces with lemon as you proceed.

Even when artichokes are to be served boiled, steamed or stuffed and whole, they will usually need to have the hard lower outside leaves snapped off first. Just pull the dark little leaves away and down from the rest, and they will snap off. Continue for two or three rows of leaves. Ways to continue cleaning, depending on the preparation desired, follow, but generally there will be some rough stuff where the leaves have been pulled away or underneath the bottom that needs to be pared away with a small knife.

If lots of artichokes are being prepared, keep the trimmed-off leaves to make a purée (see page 236), perhaps to use in soup.

All cooked artichokes except for very small ones require stripping for eating. One or more leaves are pulled away at a time and scraped between upper and lower teeth to get the soft meat at the base.

There is a great deal of confusion as to what is called what in an artichoke—what is a bottom and what is a heart. Arbitrarily, I have decided to call the very bottom with no leaves attached the "bottom" and the bottom with the finest leaves attached and the choke removed the "heart."

WASHING/WAYS OF CUTTING

GLOBE ARTICHOKES *Whole:* Cut or break off each artichoke stem flush with the bottom of the artichoke. The stems can be peeled and cooked along with the artichokes. Cut 1 1/2 inches from the top of the artichoke. Trim the pointed tips of the remaining leaves with scissors. Rub the cut surfaces with lemon juice.

Bottoms: Cut or break off the stem flush with the bottom of the artichoke. Pull off as many dark outer leaves as necessary to reach the all-yellow leaves. With the artichoke on its side, cut off yellow leaves at their base to reveal the hairy choke. Scrape out the choke with a thin-edged, usually silver, spoon or a melon baller. Trim the bottom so that none of the hard green skin remains. While working, rub the cut edges of the artichoke bottom with lemon to keep it from darkening. Keep trimmed artichoke bottoms in lemon water while preparing the rest.

The bottom from an 8- to 9-ounce artichoke will hold 1 tablespoon thick sauce or 2 teaspoons vinaigrette.

To serve bottoms raw: Cut or grate the cleaned bottoms into very thin slices. These are typically used as a salad or in pasta sauce. They are particularly good in a pale salad with thinly sliced fennel and Belgian endive. Very thin slices of Parmesan cannot go amiss.

Hearts: These are the bottoms plus the lightest green leaves, usually of smallish artichokes. To prepare, snap off several outer layers of dark green leaves to reach light green/yellow leaves. Cut off all but 1 1/2 inches of these leaves. Gently spread back leaves from center; scrape out

the choke and any violet leaves from the center. Trim and soak in acidulated water as described under *Bottoms*.

SMALL ARTICHOKES Slice off the artichoke tip, about one-third to half of the way down. Remove all tough outer leaves (generally two to three layers), leaving only the tender light green leaves. Trim stem to 1/2 inch. Or, if the recipe indicates to leave the stem, scrape off the skin and trim just the end. Remove all hard green bits from bottom and stem. Rub all cut surfaces with lemon. Keep trimmed artichokes in lemon water while preparing the rest. Cut one artichoke in half. If there is any visible choke or violet-tipped leaves, remove with an espresso spoon or the tip of a paring knife. Repeat with the remaining artichokes, returning them to the water as you work.

BABY ARTICHOKES Prepare by trimming the tips of the leaves and the bottoms of any rough patches. Continue as for small artichokes.

Preparation

BOILING

GLOBE ARTICHOKES Often some lemon juice or the lemon juice and the shells from which it has come, and even some flour, are put in the water and a largish heavy plate put on top of the artichokes to keep them submerged and the leaves as light in color as possible.

Whole: Drop prepared artichokes, and lemon or anything else being used, into boiling salted water and cook until the bottoms are pierced easily with a knife, 30 to 45 minutes, depending on size. Drain upside down.

Bottoms: Drop prepared bottoms into boiling lemon water and cook 9 to 10 minutes for bottoms that retain a slight texture (best when artichokes will be used in other preparations). Cook 15 to 20 minutes for fully done. Drain. Test by sticking point of a sharp knife into underside of the bottom.

SMALL ARTICHOKES *Trimmed and left whole:* Add to boiling salted water; weight with an otoshi-buta (see Note, page 237) or smaller pan lid to keep them submerged. Cook until thickest part of bottom is easily pierced with a paring knife, about 10 minutes. Drain.

Trimmed, quartered and choke removed: Add to boiling salted water; stir until water returns to a boil. Cook until bottoms are easily pierced with a paring knife, about 7 minutes. Drain.

STEAMING

GLOBE ARTICHOKES *Whole:* Stand prepared artichokes in a covered steamer basket. Cook medium globes (12 ounces or under) 25 to 30 minutes, large globes 30 to 40 minutes. Tightly packed artichokes may take 10 to 20 minutes longer.

Bottoms: Place prepared bottoms in a covered steamer basket. Steam 9 to 10 minutes for bottoms that retain a slight texture (best when artichokes will be used in other preparations). Steam 20 to 25 minutes for fully cooked.

SMALL ARTICHOKES *Whole:* Place prepared artichokes in a covered steamer basket. Steam 10 minutes for artichokes that retain a slight texture (best when artichokes will be used in other preparations). Steam 20 to 25 minutes for fully cooked.

BABY ARTICHOKES *Whole:* Place prepared artichokes in a covered steamer basket. Steam 5 minutes for artichokes that retain a slight texture (best when artichokes will be used in other preparations). Steam 12 to 15 minutes for fully cooked.

ROASTING

I do not recommend roasting globe or purple artichokes.

SMALL ARTICHOKES *Halves:* Cut prepared artichokes in half lengthwise. Rub with lemon juice. Use the smallest nonreactive pan that will hold artichokes comfortably in a single layer. Pour $1/4$ cup fresh lemon juice into pan. Place artichokes cut side down in pan. Slick halves with fat. Roast in center of 500°F oven for 20 minutes. Add $3/4$ cup water or stock. Cover tightly with foil. Roast 15 to 20 minutes more. (1 pound serves 3 to 4 as side dish)

BABY ARTICHOKES: Roasting these would be an unnatural act.

MICROWAVING

This may be the best way to cook artichokes, as they do not become waterlogged.

BABY ARTICHOKES *Whole* ($3/4$ ounce each, about 18 per pound): Remove round bottom leaves and trim leaf tips. Cover tightly and turn once during cooking.

1 pound artichokes with 2 cups stock or broth and $3/4$ cup olive oil ($1 1/2$-quart casserole or soufflé dish): 12 minutes

SMALL ARTICHOKES *Whole* (2 ounces each): Trim as for baby artichokes; cover tightly.

4 artichokes: 10 minutes

8 artichokes: 11 minutes

16 artichokes: 14 minutes

8 artichokes with $1 1/4$ cups liquid (2-quart casserole or soufflé dish) turned once: 13 minutes

GLOBE ARTICHOKES *Whole* (8 to 12 ounces each): Arrange in a circle on a large baking dish. Cover with microwave plastic wrap. At the end of cooking, pierce plastic to release the steam.

1 artichoke: 7 minutes

2 artichokes: 10 minutes

4 artichokes: 15 minutes

6 artichokes: 19 minutes

Bottoms (2 ounces each): Arrange in a single layer in a large soufflé dish so they are not touching. Add 1 tablespoon water; cover tightly.

4 artichoke bottoms: 6 minutes

SAUTÉING

BABY OR VERY SMALL ARTICHOKES Heat 1 tablespoon olive oil in a 10-inch skillet over medium-low heat. Add 8 ounces artichokes, trimmed, quartered and chokes removed. Cook, tossing often, until lightly browned, about 6 minutes. Add $1/4$ cup chicken stock or broth, cover and cook until tender, about 3 minutes for baby artichokes, 6 minutes for small artichokes. Uncover, add 1 tablespoon olive oil or butter and cook until liquid is evaporated and artichokes begin to sizzle.

FROZEN ARTICHOKE HEARTS For one 9-ounce box: Defrost if necessary in a colander under warm running water; drain thoroughly. Blot artichokes dry with paper towels. Heat 1 tablespoon olive oil in a 10-inch skillet over medium heat. Add 1 clove garlic, sliced, or 1 tablespoon chopped shallots. Cook 1 minute. Add artichokes and cook, stirring gently to keep them intact, until lightly browned, about 5 minutes. Add 3 tablespoons chicken stock, broth or water and cook until liquid is evaporated and artichokes begin to sizzle, about 2 minutes. Season with salt to taste. (Makes 1 1/3 cups)

PREPARATION FOR STUFFING

Artichoke shells are similar to artichoke hearts. Shells have more green leaves left in place to make a sturdier container for stuffing.

To make artichoke shells: Cut or break off each artichoke stem flush with bottom of artichoke. Strip off bottom leaves, at least three layers; all tough, dark leaves should be removed. Using a knife or scissors, cut off top 1 1/2 inches of artichoke. Rub cut areas with lemon juice to keep them from discoloring. With a stainless steel knife or grapefruit spoon, cut out and discard choke (gently spreading the leaves apart makes it easier to see and get at choke; be sure to remove it all). Keep trimmed artichokes in lemon water while preparing the rest.

Alternatively, artichokes can be prepared according to the method for whole artichokes and cooked, then have center leaves and choke removed.

Artichoke hearts (see page 527) can also be stuffed. One 2-ounce artichoke heart, cooked, holds 1 tablespoon thick sauce or 2 teaspoons vinaigrette.

To cook artichoke shells: Fill a large stainless steel or enamel pot with salted water. Add the artichokes and weigh down with a small plate or an otoshi-buta (see Note, page 237). Bring to a boil. Reduce to a simmer. Cook for 20 minutes, or until a knife easily slips into artichoke bottoms. Remove and let artichokes drain upside down on a rack or towels. To make it easier to fill artichokes, spread leaves out from center of each, making a larger opening.

Alternatively, steam artichokes on a rack or strainer over boiling water for 20 minutes (be sure artichokes do not touch water).

BAKING STUFFED ARTICHOKES

Once trimmed, cooked artichokes are filled with the stuffing of choice (see pages 491–500 for suggestions), arrange in a baking dish in which they fit snugly. Drizzle with olive oil and pour 1/4 cup stock, broth or water into dish. Bake until stuffing and artichokes are heated through, about 20 minutes.

Yields and Equivalents

The usual serving of a globe artichoke is one per person. For raw sliced or quartered artichokes, it is very hard to give a yield because of variations in size. See individual recipes.

GLOBE ARTICHOKES

1 large artichoke yields 8 to 12 ounces

One 8-ounce artichoke yields a 1-ounce bottom

One 9- to 12-ounce artichoke yields a 2-ounce bottom

6 average artichoke bottoms = 6 1/2 ounces, puréed = generous 3/4 cup

1 pound artichoke leaves, stems and trimmings = 1 1/2 cups purée (see page 236)

SMALL ARTICHOKES

1 small artichoke = 2 1/2 ounces = 1 3/4 to 2 ounces trimmed

1 pound small artichokes, trimmed, quartered and chokes removed = 3 cups

BABY ARTICHOKES

1 baby artichoke = 1 to 1 1/2 ounces = 3/4 to 1 ounce trimmed

1 pound baby artichokes, trimmed, quartered and chokes removed = 4 cups

CANNED BOTTOMS

These can be bought in jars or bottles. After thorough rinsing to remove the flavor of the brine, they can be used as cooked fresh bottoms, but obviously are nowhere near as good.

FROZEN HEARTS

Of the many frozen vegetables, these are some of the most acceptable and work very well in light-colored and -flavored stews, such as veal or chicken. Do not overcook or they will fall apart.

One 9-ounce package frozen quartered artichoke hearts, defrosted and drained = 1 1/3 cups

PICKLED HEARTS

These can be bought in jars and are a reasonable emergency addition to a mixed hors d'oeuvre.

One 12-ounce jar = 1 3/4 cups quartered artichoke hearts

CANNED WHOLE HEARTS

One 14-ounce can = 6 to 8 whole artichoke hearts = 1 1/2 cups quartered artichoke hearts

Arugula
Eruca sativa

This has become very popular in Italian restaurants, where people from different regions spell it differently. There are several strains. Those that are thinner are more tender and better in salad. They are also used cooked with or in pasta. They can be used fairly interchangeably with young dandelion greens, which they resemble in their longish narrow shape and saw-toothed outline.

Methods
BUYING AND STORING

Regular arugula runs the gamut from large, thickish, flat dark green leaves to small feathery lighter green and more delicate leaves. It is sold in bunches of various sizes. In any case, look for firm, not floppy, bright green leaves. Baby arugula is becoming widely available in cello bags. The smaller the leaves, the milder the flavor, which is pleasantly bitter. Shake the bag; the leaves should be loose and dry, not clumpy, wet or yellow. Store large or baby arugula in plastic bags in the vegetable drawer of the refrigerator.

WASHING/WAYS OF CUTTING

Wash well and dry well. If the leaves are very large, they can be torn into 2-inch lengths.

Yields and Equivalents
REGULAR ARUGULA

1 medium bunch large-leaved arugula = 6 to 7 ounces = 4 ounces trimmed = 7 cups leaves

BABY ARUGULA

4 ounces baby arugula = 5 cups = 2 cups lightly wilted = 1/2 cup fully cooked

ASIAN CABBAGES see Cabbages, Asian

Asian Greens

Asians, particularly the Chinese, are great collectors of wild herbs and growers of others. In keeping with their general attitude, the Chinese designate many of these as medicinal. The Japanese use many of the same leaves but with different attributes assigned. Once again, I am not an expert in these cuisines and can give only notes on those that I have grown or used. There is a book in the Bibliography by Dahlen and Phillipps that I recommend highly, as well as the ever-useful Charmaine Solomon's *Encyclopedia of Asian Food.*

Increasingly, some of the Japanese leaves are showing up in assorted young" salad packs" of seed or the leaves can be added to salads as they are to mesclun (young green) mixes. Also see Lemongrass, page 592.

Again, there are so many names in so many countries that it is impossible to give them all, especially as they are transliterated differently—including Cantonese and Mandarin versions.

Varieties

GINGER (*Zingiber officinale*) Ginger is really a seasoning or a spice. It is used fresh, dried, pickled and candied. The only reason that it shows up here among the leaves is that in the early spring, the rhizome—what is thought of as the root and grows underground—sends out pale lilac-pink shoots, long and thin. They are delicious in a stir-fry. Fresh ginger is best when the skin is pale, smooth and thin. Checking where knobs have fallen off will give a good idea as to whether the ginger is coarsely fibrous; if it is, do not buy it. Keep it wrapped in the refrigerator for up to a week.

MITSUBA (*Cryptotaenia japonica*) This is an almost exclusively Japanese ingredient, also called honewort. It is a member of the same family as the carrot, and it comes in both red and green. Japanese growers often blanch it so that the stems can be used. The roots are sometimes boiled and served with oil. It is used as frequently in Japan—both cooked and raw—as Westerners use parsley. I grow it, easily, to throw the leaves into salad.

MIZUNA (*Brassica rapa,* Japonica group) This is our old friend mustard (see page 593), whose youngest leaves are eaten in salad.

PERILLA OR SHISO (*Perilla frutescens*) Known in the West as beefsteak plant and in the East as shiso and egoma, perilla comes in both red and green. Many people will be most familiar with the green variety, which is tucked raw in among the fish in sushi and sashimi. It has a mysterious aroma that is not evident outside the mouth but that becomes pronounced on the palate when chewed. It has a slightly peppery taste in the front of the mouth. Its oval, jagged leaves are about 2 inches long and 1 inch across, with a slightly fuzzy surface. Perilla is a good palate cleanser.

Asparagus
Asparagus officinalis/Ornithogalum pyrenaicum

Asparagus are one of the ravishments of spring. I grow them. A well-established bed will yield forever, but it likes lots of manure and needs weeding. A new bed should be allowed to go to seed for the first three years to give it strength. The asparagus stalks should be cut beneath the ground to avoid crown rot. Asparagus are lilies, but what we cook and eat is the nascent plant before the flowers appear, even before the tops begin to open. Some of the small asparagus are called wild; they are wild only in the sense that they have escaped from gardens.

Ornithogalum is a different plant but often sold, imported from Italy or elsewhere, as wild asparagus. I like it very much. It can be replaced by pencil-thin asparagus.

Varieties

GREEN (*Asparagus officinalis*) These are the asparagus that we are used to. There are many different cultivars and they range in size, the smallest being pencil asparagus, about 1/4 inch in diameter and really the only asparagus that can be cooked without peeling. These are sometimes simply called grass, especially by country folk. They are often eaten raw by Italians, who dip them in olive oil. They are fine finger food. Larger ones should be peeled and cooked. They can be eaten cold or warm with hollandaise sauce or a vinaigrette.

AMERICAN WHITE (*Asparagus officinalis*) Cream-colored specimens with light purple shading possible toward the tip, a particularly fibrous texture, and stalks that need complete peeling before cooking. Provide knives and forks.

EUROPEAN WHITE (*Asparagus officinalis*) These are the basis of festivals and special menus in the spring. The biggest, fattest ones, from near Baden-Baden in Germany, Argenteuil in France and many parts of Spain, are a great delight. They have no lavender tips and are grown blanched either in earth or in fabric tunnels. They too are tougher than green asparagus and after peeling and cooking must be eaten with a knife and fork. They are expensive, but I would gladly give up the rest of the meal for them. They are particularly good with hollandaise or black truffles.

CANNED WHITE (*Asparagus officinalis*) One of the only vegetables that are almost as good in their preserved state as fresh. I have had them from Europe and, most recently, from China. The best have come from Spain. The large cans or jars will feed six people as a first course. They should be rinsed, and heated slightly if serving with a hot sauce.

PURPLE (*Asparagus officinalis*) Deep purple stalks that, when raw, taste slightly sweeter and lighter than green asparagus. Once cooked, though, they look and taste exactly the same.

"WILD" (*Asparagus officinalis*) The same species as regular asparagus and usually just garden escapees. They range in size from pencil-thin to quite large.

EUROPEAN WILD (*Ornithogalum pyrenaicum*) Slender and pliable stalks that are not a true asparagus but a distant relative of the onion, as evidenced by their slight onion flavor; occasionally available in specialty markets. All recipes on pages 160–162 featuring wild asparagus refer to this variety. It is also referred to as Bath asparagus, Prussian asparagus and spiked star-of-Bethlehem. It should not be picked from the wild unless very sure what one is getting; the other star-of-Bethlehem is poisonous. The one we eat looks rather like an unopened hyacinth with basal leaves. The best substitute in my recipes is pencil-thin asparagus, often called grass.

HOP SHOOTS (*Humulus lupulus*) When I was trying to track down European wild asparagus, several people suggested that they might be hop shoots, which look somewhat the same. They are floppier and are best used in stir-fries.

Methods
BUYING AND STORING
Try to buy bunches of asparagus that have stalks pretty much of equal thickness for even cooking. The tips should be tightly furled and the stalks firm, and the cut ends of the stalks should not be woody.

Asparagus should be eaten as fresh as possible so that their sweetness doesn't dissipate. If they must be stored, wrap them in damp paper towels and then in plastic wrap.

WASHING/WAYS OF CUTTING
GREEN, WHITE AND PURPLE ASPARAGUS When buying asparagus, remember that approximately half their total weight will be lost when the woody ends are snapped off and they are peeled. (For instance, 1 pound from the store will give about 8 ounces.)

To prepare, hold the asparagus stalk in both hands and break off the stem end. The stem will automatically break at the correct place, removing the rough end. Place the stalk on the work surface and run a vegetable peeler down all sides of the stem from just under the tip to the end. Repeat with the remaining spears. What is called grass, with stalks about 1/4 inch in diameter, does not need peeling; white asparagus always does.

Medium and larger stalks of asparagus can be "roll-cut": After removing the ends and peeling, place several stalks side by side on the cutting board and cut off the stem ends on a 45-degree angle. Roll the stalks a quarter turn and cut again on a 45-degree angle about 2 inches from the bottom. Repeat until all the stalks are cut; leave the tips intact. Roll-cutting exposes more surface area of the stalks and is preferred for stir-frying or sautéing.

Do not discard the peelings and snapped-off ends; save them for soup or Asparagus Stock (see page 506). **EUROPEAN WILD ASPARAGUS** These thin stalks do not need to be peeled. Just trim 1/4 inch off the stem ends.

Preparation
I generally cook asparagus in a microwave oven—fast and impeccable. Alternatively, I tie them with white string into even bunches and boil them, uncovered, in lots of salted water until the point of a knife just slips into the fat end. Pick them up by the strings, move them onto a cloth-lined plate and cut the strings. Remove from the cloth when completely drained.

Serve the spears with sauce over the middle or the tips, leaving the ends clear to pick up with fingers. If they need to be kept warm for a while, cover with a cloth. I don't like to serve them either hot or ice-cold.

BOILING
GREEN AND PURPLE ASPARAGUS *Whole spears:* Tie prepared asparagus into even bunches. Drop into boiling salted water. Cook 3 to 8 minutes, depending upon thickness, or until the point of a knife just slips into a fat end. Pick up by the strings; cut strings.
WHITE ASPARAGUS *Whole spears:* Drop prepared asparagus, tied in bunches, into a large pot of boiling water. Cook for ten minutes. Reduce heat to a low boil. Cook another 10 minutes, or until asparagus are very

tender. Rinse under cold running water if serving cold or in a salad.

JUMBO WHITE ASPARAGUS *Whole spears* (1 inch thick): Cook 20 minutes at a rolling boil, then 10 minutes at a low boil. Rinse under cold running water if serving with an enriched vinaigrette. Traditionally, white asparagus are served in linen napkins to absorb the liquid they continue to give off as they sit.

STEAMING

GREEN AND PURPLE ASPARAGUS *Whole spears:* Place prepared asparagus, preferably in a single layer, in a covered steamer basket. Steam 4 to 7 minutes, depending on thickness. Add 1 to 2 minutes to cooking time if asparagus is deeper than a single layer; if piled very deep, rearrange halfway through cooking.

WHITE ASPARAGUS *Whole spears:* Place prepared asparagus in a single layer in a covered steamer basket. Steam 1 hour, or until meltingly tender.

EUROPEAN WILD ASPARAGUS *Whole spears:* Place prepared asparagus in a single layer in a covered steamer basket. Steam 1 minute.

ROASTING

GREEN AND PURPLE ASPARAGUS *Whole spears:* Snap ends off (do not peel). Use smallest pan that will hold asparagus comfortably in a single layer. Slick asparagus and pan with olive oil. Roast in center of a 500°F oven for 6 minutes. Turn and roast for 5 minutes more.

When multiplying the recipe to use as many asparagus as pan will hold, add oil a little at a time; the asparagus don't need to be drowned. It is better to get an intense flavor from just a film of the very best olive oil. Too much can be overly assertive.

WHITE ASPARAGUS Not suited for roasting.

GRILLING

GREEN AND PURPLE ASPARAGUS *Whole spears:* See Grilling, page 518, for preparing the grill. Trim and peel medium asparagus (stalks about 1/2 inch thick). Rub with just enough vegetable oil to coat them lightly. Line spears up in a grill basket or, alternatively, line up four or five spears at a time and pass a water-soaked long wooden skewer through center of stalks. Grill over direct heat (laying skewered asparagus across the grate), turning once, until lightly browned in spots and tender, 6 to 8 minutes, depending on thickness. Season with salt and pepper and drizzle with olive oil or melted butter.

EUROPEAN WILD ASPARAGUS *Whole Spears:* I coat them with a little olive oil first and grill just as regular asparagus.

MICROWAVING

The nice thing about asparagus in the microwave oven is that they require no water (unless the covering is not tightly sealed), stay bright green, retain all their vitamins and don't have to be bunched, since they're not floating around; and the cooking time is by weight, not number of pieces. Further, it doesn't matter if that weight is composed of trimmed or untrimmed stalks, or fat or thin stalks.

When cooking whole spears, lay them 2 to 3 layers deep (pointing in same direction) in a rectangular baking dish. Cover tightly with microwave plastic wrap and cook at 100%.

Tips or short pieces, to be cooked before incorporation in another dish, should be placed, by the 8-ounce batch, in a container or containers just large enough to hold them. Cover tightly with plastic wrap. If using one container, place in the center of the oven. Several containers should be placed in a circle so they do not touch.

Prick the plastic wrap after cooking, then carefully uncover it as soon as it comes out of the oven; wrapped, the asparagus will continue to steam and can overcook very quickly. If using the asparagus tips or pieces in a dish where they will be reheated, place them in a sieve immediately after cooking and run plenty of cold water over them to keep them firm.

GREEN AND PURPLE ASPARAGUS *Whole spears:* Arrange prepared asparagus 2 to 3 layers deep in a dish just large enough to hold them. Cover tightly.

8 ounces: 2 minutes 30 seconds
1 pound: 4 minutes 15 seconds
2 pounds: 7 minutes

Tips and/or stalks, 1- to 2-inch lengths: Place in a container or containers, cover and arrange in oven as described in Microwaving.

   8 ounces: 3 minutes
   1 pound: 4 minutes 30 seconds

WHITE ASPARAGUS *Whole spears:* Arrange prepared asparagus 2 to 3 layers deep in a glass loaf pan. Add 3 tablespoons water. Cover tightly.

   1 pound: 10 minutes

SAUTÉING

PENCIL-THIN ASPARAGUS OR THIN OR MEDIUM GREEN OR PURPLE ASPARAGUS For 8 ounces, trimmed, peeled and cut into 2-inch lengths: Heat 1 tablespoon olive oil in a 10-inch skillet over medium heat. Add asparagus. Cook, tossing, until tender but still slightly crunchy, about 7 minutes for medium asparagus, 5 minutes for thin asparagus, 3 minutes for pencil asparagus. Add 2 tablespoons water, stock or vegetable broth to pan and cook, tossing, until evaporated. Season with salt and add an additional tablespoon of olive oil or butter, if desired. (Serves 2 as a side dish)

THIN EUROPEAN WHITE ASPARAGUS For 1 pound (about 30 thin spears), trimmed and peeled: This isn't really sautéing, but it happens in a pan, so here it is. Put asparagus in 10- or 11-inch skillet. Add ¹/₃ cup water and 1 tablespoon unsalted butter. Bring to a boil, reduce heat to medium-low and cook, turning asparagus once or twice, until water is evaporated. Reduce heat to lowest possible setting, cover pan and cook until tender, about 12 minutes. Turn asparagus once during this final cooking. If butter begins to brown, add 1 tablespoon water. Season with salt. (Serves 3 as a side dish)

Yields and Equivalents

PENCIL ASPARAGUS (¹/₄ inch thick or less)
   1 pound asparagus = approximately 48 stalks
THIN ASPARAGUS (¹/₄ to ³/₈ inch thick)
   1 pound asparagus = approximately 42 stalks
MEDIUM ASPARAGUS (³/₈ to ¹/₂ inch thick)
   1 pound asparagus = approximately 36 stalks

JUMBO ASPARAGUS (³/₄ to 1 inch thick)
   1 pound asparagus = approximately 20 stalks
   1 pound asparagus, trimmed, peeled and cut into
      2-inch pieces = 2 cups raw = 1³/₄ cups cooked =
      1 cup purée
WHITE ASPARAGUS, EUROPEAN AND AMERICAN
   1 pound thin white asparagus = 30 spears =
      12 ounces trimmed and peeled
   1 pound jumbo white asparagus = 12 spears =
      10 ounces trimmed and peeled
   One 11.6-ounce jar = 7 ounces drained =
      7 medium spears
   One 8.8-ounce can = 6 to 8 large spears
EUROPEAN WILD ASPARAGUS
   1 pound asparagus = approximately 48 stalks

AUBERGINE see Eggplants
AVOCADO LEAVES see Avocados
AVOCADO PEAS see Wing Beans under Peas

Avocados

Persea americana

By arrogant fiat, I declare avocados a vegetable, and one of my favorites at that.

Varieties

HASS A dark green variety with alligator-rough skin that comes primarily from California.

FLORIDA aka DUERTE Large, smooth, bright green avocados often called alligator pears, which tend to be more fibrous and watery. They usually come from Florida or from North Africa.

MINIATURE OR COCKTAIL AVOCADOS Ripe at about 2 inches long with only vestigial pits. A lengthwise half makes a super hors d'oeuvre when stuffed; peeling it may be more of a problem.

AVOCADO LEAVES Used as a seasoning, first usually brought to a boil in fresh water two times. The leaves may be put in with rice as it cooks, or small amounts of rice can be steamed wrapped in the leaves—much as banana leaves are used.

Methods
BUYING AND STORING

Avocados must be ripe but not overripe, the meat going brown and with mushy spots. The kindest way to judge Hass avocados, from the point of view of the store, is to wiggle the stem, which should be loose like a young child's tooth that is about to go. The only way to truly judge them, though, is to squeeze them ever so gently. They should give slightly. The skin of a Hass will turn from bright to dull green as it ripens but should show no brown or black parts or dents. Florida avocados are ready for eating when they yield slightly to firm pressure; they show no significant change in skin color as they ripen.

Store either type of avocado at room temperature, uncut; do not refrigerate. A rock-hard Hass avocado can take up to a week to ripen, less if put in a brown paper bag with an apple.

It is still fun to stick three toothpicks into a pit and suspend it in a glass of water, where it will gradually make a plant. I did it as a child and then for my children and now for my grandchildren. I have never been able to make it take the next step and grow into a tree.

WASHING/WAYS OF CUTTING

Twist off the stem, if any. Slice the avocado in half lengthwise. Twist the halves in opposite directions to free at least one. Remove the pit—the easiest way is often to stick the point of a sharp knife into the pit and sort of flip it out. To take off the peel, score the skin about every inch lengthwise. Bend a segment of skin back and pull it down. Avocado flesh will darken after lengthy exposure to air. A few drops of lemon or lime juice is the best way to maintain its color. The acid in combination with garlic really does impede browning. (See Guacamole, page 8.) I have not found that sticking the pit into the mushed flesh does any good: old wives' tale.

Always use a stainless steel knife to cut avocados. They have a discoloring relationship with other metals. They may be cut in chunks or cubes, or scooped out with a melon baller or a spoon.

Preparation
MICROWAVING

I really don't like cooked avocados. I buy them ripe, preferably the Hass variety, and use them raw in salads and dips. If fate has brought a hard avocado and it absolutely must be used, after cutting it in half lengthwise and removing the pit, wrap the halves and cook in the microwave oven for 1 minute. Immediately remove from the oven; run under cold water and unwrap. The avocado will be softer, and edible—but not my choice.

Yields and Equivalents
HASS

1 medium avocado = 8 ounces = $^3/_4$ cup purée

1 large avocado = 10 ounces = twelve $^1/_2$-inch-wide lengthwise slices

1 large avocado, peeled, seeded and cut into $^1/_2$-inch dice = 1 $^1/_2$ cups

Half an 8- to 10-ounce avocado will hold 2 tablespoons dressing or a generous $^1/_4$ cup stuffing

FLORIDA (DUERTE)

1 avocado = 15 to 18 ounces = 1 $^1/_4$ cups purée

COCKTAIL AVOCADOS

Can be as small as 1 ounce each, but generally approximately 2 ounces each; halves will hold 1 to 2 teaspoons stuffing

BALM see Herbs and Their Flowers

BAMBOO MUSTARD see Mustard Greens and Leaf Mustard

Bamboo Shoots

Phyllostachys heterocycla

Bamboo can grow very large and there are glorious bamboo gardens in Japan, such as those in Kyoto and Nara, which are actually forests. This is odd, as bamboo is actually a grass. There are an incredible number of different bamboos and only a few are edible.

Bamboo shoots are now being grown as a crop in California. They can be bought "fresh." What fresh means in the context of bamboo is extremely hard to define. While developing the recipes for this book and trying to learn about bamboo shoots, we found them in vacuum-packed plastic labeled as fresh. How does this differ from the bamboo shoots that are still in the leaves (which are rare even in Chinatown)? Well, it's a matter of wording. "Fresh" does not equal "raw." The bamboo still in its leaves is raw bamboo. Chinese people always boil bamboo shoots briefly to get rid of any bitterness before using them. Some sources also say that the bitterness is the result of a mild toxin, of which brief cooking rids it. All bamboo shoots must be peeled if they are actually raw and then briefly boiled. The stuff in vacuum-packed bags and loose in bins covered with water that is also known as fresh has been peeled and preboiled and is ready to use and eat.

Methods

BUYING AND STORING

Fresh bamboo shoots are extremely difficult to find, even in Chinatowns. If you come across them, look for firm, pale shoots. As for canned, look for white rather than yellow shoots that are crisp and sweet. Try several brands if necessary until you hit on one you like.

WASHING/WAYS OF CUTTING

For raw bamboo still in the leaves, remove the leaves and trim the bottoms and any tough parts. Peel. Cut into pieces according to recipe.

Preparation

BOILING

Drop pieces of trimmed and cut bamboo shoots into boiling water and cook until softened but still crunchy. Thin slices will take a minute or less; large chunks will take longer. Drain and rinse under cold running water. Canned, vacuum-packed and loose fresh bamboo shoots all come blanched and are ready for use.

Yields and Equivalents

Bamboo shoots retain their size and shape when cooked.

$1/4$ pound blanched fresh or canned bamboo shoots, cut into $1/4$-inch slices = 1 cup

$3 1/2$ ounces blanched fresh or canned bamboo shoots, cut into $1/8$-inch slices = $1/2$ cup

BANANA PEPPERS see Peppers
BANANA SQUASH see Squash, Winter
BASIL see Herbs and Their Flowers
BATATAS see Boniatos under Sweet Potatoes and Yams
BATAVIA LETTUCE see Iceberg under Lettuces
BAY LEAVES see Herbs and Their Flowers

Beans

The information in this bean section is organized in the same way as the information in the three bean chapters in the recipe section of the book: one on New World beans, starting on page 537; one on fava beans, starting on page 542; and the third on Asian beans, starting on page 543.

After much research and suffering, I have finally decided that there is no absolute distinction between beans and peas except that historically we seem to put them in one category or another. All are shells or pods containing a number of beans or peas. Some are round and cook rather rapidly; we are liable to call these peas, and, as a group, they will be found starting on page 296 in the recipe section of the book and under Peas in this section. They are sweet green peas (English peas), snow peas, pea shoots (tendrils), split peas, cowpeas, long beans and wing beans. Here, under Beans, are the New World varieties in the *Phaseolus* genus, some Asiatic beans (soy and adzuki) and one European bean, the fava.

BEANS OF THE NEW WORLD

Among the many vegetable confusions, none may be more frustrating for the writer to explain than those surrounding beans. It is easily said that all of them, from no matter what part of the world, are legumes (a collective name that includes all seeds of the Leguminosae or Fabaceae families)—but then the fun begins. The only kinds that concern me under the New World heading are the different kinds of *Phaseolus*. As beans were accepted, they were hybridized and spread far beyond their original boundaries. Different kinds of beans were also prized for their sprouts. (See Sprouts.)

Eaten in the Shell
Phaseolus vulgaris

Varieties

These are the American-sourced beans (for more information, see page 10), the kinds most usually eaten young—pod, bean and all. Many used to be called string beans because they had a string running their length that had to be removed. Newer varieties are stringless and are preferred for eating whole.

GREEN BEANS Fairly large, growing either on vines or bushes.

HARICOTS VERTS French green beans, thinner, rounder and shorter than regular green beans.

WAX BEANS Like green beans but yellow, and sometimes flattish rather than round. I find them somewhat flabby in taste and needing a fair amount of seasoning.

ROMANO BEANS Also known as Italian green beans, green but flatter and wider than green beans. They can be exchanged for green beans in recipes, with slightly longer cooking.

Methods
BUYING (OR PICKING) AND STORING

When buying beans, make sure that they feel firm. For cooking whole—in the pod—it is important that the seeds (beans on the inside) aren't bulging, indicating that the beans are overripe. The beans should be smooth without any soft or discolored spots. Try to pick beans all of one size for even cooking. If picking, search all around the places where beans are spotted, raising leaves and even vines as necessary: Beans love to hide. Green beans have great camouflage, as they look very like the vines that they grow on. If the beans are a good size, pick them immediately. They will keep raw for a day or so in the refrigerator, or they can be boiled and chilled or frozen. Don't wait; they overgrow very quickly.

Beans should be kept tightly wrapped and refrigerated and used as soon as possible after buying or picking. Like all high-carbohydrate vegetables, they will become starchier and less sweet with time. Light will change their color. If longer storage is needed, they should be briefly boiled in heavily salted water, refreshed under cold water and then frozen in amounts that are likely to be used at any one time.

WASHING/WAYS OF CUTTING

I don't wash my own beans, as they are grown organically. Store-bought beans should be washed in cold running water before snapping the ends. Trim the beans by snapping off both ends (trimmed beans are commonly referred to as having been "tipped and tailed"). It has become fashionable of late to remove only the stem end: While this is pretty, I don't think it makes for very good eating.

Before the thin French haricots verts were readily available, beans were often "Frenched." This means they were slivered lengthwise. The odd little gizmo at the end of some potato peelers was meant for forcing the beans through to sliver them. I never found it worked very well. Older beans are often cut in 2-inch lengths. They may also be roll-cut (see page 532) for stir-frying.

Preparation

BOILING

The following instructions are given only as a guideline. Larger quantities can also obviously be cooked, but it is better not to try more than a pound at a time. It takes too long for the water to return to the boil when larger amounts are added. Always use water that is at a full boil, and do not cover the pot, or the beans will discolor. Timing starts from the point at which the water returns to the boil. I detest the term "al dente," which usually means undercooked. Such beans will have a grassy taste. The best test is to actually taste a bean (don't get burned).

For 8 ounces of any of the following beans, bring 2 quarts water to a boil in a 3-quart saucepan. Add 2 tablespoons salt, then the beans.

WHOLE GREEN BEANS AND WAX BEANS, TIPPED AND TAILED Cook 6 to 8 minutes after water returns to a boil. For very small and thin beans (smaller than haricots verts), simmer 2 to 3 minutes.

HARICOTS VERTS (FRENCH GREEN BEANS), TIPPED AND TAILED Cook 4 to 5 minutes after water returns to a boil.

ROMANOS (ITALIAN GREEN BEANS), TIPPED AND TAILED Cook 7 to 8 minutes after water returns to a boil.

STEAMING

GREEN BEANS, WAX BEANS AND ROMANOS (ITALIAN GREEN BEANS), TIPPED AND TAILED Place trimmed beans, preferably in a single layer, in a covered steamer basket. Cook 7 to 9 minutes. If beans are deeper than a single layer, increase cooking time to 12 minutes and rearrange halfway through cooking.

HARICOTS VERTS (FRENCH GREEN BEANS), TIPPED AND TAILED Place trimmed beans, preferably in a single layer, in a covered steamer basket. Cook 8 to 10 minutes. If deeper than a single layer, increase cooking time to 14 minutes and rearrange halfway during cooking.

MICROWAVING

Green, wax, Romano, French (haricot vert) and other fresh pole and bush beans are quick to cook, are not watery and have a bright color when cooked in the microwave oven. Tip and tail. If the beans are very large, or if the recipe calls for it, either cut across into lengths or halve lengthwise.

GREEN BEANS AND WAX BEANS, TIPPED AND TAILED Cooking times are based on beans in 4-ounce amounts, each quantity in a container just large enough to hold it. Cover tightly. If using one container, place it in the center of the oven. More containers should be placed in a circle so that they do not touch.

Place trimmed beans in 4-ounce amounts, sprinkle with water and cover tightly.

4 ounces beans: 3 minutes 30 seconds to
    4 minutes
8 ounces beans: 4 minutes to 4 minutes
    30 seconds
1 pound beans: 6 to 8 minutes

HARICOTS VERTS (FRENCH GREEN BEANS), TIPPED AND TAILED Arrange trimmed beans in a single layer; add water. Cover container tightly with microwave plastic wrap; or use a container with a tight-fitting lid and check to see if an extra minute is needed.

4 ounces beans with 1 cup water
    (1-quart measure): 6 minutes
1 pound beans with 3 cups water
    (14 x 11 x 2-inch dish): 15 minutes

SAUTÉING

GREEN, WAX AND ROMANO (ITALIAN GREEN BEANS) For 8 ounces beans, tipped, tailed and cut into 2-inch lengths: Heat 1 tablespoon olive oil in a 10-inch skillet over medium heat. Add beans. Cook, tossing, until lightly browned and tender but firm, about 6 minutes. Add 1/4 cup water, stock or broth and season with salt and, if desired, a pinch of hot red pepper flakes. Cook until liquid is evaporated and beans start to sizzle in the fat. Add an additional tablespoon of olive oil or an equal amount of butter, if desired. (Serves 2 as a side dish)

Yields and Equivalents

GREEN BEANS AND WAX BEANS

4 ounces beans, tipped and tailed = 1 1/4 cups raw =
1 cup cooked

3 pounds beans, tipped and tailed = 14 cups raw

1 pound beans, tipped, tailed and cut into
1 1/2-inch lengths = 3 1/2 cups

HARICOTS VERTS (FRENCH GREEN BEANS)

4 ounces beans, tipped and tailed = 1 cup raw =
3/4 cup cooked

ROMANO (ITALIAN GREEN BEANS)

12 ounces beans, tipped, tailed and cut into 2-inch
lengths = 4 cups

Eaten Shelled (Dried and Fresh)

Phaseolus vulgaris, Phaseolus coccineus, Phaseolus lunatas

Varieties

There are literally thousands of bean cultivars. Each country seems to have created its own varieties. I am mentioning only the most commonly available of the *Phaseolus* here. Spanish speakers call beans "frijoles" or "habichuelas." There doesn't seem to be a significant order to what word is used when or where. The French call all beans "haricots" and usually add "verts" to mean the beans in the shell and "sec" for dried shelled beans. Indians and other Asians, many of whom are vegetarians, have so many different beans that I cannot begin to know or list them all (see page 11). Many beans are available cooked and canned; some brands are better than others. They are a real convenience that is generally quite adequate, but not as good as home-cooked. Also, canned beans should be well rinsed in a sieve and salt in dishes using canned beans used with caution.

Whether they are dried or fresh, the water for cooking these beans should not be salted: It toughens their skin. Salt after draining or after all cooking is completed.

Beans take kindly to herbs from sage to marjoram to epazote, a Mexican herb almost always added there to bean dishes. It can be scavenged; I have found it growing as a weed in Central Park in New York.

PHASEOLUS VULGARIS

BLACK BEANS Heavily used in Central America and the Caribbean. They are sometimes called turtle beans.

CANNELLINI BEANS Creamy white beans preferred in Italy, somewhat larger than most others and very good especially when freshly cooked, although canned can be used if drained and well rinsed. Be aware that the skins of these beans tend to come loose as they cook and drift around the top of the water; just skim them off. These are the beans that are found along with tuna in salads and as part of antipasti and in soup. Great beans.

CRANBERRY BEANS The most widely available of shelled beans sold fresh. Sadly, the beautiful dappled color disappears with cooking.

KIDNEY BEANS The common, dark red beans used, for instance, in chili and to make refried beans.

NAVY AND SMALL WHITE BEANS These make wonderful soup. In southwestern France, they are used for cassoulet. The most common in North America are Great Northern.

PINTO BEANS Pink to light red, lighter than kidney beans, but not quite as pink as rosadas. These are best grown at a high altitude and eaten fresh.

PINK BEANS OR ROSADAS These are a lovely pale color, and I tend to use them with fish or lightly colored greens as an elegant contrast.

FLAGEOLETS The seeds of adult haricots verts, pale green and generally served in France with roasted lamb. They are available fresh and dried. Delicate in taste, they do well with butter or the juices of the meat, usually leg of lamb. There are also white flageolets, more like a small navy bean and usually dried.

PHASEOLUS COCCINEUS

SCARLET RUNNER BEANS At their beautiful best winding their way up a garden fence; but the English like to eat them.

PHASEOLUS LUNATUS

LIMA BEANS These used to confuse me, since their shape looks so much like that of favas I thought they were a relative. They are not, but they do make a good substitute for young favas. This is one of the few beans that I often use frozen—better than canned. Look for Fordhooks, named after the farm at which they were developed.

Large beans of this variety, like the Greek gigantes, called "coronas" in Italy and "habas grandes" in Mexico, are usually translated here as giant or extra large limas, the best of which are Peruvian. Unlike favas, none of the limas need peeling.

CORONAS Large cousins of the lima bean. I have always cooked them from dried.

GIGANTES Very large flattish beans much loved in Greece, and by me. The same family as lima beans but brown in color, they are usually available dried. They have a rich meaty flavor. Aglaia Kremezi says the best come from Kastoria in Greek Macedonia.

Methods
BUYING AND STORING

Keep dried beans in a cool, dark, dry place in tightly sealed containers, preferably opaque. While it may seem that they last forever, it is best to use dried beans as soon as possible after buying them. Older dried beans will take longer to cook.

Store fresh shelled beans in the refrigerator and use as soon as possible after buying, as they tend to mold or dry out. If need be, they can be half cooked, covered with water and frozen in amounts that are likely to get used. I often do this in the fall, the only time I can get them.

WASHING/WAYS OF CUTTING

FRESH CRANBERRY BEANS AND LIMA BEANS Break open pods along their seams to remove the beans inside. Cranberry beans can be shelled a day in advance; cover them with water and store in the refrigerator to prevent drying out. Lima beans and soybeans (see page 543) can be shelled and frozen.

OTHER BEANS Except for those described here, most shelled beans are sold dried. It used to be that all recipes warned us to pick over dried beans to remove any pebbles or other detritus. Today, I find that is generally not necessary. Just rinse them under cold running water. Dried beans are commonly soaked to quicken the cooking time; see Soaking Dried Beans.

Preparation
SOAKING DRIED BEANS

Almost all dried beans are soaked before cooking. Add liquid as necessary to keep the beans covered. Some dried beans and peas, such as cowpeas (see page 622) and adzuki (see page 544), cook in under an hour with no soaking. Some cooks discard the soaking liquid and replace it with fresh for greater digestibility, but Cubans tend to use the dusky liquid from black beans to start their soups.

There are three good ways to soak beans.

Cold soak method: Place beans in a pot, add water to cover by 2 inches and refrigerate overnight. When it is time to cook, if desired, drain beans and cover with fresh water.

Hot soak method: Place beans in a pot, add water to cover by 2 inches and bring to a boil. Remove from heat and let sit for 1 hour. When it is time to cook, if desired, drain and cover with fresh water. Alternatively, simply boil for 15 minutes, then drain and cook.

Microwave method: For 2 cups dried beans: Place in a 5-quart casserole with a tightly fitting lid. Add 2 cups water, cover and cook at 100% for 15 minutes. Remove and let stand, covered, for 5 minutes. Uncover and add 2 cups very hot tap water. Re-cover and let stand for 1 hour. Drain. Cover with fresh water to cook.

BOILING

DRIED BEANS

BAKED BEANS Just about any type of soaked dried bean can be prepared following the method for Basic Boston Baked Beans (page 24). Season the beans as you like and cover them for the first 6 hours or so of cooking; make sure the beans are covered with liquid throughout the cooking.

STOVETOP BEANS Cover soaked and drained beans with an inch or two of water or broth. Season the liquid, if desired, with herbs, onions and/or garlic (no salt) and bring to a boil. Adjust the heat to simmering and cook the beans until tender, 1 to 3 hours, depending on the type of bean. Add liquid as necessary to keep the beans covered during cooking. Some beans, such as coronas, can take up to a full 3 hours or more and need several additions of water to keep them submerged. Size is usually not an indicator of how long beans will take to cook. Even a bean as small as a navy bean will take a long time. If serving the beans with their cooking liquid, let the liquid cook down to the level of the beans during the last half hour or so. When the beans are tender, add salt, remove from the heat and let stand 10 to 15 minutes.

SLOW-COOKER BEANS Thoroughly drain soaked beans before cooking. Season the beans as desired, pour in enough cooking liquid to cover by 1 inch and cook at the low heat setting 5 to 10 hours, depending on the bean. (Relatively quick-cooking beans such as black beans will take about 5 hours; slower-cooking beans such as gigantes may take a full 10 hours.)

FRESH BEANS

CRANBERRY BEANS Add shelled beans to boiling water (no salt). Simmer 20 minutes, or until tender.

FLAGEOLETS Add shelled beans to boiling water (no salt). Simmer 10 to 15 minutes, until tender.

LIMA BEANS Add shelled beans to boiling water (no salt), simmer about 5 minutes, then taste; cooking time will vary with size of beans.

STEAMING (fresh beans only)

CRANBERRY BEANS Place shelled beans in a covered steamer basket. Cook 20 to 25 minutes.

LIMA BEANS Place shelled beans in a covered steamer basket. Cook 10 to 12 minutes.

Yields and Equivalents

FRESH OR FROZEN BEANS

CRANBERRY BEANS

12 ounces cranberry beans in the shell =
1 cup shelled raw = 1 1/4 cups cooked
2 1/2 pounds beans in the shell = 1 1/4 pounds
shelled = 4 cups raw = 5 cups cooked

LIMA BEANS

One 10-ounce package frozen baby lima beans,
defrosted = 1 1/2 to 2 cups

DRIED BEANS

SMALL DRIED BEANS (such as flageolets, white flageolets, black beans)

1 cup dried beans = 7 ounces = 2 1/2 cups soaked =
scant 3 cups cooked

LARGE DRIED BEANS (such as black beans, cannellini, red and black kidney beans, pink beans, pinto beans)

1 cup dried beans = 6 to 6 1/2 ounces =
2 cups soaked beans = 2 1/2 cups cooked

GIANT LIMAS, CORONAS AND GIGANTES

1 cup dried beans = 5 1/2 ounces = 2 cups soaked =
2 1/2 cups cooked

CANNED BEANS

Canned beans are available, generally speaking, in 15 (or 15.5)-ounce cans, 19-ounce cans and 28-ounce cans.

One 15-ounce can smaller compact beans, such as
black beans = 1 1/2 cups drained and rinsed beans
One 15-ounce can larger or irregularly shaped
beans, such as red kidney beans = 2 cups drained
and rinsed beans
1 cup drained canned beans = 6 to 8 ounces,
depending on type of bean

THE BEAN OF THE OLD WORLD

Vicia faba or Faba vulgaris

Fava and broad beans were, for millennia, the only beans available in Europe. They confused life by giving their name to the entire species of beans, but this is a confusion that must be overridden. There were, of course, other legumes, such as chickpeas and lentils. All of them were used to make polenta in Roman times, before American corn arrived.

Varieties

BROAD BEANS Favas in their yellow shells, eaten shell and all. I have found them to be eaten regularly only in England. I don't like them and find them both flabby and fibrous even when cut into small pieces and boiled. I prefer to let them grow a little longer and eat the shelled beans, which are a delight.

FRESH FAVAS Spring vegetables bought in the shell. They need both to be shelled and to have the actual skin of the beans removed (see Washing/Ways of Cutting).

DRIED FAVAS All over Europe and also, by countermigration, in Central America, dried favas are a staple. For many years I wouldn't use them, as they came in their skins and were a pain to deal with. Today peeled dried favas are available.

MEXICAN FAVAS These are the most common peeled and dried favas. They come both whole, with two lobes, or split, with their lobes separated. Split cook more quickly and are good for soup, but whole beans are more satisfactory for other uses.

Methods
BUYING AND STORING
Fresh favas or broad beans should be smooth and plump in their pods. Store them in plastic bags in the refrigerator and use as soon as possible. They are starch-rich and will lose their sweetness very quickly.

Dried favas should be already shelled and peeled when bought and a light brown in color. They should not look wizened. Store as other dried beans.

WASHING/WAYS OF CUTTING
FRESH FAVAS Break open the pods to remove the beans inside. Shelled fava beans have a light-colored outer skin that, except for the very smallest beans, must also be removed. The easiest way is to quickly blanch the beans and rinse under cold running water. The beans will then easily slip from their skins.

Preparation
SOAKING
The method for soaking favas with peels is similar to that of regular shelled beans; see page 540. In "Rich" Peasant Stew with Favas (page 227), I outline an alternative method using hot water. It is ideal for favas that are being added to long-cooking soups and stews, but can be used to peel dried favas for any recipe.

Some recipes (especially Middle Eastern ones) omit the step of peeling whole dried favas. If using them, I prefer to peel, as the skin can be tough. Mexican fava beans (fabas) do not have to be peeled; buy them and save yourself the trouble. Likewise, split and dried favas need not be soaked and cook quickly.

BOILING
FRESH FAVAS For 1 pound shelled fava beans ($2^3/_4$ pounds in the shell): Drop in boiling water for 1 minute; drain and rinse under cold water. Peel outer skin. Simmer peeled beans for 5 minutes.
DRIED FAVAS Cook at a low boil in unsalted water for 30 minutes (shelled and split favas) to 1 hour (whole peeled favas).

Yields and Equivalents
FRESH FAVA BEANS
$2^3/_4$ pounds beans in the shell = 1 pound shelled = 3 cups raw = 9 ounces, or $1^1/_2$ cups, blanched and peeled

1 pound 14 ounces beans in the shell =
1 cup shelled

DRIED FAVA BEANS
1 cup dried peeled beans = 5 ounces =
2 cups cooked
1 cup dried split beans = $5^1/2$ ounces =
$1^3/4$ cup cooked

BEANS FROM ASIA

While most beans, wherever they turn up in the world, were originally American, there are a few kinds that are of African or Asian origin. Perhaps the most important bean for commercial purposes, not only directly as a food, is the soybean.

Black-eyed peas, cowpeas, long beans and wing beans are actually peas. That's where information on them will be found, both in the Cook's Guide and the recipe section of this book.

Eaten in the Shell

A little misleading, as soybeans can be cooked in the shell, but the shell is not eaten. More on fresh and dried soybeans follows.

Eaten Shelled
Vigna angularis/Glycine max

Varieties

ADZUKI, AZUKI OR ADANKA (*Vigna angularis*) Can be eaten young in the pod but are most often shelled and dried or powdered for use in desserts or sold as a sweetened paste. They are smallish and red and primarily used in Japan and China.

SOYBEANS, FRESH (EDAMAME), DRIED OR FREEZE-DRIED (*Glycine max*) Perhaps the world's largest legume crop, and not all of it for food—however, there are many forms in which it shows up as a food. If eating fresh soybeans, cook them first. Raw, they inhibit the action of trypsin, an enzyme vital to the digestion of protein. On their own and fresh, soybeans are boiled in salted water in the pod for a snack or starter. Just pop the beans out of the pod and eat. Edamame can be bought precooked; they are not as good, but fresh can be hard to find. Dried soybeans are cooked and eaten or turned into a variety of products, such as tofu, oil, milk, paste, etc. Soybeans are also sold freeze-dried, and these make a good crunch with drinks. Information on dried soybean and soybean products follow.

SOYBEAN PRODUCTS

William Shurtleff and Akiko Aoyagi are the great experts on all forms of culinary soy and soy products. See the Bibliography for their books.

TOFU Custardlike blocks or pillows of soybean curd kept stored in water. I have had, in a very good restaurant, freshly made tofu and it was as much better than that available in stores as fresh mozzarella is better than the usual kind. This goes to say that whatever kind of tofu is being used, fresher is better. There is a very soft tofu that usually comes in 3-inch blocks and is called silk. Firm tofu comes in blocks of the same size but is easier to slice and use for stir-fries. The firmest tofu comes in "pillows" that look like giant ravioli.

SOY SAUCE There are almost as many types of soy sauce as there are countries in Asia and Malaysia. It is a good idea to try to discover what kind the author of a recipe has in mind. While all good-quality soy sauces are made from fermented soybeans, most today have wheat added to them. There are wheat-free soy sauces available. My favorite is wheat-free tamari soy. I don't use Chinese black soy a great deal—it is more viscous and often sweetened, but it is worth a try in Chinese recipes. Remember that there are several different kinds of Chinese soy sauce.

SOY MILK Commonly used as a substitute for animal milk by those unable to digest animal milk. It is also used by vegans.

NATTO A gooey brown mass of fermented soybeans that is considered a great delicacy in Japan. I have found only two Americans who enjoy it.

MISO A soluble paste that comes in several colors: white, yellow, red and brown—the most common. The darker the color the deeper the flavor. It is usually sold in plastic bags and used to make soup or sauces.

FREEZE-DRIED AND SALTED SHELLED SOYBEANS These are eaten as a snack. On their own, they are packed in 9-ounce packages (about 2 cups). They also come in mixed Japanese snacks. In a sealed package, they will keep indefinitely, as they will in the refrigerator once opened.

Methods

For information on how to store, wash, soak and cook dried adzuki and soybeans, refer to the material on page 540. Information on fresh soybeans (edamame) follows here.

BUYING AND STORING

Edamame are best bought in the shell. They should be plump and unwrinkled. Store in plastic bags in the refrigerator, but use as soon as possible. Don't bother shelling them before cooking; it is too much work. Shell them once cooked. Shelled beans sold in plastic should just be stuck in the refrigerator unless they are frozen— then they go in the freezer. They are usually cooked and can be added to stir-fries for a minute or two at the end of the cooking.

Preparation
BOILING

FRESH SOYBEANS IN THE SHELL Edamame are best boiled in the shell in salted water, then eaten right from the shell or added to cooked dishes or salads. Drop whole pods into boiling salted water. Age of beans and freshness will determine cooking time: Test fresh small beans at $2^1/2$ minutes; older, larger beans at 4 minutes.

Yields and Equivalents
ADZUKI BEANS

> 1 cup dried adzuki = $6^3/4$ ounces
> 1 cup dried adzuki = $1^2/3$ cups soaked =
> $2^2/3$ cups cooked
> One 15-ounce can adzuki, drained = scant 2 cups

SOYBEANS

> 1 pound fresh soybeans, in the pod = $4^1/2$ cups =
>   1 cup shelled raw = $^2/3$ cup cooked
> 1 cup dried soybeans = 6 ounces =
> $2^1/4$ cups cooked

BEE BALM see Herbs and Their Flowers
BEEFSTEAK PLANT see Perilla under Asian Greens

Beets
Beta vulgaris

Beets are one of the most attractive and versatile of the root vegetables. Very young ones, the kind that are pulled from the row as thinnings, can be used whole. Slightly larger ones can be peeled and grated to add raw to salad. The rest must be cooked, as they are quite tannic. Beets are, botanically speaking, the same plant as chard (see page 566).

Varieties

RED The most common variety available, deep crimson, ranging in size from baby (1 inch in diameter) to very large.

GOLDEN Deep golden color, found in the same size range as red beets, with which they are fairly interchangeable though somewhat sweeter.

CHIOGGIA A less commonly found beet, originally from Italy, featuring striking red-and-white-striped flesh, much like the radicchio of the same name.

Methods

BUYING AND STORING

Look for beets that are a deep red, very firm and free of blemishes. There may be a thin light-colored soil layer around the beets; that is fine. Leaves, if attached, should be vigorous and bushy, a sign that the beets were recently pulled from the ground. Store the leaves and roots separately in plastic bags in the refrigerator. Like most greens, the leaves will last only a few days to a week. The roots have much better storage ability and will keep for several weeks. I have actually kept them for two months and used them at Thanksgiving. They were delicious. Don't wash and clean them until ready to use.

WASHING/WAYS OF CUTTING

Beets are easiest to wash after trimming. Scrub the skin well if leaving it on for cooking.

Cut off leaves about 1/4 inch above the beet. Save them for use in Beet Greens with White Beans, Bacon and Walnuts (page 173) or any mixed greens dish. They go well with collards or their relatives the chards. Trim the bottom root to 1/2 inch.

To peel raw beets, use a vegetable peeler. To peel cooked beets, allow them to cool slightly, then rub off the skins with a rough green scouring pad or the back of a knife. Handling peeled beets will temporarily stain hands. Wear rubber gloves or use paper towels if this is a concern.

Preparation

Very small beets, the ones that I thin from a row in the very early spring, can be sautéed, leaves and all, in any desired fat—bacon grease is good—and sprinkled with a little vinegar. I like malt. Salt to taste. Like red cabbage, red beets required a little vinegar or another acid during or after cooking to retain their brightness.

BOILING

Whole: Place trimmed beets in a saucepan. Cover by 2 inches with water and bring to a boil. Lower heat and simmer 30 to 45 minutes, or until a knife slips easily into flesh. Add water as necessary to keep beets covered.

Remove from the liquid and cool for about 10 minutes. Rub off skins.

STEAMING

BEETS *Whole:* Place trimmed beets in a covered steamer basket. Cook 35 to 45 minutes, or until a knife easily slips into flesh. When just cool enough to touch, rub off skins.
BEET GREENS Trim stems. Place whole leaves in a covered steamer basket. Cook 7 to 8 minutes, until tender and bright green.

ROASTING

Whole: Use smallest pan that will hold beets comfortably. Rub trimmed beets and pan lightly with vegetable oil (amount of oil will vary depending on quantity of beets). Bake in center of a 450°F oven for 40 to 50 minutes, or until a knife slips easily into flesh. When just cool enough to touch, rub off skins.

BAKING (IN FOIL)

The English and some French buy preroasted beets from the greengrocer and keep them on hand. That may be why so many English green salads have sliced beets mixed in—that and the sweetness.

Whole: Wrap each trimmed beet in foil and place in a baking pan. Bake in center of a 450°F oven for 40 to 50 minutes, or until a knife slips easily into flesh. When cool enough to touch, rub off skins.

Wedges: Trim beets. Slice lengthwise into 1-inch wedges (small beets can be sliced into quarters; large beets can be sliced into eighths). Wrap in foil and place in a baking pan. Bake in center rack of a 500°F oven: 20 minutes for small beets, 30 minutes for large ones, or until a knife easily slips into skin. When cool enough to touch, rub off skins.

MICROWAVING

When baked, beets retain a maximum of color and flavor. Microwave cooking achieves the same effect rapidly and with almost no mess.

Trim the leaves to within 1 inch of the beets. Scrub the beets well. Arrange beets in a circle on a dish or carousel. Cook as on page 546. If using immediately, cool slightly, trim the tops and slip off their skins. (You can then clean your hands with some lemon if you don't wish to be mistaken for Lady Macbeth.)

Save any juices from the dish for adding to soups and to beet purée. Precooked beets will last, well wrapped and refrigerated, for more than a week and are worth keeping on hand.

BEETS *Small whole* (2 ounces each): Put in a dish at least $1/2$ inch deep and large enough to hold them in a single layer; cover tightly.

8 ounces: 8 minutes

1 pound: 12 minutes

$1 1/2$ pounds: 16 minutes

Large whole: Place in a container just large enough to hold them; cover tightly. Turn once and re-cover.

1 beet (10 ounces): 20 minutes

6 beets ($2 1/2$ pounds): 25 to 30 minutes

BEET GREENS Cook with 1 cup liquid and, if desired, 4 ounces fatback in a 14 x 11 x 2-inch dish. Cover tightly; uncover for last 5 minutes of cooking.

2 pounds: 30 minutes

Yields and Equivalents

1 small beet = 2 ounces

1 medium beet = 3 to 5 ounces

1 large beet = 8 to 10 ounces

1 medium beet (5 ounces), trimmed, peeled, cut into $1/4$-inch dice and cooked = generous $1/2$ cup

1 medium-large beet (6 ounces), trimmed, peeled and grated = 1 cup

1 medium-large beet (6 ounces), trimmed, peeled, cut into $1/4$-inch slices and cooked = $2/3$ cup

1 pound beets, trimmed, peeled, cooked and puréed = 1 cup

Canned beets can be substituted for fresh beets in roughly equal measure. Use the weight of canned beets *after* the liquid has been drained and raw beets *after* the leaves and roots have been trimmed.

One $8 1/4$-ounce can sliced beets = 5 ounces drained = $3/4$ cup

One $14 1/2$-ounce can sliced beets = $8 3/4$ ounces drained = 1 cup

One 1-pound can sliced beets = 10 ounces drained = $1 1/2$ cups

BELGIAN ENDIVE see Endive under Chicories

BELL PEPPERS see Peppers

BERMUDA ONIONS see Onions

BETA-CARROTS see Maroon Carrots under Carrots

BIBB LETTUCE see Lettuces

BIRD PEPPERS see Peppers

BLACK BEANS see Beans of the New World under Beans

BLACK CHANTERELLES see Mushrooms, Fresh

BLACK-EYED PEAS see Peas

BLACK RADISHES see Radishes

BLACK-SEEDED SIMPSON LETTUCE see Iceberg under Lettuces

BLACK TRUMPETS see Mushrooms, Fresh

BOK CHOY see Cabbages, Asian

BOLETUS see Cèpes under Mushrooms, Fresh

BONIATOS see Sweet Potatoes and Yams

BORAGE see Herbs and Their Flowers

BOSTON LETTUCE see Lettuces

BRAZILIAN ARROWROOT see Yuca under Tropical Tubers

BRAZIL ÑAME see Yams under Sweet Potatoes and Yams

BROAD BEANS see The Bean of the Old World under Beans

Broccoli and Cauliflower

Brassica oleracea

These are basically the same vegetable. They come in different colors and shapes, and names have been arbitrarily assigned to them, with most of the green ones being called broccoli. Broccoli is a relative arriviste and was unfamiliar as late as the 1920s. This may be why George Bush said he loathed it; it was unfamiliar. It also helps to explain the famous *New Yorker* cartoon where a mother talking to a seated little girl says that what the child is eating is broccoli and the kid responds, "I say it's spinach, and I say to hell with it."

There was an old New York restaurant named Divan Parisienne, owned by a race-car driver, which served steamed or cooked broccoli with chicken breast and hollandaise on top, called chicken divan. One can see that in those days broccoli was considered a fancy novelty.

Cauliflower has been a European favorite for centuries particularly in German-speaking countries. My Viennese husband's mother made cauliflower soup (see page 257) and he likes it with little bits of whole florets swimming around. She prepared whole heads of cauliflower with butter-browned bread crumbs (page 259).

Broccoli and cauliflower tend to like fat and can be simply boiled or steamed and served hot or cold with a wide variety of sauces. Vinaigrettes, Hollandaise Sauce (page 454), Olive Oil and Garlic Sauce (page 468) and Pseudo-Indian Dressing (page 451) are just a few that are good.

Varieties

BROCCOLI Usually green, although there are some purple varieties, which are actually a supersaturated green that turns bright green with cooking. The most common type of broccoli forms heads, with more stem than cauliflower. The heads are composed of round prenascent flowers. If yellow flowers have formed, they are less desirable. After the heads are cut, a small group of individual florets will usually grow. They are very good.

The stems and the florets can be cooked and eaten separately. The stems will need peeling. Cut into $1/4$-inch-thick rounds, they are good in a stir-fry.

SPROUTING BROCCOLI (*Brassica oleracea,* Italica group, aka Italian asparagus) A group that is ready in the spring, having wintered over. The stalks are well separated with individual heads that may be green, white or purple. As their name indicates, they are a great favorite in Italy.

BROCCOLI SPROUTS New information never ceases to arrive—and in recent years, broccoli seeds have been sprouted and the sprouts deemed to be extremely healthful and nutritious.

WHITE CAULIFLOWER The most familiar form of cauliflower, a creamy white head made up of rounded knobs that are the tops of florets. The head can be separated into florets, discarding the hard core, or cooked whole. Individual florets are good for serving raw with dips.

PURPLE CAULIFLOWER As with many other vegetables, the purple is really a hyper-saturated green. When the vegetable is cooked, it will turn bright green.

ROMANESCO An unusual-looking cauliflower, shaped like an inverted cone and colored a brilliant chartreuse. Romanesco cooks faster than regular cauliflower. The florets, cut into $3/4$- to 1-inch pieces, should simmer in boiling water for just 4 to 5 minutes. Once cooked, the florets remain green and are crisper than regular cauliflower. This cauliflower does not store well. The florets are somewhat separated and not tightly formed, so mold develops easily.

Methods

There are many good ways to cook broccoli: steaming, stir-frying, boiling, frying and microwaving. Broccoli can be cooked in whole branches or with the stems and florets separated. It is rarely roasted, but if the stems are well peeled and the whole branches sliced lengthwise through the stems and the florets into pieces with a width of no more than 2 to $2^{1/2}$ inches at the floret end, the resulting strips, oil slicked, roast brilliantly in 15 minutes. They turn a toasty brown and are good on their own or as an ingredient in other recipes.

Cauliflower can be cooked in the same ways as broccoli, but is not good roasted.

BUYING AND STORING

Look for heads of broccoli and cauliflower that are firm and tightly packed, with any leaves being crisp and unwilted. Store in plastic in the refrigerator.

WASHING/WAYS OF CUTTING

CAULIFLOWER Store-bought cauliflower is very clean, often wrapped in plastic for protection. A quick rinse is all it needs. To prepare, remove the leaves. Scrape off any brown spots with a paring knife. Stand the cauliflower with the stem end in the air, cut deeply around the core and remove. Cut the florets into pieces, if desired, or cook the head whole.

BROCCOLI Rinse under cold running water. Either peel and trim the ends of the stems or separate the stems from the florets. Break up the florets into smaller sizes as called for in the recipe. Peel the stems with a vegetable peeler or, if the skin is very fibrous, by using a paring knife to pull off strips of skin beginning at the stem bottom. Trim the ends.

Preparation

BOILING

BROCCOLI *Long spears:* For 1 bunch: Bring 2 quarts water and 1 teaspoon salt to a boil. Trim broccoli: Cut off and discard leaves. Cut off and discard woody bottom part of stems. Slice lengthwise into pieces about ³/4 inch in diameter. Try to have all pieces roughly the same size so they will cook in the same time. Drop into boiling water. Let water return to boil and cook for 5 minutes. Remove with a slotted spoon to a colander. Run cold water over broccoli to stop the cooking. Serve cold with mayonnaise or another sauce, or reheat to serve warm with sauce or dressing of choice.

Florets: Cook as for spears but for slightly less time. Test with the tip of a sharp knife.

Sprouting Broccoli: Cook as for spears or as florets, depending on size of the cut.

CAULIFLOWER *1-inch florets:* Boil in salted water until a paring knife easily pierces the center of a floret, 5 to 7 minutes.

Whole head: Cut out core, leaving enough in place to hold florets together. Pour enough water to cover cauliflower halfway into a pot large enough to hold the head very comfortably and wide enough to retrieve the cooked cauliflower. Add a small handful of salt and bring to a boil. Slip cauliflower core side up into water. Return to a boil and cook until tender but not mushy, 14 to 20 minutes, depending on size. Set a colander large enough to hold cauliflower in a large bowl next to stove. Slip two wire skimmers or large slotted spoons under cauliflower and lift from water, draining as much water from cauliflower as possible. Carefully set in colander to drain and cool.

ROASTING

Consider a mild vinegar, such as rice wine or balsamic, as an alternative to water or stock as the liquid.

BROCCOLI *Florets and stems:* For 1 pound: Peel broccoli stems well and cut whole head lengthwise into strips, each being no wider at florets than 2 inches. Use smallest pan that will hold broccoli comfortably. Slick slices and pan with 3 to 4 tablespoons fat. Add ¹/4 cup liquid. Roast on lowest rack of 500°F oven for 15 minutes. If any pieces are thicker than 2 inches, they will take longer.

CAULIFLOWER I do not care for roasted cauliflower

STEAMING

BROCCOLI *Florets and/or stems cut into coins:* Place in a covered steamer basket. Cook 5 to 10 minutes until tender.

CAULIFLOWER *1-inch florets:* Place in a covered steamer basket. Cook 15 to 20 minutes, until tender.

Whole head: Cut out core, leaving enough in place to hold florets together. Place core side down in a covered steamer basket. Steam for 18 to 20 minutes, until tender.

MICROWAVING

BROCCOLI Broccoli for hors d'oeuvre rewards cooking, as it turns a bright green and has a milder, pleasanter flavor than when raw. Cooked in the microwave oven, it doesn't get waterlogged; dripping vegetables are a threat to guests' hands and clothing. Cut the florets fairly small so they go in the mouth in one bite.

Florets: Place florets in cooking dish specified and cover tightly with microwave plastic wrap or a lid. If using a lid, add a tablespoon of water for each 4 ounces of broccoli. (4 ounces raw broccoli yields 1 scant cup cooked)

   4 ounces (1 1/2-quart soufflé dish): 1 minute
      30 seconds
   8 ounces (1 1/2-quart soufflé dish): 3 minutes
   1 pound (2 1/2-quart soufflé dish): 6 minutes
   1 1/2 pounds (2 1/2-quart soufflé dish): stir once,
      8 minutes
   2 pounds (5-quart casserole): stir once,
      13 minutes
   2 1/2 pounds (5-quart casserole): stir once,
      15 minutes
   3 pounds (5-quart casserole): stir once,
      17 minutes

CAULIFLOWER *Large whole head:* Bring a pot of water to a boil and proceed in the traditional fashion; it will be too big to cook evenly in a microwave oven. Small heads, under 1 1/2 pounds with the leaves, and florets, about 2 inches long and 2 inches across at their widest, cook quickly and well in a microwave oven, either to serve alone (drizzle with a little butter or top with a sauce such as Romesco, page 63) or to be added to soups and puréed (see page 257).

   Florets: Cook in a single layer in a dish just large enough to hold them; cover tightly.

   8 ounces: 4 minutes
   1 pound: 7 minutes
   1 1/2 pounds: 9 minutes

   Whole head: Core and trim as for steaming (page 548). Cook in a dish just large enough to hold it; cover tightly.

   1 small head (1 1/2 pounds with leaves, 18 ounces
      cored and trimmed): 7 minutes

ROMANESCO Follow timing for cauliflower florets; do not cook whole heads, as they will fall apart and get too soft.

Yields and Equivalents

BROCCOLI

   1 medium bunch broccoli (3 stalks) = about
      1 1/2 pounds = about 12 ounces stems and
      12 ounces florets
   1 1/2 pounds broccoli, cut into medium florets,
      stems peeled and cut into 1-inch cubes =
      4 1/3 cups florets and 4 cups stems
   5 ounces florets = 2 cups = 1 cup cooked =
      1/2 cup purée
   1 1/2 pounds stems, peeled and cut into coins or
      matchsticks = 1 1/2 cups raw = 1 cup cooked =
      2/3 cup purée

Sprouting broccoli will give as much as is cut. It cannot be bought in this country.

CAULIFLOWER

   1 medium head cauliflower = 2 1/4 pounds,
      cut into small florets = 4 3/4 cups
   1/2 small head cauliflower = 12 ounces = 9 ounces
      with cores and outer leaves removed = 2 1/2 cups
      raw florets = 2 1/4 cups cooked = 1 cup purée

Broccoli, Chinese

Brassica algobrada

With long stalks, large green leaves and edible yellow flowers, this leafy green looks nothing like its Western counterpart. Sometimes referred to as Chinese kale, it has a hearty flavor and makes a suitable substitute for broccoli di raab. Otherwise, it can be steamed or stir-fried and sprinkled with soy sauce and rice vinegar. It can also be boiled with slices of ginger.

Methods

BUYING AND STORING

As for all leafy greens, the leaves should not be limp. The stems should not be more than about 1/4 inch thick. The yellow flowers can be shut or open. The ends of the stems should not be woody.

WASHING/WAYS OF CUTTING

To wash, rinse under cold running water. Separate the leaves and stems. Discard any tough (thick) stems. Trim the bottom ends of remaining stems. Either leave in branches—not too wide—or cut the stems, tops and leaves across into 1- to 2-inch pieces.

Preparation

STIR-FRYING

For a more involved recipe for stir-fried Chinese broccoli, see page 320.

Stalks, thick stems trimmed, cut into 2-inch pieces: For 1 pound remaining stems and leaves: Heat 1 tablespoon peanut or vegetable oil in a wok or 12-inch skillet until very hot. Add 1 clove garlic, smashed and peeled and cook until light brown. Discard. Add broccoli and stir-fry until bright green but still crunchy, about 2 minutes.

STEAMING

Whole stalks, stem ends trimmed: Cut any stalks with stems wider than 1 1/2 inches in half lengthwise. Place in a covered steamer basket. Cook until stems are pierced easily with a paring knife, 6 to 7 minutes.

Yields and Equivalents

1 bunch Chinese broccoli = 1 pound, cut into 2-inch pieces = 10 cups

1 pound Chinese broccoli, cut into 2-inch pieces and steamed or stir-fried = 5 cups

Broccoli di Raab

Brassica rapa

Also known as broccoli rabe, broccoli raab, broccoli di rape and rapini, broccoli di raab is characterized by long slender stems, ruffled green leaves and small flowers that resemble broccoli florets. It is prized for its slightly bitter taste. It is not eaten raw. It is mainly eaten in Italy and in North America, where it has become common because of Italian restaurants. My favorite way of cooking and eating it is cut across into three-inch pieces and braised. This is better done at home, as most restaurants are in too much of a hurry and send out the broccoli di raab before the stems are soft enough to eat with pleasure. This is not a time for al dente.

Broccoli di raab makes an excellent pasta sauce or accompaniment to fresh Italian sausage—the soft kind (not the air-dried kind, such as soppressata), cooked. As a simple vegetable with fish or roasted meat, it can be boiled, steamed or cooked in the microwave oven.

Methods

BUYING AND STORING

Split stem ends, yellow leaves and many open flowers are all signs of age in broccoli di raab. Look for bright green leaves, tightly closed flower buds and firm stems. Store broccoli di raab in the vegetable drawer of the refrigerator.

WASHING/WAYS OF CUTTING

Rinse under cold running water. Trim any tough pieces off the bottoms of the stems. Cut across into 1-inch pieces or as specified in recipe.

Preparation

The vegetable is done when the tip of a sharp knife easily pierces the stem.

BOILING

Whole: Bring salted (or not) water to a boil. Add trimmed broccoli di raab and simmer 10 minutes, or until tender. Drain and run under cold water.

STEAMING

2- to 3-inch pieces: Place in a covered steamer basket. Cook 10 to 15 minutes.

MICROWAVING

Cover tightly.

> 12 ounces broccoli di raab with 6 tablespoons olive oil that has been heated for 3 minutes (11 x 8 1/2 x 2-inch dish): 7 minutes
>
> 1 1/2 pounds broccoli di raab with 3/4 cup olive oil that has been heated for 4 minutes (14 x 11 x 2-inch dish): 10 minutes

BRAISING

1 bunch broccoli di raab, washed, trimmed and cut across into 2-inch pieces: Heat 2 tablespoons olive oil in a deep 12-inch pan with a cover. Add 4 smashed and peeled garlic cloves. Cook just until garlic begins to color. Add a large pinch of crushed hot pepper flakes, if desired, and broccoli di raab. Turn raab in oil until bright green and leaves are wilted. Pour in 1/2 cup chicken stock, broth or water and bring to a boil. Lower heat to medium-low. Cover and cook until stems are tender, about 8 minutes. Uncover and boil off liquid if necessary.

Yields and Equivalents

> 2 bunches broccoli di raab = 1 1/2 pounds untrimmed = 1 1/4 pounds trimmed
> 1 bunch broccoli di raab = 12 ounces = 10 ounces trimmed
> 1 bunch broccoli di raab, trimmed and cut into 1 1/2-inch pieces = 6 cups raw = 2 cups cooked
> 8 ounces broccoli di raab, trimmed and cut into 1-inch pieces = 4 packed cups

BROCCOLI RAAB, BROCCOLI RABE and **BROCCOLI DE RAPE** see Broccoli di Raab
BROCCOLI SPROUTS see Sprouts

Brussels Sprouts

Brassica gemifera

Brussels sprouts are like miniature cabbages that are amusing to watch grow. They seem to crawl up the sturdy stalks to nestle under the leaves on their way upward. They can vary enormously in size from two inches wide at the biggest down to three quarter inch wide. It is hard to say how many and how much will fit in a cup; the largest size that I've worked with fits three to four per cup. My favorite way of eating and serving them is roasted; they develop a nutty flavor. They can have their inside scooped out with a melon baller to serve with a hot stuffing or filling as an hors d'oeuvre. Smallish ones are best for this.

Varieties

GREEN The standard Brussels sprout.

RED (Rubine) Same as the regular but reddish; decorative for holidays.

Methods

BUYING AND STORING

While buying a whole stalk of Brussels sprouts at a farmers' market is fun, there is no actual advantage. If that is the way they come, make sure the stalk looks crisp and juicy. If picking, remember there is no urgency. The plant will stay healthy until the first frost. However, if any of the little cabbages start to unfurl petals, with a sharp knife cut the plant down immediately at the bottom of the stalk. Snap sprouts off the stem and discard the stems. Keep the sprouts in a paper bag in the refrigerator.

WASHING/WAYS OF CUTTING

Brussels sprouts are fairly clean, as they grow well above the ground and need only a quick rinse. Trim the ends and remove any leaves that have yellowed or browned. Cook whole or halved lengthwise.

Preparation

All instructions except braising are for whole heads.

BOILING

Brussels sprouts get soggy when boiled. Steaming and roasting are much preferred.

STEAMING

For medium Brussels sprouts: Trim and cut an X in the base of each sprout. Place in a covered steamer basket. Cook 11 to 12 minutes, or until a knife easily slips into flesh.

ROASTING

All sizes of Brussels sprouts can be roasted using either butter or olive oil. Butter will give a dark, nutty brown color and a nutty flavor.

Use pan just large enough to hold sprouts in a single layer. For each 2 cups sprouts, slick with 1 tablespoon fat. Roast in bottom third of a 500°F oven for about 20 minutes, or until a knife slips in easily; shake pan from time to time to roll sprouts around. Time will depend on size and age of sprouts.

MICROWAVING

Trim and place in a single layer in a dish just large enough to hold them; cover tightly.

6 ounces: 2 minutes

12 ounces: 3 minutes

18 ounces: 4 minutes 45 seconds

1 1/2 pounds: 6 minutes 45 seconds

BRAISING

Trimmed and cut in half: For one 1-pint container: Heat 1 tablespoon vegetable or olive oil in a 10- to 11-inch skillet over medium-high heat. Add 1/4 cup finely diced onion or 2 tablespoons finely chopped shallot, if desired, and stir for 2 minutes. Add sprouts and stir until bright green. Add 1/2 cup chicken stock, Leek Broth (page 385) or water. Season lightly with salt. Cover pan, reduce heat to medium-low and cook until liquid is gone and sprouts are tender, about 10 minutes. Make sure there is some liquid in the pan throughout cooking. If necessary, at end of cooking, increase heat to medium and boil off remaining liquid. Season with salt.

PREPARATION FOR STUFFING

Choose Brussels sprouts that are large enough for a small melon baller to fit inside. They should not be cooked before stuffing, or the shells will become mushy.

Trim sprouts. Use a small melon baller to hollow out the center of each sprout from root end, leaving a 1/8-inch-thick shell. Discard interiors or reserve for another use (see page 267 for a recipe that uses interiors as part of a stuffing). Slice a small piece from rounded side of each shell so they can stand upright.

One medium Brussels sprout will hold a rounded tablespoon of stuffing.

Stuffed Brussels sprouts will need a total of about 50 minutes baking time in a 350°F oven. See page 267 for a recipe.

Yields and Equivalents

Note: Brussels sprouts are often sold in 1-pint plastic or wax-coated paper containers labeled "net weight 10 ounces." These, as a rule, contain closer to 12 ounces.

Two 1-pint containers Brussels sprouts =
4 to 5 cups = 1 1/2 pounds = 36 medium Brussels sprouts

One 1-pint container Brussels sprouts =
18 medium sprouts; if hollowed for stuffing, coarsely chopped centers = 1 1/2 cups

12 ounces Brussels sprouts = 2 1/2 cups raw =
2 cups cooked

BUDDHA'S HANDS see Chayote under Squash, Winter

Burdock

Arctium lappa

A root that is a favorite in Japan, where it is called gobo. Burdock is easy to grow but very hard to dig up due to its long, thin pointed shape. It may be hard to buy, too, unless there is a handy Asian grocery store. In the past, it was grown in Europe as a medicinal.

Although several Japanese recipes I looked at call for peeled burdock, it tastes better if left unpeeled, having a nuttier flavor. It is commonly cut into strips or shaved like a pencil into slivers.

The fibrous center can be removed by hollowing out short pieces, but this is laborious. Smashing short lengths with the side of a heavy knife exposes the fibers, which can then be easily removed. Move quickly, as the flesh begins to darken if not soaked in acidulated water immediately.

Burdock retains its crunchiness after it's cooked, but the color is a drab gray, very unappealing. Soaking it and boiling it with a touch of vinegar as instructed by Japanese books makes it lighter but still gray.

Roasting and deep-frying bring out its sweetness.

There is also a red-skinned variety that becomes whitish when cooked. Both kinds taste the same, but the red-skinned is less mealy and floury. It can be used in place of water chestnuts.

Methods

BUYING AND STORING

Burdock can be found loose or in bundles of three, trimmed and wrapped in plastic. Stored tightly wrapped in the refrigerator, it keeps practically indefinitely.

WASHING/WAYS OF CUTTING

Burdock does not need to be peeled. Scrub clean with a stiff brush and rinse under cold running water.

If the skin is being peeled for a particular recipe or because it is damaged, have ready a bowl of water with some lemon juice in it; the flesh will darken almost immediately upon exposure to air. Remove the skin with a vegetable peeler, trim ends and immediately drop into the acidulated water.

Preparation

All times are for unpeeled burdock. Peeled burdock may cook in a minute or two less.

The common test of piercing the flesh with a knife to test for doneness is less accurate here, as cooked burdock remains crunchy; taste.

BOILING

1-inch pieces: Cover with water by 1 inch. Bring to a boil. Reduce heat and simmer 12 minutes.

STEAMING

2- or 3-inch pieces: Place in a single layer in a covered steamer basket. Cook 18 to 20 minutes, depending on thickness.

ROASTING

Roasting intensifies the flavor of burdock.

1-inch pieces: Place in smallest pan that will hold burdock comfortably in a single layer. Slick with 1 teaspoon fat per cup of burdock. Roast in center of a 500°F oven for 8 minutes. Turn. Roast 8 minutes more.

Yields and Equivalents

One 12-inch length burdock = 2 to 4 ounces

8 ounces burdock, trimmed and cut into 1-inch lengths = 1 1/2 cups raw = 1 cup cooked

1 pound burdock, trimmed and cut into 3-inch pieces = 5 cups raw = 2 1/2 cups cooked

BURNET see Herbs and Their Flowers
BUTTERCUP SQUASH see Squash, Winter
BUTTERHEAD LETTUCE see Boston under Lettuces
BUTTERNUT SQUASH see Squash, Winter

Cabbages, European
Brassica capita

Cabbages comprise a large family in which some of my favorite vegetables live. Great green cabbage got a terrible reputation during the many years that it was virtually the only green, non-root vegetable to last through the winter. It was generally old, overcooked and smelly. Let us not give up on this wonderful family that has taken such a bad rap. Young cabbage shredded and wilted (melted) with butter with seasonings is good as a vegetable dish, or as part of a recipe. Unlike the other Brassicas, cabbages form single heads with their leaves wrapped around them, which distinguishes them even from cauliflower which heads—but only its buds.

Pickled in salt as sauerkraut, cabbage also helped people last through the winter.

It has become a summer staple, shredded and dressed as coleslaw. In Germany and other regions where sauerkraut and slaw are popular, special cutters called slaw boards were developed. They consist of a wooden frame with a plate into which a sharp knife blade is angled. The cut side of half a cabbage is pushed down it to make thin strips. Today there are many alternative cutting devices, and a sharp knife still works well. I usually quarter the cabbage from top to bottom so as to be able to remove the hard white core easily.

Varieties
GREEN (WHITE) The standard green cabbage, called white when very young and pale. It is the cabbage for sauerkraut and coleslaw. It goes well with caraway, juniper and cured pork. One has only to think of choucroute garni.

RED This cabbage is a very dark red and needs to be cooked with some acid, usually vinegar, to prevent it from turning a nasty color. Raw, it had a hideous place in the history of American salads as a filler and provider of color. Cooked, it has a deep winey flavor that is often paired with game or pot roast. It is good sweet-and-sour and it loves juniper.

SAVOY The most tender of the cabbages, this has a largish firm head and pale green, crinkly leaves. If you can find it, use it. It is also made into sauerkraut. Rolls of the pickled leaves, usually from Central Europe, are sold in jars for stuffing (see Preparation for Stuffing and also Yields).

SAUERKRAUT I have a friend, Paula Frosch, who makes her own every year. She uses a ratio of 5 pounds of salt to 50 pounds of cabbage, shredded, weighted and allowed to ferment with frequent turnings—up to your elbows is the only way. I tried to do a small quantity, but it didn't work. It comes in jars, cans and plastic bags. I prefer the bags. It's quite acceptable.

PICKLED SAVOY LEAVES These can be bought and are excellent. They are generally used to make stuffed cabbage. They are fragile. Work with them carefully and overlap places where they have broken or use two leaves, one on top of the other.

Methods
BUYING AND STORING
Buy heads that are firm and seem heavy for their size. Green and red cabbage will keep indefinitely in a cool place. These used to be stored in deep holes, covered with sand. Savoy cabbage is much more fragile. Tightly wrapped in plastic and refrigerated, it will keep for under a month.

WASHING/WAYS OF CUTTING
The tightly furled leaves of a cabbage create a barrier to protect it from dirt. To wash, remove the dark or wilted outer leaves. Rinse the head under cold water.

To core a whole cabbage, place it upside down with the stem end facing up. Hold a paring knife angled towards the center and cut deeply around the core. Remove the core in a single cone-shaped piece.

The core can also be sliced out after cutting the cabbage into quarters.

For many preparations, cabbage is sliced more or less thinly across the head.

Preparation

Always cook cabbage in a nonreactive pan.

BOILING

GREEN, SAVOY AND RED *Head quartered, cored and leaves cut across into 1-inch strips:* Add to generous amount of boiling salted water. Cook, partially covered, stirring once or twice, until tender but not mushy, about 8 minutes for green and savoy, 10 minutes for red.

One 3-pound head green, 2-pound head red or 1³/₄-pound head savoy, cut through core into 8 wedges: Add to generous amount of boiling salted water. Weight with an otoshi-buta (see Note, page 237) or pot lid to keep submerged. Cook until thickest part of leaves near stem is tender, 14 minutes for green and savoy, 18 minutes for red.

STEAMING

GREEN, SAVOY AND RED *Head quartered, cored and leaves cut across into 1-inch strips:* Place in a covered steamer basket. Cook until tender, about 10 minutes for green and savoy, 12 minutes for red.

One 3-pound green or red cabbage or 1³/₄-pound savoy cabbage, cut through core into 8 wedges: Working in batches if necessary, place wedges in a covered steamer basket. Cover and steam until thickest part of leaf near core is tender, 14 minutes for green and savoy, 20 minutes for red.

Whole leaves: Core cabbage. Place entire head in a covered steamer basket. Cook several minutes to wilt the leaves slightly and make them easier to remove. Remove leaves and place in a covered steamer basket. If necessary, steam head for another few minutes after first few layers are removed, then remove remaining leaves. Steam separated individual savoy leaves 4 to 5 minutes, green or red cabbage leaves 7 to 9 minutes.

ROASTING

Throughout the Cook's Guide I have given general instructions and timings for roasting vegetables in order to accommodate whatever quantity of vegetables is on hand. Cabbage is different; it needs more specific timings.

GREEN AND SAVOY *One 2-pound cabbage, quartered, cored and cut across into ¹/₂-inch strips (about 12 cups):* Place cabbage strips, roughly in an even layer, in a large pan. Slick cabbage and pan with 3 tablespoons fat. Fat will not coat each and every piece of cabbage; that is fine. Roast in upper level of 500°F oven for 15 minutes. Toss and turn strips. They will be very moist, particularly in center of pan. Be sure to scoop up center pieces and redistribute them around pan for even cooking. Roast 15 minutes more. Cabbage should be less moist, with about half the pieces beginning to brown nicely at the end roasting. (Serves 6 as a side dish)

To double the recipe, increase the cabbage to 3¹/₂ pounds. The cooking time will remain the same.

RED *One 2-pound cabbage, quartered, cored and cut across into ¹/₂-inch strips (about 10 cups):* Roast as for green or savoy, then toss with 2 tablespoons malt or other vinegar. (Serves 8 as a side dish)

Unlike green cabbage, when quantities of red cabbage change, so do cooking times. If doubling the recipe, increase the cooking time to 1 hour and toss the cabbage every 15 minutes. Two 1-pound heads make twice as much cooked cabbage.

MICROWAVING

GREEN *Shredded:* Season with fat or liquid, if desired. Cover tightly.

2 cups (1-quart measure): 4 minutes

3 cups with 1 tablespoon water or 2 tablespoons fat (2-quart soufflé dish): 12 minutes

8 cups with 1 tablespoon water or 3 tablespoons fat (2-quart soufflé dish): 12 to 14 minutes

Whole leaves: Deeply core whole cabbage. Set uncovered on carousel or a plate.

2¹/₂ pounds cabbage: 5 minutes

Wedges: Arrange 4- to 5-ounce wedges, about 2¹/₂ to 3¹/₂ inches at the widest part, in a shallow dish in a ring, petal fashion, with core end toward outside of dish. Cover tightly.

2 wedges (8-inch dish): 8 minutes
   (12 minutes in a small oven)

4 wedges (10-inch dish): 12 minutes

6 wedges (12-inch round dish): 16 minutes

RED *Shredded:* Cover tightly.

   9 cups with 2 tablespoons plus 1 teaspoon unsalted butter and 1 1/2 cups sliced onions; add 3/4 cup water after 8 minutes (12 x 10 x 3-inch dish): 18 minutes

SAVOY *Shredded:* Cover tightly.

   2 cups cabbage (1-quart glass measure): 4 minutes

SAUTÉING

One 2-pound green or savoy cabbage, trimmed, quartered, cored and cut into 1-inch strips (12 cups): Heat 2 tablespoons olive oil or vegetable oil in a deep 12-inch pan with a cover over medium heat. Add about one-third of cabbage; cook until wilted. Add remaining cabbage in 2 batches. Season very lightly with salt and continue cooking, stirring often, until done to taste: about 10 minutes for crisp cabbage, up to 20 minutes for golden brown, tender and sweet cabbage. (Savoy cabbage will require less total cooking.) If cabbage begins to stick, add a small amount of water and stir well. Add any of the following during the last few minutes of cooking: 2 cloves garlic, smashed, peeled and minced; 1 teaspoon caraway seeds; or 16 black olives, pitted and coarsely chopped. (Makes about 4 cups)

PREPARATION FOR STUFFING

Savoy cabbages are preferred for stuffing—the leaves are generally larger and much easier to remove than those of green cabbage. If green cabbage is all that is available, if stuffing individual leaves, core and steam the entire head for several minutes (see page 555). This will make the leaves more pliable. Do not steam if the cabbage will be stuffed whole.

To prepare cabbage leaves: Bring a large pot of water to a boil. Core cabbage, taking off as many of the largest leaves as needed. Add leaves to pot and cook briefly until just softened. Drain leaves and rinse under cold running water to stop the cooking. Drain leaves.

   Remove thick center rib of each leaf by cutting out a narrow V shape. Overlap cut ends of each leaf and place stuffing in center. Tuck in sides and roll up the cabbage leaf carefully; do not roll too tightly if stuffing contains rice or any other ingredient that needs room to expand. If rolls will not stay together by simply tucking in edges, secure each roll with a toothpick.

To cook stuffed cabbage leaves on the stovetop: Choose a heavy casserole or Dutch oven that will hold the cabbage rolls in no more than 3 layers. Pour an inch or so of broth or not-too-thick sauce (such as Tomato Sauce for Stuffed Vegetables, page 461) into casserole. Arrange rolls in casserole, leaving 1/2 inch between them and stacking them as necessary. Pour in enough broth or sauce to barely cover rolls. Bring to a boil. Reduce heat to simmering, cover casserole and cook over very low heat until the filling is fully cooked, 1 1/2 to 2 hours. Check occasionally during cooking to make sure sauce isn't sticking to bottom of casserole; add broth or water if it is. Let sit off the heat 15 minutes before serving.

To bake stuffed cabbage leaves: Preheat oven to 350°F. Pour enough sauce into a baking dish large enough to hold rolls snugly in a single layer to coat bottom. Put rolls in the dish, pour enough sauce over them to cover completely and cover baking dish. Bake until filling is completely cooked, about 1 1/2 hours. Remove cover during the last 15 minutes to brown top, if desired.

To prepare a whole head of savoy cabbage: Core cabbage from stem end with a pairing knife. Remove core and cut out inside of cabbage, leaving a 1-inch-thick shell. Discard interior or reserve for another use (see page 276 for a recipe that uses the interior as part of a stuffing). Slice a small piece from rounded top so cabbage can stand upright.

To bake a whole stuffed cabbage: Stuff head of cabbage with filling of your choice (see pages 491–500). Place in a roasting pan large enough to hold it comfortably, stuffing side up. Pour in 1 1/2 cups liquid—stock, broth or a combination of broth and wine—and bake in a 350°F oven until cabbage is tender and filling is fully cooked, about 1 hour and 15 minutes.

   One medium savoy cabbage (1 3/4 pounds) will hold 2 cups stuffing.

   One savoy cabbage leaf will hold 1/3 cup stuffing; for smaller rolls, use 1/4 cup stuffing.

Yields and Equivalents

There is an odd law of diminishing returns with cabbage. While 6 cups of raw slices will make 3 cups cooked, 12 cups of raw slices does not make 6 cups cooked. Start with about 19 cups sliced red cabbage or 22 cups sliced green cabbage to make 6 cups cooked. This is not as overwhelming as it seems because a 1-pound green cabbage will make 6 cups raw slices and a 2-pound red cabbage will make more than 10 cups raw slices.

GREEN

    1 small cabbage = 2 pounds

    1 small cabbage, cored and cut into $^1/_2$-inch strips = 12 cups raw = $4^1/_2$ cups cooked

    $^1/_2$ cabbage = 1 pound = 6 cups finely shredded

    $^1/_4$ cabbage = 8 ounces = 2 cups sliced into long thin strips

RED

    1 small cabbage = 2 pounds

    One 2-pound cabbage, cored and cut into $^1/_2$-inch strips = 10 cups raw = 4 cups cooked

    One $2^3/_4$-pound cabbage, cored and cut into $1^1/_2$-inch chunks or shredded = 8 cups

SAVOY

    1 savoy cabbage = $1^3/_4$ pounds, cut into 1-inch chunks = 12 cups = 4 cups boiled or steamed

    One 46-ounce jar pickled savoy cabbage leaves = approximately 28 leaves

SAUERKRAUT

    One 16-ounce bag, drained = $1^1/_2$ cups packed

    One 14-ounce can, drained = $1^3/_4$ cups packed

Cabbages, Asian

Brassica parachinensis/Brassica rapa

Varieties

BOK CHOY (*Brassica rapa*, Chinensis group) The name is very confusing. The long, rather white-leafed cabbage that used to go by this name in the Northeast (and still does in Cantonese communities) is now called napa cabbage to avoid confusion with the Mandarin bok choy, which looks like a dark-leaved escarole with fleshy white bottoms and leaves that flourish outward. That is what I am calling bok choy here. All kinds of bok choy are very low in calories and delicious if not overcooked. It comes white or green; green bok choy is also known as Shanghai bok choy. Both the white and green come in small and baby varieties; the baby can be as small as a thumb. Check the local Chinatown; these tiny bok choy are usually available there. I much prefer the babies. They should not be overcooked. To complicate matters even further, various other cabbages are also sometimes called bok choy.

NAPA CABBAGE (*Brassica rapa*, Pekinensis group) This used to be known by its Cantonese name, bok choy. Napa cabbage has elongated oval heads of pale green, tightly packed, crinkly leaves. In Australia, it is known as Chinese cabbage.

PAK CHOY (*Brassica rapa*, Chinensis group) Pak choy, also known as choy sum and Chinese flowering cabbage, is a close relative of bok choy. Slender stalks, smooth oval leaves and colorful sprigs of edible yellow flowers make this vegetable a favorite of classic Chinese cooking.

PURPLE PAK CHOY (*Brassica parachinensis*) The purple variety not only looks different, it tastes different. The curvy green leaves and deeply purple veins and stems (it looks rather like beet greens) have a flavor reminiscent of mustard greens.

TATSOI (*Brassica rapa*) A Japanese variant, a pretty plant that is also called flat cabbage to describe its horizontal growing habit. It has celery-green stems terminated by darker green smoothish-to-puckered leaves (depending on the variety). The leaves are round at the bottom and taper to a mild point. They are often sold separate from the plant. The whole plant is harvested in many sizes, like bok choy. It appears in mesclun mixes. It is tougher and stronger tasting than the other bok and pak choys. Cooked, it mellows.

Methods

BUYING AND STORING

As with most greens, these should not be wilted. Some, like napa cabbage, will be pale in color and others various shades of green. Those having ribs should have firm ones. I pick heads that are heavy for their size, or I end up with air.

WASHING/WAYS OF CUTTING

BOK CHOY (ALL VARIETIES) Most bok choy tends to be full of dirt and sand. Make sure to soak it in a sink full of cold water for at least 30 minutes. The larger the bok choy, the longer the soaking time. The bok choy will be cleaner and the soaking time (as well as cooking time) less if the bok choy is cut lengthwise into wedges, either halves, quarters, sixths or eighths. Small bok choy (2 to 4 inches long) and tiny or baby bok choy tend to need only a quick rinse in the colander. For regular-size bok choy, the leaves and stalks are often cooked separately.

NAPA CABBAGE Dirt likes to hide inside the base, where the leaves attach to the bottom. To wash, separate all the leaves from the bottom; discard any bottom. Rinse the leaves well under cold running water.

To slice, stack several leaves together and slice crosswise into thin strips or larger pieces.

PAK CHOY Pak choy just needs a quick rinse. It can be cooked whole or in pieces.

PURPLE PAK CHOY This tends to be very dirty. Break apart the leaves and soak in cold water for several minutes. Lift out the leaves, drain and repeat.

Cut the stems and leaves (with flowers intact) into 1 1/2- to 2-inch pieces. Reserve separately. The stems will need a minute more cooking than the leaves.

TATSOI When leaves are sold loose, they need only be rinsed lightly. For smallish heads, halve or quarter, then plunge into plenty of cold water to dislodge the soil that clings to the leafstalks. Repeat as needed.

Preparation

BOILING

NAPA CABBAGE *Shredded:* For 11 ounces, add to boiling water and simmer 5 minutes.

STEAMING

WHITE BOK CHOY *Whole heads* (8 ounces each): Place in a single layer in a covered steamer basket. Cook 10 minutes.

GREEN BOK CHOY *Whole heads* (6 ounces each): Place in a single layer in a covered steamer basket. Cook 15 minutes.

SAUTÉING

BABY BOK CHOY *Whole heads:* For 8 ounces thumb-size bok choy (about 5 cups), heat 1 1/2 tablespoons oil in a large pan. Add bok choy. Cook and stir over high heat for 1 to 2 minutes, until tender-crisp.

PURPLE PAK CHOY *1 1/2- to 2-inch pieces:* For 4 ounces greens, leaves and stems reserved separately, heat 1 teaspoon oil in a large pan. Add stems. Cook, stirring, over medium heat for 1 minute. Add leaves. Cook over medium heat for 1 to 2 minutes, continuously stirring from bottom until leaves are bright green and wilted. (Makes a generous 1/2 cup)

For 13 ounces greens, increase oil to 2 tablespoons and cooking time of leaves to 5 to 6 minutes.

MICROWAVING

BOK CHOY *2 medium heads (1 1/2 pounds each):* Cook in a 14 x 11 x 2-inch dish. Cover tightly.

Ribs, cut into 2- to 3-inch lengths, with 1/2 cup liquid: 11 minutes

Leaves, cut into 1/4-inch strips, with 6 tablespoons liquid: 6 minutes

NAPA CABBAGE *2-inch lengths:* Cover tightly.

4 cups with 2 tablespoons unsalted butter (11 x 8 1/2 x 2-inch dish): 4 minutes 30 seconds

8 cups with 4 tablespoons unsalted butter (11 x 8 x 3-inch oval dish): 7 minutes

Yields and Equivalents

BOK CHOY

3 to 3 1/2 ounces bok choy, shredded = 1 cup

8 ounces bok choy, shredded = 2 cups = 3/4 cup cooked

1 $3/4$ pounds bok choy, shredded = 7 cups =
   1 $1/4$ cups cooked
1 large head bok choy = 2 pounds, shredded =
   10 cups = 3 $1/2$ cups cooked

SMALL BOK CHOY (4 inches long)
   1 white small bok choy = 4 ounces
   1 green small bok choy = 3 ounces

BABY (TINY) BOK CHOY
   1 pound bok choy in 1 $1/2$- to 2-inches pieces =
   70 pieces = 16 cups

NAPA CABBAGE
   1 extra-large cabbage = 3 $1/4$ pounds = 19 cups
      cut across in $1/4$-inch strips
   1 large cabbage = 2 $1/2$ pounds = 2 $1/4$ pounds
      trimmed = 18 to 20 cups in 2-inch pieces
   8 cups cabbage in 2-inch pieces, raw = 2 $1/4$ cups cooked
   11 ounces shredded cabbage = 2 $3/4$ cups raw =
      1 cup cooked

PURPLE PAK CHOY
   4 ounces = 3 ounces leaves, 1 ounce stems =
      2 packed cups in 1 $1/2$- to 2-inch pieces, raw =
      generous $1/2$ cup cooked
   13 ounces = 8 packed cups in 1 $1/2$- to 2-inch
      pieces, raw = 1 $3/4$ cups cooked

Cactus Pads (Nopales)
Opuntia ficus-indica

These are the cacti seen growing in large fields in Mexico
where I gather little else will grow due to the lack of
moisture. The part we eat is a sort of large oval leaf called
a pad. As they get older, beautiful reddish-purple flowers
grow at the tips of the oval leaves. It is better to get them
large, but before the flower forms and blooms. They can
be purchased in Mexican stores and can be served as a
hot vegetable or as a salad, much like a green bean salad.
They go well with most fresh Mexican ingredients and
herbs. I give only one recipe (page 29) because they are
literally a pain to clean, as they are covered with nasty
thornlike excrescences.

Methods
BUYING AND STORING
They should be bought when they are as plump as possible,
although always flat. They should be wrapped in plastic
and refrigerated and used as soon after purchase as
possible.

WAYS OF CUTTING
To clean, don rubber gloves—not the thin surgical kind,
but the sturdy kind used for cleaning. Take a pair of
eyebrow tweezers and pluck the thorns out. Cut off any
hardened tissue at the rounded end.
   They are usually cut in strips before cooking.

Preparation
BOILING
Boil in plentiful water for 15 to 20 minutes, depending on
width of strips. The water may be flavored first. Cook until
strips have the texture of a fully cooked green bean. Drain,
flavor and use. Cooked, they keep for several days.
   Traditionally bicarbonate of soda is added to the
cooking liquid to keep the nopales green (as is done in
Europe with green vegetables). I opt to leave it out, as
bicarbonate leaches nutrients from the leaves.

Yields and Equivalents
   1 pound cactus pads = 5 large pads, each around
      5 x 8 $1/2$ inches
   1 pound cactus pads, cut into $1/8$- to $1/4$-inch strips =
      2 cups

CALABAZA see Squash, Winter
CALIFORNIA POTATOES see Potatoes
CANNELLINI see Beans of the New World
   under Beans

Capers

Capparis spinosa

This plant is actually three kinds of salad ingredient. There are the small round buds that we have seen in bottles forever and sprinkled on steak tartare and other cold dishes. The best are the really small ones (nonpareil). And the best of those are salt-packed from Spain. They have a rich flavor. Salt-pack capers come in large—2.2-pound—cans, a few years' supply. There are the larger seed enclosures, buds, or caper berries, round and usually with the stem attached and pickled, which can be eaten with drinks or tossed in a mixed vegetable salad. And then there is something that I had not happened upon until a recent trip to Greece. In Santorini, the very small fleshy leaves are pickled. They make a wonderful addition to a tomato and cucumber salad.

Yields and Equivalents

One 3.5-ounce jar nonpareil capers, drained = $1/2$ cup

One 4.25-ounce jar caper berries = 25 large (about $1 1/8$ inches in diameter) berries with stems

Pickled caper leaves come in small jars holding about $1/4$ cup = about 35 leaves

Cardoons

Cynara cardunculus

Cardoons are a primitive relative of the artichoke. They are longish white heads with the leaves loosely wrapped. The jagged edges of the leaves show their thistle connection, but only the innermost are thorny and in any way ferocious. They are often baked in a béchamel sauce or made into a gratin. See pages 242 and 243 for a version of each dish.

Methods

BUYING AND STORING

Buy heads that are light in color and fairly firm. While they can be stored whole in a plastic bag in the refrigerator for 2 days, it may be preferable to wash, cut and boil them ahead so that they take up less space.

WASHING/WAYS OF CUTTING

Separate the ribs, discarding the leafy center. Be careful when handling the center ribs, as they may have small thorns. Strip the outer leaves from each rib. Rinse well. Ribs near the center may have a white fuzzy coating that can be easily removed by rubbing with fingers or a stiff brush under running water.

To peel, trim the ends, then use a vegetable peeler to remove the fibrous skin. Cut into 3-inch lengths. (Use stainless steel implements.)

Soak the pieces in water with lemon juice for 30 minutes. Drain.

Preparation

BOILING

For 2 pounds cardoons, peeled and trimmed, fill a large pot with 8 cups water, or twice the volume of cardoons. Add 1 teaspoon kosher salt plus juice and shells of 1 lemon. Bring to a boil. Add cardoons. Simmer $1 1/2$ hours, or until tender. Drain. Rinse under cold water.

This recipe can be multiplied.

SHALLOW-FRYING

Begin by peeling, cutting, soaking and boiling 3-inch lengths of cardoons as described above. Spread $1/2$ cup all-purpose flour out on a plate; beat 3 eggs in a shallow bowl and mix together 1 cup dried bread crumbs and $1/3$ cup freshly grated Parmesan cheese in a second shallow bowl. Pat cardoon pieces dry and season with salt and pepper. Roll a few pieces at a time in flour; tap off excess. Turn to coat with egg and remove, letting excess egg drip back into bowl before coating with bread crumbs. Pat the crumbs lightly to help them stick. Pour enough vegetable oil and olive oil (equal amounts) into a large heavy skillet to come to $1/2$ inch. Heat over medium heat until a breaded piece of cardoon gives off a lively sizzle. Add as many pieces as will fit without touching. Fry, turning once, until golden brown on both sides, about 8 minutes. Remove and drain. Repeat with remaining cardoons if necessary. Serve hot or at room temperature.

Yields and Equivalents

2 pounds cardoons (1 average head) =
   1 1/2 pounds peeled and trimmed

2 pounds cardoons, peeled, trimmed and cut into
   3-inch lengths = 8 cups raw = 5 cups cooked

1 bunch cardoons = 5 to 8 ribs, average weight
   5 ounces per rib

CARIBBEAN PUMPKIN see Calabaza under
   Squash, Winter

CARROT GREENS see Carrots

Carrots
Daucus carota sativa

Carrots are so common in the kitchen, so useful, that
we tend to think of them as a single flavor. In a more
thoughtful mode, we can see that carrots come in many
colors and degrees of sweetness, fibrousness, percentage
of core (the usually lighter part down the middle), age,
thickness and bitterness of skin. They range in size from
the hideous bitter giants known as chefs' specials, which
are useful mainly because—as there is less surface to
center—there is less peeling and preparation involved,
to tender and sweet baby carrots with pale greens still
attached, which often need no peeling, only scrubbing.

We are used to seeing carrots that are, no matter what
their size, orange and pointy. Carrots were originally
white and were bred to be orange to make them more
appealing. The added color also increases their vitamin
A content—that beta-carotene we hear so much about.
In various parts of the world, carrots may range from
almost purple through red to orange. There are ball-
shaped carrots, like the Planet; short conical carrots,
like the Chantenay; and carrots that are almost straight,
like the Nantes. Most of the differences in shape have to
do with gardening conditions. However, it is a shame the
Nantes type of carrot is not grown more in America. Since
they are straight and smooth, they are easier to cut into
even pieces without waste, and they have less core.

Varieties

BABY CARROTS These are simply very young and tender
carrots. They are delicious. If bought, they are usually the
pointed kind. They can be eaten raw or cooked relatively
rapidly. See Warm Spring Vegetable Salad, page 432.

DWARF CARROTS These are small carrots pretending
to be babies. They are often sold in bags, washed and
peeled. Sometimes they are not even whole carrots but
instead pieces of larger carrots cut to look as if whole.
They are convenient but not as delicious as true babies.

MAROON CARROTS Sometimes called beta-carrots,
maroon carrots are named for their striking color. Much
of this color, unfortunately, may leach out during cooking,
so serve them raw. They are very sweet.

Methods
BUYING AND STORING
It is better to buy carrots with attached tops, as the freshness
will be a good indication of the freshness of the carrots.
Remove the tops as soon as the carrots are home, to keep
the carrots moister. Usually, the greens are thrown out.
Only the youngest greens are useful as a vegetable or in
soups and even they require being briefly boiled (blanched)
twice in salted water before they can be used for cooking.
Carrots for sale that are hairy are not fresh; don't buy them.
But when they are hairy or deformed straight from the
garden, they will be fine.

Whole, raw: Tops twisted off, wrapped airtight and
refrigerated, unpeeled, carrots will keep for about a week.

Sliced: Peeled and cut for use, they will keep for about
5 days packed airtight or in water, refrigerated.

Frozen: Carrots can be frozen raw, peeled, cut into
usable sizes and covered with water, or boiled briefly
(blanched), cooled and then frozen covered with water.
They will keep for about 3 months.

Pickled: I do not like dilled carrot sticks and give no
recipe. Carrots can, however, be cut into 1/4-inch sticks,
boiled for 2 minutes in a flavored brine and then canned
(see page 91).

WASHING/WAYS OF CUTTING

REGULAR CARROTS The skins of very fresh young carrots just pulled from the ground are so thin they can be easily rubbed off with a flat green scouring pad. I find that a rotary motion, circling the carrot with the pad in my fist, is most efficient. A good stiff vegetable brush or plastic scouring pad may work as well (do not use a metallic scouring pad). The skins of carrots purchased in grocery stores will be drier and thicker. Scrub the carrots with a hard brush and peel with a potato peeler if the skin has any gritty texture or bitter taste.

Trim the root end. Depending on size, larger carrots may be cut in any way called for in the recipe. Use as large a knife as is comfortable to handle. Cut down firmly in a single motion.

The skins of carrots will also slip off easily after cooking, and the carrots will retain more vitamins that way.

BABY Cut off the bushy tops, leaving a $1/4$ inch or so of the green stems attached if the carrots are very small (otherwise the greens will be tough). The skin on baby carrots does not need peeling, but if doing so, scrape the skin off using the back of a paring knife, or as above. Small and baby carrots are not normally cut.

DWARF Nick off any remaining bits of stem; rinse lightly and drain. Check to see if they have skins; if so, peel.

Preparation

BOILING

REGULAR CARROTS *Medium carrots, in 1-inch rounds:* Cook in boiling salted water until a knife easily slips into flesh, 15 to 20 minutes, depending on freshness of carrots.

DWARF Add to a generous amount of boiling salted water. Cook until the tip of a paring knife easily pierces thickest part, 8 to 9 minutes. Drain.

BABY *Whole:* Cook in boiling salted water until a knife easily slips into flesh, about 8 to 9 minutes.

MAROON Cooking times are shorter than those of regular carrots: $1/4$-inch slices dropped into boiling water will take 3 minutes to cook, $1/2$-inch slices will take 5 minutes and 1-inch chunks will take 8 to 10 minutes.

CARROT GREENS Remove greens from stems. Bring 6 quarts water to a boil in a large pot over high heat. Add greens, return water to a boil and boil for 5 minutes. Drain and cool under cold running water. Repeat twice. (Or repeat just once if using in soup.)

STEAMING

REGULAR CARROTS *Whole:* Put unpeeled, untrimmed carrots in a covered steamer basket and steam for 15 minutes, or until a knife easily slips into flesh. Rinse under cold water until cool enough to handle. Rub skins off.

BABY AND DWARF CARROTS Put trimmed carrots (scraped or unscraped if using baby) in a covered steamer basket. Steam until a paring knife easily slips into thickest part, about 10 minutes for babies, 9 minutes for dwarves.

ROASTING

REGULAR CARROTS Carrots are excellent simply roasted, with butter or olive or canola oil as the fat. Butter browns them more darkly. Liquids to use range from orange, lemon, or apple juice to stocks or even water. Do not use milk or cream for a small quantity, as it will burn. And do not put pepper on the carrots at the beginning of roasting, as it will turn acrid with the prolonged cooking time. Do add some salt. Other seasonings that may be added—but not all together—are a pinch of cayenne pepper or somewhat more ground cumin, coriander seeds or celery seeds.

Carrots roast very well along with potato pieces.

Whole: Trimmed and peeled: Use the smallest pan that will hold carrots comfortably in a single layer. Slick carrots and pan with fat. Roast on second level from bottom of a 500°F oven for 10 minutes. Reduce oven heat to 325°F. Add $1/4$ cup liquid and roast 20 minutes. Turn and roast for 20 minutes more.

$1/2$-inch rounds: Roast on second level from bottom of a 500°F oven for 15 minutes. Turn. Add $1/4$ cup liquid. Roast for 10 minutes more.

SAUTÉING

REGULAR CARROTS *Wedges, 1 1/2 inches long, 1/2 to 3/4 inch wide:* Heat a pan wide enough to hold carrots in a single layer. Add just enough oil to coat pan bottom. Add carrots. Cook, stirring, over low heat for 7 to 10 minutes.

BABY AND DWARF CARROTS For 1 1/2 pounds (with tops) baby carrots, trimmed, or one 1-pound bag dwarf carrots

Method 1: Boil or steam carrots 1 minute less than directed in Boiling and Steaming. Drain thoroughly. Heat 1 tablespoon butter in a 10- or 11-inch skillet over medium heat. Add carrots. Cook, tossing, until tender and lightly browned, about 4 minutes.

Method 2: Put carrots, 1 1/2 tablespoons unsalted butter and 1/2 cup water in a 10- or 11-inch skillet. Bring to a boil over medium heat. Cover and cook 5 minutes. Uncover and lower heat to medium-low. Cook, stirring often, until liquid is evaporated and carrots are tender and lightly browned, about 6 minutes.

DEEP-FRYING

REGULAR CARROTS *Wedges, 1 1/2 inches long, 1/2 to 3/4 inch wide:* Pour 1 1/2 to 2 inches of oil into a deep pan. Heat oil to 300°F. Add carrots and fry 2 to 3 minutes, until lightly brown and a knife easily inserts into flesh. (See page 514 for carrot chips.)

MICROWAVING

These basic vegetables cook rapidly in the microwave oven without getting mushy. This means that they can be added to a microwave stew or soup right at the beginning of the cooking time and emerge as recognizable pieces of carrot, not orange slime.

Cooking in butter with a nice little bit of sugar is particularly good.

REGULAR CARROTS *Whole:* Arrange the carrots with the thin tips toward the center of a microwave-safe dish. If using a lid, add 2 tablespoons water to the dish. If desired, season and add butter. Cover tightly with microwave plastic wrap or a tightly fitting lid.

Matchsticks or 1/8- to 1/4-inch rounds: Arrange carrots in 2 or 3 layers in a dish just large enough to hold them. Cover tightly.

4 ounces: 4 minutes 30 seconds

8 ounces: 6 minutes 30 seconds

12 ounces: 7 minutes

1 pound: 8 minutes

2 pounds: 11 minutes

Glazed whole baby carrots (about 12 per pound): Peel. Arrange in a dish just large enough to hold them. Cover tightly.

1 pound, with 1 tablespoon each butter and sugar: 8 minutes

Yields and Equivalents

REGULAR AND MAROON CARROTS

1 small carrot = 2 ounces

1 medium carrot = 3 to 5 ounces

1 large carrot = 6 to 8 ounces

2 pounds carrots, peeled, trimmed and cut into 1-inch rounds = 6 cups

1 pound carrots, peeled, trimmed and cut into 1/4-inch dice = 3 cups

12 ounces carrots, peeled, trimmed and cut into 1-inch pieces = 2 cups

8 ounces carrots, peeled, trimmed, halved crosswise and grated on large holes of a box grater= 2 cups

6 ounces carrots, peeled, trimmed and cut into 1/4-inch rounds = 3/4 cup

5 ounces carrots, peeled, trimmed and cut into 1/2-inch dice = 1/2 cup

8 ounces carrots, peeled, stemmed, cooked and puréed = 1/2 cup

5 1/2 to 6 pounds carrots = 1 quart juice

BABY CARROTS

6 ounces baby carrots = 1 cup peeled and trimmed

1 pound baby carrots (about 4 bunches), peeled and trimmed = 2 1/2 cups

DWARF CARROTS

One 1-pound bag carrots = 3 1/2 cups

CARROT GREENS

Greens from 23 bunches baby carrots = 7 cups =
$3/4$ cup cooked

Greens from 2 bunches large carrots = 7 cups =
$1/2$ cup cooked

CASCABEL PEPPERS see Peppers
CASSAVA see Yuca under Tropical Tubers
CAULIFLOWER see Broccoli and Cauliflower
CAYENNE see Peppers
CELERIAC see Celery Root

Celery
Apium graveolens dulce

Varieties

Life doesn't always get better. Celery certainly used to be better. There were white varieties and yellow varieties. The yellow were used in combination with other aromatic vegetables to flavor soup or cut up and sautéed to be used as a flavoring in Italian, French, Spanish and Cajun dishes.

The various white varieties were bunched up and scrupulously blanched with mounded dirt to emerge as vegetables to be eaten raw or cooked. The very best was called Pascal, or Easter, celery.

Today, we have to make do with diffuse green heads that are not wonderful raw; they are better cooked.

Celery is the modern-day version of what was known as smallage. Its difference is told by its name. It was generally used as a seasoning.

Celery is commonly used as a vegetable, but it also finds plentiful use as an aromatic, part of a mixed chop of vegetables and herbs.

Chinese celery is still blanched. It has long thin stalks that are bunched rather than heading. They compensate with a wonderful aroma and an abundance of leaves that must be cooked before use, as they are tough. The stalks are too thin to be peeled, so it is essential to cut them across into very thin slices—at which point, they make a good addition to stir-fries. Both leaves and stems can be added to dishes that cook for a long time.

Celery seeds are a fine flavoring. Celery salt, which is commonly used in Bloody Marys, is a less fine ingredient.

Methods
BUYING AND STORING

Celery doesn't keep brilliantly. Buy it as close to the time it will be used as possible. Choose celery that has crisp green leaves and stalks that snap easily. At home, the leaves can be cut off and kept in a plastic storage bag in the refrigerator to use as an herb. The heads should be wrapped as close to airtight as possible and refrigerated.

WASHING/WAYS OF CUTTING

Separate celery into stalks and rinse well under cold running water. Trim the leafy tops and the rough bottoms. The stalks, especially large ones, are often fibrous. Snapping the stalks and pulling lengthwise will remove many of the strings. Remove any remaining stringy fibers with a vegetable peeler.

If using the bottoms for braising, leave the stalks attached. Trim off the root end as closely as possible. Cut the stalks off 3 to 4 inches from the stem end.

Preparation
BOILING

$1/2$-inch slices: Drop into boiling water. Simmer for 10 minutes.

Purée: For 1 medium bunch, trimmed, peeled and quartered, simmer for 20 to 25 minutes. If cut into eighths, simmer for 14 to 20 minutes. Purée. (Makes 1 cup)

STEAMING

Times are for standard celery stalks, which are fibrous. The tender inner stalks or hearts will cook more quickly.

$1 1/2$- x $1/4$-inch sticks: Place in a covered steamer basket. Cook 5 to 7 minutes, or until a knife easily slips into flesh.

2-inch pieces: Place in a covered steamer basket. Cook 15 to 20 minutes, or until a knife easily slips into flesh (pieces will not appear limp).

Whole stalks: Place in a covered steamer basket. Cook 15 to 20 minutes, or until a knife easily slips into flesh (stalks will not appear limp).

Hearts: Slice into quarters or halves and place in a covered steamer basket. If sliced into quarters, cook 10 minutes, or until a knife easily slips into flesh. If sliced into halves, cook 13 to 15 minutes.

MICROWAVING

1/4-inch slices: To steam celery, cook in a glass measuring cup in 1/2-cup quantities. Cover tightly.

 1 cup celery with 1 1/2 teaspoons water: 2 to 3 minutes
 2 cups celery with 1 tablespoon water: 5 to 6 minutes
 To sweat celery, cook in a 1-quart glass measure with unsalted butter that has been melted at
  100% for 2 minutes; cover tightly.
 1/2 cup celery with 2 teaspoons butter: 4 minutes
 1 cup celery with 1 tablespoon butter: 6 minutes
  15 seconds

Yields and Equivalents

CELERY

 1 medium bunch celery = 10 ounces
 1 large bunch celery = 2 pounds
 1 small celery stalk = 1 ounce
 1 medium celery stalk = 2 to 3 ounces
 1 large celery stalk = 4 ounces
 4 ounces celery (2 stalks), peeled and cut into
  1/4-inch slices = 1/2 cup
 8 ounces celery (4 stalks), peeled and cut into
  1/2-inch pieces = 2 cups raw = 1 cup cooked
 1 pound celery, peeled and cut into 2 x 1/4 x 1/4-inch
  slices = 2 cups
 1 pound celery, peeled and cut into 2 x 1/4 x 1/4 -inch
  strips = 3 cups

CHINESE CELERY

 1 bunch celery (3 to 4 heads) = 12 ounces
 5 celery stalks = 4 ounces = 3 ounces trimmed and
  leaves removed
 5 celery stalks, trimmed and leaves removed =
  2/3 cup thinly sliced raw = 1/3 cup cooked

Celery Root

Apium graveolens rapaceum

Celery root is not prepossessing. It is actually very ugly, with dirty brown, coarse, hairy skin. Peeling it is a bit of a problem, requiring a sharp knife and determination. The reward is the aromatic white flesh, whose texture is much like that of jicama although less starchy and not quite as crisp. If jicama is unavailable for Tex-Mex salads, celery root is a good substitute.

Varieties

I have never grown celery root and know nothing about its varieties. The major differences between them seem to be size and age.

Methods
BUYING AND STORING

This is a time when bigger is better. There will be less of the hard skin/rind in proportion to the soon-to-be revealed white interior.

 Trim off the top leaves, if any. Store celery root in the refrigerator. Protected by its tough rind, it will keep for a long time. Traditionally, for long storage, it was packed in sand and kept in a cool cellar.

WASHING/WAYS OF CUTTING

The best way to peel celery root is with a paring knife. Cut off the top leaves, if any. It is easier to peel if it is first cut into quarters lengthwise. Peel from the bottom to the top, trimming off the gnarled parts.

Preparation
BOILING

1/2-inch cubes: For 1 medium celery root, peeled and trimmed, cover with water by 1 inch. Bring to a boil. Simmer 10 minutes (20 to 25 minutes for purée).

 Wedges: For 1 medium celery root, peeled, trimmed and cut into eighths: Cover with water by 1 inch and bring to a boil. Simmer for 15 to 20 minutes.

STEAMING

3/4- to 1-inch cubes: For 1 medium celery root, peeled and trimmed, place in a covered steamer basket. Steam 15 to 20 minutes, or until a knife easily pierces flesh.

1/2-inch cubes: Steam 10 to 12 minutes.

ROASTING

1/2-inch wedges: For 1 medium celery root, peeled and trimmed, place in smallest pan that will hold celery root comfortably in a single layer. Slick celery root and pan with 2 teaspoons olive oil. Roast in center of a 500°F oven for 8 minutes. Turn. Roast 8 minutes more. Use a larger pan to multiply the recipe.

MICROWAVING

1/2-inch dice: Cook in a dish just large enough to hold the celery root in 2 layers. Cover tightly.

6 ounces celery root: 4 minutes

12 ounces celery root: 6 minutes

1 1/4 pounds celery root: 9 minutes

1 1/2 pounds celery root: 15 minutes

Yields and Equivalents

1 medium celery root = 11 ounces

1 large celery root = 1 1/4 pounds

1 medium celery root, peeled, trimmed and
cut into 1/2-inch dice = 1 1/4 cups raw = 3/4 cup
cooked = 1/2 cup purée

1 large celery root, peeled, trimmed and
cut into 1/2-inch dice = 2 1/2 cups raw =
1 1/2 cups cooked = 1 cup purée

CÈPES see Mushrooms, Fresh

CHANTERELLES see Mushrooms, Fresh

CHANTERELLES, BLACK see Trumpets of Death
under Mushrooms, Fresh

Chard
Beta vulgaris

Chard, or Swiss chard, is a member of the beet family. (See Beets, page 544.) The taste relationship will be most notable in red-stemmed chard. Both leaves and stems are cooked and eaten, often separately. The leaves are particularly popular in Italy and the South of France, where they are called, respectively, "bietole" and "blette."

The differences between chards are primarily of color. All will have green leaves, some darker, some lighter. The paler the stems, the less pronounced the beet flavor. For braising, wider stems are preferred. The stems continue as the midrib of the leaf. The designations have to do with stem color. For instance, rhubarb chard has red stems, Blonde de Lyon has a very large white stem. There are also yellow, cream- and orange-stemmed chards. Bright Lights and Rainbow chard have a mix of colors. Mixed bunches and seed packets are available (see Sources). They are a favorite of gardeners because they are decorative and grow from midsummer to frost.

Methods
BUYING AND STORING

When picking, cut whole heads or stalks at the bottom. The leaves, as with all greens, should be fresh and crisp. The stems must be firm and both need to be clear in color without spots. Separate stalks, if necessary, and rinse. Wrap loosely in damp paper towels, or prepare as below and store leaves and stalks separately.

WASHING/WAYS OF CUTTING

Remove the stems if cooking separately from the leaves. If the chard is young, the stems may simply be cut off. With older chard, it is better to fold the two sides of each leaf over the center rib and pull the leaf away from it with one hand while holding the bottom of the stem with the other hand. Alternatively, lay the leaf flat on a cutting surface. With a knife, make a V-shape cut along the rib to free it from the leaf.

Preparation

BOILING

Leaves, chopped: Cook in boiling water for 5 to 10 minutes, until tender.

Stems, in $^3/_4$-inch pieces: Bring water to a boil and add stems. Cover until water returns to a boil; uncover. Cook for 10 to 12 minutes, until a knife easily slips into flesh. Drain. Rinse under cold running water. Drain.

STEAMING

Stems: The delicate flavor of the white stems asks for a more subtle accompaniment than the hearty red. Eat them as a fall asparagus. Make up a luscious hollandaise (page 454) to go with them or serve with melted butter or, for a lighter taste, a lemony vinaigrette. Give at least 4 to 5 stems per person for a first course.

Trim stems to uniform lengths of about 7 to 8 inches. If larger and fibrous, string, like celery, with a vegetable peeler. Put stems in a covered steamer basket and cook for 12 to 15 minutes, until tender but not mushy. Drain well. Serve warm or tepid, with a sauce.

SAUTÉING/BRAISING

1 large bunch chard (about 12 ounces), leaves and stems separated; stems, if using, cut across into $^1/_4$-inch strips, leaves cut across into 1-inch strips (about 1$^1/_2$ cups stems and 6 cups leaves): Heat 1 tablespoon olive oil or vegetable oil in a deep 10-inch skillet or casserole over medium-high heat. Add stems, if using; cook, stirring constantly, until light brown, about 3 minutes. Add greens, season lightly with salt and stir until completely wilted and bright green, about 2 minutes. Add $^1/_4$ cup water, chicken stock or broth or vegetable broth and bring to a boil. Lower heat to medium, cover and cook until stems and leaves are tender, about 4 minutes. Uncover, increase heat to high and boil just until excess liquid is evaporated. Season with salt, if desired. (Makes about 1$^1/_2$ cups, including stems)

Yields and Equivalents

2 pounds chard = 1 pound leaves, 1 pound stems
1 medium bunch chard = 9 ounces = 5 cups leaves cut into 1-inch strips and 1 cup sliced stems
4 cups stems in $^3/_4$-inch pieces = 3 cups blanched = 2$^1/_2$ cups reheated or cooked longer
1 pound leaves = 1 cup cooked

CHAYOTE see Squash, Winter
CHEESE PUMPKIN see Squash, Winter
CHERRY PEPPERS see Peppers
CHERVIL see Herbs and Their Flowers
CHICKENS OF THE WOODS see Mushrooms, Fresh

Chicories

Chichorium intybus/Chichorium endivia

Chicories are not lettuces, but they are often used in salads on their own or with lettuces. Many of them are good for cooking. The names in English are confusing. What Americans call endive is what the Brits call Belgian endive or even chicory.

Many of the chicories are grown to be cut back and then blanched in a dark place, forming a second growth, a chicon. Some of these chicories, such as Belgian endive, will be white. Some of these second growths turn red, such as Verona and Treviso radicchios.

Varieties

CHICORY (*Chichorium intybus*) A green or red nonblanched chicory, which may have small thin leaves.

ENDIVE (*Chichorium intybus*) What Americans call endive is the pale green second growth of a chicory. We also call it Belgian endive, but the Belgians call it witloof and the English, chicory. We eat endive raw in salads, but it is also delicious cooked, as is common in Europe, as with other chicories, such as the red ones.

"REGULAR" RADICCHIO (*Chichorium intybus;* aka Verona) What supermarkets label as radicchio usually refers to this variety, the most commonly seen outside of Italy. It is round like a cabbage and dark red. It is often abused in the same way that red cabbage used to be, as a supplier of color in salads. Cook it or quarter it and treat with an enriched vinaigrette.

CHIOGGIA (*Chichorium intybus*) A round head that has green and red splotches. Unlike Verona and Treviso, it is not a second growth. It has rather tender leaves that are good in salad.

TREVISO (*Chichorium intybus*) My favorite variety of radicchio, Treviso has thin, pointy heads like Belgian endive, although the leaves are a good bit less tightly furled and usually longer; they are dark red. There is enormous variation in weight and length of heads among Trevisos available in the market. They do very well grilled or braised.

ESCAROLE (*Chichorium endivia*) What we call escarole is a floppy head of large leaves that are dark green with white veins. They can be tough and are often cooked in soup or with pasta rather than eaten raw.

FRISÉE (*Chichorium endivia*) A chicory popular among the French and the base of a basic bistro salad (see recipe on page 218). It grows in flattish heads. The inner leaves are white and the outer ones are green. The flattest heads are the best. Ideally, the heads are covered with little white hats as they grow to promote as much white growth as possible. The leaves are saw-toothed.

PUNTARELLE (*Chichorium intybus*) A more delicate version of frisée, eaten primarily in Italy at the end of winter. The thin—about a half inch across—leaves are almost white. They may be served simply with a dish of good olive oil, through which individual leaves are swished and eaten. If they are to be made into a salad, the individual leaves should be tossed with a minimum of a light vinaigrette to allow the flavor and texture to sing.

Methods

There are so many sorts and forms of chicory that it is hard to give general rules for buying or picking it. As with all greens, the leaves should be unblemished. The leaves of the chicon, second-growth, type should not be curling away from the head, which should be firm. The chicons should not be too large, or they will have developed too much core and not enough leaves.

WASHING/WAYS OF CUTTING

ENDIVE AND TREVISO RADICCHIO These are usually very clean. Just remove any outer wilted or browned leaves. There is a core that runs from the bottom up through the center; it can be eaten but is often discarded. Pull off whole leaves and discard the exposed core. Alternatively, slice each head in half lengthwise, and cut a V shape from each half to remove the core.

RADICCHIO (VERONA) Pull off the whole leaves and discard the stem. Alternatively, place the radicchio stem side up. With a knife, cut around the stem to remove it; discard.

FRISÉE AND ESCAROLE Pull off and discard any dark green wilted or damaged outer leaves. If the frisée leaves are large—and always with escarole—cut out the core and cut the remaining leaves into bite-size pieces. Wash, drain and spin dry in a salad spinner. Smaller frisée leaves should be used whole.

Preparation
ROASTING

ENDIVE *Whole heads:* Using a sharp small knife, trim around root end of each endive to remove any tough edges and brown spots. Place endives in smallest pan that will hold them comfortably. Slick endives and pan with fat. Roast on lowest level of a 500°F oven for 15 minutes. Turn. Roast 15 minutes more. Remove. Sprinkle endives lightly with stock or water. Serve hot or cold. (4 heads serve 2 as a side dish or first course)

TREVISO RADICCHIO Simply roasted, Treviso makes a good side dish with roasted veal, chicken or fish. One to two small halves or two to three large quarters will make a serving.

Halves or quarters: Place in smallest pan that will hold pieces comfortably in a single layer. Slick Treviso and pan generously with fat. Roast on lowest level of 500°F oven for 10 minutes. Turn. Roast 10 minutes more.

MICROWAVING

ENDIVE *Whole:* Braise in a dish just large enough to hold them. Cover tightly. You can vary the ingredients in the braising liquid (keep quantities and times the same).

2 heads with $1/3$ cup liquid: 8 minutes

8 heads with 1 cup liquid: 16 minutes

RADICCHIO (VERONA) When radicchio is cooked, it generally loses its beautiful red color. It retains more of it when cooked in the microwave oven.

Whole: Cook in a tightly sealed microwave-safe plastic bag.

1 pound radicchio: 5 minutes

2 pounds radicchio: 8 minutes

SAUTÉING/BRAISING

ESCAROLE *For 12 cups bite-size pieces escarole:* Heat 2 tablespoons olive oil or vegetable oil in a deep 10-inch skillet or casserole. Add 2 cloves garlic, smashed, peeled and sliced, if desired, and cook just until garlic starts to change color. Add escarole, season lightly with salt and cook until completely wilted and bright green, about 3 minutes. Serve as is for crunchy, slightly bitter escarole. For tender, less bitter escarole, add $1/4$ cup water, chicken stock or broth or vegetable broth and bring to a boil, then lower heat to simmering. Cook, uncovered, until liquid is evaporated and escarole is tender, about 4 minutes. Season with salt if necessary. (Makes 2 cups)

Yields and Equivalents

ENDIVE

1 large head = $3^{1}/_{2}$ ounces, cored = 2 ounces (10 leaves)

1 small head = $1^{1}/_{4}$ ounces, cored = $1/2$ ounce (4 leaves)

RADICCHIO

1 medium head = 4 ounces = 2 cups shredded

TREVISO RADICCHIO

5 small heads = $1^{3}/_{4}$ pounds

2 large heads = $1^{3}/_{4}$ pounds

FRISÉE

1 medium head = 6 ounces

1 medium head, trimmed and cut into 2-inch pieces = 8 cups

ESCAROLE

1 small head, cored and cut into 1-inch pieces = 10 ounces = 6 cups = 1 cup cooked

CHILACATE CHILIES see Peppers

CHILIES see Peppers

CHINESE BROCCOLI see Broccoli, Chinese

CHINESE CABBAGE see Napa Cabbage under Cabbages, Asian

CHINESE CELERY see Celery

CHINESE CHIVES see Chives under Herbs and Their Flowers

CHINESE EGGPLANT see Eggplants

CHINESE FLOWERING CABBAGE see Pak Choy under Cabbages, Asian

CHINESE KALE see Broccoli, Chinese

CHINESE MINIATURE CORN see Fresh Corn under Corn

CHIOGGIA BEETS see Beets

CHIOGGIA CHICORY see Chicories

CHIOGGIA RADICCHIO see Radicchio under Chicories

CHIPOTLES see Peppers

CHIVE FLOWERS see Herbs and Their Flowers

CHIVES See Herbs and Their Flowers

CHO CHO see Chayote under Squash, Winter

CHOY SUM see Pak Choy under Cabbages, Asian

CHRISTOPHENE see Chayote under Squash, Winter

Chrysanthemum Greens

Chrysanthemum coronarium

In the East, chrysanthemums are as much a vegetable as decoration. The jagged dark green leaves have a unique and intense flavor, with hints of parsley and celery, that has made it a favorite among the Chinese and Japanese.

The leaves look like those of our common garden chrysanthemum; but only the garland chrysanthemum (*Chrysanthemum coronarium*) is considered edible. It is called shungiku in Mandarin. In Cantonese, it is called tung ho. It is kikuma in Japan. The Hunanese stir-fry these leaves on their own, like spinach. Usually, though, they are eaten as part of a stir-fry unless they are very young, when they may be part of a raw dish. Bunches of leaves may look slightly sad and wilted but revive in cold water. Leaves should be removed from their stems. The smaller the leaves, the more tender. In the fall, the petals of the same flower are used to color rice and clear soup in Japan.

Methods
BUYING AND STORING

As with all fresh greens, the dark green leaves should not be spotted or very wilted. If they are slightly wilted, they will come back in cold water.

WASHING/WAYS OF CUTTING

Chrysanthemum leaves can be very dirty. Wash twice or as many times as necessary to remove all grit. Break apart the leaves and soak in cold water for several minutes. Lift out the leaves, drain and repeat.

Remove and discard the bottoms of the thick center stems. Cut leaves across into 1 1/2- to 2-inch pieces.

Preparation
SAUTÉING

1 1/2- to 2-inch pieces: For 2 packed cups (about 4 ounces): Heat 1 teaspoon oil in a pan. Add greens. Cook over medium heat for 2 to 3 minutes, continuously stirring from bottom, until leaves are bright green and wilted. (Makes 1/3 cup)

For 1 pound (about 8 packed cups): Increase oil to 2 tablespoons and cooking time to 4 to 5 minutes.

Yields and Equivalents

1 1/2 pounds chrysanthemum greens = 1 1/4 pounds leaves (12 cups packed) and 4 ounces stems

4 ounces chrysanthemum greens = 3 ounces trimmed

4 ounces chrysanthemum greens, trimmed and cut into 1 1/2- to 2-inch pieces = 2 packed cups raw = 1/3 cup cooked

CILANTRO see Herbs and Their Flowers
CIPPOLINI see Onions
COCO YAMS see Taro under Tropical Tubers

Collard Greens

Brassica acephala

Collards are a form of kale (see page 598) but with smoother leaves. They are found around the globe, but to me, they are intimately connected with the American South, where they are a long-cooking green often associated with some kind of cured or smoked pork. There is a wonderful book by Vertamae Smart-Grosvenor called *Vibration Cooking* that has a very funny story about collards. Try to find the book (see the Bibliography)—or ask me.

Methods
BUYING AND STORING

Collards should not be frayed or limp around the edges. They should be firm with a consistent green color. Store loosely wrapped in the refrigerator for up to 4 days. Since they are large, it may be preferable to stem the leaves and keep only the leaves in a bag. Do not wash or cut before storing.

WASHING/WAYS OF CUTTING

Separate the leaves from the stems either by hand or with a knife. Discard the stems; they are too fibrous to eat. Soak the leaves in cold water to remove dirt and grit. Lift out, drain and cut according to the recipe.

Preparation

Since collards are a kale, they cook in basically the same way. They also like to be cooked with fatback, bacon or other kinds of cured or smoked pork. Chris and I have included a recipe for braised collards (page 286) that is good and unconventional.

BOILING

Whole or cut: Add prepared collard leaves to boiling water and simmer 20 minutes.

STEAMING

3/4-inch strips: For 1 large bunch collards, or about 5 cups prepared leaves: Place in a covered steamer basket. Steam 15 minutes, or until wilted and tender.

MICROWAVING

Whole or cut: Cook with 1 cup liquid and 1/4 pound fatback in a 14 x 11 x 2-inch dish. (If you like your greens with ham hocks, cook the hocks first. Use 1 ham hock, along with its cooking liquid, to cook each 2 pounds of greens, and omit the fatback.) Cover tightly; uncover for last 5 minutes of cooking.

2 pounds collards: 30 minutes

PREPARATION FOR STUFFING

The leaves of collard greens are too small for stuffing in the same manner as cabbage. Layering the leaves together in a small mold or ramekin is the best technique.

Choose large leaves. Cut out center stem of each to form two leafy halves. Three to four halves are needed to line a 4-ounce ramekin. (A 4-ounce ramekin will hold 6 tablespoons stuffing.)

Bring water to a boil in a large wide pot. Add collard leaves, laying them flat in overlapping layers. Cook

15 minutes, pushing down on leaves periodically to keep them submerged. Cover, turn off heat and allow to sit 1 hour. Drain.

Oil as many 4-ounce ramekins as needed. Line each ramekin with 3 to 4 leaves, or enough to cover bottom and sides, leaving at least a 1 1/2-inch overhang. Divide stuffing evenly among ramekins, packing it down to fit. Fold leaves over toward center; stuffing should be completely covered. Brush tops with oil. Bake according to instructions for Timbale of Mushrooms, Collards and Ham on page 286. Unmold before serving.

Yields and Equivalents

2 pounds collard greens, stems removed =
   1 pound leaves
1 pound collard leaves, cut into 1 1/2- to 2-inch
   pieces = 13 cups raw = 3 cups cooked
4 ounces collard leaves, cut into 1/4-inch pieces =
   2 cups

CORAL MUSHROOMS see Mushrooms, Fresh
CORIANDER see Cilantro under Herbs and
   Their Flowers

Corn
Zea mays

Corn is a large subject, and I have had to divide the information into sections to make it at all useful. I start with fresh corn—my favorite—and go on to dried corn, dividing that into the various ways it is processed and sold. Corn may be prepared for cooking by drying, grinding or soaking in lye to remove the skin around the niblet. Thus we have cornstarch and corn flour (see page 574), grits (see page 45), and hominy. (A look at the Index may be the best way to find more information about each.) I think the only thing I have omitted is using the cobs for pipes and the silk for country kids to roll into cigarettes and smoke.

FRESH

Varieties

The corn that we eat is specially grown to be tender and sweet. There are other kinds that are used primarily for animal feed. For centuries, Europeans had a prejudice against corn for this reason. Also, they were probably confused by the fact that "corn" was the universal name for all grains. Maize, from the Central American name, is what our corn is called in Europe. Corn is actually a grass. There are also various colored corns: red and blue-black. Generally, they are more decorative than edible.

Like many other vegetables, corn hybridizes on the wind. This makes anything but the most general categories of identity hard to discuss. Now we have supersweet corns from seed companies. I loathe them—the supersweets, not the companies; but I do loathe the companies when they sell seeds that will not produce seeds that will grow in the following year.

My favorite corn is white with small niblets. My husband prefers yellow corn and eats with a care I have never seen in anybody else. He eats row by row, pulling out every last bit of the corn.

There is a disease of corn unalluringly called smuts or corn fungus. This fungus is huitlacoche, regarded as a great delicacy in Mexico. (For more information, see the Bibliography for Diana Kennedy and Rick Bayless.)

SWEET CORN Bred for consumption by humans.

FLOUR (SOFT OR SQUAW) CORN Easy to grind.

DENT CORN The most generally grown, accounting for 95 percent of production; this is the animal feed corn.

FLINT CORN Harder, as one might guess from the name, this makes good meal and stores better than other types.

POPCORN William Woys Weaver (see the Bibliography) is particularly good on all the corns, including popcorn. In Vermont, I have used dark red bear claw popcorn, named

for its shape. The easiest way to remove dried niblets from cobs is to run one up and down against the other lengthwise. They will act like graters.

BABY CORN (CHINESE MINIATURE) Ears of baby corn are not true babies but a variety of miniature corn that matures at 2 to 3 inches in length and has an edible cob. They are light and sweet with a pleasing crunch. Most of us have not cooked fresh miniature corn; instead, we use what comes jarred. Canned baby corn has long been a staple of Chinese cooking. Fresh is increasingly available.

CANNED OR FROZEN CORN I do not generally use canned or frozen corn. I never use frozen corn on the cob. However, it doesn't pay to be too snobbish; the Chinese often use canned creamed corn when making soup. I find that the small white kernels of canned shoepeg corn are a very good addition to first-course winter salads such as lobster. I avoid frozen corn unless I have put it up myself.

Methods

BUYING AND STORING

Buying or picking corn can be an iffy business. One wants the ears to be plump with kernels but not over the hill. The silk should be glossy, not dried out. Pulling down the husks is frowned upon by all merchants, as the ear will dry out or rot. The best thing to do is to feel the corn and see if it seems full. If it is your own corn, getting it before the raccoons can be iffy-er than buying. Good luck.

As for storage: Don't. Corn is only really good when freshly picked. The longer it is kept, the more the natural sugars turn to starch. If a garden yields too much or there is such a good buy that it cannot be resisted, cut off the niblets (see below) and boil for 1 minute; cool and freeze, or make relish (page 40).

WASHING/WAYS OF CUTTING

CORN The husks and silk protect the corn from dirt and damage. Unless roasting, microwaving or grilling on the cob, prepare by removing the husks. Pull off the silk. If cooking corn on the cob, it may be a good idea to snap or cut off protruding pieces of stalk—more room in the pot. If roasting or grilling whole, it may be a good idea to use the husks as insulation. Pull them back but not off, and remove the silk. If desired, slick the corn with butter (can be flavored) and gather the husk-clothes around the corn's nakedness. If the grill fire is very hot, dampen the husks with water. For more detail, see page 518.

To remove the kernels, run a thin knife down all sides of the cob from tip to base with the knife blade against the cob. Be careful not cut so deeply as to include part of the cob.

To remove the pulp without the kernels (for use in creamed corn, see page 32, and other recipes): Cut through the center of each kernel by running the knife down the center of the row, splitting the kernels in half. Then turn the knife over and, using the blunt edge, scrape the corn innards into a bowl.

To make rounds of corn for simmering in soups or stews (see Cazuela de Elsa Tobar, page 36): Shuck the corn and remove the silk. Lay each ear on a flat surface. Hold the ear steady with one hand and, with a large sharp knife, make a quick cut through corn and cob.

BABY CORN Remove the husks. Pull off the silk. Trim any stem.

Preparation

All corn should be cooked until the tip of a knife can pierce the cob, but not until it is soft.

BOILING

CORN *Corn on the cob:* Bring a large pot of water to a boil. Add husked corn and cook 2 to 3 minutes. Serve immediately. Or, if using in another recipe, rinse under cold running water and proceed with the recipe. Alternatively, bring an inch of water to a boil. Add corn, cover with a kitchen towel and the lid and cook until done. Turn off heat and leave corn in pot; serve when ready.

Kernels: Bring a pan of water to a boil. Add kernels. Cook 1 1/2 to 2 minutes.

BABY CORN *Whole:* Bring a pot of water to a boil. Add husked corn. Cook 2 minutes, or until softened but still crisp. Rinse under cold running water. Reheat if desired.

STEAMING

CORN *Corn on the cob:* Place husked corn in a covered steamer basket. Cook 10 minutes. Kernels will yield slightly to pressure.

Kernels: Place on a plate in a covered steamer basket. Cook 4 to 5 minutes. Kernels will yield slightly to pressure.

BABY CORN Corn steamed in the husk will have a slightly different flavor from corn that is husked and then steamed. Try both to decide which is preferred.

Corn in the husk: Place corn in a single layer in a covered steamer basket. Steam 3 minutes. Rinse under cold running water. Remove husks and silk. Trim stems if needed.

Husked corn: Place corn in a single layer in a covered steamer basket. Steam 2 to 3 minutes. Rinse under cold running water.

MICROWAVING

For corn on the cob, with husks and silk intact: Place in a single layer on a carousel or platter. Dampen husks slightly. Cook uncovered.

1 ear: 2 minutes

2 ears: 5 minutes

4 ears: 9 minutes

6 ears: 14 minutes

GRILLING

There are two approaches: Shuck the corn or grill it in the husk. (See Grilling, page 518, for preparing the grill.)

For shucked corn: To reproduce a favorite street food of Central America, remove husks and all traces of silk. Rub ears lightly with vegetable oil (they will be buttered and seasoned later). Grill corn over moderately hot coals until well browned on all sides and blackened in spots, about 8 minutes. Brush with butter and sprinkle with salt.

For corn grilled in the husk: The simplest way to grill corn in the husk is to soak whole ears in cold water to cover for 1 hour. Drain thoroughly and grill over moderately hot coals until husks are blackened and kernels are tender, about 30 minutes. But dealing with charred husks and silk can be tricky. A more elegant approach is to bend back corn husks one at a time, starting with the outermost pieces and being careful not to break them off. Rub off corn silk. Spread

2 teaspoons butter, plain or seasoned (see pages 35 and 443) over each ear before re-covering corn with its husks, this time working from the innermost pieces out. Secure husks in place with a piece of twine tied around tip of each ear. Soak corn in water to cover for at least 30 minutes. Grill as above until husks are well charred.

Yields and Equivalents

Corn will vary significantly in size and therefore in yield. At midsummer, my garden consistently produces corn weighing 6 to 8 ounces each. By end of summer and early fall, each fat and juicy ear weighs an average of 12 ounces—quite a difference.

CORN

1 pound corn in the husk = 2 to 3 medium ears

1 $^1/_2$ pounds corn in the husk = 2 large ears

2 medium ears corn = 6 ounces kernels = 1 cup raw

2 medium ears corn = $^1/_2$ cup pulp

1 large ear corn = 7 ounces kernels = 1 $^1/_4$ cups raw

$^1/_2$ cup kernels = scant $^1/_2$ cup cooked

One 10-ounce box frozen corn kernels = 1 $^1/_2$ cups

1 medium ear corn = $^1/_4$ to $^1/_3$ cup (depending on juiciness of the corn) raw creamed corn

1 large ear corn = $^2/_3$ cup (depending on juiciness of the corn) raw creamed corn

BABY CORN

12 baby corn in the husk = 9 $^1/_2$ ounces = 4 $^1/_2$ ounces husked and trimmed = $^3/_4$ cup

One 15-ounce can baby corn = 16 to 18 pieces

CANNED AND FROZEN CORN

Fortunately, the exact amount of canned corn used doesn't make a huge difference to a recipe. "Fortunately," because can sizes and amount in a can vary from brand to brand. This is the kind of vagary that can drive an exacting recipe writer batty.

There are basically two sizes of cans, small and large—but the amount of corn isn't consistent between brands. For creamed corn, we found weights of everywhere from 8 $^1/_4$ ounces to 15 ounces. Niblets varied between 7 ounces to just over 15 ounces. The largest can of niblets (15 $^1/_4$ ounces) yields just over 1 $^1/_2$ cups kernels.

DRIED AND HOMINY

Varieties

CORNMEAL This is simply dried corn ground to make a flour. It may be white, yellow or even blue and it varies in fineness. Italians use a relatively coarse grind to make polenta. I find that polenta works equally well made with the finer American grind. Americans used to call it cornmeal mush until we all got so sophisticated; I suppose "mush" doesn't sound as attractive as "polenta." If you think of it as mush, maybe you will think of it as hot cereal to serve with maple syrup, especially since in a microwave oven it is so quickly made without lumps or endless stirring. Becoming more prevalent is "instant" polenta, which cooks in about 5 minutes. Not bad, but it lacks the character of the traditional type.

There are various grades of cornmeal. Stone-ground is better. Rhode Island and the rest of the North prefer white cornmeal. The South prefers yellow. Blue cornmeal, actually grayish, is increasingly available. In addition to mush, cornmeal is used for pone, johnnycakes, corn dodgers, chips and various kinds of baked goods.

CORNSTARCH Extremely finely ground—to a powder—cornmeal that is used as a thickener for sauces. It is particularly useful in that it can be stirred into a small amount of hot liquid that is then stirred back into the sauce or stew. Thicken just before serving; cooking for more than a few minutes will thin the sauce. Two teaspoons cornstarch dissolved in 1 $^1/_2$ tablespoons liquid will thicken approximately 1 cup liquid, depending on how thick or thin the liquid is to begin with. It is also used by leaving an open box, as one does baking powder, in the refrigerator to absorb untoward smells. And I have known many chefs who dusted their bodies with it to help with the chafing from the extreme heat of the kitchen.

MASA The Mexican and Central American version of ground cornmeal, usually used to make tortillas. I have been in somewhat primitive tortilla factories when women arrived with baskets of dried corn niblets. These are weighed, then they are ground and turned by machine into fresh tortillas, which are again weighed and returned to the woman who brought the corn.

TORTILLAS A flat grain cake much like a crêpe in appearance. Patted out or pressed rather than rolled as cornmeal, it doesn't have the elastic properties of doughs made with wheat flour. While they can be bought fresh in commercial packages, increasingly, due to the vast Mexican populations in our cities, a search will generally find very good fresh handmade tortillas. Corn tortillas are often fried to make taco shells and tortilla chips. There are special baskets used to form and fry the taco shells. I am happy to use store-bought and reheat them slightly in the oven. Tortillas can also be made from wheat flour.

HOMINY Hominy is processed dried corn kernels. The dried kernels are soaked in lye to loosen the skin. After extensive washing to remove the skin and all traces of lye, the popped interior is dried. Hominy is extensively used in posole in the American Southwest. I use it in a fine Ecuadoran soup (page 42) as well as an invention that I really like on page 43. It is available dried, loose and cooked in cans. As a matter of convenience, I deal exclusively with canned hominy.

GRITS Grits are made by grinding dried hominy. The best is black-heart, or speckled-heart, grits that have the germ left in. Grits can be used at breakfast and as a side dish. In the South, grits take the singular verb: Grits is good.

Methods
STORAGE
Keep cornmeal, polenta and grits in sealed containers in a cool, dark place.

Yields and Equivalents
CORNMEAL
$1/2$ cup cornmeal = 2 ounces

GRITS
3 tablespoons dry grits = $2/3$ cup cooked

1 cup dry grits = 4 cups cooked
HOMINY
One 15-ounce can = approximately 2 cups drained and rinsed

CORNICHONS see Cucumbers
CORN SALAD LETTUCE see Mâche under Lettuces
CORONA BEANS see Beans of the New World under Beans
COS LETTUCE see Romaine under Lettuces
COURGETTES see Squash, Summer
COWPEAS see Peas
CRAMBE see Sea Kale
CRANBERRY BEANS see Beans of the New World under Beans
CREAMER POTATOES see Potatoes
CREMINI see Mushrooms, Fresh
CRESS SPROUTS see Sprouts
CRISPHEAD LETTUCE see Iceberg under Lettuces
CROOKNECK SQUASH see Squash, Summer
CUBANELLES see Peppers
CUBAN PEPPERS see Peppers

Cucumbers
Cucumis sativa

While most of the other members of this large family, which includes the pumpkins and squash, are American in derivation, cucumbers seem to have originated in India. (Another member of the clan—edible gourds—came from Africa and Asia.) The English hybridized cucumbers into a hothouse vegetable. America seems to have specialized in cucumbers for pickling. The French particularly like the tiny cucumbers that they call cornichons and Americans call gherkins. Those cucumbers derive from a light-colored Indian strain. Cucumbers come in many shades, from yellow (lemon cucumbers) and white to very dark green, almost black. They also may be of many shapes, although we are accustomed to seeing the longish cylindrical kind. I've grown many and like few. It may be that I like the ones I do just because I know them.

The peoples of the Germanic and Scandinavian countries like field-grown cucumbers for use in salads. India still uses a wide variety of cucumbers for a wide variety of dishes. Among the breakfast pickles served in Japan, I have sometimes found a cucumber.

Varieties

REGULAR (ORDINARY MARKET CUCUMBERS) Usually wax-coated, with shiny, smooth dark green skin and large seeds. Peel before eating.

KIRBY Bumpy pale to deep green skin with small seeds and crunchy texture. Kirbys are not waxed and have no shine; typically used for pickles.

ENGLISH Long, narrow, straight and usually unwaxed but shrink-wrapped in a glove of plastic, these should have no true seeds; also known as hothouse or seedless cucumbers.

CORNICHON A very small variety of cucumber, picked at 1 1/2 to 2 1/2 inches. They have very rough vines and I sometimes wear gloves to pick them. It is important to pick up the vines and check under the leaves or the result will quickly be large cucumbers. Cornichons are usually pickled.

Methods

BUYING (OR PICKING) AND STORING

Cucumbers should be firm, without soft spots or blemishes. It is better to go for smaller rather than longer, as the seeds will be less prominent and there will be fewer of them. When picking from the garden, it is important to search carefully so as not to let them escape and become monsters.

They need to be kept in the refrigerator to remain crisp. Use as soon as possible.

WASHING/WAYS OF CUTTING

Kirby cucumbers do not need to be peeled. To prepare, rinse well under cold running water and trim both ends. For all other cucumbers, trim both ends and remove the skin with a vegetable peeler. If the cucumber has seeds, slice it in half lengthwise and use a spoon to scoop them out. Or make a V-shaped cut toward the center of each half and pull them out. Cucumbers can be cut into chunks or thinly sliced with a knife, on a mandoline or with one of the newer cutters.

If cucumbers are to be salted, which will make them slightly limp but removes all bitterness, they are usually sprinkled with salt and allowed to sit for at least thirty minutes before being well rinsed in cold water. I find that they stay crisper if placed in fairly heavily salted water for slightly longer and then rinsed. That way, they are less limp.

To make cucumber boats for stuffing: Trim ends (thinly) and cut a medium (5- to 6-inch) Kirby cucumber in half lengthwise. Scoop out seeds with a teaspoon. Peel or not, as desired, but in either case, remove a thin strip of flesh from underside of each boat so it will sit steady on a plate before stuffing. Each half of a Kirby cucumber of this size will hold 1/3 cup filling, such as Quintessential Tuna Salad (page 499), for example.

Preparation

STEAMING

1/4-inch slices or matchsticks: Place in a covered steamer basket. Cook 5 minutes, or until cucumber is tender but retains some firmness.

SAUTÉING

Kirby cucumbers, peeled, halved lengthwise, seeded and cut across into 1/4-inch slices: For 3 cucumbers (2 1/4 cups): Heat 2 teaspoons vegetable oil in a 10-inch skillet over medium-high heat. Add cucumber and cook, tossing often, until browned in spots and crisp-tender, about 5 minutes. Season with salt and pepper. For more tender, buttery cucumbers, add 1 tablespoon unsalted butter, cut into pieces and cook and toss 1 minute longer. (Makes 1 1/4 cups)

Yields and Equivalents

REGULAR CUCUMBER

1 small cucumber = 3 ounces

1 medium cucumber = 6 ounces

1 large cucumber = 8 ounces

1 medium cucumber, trimmed, peeled, halved, seeded and cut into $^1/_4$-inch dice = $^1/_2$ cup

8 ounces cucumbers, trimmed, peeled and cut into $^1/_4$-inch slices = 1 cup

12 ounces cucumbers, trimmed, peeled, seeded and shredded = $^1/_2$ cup

3 pounds cucumbers, trimmed, peeled, halved and seeded = 1 $^3/_4$ pounds in $^1/_4$-inch dice = 5$^1/_2$ cups

KIRBY CUCUMBER

1 small cucumber = 1 to 2 ounces

1 medium cucumber = 3 to 4 ounces

1 large cucumber = 5 ounces

1 medium cucumber, cut into $^1/_8$-inch slices = $^3/_4$ cup

CORNICHONS

30 cornichons = 1 cup = about 6 ounces

CURLY LEAF PARSLEY see Parsley under Herbs and Their Flowers

CUSHA see Squash, Winter

CUSQUEÑOS see Peppers

DAIKON see Radishes

Dandelion Greens

Taraxacum officinale

Those of us who garden may find it inconceivable that the English settlers actually were so nostalgic for dandelions they imported them to America, where they have escaped from gardens to become an omnipresent pest. There are days in a damp spring when the huge golden yellow flower heads are somewhat seductive, even though I know what will happen as they go to seed, forming lighter-than-air round balls of seeds that waft as they will on any passing breeze. The best solution is the same as that for sorrel. Weed them out early, pull or cut off the roots; wash the green saw-toothed leaves and use quickly.

Dandelion greens were commonly used as a diuretic, accounting for the French name pise-en-lit, or "wet your bed." However, they are also extremely nutritious.

The younger they are, the better when used as salad greens. They are very good with endive and/or beets. Older and larger, they get more bitter and lend themselves better to cooking. Mow, and then pick the new growth. They can be used interchangeably with arugula and nettles in cooked dishes. I recently had them as a horta (see below) in a Greek restaurant.

HORTA There are probably as many kinds of horta as there are cooks in Greece—possibly even more, due to the seasonal variations of the weeds or other leaves available. In *The Foods of the Greek Islands* (see the Bibliography), the invaluable Aglaia Kremezi even mentions one made in arid summertime from amaranth shoots. While bitter greens such as the mustards are preferred—and dandelion certainly fits here—they can range from purslane to pea shoots to young spinach to orach, escarole, beet greens, chicory, watercress, nettles and other weeds.

The greens can be either boiled or, more elegantly, steamed in a pan, turned over frequently in the liquid adhering to them after washing, until they are tender. Then they are drained and the liquid saved for other cooking or drunk as a health boost. The greens shrink like crazy, so it takes about two and a half pounds to feed four. After cooking, they are dosed with olive oil, about a third of a cup for that amount of greens, lemon juice, salt, possibly a crushed clove of garlic and a sprinkling of crushed good dried oregano. Horta is usually served warm or at room temperature as a first course or as a salad.

Methods

BUYING AND STORING

Well, I have never bought a dandelion and never expect to, nor do I expect to intentionally grow them. Random gifts of nature provide me with more than I need. The only important thing is to try to find the greens at places other than the edge of the road, due to icky exhausts. Use them soon after picking, avoiding any stems or discolored leaves.

WASHING/WAYS OF CUTTING

Remove the stems. Wash several times in a sink full of water. Unless they are larger than desirable, they need not be cut or torn.

Preparation

The following methods are best for larger, more bitter dandelion greens. Eat young tender leaves in salad.

STEAMING

Remove thick tough stems and cut leaves across into 2-inch lengths or leave them whole. Wash in a sink full of cold water and drain in a colander. Do not pat them dry or spin in a salad spinner; the water that clings to the leaves provides the liquid for steaming. Transfer to a wide skillet or pan large enough to hold them and turn heat to high. When steam starts to rise from bottom, season dandelions very lightly with salt and lower heat to medium-low. Cover pan and cook 4 minutes, turning greens occasionally. Uncover and check for doneness; if still a little tough, cover and cook a minute or two more. Drain off any liquid in pan to drink separately, or raise heat to boil it off. Season with salt and any or all of the following: olive oil, crumbled dried oregano (preferably Greek), a squeeze of lemon juice and crushed garlic.

BOILING

Best for greens that will be added to other dishes, such as horta.

Stir trimmed and washed whole leaves into a large pot of boiling salted water. Cook, stirring once or twice, until tender and bright green color starts to fade, about 5 minutes, or longer for really large greens. Drain immediately.

SAUTÉING

Older, tougher leaves, thick stems removed, leaves cut across into 2-inch lengths or left whole: For 2 large bunches (about 1 pound), trimmed and cut into 2-inch pieces: Heat 1 1/2 tablespoons olive oil in an 11- to 12-inch pan over medium heat. Add 2 cloves garlic, crushed, peeled and chopped, and/or 3 anchovy fillets, if desired.

Cook, stirring, until garlic starts to brown. Add dandelions. Stir until bright green. Season lightly with salt (very lightly if using anchovies). Reduce heat to medium-low, cover and cook 4 minutes. Check for doneness. If still tough, add 1 to 2 tablespoons water, cover and cook 2 to 3 minutes longer. Season with pepper and serve. (Makes about 2 cups)

Yields and Equivalents

> 3 ounces tender young dandelion greens = 4 cups lightly packed = 1/2 cup cooked
>
> 2 bunches large, long dandelion greens = 14 ounces = 10 ounces trimmed leaves
>
> 2 bunches large, long dandelion greens, stemmed and cut across into 2-inch pieces = 8 cups lightly packed raw = 1 1/3 cups cooked

DASHEEN see Taro under Tropical Tubers
DASHIN see Yams under Sweet Potatoes and Yams
DATIL see Peppers
DELICATA SQUASH see Squash, Winter
DENT CORN see Fresh Corn under Corn
DILL see Herbs and Their Flowers

Dock

Rumex obtusifolius

This was revealed to me as an edible by Sheila, an Indian woman who cooked for the John Kenneth Galbraiths. Dock is the nasty weed in lawns with hard oval leaves of dark green. Sheila used them in a curry. I have read that they can be used in salad, but I wouldn't try them—too tough, although the other day I did find some very young leaves and they could be chewed and swallowed. They have a faintly curry taste.

Methods
WASHING/WAYS OF CUTTING

Rinse thoroughly and cut across into thin strips. Sauté to add to curries or add raw very young basal leaves, also cut up, to salad.

DUERTE AVOCADOS see Florida under Avocados

EDAMAME see Beans from Asia under Beans

EDDO see Taro under Tropical Tubers

Eggplants
Solanum melongena

I think I have run on at length on eggplants, starting on page 322. The one point I reiterate is that they must be fully cooked or they can be nauseating.

Varieties

LARGE PURPLE The kind generally available in America; they can weigh up to 5 pounds, but are best up to 1 1/2 pounds.

SMALL PURPLE Also known as Japanese eggplants, these are miniature versions of large purple eggplants. The best are 3 to 4 inches long.

CHINESE Long curved eggplants that go from a narrow stem end to a slightly wider end. They are usually bright lavender but are also available (rarely) all white, or white blushing to lavender at the thicker end.

FINGER Cylinders about 1 inch in diameter, these are about 5 inches long. They grow in clusters and follow the general rules for Chinese eggplants. Sliced across, the rounds will be more uniform.

JAPANESE Small (3 to 4 ounces each), purple and shaped like an asymmetrical pear. Substitute miniature eggplants for small Japanese eggplants and Chinese eggplants for larger ones.

MINIATURE About 2 inches long and under 1 inch in diameter, these are usually preserved in oil or pickled.

Methods
BUYING AND STORING

No matter what their color or shape, pick—from either the garden or the store—fruits that are glossy, that do not have brown spots on their skins and that feel firm to the touch; the calyx, the leaves at the top, should not be curling up but adhering to the eggplant.

WASHING/WAYS OF CUTTING

Since their skin should be intact, only the most cursory washing is needed. Recipes generally give indications for cutting.

Some recipes call for peeled eggplant. The easiest way is with a vegetable peeler. If it doesn't work well, either the peeler is old and not sharp (they are cheap; be a sport and buy a new one) or the eggplant is old. In that case, roast the eggplant for its pulp.

For roasting, frying or sautéing, halved eggplants can have their flesh scored to aid in penetration of a marinade or of seasonings that are rubbed in. Place each half skin side down. With a very sharp pointed knife, score the flesh in a diamond pattern down to the skin, being careful not to cut through the skin.

Preparation
SALTING EGGPLANTS

As they can be bitter—having many alkaloids in them—large eggplants are commonly salted and allowed to sit with a weight on top to extract moisture and bitterness. Soaking the eggplants in salt water as many Greeks and Albanians do will produce even better results. If they have been salted, rinse well and pat dry. If they are very young, still slightly green under the calyx, though, they do not need salting at all.

Slice eggplant according to the recipe. If salting, put slices in a large bowl in enough water to cover them. Generously salt the water, about a handful of kosher salt for every 2 quarts of water. Swish gently to dissolve salt. Let soak for 30 minutes. Drain, rinse and pat dry with paper towels.

ROASTING

When roasting eggplant, there is a choice of recipe and technique. Eggplants that are 3 to 4 ounces can be roasted whole or cut in half lengthwise. Eggplants from 4 to 8 ounces should be cut in half lengthwise and roasted 25 to 30 minutes. Eggplants weighing more than 8 ounces do not roast well when cut in half, as their flesh develops a custardy texture. They need to be cut across into 1/2-inch-thick slices and roasted for 30 minutes, with the slices turned over every 10 minutes for even browning. Large eggplants may be roasted whole when the puréed flesh is desired for dips and soups.

LARGE PURPLE *Whole* (1 to 1 1/2 pounds): Put eggplant (usually no more than 2 at a time if cooking more than 1) on an ungreased baking sheet. Bake in center of 400°F oven for approximately 1 1/2 hours, or until eggplant bursts and center becomes very tender. As eggplant becomes fully cooked, it will deflate like a pricked balloon and skin will char slightly. This is ugly but correct.

Remove eggplant from oven and immediately, using two forks, tear it open. Scrape out pulp onto hot baking sheet. Let it sizzle and brown slightly, to help some of the juices evaporate. Discard skin. Remove pulp to a bowl and continue to shred it finely with forks. Pulp can be puréed in a food processor or blender, but the seeds will get crushed and mixture may become bitter.

Large eggplant slices: Trim ends from eggplant. Cut across into 1/2-inch-thick slices. Place slices in smallest pan that will hold them comfortably. Slick slices and pan generously with fat. Roast in center of 500°F oven for 10 minutes. Turn. Roast 10 minutes more. (1 to 1 1/2 pounds eggplant serve 3 to 4 as a side dish)

Medium eggplant halves: It is a nice idea to add a bit of flavor to whatever fat you are using. Crushed garlic or a mixture of fresh or dried herbs would be a good addition. Citrus juice, pomegranate juice, white wine, vinegar, sherry or vermouth is delicious as a basting liquid.

Cut 8-ounce eggplants in half lengthwise, calyx removed or not. Place halves, cut side down, in smallest pan that will hold them comfortably. Slick halves and pan generously with fat; add optional seasonings, if desired. Add 2 tablespoons liquid. Roast in center of 500°F oven

for 25 minutes. (8 eggplants serve 8 as a side dish, 4 as a first course)

BABY PURPLE, JAPANESE AND CHINESE

Small eggplant halves: Cut 4-ounce eggplants in half lengthwise. Place halves, cut side down, in smallest pan that will hold them comfortably. Slick halves and pan generously with fat. Add 2 tablespoons stock, white wine, vinegar, sherry or vermouth. Roast in center of 500°F oven for 10 minutes. Turn halves over. Roast 15 minutes more. (8 eggplants serve 8 as a side dish, 4 to 5 as a first course)

Whole, small (baby or small Japanese eggplants): Place whole 3-ounce eggplants in smallest pan that will hold them comfortably. Slick eggplants and pan with fat. Roast in center of 500°F oven for 15 minutes. Shake pan to turn eggplant. Roast for 10 minutes more. (8 eggplants serve 4 to 8 as a side dish)

OVEN-GRILLED

This method gives the look of grilled vegetables without the hassle of firing up the grill. Soaking the eggplant beforehand gets rid of any bitter flavor from baking in the oven.

Cut 1 large eggplant (about 1 1/2 pounds) crosswise into 1/2-inch slices. Soak in salt water (see page 579); drain and pat dry.

Meanwhile, place a completely metal (no plastic covering at all) cooling rack with wires running parallel to one another (not a mesh rack) on a baking sheet. Heat cooling rack and baking sheet in a 500°F oven for at least 20 minutes.

When oven, wire rack and baking sheet have heated through, slick both sides of eggplant slices with 1/4 cup olive oil. Brush wire rack generously with olive oil. Place as many eggplant slices as will fit on rack. Cook, turning once, for 10 minutes on each side. Remove from oven and let cool. Repeat with any remaining slices. Season with salt and pepper to taste. (Makes about 20 slices)

BASIC OIL-BLANCHED EGGPLANT

Often the Chinese, rather than cooking eggplant entirely as part of a dish, briefly oil blanch it first without cooking it all the way through. The eggplant is then ready to be included in a dish. It can be done ahead.

Heat 3 cups canola oil in a $2^{1}/_{2}$-quart saucepan to 325°F. Meanwhile, trim 4 Chinese eggplants (about $1^{1}/_{2}$ pounds) and cut across into 1-inch rounds, or cut in half lengthwise and across into $^{1}/_{2}$-inch semicircles.

Fry eggplants in 3 batches, 2 to 3 minutes per batch if using 1-inch pieces, 1 to 2 minutes per batch if using $^{1}/_{2}$-inch pieces, or until lightly browned and a knife point slips into center. Remove to a plate or container lined with paper towels to drain. (Makes 3 cups)

FRIED EGGPLANT CUBES

Good in pasta sauces or as a nibble.

Cut off and discard stems from two 1-pound eggplants, then cut eggplants into 1-inch cubes (leaving skin on). Place in a bowl and toss lightly with kosher salt. Weight down with a plate or other heavy object for 30 minutes. Drain well and blot dry.

Fill a deep pot with vegetable oil to a depth of 4 to 5 inches. Heat to 375°F. Lightly dust eggplant cubes with cornstarch. Deep-fry for 3 minutes, or until browned on all sides. Drain on paper towels. (Serves 6 to 8)

MICROWAVING

Eggplant comes into its own in the microwave oven. Now, it is true that you will not get a charred taste cooking it this way, nor can you fry it in the microwave oven, but you will get a lightness of taste and lack of bitterness. The skin on whole eggplants—pricked a few times so the vegetables don't explode while cooking—have a nicer color than those of eggplants cooked any other way. And the flesh stays a lovely pale green that is attractive for dips.

LARGE PURPLE EGGPLANTS *Whole:* Prick each eggplant several times with tip of a knife. Put on double thickness of paper towels in bottom of the oven or on the carousel. Cook, uncovered, at 100%, or until eggplant deflates.

8 ounces: 8 minutes
1 pound: 12 minutes
$1^{1}/_{2}$ pounds: 15 minutes
2 pounds: 19 minutes
$2^{1}/_{2}$ pounds: 22 minutes
3 pounds: 45 minutes

JAPANESE EGGPLANTS *Halved and stuffed:* Cover tightly.

Six 4-inch-long eggplants, halved (9-inch pie plate); stuff after 3 minutes: 7 minutes

CHINESE EGGPLANTS *Whole:* Prick several times with a fork. Cook in a dish just large enough to hold them; cover tightly.

8 ounces: 10 to 12 minutes
1 pound: 15 minutes

MICROWAVE EGGPLANT PURÉE

Puncture a large (about $1^{1}/_{2}$ pounds) eggplant several times with a fork. Place on top of a double layer of paper towels. Cook, uncovered, at 100% for 14 minutes. Let eggplant sit for 5 minutes. Cut in half lengthwise; scoop out pulp and purée in the blender until smooth. (Makes $1^{1}/_{2}$ cups purée)

GRILLING

See Grilling, page 518, for how to prepare the grill.

LARGE PURPLE EGGPLANT Remove calyx and cut eggplant(s) lengthwise into $^{1}/_{3}$-inch slices. Rub both sides of slices with vegetable oil and season with salt and pepper. Or brush both sides with one of the marinades on pages 519–520. Let stand at room temperature 30 minutes to 1 hour before grilling.

Grill, turning once, until well browned on both sides and tender, about 8 minutes.

JAPANESE OR CHINESE EGGPLANT Leave calyx on or remove. Slice each eggplant in half lengthwise. Score flesh in a deep crosshatch pattern, but not through to skin. Rub with vegetable oil and season with salt and pepper, or brush on one of the marinades on pages 519–520. Let stand 30 minutes to 1 hour before grilling.

Grill, cut side down, until well browned, about 6 minutes. Flip eggplant halves, move to edges of grill and cover grill. Cook until tender, about 5 minutes.

PREPARATION FOR STUFFING

To make eggplant shells: Slice eggplant(s) in half lengthwise. Slice a crosshatch pattern into flesh of each eggplant half, cutting as deep as possible without piercing skin. Run a small knife (a flexible boning knife works best) along inside perimeter of each eggplant half, leaving a thin border about 1/8 inch thick all around. Scoop out flesh.

To make cooked eggplant shells in the oven: For baby and Japanese eggplant, prepare eggplant shells as above. Preheat oven to 350°F. Brush insides of shells with oil. Place on a baking sheet and bake in 350°F oven for 15 minutes. Allow shells to cool before stuffing.

For large purple eggplant, place whole eggplant(s) on baking sheet and bake in 350°F oven for 12 minutes. Flip eggplant. Bake 12 minutes. Flip eggplant. Bake another 12 minutes. Let sit until cool enough handle.

Cut eggplant(s) lengthwise in half. Remove pulp, leaving 1/4-inch shells.

To make cooked eggplant shells in the microwave: Puncture whole eggplant(s) several times with a fork. Place on a paper towel in microwave. Cook at 100% for 14 minutes. Remove from oven and let sit for 5 minutes.

Cut eggplant(s) lengthwise in half. Remove pulp, leaving 1/4-inch shells.

Each half of a small 5-inch-long Japanese eggplant (5 ounces) will hold 1/3 cup mounded stuffing.

Each half of a large (1 1/2-pound) eggplant will hold 1 1/4 cups slightly mounded stuffing.

Each quarter of a large (1 1/2-pound) eggplant will hold 1/2 cup slightly mounded stuffing.

Yields and Equivalents

LARGE PURPLE EGGPLANT

1 large eggplant = 1 1/2 pounds = 1 1/2 cups cooked purée

1 medium eggplant = 1 1/4 pounds

1 medium eggplant, peeled and cut into 1/2-inch cubes = 4 1/2 cups

1 medium eggplant, cut lengthwise into 1/8-inch slices = 12 to 14 slices

SMALL PURPLE EGGPLANT

1 small eggplant (up to 8 ounces) = about 1/2 cup cooked purée

One 8-ounce eggplant, cut lengthwise into 1/8-inch slices = about 6 slices

CHINESE EGGPLANT

4 Chinese eggplants = 1 1/2 pounds = 1 1/3 cups cooked purée

JAPANESE EGGPLANT

4 small Japanese eggplants = 12 ounces

6 large Japanese eggplants = 1 1/2 pounds

EGOMA see Perilla under Asian Greens

EGYPTIAN ONIONS see Onions

ENDIVE see Chicories

ENGLISH CUCUMBERS see Cucumbers

ENGLISH PEAS see Peas

ENOKI see Mushrooms, Fresh

ESCAROLE see Chicories

EUROPEAN WILD ASPARAGUS see Asparagus

FAIRY RINGS see Mushrooms, Fresh

FAVA BEANS see The Bean of the Old World under Beans

Fennel

Foeniculum vulgare

One is the Florence fennel (see Varieties). The other is a weed that can be cultivated; it grows along the shores of the Mediterranean and in California. Its feathery tops, which look a lot like dill, are used in fish dishes, and its dried stalks are used as fuel for fires over which fish is grilled. It isn't until either kind of fennel—or dill—flowers and goes to seed (all esteemed) that one can see the family resemblance to the other Umbelliferae.

Varieties

WILD FENNEL This is the herb form as a weed, frondy and growing as much as five feet tall. It is a common roadside plant in California, as it is in the South of France. I am always amused when people pay fairly large sums of money for packages of the dried stems to use on top of coals when cooking fish. I dry my own, hanging them upside down in bunches in a dark place.

FLORENCE FENNEL A large plant with a somewhat oval bulbous base about 3 to 4 inches across, ivory or oyster white in color with tough stalks shooting up many attractive and savory green fronds. Although the bulbous base is usually called a bulb, it is not: It doesn't grow under the ground. Think of it as an attractive goiter. The stalks can be used to stuff and flavor fish or chicken as it roasts, or they can be dried and flamed under fish that is being grilled outdoors, as is done in the South of France. Fennel is terrific raw, thinly sliced, in salads with a lemony dressing. It also makes a good and unusual cooked side dish or vegetable. If it is unavailable, try substituting celery hearts or celery root.

BABY FENNEL Not a different variety, but a smaller version of above, about 2 inches wide. These are wonderful to cook whole as a first course or as part of an antipasto.

Methods

BUYING AND STORING

Buy as close to the time of using as possible. Look for fresh fronds and firm bulbs that are not discolored or mushy. Bulbs that are heavy for their size are preferable; otherwise one is liable to be unpleasantly surprised by bulbs where the ribs are fairly separate, so one has bought air. By preference, choose those that have many green fronds, as they are a wonderful flavor booster.

WASHING/WAYS OF CUTTING

Rinse under cold water. Cut off the stalks. Remove some of the outer layers of the bulb if they are tough and thick, leaving just the heart. Trim the bottom. Peel the outer layer with a vegetable peeler if it is tough and remove any layers that have browned or discolored spots.

Remove the core if cutting fennel into chunks. If cutting into wedges, though, be sure to include part of the core with each piece; this helps them to stay intact.

Save any fronds and store in a plastic bag.

Preparation

BOILING

1-inch cubes: Drop fennel into boiling water and cook 15 to 20 minutes, or until a knife easily slips into flesh.

STEAMING

Quarters: For a 1-pound fennel bulb, quartered lengthwise through the core: Place in a covered steamer basket and cook 10 minutes, or until a knife easily slips into flesh.

ROASTING

¼-inch slices, cut through the core: Arrange in smallest pan that will hold slices comfortably. Slick the pan and fennel with fat. Roast 15 minutes in a 500°F oven. Turn fennel over. Roast 15 minutes more.

MICROWAVING

The microwave cooks fennel quickly without leaving it fibrous or turning it mushy. I have added microwave-cooked fennel to vegetable dishes (see Eggplant, Tomato and Fennel, page 211) and served it on its own.

Wedges: For 8-ounce fennel bulbs, trimmed and cut through the core into 6 wedges. Cover tightly.

    1 fennel bulb: 3 minutes 30 seconds; rest
      2 minutes
    2 fennel bulbs: 5 minutes; rest 2 minutes

SAUTÉING

2 medium fennel bulbs, trimmed and cut through the core into wedges (see Washing/Ways of Cutting; 3¾ cups): Heat 1 tablespoon olive oil or vegetable oil in a 12-inch skillet over medium-high heat. Add fennel. Cook, tossing constantly, until fennel starts to brown, about 4 minutes. Lower heat slightly; continue cooking and tossing until fennel is done to preference: 2 minutes for slightly crunchy fennel, 4 minutes for more tender fennel. Serve. Or, at any point during final cooking, add 1 tablespoon water or vegetable broth and 1 tablespoon unsalted butter, cut into pieces. Cook until liquid is evaporated and butter begins to brown, about 2 minutes. (Makes 1¾ cups)

Yields and Equivalents

1 large fennel bulb = 1 $^1/_4$ to 1 $^1/_2$ pounds (without stalks)

1 medium fennel bulb = 14 ounces to 1 pound

1 small fennel bulb = $^1/_2$ to $^2/_3$ pound

1 large fennel bulb, trimmed and cut into 1-inch chunks = 4 cups

1 medium fennel bulb, trimmed and cut into $^1/_4$-inch slices = 3 cups

1 medium fennel bulb, trimmed and cut into $^1/_4$-inch dice = 2 $^1/_2$ cups

1 small fennel bulb, trimmed and cut into 1-inch chunks = 2 $^1/_2$ cups raw = 1 $^3/_4$ cups cooked

6 trimmed baby fennel bulbs = about 1 pound

Fiddlehead Ferns
Matteuccia pensylvanica

These curled, unopened tops of ferns have become very trendy. It is important to know what one is picking, or one gets a mouthful of fuzz (see Washing/Ways of Cutting). I prefer to blanch them briefly in boiling water before putting them in a salad. Lightly stir-fried, they are very good in a flat omelet, particularly with other spring greens such as asparagus tips and finely snipped chives. When I add blanched fiddleheads to a stew, it is just for the last few minutes to heat them and let them blend in. If I am going to reheat the dish, I wait until the dish is warm to add them. To my surprise, when reading Charmaine Solomon, I found that she lists fiddleheads as an Asian ingredient as well.

Methods
BUYING AND STORING
Fiddleheads should be green and tightly furled when bought, without any black tips to the stems, although these can be cut off if necessary. Store in plastic bags in the refrigerator. Use as soon as possible; they keep badly.

WASHING/WAYS OF CUTTING
Fiddleheads require no preparation besides a quick wash and the cutting off of any discolored stem ends—unless they are the kind with cinnamon-colored fuzz on the outside. Then they need to be lightly rubbed with hands or two dish cloths to remove the fuzz.

Preparation
BOILING
For 1 pound fiddlehead ferns: Bring 3 quarts water and 1 $^1/_2$ tablespoons salt to a boil in a 4-quart pot. Add fiddleheads and cook until tender but not soft, about 4 minutes after water returns to a boil. Drain. When cooking smaller or larger quantities, keep in mind that total cooking time will vary depending on how long it takes the water to return to a boil after adding fiddleheads. Fiddleheads are done when bright green but still crunchy.

Yields and Equivalents

1 pound fiddlehead ferns = 6 cups

Cooked volume of fiddlehead ferns is the same as raw volume unless fiddleheads sit after cooking, in which case they will exude liquid and shrink.

FINGER EGGPLANTS see Eggplants
FINGERLINGS see Potatoes
FLAGEOLETS see Beans of the New World under Beans
FLAT CABBAGE see Tatsoi under Cabbages, Asian
FLAT-LEAF PARSLEY see Parsley under Herbs and Their Flowers
FLINT CORN see Fresh Corn under Corn
FLORENCE FENNEL see Fennel
FLORIDA AVOCADOS see Avocados
FLOUR CORN see Fresh Corn under Corn
FRENCH GREEN BEANS see Beans of the New World under Beans
FRENCH SORREL see Sorrel
FRIJOLES see Beans of the New World under Beans
FRISÉE see Chicories
FUSEAU ARTICHOKES see Jerusalem Artichokes

GARDEN ORACH see Spinach

GARLAND CHRYSANTHEMUM see Chrysanthemum
Greens

Garlic

Allium sativum

Although most of the garlic in America is of one variety grown in Gilroy, California, there are many different kinds. Garlic is most broadly defined by the scape or stalk that the head sends up, which is known as the "neck." The Gilroy kind is a soft-necked garlic with a white outer wrapper, which I tend to call the paper, surrounding the head and white "skins" around each clove. I recommend Chester Aaron's *Great Garlic Book* for ultimate information (see the Bibliography). He is a real authority and grower as well. He has collected garlic from all over the world and grows what he had believed to be somewhere in the low nineties of different kinds. He is currently working with a plant researcher on the DNA and thinks they will actually come up with about thirty varieties.

Different countries prefer different types of garlic with different colors and strengths, different numbers of cloves and different sizes. Some will be sweeter. The two major divisions are the soft-necked—the kind that can be made into a decorative braid—and the hard-necked, which cannot be braided. The hard-necked send up a stem that is called the scape and Aaron has found that it makes very good broth (follow directions for making Egyptian onion scape broth on page 616).

In talking with researchers, including Dr. David Mirelman of the Weizmann Institute in Rehovot, Israel, Aaron has also found that there is an element in raw garlic, allicin, that acts as an antibiotic and has various other health benefits as well. (Dr. Mirelman has done medical research with pure allicin.) Along with the other alliums, garlic has elements that work to reduce blood pressure and is an antibiotic and a fungicide. When I was a kid, we used to give garlic to dogs that had worms; it got rid of them (the worms, not the dogs).

Each individual clove can be the start of a new plant, which is nice for the gardener but more difficult for the cook. In the center of each clove is the onset of the new plant, which the French call the *germe,* and we call the sprout. It starts out, when the garlic is newly dug, as almost invisible and pale. As the clove ages, the sprout develops and becomes a darker yellow and finally green, and ready to be planted. As it ages, the sprout uses the rest of the clove as food, turning it into an unusable lacy texture of cell walls. Even before it gets that far, the sprout becomes strong in taste and should be removed. This is easy if my method of whacking the head and semi-crushing it before peeling is used, as the sprout can be picked out. If working with older cloves that are wanted for slicing, remove the skin, cut the clove in half lengthwise and pick out the sprout with the point of a sharp small knife. Garlic is a live plant. The method I recommend, whacking the whole head—covered with a kitchen towel—with a heavy pot to separate the cloves and remove the wrapper, then smashing each clove either by putting all the cloves under the towel and whacking again or smacking each clove with the broad side of a heavy knife, kills the garlic, makes the skins easier to remove if desired and makes for a milder taste if it is used raw.

Some cooks prefer to remove whole cloves before serving a dish. I don't. I love to eat the garlic. The easiest way to remove whole cloves is to stick a toothpick into each clove and then pull it out. A slotted spoon can be used.

All garlic has two very different tastes: Raw or barely cooked garlic is sharp and is tasted on the tip of the tongue. Long-cooked garlic becomes sweet and mellow. I often add garlic to a recipe twice to take advantage of these differences. Garlic has a high sugar content, so it burns easily.

Garlic is sticky on the fingers after peeling. This stickiness is very useful to the cook, especially the vegetarian cook, as it adds substance the way gelatin does to sauces and stocks. This is what makes Garlic Broth (page 507) so useful.

Correct storage of garlic is very important. It should be kept cool and in the dark to minimize the rate of sprouting. It is important that it be in a dry place, or it may become moldy. I have found that, contrary to popular custom, it stores well wrapped in a brown paper bag in the refrigerator. But don't put it in the vegetable drawer, where it will get moist; just put it on a shelf.

Elephant garlic (*Allium ampeloprasum*), a great big head often 4 inches across, was a brief fad as it was easier to peel very large cloves. It is not a true garlic, but rather a close relative of the leek and goes bad quickly.

Methods

BUYING AND STORING
See general information above.

WAYS OF CUTTING
The easiest way to chop garlic is to whack the whole clove, still in its paper, with the side of a heavy knife. Pick off the papery coating. The clove will be already half-chopped; just go from there. This also comes in handy in dishes where cloves of garlic are simmered or fried to add flavor but removed before serving. If perfect slices or whole cloves are needed, remove the paper with a paring knife, starting at the flat root (not pointy) end of the clove. The root end should always be removed.

Preparation

ROASTING
Below are directions for roasting whole heads of garlic using moderate oven heat and for peeled cloves using the microwave oven. For a high-heat method, see my book *Roasting, A Simple Art.*

Oven methods for whole heads: Cut off top $1/2$ inch from as many heads of garlic as you like. Rub off extra papery coating from heads, leaving heads intact. Put garlic cut side up in a baking dish that holds it comfortably. Drizzle about 2 teaspoons olive oil over each, and pour $1/4$ inch of water into the dish. Cover tightly with aluminum foil and bake in a 350°F oven until tender and lightly browned, about 1 hour. If desired, remove foil and continue baking until well browned, about 15 minutes.

The soft garlic can be squeezed out from the cloves either with fingers or by firmly running the back of a knife from the root end to the cut end. I often serve whole cloves of garlic and guests can drag the sweetness out with their teeth.

Microwave method for whole cloves: Any amount of garlic cloves can be microwave-roasted as desired, providing the container fits in the oven. Smash and peel garlic cloves and put in a microwavable dish. Pour in enough broth or water to cover (1 to $1\,1/2$ cups). Tightly cover with lid or plastic wrap. Microwave at 100% for 8 minutes, or until soft and sweet and liquid is lightly thickened. Prick plastic, if using, to release steam. Use broth and cloves separately or together.

SAUTÉING
Don't sauté garlic at too high a heat. If both onions or another vegetable and garlic are being sautéed, start with the onions or other vegetables and add the garlic a little later to avoid burning.

GARLIC CHIPS Crisp, golden garlic chips are good sprinkled over vegetable dishes, such as sautéed string beans, parsnip purée and a host of other purées, or on soups, into salads, etc.

Chris has found that starting garlic slices in cold oil gives a much better result than putting them into already heated oil. The oil also has a better taste and can be used in dishes wanting just a little garlic flavor.

Peel (without crushing) and thinly slice as many garlic cloves as desired (1 large clove makes about 2 tablespoons chips). Scatter them over bottom of a skillet that holds them in more or less a single layer. Pour enough vegetable oil or equal parts vegetable oil and olive oil into pan to float garlic. Place over medium-low heat and cook, shaking pan often, until garlic is medium golden brown, about 5 minutes from when it starts sizzling. Garlic should give off a nice, even sizzle; turn heat down a little if it starts sizzling wildly. When cooked, immediately remove chips to paper towels to drain. Reserve oil and use within 1 day for sautéing vegetables.

Yields and Equivalents
1 large head = $3\,1/2$ ounces = 3 ounces peeled = 6 large, 5 medium and 3 small cloves
1 small head = 2 ounces = $1\,3/4$ ounces peeled = approximately 5 large and 7 medium cloves

2 large or 3 medium garlic cloves = $1/2$ ounce =
    4 teaspoons coarsely chopped = 1 tablespoon
    finely chopped
2 large or 3 medium garlic cloves = 2 tablespoons
    thinly sliced
1 large head, roasted = 3 tablespoons garlic paste

GARLIC CHIVES see Chives under Herbs and
    Their Flowers
GHERKIN see Cucumbers
GINGER see Asian Greens
GLASSWORT see Samphire
GOA BEANS see Wing Beans under Peas
GOBO see Burdock
GOLDEN NUGGET SQUASH see Squash, Winter
GOLDEN OAK MUSHROOMS see Shiitakes under
    Mushrooms, Fresh

Gourds

One balmy winter Saturday night, I was in San Miguel de Allende. The main plaza was dominated by mariachi bands. There were three of them playing simultaneously, competitively and contrapuntally. Each had at least one pair of decorated gourds on handles with dry beans inside, maracas, shaken to be the rhythm section. Without them, none of these bands with their ornate costuming is complete. Such hard gourds native to the Americas are used in other musical instruments, as in Africa in marimbas. They are also used as spoons, scoops, drinking cups and decorations. They are not suitable for food. Africa and Asia have numerous other families of gourds that are appreciated for eating.

This is another situation where the poor food writer—me—is in the middle of a vast confusion. All gourds are members of the Cucurbitae family, which also houses the summer and winter squash, pumpkins and melons—typically American—and cucumbers—typically Asian. Africa contributes a whole other group of edible gourds, one of which, oddly to me, is the loofah. I think of the loofah as the scratchy scrubber in bath and shower, but it turns out that very small ones, about three inches long, are boiled and eaten.

Most of the edible gourds are unavailable in the Americas and Europe, even what seems to be the most popular—the very long, thin snake gourd.

The question arises, "Why mention them at all?" The answer for me is that those vegetables are spreading around the world at an accelerating pace. By the time someone reads this book, gourds may be the vegetable of the year. I am about to plant some, as the seeds are available, and I will keep everybody posted on my Web page, www.bkafka.com. As usual, I will probably find them all over menus before I get the hang of it.

In the meantime, the standard procedure gleaned from reading is to boil the gourd until tender and to avoid the seeds. Pieces of gourd can be served as a vegetable or find their way into curries.

GREEN BEANS see Beans of the New World
    under Beans
GREEN ONIONS see Scallions
GRITS see Dried and Hominy under Corn
GUAJILLO PEPPERS see Peppers
GYPSY PEPPERS see Peppers
HABANEROS see Peppers
HABICHUELAS see Beans of the New World
    under Beans
HAMBURG ROOTED PARSLEY see Parsley under
    Herbs and Their Flowers
HARICOTS VERTS see Beans of the New World
    under Beans
HASS AVOCADOS see Avocados

Hearts of Palm

Bactris gasipaes

I used to feel very guilty about my love for hearts of palm, as the whole tree had to be destroyed to get the correct section of the trunk for peeling. Today there are specialty farms growing palms just for this purpose. Most of the hearts of palm we see in stores and restaurants have been canned. Fresh are infinitely better. Canned should be washed to remove as much of the canning liquid as possible. Fresh should be used as soon as possible and can be eaten raw.

Methods

WASHING/WAYS OF CUTTING

For fresh hearts of palm, cut off any parts toughened by exposure to air. Shred lengthwise and use according to the recipe. For canned hearts of palm, rinse or soak in cold water, dry and then shred.

Yields and Equivalents

One 14-ounce can hearts of palm, drained =
8 ounces, about 6 pieces = 1 1/2 cups shredded

HEDGEHOG MUSHROOMS see Wood Hedgehogs under Mushrooms, Fresh
HENS OF THE WOODS see Mushrooms, Fresh

Herbs and Their Flowers

I'm a nut for herbs. The very first garden that I planted in Vermont was an herb garden. In New York, I have a sort of large box outside planted with herbs. In Greece and Turkey, I walk around picking wild herbs for drying. I frequent spice markets.

It used to be that a very small selection of fresh herbs was sold. Gradually, due to demand from chefs and urgings of food writers such as myself, the selection expanded. Herbs are widely available dried. Look for dried herbs that still show some of their original color and are not collapsing into a powder.

Obviously, there is a whole world of herbs and I do not anywhere near cover them all here. I have chosen those that I believe are best with vegetables. Sometimes, as in the case of Parsley Soup (page 444) or Lovage Pesto (page 442), they really become the vegetable. Even when they are less dominant, they may be used in such a quantity that they become a critical part of the dish.

A note on the herb yields that follow: By and large, fresh herbs are measured for recipes in terms of leaves, tablespoons and cups or parts thereof. Fresh herbs are very light and one needs a very sensitive postage scale to weigh them. It is hard to give exact weights and their corresponding volumes for herbs and almost impossible for their flowers. I have done my best.

Dried herbs are also light and are usually weighed only for pickling or other large-scale recipes.

Herbs should be cut from the plant with sharp scissors. Many people prefer to "snip" their herbs, cut them into small pieces with a scissors. I find that I have more control with a sharp knife.

Herbs can be dried by being placed in a single layer on several sheets of paper in an airy, not too sunny, spot. They can be put in a dehydrator (read the instructions), and they can go into the microwave oven.

The color and fragrance of microwave-dried herbs are the next best thing to fresh. Scatter 2 cups of loosely packed washed and dried herb leaves or sprigs in an even layer on a double layer (1 sheet each) of paper towels. Do not cover. Cook for 3 to 4 minutes at 100%. Store in a tightly covered container. Many herbs can be washed and dried and deep-fried.

HERBED BEANS One day when I was getting ready to have people for dinner the following night and I happened to have dried corona beans, I came up with something delicious. I soaked two cups of them overnight and boiled them for three hours the following day. They still did not please me. I drained them and put them in a smallish pot with a third of a cup of good olive oil and a half cup of tomato sauce—Paula Wolfert says that tomatoes help to make dried beans more succulent in texture. I let them simmer, and when all the liquid was absorbed, I added two cups of finely chopped herbs—young flat-leaf parsley, marjoram and lovage—another half cup of tomato sauce and a half cup of water. They simmered a bit longer, then I turned them off. Gradually they absorbed all the liquid and, with salt and pepper, were perfect.

HERB VINEGARS Herbs are often steeped in vinegar—usually white wine vinegar—either to preserve them or to flavor the vinegar. Tarragon vinegar is a favorite. Three or four sprigs in a pint container of white wine vinegar steeped in a dark place for at least two weeks will be excellent.

ANGELICA (*Angelica archangelica*) How can anyone resist an herb that is angelic? But it is little used except to be candied and cut up in sweets. It turns a lovely shade of green that is made mockery of by its replacement in fruitcakes by green-colored candied cherries. Books say that the plant is huge—as large as a man. In my garden, it is shorter, rather like a rhubarb plant in form. It grows particularly well in northern Europe and the United States. The leaf stalks used to be blanched and used like its relative celery, which only became readily available somewhat later. Angelica is a biennial but can, like its relative lovage, be made almost a perennial. However, it requires some attention to keep it going. The stalks need to be substantial to be worth candying, but the flower heads must be removed before they go to seed, or the plant will die. As it is impossible to buy fresh angelica and candying it is complicated, I give no more description or instruction. Those who have plants growing can chop the leaves and tender stems to flavor fish dishes or salads.

BALM, LEMON BALM or BEE BALM (*Melissa officinalis*) This is in the mint family. The leaves are rounder than the other mints and they are downy, like apple mint. It has a very nice lemon flavor without much acidity. The leaves are used in salads and cooked in fish sauces.

BASIL (*Ocimum basilicum*) This is a whole world of plants: tall or small, red to maroon to green, leafy or bushy, with the leaf size ranging from no bigger than a pine nut to lettuce basil, with tender leaves large enough to be put like lettuce on a sandwich. Almost every area of Italy lays claim to its own variety. It is widely grown in Greece in sawn-off olive oil cans put out on stoops, but it is almost never used there. There are basils that taste of other seasonings, such as anise basil. And there are Thai—cinnamon-tasting—and other Asian basils. One particularly nice kind is *Ocimum basilicum sacrum*—"holy" or "biblical" basil—used in Vietnamese cooking. In the West we are most familiar with the Italian basils. Best used in season, when they are most aromatic. They send up a pale violet flower spike that I try to cut off as soon as it begins to form, as the plant does not flourish after it blooms. If the flowers do escape me, I run my nails down the spike and remove the individual flowers for use in salads or omelets.

Try to find ordinary basil, tiny-leaved bush basil and lettuce basil, with its large undulating leaves, to have some idea of the range. Purple basil is attractive, but I'm not so keen on its flavor.

Basil is the plant most sensitive to cold. I can always tell when my garden has had a frost by the sudden brown death of the basil. I try to cut it just before frost. I grind up the leaves with a little oil in a food processor or blender, put two tablespoons in each hollow of an old-fashioned ice cube tray and freeze. I can then pop them out and store them in a plastic bag in the freezer. (I do not make pesto, as the nuts and garlic do not freeze well. They can be added later.)

Basil leaves, if being cut, should be sliced across. It is often easiest to roll up a bunch of the leaves and slice them all at once. If chopping, turn the pile and cut again.

BAY LEAVES (*Laurus nobilis*) I grow bay in a pot. Those in milder climates can grow it out-of-doors. It is important to grow, or use, dried Mediterranean bay leaves. They come from a bush. California bay leaves are a whole other matter, growing on trees; they can have a very nasty taste. It takes about 12 fresh bay leaves to make ¹/₄ ounce, even more if dried leaves. This shows that bay should be bought in small quantities.

BORAGE (*Borago officinalis*) Once planted, borage will live to haunt. It spreads like the weed it is and has prickly hairs. The flowers are a brilliant blue and I use them in and on tea sandwiches. According to a charming little book, *Le Erbe Aromatiche in Cucina* (*Aromatic Culinary Herbs*), soup can be made from borage. Chris has actually had this in Italy and says it is good. It takes a pound of leaves and an equal amount of green lettuce. Boil briefly in salted water. Break up with a fork or roughly in the food processor. Heat ¹/₄ cup olive oil with a mix of other herbs, such as marjoram, thyme and mint. Add stock and salt and pepper to taste, along with the greens.

BURNET aka PIMPINELLA (*Sanguisorba minor*) This is also called salad burnet. There was an old Italian saying that no salad was complete without pimpinella. It is a perennial that grows about a foot tall and has soft roundish leaves with many notches. It tastes lightly of cucumber.

CHERVIL (*Anthriscus cerefolium*) Chervil looks like a daintier, more ladylike version of parsley. In the eighties, it became the chefs' ubiquitous replacement for parsley, frilling up carefully arranged plates. As with parsley, that is an undeserved fate. It is a delightful herb, although it may be hard to find in the store. I plant it in a shady spot, as it bolts very easily. Every two weeks, I throw more seed on the bed and let the new grow in among the old—like a family. It was a wild native plant in western Asia and was first cultivated in Syria.

Chervil is a standard component of fines herbes and as such is used in omelets. Its daintiness had misled me until I started working on recipes for this book; I had always thought of it as being milder in taste than parsley. It turns out to be more robust and more complex. Aside from the sporadically munched sprig, it needs to be cooked to be fully enjoyed. Then its faint admixture of licorice and hint of its cousin coriander come to the fore. It can be prepared as a sauce to be used warm or cold, can inform a spring stew or flavor a soup.

There is really only one variety of chervil, but if it is allowed to get very leggy and go to seed, it will take on more of a coriander taste. Do not plant it close to coriander or it will tend to intermarry and taste heavily of cilantro.

Methods

BUYING AND STORING

Chervil tends to be sold in small well-wrapped packages of about 1 ounce each. It will take several to make a decent showing in any recipe. It comes with stems on. About the top inch of the stem is usable, along with the leaves.

Chervil is not usually thought to keep, but I have found that if left in its original package or loosely assembled and wrapped airtight in plastic wrap, it will keep in the refrigerator for up to a week.

WASHING/WAYS OF CUTTING

Chervil is not usually very sandy—and not at all if it comes from the market. Just rinse it lightly and shake it to dry,

then pat with paper towels. Cut off the stems, leaving the top tender inch or two. Do not wash it before refrigeration for storage; it will tend to get mushy.

Yields and Equivalents

3 ounces chervil sprigs with 1 inch of stem = about $1/2$ packed cup

3 ounces chervil sprigs with 1 inch of stem = $1/3$ cup chopped

3 ounces chervil, stems removed and chopped (but not minced) = $1/4$ cup

CHIVES (*Allium schoenoprasum*) There are several kinds, including the rather robust Chinese chives and the distinctly garlic chives, which are sometimes curly. Chives are in the onion family; see page 615. Individual leaves are sometimes used to tie bundles of vegetables for an elegant presentation. Chopped, they are nice in salads and sprinkled on all sorts of dishes. Their flowers taste good. Lobster salad is particularly beautiful with chive flowers. The chive blossom, a round ball, is actually a cluster of small flowers. Take all of the tiny little flowers that form the ball in one hand and pull them firmly away from the calyx—basal leaves—and stem.

Yields and Equivalents

$1/4$ ounce chives, cut across into small pieces = 2 tablespoons

A normal store-bought bunch chives, sliced = $1/4$ cup

$1/2$ ounce chives = about 50 = $1/4$ cup thinly sliced or $1/4$ cup 1-inch lengths

Flowers from 2 chives = 1 tablespoon

4 ounces Chinese or garlic chives = about 25 chives = 2 cups thinly sliced

CILANTRO (*Coriandrum sativum*) Here is a linguistic anomaly. The plant is coriander and its seeds, which are used for flavoring, are called coriander; they are much used in the cooking of India. The leaves, however, have come to be called cilantro, based on their almost ubiquitous use in Mexican and Central American cooking, as well as in Chinese and other Asian cookery. They can be used raw or cooked. When I was working on Ecuadoran soups, I found that Ecuadorans left about three inches of the tender stems on. The stems have a very good flavor, and I now include them when chopping up cilantro. In some cuisines, the root is used, just as is the root of Hamburg parsley. It is good, scrubbed very thoroughly, in soups and stews.

Yields and Equivalents

1 medium bunch cilantro = 5 ounces =
    1 1/2 ounces leaves = 1/2 cup chopped
1 medium bunch cilantro, with 3 to 4 inches of
    stems = 3/4 cup chopped

DILL (*Anethum graveolens*) This is a frondy plant looking much like the herb fennel. It is another of the tall herbs. Some varieties will grow a good five feet tall. Many of us know it best from its umbelliferous seed heads, which are used dried in pickle making. For pickling, pick the stalks and hang upside down to dry. Hang them over clean paper so as not to lose any seeds.

Dill is one of my favorite herbs, perhaps because I have ancestors from Byelorussia and Ukraine who used it plentifully. In Russia, it is call ukrop, in France aneth. I also like the way it looks with delicate fronds, like lace. The flavor is fresh and goes well with fish, chicken, cucumbers, lemon and, above all, soups. I add a little chopped fresh dill to tuna or chicken salad and a lot to chicken soup. It is lovely with veal. It doesn't do well with dark meats except for boiled beef.

Dill can be used fresh or dried, and its seeds are prized for pickles. The fresh herb and the seeds often combine well in a recipe to give layers of flavor. The stems, after the fronds have been removed, can be used for stuffing fish or chicken then discarded.

Botanically there is only one variety of dill, but effectively there are two kinds, and the difference between them will make a great deal of difference to both the gardener and

the cook. Salad dill is grown for its greens. It is relatively short and goes to seed much less rapidly than ordinary dill, whose greens are sparser. Ordinary dill is best grown for its seed heads used for making pickles.

In markets, one often gets the salad dill picked root and all. I have had no luck starting plants using this root material, but it does give a clue. Dill grows quickly and it is better to keep reseeding it than to try to keep plants from going to seed.

Methods
BUYING AND STORING

It is best to buy short bushy bunches rather than lanky ones—more fronds for your money. Don't buy limp dill. Look for fronds that are slender enough to be chewed.

I have a sad tale about storing dill. Many years ago, when I was new to the food business, I had the best commission I ever got, even to date. I did all the buying, prop acquisition, food prep and cooking for a photo shoot; I was young and strong and nothing seemed too much. Among the things I bought were two heroic bunches of dill. One was for cooking and the other to decorate the set. Intending to keep them as fresh as possible, I stuck them into a large glass of water and stuck it in turn into the refrigerator. To my horror, when I went to retrieve them, they were limp and dark. The photograph turned out all right, thanks to a last-minute dash to a market; but I learned that dill is best kept loosely wrapped in a cloth in the refrigerator. Don't stick it in water.

Dill that has gone to seed can be dried by hanging it in bunches upside down. Try to put it someplace where a tray or large piece of paper can be put underneath to collect any seeds that fall.

WASHING/WAYS OF CUTTING

Generally, the fronds will need to be separated from the stems. The very fastidious and frugal will carefully pinch off the fronds, removing even small bits of stem; that is the best way. However, I am often in a hurry. Then, I lay the bunch flat and run a large sharp knife down from where the fronds begin on the stems and slice off as many fronds as I can. I turn and spread out the bunch and keep on going. After that I chop. Usually the bitty bits of stem will pop to the top of the pile and I pick them out. Dill should not be too finely chopped. This is not the time for fancy French mincing. Cut that small, dill will taste gritty.

Don't add dill early in the cooking procedure; it will lose its freshness and taste grassy or bitter.

Yields and Equivalents

1 large bunch dill = 10 ounces = 7 ounces fronds =
2 1/2 cups coarsely chopped = 2 cups finely
chopped
1 small bunch dill = 3 ounces = 2 cups fronds =
1 cup coarsely chopped = 3/4 cup finely chopped
1/4 ounce dill fronds, just tops = 1 tablespoon

LEMONGRASS (*Cymbopogon citratus*) With its light lemon flavor and attractive scent but without acidity, lemongrass is used all over Asia and the Pacific islands. It prevails as well in Ecuador and other Central American countries. By now, it has become very common in North America and Europe perhaps due to the spread of Asian food.

Whacking the very fibrous stalks with the flat of a knife will make them easier to cut and somewhat edible. I serve only the most tender of interior layers cut into very thin strips. I have seen the green part of the stalks sold on their own in a number of stores. They are virtually useless.

LOVAGE (*Levisticum officinale*) This is a huge member of Umbelliferae family (it can grow to over six feet tall and make a five-foot-round clump) that has to be grown from root division. I am on a campaign to introduce it into American gardens. It is a reassuring herb, the first green up in the spring. It is best used fresh, but it can be dried by wrapping it loosely in paper towels and refrigerating it until dry.

Lovage was the most common herb in Roman times. I have tried it in everything but desserts to good effect. The stalks used to be candied like angelica. The leaves, raw and chopped, are wonderful in salads. Cooked, it makes a

fabulous soup such as I first had in Ireland. It is splendid with chicken. A small branch simmered in chicken soup may be all the flavoring that is needed; it can replace its cousin dill in this way. Lovage should be chopped—without stems—or thinly sliced across the leaves so as to reduce fibrousness.

I don't know why it isn't grown commercially, as it has two seasons, in the spring and then again in the fall.

Methods
PICKING AND STORING

Lovage cannot be bought. When picking, choose leaf fronds that are tender and youngish and bright green. It keeps well in the refrigerator with its stems wrapped in wet paper and the whole stuck into a plastic bag, or as a massive bouquet in the kitchen.

Yields and Equivalents

Lovage will give yields very much like parsley (see page 593), depending on the way it is cut.

MARJORAM (*Origanum marjorana*) This is an annual subset of oregano. The explanation is complicated and those wanting real, hard information should look in Alan Davidson's *Oxford Companion to Food* (see the Bibliography). The kind I usually grow is *Origanum marjorana,* an annual with a gentle taste. It is often mistaken for wild oregano. Marjoram is used extensively in Italy and Greece as a flavoring. What I grow, I think of as the true marjoram. Its lavender flowers can also be used stripped from the stems in salads. The leaves of the herb itself are good in salads and made dishes, often with tomatoes.

Yields and Equivalents

1 small bunch marjoram = 1 1/4 ounces =
1/2 ounce leaves = 1/2 cup chopped

MINTS (*Mentha;* there are hundreds, including the catnips) They are very invasive growers and should be put in an isolated spot of ground. I tend to prefer the large group related to peppermint rather than the one related to spearmint. My very favorite, and the one I mainly bother to grow, is apple mint, which has fuzzy leaves and is gentler in taste than the others. It is splendid in salads, drinks and sauces. Once again, Alan Davidson is a reliable guide (see the Bibliography). The various *Nepeta*s, a related group of plants, are used in North African cooking and in France as an infusion.

Of course, mint is much used as a drink or in drinks. Mint tea is ubiquitous throughout the Muslim and Arab worlds. Iced tea and mint julep are unthinkable without it, and it is a fine addition to fruit salads.

Yields and Equivalents

1 medium bunch mint = 2 ounces = 1 $^1/_2$ ounces leaves = $^1/_3$ cup chopped

MUSTARD (*Brassica*) There is a tiny plant called mustard, a sprout that is grown like cress (see page 647); otherwise, mustard is a very various plant used as a long-cooking green (see page 611), and, of course, its seeds—brown, black and white—are used as a condiment on their own in the cooking of India (usually popped in a hot pan) or made into the paste that we call mustard. In addition to being spread on sandwiches and served as a condiment with meats, it is often added—sometimes as a dry powder—to salad dressings, which it helps to emulsify. Of the pastes, both smooth and coarse, by far the best are the French. Young tender mustard leaves can be cut into strips and put in salad; I'm really not fond of this usage. See also Mizuna, page 612.

OREGANO (*Origanum vulgare*) I hardly know what I am talking about when discussing this perennial, which has a flavor like marjoram's but much stronger, and tougher leaves and stems. I pick wild oregano in Greece and its islands and it is by far superior to the others. When purchasing dried oregano, look for Greek oregano. Once again, turn to Alan Davidson (see the Bibliography) for clarification.

Yields and Equivalents

See Marjoram, page 592.

PARSLEY (*Petroselinum crispum*) This is probably the most ubiquitous herb in Western cooking. Much of it, sadly, is used purely for decoration. Evelyn (see the Bibliography) made the distinction between the flat-leaved kind and the curly kind, saying that that the curly was chiefly used for decoration. Flat-leaved parsley is commonly called Italian parsley. Some of it grows leaves that are large, tough and leathery, rather like those of its relative celery; try to avoid these. Raw in salads, they are tough; minced in hot dishes, they are somewhat lacking flavor. Young flat-leaf parsley is a delight.

Varieties

All are *Petroselinum crispum*.

FLAT-LEAF OR ITALIAN The leaves look like celery leaves but are dark green. The stems are slender but strong.

CURLY LEAF In contrast, this parsley's leaves are intensely ruffled. They need more washing, as the curls are liable to conceal and hold the dirt.

HAMBURG ROOTED PARSLEY The leaves are like those of flat-leaf parsley, but they have a longish white root like a parsnip. The root has a strong parsley taste. It used to be a staple of the greengrocer's soup bunch, but it has almost disappeared. I don't grow it, as pulling it up ends the plant.

Methods
BUYING AND STORING

Buy bunches that are vigorous and with crisp, bright green leaves and stems, not wilted or limp. Do not accept any parsley with yellow leaves. The stems should offer some resistance to bending. It is not true that the largest leaves are the best.

It is hard to know exactly how much to buy. Experience lets us eyeball the leaves and guess. I tend to buy more than I need, as I can always use it and it is better not to run short in the middle of a recipe.

Remove any strings or rubber bands that are holding the bunch together. They tend to break the stems and let juices out. Do not wash before storing, and do not stem until ready to use. Store in the refrigerator in a plastic bag for up to a week. If the kitchen isn't too warm, I like to stick the bunch in an attractive pitcher with cold water—very decorative, and a deodorizer. It should not be kept in direct sun, and the water should be changed every day.

WASHING/WAYS OF CUTTING

Don't wash parsley until ready to use it. If a packed measure is desired, wash only after measuring.

Rinse parsley, leaves only or whole bunches, under cold running water and dry thoroughly. The wet leaves can be dried in a salad spinner and then patted with a dry cloth, or layers of paper toweling can be used.

Tear the leaves from the stems. Discard the stems or save for making stock. Use the leaves whole or chop according to the recipe.

Generally I do not chop parsley in a food processor, as it turns to green mush. It is better to chop the leaves with a sharp knife, keeping the blade at a right angle to the work surface. When I'm in a hurry and don't mind a little waste, I lay the bunch of dry parsley on a cutting board and run the flat edge of a sharp chef's knife, held almost flat, from the stem end toward the leaf tips. I give the bunch a small turn and repeat. I keep going until almost all of the leaves are removed. What remains goes in the soup pot.

One of the most common uses of finely chopped parsley is what is called in French cooking "fines herbes," as in omelet aux fines herbes (see page 483), which may have other herbs or not. The term is also taken to mean a combination of parsley with chervil and tarragon and sometimes chives.

Yields and Equivalents

It is very hard to know just how much parsley one is buying in a bunch; they vary wildly in size, amount of stem and weight. Bunches can run anywhere from an ounce to 3 ounces or more. When following a recipe where the amount of parsley used matters, it is better to follow the indication in the recipes or to consult the list below.

All those parsley stems can be used alone or tied up in herb bundles to flavor soups and stews or in Vegetable Broth (page 506).

When I say "packed leaves," I mean really pushed down hard until made as compact and as level as possible.

3 1/4 ounces parsley with stems = 5 cups loosely packed, 1 1/2 cups packed

2 ounces stemmed parsley = 3 1/2 cups loosely packed, 1 cup packed = 1/2 cup chopped

11 ounces parsley leaves trimmed of all stems = 9 cups packed dry leaves

5 to 6 ounces parsley leaves trimmed of all stems = 4 1/2 cups packed dry leaves

1/4 cup packed leaves, chopped = 1/4 cup

1/4 cup packed leaves, minced = 2 heaping tablespoons

ROSEMARY (*Rosmarinus officinalis*) A popular herb that gets scant mention in this book because it is too strong to go with most vegetables. The notable exception is potatoes, especially when roasted. Rosemary can get quite large in the right climate and looks like a small evergreen bush. There is also a creeping form that grows brilliantly in California. Molly Chappellet (of the winery Chappellet) made me very envious with her garden. Rosemary is very sensitive to cold and even in the South of France it has been known to die from a rare snow. In a pot in the house, rosemary needs to be away from the kitchen; somehow the oils do it in. Use the top branches and strip as for winter savory.

SAGE (*Salvia officinalis*) There are ornamental sages that are not edible and then there are the herbs. The sages, pineapple and lemon among them, are perennial members of the mint family but not so invasive, growing in discrete plants. There are many different sorts, including clary, which is now little used. I usually pinch a few leaves from the top of a branch. The plants will continue to grow well into cold weather. The easiest way to get more plants is to bury one of the stems under the soil, just letting a little leaf stick up. After about a month, a new plant can be separated from the mother plant.

Sage has a strong flavor and is often used in stuffings along with its favorites, pork and onions. It is very good fried. It is a good friend, when cooked, to green beans and bean soups. Again, cut across the leaf. The only part of it that I regularly eat raw is its flower.

Yields and Equivalents

1 small bunch sage = 1 1/4 ounces = 3/4 ounce leaves = 6 tablespoons chopped

SUMMER SAVORY (*Satureja hortensis*) This is an annual with rather ungainly growth habits. It is good only in midsummer. However, it is worth trying in stuffings and in mushroom dishes, as well as in salads.

Yields and Equivalents

1 medium bunch summer savory = 3/4 ounce = 1/2 ounce leaves = 4 1/2 tablespoons finely chopped

TARRAGON (*Artemisia dracunculus*) There is only one good tarragon, French tarragon. It cannot be grown from seed. It is a perennial. Beg a rootling from a friend or buy some at a nursery. Plant it where it gets a lot of sun but can be well watered. Every two or three years, the clumps should be divided. Tarragon has long, thin elegant oval leaves that make a lovely topping for a simple dish. Otherwise, they are chopped and find their way into a version of many classic French dishes. Béarnaise sauce depends on them. They are good with fish, seafood and chicken, less good with heavier meats, excellent with eggs.

Methods
BUYING AND STORING
Tarragon is sold in plastic packets in the store. Look at it carefully. The leaves should not be getting black or even dark, nor should they be crumpled. Store in the refrigerator in the original packet for up to a week. When

picking, cut off about the last four inches of a branch with scissors. The plant will regrow.

WASHING/WAYS OF CUTTING
Since it is just the ends of branches that are cut, tarragon is not usually dirty. Wash just before using, or it will wilt. Whole leaves may be stripped from the stems and used as is in salads or under the skin of chicken. Otherwise, it should be chopped across with a sharp knife as called for in the recipe.

Yields and Equivalents

1 medium bunch tarragon = 1 1/2 ounces = 1 ounce leaves = 7 tablespoons chopped

THYME (*Thymus vulgaris*) There are literally hundreds of kinds of thyme. I particularly like the creeping thymes that can be grown on paths and give off a seductive aroma when trod upon. English, or common, thyme is the most usual. Do not confuse it with lemon thyme—unless a strong lemon taste is desired. Variegated thyme is beautiful, but I'm not so sure about its flavor.

Thyme has woody stems and the leaves must be removed from them, but it is not necessary to pluck them off one by one. Working against the growing pattern of the leaves, run a thumb and a fingernail down the stem to remove the leaves. They do not need to be cut when fresh. Thyme has a strong taste and is best with meats and mushrooms. It dries quite well, but it should be crumbled before use.

Yields and Equivalents

1 medium bunch thyme = 2 ounces = 3/4 ounce leaves = 1/2 cup chopped

WINTER SAVORY (*Satureja montana*) This is a small perennial bush whose leaves are much stronger in flavor than regular (summer) savory and are somewhat similar to softer small pine needles. I really don't use it in salad, although it has been used that way. It goes well with thyme and sage but not with rosemary, which it is rather like. It does best in hearty stews and in dried bean dishes.

HOMINY see Corn
HONEY MUSHROOMS see Mushrooms, Fresh
HONTAKA PEPPERS see Santakas under Peppers
HOP SHOOTS see Asparagus
HORNS OF PLENTY see Trumpets of Death under
   Mushrooms, Fresh

Horseradish
Armoracia rusticana

This is a plant that is ridiculously easy to grow. Annoyingly, it can become very invasive, growing a new plant from even the tiniest bit of root left in the ground. It has coarse ugly oval green leaves at ground level. In Vermont, I discovered a large patch of weeds that turned out to be horseradish. It is eaten only for the root, which can be enormously long. If discretion be the better part of valor, it may be preferable to buy horseradish, either fresh or grated and preserved in jars in vinegar. In jars, it can be white or red; the red color is provided by beets, which also take some of the bite away.

Horseradish is typically part of the Jewish Passover celebration (seder), where it is one of the "bitter herbs"— which tells much about its sharp, mustardlike flavor. It is used primarily in Russia, Scandinavia and England, with meats—roasted or boiled.

Cooking gentles the flavor, as does the addition of cream, sour cream or applesauce.

See also Wasabi.

Methods
BUYING AND STORING
Fresh horseradish should be firm, not pliable, and with unblemished skin. Keep whole fresh horseradish in a plastic bag in the refrigerator. It will last for several weeks. Once peeled and grated, cover it with an equal amount of vinegar and store covered in the refrigerator for about 2 weeks.

WASHING/WAYS OF CUTTING
Remove the skin with a vegetable peeler. Trim the ends. Grate horseradish on a box grater using the largest holes. Prepare to weep.

Yields and Equivalents
4 ounces horseradish, peeled and grated = $1/2$ cup
One 4-ounce bottle prepared horseradish= $1/2$ cup
   with liquid = $1/4$ cup plus 2 tablepoons drained
1 cup drained prepared horseradish = $1/2$ cup
   freshly grated horseradish

HUBBARD SQUASH see Squash, Winter
HUNGARIAN WAX PEPPERS see Peppers
ICEBERG LETTUCE see Lettuces
IDAHO POTATOES see Potatoes
INKY CAP MUSHROOMS see Mushrooms, Fresh
ITALIAN ASPARAGUS see Sprouting Broccoli under
   Broccoli and Cauliflower
ITALIAN FRYING PEPPERS see Peppers
ITALIAN GREEN BEANS see Beans of the New World
   under Beans
ITALIAN PARSLEY see Parsley under Herbs and
   Their Flowers
JALAPEÑOS see Peppers
JAPANESE EGGPLANT see Eggplants
JAPANESE PUMPKIN see Kabocha under Squash,
   Winter
JARRAHDALE SQUASH see Squash, Winter

Jerusalem Artichokes (Sunchokes)
Helianthus tuberosus

Helianthus means these are a member of the sunflower family—but not a really decorative one. They are neither artichokes nor Israeli, but rather American-Peruvian-Indian. Some root varieties are knobby, typically gnarled— as if arthritic. However, there is a variety, Fuseau, that has no knobs and is much easier to clean. If planting, try to find it.

The flavor is a bit like artichokes and slightly sweet. I like them roasted, fried as chips (see page 514) or turned into a purée.

Methods

BUYING AND STORING

Store in a plastic bag in the refrigerator. They will last up to a month.

WASHING/WAYS OF CUTTING

Their knobby shapes make peeling Jerusalem artichokes a bit of a challenge. A potato peeler will do the job. Rough bits should be trimmed away after peeling.

Jerusalem artichokes will discolor when exposed to air. Drop peeled ones into a bowl of water with lemon juice.

Preparation

BOILING

Whole: Put peeled and trimmed Jerusalem artichokes in a pot and cover with 1 inch of water. Bring to a boil. Reduce heat and simmer 20 minutes.

STEAMING

Whole: Place peeled and trimmed Jerusalem artichokes in a covered steamer basket. Cook 15 minutes, or until a knife easily slips into flesh.

ROASTING

Whole and/or halves: For 1 pound, peeled and trimmed: Cut pieces that are larger than 1 inch long in half lengthwise. Use smallest pan that will hold artichokes comfortably in a single layer. Slick artichokes and pan with 2 teaspoons olive oil. Roast in center of 500°F oven for 8 minutes. Turn. Roast 8 minutes more. This can be multiplied.

MICROWAVING

1/4-inch rounds: Peel and trim. Cut crosswise into 1/4-inch rounds. Put in a 2-quart container with 1 cup water. Cover tightly.

1 pound: 8 minutes

Yields and Equivalents

1 pound = 8 large Jerusalem artichokes

1 pound = 10 medium Jerusalem artichokes

1 pound = 16 small Jerusalem artichokes

1 pound = 24 small peeled Jerusalem artichokes (really small ones will lose more proportionately when peeled)

1 pound large Jerusalem artichokes, peeled, trimmed and cut into 1/4-inch rounds = 2 1/2 cups raw = 2 cups cooked = 1 1/3 cups purée

JEW'S MALLOW see Malokei

Jicama

Pachyrhizus erosus/Pachyrhizus tuberosus

Here we go with Sally and Alice, two names for the same girl, or, in this case, the same large tuber that looks like a giant top for a large child. "Rhizus" is for the tuber and, in my fantasy, "pachy" is for pachyderm, elephant. It is large.

It is used mainly in the Southwest, particularly in Mexico and Texas, but I find it in shops in New York and use it. I like it in salad, with or without a light boil to remove starch (cold water afterward to stop the cooking). It can easily replace water chestnuts.

Methods

BUYING AND STORING

Jicama should be firm with a dry light tan skin, without bluish-green, soft or dark spots. Choose small to medium (no larger than 1 1/2-pound) roots. They will be easier to peel and cut. Store jicama in the refrigerator for no more than a few days.

WASHING/WAYS OF CUTTING

Remove the skin with a vegetable peeler. Cut according to the recipe.

Preparation

Jicama is usually served raw. However, it can be boiled for a minute or two to remove its somewhat floury feel. Boiling jicama leaves its crunch intact and makes it a little more absorbent, nice in a salad such as the one on page 145. It might also be cut into thin slices and fried as chips (see page 514).

Yields and Equivalents

1 large jicama = 2 pounds

1 medium jicama = 1 1/2 pounds

1 small jicama = 1 pound

1 large jicama, peeled and cut into 1/4 x 1/4-inch strips = 8 cups

1 medium jicama, peeled and cut into 1/8-inch strips = 6 1/2 cups

1 medium jicama, peeled and cut into 1/4-inch dice = 4 1/2 cups

1 medium jicama, peeled and cut into 1/2-inch dice = 5 1/4 cups

KABOCHA see Squash, Winter

Kale

Brassica oleracea (Acephala group)

Kale lives happily until well after first frost, endearing it to me as the remaining leafy greens droop to their death.

Varieties

All kinds of kale are relatives of cabbages but more primitive and without heads. They are all green and fairly dark. They vary in curliness and the amount of stem. There was a time when kales were eaten mainly for their stems. Perversely, today they are eaten almost exclusively for their leaves. While kale is also known as Scots cabbage because it grows in that difficult climate, which would also explain the name Siberian kale, it is also very popular in Portugal, where a special kind, "couve," is used to make caldo verde or caldo gallego, a stew or soup.

The Italians have been busy with the kales, breeding their own varieties such as Tuscan and Lacinato. There are kales that are almost blue and others that are much less crinkly than the standard.

They all need serious cooking in terms of time, but by way of compensation, they stand up very well to prolonged cooking. They also shrink with heat, as if they were anorectic.

See also Collards. Chinese kale is a different plant; see Chinese Broccoli.

Methods

BUYING AND STORING
Do as Collards, page 570.

WASHING/WAYS OF CUTTING
Do as Collards, page 570.

Preparation

Steaming makes mushy, bland kale. Boiling, as for collards, is better. For kale with a pronounced flavor and bite, try braising as outlined below.

BRAISING
Thick stems removed, leaves cut into 2-inch pieces:
For 1 1/4 pounds kale: Heat 2 tablespoons olive oil or vegetable oil in a deep 11- to 12-inch skillet over medium-high heat. Add half of kale. Cook until wilted enough to accommodate remaining kale. Add remaining kale and stir until all kale is bright green and wilted. Pour in 1/2 cup chicken stock, broth or water. Season lightly with salt and, if desired, hot red pepper flakes. Bring to a boil, reduce heat to low and cover pan. Cook until kale is tender but firm, about 10 minutes. If necessary, raise heat to high to boil off excess liquid. Check seasoning and serve. (Makes 3 cups)

Yields and Equivalents

Raw and cooked yields for all types of kale are virtually the same.

2^1/$_2$ pounds kale, stemmed and heavy veins removed = 1^3/$_4$ pounds

1^3/$_4$ pounds kale, stemmed, trimmed and cut across into ^{1}/$_4$-inch strips = 20 cups (not packed) raw = 3 cups cooked

8 ounces Lacinato kale, stemmed and cut into 1-inch strips = 8 lightly packed cups

KELLU-UCHU see Peppers
KIDNEY BEANS see Beans of the New World under Beans
KIKUMA see Chrysanthmum Greens
KIRBY CUCUMBERS see Cucumbers

Kohlrabi

Brassica oleracea (Gongylodes group)

This is the only vegetable I know other than fennel that seems to form a bulb but actually is a swollen base of the stem. Both this base and the leaves can be used. It tastes like a cross between a mild turnip and cauliflower. My husband hates it; I can abide it, and some love it. It needs to be thoroughly cooked.

Varieties

RED AND GREEN Interchangeable, with the green being more common. The green is sometimes called white.

Methods

BUYING AND STORING

Choose bulbs that are firm and unspotted. The leaves, although shortish, should be crisp and green. Leaves may be cut away from stems and kept in a plastic bag in the refrigerator and used as collards or kale. Bulbs should be wrapped tightly and kept in the refrigerator for up to a week.

WASHING/WAYS OF CUTTING

Cut off the leaves and any remnant stems. Remove the skin with a vegetable peeler. Trim the bottom and any other tough areas. The leaves should be thoroughly washed and cut as for any leaves they are replacing.

Preparation

BOILING

Bring 2 quarts water and 1 tablespoon kosher salt to a boil in a 3-quart saucepan. Add 2 pounds peeled, diced (1-inch) kohlrabi. Cook until tip of a paring knife pierces kohlrabi easily, about 13 minutes.

STEAMING

Put peeled, diced (1-inch) kohlrabi in a covered steamer basket. Steam until easily pierced with tip of a paring knife, about 16 minutes.

MICROWAVING

Small kohlrabi: Cook 8-ounce quantities in tightly sealed measuring cups.

8 ounces: 4 to 5 minutes
1 pound: 6 minutes

PREPARATION FOR STUFFING

To make kohlrabi shells: Peel and trim kohlrabi. Using a melon baller, remove center of each kohlrabi, leaving a relatively thick shell.

Yields and Equivalents

3 large kohlrabi = 1^1/$_2$ pounds

1^1/$_2$ pounds kohlrabi, trimmed, peeled and cut into 1-inch cubes = 6 cups

6 to 10 small kohlrabi = 1 pound

3 cups cubed (1-inch) peeled kohlrabi, cooked = 1^1/$_3$ cups purée

KURI see Squash, Winer
LACINATO see Kale
LAMB'S LETTUCE see Mâche under Lettuces
LEAF MUSTARD see Mustard Greens and
    Leaf Mustard

Leeks

Allium ampeloprasum (*Porrum* group)

Leeks are among my favorite members of the onion family. The whites are sweated in small pieces to form the base of many sauces. Whole whites are cooked as a vegetable to be eaten hot, braised or at room temperature with one of the vinaigrettes (pages 448–450) or cooler with a homemade mayonnaise (page 455) with lemon juice. The greens make a good broth (page 385).

Varieties

Leeks are the same except for their size. They will keep in the ground for most of the winter, getting sweeter. However, they may be hard to dig midwinter, when the ground is frozen, and will have to wait for a spring thaw. (Some wintered-over leeks, though, may get woody in the center.) Rather than being round like a scallion, they are slightly oval. They can range in size from the earliest picked ones of half an inch in diameter to huge ones that are two inches across.

Methods
BUYING AND STORING

Try to buy leeks that are pretty much of one size for even cooking. They should be smooth without wrinkled outer layers, and it is better if the greens are unblemished so that they can be used for stock. If digging my own, I usually cut off the roots, then wash the leeks and cut off the greens. I store the greens and whites separately in plastic bags in the refrigerator. The whites will keep for 1 to 2 months. The greens need to be used within a few days. As with all onion relatives, use a stainless steel knife.

WASHING/WAYS OF CUTTING

Buy twice the weight of uncleaned leeks required in the recipe. Leeks are always dirty and sandy. As they grow in a trench, soil is piled up around them to blanch them (keep them white). To clean, remove the tops (wash and refrigerate to use in stock; see page 385), leaving about 6 to 7 inches of the white part and lightest green parts. Trim the hairy roots and a very thin slice from the bottom of each one. Make two cuts about 1 inch deep in a cross shape in the bottom of each leek; make similar cuts at the top of each one. Put the leeks to soak in a sink full of cold water for about 20 minutes. If using the greens, they can soak at the same time. Remove from the water and pat dry.

Even very young small leeks cannot be eaten raw and will need a knife and fork unless picked up and munched— messy, but I like it.

Preparation
BOILING

1/8-inch slices, white and light green parts only:
Drop into boiling water. Simmer for 10 minutes.

Whole leeks, white and light green parts only:
Drop into boiling water. Simmer for 7 to 10 minutes for small leeks, 10 to 15 minutes for medium.

STEAMING

Whole leeks, white and light green parts only: Place trimmed leeks in a covered steamer basket. Cook slender leeks for 10 to 15 minutes, until a knife easily inserts into white part of flesh. Add 5 minutes for medium leeks, 10 minutes for large leeks.

2-inch pieces, white parts: Place in a covered steamer basket. Cook for 15 to 25 minutes, depending on thickness of leeks, until a knife easily slips into flesh.

SAUTÉING

1/8-inch slices, white and light green parts only: For 4 medium leeks, trimmed and sliced: Add 2 tablespoons fat to a medium pan. Add the leeks and cook, stirring, over medium heat for 15 minutes.

ROASTING

Whole leeks: For 2 pounds (about 8 small, 6 medium or 4 large), trimmed: Use smallest pan that will hold leeks comfortably in a single layer. Slick leeks and pan with 3 tablespoons fat. Roast in center of 500°F oven for 15 minutes. Turn. Roast for another 7 minutes. Remove from oven. Add 1 cup chicken stock, Leek Broth (page 385) made from the leaves, broth or water. Roast for 10 minutes. Turn. Roast for 10 minutes more for maximum browning. (Serves 4 to 6 as a side dish or first course)

1/4-inch slices, white and light green parts only: For 3 medium leeks (about 2 cups): Use smallest pan that will hold leeks comfortably. Slick slices and pan with 2 tablespoons fat. Roast in center of 500°F oven for 6 minutes. Turn. Roast for 6 minutes more. Watch carefully so they don't burn. (Makes 1 cup, serves 4 to 6 as a topping)

GRILLING

See Grilling, page 518, for how to prepare the grill.

Whole medium leeks: Clean leeks as directed on page 600, but leave the root intact to hold leeks together during cooking. Cut each leek in half lengthwise. Steam or boil as directed above, but reduce cooking by 3 minutes if boiling, 5 minutes if steaming. Drain thoroughly. When they're cool enough to handle, squeeze excess liquid from leeks. Slick with vegetable oil and season with salt and pepper. Grill, cut side down, until well marked, about 4 minutes. Turn and cook until second side is well marked and leeks are tender, about 4 minutes.

Yields and Equivalents

1 small leek = 2 to 4 ounces

1 medium leek = 5 to 7 ounces

1 large leek = 8 ounces or more

3 medium leeks = 1 1/4 pounds

4 small leeks = 1 pound

3 medium leeks, white and green parts only, cut into 1/4-inch slices = 2 cups raw = 1 cup cooked

4 small leeks, white and light green parts only, cut into 1/8-inch slices = 2 1/2 cups raw = 1 cup cooked

LEMON BALM see Herbs and Their Flowers
LEMONGRASS see Herbs and Their Flowers

Lettuces

Lactuca sativa

Salads often contain greens other than lettuces; see also Chicories (page 567), Arugula (page 530) and Herbs and Their Flowers (pages 588–595), as well as Asian Greens (pages 530–531). Lettuces may also be cooked (see pages 418–419).

Varieties

HEADING

BIBB aka TOM THUMB This was originally an American lettuce named after a Mr. Bibb who grew it. It is like romaine (Cos) but makes a smaller, firmer head—an apple lettuce.

BOSTON aka BUTTERHEAD The lettuce the French use for the basic salade laitue topped with finely chopped parsley.

MERVEILLE DE QUATRE SAISONS This is a mottled red lettuce, sometimes called brown in earlier books. It is a little firmer than an ordinary laitue, but certainly not crisp.

ICEBERG aka CRISPHEAD, BATAVIA, BLACK-SEEDED SIMPSON This is the sine qua non of the cabbage lettuces, making a firm hard head that can be easily sliced. (See pages 415 and 420 for recipe and essay.)

ALMOST-HEADING

ROMAINE aka COS, LITTLE GEM This family of lettuces makes a loose cylindrical head that used to be tied up to blanch the interior leaves. The little ones really don't head.

NON-HEADING

SALAD BOWL This has a large, softish frilly leaf that is good in almost any mild summer salad.

OAK LEAF Its name follows its shape. It comes in green and a reddish variation. It is very decorative, especially when small. Use instead of salad bowl.

LOLLO ROSSA This is the pet peeve of my friend Paul Levy, who dislikes its stiff texture and thinks its red mottling comes from a viral infection that modified it genetically, as it did the other red (brown) lettuces. I rather like it when it is very small as part of a mesclun or cut-and-come-again group.

OTHER
MÂCHE aka LAMB'S LETTUCE, CORN SALAD The leaves, spatulate in form, dark green and about 3 inches long, grow very close to the ground in rosettes. They have to be carefully washed, but they are a delightful salad on their own or mixed in with a pale soft leaf like a Boston. Sometimes mâche is sold as a plant, in which case, it should be removed from the pot or the bag by pulling it out by the leaves so that the root can be pinched off without getting too much of the dirt into the leaves.

MESCLUN This is not an individual lettuce but a collection of lettuces and other greens to pick when small. They can be bought already mixed in seed packets. My favorite way to grow them is to prepare the soil, sprinkle the seeds on top and cover them with a thin layer of dirt that I water. They can be cut as needed from about 3 inches tall. They will grow again, but if they are getting sparse, the best solution is simply to sprinkle on some more seeds. The leaves of what we purchase in stores are a lot bigger and somewhat tougher.

Methods
BUYING AND STORING
As with all greens, lettuces should be firm and clear of aberrant color. Some, such as Boston, will have softer leaves than others. Try to find heads that are relatively heavy for their size. Lettuces should be trimmed but not washed before storing unless it is only a short time awaiting dinner. In that case, they should be washed and stored loosely in a bag.

WASHING/WAYS OF CUTTING
Bruised lettuce will darken, so handle it gently. Fill a sink with cold water. Remove the layer of outer leaves or any parts of the lettuce that are darkened or yellowed. Separate the leaves from the core, discard the core, and soak the leaves in water for several minutes to loosen the dirt. Carefully lift out the leaves and drain in a colander. Repeat if needed. With the harder lettuces, such as iceberg, it may be easier to cut out the core in a cone, as if they were cabbages.

Many people prefer their lettuce dried before putting it into a salad. A salad spinner is one easy way to dry it. Patting it dry with paper towels or a kitchen towel is another. I often don't dry lettuce and let the small amount of water remaining slightly dilute the dressing.

Yields and Equivalents
BIBB LETTUCE
1 head = 2 ounces, trimmed and shredded = 1 cup
BOSTON LETTUCE
1 large head = 9 ounces, trimmed and torn into
1 1/2-inch pieces = 5 cups
(An equal-size head of hydroponically grown
Boston lettuce will weigh less and yield less)
ROMAINE LETTUCE
1 medium head = 12 ounces, trimmed =
10 ounces, torn or cut into 1 1/2-inch pieces =
8 cups
1 large head = 18 ounces, trimmed = 15 ounces,
torn or cut into 1 1/2-inch pieces = 12 cups
ICEBERG LETTUCE
1/2 head = 8 ounces, torn or cut into 1/2-inch
squares = 9 cups
RED LEAF LETTUCE
1 medium head (7 ounces), torn into
1 1/2-inch pieces = 6 cups
1 large head = 12 ounces, trimmed = 9 ounces,
cups torn into 1 1/2-inch pieces = 16 (very loose)

LIMA BEANS see Beans of the New World under Beans

LOLLO ROSSA see Lettuces

LONG BEANS see Peas

Lotus Roots

Nelumbo lutea/Nelumbo nucifera

Lotus root is a rhizome, not a root. The *nucifera* variety has the most beautiful flowers, often seen in Chinese and other Asian art, as Buddhists consider the lotus flower a symbol of purity. The Buddha is often shown sitting on a flower or holding one. The rhizomes are segmented, looking like medium-size attached narrow yams or sausages. They have a reddish-brown skin that needs to be peeled. When cut across, the slices display the most beautiful pattern of holes that looks like lace. They do not have much flavor, but they do have a crisp texture much liked in Chinese stir-fries.

Varieties

NELUMBO LUTEA From eastern North America, this has really been used only by Native Americans, baked as a sweet potato alternative.

NELUMBO NUCIFERA From Asia, this is the beautiful one.

Methods
BUYING AND STORING

Usually one buys a single link of rhizome. It will keep for quite a long time if refrigerated. Once peeled, it needs to be immediately placed in acidulated water—usually with vinegar—or it will discolor. Then use as soon as possible, after a brief rinsing.

WASHING/WAYS OF CUTTING

Cut lotus root into segments along its natural dividing lines. Remove the skin with a vegetable peeler. Slice crosswise, either into rounds or half-moons, to best show off the decorative pattern inside. If preparing it ahead of time, keep sliced lotus root in acidulated water to maintain its crispness. Discard seed.

Preparation
STEAMING

$1/8$-inch slices: Place in a covered steamer basket. Cook for 2 minutes; lotus root will be pliable but retain its crunch. Rinse under cold running water.

Yields and Equivalents

8 ounces lotus root = $1\,1/3$ cups $1/8$-inch slices

3 ounces lotus root = $1/2$ cup $1/8$-inch slices

LOVAGE see Herbs and Their Flowers

MÂCHE see Lettuces

MAGMA MUSTARD see Mustard Greens and Leaf Mustard

MAITAKE see Hens of the Woods under Mushrooms, Fresh

MAIZE see Fresh Corn under Corn

MALANGA see Taro and Yautía under Tropical Tubers

Malokhei

Corchorus olitorius

It always amazes me when I come across an ingredient that I have never heard of before and it turns out to be very popular in another part of the world. Malokhei is one such ingredient. I am still a bit confused about its identity. One English name for it is Jew's mallow. The generic name for mallows comes from the Greek malake. It may be that it is seen as a medicinal, as its name in Greek means softening, and it was used to soften and heal. To me malake sounds a great deal like the enormously varied transliterations from Arabic and Egyptian of the ingredient I am dealing with here. I did find out that once upon a time it was assigned to the same family as okra. This made a great deal of sense to me, as the large leaves which look like hollyhock leaves and other mallows, have a slippery, thickening quality much like okra. However, Chris assures me that the Latin name given above is correct. Until I learn more, I will just enjoy it as a food.

Methods

BUYING AND STORING

While markets in Middle Eastern pockets of the country may carry fresh malokhei for a time during the summer, frozen or canned is (somewhat) more available. If found, buy several bags of the frozen. It is better to my mind than the canned and keeps quite a while in the freezer. Defrost overnight in the refrigerator right in its bag, or in minutes in a sieve—whithout removing from its bag—under warm running water.

WASHING/WAYS OF CUTTING

Do not wash frozen malokhei; it will lose some of its gelatinous quality. Simply cut into pieces—carefully, it can be slippery—and scrape into a bowl. Canned should be drained in a sieve but not rinsed.

Preparation

BOILING

Malokhei needs very light cooking, as in the recipe on page 344. To serve it as a vegetable on its own, pour enough chicken stock, broth or water over the malokhei in a saucepan to barely cover. Season lightly with salt, bring to a boil and cook until tender, a minute or two. The cumin oil made in the recipe would make a nice addition.

Yields and Equivalents

One 400-gram bag malokhei = 14 ounces =
   1 3/4 cup leaves, coarsely chopped
One 27-ounce can malokhei = 12 ounces drained =
   2 1/2 cups lightly packed

MANIOC see Yuca under Tropical Tubers
MARINA DI CHIOGGIA see Squash, Winter
MARJORAM see Herbs and Their Flowers
MASA see Dried and Hominy under Corn
MATSUTAKE see Mushrooms, Fresh
MERVEILLE DE QUATRE SAISONS see Lettuces
MESCLUN see Lettuces

MEXICAN FAVAS see The Bean of the Old World
   under Beans
MINER'S LETTUCE see Purslane and Miner's Lettuce
MINTS see Herbs and Their Flowers
MIRASOL see Peppers
MIRLITON see Chayote under Squash, Winter
MISO see Soybeans under Beans from Asia
   under Beans
MITSUBA see Asian Greens
MIZUNA see Asian Greens and see Mustard Greens
   and Leaf Mustard
MORELS see Mushrooms, Fresh and Dried
MOUNTAIN SPINACH see Garden Orach under
   Spinach
MULATO PEPPERS see Peppers
MUNG BEAN SPROUTS see Sprouts

Mushrooms, Fresh

For information on dried mushrooms, drying mushrooms and mushroom powders, see the section beginning on page 610.

I have gathered and/or cooked the mushrooms mentioned here. I have restricted the list to mushrooms usually found in stores or restaurants. There are many, many more. If this is of interest, consider taking a class or turn to one of the many excellent books available. My favorite is the beautifully illustrated—watercolor drawings—*Complete Book of Mushrooms* by Augusto Rinaldi and Vassili Tyndalo. It originally came out in Italy. Another excellent book filled with photographs and giving common English names for mushrooms is *The Encyclopedia of Mushrooms* by Colin Dickinson and John Lucas (see the Bibliography).

When using wild mushrooms, I don't really weigh them unless there is a bumper crop. I am grateful for what I find. A few chanterelles will make an omelet for two. I prefer them sautéed and added to loosely scrambled eggs.

Varieties

COMMON MUSHROOMS, FIELD MUSHROOMS
(*Agaricus campestris*) These are the type I refer to as
"mushrooms" or "common mushrooms" throughout.
Wild, they tend to grow in horse-frequented fields and
are more aromatic, larger and with darker gills than the
store-bought. While the gills start out pink, they go to a
chocolate brown as the mushrooms mature. The caps are
a light ivory color. Ideally they should be smooth on top
and the gills should not be bruised or collapsed. If the
mushrooms are less than ideal, they may be rescued. Snap
or cut off the stems, reserving them for duxelles (page 405).
If caps are dirty, turn each cap over and search for a free
bit of the skin that covers it. Pull it up gently, revealing a
clean white layer of mushroom. Continue around the
entire mushroom. I try to buy mushrooms all of one size.
Large ones are good for stuffing, small ones are very good
whole in stews and medium ones can be cut up to go in
recipes or used raw in salads.

CREMINI (*Agaricus bisporus*) These are a small, dark
brown version of the portobello, related to the common
mushroom, and were developed in Italy. They are somewhat
more intense in flavor than the common but tend to have a
tougher skin on top. They are best used cooked. Use as
common mushrooms.

PORTOBELLOS (*Agaricus bisporus*) These are nothing
but very large cremini. They grill well whole or sliced.
A stuffed cap is enough for a first course.

CHANTERELLES aka GIROLLES (*Cantharellus
formosus*) These heavenly golden yellow trumpet-shape
wild mushrooms are increasingly available in stores. The
Austrian name, eier schwarmrl, is a giveaway. The eier
(egg) in question is the yolk color. They are also given the
name because they are so good cooked with scrambled
eggs. Their stem continues up to the top of their crater
(therefore *Cantharellus*). They do not have true gills, but
rather ridges that squiggle around and divide. Girolles are
the very smallest of these mushrooms. To pick chanterelles,
as I do, begin to look for them in late spring and on into

early summer. Store-bought ones may come from different
climates and be available into fall and early winter. They
are elegant, with a gentle flavor and texture. They are best
cooked in butter over medium heat, and they like fresh
herbs, particularly tarragon, and shallots rather than
garlic or onions. A few added to duxelles (page 405) can
make a vast improvement. They are German favorites,
sometimes called Scharzwalder (Black Forest) pfifferlinge,
sautéed and even enriched with some heavy cream.

TRUMPETS OF DEATH aka TROMPETTES DU MORT
(France), **HORNS OF PLENTY** (England), **BLACK
CHANTERELLES, BLACK TRUMPETS** (*Craterellus
cornucopioides, Craterellus fallax*) The dark gray,
almost black version of the chanterelle, having the same
characteristics of form, but their flesh is thinner and I
find them less succulent.

CÈPES (*Boletus edulis*) The generic name for this
wonderful, fleshy wild mushroom is *boletus*; cèpe is the
French name. The Italians call them porcini ("little pigs"),
the Germans, *Steinpilz* ("stone mushroom") and the
Russians, belyi grib. Cèpes have a large fleshy cap whose
underside looks like a sponge with all-over pores that have
no discernable arrangement. The somewhat more fibrous
stem is shaped like a baluster leg on a Victorian piano and
is almost as thick in the middle as the cap is wide. Cèpes
are picked in the late summer and fall. When fresh, in Italy,
they are sliced lengthwise and eaten raw with a drizzle of
olive oil or grilled whole or cut up and vigorously cooked
in olive oil (done best in a heavy pan on top of the stove).
Sliced, both fresh and dried, they are a wonderful
component of sauces, soups, stews and grain dishes,
darkening and intensifying the taste.

Cèpes will do wonders added to dishes made with
common fresh store-bought mushrooms. An ounce of
dried cèpes, reconstituted, added to risotto during the
final cooking time makes a lovely dish. They do very well
with garlic and a selection of thyme, marjoram, sage,
parsley and/or savory—not all of them at once. There are
many other mushrooms in this family, but they are not
usually found in stores or restaurants. Watch out for

Boletinus species, which have the pores arranged in wedge shapes radiating from the stem. They will be slimy when cooked, as will several others of the *Boletus* family. They are good in sauces, however, and good for drying.

MORELS (*Morchella angusticeps, Morchella elata,* and *Morchella conica*) These look like oval sponges. European ones and those from the northeastern United States are very dark, almost black, and are spring mushrooms. Those from the American Northwest are honey to brown in color and usually larger. I prefer the dark ones, with their more intense flavor. One of the most expensive mushrooms, morels are most commonly available dried (they reconstitute beautifully and quickly in the microwave oven; see page 610), since they are hard to locate—you don't even tell your best friend where your patch is—and have a short season. Smaller morels, both fresh and dried, are preferred. They go well with spring vegetables such as tender asparagus or fiddlehead ferns and make fabulous sauces.

HONEY MUSHROOMS (*Armellaria melea*) These grow in clumps on the ground in the fall. They have a fuzzy center on top of their cap. They can be used like common mushrooms but have a better flavor and are worth serving on their own.

INKY CAPS (*Coprinus atramentarius*) Caution: Do not eat these when having wine; they act like Antabuse. Delicate and good with eggs, they should be eaten before they open, as they otherwise dissolve into a black mess.

SHAGGY INKY CAPS (*Coprinus comatus*) Pliny described these tallish, shaggy, ovoid-capped mushrooms as closely resembling soldiers' helmets. They must be used quickly after picking, as they dissolve into a black liquid that has been used as ink. They are delicate and delicious when young and are much admired in Haiti, where they are used with rice to make a dish resembling squid ink–colored rice and are also eaten raw in salads.

FAIRY RINGS aka SCOTCH BONNETS (*Marasmius oreades*) Sold in French markets, these mushrooms

actually grow in the grass in rings. They have light tan caps and their gills are not attached to the stems. This last trait is important, as it differentiates these delightful, light-tasting, prolific mushrooms—good with eggs—from nauseating species that are similar in appearance.

CORAL MUSHROOMS (*Clavaria*) Don't pick these unless very sure as to what variety they are; some people find some of them laxatives and an unfortunate combination with wine. They grow in the fall among pine trees, which makes them very hard to clean. As their name indicates, they look like small-branch coral. They make a particularly good soup. If I have a lot, I melt them in butter and simmer them in chicken stock, then freeze them for future use.

CHICKENS OF THE WOODS (*Laetiporus sulphureus*) When young and choice, these mushrooms, which grow in shelves on trees, are orange-y red—hence their name. They are only good young; otherwise, they are too tough. They are showing up in restaurants.

HENS OF THE WOODS (*Grifola frondosa*) In Japan, these are called *maitake* (dancing mushrooms). They have recently become very popular in restaurants. The name "hen of the woods" goes back to Roman times, when the mushroom was already highly esteemed. It forms a large, fluttery brownish tuft. It needs soaking in salt water to get rid of insects and is best eaten when young or, if larger, chopped and stewed.

MATSUTAKES and AMERICAN PINE MUSHROOMS (*Armillaria ponderosa*) While the Japanese and American forms are not exactly the same, they are similar enough to be treated in the same way. The American grows in the Northwest. The Japanese esteem theirs very highly. They cut them in thin slices and pour boiling water over them in a heavy iron teapot, where they steep. The broth is drunk and then the mushrooms are eaten. Americans are more likely to roast or broil or make them into soup. They can be bought in Japanese stores but are very expensive there, whereas the American version grows fairly profusely. Unfortunately, they do not dry or store well.

OYSTER MUSHROOMS (*Pleurotus ostreatus*) These are perfectly wonderful mushrooms. They are so good that they even reconcile me to the death of elms due to the Dutch elm blight, as these are their favorite place to grow. Until recently, they had to be picked from the wild.

Of late, they have shown up as a cultivated although less succulent mushroom that has the advantage of being cleaner. In the wild, *Pleurotus* grow in overlapping layers on the trunks of trees. They tend to pick up small insects and dirt where they join the tree; they should be briefly soaked in heavily salted water, which will drive out the mites. The mushrooms are a creamy white and shaped something like a Belon oyster. I have seen in stores a slightly yellow version, called "lemon," which seems to have somewhat more flavor than the cultivated white ones. I have also seen pictures of oyster mushrooms with pale lavender caps. I have never found or eaten one.

Generally I remove the hardish base and cut them into strips following the wedge pattern of the gills. If I am in the fortunate position of having more than I need, I cook them over low heat in a little butter for about 5 minutes and then pour on enough chicken broth to cover and bring to a boil; I freeze in usable amounts. Oyster mushrooms love butter, cream, chicken stock and tarragon. They are elegant and should not be overwhelmed by extraneous flavorings. They are best in sauces and soups.

WOOD HEDGEHOGS aka HEDGEHOGS (*Hydnum repandum*) Unlike the common mushroom, which has gills underneath the cap, and the cèpe, which has a sponge beneath the cap, the hydnums have a bottom that looks rather like the roof of a miniature stalactite-studded cave. These projections are called spines. The Italians also use the hedgehog analogy calling the mushrooms steccherini. The fresh mushrooms should be boiled before slow stewing to get rid of any bitterness.

SHIITAKES (*Lentinus edodes*) These mushrooms with dark brown tops and pale beige gills, used in Asian cooking, are often available in this country as dried Chinese mushrooms. Fresh, they are sometimes called golden oak mushrooms. If dried mushrooms are called for, do not substitute fresh;

it will change the flavor of the dish. Fresh or dry, remove the stems, which are unpleasantly fibrous. Small ones are more esteemed than large. They are beautiful when fresh, cooked and served with tatsoi (see Cabbages, Asian).

ENOKI (*Flammulina velutipes*) These very small long-stemmed white mushrooms can be bought in plastic packages in many markets and Japanese stores. They keep well when refrigerated. I find them virtually tasteless, but they are very decorative. They are generally used raw for decoration or put into a stir-fry for a short time. They can also be broken into small clumps and briefly sautéed to brown lightly on all sides and again used as a decorative touch.

STRAW MUSHROOMS (*Volvariella volvacea*) These are called straw mushrooms because they are usually grown on paddy straw mats that are kept wet. They generally come from Asia in cans as immature unopened mushrooms about $3/4$ inch across. Less expensive canned broken straw mushrooms are available as well. They should be drained and rinsed before being added to stir-fries with mild flavors.

Methods
BUYING AND STORING
Most store-bought mushrooms will be relatively clean. Buy only ones that look clean and are not mushy, and whose surface hasn't turned color or hardened. Store in paper bags and use as quickly as possible.

WASHING/WAYS OF CUTTING
All mushrooms need to be cleaned before cooking. Avoid soaking in water whenever possible, as mushrooms are like sponges and sop up the water. For roasting, the stems should be cut off close to the caps. The dirty ends of the stems should be cut off in any case, and the stems kept for stocks, stews, or sauces or drying. The palm of your hand, a paper towel or, at most, a damp paper towel wiped firmly over the mushrooms should be all that is required to clean them, although there was for a time a vogue for very soft-bristled mushroom brushes.

Preparation

ROASTING

Common white mushrooms are not suitable for roasting. Those readily available that roast well are portobellos, fresh shiitakes, whole or sliced porcini and cremini.

PORTOBELLOS *Whole caps:* Remove stems. Wipe caps clean. Use smallest pan that will hold portobellos comfortably in a single layer. Place, stem side down, in pan. Slick portobellos and pan generously with fat. Roast in center of 500°F oven for 6 minutes. Turn, changing position of each mushroom for even roasting, and roast for 6 minutes more. (Four 4-ounce mushrooms serve 4 as a side dish)

CREMINI It is better to buy cremini that are loose rather than in packages to ensure large, even cap sizes.

Whole caps: (2 to 2 1/2 ounces each, 2 1/2 to 3 inches in diameter): Remove stems. Wipe caps clean. Use smallest pan that will hold cremini comfortably in a single layer. Place, stem side down, in pan. Slick cremini and pan generously with fat. Roast in center of 500°F oven for 7 minutes. Turn, changing position of each mushroom in pan for even roasting, and roast for 5 minutes more. (2 pounds serve 3 to 4 as a side dish or a first course)

SHIITAKES AND CÈPES (PORCINI) While the large fresh shiitakes look handsome when presented as a first course and taste somewhat better since they are fleshier, smaller caps can be roasted the same way and are nice for surrounding a roasted main course. For smaller caps, use more shiitakes. Five of the largest caps, or 8 small, will fit into a 12 x 8 x 1 1/2-inch pan; 6 to 8 large, or 12 small, in a 14 x 12 x 2-inch pan; and 12 large, or 16 small, in an 18 x 13 x 2-inch pan. Larger pans require more oil, but adjust the amount accordingly: Use one and a half times as much oil for a medium pan and double the oil for the largest pan. Allow 2 large caps, or and 4 to 5 smaller ones, per person. Small ones take as long to cook as larger ones.

Fresh *Boletus* (porcini or cèpes) are too special and too expensive to waste as a garnish. Always use them as a first course or on their own or with other compatibly seasoned vegetables. The Italians eat them raw, thinly sliced lengthwise through cap and stem and dressed with a little olive oil, salt and pepper. Given the presence of beavers near the streams where the mushrooms grow, I cook those mushrooms.

Unlike portobellos and cremini, which both cook for 12 minutes total, these require 20 minutes total. Sprinkle with seasonings and lemon juice just before serving.

Whole caps or sliced: For 6 large fresh shiitakes (about 2 ounces each, 4 to 4 3/4 inches in diameter; serves 6 as a side dish), or 6 to 8 large fresh *Boletus* (each about 3 inches in diameter, 3/8 inch thick; serves 6 as a first course) or 4 large *Boletus* (serves 4 as a first course): Remove stems and wipe caps clean. If slicing, trim end of each stem and cut through cap and stem into 3/8-inch-thick slices. Use smallest pan that will hold mushrooms comfortably. Place in pan, stem side down for caps. Slick mushrooms and pan with 2 tablespoons fat. Roast in center of 500°F oven for 10 minutes. Turn. Roast for 10 minutes more.

MICROWAVING

COMMON MUSHROOMS *Sliced:* Toss with 1 teaspoon fresh lemon juice per 8 ounces. Cover tightly.

8 ounces (11 x 8-inch oval dish): 3 minutes

1 pound (11 x 8-inch oval dish): 3 minutes

2 pounds (14 x 11 x 2-inch dish): 6 minutes

Whole caps: Toss with 1 teaspoon oil per 8 ounces. Cover tightly.

8 ounces (11 x 8-inch oval dish): 8 minutes

1 pound (11 x 8-inch oval dish): 12 minutes

2 pounds (14 x 11 x 2-inch dish): 15 minutes

SAUTÉING

The time it takes to sauté mushrooms will depend on the mushrooms themselves and how they are cut. For sautéed mushroom recipes, see pages 403–405. Otherwise, here are a few pointers: Cut or slice the mushrooms into relatively small pieces, such as 1/2-inch chunks or slices. Heat the fat well before adding the mushrooms and do not overcrowd the pan. Once added, the mushrooms will soak up all or most of the fat. Do not be tempted to add more; the mushrooms will first release their own liquid, then the fat they soaked up. Finish cooking and browning in the fat that has been released. Season with salt and pepper and one or more of any number of fresh herbs, including parsley, thyme, tarragon, savory and/or chives.

GRILLING

See Grilling, page 518, for preparing the grill. Any of the marinades on pages 519–520 can be used instead of the oil, salt and pepper suggested here. Whether using oil or a marinade, resist the urge to add more than suggested. All types of mushrooms will soak up liquid and then release it during cooking. Adding more oil or marinade than suggested will cause flare-ups on the grill.

COMMON MUSHROOMS Choose large mushrooms, about 2 1/2 inches across and 1 ounce each. Trim stems flush with caps. For each pound of mushrooms, pour 1 1/2 tablespoons vegetable oil into a bowl and swirl to coat sides of bowl. Add mushrooms and toss quickly to coat. Season with salt and pepper and toss again. Let stand for up to 30 minutes before grilling. Line mushrooms up in a grill basket. Start them stem side down and cook until browned, 4 to 6 minutes. Flip and cook until browned and tender, about 3 minutes.

CREMINI Choose medium mushrooms, about 1 1/2 inches across and 1/2 ounce each. Season and cook as above, reducing cooking time by about 1 minute on each side.

PORTOBELLOS Choose medium mushrooms, about 4 ounces each. Snap off stems and, using a teaspoon, scrape off all dark brown gills. If desired, peel off skin from caps, starting at edge and peeling toward center. Brush both sides of caps lightly with oil and season with salt and pepper. Cook directly on grill.

OYSTER MUSHROOMS Choose clumps of mushrooms of about the same size. Trim tough ends of stems, leaving clumps as large as possible. Drizzle enough vegetable oil into a large bowl to coat sides lightly. Add mushrooms, season lightly with salt and pepper and toss gently to coat with oil. Line mushrooms up in grill basket. Grill, turning once, until mushrooms are tender and edges are deep brown and charred in places, about 8 minutes.

PREPARATION FOR STUFFING

To make mushroom shells: Remove stems and reserve for another use (see page 607). Turn, stem side up, to stuff.

To cook mushroom shells: For each pound of mushrooms, toss caps in a large bowl with 2 tablespoons olive oil and 1 teaspoon kosher salt. Arrange in a single layer in smallest pan that will hold them comfortably. Cover with foil. Bake in center of 350°F oven for 15 minutes for 2-inch-wide mushrooms. Smaller mushrooms will require shorter cooking; larger mushrooms may require longer cooking. Cool before using.

> 1 extra-large mushroom, 2 1/2 to 2 3/4 inches wide, will hold 3 tablespoons stuffing.
>
> 1 large mushroom, 2 1/4 to 2 1/2 inches wide, will hold 2 tablespoons stuffing.
>
> 1 medium mushroom, 2 inches wide, will hold 1 to 1 1/2 tablespoons stuffing.
>
> 1 small mushroom, 1 1/2 inches wide, will hold 1 1/2 teaspoons filling.

Yields and Equivalents

COMMON WHITE MUSHROOMS AND CREMINI

> 1 pound mushrooms = 32 medium
>
> 8 ounces mushrooms = 16 medium, sliced = 2 cups raw = 1 cup cooked, plus 3 tablespoons mushroom liquid
>
> 5 ounces mushrooms, cut into 1/4-inch slices = 2 cups raw = 1 cup cooked
>
> 8 ounces caps = 2 cups cooked, plus 1/3 cup mushroom liquid

PORTOBELLOS

> 1 pound portobellos = about 4
>
> One 4-ounce portobello, cap halved and cut into 1/4-inch slices, stem in 1/4-inch dice = 1 1/2 cups raw = 1/2 cup cooked

CHANTERELLES

> 1 pound chanterelles = 4 cups = generous 3 cups trimmed = 1 3/4 cups cooked

MORELS

> 7 large morels = scant 2 ounces
>
> 7 medium morels = 1 1/2 ounces

STRAW MUSHROOMS

> One 15-ounce can = 8 ounces drained = 1 1/3 cups

Mushrooms, Dried

Dried mushrooms make magic—not the kind that turned people on in the 1970s, but the kind that transports winter foods, giving them mystery and depth of flavor. In the West, the French, Italians, Central Europeans and Russians have used these treasured and costly morsels to boost their cooking. The most esteemed dried mushrooms in Europe are morels—black, spongelike ovals with intense flavor—and *Boletus edulis,* known in one place or another as porcini, cêpes and a dozen more regional names. In Asia, the Chinese and Japanese are the foremost epicures of dried mushrooms. The Chinese prize shiitakes and tree ears; the Japanese, shiitakes.

Dried chanterelles and oyster mushrooms have recently been added to the variety available at the market. Don't be put off by their light weight and small size. Reconstituted, they swell, and their soaking liquid is an asset in soups, stocks and sauces. To reconstitute, put them in warm water, usually three times as much water by volume as mushrooms. Tree ears (wood ears) are bought dry and reconstituted to put in stir-fries. They are reputed to be very good for the health. Their texture is much like that of thin, frilly seaweed. Tree ears swell enormously and it is better to start with five times as much water as mushrooms. In any case, allow the mushrooms to sit until they are pliable.

Depending how great my hurry—often hysterical—I have two shortcuts. The longer one is to bring the water to a boil and pour it over the mushrooms. The quicker one is to actually boil the mushrooms in the water until soft, adding more water if need be. This should take only from 5 to 15 minutes. Drain the mushrooms in a fine-mesh sieve lined with a damp cloth, reserving the liquid. If the water still seems gritty, put it through a coffee filter. They also reconstitute beautifully and quickly in the microwave oven (see Soaking).

When I just have a few dried mushrooms remaining from a batch, I have taken to powdering them in a spice mill and mixing them with other such powders as they become available. They are wonderful additions to sauces, stews and the like. See the Index for recipes.

Methods

DRYING

In the happy times when hunting has provided me with more magic than I can foresee using in the quite-near future, I dry the surplus. I spread a large table, not outdoors—the wind would blow the mushrooms away as they get lighter as they dry—and not in direct sunlight, with newspaper, which I cover with a layer of paper towels. Small mushrooms can be dried whole. Larger ones should be sliced about $1/8$ inch thick. (That goes for most mushroom stems, too. Shiitake stems are an exception.) I spread them in a nontouching single layer and turn them over several times during the course of a day or two until they are totally dry. Then they go into a jar with a tight screw top. This is a treasure for other seasons in risottos, soups and stews. They cannot be used as if fresh; the texture is wrong.

Common store-bought mushrooms, fairy rings, chanterelles and cèpes all dry successfully in the microwave as well. After wiping clean or washing only with a damp paper towel, dry mushrooms thoroughly. Slice common mushrooms or cèpes $1/8$ inch thick through the stem. Leave fairy rings whole. Cut chanterelles into quarters from top to bottom, or sixths if very large. Cover a doubled layer of paper towels (2 sheets) with a single layer of mushrooms. Cook, uncovered, at 100% for 3 minutes. Turn mushroom slices over onto fresh towels and cook for 2 minutes at 100%. If mushrooms are not light and perfectly dry, leave on a dry sheet of paper overnight. When perfectly dry, store in a tightly closed jar.

If drying in a dehydrator, follow the manufacturer's directions for each type of mushroom.

SOAKING

Most dried mushrooms, particularly sliced, do not need to be presoaked if they are being cooked for more than 3 minutes in a dish that contains liquid, such as soup, sauce or stew. When using dried shiitakes in such a dish, break them into pieces, discarding the stems and the hard places where the stems attaches to the caps. Morels must always be presoaked because they tend to contain lots of sand. Save the soaking liquid; put it through a dampened cloth in a sieve and then through a coffee filter if necessary, and use either in the dish or in another soup or stew.

See Yields and Equivalents for alternative methods of soaking various mushrooms.

MORELS Place in a measuring cup with water as indicated. Cover tightly with microwave plastic wrap and cook at 100%.

2 tablespoons mushrooms (1 ounce) with
$^1/_4$ cup water: 3 minutes

$^1/_4$ cup mushrooms (2 ounces) with $^1/_2$ cup water:
5 minutes

$^1/_2$ cup mushrooms (4 ounces) with $^3/_4$ cup water:
7 minutes

CÈPES (PORCINI) AND SHIITAKES Discard stems of cèpes or whole shiitakes (including hard part where stem attaches to cap). Swish briskly in cold water to rinse off grit. Arrange bottoms up in a single layer on an 8-inch plate with 1 tablespoon water. Cover tightly and cook at 100%, then let stand, covered, for 4 minutes.

20 small caps: 2 minutes

8 large caps: 4 minutes

Yields and Equivalents

When possible, approximate cup measures are given, but this figure can be difficult to determine because of variations in mushroom size.

CHANTERELLES

$^1/_4$ ounce dried chanterelles (about $^1/_2$ cup), boiled in 2 cups water for 2 minutes and drained =
$^2/_3$ cup mushrooms, $^1/_2$ cup liquid

$^1/_2$ ounce dried, finely ground = 2 heaping tablespoons powder

MORELS

1 ounce dried morels, boiled in 2 cups water for 2 minutes and drained = 1 cup mushrooms,
1 cup liquid

$^1/_2$ ounce dried, finely ground = 1 $^1/_2$ tablespoons powder

CÈPES (PORCINI)

1 ounce dried cèpe slices (about 1 cup), boiled in 2 cups water for 2 minutes and drained = $^3/_4$ cup mushrooms, $^3/_4$ cup liquid

$^1/_2$ ounce dried, finely ground = 2 scant tablespoons powder

OYSTER MUSHROOMS

$^2/_3$ ounce dried oyster mushroom pieces, boiled in 2 cups water for 2 minutes and drained =
1 cup mushrooms, $^3/_4$ cup liquid

$^1/_2$ ounce dried, finely ground = generous
$^1/_4$ cup powder

SHIITAKES

1 ounce dried shiitakes (about 1 $^1/_2$ cups, stems removed), boiled in 2 cups water for 3 minutes, steeped for 20 minutes and drained = $^3/_4$ cup mushrooms, $^3/_4$ cup liquid

6 medium dried shiitake mushroom caps =
1 $^1/_4$ ounces

1 ounce dried, finely ground = $^1/_3$ cup powder

WOOD EAR MUSHROOMS

$^1/_2$ ounce (about $^3/_4$ cup medium pieces), soaked in 4 cups warm water for 30 minutes and drained = about 3 cups mushrooms and
1 $^1/_2$ cups mushroom liquid

MUSTARD see Herbs and Their Flowers

Mustard Greens and Leaf Mustard

Brassica juncea/Brassica rapa

All mustards except the spice kind are members of the cabbage family. Beyond that, I must confess myself at a loss. My usual saints of research books really don't help very much. Unless I learn Chinese—unlikely—I probably will not be able to sort things out. All mustard greens seem to have originated in China, and they seemingly have hundreds of varieties, each with multiple names. In the American South, *Brassica juncea* has become a weed. It is used, as are the other coarse greens of the nonheading cabbage family, as a long-cooking pot green with liquid to be sopped up with corn bread. It is often cooked with various kinds of smoked and salted pork and sausages.

Following, I give a few of the mustard greens, but I cannot say I know much about them. Now, once again, I miss Barbara Tropp.

Varieties

WRAPPED HEART MUSTARD aka DAI GAI CHOY This is part of a group that forms a head and, according to G.A.C. Herklots (see the Bibliography), they are more esteemed and more expensive than most other mustard greens.

BAMBOO OR LEAF MUSTARD aka JUK GAI CHOY, RED-IN-SNOW MUSTARD, HSEUH LI HUNG, TOKYO BEKANA MUSTARD This small Japanese cabbage, part of a Chinese cabbage group called pe tsai, is one of the milder-tasting vegetables in the mustard family. The broad, smooth, pale green leaves and thin edible stems offer the barest hint of mustard flavor. It cooks very quickly, so add it at the last minute to soups and stir-fries.

MAGMA MUSTARD (*Brassica juncea*, var. *integrifolia*) This variety is more looks than substance. Deeply crinkled wide leaves are edged with ruffles, and a burnish of red tints the top side of the leaves. Sadly, the color disappears once it is cooked, leaving a standard-looking and -tasting mustard green.

MIZUNA (*Brassica rapa*, var. *Nipponsinica* or *Japonica*) In recent years, mizuna has become more widely available, especially in farmers' markets and specialty stores. The mildly sweet, feathery leaves are commonly used as a salad green but are equally good cooked.

PURPLE MIZUNA Purple mizuna more strongly reflects characteristics of its mustard family than its cousin, regular mizuna. The stems are purple and the green leaves broader, coarser and covered with short, fine hairs. Cooked, it has a pleasant bitterness similar to broccoli di raab and can be used similarly.

Methods

BUYING AND STORING

As with all greens, they should look fresh and unblemished; given their wide diversity, it is hard to be more exact.

WASHING/WAYS OF CUTTING

Fill the kitchen sink with cool water. Snap off the stem from each leaf. If there are any extra-large and tough-looking stems, strip them off the leaves. Put the leaves in the water, swirl around to loosen the dirt and grit and let sit so that the dirt sinks to the bottom. Scoop out the leaves and put in a colander. If the greens are very dirty, this step should be repeated.

Cut the leaves across into 1 1/2- to 2-inch pieces.

Preparation

BOILING

Thin strips: For 4 ounces: Add greens to boiling water. Simmer for 6 minutes, or until wilted and tender.

STEAMING

Whole leaves: For 1 bunch, about 6 cups: Place in a covered steamer basket. Steam for 9 to 10 minutes, until wilted and tender.

MICROWAVING

Whole or cut: Cook with 1 cup liquid and 4 ounces fatback in a 14 x 11 x 2-inch dish. (If you like your greens with ham hocks, cook the hocks first. Use 1 ham hock along with its cooking liquid to cook each 2 pounds of greens; omit the fatback.) Covered tightly; uncover for last 5 minutes.

2 pounds: 30 minutes

SAUTÉING

MAGMA *1 1/2- to 2-inch pieces:* For 4 ounces greens (about 3 cups): Heat 1 teaspoon oil in a pan. Add greens. Cook over medium heat for 2 to 3 minutes, continuously stirring from bottom until leaves are bright green and wilted. Add 2/3 cup water, or enough to barely cover leaves. Cover pan, reduce heat and simmer for 10 minutes. (Makes 2/3 cup)

For 11 ounces greens (about 10 packed cups), increase oil to 2 tablespoons and cooking time by 4 to 5 minutes.

TOKYO BEKANA *1 1/2- to 2-inch pieces:* For 4 ounces greens (about 3 packed cups): Heat 1 teaspoon oil in a pan. Add greens. Cook over medium heat for 4 minutes, continuously stirring from the bottom until leaves are bright green and wilted. (Makes 1/2 cup)

For 11 ounces greens (about 8 1/2 packed cups), increase oil to 2 tablespoons and cooking time to 6 minutes.

MIZUNA *1 1/2- to 2-inch pieces:* For 3 ounces greens (about 2 packed cups): Heat 1 teaspoon oil in a pan. Add greens. Cook over medium heat for 45 seconds, continuously stirring from bottom until leaves are bright green and wilted. (Makes 1/4 cup) For larger quantities, increase oil and cooking time slightly.

PURPLE MIZUNA *1 1/2- to 2-inch pieces:* For 2 1/2 ounces greens (about 1 1/4 cups packed): Heat 1 teaspoon oil in a pan. Add greens. Cook over medium heat for 1 to 2 minutes, continuously stirring from bottom until leaves are bright green and wilted. (Makes 1/4 cup) For larger quantities, increase oil and cooking time slightly.

Yields and Equivalents

All of these mustard greens have similar raw and cooked yields.

4 ounces mustard greens leaves = 5 cups = 3 cups packed = 1/2 to 2/3 cup cooked

12 ounces mustard greens = 1 1/2 cups stems, 5 1/2 cups packed leaves = about 1 1/2 cups cooked

MUSTARD SPROUTS see Sprouts
ÑAME see Yams under Sweet Potatoes and Yams
NAPA CABBAGE see Cabbages, Asian

Nasturtium
Tropaeolum majus

Of course we know these as flowers and there is a wonderful Monet painting of a pathway in his garden at Giverny that has nasturtiums growing from both sides, almost covering it. I grow nasturtiums for their beauty too, but also because both leaves and flowers are a delicious peppery addition to salads, used long before Evelyn's time. I usually save a few flowers to stick on top after tossing in the rest. Don't use too many; they are strong.

Methods
STORING
As these can't be bought, most likely they will be picked and used, without storing.

WASHING/WAYS OF CUTTING
I know mine are organic. Perhaps yours will need to be washed. Flowers don't stand up well to washing, so try to buy organic.

NATTO see Beans from Asia under Beans
NAVY BEANS see Beans of the New World under Beans

Nettles
Urtica dioica

There are many, many kinds of nettles, but, I venture to say, few of them are cooked or eaten. In the spring, Italian and Greek women go out by the side of the road and pick stinging nettles at the same time they pick wild dandelions and other wild greens. These are the first relief from the lack of greens in winter. The greens are usually part of Lenten meals: Horta (page 577) and torta pasqualina. They are also made into soup and used in and with pasta.

In my case, they are a by-product of gardening, weeds to be ripped out. The gardener must be careful—gloves are advised—as these nettles do sting in much the same way, but not as severely, as sea urchins. There is no barb left in the hand, but the slightly numbing tingle is unpleasant. The older the nettle is, and the taller, the worse the sting.

The leaves have an almost furry quality, rough on the tongue, so they need to be well cooked before eating. They are very dry and need moisture when cooked; boiling, steaming (boring) and sautéing are probably best. Sautéing retains flavor but water needs to be added, or they are too dry. The color is darker when sautéed, brighter when boiled. Flavor becomes almost bland when boiled for very long. The leftover liquid from boiled nettles is revered as a tonic, but it does not have much taste.

Boiled nettles bleed lots of green into the water. As it cooks, the water goes from emerald to dark, almost black.

Methods

BUYING AND STORING

I cannot imagine anybody storing nettles. They are picked and used. In many cases, they can replace spinach.

WASHING/WAYS OF CUTTING

Like all greens, nettles should be thoroughly washed in a change of cold water. They tend to grow where the soil is loose or on roadsides. Wear gloves when handling them. Their stems are riddled with small thorns. Discard the stems. Use scissors to cut the leaves off at the base. Wash leaves in cold water and drain. Gather the leaves into a bundle and slice them across to eliminate fibrousness. For cooking, choose just the tender top 10 inches of the plant.

Preparation

Nettle strips are generally cooked before being added to another preparation.

BOILING

Usually the sautéed nettle strips are boiled in soup (see page 244), but sometimes they are added as is to a stuffing, as in the Nettle and Ricotta Filling (page 245).

Whole leaves: Bring a pot of water to a rolling boil. Add nettle leaves. Boil, partially covered, for about 10 minutes, or until tender.

STEAMING

Nettles can be steamed for about 3 minutes, but I really do not see the point. Fat phobia can go only so far.

MICROWAVING

No point.

Yields and Equivalents

4 ounces nettles (top 10 inches of plant only) =
$2^3/_4$ ounces leaves = $1^1/_2$ cups packed
$1^3/_4$ ounces leaves, cut across into $^1/_4$-inch strips =
1 cup packed raw = scant $^1/_2$ cup cooked

NEW ENGLAND BLUE SQUASH see Hubbard under Squash, Winter

NEW ENGLAND PIE PUMPKIN see Sugar Pie Pumpkin under Squash, Winter

NEW POTATOES see Potatoes

NEW ZEALAND SPINACH see Spinach

NONPAREILS see Capers

NOPALES see Cactus Pads

OAK LEAF LETTUCE see Lettuces

OCA see Sorrel

Okra

Abelmoschus esculentus

Many people loathe okra, finding it slimy. When it is small and properly cooked, as in Turkey or the American South, I find it to be excellent. It is also valuable as a thickener in gumbos and soups.

The plants are attractive small bushes. After flowering, the okra form at the ends of branches like little candles. As they ripen, the candles fall over and look like Christmas tree ornaments.

Okra comes in both green and purple, which will have lavender flowers. Once again, the purple is a supersaturate of green and the okra will turn bright green when cooked. Do not overcook okra, or it will become stringy.

Methods

BUYING AND STORING

Choose okra that is all of one size for even cooking. Preferably choose those that are about 2 inches long. Cornmeal-dusted and deep-fried, though, it can be used when up to $3^1/2$ inches. The pods should be firm and consistent in color, without dark spots.

WASHING/WAYS OF CUTTING

When trimming okra for stewing, it is important not to remove the entire stem end or cut into the pod itself; if you do, you'll find that every slimy tale you've heard about it is true. If you trim carefully, though, your efforts will be rewarded with succulent, well-behaved okra. On the other hand, if you are using it in a gumbo to act as a thickener, you will want to slice it across to let out the viscous thickener.

Preparation

BOILING

Whole: Add okra to boiling water. Simmer for 8 minutes.

MICROWAVING

Stewed, whole: Trim stems (see Washing/Ways of Cutting). Cook in a 9-inch square dish, uncovered.

    8 ounces okra cooked in $1/4$ cup oil: 3 minutes; then add 2 cups thick liquid, such as tomato sauce, and cover tightly: 5 minutes

Yields and Equivalents

    1 pound okra = 40 to 50 small pods = 5 cups

    3 ounces okra, cut into $1/4$-inch slices = 1 cup raw = $1/4$ cup cooked

Onions

Allium cepa

While I know people who will not eat onions either because of the smell or because they have problems digesting them, I know of no cuisine that is without some kind, or several kinds, of onions. Hands can be cleaned with lemon juice or a new device that a friend gave me that, to my great surprise, worked. It looks like an oval stainless steel stone.

    Onions are primarily an annual that must be planted from seed (difficult) or onion sets, bundles of very small onions from nurseries. Other members of the large onion clan can be found in this guide under their own headings.

Varieties

YELLOW These may be of various kinds. Usually when referred to in a recipe without a secondary name, the regular onions bought in a grocery store are meant. Depending on their size, they will have thicker or thinner rings and therefore give different-size pieces when diced. The root end, which can be dirty, should always be trimmed. A whole unpeeled onion can be put in the soup pot. The yellow skin contributes color to chicken soup, especially if roasted first.

WHITE These tend to be smaller than yellow onions, with thinner rings, giving a smaller dice. They also tend to be somewhat sweeter than yellow onions although not as sweet as the "sweet" onions. Raw, they tend to be used in steak tartare and in Mexican cooking.

RED These are midsize onions, usually slightly flattened. They are gentler than yellow onions and make a smashing-looking contribution to salad and other dishes where they are used raw. When cooked, they pale and may in fact turn a sort of grayish, almost dirty, color.

SWEET While these are often cooked, they are particularly useful for eating raw sliced on a hamburger or in salads. When I was a child, there were only Bermudas, but the geography has billowed: Along with Bermudas, there are Hawaiian (Maui), Spanish, Vidalia from the American South and Walla Walla from Washington State.

SPECIALTY ONIONS

PEARL White and red, these are natural dwarves about ³/₄ inch across. They are good in stews and pickled. They are annoying to peel unless blanched—lightly boiled—or soaked first. See Washing/Ways of Cutting; see also Egyptian onions.

GREEN Americans use scallions (see page 640). The British use green onions that instead of being thin at the bottom have a rounded end, like an ordinary onion. The greens can be sliced and used like scallion greens. It may be my native prejudice, but I prefer scallions, particularly in Asian dishes. See also Chives (page 431).

CIPPOLINI These small, flat white onions have an August harvest in their native Italy and are really only good September through February. When cippolini are in season, roast and marinate lots of them and put them up in refrigerated jars (see page 91). They are perfect as part of a mixed hors d'oeuvre or as an accompaniment to pâté. Cippolini are now available here either loose or in 8-ounce bags, each of which holds 8 to 9 onions.

EGYPTIAN aka WALKING OR SPROUTING ONIONS These are strange plants and, unlike most onions, perennials. They have a bulb underground but are grown for the bunch of small onions that form at the top of long stalks. They are called walking onions because these top growths can set new plants and will end up anyplace. I like to have them in the garden as they are always there and tend to be early. Separate the bulbs and peel and use. Mince or pickle them. The scapes, as with garlic scapes, make a useful broth. Gently boil 1 pound in 4 quarts water, weighted with an otoshi-buta (see Note, page 237) or a small lid for 2 hours. Strain; there will be about 11 cups, which can be frozen. I used some in a risotto for a friend who drinks no wine.

Methods
BUYING AND STORING
YELLOW, WHITE, RED, SWEET AND PEARL ONIONS, CIPOLLINI AND SHALLOTS Look for firm alliums that feel heavy for their size with dry, crackly skin and no visible green or yellow shoots emerging from their centers. Store in a paper bag in a cool, dark place or, if necessary, in the refrigerator.

EGYPTIAN ONIONS Most likely these will be grown, not bought. Store them in the refrigerator up to a week.

All onions are left to paper over if being kept for any length of time.

WASHING/WAYS OF CUTTING
CIPPOLINI Cut off the root end, peel off the skin and trim off any stalk. The stalk sits in a sort of hollow in the top of the onion. It is essential to dig in slightly with the tip of a sharp knife to get it all out. Rinse.

EGYPTIAN ONIONS Despite being small like pearl onions, these have thicker skin and so are easier to peel when dry. Break up clusters into individual onions. Trim both ends. Remove the skin with a paring knife.

PEARL ONIONS Soak in warm water for 10 minutes to soften the skin. Trim the stalk and root ends, leaving just enough root to hold the onion together. Use a paring knife to remove the papery outer layer.

To blanch pearl onions for peeling, bring a saucepan of water to a boil. Cut off the root ends, leaving enough intact to hold the onions together after peeling, and trim any stalks. Drop the onions into boiling water. Boil for 2 minutes. Drain in a colander and rinse under cold water just until the onions stop steaming. Pinch the end opposite the root to squeeze the onion from the skin.

Preparation
BOILING
ALL ONIONS EXCEPT PEARL AND EGYPTIAN
1-inch chunks or coarsely chopped: Add to boiling water. Simmer for 10 to 15 minutes, until translucent and completely soft. Whole onions may also be boiled until tender. Keep water at a simmer rather than a hard boil so the onions do not get mushy.

STEAMING

PEARL ONIONS *Whole:* Place trimmed and peeled onions in a covered steamer basket. Cook for 10 to 15 minutes for small to medium onions, 15 to 20 minutes for large. Onions are cooked when a knife easily slips into flesh.

SAUTÉING

ALL ONIONS When the desire is to brown the onions, it is very important to have the onions in a shallow layer and not to crowd the pan, which makes them steam instead of brown. This is done at a fairly high heat. Butter and lard or bacon grease will brown more than oil. Sometimes onions are sautéed without coloring them to soften both their taste and texture. All onions must be thoroughly peeled for sautéing or a thin membrane will adhere and then separate.

Whole: These are seldom sautéed except for browning. My prejudice is to brown them by roasting; see Roasting. If browning in a pan, make sure that the pan is large enough and heavy-bottomed and the heat medium-high. Shake or stir from time to time until the desired color is achieved. Red onions will never brown.

Sliced: Once again, do not crowd the pan. The higher the heat, the quicker the browning, but care must be taken to not burn the sugar-rich onions. Timing will depend on the thickness of the slices. Again, the pan must not be overcrowded and the onions must be tossed or stirred. I prefer to use medium-high heat in order to get even browning of all slices and have them cooked through. I have had a mess of onions for French onion soup take a good three-quarters of an hour.

Chopped: Chopped onions are often wilted for use in a made dish. Use lowish heat. To brown, follow the directions for sliced onions, being even more careful to keep the onions moving so as not to burn them.

ROASTING

ALL ONIONS *Whole:* Whole onions vary in size and color. Large onions up to 14 ounces each can be roasted successfully. They may be peeled or not before cooking.

Place onions in smallest pan that will hold them comfortably. Slick onions and pan with fat. Roast in center of 500°F oven, turning onions in pan halfway through cooking time. Large onions (up to 14 ounces each) will take 45 minutes; medium onions (up to 10 ounces each), 40 minutes; smaller onions (from 4 to 6 ounces each), 30 minutes. Four 6-ounce onions will serve 4 as a side dish. One large onion is a portion.

Whole very small: I tend to roast small onions to use in stews and other foods. Sometimes I roast them with a chicken or a small leg of lamb. They take the same amount of time and can surround the meat in the pan. They require only 1 1/2 tablespoons fat when roasted with meats because the cooking meat will provide more. These onions may also be used in the same way as cippolini onions.

For 1 pound really small round onions (approximately 2 cups, 26 to 30 onions about 1/2 ounce each, 1/4 to 1/2 inch in diameter) or cippolini, peeled and trimmed: Place onions in smallest pan that will hold them comfortably. Slick onions and pan with 3 tablespoons fat. Roast in center of 500°F oven for 15 minutes. Shake pan vigorously to turn onions. Roast for another 15 minutes. Shake. Roast for 15 minutes more. (Serves 4 to 5 as a side dish)

1/4-inch-thick crosswise slices (4 small 4-ounce white or red onions): Place onion slices in smallest pan that will hold them comfortably. Slick slices and pan with 2 tablespoons fat. Place one rack on lowest level of oven and another rack in center. Roast on bottom rack at 500°F for 15 minutes. Turn slices. Roast for another 15 minutes. Move pan to center rack. Roast for 15 minutes more. (Serves 4 to 6 as a side dish)

When making larger quantities, divide onions between two pans on two different racks, switching pans halfway through the cooking, or use a larger pan for all slices. Cooking time will almost double.

Wedges: Of the many vegetables tested, these rank among the best glazed ones. If smaller onions are used, there will be about 4 wedges from each. If using red onions, check about 5 minutes before end of time given; they may cook more quickly.

For 2 1/2 pounds (4 onions about 10 ounces each, or 10 onions about 4 ounces each): Peel onions, keeping root ends intact. Halve from stem to root. Cut each half of larger onions lengthwise into 3 to 4 wedges. Cut each half of smaller onions into 2 wedges. Place wedges in smallest pan that will hold them comfortably in a single layer. Slick wedges and pan with 3 tablespoons fat. Roast in center of 500°F oven for 15 minutes. Remove pan and turn wedges. Return pan to oven, reversing position back to front for even browning. Roast for 15 minutes more. (Serves 6 as a side dish)

1/4-inch dice: When a large quantity of chopped onions needs to be browned to include in a dish, to flavor another vegetable or to serve as a topping for sliced roasted or grilled meats, this method is a winner. While smaller batches can be made, it is convenient to have extra on hand in a container in the refrigerator. Also, for the health-conscious, there is a saving in the amount of fat used with larger quantities. Regardless of the quantity made, less fat is used than would be used for sautéing.

This is a technique that liberates the cook from watching and stirring constantly. There is little danger of scorching the onions, which happens so easily when they are sautéed on top of the stove, and they come out golden and meltingly soft. Just remember to set the timer and to toss and turn the onions well to mix them. If using fewer onions and therefore a shallower layer, check them the last two stirrings. They may brown more quickly.

It may seem that all the onions in the world are being cut up, but they shrink away when cooked. Ten cups raw reduces to 2 cups when cooked. The work is lessened appreciably by using larger onions. While any fat can be used, half butter and half olive or canola oil is a good combination. The butter increases browning and adds flavor. The oil keeps down any smoking, reduces the amount of saturated fat and, in the case of olive oil, adds another good flavor.

For 4 1/2 pounds (5 to 6 onions about 13 ounces each): Peel onions. Roughly chop into 1/4-inch dice (about 10 cups). Place onions in smallest pan that will hold them comfortably in a thin layer. Slick onions and pan with 1/4 cup fat. Roast in center of 500°F oven for 15 minutes. Toss and turn.

Roast for another 15 minutes. Toss and turn. Roast for 15 to 20 minutes more. If using as a sauce or topping, salt and pepper to taste. (Makes 2 cups)

DEEP-FRYING

Onions are very wet and tend to splatter when fried. They are usually cut in some form and may be fried without a coating, dusted with flour and seasonings or battered. (See recipe, page 517.)

PICKLING

Aside from use in Gibsons, for which they are usually purchased, onions are not among the most pickled of vegetables unless they are little ones tucked in with another vegetable like cornichons (page 576) or are a specialty onion like cippolini (see page 616).

MICROWAVING

The sweeter the onion, the more likely it is to brown well with microwave cooking, except for red onions, which never brown well unless roasted. Unfortunately, browning onions takes a long time even in the microwave oven. The advantage is you don't have to stand and stir and worry about scorching.

Since onions vary so wildly in size and weight, I have tried in these recipes to give you the size of the onion being used, or the weight and/or the quantities of chopped onion.

PEARL ONIONS Pearl onions seem delightful until it comes time to peel them. The microwave oven makes this easy: Trim the root ends; blanch onions. If they are very young, reduce the cooking time by about 15 seconds. When cool enough to handle, simply pop them out of their skins.

Blanching times: Arrange onions in a single layer. Cook in an 11 x 8 1/2 x 2-inch oval dish, uncovered.

8 ounces onions with 1 tablespoon water: 1 minute
1 pound onions with 2 tablespoons water: 2 minutes

Pearl onions, blanched: Peel. Cook in a 1-quart soufflé dish. Cover tightly.

8 ounces onions with 6 to 8 tablespoons liquid: 8 minutes
8 ounces onions with 1/2 to 1 cup liquid: 10 minutes
1 pound onions with 1 to 2 cups liquid; stir once: 15 minutes

ALL OTHER WHITE ONIONS

Whole small (12 per pound): Peel and trim. Cook in a 10-inch quiche dish. Cover tightly.

2 pounds onions with 2 cups sauce, such as
    béchamel or tomato sauce: 10 minutes

Whole cippolini (2^1/$_4$ x 3^1/$_4$ x ^{1}/$_2$ inch): Peel and trim. Cook in a 14 x 11 x 2-inch dish. Cover tightly. Uncover for last 10 minutes of cooking time.

1^1/$_2$ pounds onions with 1^3/$_4$ cups sauce:
    25 minutes

Sliced: To caramelize, cook, uncovered.

2 cups onions with 4 tablespoons unsalted butter
    (1-quart soufflé dish): 30 minutes

4 cups onions with 8 tablespoons butter
    (14 x 11 x 2-inch dish): 40 to 50 minutes

Minced: Cook in a shallow dish with fat that has been heated for 2 minutes, uncovered.

^{1}/$_4$ cup onion with 2 tablespoons fat
    (8-inch square dish): 2 minutes

^{1}/$_3$ cup onion with 4 tablespoons (^{1}/$_4$ cup)
    fat (10-inch quiche dish): 2 minutes

^{1}/$_2$ cup onion with 4 tablespoons (^{1}/$_4$ cup)
    fat (10-inch quiche dish): 4 minutes

^{2}/$_3$ cup onion with 8 tablespoons (^{1}/$_2$ cup)
    fat (14 x 11 x 2-inch dish): 3 minutes

1 cup onion with 8 tablespoons (^{1}/$_2$ cup)
    fat (14 x 11 x 2-inch dish): 3 minutes

PREPARATION FOR STUFFING

To make onion shells: Slice about ^{1}/$_4$ inch off tops of peeled onions. Use a mellon baller to hollow out onions, leaving ^{1}/$_3$-inch-thick shells. Cut a sliver off root end of each onion so it can stand upright.

A 6- to 7-ounce onion, 2^1/$_2$ to 3 inches in diameter, will hold ^{1}/$_3$ cup stuffing.

Yields and Equivalents

CIPPOLINI

1 pound onions = 16 to 20 onions = 3^1/$_2$ cups

PEARL ONIONS

6 ounces onions = 1^1/$_2$ cups raw = 1 cup peeled
    and cooked

8 ounces onions = 2 cups

10 ounces onions, blanched and peeled = 1^1/$_3$ cups

ALL OTHER ONIONS

1 small onion = 2 ounces

1 medium onion = 5 to 6 ounces

1 large onion = 7 to 8 ounces

1 small onion = 1 cup sliced

^{1}/$_2$ medium onion = ^{1}/$_2$ cup coarsely chopped

1 medium onion = 1 cup coarsely chopped, raw =
    ^{1}/$_4$ cup cooked

1 pound onions = 2 cups sliced

1 pound really small round onions = 26 to 30 onions,
    ^{1}/$_2$ ounce each, ^{1}/$_4$ to ^{1}/$_2$ inch in diameter = 2 cups

4^1/$_2$ pounds onions (5 to 6, about 13 ounces each),
    cut into ^{1}/$_4$-inch dice = 10 cups raw = 2 cups cooked

OREGANO see Herbs and Their Flowers

OYSTER MUSHROOMS see Mushrooms, Fresh

OYSTER PLANT see Salsify under Scorzonera and
    Salsify

PADRON PEPPERS see Peppers

PAK CHOY see Cabbages, Asian

PAPRIKA see Peppers

PARSLEY see Herbs and Their Flowers

Parsnips

Pastinaca sativa

Varieties

Like many other root vegetables, these may be conical, like an exaggerated carrot, or rounder, like a turnip. The conical ones have a longer growing season and will sweeten as the ground freezes. They can be dug in the spring. The round ones are tenderer and mature more quickly. They are seldom seen in markets. I grew some and they were particularly good when young and small in the spring for frying to accompany duck. This was a dish at Chez Allard in the good old days when Madame Allard was doing the cooking.

Methods

BUYING AND STORING

Choose parsnips that are firm, not wrinkled, and unblemished. Medium-size ones are safer. If they are too big, they can be fibrous or have hollow cores.

Scrub them and store in a plastic bag in the refrigerator. They will keep for months. There is no need to freeze them.

WASHING/WAYS OF CUTTING

Scrub parsnips with a hard brush and peel with a potato peeler if the skin has any gritty texture or bitter taste. Trim the root end. If cutting parsnips into pieces, first cut the parsnip crosswise into skinny and thick halves. Slice the skinny end and halve the thicker end before slicing.

Preparation

BOILING

1/2-inch rounds: For 4 ounces parsnips: Place prepared parsnips in a saucepan and cover by 2 inches with water. Bring to a boil, lower heat and simmer for 20 minutes, or until a knife easily inserts into flesh.

STEAMING

Whole: For 1 1/2 pounds parsnips (2 1/2 to 3 ounces each): Place trimmed but unpeeled parsnips in a covered steamer basket. Cook for 15 to 20 minutes, or until a knife easily slips into flesh. When just cool enough to touch, rub off skins.

1/4-inch rounds: Place in a covered steamer basket. Cook for 9 to 10 minutes.

ROASTING

Whole: For 1 1/2 pounds parsnips (2 1/2 to 3 ounces each): Trim and peel parsnips. Place in smallest pan that will hold them comfortably in a single layer. Slick parsnips and pan with 1 tablespoon fat. Roast in center of 500°F oven for 15 minutes. Turn. Roast for 15 minutes more. (Serves 3 to 4 as a side dish)

1/2-inch-thick half-moons: For 2 pounds parsnips (about 6 cups slices): Place slices in smallest pan that will hold them comfortably. Slick slices and pan with 2 tablespoons fat. Roast in lowest level of 500°F oven for 15 minutes. Turn. Roast for 15 minutes more. (Makes 3 cups; serves 6 as a side dish)

SAUTÉING

Wedges: Cut peeled parsnips into 1 1/2-inch lengths, then into wedges 1/2 to 3/4 inch wide. Heat a pan wide enough to hold parsnips in a single layer. Add just enough oil to coat pan bottom. Add parsnips. Cook, stirring, over low heat for 7 to 10 minutes.

DEEP-FRYING

Parsnips become meltingly tender when fried.

Wedges or small whole: Cut larger peeled parsnips into 1 1/2-inch lengths, then into wedges 1/2 to 3/4 inch wide. Very small parsnips may be peeled and fried whole. Pour 1 1/2 to 2 inches of oil into a deep pan. Heat oil to 300°F. Put in parsnips and fry for 2 minutes, or until golden brown and a knife easily inserts into flesh.

MICROWAVING

1 1/2-inch chunks: Cover tightly.

    8 ounces parsnips with 1/2 cup liquid
      (1-quart measure): 5 minutes
    1 pound parsnips with 1 cup liquid
      (2-quart measure): 8 minutes
    2 pounds parsnips with 1 1/2 cups liquid
      (1-quart soufflé dish): 11 minutes

Yields and Equivalents

    1 small parsnip = 2 1/2 ounces
    9 to 10 small parsnips = 1 1/2 pounds
    12 to 13 small parsnips = 2 pounds
    1 medium parsnip = 4 ounces, cut into 1/2-inch
      rounds = 1 cup raw = 1/2 cup cooked purée
    2 medium parsnips = 7 to 8 ounces, cut into
      1/4-inch rounds = 1 1/2 cups raw = 1 cup cooked =
      3/4 cup purée
    2 pounds parsnips, halved lengthwise and sliced
      crosswise into 1/2-inch slices = 6 cups raw =
      3 cups cooked = 2 cups purée

PASILLAS see Peppers
PATTYPAN SQUASH see Squash, Summer

Peanuts

Arachis hypogaea

Peanuts are not a nut. They come from Peru and have spread around the world, particularly to Africa. They are also used in Asia, but there mainly as an oil. They are a legume and widely grown as animal food, as people food (particularly in America as a children's sandwich spread) and as a source of oil, which, once purified, is used for cooking because it can get very hot without burning. In Africa, peanuts are used as a cooking ingredient in soups and stews, often in the form of peanut butter.

The peanut has a weird growth habit. It sends up a plant, but then the shoots burrow underground, where the "nuts" are formed. Usually there are two to three in a pod.

Methods

BUYING AND STORING

Peanuts can be bought in the shell, raw or cooked. They can be bought in jars and cans, shelled, raw or roasted, salted or unsalted. They will keep for quite a long time if left in the shell and stored in a cool, dark place. If they are in jars or cans, they will keep until opened. If they are to be cooked in the shell, they should be rinsed; otherwise, they need no preparation aside from shelling after cooking.

COMMERCIAL PEANUT PRODUCTS

I would venture that most of us first became acquainted with peanuts as peanut butter used in sandwiches. At events, there were small transparent bags of shelled salted peanuts. I remember going to the circus and having bought for me a large bag of peanuts in the shell that I proceeded to feed to the elephants.

Commercial peanut butter is sold smooth as creamy or with pieces of nuts as chunky. It has more fat and salt than homemade or store-bought as organic in health food stores.

Peanut oil comes in bottles, now usually plastic. It should be kept in a dark place as, like other nut oils, it is liable to become rancid.

Preparation

ROASTING

This is best done at a moderate temperature so the heat penetrates the shells slowly and colors and cooks the nuts evenly. Spread raw peanuts in the shell out on a baking sheet in a single layer. Cook in a 350°F oven until nuts are evenly golden brown, about 20 minutes or so, depending on size. The best way to check for doneness is to shell one and rub off peanuts' papery coating. Cool to warm or room temperature before eating.

BOILING

Start with raw, not roasted, peanuts in the shell. Health food and Asian stores carry them. Timing can vary from 45 minutes for "green," or very freshly picked, peanuts, which are not widely available, to close to 3 hours for older peanuts.

First soak peanuts in plenty of cold water for 30 minutes, draining and changing water once. Weight peanuts with an otoshi-buta (see Note, page 237) or pot lid to keep them submerged during soaking. Put drained soaked peanuts in a saucepan they fill halfway. For every pound of peanuts, add 2 quarts water and 1 tablespoon salt. Bring to a boil over high heat. Reduce heat to a low boil. Weight peanuts to keep them submerged. Cook until done to taste. Some prefer them with a little bite, others with the softness of a thoroughly cooked navy bean. If water level drops to below 2 inches above the peanuts during cooking, replenish with fresh hot water. Drain and serve warm or room temperature.

PEANUT BUTTER

Place peanuts in a food processor or blender. Process to the degree of smoothness desired. Some peanut oil and salt can be added.

Yields and Equivalents

RAW PEANUTS

> 5 ounces small peanuts in the shell = 2 cups =
> $1/2$ cup shelled

PEANUT BUTTER

> 2 cups roasted and peeled peanuts = scant $2/3$ cup
> peanut butter

Peas

Pisum sativum/Vigna unguiculata/
Psophocarpus tetragonolobus

See the introduction to Beans, page 536, for definitions.

There are countless varieties, called cultivars, of sweet peas, from low-growing dwarf peas and tall climbing ones to those with smooth, pitted or wrinkled seeds. The three basic types of sweet peas are English peas, sugar snap peas and snow peas.

Additionally, there are the dried versions of peas—usually split peas green or yellow, but sometimes freeze-dried peas for snacks.

Frozen peas are a good out-of-season friend. Defrost in a sieve under warm running water. Cook briefly on their own with some butter and salt or add to made dishes.

Varieties

ENGLISH PEAS aka SWEET GREEN PEAS (*Pisum sativum*) The English have appropriated many Indian and Asian ingredients such as chutney and curry, but they have stopped short of calling them English. Here they got a winner.

SNOW PEAS (*Pisum sativum*) The thin edible pods with undeveloped peas so much seen in Chinese restaurants.

SUGAR SNAP PEAS (*Pisum sativum*) An edible-pod pea with fully formed peas inside, these have been touted as a recent innovation, but nineteenth-century strains existed. Sugar snap peas are at their best flung on top of a stew to

steam for the last 2 minutes of cooking time in the microwave oven. Do not overcook, or the pods become mushy.

FREEZE-DRIED PEAS (*Pisum sativum*) A recent addition to the food lexicon.

PEA SHOOTS aka PEA TENDRILS (*Pisum sativum*) These uppermost leaves and tendrils have been used for years in non-European, non-American cooking. Recently they have come on these markets to be treated as a delicacy or a garnish. I have found that they do not do well on their own. Even when sautéed—the best preparation—they shrink to almost nothing. They are best saved for stir-fries and added only for the last few seconds.

COWPEAS, BLACK-EYED PEAS (*Vigna unguiculata*) Actually these are two different varieties of bean, but only someone as fastidious as Herklots makes the distinction. Eaten shelled, fresh or dried and cooked. Like adzuki, they have shorter cooking times than other shelled or dried peas or beans. They are African in origin.

LONG BEANS aka YARD-LONG BEANS (*Vigna unguiculata sesquipedalis*) Similar in appearance to green beans but much longer—up to 30 inches—and with a somewhat starchier texture. Available in Asian and specialty markets, they are often cut into lengths the size of green beans before cooking. They tend to be tougher than green beans, so stand up well to stir-frying.

WING BEANS aka ASPARAGUS PEAS, GOA BEANS (*Psophocarpus tetragonolobus*) These are very popular in India and Southeast Asia, but they will grow in most climates. My friends the Levys have grown them near Oxford, England. The beans take their name from their shape, which is like a dinosaur pod with raised and scalloped ridges running down their length. They are eaten fresh in the pod. (Had the Levys' beans ripened before this book went to press, I would have given weights and yields.)

Methods

BUYING AND STORING

PEAS Buy or pick sweet green peas when they are plump in a smooth pod but before they get too large. The best way to eat them is out of hand on the way back from the garden. Short of this, they should be used as soon as possible, before their sugar turns to starch. Refrigerate in a bag.

SNOW PEAS They should be flat and smooth and fresh. Refrigerate until ready to use.

SUGAR SNAP PEAS With pods as for snow peas, but with formed peas visible and able to be felt with fingertips—not too large, though. Again, refrigerate and use as soon as possible.

SPLIT PEAS (dried; green or yellow) If possible, find out how old they are and choose those that are most recent. Store as other dried beans in a cool, dark place. I use old coffee cans.

FREEZE-DRIED PEAS Store in the original container in the refrigerator.

WASHING/WAYS OF CUTTING

SNOW PEAS AND SUGAR SNAP PEAS Snap off the tip and tail of each pod, pulling off the string along the seam. Rinse well under cold water.

Preparation

BOILING

PEAS *Shucked:* Add peas to boiling water. If very young and fresh, simmer for 3 to 4 minutes. Simmer larger or older peas for 8 to 10 minutes, or until tender. Frozen peas will take 3 to 5 minutes.

SNOW PEAS AND SUGAR SNAP PEAS *Whole:* Add prepared peas to boiling water. Simmer for 3 to 4 minutes, until cooked but retaining some crunch. I like to add a little shredded apple mint or lemon balm to the water.

WING BEANS Bring ample water to boil. Add beans and cook for 1 to 2 minutes.

STEAMING

PEAS *Shucked:* Place peas in a covered steamer basket. Cook for 8 to 10 minutes.

SNOW PEAS AND SUGAR SNAP PEAS *Whole:* Place prepared peas in a covered steamer basket. Cook for 3 to 5 minutes, until crisp-tender.

MICROWAVING

PEAS *Large winter peas (shucked):* Cover tightly.

   1 cup peas with 1 tablespoon butter
      (2-cup measure): 4 minutes
   Tiny new peas: Cover tightly.
   2 cups peas with 1 tablespoon water
      (1-quart measure): 3 to 4 minutes

SNOWPEAS AND SUGAR SNAP PEAS *Whole:* If adding them to a stew or Chinese-style dish, lay them on top, tightly covered, for the final 1 minute 30 seconds cooking time. Snow peas really should not be cooked in much water. To cook as a separate vegetable, string; heat 2 teaspoons butter or water for each 1 cup of prepared peas for 2 minutes, uncovered, at 100%. Stir in peas; cover tightly and cook as below. (1 cup will feed at least 2 people)

      4 ounces (1-quart measure): 2 minutes
      8 ounces (14 x 11 x 2-inch dish): 3 minutes

SAUTÉING

PEAS See Peas with Mint (page 301).

SUGAR SNAP PEAS *For 2 cups peas:* Heat 2 teaspoons vegetable oil or toasted sesame oil in a 12-inch skillet over medium-high heat. Add sugar snaps, season lightly with salt and cook, tossing, until peas turn bright green and shells start to blister, about 2 minutes. Season with salt and eat as is for very crunchy beans. Or, for slightly more tender beans, add 2 tablespoons water or vegetable broth and cook until liquid is evaporated, about 1 minute.

SNOW PEAS *For 2 cups peas:* Heat 2 teaspoons vegetable oil or toasted sesame oil in a 12-inch skillet over medium-high heat. Add snow peas, season lightly with salt and cook, tossing, until bright green, about 1 1/2 minutes. Eat as is for very crisp snow peas. Or, for slightly more tender peas, add 1 tablespoon water or vegetable broth and cook until evaporated, about 15 seconds. Snow peas are often cut lengthwise into strips before cooking, to eat as is or to add to other dishes.

PEA SHOOTS *For 3 ounces pea shoots (4 cups):* Heat 1 tablespoon vegetable oil or toasted sesame oil in a deep 8-inch pan over medium-high heat until a shoot sizzles when dropped in. Add all shoots. Cook, turning to prevent browning, until wilted and bright green, about 1 minute. Serve immediately. (Makes a scant cup)

Yields and Equivalents

PEAS

$1^1/_2$ pound peas in the pod = 8 ounces shelled = 2 cups raw = $1^2/_3$ cups cooked

1 pound peas in the pod = $^3/_4$ cup shelled peas plus 2 cups empty pods

One 10-ounce package frozen peas = $1^2/_3$ cups

SNOW PEAS

8 ounces snow peas = 3 cups loosely packed raw = $1^1/_4$ cups cooked

4 ounces snow peas, strung, tips and tails removed = scant 1 cup

4 ounces snow peas, strung, tips and tails removed and sliced lengthwise into thin strips = $^1/_2$ cup

4 ounces snow peas, strung, tips and tails removed and sliced on the diagonal into $^1/_4$-inch strips = $^1/_2$ cup

SUGAR SNAP PEAS

8 ounces peas = 3 cups whole

PEA SHOOTS

3 ounces pea shoots = 4 cups (not packed)

4 cups pea shoots, sautéed/stir-fried = 1 scant cup

FREEZE DRIED PEAS

One 7-ounce package = about 2 cups

LONG BEANS

1 pound long beans = about eighteen 20- to 24-inch beans, cut into 2-inch lengths = 5 cups beans

WING BEANS

Will give just about the amount that is started with

SPLIT PEAS Long before young tiny peas were eaten fresh from the pod on a regular basis, they were grown to full size, shucked and dried. It was the people of the Indian subcontinent who most likely came up with the process of steaming peas, removing their skins and splitting them before drying, as they have been cooking yellow split peas as dahl for millennia. (The Indian word "dahl," which has become synonymous with the legume being cooked or the finished dish, actually means "split," as are all the legumes that are turned into dahl.) Both green and yellow split peas are worth keeping on the shelf. Because they are peeled and split, they need no soaking and cook in 20 minutes or so—ready for service as a soup or side dish.

Yields and Equivalents

1 cup = 7 ounces, cooked and drained = $1^3/_4$ cups

PEA SHOOTS or TENDRILS see Peas
PEPERONCINI see Peppers
PEPPERMINT see Mints under Herbs and Their Flowers

Peppers

Capiscum

Many people dislike peppers or have trouble digesting them. It is usually a problem with the pepper skins. Peppers to be stuffed must retain their skins so as to hold together; otherwise, there are many ways to remove the skins. The simplest way to remove the skin for raw use is to peel them with a vegetable peeler, which works best with thick-skinned peppers, like bells. Thinner-skinned peppers, such as Italian frying peppers, are less in need of being skinned. For ways of peeling peppers that are cooked, see pages 628–629. There is one recipe in the book, Greek Garlic Roasted Peppers (page 56), that cooks the peppers without peeling them. I learned it in Greece and think it is sensational. Most people seem to be able to eat them.

Varieties

To get over heavy ground lightly, I just briefly note the following botanical details that will make no difference to the cook. Those who want more information can look in the Bibliography. All peppers are Solanaceae *Capiscum*. Most are *Capiscum annuum*. However, the following peppers are exceptions; most of them are quite spicy. Tabasco and piri piri are *Capsicum frutescens.* Kellu-uchu, ají amarillo and cusqueño, dried chilies, are *Capsicum baccatum,* as is puca-uchu. Chinchi-uchu, datil, habanero, rocotillo, Scotch bonnet and uvilla grande are *Capsicum chinense.* And finally, rocoto is *Capsicum pubescens.* For more botanical information, consult the Bibliography.

From my point of view, the most important distinctions have to do with the cook's uses for different sorts of peppers. The following list is not complete but can serve as a guideline. Numbers at the end of some of the pepper descriptions refer to the Scoville scale, named for the man who invented it. It goes from 1 to 10, 10 being the hottest. Milder peppers, such as jalapeños and serranos, vary tremendously in level of heat from pepper to pepper; it is difficult to assign them a place on the Scoville scale.

Additionally, many peppers are dried and used reconstituted, or powdered to make paprika, cayenne pepper and ground chili. There are also commercial pepper pastes—usually paprika. Another preparation worth noting and even buying if not making it at home is pepper jelly (see page 67).

Some peppers are canned or jarred, commercially or at home (see page 91).

PEPPERS USED RAW IN SALADS AND OTHER DISHES

All of these peppers also have cooked uses.

BELL PEPPERS These may be green, red, yellow, orange or purple. They vary in size but are relatively larger than other peppers, have thick skins and are sweet. Green and purple bell peppers are the least sweet and fleshy. When used raw, they are often skinned with a vegetable peeler.

CUBANELLE, GYPSY, ROMANIAN, SHEPHERD AND SZEGEDI These longer peppers, favorites of Italians and Slavs, are sweeter and more flavorful, thinner skinned and thinner fleshed than the bell type.

PIMIENTO Green or red pimientos are heart shape, pointed or tomato shape, smooth and sweet. They may be best known to us when dried and powdered or peeled and out of a jar.

SQUASH, TOMATO, CHEESE Red and flat, 2 to 4 inches in diameter. These are sweet to mildly pungent.

YELLOW WAXY PEPPERS These may be long, such as Hungarian wax or banana, or short short, such as yellow waxy or cascabella sweet. They are commonly seeded and sliced into rings for use raw.

PEPPERS FOR COOKING, FRYING, SAUTÉING AND STIR-FRYING

All of the above, plus (many of these are used as main ingredients or as seasoning):

ITALIAN FRYING PEPPERS A thin-skinned and thin-fleshed, slightly acidic pepper with steep shoulders and a tapering shape. Usually around 6 to 9 inches long, Italian frying peppers live up to their name. Cut into large pieces, as in Fried Peppers and Tomatoes (for Pasta) (page 62), or even cooked whole, as in Roasted Italian Frying Peppers and Chunky Tomatoes (for Pasta) (page 63), they love high heat and oil and cook fairly quickly. Cubanelles are a good substitute—similar in texture but with an occasional burst of mild heat. Gardeners can look for thicker-fleshed varieties in seed catalogs but that, for me, defeats the purpose. May as well use bell peppers.

PADRON PEPPERS Spanish fresh green peppers. They are generally mild, with the occasional initial burst of heat. They are delicious fried whole in olive oil for 3 minutes, then sprinkled with coarse sea salt or fleur de sel. Eat as a tapa or an accompaniment to a vegetarian meal. Pick up by the stem and eat the whole thing.

ROMESCO PEPPERS These are green to red, long and narrow, with a tapering point. Medium to hot, they are used in sauces such as Romesco, the traditional sauce of Catalonia, Spain, to be eaten with seafood or vegetables (see page 63). **5–7**

POBLANOS Dark green mildly spicy peppers, slightly longer than the wide. Their relatively large size (about 4 inches long) and thick flesh make them ideal for roasting. After roasting they can be peeled and cut into whatever shape needed or they can be stuffed (see page 630). For their dry version, see Anchos.

PEPPERS FOR HEAT, FRESH

JALAPEÑOS Usually dark green, these are about 3 inches long and frequently used in the Southwest. They vary from quite hot to almost bland. When ripe, they turn orange; these are seldom found in stores. Smoked and dried jalapeños are called chipotles; see Peppers for Heat, Dried.

SERRANOS These are green when immature, red, brown, orange or yellow when mature. They are cylindrical, similar in shape to jalapeños but slightly narrower and hotter.

HABANEROS Habaneros may be red, orange, yellow, green or white. They are short and stubby and very hot. They can also be fermented to make a sauce. **10**

SCOTCH BONNETS Shaped like a tam o'shanter, these may be orange, red or yellow. These very hot peppers from the Caribbean have found their way into much Asian food. **10+**

ROCOTOS Green to golden yellow or red, these small roundish peppers have black seeds and are very hot. **9–10**

PIQUÍN aka BIRD PEPPERS Small, slim and pointed, these grow on a sort of bush. They are hot and may be used fresh or dried. When I grow them, I pull up the whole plant when the peppers are quite red, hang the plant upside down in a cool, dry place and let the peppers dry.

PEPPERS FOR HEAT, DRIED

Use as is or reconstitute; see the section on reconstituting under Santakas.

ANCHOS (RED) and MULATOS (BROWN) These are both dried versions of the heart-shaped poblano chili. Both are fairly mild.

PASILLAS A dried form of the chilacate chili, these are brown and slender with wrinkled skin. Pasillas are commonly used in sauces.

CHIHUACLES Yellow, red or black chihuacles are bell shaped or broad shouldered tapering to a point. Medium hot, they are used in various mole sauces of Oaxaca.

CHIPOTLES Mature red jalapeños that have been smoked, chipotles are sold loose and canned in adobo, a tart tomato-based sauce.

GUAJILLOS Dried mirasol chili peppers, guajillos are dark red, long and medium hot. **5**

CATARINAS These are difficult to find, but worth the search. Catarinas are small (usually less than an inch long), pointy and deep red. They are medium-spicy; guajillos make a good substitute.

CASCABELS Cascabels are roughly the size and shape of a cherry pepper (see below) when fresh. When dried, they are wrinkled and round and the seeds rattle in the pods. They range in heat from low to medium-high. When fried, the milder ones are often cleaned, steamed and stuffed with sauerkraut. They are also pickled, like plain cucumber pickles. The hot ones were known as cherry bombs in my youth. **3–7**

SANTAKAS or HONTAKAS These are Japanese long narrow red peppers with a punch. **7**

TO RECONSTITUTE DRIED PEPPERS

Pour enough hot water over the peppers to cover them generously. Soak until pliable, from 20 minutes to an hour, depending on the pepper. Pull out the stems, tap out the seeds and, if desired, open up the peppers and cut away the ribs.

Toasting the peppers before soaking them improves the flavor: Heat a heavy (cast-iron is ideal) skillet or griddle over medium-low heat. Add the dried chilies and toast, turning occasionally, until they begin to change color on all sides. Soak and clean as above.

DRIED PEPPERS, POWDERED AND CRUSHED

Just as there are many varieties of peppers, there is a large variety of dried peppers. Preference tends to vary with nationality, as does that for fresh peppers. Unlike peppercorns, which give off their flavor only in liquid—which is why pepper steak can have so much pepper and not be burning hot—dried peppers, especially when ground, give off their essence only in some kind of fat. Always cook chili powders in a little fat to bring out their flavor—and heat. Be careful; they scorch easily and become unpleasant.

AMERICAN CHILI POWDER This has to be designated as "pure" to come without other seasonings such as cumin. It is usually made from dried New Mexican red-ripe chili peppers, the same kind hung to dry in long garlands, or ristras, in the Southwest. The immature pods of the New Mexican type are referred to as chili verde, or green chili, and the mature ones are chili colorado, or red chili. These have long been a significant part of the bill of fare in Texas and New Mexico. In Mexico, the chili colorado is known as chilacate. However, most Americans think of chili powder as the kind that has a substantial addition of other flavorings such as cumin and sometimes oregano. This is what is meant in most recipes for chili, the dish.

PAPRIKA Spanish and Moroccan paprika peppers are round and sweet. Hungarian or Balkan paprikas (pritamin paprika) are made from peppers that are longish and pointed; they, and their powders, run a gamut of flavors from sweet through spicy. Some powders are made from smoked peppers. The box or tin will designate the heat. Some paprikas are also available as a paste in tubes; I find the taste to be fresher, with more retained acidity. Use roughly twice as much paste as powder. The paste does not need precooking in fat.

CHILTEPIN and PIQUÍN POWDERS These are made from small very hot red peppers found naturally in the wild. Birds are fond of them, and they are sometimes referred to as "bird peppers." **10+**

GROUND CAYENNE PEPPER This comes from long red chilies. The name "cayenne" is less used than formerly, but still appears in recipes. **7–9**

DRIED HOT RED PEPPER FLAKES Sometimes called "pizza pepper," these contain portions of the peppers as well as membranes and seeds, which are hotter than the pepper flesh.

PEPPERS PRESERVED IN BRINE OR VINEGAR AND JARRED PEPPERS

There are basically two different ways of pickling peppers. The first uses raw peppers; see the recipe for Pickled Jalapeño Peppers on page 62. To keep these for any length of time, they should be heat-packed; see page 91. The other method uses roasted or otherwise cooked peppers, which are generally soaked in vinegar, often balsamic, and refrigerated. In addition to those put up at home, there are many kinds of pickled peppers sold in stores that are worth trying. Many of these are suitable for hors d'oeuvre selections or for stuffing. See the Index for recipes.

A wide variety of nonpickled peppers are available in jars too. On page 631, there is a list of how many to a jar of a few kinds, as well as what each will produce when cut up. The fire-roasted and peeled ones are familiar. A particular favorite of mine is the piquillo pepper, which is beloved of the Spanish and frequently used for tapas with a stuffing, as its shape is ideal. The peppers are red and conical. They are usually imported cored, seeded and peeled. Pimientos are the granddaddy of this kind of preparation and are almost tasteless.

PIMIENTOS Depending on their country of origin— usually Italy, a Spanish-speaking country, America or Central America—the actual pepper used will vary. Mostly, though, they are red and pointed. Pieces of them end up in pitted olives.

CHIPOTLES Dried smoked jalapeños, these may be preserved in vinegar as well as packed in adobo (spicy tomato sauce). Mild to hot.

JALAPEÑOS, GREEN OR RED Easy to find in stores or to pickle at home. See recipe, page 62.

SQUASH, TOMATO, CHEESE AND YELLOW WAX PEPPERS Most likely, these varieties will be pickled at home, not bought. Follow the directions for Pickled Jalapeño Peppers on page 62.

YELLOW WAX PEPPERS (pickle) Sweet.

CHERRY PEPPERS These are small, round and red or green. They are sweet to mildly pungent. Check farmers' markets or fresh produce stores in Italian-American neighborhoods during the summer for fresh cherry peppers to pickle, or buy them bottled.

CHILTEPINS aka BIRD PEPPERS These small green peppers which ripen to red are extremely hot. They are one of several small peppers also known as "bird peppers." See Piquín on page 626.

CUBAN PEPPERS AND PEPERONCINI (Italian or Greek) These are small, green, long and crinkly. They are sweet to mildly spicy. They are available in most supermarkets. Use the liquid in marinades and dressing to add acidity and heat.

SANTA FE GRANDE PEPPERS These may be green-yellow, orange or red. Long, pointed and waxy smooth, they are medium to hot and used as pickles and in sauces.

PEPPER OILS AND SAUCES IN BOTTLES

There is an almost infinite variety of prepared pepper sauces and more than a few oils. The most commonly used oil is Chinese hot pepper oil. The sauces range from red to green and will taste and be different depending on their country of origin; they vary in hotness as well as aroma. Usually they should be added at the end of cooking so as not to destroy the acid. In America, the most common sauce is Tabasco, which contains only peppers, vinegar and salt, made from the pepper of the same name. Unlike Tabasco, most of the other sauces have extra ingredients. There are green sauces from Mexico and Central America that are wonderful, and oddities like the Bermudan bird peppers pickled in sherry, which becomes moderately spicy. Sambal olek, indispensable to Indonesian cooking, is also found in Malaysia and Singapore—and, not surprisingly, in Dutch cooking. It is basically a hot chili paste but can be found in many variations, such as those that include shrimp paste and lime juice.

Add any of the above a little at a time at the end of cooking. Hot pepper sauce can be made at home using the recipe on page 629 as a guideline.

Methods
BUYING AND STORING

Fresh peppers should be shiny and unwrinkled. It is better to buy those that are not wrapped in plastic so as to be certain that they are not soft. Intense color is another good indicator of ripeness. Store them in the refrigerator in a brown paper bag. Use as quickly as possible.

Dried peppers will look like aging shoe leather, but they shouldn't be crumbling. I store them in paper bags in an old clamming basket hung from the ceiling, meaning that they have a lot of air circulating around them. If this is not a possible solution, store in a plastic box in a dark, dry place.

Jarred peppers and pepper sauces should be stored in a dark place also and used reasonably rapidly. Once opened, they can be kept, tightly closed, at room temperature, as they will be protected by their high amounts of acid. However, they will discolor with time.

WASHING/WAYS OF CUTTING

Rinse peppers well under cold running water.

Core and seed peppers from the top by cutting a circle around the stem. Remove the stem piece; this will also remove most of the seeds. Shake out any loose remaining seeds. If using the peppers whole, use a small spoon or paring knife to scrape out the ribs. If using in pieces, quarter and cut out the white ribs with a small sharp knife.

For hot peppers, such as jalapeños, removing the seeds and ribs will also lessen the heat.

Preparation
ROASTING

Recipes using roasted peppers are found on pages 55–58.

If time doesn't allow roasting, fire-roasted peppers in jars can be used. Rinse them off before proceeding. Marinated peppers will keep in the refrigerator for a week. *Note:* Fire-roasted peppers vary in size from 1 1/2 to 3 inches in length.

BELL PEPPERS If possible, choose squarish peppers; they will be easier to roast and peel.

> 6 firm medium red, yellow, orange or green bell peppers (purple peppers will lose their color when the skins come off)

Microwave Method: Core peppers and cut into squares; cut out ribs and seeds. Peel with a vegetable peeler, being careful not to remove too much flesh. Arrange pepper pieces overlapping in an 11 x 7-inch baking dish. Cover tightly. Cook at 100% for 12 minutes. Peppers should be tender but still firm, with a small amount of liquid in bottom of the dish. Cool to room temperature, tossing occasionally in the liquid.

Additional timing and yields for microwave-roasted peppers:

> 1 pound peppers (2 1/2-quart soufflé dish): 10 minutes
> 2 1/2 pounds (2 1/2-quart soufflé dish): 15 minutes
> 5 1/4 pounds (5-quart casserole): 22 minutes

Fire-Roasting Method: Leave peppers whole; rinse under cold running water and drain well. Roast peppers directly over gas burners on medium-high, rotating them until all sides are blackened and peeling. Some parts may roast more quickly than others. Check frequently and turn peppers with a pair of long tongs as necessary. As peppers are blackened, transfer them to a large bowl. Cover with cloth or plastic wrap and let stand until cool enough to handle.

Pull out cores from peppers and drain liquid carefully. (Liquid may remain hot for a while after peppers have cooled.) Gently tear each pepper into sections along its creases. Scrape seeds and blackened skin from peppers. (Avoid rinsing peppers if possible—a few remaining specks of black won't matter.) Drain on paper towels.

Broiler Method: Preheat the broiler with oven rack at its highest setting. Broil peppers, turning as necessary with a pair of long tongs, until blackened on all sides, about 8 minutes. Remove to a large bowl, cover and proceed as for fire-roasted method.

Oven-Roasted Method: Place whole peppers in smallest pan that will hold them comfortably. No fat is needed. Roast on highest level of 500°F oven for 15 minutes. Turn. Roast for another 15 minutes. Turn. Roast for 15 minutes more. Oven-roasted peppers will not char as much as those broiled or roasted over an open flame.

ITALIAN FRYING PEPPERS and large chili peppers, such as poblano *Oven-Roasted Method:* Leave peppers whole or core each pepper from the top and remove all seeds, without further cutting peppers. Place peppers in smallest pan that will hold them comfortably. Slick peppers and pan with 1/2 teaspoon fat. Roast in center of 500°F oven for 10 minutes. Shake pan to move peppers. Roast for 5 minutes more. Proceed as for fire-roasted peppers.

JALAPEÑOS *Oven-Roasted Method:* Place peppers in smallest pan that will hold them comfortably. Slick peppers and pan with 1/2 teaspoon fat. Roast in center of 500°F oven for 10 minutes. Shake pan to move peppers. Roast for 5 minutes more if leaving peppers unpeeled. If roasting peppers for peeling, cook for an additional 5 minutes (see Note).

Note: Peeling jalapeños and other hot peppers with thin skins, particularly small ones, is a great bore and I almost never do it. However, a quantity can be roasted at one time and peeled afterward, which makes it easy. As soon as the peppers come from the oven, cover loosely with a towel. When they are cool enough to touch, peel off the skins. If the peppers are large and hot, such as gypsy peppers and poblanos, that need peeling before stuffing, follow the cooking time for basic Italian frying peppers.

RED PEPPER PURÉE (OR SAUCE)

This is the way to make one's own red pepper purée, usable in many dishes. It can be frozen.

> 2 1/2 pounds red bell peppers (about 5 very large peppers), roasted (see Roasting), cored, seeded and peeled

Put peppers through a food mill fitted with a fine disc. (Makes 2 1/2 cups)

Note: To make just 1 cup, use 12 ounces peppers.

FIERY PEPPER SAUCE

Use in place of the hottest red pepper sauces from Louisiana or Thailand. This can be made with variously colored peppers, but the resulting sauce will be muddy. For a sauce as brilliant as it is strong, use hot peppers of the same color, all red or all green.

> 1 pound hot peppers, roasted (see Roasting), stemmed, seeded and peeled

Pass through a food mill fitted with a fine disc. Store in the refrigerator in a tightly covered glass jar or bottle. (Makes 1/2 cup)

STORING

Tightly pack the peppers into glass containers, removing as much of the air as possible. Cover with olive oil or balsamic vinegar, seal and refrigerate. They will keep about 1 week.

GRILLING

See Grilling, page 518, for how to prepare the grill.

Cut 6- to 8-ounce peppers into quarters. Remove cores, stems, seeds and ribs. Toss together in a bowl with vegetable oil, salt and pepper or one of the marinades on pages 519–520. Let stand at room temperature for 30 minutes to 1 hour before grilling.

Start peppers skin side down. Grill until charred in spots (if serving with skins on) or completely blackened, 5 to 8 minutes. Turn and cook until as tender as desired, 1 to 4 minutes. If skins are completely blackened, scrape them off with a knife before serving.

PREPARATION FOR STUFFING

Almost all (including hot and spicy) peppers, except for those that are very small, are suitable for stuffing.

Larger peppers such as bell peppers are usually served one per person as a first or main course.

Poblanos are a favorite for chiles rellenos.

Medium-size peppers such as piquillos or serranos are usually served two or three per person as a first course. For a tapa, one is often served.

Small peppers such as the round red cherry peppers ("bombs" if hot) beloved of the Hungarians are often part of an hors d'oeuvre or picnic spread.

BELL PEPPERS *To make bell pepper shells:* There are three ways to prepare bell peppers for stuffing, depending upon their size and shape. Look for peppers that are plump and well formed. Flatter peppers are more difficult to stuff. If the finished pepper does not stand upright, slice a small piece off the bottom to create a flat base, being careful not to cut though to the interior of the pepper, or the filling will leak out. The easiest way to remove the seeds and white ribs is to flick them out with a small knife or sharp melon baller.

For standing peppers with a lid: Cut across pepper $1/2$ inch from the top; save the lid. Remove seeds and white ribs. Best for medium-size peppers.

For standing peppers without a lid: Slice crosswise to create 2 equal-size cups for stuffing. Remove seeds and white fibers. Best for large peppers.

For peppers lying on their sides: Slice lengthwise to create 2 cups for stuffing. Keep stems intact while removing seeds and white ribs. Good for any size pepper.

To cook the shells only: Place prepared peppers in smallest pan that will hold them comfortably. Add enough water to cover bottom of pan by $1/2$ inch. Cover with foil.

Bake in center of 350°F oven for 25 minutes. Or, if peppers will not be cooked again after stuffing, bake until a knife easily slips into skin and sides have almost collapsed.

If the pepper lids are being used, add these to the pan after 10 minutes of baking. Cover with foil and continue to bake another 15 minutes if the peppers will be stuffed. If the peppers will not require additional cooking after stuffing, bake until a knife easily slips into the skin and the sides have almost collapsed.

Remove peppers from pan. Cool upside down so accumulated water will drain.

To cook stuffed peppers: For each medium pepper prepared as a standing pepper with a lid, fill with about $2/3$ cup stuffing (amount depends on size of pepper; see below) and 2 teaspoons water. Bake, without lids, in a 350°F oven for 1 hour. Add 1 tablespoon olive oil and place lids on top. Bake for 30 minutes longer.

An 8-ounce bell pepper, top sliced off, will hold a generous 1 cup level stuffing or 1 $1/4$ cups mounded stuffing.

Half an 8-ounce bell pepper, whole pepper halved crosswise, will hold $1/3$ cup level filling or a scant $1/2$ cup mounded filling.

Half an 8-ounce bell pepper, halved lengthwise, will hold a generous $1/3$ cup level filling or $1/2$ cup mounded filling.

A 6-ounce bell pepper, top sliced off, will hold $1/2$ cup level stuffing or a generous $1/2$ cup mounded stuffing.

Half a 6-ounce bell pepper, whole pepper halved lengthwise, will hold a scant $1/3$ cup level stuffing or $1/3$ cup mounded stuffing.

JALAPEÑOS *To make pepper shells:* Cut across each pepper $1/2$ inch from the top; save lids. Remove seeds and white cores by scraping them out with a small knife. If using canned jalapeños, make sure to choose fairly large peppers without cracks in their sides. Cut off tops and reserve for lids. Bake them on their sides after stuffing.

To cook stuffed jalapeños: Fill each pepper with 2 tablespoons stuffing and 1 tablespoon water. Bake at 350°F. For fresh jalapeños, cook for 1 hour. Place lids on top and cook for 15 minutes longer. For canned jalapeños, cook for 30 minutes. Place lids on top and cook for 15 minutes longer.

One jalapeño will hold 2 tablespoons stuffing.

Yields and Equivalents

BELL PEPPERS

1 small pepper = 3 to 4 ounces

1 medium pepper = 5 to 7 ounces

1 large pepper = 8 ounces

3 bell peppers (about 8 ounces each), stemmed, seeded, deribbed and cut into 2-inch chunks = about 4 1/2 cups

12 ounces peppers, stemmed, seeded, deribbed and cut into 1/4-inch strips = 3 1/4 cups

1 large pepper, cored, seeded, deribbed and cut into 1/4-inch dice = 1 1/3 cups

1 large pepper, cored, seeded, deribbed and cut into 1/2-inch dice = 1 1/2 cups

1 large pepper, roasted, peeled, seeded and cut into 1/2-inch dice = 1/2 cup

2 large peppers, roasted, peeled, seeded and puréed = 1 generous cup

SERRANOS

1 medium pepper = 1/2 ounce

1 large pepper = 3/4 ounce

6 medium peppers, stemmed and cut into 1/8-inch slices = 1/2 cup

6 medium peppers, stemmed, halved, seeded, deribbed and finely chopped = 1/4 cup

CUBANELLES

1 medium pepper = 4 1/2 ounces

1 medium pepper, cored, seeded, deribbed and cut into 1/4-inch dice = scant 1 cup

HABANEROS

1 average pepper = 1/4 ounce

2 peppers, stemmed, halved, seeded, deribbed and chopped = 2 tablespoons

POBLANOS

1 medium pepper = 4 to 5 ounces

1 large pepper = 6 ounces

1 medium pepper, roasted, peeled, seeded and cut into 1/2 inch dice = 1/3 cup

JALAPEÑOS

1 small pepper = 1/2 ounce

1 medium pepper = 1 ounce

1 large pepper = more than 1 ounce

DRIED

3 ounces pasilla chilies = eight 3 1/2- to 4-inch peppers, soaked, drained, stemmed, seeded and coarsely chopped = 1 1/2 cups = 3/4 cup plus 2 tablespoons purée

3 ounces ancho chilies = twelve 3- to 4-inch peppers, soaked, drained, stemmed, seeded and coarsely chopped = 1 2/3 cups = 1 scant cup purée = 1/2 cup sieved purée

1 ounce colorado (dried Anaheim) chilies = three 6-inch peppers, soaked, drained, stemmed, seeded and coarsely chopped = 2/3 cup (these peppers don't purée well)

JARRED ROASTED PEPPERS

One 14-ounce jar roasted peppers contains 3 medium peppers = 8 ounces drained = 1 1/2 cups chopped (to remove remaining charred skin, scrape with thumbnail)

One 12-ounce jar piquillo peppers contains about 14 peppers, ranging in size from 1 1/2 to 2 1/2 inches long and 2 to 3 inches wide

One 12-ounce jar peperoncini contains about 15 small peppers (1 1/2 to 2 inches long) or 12 medium peppers

One 20-ounce jar whole pimientos contains 4 large (about 4 inches long by 2 1/2 to 3 inches across at the widest point) or 5 smaller (about 4 inches long by 2 to 2 1/2 inches across) peppers

PERILLA see Asian Greens

PHASEOLUS see Beans of the New World under Beans

PIMIENTOS see Peppers

PIMPINELLA see Burnet under Herbs and Their Flowers

PINK BEANS see Beans of the New World under Beans

PINTO BEANS see Beans of the New World under Beans

PIQUILLOS see Peppers

PIQUÍN PEPPERS see Peppers

PIRI PIRI see Peppers

POBLANOS see Peppers

POI see Taro under Tropical Tubers

POPCORN see Fresh Corn under Corn

PORCINI see Cèpes under Mushrooms, Fresh

PORTOBELLOS see Mushrooms, Fresh

Potatoes

Solanum tuberosum

See page 70 for information on waxy, medium waxy and floury potatoes; fingerlings are so called because they are a narrow oval in shape and about the length of a small finger. I often grow my own. Come spring, the potatoes will begin to sprout from their eyes. I cut out chunks of potato with sprouts. I lay them on ground that has been well turned over and cover them with a three-inch layer of straw. They stay cleaner than if in dirt, and it is easy to lift the straw and find out if the potatoes are ready. Since I can buy standard-size potatoes, I grow unusual varieties and pick them when they are quite small, from rounds 1 inch in diameter to 2-inch-long fingerlings. Potatoes grow, underground or under straw, on rootlets that spread out in a kind of web; search. Usually they are ready when the first flowers appear. The flowers are very pretty.

Do not plant potatoes in the same bed two years in a row—they will be more prone to diseases.

Varieties

Potatoes used to be regularly sold in fifty or more varieties. A few of the old varieties, like purple and Yellow Finn, are coming back. Try them for their attractive colors and unusual flavors. Blue and pink potatoes can be floury or waxy—boil a small slice to check. Pink Firs, for instance, are waxy. Potatoes are done when a knife slips in easily.

FLOURY (MASHING)

BAKING OR IDAHO Will be mealy and are good for eating baked whole or making mashed potatoes.

WHITE Often round, with dark-brown skins. These come from Maine or Long Island. Wash well before peeling, or they can have a dirty taste.

WAXY

NEW Should really be of the season. They can be red-, blue- or brown-skinned; the smaller, the sweeter and better. Scrub clean; don't peel. Skins are good and nourishing. In the microwave oven, they should be cooked by weight, not by number. Most new potatoes are waxy but there are a few that are not, particularly among the purples.

CALIFORNIA Have the same shape as baking potatoes and yellow to pale beige skins, but they do not bake well, as they are firm rather than mealy. Use as white potatoes.

CREAMER Not a specific type of potato, but a waxy young potato (often a Yukon Gold or Red Russet) harvested when very small—about 1 inch in diameter. So called because their traditional use was in creamed potatoes, made with or without pearl onions. The name is enjoying somewhat of a comeback.

RUSSIAN BANANA Oval with a fine texture and excellent flavor.

RED FINGERLING Another oval, with red skin.

SMALL YELLOW FINN Another oval fingerling with yellowish flesh and an almost buttery taste.

Methods

BUYING AND STORING

It is essential that potatoes be stored in a cool, dark place so that they do not turn green and become poisonous. Before we had such large refrigerators, but after most of us no longer had root cellars, caves or holes deep in the ground that stayed cool and admitted no light, apartments in New York City had metal trapdoors set into an outside wall and projecting into a colder outside world. These were used for potatoes and onions.

Potatoes should be wiped clean but not washed before storing. Any moisture will tend to rot them.

WASHING/WAYS OF CUTTING

To peel, use a vegetable peeler or paring knife to remove all the skin, and dig out any dark eyes with the tip. Do not peel and cut potatoes too far ahead of time; the flesh will darken. If potatoes must be prepeeled, put them in a bowl of cold water. They will lose some starch, which will make a film on the bottom of the bowl.

If the skin is to remain on, rinse potatoes well under cold running water. Scrubbing may be needed for those that are very dirty. Be gentle with small new potatoes that have thin skins. I find that the dark green thin abrasive scrubbers work best. Do not use metal ones as bits of metal may stick in the potatoes. Plastic scrubbing pads without soap can be used as well.

Always use stainless steel knives or cutters for potatoes. Mild steel will interact with the potatoes and discolor them. (Incidentally, this makes potatoes a good cleaning tool for such knives.)

Cut potatoes following recipe instructions.

Preparation

While I give instructions for numerous ways of cooking potatoes, there is one notable exception. I give no recipe or instructions for pommes soufflés, those seductive little air-filled pillows of crisply fried potato. They are really very difficult. Recourse to a classic French cookbook should give the needed information. The difficulties are the need for very thin, absolutely even slices of potato and double-frying at two exact temperatures. If you master them, please invite me over and make extra. I love them.

BOILING

The reason that there are no times given for boiling whole—jacket—potatoes is that what seem to be the easiest things are also the hardest. Every Irish cook seems able to boil potatoes beautifully and then dry them out in an empty pot. I find it almost impossible to give general rules, since potatoes vary so much in size, age and quality of flesh. Generally, whole potatoes will take between 15 and 20 minutes in boiling water. The knife test is good here. I prefer to microwave or steam, thinking them more reliable.

FLOURY POTATOES *1/2-inch cubes:* Add to boiling water. Simmer for 10 to 15 minutes, or until a knife easily slips into flesh.

WAXY POTATOES *Whole, red or white:* Add to boiling water. Simmer for 15 to 20 minutes for very small (1- to 2-ounce) potatoes, 25 to 30 minutes for medium potatoes, or until a knife easily slips into flesh.

STEAMING

FLOURY POTATOES *1 1/2- to 2-inch cubes:* Place in a covered steamer basket. Steam for 25 minutes, or until a knife easily slips into flesh.

WAXY POTATOES *Whole:* Place in a covered steamer basket. Steam until a knife easily slips into flesh: 25 to 25 minutes for small (2- to 3-ounce) potatoes, 35 to 45 minutes for medium (4- to 5-ounce) potatoes.

1 1/2- to 2-inch cubes: Place in a covered steamer basket. Steam for 15 to 20 minutes, or until a knife easily slips into flesh.

DEEP-FRYING

See pages 78–79 for fried potato recipes.

BAKING

FLOURY POTATOES *Whole:* For 8-ounce baking potatoes: Bake in a 450°F to 500°F oven for 45 minutes to 1 hour. This produces an old-fashioned baked potato with a really crisp skin and fluffy inside.

BUTTER-STEAMING

This is a sinfully delicious way of cooking newly dug tiny to very small potatoes. Choose a heavy pan just large enough to hold the potatoes in a 2- to 3-inch layer with at least 3 inches of headroom; the pan should have a tightly fitting lid. For each 1 1/2 cups unpeeled potatoes, melt 1 tablespoon of butter. Do not raise the heat so high that it will fry the potatoes. Add the potatoes and cover. Holding the lid in place, shake and toss the potatoes every few minutes until a knife slips into them easily. Timing will depend on the size of the potatoes—anywhere from 10 to 20 minutes. Sprinkle with salt. Here is a place worth using fleur de sel, and chives or parsley, if desired. Careful. It is hard to make enough of these.

MICROWAVING

I am going to get myself in real trouble discussing potatoes, since one of the first things that everybody tries and marvels at is "baking" potatoes in the microwave oven. I have given the cooking times for microwave-baked potatoes because I think that potatoes so cooked are used in myriad preparations, such as mashed potatoes and purées. I do not think that a baking potato cooked in the microwave oven is a baked potato as I understand it: with a crisp skin and light, mealy flesh. Of course, if you've been baking potatoes wrapped in foil in a regular oven, you won't see the difference. Baking potatoes cooked for a good hour in a 400° to 500°F oven are real baked potatoes. A compromise is possible. A potato can be cooked in the microwave for 6 minutes and then put in a 500°F oven for about 10 minutes, or until the skin is crisp.

Potatoes in general do something funny in the microwave oven. When they are fully cooked, they will still have a somewhat firm, waxy texture. This is an asset when making soups or stews, where they should retain their shape rather than fall apart, but it is less wonderful for making potatoes Lyonnaise or baked potatoes. When potatoes have cooked in the microwave oven, take them out immediately and, holding them in a doubled cloth, squeeze each potato gently, which will make a lighter potato but not entirely solve the problem. Oddly, letting them cool and then reheating for about 2 minutes helps.

On the other hand, it's hard to beat the rapidity of the microwave, especially when there's no need to wait for the oven to heat or for water to come to a boil. Potatoes cooked in fat do better (probably because nobody expects them to be mealy).

For 9- to 10-ounce baking potatoes, add 1 minute to the cooking times.

FLOURY POTATOES *Whole:* For 7- to 8-ounce baking potatoes: Prick twice with a fork. Place 1 potato in the center, arrange other potatoes spoke-fashion around it; do not cover.

> 1 potato: 6 minutes
> 2 potatoes: 10 minutes
> 3 potatoes: 13 minutes
> 4 potatoes: 15 minutes

Sliced: Cover tightly.

> 8 ounces potatoes with 1/2 tablespoon unsalted butter (1-quart soufflé dish): 4 to 5 minutes
> 1 pound potatoes with 1 tablespoon butter (2-quart soufflé dish): 4 to 5 minutes

1/2-inch cubes (boiled in microwave): Cover tightly.

> 8 ounces potatoes with 1 cup water (1-quart measure): 8 minutes
> 1 pound potatoes with 2 cups water (2-quart measure): 15 minutes 30 seconds

WAXY POTATOES *Whole:* For small new potatoes: Cover tightly.

> 8 ounces potatoes with 1/2 tablespoon butter (1 1/2-quart soufflé dish); stir once: 7 minutes
> 1 pound potatoes with 3 tablespoons oil (1 1/2-quart soufflé dish); stir once: 10 to 12 minutes
> 1 pound potatoes in circle on dinner plate with 2 tablespoons water: 10 minutes
> 4 pounds potatoes with 3/4 cup oil (14 x 11 x 2-inch dish); stir once: 20 minutes

ROASTING

Poatatoes may be peeled before roasting or the skin left on and the potatoes washed.

FLOURY POTATOES Baking or other floury potatoes can be roasted cut into wedges, thick slices, or cubes and lightly coated with butter, oil, goose or duck fat or bacon drippings. I don't know if anybody else remembers a coffee can to which bacon drippings were added each morning after breakfast. Few of us eat that way anymore. The fat rendered by roasting bacon lardons (page 509) can be used, and the lardons strewn over the potatoes after roasting. Use only the amount of fat called for; save extra lardons, refrigerated, to add to a salad or stew.

Floury potatoes generally need to be cut into larger pieces or thicker slices than waxy potatoes so that they will not fall apart.

For potatoes weighing about 10 ounces each: Small roasting pan (13 x 12 x 1 1/2-inch) holds:

> 1 potato cut in 1/2-inch thick slices or
> 1 potato in 1/2-inch dice (2 cups)

Medium pan (14 x 12 x 2-inch) holds:
2 potatoes cut into 1/2-inch-thick slices or
2 potatoes in 1/2-inch dice (4 cups)

Large pan (18 x 13 x 2-inch) holds:
3 potatoes cut into 1/2-inch-thick slices or
4 potatoes in 1/2-inch dice (8 cups)

Slices: Trim ends. Cut potatoes across into 1/2-inch slices. Place in smallest pan that will hold them comfortably in a single layer. Slick potato slices and pan with fat. Roast in center of 500°F oven for 15 minutes. Turn potatoes with a spatula, scraping along bottom of pan to scoop up any slices that stick. Roast for 10 minutes more. Transfer slices to a plate lined with paper towels. (1 large potato serves 2 to 3 as a side dish)

Dice: Trim ends. Cut potato lengthwise into 1/2-inch slices. Cut slices into 1/2-inch squares. Place dice in smallest pan that will hold them comfortably in a single layer. Slick potato dice and pan with fat. Roast in center of 500°F oven for 10 minutes. Turn potatoes with a spatula, scraping along bottom of pan to scoop up any that stick. Roast for 10 minutes more. Transfer dice to a plate lined with paper towels. (1 large potato serves 2 to 3 as a side dish)

Wedges: Cut in half lengthwise, then across. Cut each section lengthwise into 3 to 4 wedges. Place potatoes in the smallest pan that will hold them comfortably in a single layer. Slick wedges and pan with fat. Roast on second rack from bottom of 500°F oven for 15 minutes. Turn potatoes with a metal spatula, scraping along bottom of pan to scoop up any potatoes that stick. Roast for another 20 minutes. Turn. Roast for 20 minutes more. (1 large potato serves 2 to 3 as a side dish)

WAXY POTATOES

Small roasting pan (12 x 8 x 1 1/2-inch) holds:
3/4 to 1 pound potatoes, halved (3 cups), or
1 pound quartered (2 3/4 cups), or
10 ounces, cut into 1/4-inch slices (2 cups) or
10 ounces potatoes, cut into 1/4-inch dice (1 1/2 cups)

Medium pan (14 x 12 x 2-inch) holds:
1 3/4 pounds potatoes, halved (6 cups), or
1 3/4 pounds, quartered (5 1/2 cups), or
18 to 20 ounces, cut into 1/4-inch slices (4 cups) or
2 pounds, cut into 1/4-inch dice (5 cups)

Large roasting pan (18 x 13 x 2-inch) holds:
2 1/2 pounds potatoes, halved (10 cups), or
2 1/4 pounds, quartered (9 cups) or
1 3/4 to 2 pounds, cut into 1/4-inch slices (7 cups)

Whole: (about 2 1/2 ounces each): Place potatoes in smallest pan that will hold them comfortably in a single layer. Slick potatoes and pan with 2 tablespoons fat. (If using butter or another animal fat, total time will be 40 minutes; if using oil, 50 minutes. Roast in center of 500°F oven for 15 minutes. Turn potatoes with a metal spatula, scraping along bottom of pan to scoop up any that stick. Roast for another 15 minutes. Turn. Roast 10 to 20 minutes more. (3 potatoes make 1 side dish serving)

Halves: Cut 2-ounce (about 2-inch) potatoes in half lengthwise. Place halves, cut side down, in smallest pan that will hold them confortably in a single layer. Slick potatoes and pan with fat. Roast in center of 500°F oven for 15 minutes. Turn potatoes with a spatula, scraping along bottom of pan to scoop up any that stick. Roast for 15 minutes more. Turn again. Roast for 5 minutes more. Transfer halves to a plate lined with paper towels. (3 potatoes make 1 side dish serving)

Quarters: Cut 1 1/2- to 2- inch potatoes lengthwise into quarters. Place wedges, cut side down, in smallest pan that will hold them comfortably in a single layer. Slick potato wedges and pan with fat. (Adjust timings for fat used; see above.) Roast in center of 500°F oven for 15 minutes. Turn potatoes with a spatula, scraping along bottom of pan to scoop up any wedges that stick. Roast for about 15 minutes more. Transfer potatoes to a plate lined with paper towels. (8 to 10 pieces make 1 side dish serving)

Slices: Trim ends from very small (about 1 1/2-inch) potatoes. Cut them across into 1/4-inch slices. Place slices in smallest pan that will hold them comfortably in a single layer. Slick potato slices and pan with fat. (Adjust timings for fat used; see above.) Roast in center of 500°F oven for

15 minutes. Turn potatoes with a spatula, scraping along bottom of pan to scoop up any slices that stick. Roast for about 5 minutes more. Transfer slices to a plate lined with paper towels. (8 slices make 1 side dish serving)

Dice: Trim ends from new potatoes. Cut them lengthwise into $1/4$-inch slices. Cut slices into $1/4$-inch squares. Place dice in smallest pan that will hold them comfortably in a single layer. Slick potato dice and pan with fat. Roast in center of 500°F oven for 10 minutes. Turn potatoes with a spatula, scraping along bottom of pan to scoop up any dice that stick. Roast for 10 minutes more. Transfer dice to a plate lined with paper towels. ($1/2$ cup makes 1 side dish serving)

Yields and Equivalents

FLOURY POTATOES

1 small potato = 4 to 6 ounces

1 medium potato = 8 ounces

1 large potato = 9 to 10 ounces

1 medium potato, cut into $1/2$-inch cubes =
    $1 1/2$ cups raw = 1 cup cooked

1 medium baking potato = $1 1/2$ cups purée

WAXY POTATOES

1 small potato = 3 to 4 ounces

1 medium potato = 7 to 8 ounces

1 large potato = over 8 ounces

VERY SMALL FIRM POTATOES
(NEW RED BLISS OR WHITE)

Average size = 1 to 2 ounces

PUMPKINS (including Cheese Pumpkin)
    see Squash, Winter

PUNTARELLE see Chicories

PURPLE MIZUNA see Mustard Greens and
    Leaf Mustard

Purslane and Miner's Lettuce

Portulaca oleracea/Montia perfoliata (Claytonia perfoliata)

Purslane, a plant with multicolored flowers, is a common ground cover. Miner's lettuce is an American weed that grows by the side of the road. Purslane leaves are about an inch and a half in diameter and more oval than round. Miner's lettuce leaves look vaguely like violet leaves, but three times as large. Both are fleshy and taste lightly of cucumber. Purslane can be bought as seed and grown in the garden. Boiled, they can be seasoned with oil, salt and pepper and served as a side dish.

Varieties

PURSLANE (*Portulaca oleracea*) Whether wild or garden grown, it will taste the same. The first time I encountered the leaves as a vegetable was when I found them being sold at Fauchon in Paris.

MINER'S LETTUCE OR WINTER PURSLANE (*Montia perfoliata,* formerly *Claytonia perfoliata*) Technically neither a lettuce nor a purslane, although it resembles purslane. Tall slender stalks are dotted with fat round green leaves. A loose handful in a vase makes for a beautiful decorative arrangement. Serve them as greens under chicken or shrimp salad. The California Gold Rush miners used them as a salad, which is how they got their name.

Methods
BUYING AND STORING

If picked from the wild, take only firm, unblemished leaves. Those bought from stores should be similar. Use rapidly. Both purslane and miner's lettuce are eaten and cooked in the same way.

WASHING/WAYS OF CUTTING

Soak the leaves in cold water to loosen any dirt. Dry thoroughly before using. Check the stalks, which are normally tender and edible but can be tough and fibrous. If the stems are tough or fibrous, discard and use just the leaves. Otherwise, trim the tough ends and break each stalk into 1-inch pieces.

Preparation

BOILING

Whole leaves or 1-inch pieces: Drop into boiling liquid and simmer for 1 to 3 minutes, until wilted and tender.

Yields and Equivalents

> 1 pound bunch purslane or miner's lettuce, roots trimmed, tough stems discarded, remaining stems cut into 1-inch pieces = 12 ounces
> 1 ounce trimmed as above = $1/2$ cup

RADICCHIO see Chicories

Radishes

Raphanus sativus

Radishes are easy to grow and can be planted early in the spring. They are very rewarding for child gardeners, as they do not require much waiting after seeded. Unfortunately, the spiciness of most radishes is not to the taste of most children. Radishes will vary enormously in spiciness from variety to variety. Live and learn, or consult seed packets.

If growing them, do not let them get too large or long. They will tend to become stringy, with hollows inside. The leaves can be used as a cooked green if not too large.

Varieties

RED Red radishes, it seems to me, are a sadly neglected ingredient. They show up on our plates mainly raw on their own or as an ingredient in salads. There are many shapes and sizes and a variety of colors. Cooked, they have a mild spiciness and, when treated with a little vinegar, a charming pink color. They can also be boiled, which gentles the flavor and softens the red color, but they should not be overdone, or they will lose all their color and become limp. Breakfast radishes, or the kind that the French regularly serve with a first glass of wine, some coarse salt and sweet butter, are oval rather than round, and bicolored with white tops and red bottoms.

WHITE Essentially there is no distinction between these and red radishes except for the color.

BLACK These are quite different from their relatives. They are larger and almost round, with black skins. They are not very spicy. They should be scrubbed but not peeled. They are commonly served sliced across into thin rounds that are crisped in very cold water, with Jewish or Russian dishes such as chopped liver. They curl somewhat when crisped, which makes them a good canapé base. I have used them with pâté.

DAIKON This is the ubiquitous Japanese radish. Finely grated into long hairlike strips, it shows up with sushi and sashimi. Again it is not very spicy, but there will be variation from root to root. The roots can be quite large, but they will be better if no more than 6 inches long and $1 1/2$ inches in diameter. Cut in pieces, as indicated by the recipe, they turn up in stir-fries and cold dishes.

Methods

BUYING AND STORING

If buying rather than picking, make sure the radishes are firm and the leaves unwilted. Store in the refrigerator and use within a few days. If desired, remove the leaves and save in a plastic bag for another use.

WASHING/WAYS OF CUTTING

RED AND WHITE Red radishes are normally eaten with the skin left on. Remove the leaves and stems, scrub the radishes under cold running water and trim the root ends.

Very small radishes may be served whole with a small amount of stem attached. Medium radishes can be either quartered lengthwise or cut across into slices. White radishes tend to have a tougher skin and may call for peeling.

DAIKON AND BLACK Large radishes may be peeled or not. I usually peel daikon but do not peel the black. Daikon can be cut either into thin crosswise slices or into sticks, 3 x ¼ inches. Black radishes are nice cut across into thin slices, leaving a tiny rim of black around the white center.

Preparation

Buttered cooked radishes make an attractive and unexpected side dish.

BOILING

RED RADISHES *⅛-inch slices:* Drop into boiling water or stock. Simmer just until center turns creamy but skin is still red, about 30 seconds.

STEAMING

RED RADISHES *⅛-inch slices:* Placed in a covered steamer basket. Cook for 2 minutes for radishes that retain their crunch (good for salads). Drain and rinse under cold running water; drain again. Add 2 to 4 minutes for fully cooked radishes.

Yields and Equivalents

RED RADISHES

1 medium bunch radishes with stems = about
   11 radishes = 8 ounces
1 medium bunch radishes, trimmed and
   quartered = 4 ½ ounces = ¾ cup
4 ounces radishes, trimmed, cut into ⅛-inch slices =
   1 cup raw = ¾ cup cooked

DAIKON, WHITE AND BLACK RADISHES

5 ounces radishes = ⅔ cup sliced
5 ounces radishes, cut into 3 inches x ¼ inch =
   22 sticks = ¾ cup

RADISH SPROUTS see Sprouts

Ramps
Allium tricoccum

Ramps are wild leeks, which can sometimes be bought. They have slender white bottoms and leaves that look like lily of the valley. They are entirely edible except for the hairy root, which must be cut off. When they're raw, many people find them offensive; they can smell and taste somewhat rank. Cooked, they are a seduction, sweet and delicious. Protect the green leaves for the early part of the cooking. Leave the leaves out of the cooking liquid and slide them down in after a few minutes. Or, if grilling, either arrange on the grill so that the leaves are not over the fire for half of the cooking time or wrap the leaves in foil for part of the time so they don't dry out.

Methods

BUYING AND STORING

As always, leaves should be fresh looking and unblemished. Ramps should be considered a fragile vegetable and used as soon as possible. Store wrapped in the refrigerator for up to 3 days.

WASHING/WAYS OF CUTTING

Ramps need washing and they need their root ends trimmed. The green part is usually left on. Sometimes there will be a barely attached thin outer layer on the white part that needs to be pulled off.

Preparation

STEAMING

Whole ramps: Place trimmed ramps in a covered steamer basket. Steam for 15 minutes, or until a knife easily slips into flesh.

SAUTÉING

¼-inch slices, white and green parts reserved separately: Heat butter or oil. Add white parts. Cook for 1 minute over medium heat. Add greens. Continue to cook and stir until greens are wilted.

BOILING

Whole: Bring a wide deep skillet of salted water to a boil. Holding ramp greens with tongs, submerge white parts of ramps in boiling water, leaving greens above water. Cook for 2 minutes. Submerge the ramps entirely and cook until fully tender, about 4 minutes. Drain.

GRILLING

See recipe, page 394.

Yields and Equivalents

1 pound ramps = 12 to 14 ramps = 14 ounces trimmed

Greens from 4 ounces ramps, cut into 1-inch pieces = 1 cup

RAPINI see Broccoli di Raab
RED FINGERLINGS see Potatoes
RED-IN-SNOW MUSTARD see Mustard Greens and Leaf Mustard
RED KURI SQUASH see Squash, Winter
RED RUSSET POTATOES see Potatoes

Rhubarb

Rheum rhaponticum

I thought I was being very creative using rhubarb as a vegetable. Imagine my surprise when I found out that it is one. It is usually eaten sweetened. As a kid, I would simply stick the end of a stalk in sugar; eat and repeat. In New England, rhubarb was called pie plant and every old garden had at least one. It was an early source of acidity in the spring after a lack in winter. In addition to liking the taste, I love the plant because it likes cold weather and doesn't die coming up early in Vermont. Don't eat the leaves; they make people very ill.

If rhubarb is cut regularly and not allowed to form flowers, the season can be prolonged.

My son, Michael, who is an excellent cook, suggested that rhubarb would make a very good chutney. I'm sorry I didn't think of that. I did think of using its acidity to counteract the fat of duck (see page 347).

Varieties

While we commonly think of bright red rhubarb as better, I suppose by association of red with ripeness as in tomatoes and strawberries, it is not true. The stems should certainly show a trace of pink, but they need not be bright red. There are different varieties, some redder than others. Sometimes they will turn red as they cook. The earliest rhubarbs of China and northern Asia were barely red at all and considered mainly medicinal. With time, they were bred to various colors and sizes. I often find that if I plunge down into the plant, I will find redder stalks toward the inside.

Methods
BUYING AND STORING

Rhubarb is usually sold as loose stalks. Look for stalks that are crisp, not limp, and without bruises.

WASHING/WAYS OF CUTTING

Rinse rhubarb under cold running water; scrub lightly if dirty so as not to remove the red. Trim off any leaves. Rhubarb should always be cut across on the diagonal. Unless counterindicated by the recipe, cut into slices about $1/8$ to $1/4$ inch wide. Rhubarb should always be cut with nonreactive stainless steel or ceramic knives and cooked in nonreactive pans.

Preparation
SIMMERING IN SYRUP

$1/8$-inch slices: Put into a pot and add 2 tablespoons sugar for every cup of rhubarb. Toss to coat. Cook over low heat until sugar is melted, pieces are limp and volume is reduced by about half.

MICROWAVING

1/8-inch slices: Cover tightly.

2 cups rhubarb with 1/4 cup sugar (1-quart measure): 3 minutes 30 seconds (serves 2 with dessert)

Yields and Equivalents

1 pound rhubarb = about 7 medium stalks, 13 to 18 inches long, cut into 1/2 or 1/4-inch diagonal slices = 4 cups

3 cups 1/4-inch thick diagonal slices raw = 1 1/2 cups cooked with sugar

ROCOTO PEPPERS see Peppers

ROMAINE see Lettuces

ROMANESCO see Cauliflower under Broccoli and Cauliflower

ROMANIAN PEPPERS see Peppers

ROMANO BEANS see Beans of the New World under Beans

ROMA TOMATOES see Tomatoes

ROMESCO PEPPERS see Peppers

ROSADAS see Beans of the New World under Beans

ROUGE D'ETAMPES see Squash, Winter

RUSSIAN BANANA POTATOES see Potatoes

RUTABAGAS see Turnips

SAGE see Herbs and Their Flowers

SALAD BOWL LETTUCE see Lettuces

SALAD DILL see Dill under Herbs and Their Flowers

SALSIFY see Scorzonera and Salsify

Samphire aka Glasswort

Salicornia europaea

I first tasted samphire in Brittany, where it grows along the shore. It is not a seaweed but is easy to mistake for one. It looks rather like green branch coral but is supple like a succulent and has a snap when bitten. I particularly like its salty flavor, which goes well with seafood.

Methods

BUYING AND STORING

Or perhaps I should say growing. If it appears in a store, grab it. Refrigerate it and use it as soon as possible so that it remains crisp.

WASHING/WAYS OF CUTTING

Pinch off any dark or woody pieces and discard. Larger pieces can be broken in half. Store-bought samphire tends to be very clean and usually does not need to be washed.

Preparation

BOILING

1 1/2- to 2-inch pieces: Add to boiling water. Simmer for 1 to 2 minutes, until just wilted.

SAUTÉING

1 1/2- to 2-inch pieces: Pour a very thin film of oil into a pan. Add samphire. Toss over high heat for 1 to 2 minutes, until just wilted.

Yields and Equivalents

3 ounces samphire = 1 cup

1 1/2 pounds samphire = 11 cups

SANTA FE GRANDE PEPPERS see Peppers

SANTAKA PEPPERS see Peppers

SAUERKRAUT see Cabbages, European

SAVORY, SUMMER and WINTER see Herbs and Their Flowers

SAVOY CABBAGES see Cabbages, European

Scallions

Allium cepa var. *aggregatum*

The Chinese, the Japanese and Americans use scallions. It was a shock when I had previous books converted for the British to find that the British do not. They happily use spring (green) onions, which form bulbs; baby leeks, which are straight like American scallions but flatter and tougher and need to be cooked, like big leeks; and wild onions or wild leeks, which many of us call "ramps" (see page 638). I think it's a shame to be deprived of the crisp freshness of raw scallions, with the white and green parts often used differently.

Roasted, green onions, ramps and scallions will cook in the same way. The only thing to keep in mind is the necessity of choosing a pan just big enough to hold them flat. And turn on the exhaust fan or open a window. Members of the onion (allium) family have a lot of sugar, which may caramelize and smoke.

The sweet brownness is delicious, which is why I bother with roasting. Also, roasting is easier and uses less fat than trying to get the same effect in a skillet. A grill can char the scallions before they cook through; be careful.

Methods

STORAGE

Rinse and wrap in plastic and store in the refrigerator. They will usually keep up to 4 days.

WASHING/WAYS OF CUTTING

Trim off root ends. Sometimes there is a thin outer membrane that needs to be pulled off. The whites can be cooked on their own as if they were small leeks. Both the green and white parts can be cut across into 1/4-inch lengths and added to cooked dishes at the end or put raw into salads.

Preparation

STEAMING

Whole scallions: Place trimmed scallions in a covered steamer basket. Steam for 15 minutes, or until a knife easily slips into flesh.

SAUTÉING

1/4-inch slices: Pour a very thin film of oil into a pan. Cook, stirring, in butter or oil for 5 minutes.

ROASTING

Whole: Trim and cut scallions into 8-inch lengths, including all of the white and some of the green. Use smallest pan that will hold scallions comfortably in a single layer. Slick scallions and pan with fat. Roast in center of 500°F oven for 8 minutes. Turn. Roast for 3 minutes more. (Serves 5 to 6 as a side dish)

GRILLING

See Grilled Ramps, page 394.

SCALLION BRUSHES AND FLOWERS

To make scallion brushes, a decorative way to brush sauces onto foods: Cut scallion across just below where stalks begin to branch out; save greens for another use. Trim off roots. Lay scallion on a cutting board and, using a paring knife, cut 1 1/2-inch slits through root end, giving scallion a slight turn after each cut. Drop brush(es) into ice water for 30 minutes to 1 hour. Drain before using.

For scallion flowers, to decorate finished dishes: Cut 2-inch-or-so pieces of scallion whites. Trim roots. Cut slits in both ends as described above, leaving about 1/2 inch uncut in center. Drop scallions into ice water for 30 minutes to 1 hour to open up cut ends. Drain thoroughly before using.

For deep-fried scallion flowers, to eat on their own or decorate finished dishes: Start with 3-inch-or-so lengths of scallion whites (some green is fine). Cut slits in both ends as described above, leaving about 1 inch uncut in center. Do not soak in ice water as above: They will splatter when fried. Pour about 1 1/2 inches of vegetable oil into a small heavy saucepan. Heat over medium heat to 325°F. Slip 6 or so flowers into oil at a time. Fry, using a wire skimmer to keep scallions submerged, just until ends turn light brown, about 45 seconds. Remove immediately and drain on paper towels. Sprinkle with salt.

Yields and Equivalents

4 bunches small scallions = about 24 = about 12 ounces
1 pound scallions, trimmed and cut across into narrow strips = 8 cups raw = 1 cup cooked

SCARLET RUNNER BEANS see Beans of the New World under Beans

Scorzonera and Salsify

Scorzonera hispanica / Tragopogon porrifolius

There is a common confusion among professional chefs between these two different plants. They have the same long, thin pointed shape. Salsify has white skin and seems to be unfindable in the market here, although it is very popular in France. Scorzonera is popular in Italy, where it is also called black salsify due to its black skin. Ours was purchased in two-kilogram bags and came from Belgium. An average one is about 12 inches long and ³/₄ to 1 inch thick. The skin resembles thin, dark tree bark. When peeled, there is a slightly sticky residue that washes off after plunging into acidulated water. Soaking it for several hours before cooking makes no difference in the discoloration of exposed flesh.

Varieties

SALSIFY (*Tragopogon porrifolius*) This is the white-skinned, sweeter one, which is a little starchier.

SCORZONERA (*Scorzonera hispanica*) This is the black-skinned, more common, slightly crisper one.

I find that the two vegetables really can be used interchangeably, although salsify is somewhat sweeter. This is a good thing, as the only way to have salsify in this country is to grow it oneself. Check seed catalogs or packets carefully for the Latin name to be sure that what is being sold is truly salsify.

Methods
BUYING AND STORING

Scorzonera, the only one I have been able to buy, is usually sold in airtight packages and, if refrigerated, will last for weeks.

WASHING/WAYS OF CUTTING

Scorzonera flesh will begin to darken immediately upon exposure to air, so before peeling, prepare a bowl of water with some lemon juice added. Remove the skin with a vegetable peeler, trim the ends and immediately drop scorzonera into the acidulated water. Allow to sit a minute. Then drain, rinse and cut as desired or as specified by recipe.

Preparation
BOILING

1-inch pieces: Cover prepared scorzonera with water by 1 inch and bring to a boil. Reduce heat and simmer for 6 to 9 minutes, or until a knife is easily inserted into flesh.

STEAMING

Whole: Place prepared scorzonera in a covered steamer basket. Cook for 12 to 18 minutes, or until a knife is easily inserted into flesh.

ROASTING

1-inch pieces: Dry soaked prepared pieces with a towel. Place in the smallest pan that will hold them comfortably. Slick with 1 teaspoon fat for every cup of scorzonera. Roast in center of 500°F oven for 8 minutes. Turn. Roast for 8 minutes more.

Yields and Equivalents

8 ounces scorzonera = 6 thin (¹/₂-inch) stalks or 2 thick (1-inch) stalks

8 ounces scorzonera, peeled, trimmed, and cut into 1-inch pieces = 1¹/₂ cups raw = 1 cup cooked (³/₄ cup if roasted)

SCOTCH BONNET MUSHROOMS
see Mushrooms, Fresh
SCOTCH BONNET PEPPERS see Peppers
SCOTS CABBAGE see Kale
SERRANOS see Peppers
SHAGGY INKY CAPS see Mushrooms, Fresh

Sea Kale
Brassica maritima/Brassica oleracea (Tronchuda group)

This was originally a wild plant growing along the shores of England and other Atlantic countries. It was gathered for eating to the point that it has almost disappeared in the wild. It is being grown by the knowledgeable French as a market crop.

Like so many, it is a confusing plant. Its familiar name is "crambe." It comes as two basic sorts, that for eating and a decorative garden flower that is large and has white flowers much like baby's breath. Gathered wild, the edible perennial was picked for its shoot. Grown, it is still used for its shoot; but this is often blanched under a cloth cover to remain white and tender. This manifestation of the plant has given rise to another name. It is cooked, eaten and sauced like asparagus. It is then called winter asparagus.

Evelyn (see the Bibliography) found it to be like cabbage but more delicate. He may have meant the leaves as they are also eaten, being members of the cabbage family classified with the savoy cabbages, meaning it has crinkly leaves. In this guise it is also known as Braganza cabbage and Portugal cabbage. It is the actual green used in the Portuguese national dish, a soup called caldo gallego.

Shallots
Allium ascalonicum

Another member of the onion (allium) family. Shallots with red-brown skins are milder that those with bluish-gray ones. They seem to have grown larger and are easier to peel than they used to be, but they are still small and persnickety, and you can't bang them first as you do garlic. They are essentially used as a seasoning that is milder than onions or garlic and are essential for Beurre Blanc (page 453) and other French sauces. The French grow some very large pointy ones. The small ones are excellent pickled like onions.

Methods
BUYING AND STORING
See Onions, page 616.

WASHING/WAYS OF CUTTING
Shallots often grow like Siamese twins and need to be separated. Use a paring knife to remove the papery outer layer and the first layer of the shallot if necessary. Trim the stalk end. The root end will hold the shallot together and make it easier to slice. Discard the root end when finished.

Preparation
ROASTING
Whole: Peel and trim shallots. Use smallest pan that will hold them comfortably in a single layer. Slick shallots and pan with olive oil. Roast on lowest level of 500°F oven for 5 minutes. Turn pan around and roast for 5 minutes more. (1 pound serves 4 to 6 as a side dish)

Yields and Equivalents
 1 pound shallots = 18 to 20 = 3 cups
 2 ounces shallots, finely chopped = scant $1/3$ cup
 $1 1/2$ ounces shallots, finely chopped = $1/4$ cup

SHEPHERD PEPPERS see Peppers
SHIITAKES see Mushrooms, Fresh
SHISO see Perilla under Asian Greens
SHUNGIKU see Chrysanthemum Greens
SIBERIAN KALE see Kale
SIMPSON LETTUCE, BLACK-SEEDED see Iceberg under Lettuces
SMALL WHITE BEANS see Navy Beans under Beans of the New World
SMALL YELLOW FINNS see Potatoes
SNAP PEAS see Peas
SNOW PEAS see Peas

Sorrel

Rumex acetosa/Rumex scutatus/Rumex acetosella

The thought of sorrel has sustained me through many hot weeding sessions. I prefer the small wild sorrel to the larger leaves of French sorrel, a garden perennial. Both have what are called shield, or lance-shaped, leaves; they look rather like arrowheads to me. Wild sorrel needs a lot of washing—rinsing in a sieve won't do the job—and both kinds of sorrel must have their stringy stems removed. When working with sorrel, it is absolutely essential that no aluminum come near it. It will not only become acrid but will also be a revolting color.

While French sorrel is a domesticated garden version, small wild sorrel is a pest in garden beds, with roots that spread underground. I used to get my children to weed by promising to make them sorrel soup, which they love even though now grown and no longer weeding. Wild sorrel can be tossed whole into salads or cooked whole. Domesticated sorrel has to be cut across into thin strips, or it will be tough. In France, it is commonly cooked with shad on the assumption that it will dissolve the numerous bones. I've never found this to be true, but its delightful acidity is a fine counterpoint to the fatty fish. Sorrel is very nice, finely shredded, with baby carrots, onions and beets, all of which are rich in sugar to balance the acidity of the sorrel. It is also used mixed into spinach purées and sauces.

I like to wilt cut-up sorrel and put it in ice cube trays to freeze. Then I pop the cubes out and store in the freezer in plastic bags, awaiting my whims.

Varieties

For the recipes in this book, use French sorrel, wild sorrel or sour grass. All have a sour lemony taste.

COMMON SORREL aka GARDEN SORREL (*Rumex acetosa*). Garden sorrel should be pinched back. If this is done, sorrel is a continuous-yield crop. A mature plant can be treated as a "cut and come again" crop. I often throw a little extra seed on the sorrel patch after the first substantial cutting so as to have young leaves. The younger—and wild—leaves will be a darker green than older ones.

FRENCH SORREL (*Rumex scutatus*) With a large shield-shaped leaf, this can be grown in the garden. French sorrel tends to be less bitter than the common.

WILD SORREL (*Rumex acetosa*) This variety has smaller leaves, also shield-shaped. It is a pestiferous weed that, once identified, may cause a gardener to look at weeding the garden with a different eye. For the wild variety, pull it up with the roots, but be sure to break off the roots and dirt before using.

SHEEP SORREL aka RED SORREL, SOUR GRASS (*Rumex acetosella*) A common sorrel that looks like a soft clover.

OCA aka WOOD SORREL (*Oxalis corniculata*) This is used for its roots in South America. I use its clover-shape leaves, slightly more bitter than ordinary sorrel, as I do those of wild sorrel.

Methods

BUYING, PICKING AND STORING

The wild greens are best gathered with a cultivator and then trimmed. Garden-grown sorrel is easiest cut with scissors. While I'm at it, I cut off any forming flower/seed heads. Bought sorrel should be green, not yellow, and not look limp or chewed.

WASHING/WAYS OF CUTTING

Trim the stems. Rinse the leaves very well under cold running water. Shake off the excess water, but do not blot dry if steaming the sorrel.

Stack together several leaves at a time, in the same direction, and cut across into $^1/_8$- or $^1/_4$-inch strips with a stainless steel knife. If it is not cut across, it will be stringy.

Preparation

STEAMING

$^1/_8$- or $^1/_4$-inch strips: After washing, shake off any excess water but do not blot dry. The water clinging to the leaves will help the sorrel cook.

Add sliced sorrel in batches to a nonreactive pan over medium-low heat, continuously turning it up from the bottom and allowing each batch to wilt before adding the next. Remove from heat as soon as all leaves have wilted and changed color.

SAUTÉING

1/8- or 1/4-inch strips: Wash and blot dry before slicing. Heat 1 tablespoon unsalted butter or oil in a nonreactive pan over medium-low heat. Add sorrel in batches and cook as directed under steaming, above.

MICROWAVING

1/8- or 1/4-inch strips: Cover tightly.

2 ounces sorrel with 1 tablespoon unsalted butter (1-quart measure): 2 minutes
8 ounces sorrel with 4 tablespoons butter (2-quart soufflé dish): 3 minutes

Yields and Equivalents

1 bunch sorrel, stemmed = 4 ounces
4 ounces stemmed sorrel, cut across into strips = 2 cups lightly packed
5 pounds sorrel, stemmed = scant 3 pounds leaves
1 pound stemmed sorrel, cut across into 1/4-inch strips = 8 cups packed = 1 1/4 cups cooked
1 cup sorrel, cut into 1/4-inch strips, raw = 3 tablespoons cooked
2 cups sorrel, cut into 1/4-inch strips, raw = 1/4 cup cooked
3/4 cup cooked sorrel = 6 frozen 1-ounce cubes for sauce

SOUR GRASS see Sorrel
SOYBEANS and SOYBEAN PRODUCTS see Beans from Asia under Beans
SOYBEAN SPROUTS see Sprouts
SPAGHETTI SQUASH see Squash, Winter
SPEARMINT see Mints under Herbs and Their Flowers

Spinach

Spinacia oleracea/Atriplex hortensis/Tetragonia tetragonioides

Varieties

All of the species listed above are thought of as spinach and used in the same way in different parts of the world or gardens. They are prepared similarly.

LEAF SPINACH (*Spinacia oleracea*) This is the true spinach. It has a great deal of oxalic acid and, like the sorrels, should never come near aluminum or another reactive metal. Cut only with a stainless steel or ceramic knife. Some varieties have smoother leaves than others.

BABY SPINACH (*Spinacia oleracea*) The small leaves of the above. Recently I have bought bags of washed greens that are called "baby spinach." I'm not quite sure what they really are, but they are tender, good in salads as well as cooked and a great labor saver.

FROZEN SPINACH (*Spinacia oleracea*) While I vastly prefer fresh spinach, it takes a lot of prep work. If I'm in a rush but want to cook spinach, I look in the freezer. The yields, in weight, for frozen and cooked fresh are the same, and the two can be used interchangeably in these recipes. However, if tough stems are a concern, buy fresh spinach and de-rib the leaves.

GARDEN ORACH aka MOUNTAIN SPINACH (*Atriplex hortensis*) As a weed, this is also known as goosefoot. Before spinach was readily available, it was used as spinach is today. It is not as good.

NEW ZEALAND SPINACH (*Tetragonia tetragonioides*) A very good substitute for spinach, particularly in the hot months when ordinary spinach will probably have bolted.

Methods
BUYING AND STORING

I try to buy leaves that are fully green, crisp and not too large.

WASHING/WAYS OF CUTTING

It does take some time to stem and wash spinach. Run a sinkful of very cold water. As the water runs, stem the spinach and tear off any nasty pieces. If the ribs are very large, fold the leaves over and, holding them with one hand, pull off as much of the rib as will come off easily. Put the good stuff in the water. Swish it around and let it soak a few minutes. Lift out the spinach, letting the water run through fingers and being careful not to stir up the dirt and sand in the bottom of the sink, and put in a colander. If the spinach is still gritty, repeat with a clean sink and clean water.

Preparation

POT-STEAMING

Whole leaves: Put washed spinach in a stainless steel pot, adding it in batches every few seconds if making a great deal. Turn spinach over either with hands or spoons. It will shrink enormously. One can start with some melted butter; but I usually prefer to add butter after cooking since spinach gives off so much juice. Spinach is cooked when it is all limp and has turned dark green.

Strips: Stem spinach and cut across in strips. Bring water to a boil. Add spinach. Turn off heat and stir. Drain.

STEAMER-STEAMING

Whole leaves: Place stemmed spinach in a covered steamer basket. Cook for 3 to 4 minutes, until leaves are wilted and bright green. Add a few minutes more for large quantities.

SAUTÉING

Whole leaves: Pour enough oil or melt enough butter to coat the bottom of a pan. Add spinach, waiting for each batch to wilt before adding more. Cook, stirring, for 2 to 5 minutes, or until leaves are wilted and bright green.

MICROWAVING

Cooking spinach, either plain (no water needed) or in melted butter, takes the same brief time in the microwave oven. It is not only quick and clean, but it also produces unusually bright green spinach. The flavor is so intense you may very well not need any salt. If you find it is too strong for you, try cooking it uncovered.

> *Whole leaves*
>
> 8 ounces stemmed spinach (14 x 11 x 2-inch dish, uncovered): 4 minutes
>
> 2 pounds stemmed spinach (2$\frac{1}{2}$-quart casserole; cover tightly): 5 minutes 30 seconds

Yields and Equivalents

> 8 ounces spinach, stemmed = 2 cups raw = $\frac{1}{3}$ cup cooked
>
> 2 pounds spinach, stemmed = 8 cups raw = 1$\frac{1}{2}$ cups cooked
>
> 12 ounces spinach, stemmed = 4$\frac{1}{2}$ cups loosely packed raw = 1 cup cooked
>
> 6 cups baby spinach = 5 ounces = 2 cups wilted = scant 1 cup fully cooked

SPLIT PEAS see Peas
SPROUTING BROCCOLI aka ITALIAN ASPARAGUS see Broccoli and Cauliflower
SPROUTING ONIONS see Egyptian Onions under Onions

Sprouts

It used to be that only Asian beans were sprouted. Now other kinds, as well as seeds, are sprouted—mustard sprouts, for example. Mung bean and alfalfa are perhaps the most commonly sprouted. The sprouts are the opening shoots of new plants and could be planted.

Varieties

Basically there are two types of sprouts, those grown from beans and those grown from (usually tiny) vegetable seeds. Both are eaten with the bean (a seed, too) or seed attached.

Under the first heading come mung, soy and adzuki bean sprouts. Both sprouts and beans are crisp. Mung and adzuki can be eaten raw or cooked. Soy sprouts must be cooked. Sprouts to be cooked should only be added during the last few seconds to keep their bite. Scatter some over Asian-y noodle dishes or clear vegetable soups.

Under the second heading come alfalfa, mustard, radish, cress and broccoli sprouts, among others. Sprouted vegetable seeds are finer than bean sprouts, and the overall texture is less crisp than it is fuzzy. These are good in sandwiches and in salads, especially those made with all raw ingredients, such as bulgur salads.

Methods

Any of the above beans or seeds can be sprouted at home. The method for doing so is the same for all: Line a baking sheet with a double thickness of blotter paper or blank newspaper (the kind used often for packing). Soak the paper thoroughly and strew the seeds or beans over the paper. Set in a sunny place and moisten often with water from a spray bottle. To use as sprouts, wait until they are about an inch to an inch and a half long, without any leaves having formed. Remove from the paper and store as directed below.

BUYING AND STORING

Whether home-sprouted or store-bought, sprouts should have no unpleasant odor. Store in paper bags in the refrigerator and use as quickly as possible.

Preparation

Most sprouts need only a very quick rinse under cold water before using. Many are best raw, in salads, sandwiches, etc. Sturdier sprouts like mung bean and soybean, however, can take a bit of heat; add to cooked dishes at the last minute or two so they retain their crunch.

Yields and Equivalents

COARSE SPROUTS (MUNG, SOYBEAN, ETC.)
  1 cup sprouts = 1 3/4 ounces
  One 4-ounce package = 3 cups

FINE SPROUTS (ALFALFA, BROCCOLI, RADISH)
  1 cup sprouts = 1 1/4 ounces
  One 4-ounce package = 5 cups fluffed, 4 cups
    lightly packed

Squash, Summer
Cucurbita pepo

Summer squash, American by origin, are vigorously growing vines that can threaten to take over the garden. If squash are not picked in timely fashion, the vegetables will get monstrously large and almost inedible, except for the Italian cucuzza (known as "gah-GOOTZ" on *The Sopranos* and by other related names in southern Italy and its islands), which simply get longer and twistier but remain edible. There is an American kind of gourd or *Curcurbita* that is commonly called bottle gourd. It may be an import.

See also Delicata in Winter Squash, page 651.

Varieties

Summer squash are mainly green or yellow, although there are said to be a few white ones, which I have not seen or used.

ZUCCHINI These narrow green squash are wonderful when small, about 5 inches long at most. They can be used smaller with their flowers still attached. They are, however, one of the great curses of summer if not picked soon enough. They get very large with big seeds. I have known people to leave a basket of them on a doorstep as if they were unwanted babies. The English call them vegetable marrow at the stage when I consider them too large to eat.

YELLOW SQUASH aka YELLOW ZUCCHINI A yellow version of zucchini; the two can be used interchangeably. They may take a little longer to cook.

CROOKNECK SQUASH These squash are also yellow, but with a somewhat warty exterior, and they can be allowed to get to 7 or 8 inches long.

PATTYPAN SQUASH Very pretty squash, white to yellow, with a scalloped top rim and a rounded top. Small ones, about 3 inches in diameter, are best, tenderest and good for stuffing.

Methods
BUYING AND STORING
All of the summer squashes should be firm without blemishes or soft places. Store in the refrigerator and use within the week.

WASHING/WAYS OF CUTTING
Generally these will be pretty clean. Zucchini and yellow squash may feel slightly hairy. All that needs to be done is to wash them, rubbing with a hand to smooth them if necessary. If they have a flower attached and are small, they can be left whole, with the flower attached, to sauté, or steamed without the flower. If cutting them up according to a recipe, save the flowers and use within the day as a final addition to risottos. Cut according to recipes.
ZUCCHINI, YELLOW SQUASH Zucchini and yellow squash both have thin edible skin. To clean, rinse well under cold running water. Do not rub too hard; the skin will come off. Trim both ends. The seeds are edible and can be kept if slicing young squash into rounds or half-moons. Scoop them out with a spoon if cutting squash into matchsticks.
CROOKNECK SQUASH Crookneck squash may or may not have skin that is pleasant to eat. I usually leave the skin on young ones and peel larger, older ones. Rinse well if not peeling. Crookneck will always take longer to cook than zucchini or yellow squash.
PATTYPAN SQUASH Pattypans are almost always used whole to show off their attractive shape. Rinse under cold running water.

Preparation
BOILING
ZUCCHINI AND YELLOW SQUASH *Matchsticks:* Add to boiling water and simmer for 9 to 10 minutes, until soft and translucent.
CROOKNECK SQUASH I do not boil these.
PATTYPAN SQUASH Add to boiling water and cook, turning squash over halfway through cooking, until softened but not too soft—about 10 to 11 minutes for 3-ounce squash, 11 to 15 minutes for 5-ounce squash, 18 minutes for 8-ounce squash, 20 to 22 minutes for 12-ounce squash. The flatter side often needs a minute longer to cook than the rounded side.

STEAMING
ZUCCHINI AND YELLOW SQUASH *Matchsticks:* Place in a covered steamer basket. Cook for 6 minutes, or until a knife easily slips into flesh.
1/4-inch slices: Place in a covered steamer basket. Cook 9 to 10 minutes, or until a knife easily slips into flesh.

GRILLING
See Grilling, on page 518, for how to prepare the grill.
ZUCCHINI OR YELLOW SQUASH. Trim stems from 6-inch (about 6-ounce) squash. Cut lengthwise into 1/3-inch-thick slices. Brush both sides of slices with vegetable oil and season with salt and pepper, or brush with one of the marinades on pages 519–520. Let stand at room temperature for about 30 minutes.

Grill until underside is marked, about 3 minutes. Turn and cook until second side is well marked and squash is tender, about 4 minutes. Serve hot, warm or at room temperature.

SAUTÉING
ZUCCHINI AND YELLOW SQUASH *1/4-inch slices or matchsticks:* For 2 small squash: Cook over medium-high heat, stirring occasionally, in 1 tablespoon unsalted butter or oil for 8 minutes. Multiply as needed.

ROASTING

CROOKNECK AND YELLOW SQUASH There is one odd thing about yellow crookneck squash; it is almost impossible to overcook it. That doesn't hold true for yellow zucchini, another squash entirely. The easiest way to remove the seeds is to scrape them out with a teaspoon. If they are obdurate, run the tip of a knife lengthwise down both sides of the seeds, then scrape.

$1^1/_2$- to 2-inch chunks: Trim squash. Cut each across in half. Cut each half lengthwise into 4 wedges. Remove seeds. Use smallest pan that will hold squash comfortably in a single layer. Slick pieces and pan with fat. Add $^1/_4$ cup water or stock. Roast on upper level of a 500°F oven for 15 minutes. Turn. Roast for 15 minutes more. (2 pounds serve 4 as a side dish)

ZUCCHINI *Halves:* Trim squash and cut in half lengthwise. Use smallest pan that will hold zucchini comfortably in a single layer. Slick zucchini and pan with fat. Roast in center of 500°F oven for 15 minutes. Turn and roast for 10 to 15 minutes more. (4 medium zucchini serve 8 as a side dish)

Slices: Trim zucchini and cut across into $^1/_2$-inch slices. Use smallest pan that will hold zucchini comfortably. Slick zucchini and pan with fat. Roast in center of 500°F oven for 10 minutes. Turn and roast for 10 minutes. Turn and roast for 10 minutes more. (2 medium zucchini serve 2 as a side dish)

$1^1/_2$- to 2-inch chunks: Cut and roast as for yellow squash, cooking for 10 minutes before and after turning.

MICROWAVING

ZUCCHINI AND YELLOW SQUASH (add 1 to 2 minutes to timings if cooking crookneck squash) Trim ends and wash well.

Times may need to be decreased for very powerful ovens; for smaller ovens, add 1 minute to cooking times.

Quartered lengthwise: Arrange in a dish just large enough to hold squash in no more than 2 layers; cover tightly.

    4 ounces: 8 minutes
    8 ounces: 8 to 9 minutes
    1 pound: 10 minutes
    2 pounds: 12 to 14 minutes

$^1/_4$-inch slices or $^1/_4$-inch matchsticks: Arrange as for quartered squash; cover tightly.

    4 ounces: 2 minutes 30 seconds
    8 ounces: 3 minutes 30 seconds
    1 pound: 5 minutes
    2 pounds: 8 minutes 30 seconds

PREPARATION FOR STUFFING

To make zucchini or yellow squash shells:

Hollowed centers This method works best with 5-ounce squashes about 6 to 7 inches long and 1 $^1/_2$ inches wide. Slice $^1/_2$ inch from stem end and reserve as a lid. With an apple or zucchini corer, carefully remove the center from squash, then hollow out squash as much as possible.

Squash boats Slice squash in half lengthwise. Run a paring knife along inside perimeter of squash, leaving a $^1/_8$-inch-thick border, then scoop out seeds. A melon baller works very well here. This can be done with squash of any size.

To cook zucchini or yellow squash shells: Preheat oven to 350°F.

Hollowed centers Prepare squash as above. Rub outside and stem caps with a little oil. Place in a baking pan. Bake for 10 minutes, or until a knife easily slips into flesh.

Squash boats Place, cut side up, in a baking pan. Rub outside with a little oil. Bake for 30 minutes, or until a knife easily slips into flesh. Allow to cool.

To make and cook miniature pattypan squash and zucchini shells: Cook whole squash in a large pot of salted boiling water for 3 minutes. Drain and rinse under cold running water until cool. Drain thoroughly. Cut a thin slice from bottom of pattypan squash or from one side of zucchini so squash can sit upright. Cut off about $^1/_4$ inch from top of each and hollow out squash with a small paring knife, keeping shells intact. Reserve tops if desired. Serve stuffed squash as an hors d'oeuvre.

To make and cook larger pattypan squash shells (for pattypans about 3 inches in diameter): Follow instructions above, cooking squash for 8 minutes. The scooped-out flesh can be drained, chopped and mixed with an equal amount of stuffing to be packed back into the hollowed shells.

One 5-ounce squash with a hollowed center will
hold 5 tablespoons stuffing.

One 4-ounce squash boat will hold $^1/_2$ cup stuffing.

One miniature zucchini will hold 2 teaspoons
stuffing.

One miniature pattypan squash will hold 1 teaspoon
stuffing.

Yields and Equivalents

ZUCCHINI

1 small zucchini = 4 to 5 ounces, cut into
matchsticks or $^1/_4$-inch slices = 1 cup raw =
$^1/_2$ cup cooked

24 miniature zucchini = 1 pound

YELLOW SQUASH

2 small yellow squash = 10 ounces, cut into
matchsticks or $^1/_4$-inch slices = 2 cups raw =
1 cup cooked

PATTYPAN SQUASH

24 miniature pattypan squash = 12 ounces

One 3-ounce pattypan = 3 tablespoons
cooked pulp

5 ounces pattypans = $^1/_4$ cup cooked pulp

8 ounces pattypans = $^1/_3$ cup plus 1 tablespoon
cooked pulp

12 ounces pattypans = $^1/_2$ cup cooked pulp

Squash, Winter

Cucurbit family/*Cucurbita moschata/Cucurbita
maxima/Sechium edule/Cucurbita pepo/Cucurbita
argyrospyrma*

Winter squash are keepers. Winter rewards for summer
growing. They vary in texture, flavor and degree of
moisture, so they cannot be used interchangeably.
There is a chart on page 653 that suggests which one
can replace another.

Varieties

ACORN (*Cucurbita maxima*) This 1- to 2-pound squash
is widely available. With a distinctive acorn shape, well-
formed ridges and smooth green skin occasionally
decorated with orange splotches, it is easy to recognize.
Regular acorn squash has a watery texture and tends to fall
apart during cooking. The orange flesh offers little flavor
other than sweetness. There is also a golden variety with
pale cream skin and light yellow flesh that is grainier, more
watery and less sweet. For either variety, the medium-thick
skin is not difficult to cut. Because acorn squash does not
hold together well, it is best baked or steamed, but it can be
braised. It will store for 1 to 2 months.

BANANA (*Cucurbita maxima*) This is a long, thin yellow
squash good for hot-weather gardeners.

BUTTERCUP (*Cucurbita maxima*) This squash typically
weighs about 3 pounds and is round, like a sat-upon
pillow. It has dark green skin, lighter green stripes and a
small turban on top. There is also another variety, similar
in size, with light orange skin and continuous gray-green
splotches, the distinctive ridges of a pumpkin and no
turban at all. Both are medium sweet, rich and nutty, with
an intense squash taste that goes well with strong flavors.
This is a good, sturdy all-purpose squash with few seeds
and lots of flesh. It will store for at least a month and can
be steamed, sautéed, baked or braised.

BUTTERNUT (*Cucurbita moschata*) This abundant squash
weighs an average of 2 to 5 pounds. It has smooth peach-
colored skin and lots of deep orange flesh. Seeds are stored
in the bulbous bottom. The flavor is lightly sweet with a hint
of nuttiness and the texture medium dense and moist. This
squash will store for 2 to 3 months and is very easy to slice
and peel. It can be steamed, sautéed, baked or braised.

CALABAZA (*Cucurbita moschata*) Also called Caribbean
pumpkin, calabazas are a tropical squash that can grow to
upwards of 10 pounds. They are commonly sold presliced
in supermarket ethnic produce sections. They have either
pale orange or mottled green skin and bright orange flesh

that cooks up moist and firm, with a light nutty flavor. Sliced calabaza should be stored in the refrigerator; it will hold for 1 to 2 weeks. This fine-textured squash is excellent steamed, sautéed, baked or braised. The name "calabaza" is also used for a nonedible gourd that is often used in the Caribbean and in Africa to make containers for food or ladles, often with intricate designs.

CHAYOTE aka CHRISTOPHENE (*Sechium edule*) This tropical squash has many regional names, including mirliton (Louisiana), cho cho (Jamaica), Buddha's hands (Asia) and vegetable pear. Vegetable pear is an apt description for the chayote. It is shaped like a plump pear with smooth green skin (some varieties have yellowish or whitish skin) neatly tucked into a pleated row at the bottom. Inside, the porous green flesh is moist and firm with a light, fresh taste that absorbs other flavors easily. Chayote is easy to slice although a little slippery to peel. It has just a single large seed that easily scoops out. Stored in the refrigerator, it will last for weeks. Chayotes can be eaten raw but are more commonly steamed, baked, sautéed or braised.

CHEESE PUMPKIN (*Cucurbita moschata*) Common in farmers' markets, this light-peach-skinned, slightly squat pumpkin is a beauty. The cantaloupe-colored flesh is extremely moist, almost watery, with a light, sometimes grassy flavor. Do not use in pies, purées or anything where starch or thickness is needed.

CHIOGGIA see Marina di Chioggia.

CUSHA (*Cucurbita argyrospyrma,* formerly *mixta*) This name can be confusing as it is sometimes applied to different sorts of squash. Ask the seller for information.

DELICATA (*Cucurbita pepo*) This small (1- to 1 1/2-pound) cucumber-shaped squash has pale yellow skin creased with green stripes. The flesh is pale yellow with a light taste reminiscent of sweet corn and a texture between that of winter and summer squash. Delicata will store for only 2 to 3 weeks. During storage, the green stripes may

turn orange; this color change will not affect the taste. Delicata slices easily and is best steamed, sautéed or baked. Its small size and its shape make it ideal for stuffing.

GOLDEN NUGGET (*Cucurbita maxima*) This is a small squash—one per person—with orange skin that makes it look like a miniature pumpkin. It is a product of recent breeding and is usually baked or roasted whole.

HUBBARD, BLUE (*Cucurbita maxima*) There are two types of Hubbard squash. The New England Blue resembles a light gray-blue football with slightly bumpy skin. It can grow quite large but is often in the 3- to 5-pound range. Inside, the deep orange flesh is dense and starchy, and it tastes like a rich sweet potato, which it can substitute for in most recipes. A thick protective rind helps the Hubbard store for many months but makes it more challenging to slice and peel (see below). Scraping out the fibers, which are slightly bitter, is a little work. Blue Hubbards are best steamed or baked. This squash will yield a large quantity of meaty white seeds, a great snack to prepare according to Basic Seeds (page 136).

HUBBARD, GOLDEN (*Cucurbita maxima*) Also shaped like a football, this variety of Hubbard is slightly smaller than its blue sibling. And despite its name, both its pebbly rind and smooth flesh are orange. This Hubbard is less flavorful and barely sweet. It is, however, moist and low in starch, so it holds together well if steamed, baked or braised. Again, the skin, which helps the squash to store for many months, can be difficult to peel.

JARRAHDALE (*Cucurbita maxima*) This large—5- to 10-pound—squash resembles a pumpkin in both looks and taste. It is sometimes called a blue pumpkin; the skin is actually light gray to celadon green. The light orange flesh is watery with a delicate grassy flavor and a fine texture that purées beautifully. Despite its sliceable thin skin, the Jarrahdale can be stored for several months. Its flesh holds together well when baked, steamed or braised. It also yields plenty of large plump seeds that, unfortunately, are too tough for snacking.

KABOCHA (*Cucurbita maxima* and *Cucurbita moschata*) Sometimes referred to as Japanese pumpkin, this squat 2- to 3-pound round squash has a deep green outer skin. The dark orange flesh is dense, meaty and very sweet, with a more pronounced squash flavor than butternut or acorn. A heavy knife is required to slice through its tough exterior, which allows the squash to keep well for a month or more. Kabocha flesh holds its shape better than most squash when cooked, making it suitable for many preparations: steaming, sautéing, baking and braising. It is one of my favorite squash and absolutely worth seeking out (see also Red Kuri).

MARINA DI CHIOGGIA (*Cucurbita maxima*) As one might guess from the name, this is an Italian favorite. A large greenish-gray turban squash, it is usually replaced in this country by Hubbard squash or Jarrahdale.

MINI PUMPKINS (*Cucurbita maxima*) This 6- to 8-ounce round, squat pumpkin is a common fall decoration. Too bad it is rarely eaten. The orange flesh is sweet and starchy with a coarse texture that makes it a good substitute for sugar pie pumpkins. It is best steamed or baked whole or stuffed.

RED KURI (*Cucurbita maxima*) A type of Kabocha squash, this is also called a Baby Red Hubbard, as it is smaller than the really large Hubbards. From 2 to 10 pounds in size, Red Kuri resembles a squat pear with wrinkly deep orange skin and orange flesh that turns reddish when cooked. The smooth-textured flesh is sweet and starchy with a bright citrus note. This squash will store well for months and is good for all manners of cooking, including steaming, sautéing, baking and braising.

ROUGE D'ETAMPES (*Cucurbita maxima*) This pumpkin-type squash looks just like the one that made Cinderella's coach. It is a great favorite in France.

SPAGHETTI (*Cucurbita pepo*) A cylindrical squash with pale yellow skin and flesh of a slightly deeper yellow. It is named for the spaghettilike strands the flesh separates into when cooked. This mild squash does not offer much flavor on it own; however, it is an excellent foil for sauces, including the many pasta sauces in this book (see pages 459–463) and the Index.

SUGAR PIE PUMPKIN (*Cucurbita maxima*) Also called New England pie pumpkin, these are the most common eating pumpkins and a favorite for pies. They are perfectly round, from 2 to 5 pounds, with dull orange skin and light orange flesh. The assertive flesh is not at all sweet but pairs well with sweet or savory accompaniments. Do not confuse eating pumpkins with the larger, decorative pumpkins such as the jack o'lantern and Big Tom.

SWEET DUMPLING This squash weighs less than a pound and resembles a mini pumpkin, with pale cream skin decorated by green stripes. Inside, the fibrous flesh is a drab mustard yellow, but it makes up for its color with an appealing sweetness and dry texture. In fact, Sweet Dumpling tastes less like squash and more like candy. The squash slices very easily and can store for months, during which time the thin edible skin may turn a richer cream color and the green stripes to orange. Sweet Dumplings are best steamed or baked. Their shape and size make them a natural for stuffing.

TURBAN (*Cucurbita maxima*) Named for the large turban-shape growth on its bottom, this very unusual-looking squash, with a smaller turban on top, is fat and squat, weighing about 4 to 6 pounds, and bright orange with patches of green and yellow. It is beautiful to look at, but inside the very tough skin is fibrous flesh that is not very flavorful. It also tends to be dry and sometimes spongy. The turban will store for months. It is very difficult to slice but the turban top (where the seeds are stored) can be easily removed by cutting along the seam. These squash are best steamed or baked whole—or avoided.

SEEDS Most winter squashes and pumpkins have edible seeds. See the recipes on page 136. After the vegetable is cut, the seeds should be removed with the fibrous material surrounding them, then put in a sieve and washed, rubbing to separate the seeds from the fiber. The amount will depend on the variety. The seeds should be allowed to dry before roasting or frying.

Methods
BUYING AND STORING
Winter squash should be firm, with no soft or mushy places. If the stem is attached, it should be firm as well. Winter squashes were bred for storage. Most can be stored in a cool place for up to 6 months. Among the exceptions are Delicata and spaghetti squash, which will need to be refrigerated and used within about 3 weeks of purchase.

SUBSTITUTING SQUASH
If a specific squash is unavailable, use one with a similar texture and moisture content.

	MOIST	MEDIUM-DRY	DRY
FINE	Jarrahdale Cheese Pumpkin		
MEDIUM	Delicata	Buttercup Butternut Calabaza Golden Hubbard Sugar Pie Pumpkin	Blue Hubbard Kabocha Red Kuri
COARSE	Acorn Spaghetti Sweet Dumpling	Mini Pumpkin Pumpkin	Turban

WAYS OF CUTTING
ACORN, CHEESE PUMPKIN AND JARRAHDALE Halve and remove the seeds and fibers. Cut the squash along the ribs into wedges. Remove the skin with a vegetable peeler or paring knife.

BUTTERNUT Slice crosswise at the point where the neck meets the bottom. With a vegetable peeler, remove the skin. Scoop the seeds and fibers from the squash bottom.

CHAYOTE/CHRISTOPHENE Cut in half. Remove the skin with a vegetable peeler. Scoop out the center seed.

DELICATA AND SWEET DUMPLING The thin skin is actually edible. Peel all or just part of the skin, if desired, with a vegetable peeler. Halve the squash and remove the seeds and fibers.

BUTTERCUP, CALABAZA, HUBBARD, KABOCHA, RED KURI AND SUGAR PIE PUMPKIN Halve and remove the seeds and fibers. Cut squash into smaller wedges. Remove the skin with a vegetable peeler or paring knife. Hubbards and other squash with thicker skin will be more difficult to peel. Use a sturdy peeler with a sharp blade or a sharp paring knife. For sugar pie pumpkins, a paring knife works best. Even better is to steam the halves. The tough rind separates from the flesh and becomes easy to remove by hand.

MINI PUMPKIN Cut around and remove the stem. Scoop out the seeds and fibers. Bake whole.

TURBAN The skin is too hard to peel. Remove the turban top by cutting along the seam. Remove the seeds and fibers. Bake or steam whole.

Preparation
BOILING
ACORN *2-inch chunks:* Add squash to boiling water. Simmer for 15 to 20 minutes, or until a knife easily slips into flesh.

STEAMING
To encourage even cooking, slice any pieces thicker than 2 inches in half. Or, if steaming whole, turn squash over halfway through cooking. Steam squash with skin on and peel after steaming, if necessary. It is easier.

ACORN *Halves:* Cut squash along ribs into wedges. Remove seeds and fibers. Place in a covered steamer basket and cook for 7 minutes, or until a knife easily cuts through flesh. Alternatively, halve squash and remove seeds and fibers. Place, cut side down, in covered steamer basket and cook for 17 to 20 minutes, or until a knife easily cuts through flesh.

BUTTERCUP *Whole:* Place whole squash in a covered steamer basket. Cook for 35 to 40 minutes, or until a knife easily cuts through flesh. Rinse under cold running water until cool enough to handle. Halve squash and scoop out seeds and fibers.

BUTTERNUT *Halves:* Cut squash in half. Remove seeds and fibers. Place, cut side down, in a covered steamer basket and cook for 23 to 25 minutes. Alternatively, separate each half into two sections—neck and the bottom. Place all 4 pieces, cut side down, in covered steamer basket and cook 17 to 20 minutes for bottom, 23 to 25 minutes for neck.

CALABAZA *Wedge:* Remove seeds and fibers. Cut squash in half if wedge is thicker than 2 inches. Place, cut side down, in a covered steamer basket and cook for 30 to 40 minutes, or until a knife easily cuts through flesh.

CHAYOTE/CHRISTOPHENE *Halves:* Cut in half lengthwise. Scoop out center seeds. Place squash, cut side down, in a covered steamer basket, and cook for 15 to 23 minutes for squash that will retain some texture and shape for stews, 40 minutes if chayote will be mashed or puréed.

CHEESE PUMPKIN *Wedge:* Remove seeds and fibers. Place the squash, cut side down, in a covered steamer basket and cook for 10 to 15 minutes, or until a knife easily cuts through flesh.

DELICATA *Whole:* Place whole squash in a covered steamer basket. Cook for 10 to 12 minutes, or until a knife easily cuts through flesh. Rinse under cold running water until cool enough to handle. Halve squash and scoop out seeds and fibers.

HUBBARD, BLUE *Whole or halves:* Place whole squash in a covered steamer basket (if squash is very large, it should be halved before cooking; see below). Cook for 30 minutes, or until a knife easily cuts through flesh. Rinse under cold running water until cool enough to handle. Halve squash and scoop out seeds and fibers. Alternatively, halve squash and remove seeds and fibers. Place, cut side down, in covered steamer basket. Cook for 23 to 25 minutes or until a knife easily cuts through flesh.

HUBBARD, GOLDEN *Halves:* Cut squash in half. Remove seeds and fibers. Place, cut side down, in a covered steamer basket. Cook for 15 to 20 minutes or until a knife easily cuts through flesh.

JARRAHDALE *Halves:* Cut squash in half. Remove seeds and fibers. Place, cut side down, in a covered steamer basket. Cook for 30 minutes, or until a knife easily cuts through flesh.

KABOCHA *Wedges:* Cut squash into 3 large wedges. Remove seeds. Place in a covered steamer basket and cook for 17 to 20 minutes, or until a knife easily cuts through flesh.

MINI PUMPKIN *Whole:* Place in a covered steamer basket. Steam for 12 to 15 minutes until a knife easily cuts through flesh. Rinse under cold running water until cool enough to handle. Cut around stem and remove. Scoop out seeds and fibers.

RED KURI *Halves:* Cut squash in half lengthwise. Remove seeds. Place, cut side down, in a covered steamer basket and cook for 15 minutes, or until a knife easily cuts through the flesh.

SPAGHETTI *Whole:* Place in a covered steamer basket. Cook for 25 minutes, or until a knife easily cuts through flesh. Rinse under cold running water until cool enough to handle. Halve squash and scoop out seeds. Using fingers or a fork, shred flesh into long strands. Serve with any of the tomato-based pasta sauces listed in the Index.

SUGAR PIE PUMPKIN *Halves:* Cut squash in half. Remove seeds and fibers. Place, cut side down, in a covered steamer basket. Cook for 15 to 20 minutes, or until a knife easily cuts through flesh. Unlike other squash, the skin will not soften during cooking, so it is important to test for doneness on the underside. Once cool, the skin will harden and separate from the flesh, making it easy to remove by hand.

SWEET DUMPLING *Whole:* Place in a covered steamer basket. Steam for 12 to 15 minutes, until a knife easily cuts through flesh. Rinse under cold running water until cool enough to handle. Halve squash and scoop out seeds and fibers.

ROASTING

ACORN *Halves:* For a 1 1/2-pound squash: Halve lengthwise and remove seeds and fibers. Brush cavity of each half with 1/2 teaspoon fat. Roast in center of 500°F oven for 40 to 45 minutes, or until squash is easily pierced with tip of a sharp knife.

SAUTÉING

ACORN *1-inch chunks (peeled):* In a small pan, heat 1 tablespoon olive oil over medium heat. Add squash and reduce heat to low. Cook, stirring regularly, for 10 minutes, or until squash is tender and lightly browned. Season with salt .

KABOCHA *1-inch chunks (peeled):* In a small pan, heat 1 tablespoon unsalted butter over medium heat. Add squash. Cook, stirring regularly, for 10 minutes, or until squash is tender and lightly browned. Season with salt.

MICROWAVING

SPAGHETTI SQUASH Cooking spaghetti squash takes approximately the same amount of time in the microwave oven as in a regular oven. I would cook the squash conventionally and make the sauce in the microwave oven.

Halves: Slice in half lengthwise. Place seeded halves side by side in a dish just large enough to hold them. Cover tightly.

One 4³/₄-pound squash: 20 minutes

ACORN AND BUTTERNUT *Halves:* Halve lengthwise. Remove seeds and fibers (wash seeds and toast in conventional oven). Place seeded halves side by side (for butternut, place a large end next to a narrow end) in a dish just large enough to hold them. Cover tightly.

4 ounces: 5 minutes

1 pound: 7 minutes

2 pounds: 15 minutes

3 pounds: 20 minutes

1-inch chunks: For 1 to 1¹/₄ pounds: Arrange in a single layer in a dish just large enough to hold them. Cover tightly. Cook for 6 minutes, stirring halfway through cooking.

CHAYOTE/CHRISTOPHENE *Whole:* Prick 4 times with a fork. Set on a paper towel and cook uncovered.

1 chayote: 6 minutes

2 chayotes: 9 minutes 30 seconds

4 chayotes: 15 minutes

PREPARATION FOR STUFFING

The best winter squash for stuffing are the small ones: acorn, Delicata, Sweet Dumpling, mini pumpkin and chayote. All of them, with the exception of chayote, have a large cavity in the middle—a perfect bowl for holding stuffing once the seeds and fibers are removed.

All of the squash flowers can be stuffed. Pinch off the inner elements. Use 1 tablespoon stuffing for small flowers, 2 tablespoons for medium and as much as ¹/₂ cup for large pumpkin flowers. Stuffed squash flowers may be steamed or sautéed.

ACORN AND DELICATA Slice in half lengthwise. Remove seeds and fibers.

SWEET DUMPLING AND MINI PUMPKIN Slice across squash ¹/₂ inch from the top; save top as a lid. Remove seeds and fibers. Alternatively, slice squash lengthwise, keeping stem intact. Remove seeds and fibers.

CHAYOTE/CHRISTOPHENE Slice chayote in half lengthwise. Steam (page 653). Scoop out the flesh from the skin, leaving a shell ¹/₄ inch thick. If drained, the watery flesh may be used as part of the stuffing.

Half of a medium acorn squash will hold ¹/₂ cup plus 3 tablespoons mounded stuffing.

Half of a small (7-ounce) Delicata squash will hold 2 tablespoons plus 2 teaspoons level stuffing or a scant ¹/₄ cup mounded stuffing.

Half of a large (14-ounce) Delicata squash will hold a scant ¹/₄ cup level stuffing or a generous ¹/₄ cup mounded stuffing.

Half of a medium chayote will hold a generous ¹/₂ cup mounded stuffing.

Yields and Equivalents

ACORN

1 squash = 1 to 1¹/₂ pounds

¹/₂ squash = 12 ounces, cut into 1-inch chunks = 2 cups raw = 1¹/₄ cups cooked = ³/₄ cup purée

BUTTERCUP

1 squash = $2^1/_2$ pounds

$^1/_2$ squash, cut into 1-inch chunks = $3^1/_2$ cups raw

1 large squash = $2^3/_4$ pounds, cut into 1-inch
chunks = 6 cups = $3^1/_2$ cups purée

BUTTERNUT

1 medium squash = $2^1/_4$ pounds, cut into 1-inch
cubes = 6 cups raw

$^1/_2$ squash = $1^1/_4$ pounds, cut into 1-inch chunks =
$2^1/_2$ cups = $1^1/_2$ cups purée

CALABAZA

One $1^1/_4$-pound wedge, cut into 1-inch chunks =
$3^1/_4$ cups raw = 3 cups cooked = $^3/_4$ cup purée

CHAYOTE

1 medium squash = 11 ounces, cut into 1-inch
chunks = $^3/_4$ cup

1 medium squash = 10 ounces, cut lengthwise into
$^1/_2$-inch sticks = 2 cups

CHEESE PUMPKIN

1 squash = $3^1/_2$ pounds

One 1-pound wedge, cut into 1-inch chunks =
$2^1/_2$ cups raw = $1^1/_2$ cups cooked = 1 cup purée

DELICATA

1 squash = 8 ounces, cut into 1-inch chunks =
$1^1/_4$ cups raw = 1 cup cooked = 6 tablespoons purée

HUBBARD, BLUE

1 squash = 4 pounds

$^1/_2$ squash, cut into 1-inch chunks = 5 cups raw
(plus $^1/_2$ cup seeds) = $3^1/_2$ cups cooked = $^1/_2$ cup purée

HUBBARD, GOLDEN

1 squash = $3^1/_2$ pounds

$^1/_2$ squash, cut into 1-inch chunks = 4 cups raw =
$3^1/_2$ cups cooked = 2 cups purée

JARRAHDALE

1 squash = 5 pounds

$^1/_2$ squash, cut into 1- to $1^1/_2$-inch chunks =
$7^1/_2$ cups cooked = $4^1/_2$ cups purée

KABOCHA

1 squash = $3^1/_2$ pounds

$^1/_2$ squash, cut into 1-inch chunks = 5 cups raw

$^1/_4$ squash = 12 ounces, cut into 1-inch chunks =
$3^1/_2$ cups cooked = $2^1/_2$ cups purée

MINI PUMPKIN

1 pumpkin = 8 ounces = generous $^1/_4$ cup purée

RED KURI

1 squash = $2^1/_4$ pounds

$^1/_2$ squash, cut into 1-inch chunks = 3 cups raw =
2 cups cooked = $1^1/_4$ cups purée

SPAGHETTI SQUASH

1 squash = 3 pounds = 6 cups shredded
cooked flesh

SUGAR PIE PUMPKIN

1 pumpkin = 2 pounds

$^1/_2$ pumpkin, cut into 1-inch chunks = $2^1/_2$ cups
raw = $1^2/_3$ cups cooked = 1 cup purée

SWEET DUMPLING

1 squash = 14 ounces, cut into 1-inch chunks =
2 cups raw

1 squash = $11^1/_2$ ounces, cut into 1-inch chunks =
$1^1/_4$ cups cooked = $^3/_4$ cup purée

TURBAN

1 squash = 4 pounds = $2^1/_2$ cups cooked,
scooped purée

SQUAW CORN see Fresh Corn under Corn

STEINPILZ MUSHROOMS see Mushrooms, Fresh

STRAW MUSHROOMS see Mushrooms, Fresh

SUGAR SNAP PEAS see Peas

SUMMER SAVORY see Herbs and Their Flowers

SUNCHOKES see Jerusalem Artichokes

SWEET GREEN PEAS see Peas

Sweet Potatoes and Yams

Ipomoea batatas/Dioscorea alata, D. bulbifera et al.

Sweet potatoes and yams are routinely confused with
each other by eaters, cooks, writers and shops. They are
quite different in texture and sweetness.

Varieties

SWEET POTATOES (*Ipomoea batatas*) These are roots, not potatoes (tubers) at all, and they are not yams either, although to add to the confusion, some kinds of sweet potatoes have been given the word "yam" as part of their common name. There are both yellow and white; the white are sweeter than the yellow and take about 3 minutes longer to cook. Both do well in purées, a use to which they are frequently put in the Caribbean, but white will take much more butter and cream to become smooth than yellow potatoes.

BONIATOS (*Ipomoea batatas*) Also called batatas. boniatos look and taste like a typical orange or yellow sweet potato, only starchier. Most have smoothly dark reddish-brown skin and white flesh that immediately darkens upon contact with air. A good deal (but not all) of this black will disappear upon cooking. Cook boniatos in their skins or work quickly and drop them into water immediately after peeling and cutting.

YAMS aka ÑAME, IGNAME (*Dioscorea alata*) Yams are not sweet potatoes even though they are often mislabeled as such in supermarkets. In fact, yams are barely sweet. There are many varieties; a few follow: White yam (called Brazil ñame at my local ethnic grocer) seems to be the most common variety. It is oval-shaped, with skin the color and texture of tree bark. The flesh is dense and coarse, dry and a little flaky. I have also tried Costa Rican yam (smooth brown skin, crisp white flesh that yellows upon air contact, coarse and moist in texture, neutral in flavor), dashin yam (rough brown skin, dry white flesh with pink swirls, very dry and starchy, almost gummy when puréed, neutral in flavor) and yellow ñame (thicker skin that is tougher to peel, moist yellow flesh that darkens upon air contact, slight sweetness followed by strong bitterness).

Methods

BUYING AND STORING

Sweet potatoes and yams should have firm, smooth skins.

WASHING/WAYS OF CUTTING

Remove the skin with a vegetable peeler. Trim the ends if fibrous. The flesh will darken when exposed to air, so work quickly. Often I microwave or bake the vegetable unpeeled so as minimize its absorption of liquid.

Preparation

BOILING

1-inch cubes, ¹/₄-inch slices or eighths: Add sweet potatoes or yams to boiling water. Simmer for 15 to 20 minutes, or until completely soft.

STEAMING

ALL TYPES *¹/₄-inch dice:* Place in a covered steamer basket. Cook for 15 minutes, or until a knife easily slips into flesh.

YAMS (ÑAME) *1-inch slices:* Place in a covered steamer basket. Cook for 20 minutes for dashin yam, 25 minutes for Costa Rican yam or yellow ñame, 30 minutes for white yam, or until a knife slips easily into flesh.

BONIATO *1-inch slices:* Place in a covered steamer basket. Cook for 15 minutes, or until a knife slips easily into flesh.

ROASTING

Do not roast yams. Roast sweet potatoes to serve on their own, perhaps with a sauce such as one of the pestos on pages 442, 443 and 467.

¹/₄-inch slices: Place slices in smallest pan that will hold them comfortably in a single layer. Slick slices and pan with fat. Place one rack in center of oven and another on second level from bottom. Roast in center of 500°F oven for 25 minutes. Remove pan and turn each slice. Return pan to lower oven rack, back to front. Roast for 25 minutes more. (1 ¹/₂ pounds serve 4 as a side dish)

Wedges: Cut sweet potato in half lengthwise, then across. Cut each section into 3 to 4 wedges. Place wedges in smallest pan that will hold them comfortably in a single layer. Slick wedges and pan with fat. Roast in center of 500°F oven for 15 minutes. Turn wedges. Roast for 15 minutes more. (1 ¹/₂ pounds serve 3 to 4 as a side dish)

MICROWAVING

SWEET POTATOES *Whole:* For purée or pie: Prick and set on paper toweling. Cook uncovered.

2 pounds (about 2 large): 13 to 15 minutes

DEEP-FRYING

See Crisp Vegetable Chips, page 514.

GRILLING

Use sweet potatoes only. See Grilling, page 518, for how to prepare the grill.

Halves: Microwave whole sweet potatoes as above until tender, or bake them directly on rack of a 375°F oven until a knife slips easily into flesh, about 1 hour 15 minutes. Cool completely. They can be cooked up to a day in advance; refrigerate until needed, then bring sweet potatoes to room temperature while grill is heating.

Cut sweet potatoes in half lengthwise and slick cut surfaces and skins generously with oil, or brush well with one of the marinades on pages 519–520. Grill, skin side down, rotating potatoes as necessary, until skins are crisp and charred in places, about 4 minutes. Turn and cook until flesh is marked and warmed through, about 5 minutes. Serve warm or at room temperature.

Yields and Equivalents

SWEET POTATOES

1 small sweet potato = 6 to 7 ounces

1 medium sweet potato = 8 to 10 ounces

1 large sweet potato = 10 to 12 ounces

2 large sweet potatoes (1 1/2 pounds) =
2 1/4 cups cooked purée

1 1/4 pounds sweet potatoes (about 2 medium),
peeled and cut into 1/4-inch dice = 3 1/2 cups

1 pound sweet potatoes, peeled and cut into
1/4-inch dice = 1 1/2 cups

YAMS

1 medium yam = 2 1/2 pounds

1 medium yam, peeled and cut into 1/2-inch
cubes = 4 1/2 cups

1 medium yam, cooked and riced = 3 1/2 cups

SWISS CHARD see Chard
SZEGEDI PEPPERS see Peppers
TABASCO PEPPERS see Peppers
TAPIOCA see Yuca under Tropical Tubers
TARO see Tropical Tubers
TARRAGON see Herbs and Their Flowers
TATSOI see Cabbages, Asian
THYME see Herbs and Their Flowers
TOKYO BEKANA see Mustard Greens and Leaf Mustard

Tomatillos

Physalis ixocarpa

These are often thought of as green tomatoes and are used interchangeably in sauces, although tomatillos have a pleasant extra edge of acidity. They are related to ground cherries and grow in a papery husks. They can be grown as far north as Vermont but are actually Central American.

Methods
BUYING AND STORING

The husks will be brown but should not look tired. Store in the refrigerator for up to 3 days.

WASHING/WAYS OF CUTTING

Remove the husks. Rinse well under cold running water; be sure to rub off any sticky residue.

Preparation
ROASTING

Slick prepared tomatillos with vegetable oil and set them core side down in a roasting pan that holds them snugly. Roast in center of 500°F oven until skin is blistered and flesh is very tender, about 14 minutes for small tomatillos, 17 minutes for large.

Quick Tomatillo Sauce: Roast 3 to 4 peeled garlic cloves along with 3/4 to 1 pound tomatillos. Pass the tomatillos, garlic and any liquid through a food mill fitted with the fine disc. Season with salt. Wonderful with grilled flank steak or fish fillets.

Yields and Equivalents

Small tomatillos = 14 per pound

Medium tomatillos = 7 to 8 per pound

Large tomatillos = 5 to 6 per pound

1 pound tomatillos, cut into $1/4$-inch dice = $1^2/_3$ cups

1 pound tomatillos = 1 cup purée (raw)

12 ounces tomatillos, cooked and puréed = 1 cup

Tomatoes

Lycopersicon lycopersicum

What is there to say about the all-American favorite? Good ones are splendid and have conquered the globe.

While there appears to be an endless number of tomato varieties, botanically speaking there is only one we eat, *esculentum*. (There may be traces of the tiny *S. pimpinellifolium* not only in the *L. esculentum,* which seems to derive from it, but more directly, in our sprays of berrylike tomatoes that, like the other variant, *L. pimpinellifolium,* have a nasty tendency to split on the vine but are mind-bogglingly sweet.) However, what we perceive is almost true. Tomatoes have been so intermarried, particularly in Italy, the Americas and Spain, that there are endless sorts with a wild range of flavors, colors, sizes and even best uses.

The Cambridge World History of Food sensibly divides tomatoes into three groups: cooking tomatoes (including the Italian-style plum tomatoes), salad tomatoes (mainly raw eating) and juice tomatoes. There is a continuum here from the fleshiest tomatoes—the cooking tomatoes—through the salad tomatoes (but I mainly cook with these) to the juice tomatoes, with the least pulp.

Generally, orange and yellow tomatoes will be sweeter than red ones. Some may be lacking in acidity—good for those who have trouble digesting raw tomatoes. Taste any finished dish cooked with them and decide if it needs a little lemon juice or vinegar. Also beware when canning, since missing acidity means lack of preservation. Recently I have combined one-third each of orange cherry tomatoes, plum tomatoes and American tomatoes to make a wonderful sauce that needs none of the sugar sometimes called for in tomato sauce recipes.

Look at page 96 to get some idea of the vast variety of tomatoes available. Within any type there will be a range of textures, flavors and apposite usages. Below I give the main categories as I use them in this book.

Varieties

AMERICAN TOMATOES These tend to be round and may be one or several of many colors: brown, green (even when ripe), yellow, orange, even purple or striped. They vary in size from the huge beefsteaks, which are rich in juice and make marvelous salads simply sliced, through to the neat cardboard supermarket rounds in cellophane. The French tomatoes with the bumpy tops and the round-topped, pointy-bottomed Italian tomatoes described as ox-heart both fit in this category but tend to be meatier.

When cooked, American tomatoes will give a fresher-tasting, more acidic purée. Meaty Italian plum tomatoes (see below) will need much less cooking time—less water to evaporate—and will give a darker red, sweeter purée.

PLUM TOMATOES Usually thought of as Italian and are even confusingly called Roma, when they are a variety developed in America. These are the kind commonly found in cans from Italy.

CHERRY TOMATOES Red, yellow or orange, these used to be used mainly in salads, as part of a raw vegetable assortment or as shells to stuff for hors d'oeuvre. Now we find that they are a good cooking tomato, especially when the only American tomatoes available are the cardboard kind.

PEAR-SHAPED TOMATOES These, what I think of as shmoos, are usually slightly larger than cherries and can be used in the same ways, but I do tend to save them for raw eating so that their shape can be enjoyed.

GRAPE TOMATOES A smaller, sweeter version of cherry tomatoes that grow in long bunches like grapes.

SUN-DRIED TOMATOES A prepared ingredient that needs to be reconstituted; see page 661. Choose tomatoes dried without chemical additives.

Methods

BUYING AND STORING

It is too bad there is no Chiquita tomato to warn us never to put tomatoes in the refrigerator. If tomatoes are less than ripe, put them in a brown paper bag with an apple. Do not store in plastic.

WASHING/WAYS OF CUTTING

Remove any stems. Rinse tomatoes under cold running water. For all tomatoes except grape and cherry, remove the core on top where the stem was attached. Use a sharp paring knife, making a conical cut to remove all the whitish pith.

A tomato knife, serrated like a small bread knife, is the best tool to use when cutting up tomatoes so that they do not get crushed as one slices through the occasionally tough skin. Large tomatoes can also be sliced with a bread knife.

PEELING

There is a classic dilemma when using tomatoes for eating raw as in salads: to peel or not to peel. I may just be lazy, but I seldom peel. Tomatoes that are wonderfully ripe fall apart easily when the skin is removed. But some tomatoes develop tough, heavy skins as they ripen and will need to be peeled.

Really ripe tomatoes do not have to be plunged into boiling water should you have a desperate desire to peel them. Simply run the back of a table knife firmly over the skin; this loosens it from the flesh. Then slip the tip of a knife under the skin and pull. The skin will come off easily in strips. I learned this trick from a farmer in the South of France who was scandalized to see me preparing the seething pot.

For less ripe tomatoes or those with thick skins, score a shallow X in the skin at the bottom of each tomato. Bring a large pot of water to a rolling boil. Put in the tomatoes and cook (blanch) for several seconds, just until the skin begins to peel back from the cut surfaces; do not overcook. Remove the tomatoes and immediately plunge into ice water—or, if only making a few, rinse under cold running water. The skin will now be loose and easy to remove.

Preparation

COOKING

Tomatoes are another vegetable that cannot be properly cooked in reactive—i.e., aluminum—pots; it's the acid.

BOILING

I don't normally boil tomato pieces; but it is useful to do so when adding cubes of tomato to cooked soup. It heats them and removes a little of the excess water.

¹/₂-inch dice: Drop into boiling liquid and simmer for 5 to 15 minutes.

ROASTING

Summer, when tomatoes are really ripe, is the best time to roast most regular tomatoes, unless they are roasted along with other ingredients to add to a stock. In a 500°F oven, 8-ounce tomatoes will cook in 20 minutes or less and need little oil. They are an excellent vegetable hot or cool, skins on or off, with roast chicken or fish. Sprinkle with salt, pepper and finely cut fresh basil, chives, dill or lemon balm. I don't think they need anything else, but butter or cream can be added when serving hot and a little olive oil when serving cold.

TOMATOES OF VARIOUS SIZES (whole, stems removed but not cored) **AND CHERRY TOMATOES** The smallest cherry tomatoes will take only 25 minutes to roast in a 500°F oven, but larger cherry tomatoes, the kind on the stem in the stores in the winter, take 25 to 30 minutes.

Use smallest pan that will hold tomatoes comfortably in a single layer. For 1 ¹/₂ pounds cherry tomatoes or 8-ounce or 1 pound tomatoes, slick tomatoes and pan with 1 tablespoon fat; for 5 pounds cherry tomatoes, use 2 tablespoons fat. Roast in center of 500°F oven for 10 minutes. Shake pan. Roast for another 10 minutes. If using larger cherry tomatoes, turn and roast for 5 to 10 minutes more.

PLUM TOMATOES Roasted plum tomatoes merit separate instructions because they are so often used in recipes and, when time is available, in sauce. When they are puréed through a food mill, the result is richly red.

In summer, when plum tomatoes are riper and sweeter, roasting may take only 20 minutes. In winter, when the tomatoes are harder, they may take 5 minutes longer. Two pounds plum tomatoes will fit in a small (12 x 8 x 1½-inch) roasting pan. Six pounds will fill a large (19 x 13 x 2-inch) pan.

Whole: Remove stems. Use smallest pan that will hold tomatoes comfortably. Slick tomatoes and pan with 1 to 3 tablespoons fat, depending on quantity (see above). Roast in center of 500°F oven for 10 minutes. Shake pan. Roast for 10 to 15 minutes more.

Note: Since I often use these as a replacement for the inferior canned plum tomatoes, I find it useful to know the yields for different sizes of canned tomatoes; see page 663.

MICROWAVING

Microwave cooking can help us with many of the pedestrian tasks involved in cooking tomatoes. It helps us make sauces and pastes quickly enough so that some of the acid freshness of the tomato remains. In addition, it is a joy to cook stuffed tomatoes in the microwave. They retain their shape and color, cooking without collapsing. See individual recipes for indications of time.

BROILING

These timings were done using store-bought "vine-ripened" tomatoes. Cooking times will most likely be shorter when using home-grown or farm stand tomatoes.

LARGE PLUM OR MEDIUM AMERICAN TOMATOES Preheat broiler with rack about 5 inches from heat. Core tomatoes. Cut plum tomatoes in half lengthwise, American tomatoes along the equator. Squeeze out seeds or remove with a small spoon, if desired (recommended if using crumb topping; see below). Slick cut surfaces with olive oil and season with salt and pepper. Put, cut side up, on broiler pan, without crowding. Broil until browned and tender but not mushy, about 8 minutes. If using crumb topping, coat cut sides of tomatoes with an even, light layer of crumbs and return to broiler until golden brown, about 1 minute. Serve hot, warm or at room temperature.

For crumb topping: Stir together ¼ cup dried bread crumbs, homemade (page 510) or store-bought, 2 teaspoons olive oil, ½ teaspoon kosher salt and freshly ground black pepper to taste. (Makes 5 tablespoons, enough to top 8 tomato halves)

OVEN-DRYING

MEDIUM TO MEDIUM-LARGE PLUM TOMATOES (3 to 4½ ounces each): Choose ripe unblemished tomatoes. Core and cut in half lengthwise. Arrange, cut side up, on a baking sheet (or sheets) that holds them comfortably. Sprinkle salt lightly and evenly over tomatoes. Let stand at room temperature for 30 to 45 minutes.

Place an oven rack in center position and preheat oven to 200°F. Or, if drying more than one baking sheet full of tomatoes, dry on two racks, switching positions halfway through drying. Place in oven and dry until firm but pliable, about 9 hours for medium, up to 12 hours for medium-large. Turn once about halfway through drying. Store in refrigerator and use within 3 weeks or freeze for up to 3 months. Southern Italians will often semi-dry bunches of grape or cherry tomatoes by hanging them outdoors in a breezy place.

RECONSTITUTING SUN-DRIED TOMATOES

Reconstituted sun-dried tomatoes can be halved and put out with toothpicks as a nice snack or turned into a dip for your next party.

A half-pound dried makes 4 cups reconstituted—about 27 pieces in each cooked cup, which, halved, will make 54 snacks (216 per ½ pound). Each cooked cup is enough for 12 to 15 people. If you pack them in oil for storage, the oil can be used for another batch.

STOVETOP METHOD

Cover tomatoes with water in a nonreactive saucepan. Bring to a boil over medium heat. Reduce heat to a simmer and cook, covered, for 22 minutes, or until plump. Allow to cool. Drain.

MICROWAVE OVEN METHOD

For 4 ounces sun-dried tomatoes: Cook with 2 cups water in a 2^1/$_2$-quart soufflé dish. Cook, covered with microwave plastic wrap, at 100% for 5 minutes. Prick plastic to release the steam. Stir and cook, uncovered, for 5 minutes.

For 8 ounces sun-dried tomatoes: Cook with 2 cups water in a 13 x 9 x 2-inch oval glass or ceramic dish. Cook, uncovered, at 100% for 8 minutes. Stir, then cook, uncovered, for 8 minutes.

For 1 pound sun-dried tomatoes: Cook with 4 cups water in a 5-quart casserole. Cook, covered, at 100% for 14 minutes. Stir, then cook, uncovered, for 14 minutes.

PREPARATION FOR STUFFING

To make tomato shells: Cut across each tomato ^{1}/$_2$ inch from the top and save top portion to make a lid. Scoop out pulp, leaving a ^{1}/$_2$-inch shell. Do not cook tomatoes before stuffing; they will become too soft.

Stuffed cherry tomatoes also make an appealing and colorful hors d'oeuvre. To prepare, slice off about ^{1}/$_4$ inch from tops and save top portions for lids. If necessary, slice a thin sliver from bottom so tomatoes can stand upright.

Cooking stuffed tomatoes: For 8-ounce tomatoes: Fill each with ^{1}/$_2$ cup stuffing and 2 tablespoons water. Bake, without the lids, at 350°F for 55 minutes. Add 1 tablespoon olive oil and place lids on top of tomatoes. Cook for 15 minutes longer.

Commercial Tomato Products

Commercially prepared tomato products are high in sodium. If time is available in season, make fresh and freeze to keep on hand. All processed tomato products will taste fresher if a little lemon juice is added to them when cooking. Canned tomato products from Italy have a nasty tendency to taste of the can. And ketchup is ubiquitous.

AMERICAN TOMATOES Those in cans are round and look like most of the tomatoes in produce departments; they are always peeled. They have a fresher, brighter flavor than the fleshier Italian plum tomatoes. I like them in stews and soups when good fresh tomatoes are unavailable. Avoid canned tomatoes packed in purée or paste, which have more salt, more calories and a less fresh flavor.

PLUM (ITALIAN) TOMATOES These are canned in Italy and America with or without basil (no problem) and with or without purée or paste added (avoid). San Marzano and Roma are the plum tomato varieties to look for. These are the tomatoes used to make paste; they have more flesh than juice.

TOMATO PURÉE AND CRUSHED TOMATOES These are a help when not making fresh (see Plum Tomato Purée, page 459, and American Tomato Purée, page 460). The best packaged purée (labeled as "strained") comes from Italy sterile-packed in cartons; see below. It has less of a cooked taste and less salt, and is less sickly sweet than the canned products. If it's not available, put American canned or crushed tomatoes through a coarse sieve or food mill. There are some salt-free products on the market.

STERILE-PACK TOMATOES This is a mainly Italian habit and a very good one it is too. These are shelf-stable and have no off taste from the can and generally are unseasoned. They come chopped and puréed (strained). Out of season, I cannot recommend them too highly. The most available brand packs strained or chopped tomatoes into 26.5-ounce containers; each yields about 3^1/$_4$ cups.

TOMATO PASTE A cooked-down concentrate of tomato purée, tomato paste can be made at home (page 459), which is preferable. If buying, look for it in tubes. It will have much less waste, as they can be closed up tightly and refrigerated. If buying in cans, freeze leftovers in 1-tablespoon amounts in ice cube trays. When frozen, remove the cubes from the trays and store in the freezer in plastic bags. They can be added to cooking foods without defrosting.

TOMATO JUICE Juice is generally made from tomatoes that are not good for cooking or eating raw—they are too liquid. Some varieties are made with other vegetables as well. Tomato juice often can be used by vegetarians as a flavorful cooking liquid when there are no vegetarian stocks (pages 506–507) on hand. When using instead of stock, a little more may be required, as it is not all liquid. Be careful about salt.

Yields and Equivalents

CHERRY TOMATOES

1 1/2 pounds cherry tomatoes, stemmed = 4 cups
The commonly available basket of cherry tomatoes weighs about 1 1/4 pounds and contains approximately 20 tomatoes. When roasting, a pound and a half fits in a small pan (12 x 8 x 1 1/2-inch), 5 pounds fills my largest pan (18 x13 x 2-inch). If puréed through a food mill for an intense red or orange-colored sauce, the larger amount of roasted tomatoes will make about 6 cups. Greater amounts of tomatoes need a little more oil. The skins pop off easily after roasting. But why bother?

AMERICAN TOMATOES

1 small tomato = 3 to 4 ounces
1 medium tomato = 5 to 7 ounces
1 large tomato = 8 to 10 ounces
4 medium-large tomatoes = 2 pounds
8 ounces tomatoes, cut into 1/2-inch dice = generous 1 cup raw = 1/2 cup cooked
12 ounces tomatoes, cut into 1/2-inch dice = 1 3/4 cups

PLUM TOMATOES

1 small tomato = 2 ounces
1 medium tomato = 3 to 4 ounces
1 large tomato = 5 ounces
2 pounds tomatoes, cut into 1-inch pieces = 6 cups

CANNED TOMATOES

One 33.5-ounce can plum tomatoes = 4 cups
   whole = 4 cups, coarse chunks = 2 1/2 cups
   drained = 2 cups purée
One 14.5-ounce can American tomatoes =
   1 1/2 cups whole = 1 1/2 cups purée

STERILE-PACK TOMATOES

One 26.5-ounce container chopped tomatoes =
   3 cups = 2 1/2 cups purée (using the finest disc
   of food mill)
One 35.25-ounce container strained tomatoes =
   4 cups

TOMATO PASTE

One 4.5-ounce tube = 10 tablespoons
   (1/2 cup plus 2 tablespoons)
One 6-ounce can = 13 tablespoons
   (3/4 cup plus 1 tablespoon)

TOM THUMB LETTUCE see Bibb under Lettuces
TREE EARS see Mushrooms, Dried
TREVISO RADICCHIO see Chicories
TROMPETTES DU MORT see Trumpets of Death
   under Mushrooms, Fresh

Tropical Tubers

*Manihot esculenta/Colocasia esculenta/Xanthosoma/
Ipomoea batatas*

This is one of the most aggravating and confusing groups, and the names can be inaccurate. The same tuber can be called a myriad of different names, and the same name may be applied to completely different tubers. Case in point, malanga and taro. We are mentioning only the most common names, but there are dozens for each variety. They are all different in starchiness and moisture content. Some darken upon exposure to air. Some are sweet, some nutty and some bitter, but most seem to be pretty neutral in flavor, or at least very light in flavor. All cook in about the same amount of time and are best boiled, since water adds moisture to these very starchy tubers.

Varieties

YAUTÍA aka MALANGA (*Xanthosoma*) The varieties of yautía, or malanga, differ greatly in looks, tastes and texture, with shapes ranging from fat and rounded to long, slender and tapered at one end. All have brown skin decorated with many small cracks and a pronounced ring pattern. A variety generally labeled as basic yautía is long and slender, with medium-moist white flesh and a taste lightly reminiscent of black beans. Another labeled yautía amarizia is large and plump. It looks and tastes very much like taro—white flesh speckled with purple, smoothly starchy and lightly nutty—and can replace taro in recipes such as Deep-fried Taro Horns (page 363). A variety labeled as plain malanga has the white flesh and purple swirls of taro, tastes slightly of coconut and is less starchy.

TARO aka COCO YAM, DASHEEN, EDDO, MALANGA (hence some of the confusion) (*Colocasia esculenta*) Taro is incredibly versatile: The Chinese use it in cakes and snacks, Hawaiians ferment it to make poi and Caribbeans eat the leafy tops known as callaloo (although other greens are also called callaloo). There are two basic varieties, large and small. Large is the more common, with a rough brown ring-patterned exterior and a white interior attractively flecked with pink-purple swirls. The texture is starchy and the flavor slightly nutty. Small taro, often called eddo, looks like a younger version of large taro. Its white flesh is more moist and less flavorful, similar to a waxy potato.

YUCA aka CASSAVA, MANIOC, BRAZILIAN ARROWROOT (*Manihot esculenta*) Yuca is long and narrow in shape, with wax-coated brown skin. A thick fiber runs through the center of its starchy white flesh. This fiber can be difficult to see when raw. Be sure to remove all of it, as it takes on the consistency of a twig when cooked. Yuca is served in Cuba much as potatoes are served in this country.

Tapioca is yuca that has been processed and formed into balls or flakes (see page 150).

Methods
BUYING AND STORING
These all keep very well in a cool, dark place.

WASHING/WAYS OF CUTTING
YUCA Trim both ends. Remove the skin with a vegetable peeler. Slice lengthwise in half or quarters. Remove the center fiber that runs through the entire vegetable.
ALL OTHER TUBERS Use a good vegetable peeler or a paring knife to remove the skin. Peel entirely and cut off any dried or brown bits. Slice as desired.

Preparation
BOILING
1-inch slices: Cover with water by 2 inches. Bring to a boil. Reduce heat and simmer for 15 to 25 minutes.
¹/₂-inch chunks: Cover with water by 2 inches. Bring to a boil. Reduce heat and simmer for 12 to 15 minutes.
¹/₄-inch dice: Cover with water by 2 inches. Bring to a boil. Reduce heat and simmer for 10 minutes.

STEAMING
YAUTÍA AMARIZIA *1-inch thick slices:* Place in a covered steamer basket. Cook for 30 minutes, or until a knife easily slips into flesh.
EDDO AND YAUTÍA *1-inch-thick slices:* Place in a covered steamer basket. Cook for 20 minutes, or until a knife easily slips into flesh.

For taro chips, see Crispy Vegetable Chips, page 514.

Yields and Equivalents
4 ounces cooked peeled tuber (any variety) =
 ¹/₂ cup purée
8 ounces cooked peeled tuber (any variety) =
 1 cup purée
1 pound any tuber, peeled and trimmed =
 14 ounces cut into ¹/₄-inch dice = 2¹/₄ cups raw
13 ounces any tuber, peeled and trimmed =
 12 ounces cut into ¹/₂-inch dice = 2 cups raw
 (and same volume cooked)

TUNG HO see Chrysanthemum Greens
TURBAN SQUASH see Squash, Winter

Turnips

Brassica rapa/Brassica napus

Young turnips are sweet, with a certain sharpness, and their greens can be used with other boiling greens. Older turnips will be stronger tasting, depending on their kind.

Varieties

WHITE (*Brassica rapa*) These vary, depending on type, from small ovals to large round turnips like the Vermont-bred Gilfeather. I prefer the sweetness of small ones.

WHITE-PURPLE (*Brassica rapa*) Basically like white turnips except that their bottom half is purple. These are the kind generally called for in French recipes.

RUTABAGA (*Brassica napus*) As a child, I thought this was "rooter-baker." It is a large, waxy yellow turnip with a sharper taste than a regular turnip. If it is to be puréed, it requires longer cooking than a regular turnip, as it will if steamed. On the other hand, cut into strips and quickly blanched, it can be used instead of celery root in a mustard vinaigrette or mayonnaise for a first-course salad.

Methods

BUYING AND STORING
Twist off the greens; if too large for use, discard. Turnips will store well in the refrigerator as long as they are firm and unblemished.

WASHING/WAYS OF CUTTING
Trim both ends and remove the skin with a vegetable peeler.

Rutabaga often comes coated with a thick protective wax that is both tough and slippery for a knife to penetrate. With a large heavy knife, carefully cut the rutabaga in half. Then peel with a small paring knife or sturdy vegetable peeler.

Preparation

BOILING
WHITE AND WHITE-PURPLE *¹/₂-inch dice:* Cover with 1 inch water and bring to a boil. Simmer for 20 to 25 minutes.

Halved (small) or quartered (large): Cover with 1 inch water and bring to a boil. Simmer for 15 to 20 minutes.

RUTABAGA *¹/₂-inch dice:* Cover with 2 inches water and bring to a boil. Simmer for 20 minutes.

STEAMING
WHITE AND WHITE-PURPLE *Small, quartered:* Place in a covered steamer basket. Cook for 10 to 12 minutes, or until a knife easily slips into flesh.

MATCHSTICKS Place in a covered steamer basket. Cook for 5 to 7 minutes, or until a knife easily slips into flesh.

SAUTÉING
WHITE *Baby, quartered:* Heat a pan wide enough to hold turnips in a single layer. Slick with just enough oil to coat pan bottom. Add turnips. Cook, stirring, over medium-high heat for 4 to 5 minutes.

Baby, whole: Heat a pan wide enough to hold turnips in a single layer. Slick with just enough oil to coat pan bottom. Add turnips. Cook, stirring, over medium-high heat for 6 minutes. Reduce heat to low. Cook, stirring, for 4 to 6 minutes, until a knife is easily inserted into flesh.

DEEP-FRYING
WHITE *Baby, peeled and quartered:* Pour 1¹/₂ to 2 inches of oil into a deep pan. Heat oil to 300°F. Put in turnips. Fry for 2 minutes, or until they are golden brown and a knife easily inserts into flesh.

ROASTING
WHITE AND WHITE-PURPLE *¹/₂-inch dice (peeled):* Use smallest pan that will hold pieces comfortably. Slick turnips and pan with fat. Roast on lowest level of 500°F oven for 10 minutes. Turn. Roast for 15 minutes more.

Wedges: Peel and trim turnips, cut in half lengthwise and cut each half in 3 wedges. Use smallest pan that will hold them comfortably in a single layer. Slick wedges

and pan with fat. Roast in center of 500°F oven for
15 minutes. Turn. Roast for another 7 minutes. Turn.
Roast for 5 minutes more.

MICROWAVING

WHITE AND WHITE-PURPLE *Diced (peeled):*
Cover tightly.

    4 turnips (1-quart measure): 6 minutes

RUTABAGA *1/2-inch cubes (peeled):* Cover tightly.

    1 1/2 pounds rutabaga with 1/2 cup water
    (2-quart measure): 15 minutes

Yields and Equivalents

WHITE AND WHITE-PURPLE TURNIPS

    1 small turnip = 3 to 5 ounces

    1 medium turnip = 6 to 7 ounces

    1 large turnip = 8 to 10 ounces

    8 ounces turnips, trimmed, peeled and cut into
      1/2-inch dice = 2 cups raw = 1 cup cooked

    2 pounds turnips, trimmed, peeled and cut into
      1/2-inch dice = 3 cups cooked

    1 pound small turnips, trimmed, peeled and
      diced = 3 cups raw = 2 1/2 cups cooked

RUTABAGA

    1 1/2 pounds rutabaga, peeled and cut into 1/2-inch
      cubes = 4 cups raw = 1 3/4 cups purée

TUSCAN KALE see Kale

UVILLA GRANDE PEPPERS see Peppers

VEGETABLE MARROWS see Squash, Summer

VEGETABLE PEARS see Chayote under
    Squash, Winter

VERONA RADICCHIO see "Regular" Radicchio
    under Chicories

WALKING ONIONS see Egyptian Onions under
    Onions

Wasabi

Eutrema wasabi

This is really a Japanese national treasure and is not to
be confused with horseradish, which is sometimes tinted
green to masquerade as the real thing. For many years
wasabi was poisonously expensive and could be bought
only imported and generally only by Japanese restaurants.
Today it is also grown in the American Northwest in
specially formulated water baths. In Japan, it is grown in
natural streams of running cold water. It is not the nasty
powder made to be mixed with water. The real thing in
paste form will not be totally homogeneous but will be a
flecked green. In Japanese restaurants, ask if they have real
wasabi (expect to be charged extra unless it is a very good
restaurant). Wasabi can be bought in tubes in Japanese
food stores or from many online sources. Once exposed
to the air, it should be used fairly quickly even though
refrigerated.

    Wasabi should be treated with respect, used raw and
not drenched in soy sauce. "A little dab will do." It is spicy
but has a pleasant sweetness and does not burn the mouth.

Watercress

Nasturtium officinale

Clear running streams will often have watercress growing
in clumps in among the stones. It is now cultivated in beds
that are flooded. Try to buy watercress that is not too large
and dark green, not yellow. In addition to being a standard
in salads, it makes a very good sauce and an excellent
soup. Watercress is related to nasturtiums.

Methods

BUYING AND STORING

Watercress is better when it is not too large and the stems
are less prominent. The leaves should be dark green and
the stems crisp. Store in the refrigerator and use within
2 to 3 days.

WASHING/WAYS OF CUTTING

As it is grown in water, watercress is generally quite clean, but a quick swish through cold water would not be amiss. The leaves can be picked off or the stems trimmed and the watercress left pretty much whole; or a knife can be run down the bunch from the stems to the top, which will provide most of the leaves.

Preparation

SAUTÉING

Lightly wilted watercress makes a nice side dish or bed for grilled vegetables, chicken or fish. Vary the oil: toasted sesame for an Asian feeling, olive oil for Mediterranean.

Whole sprigs, thick ends trimmed: For 1 good bunch, trimmed: Heat 1 tablespoon oil in a large skillet over medium heat. When rippling, add watercress and immediately stir and toss just until bright green and barely wilted, about 45 seconds. Remove from heat, season lightly with salt or soy sauce and serve warm or at room temperature.

GRILLING

Grilled watercress, tied in neat bundles, makes an unusual side for grilled dishes. Alternatively, the watercress can be spread out in an even layer in a grill basket, sprinkled lightly with oil and seasoned with salt and pepper. Tumble basket-grilled watercress into a shallow bowl and serve.

See Grilling, page 518 for information on preparing the grill.

Watercress bundles: Remove rubber band or twist tie from watercress bunch, leaving bunch as intact as possible. Trim thick ends from stems. Again keeping bunch intact, swish in a bowl of cold water to remove sand and grit. Shake out as much water as possible and roll bunch lightly in paper towels to dry. Divide into smaller bundles (about 6 bundles per average-size bunch). Tie securely with kitchen twine about 1 inch from bottom of stems. Alternatively, dip as many long chives as there are bundles into boiling water for 3 seconds; remove and cool. Use the softened chives to tie bundles.

Slick bundles very lightly with toasted sesame oil or vegetable oil. Season lightly with salt and pepper. Grill, turning once, until bright green and wilted, about 30 seconds per side.

Yields and Equivalents

1 medium bunch watercress = 7 ounces
1 medium bunch watercress, thick stems removed, sprigs left whole = 7 cups

WAX BEANS see Beans of the New World under Beans
WILD SORREL see Sorrel
WING BEANS see Peas
WINTER ASPARAGUS see Sea Kale
WINTER PURSLANE see Purslane and Miner's Lettuce
WINTER SAVORY see Herbs and Their Flowers
WOOD EARS see Mushrooms, Dried
WOOD HEDGEHOGS see Mushrooms, Fresh
WRAPPED HEART MUSTARD see Mustard Greens and Leaf Mustard
YAMS see Sweet Potatoes and Yams
YARD-LONG BEANS see Peas
YAUTÍA and YAUTÍA AMARIZIA see Tropical Tubers
YELLOW FINN POTATOES see Potatoes
YELLOW SQUASH see Squash, Summer
YELLOW WAXY PEPPERS see Peppers
YELLOW ZUCCHINI see Squash, Summer
YUCA see Tropical Tubers
YUKON GOLD POTATOES see Potatoes
ZUCCHINI see Squash, Summer

Sources

Ingredients

These are sources from which we have ordered and been made happy. We may not have tried every item from every source listed below, but we can speak for the quality of the products in general and for the service.

Buon Italia
75 Ninth Avenue
New York, NY 10011
212-633-9090
www.buonitalia.com

Several types of rice for risotto, olive oils, caviar, fruits preserved in mustard syrup

www.chefs-garden.com
Information about heirloom vegetables, sustainable agriculture and "Veggie U"

The CMC Company
P.O. Drawer 322
Avalon, NJ 08202
800-262-2780
www.thecmccompany.com

The CMC Company has an interesting site. We didn't have a chance to order before the book printed, but the site looks hopeful. It is divided into several ethnic categories. A sampling of some of the items we discuss in this book follows.

From the Chinese section Dried black mushrooms, five-spice powder, dried sesame seeds, tapioca starch, fermented black beans
From the European section Piquillo peppers, capers, caper berries, smoked paprika
From the Indian section Black mustard seed, mango powder (amchoor), fenugreek, ghee

From the Mexican section Pure chili powders, dried whole chilies, hot sauces, epazote, bottled nopales (cactus leaves), dried avocado leaves, dried posole (hominy)
From the Thai section Nam pla (Thai fish sauce), coconut milk, lemongrass powder, tamarind paste

D'Artagnan
280 Wilson Avenue
Newark, NJ 07105
800-327-8246
www.dartagnan.com

Fresh (in season) and dried mushrooms, duck and veal glaze

El Mercado Grande
Mesa, AZ 85203
480-862-2964
www.elmercadogrande.com

Several types of posole (dried hominy), paprikas, Andean popping corn, whole and ground annatto seeds

www.friedas.com
Use this site's store locator to find a store that *may* carry Frieda's cocktail avocados, heirloom tomatoes, Meyer lemons

Gustiamo, Inc.
1715 West Farms Road
Bronx, NY 10460
877-907-2525
www.gustiamo.com

All things Italian, including capers from Pantelleria, pastas and rice for risotto, saffron, polenta and oils

Hardy Farms Peanuts
Route 2, P.O. Box 2120
Hawkinsville, GA 31036
888-368-NUTS (6877)
www.hardyfarmspeanuts.com

Green (raw) peanuts, boiled or fresh

Kalustyan's
123 Lexington Avenue
New York, NY 10016
800-352-3451
www.kalustyans.com

Beans and peas including, but not limited to, adzuki, broad beans, favas, coronas, gigantes and cranberries; malokhei; herbs and spices; oils; fermented black beans; curry powders; Greek oregano, dried in bunches; amchoor (dried mango) powder; five-spice powder; fennel pollen; mustard seeds; cardamom pods and powder; juniper berries; harissa sauce; tamarind concentrate (purée); crystallized ginger; sambal olek; anchovy paste; agar-agar

Katagiri
224 East 59th Street
New York, NY 10022
212-755-3566
www.katagiri.com

Konbu for dashi, rice flour, miso (several varieties); fresh produce, including chrysanthemum leaves, shiso (perilla), lotus root, burdock root; black sesame seeds; dried soy and adzuki beans; otoshi-butas

La Tienda
3601 La Grange Parkway
Toano, VA 23168
888-472-1022
www.tienda.com

Salt-packed capers; hot, sweet and smoked paprika; fresh padron peppers; jarred white asparagus; roasted piquillo peppers; dried beans; achiote (annatto) seeds; chorizo; manchego cheese; saffron; fleur de sel

Otto's
2320 West Clark Avenue
Burbank, CA 91506
818-845-0433 (order in English or Hungarian)
www.members@aol.com/HungImprts

Paprika powders and pastes of all descriptions, letcho (called "lecsó" on the site)

Pacific Farms USA
800-927-2248 ext. 313
www.freshwasabi.com

100 percent wasabi (no horseradish, mustard or food dyes) in ½- and 1-pound packages (Be warned: It is expensive.)

www.pepperfool.com
While hot pepper sauces and other items can be ordered directly from this site, it is a terrific source of links to other pepperabilia: fresh and dried chilies, chili seeds and more

Titan Foods
25–36 31st Street
Long Island City, NY 11102
718-626-7771
www.titanfoods.com

Bottled caper leaves

Tsar Nicoulai Caviar
60 Dorman Avenue
San Francisco, CA 94124
800-952-2842
www.tsarnicoulai.com

Caviar of all stripes, including domestic and imported sturgeon caviar, paddlefish and whitefish caviar and smoked fish

Seeds

As it must be clear, I have a special affection for foods that I grow myself; I think we all do. Here are a few sources for seeds.

Baker Creek Heirloom Seeds
2278 Baker Creek Road
Mansfield, MO 65704
417-924-8917
www.rareseeds.com

Edible gourds, including luffa, cuccuzzi, Thai bottle gourd and Chinese tri-leaf; wing beans; puntarelle and other chicories, including Verona, Chioggia and Treviso radicchio; long beans; salsify; interesting chili peppers such as "chocolate habanero," bird peppers and black Hungarian; cornichons (gherkins)

www.chilternseeds.co.uk
Good source, good catalog information, also for hard-to-find plant seeds and is a wonderful search system

Flora Exotica
514-747-7618
www.floraexotica.ca

This Montreal company sells plants or seeds for all of the following: lemongrass, okra, pandan, fuzzy squash (edible gourd), amaranth, vegetable (edible) chrysanthemum, sweet potato, Chinese mustard, Egyptian walking onion, Thai basil and wing beans

www.gardenguides.com
Santaka chilies; mitsuba; Chinese celery; unusual lettuces and lettuce mixes

www.gardenlist.com
A wonderful source for seed catalogs from companies that specialize in everything from heirloom vegetable seeds to mushroom spores

www.growitalian.com
Hard- and soft-necked garlic, cardoons, many chicories and radicchios, lettuces (including quattro stagione/quatre saisons and lolla rossa), many winter squashes including Marina di Chioggia, broccoli di raab

Heirloom Seeds
P.O. Box 245
West Elizabeth, PA 15088-0245
412-384-0852
www.heirloomseeds.com

Extremely well-organized site with large selection including lovage, cardoons, favas, soybeans; Chioggia (and many other) beets; salsify; angelica; many basils; bee balm; borage; epazote

Bibliography

Books

Aaron, Chester. *The Great Garlic Book*. Berkeley: Ten Speed Press, 1997

Ali-Bab (Henri Babinsky), ed. *Gastronomie Practique*. Paris: Flammerion, 1928.

Andrews, Colman. *Catalan Cuisine*. New York: Atheneum/Macmillan, 1988.

Andrews, Jean. *The Pepper Lady's Pocket Pepper Primer*. Austin: University of Texas Press, 1998.

————. *Peppers: The Domesticated Capsicums*. Austin: University of Texas Press, 1995.

————. *The Pepper Trail*. Austin: University of Texas Press, 1999.

Antolini, Piero, and Guido Stecchi. *Les Champignons dans la Cuisine*. Adaptation d'Elisabeth Lange. Paris: Duclot, 1988.

Artusi, Pellegrino. *The Art of Eating Well*. Translated by Kyle M. Phillips III. New York: Random House, 1996.

Barr, Nancy Verde. *Make It Italian: The Taste and Technique of Italian Home Cooking*. New York: Alfred A. Knopf, 2002.

Batali, Mario. *The Babbo Cookbook*. New York: Clarkson Potter, 2002.

Batmanglij, Najmieh. *Silk Road Cooking: A Vegetarian Journey*. Washington, D.C.: Mage Publishing, 2002.

Bayless, Rick. *Rick Bayless's Mexican Kitchen*. New York: Simon & Schuster, 1996.

Better Homes and Gardens Complete Guide to Food and Cooking. Des Moines: Better Homes and Gardens Books/Meredith Corporation, 1991.

Biaggi, Vladimir, and Jean Arnaud. *Poulpes, Seiches, Calmars: mythes et gastronomie*. France: Jeanne Laffitte, n.d.

Bianchini, Francesco, Francesco Corbetta, and Marilena Pistola. *The Complete Book of Fruit & Vegetables*. New York: Crown Publishers, 1976.

Bladholm, Linda. *The Asian Grocery Store Demystified*. Los Angeles: Renaissance Books, 1999.

Bosland, P. W., and E. J. Votava. *Peppers: Vegetable and Spice Capsicums*. New York: CABI Publishing, 2000.

Bras, Michel, Colette Gouvion, and Patrick Mialon. *Bras: Laguiole, Aubrac, France*. Paris: Éditions du Rouergue, 2002.

Brennan, Jennifer. *Curries and Bugles*. New York: HarperCollins, 1990.

Buff, Sheila. *The Great Tomato Book*. Short Hills, N.J.: Burford Books, 1999.

Button, David, and Keith Miller. *The Restaurants in Barbados*. Barbados: Miller Publishing, 2002.

Cost, Bruce. *Bruce Cost's Asian Ingredients*. New York: William Morrow, 1988.

Creasy, Rosalind. *Cooking from the Garden*. San Francisco: Sierra Club Books, 1988.

Dahlen, Martha, and Karen Phillipps. *A Popular Guide to Chinese Vegetables*. New York: Crown Publishers, 1983.

Davidson, Alan. *The Oxford Companion to Food*. Oxford: Oxford University Press, 1999.

De Witt, Dave. *The Chile Pepper Encyclopedia*. New York: William Morrow, 1999.

————, and Paul W. Bosland. *Peppers of the World*. Berkeley: Ten Speed Press, 1996.

Dictionnaire Vilmorin des Plantes Potagères. Paris: Vilmorin-Andrieux, 1946.

Elon, Beth. *A Mediterranean Farm Kitchen*. Tel Aviv: Modan Publishing House, 2000.

Escoffier, Auguste. *Ma Cuisine*. New York: A&W Publishers, 1978.

Evelyn, John. *Acetaria: A Discourse of Sallets*. Devon, England: Prospect Books, 1996.

Facciola, Stephen. *Cornucopia II*. Vista, Calif.: Kampong Publications, 1998.

Fortin, Francois, ed. *The Visual Food Encyclopedia*. Montreal: Québec/Amérique International, 1996.

Forley, Diane, with Catherine Young. *Anatomy of a Dish*. New York: Artisan, 2002.

Goldman, Amy. *The Compleat Squash: A Passionate Grower's Guide to Pumpkins, Squashes, and Gourds.* New York: Artisan, 2004.

Gosetti della Salda, Anna. *Le Ricette Regionali Italiane.* Italy: Solares, 2003.

Grigson, Jane, and Sharon Knox. *Cooking with Exotic Fruits & Vegetables.* New York: Henry Holt, 1986, 1987.

Hawkes, Alex D. *A World of Vegetable Cookery.* New York: Simon & Schuster, 1984.

Heiser, Charles B. *The Gourd Book.* Norman: University of Oklahoma Press, 1979.

Herklots, G.A.C. *Vegetables in South-East Asia.* London: George Allen & Unwin, 1972.

Huang, Su-Huei. *Chinese Snacks (Wei-Chuan Cooking Book).* Taiwan: Wei-Chuan Publishing Co., 1974.

Hutchison, Frances, cons. ed. *Garden Herbs.* New York: Barnes & Noble, 2003.

Kennedy, Diana. *Recipes from the Regional Cooks of Mexico.* New York: Harper & Row, 1978.

Keoke, Dean Emory, and Kay Marie Porterfield. *Encyclopedia of American Indian Contributions to the World.* New York: Checkmark Books, 2005.

Kiple, Kenneth F., and Kriemhild Coneè Omelas, eds. *The Cambridge World History of Food.* Vols. 1 and 2. New York: Cambridge University Press, 2000.

Kremezi, Aglaia. *The Foods of Greece.* New York: Stewart, Tabori & Chang, 1993.

———. *The Foods of the Greek Islands.* New York: Houghton Mifflin Co., 2000.

———. *Mediterranean Hot.* New York: Artisan, 1996.

Labensky, Steven, Gaye G. Ingram, and Sarah R. Labensky. *Webster's New World Dictionary of Culinary Arts.* Englewood Cliffs, N.J.: Prentice Hall, 1997.

Larkom, Joy. *Oriental Vegetables: The Complete Guide for Garden and Kitchen.* Tokyo/New York: Kodansha International/Kodansha America, 1991.

Larousse Gastronomique. Paris: Librairie Larousse, 1938.

Lesem, Jeanne. *Preserving Today.* New York: Alfred A. Knopf, 1999.

Lo, Eileen Yin-Fei. *The Dim Sum Book.* New York: Crown Publishers, 1982.

McGee, Harold. *The Curious Cook: More Kitchen Science and Lore.* New York: John Wiley & Sons, 1992.

Mardan-Bey, Farouk. *Ziryab Authentic Arab Cuisine.* Woodbury, Conn.: Ici La Press, 2002.

Marks, Copeland. *Sephardic Cooking.* New York: Donald I. Fine/Penguin Publishing, 1992.

Martin, Guy. *Vegetables.* Woodbury, Conn.: Ici La Press, 2002.

Masefield, G. B. et al. *The Oxford Book of Food Plants.* Oxford: Oxford University Press, 1969, 1975.

Maximin, Jacques, with Martine Jolly. *Cuisine les Légumes.* Paris: Albin Michel, 1998.

Muenscher, Walter C., and Myron A. Rice. *Garden Spice & Wild Pot-Herbs.* New York: Comstock Publishing Associates, 1955.

Obauer, Karl, and Rudolf Obauer. *Hemmungslos Kochen.* Munich: Knaur Verlag, 2002.

Padilla, Carmella. *The Chile Chronicles: Tales of a New Mexico Harvest.* Santa Fe: Museum of New Mexico Press, 1997.

Parlavecchia, Paolo, ed. *Grande Enciclopedia Illustrata della Gastronomia.* Milan: Selezione dal Reader's Digest, 1990.

Passmore, Jackie. *The Encyclopedia of Asian Food and Cooking.* New York: Hearst Books, 1991.

Paterson, Hent Ian. *The Hot Empire of Chile.* Tempe, Ariz.: Bilingual Press, 2000.

Peterson, James. *Vegetables.* New York: William Morrow, 1998.

Phillips, Roger. *Der Kosmos Pilzatlas.* Germany: Franckh-Kosmos Verlags, 1990.

———. *Mushrooms and Other Fungi of Great Britain and Europe.* London: Pan Books, 1981.

Phillips, Roger, and Nicky Foy. *Herbs.* New York: Random House, 1990.

Plotkin, Fred. *Recipes from Paradise: Life and Food on the Italian Riviera.* New York: Little, Brown & Company, 1997.

Randelman, Mary Urrutia, and Joan Schwartz. *Memories of a Cuban Kitchen.* New York: Macmillan, 1992.

Rinaldi, Augusto, and Vassili Tyndalo. *The Complete Book of Mushrooms.* New York: Crown Publishers, 1974.

Roberts, Jonathan. *The Origins of Fruits & Vegetables.* New York: Universe Publishing, 2001.

Root, Waverley, and Richard Rochemont. *Eating in America.* New York: William Morrow, 1976.

Rosenthal, Sylvia, ed. *Fresh Foods.* New York: Tree Communications/E. P. Dutton, 1978.

Schaecter, Mordkhe. *Plant Names in Yiddish*. New York: Yivo Institute for Jewish Research, 2005.

Schiavelli, Vicent. *Many Beautiful Things: Stories and Recipes from Polizzi Generosa*. New York: Simon & Schuster, 2002.

Schneider, Elizabeth. *Uncommon Fruits & Vegetables: A Commonsense Guide*. New York: William Morrow, 1998.

———. *Vegetables from Amaranth to Zucchini*. New York: HarperCollins, 2001.

Shaida, Margaret. *The Legendary Cuisine of Persia*. New York: Penguin Books, 1994.

Shurtleff, William, and Akiko Aoyagi. *The Book of Miso*. New York: Ballantine Books, 1976.

———. *The Book of Tempeh*. New York: Harper & Row, 1985.

———. *The Book of Tofu*. Berkeley: Ten Speed Press, 2001.

Smart-Grosvenor, Vertamae. *Vibration Cooking: Or the Travel Notes of a Geechee Girl*. New York: Ballantine Books, 1970, 1992.

Smith, Alexander H., and Nancy Smith Weber. *The Mushroom Hunter's Field Guide*. Holt, Mich.: Thunder Bay Press, 1996.

Solomon, Charmaine. *Encyclopedia of Asian Food*. Melbourne: William Heinemann Australia, 1996.

Stobart, Tom. *The Cook's Encyclopedia*. New York: Harper & Row, 1981.

———. *Herbs, Spices and Flavorings*. New York: Overlook Press, 1982.

Stone, Sally. *The Essential Root Vegetable Cookbook*. New York: Clarkson Potter, 1991.

Tindall, H. D. *Vegetables in the Tropics*. London: Macmillan, 1992.

Tower, Jeremiah. *Jeremiah Tower Cooks*. New York: Stewart, Tabori & Chang, 2002.

Townsend, Doris McFerran. *The Cook's Companion*. New York: Rutledge Books/Crown Publishers, 1978.

Tropp, Barbara. *China Moon Cookbook*. New York: Workman Publishing, 1992.

———. *The Modern Art of Chinese Cooking*. New York: William Morrow, 1982.

Van Aken, Norman. *Norman's New World Cuisine*. New York: Random House, 1997.

Visson, Lynn. *The Art of Uzbek Cooking*. New York: Hippocrene Books, 1999.

Weaver, William Woys. *Heirloom Vegetable Gardening*. New York: Henry Holt, 1997.

———. *100 Vegetables and Where They Came From*. Chapel Hill, N.C.: Algonquin Books, 2000.

Weir, Joanne. *You Say Tomato*. New York: Broadway Books, 1998.

Wolfert, Paula. *Mediterranean Grains and Greens*. New York: HarperCollins, 1998.

Wood, Rebecca. *The New Whole Foods Encyclopedia*. New York: Penguin Books, 1999.

Wright, Clifford A. *Mediterranean Vegetables*. Boston: The Harvard Common Press, 2001.

Yoneda, Soei. *Good Food from a Japanese Temple*. New York: Kodansha International, 1982.

Web Resources

Today, the World Wide Web offers us an astounding resource of research information from universities, trade groups, companies and passionate individuals—it is well worth a look. For instance, Bill McKay, at growitalian.com, has a seed business that is excellent, and he also has an informational newsletter that costs nothing and is very helpful with questions.

Be careful to verify online sources—some are iffy.

Spanish products: www.tienda.com

Unusual Italian seeds: Bill McKay e-mail: bmkay@growitalian.com

Information on herbs: Gernot Katzer—you will have to do a Google search to reach this site.

Unusual vegetables: www.chefs-garden.com

Background information: Use the search option in www.floridita.com

Index

A

Aaron, Chester, 585
Acetaria (Evelyn), 416
acorn squash, 117, 118, 650, 653–55
  braised with mushrooms, 129
  -coconut-vegetable stew, 130
  and mint soup, 126
  nuggets, fried, 121–22
  purée, simple, 127–28
  purée soufflé, 488
  stew, 129–30
  stew with lamb, 131
  stuffed, 118
  Thanksgiving pudding, 135–36
  in thick potato soup with corn, 35
acras de christophene, 122
  spicy Middle Eastern tomato sauce
    for, 464
adanka, *see* adzuki
Adelle's favorite roasted seeds, 136
adzuki (azuki, adanka), 311–12, 543,
    544
  braised short ribs with celery and,
    311–12
  and rice, Japanese style, 311
adzuki bean sprouts, 646–47
Africa, African-style dishes, 340, 351,
    575
  Asia's links with, 295, 296
  black-eyed peas in, 307
  chicken peanut butter stew, 50
  gourds from, 351, 587
  peanuts in, 49, 50, 621
agar-agar, 501
aïoli, 456
  in cauliflower Bavarian, 255–56
  with potato, 456–57

alfalfa sprouts, 647
Algerian-style dish, orange and onion
    salad with cumin vinaigrette, 374
allergies, 49
allicin, 375, 585
alliums, 375
  see also garlic; leek(s); onion(s);
    shallots
almonds:
  carrot salad with currants and, 184–85
  kabocha with cumin, raisins and,
    132–33
amaranth, 525
amchoor, 451
American, American dishes, 390
  bread-and-butter pickles, 361
  corn chowder, 34–35
  long-cooked green beans, 16
  ramps in, 393
  steak-house tomato salad, 101
  stewed tomatoes, all-, 106–7
  tomato ketchup, early, 113
  see also New England, New England
    dishes; Southern dishes;
    Southwestern dishes
American Cookery Book (June), 113
American Food and California Wine
    (Kafka), 347
American pine mushrooms, 606
American tomatoes, 659, 662, 663
ancho chilies (peppers), 626
anchovy cheese vinaigrette, 450
  green beans, tuna, potatoes, Niçoise
    olives and tomatoes with (salade
    Niçoise), 14–15
anchovy(ies):
  cardoons with sauce of parsley, olive
    and, 242
  cauliflower pasta sauce with garlic
    and, 260
  in creamy potato salad, 81
  dip, 467
  with fennel marinade, 210
  garlic roasted peppers with
    mozzarella and, 57
  kale pissaladière with, 280
  paste vinaigrette, 449–50
  roasted peppers with chives and, 55
  roasted red pepper spread with, 56
  sautéed dandelion greens with, 578
  sauté of warm ruby chard stems and,
    179–80
  toasty Treviso with mozzarella and,
    219–20

yellow chard, roasted tomatoes and
    penne with, 181
Andrews, Colman, 63
angelica, 183, 589
angel potatoes, 79
anise, 183, 525
  -scented eggplant cubes, 334
annatto butter, in thick potato soup
    with corn, 35
antipasto:
  Kalamata, 209–10
  pickled vegetable, 256–57
Antonucci, Francesco, sage potatoes of,
    79–80
ants on a scallion tree, 393
Aoyagi, Akiko, 543
apple mint, 589, 593
apple(s):
  and beet strudel, 176
  in green shrimp curry, 437
  puréed celery root with, 206
applesauce, fresh, horseradish with, 413
Arabs, Arabic language, 322, 323, 593
arborio rice:
  with peas, Venetian (risi bisi), 302
  see also risotto
arctic char, roast, with braised carrots in
    orange cherry tomato sauce,
    190–91
artichoke(s), 229–41, 525–30
  à la grecque, 229–30
  à la grecque, late fall, 240
  bacon-wrapped, 233
  bottoms stuffed with duxelles,
    238–39
  filled with artichoke soufflé, 233–34
  filled with snails in cream, 231
  with garlic, roasted young, 231–32
  heart and veal stew, 440–41
  marinated, 230–31
  methods for, 526–27
  and olive pasta sauce, tangy, 238
  preparation of, 527–29
  purée, 236–37
  purée, -chervil ravioli, 239
  salad of marinated shrimp, mussel
    and, 234
  stuffed, 241
  stuffed, preparation and baking
    of, 529
  varieties of, 526
  in warm vegetable salad, 290
  whole cooked, presentation of, 232

artichoke(s) *(continued)*
    yields and equivalents for, 527–28
    young, 527
artichokes, baby, 526–29
    à la grecque, 240
    Jewish style (carciofi alla giudia),
        237–38
    and olives, tangy, 238
artichoke soup, 234–35
    hazelnut, 236
    potato and (zuppa di patate e
        carciofi), 235
Art of Eating Well, The (Artusi), 248
Artusi, Pellegrino, 248
arugula, 530
    in bitter greens with lardons, 219
    salad of fennel, hazelnut and, 429
    salad of tuna, white bean and, 429
    in "soup" of small peas with fresh
        herbs (soupe de petits pois aux
        herbes fraîches), 300–301
Asia, 351, 575, 587, 607, 610, 639
    Africa's links with, 295, 296
    beans from, *see* adzuki; bean(s),
        Asian; soybeans
    cabbage from, 315–21; *see also* bok
        choy; broccoli, Chinese; napa
        cabbage; pak choy; tatsoi
    herbs from, 589, 590, 592
    peas in, 296
Asian, Asian-style dishes:
    braised napa cabbage with lotus
        root, snow peas and bamboo,
        366–67
    braised small bok choy, 319–20
    deep-fried baby bok choy, 316
    dip, creamy, 435
    dressing, vegetable slaw with, 271
    east of the Pacific eggplant dip, 326
    -flavored red kuri purée, 128
    fried feelers, 317
    ginger and garlic baby bok choy, 319
    greens, 530–31
    kale stew with chickpeas and
        mushrooms, 285
    marinade and brushing sauce, 519–20
    quadruple soy threat, 313
    radiant bok choy, 318–19
    roasted edamame, 313
    seasoning, eggplant with, 325
    shredded napa salad, 317
    shrimp and lotus root with
        lemongrass and lime, 365–66

soothing vegetable salad, 368
spicy bamboo stir-fry, 368–69
steamed Chinese broccoli with
    mustard-soy sauce, 321
stir-fried Chinese broccoli, 320–21
tatsoi vegetarian feast, 320
very spicy vegetable salad, 318
see also China, Chinese-style dishes;
    Japan, Japanese-style dishes;
    Southeast Asia, Southeast Asian
    dishes
asparagus, 154–62, 530–34
    and beef stir-fry, 162
    colors of, 154–56
    custard, 159
    fettuccine with leeks and, 162
    with ham and vinaigrette, 157–58
    light spring soup with peas and, 157
    as lilies, 154, 373, 531
    methods for, 532
    with morels, 159
    morels with rhubarb and, 404
    with poached egg and browned
        butter, 158
    preparation of, 532–34
    risotto with sorrel, samphire and,
        424–25
    sauce, pasta with, 161
    sauté of scallops, baby corn and,
        37–38
    with sesame dressing and tofu, 158
    and shrimp with sorrel, 428
    soup with caramelized leeks, 156–57
    special dishes for, 155
    in spring vegetable gumbo, 341–42
    stock, 506–7
    and tarragon quiche, 160–61
    varieties of, 531–32
    in warm spring vegetable salad, 432
    yields and equivalents for, 534
asparagus, wild (European wild
    asparagus), 156, 532–34
    fettuccine with ramps and, 161–62
    and ramp frittata, 160
asparagus peas, *see* wing beans
aubergine, *see* eggplant(s)
Austria, Austrian-style dishes, 547
    creamy cauliflower soup, 257–58
    cucumber dill salad, 352–53
    pickles in, 359
    Viennese-style cauliflower, 259
Auxillo Rodriguez, Maria, fava bean
    soup (sopa de habas) of, 225–26

avocado leaves, 5, 535
    in Zarela Martinez's puréed black
        beans (frijoles negros colados),
        23–24
avocado(s), 4–9, 534–35
    dressing, 8–9
    guacamole, 8
    ice cream, 9
    and liver sauté, 7–8
    and lobster salad, cold, 6
    in salade less-gastronomique, 14
    salad of pink grapefruit, papaya
        and, 5
    sauce, spicy-cool, 9
    and shrimp, Chinese, 7
    and shrimp salad on lettuce and
        sorrel, 6
    tomato salad, 5–6
azuki, *see* adzuki

B

baba ganoush (eggplant caviar), 324–25
baby food tomato sauce, 461
    in ratatouille pasta sauce, 338
bacon:
    cauliflower with mushrooms and,
        260–61
    potato salad with capers and, 81
    -wrapped artichokes, 233
bacon fat, for fried tomatoes, 108
bacon lardons, 509
    beet greens with white beans,
        walnuts and, 173
    bitter greens with, 219
    in stuffed cabbage rolls, 276–77
bagna cauda, 466–67
baked, baking:
    beans, 541
    beans, basic Boston, 24
    of beets, 545
    broccoli in light cheese sauce, 264
    halibut with Jerusalem artichokes
        and leeks, 144
    of potatoes, 633
    pumpkin and onion dumplings
        (kadoo bichak), 120–21
    of stuffed artichokes, 529
baking (Idaho) potatoes, 632
    sage, 79–80
balm, *see* lemon balm
balsamic (vinegar):
    bell peppers and sardines with,
        58–59

roasted peppers in, 55
root vegetables, 140–41
in vegetable combination salad, 196
bamboo or leaf mustard (juk gai choy, red-in-snow mustard, hseuh li hung, Tokyo bekana mustard), 612, 613
bamboo (shoots), 363, 536
braised napa cabbage with lotus root, snow peas and, 366–67
-détente lamb, 369
stir-fry, spicy, 368–69
banana peppers, 625
banana squash, 650
Banker family, 342
Barbara's tomato salad, 101
barley:
mushroom soup, 400
risotto with broccoli di raab, 284
in winter mushroom soup, 401
basil, 589
freezing of, 589
okra with, 340–41
roasted cherry tomatoes with, 109
stuffed tomatoes with rice and, 111
tomato bruschetta topping, 115
tomato dipping sauce, 464
-tomato quiches, miniature, 101–2
tomato soup, 105
batata, purée de, 138
batatas, see boniatos
Batavia lettuce, see lettuce, iceberg
Batmanglij, Najimieh, 263
batters, 515, 516
Bavarian, cauliflower, 255–56
bay leaves, 589
Bayless, Rick, 572
bean cakes:
with crab or shrimp, 25
panfried, 25
bean(s), 536–44
canned, 17, 541
freezing of, 11, 12
refreshing of, 12
soaking of, 17, 540, 542
see also soups, bean
bean(s), Asian, 11, 310–21, 536, 543–44
see also adzuki; soybeans
bean(s), New World, 10–27, 537–41
bush vs. climbing, 11
corn and, 11, 31
eaten in the shell, 10–17, 537–39
eaten shelled, 10, 17–27, 539–41

methods for, 537–38, 540
preparation of, 538, 540–41
varieties of, 537, 539–40
yields and equivalents for, 539, 541
see also black bean(s); cranberry bean(s); gigantes; green bean(s); haricots verts; kidney beans; lima beans; navy bean(s); pink bean(s); Romano beans; wax beans; white bean(s)
bean, Old World, 11, 542–43
see also fava bean(s)
Beard, James, 102, 155, 444, 448, 452
onion sandwiches of, 377
"beaver fever," 397
béchamel sauce:
in eggs Florentine, 250–51
in Mexican lasagne with cilantro-jalapeño pasta, 437–38
sorrel, 428–29
sorrel, in sorrel soup with potato, 426
bee balm, see lemon balm
beef:
adzuki and celery with braised short ribs of, 311–12
and asparagus stir-fry, 162
boiled, cucumber dill salad with, 352–53
burdock kinpara, 411
glaze, stuffed cabbage rolls with, 277
in horseradish dressing, 413
in red Russian soup, 169
roast, in okroshka, 355–56
soup of chicken, vegetable and, 304–5
beef, ground:
in fake beef stock, 504
in gala meat loaf with spinach, 253
in gratin of cardoons with meat sauce, 243
in Greek stuffing, 494
in Jamaican stuffed cho cho, 119–20
in stuffed cabbage rolls, 276–77
beefsteak plant, see perilla
beef stock, 502–4
brown, 502, 503
enriched, 504
fake, 504
meat glaze from, 505
white, 502, 503
beer:
batter, 515
in okroshka, 355–56

in spicy corn relish, 40
in spinach soup, 247
beet greens, 164, 545, 546
in "rich" peasant stew with favas, 227
in vegetarian borscht, 268–69
with white beans, bacon and walnuts, 173
beet(s), 163–77, 544–46, 566
and apple strudel, 176
in balsamic root vegetables, 140–41
biscuits, 174
caraway sauce, 175
and carrot strudel, 176
chips, crisp, 514
cooking liquid from, 164
and endive salad, 165
in endive sweet-and-sour sauce, 223
flavor of, 164
ice cream, 175
orange glazed, 171–72
pickled, 170
and potato purée, 170
rainbow, with celery, capers and dill, 166
rhubarb energy, 349
shredded, salad of orange and, 165–66
sorbet, 165–66
and tuna Niçoise bâtarde, 173–74
see also borscht
beets, Chioggia, 544–46
in rainbow beets with celery, capers and dill, 166
in tuna and beets Niçoise bâtarde, 173–74
beets, golden, 544–46
in rainbow beets with celery, capers and dill, 166
soup, 171
surprise, 170–71
in tuna and beets Niçoise bâtarde, 173–74
Begnaud, Mrs. Wayne, 44
Belgian endives, see endive(s)
bell peppers, see green bell pepper(s); peppers, bell; red bell pepper, roasted; red bell pepper(s); yellow bell pepper(s)
Bermuda onions, 615–16
beta-carrots, see maroon carrots

beurre:
    blanc, 453–54
    maître d'hôtel, 443–44
Bibb lettuce, *see* lettuce, Bibb
bird peppers, 54
    see also chiltepins; piquín peppers
biscuits, beet, 174
bistro salad, 218
bitter greens with lardons, 219
black bean(s), 539–41
    and corn salad, 18
    in mushroom-vegetable stew,
        404–5
    salad, 18
    soup, Doug Rodriguez's, 19–20
    Zarela Martinez's puréed (frijoles
        negros colados), 23–24
black beans, Chinese salted (fermented
        black beans):
    in Chinese shrimp and avocado, 7
    in Chinese stewed tomatoes, 107–8
black chanterelles, *see* trumpets of death
black-eyed peas, *see* peas, black-eyed
black radishes, 637–38
black-seeded Simpson lettuce,
    see lettuce, iceberg
black trumpets, *see* trumpets of death
blood orange:
    sauce, 468
    vinaigrette, 450
    vinaigrette, poppy seed, 450
blood pressure, allicin and, 375, 585
blue cheese, 421
    dressing, iceberg lettuce wedges
        with, 415
bluefish:
    gravlax, 438–39
    roast, with braised carrots in orange
        cherry tomato sauce, 190–91
Blumenthal, Heston, 354
boiled, boiling:
    of artichokes, 527–28
    of asparagus, 532–33
    of bamboo shoots, 536
    of beans, 538, 541, 542, 544
    of beets, 164, 545
    of broccoli and cauliflower, 548
    of broccoli di raab, 550
    of Brussels sprouts, 552
    of burdock, 553
    of cabbages, 555, 558
    of cactus pads, 559
    of cardoons, 560

of carrots, 562
of celery, 564
of celery root, 565
of chard, 567
of collard greens, 571
of corn, 573
of dandelion greens, 578
of fennel, 583
of fiddlehead ferns, 584
of Jerusalem artichokes, 597
of kohlrabi, 599
of leeks, 600
of malokhei, 604
of mustard greens and leaf mustard,
    612
of nettles, 614
of okra, 615
of onions, 616
of parsnips, 620
of peanuts, 621
of peas, 623
of potatoes, 633
of purslane and miner's lettuce, 637
of radishes, 638
of ramps, 639
of samphire, 640
of scorzonera and salsify, 642
of squash, 648, 653
of sweet potatoes and yams, 657
of tomatoes, 660
of turnips, 665
variation of broccoli di raab with
    Italian sausage, 284
of yuca, 664
bok choy, 316, 557–59
    braised small, 319–20
    Provençal, 320
    radiant, 318–19
    shiitake mushrooms and scallions in
        broth, 392
    in very spicy Asian vegetable salad,
        318
bok choy, baby:
    deep-fried, 316
    in fried feelers, 317
    ginger and garlic, 318
    in shrimp and lotus root with
        lemongrass and lime, 365–66
boletus, *see* porcini mushrooms, dried;
        porcini mushrooms, fresh
boniatos (batatas), 657
borage, 589
borscht, 163

cold beef, 166–67
    jellied, 167–68
    red Russian soup—the meat version,
        169
    red Russian vegetable soup, 168
    vegetarian, 268–69
Boston baked beans, basic, 24
Boston lettuce, *see* lettuce, Boston
bouillon cubes, 502
    in fake beef stock, 504
braised, braising:
    baby fennel, double-garlic, 214
    broccoli di raab, 283, 551
    of Brussels sprouts, 552
    calabaza with mushrooms, 129
    celery, 200–201
    celery hearts, stovetop, 201
    celery hearts with meat glaze, 201
    of chard, 567
    collards with vegetables, 286
    escarole, 569
    fennel, 213–14
    kale, 284–85, 598
    lettuce, 419
    mustard greens, 287
    napa cabbage with lotus root, snow
        peas and bamboo, 366–67
    roasted leeks, then, 384
    scallions, roasted, then, 394
    scorzonera with tarragon, 412–13
    short ribs with adzuki and celery,
        311–12
    small bok choy, 319–20
    stuffed morels, 406–7
    stuffed mushrooms, 407
    wax beans with herbs, 16
    see also carrots, braised; leeks,
        braised; oven-braised;
        slow-braised
brandy:
    in spoon bread with raisins, 47
    in wild mushroom soup, 401–2
Bray, 354
Brazilian arrowroot, *see* yuca
Brazil ñame, *see* yam(s)
bread:
    with bagna cauda, 466
    carrot, 192
    in cucumber gazpacho, 354–55
    in green gazpacho with citrus fruit
        and yellow squash, 84–85
    in onion soup, 377–78
    pumpernickel, in okroshka, 355–56

in romesco sauce, 63–64
sour rye, in roast turkey with
    sauerkraut stuffing, 277–78
and tomato soup, 104
see also croutons
bread, corn:
    dressing, Lee Ann Cox's, 46
    freezing of, 46
    Lee Ann Cox's classic, 45–46
    Southwestern, 46
    spoon, 44–45
    spoon, with raisins, 47
bread-and-butter pickles, 361
bread crumbs:
    dried, 510
    Viennese-style cauliflower with, 259
breaded fried eggplant, Parmesan-,
    33–34
Brie, in braised stuffed morels, 406–7
broad beans, 542
broccoli, 254, 261–65, 546–49
    baked in light cheese sauce, 264
    in chicken and jicama salad with
        green goddess dressing, 145–46
    in coconut-Jarrahdale-vegetable
        stew, 130
    potato soup, 259
    purée, 263–64
    soufflé, 487
    soup, light and tangy, 264
    stems, roasted, with spaghettini,
        265
    stems with lemon-garlic bath,
        roasted, 264–65
    in vegetable curry, 261–62
broccoli, Chinese (Chinese kale), 316,
    549–50, 598
    steamed, with mustard-soy sauce,
        321
    stir-fried, 320–21
broccoli di raab (broccoli rabe, broccoli
    raab, broccoli di rape, rapini),
    279, 281–84, 550–51
    barley risotto with, 284
    and bean soup, 281
    braised, 283
    with Italian sausage, 283–84
    soup, creamy, 281
    soup of greens, chicken and,
        281–82
broccoli sprouts, 547, 647
brodo con stracciatelle, 248
broiling, of tomatoes, 661

broths, 506–7
    Egyptian onion scape, 616
    garlic, 507
    konbu dashi, 507
    leek, 385
    mushroom, 507
    scallions, bok choy and shiitake
        mushrooms in, 392
    vegetable, 506
Brown, Helen Evans, 452
brown rice, 490
    spicy, pink bean feijoada over, 26
bruschetta, fresh tomato basil topping
    for, 115
Brussels sprouts, 551–52
    basic roasted, 274
    braised, 552
    with caraway and sour cream, 275
    and pearl onions, creamy, 274
    roasted, 267
    roasted chestnuts and, 274–75
    stuffed, 267–68
    stuffed, preparation of, 552
bucatini:
    with hidden-depth eggplant, 334
    with tomato, pancetta and onion
        sauce (all'amatriciana), 112–13
Buddha's hands, *see* chayote(s)
bulgur:
    –chicken liver stuffing, 498
    in eggplant with confetti vegetarian
        stuffing, 330–31
    -mushroom stuffing, 497–98
    see also tabbouleh
burdock (gobo), 410, 553
    kinpara, 411
    roasted onions and, 412
    tempura, 410
burnet (pimpinella), 589
Bush, George, Sr., 254, 546
buttercup squash, 650, 653–54, 656
    basic seeds, 136
    with chili oil, roasted, 128–29
    gnocchi, 124
    muffins, Thanksgiving, 131–32
butterhead lettuce, *see* lettuce, Boston
buttermilk:
    in avocado dressing, 8–9
    batter, 516
    in beet biscuits, 174
butternut squash, 117, 650, 653–56
    with cumin, raisins and almonds,
        132–33

gnocchi, 124
muffins, Thanksgiving, 131–32
purée soufflé, 488
soup with glazed chestnuts, 126–27
butter(s), butter sauces, 453–54
    annatto, in thick potato soup with
        corn, 35
    in bagna cauda, 466–67
    basic fennel with, 215
    beurre blanc, 453–54
    beurre maître d'hotel, 443–44
    browned, 453
    browned, asparagus with poached
        egg and, 158
    clarified, 453
    flavored, 31
    hot parsley, 444
    lemon, fennel with, 215
    mint, baby carrots with tiny green
        beans sautéed in, 187–88
    parsley, radishes with, 292
    sage-, squash tortelli with, 122–23
    see also hollandaise sauce
butter-steaming, of potatoes, 633
buttery zucchini and summer squash, 87

C

cabbage, 266–73, 275–93
    Asian, 315–21, 557–59; *see also* bok
        choy; broccoli, Chinese; napa
        cabbage; pak choy; tatsoi
    European, 266–73, 275–78, 554–57;
        see also cabbage, green; cabbage,
        red; cabbage, savoy; sauerkraut
    without heads, *see* broccoli di raab;
        collard(s); kale; mustard greens
    methods for, 554, 558
    preparation of, 555–56, 558
    with roots, *see* kohlrabi; radish(es);
        turnip(s)
cabbage, green, 554–57
    in coleslaw for the slender, 270
    curried, 272–73
    Hungarian roasted, 272
    mildly cardamom, 271–72
    risotto, 269–70
    and shrimp slaw, hot, 266
    in vegetable slaw with Asian
        dressing, 271
    in vegetarian borscht, 268–69
    white noodles, string beans,
        cream and, 273

cabbage, red, 266–67, 554–57
  in coleslaw for the slender, 270
  in red Russian soup—the meat
    version, 169
  in red Russian vegetable soup, 168
  sweet-and-sour, 275
cabbage, savoy, 554–57
  with garlic, slow-braised, 272
  rolls, stuffed, 276–77
  rolls with beef glaze, 277
  stuffed whole, 276
cabbage family, 256, 554–59
  see also broccoli; cauliflower
cactus pad(s) (nopales), 28–29, 559
  salad, 29
Caesar salad, 418, 420–21
cake, coconut-yuca custard, 148–49
calabaza (squash) (Caribbean pumpkin),
    650–51, 653, 654, 656
  braised with mushrooms, 129
  nuggets, fried, 121–22
  and onion dumplings, baked (kadoo
    bichak), 120–21
  pudding, spiced, 133–34
  stew, 129–30
  stew with lamb, 131
  tortelli with sage-butter sauce,
    122–23
California potatoes, 632
callaloo, see taro
calves' liver and avocado sauté, 7–8
Cambridge History of World Food, 659
candy, candied:
  coconut-acorn squash balls, 133
  peanut brittle, 51–52
  popcorn crunch, 48
canned tomatillo sauce, 93
cannellini beans, see white bean(s)
canning, canned goods:
  bread-and-butter pickles, 361
  cippolini Riviera, 381
  cornichons, 359–60
  hot-and-sweet pepper jelly, 67
  information about, 91
  maple corn jalapeño relish, 40
  pepper relish, 66–67
  pickled Egyptian onions, 382
  pickled jalapeño peppers, 62
  pickled samphire, 424
  rhubarb strawberry jam, 349
  roasted and marinated cippolini,
    380–81
  spicy corn relish, 40

sweet-and-sharp cucumbers, 360
  zucchini bread-and-butter pickles, 90
capers, 560
  potato salad with bacon and, 81
  rainbow beets with celery, dill and,
    166
caponata, 327–28
  pizza, 475
cappelletti, making, 470
caramelized:
  leeks, asparagus soup with, 156–57
  onions, purée of split peas with, 307
  tomato sauce, roasted fennel with,
    210–11
caraway (seeds):
  beet sauce, 175
  Brussels sprouts with sour cream
    and, 275
  in roast turkey with sauerkraut
    stuffing, 277–78
carciofi alla giudia (baby artichokes,
    Jewish style), 237–38
cardamom:
  cabbage, mildly, 271–72
  in coconut-Jarrahdale-vegetable
    stew, 130
cardoons, 229, 242–43, 560–61
  with Fontina, creamy gratin of,
    242–43
  with meat sauce, gratin of, 243
  with parsley, anchovies and olive
    sauce, 242
Caribbean, Caribbean-style dishes, 142,
    363, 539
  callaloo soup with dumplings, 365
  chayotes au gratin, 119
  Jamaican stuffed cho cho, 119–20
  purée de batata, 138
  yuca con mojo criollo, 147–48
Caribbean pumpkin, see calabaza
carrot greens, 564
carrot(s), 182–96, 561–64
  in baby artichokes à la grecque, 240
  in beef stock, 502–4
  and beet strudel, 176
  in "braised" collards with vegetables,
    286
  bread, 192
  in cazuela de Elsa Tobar, 36–37
  in crisp slaw, 270
  cumin, 191
  cumin salad, 184
  frying of, 517

grated, with mustard dressing, 183
  -honey ice cream, 192–93
  juice, information about, 193
  leek soup, 186
  lemon-light, 188
  potage of turnip and, 185–86
  potato purée, 187
  purée or sauce, 186–87
  salad with currants and almonds,
    184–85
  sauce with sage, creamy, 187
  sorbet, 193
  soup, creamy, 185
  in vegetable combination salad, 196
  in vegetable curry, 261–62
  in vegetable slaw with Asian dressing,
    271
  in vegetarian borscht, 268–69
  in warm spring vegetable salad, 432
  in warm vegetable compote, 385–86
  in warm vegetable salad, 290
carrot(s), baby, 183, 561–63
  in fall vegetable sauté, 191–92
  lemon glazed, 188
  with tiny green beans sautéed in
    mint butter, 187–88
carrots, braised, 189–90
  actic char with, in orange cherry
    tomato sauce, 190–91
  in orange cherry tomato sauce,
    190–91
  oven-roasted version, 190
  and potatoes, 189
Carver, George Washington, 49
cascabel peppers, 626
  in peas with peppers and tomatoes,
    302
cashews, in stir-fried chicken and snow
    peas in mustard-soy sauce, 304
cassava, see yuca
Catalan Cuisine (Andrews), 63
Catalan dishes, romesco sauce, 63–65
Catarina peppers, 626
catfish gravlax, 438–39
cauliflower, 254–63, 546–49
  with bacon and mushrooms, 260–61
  Bavarian, 255–56
  carrot sauce for, 186–87
  Cheddar gratin, 260
  kookoo, Persian, 263
  in mushroom-vegetable stew, 404–5
  pasta sauce with anchovies and
    garlic, 260

in pickled vegetable antipasto, 256–57
purple, 547
romanesco, 547
stew with lamb, 262
in vegetable curry, 261–62
Viennese-style, 259
white, 547
cauliflower soup:
    creamy, 257–58
    light, 258
    simpler creamy, 258
caviar, eggplant (baba ganoush), 324–25
cayenne, 625, 627
    quail on a cilantro nest, 436
    in spicy rémoulade, 458
cazuela de Elsa Tobar, 36–37
celeriac, see celery root
celery, 183, 199–203, 564–65
    braised, 200–201
    braised short ribs with adzuki and,
        311–12
    fillet of sole over, 203
    frying of, 517
    hearts, stovetop braised, 201
    hearts with meat glaze, braised, 201
    purée, 202–3
    rainbow beets with capers, dill and,
        166
    salad of tiny shrimp, dill and, 500
    slaw, 201–2
    soup, 202
    soup (from celery purée), 203
    tangy artichokes and olives with, 238
    in vegetable curry, 261–62
celery root, 183, 204–7, 565–66
    with apples, puréed, 206
    chips, crisp, 514
    gratin of, 207
    and potato purée, 207
    purée, 206–7
    purée soufflé, 488
    rémoulade, 205–6
    salad, 205
    salad of smoked mozzarella,
        prosciutto and, 205
    soup, cream of, 206
Central America, 11, 31, 69, 92, 142,
    372, 539
    herbs in, 591, 592
Central Europe, pickles in, 359
cèpes, see porcini mushrooms, dried;
    porcini mushrooms, fresh
Chadwick, Eva, 205

Chadwick, Lynn, 205
Champagne:
    in fiddlehead and chanterelle
        risotto, 431–32
    in onion soup, 377–78
    in risotto with asparagus, sorrel and
        samphire, 424–25
chanterelle(s) (girolles), 604, 605, 609,
    610, 611
    black, see trumpets of death
    creamy baby corn, pea shoots and,
        305–6
    and fiddlehead risotto, 431–32
    omelet, 402
Chappellet, Molly, 594
chard (Swiss chard), 163, 177–81, 544,
    566–67
    braised, 567
    in brodo con stracciatelle, 248
    gratin, elegant, 180
    and lentil soup, 179
    timbale of mushrooms, ham and,
        286–87
    see also ruby chard; yellow (golden)
        chard
chayote(s) (Buddha's hands, cho cho,
    christophene, mirliton,
    vegetable pear), 118, 651, 653–56
    au gratin, 119
    Jamaican stuffed, 119–20
    pickled, 132
cheddar (cheese):
    braised leeks with ham and, 384
    in chilies rellenos with corn, 60–61
    gratin of cauliflower and, 260
    grits, 45
    tart dough, 478
    white, individual corn-chili soufflés
        with, 44
cheese, see specific kinds of cheese
cheese peppers, 625, 627
cheese pumpkin, 651, 653, 654, 656
cherry peppers, 627
    pork chops with bell peppers and, 61
cherry tomato(es), 659–63
    with basil, roasted, 109
    purée, roasted, 109
    risotto, stovetop, 110
    roasted, yellow chard, penne and,
        181
    sauce, orange, braised carrots in,
        190–91

stew base, 460–61
    stew base, simple stovetop, 461
chervil, 183, 590, 594
    -artichoke ravioli, 239
    chicken stew, 434–35
    pasta dough, 472
    pesto, 434
    sauce or stew base, warm, 434
chestnuts:
    in fall vegetable sauté, 191–92
    glazed, 508–9
    glazed, butternut squash soup with,
        126–27
    roasted Brussels sprouts and,
        274–75
    roasted peeled, 508
chicken:
    boiled, cucumber dill salad with,
        352–53
    carrot sauce for, 186–87
    in cazuela de Elsa Tobar, 36–37
    cold spinach sauce for, 249
    cutting up, 37
    with endive sweet-and-sour sauce,
        223
    and jicama salad with green goddess
        dressing, 145–46
    in okroshka, 355–56
    paprikás, 66
    peanut butter stew, 50
    with roasted eggplant, cumin and
        yogurt sauce, 338
    salad stuffing, curried, 499
    and snow peas in mustard–soy
        sauce, stir-fried, 304
    stew, chervil, 434–35
chicken broth, canned, gelatin in, 75
chicken liver(s):
    –bulgur stuffing, 498
    paprikás, 66
chickens of the woods, 606
chicken soup:
    beef, vegetable and, 304–5
    broccoli di raab, greens and,
        281–82
    with dill, gelled or hot, 439–40
    escarole and, 282
    light, malokhei, rice and, 344–45
chicken stock:
    basic, 501–2
    enriched, 502
    glaze from, 505
    roasted, 502

chickpea(s):
   and eggplant fritters, 328
   kale stew with mushrooms and, 285
   and lentil soup, 280–81
chicories, 217–23, 417, 567–69
   see also chicory; endive; escarole(s);
     frisée; puntarelle; radicchio
chicory, 217, 567
   potage, 221
chihuacles, 626
Chilean dish, cazuela de Elsa Tobar,
   36–37
chilacate chilies, 626
chilies, *see* peppers
chilies rellenos, 59–60
   with corn, 60–61
chili paste, in Chinese dipping sauce,
   465
chili peppers:
   in pickled chayote, 132
   in pickled okra, 341
chili (powder), 625, 626–27
   in Adelle's favorite roasted seeds,
     136
   -corn soufflé, 43–44
   -corn soufflés, individual white
     cheddar, 44
   in letcho, 65
   oil, roasted buttercup squash with,
     128–29
   in pumped-up popcorn, 41
chilled:
   cucumber soup, 355
   curried pea soup, 300
   stewed tomato soup, 107
   see also cold
chiltepins (bird peppers), 627
China, Chinese-style dishes, 297, 309,
   323, 340, 390, 525, 572, 610, 639
   bamboo shoots in, 536
   cabbage in, 315–16
   creamy baby corn, chanterelles and
     pea shoots, 305–6
   deep-fried taro horns, 363–64
   dipping sauce, 465
   greens in, 530–31, 570
   mustard greens in, 611
   sesame noodles with cucumber, 358
   shrimp and avocado, 7
   stewed tomatoes, 107–8
   Szechwan green beans, 16–17
   velvet corn soup, 34
chinchi-uchu, 625

Chinese artichokes (Japanese artichokes;
   crosne), 362, 367
Chinese broccoli, *see* broccoli, Chinese
Chinese cabbage, *see* napa cabbage
Chinese celery, 564
Chinese chives, 590
Chinese eggplants, *see* eggplants,
   Chinese
Chinese flowering cabbage, *see* pak choy
Chinese kale, *see* broccoli, Chinese
Chinese miniature corn, *see* corn, baby
Chinese soup, 423
Chioggia beets, *see* beets, Chioggia
Chioggia radicchio, *see* radicchio,
   Chioggia
Chioggia squash, *see* Marina di Chioggia
chipotles, 626, 627
chips, crisp vegetable, 514
chive flowers, 431, 590
chives, 372, 431, 590, 594
   roasted peppers with anchovies and,
     55
cho cho, *see* chayote(s)
chorizo, chrysanthemum leaves with, 430
chowder, corn, 34–35
choy sum, *see* pak choy
christophene, *see* chayote(s)
chrysanthemum leaves (greens)
     (shungiku, tung ho, kikuma), 570
   with chorizo, 430
cider vinegar:
   in cucumber dill salad, 352
   in early American tomato ketchup,
     113
   in hot-and-sweet pepper jelly, 67
   in pepper relish, 66–67
   in vegetarian borscht, 268–69
cilantro, 590–91
   chard and lentil soup with, 179
   cucumber salad, 353
   in curries, 38, 357–58, 437
   dressing, julienne of jicama, red
     peppers and pear with, 144
   -jalapeño pasta, Mexican lasagna
     with, 437–38
   -jalapeño pasta dough, 472–73
   -marinated shrimp, 436
   nest, cayenne quail on a, 436
   orzo, edamame and shrimp sauté
     with, 314
   in salads, 6, 18, 27, 29, 271, 353,
     368, 499
   salsa, 435

   in soups, 84–85, 103, 179, 225–26,
     227, 353, 356–57
   tomato salsa, fresh, 114–15
cinnamon, in sweet mustard sauce, 441
cippolini, 616–19
   Riviera, 381
   roasted and marinated, 380–81
citric acid, note about, 167
citrus (fruits):
   -garlic marinade, 520
   green gazpacho with yellow squash
     and, 84–85
   segments, preparation of, 5
   zucchini chunks with mint and, 86–87
   see also blood orange; grapefruit;
     lemon (juice); lime (juice); orange
     (juice); tahini-citrus dressing
clams, in green seafood stew with peas
   and spinach, 302–3
clarified butter, 453
coconut (milk):
   –acorn squash balls, candied, 133
   -Jarrahdale vegetable stew, 130
   peanut butter cookies, 51
   -yuca custard cake, 148–49
coco yam, *see* taro
coddled eggs, *see* oeufs mollets
cod soup:
   with fresh cranberry beans, 19
   ten-minute, 64–65
cold:
   beet borscht, 166–67
   leek and potato soup (vichyssoise),
     387–88
   Moroccan tomato soup, 103
   radish soup with cucumber, 291
   spinach sauce, 249
   see also chilled
coleslaw:
   for the slender, 270
   see also slaws
collard(s) (collard greens), 279, 570–71
   and black-eyed peas, 308
   "braised" with vegetables, 286
   "braised" with vegetables, liquid
     from, in chickpea and lentil soup,
     280–81
   in fresh greens, 288
   stuffing of mushroom, ham and, 496
   timbale of mushrooms, ham and,
     286–87
Colombe d'Or, 381
Columbus, Christopher, 3

common mushrooms (field mushrooms), 605, 609
  see also mushroom(s)
Complete Book of Mushrooms (Rinaldi and Tyndalo), 604
compote:
  fennel, 214–15
  warm vegetable, 385–86
confetti vegetarian stuffing, eggplant with, 330–31
cookies:
  cornmeal, 47–48
  oatmeal or coconut peanut butter, 51
  peanut butter, 51
  peanut-ginger lace, 50–51
cooking methods, 512–21
  see also braised, braising; deep-fried, deep-frying; fried, frying; grilled, grilling; microwave cooking; sauté(ed), sautéing; steamed, steaming
coral mushrooms, 606
coriander, 183, 590
  see also cilantro
corn, baby (Chinese miniature), 572–74
  creamy chanterelles, pea shoots and, 305–6
  sauté of scallops, asparagus and, 37–38
corn, dried, 31, 41–48, 571, 574–75
  see also bread, corn; cornmeal; cornstarch; grits; hominy; masa; polenta; popcorn; tortillas, corn
corn, European use of term, 31, 572
corn, fresh, 11, 30–40, 571–75
  beans and, 11, 31
  and black bean salad, 18
  canned or frozen, 31, 572, 574
  in cazuela de Elsa Tobar, 36–37
  chilies rellenos with, 60–61
  chowder, 34–35
  in corn-chili soufflé, 43–44
  creamed, making, 33
  crêpes, mini, 33–34
  custard, 39–40
  custard, south of the border, 40
  and feta cheese omelet, 36
  fritters, 32
  in hominy soup, 42–43
  in individual white cheddar corn-chili soufflés, 44
  pudding, summer, 38–39

relish, maple jalapeño, 40
relish, spicy, 40
salad, Santa Fe, 36
in seafood succotash, 22–23
selection of, 31, 572
and shrimp curry, 38
soup, velvet, 34
Southwestern, 36
in succotash, 20–21
in summer vegetable gumbo, 343–44
thick potato soup with, 35
and tomato soup, Southwestern, 105–6
  see also corn, baby
corn flour, 31, 571
  see also cornmeal; masa
cornichons (gherkins), 351, 575, 576, 577
  recipe for, 359–60
  in rémoulade sauce, 458
  in salade Russe, 82
  in tartar sauce, 457
cornmeal, 31, 41, 574, 575
  cookies, 47–48
  crumb coating, for fried tomatoes, 108
  see also polenta
corn salad lettuce, *see* mâche
corn shoots, creamy baby corn, chanterelles and pea shoots with, 305–6
cornstarch, 31, 41, 571, 574
corona beans, 11, 540–41
  herbed, 588
Cos lettuce, *see* lettuce, romaine
cottage cheese:
  in chilies rellenos with corn, 60–61
  in creamy carrot sauce with sage, 187
  in fennel soup, 212–13
  in parsley soup, 444–45
  in summer corn pudding, 38–39
Courtine, Robert, 98
couscous, in Moroccan stuffing, 494–95
cowpeas, 296–97, 536, 543, 622
  see also peas, black-eyed
Cox, Lee Ann:
  classic corn bread, 45–46
  corn bread dressing, 46
crab:
  bean cakes with, 25
  and cucumber curry, 357–58
crambe (sea kale), 642–43

cranberry:
  tapioca parfait, 151
  tomato salsa, 114
cranberry bean(s), 11, 539–41
  curry stew with lamb and, 21
  fresh, cod soup with, 19
  in hominy soup, 42–43
  soup, fresh, 18–19
  in summer vegetable gumbo, 343–44
cream:
  artichokes filled with snails in, 231
  in cauliflower Bavarian, 255–56
  in custards, 39–40, 85, 159, 410–11
  in gratins, 79, 180, 260, 387
  in morels in rich lamb sauce, 406
  in parsnip flan, 197–98
  in puddings, 133–34, 135–36
  in purées, 198, 202–3
  in quiches, 388, 399–400
  in salmon with sorrel soup, 426
  in seafood succotash, 22
  shirred eggs with herbs, tomatoes and, 102
  in spinach and mushroom lasagna, 251–53
  in succotash, 20–21
  in sweet potato pie, 141
  white noodles, green cabbage, string beans and, 273
  see also crème fraîche; ice cream; sour cream
cream cheese, parsley and scallion dip, 391
creamed:
  corn, crêpes, mini, 32–33
  corn, fresh, 33
  onions, 381–82
creamed spinach, 249–50
  in easy eggs Florentine, 251
  polenta sandwiches, 250
  sorrel and, 428
creamer potatoes, 632
cream sauces:
  cremini mushroom with tarragon, 408
  horseradish, 413
  leek, 388
creamy:
  Asian dip, 435
  baby corn, chanterelles and pea shoots, 305–6
  Brussels sprouts and pearl onions, 274

creamy (continued)
    carrot sauce with sage, 187
    gratin of cardoons with Fontina,
      242–43
    potato salad, 81
creamy polenta, 41–42
    Gorgonzola, 42
    microwave variation of, 42
cream(y) soups:
    artichoke hazelnut, 236
    artichoke soup, 234–35
    broccoli di raab, 281
    carrot, 185
    carrot leek, 186
    cauliflower, 257–58
    cauliflower, simpler, 258
    celery root, 206
    corn chowder, 34–35
    curried onion, 378
    green, 282–83
    Hubbard squash silk, 125–26
    leek and potato (potage Parmentier
      if hot, vichyssoise if cold),
      387–88
    nettle, 244
    pea pod, 298
    rich sorrel, 425
    sorrel, with potato, 426
    spinach, 247
    spinach potato, 247–48
    three-vegetable winter, 207
crème fraîche:
    haricots verts with, 15
    tomato and dill soup with, 104
cremini mushroom(s), 605, 608, 609
    in mushroom-vegetable stew, 404–5
    sauce with tarragon and cream, 408
    soufflé, 487
    in wild mushroom soup, 401–2
crêpes, mini corn, 33–34
    curry, 32, 33
    Southwestern, 33
cress sprouts, 647
Crisphead lettuce, see lettuce, iceberg
crookneck squash, 648–49
croquettes, yuca, 146–47
crosne, see Chinese artichokes
croutons:
    cubed, 511
    fried bread or crostini, 510–11
    garlic, 511
crustless spring quiche, 399–400
cubanelle peppers, 625, 631

Cuban peppers, 627
Cuban-style dishes, 540
    Doug Rodriguez's black bean soup,
      19–20
cucumber(s), 350–61, 575–77
    cod soup with, 19
    cold radish soup with, 291
    cornichon, see cornichons
    dill salad, 352–53
    in gazpacho, 102–3
    granita, 361
    in green gazpacho with citrus fruit
      and yellow squash, 84–85
    hot dilled, 441
    pachadi, 353
    in pot cheese and vegetable salad,
      439
    purée, 357
    salad, 353
    salting of, 351, 360, 576
    sweet-and-sharp, 360
    tzatziki, 352
    in warm vegetable compote,
      385–86
cucumber(s), Kirby, 350, 351, 576, 577
    in bread-and-butter pickles, 361
    and crab curry, 357–58
    in garlic or dill pickles, 358–59
    gazpacho, 354–55
    salting of, 360
    sesame noodles with, 358
    sweet-and-sharp, 360
cucumber soup:
    chilled, 355
    curry, 356–57
    elegant bean, 356
    gazpacho, 354–55
    general information about, 354
    okroshka, 355–56
    vichyssoise, 354
Culinary Herbs and Condiments (Grieve),
    417
cumin, 183
    carrots, 191
    carrot salad, 184
    creamy carrot soup with, 185
    kabocha with almonds, raisins and,
      132–33
    mushrooms, 403
    sauce of roasted eggplant, yogurt
      and, 338
    vinaigrette, orange and onion salad
      with, 374

Curious Cook, The (McGee), 455
curly leaf parsley, 442, 593
currants:
    carrot salad with almonds and,
      184–85
    in eggplant with confetti vegetarian
      stuffing, 330–31
    in rice pilaf, 489–90
curry(ied):
    cabbage, 272–73
    chicken salad stuffing, 499
    corn crêpes, 32, 33
    cucumber soup, 356–57
    green shrimp, 437
    lamb stuffing, 493–94
    lamb stuffing, acorn squash stuffed
      with, 118
    lamb stuffing, for mushrooms, 406
    lima beans, 20
    onion soup, 378
    pea soup, chilled, 300
    shrimp and corn, 38
    stew with lamb and cranberry beans,
      21
    of summer squash, green, 87–88
    tomato sauce, 105
    vegetable, 261–62
cusha squash, 651
cusqueños, 625
custard(s):
    asparagus, 159
    cake, coconut-yuca, 148–49
    corn, 39–40
    horseradish, 410–11
    horseradish, in ramekins, 411
    south of the border corn, 40
    zucchini, 85

D

dahl, 296, 624
    purée of split peas with caramelized
      onions, 307
dai gai choy (wrapped heart mustard),
    612
daikon, 637, 638
    pickles, 293
    in shredded napa salad, 317
    spicy papaya salsa with, 293
    in very spicy Asian vegetable salad, 318
    in warm vegetable compote, 385–86
dandelion greens, 422, 577–78
    in bitter greens with lardons, 219
    penne with garlic and, 430

dasheen, *see* taro

dashin yam, 657

datil, 625

Davidson, Alan, 592, 593

deep-dish pizza, 474–75

deep-fried, deep-frying, 512–13
  baby bok choy, 316
  of carrots, 563
  crisp vegetable chips, 514
  fritto misto, 516–17
  onion rings, 517–18
  of onions, 618
  parsley, 445
  of parsnips, 620
  of potatoes, 633
  scallion flowers, 641
  suggested items for, 517
  of sweet potatoes, 658
  taro horns, 363–64
  of turnips, 665
  zucchini, 515

delicata squash, 118, 651, 653–56
  with mixed fresh herbs, 128
  with shrimp, 118–19

deli pizza, 273

demi-glace, information about, 7

dent corn, 572

desserts:
  beets for, 175
  coconut-yuca custard cake, 148–49
  cranberry tapioca parfait, 151
  curry corn crêpes, 32, 33
  kabocha with cumin, raisins and almonds, 132–33
  spoon bread with raisins, 47
  see also cookies; granita; ice cream; pie(s); pudding, dessert; sorbet; strudel

Diat, Louis, leek and potato soup (potage Parmentier if hot, vichyssoise if cold) of, 387–88

Dickinson, Colin, 604

dill(ed), 183, 591–92
  cucumbers, hot, 441
  cucumber salad, 352–53
  mushrooms with yogurt and, 398
  pickles, 358–59
  rainbow beets with celery, capers and, 166
  salad of tiny shrimp, celery and, 500
  and tomato soup with crème fraîche, 104
  zucchini sautéed with, 86

Dim Sum Book, The (Yin-Fei Lo), 363

dipping sauces, 463–67
  anchovy, 466
  bagna cauda, 466–67
  Chinese, 465
  harissa, 465–66
  Japanese, 465
  Pacific tomato, 463
  peanut, 464
  plum tomato base for, 462
  Southeast Asian, 465
  spicy Middle Eastern tomato, 464
  tomato basil, 464

dips:
  creamy Asian, 435
  cucumber tzatziki, 352
  parsley and scallion, 391

dips, eggplant:
  with Asian seasonings, 325
  caponata, 327–28
  caviar (baba ganoush), 325–26
  caviar with onions and peppers, 324–25
  classic appetizer, 325
  east of the Pacific, 326
  Moroccan, 326–27
  Romanian, 325
  Russian, 325
  Russian orientale, 325

Divan Parisienne, 547

dock, 422, 578

doughs:
  basic focaccia, 475–76
  basic focaccia, pissaladière with, 376
  for kale pissaladière, 280
  pizza, 473–76

doughs, pasta, 469–73
  basic, 469
  chervil, 472
  cilantro-jalapeño, 472–73
  cilantro-jalapeño, Mexican lasagna with, 437–38
  green, 472
  rolling out, shaping and filling of, 470–71

doughs, pastry and pie, 476–78
  basic crust, 476–77
  basic tart, 477
  in beet and apple strudel, 176
  cheddar cheese tart, 478
  flaky tart, 477–78
  flamiche crust, 481–82
  quiche crust, 480

Dim Sum Book, The (Yin-Fei Lo), 363

Doug Rodriguez's black bean soup, 119–20

dressings:
  horseradish, beef in, 413
  Lee Ann Cox's corn bread, 46
  see also salad dressings

duck breast with rhubarb sauce, 347–48

Duerte (Florida) avocados, 534–35

dumplings:
  baked pumpkin and onion (kadoo bichak), 120–21
  callaloo soup with, 365
  mushroom, 398–99

duxelles, mushroom, 405–6, 605
  artichoke bottoms stuffed with, 238–39
  poached eggs on, with hollandaise sauce, 407
  in stuffed eggplant, 329–30
  stuffing of collard, ham and, 496

E

east of the Pacific eggplant dip, 326

Ecuador, Ecuadoran dishes, 36, 70
  herbs in, 591, 592
  hominy soup, 42–43
  thick potato soup with corn, 35

edamame, 310, 312, 313, 543, 544
  in acorn squash stew, 129–30
  in quadruple soy threat, 313
  roasted, 313
  sauté of orzo, shrimp and, 314

eddo, *see* taro

egg noodles:
  with asparagus sauce, 161
  ratatouille pasta sauce for, 338

eggplant, stuffed, 329–30
  with confetti vegetarian stuffing, 330–31
  general information about, 330
  with Greek or Moroccan stuffing, 329–30
  with Italian sausage stuffing, 332
  with lamb and orzo, 330
  with Middle Eastern spiced rice, 332–33
  with minted rice, 331–32
  preparation of, 581–82

eggplant(s), 97, 295, 329–30, 579–82
  basic oil-blanched, 580–81
  and chickpea fritters, 328

eggplant(s) *(continued)*
 cubes, anise-scented, 334
 hidden-depth, pasta with, 334
 lasagna, 336
 marinated roasted baby, 328–29
 microwave purée, 581
 in mysterious pasta sauce, 343
 and okra stew, 342–43
 and okra stew, Middle Eastern, 343
 oven-grilled, 580
 Parmesan, mock, 336–37
 Parmesan-breaded fried, 333–34
 in ratatouille pasta sauce, 338
 roasted, sauce of cumin, yogurt and,
  339
 rollatini, 337–38
 in summer vegetable bonanza, 88–89
 tomato and fennel, 211
 winter-y lamb stew with red peppers
  and, 335
 see also dips, eggplant
eggplants, Chinese, 323, 324, 579–82
 in Chinese soup, 423
 marinated roasted baby, 328–29
 in party frittata (tortilla), 485–86
 stuffed, 329–30
 in summer's bounty stew, 334–35
eggplants, Japanese, 323, 324, 579–82
 marinated roasted baby, 328–29
 stuffed, 329–30
egg(s), 479–88
 in brodo con stracciatelle, 248
 Florentine, 250–51
 Florentine, easy, 251
 with herbs, tomatoes and cream,
  shirred, 102
 white batter, 516
 see also custard(s); frittatas; hollandaise
  sauce; kookoo; mayonnaise,
  mayonnaise-based sauces; oeufs
  mollets; omelets; quiches; soufflés
egg(s), hard-boiled:
 in creamy potato salad, 81
 green beans, tuna, potatoes and
  Niçoise olives with tomatoes and
  anchovy cheese vinaigrette
  (salade Niçoise), 14–15
 in okroshka, 355–56
egg(s), poached, 479–80
 asparagus with browned butter and,
  158
 on mushroom duxelles with
  hollandaise sauce, 407

egoma, *see* perilla
Egyptian onions, *see* onions, Egyptian
Elaine's (restaurant), 232
Emerson, Ralph Waldo, 422
Emmenthaler cheese:
 in spinach and mushroom lasagna,
  251–53
 in vegetable purée soufflé (without
  flour), 488
 -vegetable soufflé, 486–87
Encyclopedia of Asian Food (Solomon),
  373, 530
Encyclopedia of Mushrooms, The
  (Dickinson and Lucas), 604
endive(s) (Belgian endives), 567–69
 with anchovy dip, 467
 and beet salad, 165
 with blood orange vinaigrette, 450
 mahogany roasted, 221–22
 and scallop soup, 220–21
 sweet-and-sour sauce, 223
 in white salad, 230
England, 11, 70, 224–25, 545, 575, 596
English cucumbers, 576
English peas, *see* peas, sweet green
enokis, 607
epazote, 539
*Erbe Aromatiche in Cucina, Le (Aromatic
  Culinary Herbs)*, 589
escarole, 217, 568, 569
 in bitter greens with lardons, 219
 braised, 569
 and chicken soup, 282
 in julienne of five lettuce soup, 418–19
Escoffier, 482
European wild asparagus, *see* asparagus,
  wild
Evelyn, John, 397, 410, 416–17, 433,
  593, 613, 643
evergreenseeds.com, 316

F

fairy rings (Scotch bonnets), 606, 610
fall vegetable sauté, 191–92
Family Food, a New Approach to Cooking
  (Blumenthal), 354
farmer cheese, in chilies rellenos with
  corn, 60–61
fatback, in hoppin' John, 308–9
Fat Duck (restaurant), 354
faux pho, 43
fava bean(s), 11, 224–28, 536, 542–43
 dried, preparation of, 226, 542

fritters, great green, 228
 omelet, Persian (kookoo-ye baghala),
  226
 "rich" peasant stew with, 227
 soup, Latin-style golden, 227
 soup (sopa de habas), 225–26
 in summer vegetable gumbo,
  343–44
fennel, 183, 208–16, 582–84
 with anchovy dip, 467
 braised, 213–14
 with butter, basic, 215
 compote, 214–15
 double-garlic braised baby, 214
 eggplant and tomato, 211
 large lima beans with garlic and,
  26–27
 with lemon butter, 215
 marinade, anchovies with, 210
 with olive oil and lemon, 215
 and pepper salad, roasted, 211–12
 roasted, with caramelized tomato
  sauce, 210–11
 roasted sliced, 213
 salad, 212
 salad of arugula, hazelnut and, 429
 sardine sauce, 215–16
 sauce, 216
 soup, 212–13
feta cheese and corn omelet, 36
fettuccine:
 with asparagus and leeks, 162
 with asparagus sauce, 161
 making, 470
 with mushroom duxelles, 405–6
 mysterious pasta sauce for, 343
 with roasted scallion and tomato
  sauce, 395
 Virginia ham, spinach and, 253
 white, green cabbage, string beans,
  cream and, 273
 with wild asparagus and ramps,
  161–62
fiddlehead(s) (ferns), 584
 and chanterelle risotto, 431–32
 light spring soup with peas and, 157
 in warm spring vegetable salad, 432
fillings:
 nettle and ricotta, 245
 pasta, 471
 for yuca croquettes, 146–47
fines herbes, 594
finger eggplants, 579

fish:
    beet caraway sauce for, 175
    carrot sauce for, 186–87
    cold spinach sauce for, 249
    fresh greens as base for, 288
    in fritto misto, 516–17
    in green seafood stew with peas and
      spinach, 302–3
    roast arctic char with braised carrots
      in orange cherry tomato sauce,
      190–91
    soup, ten-minute, 64–65
    swimming in vegetables, 93–94
    velvet smoked trout stuffing, 500
    see also anchovy(ies); bluefish; cod
      soup; halibut; sardine(s); sole;
      tuna
fish sauce, Thai or Vietnamese:
    in semi-Thai sauce, 467
    in Southeast Asian dipping sauce,
      465
fish stock:
    basic, 505–6
    roasted, 506
flageolets, 11, 18, 539–41
flamiche crust, 481–82
flan, parsnip, 197–98
flat-leaf (Italian) parsley, 442, 593
flint corn, 572
Florence fennel, 208, 582, 583
Florida (Duerte) avocados, 534–35
flour (soft or squaw) corn, 572
focaccia:
    basic, 475–76
    dough, basic, pissaladière with, 376
Fontina, creamy gratin of cardoons
    with, 242–43
Food for Friends (Kafka), 281
food processor method:
    for cucumber dill salad, 352–53
    for cucumber pachadi, 353
Foods of the Greek Islands, The (Kremezi),
    577
Foote, Nicole Kafka, 377
Four Columns Inn, 401
France, French-style dishes, 30, 70, 150,
    224, 531, 545, 642, 643, 644
    basic potage, 71–72
    basic tomato salad, 100
    beans in, 11, 539
    beet and endive salad, 165
    bistro salad, 218
    celery root rémoulade, 205–6
    cippolini Riviera, 381

cornichons in, 351, 359–60, 575
cubed croutons, 511
eggplants in, 322, 323
everyday vinaigrette, 449
herbs in, 591, 593, 594
Jerusalem artichokes in, 143
kale pissaladière, 280
mushroom duxelles, 405–6
mushrooms in, 397, 605, 606, 610
okra in, 340
omelet in, 482–83
onion soup, 377–78
parsnips in, 195
peas with mint, 301
pissaladière, 374–76
pistou (pesto sauce), 467–68
pommes à l'huile, 80
pommes lyonnaise (potato gratin), 79
potato and truffle salad, 80
rémoulade sauce, 458
rouille, 457
salade less-gastronomique, 14
salade Niçoise (green beans, tuna,
    potatoes and Niçoise olives with
    tomatoes and anchovy cheese
    vinaigrette), 14–15
salade Russe, 82
"soup" of small peas with fresh herbs
    (soupe de petits pois aux herbes
    fraîches), 300–301
tomatoes in, 96, 98
tuna and beets Niçoise bâtarde,
    173–74
see also Provence, Provençal
frankfurters, in split pea soup, 306
frappé:
    green bean, 17
    tomato, 452
freeze-dried peas, 622–24
freezing:
    of basil, 589
    of beans, 11, 12
    of beef stock, 502
    of corn bread, 46
    of filled pasta, 471
    of rhubarb, 347
    of tortelli, 123
French Chef Cooks at Home, A (Pépin), 377
French fries, 71
    art of, 78
    basic recipe for, 78
    shoestring, 78
    steak-house, 78

French green beans, *see* haricots verts
French sorrel, 644
fried, frying, 512–18
    of eggplant, 581
    eggplant, Parmesan-breaded,
      333–34
    feelers, 317
    five batters for, 515–16
    naked, 514
    okra, 341
    peppers and tomatoes, 62–63
    polenta, 42
    squash nuggets, 121–22
    tomatoes, 108
    see also deep-fried, deep-frying;
      shallow-frying; stir-fry(ied)
frijoles, 539
    negros colados (Zarela Martinez's
      puréed black beans), 23–24
frisée, 217, 568, 569
    in bistro salad, 218
    with walnuts and walnut oil, 218–19
frittatas, 482–86
    basic technique for, 483–84
    party (tortilla), 485–86
    vegetable, 484
    wild asparagus and ramp, 160
fritters:
    chickpea and eggplant, 328
    corn, 32
    great green fava bean, 228
    yautía, 146
fritto misto, 516–17
Frosch, Paula, 266, 554
frying peppers, *see* peppers, Italian
    frying
Fuseau, 596

G

Gagnaire, Pierre, "soup" of small peas
    with fresh herbs (soupe de petits
    pois aux herbes fraîches) of,
    300–301
gala meat loaf with spinach, 253
gardening and growing information, 31,
    54
    for artichokes, 230
    for asparagus, 154, 155–56, 531
    for beans, 11
    for carrots, 183, 561
    for cucumbers, 351
    for eggplants, 324

gardening and growing information
(continued)
for fennel, 209
for parsnips, 194–95, 619
for peppers, 625
for potatoes, 70, 632
for sage, 594–95
for tomatoes, 96–97
garden orach (mountain spinach),
645
garden sorrel (common sorrel), 644
garland chrysanthemum, 570
garlic, 372, 375, 585–87
braised baby fennel, double-, 214
broth, 507
cauliflower pasta sauce with
anchovies and, 260
chips, 586
-citrus marinade, 520
croutons, 511
giant lima beans simmered with
onion and, 21–22
and ginger baby bok choy, 319
kale with yogurt, 285
large lima beans with fennel and,
26–27
-lemon bath, roasted broccoli stems
with, 264–65
marinade, roasted portobello
mushrooms with, 402–3
"mayonnaise," sweet, 456
and olive oil sauce, 468
or dill pickles, 358–59
oven-braised turnips with, 292
and parsley stuffing, 498–99
penne with dandelion greens and,
430
roasted pepper purée, 57
roasted peppers, Greek, 56–57
roasted peppers with mozzarella
and anchovies, 57
roasted red new potatoes with
rosemary and, 73–74
sauce, yuca with (yuca con mojo
criollo), 147–48
slow-braised cabbage with, 272
-tamari kale, 285
garlic chives, 590
gazpacho, 102–3
cucumber, 354–55
green, with citrus fruit and yellow
squash, 84–85
gelatin, canned broth enriched with, 75

Germany, German-style dishes, 224,
359, 531, 554, 576, 605
cauliflower with bacon and
mushrooms, 260–61
crisp slaw, 270
gherkins, see cornichons
gigantes (giant lima beans), 11, 540–41
with garlic and fennel, 26–27
salad with Mexican flavors, 27
simmered with onion and garlic, 21–22
soaking of, 17
ginger, 530
and garlic baby bok choy, 319
juice, 509–10
-peanut lace cookies, 50–51
girolles, see chanterelle(s)
glasswort, see samphire
glaze(d):
chestnuts, 508–9
chestnuts, butternut squash soup
with, 126–27
maple mustard, 520
roasted sweet potatoes, maple-, 140
gnocchi, buttercup squash, 124
Goa beans, see wing beans
goat cheese:
polenta, creamy, 42
in ruby chard tart, 178–79
gobo, see burdock
golden fava soup, Latin style, 227
golden nugget squash, 651
golden oak mushrooms, see shiitake
(mushrooms)
golden pepper ice cream, 67–68
golden pepper potato purée, 59
golden soup, 171
golden surprise, 170–71
Gorgonzola polenta, creamy, 42
gourds, edible, 295, 351, 575, 587
grana padano, in white salad, 230
Grande Enciclopedia Illustrata della
Gastronomia, 123, 124
granita:
cucumber, 361
tomato, 116
grapefruit:
juice, in julienne of jicama, red
peppers and pear with cilantro
dressing, 145
pink, salad of avocado, papaya and, 5
grape tomatoes, 660
gratin:
of cardoons with Fontina, creamy,
242–43

of cardoons with meat sauce, 243
cauliflower cheddar, 260
of celery root, 207
chayotes au, 119
elegant chard, 180
leek, 387
potato (pommes lyonnaise), 79
of radicchio, 222
gravlax, 438–39
Great Britain, 69, 390, 640
see also England; Ireland
Great Garlic Book, The (Aaron), 585
Great Northern beans, 539
see also navy bean(s)
Greece, Greek-style dishes, 54, 540, 560,
613
artichokes à la grecque, 239–40
cucumber tzatziki, 352
garlic roasted peppers, 56–57, 624
green split pea soup, 307
herbs in, 589, 592, 593
horta, 423, 525, 577
island potatoes, 75–76
large lima beans with garlic and
fennel, 26–27
late fall artichokes à la grecque, 240
minted rice stuffing, 496
nettles with olive oil and lemon, 245
stuffed, 329
stuffing, eggplant stuffed with,
329–30
Greek Salonika peppers, in chilies
rellenos, 59–60
green bean(s), 10–17, 537–39
in coleslaw for the slender, 270
cucumber soup, elegant, 356
frappé, 17
French, see haricots verts
frying of, 517
Italian, see Romano beans
long-cooked American, 16
Romanos, see Romano beans
in salade Russe, 82
salad with vinaigrette, 13
sautéed, 538
Szechwan, 16–17
in warm vegetable compote, 385–86
white noodles, green cabbage, cream
and, 273
green bell pepper(s), 625
eggplant caviar with onions and,
324–25

in gazpacho, 102–3
    in green gazpacho with citrus fruit
        and yellow squash, 84–85
    strips, silky, 58
    in vegetable frittata, 484
green curry of summer squash, 87–88
green gazpacho with citrus fruit and
    yellow squash, 84–85
green goddess dressing, 452
    chicken and jicama salad with,
        145–46
green onions, *see* spring (green) onions
green pasta dough, 472
greens:
    Asian, 530–31
    bitter, with lardons, 219
    fresh, 288
    soup of broccoli di raab, chicken
        and, 281–82
    see also specific kinds of greens
green seafood stew with peas and
    spinach, 302–3
green shrimp curry, 437
green soup, 282–83
gremolata, 443
Grieve, M., 417
grilled, grilling, 518–20
    of asparagus, 533
    baby leeks or large scallions,
        386–87
    of corn, 573–74
    of eggplant, 581
    of leeks, 601
    marinades for, 519–20
    method of, 518–19
    of mushrooms, 609
    of peppers, 629–30
    polenta, 42
    ramps, 394
    of squash, 648
    of sweet potatoes, 658
    of watercress, 667
    see also oven-grilled
grits, 31, 41, 571, 575
    basic recipe for, 45
    cheese, 45
Gruyère cheese:
    in gratins, 119, 180, 207, 387
    in quiches, 160–61, 388, 399–400
    quiche with leeks, ham and, 388
    in soufflés, 250, 486–87, 488
    -vegetable soufflé, 486–87
guacamole, 8
guajillo peppers, 626

gumbo:
    spring vegetable, 341–42
    summer vegetable, 343–44
gypsy peppers, 625

H

habaneros, 625, 626, 631
habichuelas, 539
Haiti, shaggy ink caps in, 606
halibut:
    baked with Jerusalem artichokes
        and leeks, 144
    in green seafood stew with peas and
        spinach, 302–3
    soup, ten-minute, 64–65
ham:
    asparagus with vinaigrette and,
        157–58
    braised leeks with cheddar and, 384
    in okroshka, 355–56
    quiche with leeks, Gruyère and, 388
    Smithfield, in leek gratin, 387
    in stuffed onions, 376
    stuffing of collard, mushroom and,
        496
    timbale of collards, mushrooms and,
        286–87
    in velvet corn soup, 34
    Virginia, spinach and rosemary
        pasta, 253
    in yuca croquettes, 146–47
ham, serrano:
    in leek gratin, 387
    in piselli alla romana, 301
Hamburg rooted parsley, 183, 593
ham hock(s):
    in black-eyed peas and collard
        greens, 308
    and yellow split pea soup, 306–7
haricots verts (French green beans), 11,
    537–39
    with baby carrots sautéed in mint
        butter, 187–88
    in chervil chicken stew, 434–35
    with crème fraîche, 15
    salad, 12
    salad, midsummer, 13
    in salade less-gastronomique, 14
    small shelled, *see* flageolets
    tuna, potatoes and Niçoise olives
        with tomatoes and anchovy
        cheese vinaigrette (salade
        Niçoise), 14–15

use of term, 12
    in warm spring vegetable salad, 432
hash, meatless red flannel, 172
Hass avocados, *see* avocado(s)
hazelnut(s):
    artichoke soup, 236
    in romesco sauce, 63–64
    salad of arugula, fennel and, 429
    skinning of, 236
hearts:
    of artichokes, 527
    of palm, 363
    see also bamboo (shoots)
hearts of palm, 363, 587–88
    salad, 367
hedgehogs (wood hedgehogs), 607
Heirloom Vegetable Gardening (Weaver),
    375
hens of the woods (maitake), 606
herbed:
    beans, 588
    rice, 490
    tomato sauce, 462
herb(s) (and their flowers), 417, 431–45,
    588–95
    braised wax beans with, 16
    fresh, "soup" of small peas with
        (soupe de petits pois aux herbes
        fraîches), 300–301
    in fritto misto, 516–17
    leek sauce with, 388
    marinade, fresh, 519
    mixed fresh, delicata with, 128
    in rémoulade sauce, 458
    shirred eggs with tomatoes, cream
        and, 102
    vinegars, 588
    see also specific herbs
Herklots, G.A.C., 323, 417, 524, 612, 622
hollandaise sauce, 454
    horseradish, 413
    poached eggs on mushroom
        duxelles with, 407
hominy, 31, 571, 575
    canned, 41
hominy soup, 42–43
    faux pho, 43
    rich lamb and, 43
honey-carrot ice cream, 192–93
honey mushroom(s), 606
    sauté, 405
hontaka peppers (santakas), 626
hoppin' John, 308–9
hop shoots, 532

horns of plenty, *see* trumpets of death
hors d'oeuvre:
    acras de christophene, 122
    artichokes à la grecque, 239
    baby artichokes à la grecque, 240–41
    burdock kinpara in beef, 411
    burdock tempura, 410
    cippolini Riviera, 381
    fried squash nuggets, 121–22
    James Beard's onion sandwiches,
        377
    miniature mushroom quiches, 399
    miniature scallion-pea quiches,
        297–98
    miniature tomato-basil quiches,
        101–2
    mini corn crêpes, 32–33
    red kuri rice paper packets, 121
    tiny chard tarts for, 178, 179
horseradish, 410, 596
    chicken, beef and vegetable soup
        with, 304–5
    custard in ramekins, 411
    custards, 410–11
    dressing, beef in, 413
    fresh applesauce with, 413
horseradish sauce, 413
    hollandaise, 413
horta, 423, 525, 577
hot-and-sweet pepper soufflé, 487
hot dilled cucumbers, 441
hot parsley butter sauce, 444
hot peppers, *see* peppers, hot
hot red pepper flakes, dried, 627
hot shrimp and cabbage slaw, 266
hseuh li hung, *see* bamboo or leaf
    mustard
Hubbard squash, 651–54
    basic seeds, 136
    blue (New England Blue), 651, 653,
        654, 656
    golden, 651, 653, 654, 656
    risotto, 124–25
    silk, 125–26
Hungarian-style dishes, 372
    Brussels sprouts with caraway and
        sour cream, 275
    chicken livers paprikás, 66
    chicken paprikás, 66
    letcho, 65
    roasted cabbage, 272
Hungarian wax peppers, 625

I

iceberg lettuce, *see* lettuce, iceberg
ice cream:
    avocado, 9
    beet, 175
    carrot-honey, 192–93
    golden pepper, 67–68
    parsnip, 198
    sweet pea, 303
Idaho potatoes, *see* baking (Idaho)
    potatoes
igname, *see* yam(s)
India, Indian-style dishes, 340, 423,
    539, 575, 591, 593
    cucumber pachadi, 353
    dahl in, 296, 624
    dressing, pseudo-, 451
    eggplants in, 323
    mildly cardamom cabbage, 271–72
    raitas in, 350, 351
    taro in, 363
inky cap mushrooms, 606
insalata caprese, 99, 205
    recipe for, 100
Ireland, potatoes in, 31, 69, 70
Italian asparagus (sprouting broccoli),
    547–49
Italian (flat-leaf) parsley, 442, 593
Italian frying peppers, *see* peppers,
    Italian frying
Italian green beans, *see* Romano beans
Italian pickled peppers, *see* peperoncini
Italian sausage:
    broccoli di raab with, 283–84
    stuffing, 493
    stuffing, eggplant with, 332
Italy, Italian-style dishes, 218, 372, 423,
    502, 613, 642
    baby artichokes, Jewish style, 237–38
    bagna cauda, 466–67
    basic focaccia, 475–76
    basic tomato salad, 100
    beans in, 11, 12, 540
    braised broccoli di raab, 283
    braised mustard greens, 287
    broccoli di raab, greens and chicken
        soup, 281–82
    broccoli in, 254
    brodo con stracciatelle, 248
    bucatini with tomato, pancetta and
        onion sauce (all'amatriciana),
        112–13
    buttercup squash gnocchi, 124

    caponata, 327–28
    cauliflower pasta sauce with
        anchovies and garlic, 260
    creamy polenta, 41–42
    eggplant in, 322, 324
    favas in, 224
    fried peppers and tomatoes, 62–63
    fritto misto, 516–17
    gratin of cardoons with meat sauce,
        243
    herbs in, 99, 589, 592
    Hubbard squash risotto, 124–25
    insalata caprese, 99, 100
    mushrooms in, 605, 607, 610
    parsnips in, 195
    pesto sauce (pistou), 467–68
    pickled vegetable antipasto, 256–57
    piselli alla romana, 301
    polenta in, 30, 41
    potato and artichoke soup (zuppa di
        patate e carciofi), 235
    roasted frying peppers and chunky
        tomatoes, 63
    squash tortelli with sage-butter
        sauce, 122–23
    stovetop tomato risotto, 110
    tomatoes in, 96, 98–99
    see also frittatas; pizza; Sicilian-style
        dish; Venice, Veneto, Venetian-
        style dishes

J

jalapeño (peppers), 625, 626, 627, 629,
    630, 631
    -cilantro pasta, Mexican lasagna
        with, 437–38
    -cilantro pasta dough, 472–73
    pickled, 62
    preparation for stuffing of, 630
Jamaican stuffed cho cho, 119–20
James Beard's onion sandwiches, 377
Jamin, 255
jams and jellies:
    hot-and-sweet pepper, 67
    rhubarb strawberry, 349
    tomato, 116
Japan, Japanese-style dishes, 390, 536,
    570, 666
    burdock kinpara, 411
    burdock tempura, 410
    dipping sauce, 465
    eggplants in, 322, 323
    greens in, 530–31

miso soup with shiitake and shiso, 367–68
mushrooms in, 606, 610
red beans and rice, 311
tempura batter, 516
Japanese artichokes, *see* Chinese artichokes
Japanese eggplants, *see* eggplants, Japanese
Japanese pumpkin, *see* kabocha
Jarrahdale (squash), 651–54, 656
-coconut vegetable stew, 130
-lemongrass soup, 127
jellied borscht, 167–68
Jerome, Carl, 102
Jerusalem artichokes (sunchokes), 142–44, 362, 596–97
baked halibut with leeks and, 144
chips, crisp, 514
in tomato-olive sauce, roasted, 143–44
Jewish-style dishes, 268, 596
baby artichokes (carciofi alla giudia), 237–38
potato pancakes, 76–77
young artichokes, 237–38
Jew's mallow, *see* malokhei
jicama, 143, 597–98
and chicken salad with green goddess dressing, 145–46
red peppers and pear with cilantro dressing, julienne of, 145
spicy papaya salsa with, 293
Jones, Bob, 155–56
juk gai choy, *see* bamboo or leaf mustard
julienne of five lettuce soup, 418–19
julienne of jicama, red peppers and pear with cilantro dressing, 145
June, Jennie, 113

K

kabocha (Japanese pumpkin), 652–56
with cumin, raisins and almonds, 132–33
purée, simple, 127
kadoo bichak (baked pumpkin and onion dumplings), 120–21
Kafka, Ernest, 254, 259, 547
Kafka, Hanni, 257, 259, 547
Kafka, Jill Gaydosh, 267
Kafka, Michael, 383, 639

Kalamata antipasto, 209–10
kale, 279, 282–87, 598–99
braised, 284–85, 598
in filling for yuca croquettes, 146–47
garlic, with yogurt, 285
in green soup, 282–83
pissaladière, 280
stew with chickpeas and mushrooms, 285
in summer vegetable gumbo, 343–44
tamari-garlic, 285
timbale of mushrooms, ham and, 286–87
Kalustyan's, 340
kellu-uchu, 625
Kennedy, Diana, 572
ketchup, 112
better than, 114
early American tomato, 113
kidney beans, 539–41
thick potato soup with corn and, 35
kidney stones, 346
kielbasa:
roasted vegetable combination with, 196
in split pea soup, 306
kikuma, *see* chrysanthemum leaves
kinpara, burdock, 411
Kirby cucumbers, *see* cucumber(s), Kirby
kitchen sink sandwiches, 99
kohlrabi, 599
stuffed, 290–91
konbu dashi, 507
in miso soup with shiitake and shiso, 367–68
kookoo, 482
Persian cauliflower, 263
-ye baghala (Persian fava bean omelet), 226
Kremezi, Aglaia, 540, 577
large lima beans with garlic and fennel of, 26–27

L

lace cookies, peanut-ginger, 50–51
Lacinato kale, 598
lamb:
bamboo-détente, 369
chops, roasted eggplant, cumin and yogurt sauce for, 338

curry stew with cranberry beans and, 21
and hominy soup, rich, 43
winter-y stew of eggplant, red peppers and, 335
lamb, ground:
calabaza stew with, 131
cauliflower stew with, 262
curry stuffing, 493–94
curry stuffing, acorn squash stuffed with, 118
curry stuffing, for mushrooms, 406
in Greek stuffing, 494
in Moroccan stuffing, 494–95
sauce, morels in, 406
in stuffed Brussels sprouts, 267–68
stuffed eggplant with orzo and, 330
in stuffed whole cabbage, 276
-tomato stuffing, 496–97
lamb's lettuce, *see* mâche
La Ratte(s), 70
lardons, *see* bacon lardons
lasagna:
with cilantro-jalapeño pasta, Mexican, 437–38
eggplant, 336
with mushroom duxelles, 405–6
spinach and mushroom, 251–53
La Tienda, 156
Latin-style dishes:
golden fava, 227
golden fava soup, 227
see also specific countries
leaf mustard, *see* mustard greens and leaf mustard
Lebanon, 340
Lee Ann Cox's classic corn bread, 45–46
Lee Ann Cox's corn bread dressing, 46
leek(s), 372, 383–90, 600–601
in asparagus stock, 506–7
baked halibut with Jerusalem artichokes and, 144
broth, 385
caramelized, asparagus soup with, 156–57
carrot soup, 186
fettuccine with asparagus and, 162
gratin, 387
grilled baby, 386–87
and potato soup (potage Parmentier if hot, vichyssoise if cold), 387–88
quiche with, 388

leek(s) (*continued*)
   quiche with ham, Gruyère and, 388
   sauce, 388
   sauce with red wine, 389
   storage of, 375
   in summer soups, 377
   vinaigrette, 385
   in warm vegetable compote, 385–86
   wild, *see* ramps
leeks, braised, 384
   anecdote about, 383
   with lemon, 385
   with lemon, microwave variation, 385
   roasted, then, 384
lemon balm (balm, bee balm), 589
   beans with, 11
lemongrass, 592
   shrimp and lotus root with lime and, 365–66
lemon (juice), 448
   braised leeks with, 385
   butter, fennel with, 215
   fennel with olive oil and, 215
   -garlic bath, roasted broccoli stems with, 264–65
   glazed carrots, 188
   -light carrots, 188
   nettles with olive oil and, 245
   -parsley sauce, scorzonera in, 412
   sautéed mushrooms with mustard and, 403–4
lentil:
   and chard soup, 179
   and chickpea soup, 280–81
Leroy, Jeanette, 108
Leslie, Eliza, 31
letcho, 65
   in chicken paprikás, 66
lettuce, 414–21, 601–2
lettuce, Bibb (Tom Thumb), 601, 602
   in okroshka, 355–56
   with soy-sesame vinaigrette, 415
lettuce, Boston (butterhead), 601, 602
   braised, 419
   salmon wrapped in leaves of, 415, 418
lettuce, iceberg (Crisphead, Batavia, black-seeded Simpson), 420–21, 601, 602
   wedges with blue cheese dressing, 415
lettuce, romaine (Cos, Little Gem), 601, 602
   with anchovy dip, 467

shrimp and avocado salad on sorrel and, 6
Lettuce and Lovage (Shaffer), 417
Levy, Paul, 154, 156, 205, 602, 622
Levy, Penny, 154, 524, 622
Liguria (Italy), 177
lilies, 154, 373, 531
lima beans, 225, 540–41
   in chicken, beef and vegetable soup, 304–5
   curried, 20
   Fordhooks, 20
   giant, *see* gigantes
   in green shrimp curry, 437
   in hominy soup, 42–43
   in seafood succotash, 22–23
   in succotash, 20–21
   in summer vegetable gumbo, 343–44
lime (juice), shrimp and lotus root with lemongrass and, 365–66
linguine, fried peppers and tomatoes for, 62–63
Little Gem lettuce, *see* lettuce, romaine
liver, *see* calves' liver; chicken liver(s)
lobster:
   and avocado salad, cold, 6
   in seafood succotash, 22–23
lollo rosa lettuce, 602
Long, Kathi, 24
long beans (yard-long beans), 296, 297, 309, 537, 543, 622, 624
   shelled, *see* cowpeas
lotus root, 362, 365–67, 603
   braised napa cabbage with snow peas, bamboo and, 366–67
   and shrimp with lemongrass and lime, 365–66
lovage, 183, 589, 592
   green bean salad with, 12
   pesto, 442–43
Lucas, John, 604

M

McGee, Harold, 455
mâche (lamb's lettuce, corn salad), 602
   julienne of jicama, red peppers and pear with cilantro dressing with, 145
mackerel gravlax, 438–39
magma mustard, 612–13
maitake (hens of the woods), 606
maize, use of term, 31, 572

malanga, *see* taro; yautía
malokhei (Jew's mallow), 340, 603–4
   light soup of chicken, rice and, 344–45
Manchego cheese, in Mexican lasagna with cilantro-jalapeño pasta, 437–38
manicotti, nettle and ricotta filling for, 245
manioc, *see* yuca
Many Beautiful Things (Schiavelli), 238
maple (syrup):
   corn jalapeño relish, 40
   -glazed roasted sweet potatoes, 140
   mustard glaze, 520
Marina di Chioggia (Chioggia), 652
marinade(s), marinated, 519–20
   artichokes, 230–31
   Asian, and brushing sauce, 519–20
   cippolini, roasted and, 380–81
   citrus-garlic, 520
   fennel, anchovies with, 210
   fresh herb, 519
   garlic, roasted portobello mushrooms with, 402–3
   roasted baby eggplant, 328–29
   roasted peppers, 55
   shrimp, cilantro-, 436
   shrimp, mussel and artichoke salad, 234
marjoram, 592
   beans with, 11
Marks, Copeland, 120
maroon carrots (beta-carrots), 561–63
Martinez, Zarela, puréed black beans (frijoles negros colados) of, 23–24
masa, 31, 574–75
mashed potato(es), 70, 71
   basic recipe for, 73
   cakes, 77
   microwave olive oil, 73
   microwave variation for, 73
matsutakes, 606
May, Tony, 218
mayonnaise, commercial, 420, 421
   in iceberg lettuce wedges with blue cheese dressing, 415
mayonnaise, mayonnaise-based sauces, 455–59
   aïoli with potato, 456–57
   classic, 455
   cooked-yolk, 455
   rouille, 457

in salads, 81, 82, 499
sweet garlic, 456
tartar, 457
see also rémoulade (sauce)
meat:
glaze, 505
glaze, braised celery hearts with, 201
loaf with spinach, gala, 253
see also bacon; beef; beef, ground; ham; lamb; lamb, ground; pork; prosciutto; sausage; veal
meatless red flannel hash, 172
meat sauces:
beef glaze, stuffed cabbage rolls with, 277
gratin of cardoons with, 243
rich lamb, morels in, 406
melting potatoes, 74–75
seaside, 75
melting tomatoes Provençal, 99, 109–10
Memories of a Cuban Kitchen (Randelman and Schwartz), 147
merveille de quatre saisons, 601
mesclun, 602
Mexican favas, 225, 542
Mexico, Mexican-style dishes, 539, 540, 559, 587, 591
Adelle's favorite roasted seeds, 136
chayotes in, 118
chilies rellenos, 59–60
chilies rellenos with corn, 60
fava bean soup (sopa de habas), 225–26
giant lima bean salad with flavors of, 27
guacamole, 8
lasagna with cilantro-jalapeño pasta, 437–38
Zarela Martinez's puréed black beans (frijoles negros colados), 23–24
microwave cooking, 521
for aïoli with potato, 456–57
for all-American stewed tomatoes, 106–7
for artichokes, 528
for asparagus, 155, 533
for avocados, 535
for bacon lardons, 509
for bagna cauda, 466–67
for beans, 538, 540
for beets, 545–46
for braised leeks with lemon, 385
for broccoli and cauliflower, 548–49

for broccoli di raab, 551
for Brussels sprouts, 552
for cabbage risotto, 270
for cabbages, 555–56, 558
for carrot leek soup, 186–87
for carrot purée or sauce, 187
for carrots, 563
for celery, 565
for celery purée, 202
for celery root, 566
for celery root purée, 207
for Chinese stewed tomatoes, 107–8
for collard greens, 571
for corn, 573
for corn custard, 39
for creamed onions, 381
for creamy carrot soup, 185
for curried cabbage, 272–73
for eggplant, 581
for eggplant lasagna, 336
for endive, 569
for fennel, 583
for garlic, 586
for herbed tomato sauce, 462
for Jerusalem artichokes, 597
for kohlrabi, 599
for letcho, 65
for mashed potatoes, 73
for mushrooms, 608
for mushroom-vegetable stew, 405
for mustard greens and leaf mustard, 612
for okra, 615
olive oil mashed potatoes, 73
for onions, 618–19
for orange glazed beets, 171–72
for parsnip flan, 197–98
for parsnips, 620
for peanut brittle, 51–52
for peas, 623
for polenta, 42
for potatoes, 634
for pseudo-Indian dressing, 451
for pumpkin pudding, 135
for radicchio, 569
for rhubarb, 639
for roasted peeled chestnuts, 508
for shrimp and corn curry, 38
for sorrel, 645, 646
for spinach, 646
for squash, 649, 655
for stuffed artichokes, 241
for summer corn pudding, 38

for summer vegetable bonanza, 89
for sweet potatoes, 138, 658
for Szechwan green beans, 17
for tomatoes, 661, 662
for turnips, 666
for vegetable curry, 262
Microwave Gourmet (Kafka), 51
Microwave Healthstyle Cookbook (Kafka), 200
Middle Eastern-style dishes, 491
eggplant and okra stew, 343
eggplant with spiced rice, 332–33
tomato sauce, spicy, 464
midsummer green bean salad, 13
midsummer squash, 89–90
millet, polenta made with, 30
miner's lettuce (winter purslane), 636–37
mini corn crêpes, 32–33
curry, 32, 33
Southwestern, 33
mini pumpkins, 652–56
mint(ed), 589, 592–93
and acorn squash soup, 126
braised carrots, 189–90
butter, baby carrots with tiny green beans sautéed in, 187–88
pastina salad with radish and, 291
peas with, 301
rice, eggplant stuffed with, 331–32
rice stuffing, 496
roasted yellow squash in a bath of, 86
tomato salsa, fresh, 114–15
zucchini chunks with citrus and, 86–87
mirasol chili peppers, 626
Mirelman, David, 585
mirliton, *see* chayote(s)
miso, 544
soup with shiitake and shiso, 367–68
mitsuba, 531
mizuna, 524, 531, 612, 613
mock eggplant Parmesan, 336–37
mojo criollo, yuca con, 147–48
Monterey Jack:
-olive stuffing, piquillo peppers with, 150–51
polenta, creamy, 42
Moonen, Rick, 149, 150
morels, 606, 609, 610, 611
asparagus with, 159

morels *(continued)*
  braised stuffed, 406–7
  with rhubarb and asparagus, 404
Moroccan-style dishes:
  cold tomato soup, 103
  eggplant, 326–27
  harissa sauce, 465–66
  orange and onion salad with cumin
    vinaigrette, 374
  stuffing, 494–95
  stuffing, eggplant stuffed with,
    329–30
mountain spinach (garden orach), 604
moussaka stuffing, 497
mozzarella (cheese):
  in basic pizza, 474
  buffalo, 99
  in deep-dish pizza, 474–75
  garlic roasted peppers with
    anchovies and, 57
  sauce, light, broccoli baked in, 264
  smoked, salad of celery root,
    prosciutto and, 205
  toasty Treviso with anchovies and,
    219–20
Muenster cheese, in eggplant rollatini,
  337–38
muffins, Thanksgiving squash, 131–32
mulato peppers, 626
mung bean sprouts, 646–47
  in quadruple soy threat, 313
mushroom(s), 396–408, 604–11
  braised calabaza with, 129
  broth, 507
  -bulgur (or quinoa) stuffing, 497–98
  cauliflower with bacon and, 260–61
  cumin, 403
  dried, 610–11
  drying of, 397
  dumplings, 398–99
  duxelles, 405-6
  fresh, 604–9
  kale stew with chickpeas and, 285
  methods for, 607, 610–11
  preparation of, 608–9
  quiche, large, 399
  quiches, miniature, 399
  and roasted red pepper salad, 56
  sautéed, with lemon and mustard,
    403–4
  soufflé, 487
  and spinach lasagna, 251–53
  stems, in stuffed onions, 376
  timbale of collards, ham and, 286–87

varieties of, 605–7
  -vegetable stew, 404–5
  with yogurt and dill, 398
  see also specific kinds of mushrooms
mushrooms, stuffed, 406
  braised, 407
  braised morels, 406–7
  preparation of, 609
mushroom soup:
  barley, 400
  wild, 401–2
  winter, 401
mussel(s):
  in green seafood stew with peas and
    spinach, 302–3
  salad of marinated shrimp, artichoke
    and, 234
  in seafood succotash, 22–23
mustard, 593
  chicken, beef and vegetable soup
    with, 304–5
  dressing, grated carrots with, 183
  maple glaze, 520
  sauce, sweet, 441
  sautéed mushrooms with lemon and,
    403–4
  –soy sauce, steamed Chinese broccoli
    with, 321
  –soy sauce, stir-fried chicken and
    snow peas in, 304
mustard greens and leaf mustard, 279,
  611–13
  braised, 287
mustard sprouts, 647
mysterious pasta sauce, 343

N

naked frying, 514
ñame, *see* yams
napa cabbage (Chinese cabbage),
  315–16, 557–59
  braised, with lotus root, snow peas
    and bamboo, 366–67
  salad, shredded, 317
  in very spicy Asian vegetable salad,
    318
Nassikas, James, 234, 377
nasturtium, 613
natto, 544
navy bean(s) (small white beans), 539–41
  basic Boston baked, 24
  and broccoli di raab soup, 281
  salad of arugula, tuna and, 429

nettle(s), 229, 244–45, 613–14
  with olive oil and lemon, 245
  and ricotta filling, 245
  soup, 244
New England, New England dishes,
  347, 639
  basic Boston baked beans, 24
  long-cooked American green beans,
    16
  succotash, 20–21
New England Blue, *see* Hubbard squash,
  blue
New England pie pumpkin, *see* sugar
  pie pumpkin
New Orleans:
  pickled chayote, 132
  spicy rémoulade, 458–59
new potato(es), 632–36
  with garlic and rosemary, roasted
    red, 73–74
  Niçoise olives, green beans and tuna
    with tomatoes and anchovy
    cheese vinaigrette (salade
    Niçoise), 14–15
  salad, creamy, 81
  salad with capers and bacon, 81
  and truffle salad, 80
New World Cuisine (Van Aken), 147
New Year's Day, 307
  hoppin' John for, 308–9
New York City, restaurants in,
  101, 214–15, 218, 232, 301,
  387, 547
New Zealand spinach, 645
Niçoise olives, *see* olives, Niçoise
nonpareil capers, 560
noodle(s):
  baby food tomato sauce for, 461
  leek sauce with red wine over, 389
  sesame, cucumber with, 358
  soup, faux pho, 43
  white, green cabbage, string beans,
    cream and, 273
  see also egg noodles; pasta
nopales, *see* cactus pad(s)
North Africa, North African cooking,
  593
  see also Moroccan-style dishes
nuts, *see specific kinds of nuts*

O

oak leaf lettuce, 602–3
oatmeal peanut butter cookies, 51

oca (wood sorrel), 644
octopus:
    to clean, 317
    in fried feelers, 317
oeufs mollets (coddled eggs), 480
    salad of potatoes and purslane with
        a tahini-citrus dressing and, 423
    tuna and beets bâtarde with, 173–74
okra, 339–44, 603, 615–16
    with basil, 340–41
    and eggplant stew, 342–43
    and eggplant stew, Middle Eastern,
        343
    fried, 341
    pickled, 341
    and roasted pepper stew with rice,
        342
    selection of, 340
okroshka, 355–56
olive oil:
    fennel with lemon and, 215
    and garlic sauce, 468
    mashed potatoes, microwave, 73
    nettles with lemon and, 245
    roasted peppers in (sott'olio), 55
    for tomato salad, 99
    in vinaigrettes, 448–50
olive(s):
    and artichoke pasta sauce, tangy, 238
    and artichokes, tangy, 238
    in caponata, 327–28
    -cheese stuffing, piquillo peppers
        with, 150–51
    pimento-stuffed, in corn-chili
        soufflé, 43–44
    -tomato sauce, roasted Jerusalem
        artichokes in, 143–44
olive(s), Kalamata:
    antipasto, 209–10
    cardoons with sauce of parsley,
        anchovies and, 242
olives, Niçoise:
    in bok choy Provençal, 320
    in green beans, tuna and potatoes
        with tomatoes and anchovy
        cheese vinaigrette (salade
        Niçoise), 14–15
    in orange and onion salad with
        cumin vinaigrette, 374
    in pissaladière, 374–76
omelets, 482–84
    chanterelle, 402
    corn and feta cheese, 36
    fillings for, 483

flat, 483–84
Persian fava bean (kookoo-ye
    baghala), 226
rolled (or folded), 482–83
onion(s), 372–82, 615–19
    bucatini with sauce of tomato,
        pancetta and (all'amatriciana),
        112–13
    eggplant caviar with peppers and,
        324–25
    methods for, 616
    preparation of, 616–19
    and pumpkin dumplings, baked
        (kadoo bichak), 120–21
    stuffed, 376
    varieties of, 615–16
    in winter soups, 377
    yields and equivalents for, 619
    see also cippolini
onions, Egyptian (walking or sprouting
    onions), 616–19
    pickled, 382
    scape broth, 616
onions, pearl, 616–19
    creamed, 381–82
    creamy Brussels sprouts and,
        274
    roasted burdock and, 412
    sweet-and-sour, 382
onion(s), red, 615–19
    Doug Rodriguez's black bean soup
        with, 19–20
    flowers, roasted, 379–80
    and orange salad with cumin
        vinaigrette, 374
    puffed sweet potato slices with crisp
        rings of, 139–40
    rings, crisp, 380
    rings, fried, 517–18
onion(s), sweet, 373, 615–19
    in parsley salad, 444
onion(s), Vidalia, 372, 373
onion(s), white, 373, 615–19
    flowers, roasted, 379–80
    giant lima beans simmered with
        garlic and, 21–22
    rings, fried, 517–18
    sandwiches, James Beard's, 377
onion(s), yellow, 373, 615–19
    caramelized, purée of split peas
        with, 307
    long-cooked Italian green beans,
        15–16
    sandwiches, James Beard's, 377

onion soup, 377–78
    curried, 378
    roasted, with cannellini beans, 379
orange (juice):
    glazed beets, 171–72
    and onion salad with cumin
        vinaigrette, 374
    and shredded beet salad, 165–66
    sour, in tahini-citrus dressing, 452
    wheat germ dressing, 451
    see also blood orange
oregano, 593
orzo:
    sauté of edamame, shrimp and, 314
    stuffed eggplant with lamb and, 330
    stuffing, 495–96
otoshi-buta, 237, 503
oven-braised:
    parsnips, 196–97
    turnips with garlic, 292
oven-drying, of tomatoes, 661
oven-grilled:
    eggplant, 580
    zucchini, 87
oven-roasted:
    peppers, 629
    version of braised carrots, 190
Oxford Companion to Food (Davidson),
    592
oyster mushrooms, 607, 609, 610, 611
    asparagus and beef stir-fry with, 162
    mushroom-vegetable stew, 404–5
oyster plant, *see* salsify
oysters, a satin of tapioca and, 149–50

P

Pacific tomato dipping sauce, 463
"packed leaves," 594
pak choy (choy sum, Chinese flowering
    cabbage), 316, 557–59
pancakes, potato, *see* potato pancakes
pancetta, bucatini with sauce of tomato,
    onion and (all'amatriciana),
    112–13
pandan, in coconut-yuca custard cake,
    148–49
panfried bean cakes, 25
papaya:
    avocado and pink grapefruit salad, 5
    salsa with daikon, spicy, 293
paprika, 625, 627
parfait, cranberry tapioca, 151
Parks, Greg, 401

Parmesan (cheese):
   anchovy dressing, 450
   -breaded fried eggplant, 333–34
   in gratins, 207, 222, 243, 387
   in pizzas, 474–75
   in risotto, 110, 220, 269–70, 424–25,
      431–32
   in salads, 230, 429
   in soufflés, 43–44, 250, 486–87, 488
   in soups, 248, 377–78, 379
   in stuffings, 493, 497
parsley, 183, 442–45, 593–94
   butter, radishes with, 292
   cardoons with sauce of anchovies,
      olive and, 242
   deep-fried, 445
   and garlic stuffing, 498–99
   general information about, 442
   lemon sauce, scorzonera in, 412
   pesto, 443
   salad, 444
   and scallion dip, 391
   soup, 444–45
parsnip(s), 182, 183, 195–98, 619–20
   flan, 197–98
   ice cream, 198
   oven-braised, 196–97
   potato purée, 198
   purée, 198
   soup, 195
Party Food (Kafka), 391, 438
party frittata (tortilla), 485–86
pasillas, 626
pasta:
   doughs, *see* doughs, pasta
   rosemary, Virginia ham, spinach
      and, 253
   see also specific kinds of pastas
pastina:
   in broccoli di raab, greens and
      chicken soup, 281–82
   salad with radish and mint, 291
pattypan squash, 648–50
   –potato soufflés, 84
peach sauce, chunky, for mini corn
      crêpes, 32–33
peanut butter, 621, 622
   chicken stew, 50
   cookies, 51
   cookies, oatmeal or coconut, 51
peanut(s), 49–52, 621–22
   allergies to, 49
   brittle, 51–52
   dipping sauce, 464

   -ginger lace cookies, 50–51
   in Southeast Asian dipping sauce,
      465
pear, jicama and red peppers with
      cilantro dressing, julienne of, 145
pearl onions, *see* onions, pearl
pear-shape tomatoes, 659
peas, 225, 296–309, 536, 622–24
   see also cowpeas; long beans;
      pea shoots; snow peas;
      sugar snap peas
peas, black-eyed, 296–97, 543, 622
   and collard greens, 308
   in hoppin' John, 308–9
   soup, smooth, 308–9
peas, split, 296, 536, 622–24
   caramelized onions with purée of,
      307
   see also pea soup, split
peas, sweet green (English peas),
      296–303, 536, 622–24
   green seafood stew with spinach
      and, 302–3
   ice cream, 303
   with mint, 300
   with peppers and tomatoes, 302
   piselli alla romana, 301
   scallion quiche, large, 298
   scallion quiches, miniature, 297–98
   small, "soup" of fresh herbs with
      (soupe de petits pois aux herbes
      fraîches), 300–301
   Venetian rice with (risi bisi), 302
   see also pea soup
pea shoots (pea tendrils), 296, 303, 536,
      622, 624
   creamy baby corn, chanterelles and,
      305–6
pea soup:
   with asparagus, light spring, 157
   base, fresh, 299
   chilled curried, 300
   pod, 298
   quick, 299
   smooth black-eyed, 308
pea soup, split:
   green, Greek style, 307
   yellow, and ham hock soup, 306–7
   yellow, with smoked turkey, 307
pecans, in popcorn crunch, 48
penne:
   with dandelion greens and garlic, 430
   with tomato, pancetta and onion
      sauce, 112–13

yellow chard, roasted tomatoes and,
      181
peperoncini (Italian pickled peppers),
      627
   in chilies rellenos, 59–60
   pickled vegetable antipasto, 256–57
Pépin, Jacques, 377, 482
pepper(corns), 55
   in vinaigrette, 448
peppermint, 593
peppers, 53–68, 624–31
   cherry, *see* cherry peppers
   for cooking, frying, sautéing and
      stir-frying, 625
   methods for, 628
   mini, in fish swimming in vegetables,
      93–94
   preparation for stuffing of, 630
   preparation of, 628–30
   preserved in brine or vinegar,
      627–28
   roasted, *see* roasted pepper(s)
   used raw in salads and other dishes,
      625
   varieties of, 624–28
   yields and equivalents for, 631
peppers, bell, 3, 53, 54, 625, 631
   with confetti vegetarian stuffing,
      330–31
   pork chops with cherry and, 61
   relish, 66–67
   roasting of, 628–29
   and sardines with balsamic vinegar,
      58–59
   strips, silky, 58
   see also green bell pepper(s); red bell
      pepper, roasted; red bell
      pepper(s); yellow bell pepper(s)
peppers(s), hot, 54, 55
   bottled oils and sauces, 628
   dried, 626
   dried, powdered and crushed,
      626–27
   dried, reconstituting of, 626
   fresh, 626
   sauce, fiery, 629
   tabbouleh with red peppers and,
      61–62
   -and sweet pepper soufflé, 487
   see also ancho chilies; cascabel
      peppers; Catarina peppers; chili
      peppers; chili (powder); jalapeño
      (peppers); poblano chilies;
      serrano pepper(s)

peppers, Italian frying, 54, 624, 625, 629
 roasted, and chunky tomatoes, 63
Pepys, Samuel, 416
perciatelli with tomato, pancetta and onion sauce, 112–13
perilla (beefsteak plant, shiso, egoma), 531
 miso soup with shiitake and, 367–68
Persian-style dishes, 482
 cauliflower kookoo, 263
 fava bean omelet (kookoo-ye baghala), 226
Peru, 621
pesto (sauce):
 chervil, 434
 in green soup, 282–83
 lovage, 442–43
 parsley, 443
 (pistou), 467–68
Peter Luger, 101
pets, poisoning of, 97
Phaseolus, 11, 537
phyllo dough, in beet and apple strudel, 176
pickled, pickles, 358–61
 beets, 170
 bread-and-butter, 361
 chayote, 132
 cornichons, 359–60
 dill, in spinach soup, 247
 Egyptian onions, 382
 garlic or dill, 358–59
 general information about, 359
 jalapeño peppers, 62
 okra, 341
 onions, 618
 radish, 293
 salting of, 360
 samphire, 424
 sweet-and-sharp cucumbers, 360
 vegetable antipasto, 256–57
 zucchini bread-and-butter, 90
pie(s):
 crust, basic, 476–77
 rhubarb strawberry, 349
 spiced squash, 134
 sweet potato, 141
pimientos, 55, 625, 627
pimpinella (burnet), 589
pink bean(s) (rosadas), 24–25
 cakes, panfried, 25
 cakes with crab or shrimp, 25

feijoada over spicy rice, 26
pinto beans, 539–41
piquillo peppers with olive-cheese stuffing, 150–51
piquín peppers (bird peppers), 626, 627
piri piri, 625
piselli alla romana, 301
pissaladière, 374–76
 with basic focaccia dough, 376
 kale, 280
pizza, 473–75
 amalfitana, 475
 basic, 474
 caponata, 475
 deep-dish, 474–75
 deli, 273
 dough, 473–74
 vegetable, 474
pizza sauce:
 basic, 463
 even-more-basic, 463
 tomato sauce for stuffed vegetables as, 461
plum tomato(es), 99, 659, 661–63
 –basil quiches, miniatures, 101–2
 basil soup, 105
 in braised wax beans with herbs, 16
 and bread soup, 104
 and corn soup, Southwestern, 105–6
 dipping sauce, basil, 464
 dipping sauce, Pacific, 463
 dipping sauce, spicy Middle Eastern, 464
 fennel and eggplant, 211
 -lamb stuffing, 496–97
 risotto, stovetop, 110
 sauce, 462
 sauce, in winter-y lamb stew with eggplant and red peppers, 335
 soup, curry, 105
plum tomato purée, 459
 in basic pizza sauce, 463
 fresh tomato paste from, 459
 Italian, 459
poblano chilies (peppers), 625, 631
 -and-sweet pepper soufflé, 487
 rellenos with corn, 60–61
poisonous plants, 69, 95–96, 97, 143, 322, 346
polenta, 30, 41, 574
 creamed spinach sandwiches, 250
 creamy, 41–42

creamy Gorgonzola, 42
 fried or grilled, 42
 microwave variation for, 42
pomegranate seeds, in butternut squash soup with glazed chestnuts, 126–27
pommes:
 à l'huile, 80
 lyonnaise (potato gratin), 79
 vapeur, 72
popcorn, 31, 41, 572
 crunch, 48
 pumped-up, 41
poppy seed blood orange vinaigrette, 450
porcini mushrooms, dried (cèpes, boletus, Steinpilz), 610, 611
 braised calabaza with, 129
 spinach and mushroom lasagna, 251–53
porcini mushrooms, fresh (cèpes, boletus, Steinpilz), 605–6, 608
pork:
 chops, with cherry and bell peppers, 61
 with endive sweet-and-sour sauce, 223
 roast, with rhubarb sauce, 248
 roasted vegetable combination with kielbasa, 196
 smoked, neck bones, in black-eyed peas and collard greens, 308
 see also bacon; ham; pancetta; prosciutto; sausage
pork, ground:
 in ants on a scallion tree, 393
 stuffing, 493
portobello mushroom(s), 605, 608, 609
 with garlic marinade, roasted, 402–3
 sauce with cream and tarragon, 408
Portugal cabbage, 598, 643
Poses, Lillian, 387
potage:
 basic, 71–72
 chicory, 221
 Parmentier (hot leek and potato soup), 387–88
 of turnip and carrot, 185–86
potato(es), 69–82, 632–36
 aïoli with, 456–57
 angel, 79
 and beet purée, 170

potato(es) (continued)
  braised carrots and, 189
  carrot purée, 187
  and celery root purée, 207
  chips, crisp, 514
  gratin (pommes lyonnaise), 79
  Greek island, 75–76
  melting, 74–75
  methods for, 633–34
  parsnip purée, 198
  -pattypan soufflés, 84
  pepper purée, golden, 59
  preparation of, 633–36
  seaside melting, 75
  varieties of, 70, 632
  yields and equivalents for, 636
  see also baking (Idaho) potatoes;
    French fries; mashed potato(es);
    new potato(es)
potato pancakes:
  basic recipe for, 76
  Jewish, 76–77
  Swiss (rösti), 77
potato salad:
  with capers and bacon, 81
  creamy, 81
  pommes à l'huile, 80
  with purslane and a tahini-citrus
    dressing, 423
  salade Russe, 82
  with sweet mustard sauce, 441
  truffle and, 80
potato soup, 71, 72
  artichoke and (zuppa di patate e
    carciofi), 235
  broccoli, 259
  with corn, thick, 35
  creamy broccoli di raab, 281
  creamy cauliflower, 257–58
  nettle, 244
  radish, 291
  with sorrel, 426
  Southwestern corn and tomato,
    105–6
  spinach, 247–48
  see also potage; vichyssoise
pot cheese and vegetable salad, 439
pot-steaming, of sorrel, 646
Potter, Beatrix, 417
prosciutto, salad of celery root, smoked
    mozzarella and, 205
Provence, Provençal, 177
  aïoli in, 456

anchovy dip, 467
bok choy, 320
melting tomatoes, 99, 108–9
Prudhomme, Paul, 132
pseudo-Indian dressing, 451
puca-uchu, 625
pudding, dessert:
  pumpkin, 134–35
  spiced squash, 133–34
  Thanksgiving, 135–36
pudding, summer corn, 38–39
puffed sweet potato slices with crisp red
    onion rings, 139–40
puff pastry, in pissaladière, 374–76
pumped-up popcorn, 41
pumpkin(s), 117–18, 575, 651–56
  basic seeds, 136
  and onion dumplings, baked (kadoo
    bichak), 120–21
  pudding, 134–35
  pudding, spiced, 133–34
puntarelle, 217, 218, 568
purée(d):
  artichoke, 236–37
  Asian-flavored red kuri, 128
  beet and potato, 170
  black beans, Zarela Martinez's
    (frijoles negros colados), 23–24
  broccoli, 263–64
  carrot, 186–87
  carrot potato, 187
  celery, 202–3
  celery root, 206–7
  celery root and potato, 207
  celery root with apples, 206
  cucumber, 357
  de batata, 138
  garlic roasted pepper, 57
  golden pepper potato, 59
  golden surprise, 170–71
  parsnip, 198
  parsnip potato, 198
  plum tomato, see plum tomato
    purée
  roasted cherry tomato, 109
  simple acorn squash, 127–28
  simple kabocha, 127
  of split peas with caramelized
    onions, 307
  vegetable, soufflé (without flour),
    488
  winter vegetable, 207
purple mizuna, 612, 613

purslane, 636–37
  and potato salad with a tahini-citrus
    dressing, 423
  simple soup with, 424

Q
quadruple soy threat, 313
quail, cayenne, on a cilantro nest,
    436
Queen Anne's lace, 183
queso blanco (white cheese), in thick
    potato soup with corn, 35
queso fresco (fresh cheese), in Mexican
    lasagna with cilantro-jalapeño
    pasta, 437–38
quiche(s), 480–82
  asparagus and tarragon, 160–61
  crust, 481
  crustless spring, 399–400
  flamiche crust for, 481–82
  large scallion pea, 298
  with leeks, 388
  with leeks, ham and Gruyère, 388
  miniature mushroom, 399
  miniature scallion-pea, 297–98
  miniature tomato-basil, 101–2
quick pea soup, 299
quinoa-mushroom stuffing, 497–98

R
radiant bok choy, 318–19
radicchio, Chioggia, 218, 567, 568
  gratin of, 222
radicchio, Treviso, 218, 567, 568–69
  gratin of, 222
  with mozzarella and anchovies,
    toasty, 219–20
radicchio (Verona radicchio), 218, 267,
    567–69
  risotto with vermouth and, 220
radish(es), 289, 637–38
  with anchovy dip, 467
  with parsley butter, 292
  pastina salad with mint and, 291
  pickles, 293
  in rhubarb sauce, 348
  and scallion soup, 392
  soup, 291
  soup with cucumber, cold, 291
  see also daikon
radish greens pasta sauce, 292–93
radish sprouts, 647

rainbow beets with celery, capers and
    dill, 166
raisins, golden:
    in cippolini Riviera, 381
    in eggplant Moroccan, 326–27
    spoon bread with, 47
raisins, kabocha with cumin, almonds
    and, 132–33
raitas, 350, 351
ramp(s) (wild leeks), 390, 393, 638–39
    fettuccine with wild asparagus and,
        161–62
    grilled, 394
    and wild asparagus frittata, 160
Randelman, Mary Urrutia, 147
rapini, see broccoli di raab
ratatouille pasta sauce, 338
ravioli:
    artichoke-chervil, 239
    making, 471
    nettle and ricotta filling for, 245
"Recipe for Salad, A" (Smith), 417
red beans and rice, Japanese style, 311
red bell pepper, roasted:
    and mushroom salad, 56
    and okra stew with rice, 342
    and roasted fennel salad, 211–12
    spread, 56
    spread with anchovies, 56
red bell pepper(s), 625
    jicama and pear with cilantro
        dressing, julienne of, 145
    purée or sauce, 629
    sorbet, 68
    strips, silky, 58
    tabbouleh with hot peppers and,
        61–62
    winter-y lamb stew with eggplant
        and, 335
red cabbage, see cabbage, red
red fingerlings, 632
red-in-snow mustard, see bamboo or
    leaf mustard
red kuri, 652–54, 656
    purée, Asian-flavored, 128
    rice paper packets, 121
red leaf lettuce, 602
red onions, see onion(s), red
red runner beans, 11
Red Russet potatoes, 632
red Russian soup:
    the meat version, 169
    vegetable, 168

red snapper
    in swimming in vegetables, 93–94
red sorrel, see sheep sorrel
red wine:
    leek sauce with, 389
    in pasta with hidden-depth
        eggplant, 334
    in pickled beets, 170
    in pickled vegetable antipasto,
        256–57
    in pork chops with cherry and bell
        peppers, 61
    in "rich" peasant stew with favas, 227
    in stuffed whole cabbage, 276
red wine vinegar:
    in anchovy vinaigrette, 449–50
    in everyday vinaigrette, 449
    in pasta with hidden-depth
        eggplant, 334
    in pickled beets, 170
    in pickled vegetable antipasto,
        256–57
    in red Russian soup—the meat
        version, 169
    in red Russian vegetable soup, 168
    in rhubarb sauce, 348
    in roasted and marinated cippolini,
        380–81
    in summer vegetable gumbo, 343–44
    in sweet-and-sour red cabbage, 275
relishes:
    maple corn jalapeño, 40
    pepper, 66–67
    spicy corn, 40
Remi (restaurant), 79
rémoulade (sauce), 458
    celery root, 205–6
    New Orleans spicy, 458–59
    spicy, 459
Restaurant 1810, 225
rhubarb, 346–49, 639–40
    energy beets, 349
    freezing of, 347
    morels with asparagus and, 404
    strawberry jam, 349
    strawberry pie, 349
rhubarb sauce, 348
    basic, 348
    duck breast with, 347–48
rice, 362, 489–90
    bamboo-détente lamb with, 369
    basic white, 489
    with green seafood stew with peas
        and spinach, 303

    herbed, 490
    Middle Eastern spiced, eggplant
        with, 332–33
    minted, eggplant stuffed with,
        331–32
    okra and roasted pepper stew with,
        342
    pilaf, 489–90
    and red beans, Japanese style, 311
    stuffed tomatoes with basil and, 111
    stuffing, basic, 491
    stuffing, minted, 496
    see also arborio rice; brown rice;
        risotto
rice paper packets, red kuri, 121
"rich" peasant stew with favas, 227
ricotta (cheese):
    in broccoli potato soup, 259
    in buttercup squash gnocchi, 124
    in creamy carrot sauce, 185
    in eggplant rollatini, 337–38
    in fennel soup, 212–13
    in moussaka stuffing, 497
    in mushroom dumplings, 398–99
    and nettle filling, 245
rigatoni:
    with fennel sardine sauce, 215–16
    with hidden-depth eggplant, 334
    with tomato, pancetta and onion
        sauce, 112–13
Rinaldi, Augusto, 604
risi bisi (Venetian rice with peas), 302
risotto:
    with asparagus, sorrel and samphire,
        424–25
    cabbage, 269–70
    fiddlehead and chanterelle, 431–32
    Hubbard squash, 124–25
    with radicchio and vermouth, 220
    stovetop tomato, 110
risotto, barley, with broccoli di raab,
    284
Ritz, 387
roast(ed), roasting:
    arctic char with braised carrots in
        orange cherry tomato sauce,
        190–91
    artichokes, 528
    asparagus, 533
    beets, 164, 545
    broccoli and cauliflower, 548
    broccoli stems with lemon-garlic
        bath, 264–65

roast(ed), roasting (continued)
  broccoli stems with spaghettini, 265
  Brussels sprouts, 267, 552
  Brussels sprouts, basic, 274
  Brussels sprouts and chestnuts, 274–75
  of burdock, 553
  burdock and onions, 412
  buttercup squash with chili oil, 128–29
  cabbage, Hungarian, 272
  of cabbages, 555
  of carrots, 562
  of celery root, 566
  cherry tomatoes with basil, 109
  cherry tomato purée, 109
  chicken stock, 502
  edamame, 313
  of eggplant, 580
  eggplant, cumin and yogurt sauce, 338
  of endive, 568
  endives, mahogany, 221–22
  of fennel, 583
  fennel and pepper salad, 211–12
  fennel with caramelized tomato sauce, 210–11
  fish stock, 506
  of garlic, 586
  of Jerusalem artichokes, 597
  Jerusalem artichokes in tomato-olive sauce, 143–44
  of leeks, 601
  marinated baby eggplant, 328–29
  and marinated cippolini, 380–81
  of mushrooms, 608
  onion flowers, 379–80
  of onions, 617–18
  onion soup with cannellini beans, 379
  of parsnips, 620
  of peanuts, 621
  peeled chestnuts, 508
  portobello mushrooms with garlic marinade, 402–3
  of potatoes, 634–36
  of radicchio, 568–69
  ramps, 391
  red new potatoes with garlic and rosemary, 73–74
  scallion, fettuccine with tomato sauce and, 395
  of scallions, 391, 641
  of scorzonera and salsify, 642
  seeds, Adelle's favorite, 136
  of shallots, 643
  sliced fennel, 213
  of squash, 649, 654
  of sweet potatoes, 657
  sweet potatoes, maple-glazed, 140
  then braised leeks, 384
  then braised scallions, 394
  of tomatillos, 658–59
  of tomatoes, 660–61
  tomatoes, yellow chard and penne, 181
  turkey with sauerkraut stuffing, 277–78
  of turnips, 665–66
  vegetable combination, 195–96
  yellow squash in a mint bath, 86
  young artichokes with garlic, 231–32
  see also oven-roasted
roasted pepper(s), 54–58, 630–31
  with anchovies and chives, 55
  with fresh thyme, 55
  garlic, with mozzarella and anchovies, 57
  garlic purée, 57
  garlic purée, in ratatouille pasta sauce, 338
  Greek garlic, 56–57
  Italian frying, and chunky tomatoes, 63
  jarred, 627–28, 631
  marinated, 55
  in oil (sott'olio), 55
  in vinegar, 55
  yellow bell, and tomatoes, 57–58
  see also red bell pepper, roasted
Roasting: A Simple Art (Kafka), 267, 347, 586
Robuchon, Joël, 70, 73
  cauliflower soup of, 255
rocoto peppers, 625, 626
Rodriguez, Doug, black bean soup of, 19–20
roll-cutting, 532
romaine lettuce, *see* lettuce, romaine
romanesco cauliflower, 547, 549
Romanian peppers, 625
Romanian-style dishes:
  eggplant dip, 325
  stuffed cabbage rolls, 276–77
Romano beans (Italian green beans), 12, 537–39
  long-cooked, 15–16
  sautéed, 538
Roman-style dishes:
  baby artichokes, Jewish style (carciofi alla giudia), 237–38
  piselli alla romana, 301
romesco peppers, 625
romesco sauce, 63–65
root vegetables, 409–13
  American, 142–51; *see also* Jerusalem artichokes; jicama; yautía; yuca
  Asian, 362–66; *see also* lotus root; taro
  see also burdock; horseradish; salsify; scorzonera
rosadas, *see* pink bean(s)
rosemary, 594
  in fresh herb marinade, 519
  pasta, Virginia ham and spinach, 253
  roasted red new potatoes with garlic and, 73–74
rouge d'etampes, 652
rouille, 457
ruby chard, 177
  stems and anchovy sauté, warm, 179–80
  tart, 178–79
Russia, Russian-style dishes, 163, 346, 359, 591, 596
  cornichons in, 351
  eggplant dip, 325
  eggplant orientale, 325
  mushrooms in, 605, 610
  okroshka, 355–56
  red soup—the meat version, 169
  red vegetable soup, 168
  spinach soup, 247
  vegetarian borscht, 268–69
Russian banana potatoes, 632
rutabaga, 665–67
  chips, crisp, 514

S

sage, 594–95
  bacon-wrapped artichokes with, 233
  beans with, 11
  -butter sauce, squash tortelli with, 122–23
  creamy carrot sauce with, 187
  potatoes, 79–80
  and salt pork stuffing, 498
St. Paul-de-Vence, 381
salad bowl lettuce, 601

salad dill, 591
salad dressings, 450–52, 593
    anchovy, 467
    Asian, vegetable slaw with, 271
    avocado, 8–9
    blue cheese, iceberg lettuce wedges
      with, 415
    cilantro, julienne of jicama, red
      peppers and pear with, 145
    for crisp slaw, 270
    for iceberg lettuce, 420, 421
    mustard, grated carrots with, 183
    orange wheat germ, 451
    for pastina salad with radish and
      mint, 291
    pseudo-Indian, 451
    semi-Thai, 467
    Southeast Asian, 465
    tomato frappé, 452
    for very spicy Asian vegetable salad,
      318
    walnut oil, frisée with walnuts and,
      218–19
    yogurt, 450
    see also green goddess dressing;
      tahini-citrus dressing; vinaigrettes
salade:
    less-gastronomique, 14
    Niçoise (green beans, tuna, potatoes
      and Niçoise olives with tomatoes
      and anchovy cheese vinaigrette),
      14–15
    Russe, 82
    tomate, 98
salads:
    arugula, fennel and hazelnut, 429
    arugula, tuna and white bean,
      429
    avocado, pink grapefruit and
      papaya, 5
    beet and endive, 165
    Bibb lettuce with soy-sesame
      vinaigrette, 415
    bistro, 218
    bitter greens with lardons, 219
    black bean, 18
    cactus pad, 29
    Caesar, 418, 420–21
    carrot, with currants and almonds,
      184–85
    carrot cumin, 184
    celery root, 205
    celery root, smoked mozzarella and
      prosciutto, 205

cold lobster and avocado, 6
corn and black bean, 18
cucumber, 353
cucumber dill, 352–53
fennel, 212
giant lima bean, with Mexican
    flavors, 27
green bean, 12
green bean, with vinaigrette, 13
hearts of palm, 367
iceberg lettuce wedges with blue
    cheese dressing, 415
jicama and chicken, with green
    goddess dressing, 145–46
julienne of jicama, red peppers and
    pear with cilantro dressing, 145
marinated shrimp, mussel and
    artichoke, 234
midsummer green bean, 13
orange and onion, with cumin
    vinaigrette, 374
parsley, 444
pastina, with radish and mint, 291
potato, *see* potato salad
roasted fennel and pepper, 211–12
roasted red pepper and mushroom,
    56
Santa Fe corn, 36
shredded beet and orange, 165–66
shredded napa, 317
shrimp and avocado, on lettuce and
    sorrel, 6
tomato avocado, 5–6
white, 230
see also slaws; vegetable salads
salad stuffings, cold:
    curried chicken, 499
    quintessential tuna, 499–500
    tiny shrimp, celery and dill, 500
salmon:
    cucumber dill salad with, 352–53
    fennel sauce for, 216
    gravlax, 438–39
    roast Atlantic, with braised carrots in
      orange cherry tomato sauce,
      190–91
    roasted eggplant, cumin and yogurt
      sauce for, 338
    smoked, sweet mustard sauce with,
      441
    with sorrel soup, 426
    wrapped in lettuce leaves, 415, 418
salsa:
    cilantro, 435

fresh tomatillo, 93
fresh tomato mint, 114–15
papaya with daikon, spicy, 293
tomato cranberry, 114
salsify (oyster plant), 410, 642
salt, salting:
    of beans, 12
    in celery, 200
    of cucumbers, 351, 360, 576
    of eggplant, 579
    in pickle making, 360
    in vinaigrette, 448
salt pork:
    in callaloo soup with dumplings, 365
    in hoppin' John, 308–9
    and sage stuffing, 498
sambal olek, 628
samphire (glasswort):
    pickled, 424
    risotto with asparagus, sorrel and,
      424–25
    in stir-fried chicken and snow peas
      in mustard-soy sauce, 304
sancocho, 36
San Domenico, 218
    fennel compote, 214–15
sandwiches:
    creamed spinach polenta, 250
    James Beard's onion, 377
    kitchen sink, 99
San Francisco, Calif., 234, 312, 377, 444
San Miguel de Allende, 587
Santa Fe corn salad, 36
Santa Fe grande peppers, 628
santaka peppers (hontakas), 626
sardine(s):
    bell peppers with balsamic vinegar
      and, 58–59
    fennel sauce, 215–16
satin of oysters and tapioca, a, 149–50
sauces, 453–68
    beet caraway, 175
    blood orange, 468
    canned tomatillo, 93
    carrot, 186–87
    chunky peach, for mini corn crêpes,
      32–33
    cold spinach, 249
    creamy carrot, with sage, 187
    endive sweet-and-sour, 223
    fennel, 216
    fiery pepper, 629
    garlic, yuca with, 147–48
    green bean frappé, 17

sauces *(continued)*

horseradish, *see* horseradish sauce

leek, with red wine, 389

lemon-parsley, scorzonera in, 412

letcho, 65

light cheese, broccoli baked in, 264

olive oil and garlic, 468

parsley, anchovies and olive, cardoons with, 242

for pink bean feijoada over spicy rice, 26

quick tomatillo, 658–59

red pepper, 629

rhubarb, *see* rhubarb sauce

roasted eggplant, cumin and yogurt, 338

romesco, 63–65

semi-Thai, 467

spicy-cool avocado, 9

sweet mustard, 441

warm chervil, 434

see also béchamel sauce; butter(s); butter sauces; cream sauces; dipping sauces; hollandaise sauce; mayonnaise, mayonnaise-based sauces; meat sauces; pesto (sauce); salsa; tomato sauce

sauces, pasta:

asparagus, 161

baby food tomato, 461

caponata, 327–28

cauliflower, with anchovies and garlic, 260

cremini mushroom, with cream and tarragon, 408

eggplant and chickpea fritters in, 328

eggplant and okra stew as, 342–43

eggplant Morrocan, 326–27

endive sweet-and-sour, 223

fennel sardine, 215–16

fried peppers and tomatoes, 62–63

Greek garlic roasted peppers, 56–57

herbed tomato, 462

leek, with red wine, 389

letcho, 65

midsummer squash, 89–90

morels with rhubarb and asparagus, 404

mushroom duxelles as, 405–6

mysterious, 343

pesto, 467–68

plum tomato, 462

radish greens, 292–93

ratatouille, 338

roasted broccoli stems, 265

roasted Italian frying peppers and chunky tomatoes, 63

sage-butter, squash tortelli with, 122–23

tangy artichoke and olive, 238

tomato, pancetta and onion, bucatini with (all'amatriciana), 112–13

sauerkraut, 266, 554, 557

stuffing, roast turkey with, 277–78

sausage:

Chinese pork, in stir-fried Chinese broccoli, 320–21

chrysanthemum leaves with chorizo, 430

Italian, *see* Italian sausage

see also kielbasa

sauté(ed), sautéing, 520

of artichokes, 528–29

of asparagus, 534

baby carrots with tiny green beans in mint butter, 187–88

of beans, 538

of cabbages, 556, 558

of carrots, 563

of chard, 567

of chrysanthemum greens, 570

of cucumbers, 576

of dandelion greens, 578

defined, 520

of escarole, 569

fall vegetable, 191–92

of fennel, 583

of garlic, 586

honey mushroom, 405

of Jerusalem artichokes, 597

of leeks, 600

liver and avocado, 7–8

method of, 520

of mushrooms, 608

mushrooms with lemon and mustard, 403–4

of mustard greens and leaf mustard, 612–13

of onions, 617

orzo, edamame and shrimp, 314

of parsnips, 620

of peas, 623–24

of ramps, 638

of samphire, 640

of scallions, 641

scallops, baby corn and asparagus, 37–38

of sorrel, 645, 646

spinach and sorrel, 427–28

of squash, 648, 655

of turnips, 665

warm ruby chard stems and anchovy, 179–80

of watercress, 667

zucchini with dill, 86

savory:

summer, 595

summer, in braised wax beans with herbs, 16

winter, 595–96

savoy cabbage, *see* cabbage, savoy

scallion(s), 372, 390–95, 616, 640–41

brushes and flowers, 641

grilled large, 386–87

and parsley dip, 391

-pea quiche, large, 298

-pea quiches, miniature, 297–98

roasted, fettuccine with tomato sauce and, 395

roasted, then braised, 394

tree, ants on a, 393

scallion soup, 391

bok choy, shiitake mushrooms and, 392

radish and, 391

scallop(s):

and endive soup, 220–21

fennel sauce for, 216

fresh greens as base for, 288

sauté of baby corn, asparagus and, 37–38

stew, chervil, 434–35

Scandinavia, Scandinavian dishes, 576, 596

gravlax, 438–39

scarlet runner beans, 540

Schiavelli, Vincent, 238

Schneider, Elizabeth, 70, 316

Schwartz, Joan, 147

scorzonera, 410, 642

braised, with tarragon, 412–13

Scotch bonnet mushrooms, *see* fairy rings

Scotch bonnet peppers, 54, 625, 626

Scots cabbage, 598

Scoville scale, 54, 625

seafood:

in fritto misto, 516–17

stew with peas and spinach, green,
302–3
succotash, 22–23
*see also fish; shellfish; specific kinds of
fish and shellfish*
sea kale (crambe), 642–43
seaside melting potatoes, 75
seeds, caraway, *see* caraway (seeds)
seeds, squash, 652–53
Adelle's favorite roasted, 136
basic, 136
semi-Thai sauce, 467
Sephardic Cooking (Marks), 120
serrano ham, *see* ham, serrano
serrano pepper(s) (chili), 53, 625, 626,
631
sesame:
dressing, asparagus with tofu and,
158
noodles with cucumber, 358
-soy vinaigrette, 449
-soy vinaigrette, Bibb lettuce with,
415
Shaffer, Peter, 417
shaggy inky caps (mushrooms), 606
shallots, 372, 375, 643
shallow-frying, 513
of cardoons, 560
sheep sorrel (red sorrel, sour grass), 644
shellfish, *see* clams; crab; lobster;
mussel(s); oysters; shrimp; snails
shells:
baked stuffed, nettle and ricotta
filling for, 245
Virginia ham, spinach and, 253
shepherd peppers, 625
shiitake (mushrooms), 607, 608, 610,
611
miso soup with shiso and, 367–68
scallions and bok choy in broth, 392
shirred eggs with herbs, tomatoes and
cream, 102
shiso, *see* perilla
shoestring fries, 78
shredded beet and orange salad, 165–66
shredded napa salad, 317
shrimp:
and asparagus with sorrel, 428
and avocado, Chinese, 7
and avocado salad on lettuce and
sorrel, 6
bean cakes with, 25
and cabbage slaw, hot, 267

cilantro-marinated, 436
and corn curry, 38
curry, green, 437
delicata stuffed with, 118–19
frying of, 517
and lotus root with lemongrass and
lime, 365–66
in salade less-gastronomique, 14
salad of marinated mussel, artichoke
and, 234
sauté of orzo, edamame and, 314
in seafood succotash, 22–23
stew, chervil, 434–35
tiny, salad of celery, dill and, 500
shungiku, *see* chrysanthemum leaves
Shurtleff, William, 543
Siberian kale, 598
Sicilian-style dish, fennel sardine sauce,
215–16
Silk Road Cooking (Batmanglij), 263
Simpson lettuce, black-seeded, *see*
lettuce, iceberg
Sistina (restaurant), 301
slaves, 297, 307
slaw boards, 554
slaws:
celery, 201–2
crisp, 270
hot shrimp and cabbage, 267
vegetable, with Asian dressing, 271
slow-braised cabbage with garlic, 272
slow-cookers, 501–4, 541
small white beans, *see* navy bean(s)
small yellow Finn potatoes, 632
Smart-Grosvenor, Vertamae, 286, 570
Smith, Sidney, 417
Smokin' (Styler), 9
snails in cream, artichokes filled with,
231
snap peas, *see* sugar snap peas
snow peas, 303, 536, 622–24
braised napa cabbage with lotus
root, bamboo and, 366–67
and chicken in mustard-soy sauce,
stir-fried, 304
in soothing Asian vegetable salad,
368
in very spicy Asian vegetable salad,
318
Solanaceae, 97, 322, 624
sole:
fillet of, over celery, 203
stew, chervil, 434–35

Solomon, Charmaine, 373, 524, 530,
584
sopa de habas (fava bean soup), 225–26
sorbet:
beet, 165–66
carrot, 193
red pepper, 68
sorrel, 644–45
béchamel sauce, 428–29
creamed spinach and, 428
in green soup, 282–83
risotto with asparagus, samphire
and, 424–25
sautéed spinach and, 427–28
shrimp and asparagus with, 428
shrimp and avocado salad on lettuce
and, 6
in spinach soup, 247
spring vegetable stew with, 427
sorrel soup:
with potato, 426
rich, 425
salmon with, 426
sott'olio (roasted peppers in oil), 55
soufflés, 486–88
artichoke, artichokes filled with,
233–34
broccoli, 487
corn-chili, 43–44
corn-chili, individual white
cheddar, 44
hot-and-sweet pepper, 487
mushroom, 487
pattypan-potato, 84
spinach, 250
vegetable-cheese (master recipe),
486–87
Soup, A Way of Life (Kafka), 71, 385
"soup" of small peas with fresh herbs
(soupe de petits pois aux herbes
fraîches), 300–301
soups:
acorn squash and mint, 126
artichoke, *see* artichoke soup
asparagus, with caramelized leeks,
156–57
borage, 589
butternut squash, with glazed
chestnuts, 126–27
callaloo, with dumplings, 365
cauliflower, *see* cauliflower soup
celery, 202, 203
chard and lentil, 179

soups (*continued*)
    Chinese, 423
    cold radish with cucumber, 291
    faux pho, 43
    fennel, 212–13
    golden, 171
    hominy, 42–43
    Jarrahdale-lemongrass, 127
    lentil and chickpea, 280–81
    light and tangy broccoli, 264
    miso, with shiitake and shiso, 367–68
    mushroom, *see* mushroom soup
    onion, *see* onion soup
    parsley, 444–45
    parsnip, 195
    pea, *see* pea soup; pea soup,
      split
    with purslane, simple, 424
    radish, 291
    rich lamb and hominy, 43
    a satin of oysters and tapioca,
      149–50
    scallion, *see* scallion soups
    scallop and endive, 220–21
    smooth black-eyed pea, 308
    spinach, *see* spinach soup
    tomato, *see* tomato soup
    tomato base for, 460
    velvet corn, 34
    see also borscht; chicken soup;
      cream(y) soups; gazpacho;
      gumbo; potage; vegetable soup
soups, bean:
    Doug Rodriguez's black bean, 19–20
    fava, Latin-style golden, 227
    fava (sopa de habas), 225–26
    fresh cranberry, 18–19
soups, fish:
    cod, with fresh cranberry beans, 19
    ten-minute, 64–65
sour cream:
    Brussels sprouts with caraway and,
      275
    cold beet borscht with, 166–67
    Doug Rodriguez's black bean soup
      with, 19–20
    in green goddess dressing, 452
sour grass, *see* sheep sorrel
sourovetz, 355–56
South America, 31, 372
    see also specific countries
Southeast Asia, Southeast Asian dishes:
    coconut-yuca custard cake, 148–49

dipping sauce, 465
    eggplant in, 323
    peanut dipping sauce, 464
    see also Vietnamese-style dishes
Southern dishes, 611, 614
    corn custard, 39–40
    hoppin' John, 308–9
    long-cooked American green
      beans, 16
    maple-glazed roasted sweet potatoes,
      140
    New Orleans spicy rémoulade,
      458–59
    pickled chayote, 132
    spicy rémoulade, 458
    spring vegetable gumbo, 341–42
    summer vegetable gumbo, 343–44
south of the border corn custard, 40
southwestern dishes:
    corn, 36
    corn and tomato soup, 105–6
    corn bread, 46
    mini corn crêpes, 33
    Santa Fe corn salad, 36
soybeans, 11, 310, 312–14, 362, 543–44
    freeze-dried and salted shelled, 544
    fresh, *see* edamame
    in quadruple soy threat, 313
    see also tofu
soybean sprouts, 646–47
    in quadruple soy threat, 313
soy milk, 312, 543
soy (sauce), 312, 543
    in Chinese dipping sauce, 465
    in Japanese dipping sauce, 465
    -mustard, steamed Chinese broccoli
      with, 321
    in quadruple soy threat, 313
    -sesame vinaigrette, Bibb lettuce
      with, 415
    in very spicy Asian vegetable salad,
      318
    vinaigrette, 449
    see also tamari
spaghetti, eggplant and okra stew over,
    342–43
spaghettini:
    fried peppers and tomatoes for,
      62–63
    with pesto sauce, 467–68
    roasted broccoli stems with, 265
    Virginia ham, spinach and, 253
spaghetti squash, 117, 652–56

Spaniards, Spain, 31, 69, 96, 224, 322,
    531
Spanish-style dishes, 372, 482
    gazpacho, 102–3
spearmint, 593
spiced:
    squash pie, 134
    squash pudding, 133–34
spicy:
    Asian vegetable salad, very, 318
    bamboo stir-fry, 368–69
    -cool avocado sauce, 9
    corn relish, 40
    Middle Eastern tomato sauce, 464
    papaya salsa with daikon, 293
    rémoulade, 459
    rémoulade, New Orleans, 458–59
    rice, pink bean feijoada over, 26
spinach, 246–53, 645–46
    aglio olio, 249
    in chicken peanut butter stew, 50
    creamed, *see* creamed spinach
    in eggs Florentine, 250–51
    gala meat loaf with, 253
    goyesca, 249
    in green curry of summer squash,
      87–88
    in green pasta dough, 472
    green seafood stew with peas and,
      302–3
    in green shrimp curry, 437
    and mushroom lasagna, 251–53
    in party frittata (tortilla), 485–86
    sauce, cold, 249
    sautéed sorrel and, 427–28
    soufflé, 250
    timbale of mushrooms, ham and,
      286–87
    Virginia ham, rosemary pasta and,
      253
spinach soup, 247
    brodo con stracciatelle, 248
    jade, 249
    potato, 247–48
spoon bread, 44–45
    with raisins, 47
spreads:
    roasted red pepper, 56
    roasted red pepper, with anchovies, 56
spring (green) onions, 390, 391, 616–19,
    640–41
spring soup with peas and asparagus,
    light, 157

spring vegetable gumbo, 341–42
spring vegetable stew with sorrel, 427
sprouting broccoli (Italian asparagus),
   547–49
sprouting onions, *see* onions, Egyptian
sprouts, 646–47
   see also mung bean sprouts; soybean
     sprouts
squash, 575
   see also summer squash; winter
     squash; *specific kinds of squash*
squash peppers, 625, 627
squaw (flour or soft) corn, 572
Stanford Court Hotel, 234, 377, 444,
   448–49
steak-house fries, 78
steamed, steaming, 521
   of artichokes, 528
   of asparagus, 533
   of beans, 538, 541
   beets, 164, 545
   of broccoli and cauliflower, 548
   of broccoli di raab, 550
   of Brussels sprouts, 552
   of burdock, 553
   of cabbages, 555, 558
   of carrots, 562
   of celery, 564–65
   of celery root, 566
   of chard, 567
   of Chinese broccoli, 550
   Chinese broccoli with mustard-soy
     sauce, 321
   of collard greens, 571
   of corn, 573
   of cucumbers, 576
   of dandelion greens, 578
   of fennel, 583
   of Jerusalem artichokes, 597
   of kohlrabi, 599
   of leeks, 600
   of lotus roots, 603
   of mustard greens and leaf
     mustard, 612
   of nettles, 614
   of onions, 617
   of parsnips, 620
   of peas, 623
   of potatoes, 633
   of radishes, 638
   of ramps, 638
   of scorzonera and salsify, 642
   of sorrel, 644–45, 646

of squash, 118, 648, 653–54
of sweet potatoes and yams, 657
of turnips, 665
of yuca, 664
Steinpilz mushrooms, *see* porcini
   mushrooms
stewed tomato(es):
   all-American, 106–7
   Chinese, 107–8
   soup, chilled, 107
stews:
   acorn squash, 129–30
   calabaza-lamb, 131
   cauliflower, with lamb, 262
   cazuela de Elsa Tobar, 36–37
   cherry tomato base for, 460–61
   chervil chicken, 434–35
   chicken peanut butter, 50
   coconut-Jarrahdale vegetable, 130
   curry, with lamb and cranberry
     beans, 21
   eggplant and okra, 342–43
   eggplant and okra, Middle Eastern,
     343
   with favas, "rich" peasant, 227
   green seafood, with peas and
     spinach, 302–3
   kale, with chickpeas and
     mushrooms, 285
   mushroom-vegetable, 404–5
   okra and roasted pepper, with rice,
     342
   seafood succotash, 22–23
   simple stovetop cherry tomato base
     for, 461
   spring vegetable, with sorrel, 427
   succotash, 20–21
   summer's bounty, 334–35
   veal and artichoke heart, 440–41
   warm chervil base for, 434
   winter-y lamb, with eggplant and
     red peppers, 335
stir-fry(ied):
   asparagus and beef, 162
   chicken and snow peas in mustard-
     soy sauce, 304
   Chinese broccoli, 320–21, 550
   spicy bamboo, 368–69
stocks, 501–7
   asparagus, 506–7
   basic chicken, 501–2
   basic fish, 505–6
   beef, 502–4

enriched beef, 504
enriched chicken, 502
fake beef, 504
meat or chicken glaze from, 505
roasted chicken, 502
roasted fish, 506
vegetarian, giving body to, 501
stovetop (method):
   for beans, 541
   braised celery hearts, 201
   cherry tomato stew base, 461
   for reconstituting sun-dried
     tomatoes, 662
   for Szechwan green beans, 17
   tomato risotto, 110
strawberry:
   rhubarb jam, 349
   rhubarb pie, 349
straw mushrooms, 607, 609
string beans, *see* green bean(s);
     haricots verts; Romano beans;
     wax beans
strudel:
   beet and apple, 176
   beet and carrot, 176
stuffed vegetables, 491–500
   acorn squash, 118
   artichoke bottoms with duxelles,
     238–39
   artichokes, 241
   Brussels sprouts, 267–68
   cabbage rolls, 276–77
   cabbage rolls with beef glaze, 277
   cho cho, Jamaican, 119–20
   delicata with shrimp, 118–19
   eggplant, *see* eggplant, stuffed
   kohlrabi, 290–91
   mushrooms, *see* mushrooms, stuffed
   onions, 376
   pointers for, 492
   preparation for, 529, 552, 556, 571,
     581–82, 609, 619, 630, 649–50,
     655, 662
   spicy Middle Eastern tomato sauce
     for, 464
   tomatoes with rice and basil, 11
   tomatoes with tabbouleh, 111–12
   tomato sauce for, 461
   whole cabbage, 276
stuffings:
   basic rice, 491
   bulgur-chicken liver, 498
   cold, 492, 499–500

stuffings *(continued)*
    collard, mushroom and ham, 496
    curried chicken salad, 499
    fully cooked, 492, 495–99
    garlic and parsley, 498–99
    Greek, 494
    Italian sausage, 493
    lamb curry, 493–94
    lamb curry, acorn squash stuffed
        with, 118
    lamb-tomato, 496–97
    minted rice, 496
    Moroccan, 494–95
    moussaka, 497
    mushroom-bulgur (or quinoa),
        497–98
    olive-cheese, piquillo peppers with,
        150–51
    orzo, 495–96
    partially cooked/raw, 491–95
    pork, 493
    quintessential tuna salad, 499–500
    salt pork and sage, 498
    sauerkraut, roast turkey with,
        277–78
    velvet smoked trout, 500
Styler, Chris, 340, 586, 589, 603
    ants on a scallion tree of, 393
    beet and apple strudel of, 176
    spicy-cool avocado sauce of, 9
succotash, 20–21
    seafood, 22–23
sugar pie pumpkin (New England pie
    pumpkin), 652–54, 656
sugar snap peas, 303, 622–24
    in chicken, beef and vegetable soup,
        304–5
summer corn pudding, 38–39
summer's bounty stew, 334–35
summer squash, 83–91, 117, 647–50
    buttery zucchini and, 87
    green curry of, 87–88
    methods for, 648
    preparation of, 648–50
    in summer's bounty stew, 334–35
    varieties of, 647–48
    yields and equivalents for, 650
    see also pattypan squash; yellow
        squash; zucchini
summer vegetable bonanza, 88–89
    microwave variation of, 89
summer vegetable gumbo, 343–44
sunchokes, *see* Jerusalem artichokes

sun-dried tomatoes, 660
    reconstituting of, 661–62
Sutton's, 217
sweet-and-sharp cucumbers, 360
sweet-and-sour:
    onions, 382
    red cabbage, 275
    sauce, endive, 223
sweet dumpling squash, 652–56
sweet garlic "mayonnaise," 456
sweet onions, *see* onion(s), red; onion(s),
    sweet; onion(s), Vidalia
sweet peas, *see* peas, sweet green
sweet potato(es), 137–41, 656–58
    in balsamic root vegetables,
        140–41
    chips, crisp, 514
    crisp red onions with puffed slices
        of, 139–40
    maple-glazed roasted, 140
    pie, 141
    purée de batata, 138
    purée soufflé, 488
    terrine, 138–39
sweet tomato tart, 115
Swiss chard, *see* chard
Swiss cheese:
    in deep-dish pizza, 474–75
    in deli pizza, 273
    in spinach soufflé, 250
    in vegetable purée soufflé
        (without flour), 488
    -vegetable soufflé, 486–87
Switzerland, Swiss-style dishes:
    grated raw vegetables salads in, 183
    potato pancakes (rösti), 77
syrup, one-to-one simple, 511
    in cucumber granita, 361
    in tomato granita, 116
syrup, rhubarb simmered in, 639
Szechwan green beans, 16–17
Szegedi peppers, 625

T

Tabasco peppers, 625
Tabasco sauce, 628
tabbouleh:
    big, 109–10
    with red and hot peppers, 61–62
    tomatoes stuffed with, 111–12
tahini-citrus dressing, 452
    salad of potatoes and purslane
        with a, 423

Tale of Flopsy Bunny, The (Potter), 417
Talk About Good (Service League of
    Lafayette, La.), 44
tamari, 312
    -garlic kale, 285
tamarind:
    concentrate, in better than ketchup,
        114
    paste, in crab and cucumber curry,
        357–58
    paste, in curry stew with lamb and
        cranberry beans, 21
tangerines, in oven-braised parsnips,
    196–97
tapioca, 150
    parfait, cranberry, 151
    in piquillo peppers with olive-cheese
        stuffing, 150–51
    a satin of oysters and, 149–50
    in vegetarian stocks, 501
taro (callaloo, coco yam, dasheen, eddo,
    malanga), 143, 362–65
    horns, deep-fried, 363–64
    soup with dumplings, 365
tarragon, 594, 595
    and asparagus quiche, 160–61
    braised scorzonera with, 412–13
    cremini mushroom sauce with cream
        and, 408
tarragon vinegar, 588
    in beurre blanc, 453–54
    in cornichons, 359–60
    in everyday vinaigrette, 449
    in green goddess dressing, 452
    in New Orleans spicy rémoulade,
        458–59
    in pickled okra, 341
    in pickled samphire, 424
    in radish pickles, 293
    in soy-sesame vinaigrette, 449
tartar sauce, 457
tartlet shells, making, 478
tart(s):
    basic dough for, 477
    cheddar cheese dough for,
        478
    flaky dough for, 477–78
    ruby chard, 178–79
    sweet tomato, 115
    tiny chard, for hors d'oeuvre, 178,
        179
tatsoi, 316, 557, 558
    vegetarian feast, 320

tempura:
    batter, 516
    burdock, 410
    Japanese dipping sauce for, 465
    Pacific tomato dipping sauce for, 463
ten-minute fish soup, 64–65
terrine, sweet potato, 138–39
Thanksgiving, 383
    meatless red flannel hash, 172
    pudding, 135–36
    pumpkin pudding for, 134–35
    squash muffins, 131–32
thistles, 229–45
    see also artichoke(s); cardoons;
        nettle(s)
three-vegetable winter cream soup, 207
thyme, 595
    fresh, roasted peppers with, 55
timbale of collards, mushrooms and
        ham, 286–87
tofu, 312, 543
    asparagus with sesame dressing and,
        158
    in Chinese soup, 423
    in creamy Asian dip, 435
    in miso soup with shiitake and shiso,
        367–68
    in quadruple soy threat, 313
    in soothing Asian vegetable salad,
        368
Tokyo bekana mustard, *see* bamboo or
    leaf mustard
tomatillo(s), 92–94, 658–59
    in fish swimming in vegetables,
        93–94
    salsa, fresh, 93
    sauce, canned, 93
    sauce, quick, 658–59
tomato base:
    cherry, for stew, 460–61
    chunky, 460
tomato dipping sauce:
    basil, 464
    Pacific, 463
    spicy Middle Eastern, 464
tomato(es), 95–116, 659–63
    as accompaniment to guacamole, 8
    broiled crumb-topped, 661
    canned, 100
    in caponata, 327–28
    chunky, roasted Italian frying
        peppers and, 63
    commercial products, 662–63

in corn and feta cheese omelet, 36
in fava bean soup (sopa de habas),
    225–26
frappé, 452
fried, 108
fried peppers and, 62–63
granita, 116
green beans, tuna, potatoes and
    Niçoise olives with anchovy
    cheese vinaigrette (salade
    Niçoise), 14–15
growing of, 96–97
in harissa sauce, 465–66
jam, 116
in letcho, 65
methods for, 660
peas with peppers and, 302
poison in, 95–96, 97
preparation of, 660–62
Provençal melting, 99, 108–9
in red Russian soup—the meat
    version, 169
in red Russian vegetable soup, 168
risotto, stovetop, 110
roasted, yellow chard, penne and,
    181
roasted yellow bell peppers and,
    57–58
in romesco sauce, 63–64
shirred eggs with herbs, cream and,
    102
stewed, *see* stewed tomato(es)
stuffed, preparations for, 662
stuffed with rice and basil, 11
stuffed with tabbouleh, 111–12
tart, sweet, 115
varieties of, 96, 659–60
yields and equivalents for, 663
see also plum tomato(es)
tomato juice, 663
    in gazpacho, 102–3
    in harissa sauce, 465–66
    in vegetable curry, 261–62
tomato paste:
    commercial, 662, 663
    fresh, 459
tomato peppers, 625, 627
tomato purée, 112, 662
    American, 460
    American, in eggplant and okra
        stew, 342–43
tomato salads:
    avocado salad, 5–6

Barbara's, 101
basic French, 100
basic Italian, 100
general information about, 98–99
insalata caprese, 99, 100
steak-house, 101
tomato sauce, 112
    baby food, 461
    baby food, in ratatouille pasta sauce,
        338
    basic pizza, 463
    better than ketchup, 114
    caramelized, roasted fennel with,
        210–11
    cranberry salsa, 114
    in deep-dish pizza, 474–75
    early American ketchup, 113
    in eggplant lasagna, 336
    even-more-basic pizza, 463
    fettuccine with roasted scallion and,
        395
    herbed, 462
    for miniature tomato-basil quiches,
        101–2
    mint salsa, fresh, 114–15
    in mock eggplant Parmesan, 336–37
    olive-, roasted Jerusalem artichokes
        in, 143–44
    orange cherry, braised carrots in,
        190–91
    orange cherry, roast arctic char with
        braised carrots and, 190–91
    with pancetta and onion, bucatini
        with (all'amatriciana), 112–13
    plum, 462
    for stuffed vegetables, 461
tomato soup:
    basil, 105
    bread and, 104
    chilled stewed, 107
    cold Moroccan, 103
    curry, 105
    with dill and crème fraîche, 104
    gazpacho, 102–3
    Southwestern corn and, 105–6
Tom Thumb lettuce, *see* lettuce, Bibb
torta pasqualina, 423
tortelli, making, 470
tortelli, squash:
    with endive sweet-and-sour sauce,
        223
    with sage-butter sauce, 122–23
tortelloni, chard and veal, 180–81

tortillas, corn, 31, 574–75
tortillas, egg, 482
    party frittata, 485–86
Trader Vic's, 449
tree ears, *see* wood ears
Treviso radicchio, *see* radicchio, Treviso
Troisgros family, 452
trompettes du mort, *see* trumpets of
    death
Tropp, Barbara, 312, 323, 373, 393, 612
trout, velvet smoked, 500
truffle(s):
    creamy gratin of cardoons with
        Fontina and, 242–43
    and potato salad, 80
trumpets of death (black chanterelles,
    black trumpets, trompettes du
    mort, horns of plenty,), 605
tuiles, 50
tuna:
    and beets Niçoise bâtarde, 173–74
    green beans, potatoes, and Niçoise
        olives and green beans with
        tomatoes and anchovy cheese
        vinaigrette (salade Niçoise), 14–15
    salad of arugula, white bean and,
        429
salad stuffing, quintessential, 499–500
tung ho, *see* chrysanthemum leaves
turban squash, 652, 653, 656
turkey:
    with sauerkraut stuffing, roast,
        277–78
    smoked, yellow split pea soup with,
        307
Turkey, 295, 376, 491, 614
turnip greens, in bitter greens with
    lardons, 219
turnip(s), 665–67
    chips, crisp, 514
    frying of, 517
    with garlic, oven-braised, 292
    potage of carrot and, 185–86
    in spring vegetable stew with sorrel,
        427
    in vegetable combination salad, 196
    in warm vegetable compote, 385–86
    in warm vegetable salad, 290
Tuscan kale, 598
Tyndalo, Vassili, 604
tzatziki, cucumber, 352

U

Umbelliferae family, 183, 582
ume-boshi vinegar, in tuna and beets
    Niçoise bâtarde, 173–74
uvilla grande peppers, 625

V

V-8 vegetable juice, in mushroom-
    vegetable stew, 404–5
Van Aken, Norman, 147
veal:
    and artichoke heart stew, 440–41
    and chard tortelloni, 180–81
    knuckle, in beef stock, 502–4
    in okroshka, 355–56
vegetable marrow, 647
vegetable pear, *see* chayote(s)
vegetable(s):
    antipasto, pickled, 256–57
    with bagna cauda, 466
    balsamic root, 140–41
    bonanza, summer, 88–89
    "braised" collards with, 286
    broth, 506
    chips, crisp, 514
    coconut-Jarrahdale stew, 130
    combination, roasted, 195–96
    combination salad, 196
    compote, warm, 385–86
    curry, 261–62
    dangerous, 97
    fish swimming in, 93–94
    frittata, 484
    in fritto misto, 516–17
    gumbo, spring, 341–42
    -mushroom stew, 404–5
    pizza, 474
    and pot cheese salad, 439–40
    purée, winter, 207
    purée soufflé (without flour), 488
    sauce, in Mexican lasagne with
        cilantro-jalapeño pasta, 437–38
    sauté, fall, 191–92
    slaw with Asian dressing, 271
    stew with sorrel, spring, 427
    stuffed, tomato sauce for, 461
    see also specific vegetables
vegetable salads:
    combination, 196–97
    pot cheese and, 439
    soothing Asian, 368
    very spicy Asian, 318
    warm, 290

Vegetables from Amaranth to Zucchini
    (Schneider), 316
Vegetables in South-East Asia (Herklots),
    323, 417
vegetable soup:
    basic potage, 71–72
    chicken, beef and, 304–5
    red Russian, 168
    three-, winter cream, 207
vegetarian borscht, 268–69
velvet corn soup, 34
velvet smoked trout, 500
Venice, Veneto, Venetian-style dishes:
    radicchio in, 218
    rice with peas (risi bisi), 302
    risotto with radicchio and vermouth,
        220
vermicelli, sesame, cucumber with, 358
vermouth:
    in Hubbard squash risotto, 124–25
    risotto with radicchio and, 220
Verona radicchio, *see* radicchio
*Vibration Cooking or the Travel Notes of a
    Geechee Girl* (Smart-Grosvenor),
    286, 570
vichyssoise:
    (cold leek and potato soup), 387–88
    cucumber, 354
Vico (restaurant), 235
Vidalia onions, *see* onion(s), Vidalia
Viennese-style dishes:
    cauliflower, 259
    creamy cauliflower soup, 257–58
Vietnamese-style dishes, 589
    faux pho, 43
Vilmorin, 323
vinaigrettes, 448–50
    anchovy, 449–50
    anchovy cheese, *see* anchovy cheese
        vinaigrette
    asparagus with ham and,
        157–58
    blood orange, 450
    cumin, orange and onion salad with,
        374
    everyday, 449
    green bean salad with, 13
    leek, 385
    poppy seed blood orange, 450
    soy-sesame, 449
    soy-sesame, Bibb lettuce with, 415
    for tomato avocado salad, 5–6
    walnut, 450

vinegar(s), 448–49
        batter, 516
        herb, 588
        ume-boshi, in tuna and beets Niçoise
                bâtarde, 173–74
        see also balsamic (vinegar); cider
                vinegar; red wine vinegar;
                tarragon vinegar; white vinegar;
                white wine vinegar
Virginia ham, spinach and rosemary
        pasta, 253
vitamin C, 71, 167, 346–47

W

walking onions, *see* onions, Egyptian
walnut oil:
        frisée with walnuts and, 218–19
        vinaigrette, 450
walnuts:
        in beet and apple strudel, 176
        beet greens with white beans, bacon
                and, 173
        frisée with walnut oil and, 218–19
        in lovage pesto, 442–43
warm chervil sauce or stew base, 434
warm ruby chard stems and anchovy
        sauté, 179–80
warm spring vegetable salad, 432
warm vegetable compote, 385–86
warm vegetable salad, 290
wasabi, 666
water chestnuts, in soothing Asian
        vegetable salad, 368
watercress, 666–67
wax beans, 537–39
        with herbs, braised, 16
        sautéed, 538
Weaver, William Woys, 375, 572
weeds and odd leaves, 422–32
        see also amaranth; arugula;
                chrysanthemum greens;
                dandelion greens; fiddlehead
                (ferns); miner's lettuce; purslane;
                samphire; sorrel
Wei Chuan Chinese Snacks, 363
wheat germ orange dressing, 451
white beans, small, *see* navy bean(s)
white bean(s) (cannellini), 539–41
        beet greens with bacon, walnuts and,
                173
        roasted onion soup with, 379
        in summer vegetable gumbo, 343–44

whitefish, roast, with braised carrots
        orange cherry tomato sauce,
        190–91
white noodles, green cabbage, string
        beans and cream, 273
white onions, *see* onion(s), white
white salad, 230
white vinegar:
        in bread-and-butter pickles, 361
        in hot-and-sweet pepper jelly, 67
        in maple corn jalapeño relish, 40
        in pickled chayote, 132
        in pickled Egyptian onions, 382
        in pickled jalapeño peppers, 62
        in zucchini bread-and-butter pickles,
                90
white wine:
        in artichokes filled with snails in
                cream, 231
        in baked halibut with Jerusalem
                artichokes and leeks, 144
        in basic fish stock, 505–6
        in beurre blanc, 453–54
        in cod soup with fresh cranberry
                beans, 19
        in fiddlehead and chanterelle
                risotto, 431–32
        in hearts of palm salad, 367
        in large lima beans with garlic and
                fennel, 26–27
        in mildly cardamom cabbage, 271–72
        in onion soup, 377–78
        in potato and truffle salad, 80
        in risotto with asparagus, sorrel and
                samphire, 424–25
        in stuffed Brussels sprouts, 267–68
        in tomato sauce for stuffed
                vegetables, 461
white wine vinegar:
        in cippolini Riviera, 381
        in cornichons, 359–60
        in garlic or dill pickles, 358–59
wild asparagus, *see* asparagus, wild
wild fennel, 208, 582
wild sorrel, 644
Williams, Chuck, 448
wine, *see* Champagne; red wine;
        vermouth; white wine
wing beans (asparagus peas; Goa beans),
        537, 543, 622–24
winter mushroom soup, 401
winter purslane (miner's lettuce),
        636–37

winter savory, 595–96
winter squash, 117–36, 650–56
        Adelle's favorite roasted seeds, 136
        basic seeds, 136
        methods for, 653
        muffins, Thanksgiving, 131–32
        nuggets, fried, 121–22
        pie, squash, 134
        preparation of, 653–55
        pudding, spiced, 133–34
        substitutions for, 118
        texture of, 118
        varieties of, 650–53
        yields and equivalents for, 655–56
        see also acorn squash; buttercup
                squash; butternut squash;
                calabaza (squash); chayote(s);
                delicata squash; Hubbard squash;
                Jarrahdale (squash); kabocha;
                pumpkin(s); red kuri
winter vegetable purée, 207
winter-y lamb stew with eggplant and
        red peppers, 335
Wolfert, Paula, 588
wood ears (tree ears), 610, 611
wood hedgehogs (hedgehogs), 607
wood sorrel (oca), 644
wrapped heart mustard (dai gai choy),
        612

Y

yam(s) (ñame, igname), 137–38, 143,
        656–58
        chips, crisp, 514
yard-long beans, *see* long beans
yautía (malanga), 143, 663–64
        in chicken, beef and vegetable soup,
                304–5
        fritters, 146
yellow bell pepper(s), 625
        in fried peppers and tomatoes, 62–63
        in golden pepper potato purée, 59
        in hot-and-sweet pepper jelly, 67
        and hot pepper soufflé, 487
        ice cream, golden, 67–68
        in Mexican lasagna with cilantro-
                jalapeño pasta, 437–38
        in pepper relish, 66–67
        in pork chops with cherry and bell
                peppers, 61
        roasted tomatoes and, 57–58
        strips, silky, 58

yellow Finn potatoes, 632
yellow (golden) chard, 176–77
    roasted tomatoes, penne and, 181
    and veal tortelloni, 180–81
yellow onions, *see* onion(s), yellow
yellow squash (yellow zucchini), 647–50
    buttery zucchini and, 87
    in eggplant with confetti vegetarian
      stuffing, 330–31
    in green curry of summer squash,
      87–88
    green gazpacho with citrus fruits
      and, 84–85
    midsummer, 89–90
    in a mint bath, roasted, 86
    in vegetable slaw with Asian
      dressing, 271
yellow waxy peppers, 625, 627
Yin-Fei Lo, Eileen, 363
yogurt:
    chilled cucumber soup with, 355
    in chilled curried pea soup, 300
    in cold radish soup with cucumber,
      291
    in cucumber curry soup, 356–57

    in cucumber pachadi, 353
    in cucumber salad, 353
    in cucumber tzatziki, 352
    dressing, 450
    garlic kale with, 285
    mushrooms with dill and, 398
    sauce of roasted eggplant, cumin
      and, 338
    in spinach soup, 247
    strained, 511
yuca (Brazilian arrowroot, cassava,
      manioc), 143, 146–51
    -coconut custard cake, 148–49
    con mojo criollo, 147–48
    croquettes, 146–47
    with olive oil and garlic sauce, 468
    see also tapioca
Yuca (restaurant), 143
Yukon gold potatoes, 632

Z

Zarela Martinez's puréed black beans
    (frijoles negros colados), 23–24

ziti:
    with eggplant Moroccan, 326–27
    roasted Italian frying peppers and
      chunky tomatoes for, 63
zucchini, 647–50
    bread-and-butter pickles, 90
    buttery summer squash and, 87
    chunks with citrus and mint, 86–87
    with confetti vegetarian stuffing,
      330–31
    custard, 85
    in eggplant with Middle Eastern
      spiced rice, 332–33
    fried, 515
    in green curry of summer squash,
      87–88
    in green soup, 282–83
    in Mexican lasagna with cilantro-
      jalapeño pasta, 437–38
    oven-grilled, 87
    in party frittata (tortilla), 485–86
    sautéed with dill, 86
zucchini, yellow, *see* yellow squash
zuppa di patate e carciofi (potato and
    artichoke soup), 235